D0207464

BIOGRAPHICAL DICTIONARY OF MODERN PEACE LEADERS

BIOGRAPHICAL DICTIONARY OF MODERN PEACE LEADERS

Editor-in-Chief
HAROLD JOSEPHSON

Associate Editors
SANDI E. COOPER
SOLOMON WANK
LAWRENCE S. WITTNER

Regional Editors
Donald S. Birn (England)
Robert H. Claxton (Latin America)
Sandi E. Cooper (Western Europe)
Ainslie T. Embree (South Asia)
William D. Hoover (China and Japan)
Harold Josephson (Africa, Australia, 19th-Century America)
Thomas Socknat (Canada)
Solomon Wank (Central and Eastern Europe, Scandinavia)
Lawrence S. Wittner (20th-Century America)

Greenwood Press
Westport, Connecticut • London, England

Library of Congress Cataloging in Publication Data

Main entry under title:

Biographical dictionary of modern peace leaders.

Bibliography: p.
Includes index.
1. Pacifists—Biography—Dictionaries. I. Josephson, Harold, 1942-
JX1962.A2B56 1984 327.1'72'0922 83-26514
ISBN 0-313-22565-6 (lib. bdg.)

Library of Congress Catalog Card Number: 83-26514
ISBN: 0-313-22565-6

First published in 1985

Greenwood Press
A division of Congressional Information Service, Inc.
88 Post Road West
Westport, Connecticut 06881

Printed in the United States of America

10 9 8 7 6 5 4 3 2

For Merle Curti
and the pioneer historians in peace research

CONTENTS

INTRODUCTION

In recent years, there has been a surge of peace activism and a growing debate over the nature of war in the nuclear age. Around the world, individuals and groups have protested against the escalating nuclear arms race, the ethnocentrism that threatens global survival, and the inflexibility of great power leadership. There has been a sense of urgency and determination on the part of those challenging the arms race. In May 1983, the Roman Catholic bishops of the United States approved an unprecedented pastoral letter denouncing nuclear war and calling upon Catholics to help rid the world of nuclear weapons. "The nuclear age is an era of moral as well as physical danger," they declared. "We are the first generation since Genesis with the power to virtually destroy God's creation. We cannot remain silent in the face of such danger."[1]

Neither the bishops' moral outrage nor their sense of urgency was entirely new. Throughout the 19th and 20th centuries, peace activists sought to mobilize public opinion against war and to find alternatives to international conflict. Although individual voices had been raised against war since antiquity, it was not until after the Napoleonic wars that organized peace efforts began to take hold in the United States and Europe. The first organized peace societies sprang up in the United States in 1815, first in New York and then in Massachusetts and Ohio. The following year the Society for the Promotion of Permanent and Universal Peace (later known as the Peace Society) was established in England. Peace societies were founded in Paris in 1821 and in Geneva in 1830, but during the first half of the 19th century most organized peace activity took place in the United States and England.[2]

The Anglo-American peace movements were deeply rooted in Christian pacifism with Quakers among the most active Christian sects protesting violence and war. Nevertheless, peace leaders did not necessarily agree on all issues. In the United States, Quakers and nonresistant followers of William Lloyd Garrison rejected all war, including defensive war, while their more moderate colleagues opposed only wars of aggression. This division plagued the leadership of the American Peace Society (founded in 1828) as well as other antiwar organizations.

In England, the peace movement was based both on religious principles and upon the tradition of liberal economics as articulated by Richard Cobden and John Bright. Whereas Christian pacifists rejected war as an activity incompatible with the life and teachings of Jesus Christ, liberals viewed war as destructive to the health and prosperity of all nations. They wished to substitute international trade for war, thereby tying people together in a network of commercial interdependence.

Through a series of international peace congresses, American and English peace leaders sought to interest continental Europeans in the peace effort. The first international peace congress was held in London in 1843, with subsequent ones held in Brussels (1848), Paris (1849), and Frankfurt (1850). On the Continent, peace leaders generally ignored nonresistant and Quaker elements, emphasizing instead the secular arguments favoring peace. Belgian and French peace leaders such as Emile de Lavaleye, Gustave de Molinari, Frédéric Bastiat, and Frédéric Passy appealed to their contemporaries by emphasizing the pragmatic aspects of the peace position. Peace, they argued, was the logical concomitant of a modern economy and was a requirement for a progressive and prosperous world order.[3] Radical republicans went beyond the economic advantages of peace and argued that the militarization of society retarded the emancipation of peoples, the growth of democratic values, and the abolition of reactionary authority.

To a considerable extent, the peace movement was eclipsed during the middle decades of the 19th century, first by the Crimean War, then by the Civil War in the United States, and later by the wars of national unification. With its emphasis on Christian pacifism and liberal economics, the peace movement largely ignored the political climate in places like Italy, Germany, and the Slavic areas that had not yet achieved national unity. Still, even before nationalist movements had proven successful, pacifism added a new "radical bourgeois" element, articulated by individuals such as Marie and Armand Goegg and Charles Lemonnier. They connected the issue of peace with political and social justice, insisting that peace and liberty were interconnected, that the church and state should be separated, and that the emancipation of women and mass public education were essential to a just social order. Believing also that peace and nationalism were compatible, they argued that the end of war would result from the political organization of mankind into democratically governed national societies.

Marxian socialism provided yet another way of thinking about peace. Viewing war as the result of either dynastic ambitions or of capitalist machinations, socialists argued that a world order controlled by the working class would naturally be peaceful. Although opposed to capitalism, socialists often found grounds upon which to collaborate with middle class pacifists. These included the reduction in military budgets, substitution of armed militias for standing armies, and, to a lesser extent, the development of peace machinery such as the Hague tribunal. After 1899, socialists tended more towards antimilitarism than towards liberal or legal internationalism.

A major resurgence in peace activism developed during the final quarter of the 19th century and lasted until the outbreak of war in 1914. Based largely on the increased contacts between western nations and the growing interdependence of European economies, the peace movement entered a more sophisticated and developed state in both Europe and the United States. New and more durable peace societies were founded on the continent beginning in 1867 with the establishment of Frédéric Passy's Paris-based Ligue internationale et permanent de la paix and the Geneva-based Ligue internationale de la paix et de la liberté, which was founded by republican radicals. Beginning in 1889 annual meetings of the Interparliamentary Union and revived gatherings of the Universal Peace Congresses brought together hundreds of delegates from countries all over Europe, the United States, and occasionally from non-European nations to discuss a variety of international issues. Moreover, a lively network based on correspondence, journals, and other publications linked peace leaders together, while international headquarters were established in Switzerland and Belgium to coordinate the activities of a diverse group of peace organizations.

Despite continued and strong opposition to the peace movement in many European nations, antiwar organizations grew in number and activity. New national peace groups sprang up in nations like Germany, Austria-Hungary, and even Japan and Australia, which never had an organized peace movement before. The publication of Bertha von Suttner's antiwar novel, *Die Waffen Nieder*, in 1889 mobilized a strong base of popular support for the peace effort, while the convocation of the Hague Peace Conferences in 1899 and 1907 provided a certain amount of respectability for the cause. Emphasizing less the Christian values of the past, the peace effort called for specialized machinery that would limit international conflict and lessen the chances of war. These included arbitration agreements, the codification of international law, the establishment of an international judicial tribunal, and the development of an association of nations. In the United States a similar emphasis on peace machinery and respectability dominated the peace movement. Organizations such as the American Association for International Conciliation, the American Society for International Law, and the Carnegie Endowment for International Peace attracted men of wealth and political connections to the peace effort. In both the United States and Europe, then, peace reform became both more cosmopolitan and more respectable than it had been in earlier years.[4]

World War I created a crisis in the peace movement. In all belligerent nations, most middle class and socialist peace workers initially shared the view that their nation had been attacked and supported the call to arms. During the war, however, peace activists began to regroup. The horrors of the conflict convinced many that it was a tragic mistake and that future conflicts had to be avoided at all costs. French and German pacifists sought to convince their fellow citizens that their own national leaders were largely responsible for the death and destruction. In both the United States and Europe, internationalists who had supported the war retained their vision of a new international system based on world order machinery. In subsequent years, they rallied behind the League of Nations and the World Court.

During the interwar period the peace movement in both the United States and Europe remained divided between those who supported collective security and those who saw any organized violence as an evil to be avoided. Pacifists also divided among those who continued to define peace negatively as the absence of war and those who defined it positively as international harmony and the existence of social justice. None of these groups, however, formed a unified whole. Each represented a loose and shifting coalition. Sometimes they agreed on alternatives and sometimes they sharply divided. New organizations were created that sought to promote a particular internationalist scheme or to find means to avoid all war and violence. In Germany, peace workers divided between those who saw the primary task as combating Germany's militaristic tradition and convincing German citizens to accept their nation's responsibility for the First World War and those who retained a more traditional antiwar commitment and concentrated on international rather than domestic affairs. In the United States a variety of alternative strategies emerged, some leading towards international organization and law and others focusing on opposition to all conflict, even sanctions designed to limit aggression.

New developments in the 1930s presented deeply troubling choices for the peace movement. Heightened calls for class warfare eroded communist and socialist support for peace efforts. Furthermore, the rise of fascism—which pacifists naturally found exceptionally repugnant—once more divided peace activists over the question of their response to injustice and to aggressive war. Pacifists had always debated the dilemma of whether a time comes when something is worth fighting for, and during the 1930s many found it difficult to counsel peace in the face of fascist injustice, persecution, and cruelty. By the time World War II broke out, most peace activists had concluded that the defeat of fascism was a necessity and that pacifist ideals had to be surrendered, at least temporarily. Although conscientious objection appealed to many draft-age pacifists, just as it had during previous wars, most internationalists and pacifists backed their nations' call to arms.

Up through the Second World War the peace movement was dominated by Americans and Europeans and was hardly an issue in most other nations. The explanation for this lies to some extent in the varying political and social cultures of nations. Africa and Asia did not have the long tradition of Christianity that made the Christian call against war meaningful. In Latin America, the primary political theme throughout the 19th century was nationalism. As Roger Chickering has shown, even relatively similar nations responded differently to the quest for peace because of differences in culture and political tradition. In France, with its tradition of radical republicanism, Jacobin nationalism, and labor reformism, the peace movement was more extensive, had access to those in power, and found friends in the press, education, and the churches. This was much less true in pre-World War I Germany, with its authoritarian and strong military tradition which mitigated against peace activism.[5]

The even sharper differences between the nations of Europe and the United States and those in Asia, Africa, the Middle East, and Latin America accounted for the relative absence of an organized antiwar effort in the developing world. The political and cultural climate of these nations simply did not spawn pacifism as a political ideology and did not provide a fertile environment for peace activities. The absence of pacifism in the Third World was also the result of the priority given by the nations of Africa and Asia to state formation and/or national independence which has often been incompatible with an ideology that rejects armed resistance under any circumstances. In fact, western ideas of internationalism and rejection of violence frequently were used against national liberation movements and for the continuation of domination and exploitation. Believing that the ideology of peace was pursued by western politicians at the expense of social justice and respect for human dignity, the developing world did not rally around the banner of pacifism.[6]

Immediately following World War II, pacifism in the western world fell victim to the Cold War. Some of its earlier ideas were preserved in limited international institutions connected with the United Nations, but the emergence of the Cold War confrontation between the United States and the Soviet Union made pacifism suspect in the nations within their orbit. Still, the development of nuclear arms gradually reinvigorated the peace movement. The prospect of world annihilation led to the formation of such groups as the Committee for Non-Violent Action, the Committee for a Sane Nuclear Policy, and the Campaign of Nuclear Disarmament. In the United States the war in Vietnam swelled the ranks of the peace movement, although its intensity and depth of conviction ebbed following the American pullout in the early 1970s. Peace research, which had begun seriously between the two world wars, gained respectability and sophistication as an academic discipline.

The American-European monopoly on the peace movement, moreover, ended in the aftermath of the Second World War. In Japan pacifism came to dominate the intellectual and political life of the nation. Whereas Japanese antiwar sentiment prior to 1945 consisted mainly of isolated expressions of individual conviction, postwar pacifist views were strong and well organized. In India, Gandhi's nonviolent principles, which had gained a following before World War II, swept across the country and strongly influenced peace leaders elsewhere. Indian advocates of nonviolence, however, were not pacifists in the western sense, not even Gandhi. The central concern of the nonviolent movement was internal problems—the struggle for independence, Hindu-Muslim relations, and attitudes towards untouchables—and not primarily international relations. Similarly, nonviolent principles gained some adherents in Africa. Opposition to French atomic bomb tests in the Sahara led to the calling in 1960 of the All-African Conference on Positive Action for Peace and Security of Africa in Accra, Ghana, and efforts were made by pacifists like the American A. J. Muste to spread the principles of peace in such nations as Ghana, Tanganyika (now Tanzania), and Northern Rhodesia, but nonviolence did not become a significant force in African politics or intellectual life.

The rebirth of peace activism in the 1980s focused largely on the issue of nuclear war and arms reduction. The American Catholic bishops' pastoral letter was but one expression of a worldwide movement to prevent the use of nuclear weapons. Supporters of a nuclear freeze and arms limitation raised their voices around the globe, demanding an end to militarism and the arms race. Although the forces of peace did not control national or international policy, they had become important actors in world affairs.

This biographical reference volume seeks to define the parameters of peace advocacy, present and clarify the wide variety of ideas and approaches that comprised the antiwar effort, and offer information about the many individuals who either contributed to the organized peace effort or who influenced others to question war and organized violence through their writings or personal activity. Some of the individuals included in this volume are well known, but most are not. Peace leaders are relatively obscure because most have not held political power; indeed, many have been sharp social critics or dissidents. Nevertheless, their relative obscurity does not make these individuals less significant. Frequently their analysis of international relations, their perception of reality, and the policy prescriptions they offered were far more sophisticated and accurate than those who held political power.

Just as the peace movement itself was diverse, not all peace leaders were consistent. This should not be surprising, for human beings are sometimes contradictory and many-sided. Often, their views change over time. The biographical sketches in this volume do not seek to label individuals, but rather to show them as they were—men and women wrestling with questions of war and peace and reacting to specific events. That their outlook sometimes changed should be expected, as should the fact that they reacted differently to different situations. That some peace leaders supported the American Civil War or World War II does not necessarily invalidate their overall distaste for war or their longterm efforts for peace. Instead, it highlights what have sometimes appeared as tragic alternatives: a civil war or the continuation of slavery; world war or fascist triumph. Given these choices, some pacifists subordinated their opposition to war and violence in order to eliminate a greater evil.

The concept of peace leadership is a loose rubric that includes a number of approaches to peace, not all of them harmonious. Some of the individuals included in this volume were absolute pacifists who opposed wars and the use of violence under all circumstances. For them war was always morally wrong and should be avoided no matter what the consequences. Others were peace-oriented non-pacifists who viewed war as a conceivable possibility, although always a fundamentally irrational and inhumane way to solve disputes. The point at which warfare became a necessary evil varied tremendously from individual to individual. Moreover, their diversity in approach and program was often more startling than their similarity. Some favored arbitration, others the codification of international law, still others a world court or a congress of nations. Some believed that an end to warfare had less to do with the structure of the international system than with rechanneling human nature and eliminating violence in interpersonal relations. Some of those included in this volume did not oppose war as a matter of principle and, therefore, cannot be viewed as pacifists or peace activists in an absolute sense. They were included, however, because they took a particularly strong stand against a specific war or helped to end a war already begun and, consequently, furthered the cause of peace or influenced others.

Because of the diversity of peace advocacy, historical definitions pose a serious problem. Throughout most of the 19th century those active in the peace movement referred to themselves as "peace advocates," "peace workers," or simply "friends of peace." In the 1890s, with the peace movement expanding and a desire to establish a clearer perspective, Emile Arnaud coined the term "pacifism" to describe the doctrine and the program of the antiwar effort. Increasingly those in the movement referred to themselves as "pacifists." Debates arose over the scope and meaning of the term, but these were largely resolved with the outbreak of World War I when the movement divided between those who supported the war efforts of their respective countries and those who did not. After the war the term "pacifist" was reserved for those who unconditionally opposed all forms of international violence. Those who proposed to eliminate war through specific peace machinery such as arbitration or international organization, but who countenanced defensive warfare or the use of collective sanctions were known as "internationalists," "world federalists," or "pacificists."[7]

In this volume the word "pacifism" is used somewhat more loosely. It refers to "either the absolute renunciation of war or the refusal to participate in or opposition in principle to a specific war or governmental military program on religious, philosophical, humanitarian, or social justice grounds." More important than the motivation for adopting a pacifistic stance are the values held in advocating peace as more desirable than war.[8] Other terms also appear in many of the biographical sketches. A "peace advocate" refers to anyone who actively promoted "ideas and publicly manifested a concern for eliminating, avoiding, or minimizing the unilateral use of force by nation-states, usually suggesting alternative proposals which would modify national policy or behavior." A "peace worker" refers to anyone who contributed time and energy in supporting programs or organizations seeking to end war or oppose militarism. A "peace activist" refers to any individual "with clearly stated goals involved in antiwar protest through group action or public activity directed toward policy change." Finally, "peace leadership" refers broadly to anyone active in the antiwar effort, either through an organized movement or through individual actions, who influenced contemporary thinking about peace and war. These terms, of course, are not mutually exclusive. Pacifists may be counted among the ranks of the peace activists, peace workers, and peace advocates, but must be distinguished from those who simply opposed a specific war or favored a particular alternative to war such as arbitration or the codification of international law.

Given the diversity of peace leadership and the broad range of perspectives, the process of deciding who should be included in a biographical dictionary of modern peace leaders proved challenging. Members of the Conference on Peace Research in History, the organization that initiated this volume, felt that representatives from all camps should be included, but that they should be individuals who significantly contributed to the creation of alternatives to war, violence, and traditional power politics as ways of dealing with international conflict. The editorial committee agreed that peace leaders must have sought to disseminate their ideas through speeches, writings, and/or direct action. Specifically, the editors agreed that individuals should be included who:

(a) publicly advocated the elimination of the unilateral use of force in nation-state relations or consistently took an antimilitarist stand and demonstrated opposition to the use of force;
(b) held important or leadership positions in organizations devoted to world peace and who played active rather than honorary roles in these organizations;
(c) worked to prevent a particular international conflict from developing into an armed conflict;
(d) took public stands in opposition to a particular war during that war or sought to shorten that war;
(e) advocated the cause of peace and nonviolence in social relations;
(f) maintained a commitment to transnational values;
(g) projected ideas or visions of peace in art and literature;
(h) sought to limit national sovereignty and elevate international organization or other means as a substitute for national sovereignty.

Activity in any of these categories made an individual eligible for inclusion, but did not necessarily guarantee inclusion. The editors wished to include only those whose contribution was significant, those whose role in any one of these categories was dominant, or those who played an important role in more than one of the categories.

Effort also was made to have representative figures from many countries. This was not an easy task, for as stated previously peace activities were much more prominent in the United States and Europe than in other areas of the world. Consequently, Asia, Africa, and Latin America have relatively few representatives and many are controversial. One Chinese scholar, for example, felt that pacifism was "monumentally irrelevant to the main lines of development in China." African and Latin American scholars frequently concurred in this sentiment when commenting about peace activities in those areas.

The editors agreed to include only deceased persons, thereby giving the volume an historical dimension and avoiding the onerous task of deciding which of the current peace activists should be included. Seeking to confine the volume to the modern period, when an organized peace movement became a reality, the editors further decided to include only individuals alive after 1800. Regional editors then drew up lists of peace leaders in various countries following the guidelines agreed upon. These were discussed by the editorial board and sent to scholars in the field. The lists were refined, with additions and deletions recommended. Finally, as assignments were made, authors suggested additional subjects for inclusion and sometimes concluded that a given individual did not merit treatment.

Since internationalism and world order concerns were a major factor in peace thinking during the late 19th and 20th centuries, the editors of this volume worked closely with Professor Warren Kuehl, the editor of the *Biographical Dictionary of Internationalists*. It was agreed that instead of having two sets of entries for internationalists/peace leaders, the two volumes would be cross-referenced. The general rule followed by the editors was to ask where the subject might have preferred to be listed and, if doubt arose, to follow the recommendation of the author of the sketch. Cross-references appear both in major name entries and internally within essays by symbol. A "+" prior to a person's name indicates an entry in the *Biographical Dictionary of Internationalists*; a "*" denotes an essay in the *Biographical Dictionary of Modern Peace Leaders*.

Each entry follows a set format. An introductory paragraph includes basic data about birth, death, education, and career. Titles, honorary degrees, and standard family data regarding spouses and children have not been included. Although every effort was made to provide full information, it has not always been possible. Since records vary in precision and since some of the subjects did not acquire public prominence during their lifetimes, it sometimes was not possible to determine exact dates or places of birth and death. This is especially true for figures born in countries other than the United States, because formal record keeping in many of these nations has not been standardized, and for certain women where older ideas of propriety meant that their identity was hidden in a husband's name. In some cases, especially many of the German peace leaders included in this volume, very little previous work had been done, and authors have included a bit more biographical information than is contained in those essays dealing with better-known individuals. Where a subject cannot be found in other biographical reference volumes, the authors and editors agreed to include additional information when available. Information relating to education often defied standardization, particularly outside England, Canada, and the United States. In all cases, however, the authors and editors have gone to considerable effort to verify the facts that are included.

The main part of each sketch concentrates on the subject's work, thought, and activity as a peace leader. Although other aspects of the subject's career are not totally ignored, authors were asked to focus on his or her contribution to the cause of peace. Authors were asked not only to describe the person's involvement but also to interpret, where possible, what motivated the individual and what unique or special features marked his or her efforts.

The third section of each essay consists of a bibliography that is divided into three parts. Part A consists of works by the subject. No attempt was made to compose a definitive list of writings; included instead are those books, pamphlets, and articles relating to questions of war, peace, and international relations. Part B consists of works about the subject as well as biographical sketches and obituary notices. Part C notes the location of personal manuscript collections of the subject. These are limited to collections publicly accessible to scholars; papers yet in private or family hands have not been included.

The work of the editorial board has been central to the planning and completion of this volume. Sandi E. Cooper, Solomon Wank, and Lawrence S. Wittner, the associate editors, helped with all phases of the project. They also served as regional editors for Western Europe, Central and Eastern Europe, and the 20th century United States respectively. The remaining members of the editorial board consisted of the following individuals who also served as regional editors: Donald Birn (England); Robert Claxton (Latin America), Ainslie Embree (South Asia), William D. Hoover (China and Japan), and Thomas Socknat (Canada). As regional editors they drew up initial national lists, corresponded with and identified authors, provided the initial editing for the various essays in their field, occasionally translated essays, and provided enthusiastic support for the project. The editor-in-chief had final editorial responsibility and served as regional editor for Africa, Australia, and 19th century United States (with help from Peter Tolis).

As with most volumes of a similar nature, this reference work was a cooperative effort of scholars. The Council of the Conference on Peace Research in History not only provided the initiative for the volume, but helped guide it through to completion. In addition special help came from Warren F. Kuehl, Peter van den Dungen, Karl Holl, Helmut Donat, Nadine Lubelski-Bernard, Charles Chatfield, Charles DeBenedetti, Ilkka Taipale, K. David Patterson, Robert Rieke, Paul Escott, and Roy Moose. Since many of these essays were not written in English, translations had to be provided. All translators are credited at the end of each essay where appropriate, but a few language scholars deserve special recognition. These include William H. Hopkins, Ruthann Richards, Peter Seadle, Robert Reimer, and Judith Suther.

Mary Bottomly accepted the main responsibility for typing the manuscript, and she was assisted by Sandy Bergo, Linda Owensby, and Cindy Carter. Kay Starnes assisted with the proofreading and prepared the index. I would like especially to thank the Department of History of the University of North Carolina at Charlotte for its generous support of this project.

Harold Josephson

NOTES

1. U.S. Catholic Bishops, "The Challenge of Peace: God's Promise and our Response," in *Origins: NC Documentary Service*, 13 (May 19, 1983), 30.

2. The best surveys of the peace movement in the 19th century are A.C.F. Beales, *The History of Peace: A Short Account of the Organised Movements for International Peace* (New York, 1931); Peter Brock, *Pacifism in the United States: From the Colonial Era to the First World War* (Princeton, NJ, 1968); Merle Curti, *The American Peace Crusade, 1815-1860* (Durham, NC, 1929) and *Peace or War: The American Struggle, 1636-1936* (New York, 1936); Charles DeBenedetti, *The Peace Reform in American History* (Bloomington, IN, 1980); and Christina Phelps, *The Anglo-American Peace Movement in the Mid-Nineteenth Century* (New York, 1930).

3. Professor Sandi E. Cooper was very helpful in providing material and a perspective on the continental European peace effort.

4. Among the more important books on the peace movement during the late 19th and 20th centuries are: Nobuya Bamba and John F. Howes, eds., *Pacifism in Japan: The Christian and Socialist Tradition* (Vancouver, 1978); Peter Brock, *Pacifism in Europe*

to 1914 (Princeton, NJ, 1972); Martin Ceadel, *Pacifism in Britain 1914-1945: The Defining of a Faith* (Oxford, 1980); Charles Chatfield, *For Peace and Justice: Pacifism in America, 1914-1941* (Knoxville, TN, 1971); Roger Chickering, *Imperial Germany and a World Without War: The Peace Movement and German Society, 1897-1914* (Princeton, NJ, 1975); Sandi E. Cooper, ed., *Internationalism in Nineteenth-Century Europe: The Crisis of Ideas and Purpose* (New York, 1976); Warren F. Kuehl, *Seeking World Order: The United States and International Organization to 1920* (Nashville, TN, 1969); C. Roland Marchand, *The American Peace Movement and Social Reform, 1898-1918* (Princeton, NJ, 1972); David S. Patterson, *Towards a Warless World: The Travail of the American Peace Movement, 1887-1914* (Bloomington, IN, 1976); Solomon Wank, ed., *Doves and Diplomats: Foreign Offices and Peace Movements in Europe and America in the Twentieth Century* (Westport, CT, 1978); Lawrence S. Wittner, *Rebels Against War: The American Peace Movement, 1941-1960* (New York, 1969).

5. Chickering, *Imperial Germany and a World Without War*, 382-83. See also Friedrich-Karl Scheer, *Die Deutsche Friedensgesellschaft (1892-1933): Organisation, Ideologie, Politische Ziele* (Frankfurt am Main, 1981).

6. Sibusiso Bengu, "Commentary: 'Peace at the Expense of Justice and Humanitarian Principles,' " *Peace and Change: A Journal of Peace Research*, 8 (Fall, 1982), 35-38.

7. Chickering, *Imperial Germany and a World Without War*, 14-15. *See also* Ceadel, *Pacifism in Britain*, 1-17 and Wank, *Doves and Diplomats*, 10-12.

8. These and subsequent definitions were worked out at a conference on peace and internationalism sponsored by the Center for Peace Studies at the University of Akron on May 23-25, 1974. A transcript of the meeting entitled "Peace Research in History: Scope, Meaning, Problems" is held by the Center for Peace Studies.

CHRONOLOGY OF THE PEACE MOVEMENT

This chronology is selective and reflects an effort to provide a useful reference. Before an accurate and meaningful inventory can be developed much additional research must be done on both the international peace effort and on the various national and local movements. The study of the history of peace organizations and peace efforts is still somewhat underdeveloped and needs to be expanded. During the 19th and 20th centuries peace organizations blossomed in great multitudes (the most recent *Guide to the Swarthmore College Peace Collection* lists over 1500 organizations from nearly 50 nations). Just how significant some of these organizations were still needs to be determined. Moreover, a major problem in trying to develop a chronology is that peace organizations were constantly changing their names, combining with other groups to form new bodies, and producing regional and local offshoots, which sometimes became more important than the original organization. Some of these changes are indicated here, but it is only a partial accounting.

1815	New York Peace Society Massachusetts Peace Society
1816	Society for the Promotion of Permanent and Universal Peace (England, later, known as Peace Society)
1821	Société de la morale chrétienne (France)
1828	American Peace Society
1830	La société de la paix de Genève
1838	New England Non-Resistance Society
1843	Universal Peace Congress (London)
1846	League of Universal Brotherhood (England and the United States)
1848	World Peace Congress (Brussels)
1849	World Peace Congress (Paris)
1850	World Peace Congress (Frankfurt)
1851	World Peace Congress (London)
1858	Ligue de bien public (Belgium)
1866	Universal Peace Society (United States, later renamed Universal Peace Union)
1867	Ligue internationale et permanente de la paix (Paris, becoming in 1872, Société des amis de la paix, and in 1888, Société français pour l'arbitrage entre nations) Ligue internationale de la paix et de la liberté (Geneva)

	Union de la paix (Le Havre)
1868	Association internationale des femmes (Geneva)
1869	Lega della pace e della libertà (Turin)
1871	Algemeen Nederlandsche Vredebond (Dutch Peace Society, after 1901, Vrede door Recht) Workmen's Peace Association (England, became International Arbitration League)
1873	Institute of International Law (Ghent) Association for the Reform and Codification of the Law of Nations (Brussels, reorganized as International Law Association in 1895)
1877	International Arbitration and Peace Association (England)
1878	Congres international des amis de la paix (France) Lega di libertà, fratellanza e pace (Milan)
1879	Women's Local Peace Association (England, became the Wisbech Local Peace Association in 1881)
1880	International Arbitration and Peace Association of Great Britain and Ireland
1882	National Arbitration League (United States) Society for Promotion of Danish Neutrality (first Danish peace society, later became Danish Peace Society, and still later Danish Peace and League of Nations Society)
1883	Swedish Peace and Arbitration Society
1884	Groupe des amis de la paix du Puy de Dôme (France)
1886	Christian Arbitration and Peace Society (United States) Liverpool and Birkenhead Women's Peace and Arbitration Association (England) Société de la paix du familistère du guise (France) Ligue internationale des femmes pour le désarmement général (Paris, became in 1900 Alliance universelle des femmes pour la paix par l'éducation)
1887-88	Association des jeunes amis de la paix (France, later La Paix par le droit) Società per la pace e l'arbitrato internazionale-Unione Lombarda (Milan) Associazione per l'arbitrato e per la pace internazionale (Rome) Friends Peace Committee (England)
1889	Première Conférence interparlementaire (Paris; later the Interparliamentary Union, annual meetings held until World War I) World Peace Congress (Paris; peace congresses met annually with only five interruptions until World War I) Nihon Heiwa-kai (first Japanese peace society) Société suisse de la paix (Switzerland) Publication of Bertha von Suttner's *Die Waffen Nieder* Società della pace (Florence) Società della pace (Venice)
1889-90	First Pan American Conference (Washington)

1890	Società della pace (Palermo)
1891	Österreichische Friedensgesellschaft (Austrian Peace Society) International Peace Bureau (Berne) Società della pace e l'arbitrato internazionale (Perugia)
1892	Deutsche Friedensgesellschaft (German Peace Society) Alliance des savants et des philanthropes (France)
1894	Société chrétienne pour la propagande de la paix (Switzerland)
1895	First Lake Mohonk Arbitration Conference (United States) Norwegian Peace Association Hungarian Peace Society Union internationale des femmes pour la paix I (Paris and London)
1896	National Arbitration Conference (Washington) Bureau française de la paix Ligue des femmes pour la paix et pour le désarmement international (France, later called L'Alliance universelle des femmes pour la paix et pour le désarmement)
1898	Anti-Imperialist League (United States) Swedish Women's Peace Association Association "Le paix et le désarmement par les femmes" (Paris)
1899	First Hague Peace Conference Association des femmes du suède pour la paix (Sweden) Société chrétienne des amis de la paix (France)
1900	Peace and Humanity Society (Melbourne, Australia)
1901	First Nobel Peace Prize awarded Société de l'éducation pacifique (France and Belgium) Société castraise de la paix (France)
1902	Délégation permanente des societes françaises de la paix League of Peace (Romania) International Museum of War and Peace (Lucerne)
1903	Groupe de l'arbitrage international (France)
1904	National Council of Peace Societies (England, became National Peace Council in 1908) International Anti-Militarist Union (Netherlands) Canadian Peace and Arbitration Society
1905	Zurich Anti-Militarism League
1906	Japan Peace Society Melbourne Peace Society (Australia) Victorian Peace Society (Australia) American Association for International Conciliation American Society of International Law
1907	Second Hague Peace Conference National Arbitration and Peace Congress (Washington) New South Wales Peace Society (Australia) Peace Union (Finland)

1908	Creation of Central American International Court of Justice
1909	Ligue des Catholiques français pour la paix (France)
1910	Carnegie Endowment for International Peace (United States) World Peace Foundation (United States) National Peace Council (New Zealand) American Society for the Judicial Settlement of International Disputes Publication of Norman Angell's *The Great Illusion* Catholic Peace Association (London)
1911	Swedish Peace Association Commission on International Justice and Goodwill (United States) Ligue internationale des pacifistes Catholiques (France)
1913	Northern Friends Peace Board (England)
1914	Church Peace Union (United States) No-Conscription Fellowship (England) Australian Peace Alliance Dutch Anti-War Council World Alliance for International Friendship Through the Churches (Geneva) Union of Democratic Control (England)
1915	Woman's Peace Party (United States) League to Enforce Peace (United States) Fellowship of Reconciliation (England) League of Nations Society (England) Canadian Women's Peace Party Women's Peace Army (Australia) Henry Ford's Peace Expedition (1915-16) Central Organization for a Durable Peace (The Hague) International Congress of Women (The Hague, led in 1919 to formation of Women's International League for Peace and Freedom)
1916	National Conference for Continuous Mediation (Stockholm) American Union Against Militarism
1917	American Friends Service Committee People's Council of America for Peace and Freedom No-Conscription League (New York)
1918	League of Nations Union (England) Friedensbund Deutscher Katholiken (Germany)
1919	Nie Wieder Krieg! (Never Again War!, Germany) League of Nations established Women's International League for Peace and Freedom (Zurich)
1920	Peace Union of Finland Peace Organization of Swedish Teachers League of Nations Association of Japan Gandhi starts first nonviolent civil disobedience campaign
1921	Women's Peace Society (United States) No More War Movement (England)

	War Resisters' International (originally established as PACO; became WRI in 1923) Washington Naval Disarmament Conference (1921-22) Women's Peace Society (Japan) International Anti-Militarist Bureau (Netherlands) National Council for Prevention of War (United States)
1922	Deutsche Liga für Menschenrechte (Germany)
1923	Announcement of Edward M. Bok's American Peace Award League of Nations Non-Partisan Association (United States, changed name to League of Nations Association in 1929) Antimilitaristic Union (Finland) Woodrow Wilson Foundation (United States) War Resisters League (United States)
1924	National Conference on the Cause and Cure of War (United States)
1925	Nordic Teachers' Peace Organization (Denmark) Union of Antimilitary Ministers in Switzerland
1927	Geneva Naval Disarmament Conference Catholic Association for International Peace (United States)
1928	National Anti-War League of Japan No More War Movement (New Zealand) Kellogg-Briand Peace Pact [Pact of Paris]
1929	Anti-War Congress of Intellectuals (Frankfurt)
1930	London Naval Disarmament Conference Second all-India nonviolent civil disobedience campaign starts
1931	Emergency Peace Committee (United States) Interorganization Council on Disarmament (United States) Ligue internationale des combattants de la paix (France)
1932	National Peace Conference (United States) General Disarmament Conference (Geneva, 1932-34) Co-operative Commonwealth Federation (Canada)
1933	Argentine Anti-War Pact Catholic Worker Movement (United States) American League Against War and Fascism (later, American League for Peace and Democracy)
1934	Peace Ballot (England)
1936	International Mennonite Peace Committee Peace Pledge Union (England) First World Peace Congress (Brussels) PAX (England) Emergency Peace Campaign (United States)
1937	No-Foreign-War Crusade (United States) Christian Peace Union of Switzerland Rassemblement international contre la guerre et le militarisme (Paris)
1938	Keep America Out of War Congress

1939	Commission to Study the Organization of Peace (United States)
1942	Congress of Racial Equality (United States) Publication of Quincy Wright's *A Study of War*
1943	Publication of Wendell Willkie's *One World*
1944	Pax Christi (France)
1945	French Institute of Polemology (Paris) Republication of Emery Reeves' *The Anatomy of Peace* United Nations Organization established
1946	Swiss Peace Council
1947	United World Federalists (United States)
1948	Canadian Peace Congress
1949	Finish Peace Committee Australian Peace Council First World Congress of Peace Partisans (Paris, launched World Council of Peace)
1951	Medical Association for Prevention of War (England)
1955	Japan Council Against Atomic Weapons Bertrand Russell-Albert Einstein Manifesto
1957	National Committee for a SANE Nuclear Policy (United States) Committee for Nonviolent Action (United States) (First) Pugwash Conference (on Science and World Affairs) (Pugwash, Canada) *Journal of Conflict Resolution* begins publication (United States)
1958	Campaign for Nuclear Disarmament (England)
1959	Student Peace Union (United States) Peace Research Institute (Oslo) Center for Research on Conflict Resolution (Ann Arbor, MI)
1960	Voice of Women (Canada) Women Strike for Peace (United States) Committee of 100 (England)
1961	Turn Toward Peace (United States) Canadian Peace Research Institute
1962	Canadian Campaign for Nuclear Disarmament
1963	Encyclical *Pacem in Terris*
1964	*Journal of Peace Research* begins publication (Norway)
1965	International Peace Research Association Inaugural Conference (Netherlands) Japanese Congress Against A- and H-bombs
1966	Stockholm International Peace Research Institute Interchurch Peace Council (Netherlands)
1967	World Without War Council (United States)
1970	Comité national d'action pour la paix et le développement (Belgium)

1973	Nihon heiwa gakkai (Peace Studies Association of Japan)
1974	Samarbejdskomiteen for Fred og Sikkerhed (Liaison Committee for Peace and Security, Denmark)
1975	Overleg Centrum voor Vrede (Belgium)
1979	World Disarmament Campaign (England) Vlaams Aktic Komitee Tegen Atoomwapeds (Belgium)
1980	European Nuclear Disarmament Campaign (England) Kvinder for Fred (Women for Peace, Denmark) Nej til Tomvaben (No to Nuclear Weapons, Denmark)
1981	European Nuclear Disarmament (England) Movement for National Independence, International Peace and Disarmament (Greece)
1982	European Nuclear Disarmament Convention (Brussels) Comité pour le désarmement nucléaire en France
1983	Second European Nuclear Disarmament Convention (Berlin)

ABBREVIATIONS

Abbreviations for frequently cited reference sources

DAB	*Dictionary of American Biography*
DNB	*Dictionary of National Biography*
LT	London *Times*
NAW	*Notable American Women*
NCAB	*The National Cyclopaedia of American Biography*
NYT	*New York Times*

OTHER ABBREVIATIONS

AL Alabama
AK Alaska
AZ Arizona
AR Arkansas
CA California
CO Colorado
CT Connecticut
DE Delaware
FL Florida
GA Georgia
HI Hawaii
ID Idaho
IL Illinois
IN Indiana
IA Iowa
KS Kansas
KY Kentucky
LA Louisiana
ME Maine
MD Maryland
MA Massachusetts
MI Michigan
MN Minnesota
MS Mississippi
MO Missouri
MT Montana
NE Nebraska
NV Nevada
NH New Hampshire
NJ New Jersey
NM New Mexico
NY New York
NC North Carolina
ND North Dakota
n.d. no date
n.p. no publisher
n.s. new series
OH Ohio
OK Oklahoma
OR Oregon
PA Pennsylvania
RI Rhode Island
SC South Carolina
SD South Dakota
TN Tennessee
TX Texas
UT Utah
VT Vermont
VA Virginia
WA Washington
WV West Virginia
WI Wisconsin
WY Wyoming

BIOGRAPHICAL DICTIONARY OF MODERN PEACE LEADERS

A

ABBOTT, Lyman (18 December 1835, Roxbury, MA—22 October 1922, New York). *Education*: B.A., New York Univ., 1853. *Career*: Congregational minister, author, editor, *Outlook*.

Lyman Abbott's long and rewarding career coincided with a vast upheaval in American life. Spending his early adulthood amidst sectional strife and civil war, he was to witness the strains of rapid industrialization, unparalleled urban growth, and the nation's ascent to world power. As a clergyman, author, and editor, Abbott worked hard to understand these events and to interpret them for a frequently bewildered public.

Although quite successful, Abbott's preparation for this self-appointed task was by no means extraordinary. He graduated from New York University in 1853 and worked for several years in his brothers' law office before fulfilling a childhood desire to enter the ministry. Meanwhile he had begun to write for several periodicals, and in 1881 he replaced Henry Ward Beecher as editor of the *Christian Union*, subsequently renamed the *Outlook*. On Beecher's death six years later, Abbott also succeeded him as pastor of Brooklyn's fashionable Plymouth Church.

Always liberal in his theology, Abbott had little trouble accepting the new scientific revelations, including the unsettling theory of evolution. He merely asserted that God had ordained the evolutionary process. Jesus himself had been sent as an instrument of social progress, and it was the duty of his followers to accelerate social evolution by obeying the Master's commandments.

In his *Christianity and Social Problems* (1896), a collection of essays which had appeared in the *Outlook*, Abbott applied his evolutionary social gospel to a host of modern problems, including the question of war and peace. He had no doubt that war was contrary to divine plans for social progress: Jesus had refused to lift a hand against those who arrested and tormented him, and he repeatedly counseled passive resistance in response to individual persecution. Yet it was quite acceptable to use force on behalf of others, as Jesus did when he drove the money changers out of the Temple with a whip. In the modern world, however, governments had assumed the charge of protecting others; only the state could legitimately employ force against violence and evil.

Unfortunately, this civilized arrangement usually did not extend beyond national boundaries, each country continuing to exist in a state of nature with regard to its neighbors. The only solution, according to Abbott, was international law and compulsory arbitration of disputes. He accordingly took an active part in the annual Conferences on International Arbitration at Lake Mohonk, New York, and was quite enthusiastic over the establishment of The Hague Tribunal.

Until the advent of universal law, however, individual governments were obliged to uphold justice and order as best they could. The United States had been impelled to wage a pittiless war against slavery and disunion, just as it launched a crusade three decades later against Spanish brutality in Cuba. And when World War I broke out in 1914, Abbott loudly proclaimed that his country had a Christian duty to join the resistance against German barbarism. He had worked earnestly for peace so long as he thought it possible, but he was no pacifist. Until a gentler day had dawned, the righteous nations of the earth would continue to act as God's avenging angels.

Bibliography:

A. *Christianity and Social Problems* (Boston, 1896); *The Evolution of Christianity* (Boston, 1892); *Reminiscences* (Boston, 1915); *The Theology of an Evolutionist* (Boston, 1897); *What Christianity Means to Me* (New York, 1921).

B. Ira V. Brown, *Lyman Abbott, Christian Evolutionist* (Cambridge, MA, 1953).

C. Abbott Manuscript Collection, Bowdoin College.

David R. Contosta

ABE Isō (4 February 1865, Fukuoka, Japan—10 February 1949, Tokyo). *Education*: B.A., Dōshisha Univ., 1884; B.D., Hartford Theological Seminary, 1894. *Career*: pastor, Okayama Congregational Church, 1887-91, faculty member, Dōshisha, 1895-99, Tokyo Semmon Gakkō (Waseda Univ.), 1899-1949; author, antiwar activist, and political leader.

Known as the Father of Socialism in Japan, Abe Isō helped in 1901 to found the first socialist party whose platform established a tradition of pacifism and antimilitarism on the left which remains to this day. He participated in a campaign against the Russo-Japanese War at the beginning of his career and, nearly forty years later, climaxed his political life by resigning in protest against his party's compromise with the increasingly warlike policies of the government. He also worked for urban, industrial, and agricultural reform, promoted temperance and women's rights, and even introduced baseball to his country.

Soon after Abe's return from study in the United States in 1895, he began to cooperate with other intellectuals and labor leaders to form a political party that would represent the interests of working people. In the face of strong government opposition they published a newspaper, *Heimin Shimbun* (*People's News*), but with the end of the Russo-Japanese War the coalition split into materialist and Christian-pacifist parties. Although Abe struggled to maintain connections with both groups, his sympathies clearly lay with the pacifists. After 1918 he emerged as one of the most able leaders of the non-Marxist left in labor and politics. In 1928 he was elected to the Diet as a Social-Democratic member, a post he held with one short interruption until his resignation twelve years later. Already in his seventies, he retired from political life to emerge again briefly after the Pacific War as an advisor to the revived Socialist party.

Abe's antiwar ideas appeared in three main areas. First, they surfaced in the strongly antimilitaristic stand taken by the first socialist party, whose manifesto was largely written by him. Secondly they emerged in the speeches and articles he wrote for the campaign against the Russo-Japanese War, which appeared mainly in the *Heimin Shimbun* and its Christian-pacifist successor, *Shin Kigen* (*New Age*). And finally they appeared in a series of articles he wrote for the journal of the Tokyo Unitarian Association, *Rikugō Zasshi* (*Cosmos*), which he edited between 1899 and 1911. These ideas were characterized by a strongly cosmopolitan and humanitarian tone. War, he believed, was evil because it leads to exploitation of weak nations by strong and of the lower classes by the upper. Moreover armaments created a financial burden on the common people and diverted funds away from social welfare.

The rugged individualism of Dōshisha's founder, Niijima Jō, combined with *Leo Tolstoy's gospel of nonresistance, seem to have been the earliest influences in forming Abe's pacifism. Later, his reading of Ivan Bloch and the Christian socialists led him to build up certain economic arguments against war. But economics always remained for Abe an auxiliary to morality. While his ideas remained utopian and idealistic, his activity on the other hand exhibited a high degree of pragmatic realism. This latter bent allowed him to survive (in spite of one attempted assassination) at a time when many leftists fell victim to police brutality or direct action.

Abe's pacifism, like his socialism, exhibited certain ambiguities and inconsistencies, of which he himself was clearly conscious. Yet he stood throughout his life as a symbol of integrity with which powerless people could identify, though they themselves might remain impotent in the face of a militaristic society. When war resisters in Japan today express opposition to the alteration of their "Peace Constitution," it is to the tradition founded by people like Abe that they look.

Bibliography:

A. "The Second Restoration," in Ryusaku Tsunoda, ed., *Sources of Japanese Tradition* (New York, 1958), 816-20.

B. Cyril H. Powles, "Abe Isoo: The Utility Man," in Nobuya Bamba and John F. Howes, ed., *Pacifism in Japan: The Christian and Socialist Tradition* (Vancouver, 1978), 143-67; Katayama Tetsu, *Abe Isō den* (Tokyo, 1958); Takano Zen'ichi, *Nihon shakai shugi no chichi Abe Isō* (Tokyo, 1970).

Cyril Powles

ADDAMS, Jane (6 September 1860, Cedarville, IL—21 May 1935, Chicago). *Education*: B.A., Rockford Coll.,1881. *Career*: co-founder and head resident, Hull House, 1889-1935; international president, Women's International League for Peace and Freedom, 1915-29; reformer, pacifist author, and lecturer.

As an organizer and leader of the international women's peace movement, Jane Addams envisioned a world community in which the peaceful arbitration of conflict would promote a more just and democratic order. Only through international cooperation in the economic, political, and social spheres and with the establishment of a lasting peace would nations be able to devote their resources to the basic needs of all of their citizens. According to Addams, women—because of their historic role in protecting, nurturing, and conserving human life—brought a special perspective to these spheres. By extending these traditional values to the international arena, women added a new dimension to the voice of internationalism and a potentially powerful force for promoting peace.

Addams determined from her work at Chicago's Hull House that the changing conditions wrought by industrialization and urbanization demanded the creation of a new set of social values. Rejecting the ethic of individualism as unsatisfactory, she promoted the alternative of cooperative endeavor. Society had to refrain from depending on the "old warlike virtues" and seek to establish William James' "moral equivalent of war." Addams ultimately saw the immigrant neighborhood surrounding Hull House as a microcosm of the world community. Nations, like cities, needed a new approach to solving increasingly complex problems, and Addams often pointed to the international organizations of labor and women, as well as to The Hague Court, as evidence of a growing internationalist spirit. For Addams, as for other pre-World War I peace leaders, the establishment of The Hague Court was the clearest demonstration of the progress from war to the principle of arbitration.

The outbreak of the First World War, however, challenged Addams' progressive ideals. Through the fall of 1914, Addams, as chair of the Chicago Emergency Peace Federation and as a member of the Round Table Conference on the War meeting in New York's Henry Street Settlement, formulated a plan for neutral mediation. Dissatisfied with existing peace groups, she also considered the desirability of a separate woman's peace organization. With suffragist *Carrie Chapman Catt, Addams called for a meeting of women's organizations in Washington, D. C. Convening on January 10, 1915, the group formally created the Woman's Peace party (WPP) and elected Addams chair. The WPP articulated plans for the immediate concern of stopping the fighting as well as for the long range principles for a new international order, including the nationalization of armaments, democratic control of foreign policy, and woman suffrage.

Addams recognized the necessity of extending and creating new contacts with European women. Therefore, she quickly agreed to preside over an International Congress of Women which met at The Hague in April 1915. The Congress created the International Committee of Women for Permanent Peace (ICWPP), with Addams as international president. Resolutions adopted by the Congress charged the ICWPP with arranging a second congress to be held at the time and place of the peace negotiations and appointed two delegations to travel to the European capitals to advance the cause of continuous mediation. As a member of one of the delegations, Addams interviewed high ranking statesmen in the belligerent governments to find the conditions under which mediation would be acceptable.

While traveling, Addams saw, first hand, the destructiveness of war and heard the genuine desire for peace expressed by many citizens. In several essays appearing in *Women at The Hague* (1915), she maintained that the all-pervasive war mentality effectively kept people from uniting and identifying common interests. Developing an effective peace lobby was highly unlikely if people were unduly influenced by nationalistic voices. She concluded that war not only challenged man's moral sensibilities but also challenged women's deepest instincts for survival.

After her return from Europe, Addams continued to lobby for a conference of neutral nations, privately meeting with +Woodrow Wilson and +Edward House. She also supported Henry Ford's plan for a conference of unofficial delegates from the neutral countries. Illness, however, prevented her from sailing on Ford's peace ship in December 1915 and from attending the conference meetings in Europe. At home, she testified, as chair of the Woman's Peace party, against proposals for conscription and rearmament, and organized, with other pacifist groups, such as the American Union Against Militarism, resistance against the call for preparedness. Even when America's entry in the war became imminent, Addams helped to organize a new Emergency Peace Committee in February 1917, convinced that public opinion could still be aroused.

With the declaration of war, Addams' pacifism isolated her from many of her former colleagues in the progressive reform and peace movements. Working with *Roger Baldwin and the National Civil Liberties Bureau, she protested the passage of the Espionage Act and the state syndicalist laws, monitored the treatment of conscientious objectors, and lobbied for provisions in the conscription law for nonreligious objectors. Her moral outrage against the hardship and destruction caused by the war similarly impelled her to lecture for the U. S. Food Administration in 1917 and 1918 on conservation and the conditions of a starving Europe. From the squalor and deprivation of Chicago's west side to war-ridden Europe, people's basic needs and rights always required protection.

In July 1919, Addams presided over the second International Congress of Women, held in Zurich, where she was chosen as international president of the newly formed Women's International League for Peace and Freedom (WILPF). Following the meetings, she personally delivered the Congress' resolutions condemning the terms of the Treaty of Versailles and the proposed League of Nations to the American delegation in Paris. Particularly concerned with the effects of the Allied blockade, Addams also traveled with her colleague, *Alice Hamilton, through Germany under the auspices of the American Friends Service Committee in order to assess and publicize the plight of the starving European population.

As international president of the WILPF from 1919 to 1929, Addams worked tirelessly to raise funds, developed organizational procedures, and often mediated internal conflicts. She presided over the four International Congresses held in the 1920s, attended Executive Committee meetings when possible and, in the interim, maintained close contact with the International Office in Geneva. Her speeches and published writings contributed to the visibility of the WILPF and publicized its goals and principles. Above all, her persuasive moral voice guided the WILPF through difficult choices as it matured as an organization. With reluctance, she resigned her position in 1929 due to poor health; yet, she remained involved and informed as honorary president, and the WILPF continued to call upon her for advice.

Addams' international reputation was further enhanced in 1931 when she shared the Nobel Prize with +Nicholas Murray Butler. A woman of deep conviction, she articulated those inviolate principles upon which international relationships should be based. Only through disarmament and a continuing process of arbitration would the world avoid the terrible catastrophe of war and its consequences. Through her leadership of the WILPF, Addams advanced an internationalist perspective that called for the participation of all citizens in the search for an order that valued life over death and liberty over coercion.

Bibliography:

A. *Newer Ideals of Peace* (New York, 1907); *Peace and Bread in Time of War* (New York, 1922).

B. Allen Davis, *American Heroine* (New York, 1973); John Ferrell, *Beloved Lady: A History of Jane Addams' Ideas on Reform and Peace* (Baltimore, 1967); Sondra Herman, "Jane Addams: The Community as a Neighborhood," in *Eleven Against War* (Stanford, 1969).

C. Jane Addams Memorial Collection, University of Illinois at Chicago Circle; Jane Addams Papers, Swarthmore College Peace Collection.

Nancy Ann Slote

ALAIN [CHARTIER, Emile-Auguste] (3 March 1868, Mortagne-au Perche, France—2 June 1951, Vésinet). *Education*: Lycée d'Alençon, 1881; Lycée de Vanves, 1886-89; Agrégé in philosophy, Ecole normale supérieure, 1892. *Career*: lycée professor, philosopher, literary critic, journalist, and pacifist propagandist.

Alain was the principal French philosophical spokesman for radicalism in the twentieth century. In the period between the wars, he linked his radical politics and Cartesian rationalism with integral pacifism, that is, with an absolute opposition to warfare.

Alain attended the Ecole Normale Superieure from 1889-92 and taught as a lycée professor for the remainder of his career. His politics were formed during the Dreyfus Affair, when he defended the Republic, taught at the popular universities, and joined the struggle against the army, church, and higher administration of France. The core of Alain's political philosophy was a fundamental distrust of power, specifically of a strong executive. He connected his opposition to tyranny to protection of the individual, respect for laws and constitutions, faith in the principles of economic liberalism, and a generalized optimism about secular education. At age 46 Alain was mobilized to fight in the heavy artillery during World War I.

Historians view Alain as one of the illustrious teacher-philosophers of the Third Republic; he influenced generations of French students, including *Simone Weil, Jean Prévost, Pierre Bost, Henri Massis, Maurice Schumann, and the pacifist professor, *Michel Alexandre. He wrote thousands of *Propos* for newspapers, journals, several collections of which became best-sellers. The *Propos* were concise, elegant, ironic observations, usually with an elevated philosophical twist or moralist turn to them. Alain wrote numerous books on aesthetics, literature, fine arts, music, mythology, and philosophy. In literature his heroes were Balzac, Stendhal, and Dickens. Philosophically, he was drawn to Plato, Descartes, Kant, and Comte. Alain placed his hopes for a democratic Republic on secular education and elite building through the school system; the lycée would function to make French citizens self-conscious and rational. Education was synonymous with a moral and mental discipline. Its goal was to train the will, thereby encouraging the individual toward hard work and self-control. The school aimed to remedy the defects of family education, to liberate children from animality, and to lead them to high intellectual and ethical attainments.

In 1921, Alain published *Mars, ou la guerre jugée*, a severe indictment of the First World War. Alain condemned war as a passionate crime. His pacifism was intransigent and militant though he never espoused conscientious objection or the doctrines of *Gandhi. His opposition to war remained a protest, never a springboard for rebellion. His antimilitarism went with his opposition to bureaucracy and to authority. He saw war as a destructive alloy of mysticism, drunkenness, and madness. War was a modern psychosis. Rejecting the Marxist or nationalist explanations for war, Alain felt that wars were neither motivated by class interests nor by reasons of sovereignty. Despite his total dismissal of Sigmund Freud's views, his stress was on the psychology of the warrior, on the soldier's enthusiasm and resignation, his anger and fear. With World War I as his paradigm, Alain held that war was a collective narrative of massacres, atrocities, and untold suffering. His basic critique of modern warfare stressed the ways in which violence masked itself in right, law, and force; the biggest injustice of war was hypocrisy. War abolished all individual liberties: press, expression, assembly, the right to think critically, and to question authority. Alain's antiwar writings vilify army officers, army discipline, and regimentation. He also had harsh remarks about the French bourgeoisie, safe at home in their armchairs, while the soldiers at the front were reduced to cannon fodder. War simply degraded man into a slave, a means, an object. By the 1930s Alain came to see all wars as wars of religions; all became legitimized as sacred crusades. Likewise, he judged all wars to be fascist, in the sense that fascist movements were born from or worked to prepare future wars.

In 1934 Alain joined with two other distinguished Parisian academics, Paul Rivet and Paul Langevin, to launch the Comité de vigilance des intellectuels antifascistes (Vigilance Committee of Antifascist Intellectuals). Alain's pacifistic antifascism was only temporarily consistent with Popular Front politics. His absolute pacifism moved in the direction of appeasement, not toward left-wing coalitions and a strong "no" to fascism, either in Spain or in France. Alain called for immediate peace until 1939, underestimating the Hitlerian danger. He argued that the only way to save peace was to renounce all preparation for war.

Alain systematically ignored fascist intentions, always calling for conciliation and negotiation with Hitler. He viewed the struggle for peace as the same struggle as the one to reduce power. Clearly, this type of refusal was abstract and purely negative; peace depended on the conscience and courage of the individual resister. Peace became elevated into a supreme value—the work of reason and will.

Alain's pacifistic writings reflect a form of politics that refuses to recognize history. He never realized that World War I might not be universal, that other wars might have different causes, modalities, and consequences. He never challenged his own optimistic faith in education, in progress, and in the individual's capacity to resist powerful irrational currents. As a rational humanist and Kantian, Alain always wrote as a philosopher of freedom and a philosopher of the mind; he tenaciously held onto a view of the power of the human will. His blend of pacifism and self-styled "petty-bourgeois radical politics" stands out in the interwar period both for its forceful expression of a moral view and for its conspicuous illusion and weakness.

Bibliography:

A. *Eléments d'une doctrine radicale* (Paris, 1925); *Histoire de mes pensées* (Paris, 1936); *Mars, ou la querre jugée* (Paris, 1921); *Propos* (Paris, 1956); *Souvenirs de guerre* (Paris, 1937).

B. André Maurois, *Alain* (Paris, 1951); Georges Pascal, *L'Idée de philosophie chez Alain* (Paris, 1970); Olivier Reboul, *L'Homme et ses passions d'après Alain* (Paris, 1968).

David James Fisher

ALBERDI, Juan Bautista (29 August 1810, Tucumán Province, Argentina—18 June 1884, Paris). *Education*: Diploma, Collegio de Ciencias Morales, 1831; B.A., Univ. of San Carlos, 1834; studies in law, Academia Practica de Buenos Aires, 1835-36. *Career*: Argentine plenipotentiary, political thinker, writer, lawyer, and congressional delegate.

Juan Bautista Alberdi was one of the most important nineteenth century Argentine political thinkers. After joining the Association of May, a group opposed to the dictator Juan Manuel Rosas, Alberdi was forced into exile in Chile where he wrote his major work, *Bases* (1852). There he argued for a central, federal government with a constitution similar to that of the United States, increased migration, and foreign capital.

In the 1850s after Justo José de Urquiza overthrew Rosas, he appointed Alberdi as Argentina's plenipotentiary to Paris, Madrid, Washington, and London. Alberdi helped to gain recognition for Argentina's independence from Spain and acceptance of Urquiza's government as the federation's legitimate one. Soon, however, Alberdi's adversary, Bartolomé Mitre, assumed power. This, coupled with Alberdi's opposition to the War of the Triple Alliance, in which Argentina, Brazil, and Uruguay were allied against Paraguay, again forced him into exile. He died in Paris in 1884.

Alberdi viewed peace from a traditional Spanish legal viewpoint rather than an English judicial or pacifist one. He opposed Argentina's participation in the

War of the Triple Alliance as a violation of Paraguay's international rights and charged that Argentina's alliance with the Brazilian monarchy was alien to the American system. He also chose to ignore the dictatorial aspects of the Francisco Solano Lopez regime.

As early as 1844 Alberdi called for the organization of a general American congress. He urged such a congress to discuss arms limitation, establish an international peace tribunal, codify American international law, and examine ways to regulate and prevent future warfare. He also championed immigration of an educated, civilized population to strengthen the economic sector and supersede the military as a national foundation. Alberdi believed that Pan Americanism and international peace consisted of a community of mutual interests among the American nations, while the independence of each state was respected. These ideas, the forerunner of the Organization of American States, differed from the purely defensive nature of the Monroe Doctrine, which divided the world into two systems.

Alberdi's internationalist ideas matured over the years, and in 1870 he submitted a prize winning essay to a French peace society. It was published posthumously as *El Crimen de la Guerra* (1915), calling for a new world order based upon the renunciation of war as an instrument of policy and the gradual evolution of the body politic toward world government. Alberdi saw territorial expansion and personal ambition as the key motives for warfare and argued that national leaders who initiated wars must be held responsible for their consequences. He also believed that public revenues financed military power and reduced a nation's productivity. The military, munitions industries, and professionals who taught warfare were key segments profiting from conflict. Alberdi claimed that financing the nonproductive military sector enslaved the population through conscription and impoverished the nation with increased public debt. Conflict depressed agriculture, trade, and industry. Population losses which, through battle casualties or emigration or reduced immigration of "civilized" people, were a major war "crime." Reduced immigration was especially disastrous for the developing South American republics.

Alberdi asserted that neutrality supplemented by popular participation in government was the most significant peace agent. Peace signified order as long as liberty was not equated with power. Alberdi rejected opportunistic alliances and promoted arbitration to relieve Argentina's military burden.

Bibliography:

A. *Bases y punto de partida para la organización política de la República Argentina* (Santiago, 1852); *El Crimen de la Guerra* (Buenos Aires, 1915); *Las Disensiones de las Repúblicas del Plata y las Maquinaciones del Brasil* (Buenos Aires, 1865); *Interés, peligros y garantías de los estados del Pacífico en las regiones orientales de la América del Sud*, (Buenos Aires, 1866); *Memoria sobre la conveniencia y objetos de un congreso general americano* (Santiago, 1844).

B. Harold Eugene Davis, "Juan Bautista Alberdi, Americanist," *Journal of Inter-American Studies*, 4 (January 1962), 53-65; Juan Carlos Gómez Haedo, *Las Ideas políticas de Alberdi* (Montevideo, 1924); Leopold Kanner, *El Concepto de patria en Alberdi* (Rosario, 1960); José Nicolas Matienzo, *La Politica Americana de Alberdi* (Buenos Aires, 1910); Ernesto Quesada, *La Figura histórica de Alberdi* (Buenos Aires, 1919); Pablo Rojas Paz, *Alberdi, el ciudadano de la soledad* (Buenos Aires, 1941); Idalia Flores G. de Zaraza, *Juan Bautista Alberdi y la defensa del Paraguay en la guerra contra la Triple Alianza* (Buenos Aires, 1976).

John A. Jackson, Jr.

ALBUQUERQUE, Antônio Coelho de Sá e (1821, Guararapes, Pernambuco, Brazil—1868, at sea off the Brazilian coast). *Career*: Brazilian senator; minister of agriculture, commerce and public works, 1861-62; minister of foreign affairs and secretary of state, 1861, 1866-67; diplomat, politician, and administrator.

A number of capable public servants represented the nineteenth-century Empire of Brazil. Antônio Coelho de Sá e Albuquerque was one who enhanced international amity while his nation engaged in a destructive international conflict.

Albuquerque first won plaudits as a peacemaker when, as a provincial administrator during the 1850s, he calmed local unrest by failing to enforce a hated regulation. He also represented the province of Pernambuco in the Brazilian Senate and was twice foreign minister in the subsequent decade. Albuquerque enjoyed a brief tenure in the Foreign Affairs Office during 1861, receiving experience in attempting to resolve claims and boundary questions. He assumed the post again on April 21, 1866, as part of a government headed by the brilliant Liberal party leader, Zacharias de Góes e Vasconcellos.

Two international conflicts subsequently claimed his attention. Brazil allied herself to Argentina and Uruguay in a savagely fought conflict with Paraguay from 1865 to 1870. A quadruple alliance of Peru, Chile, Ecuador, and Bolivia simultaneously faced Spain in a naval war. Albuquerque firmly upheld Rio's neutrality in the Pacific conflict. He insisted that Spanish war vessels visiting Brazil not engage in further hostilities but refused to allow their detention by Peru. This stand won applause from neither side but contributed to peace by depriving a belligerent of a potential base and promoting Brazilian noninvolvement.

Brazil could ill afford diplomatic wrangles. The Pacific allies felt that Paraguayan War would produce Brazilian territorial expansion. Brazil, however, feared the Paraguayan dictator, Francisco Solano López, and insisted on his overthrow. Declaring that Brazil desired peace with her neighbors, but not at the cost of safety, Albuquerque turned down mediation offers. Bolivia, fearing a loss of territory, massed troops at her Argentine border in 1866. Albuquerque responded by promulgating a liberal boundary treaty with La Paz on the basis of *uti possedetis* or giving title to the nation actually controlling disputed lands. Bolivia also gained an arbitral commission and Atlantic access. Negotiations for a boundary treaty with Peru, however, were not continued by Albuquerque's successor.

The Bolivian treaty of 1867 promoted the principle of free navigation of rivers in southern South America. Albuquerque also reversed the longstanding Brazilian policy of excluding foreign vessels from the Amazon. This removed another potential source of international disputes.

Albuquerque died soon after leaving office in 1867. Though not a consistent advocate of peace, his actions, on balance, lessened international tensions in South America.

Bibliography:

B. José Manuel Cardoso de Oliveira, *Actos diplomáticos do Brasil, tratados do periodo colonial e varios documentos desde 1493* (Rio de Janeiro, 1912); Argeu de Segadas Machado-Guimarães, *Diccionario bio-bibliográphico Brasileiro, de diplomacia, política externa e direito internacional* (Rio de Janeiro, 1938), 19-20.

Robert C. Hersch

ALESSANDRI PALMA, Arturo (20 December 1868, Hacienda Longaví, Chile—24 August 1950, Santiago). *Education:* Law Degree, Univ. of Chile, 1893. *Career*: member of House of Deputies, 1897-1915, senator, 1915-20, 1944-50, president, 1920-25, 1932-36.

Arturo Alessandri first attained national prominence in his defense of mine workers during the 1915 senatorial campaign in the nitrate region of Tarapacá. He drew large crowds as he championed labor reforms and introduced Chile to charismatic politics. Soon touted as the ''Lion of Tarapacá,'' not only did he win the senatorial race, but he gained such stature that five years later he captured the presidency. As chief executive he promised a program of social benefits, a labor code, political reform, and more government economic controls. Parliamentary bickering, however, stifled his initiatives and eventually contributed to military intervention in September 1924. The president chose self-exile in Italy, but three months later a reformist wing of the military empowered Alessandri's confidant, Emilio Bello Codesio, to enact most of the president's original program. Don Arturo himself resumed office in March 1925 and immediately began to draft a new constitution intended to increase executive authority. A national referendum approved the constitution which governed Chilean affairs for the next fifty years.

When Alessandri once again won the presidency in 1932, he encountered a nation of high unemployment, social unrest, military meddling, and financial prostration. Following the advice of his conservative finance minister, Gustavo Ross, he reduced government expenditure and cut business taxes. To better handle labor problems, he institutionalized collective bargaining. When necessary, however, he used force to keep both labor and the armed forces in line. The policies worked: Chile returned to full employment and solid finances. Not surprisingly the spartan measures created a backlash, with imprisoned military leaders and the Popular Front forming a coalition which won the next presidential election.

In the international sphere Alessandri made a concerted effort during his first term of office to resolve the festering problem of the Tacna-Arica boundary dispute. He encouraged United States arbitration and supervision of a plebescite. Negotiations broke down, nevertheless, and the dispute was resolved by a later administration. During his second term he helped initiate the negotiations which finally ended the Chaco War, he remained impartial in a Colombia-Peruvian dispute, and he supported the use of the Chilean embassy as a refugee haven during the Spanish Civil War.

Both progressive and conservative, democratic and authoritarian, Alessandri directed Chile through the crises of the early twentieth century. Historians usually prefer his liberal first administration to his more conservative second. Still, during this latter term his discouragement of military intervention and his resolution of socioeconomic problems gave extra life to Chilean democracy. Viewed in perspective of events four decades later, Alessandri's leadership in the 1920s and 1930s illustrates the work of a master politician and statesman who helped his country travel the difficult middle road.

Bibliography:

A. *Rectificación al tomo IX de la historia de América* (Santiago, 1941); *Recuerdos de gobierno*, (3 vols., Santiago, 1967).

B. Ricardo Donoso, *Alessandri, agitador y demoledor: cincuenta años de historia política de Chile*, (2 vols., Mexico, 1952, 1954); Luis Durand, *Don Arturo* (Santiago, 1952); Augusto Iglesias, *Una Etapa de la democracia en América* (Santiago, 1960); Frederick M. Nunn, *Chilean Politics 1920-31* (Albuquerque, 1970).

John L. Rector

ALEXANDRE, Michel (27 March 1888, Dieppe, France—14 December 1952, Paris). *Education*: licence ès-lettres, Univ. of Paris, 1905, agrégation de philosophie, 1912. *Career*: teacher of philosophy, 1913-40, 1944-52.

Two strong influences determined Michel Alexandre's life—his youthful illness that made him a contemplative rather than an active man, and his friendship with the thinker *Alain, who encouraged him in his commitment to philosophy and pacifism. From 1892 to 1903, Alexandre was bedridden with a painful hip ailment that required him to be tutored at home. His condition left him a reflective person sensitive to the misfortunes of others. When his health improved, he started his formal education and demonstrated intellectual brilliance, passing his *agrégation* in philosophy in 1912. In 1908 he made the friendship of the eminent philosopher Alain, whose quiet wisdom captivated the young Alexandre for the rest of his life. He absorbed the older man's aversion to war and violence as well as his calm understanding of human behavior. Becoming a teacher of philosophy, Alexandre taught at various provincial schools before rising to the lycée Henri IV in Paris.

Alexandre's poor health prevented him from serving in World War I. His hatred of armed conflict led him to become an active pacifist. He joined the Ligue des droits de l'homme (League for the Rights of Man) and the Société d'études documentaires et critiques sur la guerre (Society for the Documentary and Critical Study of the War), formed to examine and document the causes of war. At the same time he supported the International Committee of Women for a Permanent Peace, one of whose members, Jeanne Halbwachs, he soon married. The couple shared the same ideals and commitment to peace, working together closely to try to attain them. Alexandre believed that if each citizen actively sought to prevent war, public opinion could prevent a conflict even before it developed. He submitted to the Ligue des droits de l'homme a plan for peace with Germany through arbitration, but the patriotic organization rejected the scheme. Alexandre, who welcomed Russia's withdrawal from the war in 1918, displayed no enthusiasm for Bolshevism and unlike many other intellectuals, did not join the Communist party in 1920.

During the 1920s, Alexandre quietly labored on behalf of peace. He helped to send assistance to suffering families in Austria and Germany. He signed the "Appeal to Consciences" in 1926 which called for revision of the Treaty of Versailles as well as the "Appeal to Good Sense" in 1928 which demanded international disarmament. He established the *Libres propos*, a review devoted to peace and the ideas of Alain.

In 1934 Alexandre and his wife joined the Comité de vigilance des intellectuals antifascistes (Vigilance Committee of Antifascist Intellectuals), a group dedicated to fighting fascism at home and striving for international understanding. The organization supported the Popular Front in the elections of 1936 but split over the policy to be followed in regard to Nazi Germany. Unlike some members who sought a hard line against Hitler, Alexandre favored reconciliation with Germany through revision of the peace of 1919. At the time of the Munich crisis of 1938, the two Alexandres mobilized public opinion against war through meetings and manifestos. So well known was their pacifism that when *Louis Lecoin circulated his tract *Paix immédiate* in September 1939, he included their names without consulting them.

During World War II, Alexandre, who was a Jew, was barred from teaching and was briefly interned at a prison camp near Compiègne in 1941. Upon his release, he and his wife retired to the Unoccupied Zone where they remained throughout the war. After the Liberation, Alexandre resumed his teaching, winning the affection and admiration of his students, until his premature death. Few pacifists have remained as faithful to their ideals and as philosophical in their approach to war as Michel Alexandre.

Bibliography:

A. *En souvenir de Michel Alexandre. Leçons, textes, lettres* (Paris, 1956).

B. "Michel Alexandre," *Revue de métaphysique et de la morale*, 57 (October-December, 1952), 472; Nicole Racine-Furlaud, "Le Comité de Vigilance des Intellectuels Antifascistes (1934-1939). Antifascisme et pacifisme," *Le Mouvement social*, 101 (October-December, 1977), 87-113.

James Friguglietti

ALFARO, Ricardo Joaquin. See *Biographical Dictionary of Internationalists*.

ALLEN, Devere (24 June 1891, Providence, RI—27 August 1955, Wilton, CT). *Education*: B.A., Oberlin Coll., 1917. *Career*: editor, *The Rational Patriot*, 1917-18, *The Young Democracy*, 1918-21, *The World Tomorrow*, 1921-31, 1932-33, *Worldover Press*, 1933-55; pacifist author and historian.

With the outbreak of World War I, Devere Allen became a leader in a group of young pacifists at Oberlin and editor of their paper. He thus began a career as editor, journalist, and historian. A pacifist and socialist, he promulgated a reformist philosophy of nonviolent action; an internationalist, he promoted a transnational peace movement. He stood against parochialism and factionalism. Intellectually, he was of the lineage of *Elihu Burritt.

His writing at Oberlin came to the attention of pacifists on the East Coast, and in April 1918 he became the executive secretary of The Young Democracy and editor of its journal. In 1921 he joined *The World Tomorrow* as its managing editor, and he remained with the journal until 1933, except for a brief stint as an editor of *The Nation*. Working with leaders in the Fellowship of Reconciliation such as *John Nevin Sayre, *Kirby Page, and *Reinhold Niebuhr, Allen helped to make *The World Tomorrow* independent and creative, the chief journal of liberal social gospel and radical religious critique between the world wars. In this period he joined other liberal pacifists to support the *Norman Thomas wing of the Socialist party. He ran for senator in Connecticut in 1932 and was active in the national councils of the party.

Allen left *The World Tomorrow* in 1933 to establish the No-Frontier News Service, subsequently Worldover Press. This independent news service run by Allen and his wife, Marie, tapped radical and pacifist contributions in the United States and Europe, providing news of social movements and analyses of world events to the religious and labor press and to rural and small-town papers. In 1939 the Allens moved their service to Belgium, and, upon the German invasion, they moved again to Mexico. Following the war, they returned to their lifelong home in Wilton, Connecticut. Now largely forgotten, The Worldover Press had subscribers among major newspapers and received commendations for its vision of transnational understanding. It sought to be an agent linking worldwide peace movements and relating them to the general public. It did not outlast Allen's death in 1955.

Allen was a writer of broad interests: natural history, humor, genealogy, biography, and the history of peace movements. In addition to writing many articles and editorials, he edited an anthology of intimate biographical sketches of contemporary reformers, *Adventurous Americans*, and an anthology of essays on applied nonviolent action, *Pacifism in the Modern World*. Allen tried to define pacifism as an active strategy for the peaceful resolution of conflict and for justice at a time when the perimeters of that philosophy were first explored. He carried that approach to his most important work, *The Fight for Peace*, a history of the American peace movement from about 1815 to the postwar period. Allen strove for accuracy, but the hallmark of his book was its analysis of the social dynamics of peacemaking rather than descriptive narrative.

As a journalist, editor, and historian, Devere Allen sought to develop a peace philosophy that would transcend sectarian, ideological, and natural boundaries. He strove to define a kind of pacifism that would be reformist, coupling the values of peace and justice. In his writings he realistically assessed the foibles of peace advocates and the failure of militarist society. He viewed the cause of peace an an ongoing struggle in which he tried to contribute both specific instruments of action and a broader perspective.

Bibliography:

A. *Above All Nations* (London, 1945); *Adventurous Americans* (New York, 1932), *The Fight for Peace* (New York, 1930); *Pacifism in the Modern World* (New York, 1929).

B. Charles Chatfield, "The Life of Devere Allen," in Chatfield, ed., *Devere Allen: Life and Writings* (New York, 1976).

C. Devere Allen Papers, Swarthmore College Peace Collection.

Charles Chatfield

ALLEN, R. Clifford, Lord Allen of Hurtwood (9 May 1899, Newport, Monmouthshire, England—3 March 1939, Lausanne, Switzerland). *Education*: Berkhamstead School, 1902-5; University Coll., Bristol, 1905-8; B.A., Peterhouse Coll., Cambridge Univ. *Career*: secretary and general manager, *Daily Citizen*, 1911-15, chairman, No-Conscription Fellowship, 1914-19; treasurer and chairman, Independent Labour Party, 1922-25; chairman, *New Leader*, 1922-26; director, *Daily Herald*, 1926-30; chairman, Next Five Years Group, 1935-39; Executive Committee, League of Nations Union.

While he was at Cambridge, Clifford Allen shocked his Conservative Anglican family by declaring himself a socialist and enlisting in the Fabian Society. Allen's conversion to socialism marked the beginning of a life-long commitment to peace and social justice. For him, socialism and pacifism were always inexorably intertwined. Allen's debut in the peace movement was an anonymous article attacking the idea of compulsory military training at Cambridge, but his anonymity did not last. With the outbreak of World War I, Allen quickly became identified as one of Britain's leading "peace cranks," joining with Fenner Brockway and others in November 1914 to form the No-Conscription Fellowship (NCF).

As NCF Chairman, Allen needed all of his considerable charm and administrative ability to weld the Fellowship's widely diverse elements into Britain's largest and most effective anticonscription organization. As an absolutist conscientious objector, Allen refused all compromise with the authorities and eventually served sixteen months at hard labor. He was released only after suffering irreparable physical damage which made him a semi-invalid for the rest of his life.

The NCF disbanded in 1919, and during the succeeding decade Allen had little direct association with the peace movement. Because he believed that peace and social justice could best be realized through the electoral triumph of a resolutely socialist Labour party, Allen pursued a political career in the Independent Labour party (ILP). But his hopes for himself and for Labour were generally frustrated. Ill-health denied him a safe seat in the House of Commons, moderation cost him the leadership of the ILP, and the Parliamentary Labour party refused to embrace a full socialist program. Finally, when in 1931 he supported +Ramsay MacDonald's National Government, his connections with official Labour were irrevocably severed. MacDonald, however, did reward him with a peerage; and as Baron Allen of Hurtwood he reentered the mainstream of the peace movement at a time when its influence on the British public was most significant.

Though Allen had been long inactive in pacifist circles, his heroic wartime resistance assured him a respectful hearing. Moreover, his ability as public speaker, his access to the BBC, and his journalistic connections provided a considerable forum. Allen's reflections on his experiences as a conscientious objector inspired him to formulate a method of peace advocacy very different from his previously defiant absolutism. During the war years, many resisters had assumed that their witness on behalf of pacifist convictions could be transformed into a political instrument for stopping the war. Allen, however, had come to realize that pacifism was a personal testimony, not a political force. Pacifists may have emerged from the Great War with a sense of righteousness, but their stand had largely alienated public opinion without having any discernible effect on the war.

If the revived peace movement was to achieve meaningful results, Allen said, pacifists had to develop stratagems based, not on proving the efficacy of personal convictions, but on demonstrating reasonable and realistic ways to control the scourge of war. Allen called for a policy of "constructive pacifism" aimed at mobilizing public support behind armed collective security as embodied in the League of Nations. Support for an armed League seemed an odd, even contradictory, stance for one who still claimed to be a pacifist, but Allen believed that so long as most people were not pacifists and most nations remained armed, the League's use of force on behalf of international justice was the only reasonable alternative to international anarchy.

Although his health was always precarious, Lord Allen threw himself into the peace campaign with remarkable vigor. In addition to his prominent role in the British peace movement, he became involved in direct, private negotiations with the government of Nazi Germany. As much as he detested the Nazis, Allen was convinced that peace could be assured only through the removal of German grievances arising from the "wicked" Treaty of Versailles. In his efforts to establish the basis for an effective European settlement, Allen made three trips to Germany as an "unofficial interpreter of British opinion." These private diplomatic ventures garnered considerable publicity but achieved few results. Shortly after Allen returned from his last peace mission, he broke down completely. His death six months later at least spared him the anguish of the war he had struggled so courageously to prevent.

Clifford Allen's career points up many of the dilemmas facing twentieth-century peace leaders. He was always an absolutist, but recognized early what many of his fellow pacifists would never admit—that pacifism is a personal belief, not a political creed. Therefore, the pacifist must decide whether to retain the purity of his faith by withdrawing from the political world or to compromise by collaborating with nonpacifists to achieve desirable political ends. Because he chose the latter course, Allen was simultaneously attacked by hardliners as an impossible idealist and by pacifists as a backsliding fraud. Such criticism troubled him deeply but never destroyed his vision of a peaceable world guided by reason and good will.

Bibliography:

A. *Britain's Political Future* (London, 1934); *Peace in Our Time* (London, 1936); *Putting Socialism into Practice* (London, 1924); *Why I Still Resist* (London, 1917).

B. Martin Gilbert ed., *Plough My Own Furrow* (London, 1965); Arthur Marwick, *Clifford Allen* (London, 1964).

C. Clifford Allen Papers, University of South Carolina, Columbia.

Thomas C. Kennedy

ALLEN, William (29 August 1770, Spitalfields, London—30 December 1843, Lindfield, Sussex). *Education*: largely self-taught, although attended W. Alexander's school, Rochester, Kent, for a short time. *Career*: pharmaceutical chemist; lecturer in chemistry at Guy's Hospital in London, 1802-26; fellow of the Royal Society, 1807; Quaker philanthropist; clerk of Meeting for Sufferings, 1810-15.

William Allen was active in most of the humanitarian campaigns that proliferated in Britain in the early nineteenth century. He was involved early in the antislavery agitation; energetically conducted projects for the relief of poverty; promoted Joseph Lancaster's plan for popular education (helping to found the British and Foreign Schools Society); took a keen interest in various associations to improve the prison system and treatment of offenders; helped Robert Owen at a crucial moment to continue his enlightened management of the cotton mills at New Lanark; and undertook a somewhat similar scheme for agricultural workers in a colony near his Sussex home. He was also actively involved in the British and Foreign Bible Society. He traveled widely in Europe studying social institutions and imparting his own ideas. He edited a journal called *The Philanthropist* (1811-19). And among these other concerns he supported the society formed in London at the end of the Napoleonic wars to promote "permanent and universal peace," and discourage resort to arms, including defensive war.

Allen's most significant contribution to the peace movement arose out of his acquaintance with Alexander I, Czar of Russia. As clerk of Meeting for Sufferings (the principal Quaker committee in Britain) he formed part of the deputation presenting a Quaker Address to the Czar and the King of Prussia when they visited London in 1814. The king was not impressed by Quaker principles, remarking curtly that "war was necessary to peace." But Alexander appeared much interested, conversed an hour with Allen, Stephen Grellet, and John Wilkinson, and attended Westminister meeting for worship. Allen met Alexander again on two further occasions in Russia in 1819 and in Austria in 1822. In 1823, disturbed at reports of Russian encouragement of French intervention in Spain, he wrote a letter to Alexander arguing in a firm but friendly manner the case against such interferences drawing a comparison with the allied attempts to crush the French Revolution in 1792. This was an embryonic example of the kind of direct Quaker intervention in an international crisis which was more conspicuously attempted in the Quaker mission to Russia on the eve of the Crimean War, and which has been considerably developed in the present century.

Bibliography:

A. *Life of William Allen, with Selections from his Correspondence* (3 vols., London, 1846).

B. L. Hugh Doncaster, *Friends of Humanity, with Special Reference to the Quaker William Allen* (London, 1965); Joshua Fayle, *The Spitalfields Genius. The Story of William Allen* (London, 1884); Helena Hall, *William Allen, 1770-1843* (Haywards Heath, 1953).

C. Some Allen Papers are in the records of Allen and Hanbury, pharmaceutical chemists, Bethnal Green, London.

Geoffrey Carnall

ALLEN, William, D.D. (2 January 1784, Pittsfield, MA—16 July 1868, Northampton, MA). *Education*: B.A., Harvard Coll., 1802. *Career*: assistant librarian and regent, Harvard 1805-10; Congregational pastor 1810-17; president of the short-lived Dartmouth Univ., 1817-19; president of Bowdoin College, 1819-39; a renowned man of letters and still recognized for his monumental work, *The American Biographical Dictionary*; clergyman, educator, and author.

After graduating from Harvard College in 1802, William Allen studied theology for two years and in 1805 accepted the position of assistant librarian and regent at Harvard. In 1810 Allen succeeded his father as pastor of the First Congregational Church, Pittsfield, MA. In 1813 he married the daughter of John Wheelock, second president of Dartmouth College. Upon the death of Wheelock, Allen assumed the presidency of the ill-fated Dartmouth University. Finally in December 1819, Allen ascended to the presidency of Bowdoin College. While president of Bowdoin, Allen not only established the Medical School of Maine and introduced the study of modern languages into the curriculum but also appointed a number of notables to the faculty—among them were Henry W. Longfellow and *Thomas C. Upham.

William Allen joined the American Peace Society shortly after its inception in 1828. Allen was a man of peace but not a pacifist. Indeed, he believed that defensive war was lawful and even sanctioned by Holy writ since it possessed no lustful "war-spirit" or premeditative intent. Admittedly, he found all war evil, and he honestly abhorred it. Allen held that war remained at best a cruel political expediency, a valueless hoax, a passage into carnage, which needlessly impeded universal peace. Nevertheless, he stressed that a strictly defensive war fought against pirates or murderous barbarians invading native soil should never be condemned by men of the gospel. In fact, Allen emphasized throughout his apologetics on defensive warfare that in his study of the early Christians he found no proof that defensive war was considered unlawful by the early Church fathers.

*William Ladd, the founder of the American Peace Society, welcomed non-pacifists like Allen into his association. After all, the society neither condemned nor sanctioned defensive war. Curiously, the leadership of the American Peace Society sought to avoid the question of defensive war altogether and soon relegated the distasteful subject to a place of limbo in the society's constitution. Thus did Allen and others who shared his views find their way into the society. So enthused was Allen over his initial exposure to the work of the society that he devoted his 1833 Phi Beta Kappa address at Bowdoin to the topic of world peace. Allen became a life-member of the society; contributed generously to its funds; wrote for its periodicals; served as a director for three years and shortly before his abrupt resignation from the society in August, 1837, became one of its vice-presidents.

In a public letter dated August 4, 1837, Allen tendered his resignation to William Ladd. He stated that his resignation was a formal protest against the newly revised constitution of the society which outrightly condemned both offensive and defensive warfare as utterly wrong and against the spirit of the Christian gospel. This pernicious radicalization of the ethos of the American Peace Society was faith shattering for the disgruntled Allen, who only three years before had skillfully rebutted the arguments of the radical pacifist *Thomas S. Grimké on the unlawful nature of defensive war. In 1834 Allen's article "Defensive War Vindicated" appeared in the *Calumet*, the official organ of the American Peace Society. Allen's scholarly apologia sought to stave off the radicalization of the society. However, Allen's intellectual efforts on behalf of defensive war were to no avail. In June 1837 a committee of the society revised the constitution. The forces of the deceased Grimké proved victorious. Allen believed that Grimké's polemic against all war had fundamentally changed the tenor of the society and converted Ladd, a moderate pacifist, into an ultrapacifist. By the time Allen resigned from the society his ideological rift with Ladd could no longer be mended. Thus, Allen, an early and avid supporter of the American Peace Society, bitterly attacked the society's revised constitution as antithetical to the society's philosophical roots and even predicted its early demise.

Ironically, during this same period things fared no better for Allen at Bowdoin College. The late 1830s found Bowdoin a hot-bed of student radical pacifism. Moreover, Thomas C. Upham, the man Allen appointed as Professor of Moral Philosophy became a pacifist in the Grimké mold. In fact, Upham's 1836 *Manual of Peace* was lauded and vigorously promoted by the leadership of the American Peace Society. Significantly also, Bowdoin's Boards of Trustees and Overseers had, since 1831, waged a seven-year battle to remove the inflexible Allen as president of the college. Unpopularity with the school's Boards of Trustees and

Overseers and the student body forced Allen to resign in 1839. Allen left Bowdoin as he had left the American Peace Society—in a cloud of discontent. Paradoxically, in August 1849, twelve years after his impassioned resignation from the American Peace Society, Allen attended a World Peace Conference in Paris as one of the society's representatives.

Bibliography:

A. "Defensive War Vindicated," *The Calumet* (January and February, 1834, and May and June, 1834); "Dr. Allen's Letter to Mr. Ladd" and "Mr. Ladd's Answer to Dr. Allen's Letter," *The Advocate of Peace* (December 1837); "Dr. Allen's Second Letter to Mr. Ladd," *The Advocate of Peace* (June 1838); "Address To The Friends of Peace," *The Advocate of Peace* (June 1837).

B. Devere Allen, *The Fight For Peace* (New York, 1930); Peter Brock, *Pacifism in The United States* (Princeton, 1968); Merle Eugene Curti, *The American Peace Crusade 1815-1860* (Durham, NC, 1929); Edson L. Whitney, *The American Peace Society* (Washington, DC, 1929); DAB, I, 209-10.

C. A small collection of William Allen's correspondence is housed in Special Collections, Bowdoin College Library.

Frederick J. Stefon

ALVARADO QUIRÓS, Alejandro (18 August 1876, San José, Costa Rica—20 May 1945, San José). *Education*: Licenciatura, Escuela de Derecho de Costa Rica. *Career*: educator, diplomat, politician, and jurist.

The contributions of Alejandro Alvarado Quirós to the cause of international peace included a vigorous opposition to foreign intervention in Latin America in general and in Central America in particular. A citizen of Costa Rica, which respected the right of freedom of expression, Alvarado was able to develop his anti-interventionist views in an atmosphere unfettered by political persecution, government censorship, and enforced exile —conditions which severely limited the activities of outspoken anti-interventionists in Cuba, Peru, and Honduras. Moreover, as one of Costa Rica's leading politicians and diplomats, he was able to promote the anti-interventionist cause by working directly within the established national and international power structures.

Alvarado's initial statement against outside intervention in Central American affairs appeared in an essay published in 1914. As Alvarado's political and diplomatic career progressed, however, he was able to find much more effective vehicles for his anti-interventionist views. The 1920-21 Central American Conference held in San José, Costa Rica, for example, provided Alvarado with an excellent forum for an attack on foreign intervention in isthmian affairs. He served as chairman of the conference and attempted to convince the assembled delegates that an isthmian political federation was essential for the maintenance of Central American sovereignty. In Alvarado's view only a strong Central American union could effectively turn aside the threat of North American intervention. When currents of isthmian separatism proved too strong to allow the formation of such a union, Alvarado took his anti-interventionist case to a higher authority. Representing Costa Rica at the 1923 Inter-American Conference in

Santiago, Chile, Alvarado proposed the formation of a permanent Pan American International Court of Justice that would dedicate itself exclusively to the resolution of hemispheric conflicts and disputes. The tribunal would provide for mandatory arbitration of any international differences involving members of the Pan American community. Given its hemispheric-wide jurisdiction and membership, Alvarado hoped that the tribunal would command the influence and prestige necessary to ensure the maintenance of peace and respect for sovereignty throughout the Americas. The United States delegation, however, refused to accept the concept of compulsory arbitration and succeeded in defeating Alvarado's initiative. Despite such setbacks, Alvarado, for the remainder of his life, worked consistently for the creation of such a Pan American tribunal.

Alvarado's concern for isthmian sovereignty also served as the inspiration for his efforts as a peacemaker in Nicaragua. When civil war erupted there in 1926, Alvarado sought to spare Nicaragua the humiliation of foreign intervention and introduced a resolution in the Costa Rican Congress calling upon the Costa Rican government to offer its services as a mediator in the conflict. The Costa Rican executive branch, however, insisted upon maintaining a policy of absolute neutrality, refusing to act on Alvarado's initiative. In January 1927, when United States Marines landed in Nicaragua, Alvarado appealed to the ABC (Argentina, Brazil, and Chile) powers to lend their good offices. The following month, he pushed through a resolution in the Costa Rican Congress calling upon the U.S. Senate and the legislative bodies of all the other Latin American nations to express their opposition to the North American military intervention in Nicaragua. Other Latin American legislatures responded to Alvarado's initiative by passing similar resolutions which in turn served to focus a considerable amount of international attention on the interventionist role that the United States had adopted in Nicaragua. Thus, like his advocacy of the Pan American tribunal concept, Alvarado's efforts to preserve Nicaraguan sovereignty reflected his concern for and commitment to the cause of international peace.

Bibliography:

A. *Bric-a-brac* (San José, 1914); *La Democracia: Una Conferencia y varios artículos del Licenciado Alejandro Alvarado Quirós* (San José, 1939); *Ecos de la vida parlamentaria: proyectos, iniciativas y discursos* (San José, 1930); *Nuestra tierra prometida* (San José, 1925).

B. Richard V. Salisbury, "The Anti-Imperalist Career of Alejandro Alvarado Quirós," *Hispanic American Historical Review*, 57 (November 1977), 587-612.

C. Costa Rican Foreign Ministry Archives, San José, Costa Rica.

Richard V. Salisbury

ANDERSON MORÚA, Lúis (8 June 1875, Cartago, Costa Rica—15 June 1948, Cartago). *Education*: Licenciatura, Escuela de Derecho de Costa Rica. *Career*: educator, jurist, diplomat, and politician.

Lúis Anderson Morúa, the Costa Rican diplomat and international jurist, was one of Latin America's leading advocates of peace and international law. He served as a mediator in various international disputes, opposed foreign intervention in Latin America, and helped create the Central American International Court of Justice.

The Central American International Court of Justice developed out of the Central American Conference held in Washington, D.C., in November and December of 1907. Political turmoil and the threat of international conflict on the isthmus prompted the United States and Mexico to co-host the meeting. Once the deliberations began, however, the representatives of the United States and Mexico assumed a passive role, allowing the Central American delegates to resolve their outstanding differences without any outside interference. The delegates elected Anderson as president of the conference and he, in turn, pushed for the acceptance of the principle of obligatory arbitration of international disputes. With the support of the Salvadoran delegation, he won support for the creation of a Central American International Court of Justice. The Court, which functioned from 1908 to 1918, was the first international tribunal requiring mandatory rather than voluntary adjudication of international disputes among the contracting parties and, thereby, represented a precedent-breaking step in international jurisprudence.

As Anderson's reputation as an international jurist increased, he was called upon to render his opinion on various international disputes, including the Colombian-Peruvian dispute over Leticia, the Nicaraguan-Honduran and the Costa Rican-Panamanian boundary conflicts, the Guatemalan controversy with Great Britain over Belize, the Bryan-Chamorro Treaty, and the issue of *de facto* as opposed to *de jure* recognition policy. Anderson also struck a major blow for the forces of nonintervention when, as the Costa Rican delegate to the 1927 meeting of the Rio Commission of Jurists, he called for, on his own initiative, the acceptance of the principle of absolute nonintervention by all members of the Pan American community. The report of the Rio Commission, with Anderson's resolution intact, strongly influenced the agenda of the 1928 Inter-American Conference held in Havana, Cuba. Accordingly, Anderson was in part responsible for the tremendous amount of publicity that the issue of nonintervention generated at the Havana Conference and the concomitant embarrassment that the United States suffered as it endeavored to justify its interventionist policies at the conference.

Bibliography:

A. *Estudio jurídico, acerca de la controversia entre Guatemala y la Gran Bretaña, relativa a la convención de 30 de abril de 1859, sobre asuntos territoriales* (Havana, 1939); *El Gobierno de facto* (San José, 1925); *El Tratado Bryan-Chamorro, una cuestión vital para Centroamérica* (San José, 1917).

C. Costa Rican Foreign Ministry Archives, San José, Costa Rica.

Richard V. Salisbury

ANDREEN, Ellenor Andrea (11 July 1888, Örby, Älvsborgs län, Sweden—20 April 1972, Stockholm). *Education*: medical studies, Uppsala and Stockholm universities; licensed physician 1919; doctorate in medicine, Univ. of Stockholm, 1933. *Career*: physician, Sabbatsberg Hospital, various clinics and private practice, 1919-58; school doctor and instructor in physiology and hygiene at schools in Stockholm, including Higher Seminary for Women Teachers, 1921-41; Clinical Laboratory of the Stockholm Board of Health, 1925-45; senior physician at Stockholm's Central Clinical Laboratory, 1945-53; medical researcher, author and lecturer, peace activist.

From 1919 Ellenor Andrea Andreen was engaged in medical practice and research, publishing articles on diabetes and related problems and lecturing on personal hygiene. She pursued studies in Berlin (1921), Britain (1923), and at Harvard Medical School (1926, 1929-30). In the 1920s she joined the group of gifted feminist leaders around Elizabeth Tamm at Fogelstad. She worked for improved public health, better sex education, and a more inclusive family welfare system. Until 1928 she held leadership positions in the Swedish Red Cross. In 1935 she was appointed to the Commission on Population. She chaired the Stockholm Commission on Maternal Assistance (1938-41).

Andreen's involvement in the peace movement began in the early 1920s in association with the feminist journalist *Elin Wägner. In 1924 Andreen led the National Federation of Liberal Women in adopting a strong antiwar position. Her efforts in the 1930s were concentrated on warning against the threat of chemical and biological weapons for use against civilian populations. She was a leading promoter of the ''Women's Non-Violent Revolt against War'' by which 20,000 women pledged to refuse the protection of bomb-shelters in time of war. A member of the delegation carrying this declaration to the League of Nations in 1935, Andreen was chosen to make the formal presentation to the Assembly president, +Eduard Beneš.

In the 1940s Andreen worked in the Swedish Peace Committee and the Swedish Women's Left Federation, which she chaired. At the international women's congress in Paris in November 1945 she helped found the International Democratic Federation of Women, of which she became an honorary vice president. In 1950 she gave vigorous support to the World Peace Council's ''Stockholm Appeal'' calling for a ban on atomic weapons and condemning their first use as a crime against humanity. In 1952 she traveled to China and Korea as a member of the international scientific commission to investigate the use of germ warfare in the Korean War. Her report, accusing the United States of employing bacteriological weapons, was the subject of much controversy. The following year Andreen was awarded the Lenin Peace Prize, the money from which she contributed to peace organizations. Into her advanced years, she remained an active peace advocate, lecturing, writing and participating in conferences and demonstrations.

Bibliography:

A. *Bakteriekrig i Korea och Kina* (Stockholm, 1952); *Karolina Widerström—Sveriges första kvinnliga läkare* (Stockholm, 1956).

B. Ulla Isaksson and Erik Linder, *Elin Wägner 1922-1949* (Stockholm, 1980); *Svenska män och kvinnor* (Stockholm, 1942) I;106; *Sveriges läkarehistoria*, 4th Series (Stockholm, 1930) I:77-78.

Howard T. Lutz

ANDREWS, Charles Freer (12 February 1871, Newcastle-upon-Tyne, England—5 April 1940, Calcutta, India). *Education*: B.A., Pembroke Coll., Cambridge Univ., 1895. *Career*: priest and missionary, Church of England; fellow of Pembroke Coll., 1899-1904; lecturer, St. Stephen's Coll., Delhi, 1904-14; writer and negotiator.

Born into a Nonconformist church family, Charles Andrews won scholarships to secondary school and Pembroke College, Cambridge, where he came under Anglican influence. He was secretary to the local Christian Social Union and upon graduation took a missionary parish in Walworth, a south London slum. Theologically, he was then a strict high churchman and a conventional patriot concerning imperialism but imbued with a concept of paternalistic service to the needy. After three years he returned to Cambridge as a Fellow of his college and in 1904 was appointed to the Cambridge Mission's college in Delhi, St. Stephen's. He went to India full of hope that a great Indian Christian Church would regenerate a heathen nation and reconcile India's variety of peoples and religions. Soon after his arrival in India, however, he came to recognize that this dream was spoiled by the church's association with the imperial power.

His first action in a new direction was to suggest the appointment of an Indian principal for St. Stephen's, which was done after prolonged struggle. When Indian Christians formed their own Anglican missionary society for India, Andrews became the only non-Indian member of its advisory board. Developing his associations with Indian friends, he attended the meetings of the Indian National Congress in 1906 and published frequent criticisms of British arrogance and racism, becoming a regular contributor to *The Modern Review* (Calcutta), and championing Indian nationalism in his book, *The Renaissance in India* (1912). That same year he met *Rabindranath Tagore, the Bengali poet and literary giant, beginning one of the friendships that would dominate his life. He also was intimate with Viceroy Hardinge and became known in the highest reaches of Indian government, establishing a unique position as close friend to leading Indians and Britons at the same time, preparing him for a long role as mediator and conciliator. Thus it came about that an Indian politician, Gokhale, asked him to go to South Africa in 1913, where he helped *Mohandas Gandhi negotiate an end to the passive resistance struggle. This began his intimate involvement with the Mahatma.

Resigning his missionary position in 1914, as his theology broadened to see the oneness of all faiths, he devoted himself to writing and helping both Tagore and Gandhi. He was sent to Fiji in 1915 to report on conditions among Indian indentured laborers, and his work was influential in ending the indenture system there within five years. He returned to Fiji twice, to South Africa four times, and also examined Indian overseas communities in East Africa, Canada, and British Guiana. Within India he fought the government-sponsored opium trade and took an interest in industrial and labor disputes, earning the popular title ''Deenabandhu'' (Friend of the Poor). During Gandhi's work in England at the Round Table Conference in 1931, Andrews helped establish the India Conciliation Group with Quaker assistance and thereafter served on many occasions as a spokesman for Gandhi to the British press and government. He published three volumes on Gandhi and a number of books of Tagore's letters and translations, and he wrote a stream of books on India, social issues, and religion.

Perhaps more than anything else, he won a place by his remarkable indentification with India, his renunciation of the honors and privileges of racial superiority, and his constant exertions on behalf of oppressed Indians in India and overseas. Few have identified so selflessly with a people other than their own.

Bibliography:

A. *Mahatma Gandhi's Ideas*, (London, 1930); *The Renaissance in India*, (London, 1912); *What I Owe to Christ* (London, 1932).

B. B. Chaturvedi and M. Sykes, *Charles Freer Andrews* (London, 1950); H. Tinker, *Ordeal of Love* (New Delhi, 1979).

James D. Hunt

ANDREWS, Fannie Fern Phillips. See *Biographical Dictionary of Internationalists*.

ANGELL, Norman (b. Ralph Norman Lane) (26 December 1872, Holbeach, Lincolnshire, England—7 October 1967, Croyden, Surrey). *Education*: Lycée de St. Omer, Pas-de-Calais, France, 1884-87; business school, London and Univ. of Geneva; 1887-89. *Career*: journalist, homesteader in California; editor, Northcliffe's Paris *Daily Mail*; owner-editor, *Foreign Affairs* (London), 1928-31; Labour party politician, 1919-31; member of Parliament, 1929-31; Knighthood, 1931; Nobel Peace Prize recipient, 1934 (for 1933); internationalist and peace advocate.

Norman Angell was one of the most influential publicists of the international peace movement in the first third of the twentieth century. His principal notoriety was derived from the argument of his most popular book, *The Great Illusion* (1910, originally published in 1909 as *Europe's Optical Illusion*), the chief thesis of which centered upon the international interdependency of national economic interests and thus the impossibility of nations achieving any sustained profitable gain through war.

Essentially a condensation and transformation of the free trade ideas of *Richard Cobden and the British school of liberal internationalism, Angell's reformulation also incorporated the contemporary ideas of *Jacques Novicow. He successfully presented his case with numerous examples of the dangers caused by nationalist irrationality, the latter being the subject of his first book, *Patriotism under Three Flags* (1903). Angell's examples were often simplistic and frequently lifted out of historical context. But they were cogently phrased and enormously persuasive—so much so, that *The Great Illusion* generated a widespread peace movement in its own right between 1912 and the outbreak of World War I.

Norman Angellism had a considerable impact beyond Great Britain. Important segments emerged in France. In the United States, where the Carnegie Endowment for International Peace under +Nicholas Murray Butler became interested, it nourished a growing body of peace opinion, especially in the educational circle headed by Stanford University president *David Starr Jordan. While limited as a bona fide movement in Germany, by 1914 Angell's *Great Illusion* sold in greater numbers there than in any other country outside of Britain.

In England itself, Angell's ideas captured the minds of an important portion of the British establishment. His success in that sector was vital to the overall achievement of Norman Angellism. *The Great Illusion*, as promoted by Angell's oratorical and debating skills, led to the creation of a solid phalanx of youthful supporters at Cambridge in March 1912. Angell's dynamic personal, positive qualities also enabled him to reach the British establishment. Lord Esher, the confidant of King Edward VII and chairman of the Imperial Defence Committee, brought over Conservative ex-Prime Minister +Arthur James Balfour to support the cause. Through them Angell reached industrialist Sir Richard Garton, who put up the necessary money to form the Garton Foundation—a study group designed to propagate Angell's ideas. With the coming of World War I, however, the Norman Angell peace movement died abruptly.

Angell increasingly came to view himself and his movement as a failure. Toward the end of the prewar conflict, he tried to halt the war by creating a Neutrality League, but national fervor prevented the resolution of the conflict by peaceful means. Angell was frustrated, as were other internationalists, by the failure of reason to prevail among the various national leaders. He Joined +Ramsay MacDonald, *Arthur Ponsonby, *E. D. Morel, *Charles Trevelyan, *Bertrand Russell, and others to form the Union of Democratic Control (UDC). It was a step leftward; these men were labeled "pacificists" (internationalists), and, because of their call for a negotiated peace with Germany, they were castigated as unpatriotic German-lovers.

Although in reality he was very patriotic, Angell was tarred by the government with the same brush. The press, especially the *Times*, interpreted his movement's position as not only maintaining that war did not pay but also that all war was wrong. This interpretation of Angell's ideas persisted from that time forward. Similarly Angell was erroneously deemed a pacifist in the absolutist sense that the term later acquired. He spent the rest of his life unsuccessfully trying to counter that label as well.

After the war Angell resumed his journalist career, but his association with Labour left him totally frustrated: he could never speak to the same forum he had spoken to before the war. In the beginning he thought that Labourites would give him entrée to a new world, but he quickly found that they simply were part of the old one. Although he condemned the Treaty of Versailles, and the subsequent reparations debacle proved his ideas valid, Angell had little success. In two attempts at Parliament in 1922 and 1923 he failed to win a seat. He then drew inward, bought an island in Essex, near Maldon, and retired there to raise pigs.

Angell was brought back into the center of things when E. D. Morel put him in charge of the UDC publication *Foreign Affairs* (London). He thus had an independent forum, which he acquired as his own upon Morel's death in 1924 and which he kept until he refashioned it as supplement to *Time and Tide* in 1931.

Norman Angell's role in internationalist politics in the 1920s was peripheral. But he was noteworthy because of his ability to transform Morel's foreign policy pronouncements into an internationalist polity that the Labour party leadership could accept. He also did much to steer Ramsay MacDonald into a pro-League of Nations position and helped plant the seed for the Geneva Protocol plans of the first Labour government. The subsequent debate over the use of the League as an instrument of foreign policy, the repudiation of the Versailles Treaty, the Locarno Pact, and the emerging disarmament and peace sentiment during the last half of the 1920s brought Angell once more into center stage of British politics. He was elected to Parliament in the Labour victory of May 1929. While very disappointed in not obtaining a cabinet post, he was appointed to a number of parliamentary Labour party leadership and foreign policy committees. He also accompanied MacDonald to Virginia for the disarmament talks with +President Herbert Hoover.

Angell resigned from Parliament in September 1931 when MacDonald called for a National Government in order to devote himself entirely to the peace movement in support of the League and preparations for the 1932 Disarmament Conference. True to his word, he spent a great deal of energy helping to promote the disarmament proposals of the No More War Movement, the National Peace Council, and the League of Nations Union. In these efforts he worked very closely with internationalists and even the war-resister pacifists and Quakers. Whatever unity existed between the various branches of the peace movement broke down, however, with the Japanese invasion of Manchuria in September 1931. Pacifists sharply disagreed then with those antiwar leaders who called for League sanctions against Japan. Angell strongly sided with the internationalist, collective security, and enforcement side of the peace movement and supported Lord David Davies' idea of an international police force. He quickly found himself in the middle between the traditionalists on one side and the absolute pacifists on the other. Still, in 1934 the Nobel Peace Prize Committee announced that he had won the prize for 1933.

This was the crossroad of Norman Angell's career. Increasingly he stressed the need for collective defense. He wrote a small tome, the first really different work on internationalism since he had formulated *The Great Illusion* twenty-five years before. *The Menace to Our National Defense* (1934) was not concerned with pacifism or even peace but was an attempt to formulate a practical plan for the internationalization of air power. In 1935, after the League's pitiful performance during the Abyssinian crisis and when it was clear that it was no longer a viable instrument for pooled international security, Angell quickly moved over to a more traditional form of foreign policy and condemned appeasement. Despite his writings against patriotism, Angell always had a strong patriotic zeal. He also had an equally pronounced imperialist bent and even an Anglo-Saxon racialist side. Although discernible in some of his earlier books, the nationalist, imperialist, and racist aspects of his character came to the fore in the late 1930s, during World War II which he spent in the United States, and the postwar years. He retained his internationalism only in a formal, perfunctory way.

As a peace advocate Angell always felt himself a failure. At the height of his advocacy of the unprofitability of war, World War I broke out. A generation later at the height of his advocacy of disarmament the entire internationalist structure he had touted as the hospital for the world's ills came crumbling down, and he quickly had to face up to the power political realities of nation states arming for war. He immediately abandoned disarmament and talked of arming the League, and, when that failed to be a viable alternative, he championed a Western alliance. He severely criticized appeasement, but he had to face the fact that it was an outlook that was partly derived from his previous position. He was thus responsible for his own failure to win the peace movement over to the new defense and armaments position. Quite simply, if the British peace movement had followed him, it would not have been much of a peace movement.

Angell wrote, lectured, broadcast, and championed what amounted to an Anglo-American condominium of power right up until his death in 1967. But his role and significance as a "peace leader" ended when he wrote *The Menace to Our National Defence* and *Pacifism Is Not Enough* thirty-three years earlier. By this time it was also obvious that Norman Angellism was the greatest of illusions and, of itself, quite clearly not enough.

Bibliography:

A. *After All* (New York, 1951); *The Defence of the Empire* (London, 1937); *Defence of the English-Speaking Role* (London, 1958); *Europe's Optical Illusion* (London, 1909); *For What Do We Fight*? (New York, 1939); *Foreign Policy and Our Daily Bread* (London, 1925); *The Foreigner's Turn to Disarm?* (London, 1931); *The Great Illusion* (London, 1910); *The Great Illusion—A Reply to Rear Admiral A. T. Mahan* (New York, 1912, reprint, 1973); *The Great Illusion, 1933* (London, 1933); *The Great Illusion—Now* (Harmondsworth, Middlesex, 1938); *The Menace to Our National Defence* (London, 1934); *Must Britain Travel the Moscow Road?* (London, 1926); *Must It Be War?* (London, 1939); "Pacifism," and "Peace Movements," in *Encyclopaedia of the Social Sciences* (New York, 1930-35); "Pacifism Is Not Enough," in Geneva Institute of International Relations, *Pacifism Is Not Enough* (London, 1935); *The Peace Treaty and the Economic Chaos of Europe* (London, 1919); *Peace with the Dictators?* (London, 1938); *Preface to Peace* (London, 1935, reprinted as *Peace and the Plain Man*, New York, 1935); *This Have and Have-Not Business* (London, 1936); *The Unseen Assassins* (London, 1932); *We Can Abolish War* (London, 1933); *What Causes War*? (New York, 1933); *Will Disarmament Increase Unemployment*? (London, 1931).

B. Louis Bisceglia, *Norman Angell and Liberal Internationalism in Britain, 1931-1935* (New York, 1982); Louis Bisceglia, ''Norman Angell and the 'Pacifist' Muddle,'' *Bulletin of the Institute of Historical Research*, 45 (May 1972), 104-21; Louis Bisceglia, ''The Politics of a Peace Prize,'' *Journal of Contemporary History*, 7 (July-October, 1972), 263-73; Martin Ceadel, *Pacifism in Britain, 1914-1945* (Oxford, 1980); Alfred Thayer Mahan, ''The Great Illusion,'' *North American Review*, 195 (March 1912), 318-32; Albert Marrin, *Sir Norman Angell* (Boston, 1979); Howard Weinroth, ''Norman Angell and *The Great Illusion*: An Episode in Pre-1914 Pacifism,'' *Historical Journal*, 17 (September 1974), 551-74.

C. Norman Angell Papers, Ball State University Library and Archives; Columbia University Library.

Louis Bisceglia

ANTHONY, Susan Brownell (15 February 1820, Adams, MA—13 March 1906, Rochester, NY). *Education*: Informal, home and district school (Battenville, NY); Friends' Seminary (near Philadelphia). *Career*: teacher, 1839-49; temperance worker, abolitionist, and woman's suffrage leader; president, National American Woman's Suffrage Association, 1892-1900; co-founder, International Council of Women, 1899 and International Woman's Suffrage Alliance, 1904; feminist, reform activist, and pacifist.

Susan B. Anthony's Quaker heritage predisposed her stand against individual and collective violence as well as her lifelong commitment to women's rights. Best known as a feminist and a leader in the woman's suffrage movement, Anthony's sincere concern for peace sprang naturally from her family's commitment to the principles of human equality and nonviolence. In fact, she had to be converted to the cause of woman's suffrage, because she was initially reluctant to seek participation in a government that practiced violence. Like many other pre-Civil War advocates of peace, she had to struggle with her conscientious objections to war and her belief that the northern effort would lead to the abolition of slavery and the promotion of human rights.

As an activist woman, Anthony and her colleagues in the Universal Peace Union and the Universal Peace Society forced those organizations to permit women to hold elective office after 1870. During the last quarter of the nineteenth century she helped open the way for an increased and acknowledged role for women in the organized effort for peace.

Anthony's opposition to the Spanish-American War in 1898 reflected her censure of war generally and of this conflict in particular. She regarded belligerent policies as direct consequences of the lack of social justice under a political system that excluded women from equally participating in the political process. Anthony publicly decried the incompetence of the army medical command in Cuba that had contributed to the suffering and mortality among the wounded. Moreover, she knew that wars resulted in setbacks for the cause of woman's rights and especially of woman's suffrage.

Susan B. Anthony was committed to peace and arbitration as the only appropriate means to assure the prosperity of the human race.

Bibliography:

A. (Edited with Elizabeth Cady Stanton and Matilda Joslyn Gage), *The History of Woman Suffrage* (6 vols., New York, 1881-1922).

B. Katharine Susan Anthony, *Susan B. Anthony: Her Personal History and Her Era* (Garden City, NY, 1954); Rheta Louise Childe Dorr, *Susan B. Anthony, The Woman Who Changed the Mind of a Nation* (New York, 1928); Ida H. Harper, *The Life and Work of Susan B. Anthony* (3 vols., Indianapolis and Kansas City, 1898-1908); Alma Lutz, *Susan B. Anthony: Rebel, Crusader, Humanitarian* (Boston, 1959).

C. Scattered manuscripts in Library of Congress; Schlessinger Library, Radcliffe College; Vassar College Library; Susan B. Anthony Memorial, Rochester, NY; University of Rochester Library; Seneca Falls, (NY) Historical Society; Henry E. Huntington Library, San Marino, CA; New York Public Library; Boston Public Library; American Antiquarian Society, Worcester, MA.

Angela Howard Zophy

ANTTILA, Selma (16 December 1867, Orimattila, Finland—15 May 1942, Helsinki). *Education*: Tampere Teachers' Coll,. *Career*: director of Tampere elementary school; founder, Peace Union of Finland, 1920; author and lecturer.

Working as a teacher in Tampere at the turn of the century, Selma Anttila participated actively in social reform movements. She was especially interested in the emancipation of women and in social questions. In addition, she strongly supported the awakening labor movement and its call for greater social equality. She participated in labor organizations as a lecturer and as an instructor of leisure activities. She founded and chaired a union of labor women in Tampere and wrote about the town's sharp social contrasts in her first collection of short stories, *Pictures from a Labour Town* (1904).

For Anttila, the First World War and the Finnish civil war of 1918 meant a shocking collapse of values and ideals. The war forced her to reassess her relationship to the labor movement, Western humanism, and the Christian church. None of these had prevented the vast destruction and cruelty of World War I, and Anttila concluded that mankind could not withstand another conflict of a similar kind. Educated people opposed to war, she believed, had to unite and make their position known. In the spring of 1920, in Helsinki, she called together a meeting in which a group of well-known artists, authors, and scientists participated in the founding of the Peace Union of Finland, the nation's oldest antiwar organization. From 1920 until 1926, Anttila acted as its secretary.

Between the two World Wars, peace was the central theme of Anttila's literary production. She depicted the consequences of the civil war in her novel *The Victim*, (1922), and in many of her poems she warned of the rise of fascism and the growing threat of war. She firmly believed that writers had an obligation to act for peace and that literature should never submit to the service of hate and violence. She opposed the image of writers as passive figures, calling on them to participate directly in resolving social questions. Anttila followed her own advice and actively participated in the activities of Finland's Peace Union. In 1935 she gave her support to the committee opposed to the death penalty and later joined the Union of Human Rights founded by Väinö Lassila and the Relief Committee for Jewish Refugees.

Selma Anttila helped unite the message of Christian love and Western humanism in the Finnish peace movement. She emphasized the significance of the role of intellectuals in peace work but realized that they alone could not create permanent peace. "The peace movement is communal work," she said, but she also believed that efforts toward mitigating social differences and tensions would further the cause of peace. Much of Anttila's literary efforts are now out of fashion, but her activity in creating a broadly based peace movement and her concern about reducing armaments are still relevant.

Bibliography:

A. *Rauhaa Kohti*, (*Towards Peace*) (Hämeenlinna, 1922).

Kalevi Kalemaa
Trans. by Oliver and Rita Whitehead

APPONYI, Albert (29 May 1846, Vienna—7 February 1933, Geneva). *Education*: Dr. jur., Univ. of Budapest and Univ. of Vienna, 1868. *Career*: politician, member of Parliament, cabinet minister, author, active participant in pacifist movements.

The scion of one of Hungary's most prominent aristocratic families, Count Albert Apponyi embarked upon a political career in his mid-twenties. First, he joined the governing Deák party, then the short-lived Conservative party, and emerged as the leader of the moderate opposition which reconstituted itself as the National party in 1892.

In the 1890s, Apponyi became active in the establishment of contacts between legislative bodies on an international scale in order to promote peace and understanding. He was instrumental in getting the Interparliamentary Union to hold its 7th Congress in Budapest in 1896. Apponyi was the head of the Hungarian delegation in 1899, at the Congress in Christiania (Oslo, Norway), where he was also elected to the supreme council of the organization. At the Paris Congress in 1900, Apponyi's suggestion to create an international union of the world press in the interest of peace was enthusiastically received and approved unanimously. Unfortunately, no practical result followed from the resolution.

At the Congress of St. Louis, in 1904, which Apponyi judged one of the most important, he expressed strong support for the reconvening of a second Hague Congress. In 1905, in Brussels, his motion to streamline the legal procedures of The Hague Tribunal was adopted. In all these congresses, Apponyi excelled as a brilliant speaker, championing the cause of world peace, international solidarity, and justice.

Throughout this period, Apponyi remained head of the Hungarian parliamentary delegations to the Interparliamentary Union, even during the period of 1906-10, when he served as minister for religious and educational affairs in the Hungarian cabinet. In 1910, the Party of Independence, to which Apponyi belonged since 1905, was defeated at the polls, and Apponyi became one of the opposition leaders in the Hungarian Parliament. Relations between the governing Party of National Work and the opposition deteriorated rapidly, and the former resorted to the use of force to maintain parliamentary order on its own terms. Apponyi was involved in that struggle, and he felt that under the circumstances he could not continue as the head of the Hungarian delegation to the Interparliamentary Union; he submitted his resignation in 1912.

Apponyi maintained his interest in the cause of peace nevertheless. In the April 1914 issue of the Catholic journal, *Magyar Kultúra*, Apponyi strongly endorsed the peace movement which he depicted as the outgrowth not only of humanitarian sentiments but of sober reasoning as well. He described the preservation of peace as a historical process that should not be subjected to the whims of individual statesmen but, rather, should be stabilized through the institutions of the peace movement itself. The only allowance Apponyi made for war was the case of national self-defense. When World War I broke out, Apponyi, a dedicated Hungarian nationalist, used just such a justification for his unconditional support for the war, which he characterized, in the September 1914 issue of the *Magyar Kultúra*, as "our war," "just and sacred, fought in God's name for justice, right, a moral order, and for peace." Apponyi persisted in his support of Hungary's war effort to the bitter end, until 1918.

In the postwar era, Apponyi headed the Hungarian delegation to the Paris Peace Conference. Subsequently, he became an eloquent spokesman for the treaty's revision, aiming the reversal of Hungary's territorial losses. Apponyi resumed his pacifist activities at the Congress of the Interparliamentary Union in Vienna, in 1922, where he was elected to the executive committee. He attended the Congress in Copenhagen, in 1923, for the last time, because his official duties as head of the Hungarian delegation to the League of Nations occupied most of his time and attention.

Apponyi was an outstanding example of a statesman who genuinely wished and worked for an international order of peace. The adoption of this position stemmed from his deep religious feelings, compassion, and political moderation. However, the broad principles he believed in clashed with his intransigent Hungarian nationalism. When the choice had to be made in 1914, Apponyi opted for the latter without a moment's hesitation.

Bibliography:

A. *Élmények és Emlékek* (Budapest, 1933; English trans., *Experiences and Reminiscences*, London, 1935, German trans., Berlin, 1933); *Emlekirataim* (2 vols, Budapest, 1922-34); *Lectures on the Peace Problem and the Constitutional Growth of Hungary* (Budapest, 1911).

B. Ágoston Ambrózy, *Apponyi* (Budapest, 1937); *Apponyi Emlékkönyv* (Budapest, 1926); József Kerekesházy, *Apponyi* Budapest, 1937); Sándor Pethö, *Gróf Apponyi Albert* Budapest, 1926); NYT, February 8, 1933, 19.

Gabor Vermes

ARCO, Georg Wilhelm Alexander Hans von (30 August 1869, Grossgorschütz near Ratibor, Upper Silesia, Germany [now Poland]—7 May 1940 Berlin).

Education: gymnasium, Breslau, abitur (school leaving certificate), 1889; Univ. of Berlin and Charlottenburg Technical Institute, 1889-90; 1893-96. *Career*: army officer, 1890-93; engineer, Allgemeinen Elektrizitäts-Gesellschaft (German General Electric Co.), 1898-1903; technical director, Telefunken Co., 1903-30; physicist and pacifist.

Count Georg von Arco was born into a Silesian aristocratic family whose origins went back to the South Tyrolean town of Arco in the twelfth century. (Count Arco-Valley, the right-wing assassin of *Kurt Eisner, was a descendant of the Italian branch of the Arco family). Georg Arco's life traveled a course from the Prussian military to an engineering profession, to becoming a monist, pacifist, and cosmopolitan. By 1914, Arco was already known and respected as a pioneer of radio engineering and developer of wireless telegraphy in Germany. He also enjoyed great prestige abroad for his efforts to establish international cooperation in radio telegraphy.

Arco's opposition to World War I led him early in 1915 to join the antimilitaristic Bund Neues Vaterland (New Fatherland League) (BNV), founded a few months previously by *Otto Lehmann-Russbüldt and *Kurt von Tepper-Laski. Arco was elected co-chair of the BNV. In particular, he directed his efforts during the war against German chauvinism. Likewise, he firmly rejected the politics of annexation of the Pan-German and high-level military groups and demanded, instead, both a quick end to the war based on a peace of understanding and a free public discussion concerning Imperial Germany's war aims. His commitment to peace, his opposition to the useless continuation of the war, as well as his efforts on behalf of the goals of the BNV, which supported the establishment of a democratic German political system as a precondition for the creation of a peaceful Europe, brought Arco into conflict with the military authorities. He only barely escaped imprisonment.

After the crippling of the BNV and the Deutsche Friedensgesellschaft (German Peace Society) (DFG) by the military authorities, Arco took part on June 14, 1916, in the establishment of the Vereinigung Gleichgesinnter (Union of Like-Minded People), a Berlin circle of pacifist intellectuals, who called for international rapproachement. The organization condemned all political force, rejected government by coercion and nationalism, expressed concern about the danger of a further intellectual isolation of Germany, and demanded a new politics based on ethical principles. When military censorship ended in the autumn of 1918, Arco again became active in the BNV. On October 8, in a telegram to the imperial chancellor also signed by A. Holitscher, *Max Lehmann, and Kurt von Tepper-Laski, Arco demanded the immediate release of all persons imprisoned because of their activities for peace and democracy. After the proclamation of the republic in November, he became a confidante of the Unabhängige Sozialdemokratische Partei Deutschlands (Independent German Social Democratic party) (USPD) in the revolutionary government and, although not a party member, was made their representative in the Prussian Ministry of Commerce with full powers of an authorized representative. However, because the USPD was excluded early from the government, Arco was denied the opportunity to make use of his exceptional organizational skills.

In December 1918, he supported the founding of the Deutsche Liga für Völkerbund (German Union for a League of Nations) and became a member of its board of directors. Likewise, he numbered among other German representatives, such as *Eduard Bernstein, *Wilhelm Foerster and *Georg Gothein, who belonged to the post-World War I Internationaler Ehrenausschuss (International Honorary Commission) of the Bund für Menschheitsinteressen (Alliance for the Interests of Humanity) directed by Rudolf Broda. With other members of the BNV, Arco worked diligently in June 1919 for the acceptance of the peace treaty of Versailles by the Weimar National Assembly.

In addition to his work with the BNV during the war, Arco, the former military officer, played an important role in the adoption of peace ideas by the Deutscher Monistenbund (German Monist League) (DMB). He helped lead the Berlin branch of the DMB into altering its bylaws, subscribing to pacifism, and corporately joining the German Peace Society. In 1920 Arco became chairman of the International Committee for Monism, which strove for a world community that would provide all peoples with opportunity to develop their economic and cultural potentials and that would render world war impossible in the future. The following year, Arco took over as president of the DMB and led the organization into the Deutscher Friedenskartell (German Peace Cartel) and into the Deutsche Liga für Menschenrechte (German League for Human Rights), formerly the BNV.

After 1924 Arco withdrew from political life and concentrated on his professional responsibilities. He remained associated, however, with the peace movement and helped edit *Die Friedenswarte*, a peace journal, and the *Monistische Monatshefte*, the organ of the DMB. In 1930 he was one of the signers of a "Call to the German People" which spoke out sharply against the demagoguery of the National Socialist press by characterizing its open threats of anti-Jewish pogroms as the "cultural shame of anti-Semitism."

Bibliography:

A. (With, among others, A. Einstein, H. v. Gerlach, and M. Harden) *Lille* Beiträge zur Naturgeschichte Krieges (vol. 1, Berlin, 1920).

B. M.D. "Graf Arco—60 Jahre alt," *Monistische Monatshefte*, 14 (October, 1929), 229ff; Karl Holl, "Die 'Vereinigung Gleichgesinnter' Ein Berliner Kreis pazifistischer Intellekueller im Ersten Weltkrieg," *Archiv für Kulturgeschichte*, 54 (1972), 364-84; Felix Linke, "Die Gross-Station Nauen und ihr Schöpfer Graf Arco. Zur Einweihung des neuen Gebäudes von Muthesius und zum 50. Geburtstag des Grafen Arco," *Die freie Welt. Illustrierte Wochenschrift der USPD*, 1 (September 6, 1919), 6 ff; Hans Wehberg, "Die Toten unseres Jahres 1940," *Die Friedenswarte*, 40 (1940), 232 ff; *Neue Deutsche Biographie*, I, 337ff.

Helmut Donat
Trans. by William L. Hopkins

ARNAUD, Emile (1864, Vizelle, France—? October 1921, Luzarches). *Education*: l'Ecole Professional du Vaucanson; Lycée de Grenoble; Lycée Saint-

Louis; Faculty of Law, Univ. of Grenoble, 1885-88. *Career*: notary, journalist, author, president, Ligue internationale de la paix et de la liberté, 1891-1921.

Descended from a family of farmers and son of a man who rose to the position of justice of the peace, Emile Arnaud grew up in a small town in Dauphiny where he was given his primary education. As a young man he studied law in Grenoble, became active in local politics, and learned about the peace movement from *Charles Lemmonier, president of the Ligue internationale de la paix et de la liberté (International League of Peace and Freedom), who came to give a lecture. Arnaud joined a local chapter of the League and was sent in 1889 to represent it in Paris at the founding meeting of the Universal Peace Congress. Two years later, at Lemmonier's death, he was elected president of the League, a post he held through election until his death.

Arnaud moved to Luzarches (Seine-et-Oise) where he married, established himself in a notarial practice, was eventually elected head of his professional association, and continued to give unstintingly of time and personal wealth to the peace cause. He contributed articles to *Siècle*; edited *Les Etats-Unis d'Europe*. (organ of the League), and wrote for *L'Indépendance Belge* (which he owned in community with a number of French peace activists after 1895). Further, he was elected to committees and the Council of the Universal Peace Congress and to the central council of the Délégation permanente des sociétés françaises de la paix, a national council of French peace societies. During the 1890s he delivered approximately 500 lectures on peace themes around France, in six other European countries, as well as in Tunisia and Morocco. A gifted lecturer, he was much in demand. Moreover, he spent ceaseless hours lobbying Italian and French universities to include and expand the study of public international law in their curricula. Among the themes of his lectures was his courageous stand on Alsace-Lorraine which challenged ultranationalist and militarist sentiment frontally. Arnaud argued that no permanent solution to that nagging issue would be achieved even by a victorious war; rather, it would only be settled under the umbrella of a European federation when the rule of law had become accepted practice. His belief in international law and its potential was the keystone of his pacifism. Arnaud drafted the principles of law which the international peace movement adopted in 1891 and refined them for popular dissemination in 1910.

To promote peace Arnaud did not hesitate to lobby directly with French and European officials. In 1899, with *Frédéric Passy, he visited French Foreign Minister Théophile Delcassé in an effort to prevent the Fashoda crisis from becoming a war. Later he worked to develop Franco-British understanding into a permanent arrangement (before the Entente of 1904). At the outbreak of the Boer War, he led his group to write directly to the English queen and the South African leadership to take up arbitration. Such activity continued until 1914.

Arnaud invented the word "pacifism" to describe the activities which he and the other Europeans were engaged in at the opening of the nineteenth century. In an article in *L'Indépendence Belge* (August 1901), he wrote that he and his colleagues were not only "passive types," peace makers, and negotiators; they were all those things but also something more. They were "pacifists," and their ideology was "pacifism." The word was adopted quickly by the movement and eventually by the media.

Arnaud's activities continued with undiluted energy until August 1914 when, at age 50, he joined the Army and opted for active duty. His only son, Maxime, also joined; both father and son saw themselves as participating in a just war in defense of an invaded and occupied nation. Maxime was killed and Arnaud really never recovered. For his bravery and devotion, Arnaud was awarded the Croix de Guerre and was made a Chevalier in the Legion of Honor. After the war, when the first draft of the League of Nations project was circulated, he wrote a fine criticism of its probable shortcomings. He took up his peace work after the war but never with the emotional drive which was once his hallmark.

At his death, several thousand mourners marched past shuttered and draped shops in Luzarches where he was much loved and had been very active in local causes. He left a shocked collection of peace colleagues who had anticipated he would lead the French peace movement for years to come.

Bibliography:

A. *Code international public (code de la paix), notes et commentaires* (Paris, 1913); *Le Mouvement pacifiste* (n.p., 1904); *L'Organisation de la paix* (1893; Berne, 1899); *Un Traité d'arbitrage permanent entre la France et l'Angleterre* (Paris, 1903); *Les Traités des arbitrages permanentes entre peuples* (n.p., 1895).

B. *Les Etats-Unis d'Europe* (Paris), 1922, p. 35, 1924, pp. 37-38; 1925, pp. 69-71; *La Paix par le droit*, 21 (November-December, 1921), 431-33.

C. Autobiographical notes, Archives of the Bureau International de la Paix, United Nations Library, Geneva.

Sandi E. Cooper

ARNHOLD, Georg (1 March 1859, Dessau, Principality of Anhalt, Germany—25 November 1926, Innsbruck, Austria). *Education*: attended Städtische Realschule, Berlin. *Career*: banker and pacifist.

The German Peace Society could hardly have developed its modest activities to any degree had it not been able to count on support from a few wealthy patrons. Among those generous supporters of the peace movement in Germany, such as *Edouard de Neufville and the Frankfort industrial magnate Heinrich Rössler, Georg Arnhold, a Jewish banker, deserves special mention.

In 1875 Arnhold became co-owner of the bank in Dresden that his brother had founded. This banking firm, which provided financial backing for the electrical and brewery industries, developed so favorably that a Berlin branch could be opened in 1911. A measure of the importance of Arnhold's bank was his membership on 119 boards of supervisors. Arnhold became a royal Saxon privy commercial councillor, a royal Bavarian commercial councillor, and a royal Württemberg consul, all indications of the high esteem that he enjoyed within and beyond the borders of Saxony. In Dresden Arnhold was extolled for his generous support of charitable institutions.

On the basis of his economic experience, Arnhold had learned to recognize war as a disaster. His deep commitment to humanity led him and his wife into the peace movement. The final impetus for the decision at the turn of the century was the reading of a "Summons to the Nations," produced by one of the international peace congresses. Soon thereafter, Arnhold joined the German Peace Society and established a local group in Dresden. For years he was chairman of this local group and took part in numerous international peace congresses, such as Paris (1900), Boston (1904), and Munich (1907), as well as in numerous German congresses. Up until the time when a subsidy from the Carnegie Foundation (1911-16) made possible the publication of *Die Friedenswarte*, the journal was almost totally dependent on Arnhold for its financing. Likewise, Arnhold supported *Alfred H. Fried's *Handbuch der Friedensbewegung* (*Handbook of the Peace Movement*) and gave generously to the Association for European Understanding, the German-French Rapprochement Committee, and the Esperanto movement. Arnhold combined an active interest in the peace movement with membership on the board of directors of Die Deutsche kolonialgesellschaft (German Colonial Society). In Eurocentered bourgeois, left-liberal, and, even pacifist, circles this combination was not considered contradictory because the members of those circles saw nothing wrong with German participation in colonial activities within the framework of economic imperialism.

Although shaken by the outbreak of the First World War, Arnhold still believed firmly in the breakthrough of the peace movement to a broader public after the war. Thus he participated vigorously in the establishment of the Bund Neues Vaterland (New Fatherland League), while warning, quite in keeping with older socially conservative pacifism, against a discussion of domestic political problems. He came to believe, however, that the German peace movement was moving in too radical a direction after the pacifist congresses of 1919 in Berlin and 1920 in Brunswick, both of which he attended. Thereafter he curtailed his practical participation in the German Peace Society, without, however, losing interest in its activities. He died of a heart attack on a return trip from Meran.

Bibliography:

B. Hans Wehberg, "Georg Arnhold als Pazifist," *Die Friedenswarte*, 27 (1927), 14-15.

Karl Holl
Trans. by William L. Hopkins

ARNOLD-FORSTER, William Edward. See *Biographical Dictionary of Internationalists*.

ARNOLDSON, Klas Pontus (27 October 1844, Göteborg, Sweden—20 February 1916, Stockholm). *Education*: formal education in public schools of Göteborg until 1860, then self-educated. *Career*: railroad clerk and station inspector, 1860-80; member of Parliament, 1882-87; editor of newspapers and peace periodicals, 1870-94.

Klas Arnoldson adopted and advocated "practical Christianity" which largely inspired his work for peace. This movement strove to liberate religion from its dogmatic and intolerant aspects, and aimed to put the pacifist witness back into the center of the faith. The Prussian-Danish War of 1864 and especially the Franco-Prussian War of 1870-71 only intensified his abhorrence of war. These and other events of European high politics of his time convinced him of the need for a guaranteed neutrality of the Nordic states to maintain their independence; their military means were no longer adequate in the face of overwhelming military strength of big powers. The formation of a Scandinavian union would also help promote the cause of peace.

When, largely on the strength of his peace proposals, Arnoldson was elected to Parliament, he put forward, in 1883, a proposal inviting the country to seek permanent neutrality status. He believed that the rivalry of the great powers ensured that they had a common interest in respecting such a status, and that its implementation and international recognition was a realistic possibility. He carefully analyzed and answered the various objections leveled against his proposal in the debates in the Lower House of the Swedish Parliament; ultimately it adopted the plan, albeit with major amendments.

In 1883 Arnoldson also helped to found the Swedish Peace and Arbitration Society which initially consisted entirely of members of Parliament. He edited its paper and for the first few years served as secretary which greatly assisted him in his campaign advocating neutrality and arbitration. An important preoccupation of the Society was the deteriorating relationship between Sweden and Norway; their union became increasingly the subject of disputes and dissension in the late 1880s as Norway's political development stimulated demands for greater equality with Sweden. Arnoldson supported Norwegian claims, arguing that their acceptance could only strengthen the union and the cause of peace. Although in 1883 he had sent a copy of his neutrality resolution to the leader of the Liberal party in Norway, he had excluded that country from his proposal, since he believed that this was an issue to be decided by Norway's own Parliament.

In 1888 Arnoldson launched a campaign urging arbitration agreements with other nations. This campaign he extended to Norway, and it was largely as a result of the links which he had established with Norwegian political leaders that the Norwegian Parliament adopted a resolution in favor of arbitration in 1890. In the period 1895-1905, the last and much-troubled decade of the union's existence, Arnoldson advocated its dissolution if the price for its preservation was the use of Swedish armed force. This position met with much opposition and hostility in Sweden.

In 1908 Arnoldson received the Nobel Peace Prize (which he shared with *Fredrik Bajer). His candidacy received the unanimous approval of the Swedish group of the Interparliamentary Union, which thus honored his tireless efforts for peace in and out of Parliament and his countless speeches and writings.

Bibliography:

A. *Fred med Norge* (Stockholm, 1895); *Neutralitetsfråagan* (Stockholm, 1883); *Pax Mundi: A Concise Account of the Progress of the Movement for Peace by Means of Arbitration, Neutralization, International Law and Disarmament* (London, 1892; Swedish ed., Stockholm, 1890); *Seklernas hopp: En bok om världsfreden* (Stockholm 1901); "World Referendum," Nobel Lecture, in Frederick W. Haberman, ed., *Nobel Lectures-Peace* (Amsterdam, 1972), I, 175-87.

B. Alfred H. Fried, *Handbuch der Friedensbewegung* (2nd ed., Berlin 1911-1913, reissued, New York, 1972) 2, 319-20; August Schou, *Histoire de l'internationalisme* (Oslo, 1963), III, 516-19; Axel Svenson, *En lifsgerning för freden* (Stockholm, 1904); NYT, February 21, 1916.

Peter van den Dungen

ASSER, Tobias Michael Carel. See *Biographical Dictionary of Internationalists*.

AUCLERT, Marie-Anne-Hubertine (10 November 1848, Tilly, Allier, France—8 April 1914, Paris). *Education*: Convent of Montluçon. *Career*: founder and secretary-general, Le Droit des femmes (Women's Rights), later renamed Suffrage des femmes (Women's Suffrage), 1876-88, 1892-1914; founder and editor, *La Citoyenne*, 1881-88; columnist ("Le Féminisme"), *Le Radical*, 1896-1909; feminist organizer and journalist.

The great interest of Hubertine Auclert's life was the campaign for women's suffrage, which she founded in France and led for almost forty years. Auclert championed many other causes, but she correlated them with her vision of a society in which women were full and equal partners. Her commitment to social and international peace, her interest in disarmament, and her opposition to militarism all developed as aspects of her feminism. Auclert did not seek immediate disarmament; she accepted the concern of nations for their security. True peace, Auclert believed, could only be obtained by first winning women's rights: war existed between individuals, classes, and nations because it first existed between the sexes.

Auclert chiefly developed her peace theories in her writings, especially *Le Vote des femmes* (1908) and her posthumous *Les Femmes au gouvernail* (1923). Her recurring theme was that the emancipation of women will produce the progress of all humankind, especially peaceful relations. She argued that women were certainly the moral equals of men; circumstances had possibly made them moral superiors. Emancipated women, by the sheer numbers of their ballots could make reason triumph over such masculine folly as militarism. When women were at "the rudder of state," peace would result. Auclert also reasoned that the war of the sexes within the home was the first and foremost manifestation of atavistic aggression. Children witnessed the oppression and degradation of women at home and carried this lesson of social relations into their later public life. Thus, one must disarm men and abolish marital war before one could successfully apply such ambitions to the family of nations.

Hubertine Auclert also disseminated these ideas through her organization, Suffrage des femmes. There, she was an energetic activist, employing the lectures, posters, pamphlets, and petitions that characterize nineteenth-century bourgeois feminism. Auclert occasionally went further and staged demonstrations. In 1880, she refused to pay her taxes; in 1904, she attempted a public burning of the French Civil Code; in 1908, she interrupted French elections and smashed the ballot box at one poll.

Bibliography:

A. *L'Argent de la femme* (Paris, 1905); *Le Droit politique des femmes* (Paris, n.d.); *Egalité sociale et politique des femmes* (Paris, n.d.); *Les Femmes arabes en Algérie* (Paris, 1900); *Les Femmes au gouvernail* (Paris, 1923); *Le Nom de la femme* (Paris, 1905); *Le Vote des femmes* (Paris, 1908).

B. Patrick K. Bidelman, *Pariahs Stand Up! The Founding of the Liberal Feminist Movement in France, 1858-1889* (Westport, CT, 1982); Steven C. Hause and Anne R. Kenney, "The Limits of Suffragist Behavior: Legalism and Militancy in France, 1876-1922," *American Historical Review*, 86 (1981), 781-806; Georges Lhermite, "Necrologie—Hubertine Auclert," *Le Droit des femmes,* April, 1915; Jane Misme, "Les Grands figures du féminisme—Hubertine Auclert," *Minerva*, October 19, 1930.

Steven C. Hause

AUGSPURG, Anita (22 September 1857, Verden a.d. Aller, Hanover, Germany—20 December 1943, Zurich). *Education*: Dr. jur., Univ. of Zurich, 1897. *Career*: actress; co-founder of a photography studio; feminist activist; farmer; editor, *Parlamentarische Angelegenheiten und Gesetzgebung*, 1899-1907, and *Zeitschrift für Frauen-Stimmrecht,* 1907-12, both supplements to *Die Frauenbewegung; Frauenstimmrecht: Monatsheft des deutschen Verbandes für Frauenstimmrecht,* 1912-14; co-editor, *Die Frau im Staat*, 1919-33.

Anita Augspurg came from a family of left-liberal professional men who did not discuss politics with their women. She left home for Berlin to prepare for the teaching career acceptable for girls with intellectual pretensions. Once on her own, supported by a modest inheritance, she embarked on a peripatetic and unconventional life. After traveling about German-speaking Europe as an actress, she moved to Munich, where she ran the famous Atelier "Elvira" with photographer Sophie Goudstikker. Although German women could not practice law until the Weimar Republic, in 1893 Augspurg went to Zurich to study law, meanwhile using her knowledge in the campaign to reform women's treatment in the German Civil Code. With her actress' voice and stage presence, Augspurg appeared before feminist audiences throughout Germany, speaking on a variety of subjects and becoming a leader of the bourgeois feminist "left-wing." Her short-cropped hair attracted the attention of cartoonists looking for a prototypical feminist. In 1902 Augspurg and *Lida Gustava Heymann founded Germany's first women's suffrage organization. The two feminists were already living companions, and they remained together, in Munich, on a series of farms (Augsburg also studied scientific agriculture) in Bavaria, and then in exile.

Augspurg's first active involvement in pacifism came in 1899, at the time of the first International Peace Conference at The Hague. Margarete Selenka of Munich initiated contact with feminists throughout the world to organize supportive demonstrations by women. Augspurg handled the German events. Augspurg's journals during the Wilhelmine years regularly attacked German militarism and imperialism. Augspurg's and Heymann's revulsion at the bloodshed of World War I led them to propose a women's peace conference in the winter of 1914-15. Their idea meshed with that of Dr. *Aletta Jacobs of Holland. Augspurg served as secretary of the Women's Peace Conference at The Hague in April 1915, which demanded an immediate end to fighting, proposing terms that prefigured +Woodrow Wilson's Fourteen Points, and women's political activity as a means to lasting peace.

During Munich's revolutionary upheavals in 1918-19, Augspurg and Heymann worked to find a place for women in the council system. They also forcefully opposed the death penalty as a tool of revolutionary justice. In May 1919 Augspurg participated in the creation of the Women's International League for Peace and Freedom (WILPF) from a post-Hague committee. German women having been enfranchised, her own suffrage organization became a branch of WILPF. In 1919, Augspurg and Heymann began publishing *Die Frau im Staat*, which aimed to promote women's political participation, international understanding, and an end to violence. It opposed the Versailles Treaty as more male politics of "plunder and revenge." It approved passive resistance as a pacifist tool when used by the local population during French occupation of the Ruhr in 1923, while criticizing its nationalist exploitation. Augspurg promoted many reconciliatory gestures toward Germany's former enemies, including tree-planting and village repair in devastated France. Domestically, she attacked the militarism of Weimar society, notably the reliance by right and left on paramilitary formations. Finally, her journal promoted international disarmament.

Augspurg and Heymann were traveling outside Germany when Hitler assumed power in January 1933. Knowing they were on the enemy list, they never returned and their property was confiscated. They took refuge in Switzerland.

Bibliography:

A. *Erlebtes-Erschautes: Deutsche Frauen kämpfen für Freiheit, Recht und Frieden, 1850-1940,* with Lida Gustava Heymann, ed. by Margrit Twellmann (Meisenheim/Glan, 1972).

B. Gisela Brinker-Gabler, ed., *Frauen gegen den Krieg* (Frankfurt, 1980).

Amy Hackett

AYLES, Walter Henry (24 March 1879, London—6 July 1953, Invernesshire, England). *Education*: State elementary school; engineer apprentice, 1894. *Career*: engineer; trade union official, Amalgamated Society of Engineers; founding member, No-Conscription Fellowship, 1914-19; M.P. (Labour) North Bristol, 1923-24, 1929-31, Southall, 1945-53; organizing secretary, No More War Movement, 1926-32; general secretary, British Commonwealth Peace Federation, 1932-53.

Walter Ayles joined the Independent Labour party (ILP) soon after he was apprenticed as an engineer at age fifteen and immediately began to display the dedication, energy, and eloquence which served him so well in his careers as trade union official, socialist politician, and peace leader. Even as a very young man, Ayles followed the example of ILP leader *Keir Hardie and adopted a position of absolute pacifism. His outspoken opposition to the Anglo-Boer War did not prevent him from being elected as a Poor Law Guardian in Birmingham. After he moved to Bristol, he climbed a notch on the political ladder by successfully contesting a seat on the borough council. During the same period, Ayle's vigor, popularity, and willingness to work earned him an appointment as general secretary to the Bristol Branch of the ILP and membership on the ILP National Council. He was also selected as prospective Labour candidate for the parliamentary constituency of East Bristol.

When World War I began in 1914, Ayles immediately and characteristically condemned it as an abomination in which working class comrades from belligerent nations were to be tricked into killing one another to serve the interests of their capitalist oppressors. In November 1914, Ayles was, with Fenner Brockway, *Clifford Allen, and three others, one of the founding members of the No-Conscription Fellowship (NCF). After the government introduced compulsory service in early 1916, Ayles and five other members of the Fellowship's executive body were prosecuted for the production of a "seditious" pamphlet and sentenced to two month's imprisonment. This prison experience did not dampen his ardor for war resistance. Indeed, Ayles, who eventually served three additional sentences at hard labor as a conscientious objector, was a leader of the NCF's "absolutist" faction. This group believed that if a sufficient number of conscientious objectors (COs) refused all cooperation with the authorities, the NCF might actually defeat the conscription system and cause its repeal. Thus, when the majority of COs avoided prison by accepting some form of alternative service, Ayles felt that these "alternativists" were letting down the entire peace movement. He even rejected attempts by some NCF leaders to mitigate the suffering of imprisoned COs. Ayles's position may have been inflexible and doctrinaire, but he proved the courage of his convictions. For when the government attempted to silence complaints about the treatment of absolutists by collecting them in Wakefield prison under less harsh conditions, Ayles, as elected chairman of the prisoner's council, successfully argued for the collective refusal of any concessions other than unconditional release. The Wakefield COs were all returned to hard labor.

Upon his release from prison in 1919, Ayles returned to a political career, winning the North Bristol seat for Labour in 1923. During his first Parliamentary session, Ayles led an unsuccessful ILP attempt to reduce the size of the British Army by 150,000. National security through armaments, Ayles said, was an impossibility. After losing his seat in 1924, Ayles was appointed organizing secretary for the No More War Movement (NMWM), a body formed in 1921 by ex-NCFers and associated with the War Resisters' International. Despite his unwavering adherence to absolute pacifism, Ayles attempted to steer the NMWM along a moderate, if somewhat contradictory, course of support for the League of Nations (and presumably for sanctions) as well as total rejection of force in international affairs. Ayles' position resembled that of the Labour party which he again represented in Parliament from 1929 to 1931. However, many of Ayles's old pacifist colleagues came to believe that he had softened his pacifism for reasons of political expediency. Disagreements within the NMWM came to a head in 1932 when Ayles, who had lost his Parliamentary seat, resigned from the NMWM under the cloud of an inquiry into the movement's financial status. After leaving the NMWM, Ayles became general secretary of the British Commonwealth Peace Federation, an organization which seems to have served no clear purpose other than providing a salary for Walter Ayles. Although Ayles drifted outside the mainstream of the peace movement, he retained both his pacifist convictions and his political acumen. In 1945 he was again returned to Parliament, serving as Labour M.P. for Southall (Hayes and Harlington) until 1953 when he resigned due to ill health.

Walter Ayles was an eloquent platform speaker with a strong and magnetic personality; however, in the view of some critics, he would have been more successful, both as a politician and peace leader, had he been less dogmatic. Still, Ayles labored long and hard for peace and suffered for his beliefs not only due to his imprisonment in World War I and the controversies of the interwar period, but also in the bitter irony of his only son's dying in action during the Second World War. Ayles endured this loss with the aid of the Quaker faith he had adopted after his experiences as a conscientious objector and his abiding belief that Christian socialism could somehow bring peace and goodwill to humanity.

Bibliography:

A. *The Case for Disarmament* (n.p., n.d.); *Militarism Unmasked* (n.p., n.d.); *Why I Am a Conscientious Objector* (London [1916]).

B. Martin Ceadel, *Pacifism in Britain, 1914-1945: The Defining of a Faith* (Oxford, 1980); Jo Vellacott, *Bertrand Russell and the Pacifists in the First World War* (New York, 1981); LT, July 7, 1953.

Thomas C. Kennedy

B

BAART DE LA FAILLE, Samuel (20 May 1842, Leeuwarden, Netherlands—26 December 1917, The Hague). *Education*: Univ. of Groningen, 1860-64; Dr. of Theology, Univ. of Leyden, 1867. *Career*: minister, Dutch Reformed Church, 1868-86; peace activist.

Samuel Baart de la Faille served as minister in four parishes until his retirement in 1886 to devote the rest of his life to charitable labors, in particular, to peace activities. Together with his wife, Marianne Carolina Francesca Bachiene (1847-1912), daughter of a founder of the major Dutch peace movement, Baart de la Faille attended numerous peace congresses and participated actively on the national and international level. He was the first Dutch representative to be selected to serve on the Council of the International Peace Bureau (Berne), following a Universal Peace Congress meeting in 1896 at Budapest. Thereafter he participated in congresses until 1911 and provided articles for the national yearbook of the Dutch peace movement describing the congresses.

The Dutch movement, renamed Vrede door Recht in 1901, had been created in 1871. Baart de la Faille served as an officer from 1897-1915 and to most Europeans, he became the personification of the movement. During the Hague Peace Congress of 1899, he provided a meeting place for the numerous European peace leaders who had come to "lobby" the diplomats on behalf of international arbitration and arms limitation.

While many of his colleagues found him an exacting taskmaster, his intelligence and understanding of peace issues usually led all to defer to his advice. In 1915, on his retirement from the society, he was named an honorary member, an unusual status only awarded to *Andrew Carnegie.

Bibliography:

B. "Levensbericht van Dr. S. Baart de la Faille," in *Levensberichten van de afgestorven leden van de Maatschappij der Nederlandse Letterkunde te Leiden, 1917-1918* (Leyden, 1918).

J. H. Rombach

BAILEY, Vernon Gerald (4 July 1903, Manchester, England—11 May 1972, Bramley, Surrey). *Education*: B.A., Clare Coll., Cambridge Univ., 1925, M.A., 1929. *Career*: secretary (later director), National Peace Council, 1930-49; secretary (later vice-chairman), Friends East-West Relations Committee, 1950-62; vice-chairman, Friends Peace and International Relations Committee, 1965-72; politician, lecturer, editor, and peace activist.

Gerald Bailey was born into a Quaker family and educated at Friends' schools in Yorkshire. His interest in politics developed while a student in the 1920s. He was twice a Parliamentary candidate in Hampshire, standing as a Liberal in 1929 and an Independent in 1935; but it was above all as an organizer and lecturer, working through Quaker and other nonparty organizations, that he made his contribution to the cause of peace.

For nineteen years he ran the National Peace Council and took it to the zenith of its strength and influence as a coordinating body. Granted unconditional exemption as a conscientious objector in the Second World War, Bailey organized the Peace Aims Conferences at Oxford which, with their carefully selected participants, gained widespread recognition and led to the publication of a series of influential Peace Aims Pamphlets and, in 1945, the National Petition for a Constructive Peace. He played a leading part in the creation of the World Union of Peace Organizations (later known as ILCOP) and presided at its first assembly, at Geneva, in 1948. The United Nations Association also enjoyed his wholehearted support. For many years he was a member of its Executive Committee, chairman of its Guildford (Surrey) branch, and a frequent visitor to UN sessions.

Bailey sought to promote international understanding and world accord in other ways. Throughout the 1950s he worked with Quaker groups to ease East-West relations. He helped organize the historic Quaker mission to Moscow in 1951, taking part in that and subsequent Quaker missions to China in 1955 and Poland in 1958. He also worked with government-sponsored organizations, such as the Great Britain-East Europe Centre and the Great Britain-USSR Association, which sought to promote better relations between communist nations and the West. He edited *The Great Britain-USSR Handbook* as well as two internationalist journals, *Britain-USSR* and *World Issues*. Even more than many of his Quaker colleagues, Bailey was suspicious of the pro-Soviet line on peace and avoided ''front'' organizations that criticized the West at every opportunity. Conversely, he was more inclined to appreciate the merits of British government policies. Arguing robustly against extreme or simple-minded attitudes, his provocatively phrased insistence that Friends think about world issues realistically commanded respect and admiration, if not always assent.

Deeply and constantly aware of the moral dilemma of pacifism, he gave himself unstintingly to the betterment of international relations. His high sense of civic responsibility not only helped him to sympathize with diplomats and politicians in their various predicaments, but also motivated him to educate his fellow-countrymen, especially the young, in the realities of their world—as a lecturer, organizer, and perhaps most eloquently in 1970 in a book for schoolchildren, entitled *Problems of Peace*.

Bibliography:

A. *The East-West Problem: A Re-Assessment* (London, 1960); *The Politics of Peace: The Lilly Lectures in Religion* (Richmond, IN, 1963); *Problems of Peace* (London, 1970).

B. B. Leslie Metcalf and Eric S. Tucker, ''Dear Gerald. . .,'' *The Friend*, 130 (May 26, 1972), 629-30; ''Testimonies to the Grace of God as shown in the Lives of Deceased

Friends . . . Vernon Gerald Bailey," *Proceedings of London Yearly Meeting of the Society of-Friends, 1973* (London, 1973), 207-9.

Nicholas A. Sims

BAJER, Fredrik (21 April 1837, Vester Egede, Denmark—22 January 1922, Copenhagen). *Education*: Danish military schools, 1854-56. *Career*: lieutenant, Danish Army, 1856-65; study of foreign languages, school teacher, translator, Copenhagen, 1865-72; member of parliament, 1872-95.

In the 1864 war against Prussia, Fredrik Bajer, a professional soldier, gained promotion to the rank of first lieutenant because of his able command of Danish troops. He was discharged, however, the following year when the end of the war led to a general reduction in the army establishment. He took up the study and teaching of languages and in the course of this became interested in pacifist and internationalist ideas.

Although he established contacts with *Frédéric Passy in 1867 and took a great interest in the Frenchman's work, Bajer's own efforts were concentrated initially on advancing the cause of Nordic unity. In 1870 he founded the Society of Nordic Free States to promote the formation of a community of Denmark, Norway, and Sweden. He expected that the coordination of their policies, under a republican constitution, would go hand in hand with the maintenance of their individual independence. This latter condition would require also that the Nordic countries adopt a policy of permanent neutrality and obtain from the international community firm guarantees respecting this status.

When Bajer founded the first Danish peace society in 1882, its name—Society for Promotion of Danish Neutrality—reflected the importance that he attached to neutrality as a requirement for peace. For the next ten years he served as president of the Society, which later became the Danish Peace Society and still later the Danish Peace and League of Nations Society. Towards the end of the decade, when the international organization of the peace movement gathered momentum, Bajer's international involvement and reputation greatly increased. He attended the first World Peace Congress, held in Paris in 1889, and represented the Danish Peace Society in subsequent annual congresses until 1914. The third congress, at Rome in 1891, approved his proposal, made the previous year at the London congress, for the creation of a permanent bureau to serve the international peace movement. He was appointed president of the governing board of this International Peace Bureau (initially located in Bern, Switzerland, and now in Geneva) from its inception until 1907, when deteriorating health led to his resignation; in recognition of his services he was made honorary president. Bajer was also present when the first meeting of the Interparliamentary Union took place in Paris in 1889. Two years later he founded the Danish Interparliamentary Group, of which he was the secretary for the next twenty-five years, and in 1908 he helped organize a Scandinavian Interparliamentary Union.

Apart from being Denmark's foremost pacifist and internationalist, Bajer was one of its leading advocates of women's rights. In 1871 he founded with his wife, Mathilde Schluter Bajer, a peace leader in her own right, the Danish Women's League. He also played a significant part in the development of the education system of his country.

In 1908 Bajer received, together with *Klas Arnoldson, the Nobel Peace Prize. In his lecture, in which he made some critical observations about the organization of the peace movement, he identified three "columns" amongst the forces working for peace—peoples, parliaments, and governments whose respective activities for peace were embodied in the international peace congresses, the interparliamentary union conferences, and the intergovernmental peace conferences. Bajer not only played a major role in the first two of these organizations for peace, but also advanced the goals of the Hague Conferences by his lifelong dedication to the cause of Nordic cooperation, neutrality, and arbitration.

Bibliography:

A. *Dansk Fredsforenings Historie* (København, 1894); *Forespörgsel i Folketinget angaaende Danmarks Neutralisering* (Aarhus, 1885); *Idéen til Nordens, Saerlig Danmarks vedvarende Neutralitet* (København, 1900); *Nordiske Neutralitetsforbund* (København, 1885); "Un nouvel organe de pacigérance," *Revue de droit international et de législation comparée* (1906), 57-63; *Om Årsager til Krig og Voldgift i Europa siden År 1800* (København, 1897); "The Organization of the Peace Movement," in Frederick W. Haberman, ed., *Nobel Lectures-Peace* (Amsterdam, 1972), I, 190-208; A *Serious Drama of Modern History: How Danish Slesvig Was Lost* (London, 1897, Danish ed., København, 1896); *Tactics for the Friends of Peace* (Wisbech, U.K., 1891).

B. Alfred H. Fried, *Handbuch der Friedensbewegung* (2nd ed., Berlin, 1911-13, reissued, New York, 1972), II, 238; *Privatarkiver Politikeren Fredrik Bajer og Hustrus Arkiv* (København, 1963); August Schou, *Histoire de l'internationalisme* (Oslo, 1963), III, 510-16.

Peter van den Dungen

BALCH, Emily Greene (8 January 1867, Jamaica Plain, MA—9 January 1961, Cambridge, MA). *Education*: B.A., Bryn Mawr Coll., 1889; study at Sorbonne, 1890-91; graduate work at Harvard Univ. Annex (later Radcliffe Coll.), 1893, Univ. of Chicago, 1895, Univ. of Berlin, 1895-96. *Career*: social worker, Children's Aid Society, Boston, 1891; co-founder, Denison House Settlement, Boston, 1892-93; faculty, Wellesley Coll. 1896-1918; editorial staff, *Nation*, 1918-19; international secretary, Women's International League for Peace and Freedom, 1919-22, 1934-35; president of American section of WILPF, 1931; peace society executive and economist.

Although Emily Greene Balch only reached international fame in 1946, when she received the Nobel Peace Prize, she had long been revered within the peace movement. Indeed, her name was held synonymous with the Women's International League for Peace and Freedom, which she helped found and guide in its early years.

Until she was fifty-two years old, the career of Emily Balch centered on settlement work, state regulatory commissions, and the teaching of economics at Wellesley College. A true child of the Progressive era, her initial interests were immigration, relief, and the economic role of women, and she wrote prolifically on these topics.

Although she had been a pacifist since the Spanish-American War, her peace movement involvement began with World War I. In 1915 she was one of forty American delegates to the International Congress of Women at The Hague. Here she served as part of a small delegation that sought to attain peace by continuous mediation. She first visited various neutral Scandinavian countries and Russia, then conferred with +Sir Edward Grey and +Woodrow Wilson. Though her efforts ended in failure, for which she blamed President Wilson, in 1916 she was optimistic enough to become one of the twelve members of Henry Ford's Stockholm Neutral Conference for Continuous Mediation. She made two studies for the Stockholm group's Committee on Constructive Peace: one outlined a postwar rehabilitation fund, to be contributed by neutral powers; the other proposed an international administration of colonies that resembled the mandate system. In 1916-17 she took a sabbatical leave to work in New York against American intervention in the world war. She was active in such groups as the American Union Against Militarism, the Fellowship of Reconciliation, and the Women's Peace party.

Once the United States entered the conflict, Balch became a vigorous left-wing opponent of American policy and a strong supporter of the left-wing People's Council of America. Yet she disavowed her former socialism, finding loopholes in its theories of class struggle and surplus value. In 1918, because of her antiwar activities, the Wellesley trustees refused to renew her contract.

When the International Congress of Women again met in 1919, this time in Zurich, Balch played a prominent role. The organization established itself on a permanent basis, changed its name to the Women's International League for Peace and Freedom (WILPF), and moved to Geneva. Balch became its first international secretary-treasurer, in which capacity she established the Geneva headquarters, set up organization guidelines, and focused the group's attention on eliminating the causes of war. Even after she resigned because of ill health in 1922, she served the WILPF in numerous other capacities. In 1934 she assumed her post again, doing so without pay to see the organization through a financial crisis. A woman of gaunt appearance but of tremendous energy, she sponsored summer schools on peace education, helped develop branches in some fifty countries, and acted in a sense as the WILPF's minister without portfolio. Although the WILPF housed many pacifists within it, particularly in the United States, Balch used her tact and gentle wit to keep the body pluralistic and inclusive.

In dealing with issues of world peace, Balch was fundamentally a pragmatist, one who favored piecemeal reform over sweeping but impractical change. She deplored the Versailles settlement, attacked the Allied blockade of Germany, and criticized the coercive bases of the League Covenant. Although she had no illusions concerning the League's ability to solve major conflicts, she found it able to promote economic, scientific, and cultural cooperation. Her personal activities included League work relating to drug control, admission of Albania, protection of refugees, and the internationalization of aviation.

One of Balch's major efforts concerned Haiti, occupied by United States marines in 1915. In 1926 she was part of a six-person task force that included economist Paul Douglas. Finding the situation there highly explosive, she drafted a long report that called upon America to maintain its social services while removing its troops and turning over the government to its black population.

During the interwar period, she backed disarmament agreements and the Kellogg-Briand Pact and claimed that Germany had a right to rearm. When Japan attacked Mukden in 1931, she called for an international administration of Manchuria that would insure treaty rights to all nations. She recommended mediation in the Spanish Civil War, outlining a scheme wherein a moderate Republican government would have ten years to plan in such sensitive areas as religion, education, and land reform. Declaring that it was morally impossible to treat agressor and victim alike, she endorsed such nonmilitary forms of international coercion as moral, diplomatic, and economic pressure. (She would not, however, support a food blockade). She also worked laboriously for the admission of European refugees, claiming that immigration would benefit the United States economically and culturally.

When World War II broke out, she hoped for an allied victory, although she did not want the United States to enter the conflict. Once Japan attacked Pearl Harbor, she claimed that fighting was America's only option and contributed to community war funds. She did, however, oppose the unconditional surrender policy, asserting that it would only prolong the war. She sought to alleviate the plight of interred Japanese-Americans, backed the rights of conscientious objectors, and condemned Hitler's efforts to annihilate Europe's Jews. In 1946 she shared the Nobel Peace Prize with the ecumenical churchman John R. Mott. In that year she also called for a women's peace party that would cooperate for peace across national lines.

During the Cold War, she claimed that any war against communism, even if successfully fought, would leave conditions that would make more drastic oppression and collectivism inevitable. She lauded the specialized agencies of the United Nations, but opposed the application of majority rule to international organization. As she had considerable distrust of government as such, she found no reason to believe that a world government, even a federal one, would be run differently than a national state. She placed her major hope in international administration—run independently of participating governments—to control world agriculture, underdeveloped areas, airways, nuclear energy, the high seas, strategic bases, polar regions, and international waterways, including Panama, Suez, and the Mediterranean.

In some ways, Balch always remained the progressive reformer, looking for administrative mechanisms that utilized techniques of planning by experts in the greater cause of international justice. While always a woman of great principle, she was seldom dogmatic in her views, and her tact helped the WILPF weather storms that might otherwise have destroyed it.

Bibliography:

A. *Approaches to the Great Settlement* (New York, 1918); *Women at The Hague* (with Jane Addams and Alice Hamilton; New York, 1915).

B. Mercedes M. Randall, ed., *Beyond Nationalism: The Social Thought of Emily Greene Balch* (New York, 1972); Mercedes M. Randall, *Improper Bostonian: Emily Greene Balch* (New York, 1964); NAW: The Modern Period, 41-45.

C. Emily Greene Balch Papers, Swarthmore College Peace Collection.

Justus D. Doenecke

BARBUSSE, Henri (17 May 1873, Asnières, Seine, France—30 August 1935, Moscow, USSR). *Education*: Bachelor of science and arts, Collège Rollin, 1891, licence ès-lettres, Sorbonne, 1893. *Career*: poet, editor, novelist, biographer, journalist, political organizer, Communist intellectual.

Henri Barbusse was France's most visible Communist intellectual in the period between the wars. He began his literary career as a neo-symbolist poet; he worked for Éditions Pierre Lafitte as an editor from 1902 and in 1912 he was named literary director of Hachette Publications. As a *fin-de-siècle* Parisian man of letters, Barbusse published essays and a novel before the Great War. A prewar pacifist, he wrote for the *Revue de la Paix*, which held that international arbitration was the way to prevent war.

Barbusse enlisted for combat in 1914 and spent 22 months at the trenches as a common soldier. The Great War decisively changed his life and work. His masterpiece, *Le Feu (Under Fire)*, first serialized in 1916 and published in 1917 (winner of the prestigious Prix Goncourt in 1916), remains one of the most powerful pieces of literature to emerge from the war. *Le Feu* unambiguously ruptures with the literary convention of praising warlike heroism and patriotism. The novel vividly depicts trench life while empathically portraying the life of the soldier. The reader experiences the text as an eloquent denunciation of the war. *Le Feu* demonstrates that the war was stupid, futile, bestial, an unending savage massacre.

After the war, Barbusse concentrated on recruiting veterans to the cause of international communism. He was the head of the Republican Association of Ex-Servicemen, where he collaborated with *Raymond Lefebvre and *Paul Vaillant-Couturier. As founder and editor of the review *Clarté*, and spearhead of the Clarté movement, Barbusse was instrumental in making the communist cause comprehensible to a generation of French intellectuals in the early 1920s. The politics of *Clarté* were internationalist, pacifist, supportive of the Russian Revolution, independent from political parties, and without strong links either to Marxism or Jaurèsian socialism. Barbusse's idealism spilled over into the doctrinal vagueness and humanism of *Clarté*—for instance he served as honorary president of the Esperanto movement in 1921. Barbusse's key reference point was the crimes and butchery of the First World War.

After publishing communist inspired manifestoes and appeals, the most significant of which was the rhetorical brochure, *The Knife Between the Teeth* (1920), after repudiating +Woodrow Wilson in 1920, and after engaging the pacifist-idealist *Romain Rolland in a celebrated controversy over the role and responsibility of the postwar intellectual (1922), Barbusse joined the French Communist party in 1923. He was the literary director of *L'Humanité* from 1926-29; he directed the Communist oriented but ostensibly independent weekly, *Monde*, from 1928-35; and in 1932 became one of the directors of *Commune*, the organ of the Revolutionary Association of Artists and Writers. As an activist, orator, and journalist for the Communist International, and as a leading figure in Communist front organizations, Barbusse took public positions against colonialism, militarism, and fascism. He argued for a proletarian form of literature, for a literature of commitment, and he propagandized for an appreciation of the social and educational experiment in the Soviet Union. With Romain Rolland he initiated and coordinated the Amsterdam-Pleyel Movement in 1932, itself a forerunner and subsequently a constituent part of the French Popular Front. From 1933 till his death, Barbusse was the president of the World Committee Against War and Fascism. His final years were spent in exhausting propaganda activity in which he campaigned for the Soviet Union, for peace, for Popular Front governments, and against international fascism. His biographies reveal a strong sentimental if not mawkish streak; his two studies of Jesus in 1927 betray a vague religious mysticism, a non-secular component to Barbusse's world vision. His final work, *Stalin* (1935) was a hagiography of the Soviet dictator; unreadable today, Barbusse wrote it as an act of spiritual and political devotion. It stands as a tribute to Stalin's omnipotence and omniscience.

Barbusse's Marxism was unsophisticated. He rarely cited Marx's texts, nor was he knowledgeable about the classics in the Marxist or socialist tradition. He was convinced that communism, following the Bolshevik model, could eradicate the social and economic roots of war. For Barbusse communism meant egalitarian internationalism, that is fraternity between intellectual and manual workers, and the liberation of working people from cultural deprivation and material poverty. His optimism about the "new man" and the "new society" being built in the Soviet Union went hand in hand with his amorphous, poorly digested ideas about communist theory. Barbusse saw Marxism as simply a scientific, rational, and mathematical ideology; it issued from republicanism, and it culminated the traditions begun by Rousseau and the utopian socialists. He felt that corporate capitalism engendered war, imperialism, and fascism and that communism was the only bulwark against these evils.

Barbusse represented a first generation of French literary men who came to French Communism with a blend of confusion, grandiose expectations, generosity of spirit, and a search for simple solutions to complex social and cultural issues. There was a dialectical relationship between his disgust for the butchery of World War I and his attraction to international communism. Poorly versed in theory or in philosophy, not well tutored in history, not terribly self-critical or self-reflexive, Barbusse sacrificed his health, literary reputation, and personal integrity to work for the "great cause" of the Soviet Union. A Stalinist intellectual, Barbusse died before realizing that his "god" had failed. True to party discipline he never repudiated his faith, despite his knowledge of practical as well as theoretical excesses, even aberrations, within the communist movement.

Bibliography:

A. *Clarté* (Paris, 1917); *Le Couteau entre les dents* (Paris, 1920); *Le Feu* (Paris, 1917); *Jésus* (Paris, 1927); *Judas de Jésus* (Paris, 1927); *La Lueur dans l'abime* (Paris, 1920); *Staline* (Paris, 1935); *Zola* (Paris, 1932).

B. Vladimir Brett, *Henri Barbusse sa marche vers Clarte son mouvement Clarté* (Prague, 1963), David James Fisher, "The Rolland-Barbusse Debate," *Survey* 20 (July, 1974), 121-59; Guessler Normand, "Henri Barbusse and his *Monde* (1928-1935): Progeny of the Clarté Movement and the Review Clarté," *Journal of Contemporary History*, II (July, 1976), 173-97; Annette Vidal, *Henri Barbusse, Soldat de la paix* (Paris, 1953).

David James Fisher

BASCH, Victor (18 August 1863, Budapest, Hungary—10 January 1944, Lyons, France). *Education*: agrégation, Sorbonne, 1889, Doctorat d'état, 1897. Career: professor, universities of Nancy and Rennes, Sorbonne; vice president and president, Ligue des droits de l'homme, 1909–40; educator, reformer, and peace activist.

In 1898 Victor Basch was jolted out of the protected world of academia and family by the case of Captain Alfred Dreyfus, (victim of anti-Semitism and militarism), and galvanized into action. The Basch house in Rennes became the headquarters of Dreyfus' partisans and lawyers, as well as the site of many violent anti-Dreyfus demonstrations. From that period until the end of his life, motivated by "a boundless love of justice," Basch fought for the realization of humanitarian ideals, an idealism which he combined with a clear analysis of the role of capital and the ruling classes in world affairs.

A member of the Socialist party, Basch remained committed all his life to the Ligue des droits de l'homme (League for the Rights of Man), an organization born of the Dreyfus case. Vice president from 1909, he was president of the Ligue from 1926 until 1940. Basch defined the Ligue's main goals as the defense of human rights and the promotion of self-determination, peace, democracy, and the rights of women and children. Throughout the interwar period, Basch and the Ligue defended a host of causes involving the rights of individuals: Nicola Sacco and Bartolomeo Vanzetti in the United States, the rights of colonial peoples and of foreigners in France, the rights of political asylum, and women's suffrage.

For forty years Victor Basch and the Ligue dedicated themselves to the struggle for justice and for peace among nations. An admirer of German culture, he tried relentlessly to counter militaristic forces within and to promote understanding between, France and Germany. He was convinced that the responsibility for World War I rested with Germany, which therefore owed France reparations. He felt, nonetheless, that excessive Allied demands and the threat of military occupation would discourage German democrats and Socialists and lead to future conflicts. He had faith in the international peace effort and in the League of Nations. When the Allies marched into the Rhineland in 1923, Basch condemned the occupation and continued traveling to Germany for peace discussions, running many personal risks. (In Potsdam in 1924, he barely escaped kidnapping by nationalist thugs.)

The years between the wars saw the irresistible ascent of fascism in Europe. As a Jew, a German scholar, and a sophisticated observer of world politics, Basch had no illusions about the evil, totalitarian nature of fascism. Even before 1933 he began warning the French about the horrors of Adolf Hitler's Germany, adding to his own information the gruesome stories of the many refugees in contact with the Ligue. No longer could any democratic nation close its eyes to the real nature of a regime that threw its opponents into concentration camps and that deprived the Jews and other minorities of their livelihood, their education, and, more and more systematically, of their lives. Basch's confidence in the power of moral persuasion and in the League of Nations was severely shaken when in 1935 Benito Mussolini's invasion of Ethiopia was met with international apathy. The following year, with the start of the Spanish Civil War, Basch became convinced that official "nonintervention" policies were only serving the goals of Germany and Italy. He visited Spain and then went to England, vainly attempting to convince the government that without support Republican Spain would succumb to the fascist conspiracy.

During these years dormant disagreements within the ranks of the Ligue came to a head and divided the absolute pacifists, who advocated peace at all costs, from those who, like Basch, insisted on taking a stand against the totalitarian ideology intent on world conquest. Basch opposed the fascist factions which emerged in France and became the head of the Rassemblement démocratique (Democratic Assembly). He was particularly active in the 1936 Popular Front government and in 1938, when England and France delivered Czechoslovakia into Hitler's hands at Munich, he protested once more, knowing that selling out the Czechs was both morally shameful and politically useless.

After the fall of France in 1939, Basch, then nearly 80, went to live in Lyons with his wife, Hilona. Although his life was in danger, he refused to leave the country or go into hiding. On the night of January 10, 1944, Basch and his wife were taken and executed by a commando of German Gestapo and French "Milice," headed by an extreme rightwing French naval officer. Victor Basch died for his ideas and for his ideals. But more important he lived and fought for them.

Bibliography:

A. *L'Aube, proses de guerre* (Paris, 1918); *Guernica, la mainmise—hitlérienne sur le pays Basque* (Paris, 1937); *Le Guerre de 1914 et le droit* (Paris, 1915); *L'Individualisme anarchiste Max Stirner* (Paris, 1904).

B. G. Langevin et al, *Victor Basch, 1863–1944* (Paris 1945); Michel Lenine, *Affaires non classées* (Paris, 1973).

Françoise Basch

BASTIAT, Claude Frédéric (30 June 1801, Bayonne, France—24 December 1850, Rome). *Career*: farmer, businessman; justice of the peace, Mugron, 1831–44; counselor general of Landes, 1832; editor, *Le libre-échange*, 1846; member of the Constitutional Assembly and vice-president of the Commission of Finances, 1848–50.

There was a broad range of efforts during the nineteenth century to connect the phenomena of peace and war with economics. One of the earliest and most influential people involved in these efforts was Frédéric Bastiat. He argued that peace and economic progress went hand in hand, as did war and economic stagnation. The key to economic progress was classical liberalism, particularly policies of free trade and laissez faire. These policies would inevitably lead to prosperity and a recognition by all that prosperity required internal and international interdependence, and thus avoidance of war.

He developed and propagated these views in three ways. First, as an economist he was primarily a pamphleteer and journalist who became known as a champion of free trade and an opponent of socialism. He drew ideas from theorists such as Adam Smith, J. B. Say, and David Ricardo and wrote extensively on classical liberalism, particularly for the *Journal des économistes* and his own journal, *Le Libre-échange*. His clearest statement on the connections between peace, liberty, and economic policies came in 1849 with the publication of *Paix et liberté ou le budget républicain*. By this time he had become convinced that men, social classes, and nations were tied together by economic interests. Second, as a minor governmental official under the July Monarchy (1830–48), as a member of the Constitutional Assembly in 1848, and as vice-president of the Commission of Finances during the Second Republic, he attempted to direct governmental policy toward more liberal and pacific ends. Finally, he became directly involved in peace movements, participating actively in the Peace Congress of Paris (1849).

As a French republican and admirer of England, he saw liberalism and industrialism inevitably and triumphantly on the rise. This fit well with his belief that the moral, intellectual, and especially the economic enlightenment of man would lead to the elimination of war, a belief that would persist among many through the nineteenth century. His early death in 1850 prevented him from witnessing events that might have altered his optimism about the course of history.

Bibliography:

A. *Cobden et la ligue* (Paris, 1845); *Les Harmonies économiques* (Paris, 1850); *La Loi* (Paris, 1850); *Paix et liberté ou le budget républicain* (Paris, 1849); *Propriété et loi* (Paris, 1848); *Sophismes économiques* (Paris, 1845–1848).

B. Louis Bruel, *Bastiat et le libre échange* (Paris, 1931); George Charles Roche, *Frédéric Bastiat: A Man Alone* (New Rochelle, NY, 1971); Dean Russell, *Frédéric Bastiat: Ideas and Influence* (New York, 1969).

Dennis M. Sherman

BAXTER, Archibald McColl Learmonth (13 December 1881, Brighton, near Dunedin, New Zealand—10 August 1970, Dunedin). *Career*: laborer, farmer, and peace activist.

Archibald Baxter's father was a farmworker who had migrated from Scotland to the Scottish settlement of Otago in 1860. Baxter, like many in his circumstances, left school at an early age to become a farmhand, later taking on assorted work as a carter, roadbuilder, rabbiter, and shearer. During the 1920s he farmed on his own account but sold out in 1930.

Baxter came to pacifism as a young man largely on his own, having no contact with any antimilitarist organization. Initially he was deeply impressed with the case against the Boer War, and this distaste for war soon developed into a personal commitment to refuse military service. Arrested and sent to camp when conscription was introduced in 1916, he spent several months in detention barracks and prison for disobedience before being shipped overseas aboard a military transport. In England he was kept handcuffed and forced into uniform. On his transfer to France the army tried every means to break his resistance; he was brutally treated in a punishment camp, sent to exposed parts of the front line, and deprived of food and proper medical aid. In the end he collapsed from the ordeal, was treated as a "mental case," and repatriated to New Zealand. The army granted him a discharge, which he had to accept or remain under its control.

Baxter became New Zealand's most prominent World War I conscientious objector, though many others, including Baxter's own brothers, also suffered severely. At the time his case became well-publicized, especially through the efforts of the Labour party which was emphasizing its antimilitarism in an attempt to broaden its electoral appeal. Over the years, however, Baxter developed into a significant martyr and hero-figure. His book recounting his wartime ordeal, first published in 1939, remains an important statement quite apart from its considerable literary merit. It is a telling portrayal of men at war and their response to the demands of the "military machine." It poses a challenge to the idea of the progressive society by pointing out what repression and brutality lurked in a democracy that prided itself on its record of enlightened reform. It focuses on the condemnation of war, not as the product of ideology, but as a simple moral impulse. Baxter viewed war as evil, and he once told an army chaplain that he was prepared to oppose it even if it meant death for himself.

Baxter remained active in the peace movement after World War I. He was a local leader of the No More War Movement and while on an overseas trip in 1937 he represented New Zealand at the War Resisters' International conference in Copenhagen. During World War II he interceded with the authorities on behalf of pacifists and conscientious objectors. But his enduring contribution to the cause of peace lies in his standing forth as an ordinary man acting according to his conceptions of what is right and necessary.

Bibliography:

A. *We Will Not Cease* (London, 1939; reprinted in New Zealand, 1968 and 1980.)

B. Millicent Baxter, *The Memoirs of Millicent Baxter* (Whatamongo Bay, NZ, 1981); H. E. Holland, *Armageddon or Calvary: the Conscientious Objectors of New Zealand and the 'Process of their Conversion'* (Wellington, NZ, 1919).

J. E. Cookson

BEALES, Edmond (3 July 1803, Newnham, Cambridge, England—26 June 1881, London). *Education*: B.A., Trinity Coll., Cambridge Univ., 1825, M.A.,

1828. *Career*: barrister; judge; reformer and pamphleteer for domestic and foreign causes.

The son of a merchant, himself a political reformer, Edmond Beales' own work in reform began with his enduring interest in foreign affairs. He took a leading role in organizations on behalf of Polish independence and Polish refugees, and in the 1830s and 1860s wrote several pamphlets on the Polish question. Beales became particularly active in radical causes in the turbulent 1860s. He joined the Emancipation Society during the American Civil War and championed the radical nationalist movement underway in Italy.

Though not a promoter of violent or illegal activities, Beales relied upon popular protest and working-class support in his pursuit of reform. In 1864 he supported a demonstration, despite police opposition, to protest the British government's curtailment of Giuseppe Garibaldi's tour, and later published a pamphlet defending the right of public meeting. Immediately following the demonstration, its organizers established the Reform League and elected Beales as president. His efforts in the League, for which he became best known, were directed towards securing manhood suffrage. Although he supported mass demonstrations in support of the reform movement, he eschewed violence and promoted public order. The passage of Benjamin Disraeli's reform bill in 1867 signified the League's victory. Two years later, Beales resigned as president and, lacking further purpose, the Reform League dissolved.

Beales, however, remained politically active as an antiwar activist, assuming the presidency of the League of Peace and Liberty (later the International Arbitration League) when *William Randal Cremer established a London branch in 1867. He held the presidency until his death.

Beales opposed militarism because it violated Christian morality, not because it distracted the workers from class consciousness. He was a respectable, though radical, middle-class, Victorian reformer. Due to his political activities, the lord chief justice declined to reappoint him in 1866 to his post of chancery barrister. But in 1870 the lord chancellor, amid Tory denunciations, made him a county court judge.

Bibliography:

A. *Poland: Address to Working Men* (London, 1863?); *Poland, France, and England* (London, 1864?); *The Polish Question Briefly Stated* (London, 1835?); *Representative Reform* . . . (London, 1868).

B. A. C. F. Beales, *The History of Peace: A Short Account of the Organised Movements for International Peace* (London, 1931); George Jacob Holyoake, *Sixty Years of an Agitator's Life* (2 vols., London, 1900); DNB, II, 9; LT, June 28, 1881.

Stanley M. Max

BEARD, Charles Austin (27 November 1874, Knightstown, IN—1 September 1948, New Haven, CT). *Education*: Ph.B. DePauw Univ., 1898; M.A.; Columbia Univ., 1903, Ph.D., 1904. *Career*: lecturer in History and Public Law, Columbia Univ., 1904–7; professor of Politics, Columbia Univ., 1907–17; director of Training School for Public Service, New York City, 1917–22; governmental consultant and adviser, visiting professor and lecturer, author and historian.

Charles A. Beard made his greatest contribution to peace through his writings. One of the most distinguished and widely read historians of our time, his works, including popular textbooks, exercised a tremendous influence, especially in the era between the world wars. For Beard, questions of peace or war were vital to an understanding of the history which he analyzed so eloquently in his classic *Rise of American Civilization*.

Beard was born in the midwest, where his family enjoyed a comfortable upper-middle-class status that enabled the young Charles to travel abroad before he completed his formal education. Populism, visits to Hull House in Chicago, the Spanish-American War, and his growing anti-imperialism, as well as contacts with the labor movement in England, all stirred his youthful idealism. But Beard was never a pacifist in a formal sense, and he supported +Woodrow Wilson's foreign policy. Although he had considerable nostalgia for the Jeffersonian agrarian tradition, Beard's isolationism was not the result of naiveté or a rural midwestern background. Few scholars have matched him in the breadth of his historical understanding, and he was throughout his career a sophisticated, cosmopolitan intellectual.

Despite Beard's support for American entrance into the First World War and for the League of Nations, he was not optimistic about the prospects of international cooperation and world peace. His adherence to an economic interpretation of history made him suspicious of the militarism and imperialism which he saw as both a cause and result of the war. At the same time, his concern over postwar violations of civil liberties, and later the revelations of the Senate munitions investigation and the economic crash of 1929, strengthened his growing disillusionment. During the early New Deal, he believed that social and economic planning, by creating a self-contained society, might enhance American security and isolation from the danger of foreign war. But Beard also feared that +Franklin D. Roosevelt would turn to intervention abroad as a means of solving the domestic problems of the depression.

Beard strongly supported the neutrality legislation of the 1930s. He also evolved his concept of "continentalism" as a means of self-protection for the Americas. He actively expounded his views in dozens of magazine articles and in testimony at Congressional hearings in which he opposed naval expansion and conscription. But following the Japanese attack on Pearl Harbor, he retreated to his study to write the history of how President Roosevelt and the interventionists had provoked America's entrance into yet another global struggle for international power.

On September 1, 1948, the year of the publication of his final work, *President Roosevelt and the Coming of the War*, Beard died as he neared the age of 74. A critic of the imperial presidency and apprehensive of "the headlong trend in the direction of war and national collapse," he remained to the end of his life the thoughtful iconoclast who had once scornfully remarked of America's militarists that they "will want to annex the moon."

Bibliography:

A. *American Foreign policy in the Making 1932–1940* (New Haven, CT, 1946); *The Idea of National Interest* (New York, 1934).

B. Howard K. Beale, ed., *Charles A. Beard: An Appraisal* (Lexington, KY, 1954); Thomas C. Kennedy, *Charles A. Beard and American Foreign Policy* (Gainesville, FL, 1975).

Arthur A. Ekirch, Jr.

BEBEL, Ferdinand August (22 February 1840, Deutz [now part of Cologne] Germany—13 August 1913, Churwalden/Passug, Switzerland). *Education*: completed primary school, 1854; apprenticeship as wood-turner, 1854–57, journeyman, 1858–60. *Career*: wood-turner, writer, socialist politician, and Reichstag deputy.

August Bebel's rise within the German socialist movement to chairman of the German Social Democratic party and leader of its Reichstag faction (1892–1913) coincided with the rise of Imperial Germany to great power status in European politics under Bismarck and the Hohenzollern dynasty. His contribution to the development of German socialism is less to be found in theoretical formulations than in his talent for organizing German workers and his courageous opposition to the policies, internal and foreign, of the Imperial government as well as to the predominance of the Prussian military in German life. His opposition to the undemocratic and militaristic German state began with his strong condemnation of the Austro-Prussian War which led to the creation of the North German confederation under Prussian hegemony. The program of the Saxon People's party, which Bebel helped to found in 1866, proclaimed "inexorable war against the political conditions created in Germany by the war."

From the forum of the German Reichstag, he led the fight for better social and political conditions for the German workers. This fight took the form of a three-pronged attack against: (1) the *Gesindeordnung*, a Prussian law which accorded household servants and farm workers the status of chattel; (2) the oppression of women and their exclusion from public life; and (3) the prevalence of militarism in German society. It was his relentless denunciation of the latter which on several occasions gained him convictions for high treason and lese majesty. Thus he spent more than two and a half years in jail, from 1872 to 1875, for refusing as a Reichstag member to vote further military funds during the Franco-Prussian War after Louis Napoleon had been captured. In a courageous speech in the Reichstag on November 26, 1870, he maintained that the continuation of the war against the French nation and plans for sizeable annexations of territory proved that this was not a defensive war but a war of conquest. Any further support would therefore be unconscionable. He demanded peace with the French nation and renunciation of all annexations.

Despite his ardent antimilitary and antiwar stance, Bebel was not a pacifist in the conventional sense. As a dedicated Marxist, he believed that the attainment of socialism would, itself, entail a state of permanent peace among nations. But he also believed, and here he differed from other bourgeois pacifists, that the goals of socialism, including peace, could not be reached without armed struggle with the capitalist ruling class. Bebel's antimilitarism thus derived as much from hostility toward the established order as from an abhorrence of war. Nevertheless, he strengthened and affirmed the antimilitarist tradition of nineteenth-century socialism.

Bibliography:

A. *Antrag und Reden der Reichstagsabgeordneten Bebel and Liebknecht gegen die preussische Annexionsanleihe von 100 Millionen Thalern*. (reprinted from Reichstag minutes, Leipzig, n.d.); *August Bebel. Politik als Theorie und Praxis. Ausgewählte Texte aus Reden und Schriften*, Albrecht Langner, ed., (Cologne, 1967); *Die Frau und der Sozialismus* (Zurich, 1879, Eng. trans., *Woman Under Socialism*, New York, 1971); *Nicht stehendes Heer sondern Volkswehr*! (Stuttgart, 1898); *Die Reden Bebels. Gehalten in der ersten Session des deutschen Reichstags, April und Mai 1871*. (reprinted from the Reichstag minutes, Leipzig, n.d.).

B. Horst Bartel, ed. *August Bebel. Eine Biographie*. (Berlin [East], 1963); Helmut Hirsch, *August Bebel* (Cologne, 1973); Max Hochdorf, *August Bebel. Geschichte einer politischen Vernunft* (Berlin, 1932); William H. Maehl, *August Bebel—Shadow Emperor of the German Workers* (Philadelphia, 1980); Ernst Schraepler, *August Bebel-Bibliographie* (Duesseldorf, 1962); Ernst Schraepler, *August Bebel—Sozialdemokrat im Kaiserreich* (Goettingen, 1966); NYT, August 14, 1913, 9.

Brigitte M. Goldstein

BECCARI, Alaide Gualberta (7 May 1842, Padua, Austrian Empire [now Italy]—26 September 1906, Bologna, Italy). *Education*: self-educated. *Career*: journalist, editor, playwright, suffragist, feminist, pacifist.

In nineteenth-century Italy, Alaide Gualberta Beccari was one of the few women who struggled for peace and women's rights, including the suffrage. She became convinced of these missions as a young woman and pursued them throughout her life, despite enormous personal and family difficulties.

When Beccari was six, her father, Gerolamo, a civil servant in Padua, then part of the Austrian Empire, participated in the 1848 Revolution for Italian unity and self government. With the return of Hapsburg power the next year, he was forced into exile and fled with his family to Turin where Cavour opened the doors to refugees from other sections of Italy. Here, the young girl, the only survivor of 12 children, remained with her parents and learned to help her father in his work as a scribe. She also launched her own career as a journalist. Later in her life, she demanded that all women be given the chance to study and develop intellectually.

After the liberation of Lombardy-Venetia, the Beccari family returned to Padua. There, in 1868, she founded *La Donna*, the first Italian journal devoted to women's rights. Beccari had already participated in a petition campaign on behalf of women's suffrage but not until 1877 did she succeed in collecting 2000 signatures on a circular demanding the vote for women. Considering the largely illiterate condition of Italian women then, this was a remarkable achievement.

In *La Donna*, which appeared every two weeks, Beccari began to publicize the European crusade for peace. The first example of this new interest of hers was an article, "La guerra" on August 7, 1870, which carried news of the creation of the International Association of Women for Peace, a society established in Geneva by *Marie Goegg. From then on, the pages of *La Donna* remained very hospitable to peace activities, particularly those of women, from Europe and the United States. Beccari published an appeal from American women during the Franco-Prussian War and news of an English women's peace society contest for the best prize essay by a woman on peace and disarmament. Reports of conferences and societies in Paris and Geneva were regularly aired. Despite the general disinterest in peace campaigns in Italy, Beccari persevered. Until 1880 she served as the Italian representative of Goegg's international association.

Beccari also labored alongside Anna Maria Mozzoni, Italy's leading suffragist and feminist, campaigning in the press for women's rights and equal pay for women workers. Due to a progressively debilitating illness, however, Beccari finally gave up publishing *La Donna* in 1891. She was nearly impoverished, too, by then. Nonetheless, she continued working with young women authors and teachers to help them begin. She also founded a children's magazine, *Mamma*, and wrote children's plays. Though ill and poor, her energies never flagged. She died from German measles, contracted while caring for a poor child who had the disease.

Beccari's commitment to the crusades for peace and women's rights sprung more from the "heart" than from intellectual and legalistic perspectives such as motivated Mozzoni. Among Italian women, Beccari was a major figure in the defense of peace, the sisterhood of women, and civil rights, battles which she waged with small personal means but with great strength and perseverance.

Bibliography:

B. Franca Pieroni Bortollotti, *Alle origini del movimento femminile in Italia: 1848–1892* (Turin, 1963); Judith Jeffrey Howard "Patriot Mothers in the Post-Risorgimento: Women after the Italian Revolution," in Carol R. Berkin and Clara M. Lovett, eds., *Women, War and Revolution* (New York, 1980), 237–58; Beatrice Pisa, *Alaide Gualberta Beccari e la rivista 'La donna'* (Rome, 1981).

Franca Pieroni Bortolotti

BECKWITH, George Cone (1800, E. Haddam, CT—12 May 1870, Boston). *Education*: B.A., Middlebury Coll., 1819; D.D., Andover Theological Seminary, 1823. *Career*: secretary, American Peace Society, 1837–70; editor, *Advocate of Peace*; minister and peace activist.

As a Congregationalist pastor and professor at Lane Theological Seminary, George C. Beckwith stood at the center of the antebellum reform movement. Shortly after the founding of the American Peace Society in 1828, Beckwith joined and became an active member. He traveled and lectured for the Society in 1835–36 and became the organization's secretary in 1837, succeeding *William Ladd. Beckwith was a skillful writer, and in the 1840s he published numerous works on the peace effort, including *Eulogy on William Ladd*, *Book of Peace*, and *The Peace Manual*. In addition, he edited the American Peace Society's journal, *The Advocate of Peace*.

Almost from the beginning, the American Peace Society was fraught with dissension concerning the concept of "defensive war." *William Lloyd Garrison led a faction of radical pacifists who denounced all war, while Beckwith maintained the more conservative position, upholding the right of self-defense. The Society's convention in May 1837 witnessed a showdown between the radicals and the conservatives on the issue of defensive war. A compromise was reached by a majority of the delegates who voted to amend the constitution to read that "all war is contrary to the spirit of the Gospel." Neither side, however, was completely satisfied and the radicals attacked the Society for allowing nonpacifists to become members.

Beckwith tried to ease the tension within the organization by passing two resolutions at the 1838 convention which clarified the amendments to the constitution made the previous year. This only made matters worse and Garrison and others called for a general convention in September 1838 that would explore the peace issue thoroughly and clear up the confusion. Approximately 200 delegates attended, but when voting rights for women were granted, Beckwith and his followers withdrew in protest. With the moderates gone, Garrison and the more radical pacifists formed the New England Non-Resistance Society.

Beckwith wanted to focus the time and energy of the American Peace Society on peace reform and omit other issues such as abolition and women's rights from its agenda. Although he personally supported numerous reform efforts, he felt that the Society could be more effective if it concentrated exclusively on practical solutions to the problems of peace. Among the plans he advocated were William Ladd's concept of a congress of nations, disarmament agreements, and arbitration treaties. Along with *Amasa Walker, he represented the Society at the international peace congress in London, where he spoke in favor of the congress of nations idea.

The conflict between the absolute pacifists and those who accepted the concept of self-defense continued to divide both the leadership and the membership of the American Peace Society. Although Beckwith tried mightily to keep the issue submerged, it rose to the surface again in the mid–1840s and seriously divided the organization. In 1846 Beckwith supported the decision to keep the annual convention open to all peace advocates, without regard to their views concerning defensive war. This angered the radicals, led this time by *Elihu Burritt, who, along with his supporters, resigned from their official positions within the organization, but not from the membership in the Society. Beckwith sought to keep the weak and divided organization alive by promoting alternative means for settling international disputes and by seeking to influence public opinion against international war.

As the United States moved closer to Civil War in the 1850s the American Peace Society grew even weaker and more fragmented. Since most peace advocates also opposed the institution of slavery, they found themselves faced with the possibility that only war would lead to the abolition of human bondage. Having to choose between the lesser of two evils, Beckwith and most of his colleagues in the peace movement chose to support the Union cause. It was a difficult decision and one not made easily. After the war Beckwith tried to revive the American Peace Society, but with little success. He died in 1870 having devoted a lifetime in the pursuit of peace.

Bibliography:

A. *The Book of Peace: A Collection of Essays on War and Peace* (Boston, 1845); *Eulogy on William Ladd, late President of the American Peace Society* (Boston, 1841); *The Peace Manual: or War and its Remedies* (Boston, 1847); *A Universal Peace Society, with the Basis of Co-operation in the Cause of Peace* (Boston, 1844).

B. Peter Brock, *Pacifism in the United States: From the Colonial Era to the First World War* (Princeton, NJ, 1968); Merle Curti, *The American Peace Crusade, 1815–1860* (Durham, NC, 1929); Charles DeBenedetti, *The Peace Reform in American History* (Bloomington, IN, 1980).

Kay Clontz Starnes

BEERFELDE, Hans-Georg von (12 August 1877, Schloss Sommerfeld, Crossen on the Oder, Germany [now Poland]—25 September 1960, Berlin-Nikolasee, Federal Republic of Germany). *Education*: Potsdam Cadet School. *Career*: army officer, 1897–1918; director, Institut für Körperbildung (Institute for Physical Culture), Berlin, 1927–33; founder and director, Arbeitsstätte für Verständigung, Frieden und schöperische Kultur (Workshop for Understanding, Peace and Creative Culture), Munich, 1951–60; editor, journalist, author, and pacifist.

Hans-Georg von Beerfelde, descended from an old landed aristocratic officer's family, resigned his army commission in June 1914, because of his abhorrence of servile militarism. After the outbreak of World War I, he volunteered for duty in the belief that Germany was fighting a defensive war. Until the spring of 1917, he served on the Western Front as a company commander and as an adjutant on the staff of the front commander.Transferred to the headquarters of the Supreme German Command in Berlin, Beerfelde became attached to its communications division.Through *Richard Witting, he came into possession of a copy of the 1915 memorandum of Prince Karl Max von Lichnowsky, the former German ambassador at London, attacking the German foreign office for its rejection of a negotiated solution to the July 1914 crisis. Deeply shocked by this revelation of German culpability in the outbreak of the war, Beerfelde hectographed Lichnowsky's memorandum and had copies sent to leading politicians, military men, and even the Kaiser. He brought Lichnowsky's memorandum to international attention by inducing a German-Danish parliamentary representative to reprint it in the Danish newspaper *Politiken*. As a result of his action, Beerfelde was indicted in 1917, but later acquitted.

In March 1918 Beerfelde was taken into custody again when he tried to incite the Berlin munitions workers to broaden their strike of January 1918, into one paralyzing the war industry. He saw this as one way of abrogating the dictatorial power of the Supreme Command and bringing an end to the war. During his detention pending investigation, Beerfelde wrote the accusatory document, *Eine notwendige Richtigstellung des deutschen Weissbuchs* (*A Necessary Correction of the German White Book*). On the basis of published documents on the July

1914 crisis, Beerfelde denounced the expedient lie made to the German people about the defensive character of the war. Furthermore, he demanded that the state of siege and political censorship be lifted and, referring to laws concerning the falsification of documents, demanded the arrest and trial of chancellor Theobald von Bethmann-Hollweg and other political figures who had "wantonly desired and fomented war." Through the efforts of his wife the document was put before the German Reichstag which refused his demands, as did the National Assembly in 1919.

On November 9, 1918, Beerfelde was released from prison by revolutionary sailors and elected head of the executive committee of the revolutionary Council of Workers and Soldiers, at that time one of the most powerful positions in Germany. In keeping with his earlier document, he demanded the imprisonment and condemnation of the "war-criminals." The leaders of the German Social Democratic party refused this demand, and after one week Beerfelde resigned from his position. He joined the pacifistic Bund Neues Vaterland (New Fatherland League) and became a member of its executive committee (1918–19). As a result of his efforts to inform the public of Germany's responsibility for the war, he was slandered, prevented from speaking by threats of arrest, and arrested several times.

Beerfelde's peace program for the entire period following 1918 rested upon the acknowledgement of German responsibility for the war. He was of the opinion that a denial of this guilt would necessarily lead to a renewed European and world conflict. He considered neither Spartacism nor the ideas of socialism, whose humane and ethical goals he represented, capable of eliminating the "taproot of the German problem." He saw the underlying reason for the outbreak of World War I in a dearth of morality and honesty on the part of the leaders as well as of large segments of the German people. Therefore, Beerfelde called for "truthfulness in one's personal life, truthfulness and clarity in politics and all public matters" to bring about a spiritual-moral and political-religious renewal of Germany. He rejected political life dictated by class and party interests. Only a return to honesty would enable the Germans to free themselves from "politics designed to defraud the people."

Beerfelde's pacifist convictions also were conditioned by the religious tenets of his Christian upbringing. He appealed for a world revolution of the soul on this earth to be fanned "into flames of overwhelming proportions." He advocated a "revolution of the ego, of sexual life, of voluntary poverty, of a natural way of life, and of truth." Jesus, the "perfect person," was his model and gave humanity an example of how to overcome its burden of guilt by a readiness for contrition and penance. The political content of his religio-mystical and idealistic philosophy for peace was misconstrued or overlooked. Only the pacifistic weekly publication *Die Menschheit* and *Hellmut von Gerlach's *Welt am Montag* gave heed to Beerfelde's course of action.

Although Beerfelde's insights into German political and spiritual life were confirmed by events after 1918, the retired army captain found himself isolated.

Disappointed by the apathy of a large part of the German people, Beerfelde moved to the South Tyrol in 1920. Shocked by the right-wing assassination of the German foreign minister, Walther Rathenau, Beerfelde returned to Germany in 1922, but his attempts to influence politics were in vain. Not only was he exposed to personal danger and had to endure the disruption of his meetings, but a clarification of the question of German war-guilt seemed increasingly hopeless to him. Distressed by the disaster toward which he saw German politics heading, he wrote open letters to German Chancellor Wilhelm Marx (1924) and President Paul von Hindenburg (1925) in the hope of moving them toward "truth and clarity in the matter of war-guilt;" neither replied.

Adolf Hitler's provocative politics were regarded by Beerfelde as a prelude to a new world war. In 1932 he published an open letter addressed to the Nazi leader in *Jakob Stöcker's *Dortmunder General-Anzeiger*. He tried to convince him that the premise of Germany's innocence in the outbreak of World War I, which was basic to Nazi propaganda, rested upon "a catastrophic historical mistake." After Hitler became Chancellor on January 30, 1933, Beerfelde tried once more to persuade him to undertake a thoroughgoing revision of his political course. When Beerfelde was subsequently threatened, he wrote again to the Chancellor and branded him as the person who would in the future be seen not as "Germany's savior," but as its "greatest betrayer."

Although well aware of the consequences of this action, Beerfelde refused to flee from Germany. After the burning of the Reichstag, he was arrested by Nazi storm troopers, condemned as a "betrayer of the people" and "communist agitator," and beaten to the point of becoming crippled. He was released after several months of imprisonment. Impressed by his great idealism, some Nazi leaders tried, unsuccessfully, to win him over to their side. To escape further persecution, Beerfelde moved to Garmisch-Partenkirchen in south Germany.

After 1945 Beerfelde cooperated for a while with the American occupation authorities in the political reeducation of the German people, but this came to an end when the organization he had formed for this purpose was banned on the basis of unspecified denunciation, and he was arrested. Cleared of the charges against him, Beerfelde declined to resume his work because he could not reestablish his confidence in the American military government. In October 1946 and again in the winter of 1948, uneasy over the growing East-West conflict and lacking a political base, he turned to the United Nations, Joseph Stalin, and to the leading statesmen of the West with personal appeals. He implored them to support his proposal of general disarmament based on a worldwide plebiscite as the only viable way to ensure peace. In July 1951, in letters to President Harry S. Truman of the United States and Stalin, Beerfelde renewed his call for disarmament. His exhortations to prevent a further decay of culture ruined by two world wars did arouse some public interest, but only for a short time. Even so, he continued to warn against the growing potential for war and stressed that "bombs and fortifications can destroy continents," but could not solve political, economic, or social problems.

Bibliography:

A. *Das grosse Geheimnis der Weltrevolution* (Berlin, 1919); *Kurzbericht über meinen Kampf um Deutschlands Erneuerung* (Berlin, 1958); *Michel wach auf! Mahnruf an das deutsche Volk (Flugschriften des Bundes Neues Vaterland, Nr. 1* (Berlin, 1918); *Der verbrecherische Schwindel im deutschen Weissbuch. Dem Deutschen Reichstag am 1. Juli 1918 vorgelegt* (Jena, 1918); *Wer sind die Schuldigen am Weltkrieg—Völkermord* (Cologne, 1919).

B. Andreas Weitenweber, "Aus dem Generalstab zum Arbeiter—und Soldatenrat. Hauptmann von Beerfelde eine Figur der Zeitgeschichte," *Der Tagesspiegel* (Berlin), October 9, 1960 [see also Hubert Krantz' letter in response, *Der Tagesspiegel*, December 22, 1960].

Helmut Donat
Trans. by Irene Seadle

BEERNAERT, Auguste Marie François (26 July 1829, Ostend, Belgium—6 October 1912, Lucerne, Switzerland). *Education*: Collège de Namur; Dr. jur., Univ. of Louvain, 1849; studies at the universities of Paris, Berlin, Heidelberg, Leipzig, and Strasbourg, 1851–53. *Career*: lawyer; Minister of Public Works, 1873–78; Minister of Finances and Chief of the Cabinet, 1884–94; member, Chamber of Representatives, 1874–1912; president, Chamber of Representatives, 1895–1900; Minister of State, 1894; delegate, Hague Conferences, 1899 and 1907; member, Permanent Court of Arbitration, 1900; president, Interparliamentary Union, 1909–12.

Auguste Beernaert, a Catholic statesman and an advocate of free trade in economic matters, was a major figure in Belgian politics as well as an internationalist, inspired by a belief in law and by the need to preserve the peace. In the Interparliamentary Union, over which he presided between 1909 and 1912, he worked actively for the development of international arbitration and disarmament. Because of his labors on behalf of the maintenance of peace, he was awarded the Nobel Peace Prize in 1909.

Beernaert played a major role at both Hague Conferences. In 1899, as chair of the committee concerned with arms limitation, he labored as an advocate of a cause that was unanimously unwanted and opposed. In 1907, he presided over the committee which studied means to improve the laws and customs of land warfare, the rights and duties of neutrals, and the formal opening of hostilities. However, it was in another arena—that of obligatory arbitration—where Beernaert took issue with the Belgian government itself. During an Interparliamentary Union conference in 1906 in London, he had supported a proposal for obligatory arbitration without reservations or restrictions, to be applied in a limited series of cases that governments would accept. That principle was taken up at The Hague in a proposal emanating from the Portuguese delegate. Belgian instructions ordered Beerhaert to oppose it. Refusing to vote against his convictions, he offered to resign. The Belgian government avoided embarrassment by giving him the freedom to publicly defend his own view and not participate in the vote.

As honorary president of two Catholic peace organizations, the Catholic League for Peace and the International League of Catholic Pacifists, Beernaert labored for the establishment among nations of law based upon Christian morality and tradition, principles originally articulated by theologians in the middle ages. Just before his death, he attended the 1912 Geneva meeting of the Interparliamentary Union and strongly supported a report prohibiting aerial warfare.

Bibliography:

B. Académie royale de Belgique, *Notices biographiques et bibliographiques*, 1907–9, 315–325; H. Carton de Wiart, *Beernaert et son temps* (Brussels, 1945); F. Passelecq, *Auguste Beernaert, sa carrière et son oeuvre politique* (Brussels, 1912); E. Van der Smissen, *Léopold II et Beernaert d'après leur correspondance inédite de 1884 à 1894* (2 vols., Brussels, 1920); (Complete bibliography), *Annuaire de l'académie royale de Belgique* (1939) 293–364; *Biographie Nationale*, 33, cols., 69–105.

Nadine Lubelski-Bernard
Trans. by Sandi E. Cooper

BELLEGARDE, Dantès. See *Biographical Dictionary of Internationalists*.

BELLO LÓPEZ, Andrés (29 November 1781, Caracas, Captaincy General of Venezuela—15 October 1865, Santiago, Chile). *Education*: B.A., Royal and Pontifical Univ. of Caracas (now Universidad Central de Venezuela), 1800. *Career*: journalist, diplomat, educator, legislator, jurist, philosopher, and poet.

Andrés Bello López, one of the few internationalists the eighteenth century produced, enjoyed a career that placed him in the forefront of intellectual life in the Americas during the nineteenth century. Born and educated in Venezuela on the eve of New World independence movements, his life encapsulized the practical approach to problems of political identity in the chaotic aftermath of revolution. Bello was a progressive realist; he rejected the imposition of any imported theory that refused to consider the realities of Latin American societies. He believed the new nations had to follow a moderate and gradual path, blending their historical experience with new social aspirations.

Because Bello did not accept the political utopias proposed by many post-independence Latin American leaders, his contributions went unrecognized until recently. Nevertheless, his support of Pan American principles was made clear in his *Gramática de la lengua castellana destinada al uso de los americanos* (1847). Although now over a century old, this brilliant exercise in Spanish grammar had as its objective the preservation of a common idiom throughout the Americas. It was an eloquent plea for cultural unity, the foundation of an alternative to violence and dissension among peoples of a common heritage.

Another example of Bello's evolutionary approach is the 1855 civil code he drafted for Chile. Since it was widely circulated, it fostered the idea that each independent Latin American nation should have a similar modern code. Such unanimity in law, it was thought, would encourage additional international co-operation. Bello was also an early advocate of international law.

In his *Principios de derecho internacional* (1832), Bello laid a groundwork for inter-American relations while positing many of the major features of modern international law. He decried the use of diplomatic recognition as a political ploy. Instead, he argued that any society that exercised acts of sovereignty should, by its actions, receive recognition as a sovereign state. In so doing, Bello anticipated the idea of "self-determination of peoples." In a similar vein, Bello condemned the possibility of "intervention" by one state in the internal affairs of another. In his opinion, although the internal affairs of one state might create circumstances threatening the security of another, subversion by outside forces lacked any legal foundation.

Bibliography:

A. *Obras completas de don Andrés Bello* (15 vols., Santiago, 1881–93); *Obras completas de Bello* (23 vols., Caracas, 1950–69).

B. Rafael Caldera, *Andrés Bello* (London, 1977).

Diego D. G. Rivero

BENDER, Harold Stauffer (19 July 1897, Elkhart, IN—21 September 1962, Chicago). *Education*: B.A., Goshen Coll., 1918; B.D., Garrett Biblical Institute, 1922; Th.M., Princeton Theological Seminary, 1923; M.A., Princeton Univ., 1923; studies at Tübingen Univ., 1923–24; Dr. of Theology, Heidelberg Univ., 1935. *Career*: high school teacher, Thornton, IN, 1916–17; instructor, Hesston Coll., 1918–20; professor of Bible and Church History and administrator, Goshen Coll., 1924–62; dean, Goshen Coll. Biblical Seminary, 1944–62; peace churchman, educator, historian, and theologian.

Harold S. Bender, foremost Mennonite scholar of his time, was the main progenitor from the mid-1920s onward of a "Recovery of the Anabaptist Vision" school of thought. "Anabaptist Vision" scholars emphasized literal discipleship and being the faithful church—including teaching and living a practical "Gospel of Peace." Therefore, Bender also became a leader in peace church circles, and a shaper of peace institutions.

In 1931 Bender joined the executive committee of North American Mennonites' chief agency for peace service and advocacy, the Mennonite Central Committee (MCC). Thereafter he did much to shape its policies. Meanwhile, from 1936 to 1952, he was chairman of the Peace Problems Committee of his particular Mennonite branch. In the 1930s, he was a leader in the Conference of Historic Peace Churches, a member of his church's relief committee, and, in 1936, one of the founders of a European-based International Mennonite Peace Committee. In 1944–45, he helped found Mennonite Voluntary Service, and in 1951, MCC's Pax Service. Thus he aided Mennonites and others to retain a biblical pacifist heritage and to translate peace into service.

Beginning in 1935, the year of an important Historic Peace Churches conference, Bender helped create U. S. programs of alternative service for conscientious objectors. He became chairman of the Mennonite Central Peace Committee (later MCC's Peace Section) at its founding in 1940, and worked closely with other peace-church leaders in the National Service Board for Religious Objectors. With the exception of his "Anabaptist Vision" scholarship, Bender's creative role in developing alternative service was no doubt his greatest single contribution in the peace field.

Outside peace-church circles, Bender promoted pacifism internationally, especially after World War II. He worked with the International Fellowship of Reconciliation, attended an "All-Christian Peace Assembly" in Prague in 1961, and participated in other ventures for world peace. As in his Mennonite activities, Bender worked for peace concepts based solidly in biblical teaching and in church life.

Bibliography:

A. "The Anabaptist Vision," *Church History*, 13 (March, 1944), 3–24.

B. Guy F. Hershberger, "Harold S. Bender and His Time," *Mennonite Quarterly Review*, 38 (April, 1964), 83–112; Guy F. Hershberger, ed., *The Recovery of the Anabaptist Vision: A Sixtieth Anniversary Tribute to Harold S. Bender* (Scottdale, PA, 1957); Nelson P. Springer, "A Bibliography of the Published Writings of Harold S. Bender," *Mennonite Quarterly Review*, 38 (April, 1964), 212–28; J. C. Wenger, "Harold S. Bender: A Brief Biography," *Mennonite Quarterly Review*, 38 (April, 1964), 113–120.

C. Harold S. Bender manuscripts in various collections in Archives of the Mennonite Church and the Goshen College Archives, Goshen College, Goshen, IN; additional material in National Inter-Religious Service Board for Conscientious Objectors (formerly NSBRO) Papers, Swarthmore College, Swarthmore, PA.

Theron F. Schlabach

BENEDICT XV (DELLA CHIESA, Giacomo) (21 November 1854, Genoa, Italy—22 January 1922, Rome). *Education*: Doctorate in Civil Law, Royal Univ. of Genoa, 1875. *Career*: papal election, September 3, 1914.

Della Chiesa came to power as Pope Benedict XV shortly after the outbreak of World War I. From the beginning, Benedict called upon the warring leaders to end the fighting. In his first encyclical, *Ad Beatissimi*, he took an unequivocal stand against the war, associating war with Satan's envy of the Kingdom of Peace. Thereafter, Benedict strove unfaltering to end the conflict and to prevent Italy's intervention in the conflagration.

Although Pope and Church were accused by many of pro-Austrian neutralism, Italy's Catholics overwhelmingly supported Benedict's stance. Moderate and liberal Catholic laymen and the radical peasant White Leagues of the Po valley joined Austrophile aristocrats in demanding an end to the war and Italy's absolute neutrality. They were joined in Italy by the vast majority of socialists and by most liberals as well. Yet, owing largely to the inability of Benedict and the Church to act in any but the most conservative political manner, Italy's intervention and the resulting widening of the war could not be prevented.

To Benedict XV and the Church hierarchy, "politics" meant chiefly the use of lobbying and diplomatic procedures within the context of an overriding concern for the social status quo. Consequently, almost no Catholics adhered to larger antiwar coalitions or undertook mass action on their own, either before or after Italy's entry into the war in May 1915. To have sponsored such action, Benedict would have risked his position in relation to the Italian and other governments at a time when the Vatican sought to be accorded a seat at the postwar peace conference. Moreover, the display of too powerful a peace sentiment, it was thought, could actually increase the chances of war by persuading Austria that discussions with Italy were unnecessary to avoid Italian intervention. Finally, mass action would have flown in the face of papal and Church tradition.

Benedict did maintain a rigorously antiwar position throughout the conflict and sought on several occasions to facilitate diplomatically a settlement. Most notably, the Pope offered in August 1917 a plan based upon a return to the prewar status quo. In that text, he referred to the "useless carnage" of the war. While the plan won few converts in ruling circles, it is credited with helping to inspire an insurrection in the city of Turin later the same month. As the war approached its conclusion, Benedict XV lost the peace-making mantle to +Woodrow Wilson. Later years found the Pope supporting the Washington Naval Disarmament Conference and calling for aid to reduce the suffering in war-torn Russia.

Bibliography:

A. *Acta Apostolicae Sedis* (vols. 6–14, Vatican City, 1914–22); *Ad Beatissimi* (Vatican City, 1915); *Humani Generis* (Vatican City, 1917).

B. Walter H. Peters, *The Life of Benedict XV*, (Milwaukee, 1959); Henry E. G. Rope, *Benedict XV; The Pope of Peace* (London, 1940); Ernesto Vercesi, *Il movemento cattolico in Italia (1870–1922)* (Florence, 1923).

James A. Young

BENEŠ, Eduard. See *Biographical Dictionary of Internationalists*.

BERGER, Victor Louis (28 February 1860, Nieder-Rehbach, Austria-Hungary—7 August 1929, Milwaukee, WI). *Education*: studies at the universities of Vienna and Budapest. *Career*: socialist activist and leader, Socialist Party of America, 1901–29; editor, *Wisconsin Vorwärts*, 1892–98, *Social Democratic Herald*, 1900–13; *Milwaukee Leader*, 1911–29; congressman, U. S. House of Representatives, 1911–13, 1923–29.

Victor Berger, a leader of American socialism and a newspaper editor, was educated in Vienna and Budapest. In 1878 he emigrated to the United States, settling in Milwaukee. After schoolteaching and involving himself in third party politics, he became a founder of the Socialist Party of America and edited a number of socialist newspapers. For three decades, he headed the Socialist political machine that dominated Milwaukee. He was elected in 1910 to the U.S. House of Representatives as its first Socialist, and was also elected in 1918 and 1919. He served again from 1923 to 1929. A revisionist Marxist who advocated an evolutionary brand of socialism through the ballot box, Berger served as a perennial member of the Socialist party's executive committee.

As an internationalist Berger actively opposed militarism and attempted to develop a structure for peace. Based on his socialism, he believed that the fundamental cause of modern war was capitalism, with its drive for fresh markets, and that only the elimination of that system would undermine war. Militarism as a byproduct of capitalism had to be confronted, and therefore he opposed the pre-World War I arms race, deplored the inadequacy of existing machinery for international arbitration, and condemned standing armies and the American national guard. He espoused cooperation between socialists and middle-class peace groups, despite his party's official criticism of such class collaboration, and he participated in such organizations in order to educate the public on issues of war and peace.

Berger was not a pacifist and he accepted certain types of war as legitimate. Because of his socialist ideology, he supported wars of national liberation and of social revolution. In addition, however, he endorsed wars of national self-defense. Unlike many of his Socialist comrades, he maintained that socialism harmonized with a type of nationalism that would blend ultimately into internationalism. He described socialism as nationalistic and patriotic, and termed it a force that would give workers a stake in their societies. He argued that workers already identified with their nations, a position challenged by his fellow Socialists. The future worldwide proletarian triumph would lead to internationalism and peace as workers everywhere would join hands. For the present, however, in the name of national self-defense, he espoused citizen-armies, such as the armed citizenry of Switzerland, in order to insure a people from external aggression and from internal oppression. Accordingly, he even supported public service in which young people were conscripted to serve their countries for one year in civilian capacities, working in conservation and public health and also receiving training in weaponry. These national service views, reminiscent of William James's ideas, meant that Berger's position in support of this type of "preparedness" was unique and controversial among Socialist peace activists, and nearly cost him his seat on the party's executive.

Berger consistently promoted peace as a congressman and as an editor. Prior to the World War, he introduced a resolution before the House of Representatives demanding withdrawal of American troops from Mexico. He was also an honorary member of a group promoting the possibility of a third Hague Peace Conference. After the war started, he became a vice-president of the League to Enforce Peace. In 1914, as a former congressman, he attempted to persuade President +Woodrow Wilson to assume an active peacemaking role in the first months of the war. Within the Socialist party, his newspapers publicized the slogan "Starve the War and Feed America," he promoted the idea of a peace congress of socialist parties worldwide to convene in Washington, and he helped construct his party's wartime policy statement of 1915. In that declaration, he favored immediate peace, universal disarmament, and the establishment of an international federation of nations and arbitrational machinery—a program virtually identical to those of non-socialist peace groups. When the United States declared war on Germany, he signed his party's resolution condemning U.S. entry into the war and conscription. Subsequently, he became a founding member of the People's Council, a socialist-dominated group inspired by the Russian Soviets which sought to link peace proponents throughout the nation. Berger also ran strong campaigns as a peace candidate for both the U.S. Senate and the House of Representatives in 1918, and was elected to the House. His conviction for conspiracy to violate the Espionage Act, eventually reversed by the Supreme Court, led to his exclusion from Congress. When he won the special election to fill that vacated post, he was excluded once again.

As a political leader committed to the cause of peace, Victor Berger stood for the establishment of national and international institutions that would provide for a peaceful environment. He believed in the possibility of a rational world order and social progress despite the existence of the capitalist system which, he maintained, promoted war. In his effort to build that structure for peace, he worked tirelessly with fellow socialists and non-believers as well.

Bibliography:

A. *Broadsides* (Milwaukee, 1912); *Voice and Pen of Victor L. Berger* (Milwaukee, 1929).

B. Sally M. Miller, *Victor Berger and the Promise of Constructive Socialism* (Westport, CT, 1973); DAB, Supp. 1, 72–75.

C. Victor L. Berger Papers, Milwaukee County Historical Society; Victor L. Berger Collection, Milwaukee Public Library; Victor L. Berger Collection, Tamiment Library, New York University, New York.

Sally M. Miller

BERNADOTTE, Folke. See *Biographical Dictionary of Internationalists.*

BERNSTEIN, Eduard (6 January 1850, Berlin—18 December 1932, Berlin). *Education*: attended gymnasium, Berlin. *Career*: bank employee, Berlin, 1870–78; literary secretary to Karl Höchberg, 1878–80; editor *Der Sozialdemokrat*, 1881–90; Reichstag deputy, 1902–7, 1912–18, 1920–28; author.

Unlike many of his revisionist friends within the German Social Democratic party (SPD), Eduard Bernstein became increasingly active during the decade before 1914 as an advocate of international understanding and a critic of the chauvinist tendencies that were gaining ground in Germany. In books and articles he vigorously attacked the widespread belief in Germany's encirclement and argued that the growing fear of England was both dangerous and artificially created.

Bernstein's internationalism, like his revisionism, was a product both of his essentially ethical approach to socialism and of his long exile experience, first in Switzerland and then in England. He was not, however, a pacifist. He believed that a nation must be prepared to defend itself against aggression. It was his conviction that Germany was being attacked by Tsarist Russia that led him to support the German war effort in August 1914. It was not long, however, before careful study of the documents published by the belligerents persuaded Bernstein that he had been wrong. As early as September 1914, he launched a series of attacks upon the uncritical nationalist enthusiasm exhibited by many Social Democrats. By June 1915 he had become so convinced of Germany's responsibility for the outbreak and continuation of the war that he joined the party's co-chairman *Hugo Haase and its most influential orthodox Marxist theoretician Karl Kautsky in publishing a manifesto urging the SPD to assert its opposition to the policies of the German government.

Bernstein's increasingly active involvement in the antiwar movement led to his isolation from most of his old revisionist friends. On the other hand, the new Independent Social Democratic party, which he reluctantly joined when it broke away from the SPD in April 1917, was dominated by committed Marxists and thus provided few opportunities for leadership for someone of Bernstein's views. He continued to speak out against the war, however, and to advocate, in almost Wilsonian terms, the establishment of an international league of peoples based on principles of freedom and equality.

After Germany's defeat he refused to abandon his conviction that his country bore the heaviest burden of responsibility for the war and criticized those Social Democrats who joined in the unbridled assaults upon the Allies which were so widespread during the early years of the Weimar Republic. It was in large measure because of the unpopularity of these views that Bernstein was unable to regain his influential position in the SPD when he rejoined it early in 1919, in spite of the fact that it now pursued a reformist domestic policy which had much in common with the revisionism he had long preached.

Bibliography:

A. *Die englische Gefahr und das deutsche Volk* (Berlin, 1911); *Die Internationale der Arbeiterklasse und der Europäische Krieg* (Tübingen, 1916); *Aus den Jahren meines Exils* (Berlin, 1917); *Völkerbund oder—Staatenbund* (Berlin, 1918); *Der Völkerbund* (Basel, 1919); *Völkerrecht und Völkerpolitik* (Berlin, 1919); *Die Wahrheit über die Einkreisung Deutschlands* (Berlin, 1919).

B. Peter Gay, *The Dilemma of Democratic Socialism: Eduard Bernstein's Challenge to Marx* (New York, 1952); Paul Kampfmeyer, *Eduard Bernstein und der sozialistische Aufbau* (Berlin, 1930); Thomas Meyer, *Bernsteins Konstruktiver Sozialismus* (Bonn, 1977); *Biographisches Lexikon des Sozialismus* (Hannover, 1960), I, 21–23; *Neue deutsche Biographie* (Berlin, 1955), II, 133–34.

Kenneth R. Calkins

BESKOW, Fredrik Natanael (9 March 1865, Hallingberg parish, Kalmar län, Sweden—8 October 1953, Djursholm). *Education*: theological degrees, Univ. of Uppsala, 1884, 1895; Stockholm Academy of Fine Arts, 1888–93. *Career*: preacher, Djursholm Chapel, 1896–1932; teacher and headmaster, Djursholms samskola (co-educational secondary school), 1896–1909; director, Birkågarden Settlement House, 1912–46; Birkågardens folkhögskola (People's College), 1916–30; author, theologian, hymnologist, painter.

Coming from a prominent pietistic family, Natanael Beskow was a leader in religious and mission activities in his school and university years. Upon completion of his theological studies he felt unable to subscribe to the doctrinal formulae of the state church and declined to be ordained. He accepted a post as preacher at a nondenominational chapel near Stockholm where his sermons attracted many young people from academic and labor circles. He taught at a private coeducational school and was its headmaster from 1897 to 1909.

In his preaching and writing Beskow advocated an undogmatic, ethically rigorous and socially active Christianity. He urged religious people to show greater sympathy toward the working class movement, especially during the intense labor conflicts of 1908–9. Drawing upon English and American experience, Beskow co-founded Sweden's first settlement house, Birkågarden in Stockholm in 1912. Here he established in 1916 a people's college (adult education school), the first devoted to the needs of urban industrial workers.

Beskow emerged gradually as a peace leader. In his sermons he opposed military coercion of Norway in the union crisis of 1905. His antimilitarism increased in reaction to the state church's defense agitation in 1914, and during the First World War he became a pacifist. In 1918 he organized Förbundet för kristet samhällsliv (League for Christian Citizenship) which in 1921 joined the International Fellowship of Reconciliation (IFOR). For many years Beskow chaired the IFOR Council and was an active participant in international peace conferences. He promoted measures for relief of war victims and refugees, especially the Armenians and those fleeing Nazi persecution. He worked for legal recognition of conscientious objectors, the abolition of conscription, and general disarmament. Ecumenical in spirit, independent of denominational or partisan political ties, Beskow in the interwar years was the principal spokesman for radical Christian pacifism in Scandinavia.

Bibliography:

A. *Den kristna människan i världskrisen* (Uppsala, 1937); *Kristendom och krig* (Stockholm, 1919); *Kristendom och pacifism* (Stockholm, 1924); *Predikningar* (7 vols., Stockholm, 1907–26).

B. *Natanael och Elsa Beskow. Studier och minnesbilder* (Stockholm, 1954); Öyvind Sjöholm, *Samvetets politik. Natanael Beskow och hans värld intill 1921* (Uppsala, 1972); Samuel Thysell, ed., *Natanael Beskow som kristen-social banbrytare*, (Stockholm, 1958); Lydia Wahlström, "Natanael Beskow," in Wahlström, *Glada givare*, (Stockholm, 1929), 125–58.

C. Beskow Samlingen G21, Uppsala University Library.

Howard T. Lutz

BHAVE, Vinayak (Vinoba) Narahari (11 September 1895, Gagoda, Maharashtra, India—15 November 1982, Paunar, Maharashtra). *Education*: Baroda Coll. *Career*: joined Gandhi's ashram at Ahmedabad, 1916, directed his own ashram at Wardha from 1921; leader of Bhoodan and Gramdan land reform movement, 1951–69.

Vinoba Bhave was born to a well-educated landowning family of the Chitpavan Brahmin caste in Maharashtra, near Bombay. After attending Baroda College, where he excelled in mathematics and languages, he joined *Mohandas Gandhi's ashram (community) in June 1916 and in 1921 was sent to lead a new ashram at Wardha, near the geographical center of India. He took part in the Gandhian liberation and reform movement, and was noted for his intellect and the purity of his devotion.

After the death of Gandhi in 1948, many expected Vinoba to be his successor. He headed the new Sarvodaya (Service of All) Association, and offered assistance to the large refugee communities created by the partition of India and Pakistan. In 1951 he devised a new program to deal with landlessness and rural poverty in a nonviolent manner. In Hyderabad (now Andhra Pradesh), after a Communist revolution and violent police reaction, Vinoba was approached by 40 landless Harijan (Untouchable) families in the village of Pochempelli. When he put the problem of the 40 families to the villagers, a landowner presented him with 100 acres, thus beginning the Bhoodan (land-gift) movement on April 18, 1951. Before Vinoba left the state a few days later, he had received gifts of 12,000 acres.

When called by Prime Minister *Nehru to Delhi in September 1951 to review proposals for the first Five Year Plan, Vinoba walked the 795 miles, collecting an additional 25,000 acres in villages along the way. This began his great walking pilgrimage, which was to last fourteen years and take him to most parts of India. Breaking camp before dawn, he would walk to the next village in the cool hours. There he would conduct meetings and ask for land. "I have come to loot you with love," he would say, and few could refuse him. Eventually 4.2 million acres were collected from 569,000 donors. Of these, some 1.85 million acres were unsuitable or not legally available, and distribution of the rest proceeded slowly. In 1956 Vinoba redirected the movement from individual gifts to a community program named Gramdan (village-gift), for which a certain percentage of owners must give land. By 1969 one-quarter of India's villages (140,000) had been "declared gramdan," but little development or social reconstruction followed these declarations. Vinoba ended his walking tours in 1965, his 70th year, and settled in Bihar, the large and poor North Indian state that had been the focus of much of his work. Retiring from active leadership in 1969, he returned to his ashram at Paunar near Wardha.

For Vinoba, land redistribution was only a step toward a nonviolent and just social order. He asked the landowners to see that their well-being lay in sharing land and power. He hoped that the voluntary sacrifices and new community responsibilities of administering these gifts would lay the foundation for the social and economic transformation of the whole village. It would be a nonviolent revolution of the whole nation based on the Gandhian economic principles of trusteeship and the self-sufficiency of the villages. He refrained from using nonviolent resistance, believing that this method, which had been so effective in the independence movement, was now largely inappropriate in a free nation. Stressing cooperation rather than conflict, he called his method "nonviolent assistance."

Vinoba followed the Vedanta philosophy in stressing the priority of unity over individuality, and declared it inconceivable that the interests of one person or group could be against the interests of another. At the deepest level, the good of all must reside in the good of each. Conflicts thus have their origins in wrong attitudes and misperceptions, and the illusion of separation and difference must be overcome. When human society as the expression of the totality of being becomes the object of all devotion, conflicts will be seen as errors, and thought will be purified.

Vinoba also directed his attention to the settlement of violent conflicts, and in 1957 established the Shanti Sena (Peace Army) under the direction of Narayan Desai. It was to consist of a trained corps of persons ready to intervene in crisis situations, and to engage in "constructive work" at other times. The Shati Sena was solely for employment within the nation, preferably in the home districts of the members where their peacemaking abilities would be at their greatest. It did notable service in religious and linguistic riots, and provided relief in natural disasters, but did not venture into international conflicts.

Vinoba and many Gandhians were reluctant to criticize the state they had helped to create and did not condemn India's wars. The Bhoodan/Gramdan movement accepted a high level of government patronage and relied on the government to supervise the distribution of land. After Vinoba's retirement, the leadership in Bihar passed to the former Marxist *Jayaprakash Narayan, who at first followed Vinoba's method of economic reform with government sponsorship, but later perceived government as an obstacle to reform. Vinoba urged Narayan not to challenge the government of Indira Gandhi, and during the Emergency (1974–75) when she suspended civil liberties and jailed Narayan, Vinoba tried to induce agreement between them. He did not protest her autocratic rule but called it "an era of discipline." After a heart attack in November 1982, he fasted unto death and in accordance with his belief in the equality of women had his prayers led by women and the funeral pyre lit by his adopted daughter.

At the height of his public career, 1951–69, Vinoba was the center of a mass movement to establish social peace by a nonviolent revolution. He sought harmony through a voluntary and sacrificial solution to the land crisis, in keeping with his integral philosophy: "the good of all resides in the good of each."

Bibliography:

A. *Revolutionary Sarvodaya* (Bombay, 1964); *Talks on the Gita* (Varanasi, 1932).

B. J. J. Lanza del Vasto, *Gandhi to Vinoba* (London, 1956); G. Ostergaard and M. Currell, *The Gentle Anarchists* (London, 1971); Suresh Ram, *Vinoba and His Mission* (Kashi, 1958).

James D. Hunt

BING, Harold Frederick (20 September 1897, Croyden, Surrey, England—4 June 1975, East Leakes, Leicestershire). *Education*: Croyden Secondary School; teaching certificate through state administered external examination; M.A., state administered external examination. *Career*: head, National Committee and Youth Section, No More War Movement, 1923–37; International Advisory Council, War Resisters' International, 1925–75; sponsor, Peace Pledge Union, 1937–75; teacher, lecturer, and pacifist.

Harold Bing was Britain's youngest conscientious objector in World War I. He was also an absolute pacifist who refused the alternatives offered because acceptance sanctioned the state's trespass of an individual right. To maintain this principle he went to prison for two years. Thus, as an uncompromising anarcho-pacifist, he grew to adulthood with the modern British peace movement after the war. He was in the forefront of the anarcho-nonviolent wing, and he made a strong mark as the movement's youth leader and doctrinal conscience.

The minutes and journals of the No More War Movement (NMWM) and War Resisters' International (WRI) show him always striving to keep the movement tied to what he called "pure" and "applied pacifism." As such, he headed off numerous attempts to bring the war resistance wing of the peace movement behind partisan efforts of Labourites and pro-League of Nations advocates. He was the main opponent of *Walter Ayles and Lucy Cox and their attempt to push the NMWM and the WRI into support for the Geneva Protocols and League sanctions. Thus he also frequently crossed swords with *Norman Angell and the League of Nations Union over similar issues in the 1930s—a battle from which the diminutive Bing did not shrink, while personally retaining the utmost civility toward his opponent.

At the same time Bing fought the right of the peace movement, he was even more combative towards the left-leaning revolutionary socialist war resisters, such as Fenner Brockway and Reginald Reynolds, who tried to steer the NMWM and WRI into a more overtly militant, class-war type of resistance in the 1930s. Several times he was instrumental in keeping both groups from moving into overtly partisan and rigidly ideological directions. This was especially difficult to do against the heady enthusiasm engendered by the British antiwar movement stir of 1932–33. A supporter of *Mohandas Gandhi, Bing held firm for nonviolent action. But he could not prevent the rupture in the NMWM caused by the Spanish Civil War. He was often allied to NMWM colleagues *Carl Heath, *Wilfred Wellock, Muriel Nichol, and J. A. Skinner. Thus he was part of that core that brought the rump of the NMWM into the Peace Pledge Union in 1937.

After World War II Bing remained active. Always an articulate speaker, very good with languages, and with extensive contacts abroad, he was in great demand; he was popular and valued as a resource, a custodian of the war resistance candle. He increased his oracular status shortly before his death with a history of the war resistance international movement in the pages of *The Pacifist*. Bing showed he was ever the sensitive teacher. With an eye to the future he laid claim to the past.

Bibliography:

A. "Application of Pacifism to Politics," *No More War*, 3 (October 1924), 2+; "Herbert Runham Brown," *The War Resister*, 57 (Spring, 1950); 3–6; *The Historical and Philosophical Background of Modern Pacifism* (London, 1927); *Pacifism and the General Strike: A Constructive Alternative to Collective Security* (London, 1935); "Pacifism and the Revolution," *The New World,* 3 (December 1932), 3+; "Pacifism in France," *No More War*, 3 (June 1924), 2+; "Pacifism in India," *The New World,* 1 (April 1930), 6; *Pacifists over the World* (London, 1943); *Problem of Palestine* (Enfield, Middlesex, 1937).

B. Grace Beaton, *Twenty Years' Work in the War Resisters' International* (Enfield, Middlesex, 1945); Louis Bisceglia, "Norman Angell and the 'Pacifist' Muddle," *Bulletin of the Institute of Historical Research*, 45 (May 1972), 104–21; Martin Ceadel, *Pacifism in Britain 1914–1945* (Oxford, 1980).

Louis Bisceglia

BIRYUKOV, Pavel Ivanovich (15 November 1860, Ivanovskoye, Kostroma Province, Russia—10 October 1931, Geneva). *Education*: Corps of Pages, St.

Petersburg [now Leningrad], 1872–79; graduated, Naval Academy, St. Petersburg, 1884. *Career*: author and Tolstoyan publicist.

The son of a well-to-do Russian general, Pavel Ivanovich Biryukov was destined to follow in his father's foot-steps with a career in the Russian military service; but his deeply religious nature, nourished within the Orthodox Church, led him as early as 1877–78, while he was still a naval cadet, to the conviction that military service was incompatible with Christian doctrine.

The reading of *Leo Tolstoy's religious works, particularly his *Confession* and *What I Believe*, gave his life new direction. In the winter of 1883–84, he became acquainted with *Vladimir Chertkov, who introduced him to Tolstoy a few months later. From then on, Biryukov lived out his life as a humble, industrious, and devoted follower of Tolstoy. He collaborated with Chertkov in 1884 in the founding of The Intermediary, the Tolstoyan publishing house devoted to making good reading materials available to the masses; and from 1886 to 1888 he directed the enterprise. After several years of practical work among the peasants and of Tolstoyan publishing activity in Russia and abroad, he was arrested along with Chertkov in 1897 and condemned to forced residence in the Baltic region for publishing an appeal to the government to halt its persecution of the pacifist religious sect of Dukhobors. Chertkov's influential family got his sentence changed to exile abroad, and a few months later Biryukov was also allowed to leave Russia.

After working for a while with Chertkov in England, he went to Cyprus to help Dukhobor émigrés from Russia settle there; and then from 1899 to 1904 he lived in Switzerland, where he published a Tolstoyan Journal in Russian, *Svobodnaya mysl* (*Free Thought*) and began work on his monumental biography of Tolstoy. From 1904 on, when his banishment from Russia was lifted, he divided his time between his homeland and western Europe. After spending the period of World War I in Switzerland he settled in Russia in 1918 and remained until 1926. He then went to Canada and lived for some time among the Dukhobors, returning to Switzerland shortly before his death in 1931.

Among his voluminous Tolstoyan writings Biryukov is remembered above all for his four-volume biography of Tolstoy, which was authorized by Tolstoy himself and upon which Biryukov worked for twenty years. While written from the point of view of an uncritical follower of Tolstoy, this work has a permanent place in Tolstoy studies because of the wealth of information presented in it by a man who was closely associated with Tolstoy for 26 years.

Bibliography:

A. *Biografiya L. N. Tolstogo* (4 vols., Moscow, 1922–23); *Tolstoi und der Orient: Briefe und sonstige Zeugnisse über Tolstois Beziehungen zu den orientalischen Religionen* (Zurich and Leipzig, 1926).

B. Aylmer Maude, *Life of Tolstoy; Later Years* (Oxford 1930); Ernest J. Simmons, *Leo Tolstoy* (Boston, 1946); *Socialisme et christianisme: Correspondance Tolstoï-Birioukof* (Paris, 1957).

William B. Edgerton

BJØRNSON, Bjørnstjerne Martinius (8 December 1832, Kvikne, Norway—26 April 1910, Paris). *Education*: secondary school, Molde; studies at the Univ.

of Christiania [now Oslo] *Career*: novelist; poet, journalist, orator, theater director, and dramatist; Nobel prize in literature, 1903.

As a sixteen-year old, Bjørnstjerne Bjørnson wrote his first newspaper article and for sixty years thereafter was a brilliant journalist writing on all political, social, and moral issues of the day. He began appearing as a public speaker in 1859 and was considered Scandinavia's greatest orator. His early writings are characterized by an intense Norwegian nationalism. His poem *Ja, vi elsker dette landet* (*Yes, we love this country*) was set to music by Rikard Nordraak and became Norway's national anthem. Progressively, he extended his patriotic ideals to embrace all of Scandinavia, the German speaking areas of Europe, and all of Europe in a pan-European sense. His ideals were truly internationalistic and he may be considered one of the forerunners of the idea of One World.

Bjørnson's development as a pacifist can be traced back to the 1850s, but it was an inconsistent development. During the Danish-German war of 1864, Bjørnson urged that Norway and Sweden enter the war on Denmark's side, and even volunteered to fight himself although his poor eyesight precluded his becoming a soldier. However, his growing internationalist spirit overcame his Scandinavian nationalism and he progressively grew more pacifist. His formal debut as a pacifist took place on October 27, 1890, when he wrote in the foreword to *Klas P. Arnoldson's *Lov-ikke krig mellem folkene* (*Law not War between Peoples*), "We must teach people that war never has advantages either economic or cultural." Twelve days later, Bjørnson was principal speaker at a large peace meeting in the Concert-Palace of Copenhagen. Thereafter, Bjørnson supported the cause of peace through newspaper articles, speeches, and letters. One of these letters was sent to Carl Schurz, the influential American political leader, writer, and orator. The letter, reprinted in the *New York Herald*, begs America not to isolate itself, but to work together with the European peace movement. Following the fourth World Peace Congress held in Berne in 1892, Bjørnson instigated a worldwide petition movement for peace. Living in Denmark at the time, Bjørnson succeeded in persuading nearly a quarter of a million Danes to sign the petition, more people than had ever signed a petition in Denmark. The petition was presented to the Danish parliament and later to the king. It was cordially received, but the response was that because of Denmark's position and size, it could not take an initiative in the matter.

Bjørnson called himself a socialist, although he had no sympathy with the class struggle. He identified socialism with liberal social and political reforms which, along with the tradition of Humanism became the sources of his pacifist views. These views were reflected throughout his writings and were prominent in the text of a peace cantata written for Edvard Grieg. At the time of his death Bjørnson was working on a poem to be called *Good Deeds Save the World*. *Alfred Nobel valued Bjørnson as a poet and idealist. This probably had something to do with Nobel's deciding that a committee of the Norwegian parliament would determine the peace prize. Bjørnson was a member of the first Nobel committee.

Bibliography:

A. *En Fallit* (Copenhagen, 1875; Eng. trans., *The Bankrupt*, New York, 1914); *Geografi og Kjaerlighet* (Copenhagen, 1885; Eng. trans., *Love and Geography*, New York, 1914); *Over æAevne* (Copenhagen, 1883; Eng. trans., *Beyond Human Power*. Boston, 1915); *På Guds veje* (Copenhagen, 1889; Eng. trans., *In God's Way*, New York, 1890).

B. Harold Beyer, *A History of Norwegian Literature* (New York, 1956); Astrid Finsland, *Bjørnstjerne Bjørnson og fredsaken inntil 1900* (Oslo, 1948); Harold Larson, *Bjørnstjerne Bjørnson: A Study in Norwegian Nationalism* (New York, 1944).

William Shank

BLANC, Alexandre (14 September 1874, Camps-la-Source, Var, France—26 August 1924, Alfortville, Seine). *Education*: teaching certificate, École normale, Avignon, 1893. *Career:* schoolteacher, 1893–1906 and 1910–14; syndicalist and socialist militant, 1900–20; socialist deputy from the Vaucluse, 1906–10 and 1914–20; member of the Communist party, 1921–24.

Blanc's career incorporated the features of a number of prominent French pacifists of the early twentieth century. He was a schoolteacher from the provinces; a union militant during a period when public employees were barred from forming unions; a member of the socialist movement before the founding of a unified Socialist party in France; active in antimilitarist campaigns in the decade before the First World war; gained public office as a Socialist deputy and notoriety as a political journalist.

During the First World War, Blanc joined two other Socialist deputies and former schoolteachers, *Pierre Brizon and *Jean-Pierre Raffin-Dugens, in spearheading a movement for a compromise peace—a settlement of the war without victors or vanquished to be imposed on the governments of Europe by their peoples. It was in pursuit of this ideal that all three men took part in the Kienthal Conference (April 24–30, 1916) which brought together European socialists in a common quest for peace. Thereafter, Blanc joined the other "Kienthalians" in June 1916 in voting against war credits in the Chamber of Deputies. He remained steadfast in his opposition to the Socialist party's collaboration in wartime governments, since he rejected the thesis that France was fighting a defensive war. Though reelected a Socialist deputy in November 1919, he could not abide the reformism of his party in a revolutionary era. After the Congress of Tours (December 25–30, 1920), Blanc joined the newly-formed Communist party and remained active as a Communist deputy until his death in 1924.

Bibliography:

B. Jean Charles *et al.*, eds., *Les Congrès de Tours* (critical edition, Paris, 1980); Max Ferré, *Histoire du mouvement syndicaliste révolutionnaire chez les instituteurs* (Paris, 1955); Jean Maitron, ed., *Dictionnaire biographique du mouvement ouvrier français* (vol. 10, Paris, 1973); Alfred Rosmer, *Le Mouvement ouvrier pendant la première guerre mondiale* (vol. 2, Paris, 1959).

Ioannis Sinanoglou

BLANCHARD, Joshua Pollard (1782—3 October 1868, Boston, MA). *Education*: Friends' School at Westtown, PA. *Career*: bookkeeper, author, and peace activist.

Little is known about the personal life of Joshua Pollard Blanchard, though he was certainly one of the more important pacifists in nineteenth-century America. He was among the first non-clerical peace leaders in the country. It would seem that he was from humble origins in contrast to the more privileged beginnings of some of the men who were publicly active in the peace movement. An obituary described his occupation as a bookkeeper for the Eagle Bank for over thirty years. His conversion to pacifism was not a product of a traumatic experience or a sudden moment of revelation. He recalled that until the age of 25 or 26 he was inclined toward a military nature, but he did not remember what persuaded him to become a peace advocate. He suspected that his attitude changed around 1809 or 1810, and during the War of 1812 he refused military service.

His first attendance at the meeting of the newly formed Massachusetts Peace Society in 1816 was still vivid in his mind 28 years later. From that moment until his death, he became a devoted and loyal worker in the peace movement. In 1828 the Massachusetts Peace Society voted to become an affiliate of *William Ladd's American Peace Society. The latter organization was a national association for the promotion of peace, pulling together many of the local peace societies that sprang up in the early decades of the nineteenth century. Blanchard was a member of the American Peace Society, at one point serving as its treasurer.

Blanchard's pacifist philosophy was deeply influenced by the Quaker principle of opposing everything that supported war. On the issues that divided American pacifists (for example, the moral correctness of defensive wars) Blanchard habitually took the position that all wars were wrong. During the Civil War many advocates of peace retreated from their nonviolent principles for what they saw as the greater good—the elimination of racial slavery. Some took comfort in the argument that civil wars were not conflicts between nations but the police actions of a single state, and hence could be supported. Blanchard refused to compromise. He argued for peace between the warring regions of the country.

Blanchard's views brought him close to the moderate pacifism of *Elihu Burritt. Indeed, Blanchard was a member of the latter's League of Universal Brotherhood. Believing that all wars were inconsistent with the Christian spirit, it was an organization that promoted international human brotherhood. Blanchard did not share the extreme radical views of *William Lloyd Garrison's New England Non-Resistance Society which refused to recognize the validity of state and civil government as long as they maintained the slightest connection with coercive power.

During the course of his life, Blanchard authored several tracts that urged the renouncement of all wars (offensive and defensive). He was a mainstay of the American peace movement.

Bibliography:

A. *Address delivered at the Thirteenth Anniversary of the Massachusetts Peace Society, December 25, 1828* (Boston, 1829); *Communications on Peace Written for the Christian Citizen* (Boston, 1848); *Plan for Terminating the War, by Division of the United States without Concession of Principle or Right on the Part of the North* (n.p., [1861]); *The War of Secession* (Boston, 1861).

B. Peter Brock, *Pacifism in the United States* (Princeton, 1968); Merle Eugene Curti, *The American Peace Crusade* (Durham, NC, 1929); *Appletons' Cyclopaedia of American Biography* (New York, 1888), I, 287–88.

C. Testimony of J. P. Blanchard, Samuel E. Coues Peace Album, Harvard University Library.

Gary Puckrein

BLOCH, Jean de (24 August, 1836, Radom, Russian Poland—7 January 1902, Warsaw). *Education*: Realgymnasium, Warsaw; studies at the Univ. of Berlin, 1860s. *Career*: industrialist, philanthropist, and publicist.

Jean de Bloch's claim to fame rests on his astonishingly accurate prediction of what would happen in the event of an early twentieth century general European war. A practical genius, his brand of pacifism was pragmatic and essentially conservative.

Bloch was a converted Polish Jew who constructed railways in European Russia and amassed vast wealth and influence in the enterprising climate of the 1860s and 1870s. He controlled railway transports in the Russo-Turkish War of 1877, and played a backstage role in St. Petersburg politics until the assassination of Alexander II in 1881. Following that event, which narrowed the worldly opportunities for men of his class and race, he became a keen student of military theory. He had a passion for research and a gift for grasping the broad consequences of facts.

In the 1880s and 1890s it was obvious to most that the ever growing deadliness of fire power, coupled with the unwieldiness of modern mass armies, was shifting the natural advantage in warfare increasingly to the side of defensive tactics and strategy. Armed with powerful modern weapons, any force that stayed where it was and dug itself in could throw back or destroy all save a vastly superior attacking force. Bloch was one of the very few thinkers (another was the German General Colmar Von Der Goltz) to grasp the terrible logical implication of this: that there would be no decisive victories in future land wars between Great Powers; that armies, unable to get at each other, would entrench themselves; that the ensuing deadlock would last for years; and that armed conflict would be determined not by success in the field but the eventual economic collapse of societies.

Bloch published his conclusions in 1898 in six huge statistical volumes entitled *The Future of War in its Technical, Economic and Political Relations*, subsequently rendered more digestible in the writings of such pacifist journalists as +W. T. Stead. This work attracted the attention of the *Emperor Nicholas II, who is said to have been influenced by it in his decision to convene the First Hague Peace Conference (May-July 1899). At the time of the Conference (which he considered to have more of a moral than a practical significance) Bloch's widely publicized theories achieved an immense vogue all over Europe, and he created a sensation by going to London the following year to show how they were being borne out by the course of the Boer War. But his international renown as a polemicist did not long survive his death in 1902.

A tycoon, Bloch argued that war was valueless. It was not just that the destruction outweighed the objectives to be attained. Under prevailing technical conditions, political objectives could no longer be attained at all. Uncontrollable, monstrous force that it had become, war could only destroy the economic and social fabric of a belligerent. It had become "impossible"—impossible, that is, in its old Clausewitzian sense of "a continuation of policy by other means." Hopeful that reason would prevail, he sought (like *Bertha von Suttner and her followers) to persuade the ruling classes of Europe that the preservation of "the old order" rested on the prevention of war, and to educate the masses in facts that any schoolboy might understand. Just before his death he founded the Museum of War and Peace in Lucerne to further this instructive purpose, but to little ultimate effect.

Bibliography:

A. *The Future of War in its Technical, Economic, and Political Relations* (Russian ed., 6 vols. St. Petersburg, 1898; trans. by R. C. Long, Boston, 1903, reprinted, New York, 1973; abridged ed., Boston, 1903, reprinted, New York, 1972); *Is War Now Impossible*, trans. by R. C. Long (London, 1899); *Modern Weapons and Modern War*, trans. by R. C. Long (London, 1900); *The Work of the Peace Societies: How To Widen Their Programme* (Chatham, 1901).

B. Peter van den Dungen, *A Bibliography of the Pacifist Writings of Jean de Bloch* (London, 1977); Peter van den Dungen, "The International Museum of War and Peace at Lucerne," *Schweizerische Zeitschrift für" Geschichte*, 31 (1981), 185–202; Peter van den Dungen, "Ein interessant probleem—Jean de Bloch en de eerste Haagse Vredes-conferentie," *Transaktie* (Univ. of Grönigen), 81/3 (September, 1981), 291–335; Peter van den Dungen, *The Making of Peace: Jean de Bloch and the First Hague Peace Conference*, Occasional Paper #12, Center for the Study of Armament and Disarmament, California State University, Los Angeles (Los Angeles, 1983).

Michael Bloch

BLOH, Friedrich Wilhelm Gerhard (23 October 1854, Wardenburg, Grand Duchy of Oldenburg, Germany—19 June 1941, Hamburg). *Education*: Grossherzogliches Seminar (grand-ducal college for elementary school teachers), Oldenburg, 1869–71. *Career*: elementary school teacher in various places in the Grand Duchy of Oldenburg, 1871–85; elementary school teacher, Hamburg, 1885–89; school principal, Hamburg, 1889–1921; pacifist.

For decades Friedrich Bloh sought to promote pacifist ideas at the same time that he opposed German militarism and nationalism. Prior to the outbreak of World War I, he was recognized far beyond Hamburg educational circles for his efforts to improve the living conditions and education of poor children. These efforts as well as his political work on behalf of the poor and propertyless inhabitants of Hamburg led to his being viewed as a representative of "social democratic tendencies." He was a strong opponent of corporal punishment, and as president of the Hamburger Jugendbund zum Schutze der Tiere und Pflanzen (Hamburg Youth League for the Protection of Animals and Plants), which was founded in 1897, he worked for the protection of animals and nature. In the 1890s he was chairman of the Egidy Association of Hamburg which tried to spread the ideas of *Moritz von Egidy. In addition, Bloh represented Hamburg teachers at numerous conventions, and from 1910 to 1913 he was the representative of Hamburg elementary school teachers in the city school administration, which was the highest honorary office which the Hamburg teacher's association could grant.

From 1900 to 1930 Bloh served as chairman of the Hamburg-Altona branch of the Deutsche Friedensgesellschaft (German Peace Society) (DFG). Under his leadership it developed into one of the most active branches in the nation. In lectures given in 1907 he criticized the unqualified glorification of Otto von Bismarck, whose foreign policy he attacked as being "one-sided" and "without consideration" for the international interests of Germany. He condemned war as the height of senselessness and of brutality and as the most serious obstacle to the well-being of mankind. To work for the elimination of war, he believed, was the "highest patriotic duty." During the Kaiser's regime, he criticized German foreign policy for rejecting armament reduction and obligatory arbitration, leading to the failure of the Second Hague Peace Conference (1907). Reflecting the goals of the peace movement of his time, Bloh called for international understanding and condemned both the hate campaign against England and the German arms buildup. In 1913–14 he urged a German-English agreement and autonomy for Alsace-Lorraine. His agitation against the army bill of 1913 earned him the antipathy of military circles. On May 3, 1913, the *Hamburger Schulzeitung* (*Hamburg School Newspaper*) called upon teachers to "shake off people like Mr. Bloh" in order to prevent "the spirit and the attitudes" of men like him from infecting the teaching profession.

During World War I Bloh remained true to his pacifist ideals and after the war he served as chairman of the Norddeutschen Arbeitsgemeinschaft (North German Study Group) of the DFG, which supported the radical antimilitarist views of *Fritz Küster and the West German Regional Association of the DFG. Bloh also shared *Richard Grelling's conviction that Germany was largely to blame for the outbreak of World War I. In the pages of the *Deutsche Zukunft* he attacked the nationalist campaign that sought to absolve the pre–1914 imperial government of any responsibility in this regard. Like Gerhart Seger, Bloh proposed the neutralization of Germany as a prerequisite for the political unification of Europe. He worked for the dismantling of the armed forces of Germany and called upon his fellow citizens to refuse military service. He rejected as "utopian" the attempt by the German Social Democratic party in the 1920s to republicanize the army.

Bloh lectured often and published many articles propagating his pacifist views. He wrote especially for *Das Andere Deutschland, Die Menschheit, Junge Menschen, Die Friedenswarte*, and the *Monistischen Monatshefte*. A member of the German Social Democratic party since 1919, he resigned from the party in 1931 when it declared that membership in the DFG was incompatible with membership in the party.

With great fervor, Bloh turned against the chauvinistic textbooks used in German schools by referring to paragraph 148 of the Weimar constitution which mandated an education "consistent with the idea of the brotherhood of nations." Being himself a champion of an "ethical form of life," Bloh proposed a pacifist education of youth and a "pacifist pedagogy." He offered a practical example of peace education with his book, *Krieg*! (*War!*) (1929). The book, intended primarily for young people, incorporated excerpts from the works of *Erich M. Remarque, John Galsworthy, Max Barthel, and a proclamation against war by the American socialist, *Eugene V. Debs. At the beginning of the 1930s, illness forced Bloh to curtail his activities after almost fifty years of service to the peace movement.

Bibliography:

A. *Die Erziehung der verwahrlosten Jugend in Hamburg* (Hamburg, 1903); *Krieg*! (Hamburg, 1929).

B. "F. Bloh 75 Jahre," *Deutsche Zukunft*, November 1, 1929, 2; Ingeborg Küster, "Ein treuer Freund in der Not," *Das Andere Deutschland*, nr. 13 (July, 1960), 8; Hans Wehberg, "Friedrich Bloh," *Die Friedenswarte*, 24 (1924), 293; Hans Wehberg, "Friedrich Bloh 75 Jahre alt," *Die Friedenswarte*, 29 (1929), 375.

Helmut Donat
Trans. by Karl M. Gabriel

BLUM, Léon. See *Biographical Dictionary of Internationalists*.

BLYDEN, Edward Wilmot (3 August 1832, St. Thomas, Virgin Islands—2 February 1912, Freetown, Sierra Leone). *Education*: Alexander High School, Monrovia, Liberia. *Career*: high school teacher; editor, *Liberia Herald*, 1858–60, *The Negro*, 1872–74; professor, Liberia Coll. 1860–71, 1890–92, 1900–1; president, Liberia Coll. 1880–84; secretary of state, 1864–66; Liberia's ambassador to Great Britain, 1877–79, 1892; minister of interior, 1880–82; minister to Great Britain and France, 1905.

Edward Blyden was born towards the end of the slave trade in the Americas and at the very beginning of the colonization of Africa. He was one of the young enthusiasts who willingly embraced the American Colonization Society's offer of settlement in Liberia. A determined young man, he went to this promised land with hope and dedication. His intelligence and hard work prepared him for a rich life of activity and literary productivity. His deep sense of commitment to the African cause and his determination to make his contemporaries better aware of the true nature of African life and civilization brought him into contact with some of the most sophisticated and learned men of his day.

Believing that racial harmony and black self-development could take place only in Africa, he sought to convince blacks still living in the New World that their fate under white segregation was a futile and doomed one, for they would never be able to realize their full potential. He subscribed to the notion that the racial turmoil of his day could be resolved peacefully only when people of African descent established their own government and civilization in the African continent. Throughout his life he worked to see Africa develop into a society where peace and harmony between the races were furthered through African self-development and mutual cooperation with Western peoples and cultures.

Both in his writings and speeches Blyden tried to project a positive image of Africa and her cultures. He spoke before congregations, wrote articles for American journals, engaged in pamphlet writing and hobnobed with royalty and members of the second and third estates of the Western world. His association with literary and humanitarian groups in the West enhanced his status and prestige and many an intellectual sought his company. Because of these close ties with leaders of thought in the West, the Liberian government found him politically and intellectually useful to conduct diplomacy on its behalf. Hence his appointment as negotiator for Liberia during the discussions over the protracted border dispute with France and Britain. Though Blyden did not accomplish his peace mission, his efforts marked him as a man of peace who would rather talk to the imperial powers through the peaceful medium of words than engage them in a futile military warfare.

This same commitment to peace and compromise governed his response to the racial question of his day. Peace between the races, he argued, lay in African self-development and black control of their ancestral continent. But Blyden also believed in the peaceful and harmonious relations between African peoples. To his end, he tried his best to create structures of peaceful relations between the African Muslims and their Christian brethren. His deep knowledge of Islam and Arabic put him in good stead and he died in good standing among the Muslims of West Africa with whom he made peace and developed confidences.

Bibliography:

A. *Black Spokesman, Selected Published Writings of E. W. Blyden*, Hollis R. Lynch, ed. (New York, 1971); *Selected Letters of Edward Wilmot Blyden* (New York, 1978).

B. Edith Holden, *Blyden of Liberia* (New York, Washington, Hollywood, 1966).

Sulayman S. Nyang

BOEKE, Cornelis (Kees) (25 September 1884, Alkmaar, Netherlands—3 July 1966, Amsterdam). *Education*: studied civil engineering, Polytechnic Coll., Delft; further engineering studies, London and Birmingham (Kingsmead Training Center), England. *Career*: high school principal, Brummana, Syria; teacher, England, 1915–16; peace activist; founder of the Werkplaats Kindergemeenschap, 1934–54.

As a young man, Kees Boeke pursued an education in mathematics and physics but was equally attracted to music and to the organized student movement. As a delegate to an international student meeting in Edinburgh in 1904, he made his first contact with Quaker ideas, a connection that he revived when he returned to Britain as an advanced graduate student in engineering. Boeke decided to give up his plans for a doctorate and instead applied for a post in a Quaker school in Syria (now Lebanon). During his training year at Kingsmead (1911), he met and later married Beatrice (Betty) Cadbury who shared his pacifist, and later anarchist, commitments.

When the First World War broke out, the couple returned to England where

Boeke began to work for the Fellowship of Reconciliation. His Dutch nationality permitted him to travel on the continent, including Germany, but his increasingly radical antiwar positions finally led to his deportation from England. The Boekes went to the Netherlands where they joined the circle that included *Bart de Ligt around the journal *Opwaarts*. Writing and editorial work seemed insufficient to Boeke who preferred a more active commitment to principles of nonviolence and social justice. Kees and Betty Boeke then went on to build a ''Brotherhood house'' at Bilthoven (near Utrecht) from which three important movements emanated: the creation (with *Pierre Ceresole) of a Christian International (now the International Fellowship of Reconciliation); the International Civil Service; and PACD (the International War Resisters League). There also was published the militant periodical, *A Fighter for God's Kingdom*, which made its debut in November 1919.

Increasingly troubled by a lifestyle that depended on the unearned income from the Cadbury factory, the Boekes chose to relinquish their wealth to the Worker's Council of Cadbury Bros., Ltd. Boeke grew increasingly uncomfortable with being a ''citizen'' and in the 1920s, withdrew from all tax paying, from all use of public services such as rails and mails, and from using money. The family, including seven children, was kept alive by friends. Boeke became increasingly isolated from all activity, cut off from writing and lecturing as the government sought to minimize and contain this form of total civil disobedience. The need to educate his own children, however, led Boeke to discover a new form of social action consonant with his principles. He began an experimental school that was guided by principles of pure democracy. Children and teachers who were viewed as helpers were to participate in every decision about their education and lives. Compulsion was eliminated. Thus began the Werkplaats.

Through his involvement in experimental education, Boeke slowly returned to participation in public and organizational life, compromising realistically with his antistate principles. His book, *Kindergemeenschap* (1934) publicized the new communal principles of education which he saw as crucial to the building of a new society.

During the Second World War the Boekes struggled to keep their school alive and restrict German control. Following the war he led a movement to attempt to extend the educational ideas of his democratic school to the world of politics, arguing for a principle of ''sociocraty'' which involved total participation of each community in political decision making. His school was selected by the future Queen for her daughters, and eventually the school had to accept some public financing to keep it alive. Boeke's labors in the fields of peace activism eventually had come to focus on the education of young children, of a new generation, in principles of democracy and nonviolence.

Bibliography:

A. *Kindergemeenschap* (Utrecht, 1934); *De vergetenen,* with L. van Mierop, (Blaricum,1920); *Wij in het heelal, het heelal in ons* (Utrecht, 1959).

B. Beatrice Boeke-Cadbury, *Het leven van Kees Boeke* (Purmerend, 1971); Hilbrandt Boschma, ''Kees en Betty Boeke,'' *Licht en Liefde*, 2–3 (February-March, 1925); Wyatt

T. Rawson, "Kees and Betty Boeke. A Short Account of Their Lives and Work" in *Aan Kees Boeke—25 Sept., 1954* (Purmerend, 1956), 1–81; Wyatt T. Rawson, *The Werkplaats Adventure: An Account of Kees Boeke's Great Pioneer Comprehensive School: Its Methods and Psychology* (London, 1956); *Biografisch Woordenboek van Nederland* (The Hague, 1979), I, 60–62.

J. H. Rombach

BOGANDA, Barthélemy (4 April 1910, Boubangui, Ubangui-Shari—29 March 1959, Boda, Central African Republic). *Education*: Roman Catholic seminaries in Brazzaville, Yaoundé, and Kisantu; ordained 1938. *Career*:—Roman Catholic priest until 1946; deputy, French National Assembly, 1946-56; founder, Mouvement d'Evolution Sociale d'Afrique Noire (MESAN), 1949; mayor of Bangui, 1956; president, Grand Conseil of French Equatorial Africa, 1957; president, Conseil de Gouvernement of the Central African Republic, 1958; antiracialist, peacemaker, and supporter of African unity.

Until 1946 when he was urged to run for a seat in the French National Assembly by Bishop Grandin of Bangui, Barthélemy Boganda had never expressed particularly strong political views. Yet, once elected to the assembly he, as one of the first Ubanguians to visit Paris, was struck by the very different attitude and behavior of French people in France and the colonists in Ubangui-Shari. Almost immediately Boganda began to demand an end to racism and to seek equal rights for the Ubanguian people as citizens of France. Accused by the colonial party of being a Communist although he was a member of the Mouvement Republicain Populaire (MRP), he nevertheless continued to speak out against colonial abuses. In his life long struggle against injustice and racial oppression, Boganda never succumbed to the belief that the struggle was one of black versus white. He always distinguished between the evils of the colonial system in his homeland and the more universal values he found in the best of Western civilization.

In 1948 Boganda established the Société cooperative de la Lobaye-Lessé (Socoulolé), a consumer and producer cooperative which he hoped would help his constituents obtain some measure of relief from their poverty-stricken status. Unfortunately, poor management, lack of experience and knowledge, along with opposition from the big commercial companies caused the failure of this movement by 1949. For Boganda, political solutions henceforth seemed to be the only means of achieving the goals of social justice which he sought. On September 28, 1949 Boganda founded the Mouvement d'evolution sociale d'Afrique Noire (MESAN). This and his marriage in 1950 to a French parliamentary secretary, Michelle Jourdain, signaled his final break with a priestly career and his absolute commitment to the pacific and progressive liberation of the African people. It also caused an increasingly hostile reaction on the part of the colonial administration and the majority of colonists.

Stepping up his outspoken opposition to the abuses of the colonial regime, Boganda soon ran into direct conflict with the authorities and was arrested when he went to aid members of the Socoulolé in their dispute against a number of Portuguese traders in the village of Bohanga in January 1951. Sentenced to jail,

Boganda became a national hero of the Ubanguian people and was assured of reelection as deputy. By 1953 a shift in French attitudes and Boganda's careful cultivation of good relations with the private sector had led to more amicable relations between Boganda's supporters and both the colonial officials and the European business community.

On April 3, 1954 a riot broke out in Berberati following the death of a domestic servant and his wife who were in the service of a French official known for his brutal treatment of Africans. Unable to handle the growing popular unrest, the governor called upon Boganda to intervene. Though he previously had no popular following in the area, Boganda was nevertheless able to persuade a large throng of Baya people to disperse peacefully on May 1. This clearly marked him as a national leader rather than simply an ethnic or regional figure, since he was able to quell the riot even though, shortly before his arrival, the crowd had stoned and wounded the head of the region and killed a passing Frenchman. During the next two years MESAN grew while Boganda's conciliatory attitude led to generally harmonious relations throughout Ubangui-Shari. Boganda received 84.7 percent of the votes cast in the January 1, 1956 election. He was also elected mayor of Bangui in November of that year in spite of opposition from the colonialists.

With the institution of the 1956 *loi-cadre* from February to May 1957, Ubangui-Shari became a semi-autonomous territory with Boganda as its major African spokesman. Resisting pressure toward racism, Boganda succeeded in establishing a broadly based government and then went on to become president of the Grand Conseil of French Equatorial Africa in 1957 in order to realize his plan for a greater African federation. Faced with mismanaged development schemes and divisive political maneuvering in Ubangui-Shari, Boganda spent most of March 1957 touring the especially disaffected eastern part of the country attempting to both sort out and explain his own ideas on politics and economics for Ubangui-Shari.

Returning from Paris in July 1958, Boganda broached the subject of independence but pragmatically worked to deliver a resounding 98.1 percent vote in favor of autonomous status within the French community. Then, as president of the Grand Conseil, he attempted to push through a proposal for a united state in Central Africa with the final goal of a United States of Latin Africa to include what is today Congo, Gabon, Chad, the Central African Republic, Zaire, Rwanda, Burundi, Angola, and Cameroon. Finally, however, opposition from French companies, colonists, other African leaders, and the French high commissioner dashed these hopes and Boganda formed a government on December 8, 1958 for a much reduced Central African Republic which included only the single territory of Ubangui-Shari. The constitution adopted on February 16, 1959 included all the basic principles of democracy and Boganda carefully planned a multi-ethnic, nonracist election to be held on April 5. Unfortunately for the Central African Republic and its people, on March 29, 1959, Easter Day, Boganda died in an airplane accident for which no clear cause has ever been ascertained. With him died his dreams of a multiterritory federation.

Boganda was not only the father of the present-day Central African Republic, he also remains one of the African continent's great spokesmen for human rights. Opposed to racism and ethnic divisions, Boganda's hopes for a large scale Central African federation was one of the most grandiose schemes for peaceful unity ever to be discussed seriously in Africa.

Bibliography:

A. *Enfin on decolonise* (Brazzaville, 1958); ''Faisons le point,'' *France-Outre-Mer*, Nos. 334-5 (September-October, 1957), 46-49; ''Logique, Justice et raison,'' *Terre Africaine*, No. 4 (November, 1958), 4-5.

B. Philippe Decraene, *Le Panafricainism* (Paris, 1959); Pierre Kalck, ''Barthélemy Boganda, tribu et visionnaire de l'Afrique centrale,'' *Les Africaines* (Paris, 1977), 105-37; Pierre Kalck, *Central African Republic* (New York, 1971).

Thomas E. O'Toole

BONGHI, Ruggiero (21 March 1826, Naples, Italy—22 October 1895, Torre del Greco). *Education*: Collegio degli scolopi di San Carlo à Mortella, 1837-41; studies at Univ. of Naples, 1842-46 and Univ. of Florence, 1848. *Career*: member, Chamber of Deputies; minister of public instruction, 1874-76; founding member, Comitato per l'arbitrato e per la pace, 1888; founding member, Italian section, Interparliamentary Union, 1890-95; professor, scholar, publisher, journalist, and lecturer.

In the last seven years of his life when Ruggiero Bonghi joined the Italian peace movement, he was already a famous scholar, prolific lecturer and author (between 1866-95, he contributed over 160 articles to *Nuova Antologia*, alone), founder of two major newspapers (*Il Nazionale* and *La Stampa*), defender of public education and the separation of Church and State, and government minister (belonging to the ''historical right''). Partly inspired by a visit from the crusading English peace activist, *Hodgson Pratt (1888), he created a committee to study and popularize ideas of peace and international arbitration (Comitato per l'arbitrato e per la pace). This group, collaborating with sister societies elsewhere in Italy, convened the first national Italian peace congress in 1889 in Rome where Bonghi played a leading part. By that time, he was also severely worried about the course of Italian foreign policy under Francesco Crispi's leadership. Bonghi attacked the tightened ties of his nation to the German and Austro-Hungarian alliance and the concomitant dangerous deterioration of Italian-French relationships. He was also perturbed by Crispi's imperial ambitions, convinced that Italy needed to develop its own backward sectors prior to engaging in overseas projects.

At the Rome congress, Bonghi appealed for the creation of a permanent nationwide movement such as was developing in England and France. He argued that local committees needed to be set up which published journals and held frequent meetings to create a consensus of public opinion in favor of organized international institutions. Others at the congress argued for a defensive militia in place of a professional army and discussed the true needs of national security that would not bankrupt the nation. Bonghi feared that ''the continuous increase of armaments'' assured ''only the continued increase of the national budget but not the provision of security nor the guarantee that arms will, one day, not be used.'' Thus, he turned toward the newly reorganized peace movement.

He persuaded the leaders of both the Interparliamentary Union and the Universal Peace Congress to hold their 1891 meetings in Rome. There, Bonghi convinced European delegates to establish a permanent headquarters for the Universal Peace Congress, which, in turn, appointed the Swiss peace activist, *Elie Ducommun, to serve as first general secretary. It was Bonghi's hope, too, that the Interparliamentary Union, whose membership was composed of elected parliamentarians from many European nations (later U.S. members joined), might serve as the nucleus of a European parliament. At least, the Union's annual assemblies provided a place for discussion among parliamentarians from officially hostile nations, giving them an opportunity to meet and work out resolutions that might be supported in their respective national legislatures. Bonghi argued the necessity of continuously expanding these contacts if Europe was to avoid a path of permanent progression toward barbarism and all out war. The participation of an individual with his reputation, credentials, and stature in a new born national movement was of crucial consequences to the growth of the late 19th century Italian peace movement. With Bonghi's death, the Rome Committee for Arbitration and Peace lost its position of eminence which was taken up by the Milanese group under *E. T. Moneta.

Bibliography:

A. ''Dei modi pratici di rinvigorire e di organizzare in Italia il movimento della opinione versa la pace e verso l'arbitrato internazionale,'' in *Atti del congresso di Roma per la pace e per l'arbitrato internazionale 12-16 maggio, 1889*, C. Facelli and L. Morandi, eds., (Rome, 1889), 183-86; *Discorsi parlamentari pubblicati per deliberazione della Camera dei deputati*, (Rome, 1918); *I discorsi di Ruggiero Bonghi per la società Dante Alighieri con una introduzione storica di P. Boselli* (Rome, 1920); Letters to A. Rosmini, ed. by G. Gentile in *Nuova Antologia*, June 1, 1944, 65-81; *Opere*, (14 vols, Rome, Milan, Florence, 1933-58); *La Situazione Europea e la pace*, (Rome, 1891).

B. F. Ermini, *Ruggiero Bonghi* (Prato, 1895); A. H. Ghisalberti, ed., *Dizionario biografico degli Italiani*, XII, 42-51; E. Gianturco, *Commemorae di Ruggiero Bonghi, In memoria di Ruggiero Bonghi, la società Dante Alighieri* (Rome, 1896); C. Morandi, ''Il Pensiero politico di Ruggiero Bonghi'' in *Annali di scienze politiche* II (1929) 231-7; F. D'Ovidio, *L'Avversione di Ruggiero Bonghi alla Triplice Alleanza*, (Campobasso, 1915).

C. Ruggiero Bonghi Papers, Istituto per la Storia moderna e contemporanea, Rome; various letters, Biblioteca Nazionale, Florence and Bureau International de la Paix, Archives, United Nations Library, Geneva.

Sandi E. Cooper

BONHOEFFER, Dietrich (4 February 1906, Breslau, Germany—9 April 1945, Flossenburg). *Education*: Lic. (Ph.D.), Univ. of Berlin, 1927. *Career*. theologian.

Dietrich Bonhoeffer's career as one of Germany's most significant theologians of this century was cut short by his murder at the hands of the Nazis at the age of 39. Ordained in the Berlin diocese of the German Evangelical Church, he was appointed lecturer in the Theological Faculty of Berlin University in 1929. He was first drawn to the ideas of pacifism by a fellow-student, Jean Lasserre, while both men were on an exchange visit to Union Theological Seminary in New York in 1930–31. Following his return to Europe, Bonhoeffer attended the 1931 international conference of the World Alliance for Promoting International Friendship through the Churches, and was appointed one of the three Youth Secretaries, with responsibility for central Europe. This part-time activity widened his contacts with Christian pacifism and with the leading personalities of the international ecumenical movement, such as Bishop Bell of Chichester, England. Bonhoeffer warmly supported the World Alliance campaign for international reconciliation and peace, though he was critical of its lack of an adequate theological base.

Recognizing the dangers of national extremism, he expressed his opposition to the totalitarian and racial tendencies of the new Nazi regime in Germany as early as February 1933. He equally opposed the pro-Nazi "German Christians" whose activities led to the creation of the opposition Confessing Church. At the World Alliance conferences of 1933–34, he actively sponsored resolutions critical of the new German regime and sought to mobilize support for the Confessing Church. In 1935 Bonhoeffer, who had been pastor of two German-speaking congregations in London since 1933, returned to Germany to organize training courses for ordinands to the Confessing Church, which were held irregularly (and later illegally) on various country estates in Pomerania. Here Bonhoeffer wrote his influential book *The Cost of Discipleship* (1948).

Close family connections with many of the leaders of the anti-Nazi opposition drew Bonhoeffer into the conspiracy of resistance against Hitler in which he abandoned his earlier hopes for a nonviolent solution along Gandhian lines. On a brief visit to the United States in 1939, he was offered asylum, but chose to share the fate of his fellow Germans. After the outbreak of war, Bonhoeffer was given secret assignments by the resistance movement to gain support among churchmen abroad for the proposed overthrow of the Nazi regime. In May 1942, in Sweden, he outlined to Bishop Bell the plans of the German resistance movement, which included the recognition of a "penitential" peace settlement by Germany and the violent overthrow or assassination of Hitler. Like his fellow conspirators, Bonhoeffer was confronted by a dilemma: a victory for Germany would be fateful for the church and the world; on the other hand, Germany's defeat would probably mean its end as a nation. His incompleted *Ethics* was an attempt to resolve this dilemma.

Bonhoeffer was arrested by the Gestapo in April 1943 for suspected anti-Nazi activities, and, in the aftermath of the failure of the July 20, 1944 plot against Hitler's life, was executed in April 1945 at Flossenburg concentration camp. Before his death, Bonhoeffer was able to smuggle out letters that were posthumously published as *Letters and Papers from Prison* (1953), a series of challenging reflections on the role of the church and religion. Bonhoeffer was the only leading German theologian to draw practical political conclusions from his theological reflections in opposition to Nazism. His status as a martyr in the cause of anti-Nazi resistance, and his writings reflecting the dilemmas of a committed Christian in a totalitarian state, gained him a significant reputation and influence in the post–1945 world.

Bibliography:

A. *Ethik* (Munich, 1949, English trans., *Ethics*, London, 1955); *Nachfolge* (Munich, 1937, English trans., *The Cost of Discipleship*, London, 1948); *Sanctorum Communio* Berlin, 1929); *Widerstand und Ergebung. Briefe und Aufzeichnungen aus der Haft* (Munich, 1951, English trans., *Letters and Papers from Prison*, London, 1953).

B. E. Bethge, *Dietrich Bonhoeffer. Eine Biographie* (Munich, 1967).

John S. Conway

BOSS, Charles Frederick, Jr. (22 July 1888, Washington—13 December 1965, Alexandria, VA). *Education*: George Washington Univ., 1915–16; B.R.E., Boston Univ., 1922; Harvard Graduate School, 1921; American Univ., 1923–24; Northwestern Univ., 1928–29. *Career*: director of religious education, Baltimore Conference, 1922–26; superintendent, Church School Administration of the General Board of Education, 1926–28; director, Bureau of Research of the General Board of Education, 1928–33; executive secretary and later general secretary, Methodist Commission (later Board) of World Peace, 1936–57; secretary for UN and Intergovernmental Affairs, 1957–60; Methodist minister and church leader.

Charles Boss entered the Methodist ministry in 1916 and served several pastorates in Maryland before beginning a long career as a denominational leader and spokesman. He was one of a new generation of Protestant churchmen who unabashedly thrust themselves into the political arena. Among his many interests, Boss emphasized two—military conscription and the United Nations.

As World War II loomed, Boss participated in the evolution of the Civilian Public Service (CPS) program of alternate service for conscientious objectors, and he served on the National Service Board for Religious Objectors (NSBRO) which directed CPS during the war. The Methodist Commission on World Peace was the only nonhistoric pacifist group in the NSBRO. Boss raised funds and provided other support for the large number of Methodists who participated in CPS. In the postwar period, Boss was one of the major church spokesmen against universal military training. He advocated world disarmament and international abolition of conscription under the UN framework.

Boss was a committed internationalist. He served as a leader at the World Conference of Christian Youth at Amsterdam in 1939 and Oslo in 1947; he was a member of the National Council of Churches' Department of International Affairs for many years; and he was instrumental in bringing together European Methodists to discuss international issues. Above all, Boss was a fervent proponent of the UN. He was an accredited observer at the UN Charter Conference, and he spoke and wrote in the organization's behalf throughout his career. In several appearances before Congressional committees, he consistently expressed his faith in the UN, and he called for the subordination of unilateral actions to cooperative UN ventures. In 1953 Boss established a Methodist UN office at the Carnegie Peace Center. In recognition of long dedication, a Boss Room is named in his honor at the UN Church Center.

Charles Boss maintained a total commitment to international solutions of world problems. He refused to accept the Cold War, and he repeatedly advocated cultural exchange and rapprochement with the Soviet Union. If some thought he exhibited a degree of political naïveté, his zeal and spirit never waned, and he was a spokesman for detente and international cooperation during their darkest hours.

Bibliography:

B. Joe P. Dunn, "Charles F. Boss Jr., The Methodist Commission on World Peace, and the Anti-Conscription Campaigns, 1940–1948," *The Proceedings of The South Carolina Historical Association*, 1983; Herman Will, "Boss, Charles Frederick, Jr.," Nolan B. Harmon, ed., *The Encyclopedia of World Methodism* (Nashville, 1974).

Joe P. Dunn

BOUET, Gabrielle Dechézelles (24 September 1885, Assi-Bou-Nif, Algeria—15 January 1977, Biarritz, France). *Education*: high school diploma. *Career*: primary school teacher in several towns in Maine-et-Loire, France, c. 1904–32. founding member of the National Federation of Elementary School Teachers' Trade Unions (FNSI), 1905; editorial board, *L'Ecole Emancipée*, 1921–36.

Gabrielle Bouet's career was closely intertwined with that of her husband *Louis Bouet, a primary school teacher in Maine-et-Loire. Although never arrested or dismissed for their activities, the Bouets were persecuted. In 1912 the FNSI voted to join the Soldier's Penny, an organization of trade unionists that sent money to soldiers and urged them not to shoot "their working class brothers" when called upon to control strikes and to wage war. A rain of criticism fell upon the Federation and the government began proceedings to dissolve the teachers' trade unions. The Bouets, with others, organized the resistance to dissolution and launched the famous "Manifesto of Unionized Primary Teachers" of September 12, 1912. The manifesto affirmed the teachers' pacifism. It asserted their belief in the ability of concerned peoples to settle their conflicts without bloodshed and protested against the chauvinistic excitations and maneuvers of politicians and financiers that risked provoking a general conflagration. The manifesto declared that the teachers were not antipatriotic if patriotism meant a France always more prosperous, more humane, and more just. The attempts to dissolve the Federation were foiled.

From the beginning, Bouet opposed World War I. Mobilization decimated the editorial staff of the Federation's periodical and Bouet's contributions helped keep it from collapsing. On October 3, 1914, she published an appeal to women school teachers entitled, "Aux Institutrices" that invited them not to let their trade union activity cease and urged them not to founder in chauvinism. In a letter denied publication by the censor, she criticized a colleague for placing the sole responsibility for the war on Germany and for making no distinctions between the German people, blaming them all indiscriminately. She affirmed that Germany, too, had its "generous spirits," people who hated to fight other exploited people and who were waiting for the right time to turn upon their oppressors. Throughout the war Bouet disseminated the antiwar tracts and brochures issued by minority organizations. She raised money and organized campaigns on behalf of those imprisoned or persecuted for their pacifism. She fought vigorously against censorship and the introduction of prowar propaganda into the classroom. She condemned l'Union sacrée (the concept that all Frenchmen should bury their class antagonisms and ban together in a sacred union against the enemy) and subscribed to the international peace conferences of Zimmerwald and Kienthal. Bouet gave support to all those who fought for peace during the 1914–18 war, and she was unsparing of herself in the effort to achieve it.

After the war Bouet was a dedicated member of the editorial board of the Federation's periodical, *L'Ecole Emancipée*. She was also a specialist on textbooks and was responsible for the publication of new and improved ones by the Federation's press. The Bouets managed this small publishing company. Gabrielle Bouet was much less publicly vocal than her husband during the 1930s about rearmament, the Soviet Union, and World War II, but she most likely shared his syndicalist and antiwar views.

Bibliography:

B. François Bernard, Louis Bouet, Maurice Dommanget, Gilbert Serret, *Le Syndicalisme dans l'enseignement* (3 vols., Grenoble, [1966]); Louis Bouet, *Trente ans de combat* (Blainville-sur-mer, [1973]); Max Ferre, *Histoire du mouvement syndicalist chez les instituteurs* (Paris, [1955]).

Jane Bond-Howard

BOUET, Louis (6 April, 1880, Montfaucon-sur-Maine, Maine-et-Loire, France—9 July 1969, Saumur, Maine-et-Loire). *Education*: graduated from the Normal School of Angers, 1900. *Career*: primary school teacher, Maine-et-Loire, 1900–32; founder, National Federation of Elementary School Teachers' Trade Unions (FNSI), 1905; general secretary of the Federation, 1919–21; edited, with wife *Gabrielle Dechézelles and others, *L'Ecole Emancipée*, 1921–36; member of the French Socialist party, 1906–20; founding member of the French Communist party, 1920.

Louis Bouet, as a member of the FNSI, felt close to the working class, believing in the right of teachers to unionize, to join working class organizations, and to support their causes. His pacifism during World War I emerged from the revolutionary syndicalist tradition of the pre–1914 and antiwar positions of his Federation as well as of France's national confederation of trade unions. On June 13, 1915, the FNSI held its first meeting since the war began and voted to oppose its continuation. Bouet characterized the war as "the massacre of some working people by other working people for the glory and profit of those who exploit them."

Despite his strong antiwar position, Bouet did not anticipate that the FNSI could accomplish much through political activity. He saw the fight for a peace without annexations or indemnities as difficult and perilous and believed that this fight, linked with the struggle for the defense of the workers' standard of living, the defense of those persecuted for pacifism, and the struggle for trade union demands, was all that could be undertaken. Social revolution as a means of imposing peace, though desirable, was not possible.

Bouet denounced chauvinism and nationalism. He labored for an assemblage of proletarian organizations from the belligerents. Thus he supported the international peace conferences of Zimmerwald and Kienthal. He wrote numerous articles against the war in the Federation's periodical, attacking those leaders who had disavowed the prewar socialist and syndicalist resolutions against war. He urged a constant battle against government censorship and resisted the teaching of prowar propaganda in the classroom. Bouet supported the antiwar efforts of minoritarian organizations such as the Committee for Syndicalist Defense, and the Committee for the Resumption of International Relations, along with radical antiwar periodicals such as *L'Union des Métaux* and *La Verité*. He remained a source of inspiration to his colleagues during the dark days of the war. As a teacher, he was continuously disciplined, transferred, and even imprisoned for his activism.

After the war Bouet continued to be a leader in the Federation and edited its periodical, *L'Ecole Emancipée*. In 1921 the Federation affiliated with the CGTU, the procommunist confederation of French trade unions. Though procommunist, the majority of the members of the Federation including Bouet, continued to believe in trade union autonomy. A dispute that began in 1928 with the Communist party over this issue led to Bouet's break with the party. The Federation and Bouet remained in the CGTU until the merger between it and the CGT in 1936. After 1936 Bouet lived in retirement. He never abandoned his syndicalist, antiwar position. Throughout the thirties he condemned rearmament and any rapprochement between France and the USSR to fight Nazi Germany. He did not agree with the World War II alliance between the U.S., England, and the Soviet Union for the purpose of fighting Germany. He believed these major powers to be imperialists. Bouet did not support the French Resistance Movement because he thought that by doing so one supported imperialism, both Soviet and Western. He equally condemned the German occupation.

Bibliography:

A. *Les Militants du syndicalisme universitaire* (Avignon, n.d.); *Les Pionniers du syndicalisme universitaire* (Avignon, 1951); *Le Syndicalisme dan l'enseignement* (Saumur, 1924); *Le Syndicalisme dans l'enseignement* (with François Bernard, Maurice Dommanget, Gilbert Serret, Grenoble, [1966]); *Trente ans de combat* (Blainville-sur-mer, [1973]).

B. Max Ferre, *Histoire du mouvement syndicaliste chez les instituteurs* (Paris, [1955]).

Jane Bond-Howard

BOURASSA, Henri (1 September 1868, Montreal, Canada—31 August 1952, Montreal). *Education*: attended Holy Cross Coll., Worcester, MA in 1886. *Career*: federal Member of Parliament, 1896–1907, 1925–35; member, Quebec Assembly, 1908–12; editor, *Le Devoir*, 1910–32; author and politician.

Henri Bourassa first came to public attention in October 1899 when he resigned his seat in the Canadian House of Commons. He was protesting the decision of his leader, Sir Wilfrid Laurier, then prime minister to send troops to aid the British in South Africa in their war against the Boers without first consulting Parliament. Bourassa believed that such action created a precedent by which Canada would be compelled to participate automatically in all British wars. By January 1900 he was back in the House having won his by-election by acclamation. Still he continued to warn that British imperialists would be forever demanding Canadian men and money for their military purposes.

In 1910, as editor of the influential daily, *Le Devoir*, (he was now no longer a member of the federal House) Bourassa opposed the Laurier government's naval bill which would have allowed it to turn the Canadian navy over to British authorities in times of emergency and thereby make it possible for Canada to become involved in another imperial war without a debate in Parliament. Bourassa went so far as to claim that under the proposed law a government minister at Ottawa would have the power to make a personal decision to dispatch Canadians to fight for England "in the five parts of the world." His opportunity to nullify the naval bill came in the federal elections of September 1911 when he helped defeat the Laurier government.

In August 1914 Bourassa, who as an ardent Catholic was naturally influenced by the Quebec Hierarchy, initially accepted the Canadian entry into the war. But he soon became one of its bitterest opponents. He could see no Canadian interest in the conflict. He feared Canadian participation would only strengthen the claim of British imperialists that Canada should take part in all imperial military efforts. He hated all empires, including the British and he believed that the great powers were taking advantage of the war to crush all the small nationalities.

As the war went on Bourassa was increasingly revolted by the carnage. "The sun of the year 1915 rose in a cloud of fire," he mourned, "It is setting in a sea of blood." He supported the British Union for Democratic Control which demanded a negotiated end to the war and he applauded the proposal of Pope *Benedict XV in 1917 to end the war by arbitration. But the great powers paid no heed to Rome's attempt to exercise moral leadership. The continuation of the slaughter only confirmed Bourassa's belief in the wickedness of empires. At home he consistently opposed all war measures including conscription.

In the years following World War I, Bourassa remained wary of imperialist plots. His worst fears seemed to be confirmed when Canada entered the Second World War; once again his country had been drawn into the European vortex because of the British connection. Although now an old man of seventy-five, Bourassa took up the fight and on public platforms opposed conscription and expounded his scepticism of the war aims of the Allies. His conviction that Canada should withdraw only deepened when the Soviet Union, a country whose political system he detested, joined the Anglo-Canadian side. So profound was his opposition to the conflict that despite his strong religious beliefs he openly criticized the Hierarchy for their support of Canadian participation in the war.

Although opposed to senseless killing, Bourassa was not a pacifist. In theory he was ready to support a war in the Canadian national interest, but because his country was separated from Europe by the Atlantic ocean and was protected by the United States, he could conceive of no situation where such drastic action would be necessary. Yet during his lifetime he witnessed Canadian troops fighting in three overseas conflicts. His belief that this needless sacrifice of Canadian blood and treasure was due to the British influence led him repeatedly to urge his fellow citizens to become psychologically independent of the Mother country and to agree that only it's own Parliament could decide that Canada should go to war.

Bibliography:

A. *Le Canada et la paix* (Montreal, 1935); *Conscription* (Montreal, 1917); *Discours sur la guerre du Sud-Africain* (Ottawa, 1901); *Grande-Bretagne et Canada; questions actuelles* (Montreal, 1901); *Le Pape arbitre de la paix* (Montreal, 1918); *Que devons-nous a l'Angleterre*? (Montreal, 1915). *Religion, langue, nationalité* (Montreal, 1910).

B. Joseph Levitt, *Henri Bourassa and the Golden Calf* (Ottawa, 1969).

C. Henri Bourassa correspondence, Public Archives of Canada, Ottawa.

Joseph Levitt

BOURDERON, Albert Henri (26 November 1858, Corbeilles-en-Gatinais, Loiret, France—2 April 1930, Paris). *Career*: barrel-maker; socialist and syndicalist militant; founder and secretary of the Federation du tonneau (barrel-makers' union), 1903–29; active in the cooperative movement, 1896–1911.

In war and in peace, Albert Bourderon's career was remarkable for bridging the ideological divide between the syndicalist and socialist movements in France. At the very outset of the First World War he defied the leaders of both the Confédération générale du travail (CGT) and of the Socialist party by declaring his opposition to wartime collaboration between working-class organizations and a bourgeois government. Speaking for the minority factions of the labor confederation as well as the Socialist party, Bourderon claimed that the interests of the working class would be best served by a negotiated end to the war—a peace without victors or vanquished.

In an attempt to revive the French labor movement as an organized political force, Bourderon urged the convening of the first wartime meeting of the CGT (Paris, August 15, 1915) where he cosponsored a resolution that would become the watchword of antiwar activists. The text aptly summarized the viewpoint of the syndicalist minority: it denied the governments of Europe the liberating role which they had arrogated to themselves in their wartime propaganda; it pointed to the conflicting national imperialisms which had prepared a war whose continuation would profit only those in a position to enrich themselves through speculation; and it called attention to the peace efforts of the socialist minority in Germany, the Independent Labour party in Britain, and the socialists in Italy and Russia.

Bourderon was the only member of the French Socialist party to attend the Zimmerwald Conference (Switzerland, September 5–8, 1915). The conference brought together dissident socialists from eleven countries. Participants pledged themselves to help end the conflict through working-class pressure on the warring governments of Europe. Accordingly, Bourderon and *Alphonse Merrheim (secretary of the metalworkers' union and the only other Frenchman at Zimmerwald) formed a committee of action which soon became the Comité pour la reprise des relations internationales (CRRI). The CRRI formed the nucleus of a nascent pacifist movement in France and the message of Zimmerwald was brought to a wider public in an uncensored pamphlet co-authored by Bourderon and Merrheim.

Throughout the war Bourderon and his comrades in the CRRI constituted the most important and active pressure group on the left of the Socialist party. While French "Zimmerwaldians" rejected the Bolsheviks' "revolutionary defeatism" as a means of ending the war, they did strengthen the hand of those socialists who favored a compromise peace. At wartime meetings of the Confédération Générale du Travail, Bourderon attacked CGT leaders relentlessly for their abandonment of the internationalist ideals of the prewar syndicalist movement. In his view, an abdication which may have been excusable in the aftermath of the sudden mobilization in the summer of 1914 could no longer be justified in the context of a prolonged war that directly threatened the interests of the working class.

While the issues of war and peace had propelled Bourderon to the left wing of the French working-class movement, his self-confessed reformism reemerged at the end of the war. He admired the Bolshevik revolution and championed its cause throughout the late war years. But the organizational unity of the CGT became his major preoccupation by the end of the war. Bourderon never saw his pacifism as a revolutionary act. In 1920 he admitted that France lacked leaders of the type that had directed the Russian Revolution. Thus, they had had to promote the cause of peace "without assuming responsibilities that were too heavy for our shoulders."

Bibliography:

A. *La Conference socialiste internationale, Zimmerwald*, preface by Albert Bourderon and Alphonse Merrheim: "Pourquoi nous sommes allés à Zimmerwald" (Paris, 1915).

B. Robert Brécy, *Le Mouvement syndical en France, 1871–1921* (Paris, 1963); Bernard Georges and Denise Tintant, *Léon Jouhaux: Cinquante ans de syndicalisme*, vol. I: *Des Origines à 1921* (Paris, 1962); Annie Kriegel, *Aux Origines du communisme français, 1914–1920* (Paris, 1964); Jean Maitron, ed., *Dictionnaire biographique du mouvement ouvrier français* (vol. 11, Paris, 1973); Alfred Rosmer, *Le Mouvement ouvrier pendant la guerre* (2 vols., Paris, 1936 and 1959).

Ioannis Sinanoglou

BOURGEOIS, Léon Victor Auguste. See *Biographical Dictionary of Internationalists*.

BOURNE, Randolph Silliman (30 May 1886, Bloomfield, NJ—22 December 1918, New York) *Education*: B.A., Columbia Univ., 1912, M.A., 1913. *Career*: associate editor, *The New Republic*, 1914–17, *Seven Arts*, 1917, *The Dial*, 1916–18; cultural and political critic.

Raised in a middle-class family of declining fortunes and of uncertain faith in the career prospects of a dwarfed and severely hunchbacked youth, Randolph Bourne began to earn a living as a piano accompanist in silent movie theaters and as a sweatshop worker making music rolls for player pianos. He sought a college education as the only sure escape from a future of almost certain economic and cultural depravation. By the age of twenty-three he saved enough funds to enter Columbia College on a partial scholarship. Here he found an intellectual haven and formed most of the intense personal friendships that would sustain him through the rest of his life. While still an undergraduate, Bourne published his first essays in the *Atlantic Monthly* and within a year of graduation, his first anthology, *Youth and Life*. During a year of extensive European travel funded by a Columbia fellowship, Bourne met some of the leading figures of European socialism, including Sydney and Beatrice Webb, +H. G. Wells, George Bernard Shaw, and Jules Romains. Following the German declaration of war, he fled Berlin and returned to America to assume a position secured for him by *Charles Beard, as educational editor of *The New Republic*. In the remaining four years of his life he published in that journal and in *The Dial*, *The Seven Arts*, and elsewhere a total of about one hundred and fifty articles, essays, and reviews.

Wary of the paternal benevolence underlying the progressive reform movements, sceptical of the Marxist belief in proletarian revolution, Bourne spent almost all his intellectual energies seeking a fulcrum on which to rest the levers of social transformation. His first essays, Emersonian in spirit, diction, and form, placed hope in the nonconformity of the younger generation. His subsequent educational columns, deeply influenced by *John Dewey, excoriated the conventions of the American schoolroom and its factory-like atmosphere which depleted all youthful desire for intellectual adventure and social cooperation. Under the tutelage of *Max Eastman, Van Wyck Brooks, and +Walter Lippmann, Bourne then increasingly turned to literary and cultural criticism, calling poets and artists to "sting people into new ideals and tastes" and to awaken the sleeping giant of American social democracy. By 1917 he was recognized as one of the clearest spokesmen of the cultural rebellion concentrated in New York's Greenwich Village.

Six brief articles published between April and October 1917 in the *Seven Arts* established Bourne as the foremost intellectual critic of America's entry into World War I and of allied war policy. Eschewing mechanistic indictments of munitions-makers and bankers, he exposed the tenuous, fragile character of wartime idealism. His most brilliant passages were directed against colleagues on *The New Republic* and against those former cultural rebels who now supported the war. Succumbing to the herd-instinct, collapsing before the seductive powers of the state, American intellectuals, he charged, had betrayed their philosophic heritage. These themes were given theoretical elaboration in "The State," a posthumous, unfinished essay. This important document—as Bourne himself, who died in the flu epidemic of 1918—is best remembered for the provocative phrase, "War is the health of the state."

Bibliography:

A. *History of a Literary Radical*, Van Wyck Brooks, ed. (New York, 1956); *Untimely Papers*, James Oppenheim, ed. (New York, 1919); *War and the Intellectuals*, Carl Resek, ed. (New York, 1964).

B. Sherman Paul, *Randolph Bourne* (Minneapolis, MN, 1966).

C. Randolph Bourne Papers, Columbia University.

Carl Resek

BOWLES, Gilbert (16 October 1869, Stuart, IA—10 September 1960, Honolulu) *Education*: B.A. Penn Coll., IA, 1898, M.A., 1900. *Career*: missionary to Japan, 1901–41; pacifist organizer and promoter.

Son of a devout Iowa Quaker family, Gilbert Bowles grew up in Jewell County, Kansas. At Penn College the strong pacifist views of *Benjamin F. Trueblood deeply influenced Bowles. In 1898 he married Minnie Pickett who had already taught for five years in Japan. Beginning in 1901 Bowles served for forty years as a Quaker missionary in Japan. A teacher, leader, and administrator of the Tokyo Friends Girls School, he helped lay the foundation of the present Tokyo Friends Center program.

Gilbert Bowles is probably best known for his efforts at internationalism in Japan. He devoted considerable attention to the issues of justice, peace, and race. He approached the promotion of peace and positive internationalism with a spirit of conciliation, justice, imagination, and deep devotion. He strongly believed that international problems could be solved through concerted peaceful efforts. Yet, however optimistic he was, he saw peace as the ultimate but not necessarily the immediate goal. Bowles hoped that the peace movement in Japan would place less emphasis on theoretical interpretations of peace principles and more on organizing efforts for the peaceful solution of Japan's actual international problems.

The founding of the Japan Peace Society owed much to the imagination, vigor, and tenacity of Bowles. In 1906 Bowles brought together thirty influential Japanese businessmen, religious figures, academicians, newsmen, and jurists to create the Japan Peace Society. He served the Society as corresponding secretary and director and frequently wrote and spoke for the group. The Society spread the principles of international peace through public lectures, publishing and distributing literature, sponsoring "Peace Sunday" and Hague Day celebrations, and maintaining liaison with international organizations. Following Bowles's lead, it promoted friendly relations between races and nations, encouraged the solution of international problems through peaceful means, and worked to preserve world peace. In 1924 the Japan Peace Society transferred its work to the League of Nations Association of Japan. Bowles served as the Executive Secretary of the Foreign Section of this organization. Although not strictly a pacifist organization, Bowles considered the League of Nations Association of Japan an effective agency for international education.

Bowles promoted peace through the Japan branch of the Fellowship of Reconciliation. Although predominantly a foreign organization in its early days, the

Fellowship had dedicated Japanese leadership by the mid 1920s. Bowles recognized, however, that even in this organization it was very difficult for Japanese to promote an absolute pacifism. He constantly strived to reduce Japan's differences with Korea, China, and the United States. Shortly prior to the adoption of the U. S. Immigration Act of 1924, he testified before committees in Washington that this legislation would be a severe blow to Japanese pride and would strengthen the military cult.

In 1941 Bowles and his wife retired to Hawaii where they helped Japanese who suffered from internment policies. They demonstrated the principle that "Although our countries are at war, we are not." In the postwar period Bowles assisted Japan with various relief and rehabilitation projects. He also helped organize the Hawaiian branches of the Fellowship of Reconciliation and the United Nations Association.

Bowles's epitaph was "a bridge of peace," a most fitting designation since he worked tirelessly for the cause of international peace. Patient and self-effacing, he was an effective practitioner of the methods of international conciliation. Peace was a way of life for him, not an elusive, never to be achieved dream.

Bibliography:

A. "The Japan Peace Society" (titles vary yearly) in *The Christian Movement in Japan* (1907–17); "The Peace Movement in Japan," in *The Friend* (Nov. 23, Dec. 7 and 21, 1944).

B. Errol T. Elliott, "Gilbert Bowles," in *Quaker Profiles from the American West* (Richmond, IN, 1972).

C. Papers of Gilbert Bowles, Quaker Manuscript Collection, Haverford College Library.

William D. Hoover

BOWMAN, Rufus David (23 January 1899, Dayton, VA—19 August 1952, Emporia, KS). *Education*: B.A., Bridgewater Coll., 1923; B.D., Yale Divinity School, 1926; graduate study, Catholic Univ., 1937; Ph.D., Northwestern Univ., 1944. *Career*: pastor, Roanoke, VA, 1926–29; general secretary, Board of Christian Education, Church of the Brethren, Elgin, IL, 1929–34; pastor, Washington, DC, 1934–37; president and Professor of Practical Theology and Christian Education, Bethany Biblical Seminary, Chicago, 1937–52; educator, author, peace advocate.

Born in a Brethren enclave in the Shenandoah Valley, Rufus D. Bowman imbibed early peace teachings in his home. After collegiate and theological education, he had a successful first pastorate in his native Virginia. He was called at age thirty to a national post in denominational offices in Elgin, IL, to direct the program in Christian education. Bowman was among younger leaders in the Church of the Brethren—one of the Historic Peace Churches—disappointed at its ambivalent reaction to World War I. He determined to use his office to encourage Brethren laity to maintain and advance the traditional peace position.

During his tenure at Elgin and in the following pastorate in Washington, DC, Bowman was active in interdenominational peace movements. He served on the executive committee of the Emergency Campaign for Peace, involved himself in the National Council for Prevention of War, worked with Mennonites and Friends in Historic Peace Church meetings, and wrote articles on peace. In 1936 he attended international peace conferences in Cambridge and Geneva. He was on denominational committees preparing structures for alternative forms of national service in the war he saw on the horizon. In 1937 and 1940 he was a spokesman for the Brethren in delegations of Friends, Mennonites, and Brethren which called on President +Franklin D. Roosevelt, seeking more acceptable government provisions for conscientious objectors than had existed during World War I. The result of these efforts was the Civilian Public Service (CPS) program, which Bowman helped to establish.

During the war years Bowman also wrote a dissertation, *The Church of the Brethren and War, 1708–1941*, an historical study of Brethren response to war that was published in 1944 and remains the definitive work on the subject. He wrote a second book, *Seventy Times Seven* (1945), which was designed for peace education in congregations. He collected materials for a study of the CPS program, but his early death, at age fifty-three, prevented its completion.

Besides his peace activities, Rufus Bowman played leading roles in missions, administration, and education in his own denomination and was well known in broader circles. He was on the executive committee of the American Association of Theological Schools and in 1952 was named president of the Association of Seminary Professors in the Practical Field.

Bibliography:

A. *The Church of the Brethren and War, 1708–1941* (Elgin,IL, 1944, reprinted New York, 1971); *Seventy Times Seven* (Elgin, IL, 1945).

B. Philip R. Bishop, "The Peace Activities of Rufus D. Bowman," *Brethren Life and Thought*, 20 (Spring, 1975), 97–103; Paul H. Bowman, "Rufus David Bowman: The Man," *Gospel Messenger* (Oct. 18, 1952) 12–13; D. F. Durnbaugh, "Introduction," *The Church of the Brethren and War* (Garland edition, New York, 1971) 10–17; John W. Lowe, Jr., "Rufus David Bowman: A Brethren Witness for Peace," *Brethren Life and Thought*, 16 (Spring, 1971), 89–95.

C. R. D. Bowman Papers, Bethany Theological Seminary Archives, Oak Brook, IL.

D. F. Durnbaugh

BRAILSFORD, Henry Noel. See *Biographical Dictionary of Internationalists*.

BRANTING, Karl Hjalmar. See *Biographical Dictionary of Internationalists*.

BREMER, Fredrika (17 August 1801, ÅAbo, Finland—30 December 1865, Stockholm) *Education*: private tutors. *Career*: author, feminist.

Born of a wealthy Finnish father and a Swedish mother, Fredrika Bremer grew up on the family's estate at Årsta, not far from Stockholm, to which the Bremer family moved in 1804 from Finland. Fredrika and her sisters were brought up strictly, but were given good educations if only to prepare them to become good wives and hostesses. When the rest of the family moved to Stockholm, Fredrika remained at Årsta to nurse her younger sister. She began taking care of sick and neglected people on the estate and started writing in order to earn the money she needed for that work. Her first book *Teckningar ur vardagslivet* (*Sketches from Everyday Life*) was published in Stockholm in 1828. The death of her father in 1830 left her free to devote herself to her literary interests and to pursue literary studies. She came into contact with literary circles and a very productive period followed. Between 1833 and 1849 Bremer wrote ten books. Feeling the need to broaden her views, she visited the United States and traveled in Europe and Palestine, publishing her travel impressions in several books.

The question of equality, especially equality for women, had concerned Bremer from an early age. In her novels, she often pointed to women's lack of freedom and social rights. She advocated a woman's right to a comprehensive education and took part in the debate over establishing an age of majority for women at which they would acquire independence. Her wish to make women more aware of what was going on in the world outside their homes led her into peace work. In 1854, while the Crimean War was raging and Bremer was deeply shaken by the reports from the battlefield, she got the idea of addressing an appeal to all women of the world "to join hands as sisters." The appeal, couched in Christian ideas of love and charity, was first published in the *London Times* on August 28, 1854 under the title, "Appeal to the Women of the World to Form an Alliance." It was later published in Swedish and other newspapers. Bremer's call to the women of the world in 1854 was so novel an idea and so far ahead of its time that it was impossible for her contemporaries to understand it or take it seriously. This was the case despite the fact that the alliance was well planned and meant to function with a central committee and corresponding branches and secretaries in different countries. The *Times* called it "the mere illusion of an amiable enthusiast," and stated that women's place was in the home and not in the organization of international associations. The plan for the alliance was soon forgotten. Bremer deeply resented the lack of understanding and interest. She fervently believed that people longed for peace and had hoped to arouse interest, at least among women, in building a peaceful world.

In Sweden, Bremer's books remained popular and continued to influence the political debate over equality and women's rights. The existence of the Fredrika Bremer Association in Stockholm, a research institute on the problems of women in society, attests the importance of her legacy for the women's emancipation movement. But her pioneering sense of internationalism, cooperation, and social justice, and her efforts to found an alliance of women to foster peace were soon forgotten, even by her female admirers. The founding of the Women's International League of Peace and Freedom during World War I, however, is testimony to her farsightedness as a peace advocate.

Bibliography:

A. *Familjen* (Stockholm, 1831, English trans., *The Family*, London, 1843); *Hemmen i den nya världen* (Stockholm, 1853–54, English trans., *Homes in the New World,* London, 1853); *Hertha* (Stockholm, 1856, English trans., *Hertha*, London, 1856); *Livet i gamla världen* (4 vols., Stockholm, 1860–62, English trans., *Life in the Old World* (London, 1862); *Strid och frid* (Stockholm, 1848; English trans., *Fight and Peace*, London, 1853); *Syskonliv* (Stockholm, 1848, English trans., *Brothers and Sisters*, London, 1848).

B. A. B. Benson, *America of the Fifties: Letters of Fredrika Bremer* (New York, 1914); Charlotte Bremer, *Life, Letters and Posthumous Works of Fredrika Bremer* (New York, 1884); Ellen Kleman, *Fredrika Bremer* (Stockholm, 1925); Gunnar Qvist, *Fredrika Bremer och kvinnans emancipation* (Göteborg, 1969); Elin Wägner, *Fredrika Bremer* (Stockholm, 1949).

Elisabeth Ståhle

BRETON, André (18 February, 1896, Tinchbray, Orne, France—28 September, 1966, Paris). *Education*: graduated Collège Chaptal, 1913; studied medicine at Univ. of Paris, 1914–15, no degree. *Career*: poet; essayist; polemicist; cofounder Dada, 1919; founder, leader, and principal theoretician of Surrealism; antiwar activist; internationalist; author; and editor.

Surrealism, founded by a group of antiwar artists and writers, among them, Louis Aragon, *Paul Eluard, Benjamin Pèret, Philippe Soupault, Jean Arp, and Max Ernst, began with Breton's *Manifesto of Surrealism* of 1924. Breton, who worked in a mental hospital in World War I, studied Freud and incorporated the ideas of the dream and the unconscious into Surrealism. In its pure form, Surrealism stressed automatic writing and its counterpart in painting, collage, thereby abolishing the conscious, critical role of the artist. Like the Dadaists, the Surrealists were antiwar, antinationalist, anticlerical and antibourgeois culture, and their ideology combined Freud, Marx, and Surrealist irrationalism.

Their hatred of war forced the Surrealists into political consciousness and Breton persuaded his friends to collaborate with *Clarté*, a left-wing pacifist journal on a manifesto, *La Révolution d'abord et toujours*, against the French colonialist war in Morocco. They also signed a protest in *L'Humanité* against the Moroccan war, *Les Intellectuels contre la guerre de Maroc*. Breton then led the Surrealists to join the French Communist party, which they did as a group in 1927, but they never really accepted party discipline and they left the party in 1935.

In their journal, *Le Surréalisme au service de la Révolution*, the Surrealists continued to condemn war and aggression, whether Nazi violence against the Jews or French imperialism in Indo-China. They also supported the Amsterdam-Pleyel peace congresses of 1933, sponsored by the Communist party under the leadership of *Henri Barbusse and *Romain Rolland. In 1934, because of a manifesto he wrote against the French fascist riots, Breton was asked by +Léon Blum to help plan the counter-demonstration in support of the Republic. He joined the Comité de vigilance des intellectuels antifascistes, founded by André Malraux and Jean-Richard Bloch, and, even after leaving the party, Breton and his friends remained on the left and remained consistently antimilitarist. In 1935–36 Breton helped to organize the short-lived movement, Contre-attaque, which had a noncommunist, left pacifist ideology. He also wrote several Surrealist manifestoes in support of the Spanish Republic and denounced the French policy of nonintervention.

In 1938–39 Breton went to Mexico and, with Leon Trostky, founded a "popular front" group for artists, opposed to both fascism and Stalinism, called the

Fédération internationale de l'art révolutionnaire indépendant. Groups were actually organized in several countries and a journal was published but it collapsed with the outbreak of World War II. Breton spent the war years in New York and published the journal, *VVV*. On his return to France, he published a manifesto against the war in Indo-China. He supported the Front humain, a world disarmament movement, demanded freedom for conscientious objectors, and supported the Garry Davis Citizen of the World movement. He opposed the Soviet intervention ln Hungary in 1956 and in 1960, signed the *Declaration des 121* against the Algerian war, for which the signers were threatened with arrest. Until the end of his life, Breton maintained his commitment to peace and freedom.

Bibliography:

A. *L'Amour fou* (Paris, 1937); *Anthologie de l'humour noir* (Paris, 1940); *La Clé des champs* (Paris, 1953); *Perspective cavaliere* (Paris, 1970); *Position politique du surre-́alisme* (Paris, 1935); *Légitime défense* (Paris, 1926); *Nadja* (Paris, 1928); *Les Lettres de guerre de Jacques Vaché* (Paris, 1919); *Manifeste du surréalisme* (Paris, 1924); *Seconde manifeste du surréalisme* (Paris, 1930).

B. Maxime Alexandre, *Mémoires d'un surréaliste* (Paris, 1968); Ferdinand Alquié, *The Philosophy of Surrealism* (Ann Arbor, MI, 1965); Anna Balakian, *André Breton; Magus of Surréalism* (New York, 1971); Jacques Baron, *L'An I du surréalisme suivi de l'an dernier* (Paris, 1969); Jean-Louis Bédouin, *Vingt ans du surréalisme, 1939–1959* (Paris, 1961); Marguerite Bonner, *Les Critiques de notre temps et Breton* (Paris, 1974); Clifford Browder, *André Breton, Arbiter of Surrealism* (Geneva, 1967); Victor Crastre, *André Breton* (Paris, 1952); J. H. Matthews, *André Breton* (New York, 1967) Maurice Nadeau, *Histoire du surréalisme augmentée de documents surréalistes* (Paris, 1964); Georges Ribemont-Dessaignes, *Déjà jadis ou du mouvement dada à l'espace abstrait* (Paris, 1958); André Thirion, *Révolutionnaires sans révolution* (Paris, 1972).

Helena F. Lewis

BRIAND, Aristide Pierre Henri. See *Biographical Dictionary of Internationalists*.

BRIGHT, John (16 November 1811, Rochdale, Lancashire, England—27 March 1889, Rochdale). *Education*: Quaker schools in Ackworth, York, and Lancaster, 1822–25. *Career*: Member of Parliament, 1843–89; politician, statesman, and Quaker leader.

John Bright became well known during his lifetime as a controversial figure in the political life of Victorian England. His followers and fellow workers loved and respected him highly, but his opponents villified and caricatured him without mercy. A man of high moral principles, Bright devoted his energy and his considerable talents as an orator to the task of bringing about certain changes in English political and social institutions of his day. He worked assiduously to achieve his objectives, and he had the satisfaction of seeing many of them successfully realized before his death.

Born into a staunch Quaker family, Bright received all of his formal education in various Quaker schools. At the age of fifteen he left school and went to work for his father, a man who had started out poor and who had become a successful cotton manufacturer in Rochdale. He learned the details of his family's cotton business, and the close contact which he had with the mill employees made a deep impression on his character. His manual labors helped to give a certain democratic bent to this thought, and he developed a firm belief in the essential equality of all men. Also his work experience provided him with an insight into the complexities of manufacturing society and an appreciation of the needs, difficulties, and sufferings of the working classes.

Bright's interest in politics increased in the early 1840s, after the unexpected death of his first wife. He joined his friend *Richard Cobden as a junior collaborator in the anti-Corn Law campaign, which led to a major debate over Britain's protectionist policies and the ultimate repeal of the Corn Laws in 1846. In 1843 he began his parliamentary career when he took his seat in the House of Commons as one of the members for Durham City. He remained in Parliament until his death, first representing Manchester and later Birmingham.

In Parliament Bright supported parliamentary reforms and gained considerable attention by his strong opposition to the Crimean War, a conflict that England entered in 1854. Bright condemned the war as an act of folly that would endanger the economic interests of Great Britain. His many speeches on the subject made him an unpopular figure in his own country. Both national and provincial newspapers bitterly denounced him, and even in his own constituency of Manchester he was burned in effigy.

Although he never visited the United States, Bright took a keen interest in the American Civil War, delivering on various occasions eloquent addresses on this topic. He proclaimed his admiration for the Northern states in this conflict and sharply criticized those British colleagues who were sympathetic with the Confederacy and who pressed for intervention on behalf of the South. Unlike many of his English contemporaries, Bright had a high regard for Abraham Lincoln especially after the American president had issued a preliminary Emancipation Proclamation in September 1862. In Bright's opinion this document marked a significant turning point in the war because he thought the proclamation would give an impetus to the antislavery sentiment in England. Even after armed hostilities had finally ended in 1865, Bright continued to be concerned with the course of domestic events in the United States and the numerous problems that arose during the process of reconstruction. He did not believe that the Confederate leaders should be executed, for he strongly disapproved of capital punishment for any reason. He did, however, hold firmly to the view that these leaders should be banished permanently from their native land and that the Congress of the United States should enact appropriate legislation to guarantee to the freed population their civil rights and liberties.

In addition to his parliamentary career, Bright also served in the British cabinet under William E. Gladstone. From 1868 to 1870 he held the post of President of the Board of Trade, an appointment which gave him the title of "Right Honourable." He also served as Chancellor of the Duchy of Lancaster from 1873 to 1874 and again from 1880 to 1882. He supported Gladstone in his move for the disestablishment of the Church of Ireland (1869) and in the program for

Irish land reform, but he disapproved of Home Rule for Ireland which Gladstone backed after 1885. In 1882 he resigned his position as Chancellor in protest to the government's policy of intervention in Egyptian affairs and the British bombardment of Alexandria, actions which he considered unnecessary and unjust.

Bright's health and customary vigor declined during his last years, but this period was also marked by some heartwarming signs of recognition and respect which he received. Contemporaries now regarded him as a veteran statesman of the Victorian age, and colleagues tended to treat him with a certain deference, even though they might not agree with his ideas. The animosities engendered during many years of political agitation had finally softened with the passing years. Bright's many years of loyal service, his love of peace, and his moral integrity and courage provided a worthy example for future public leaders to follow.

Bibliography:

A. *The Diaries of John Bright*, ed. by Robert Alfred John Walling (New York, 1931); *Public Addresses by John Bright, M.P.*, ed. by James Edwin Thorold Rogers (London, 1879); *Speeches on Questions of Public Policy by John Bright, M.P.*, ed. by James Edwin Thorold Rogers (2 vols., London., 1868).

B. Herman Ausubel, *John Bright: Victorian Reformer* (New York, London, and Sydney, 1966); George Macaulay Trevelyan, *The Life of John Bright* (Boston, 1925); Arthur Stanley Turberville, *John Bright—His Character and Career* (Swindon, Eng., 1945).

Bernerd C. Weber

BRION, Hélène (27 January 1882, Clermont-Ferrand, Puy-de-Dôme, France—31 August 1962, Ennery, Seine-et-Oise). *Education*: prepared as an *institutrice* at the Ecole Primaire Supérieure Sophie German; *docteur en droit*, Sorbonne, 1931. *Career*: *institutrice*; secretary, Fédération nationale des syndicats des institutrices et instituteurs (FNSII); delgate, Confederal Committee, Confédération générale du travail (CGT), 1909–14; member of editorial board, *L'Action Feministe*, 1914; secretary, Workers' Orphanage l'avenir social, Epône from 1917; feminist.

Daughter of an army officer and orphaned at an early age Hélène Brion was reared by her grandmother in the Ardennes. Almost immediately upon her appointment as an *institutrice*, she threw herself vigorously into the work of organizing *amicales* of teachers, and later—when it was still illegal to do so—into unionizing them. At first active principally in the syndical movement, she joined the Socialist party and in 1913 (with three other women) was elected to the Executive Committee of the Unified Socialist party (SFIO). Early an advocate of women's rights, both as a cause and in her personal life, she bore two children but refused to marry. The feminist conviction was the dominant force in her life, and though she found it sometimes opposed to her principles relative to the class struggle and to pacifism, it nevertheless provided a foundation for both. Before the war of 1914, she was a member of the Groupe féministe universitaire (University Feminist Group) and several other feminist organizations, and a contributor to a number of feminist periodicals.

Among the latter were *L'Equité*, founded in February 1913 by *Marianne Rauze, and *La Femme Socialiste*. Through the summer of 1913 Brion carried on an extended debate with *Louise Saumoneau over the question of the relationship of feminism and socialism, Saumoneau arguing that women socialists should not join feminist organizations (which included bourgeois women) but should subordinate their feminist interests to their class interests. Brion's response was that proletarian women should find allies where they could, even among the bourgeoisie, in order to make prevail "the feminist way of thinking" in society.

With the outbreak of war in 1914, Brion and Louis Loriot (secretary and treasurer of the FNSII) led the teachers' union in support of the Union Sacrée, following the lead of the SFIO and the CGT. In October 1914 she declined to support the action of the Bureau Fédéral of the FNSII in defense of Julia Bertrand, a teacher who had been dismissed from her post for her "anti-patriotic" activities. And in February 1915 she opposed the position of several Dutch socialist women calling on all socialists to support *Clara Zetkin's Peace Appeal; in the February issue of *L'Equité* appeared a statement, drafted by Brion and signed by Marianne Rauze and several others from the Groupe Féministe Universitaire, opposing any pacifist stand.

However, by April 1915 Brion's position was changing. At a meeting of the Ligue Nationale des Femmes Françaises (National League of French Women), she protested against a resolution to oppose any "premature peace," and a month later at a session of Fédération des Instituteurs (Federation of School Teachers) in Paris she declared herself in favor of pacifist propaganda, recommending to women that they support such efforts as being "more sympathetic than men to such ideas." When, however, the Charente federation of the *syndicat*, under the influence of *Marie Mayoux, passed a resolution calling for immediate peace, Brion and the Federal Council of the union adopted an equivocal position. In February 1917, her conversion complete, she was elected to the Central Committee of the Comité pour la reprise des relations internationales (Committee for the Renewal of International Relations), successor to the Comité d'action internationale formed after Zimmerwald. In May 1917 the Mayoux couple, both teachers, produced a pacifist tract, *Les Instituteurs syndicalistes et la guerre* (*Syndicalist School Teachers and the War*), without approval of the censors; Brion assisted in its dissemination and in the distribution of *papillons* reading "Women want women's rights! and Peace!" This event took place against a background of army mutinies, strikes in several industries, and a general mood of "defeatism." The government took stern repressive measures, and Brion could not escape the campaign; suspended from her teaching post and arrested in November, she was tried before a military court and received a suspended sentence of three years. She became while under suspension, a teacher at—and secretary of—the orphanage at Epône.

After the war Brion became a sympathizer with the left wing at the Congress of Tours in 1921, having in the interim joined the Committee for the Third International, but she never became a member of the Communist party. With

Marianne Rauze, she planned a trip to Russia (which never materialized) to distribute aid to victims of the Civil War. By 1923 she had abandoned active political life but continued her activity in feminist groups, becoming president of the Femmes de la Libération Humaine (Women for Human Liberation) in 1945. In the same year she wrote to +Eleanor Roosevelt, asking her aid in achieving women's representation at international conferences. In 1945 she wrote also to General de Gaulle, protesting the authoritarian nature of his policies.

Bibliography:

A. *Déclaration lue au premier conseil de guerre le 29 Mars 1918* (Courbevoie, 1918); *La Voie féministe; les partis d'avant-garde et le féminisme* (Epône, 1917).

B. Madeleine Vernet, *Hélène Brion: Une belle conscience et une sombre affaire* (Levallois-Perret, 1917).

Albert S. Hill

BRITTAIN, Vera (29 December 1893, Newcastle under Lyme, England—29 March 1970, London). *Education*: St. Monica's, Kingswood; M.A., Somerville Coll., Oxford Univ., 1921. *Career*: author, lecturer, and pacifist.

Vera Brittain grew up in a comfortable middle-class family in the north of England. A bright and eager student, she obtained permission to continue her studies at Oxford after much domestic conflict only to have the outbreak of war in Europe interrupt her academic career. She left Oxford in 1915 to enlist as a nurse, serving throughout the war in London, in Malta, and at the front in France. During the war both Brittain's only brother and her fiancé were killed in action. After the war Brittain first returned to Oxford to finish her degree and then moved to London to pursue a literary career.

In 1921, as she was struggling to establish herself as an author, she offered her services as a speaker to the League of Nations Union. With this gesture Brittain began her lifelong involvement in the peace movement. Brittain's view of pacifism and her relationship to the peace movement underwent a dramatic change in 1936 when she came under the influence of *Dick Sheppard, founder of the Peace Pledge Union. Sheppard, after hearing Brittain speak at a large open-air peace rally, asked her to become a sponsor of the Peace Pledge Union. This invitation caused a crisis of conscience which ultimately led her from an antiwar stance associated with her support of the League of Nations and collective security to an absolute pacifism based on Christian principle.

Brittain's commitment to pacifism remained firm even after the outbreak of World War II. Unlike many of her contemporaries, Brittain continued to work for the cause of peace, work which almost completely absorbed her literary efforts during the war. In 1939 she began to write a biweekly newsletter entitled *Letter to Peace-Lovers*. Circulation of the *Letter*, which appeared every two weeks until 1947, hovered at just under two thousand throughout the war. She also wrote a book of short essays in the form of letters to her son John. Entitled *Humiliation with Honour* (1942), these essays elaborated Brittain's conception of redemptive suffering by treating the various types of victims of war. In 1944 she published *Seeds of Chaos*. Written for and published by the Bombing Restriction Committee, this monograph attacked the strategy of saturation bombing.

The end of the war did not end Vera Brittain's efforts on behalf of peace. Brittain served as chair of the Peace Pledge Union between 1949 and 1951. She participated in the demonstrations organized by the Campaign for Nuclear Disarmament in the 1950s. Finally, in 1964 she published a history of the International Fellowship of Reconciliation entitled *The Rebel Passion*.

Vera Brittain's pacifism first grew out of her reaction to her experiences during the First World War. She differed irom her contemporaries in that her commitment to pacifism grew from a bitter disenchantment with the efficacy of war to a principled rejection of the use of force under any circumstances. Brittain's pacifism fueled her inexhaustible activity as a speaker and essayist, but she made her greatest contribution to the cause of peace through her autobiographical writings. *Testament of Youth* (1937) recorded her experiences in World War I. An immediate best-seller, Brittain's memoir ranks with Robert Graves' *Goodbye to All That* and Edmund Blunden's *Undertones of War* as a rendering of the impact of World War I on a generation of English youth. *Testament of Experience* (1957) continued the story of Brittain's intellectual development, giving a moving and persuasive account of the evolution of her deepening commitment to pacifism and the trials she underwent during World War II as a consequence of her adherence to her beliefs. Vera Brittain was neither a literary artist of the first rank or a great political leader, but her autobiographical writings provide invaluable insights into the psychological and social processes that shaped English pacifism after World War I.

Bibliography:

A. *Humiliation with Honour* (London, 1942); *Poems of the War and After* (London, 1934); *The Rebel Passion* (London, 1964); *Seed of Chaos; What Mass Bombing Really Means* (London, 1944); *Testament of Experience* (London, 1957); *Testament of Youth* (London, 1933); *War-Time Letters to Peace Lovers* (London, 1940).

B. Martin Ceadel, *Pacifism in Britain, 1914–1945: The Defining of a Faith* (Oxford, 1980); DNB, 1961–1970, 139–40; LT, March 30, 1970.

C. Vera Brittain Papers, McMaster University, Hamilton, Ontario; Bodleian Library, Oxford University.

Gail L. Savage

BRITTEN, Edward Benjamin (22 November 1913, Lowestoft, England—4 December 1976, Aldeburgh). *Education*: Gresham's School, Holt; Royal Coll. of Music, London, 1934. *Career:* pianist and musical composer.

Benjamin Britten was born on St. Cecilia's day, the son of a dentist. The boy showed a precocious talent at composing music and attracted the attention of, among others, Frank Bridge, who had been a pacifist during World War I. Britten and his friend the singer Peter Pears, with whom he joined in many recitals, similarly held that war was at all times wrong. The antiwar theme became an important aspect of Britten's music.

During the 1930s, Britten wrote his famous *Variations on a Theme of Frank*

Bridge (1937) and *Ballad of Heroes* (1939), a tribute to those who had volunteered to fight with the Republicans in Spain. Especially important was his *Sinfonia da Requiem* (1940), inspired by his father's death and written for Japan, though rejected there. He also wrote music for documentary films.

In 1939 Britten emigrated to the United States, but returned to a war-torn England in 1942 as a conscientious objector, certain that he could best serve his country through his music. During the impossible postwar period he recreated English opera through *Peter Grimes* (1945) and its successors, wrote music for the young, and created the Aldeburgh festivals. His lively settings of folk song took further the work of Cecil Sharp and others. His recitals with Pears set the country aglow.

In 1962 came the greatest of all his musical contributions to peace, *War Requiem*. Coventry Cathedral, destroyed by bombing in the war, was rebuilt in glory. *War Requiem* was commissioned to express the purpose of the new cathedral. Britten prefaced the work with *Wilfred Owen's words "My subject is War, and the pity of War. The poetry is the Pity. . . . All a poet can do today is warn." He interspersed some of Owen's poetry with the Latin words of the Requiem Mass with great sensitivity. There are few finer moments in all music than the baritone's quiet "I am the enemy you killed, my friend." It was more poignant in that the first baritone was a German, Dietrich Fischer-Dieskau.

Bibliography:

B. P. M. Young, *Masters of Music: Britten* (London 1966).

John Ferguson

BRIZON, Pierre (16 May 1878, Franchesse, Allier, France—1 August 1923, Paris). *Education*: teaching certificate, Ecole normale supérieure, Saint-Cloud, 1899. *Career*: socialist deputy from Moulins (Allier); publisher and editor of *La Vague*, 1918–23; schoolteacher, syndicalist, and socialist militant.

Brizon owed his prominence during the First World War to his outspoken and unrelenting antiwar campaign. His pacifist struggle was conducted on many fronts—in the French Chamber of Deputies; in the Socialist party; in the press; and among the peasants of the Allier. He took an active part in the Kienthal Conference (April 24–30, 1916) which brought together European Socialists from the major belligerents in an attempt to end the war through popular pressure on the governments of Europe. Brizon was one of three deputies to vote against war credits in the French chamber in June 1916. He responded to his many critics within the Socialist party by reminding them that his militant pacifism was in accord with both the letter and the spirit of prewar international Socialist conferences.

Brizon's pacifism antedated the war and formed a part of a broader combative radicalism. In the decade before World War I he had opposed the French government's colonial ventures. As a socialist and syndicalist militant Brizon had come into conflict with public authorities wherever he taught and had been rewarded with frequent transfers from one region to another. As a Socialist deputy after 1910, Brizon distinguished himself not only by his antimilitarism but also by his defense of the sharecroppers and smallholders of the district which he represented.

The war brought about a fusion of these two causes: Brizon was considered responsible for encouraging peasant proprietors and sharecroppers to abandon wheat farming in the Allier as a means of ending the war. An ardent advocate of a peace settlement without victors or vanquished, Brizon opposed his party's participation in wartime governments and its general promotion of the war effort. He was among the founders of the Comité pour la reprise des relations internationales (Committee for the Restoration of International Relations) in November 1915—the most important and active French group working in favor of a compromise peace. In April 1916 Brizon drafted the final declaration of the Kienthal Conference which called on the peoples of Europe to end the war by seizing power from their governments. As for the patriotic leaders of the French Socialist party, Brizon reminded them aptly that their party was to be found not in parliament but rather in the trenches. He believed that the international Socialist conferences at Zimmerwald and at Kienthal spoke more accurately to the concerns of the front-line armies than did the patriotic oratory of the Chamber of Deputies. Brizon's isolation from his parliamentary colleagues was dramatized by their vote to expel him from the Chamber in December 1916 for his attempt to make public the magnitude of human and material losses caused by the war.

Brizon's pacifist weekly, *La Vague*, attained a circulation of some 300,000 copies during the last year of the war despite frequent censorship and attempts to keep it from reaching the front. Brizon joined the Communist party in 1920 and was expelled two years later. He continued to work for a Socialist-Communist entente until his death in 1923.

Bibliography:

A. *Le Blé Rouge* (Montluçon, 1909); "La Cooperation," *Encyclopédie socialiste, syndicale, et cooperative de l'Internationale ouvrière* (with E. Poisson, vol. 8, Paris, 1913); *Histoire du travail et des travailleurs* (Paris, 1906).

B. Simone Derruau-Boniol, "Le Socialisme dans l'Allier de 1848 à 1914," *Cahiers d'Histoire* 2 (Lyon, 1957), 115–161; Annie Kriegel, *Aux Origines du communisme français, 1914–1920* (Paris, 1964); Jean Maitron, ed., *Dictionnaire biographique du mouvement ouvrier français* (vol. 11, Paris, 1973); Alfred Rosmer, *Le Mouvement ouvrier pendant la Guerre* (vol. 2, Paris, 1959); Hubert Rouger, "La France socialiste," *Encyclopédie socialiste, syndicale, et cooperative de l'Internationale ouvrière* (vol. 3, Paris, 1912).

Ioannis Sinanoglou

BROOMÉ, Emilia Lothigius (13 January 1866, Jönköping, Sweden—2 June 1925, Stockholm). *Education*: medical and philosophical studies, Uppsala Univ.. *Career*: teacher, Whitlock School, 1886–91, 1894–1904; founder and president, Swedish Women's Peace Organization, 1898–1911; president, Women's Liberal Association, 1914–20; member, Stockholm Town Council, 1911–24; director, Central Association for Social Work, 1904–14; member, Board of Elementary Schools, 1912–17; first woman member, Law-Drafting Board, 1914–18; member, Commission on Family Law 1919–23; member, Committee on Wages, 1921; politician, women's rights' activist, and peace advocate.

Emilia Broomé had to interrupt her medical studies when her mother died and she had to return to Jönköping to take care of her father. In Jönköping she became active in the local branch of the Swedish Peace and Arbitration Association. One of its leaders, the parliamentarian Edvard Wavrinsky, approached her and proposed that she establish a peace organization for women in Sweden. Broomé took up the proposal and, after moving to Stockholm in 1897, she issued in her own name, and those of fifty other prominent Swedish women, her great appeal "To Swedish Women." The appeal aroused some interest but also criticism, especially from conservative and patriotic circles. The negative reactions did not prevent Broomé from continuing her efforts, and in 1898 the Swedish Women's Peace Association was founded with Emilia Broomé as its president.

The activities of the new organization were mainly concentrated on peace education and its established contact with others working along the same lines, such as the American School Peace League. Parents and teachers were approached and efforts were made to introduce new ways of teaching history and literature. The literature section published brochures and pamphlets on issues such as *Woman and Peace*, *Scandinavian Neutrality*, *The Costs of War*, etc. After a little more than a decade, unable to attract broad support, the Swedish Women's Peace Association ended its independent existence. It merged with the new Swedish Peace Association, co-founded by Carl Carlsson Bonde, chairman of the peace group in the Swedish parliament. Broomé continued her work for peace as a member of the new organization's Executive. In 1919 the Swedish Peace Organization was incorporated into the Swedish Association for the League of Nations. When, in that same year, the Swedish section of the Women's International League for Peace and Freedom came into being, Broomé became an active member. Her previous work in a similar field proved highly beneficial to the new women's organization. In 1916 Broomé was awarded the Illis Quorum Meurere Labores, a Swedish royal medal given to distinguished persons.

Bibliography:

A. *Fredssaken och kvinnan* (Stockholm, 1899); *Kvinnorna och politiken* (Stockholm, 1922).

B. P. A. Fogelström, *Kampen för fred* (Stockholm, 1971); Margareta Larsson, "Kvinnoföreningar i Sverige med fred på sitt program" (Ph.D. dissertation, Univ. of Stockholm, 1970); *Svenska män och Kvinnor* I, 481–82; *Svensk uppslagsbok*. 5, 11–12.

Elisabeth Ståhle

BROWN, Herbert Runham (1879, London—19 December 1949, Enfield, England). *Career*: chairman, Enfield Branch, No-Conscription Fellowship, 1915–19; National Committee, No More War Movement, 1921–36; honorary secretary, War Resisters' International, 1923–49; Christian pacifist; businessman.

H. Runham Brown's lifelong pacifism had its roots in both the Congregationalist faith in which he was raised and the socialist creed to which he was converted. Brown joined the No-Conscription Fellowship (NCF) soon after its formation in November 1914. He subsequently helped to establish an NCF branch in Enfield and was selected as its chairman. An indefatigable and effective organizer, Brown arranged a scheme to provide work for NCF members who were "on the run" in attempting to avoid arrest or imprisonment as conscientious objectors (CO's). However, Brown himself ran afoul of the authorities when he printed and distributed part of a letter from a CO in France who was fearful of being shot. Representatives of the army claimed that this letter, the authenticity of which was never in doubt, was calculated to undermine recruitment and discipline. Brown was convicted; but before his appeal could be heard, he was arrested as a CO, court-martialed and sentenced to the first of three terms of imprisonment (nearly two and a half years) as an "absolutist" who would accept no compromise short of total exemption from all forms of war service.

After his release from prison, Brown renewed his vigorous work for the NCF, agitating for the release of still-imprisoned war resisters, supervising the rehabilitation of ex-CO's and finally, organizing local arrangements for the Fellowship's farewell convention in late 1919. Following the dissolution of the NCF, Brown's determination to maintain communications with antimilitarists in other countries brought him into contact with PACO (Esperanto for peace), a pacifist group formed in Holland in 1921. Within two years PACO had transferred its headquarters to Britain and for the next quarter century operated out of Brown's home in Enfield as the War Resisters' International (WRI). Brown was also one of the founding members of the WRI's British affiliate, the No More War Movement (NMWM), a direct descendent of the NCF. Because both the WRI and the NMWM required a pledge of absolute pacifism, they remained small, devoted to the purity of their principles rather than to the development of a mass following. In these circumstances, Brown's organizational ability and financial acumen made him an invaluable asset. He was not only secretary to the WRI and a member of the NMWM National Committee throughout much of the interwar period, but in 1932 he was placed in charge of the faltering finances of the NMWM as well.

Indispensable as H. Runham Brown proved to be, he was not always popular, especially with certain factions of the No More War Movement. During the early 1930s, Brown opposed the growing militancy of some socialist members of the NMWM, yet his insistence on correct constitutional procedures caused him to be labeled a political manipulator by some of the group's apolitical purists. In the end, the Movement's militants prevailed; their determination to reject pacifism in order to fight fascism in Spain brought about the demise of the NMWM in 1936. Brown, however, remained in the British pacifist camp by attaching himself to *Dick Sheppard's newly formed Peace Pledge Union (PPU). Within the PPU Brown proved to be just as hard working, and controversial, as he had been in the NMWM. *Max Plowman, to whom Brown's maneuverings in committee were especially distasteful, referred to him as "Run 'em Down" and cordially disliked him. Despite these personal difficulties, Brown played a key role in the PPU while also devoting part of his considerable energy to the

Embassies of Reconciliation, a pacifist group that attempted to stave off war through direct negotiations, largely by *George Lansbury, with European dictators.

Neither the outbreak of the Second World War nor even the smashing Nazi victories in the spring of 1940 could bring Runham Brown out of the pacifist camp. He kept the WRI alive in Enfield until his death in 1949, continuing to insist that, despite Hitler, the war might have been prevented if more persons had devoted themselves more vigorously to the pursuit of peace. Whether or not Brown's assessment of the political possibilities of pacifist activity was accurate or realistic, few have worked more relentlessly or resourcefully to achieve peace by political means.

Bibliography:

A. *Cutting Ice* (Enfield, 1930); ''Pioneers O! Pioneers,'' *The Tribunal*, July 25, 1918; *Why Hitler*? (Enfield, 1940).

B. Martin Ceadel, *Pacifism in Britain, 1914–1945: The Defining of a Faith* (Oxford 1980); Hem Day, *Historie d'une idee . . . H. Runham Brown et la resistance á la guerre* (Paris [1949]).

C. The Papers of the War Resisters' International, located in the Swarthmore College Peace Collection, have considerable Brown correspondence.

Thomas C. Kennedy

BROWN, Moses (23 September 1738, Providence, RI—6 September 1836, Providence). *Education*: left school at the age of thirteen. *Career*: merchant, manufacturer, philanthropist, and peace activist.

For Moses Brown, whose name is closely linked to the founding of Brown University, the death of his first wife, his cousin Anna Brown, in 1773 was a shattering experience. He interpreted it as evidence of ungodly living which had brought him to the sad point of investing in the trans-Atlantic slave trade. He sought council among the Society of Friends and ultimately converted to the Quaker faith. In joining the Quaker movement, Brown became a pacifist; for the remainder of his life he advocated peace and nonviolence.

In trying to live true to his principles in a world which accepted political violence as an unchangeable fact of nature, Brown found himself involved in many of the major political controversies of his age. As a leading Quaker spokesman in New England, he steadfastly championed the cause of peace in the early American republic. Although some Quakers were loyalists during the American Revolution, Brown was sympathetic to the colonial cause, but he would not act against his commitment to nonviolence. His refusal to pay all taxes expressly collected for the support of war earned him the suspicion of his patriot neighbors.

Brown was a strident abolitionist. He saw slavery as the sinful product of war and freed his own servants. He became a central force in the abolition movement in Rhode Island. Recognizing that many non-Quakers might not share his religious views about slavery, he couched his public criticism of the institution in terms of the natural rights philosophy that dominated the political thinking of the colonists. In 1774 he authored a bill that slowed the importation of slaves into the colony, and later led the fight that ended Rhode Island's prominence as a slave trading center.

During the War of 1812 he once again urged nonviolence. At the age of seventy he was still campaigning against war. In 1818 he, along with Thomas Arnold and George Benson, organized the Rhode Island Peace Society and became the society's treasurer in 1822. Brown wrote and helped to finance the printing and distribution of thousands of pamphlets that promoted peace. His life stands as an example of the social and political difficulties that a pacifist faced in the early years of the American republic.

Bibliography:

B. Robert Morton Hazelton, *Let Freedom Ring*! (New York, 1957); Augustine Jones, *Moses Brown: His Life and Services* (Providence, 1892); Mack Thompson, *Moses Brown* (North Carolina, 1962); DAB, II, 146–47.

C. Moses Brown Papers, Rhode Island Historical Society; Austin Manuscripts, Moses Brown School Library.

Gary Puckrein

BRUCK, Elsbeth (17 November 1874, Ratibor, Silesia, Germany—20 February 1970, Berlin, German Democratic Republic). *Career*: actress, reciter, pacifist.

Born the daughter of a prosperous hotel owner, Elsbeth Bruck early separated herself from the world of middle-class security in order to become an actress. Her talent soon revealed itself and brought her an engagement at the Deutsches Theater in Berlin. However, the established theater left her unsatisfied and, turning her back on a promising acting career, she became a giver of recitations and a teacher at an independent acting school in Berlin and later in Munich. In early 1914 she learned Carl Hauptmann's drama, *Krieg* (*War*), which touched her and led her to present recitations of it throughout World War I.

Bruck returned to Berlin at the outbreak of the war and soon came into contact with the Bund Neues Vaterland (New Fatherland League) (BNV). The following year she began to work in the league's office and became office manager after the arrest of *Lilli Jannasch in 1916. As manager of the daily affairs of the BNV, Bruck was subject to repeated house searches and interrogations for alleged treason, all of which were part of the general persecution of pacifists. In February 1918 she was arrested in connection with the circulation of a memorandum of Prince Linchnowsky on Germany's culpability for the outbreak of the war. The charges against her, however, were dropped at the time of the November Revolution of 1918.

During the revolution Bruck alienated many Germans by demanding that food supplies and clothes stored in the villas of wealthy Berliners be distributed among the starving population and returning soldiers. Even pacifist friends had misgivings about her position. Bruck also called for imbuing culture and education with ethical-pacifist ideals. The danger of a new arrest and murder threats by members of extreme right-wing groups caused her to flee to Munich at the beginning of 1919. She felt more protected there by the left-wing government of *Kurt Eisner. In keeping with her humanistic convictions, she became active in cultural and educational efforts, especially among workers and the unemployed. At the end of January 1919, she became a member of the Gesellschaft für neue Erziehung (Society for New Education) and critic for the Communist party newspaper *Neue Zeitung* without becoming a member of the party.

After the fall of the left-wing government led to a turn to the right in Bavaria, Bruck returned to Berlin in the summer of 1921. There, and in Magdeburg in 1923, she continued her social and cultural work undaunted by the constant police surveillance. In 1931 she became a member of the executive committee of the newly founded German section of the Ligue Internationale des Meres et des Educatrices, founded by *Constanze Hallgarten and which in German was called Weltfriedensbund der Mütter und Erzieherinnen (World Peace League of Mothers and [Women] Teachers). Bruck served as secretary of the Berlin group of the Mütterliga (Mother's League). Faced with new threats of arrest after the Nazi accession to power in January 1933, Bruck moved to Heidelberg and then to Stuttgart.

In 1934 Bruck left Germany and settled in Prague where she remained until 1938 when she moved to England. While in Prague, she had contact with *Ludwig Quidde in Geneva who provided her with some financial support. During her exile in Britain, Bruck joined the Freie Deutsche Kulturbund (Free German Cultural League) and was active in relief work among European refugees. Returning to Berlin at the end of the war, she continued to work for peace well into her old age.

Karl Holl
Trans. by Solomon Wank

BRYAN, William Jennings (19 March 1860, Salem, IL—26 July 1925, Dayton, TN). *Education*: B.A., Illinois Coll., 1881, M.A., 1884; LL.B., Union Coll. of Law, Chicago, 1883. *Career*: lawyer, politician, statesman; editor, *The Commoner*, 1901–23; lecturer and author.

William Jennings Bryan was taught by his parents to follow the dictates of the Bible in his temporal as well as in his spiritual life. Though never a conscientious objector or nonresistant, he did become a firm believer in progress by peaceful means.

During his early political career, Bryan showed little interest in foreign policy. While in Congress, 1891–95, he sought to solve the nation's political and economic ills. As a supporter of the Monroe Doctrine, he approved President Grover Cleveland's Venezuelan message of December 19, 1895. Yet he gave little attention to foreign affairs in his presidential campaign of 1896.

Bryan's stand with respect to Cuba in 1898 has often been misunderstood. As he saw it, war was a terrible thing but sometimes must be used as a means to an end. Consequently, in this case, he let his humanitarianism overcome his pacifism. But he opposed the McKinley administration's shift from humanitarian to territorial aims, and sounded a clarion call to follow the dictum in Holy Writ that some day swords would be beaten into plowshares. To many persons, therefore, his support for the Treaty of Paris was suspect, for by it the United States would acquire a colonial empire. The difficulty disappears when one understands that he wanted the treaty approved so that the war would end and

Congress could free the Philippines, for by the treaty Cuba went free, and he had no objection to America's acquiring Guam and Puerto Rico.

After 1900 Bryan played on the theme that morality, love, and the Christian brotherhood of man could solve international problems. From the latter emanated an advocacy of arbitration, "cooling off" treaties, and neutralism if not pacifism in international affairs. Bryan constantly berated +Theodore Roosevelt for his militarism and "big stick" diplomacy, although he agreed with him on prohibiting Asiatic "coolie" immigration and applauded his receipt of the Nobel Peace Prize for the results of the Portsmouth Conference ending the Russo-Japanese War (1905). Roosevelt would keep the United States strong and thus able to avoid threats to world peace; Bryan would have the United States live such a virtuous life that its example would be followed by other nations.

From visits to The Hague and to *Leo Tolstoy in 1903, Bryan strengthened his faith in the principle that love alone could conquer force and violence. Another visit to Europe, in 1906, deepened his devotion to peace, proscription of war, and opposition to imperialism. In subsequent addresses to American peace organizations, he avidly supported the principle of international conciliation, saying that war decided issues on the basis of brute strength, not on the basis of right or wrong, and that force should not be used to collect private debts held abroad. After 1913, when he was appointed Secretary of State by +Woodrow Wilson, he tried to put his principles into practice.

In dealing with Mexico's civil war, Bryan found that idealism and morality did not square with reality, even if they meshed with Wilson's application of the test of constitutionality before granting recognition to a government. Unable to get his way, Wilson intervened in Mexico during the spring of 1914. As for the Caribbean, Bryan believed that it must be made safe from any challenge to the security of the Panama Canal. Ingenious and inventive as Bryan's methods were to help less privileged peoples in Central American and Caribbean lands, and repeated though his protestations were that he opposed imperialism and dollar diplomacy, he made the Caribbean ever more an American lake. Thus, while demanding self-determination for the Filipinos and home rule for Puerto Ricans, he undermined his own record as an anti-imperialist.

To avoid war, Bryan supported a multilateral Western Hemispheric defense alliance and acted upon Japan's complaints about discrimination against her people. Responding to Japan's Twenty-one Demands on China he asserted that while propinquity granted Japan "special interests" in Manchuria, the United States could not consent to any violation of the open door.

Bryan's ideas for treaties of conciliation stemmed from his interest in solving labor troubles. The mere ascertaining of the facts, he believed, might lead to a settlement. Nevertheless, he would not force a solution upon the parties. On April 24, 1913, he recommended that nations establish bilateral commissions that would immediately and automatically start solving any disputes that had resisted solution by other methods. These commissions would have a year in which to work—a year during which the parties would not go to war or augment their arms. During the year, tempers would "cool off" and war would be avoided. The thirty treaties written by nations containing three fourths of the world's population were his monument to peace. Although they were criticized by self-professed realists, who said that a strong military force would deter war, others have claimed that their acceptance by the Central Powers would have prevented World War I. In any event, Bryan had given eloquent expression to his faith that an un-Christian world could be run according to the literal tenets of Christianity and had gone further than any other American in the direction of the pacific settlement of disputes. Conciliation appeared in the Covenant of the League of Nations, the Four-Power Treaty of 1921, the Kellogg-Briand Pact of 1928, and the Charter of the United Nations.

Unfortunately for Bryan, Wilson so strongly supported the principle of freedom of the seas that during the Great War, he declined Bryan's suggestion of strict neutrality and his recommendations for mediating between the contending powers. In consequence, on June 8, 1915, Bryan resigned his government post—a martyr to his ideas. Ironically, he supported Wilson's renomination and reelection on the basis that he had "saved the country from the horrors of war," and in December applauded Wilson's attempt to mediate the conflict.

Bryan's dilemmas, however, were only beginning. A prominent personage in the peace crusade to April 6, 1917, he loyally supported the administration after it entered the war. Although he told Wilson that he would be pleased to serve on the peace commission, Wilson brushed him off. Despite this rebuff, Bryan supported the Fourteen Points and accepted the League of Nations, which he urged the Senate to approve with or without reservations. For the last five years of his life Bryan continued his association with numerous peace societies. Opposing universal military training, he also advocated a popular referendum on war, disarmament, and the outlawry of war.

Bryan's record as a man of peace was inconsistent. He supported the Monroe Doctrine, saw war as a means to an end when all other methods failed, and volunteered for service in the Spanish-American War in the name of justice and right. Thereafter, however, he believed that war would be exorcized by the spread of democracy, increased popular educational standards, and heightened moral criteria emanating from the work of churches and peace societies. On the issue of guns or butter, Bryan clearly preferred the latter; he held that armaments helped cause war and that preparedness was advocated by those who sought financial profit. A cure for war lay in a popular referendum on war and the enlisting of those who voted aye. And he supported woman suffrage in part because he believed that women would vote against war. In sum, on economic, national, humanitarian, and especially on moral and religious grounds, Bryan opposed war. He remained to his death in 1925 a visionary who sought to apply biblical precepts of friendship, good will, and cooperation to the solution of everyday problems. Symptomatically, though, this prime supporter of the Prince of Peace asked to be buried in Arlington National Cemetery, a last resting place for military heroes.

Bibliography:

A. "The Forces that Make for Peace," *Address at the Mohonk Conferences on International Arbitration, 1910 and 1911* (New York, 1911); *The Memoirs of Williams Jennings Bryan*, with Mary Baird Bryan (Philadelphia, 1925); *World Peace: A Written Debate between William Howard Taft and William Jennings Bryan*, with William H. Taft (New York, 1917).

B. Paolo E. Coletta, *William Jennings Bryan* 3 vols., Lincoln, NA, 1964–69); John Nelson, *The Peace Prophets: American Pacifist Thought 1919–1941* (Chapel Hill, NC, 1967); Willard H. Smith "The Pacifist Though of William Jennings Bryan," *Mennonite Quarterly Review*, 45 (January 1971), 33–81 and (April 1971), 152–81; Willard H. Smith, "William Jennings Bryan: A Reappraisal," Indiana Academy of the Social Sciences *Proceedings*, 1965, N.S. 10 (April 1966), 56–69.

C. William Jennings Bryan Papers, Manuscript Division, Library of Congress.

Paolo E. Coletta

BUISSON, Ferdinand Edouard (20 December 1841, Paris—16 February 1932, Thieuloy-Saint-Antoine, Oise, France). *Education*: Collège d'Argentan (Orne); Lycée de Saint-Etienne; License ès lettres and agrégation de philosophie, Ecole normale supérieure, 1868; Doctorat ès lettres, Sorbonne, 1891. *Career*: professor of philosophy, Académie de Neufchatel, Switzerland, 1866–70; inspector of primary schools, Paris, 1871–72; secretary, Statistical Commission on primary education, 1872–78; Inspector General of Public Instruction, 1878, and director of primary education, 1879; professor of pedagogy, Sorbonne, 1896; elected Radical-Socialist deputy from Paris, 1902–14, 1919–24; municipal counsellor, Thieuloy-Saint-Antoine from 1924; honorary president, Socialist Federation of the Oise; founder (with Alphonse Aulard) of *La Lumière*, 1927.

An educator and a political figure, Ferdinand Buisson was active in support of a number of causes: humanitarian, civil rights, anti-clerical, feminist, and pacifist. A lifelong member of the Radical-Socialist party, his pacifism was attenuated by his Jacobin-patriotic faith. As a consequence, he supported vigorous prosecution of the war against Germany in 1914–18, and refused to accept the advanced positions of more militant pacifists both during and after the war.

Combining a career in politics with a career in teaching philosophy and pedagogy, his expertise in these fields brought him appointment to a succession of administrative posts in educational affairs from the 1870s through the 1890s. He collaborated with Jules Ferry in drafting the secular school laws. Among the earliest advocates of revision of the Dreyfus trial, Buisson assisted in the founding of the League of the Rights of Man, of which he was president from 1913 to 1926. In 1902 he was elected to the Chamber of Deputies, where he continued to espouse a variety of causes dear to him, including educational reform and women's suffrage. His humanitarian sentiments were manifested in his membership on the Committee on Oversight of the orphanage of Cempuis, in his vice-presidency of the Chamber Committee on Insurance and Social Security, and in his membership on the Chamber Committee on Public Hygiene after 1902. As president of the Ligue des droits de l'homme (League for the Rights of Man) he defended the rights of minorities—Poles, Russian revolutionaries, Slavic and Italian citizens of Austria, and Jews.

Buisson's pacifism began early in his life. In 1867 when he was a newly appointed professor at the Académie de Neufchatel, he attended the first international Congress of Peace at Geneva, where he advocated the formation of a United States of Europe, a position which he never entirely abandoned. Two years later, at the second Congress of Peace at Lausanne, he called for the abolition of "all armies, the god of the Caesars and the Napoleons." Occupied with other matters, he devoted less attention to peace issues in the latter years of the nineteenth century, although he did participate in several national peace congresses after 1902. In 1918, however, he strongly endorsed the formation of a League of Nations and shortly thereafter became a member of the executive committee of the Association française pour la société des nations, formed from eight previous organizations. Among his associates on the committee were +Leon Bourgeois, *Charles Richet, *Paul Henri d'Estournelles de Constant and *Jules Prudhommeaux. In 1923, at the 10th National Peace Congress, Buisson was appointed to the Délégation Permanente des Sociétés françaises de la paix (Permanent Delegation of French Peace Societies), an office which he held until his death. He was a delegate of the League for the Rights of Man to the 24th National Peace Congress, and continued in subsequent years.

Buisson's pacifism tended toward the patriotic and legalistic. He opposed the more advanced pacifism of those who proposed the disarmament of France or upheld conscientious objection, and he firmly rejected the doctrine of those who saw capitalism as the principal cause of war. He continued to support the League of Nations, and proposed that it be strengthened. However, from 1920 to about 1927, when the League for the Rights of Man was particularly active on peace issues (having retreated from support of the Union sacrée), Buisson was usually aligned with the more moderate leaders of the League. As a rule, he supported compromise resolutions on such issues as opposition to the occupation of the Ruhr, support for conscientious objection, and reduction of the term of military service—proposals advocated by more militant members and often supported by the majority of the rank-and-file members. Nevertheless, Buisson remained committed to the cause of peace, though within a framework of patriotism and of concern for the security of France. In 1927, in recognition of his efforts Buisson received—jointly with *Ludwig Quidde of Germany—the Nobel Peace Prize.

Bibliography:

A. *L'Organisation de la société des nations* (Paris, 1917); *Sebastien Castellion; Sa vie, son oeuvre* (Paris, 1891); *La Vote des femmes* (Paris, 1911).

B. E. Roussel, *La Vie et l'oeuvre de Ferdinand Buisson* (Montpelier, 1931).

Albert S. Hill

BURRITT, Elihu (10 December 1810, New Britain, CT—6 March 1879, New Britain). *Education*: district schools, self-educated. *Career*: blacksmith; editor, *Christian Citizen*, *Bond of Brotherhood*, *North and South*; linguist and peace reformer.

Elihu Burritt held a leading position among the nineteenth century peace reformers. Although he was involved for a time with the abolition movement, he came to believe that if the goals of the peace reformers were reached, other problems in society would correct themselves. Like many of his contemporaries, he believed in mankind's ability to attain perfection and to usher in a new age of peace and brotherhood. His unique contributions to the movement, however, are to be found in his confidence that the working class could be instrumental in attaining universal peace, his talent for finding practical solutions for bringing this dream to fruition, and his capacity to transcend the barriers of nationality, sex, and race in his quest.

Burritt's philosophy was forged in a working class home by parents who provided examples of deep religious faith and compassion for those less fortunate. There was no money for Burritt to pursue an academic career, so he became a blacksmith and taught himself languages at night. To supplement his income, he wrote a letter to William Lincoln, who had some literary connections, outlining his background and asking if he knew anyone who needed German translations. The letter so impressed Lincoln that he had it published in a newspaper and Burritt's reputation as the "Learned Blacksmith" grew. He wrote some short sentimental pieces for local publications like "My Brother's Grave," and did some translation for periodicals, but these ventures were never profitable and he was forced to continue working at other jobs to earn a living.

The lyceum circuit offered Burritt opportunities to speak. While writing a lecture on "The Anatomy of the Earth," he was so impressed by the interdependency of its parts that he ended with a plea for international peace. This became his lifelong passion. He became acquainted with other social reformers and began his career as a prophet for peace.

Burritt joined the American Peace Society in 1843, but quickly took issue with its direction and approach. He opposed what he saw as the Society's overemphasis on converting influential citizens to the peace effort and tried to carry the antiwar message to the masses. He quickly aligned with the radical element in the Society, rejecting all war, including defensive war. He stopped short, however, of rejecting government coercion. He willingly worked with Congressmen who sought to introduce measures to advance the cause of peace, a policy rejected by *William Lloyd Garrison and those who viewed almost all government institutions as corrupt.

Burritt was a radical pacifist opposed to physical force in theory, yet he struggled to reconcile his theory with practical realities. It was not until after the European revolutions of 1848 that he found a resolution of the dilemma in the concept of passive resistance. In the mid–1840s, however, his public speeches, his writings, and his organizational work brought him recognition as one of the most dynamic peace leaders in the nation. In 1846 he edited the *Advocate of Peace*, the journal of the American Peace Society. He shifted the editorial policy of the journal in the direction of opposing all war and virtually every form of human violence. He increasingly challenged the leadership of the Society and when it justified the Mexican War as a defensive action, Burritt and several of his colleagues resigned from the executive committee.

From 1844–51 Burritt edited the *Christian Citizen*, a magazine devoted to reform efforts especially those concerning peace. This periodical had a section for children through which Burritt hoped to mold the minds of youth to oppose war. He made no attempt to sugar coat the subject for the young and provided math problems for them to compute using war casualties and blood loss to find the answers. He also warned against blind nationalism, calling it ''Monstrous idolatry! Whose Christian name is Patriotism.''

Burritt firmly believed that war would cease when Christian men refused to fight. To reach a wide audience he proposed in 1845 that brief statements written by peace reformers be sent to newspapers in Europe and America. Known as ''Olive Leaves,'' hundreds of papers carried the articles and were read by an estimated 2,000,000 people. In 1846 he expanded his idea of international co-operation in the movement by organizing the ''Friendly Address'' program. This concept paired cities of the same name in England and America to exchange greetings and expressions of goodwill.

That same year Burritt went to England to begin a League of Universal Brotherhood. Anyone, male or female over the age of twelve, could join the League by signing a pledge to renounce all war and abstain from military service. Eventually some 50,000 joined the League in Britain and the United States. Branches were established in other European countries as well. It served more as a moral commitment than anything else, for it lacked direction and leadership. Burritt also promoted the concept of penny postage on transatlantic mail to make it less expensive to foster international friendship.

In the 1840s and 1850s Burritt helped organize numerous peace congresses held in Europe. He almost singlehandedly organized the Brussels Peace Congress in 1848. At these meetings, he urged the formation of a Congress and a Supreme Court of Nations. The Congress would formulate an international code of law and the Court would be the final arbiter in international disputes. This he saw as the best hope for permanent world peace.

The Crimean War in Europe and the American Civil War shattered the international peace movement. During the Civil War, many who had opposed armed conflict in any form changed their position to support the Union. Believing that war was a lesser evil than the continuation of slavery, peace leaders abandoned their well developed arguments and principles. Burritt was saddened by this compromise with the evil of war. He felt the hostility of his peers and was branded a secessionist and traitor for holding fast to his principles.

Throughout his life as a peace reformer, Burritt urged the working class on both sides of the Atlantic to join the antiwar cause. He made eloquent and practical appeals to this group reminding them that it was always the working class who bore the financial and physical burden of war. Americans were urged to vote only for peace candidates. In the 1860s he hoped that working men would form one vast Trades Union and make a universal and simultaneous strike against the whole war system.

Elihu Burritt, more than any other of his generation, was the United States' and perhaps the world's most consistent and powerful voice for world peace.

Bibliography:

A. *Lectures and Speeches* (London, 1869); *Miscellaneous Writings* (Worcester, MA, 1850); *Sparks From The Anvil* (Worcester, MA, 1846); *Thoughts and Notes at Home and Abroad* (London, 1868); *Thoughts and Things at Home and Abroad* (Boston, 1854); *The Year-Book of the Nations* (London, 1858).

B. Merle Curti, *The Learned Blacksmith* (New York, 1937); Peter Tolis, *Elihu Burritt: Crusader for Brotherhood* (Hamden, CT, 1968).

Kay Clontz Starnes

BURT, Thomas (12 November 1837, Murton Row, Northumberland, England—13 April 1922, Newcastle). *Education*: informal. *Career*: pit worker in Northumberland coal mines 1847–65; secretary and full time agent, Northumberland Miners Association, 1865–75; Member of Parliament for Morpeth, 1874–1918; president, Workmen's Peace Association and International Arbitration League, 1882–1917.

A coal miner elected to represent his fellow workers in 1874, Thomas Burt was for more than forty years a leading member of the "Labour" bloc in the House of Commons. A dedicated if conservative trade unionist, Burt was also a prominent "Little Englander," frequently taking the floor of the House to denounce British imperialism and its "little wars" such as those against Afghans (1879), Zulus (1879), Egyptians (1882), and Sudanese (1885). He was a critic of militarism throughout his tenure, voting consistently against increases in military appropriations and opposing the introduction of cadet corps into London schools as a possible forerunner of conscription.

Though never a pacifist, Burt was deeply committed to the goals of the peace and arbitration movement, serving for thirty-four years as president of the Workmen's Peace Association and International Arbitration League, an organization founded in 1871 to mobilize working class opposition to the use of force in international disputes. During the Boer War (1899–1902) Burt was one of a bloc of fifty-five "pro-Boer" Liberals who steadfastly opposed the conflict in Commons. Although Burt later expressed regret that he had not protested more emphatically against "the most disgraceful war in our history," on numerous public occasions he characterized the conflict as "unjustifiable," and as an "abomination" certain to defer social reforms that were needed by the working class. Reelected in 1900 despite the high level of attrition among antiwar Liberals, Burt intensified his commitment to the arbitration movement, convinced that "bloodless arbitration" must inevitably replace war as a means of settling international disputes. He supported the ratification of the Anglo-French Treaty of 1903 which marked, in his view, the emergence of the arbitration movement and he hailed the establishment of The Hague Tribunal as proof of its growing maturity. Though a lifelong opponent of the "arbitrement of the sword," in August 1914 Burt supported the decision of the British government to declare war on Germany, a nation that had violated Belgian neutrality and had thus undermined the very foundation of that system of law and order which he hoped would replace the present armed anarchy.

In his lengthy career as labor leader, M.P., and peace activist, Thomas Burt sought to apply to international issues the methods used to resolve industrial disputes. An advocate of cooperation between British and continental miners, Burt saw the growth of international labor congresses, in which he frequently participated, as a model for sovereign states to emulate. Viewing arbitration treaties as the equivalent among nations of the domestic agreements negotiated to ensure peace between workers and employers, Burt remained for much of his life an advocate of disarmament, a spokesman for international cooperation, and a champion of "the fights of smaller weaker nations against the military domination of the strong."

Bibliography:

A. *Thomas Burt ... Pitman and Privy Councillor. An autobiography with supplementary chapters by Aaron Watson* (London, 1928).

B. T.C. Meech, *From Mine to Ministry: The Life and Times of the Right Honourable Thomas Burt* (London, 1908); A. Watson, *A Great Labour Leader: Being a Life of the Right Honourable Thomas Burt* (London, 1908).

Claire Hirschfield

BURTON, Ormond Edward (16 January 1893, Auckland, New Zealand—7 January 1974, Otaki, New Zealand. *Education*: B.A., Univ. of New Zealand, 1915, M.A., 1921. *Career*: teacher, Methodist minister, and antiwar activist.

Nurtured in the Methodist and Presbyterian Churches, Ormond Burton became a Christian in 1913. When World War I broke out, he volunteered for the Medical Corps and served in the First Field Ambulance in the Gallipoli campaign. Later, in France, he joined the infantry. Following the war, he engaged in YMCA work, lectured for the New Zealand Alliance in the prohibition campaign, and stood unsuccessfully for Parliament as a Christian Socialist. A country school teacher before the war, he returned to his original profession and spent six years at Wesley College. Becoming a Methodist minister he served the Webb Street Church in the Wellington Central circuit from 1935 until 1942. Here his humanitarianism found expression in social work for the outcasts of society and his proclamation of faith in open-air preaching each Sunday afternoon.

Following World War I, his idealism shattered by the vengeful Treaty of Versailles, Burton became a convinced Christian pacifist. As World War II approached, he became a leader in the newly formed Christian Pacifist Society. On the very first day of the war, he spoke out against the conflict in front of the New Zealand Parliament and was arrested. Continued public protests led to his being imprisoned five times during the war. His time in jail totalled two years and eight months.

Burton's uncompromising condemnation of the war on Christian grounds led him into conflict with the more conservative Church leaders. Refusing to obey a manifesto drawn up by the Methodist Church restraining preachers from speaking from the pulpit either for or against the war, he was dismissed from the ministry in 1942. He campaigned vigorously for the retrial of the 700 conscientious objectors detained during the war and as a result many were released. He also campaigned for prison reform and his book *In Prison* (1945) helped improve conditions for those who remained in jail.

During the war Burton returned to teaching. First employed as a cleaner at the Wellington Technical College, he became a teacher, then a Departmental head, and finally acting-Headmaster. In 1956 he sought readmission into the Methodist ministry and was accepted. Appointed superintendent of the Otaki Circuit, he remained there until his retirement in 1960.

In retirement Burton retained his interest in the peace movement and played a prominent role in the Christian Pacifist Society. He publicly protested against the Korean War and in 1962 called for civil disobedience to protest the nuclear arms race. The following year he lectured in the United States and Great Britain as a member of the Council of the International Fellowship of Reconciliation. He continued his historical and theological writing, publishing *To Whom Shall We Go*? (1972) at the age of 79.

Ormond Burton was one of New Zealand's leading critics of war. Insisting on the solidarity of the human race and the sanctity of human life, he both proclaimed and practiced the gospel of love.

Bibliography:

A. *The Auckland Regiment* (Auckland, 1922); *The Conflict of the Cross* (London, 1940); *In Prison* (Wellington, 1945); *In the Way of Peace* (Auckland, 1951); *The New Zealand Division* (Auckland, 1936); *Shall We Fight*? (Auckland, 1923; *The Silent Division; New Zealanders at the Front, 1914–1919* (Sydney, 1935); *A Testament of Peace* (Wellington, 1940); *To Whom Shall We Go*? (Auckland, 1973); *The Ways of God to Men* (Auckland, 1966).

B. Norman Bennett, "Ormond Burton and the Price of Peace," *Auckland Star*, January 19, 1974.

C. "A Rich Old Man" (unpublished autobiography), The Alexander Turnbull Library, Wellington, NZ.

Ernest A. Crane

BURTON, Theodore Elijah (20 December 1851, Jefferson, OH—28 October 1929, Washington). *Education*: Grinnell Coll.; B.A., Oberlin Coll., 1872; read law in Chicago, 1874–75. *Career*: lawyer, Cleveland, OH, 1875–89, 1890–95, 1915–17; councilman, Cleveland, 1886–89; Republican congressman, 1889–90, 1895–1908, 1921–28; U. S. Senator, 1909–15, 1928–29; president, Merchants National Bank, New York, 1917–19.

Integrity, ability, dedication, loyalty, and practicality emerged as dominant qualities in Theodore Burton's forty-one years as a congressman and senator. He did not hesitate to resist political machines bosses, or special interest groups, but his convictions appeared most strongly in his positions on peace and international questions.

His interest in resolving disputes without force preceded his election to Congress in 1889, the year of the creation of the Interparliamentary Union, and in ensuing decades he became its warm supporter, serving on its Executive Council (1904–14, 1921–29). The Interparliamentary Union sought to involve legislators from national law-making bodies in discussions of the peaceful resolution of controversies. With +Richard Bartholdt, he helped create an American Branch. While Burton recognized that the Union could not achieve miracles, he saw it as an important means for building bridges among nations and getting legislators to think internationally.

Burton was more than a theorist of conflict resolution. He supported arbitration and conciliation accords and favored dropping clauses which excluded questions of national honor and vital interests. He became a voice of reason during the Panama Canal tolls controversy and ardently advocated U. S. membership in the Permanent Court of International Justice. Although the House of Representatives had no formal voice in that decision, Burton introduced a bill into the House in 1925 that gained an overwhelming vote of endorsement. He also served as a delegate to the 1926 League of Nations Conference on the Control of Opium. During the 1920s he opposed his party by resisting high tariff bills. The renunciation of war idea, embodied in the Kellogg-Briand Pact, also received his support. After ratification of the Pact, he sought Congressional action to ban the shipment of arms to nations which violated the accord or arbitration treaties.

Many other interests involved Burton in peace-related activities. He challenged +Theodore Roosevelt on naval appropriations and opposed most preparedness bills. His position against a naval cruiser building program in 1926 stimulated considerable publicity, which Burton enjoyed. He believed the U.S. should set an example as a peace leader through restraint. He advocated sufficiency, not continual expansion that led to armaments races. Burton's respected and rational position led to his appointment by Calvin Coolidge as a delegate to the League of Nations Conference on the Traffic in Arms (Geneva, 1925). There he became a leading voice for outlawing poison gas. Burton also became involved in the war debt question in the 1920s after he served on the World War Foreign Debt Commission (1922). There he stood for a reasonable approach based on capacity to pay, not cancellation, and thereafter in Congress he steered the settlement bills of several countries through the House.

Burton served as president of the American Peace Society, 1911–16 and 1924–28. He was often referred to as a pacifist, but that word does not properly describe him. While he abhorred war, he supported involvement in World War I and he believed in a need for arms. His real hope lay in a more enlightened world where people would respond rationally, accept responsibilities to resolve differences peacefully, and build the legal machinery needed to insure peace. An elaborate World Conference on International Justice, held in Cleveland in 1928 to celebrate the centennial of the American Peace Society, fully reflected his hopes.

Bibliography:

A. *Modern Political Tendencies and the Effect of the War Thereon* (Princeton, NJ, 1919).

B. Forrest Crissey, *Theodore E. Burton: American Statesman* (Cleveland, 1958); DAB III, 141; NCAB XXI, 50–51.

C. Theodore Burton Papers, Western Reserve Historical Society, Cleveland, OH.

Warren F. Kuehl

BUTLER, Nicholas Murray. See *Biographical Dictionary of Internationalists*.

BUXTON, Charles Roden (27 November 1875, London—16 December 1942, Peaslake, Surrey, England). *Education*: Harrow; B.A., Trinity Coll., Cambridge Univ., 1897; called to the Bar of Inner Temple, 1902. *Career*: private secretary to the governor of South Australia, 1897–98; principal, Morley Coll. for Working Men and Women, 1902–10; editor, *Albany Review*, 1906–8; Member of Parliament, (Ashburton), 1910, (Accrington), 1922–23, (Elland), 1929–31; treasurer, Independent Labour party, 1924–27; chairman, Advisory Committee on International Questions, Labour party, 1926–37; chairman, Advisory Committee on Imperial Questions, Labour party, 1926–40; author.

Charles Roden Buxton was one of a group of Liberal politicians who joined the Labour party during World War I and played an important role in shaping that party's policies in the interwar period. Although he never held high government office and was out of Parliament more often than not in these years, he still exercised considerable influence as an advisor on foreign policy, with an intense interest in the empire.

Buxton was born into a wealthy family with a tradition of public service. Along with his older brother *Noel, he studied life among the London poor while still a student. Charles worked for his father, who was governor of South Australia, and traveled widely in his early years. Although he was called to the bar, he chose not to practice law. He ran for Parliament as a Liberal in 1906 and 1908 without success, finally winning a seat in 1910 which he held for less than a year. Opposed to British intervention in the war in 1914, he still volunteered for active service only to be rejected because of ill health. He also agreed to go with Noel to the Balkans to recruit for the Entente in September. Both brothers were wounded in an assassination attempt and their mission failed. In 1915 they published *The War and the Balkans* which called for the creation of a Balkan federation.

Gradually, Buxton's opposition to the war and the institutions that fostered it mounted. He became one of the most active members of the Union of Democratic Control and in 1915 helped to set up a committee to help Germans and other enemies interned in Britain. The Hackney Liberal Association expelled him because of his outspoken opposition to the government's war policy. He broke with the Church of England and joined the Society of Friends, making it clear that while he was not an absolute pacifist he wanted to take a stand against the war. In August 1915, with *Clifford Allen and others, he issued the ''Peace Mandate,'' a call for neutral countries to mediate a negotiated peace.

In 1917 Buxton joined the Independent Labour party (ILP), whose leaders generally shared his views on foreign affairs, and he tried without success to reenter the Commons as an ILP candidate in the ''Khaki Election'' of 1918. He remained in the IlP until 1930, serving as the party's treasurer for several years and representing it at meetings of the International in Vienna in 1923. In 1920 Buxton became an advisor to the Labour party on foreign affairs. From this position, and as a delegate to the League of Nations in 1924 and 1930, he was able to put his stamp on the party's policies. He was critical of the Versailles peace settlement as overly harsh towards Germany, but he did support the work of the League of Nations which grew out of that settlement. His support for the League was conditional, however. Like many in the peace movement, he wanted it used as an instrument of reconciliation, but not of coercion. Buxton worked to improve relations with Germany in the 1930s and persisted in his efforts to negotiate a satisfactory relationship with Germany even after World War II had begun.

Bibliography:

A. *The Alternative to War* (London, 1936); *The World After the War*, with Dorothy Frances Buxton (London, 1920).

B. Victoria A. de Bunsen, *Charles Roden Buxton; A Memoir* (London, 1948).

C. C. R. Buxton Papers, Rhodes House, Oxford.

Donald S. Birn

BUXTON, Noel Edward, 1st Baron Noel-Buxton of Aylsham (9 January 1869, London—12 September 1948, London). *Education*: Harrow, B.A., Trinity Coll., Cambridge Univ., 1889. *Career*: brewer, Spitalfields, 1889–1904; aide to Governor of South Australia, 1896; Member of Parliament, (Whitby) 1905–6; (North Norfolk), 1910–18, 1922–30; created Baron Noel-Buxton of Aylsham, Norfolk, 1930; author.

Noel Buxton was a politician who worked for peace as a Liberal before 1918 and then as an important leader in the Labour party. Born into a wealthy family, he began his career in the family brewery, where he soon became a director. He traveled widely in the 1890s, serving in 1896 as an aide to his father, then Governor of South Australia, and developed a particular interest in the Balkans. After contesting an election for parliament and losing in 1900, he was successful in 1905 only to lose his seat in the general elections of 1906. In 1910 he won North Norfolk as a Liberal. His long association with this district was helped by his extensive philanthropy and his championship of farm workers.

Buxton quickly won distinction in Parliament as an opponent of the Liberal government's foreign policy, which he felt was needlessly provoking Germany and threatening the peace. Alarmed by the handling of the Agadir Crisis of 1911, he became chairman of the Liberal Foreign Affairs Group which backed what it saw as the legitimate hopes of Germans for territory overseas. He was also active in the Anglo-German Friendship Committee which worked to reduce tensions between the two nations.

When war came in 1914, Buxton first hoped for a quick allied victory. Along with his brother *Charles he went to the Balkans in September to win Bulgarian support for the Entente. Both brothers were wounded in an assassination attempt and their mission failed. In 1915 he worked with the Admiralty on Balkan policy, but he also supported the work of the Union of Democratic Control, which opposed Britain's war policy. In 1916 he visited the United States to establish an Armenian Relief Fund, and while there he encouraged American mediation efforts to end the war. In Parliament, he sided with dissenters who wanted a negotiated peace based on a return to the situation in 1914.

Increasingly dissatisfied with the Liberal party, he sought election as a Liberal-Labour candidate in 1918 and lost to a supporter of the coalition government. He joined the Labour party the following year and was returned to the house in 1922. In the 1924 Labour government he was appointed Minister of Agriculture and managed to secure passage of the Agricultural Wages Act, one of the few achievements of the short-lived government. He took the agriculture post again in 1929 when Labour returned to office but retired because of ill health in 1930 and accepted a peerage.

Buxton worked throughout his career for international peace. Never a pacifist, he was driven in part by his deep commitment to Christianity. An Anglican, he continued his peace work even after he retired from politics. During the 1930s he supported efforts to maintain an understanding of German policy and revise the Versailles settlement. These attitudes brought him into conflict with many of his fellow Labourites and into supporting Prime Minister Neville Chamberlain's appeasement policies. Even after the onset of World War II, he continued to hope for a negotiated peace and circulated a memorandum on war crimes in the House of Lords.

Bibliography:

A. *England and Germany* (London, 1911); *With the Bulgarian Staff* (New York, 1913).

B. Mosa Anderson, *Noel Buxton, A Life* (London, 1952); T. P. Conwell-Evans, *Foreign Policy from a Back Bench 1904–1918* (Oxford, 1932).

Donald S. Birn

C

CADBURY, Barrow (27 September 1862, Edgbaston, England—9 March 1958, Birmingham). *Education*: Owens Coll., Manchester, 1878-80. *Career*: industrialist; public benefactor and philanthropist; Quaker activist and pacifist.

Barrow Cadbury was born into a wealthy Quaker family, well known for its manufacture of chocolate and cocoa and for producing a number of men and women who have made important contributions to the cause of social justice and international harmony. A gentle, gracious, simple man, Cadbury had that Victorian capacity to combine shrewd business acumen with personal integrity and deep spirituality. He approached his wealth with a sense of stewardship, believing that money should be used for enlightened and ennobling purposes. He helped to create model working conditions in his factories, donated much valuable property to the city of Birmingham, involved himself with the adult school movement, and richly participated in the spiritual life of the Society of Friends.

Throughout his life, Cadbury demonstrated an interest in the pacifist cause. He supported the Society of Friends in its peace efforts by serving on relevant committees and helped fund the numerous Quaker relief agencies that sprung up during and after World War I. He also supported many other peace organizations during the interwar period, particularly the Fellowship of Reconciliation. After World War II he proposed to the British Government a ''budgetary'' solution to the problem of a renewed arms race. He suggested that Britain, hopefully in conjunction with other nations, reduce its armaments expenditures by a predetermined percentage annually, leading towards a significant reduction of a period of years. Near the end of his life, he proposed to several governments that they create a Ministry of Peace and Goodwill.

Perhaps Cadbury's major contribution was his emphasis upon the value of personal contact in reducing international tension. Prior to World War I, he encouraged the exchange of delegations (students, clergymen, and civic leaders) between Germany and Britain in the hope that this would reduce mistrust and promote understanding. During the 1930s, he gave vigorous moral and financial support to the Embassies of Reconciliation, a group of dedicated pacifists who wanted to present the Christian program of peacemaking directly to the leaders of Europe. The Embassies, thanks to Cadbury's generous support, sponsored a number of visits by *George Lansbury to the continent, where he conferred with kings, dictators, and prime ministers. Undoubtedly, Lansbury's most famous visits occurred in 1937, when he had interviews with Adolf Hitler and Benito Mussolini, and received much favorable publicity for the Embassies in the process. While such projects as promoting personal peace missions and Ministries of Peace did not achieve the success intended, they attracted a good deal of interest and helped promote the idea that there were alternatives to war.

Barrow Cadbury rarely mouthed platitudes nor did he give money simply to buy relief from guilt. Contemporaries noted how much he gave of himself, his time, his energy, and his concern. Much of his life involved the quest for peace, but he defined that term in its most expansive sense: industrial peace, class harmony, spiritual contentment, and international goodwill.

Bibliography:

B. Percy W. Bartlett, *Barrow Cadbury* (London 1960); Janet Whitney, *Geraldine Southall Cadbury: 1865-1941* (London, 1948); LT, March 10, 1958.

David C. Lukowitz

CADBURY, Henry Joel (1 December 1883, Philadelphia, PA—7 October 1974, Haverford, PA). *Education*: B.A., Haverford Coll., 1903; M.A., Harvard Univ., 1904, Ph.D., 1914. *Career*: professor of Biblical Studies; Quaker activist; founding member, American Friends Service Committee, 1917.

Henry Cadbury was suspended from his teaching position at Haverford College in 1918 after he published a letter in the Philadelphia *Public Ledger* denouncing the "orgy of hate" against the German people which held sway in the United States. During the following months he gave most of his time to the budding American Friends Service Committee (AFSC), which had been founded in 1917. Later he served as Chairman of the AFSC from 1928-34 and 1944-60. Cadbury represented the AFSC in Oslo in 1947 when it shared the Nobel Peace Prize with the Friends Service Council in London.

A noted Biblical scholar, Cadbury was Hollis Professor of Divinity at Harvard for two decades, in addition to teaching at Bryn Mawr and Haverford. His books included *The Making of Luke-Acts* (1927), and *The Perils of Modernizing Jesus* (1937), and he served on the editorial committee which prepared the Revised Standard Version of the New Testament. He also published several volumes and numerous articles on Quaker history, with an emphasis upon the peace testimony as well as obscure issues which had been ignored by others.

An active participant in the peace conferences held by Friends early in the century, Cadbury was named chairman of the Friends National Peace Conference in 1915 and began to publish pamphlets and articles about pacifism the same year. He continued to write about the peace testimony during his lifetime, publishing in the *Christian Century*, *Fellowship*, and theological journals as well as in Quaker publications on both sides of the Atlantic.

After he retired from Harvard in 1954, he returned to live at Haverford and gave much time to the work of the AFSC and Philadelphia Yearly Meeting of Friends. The Quaker initiative against the Cold War came during his second period as chairman of the AFSC, and he warmly supported efforts to reopen communciations with China and to find a peaceful solution in the Middle East.

Bibliography:

A. *The Perils of Modernizing Jesus* (New York, 1937); "Toward a Bibliography of Henry J. Cadbury (1910-1974)," typescript in the Quaker Collection, Haverford, College.

B. Edwin B. Bronner, "Henry Joel Cadbury," *Year Book* of the American Philosophical Society, 1975 (Philadelphia, 1975), 123-29; Mary Hoxie Jones, "Henry Joel Cadbury: A Biographical Sketch," *Then and Now* (Philadelphia, 1960), 11-70.

C. Henry J. Cadbury Papers, Quaker Collection, Haverford College.

Edwin B. Bronner

CADOUX, Cecil John (24 May 1883, Smyrna [now Izmir], Ottoman Empire [now Turkey]—16 August 1947, Oxford, England). *Education.* B. A. Univ. of London, 1909, M. A., 1911, D. D., 1918; B.A., Mansfield Coll., Oxford, 1914; M.A., Univ. of Oxford, 1918, D. Litt., 1939. *Career*: teacher, Congregational theological colleges in Bradford and Oxford; Congregational minister, theological scholar and writer, pacifist.

Cecil John Cadoux was a prominent British Christian pacifist in the first half of the twentieth century. His work as a theological teacher specializing in New Testament exegesis and early church history reinforced his conviction that a Christian could not participate in war, and he taught, preached, and wrote about this conviction throughout his life.

Although born in Smyrna, Cadoux was brought up and educated in south London. In 1902 he entered the Admiralty as a civil servant. He read voraciously in his spare time, and as he read *Leo Tolstoy and studied the synoptic gospels, his pacifist convictions were formed. He served as an officer in the Boys' Brigade and taught in the local Congregational Sunday School. The Christian attitude to war was a frequent topic for discussion in his classes, and he helped to form the pacifist convictions of a number of young men who became conscientious objectors during the First World War.

His decision to enter the Congregational ministry and enrollment as a student at Mansfield College, Oxford, in 1911 resolved the contradiction between his principles and his work at the Admiralty. A few months after his accreditation as a Congregational minister and appointment as tutor at Mansfield in 1914 World War I broke out. He opposed the war from the beginning and got into trouble for preaching pacifism on Sunday engagements in Congregational churches, but was not easily silenced on the subject. In December 1914 he attended the Cambridge conference which resulted in the foundation of the Fellowship of Reconciliation (FOR). He was a member from that moment until the end of his life. Early in 1915 he received permission to take three months' leave of absence from Mansfield in order to serve with the Friends' Ambulance Unit. He went to France in April 1915, served in the FAU hospital in Dunkirk, and experienced the second battle of Ypres on a tour inland.

On returning to Oxford he married Marguerite Asplin and began research, alongside some teaching, into the attitude of the early Christian Church to society and the state (including the attitude to war). When conscription was introduced in 1916, he defended friends and associates called before military service tribunals and served on the Oxford Joint Advisory Committee to conscientious objectors. He wrote several articles for the FOR magazine *The Venturer*.

In 1919 he published his first major work, *The Early Christian Attitude to War*, a thorough, scholarly account of the attitude to war revealed in the New Testament and in the writings and experience of early Christian leaders before the time of Constantine. The material in the book was later incorporated in *The Early Church and the World* (1925), which became one of the standard books on the subject.

In 1919 Cadoux moved to Bradford as Professor of New Testament Criticism, Exegesis and Theology at the Yorkshire United Independent College, a college, like Mansfield, for the training of Congregational ministers. Here he established his reputation as one of the foremost leaders of the Liberal Protestant school of theology, especially with his volume *Catholicism and Christianity* (1928).

He continued his work for the FOR, urging strongly that the Fellowship had a continuing role to play in the postwar world. His pamphlet on behalf of the Fellowship, *An Appeal to the People of the Christian Church*, was published in 1919. He contributed to *Reconciliation*, served as a member of the national FOR Council, and became chairman (1927-33). He was leader of the Bradford branch of the FOR and was a regular speaker on pacifism in Yorkshire and Lancashire.

In 1933 Cadoux returned to Oxford as Mackennal Professor of Church History and Vice-Principal at Mansfield College. By this time his health was deteriorating and he was forced to limit his external commitments, but his pen remained active in the pacifist cause.

The international events of the later 1930s compelled him to rethink his pacifist beliefs. The outbreak of war in September 1939 stimulated him to write a new defense of the pacifist position in the light of the existing situation. The book was published in September 1940 as *Christian Pacifism Re-examined*. Cadoux recognized that the evil nature of the Nazi regime presented the Christian pacifist with a profound challenge. While insisting that the Christian pacifist case had not been answered, he attempted to find some synthesis between pacifist and nonpacifist viewpoints. He expounded the theory of the relative justification of war, a theory he had already put forward in 1917. He argued that faced with a state of war, a man ought to choose that course of action which he believes will lead to the best consequences, and that those who reach different conclusions about the best course of action must yet respect each other's contribution to the general good, since it is best that a man should act by his conscience. The book probably converted few people to pacifism, but reinforced many already committed to nonviolence.

Cadoux believed that Christian pacifists had positive contributions to make even in a time of war, in working for the better treatment of refugees, opposing air attacks on civilians, and in stressing the need for a "healing peace" when the war was over. During World War II he served as an air-raid warden in Oxford.

After the war his health deteriorated seriously and he died in 1947, a year before he was due to retire.

Bibliography:

A. *Christian Pacifism Re-examined* (Oxford, 1940); *The Early Christian Attitude to War* (London, 1919); *The Early Church and the World* (Edinburgh, 1925).

C. Cadoux Archives, are in the possession of Dr. T. J. Cadoux of the University of Edinburgh.

Elaine Kaye

CALVO, Carlos. See *Biographical Dictionary of Internationalists*.

CAPEN, Samuel Billings (12 December 1842, Boston, MA—29 January 1914, Shanghai, China). *Education*: high school graduate, 1858. *Career*: businessman.

Samuel Billings Capen was a leader in the Protestant foreign missions movement and an advocate of peace and international arbitration. His career illustrates the close connection between Protestant missionary activity and the peace movement. While achieving moderate success as a carpet manufacturer in Boston, Capen became active in Congregationalist Sunday school and missionary work. In 1899 he was elected president of the American Board of Commissioners of Foreign Missions, the largest Protestant missionary organization. At the same time, he became involved in a number of peace organizations. With such peace leaders as *Benjamin Trueblood, Robert Treat Paine, and Edward Everett Hale, Capen participated in the annual Lake Mohonk Conferences on International Arbitration held at Lake Mohonk, New York, beginning in 1895. He was also a president of the Massachusetts Peace Foundation, vice-president of the American Peace Society, and a director of the World Peace Foundation.

As a devout Congregationalist, Capen combined a missionary zeal with the vision of a peaceful, Christian world. The crusade for world peace, he declared in 1914, was merely an effort to make Christianity "practical to every nation." Capen not only considered great military expenditures "a travesty on our Christianity," but also believed that disputes between "Christian nations" should be settled in a peaceful manner. Like other participants in the Mohonk Conferences, Capen called for the establishment of a permanent international court of arbitration. On the eve of the Spanish-American War, he backed William McKinley's peace efforts and won the endorsement of several Boston business and civic groups for a peaceful resolution of the crisis. After the turn of the century, Capen worked to secure support, particularly among businessmen, for arbitration treaties with Great Britain and several other nations.

It was primarily through his Congregationalist missionary activity, however, that Capen attempted to promote peace. In Capen's mind, peace and missionary activity were inextricably linked. As the head of the American Board of Foreign

Missions he worked to increase missionary funding, arguing that Christian missionaries were the most important force for peace in the world.

Capen's efforts for peace were clearly rooted in his wish to extend what he called ''Christian institutions'' throughout the world within one generation. Yet his desire to spread Christianity often verged uncomfortably close to a call for the extension of American power and influence in the world. Although he opposed the annexation of the Philippines, Capen lauded the rise of the United States as a ''world power.'' In addressing businessmen, moreover, Capen often based his appeal for peace upon the argument that war disrupted commercial activity overseas. Even up to his death in 1914, Capen never doubted that the spread of ''Christian institutions'' would lead naturally to a *pax Christiana* rather than to the national rivalry and warfare which he abhorred. Appropriately enough, when he died in China, Capen was on a world tour as a representative of both the World Peace Foundations and the American Board of Foreign Missions.

Bibliography:

A. ''Foreign Missions and World Peace,'' *World Peace Foundation Pamphlet Series*, No. 7 (Boston, 1912); ''Four Years of the Laymen's Movement,'' *Missionary Review* (May, 1911); ''What Christianity Is Doing for the World,'' *Missionary Review* (June, 1914).

B. Chauncy J. Hawkins, *Samuel Billings Capen* (Boston, 1914); C. Roland Marchland, *The American Peace Movement and Social Reform 1898-1918* (Princeton, 1972); David S. Patterson, *Toward a Warless World: The Travail of the American Peace Movement, 1887-1914* (Bloomington, 1976).

John E. Hollitz

CAPITINI, Aldo (23 December 1899, Perugia, Italy—19 October 1968, Perugia). *Education*: Univ. of Pisa. *Career*: author, university teacher and administrator, political organizer.

The son of a bell-ringer, Aldo Capitini attended school irregularly in his youth and did not take a university degree until he was nearly thirty. He studied philosophy at the University of Pisa, but could find no teaching job because of his refusal to join the Fascist party. Forced to return to his home in Perugia, Capitini passed the decade of the 1930s in deep economic distress and became a member of the anti-fascist underground, furtively debating with other dissident intellectuals—notably Guido Calogero—the best means of restoring Italy to political sanity. Out of these activities the legendary Partito d'Azione would emerge in the early 1940s, but by that time Capitini had renounced direct political action in favor of a more broadly based cultural reform.

Capitini's first book, *Elementi di un'esperienza religiosa* (1937), which Benedetto Croce read with genuine admiration, already had revealed his Gandhi-inspired preoccupation with nonviolence and religious values. However, after the war he could state unequivocally how the triumph of fascism and the complicity of both liberalism and Catholicism in that triumph had made it imperative for Italians to find completely novel answers to the country's political problems.

The palpable failure of the right and the inability of the center to offer Italy anything new made a turn to the left unavoidable, but Capitini abstained from an open avowal of either communism or socialism. In the strict sense of the word he was a political agnostic, believing in no party line. Instead, following national liberation and his own release from a Fascist prison in 1943, Capitini established Centri di orientamento sociale (Centers for Social Thought) (COS), in numerous Italian cities. These centers became assemblies for the discussion of the political, moral, and cultural issues facing postwar Italy; in them he hoped to hear the true voice of a free and democratic Italy, but the din of the Cold War soon rendered that voice inaudible.

He then turned his boundless energies as a publicist and political organizer to the problem of the Cold War. With the fall of fascism, Capitini was able at last to find work in the university, becoming secretary of Pisa's Scuola Normale and free docent in moral philosophy there as well. In 1956, the same year that he won the Premio Salenta for poetry, the long frustrated and underemployed professor was awarded a chair of pedagogy, first in Cagliari and then, for the last three years of his life, in Perugia. From this increasingly secure professional base he was able to pursue the broad reform objectives outlined in *Elementi di un'esperienza religiosa*, now made incalculably more pressing by Italy's wartime catastrophe and by the icy presence of the Cold War. After founding the Centro di orientamento religioso (Center for Religious Thought) (COR) in 1952, which became the vehicle for a spirited public campaign against the conservative policies of the Catholic Church, Capitini established the Center for Nonviolence along with a review based on its principles, *Azione nonviolenta*. He became deeply involved in numerous reform movements, including Danilo Dolci's work with the disinherited of Sicily, but the threat of global conflict took precedence over all of his other concerns. To alert the public to its mortal danger, he organized a peace march on September 24, 1961 from Perugia to Assisi. In his last years Capitini enjoyed a growing celebrity as the head and soul of Italy's peace movement, a living link between the antifascism of the 1930s and the antimilitarism of the 1960s. He continued to write and to campaign tirelessly for peace until his death in 1968.

Bibliography:

A. *Discuto la religione di Pio XII* (Milano, 1957); *Elementi di un'esperienza religiosa* (Bari, 1937 and 1947); *Italia nonviolenta* (Bologna, 1949); *L'Obbiezione di conscienza in Italia* (Manduria, 1959); *Il Potere di tutti* (Florence, 1969); *Le Tecniche della non violenza* (Milan, 1967); *Vita religiosa* (Bologna, 1942).

B. F. Alasia, ed., "Lettere di Aldo Capitini a Danilo Dolci" in *Il Ponte*, 25 (1969); Giovanni Cacioppo, ed., *Il Messaggio di Aldo Capitini* (Manduria, 1977); Carlo Francovich, *La Resistenza a Firenza* (Florence, 1961).

Richard Drake

CAPY, Marcelle (16 March 1891, Cherbourg, Manche, France—6 January 1962, Pradines, Lot, France). *Education*: Lycées of Cahors and Toulon, Univ. of Toulouse. *Career*: journalist, novelist, and public speaker.

The daughter of a naval officer, Marcelle Capy became one of France's most ardent feminists and socialists. Her childhood, spent on her maternal grandfather's farm, left her with lifelong memories of the joy of nature and the pleasures of rural ways. While a student at the University of Toulouse, she fell under the influence of France's most eloquent socialist, *Jean Jaurès, who spoke there in 1911 on the work of *Leo Tolstoy. After graduation, she moved to Paris where she established her reputation as a journalist who specialized in exposing the plight of the working class. She visited factories and shops and talked with employees firsthand. Her lengthy series of articles for the labor newspaper *La Bataille syndicaliste* in 1913–14 revealed the harsh working conditions, low wages, wretched housing, and blighted lives that the female proletariat endured.

With the outbreak of war in 1914, Capy turned her attention to the hardships that the conflict produced on working class women deprived of their husbands. Even though many of her moving articles were heavily censored, she brought home to a wide audience how great the cost of war was to the civilian population. Capy also insisted that the German people suffered no less as a result of the fighting. Her strong sense of internationalism led her to break publicly with *La Bataille syndicaliste*, which supported the war effort of the Union sacrée government. She identified herself completely with the pacifism of *Romain Rolland, who contributed a preface to her collection of articles, *Une Voix de femme dans la melée* (1916). Capy continued her attack on the war in *Le Journal du peuple* and *La Vague*, a socialist and feminist newspaper which she founded along with the deputy *Pierre Brizon, whom she later married.

Peace saw no end to her compaign against war. In the daily press and in her many novels, Capy stressed the painful effects that international conflicts had upon women. Her numerous speaking engagements in the 1920s and 1930s took her to all parts of France, western Europe, North Africa, and the United States. She won the reputation of being an eloquent advocate of peace and international disarmament. An early member of the Ligue internationale des combattants de la paix (International League of Fighters for Peace) founded by *Victor Meric, she became its president and used its newspaper, *La Patrie humaine*, to rally people of good will to the cause of peace.

During World War II she retired to the quiet of her childhood home in southwestern France. Only in 1944 did Capy return to journalism when she contributed to the weekly newspaper *Germinal*, which attempted to build understanding between Frenchmen and Germans. After the Liberation, she turned her full attention to the struggle for women's rights and to efforts designed to improve human morality. Her frequent lecture tours showed that she had lost none of her eloquence. In her last years she took no further role in the pacifist movement.

Bibliography:

A. *L'Amour roi* (Paris, 1925); *A bas les armes*! (Paris, 1933); *De l'amour du clocher à l'amour du monde* (Paris, 1932); *Des hommes passèrent* (Paris, 1930); *La Defense de la vie* (Paris, 1920); *Femmes seules* (Paris, 1938); *L'Homme et son destin* (Paris, 1950); *Une Voix de femme dans la melée* (Paris, 1916).

B. Henri Temerson, *Biographie des principales personnalitiés françaises décédées au cours de l'année 1962* (Paris, 1964); *Le Monde*, January 10, 1962.

James Friguglietti

CARNEGIE, Andrew (25 November 1835, Dunfermline, Scotland—11 August 1919, Lenox, MA). *Education:* five years, Rolland Street grammar school, Dunfermline. *Career*: telegrapher, 1849–53; Pennsylvania Railroad official, 1853–65; iron and steel industrialist, 1864–1901; philanthropist, 1901–11.

Born into a radical Chartist family of shoemakers and weavers, Andrew Carnegie regarded himself as a pacifist and internationalist from his earliest youth. Emigrating from Scotland to Pennsylvania with his parents when he was twelve after the failure of the great Chartist demonstration in 1848, young Carnegie wrote letters to his relatives in Scotland extolling America's republicanism and lack of militarism, claiming that the United States had the Charter that British radicals had sought for in vain.

Having served briefly in the Civil War, Carnegie would later claim that "I am not a 'peace at any price' man much as I would like to be. I believe it was my duty to be on the field at Bull Run." Nevertheless his interest in world peace through international accord remained a fixed tenet of his personal philosophy during the thirty years that he developed his company into the largest steel manufactory in the world. In the 1880s he became an enthusiastic supporter of the Continental Union movement, founded by Goldwin Smith. He went beyond Smith's proposal for a union of Canada and the United States, however, and envisioned a day in which England, Scotland, Ireland, and Wales would also become states in the Union—a true "reunion of race," which would establish an everlasting *pax Anglicae*. To achieve this goal, Britain must first dispense with the monarchy and the nobility and disestablish the Anglican church. Carnegie hoped to propagandize these revolutionary international ideas through a chain of newspapers which he purchased in England in 1884. Under the general management of Samuel Storey, the network proved a dismal business failure and Carnegie scuttled the project in 1886. He did not, however, abandon his dream of a world order in which war would be forever banished through a permanent entente of the great powers.

By 1900 Carnegie was moving ever closer to becoming a "peace at any price man." He had vigorously supported Edward Atkinson's Anti-Imperialist League in opposition to the United States' acquisition of the Philippine Islands and Puerto Rico, even offering to buy the Philippines from the United States to give the islands their independence. After selling Carnegie Steel in 1901, Carnegie was to use a large portion of his fortune in a quest for world peace. From 1903–14 he endowed four trusts or foundations and built three imposing buildings, "temples of peace," as he liked to call them, all in the cause of international peace, at a cost to himself of over twenty-five million dollars. Two of these foundations, to be sure, the Simplified Spelling Board under the direction of Melvil Dewey, and the Hero Fund, seemed quite peripheral to the cause of peace by many of Carnegie's pacifist friends. He, however, regarded them as central. By simplifying the spelling of the English language, he hoped to make English the *lingua franca* of the world. And through his Hero Fund, with separate organizations in most of the countries of western Europe and the United States, he hoped to replace the heroes of the battlefield with the civilian heroes who saved lives rather than taking them. His other two foundations, the Carnegie Endowment for International Peace, endowed in 1910 with ten million dollars, and the Church Peace Union, founded in 1914 with two million, were to make more significant contributions to the cause. The former under the initial direction of +Elihu Root and +Nicholas Murray Butler was much more conservative in its objectives than many of the radical pacifists of the day would have liked. The Endowment has persistently emphasized peace through education, international understanding, and the development of international law.

Carnegie's three ''temples of peace,'' were the Pan-American Union Building in Washington, the Palace of Peace at The Hague, and the Central American Court of Justice in Cartago, Costa Rica. All three buildings were a tangible expression of Carnegie's faith in arbitration and international law. The high point of his lifelong campaign for international peace, Carnegie believed would come in an international summit meeting which would be held in May 1910 at Wrest Park with Kaiser Wilhelm II, King Edward VII, and former president +Theodore Roosevelt. Carnegie, who had through extraordinary efforts arranged for this meeting, had the naive belief that by getting these three men to sit down at a table, world peace could be forever guaranteed. The unexpected death of Edward VII only a week before the scheduled conference dashed Carnegie's hopes for an immediate realization of his dream.

The outbreak of World War I four years later was the final blow to Carnegie's optimistic belief that war would ''soon be discarded as disgraceful to civilized men.'' Even then, however, Carnegie did not give up all hope. He had presented a proposal for a ''league of peace'' in 1905, later suggested the need for an international police force for a league of nations, and he supported conferences and educational programs prior to 1914 that called for arbitration and the advancement of law. He thus enthusiastically supported +Woodrow Wilson's concept of an international organization and was delighted that Wilson had accepted Carnegie's suggested name for such a body. Mercifully for Carnegie, he died three months before the U.S. Senate rejected the treaty which had incorporated Wilson's and Carnegie's best hopes for world peace.

Bibliography:

A. *Autobiography of Andrew Carnegie* (Boston, 1920); *Empire of Business* (New York, 1902); *The Gospel of Wealth* (New York, 1901); *Problems of To-Day* (New York, 1908); *Round the World* (New York, 1884); *Triumphant Democracy* (New York, 1893).

B. Burton J. Hendrick, *The Life of Andrew Carnegie* (2 vols., New York, 1932);

Harold Livesay, *Andrew Carnegie and the Rise of Big Business* (Boston, 1975); Joseph F. Wall, *Andrew Carnegie* (New York, 1970).

Joseph Frazier Wall

CASGRAIN, Therese Forget (10 July 1896, Ste Irenne-les-Bains, Quebec, Canada—3 November 1981, Montreal). *Education*: Convent of the Dames du Sacré-Coeur, Sault-aux-Récollets. *Career*: suffragist, feminist, politician, senator, and peace activist.

Therese Casgrain was born and raised within the economic and political elite of Quebec. Her father, Rodolphe Forget, was one of the province's most prominent financiers and a Conservative member of the federal parliament. Piérre Casgrain, whom she married in 1916, became a Liberal member of the House of Commons, Speaker of the House, and a judge of the Quebec Superior Court. Therese Casgrain became a political activist when, in 1921, she joined the suffrage movement in Quebec. Although women had gained the federal franchise in 1918 and in all other provinces by 1922, conservative Quebec resisted the tide. In 1928 she became president of La Ligue des droits de la femme (League for the Rights of Women) which she led through the successful conclusion of the suffrage battle in 1940. She also led the League in battles for women's rights in the professions, changes in the Civil Code, and the defense of striking textile workers.

Although she first ran for office as an independent Liberal in 1942, she had already established ties to the social democrats of the Co-operative Commonwealth Federation (CCF). She joined the CCF in 1946, became a national vice-president in 1948, Quebec leader in 1951, and was a member of the first National Council of the CCF's successor, the New Democratic party (NDP).

Casgrain did not become a leader in the antiwar effort until the summer of 1960 when the Voice of Women (VOW) was founded as a broadly based, women's peace group. She organized the Quebec branch in February 1961 and the following year was elected national president of VOW. Although she served for less than a year, her term was significant in the organization's history. The VOW strongly opposed acquisition of nuclear weapons by Canada and condemned the Liberal party of +Lester Pearson when it changed course and favored acquisition of nuclear warheads for the Bomarc missiles. Some of VOW's founders resigned either because of their close links to the Liberal party or because they believed this was a break with the peace group's nonpartisan basis. Although Casgrain's firm antinuclear position was sustained by the vast majority of VOW members, the organization itself became the target of red-baiting and never again received the general acclaim which had greeted its initial formation.

Casgrain resigned as VOW president to stand as an NDP peace candidate in the federal election of April 1963. Following her defeat she continued to work with VOW and was a delegate to several international meetings. In 1964 she was among a group of antinuclear demonstrators arrested in Paris. She was also an early opponent of American intervention in Vietnam and assumed the role of president of Quebec Medical aid for Vietnam. When her old friend Pierre Trudeau named her to the Senate in October 1970, she used her new position to question his government's policy on the use of Canadian-made defoliants and napalm in Vietnam.

Therese Casgrain made good use of her wit, charm, and femininity in a wide range of social causes. She contributed these qualities along with aristocratic respectability to some of the most important protest movements of modern Canada, especially the campaign against war.

Bibliography:

A. *A Woman in a Man's World* (Toronto, 1972).

Stephen Jay Scheinberg

CATCHPOOL, Thomas Corder Pettifor (15 July 1883, Leicester, England—16 September 1952, Monte Rosa, Switzerland). *Education*: Sidcot (1898–1900) and Bootham (1900–02) Schools; B.Sc. in Engineering, Univ. of London, 1908. *Career*: inspector and superintendent, Great Eastern Railway, 1905–11; architect, planner, business manager, Greenfield Garden Village, 1912–14, 1920–31; secretary, Friends Service Council, Berlin, 1931–36; treasurer, Peace Pledge Union, 1944–48.

Pacifism was for Corder Catchpool a natural by-product of his traditional Quaker upbringing, though he does not seem to have actively participated in antimilitarist campaigns in his youth. When the Great War began, his desire to aid its victims drew him into the Friends Ambulance Unit (FAU), a volunteer corps organized and financed by Quakers.

After serving eighteen months in France—during which time he was awarded the Mons Star and became FAU Adjutant—Catchpool resigned from the Unit as a protest against the introduction of compulsory military service. Returning to Britain, he joined the No-Conscription Fellowship and became active in the war resistance movement. Called to the colors in January 1917, Catchpool declared himself a conscientious objector and asked for absolute exemption from all military service. When this was denied and he refused to accept any form of alternative service, he was, despite his past record, sentenced to four prison terms, serving two years at hard labor before his release in April 1919.

A brief postwar stint with a Quaker relief mission in Germany ended in serious illness, compensated for by the fact that he married his nurse, Gwendolen Southall. The Catchpools spent the next decade quietly, developing and managing the Greenfield Garden Village at Darwen. But in 1931, with their four young children, they moved to Berlin where Catchpool became joint-secretary of the Friends International Centre. They remained in Germany until 1936, witnessing the rise and triumph of Adolf Hitler, attempting, unsuccessfully, to establish a dialogue with the Nazis, and working on behalf of the victims of persecution.

Returning to England for his children's sake, Catchpool continued his efforts to reconcile, and perhaps civilize, Nazi Germany. He served as interpreter for both *George Lansbury's peace mission in 1937 and, a year later, for *Clifford Allen's attempt to resolve the German-Czech crisis by personal intervention. During this period, he also engaged in relief work among the destitute populace of the Sudeteland, receiving the Order of the White Lion from the Czech Government for his humanitarian labors.

The invasion of Poland brought a bitter end to Catchpool's efforts to preserve the peace, but he never waivered in either his pacifism or his desire for service. The latter found expression in volunteer work for bombing victims and the former through a place on Central Committee for Conscientious Objectors, a major role in organizing the Bombing Restriction Committee, and a term as treasurer of the Peace Pledge Union (1944–48).

After 1945 the Catchpools again took up relief work in Germany. Corder also returned to peace work, serving with the National Peace Council, the Friends Peace Committee, and the Fellowship of Reconciliation until his untimely death while climbing Monte Rosa in September 1952.

Corder Catchpool's witness for peace was largely expressed through his "extraordinary power of loving and caring." His chief emphasis as a peacemaker was on the development of personal relationships as a means of illustrating that nations like individuals could overcome barriers of language, culture, religion, and politics to unite in common humanity. Thus his leadership in the international peace movement was based not primarily upon organizations he founded or directed, but upon the example of his quiet, gentle "living out" the message of peace in the brotherhood of man.

Bibliography:

A. *Letters of a Prisoner* (London, 1941); *On Two Fronts* (London, 1918).

B. Jean M. Greaves, *Corder Catchpool* (London, 1953); William R. Hughes, *Indomitable Friend* (London, 1956).

C. T. Corder Catchpool Collection, Swarthmore College Peace Collection, Swarthmore College.

Thomas C. Kennedy

CATT, Carrie Chapman (9 January 1859, Ripon, WI—9 March 1947, New Rochelle, NY). *Education*: B.S., Iowa State Coll., 1880. *Career*: principal, Mason City, Iowa High School, 1881–83, superintendent of schools, Mason City, 1883–85, assistant editor, *Mason City Republican*, 1885–86, chair, Organization Committee, National American Woman Suffrage Association, 1900–4, 1915–20, chair, Committee on the Cause and Cure of War, 1925–32; educator, women's suffrage leader, and pacifist.

Although best known as a preeminent leader of the struggle for women's suffrage in the United States, Carrie Chapman Catt was also an activist in the cause of peace.

During World War I Catt took a stand that pleased neither super-patriots nor pacifists. In January 1915 she assisted *Jane Addams in founding the Woman's Peace party. Nevertheless, when the United States entered the war, she urged women to support it. Her reasoning seems to have been that women's backing for the U.S. role in the conflict would advance the prospects for their obtaining the vote, both because they would be viewed as responsible and because a war for "democracy" would lead inevitably to extension of the suffrage. Even so, Catt refused to bow to the war hawks by scuttling the suffrage issue "for the duration," as had been done in Great Britain. For insisting that suffrage was the "number one war job" of the National American Woman's Suffrage Association, Catt was publicly attacked as unpatriotic and pro-German.

Those who suspected that Catt was suspiciously pro-peace could find considerable evidence in subsequent years. Dismayed by American rejections of the League of Nations, Catt told a 1921 meeting of the new League of Women Voters that women must use their political power to put an end to war. In 1924 she was instrumental in securing the backing of nine women's organizations for a Conference on the Cause and Cure of War, which met in Washington the following year. The conference created a Committee on the Cause and Cure of War, which continued to carry on peace agitation in the United States until its demise in 1939. Catt served as its chair from 1925 to 1932.

For helping to meld the women's movement with the peace movement, Catt once again stirred up considerable opposition. She was accused of Communist leanings and faced new difficulties in her dealings with politicians. Nevertheless, Catt persisted with her peace concerns and helped organize the National Peace Conference, an antiwar coalition of some thirty men's and women's organizations. Beginning in the mid–1930s, she participated in efforts to protest against the policies of Germany's Nazi government, particularly its persecution of the Jews.

In ill health, she spent her final days reflecting upon and writing about women's role in the peace movement.

Bibliography:

B. Mary Gray Peck, *Carrie Chapman Catt* (New York, 1944); NAW, I, 309–13; NYT, March 10, 1947.

C. Carrie Chapman Catt Papers, Library of Congress, Washington, D. C.

Ann Gleeson-Lindenfelder

CATTANEO, Carlo (15 June 1801, Milan, Italy—5 February 1869, Castagnola di Lugano, Switzerland). *Education*: graduated, Liceo Santo Alessandro, Milan, and Univ. of Pavia, 1824. *Career*: teacher; publicist; revolutionist of 1848; editor, *Il Politecnico*, 1839–44, 1861–63; and author.

Before the Revolution of 1848, Carlo Cattaneo was a moderate liberal reformer, willing to cooperate with the Habsburg government. But the collapse of the Habsburg administration in Lombardy cast him in the role of revolutionary leader and of opponent of Sardinian aims in northern Italy. Distrusted by Milanese patricians who favored union with the Kingdom of Sardinia, he left the revolutionary government. The restoration of Habsburg military power forced him into exile in nearby Switzerland. He supported himself by teaching and writing, and together with the publisher Alessandro Repetti, he set up a major center of revolutionary propaganda, the Tipografia Elvetica. Cattaneo and his collaborators edited and published scores of works on the Revolution of 1848 in Italy as well as the works of leading democratic thinkers in other countries.

The experiences of 1848–49 brought Cattaneo closer to the militants of Italy's nationalist movement, but he never accepted Giuseppe Mazzini's notion of a centralized republic. Like his friend and fellow Lombard Giuseppe Ferrari, Cattaneo argued that the finest chapter in Italy's history had been the independent city-states of the Renaissance. Lacking a tradition of monarchical, centralized government, an independent Italy could best flourish, he thought, in the form of a federation of autonomous republics of the Swiss type.

Those same practical experiences and historical considerations led Cattaneo to argue that a new, independent Italy must not have a standing army such as those of the Habsburg and other nondemocratic states. Instead, he advocated for the new Italy a militia of the Swiss type. This was to be a force in which all adult male citizens would serve for a limited period of time, thus acquiring the necessary skills to defend their country, but without ever becoming professional soldiers divorced from the values and customs of the civilian population.

In the 1850s, Cattaneo also developed the concept of European federation of democratic republics, which he called "the United States of Europe." Despite the failure of the revolutions of 1848 in Italy, Germany, and Hungary, Cattaneo was convinced that European society was moving inevitably in a democratic direction and that newly independent nations, having broken away from multinational, dynastic empires, would choose democratic and republican forms of government. The new republics, however, would need to provide for common defense against reactionary powers. They would also need to pool and integrate their economic resources in order to bring about economic development and to provide for all citizens that minimum level of economic security and well-being without which a democratic policy could not sustain itself.

Cattaneo's views were widely known among Italian intellectuals both before and after the unification of Italy. However, he declined the opportunity to influence directly the political system of united Italy. Elected to Parliament in 1860, he refused to take his seat, partly because he did not wish to leave his teaching position in Lugano and partly because, as a confirmed republican, he did not wish to take the required oath of loyalty to the new King of Italy. In the latter part of the nineteenth century, however, Cattaneo's federalist and democratic ideas were kept alive by his intellectual disciples Mauro Macchi, Gabriele Rosa, and Arcangelo Ghisleri. The political philosophy of Cattaneo became a source of inspiration and a rallying point for all Italian intellectuals who advocated more democratic political institutions for their country within the context of a secular and cosmopolitan European culture.

Bibliography:

A. *Epistolario*, ed. by Rinaldo Caddeo (4 vols., Florence, 1949–56); *Scritti economici*, ed. by Alberto Bertolino (3 vols., Florence, 1956); *Scritti filosofici, letterari e vari*, ed. by Franco Alessio (Florence, 1963); *Scritti politici*, ed. by M. Boneschi (4 vols., Florence,

1964–65); *Scritti storici e geografici*, ed. by Gaetano Salvemini and Ernesto Sestan (4 vols., Florence, 1957–67).

B. Luigi Ambrosoli, *La Formazione di Carlo Cattaneo* (Milan and Naples, 1959); Alessandro Levi, "Il pensiero federalistico di Cattaneo," *Il Ponte*, (1946), II, 110–19. Clara M. Lovett, *Carlo Cattaneo and the Politics of the Risorgimento* (The Hague, 1972).

Clara M. Lovett

CECIL, Edgar Algernon Robert Gascoyne. See *Biographical Dictionary of Internationalists*.

CERESOLE, Pierre (17 August 1879, Lausanne, Switzerland—23 October 1945, Le Daley-Lutry, Vaud, Switzerland). *Education*: engineering diploma, ETH (Technical Institute), Zurich, 1901; Ph.D., Univ. of Zurich, 1903; additional studies in Göttingen and Munich, 1903–8. *Career*: engineer, Brown-Boveri, Baden, 1915–18; secondary school teacher, mainly in La Chaux-de-Fonds, 1918–45; pacifist organizer, writer, and lecturer.

Rejecting a professorship at the Technical Institute in Zurich in 1909, Pierre Ceresole lived abroad until 1914 in the United States, Hawaii, and Japan. His pacifist sentiments crystallized after his return to Europe. A major factor in Ceresole's decision to support the peace movement was the imprisonment of John Baudraz in 1915 for his religiously motivated draft evasion. Although he had privately reflected on the problems of the State and established Christianity, the Baudraz conviction convinced Ceresole that the Christian commandment of brotherly love forbade any use of violence and that he should henceforth publicly and without compromise stand up for peace. Desiring to act upon this conviction, he refused to pay the tax required of those exempted from military duty, and he continued to refuse to pay the tax until his death, despite spending many weeks in prison for his action.

During World War I, Ceresole recruited others to his pacifist cause with lectures. In 1917 he gave a talk entitled "Religion et patriotisme" at the annual meeting of Christian Socialists in which he condemned Switzerland's policy of armed neutrality as an expression of national egoism. He demanded in its place a "peaceful revolution" sustained by the spirit of authentic Christianity and leading to an immediate and unilateral disarmament.

His reading of *Ralph Waldo Emerson and William James led Ceresole to think about alternative military service in which opponents of war could perform constructive work for peace. At meetings of the Fellowship of Reconciliation in Holland, he found followers who helped him put his ideas into practice. The first international alternative service program took place at Esnes near Verdun at which men from various European countries performed reconstruction work. On the national level, Ceresole worked with *Leonhard Ragaz in 1922 to introduce a petition (later rejected by Parliament) which demanded alternative civilian service for conscientious objectors. From 1924–26 Ceresole served as secretary of the newly founded Schweizerischen Zentralstelle für Friedensarbeit (Swiss Coordinating Office for Peace), but his primary interest was in the International Civilian Service which he tirelessly continued to build during the interwar period. After 1924 Ceresole regularly organized civilian service with international participation: first in Switzerland, then also in Liechtenstein, France, and England and from 1934–37 in India, with *Mohandas Ghandi's support.

The Second World War curtailed the activity of the International Civilian Service, but Ceresole again questioned the policy of neutrality and national defense, as he had done 25 years earlier, undeterred by his prison sentences.

Bibliography:

A. *L'Armée suisse–42 questions* (Basel, 1931); *Une Autre Patrie* (Lausanne, 1918); *Religion et patriotisme* (Lausanne, 1917); *Vivre sa vérité* (Neuchâtel, 1950; 2nd. rev. ed., Neuchâtel, 1967).

B. Daniel Anet, *Pierre Ceresole la passion de la paix* (Neuchâtel, 1969); Alfred Bietenholz-Gerhard, *Pierre Ceresole* (Bad Pyrmont, 1962); Hélène Monastier, et. al., *Pierre Ceresole d'apres sa correspondance* (Neuchâtel, 1960).

Urs Zwahlen
Trans. by Robert C. Reimer

CHACE, Elizabeth Buffum (9 December 1806, Providence, RI—12 December 1899, Central Falls, RI). *Education*: attended local schools in Smithfield, RI and Pomfret, CT; Friends Boarding School, Providence, RI, 1822. *Career*: vice-president, American Anti-Slavery Society, 1865–70; president, Rhode Island Woman Suffrage Association, 1870–92; president, American Woman Suffrage Association, 1882; abolitionist, woman suffrage advocate, and pacifist.

Elizabeth Chace was an abolitionist who advocated peaceful means in achieving emancipation. Influenced by her father, Arnold Buffum, founder and first president of the New England Anti-Slavery Society, *William Lloyd Garrison, and Wendell Phillips, Chace developed her abolitionist pacifism in the 1830s. As president of the Female Anti-Slavery Society of Fall River (MA), she steered the society toward "moral, peaceful and lawful means" in eradicating human bondage. In 1843 she resigned her membership in the Society of Friends because of its hostility to Garrisonian abolitionism and slowly drifted away from organized religion. She joined Garrison's New England Non-Resistance Society and derided those who claimed righteous authority in serving the state as a soldier. In 1846 her irenic views carried her toward vitriolic criticism of capital punishment which she described as a relic of barbarism.

Except for ambivalent support of John Brown's 1859 raid at Harper's Ferry, Virginia, Chace's pacifism fully emerged during the Civil War years. Unlike most antebellum peace advocates, she did not embrace the Civil War as just means toward noble ends. Her antiwar advocacy perdured throughout the carnage. She engaged in poignant correspondence with William Lloyd Garrison in 1862 in which they discussed parental strategy in keeping their sons from enlisting or being drafted. Chace prevented her two unionist sons, Samuel and Arnold, from joining the muster. She was not a supporter of Abraham Lincoln as long as abolition was eschewed as a war aim and depicted the president as a tool of ambitious, intriguing men who tolerated union with slavery. Early in the war she sent petitions to Lincoln urging him to proclaim liberation of the slaves as a war aim. In *My Anti-Slavery Reminiscences* (1891), she bemoaned the senselessness of the Civil War in which "millions of treasure were wasted, young manhood bled on the battlefield, and mothers' hearts were rent and torn."

After the war Elizabeth Chace continued to take an interest in a variety of reforms. She served as vice-president of the American Anti-Slavery Society (1865–70) and as president of both the Rhode Island Woman Suffrage Association (1870–92) and the American Woman Suffrage Association (1882). Her antiwar activism also deepened and intensified. She joined the Rhode Island Radical Peace Society and convoked antiwar assemblies throughout the state. She strongly supported the efforts of *Alfred H. Love to launch a nationwide peace movement and became a champion of his Universal Peace Union. She maintained her pacifism until her death at the age of ninety-three.

Bibliography:

A. *Two Quaker Sisters*, with Lucy Buffum Lovell (New York, 1937), includes *My Anti-Slavery Reminiscences* (1891).

B. Lillie Buffum Chace Wyman and Arthur Crawford Wyman, *Elizabeth Buffum Chace 1806–1899: Her Life and Environment* (2 vols., Boston, 1914).

C. Elizabeth Buffum Chace (selected documents), Brown University Library.

Peter N. Kirstein

CHALLAYE, Félicien (1 November 1875, Lyon, Rhône, France—26 April 1967, Paris). *Education*: Lycée of Lyon; licence ès-lettres, Univ. of Lyon, 1894; agrégation de philosophie, Ecole Normale Supérieure, 1897; Univ. of Berlin, 1898–99. *Career*: teacher, journalist, and polemicist.

Few individuals spent as many years fighting for peace as Félicien Challaye, whose long life, enormous energy, literary ability, and oratorical power made him one of France's leading pacifists.

Born into a middle-class Protestant family, Challaye early showed signs of promise and expressed his desire to become a philosopher. His ascent through the French school system was capped by his studies at the Ecole Normale Supérieure, where he made friends with Charles Peguy and was converted to socialism. After passing his agrégation in philosophy, Challaye was rewarded with a scholarship to the University of Berlin (1898–99) and a travel grant that took him around the world (1899–1901), enabling him to visit the Orient. He returned to France an ardent devotee of Japanese culture and an ardent foe of French imperialism. Challaye then began his teaching career, but he also devoted himself to popular education, socialism, and anticolonialism. A mission to the French Congo in 1905 further convinced him of the evils of European rule over native peoples, whose demands for independence he championed throughout his life. A loyal follower of *Jean Jaurès, Challaye was deeply shocked by the Socialist leader's assassination in 1914.

Mobilized in 1914, he spent two years at the front, fighting bravely in the trenches. His wartime experiences left him with an abiding horror of war. His combat was cut short when the government sent him on a mission to the Orient in 1917 and again in 1919. With the return of peace, Challaye returned to the classroom, published widely on philosophy, and devoted himself to preventing a new war. He firmly believed that it was essential to eliminate national hatred and establish fraternity among peoples, especially the French and Germans. He condemned the Treaty of Versailles and the harsh policies of Raymond Poincaré. Becoming one of the most eloquent speakers for peace, Challaye presented countless talks and wrote innumerable articles for a wide variety of newspapers. In 1931 he joined the Ligue internationale des combattants de la paix (International League of Fighters for Peace) and later served as its president. When the Nazis came to power in Germany, Challaye more than ever grew concerned about maintaining peace and removing all causes of conflict between France and the Reich. He accepted German reoccupation of the Rhineland, the Austrian Anschluss, and the takeover of Czechoslovakia on the grounds that Hitler was only seeking justice for his people and undoing the inequitable settlement of 1919. An integral pacifist, Challaye believed that even a bad peace was preferable to a new war and that everything possible should be done to avoid bloodshed. He did not hesitate to sign the manifesto *Paix immédiate* in September 1939, calling for an end to hostilities. For this he was threatened with prosecution by the Edouard Daladier government but escaped prison.

During World War II, Challaye contributed to several newspapers, among them *L'Atelier* and *Germinal*, praising the internationalism of Jean Jaurès, denouncing colonialism, and calling for Franco-German understanding. After the Liberation, Challaye was tried for collaboration, but eventually acquitted. He was, however, blacklisted by the National Council of Writers. Undaunted, he resumed his work on behalf of world peace, contributing to such pacifist organs as *La Voie de la paix* and *L'Union pacifiste*. He vigorously protested against France's involvement in colonial wars and campaigned strenuously for disarmament. Challaye remained active until his death, leaving behind an enviable record of achievement.

Bibliography:

A. *La Chine, le Japon et les puissances* (Paris, 1938); *Le Congo français* (Paris, 1906); *Jaurès* (Paris, 1936); *Les Origines de la guerre mondiale, Les Responsabilitiés russes et françaises* (Paris, n.d.); *Péguy socialiste* (Paris, 1954); *Pour la paix désarmée même en face de Hitler* (Paris, 1933); *Pour la paix sans aucune réserve* (Paris, 1933); *La Signification morale de la guerre actuelle* (Paris, 1916).

B. A. Alba, "Félicien Challaye," *Annuaire de l' Association amicale des anciens élèves de l'Ecole Normale Supérieure* (Paris, 1958).

James Friguglietti

CHAMBERLAIN, William Joseph (1884, London—25 July 1945, Enfield, England). *Education*: state schools. *Career*: journalist, *The Daily Citizen*, 1912–

15; editor, *The Tribunal*, 1916; owner-editor, *The Town Crier* (Birmingham), 1920–45; lobby correspondent, Labour Party Press Department, 1931–45; author and Christian pacifist.

William J. (Will) Chamberlain was born into appalling poverty, his entire family occupying one room of a slum dwelling. Although his formal education was brief and erratic, Chamberlain satisfied his keen mind and driving ambition to learn by voracious reading. Among the books that most influenced him, Chamberlain gave precedence to the *New Testament* and the works of *Leo Tolstoy, the combination of which converted him to both Christian pacifism and socialism.

Despite his educational handicaps, Chamberlain embarked upon a career in journalism and, in 1912, he joined the staff of *The Daily Citizen*, the first official Labour party newspaper. Among Chamberlain's coworkers was *Clifford Allen who, though of markedly different background (he was a Cambridge man), shared both Chamberlain's pacifism and his membership in the Independent Labour party (ILP). Allen and Chamberlain were among the first to enlist in the No-Conscription Fellowship (NCF), an anticonscription, antiwar organization founded in November 1914 chiefly composed of younger socialists. After the *Daily Citizen* shut down in 1915, Chamberlain's energy and organizational skills were employed as both national organizer for the NCF and editor of its newspaper, *The Tribunal*.

Soon after the introduction of conscription in early 1916, Chamberlain ran afoul of the law when he and others members of the NCF national committee were prosecuted for the publication of a "seditious" leaflet. The two-month sentence Chamberlain eventually served for this conviction was the basis for a rather impish and jocular account of prison life, *A.C.O. in Prison* (1916). But, as time passed and more and more conscientious objectors were consigned to His Majesty's prisons, Will Chamberlain's tone as well as his situation became considerably more serious.

After a brief period at liberty, Chamberlain was returned to jail as an "absolutist" conscientious objector who would accept no exemption from military service that did not permit him to continue his war-resistance activities. Because of this uncompromising stance, Chamberlain spent a total of two and a half years at hard labor. He never judged the period a total loss, however, for it was during this time that he joined the Society of Friends, a religious connection to which he adhered until his death.

After his release, Chamberlain settled in Birmingham where he continued to work in Labour journalism, maintaining close ties with a group which published *The Crusader*, a Christian-socialist pacifist journal. Early in 1921 he became one of the founding members of the No More War Movement (NMWM), a direct successor to the NCF which associated itself with the War Resisters' International. As first NMWM chairman, Chamberlain had to wrestle with the question of whether the organization ought to maintain the purity of its absolute, and isolated, pacifism or cooperate with nonpacifists for the fulfillment of mutually desirable goals. The inability to resolve this dilemma ensured not only that the NMWM would remain small in numbers but that even the relatively few who did join could not agree on the nature of "true" pacifism. Seeing the interwar peace movement divided by the same sort of disputes that had so weakened wartime resistance, Chamberlain eventually opted for the idea of collaboration among peace advocates who followed the dictates of their individual consciences while working to prevent war. Such a view was far too permissive for many of Chamberlain's pacifist comrades and he gradually drifted away from the extreme left of the peace movement toward the rather nebulous center which could be supported by so disparate a body as the Labour party. Indeed, by the mid–1930s, after Chamberlain joined the Labour Party Press Department, he came to believe that collective security under the League of Nations was the best means to world peace.

Although Will Chamberlain played no significant part in pacifist activities during the last decade of his life, he remained a strong and sincere peace advocate. Certainly, his courage, energy, and organizational ability contributed much to the shaping and growth of a meaningful modern British peace movement.

Bibliography:

A. *A.C.O. in Prison* (London, [1916]) *Fighting for Peace. The Story of the War Resistance Movement* (London, [1929]); *The Futility of Punishment* (Manchester, 1919).

B. Martin Ceadel, *Pacifism in Britain, 1914–1945* (Oxford, 1980); Thomas C. Kennedy, *The Hound of Conscience* (Fayetteville, AR, 1981); Jo Vellacott, *Bertrand Russell and the Pacifists in the First World War* (New York, 1981).

Thomas C. Kennedy

CHANG Chün-mai (Carsun Chang) (18 January 1887, Chiating, China—23 February 1969, Berkeley, CA). *Education*: B.A., Waseda Univ., 1910; chin-shih (highest state awarded degree), 1910. *Career*: chairman, Chinese Democratic Socialist party, 1932–69; People's Political Council, 1938–47; author, journalist, professor and college president, philosopher, and politician.

Although in 1912 Chang Chün-mai saw the world in Social Darwinist terms, he envisioned a future "state of tranquillity" when relations between nations would be both peaceful and governed by international law. World peace, he wrote, was "not necessarily Utopian." In 1918 Chang translated and published documents involving European peace feelers. He was very much interested in the League of Nations and published +Woodrow Wilson's Fourteen Points speech in Chinese. He attended the Versailles Peace Conference as an unofficial observer, participated in the Conference of Allied Societies for a League of Nations in London in 1919, and joined in the League of Nations Association gathering in Milan. In 1928, he wrote to a German friend that he would be glad to serve as China's representative at the upcoming Conference of the Peace Society.

During World War II Chang occasionally published articles on the prospects for peace. Some of these included a piece on peace feelers, an article on the question of postwar international peace, and a review of Nathaniel Pfeffer's

Basis for Peace in the Far East, all of which appeared in *Tung-fang tsa-chih*. In 1945 he was selected as one of China's delegates to the San Francisco Conference of the United Nations. The Chinese Democratic Socialist party, which he headed, advocated "full participation in the United Nations in order to secure world peace."

Chang saw international questions through the eyes of one primarily concerned with China's "national salvation." In 1907 he helped found the Political Information Society, which called for equal rights for China in foreign relations. When World War I broke out, rather than join a peace movement, he viewed the war's military, diplomatic, and financial aspects as lessons for China. He called for China to join the Allies against Germany, so that she could participate in the future peace conference. When the conference confirmed Japan's hold on Shantung Province, Chang became deeply disillusioned with international law and protested to President Wilson. In the 1930s and 1940s, he fervently opposed Japanese aggression in China.

Although his support of international peace was weakened by his nationalism, this patriotism strengthened his advocacy of domestic peace. He believed in constitutional government with its provisions for peaceful, orderly change. He favored gradualist political solutions and opposed revolution. Revolution, he felt, could only lead to disorder and foreign intervention. During the warlord period, he sought ways to eliminate the military man's political influence and end the constant civil wars. In the 1930s he opposed the Kuomintang's militarism and factionalism. During World War II he joined the united front between the Kuomintang and other parties and criticized Mao Tse-tung and the Chinese Communists for not giving up their separate army and territory. He also participated in efforts to mediate the differences between the Communist party and the Kuomintang that threatened China's peace.

Except for brief periods around 1919 and 1945, Chang was much more of a domestic peace leader than an international one. In an environment racked first by the many battles among the warlords and subsequently by the bloody struggle between the Kuomintang and the Chinese Communists, he was vitally concerned with China's revival and resistance to foreign aggression. Throughout his life, he consistently opposed armed strife and revolution and argued for peaceful, moderate, and gradual solutions to China's problems.

Bibliography:

A. *China and Gandhian India* (Calcutta, 1956); *Chung-hua min-kuo tu-li tzu-chu yü Ya-chou ch'ien-t'u* (Kowloon, 1955); *K'ai-kuo ch'ien-hou yen-lun chi* (Taipei, 1971); *Kuo hsien i* (Shanghai, 1922); *Kuo-nei chan-cheng liu-chiang* (Shanghai, 1924); *Min-tsu fu-hsing chih hsüeh-shu chi-ch'u* (Peip'ing, 1935); *The Third Force in China* (New York, 1952).

B. *Chang Chün-mai chuan-chi tzu-liao* (2 vols., Taipei, 1978); *Chang Chün-mai chuan-chi tzu-liao*, (4 vols. Taipei, 1979); *Chang Chün-mai hsien-sheng ch'i-shih shou-ch'ing chi-nien lun-wen chi* (Taipei, 1956); Chiang Yung-chen, "Chang Chün-mai," in Hu

P'ing-sheng, et al., eds., *Chung-kuo li-tai ssu-hsiang-chia* (Taipei, 1978), 10, 6231–6352; Roger B. Jeans, "Syncretism in Defense of Confucianism: An Intellectual and Political Biography of the Early Years of Chang Chün-mai, 1887–1923," Ph.D. dissertation, The George Washington University, 1974; Chester C. Tan, *Chinese Political Thought in the Twentieth Century* (Garden City, NY, 1971); Wang Hsiao-p'o, gen. ed., *Hsien-tai Chung-kuo ssu-hsiang-chia*, vol. 6: *Ting Wen-chiang yü Chang Chün-mai* (Taipei, 1978).

Roger B. Jeans

CHANNING, William Ellery (April 7, 1780, Newport, RI—October 2, 1842, Boston, MA). *Education*: B.A. Harvard Univ., 1798, D.D., 1804. *Career*: minister, author, abolitionist, and peace leader.

In the turbulent years of reform following the War of 1812, the prominent Unitarian minister, William Ellery Channing, emerged as a leading spokesman for world peace. As one of the most effective writers and lecturers of his generation, he influenced many of his contemporaries to adopt his positions on the subjects of slavery, women's rights, prison reform, education for the masses, and peace. His writings, inspired not only fellow clergymen and intellectuals, but also Senator *Charles Sumner, who was a disciple and espoused many of Channing's causes.

His philosophy about the evil of war and man's proper response to it was a logical outgrowth of his religious beliefs. Believing in the dignity and divinity of man as well as the perfectability of society, Channing sought to translate the teachings of Jesus into concrete action. Aiding *Noah Worcester, he helped to organize the Massachusetts Peace Society in 1815. Other organizations for peace were springing up simultaneously throughout the United States, leading to the formation of a national organization, the American Peace Society, in 1828.

Discourses on War written by Channing in 1816, 1835, and 1838 were widely read and discussed. He wrote in a clear and compelling style dividing his subject into three sections—the miseries, causes, and remedies of war. He departed from more radical peace advocates, like *William Lloyd Garrison, by supporting the concept of defensive war. The radicals believed in the literal interpreation of the scripture, "Resist not evil." Therefore, in their view, no war was justified. This issue split the American Peace Society. Channing articulated the moderate position by stating that while war is a tremendous evil, "national subjugation is a greater evil than a war of defence." A community had the right to defend itself after all other methods of arbitrating a dispute had failed.

Combining Enlightenment practicality with Unitarian idealism, William Ellery Channing, perhaps more than any other of his day, spoke for the majority of Americans seeking to reform society.

Bibliography:

A. *Discourses on War*, ed. by Edwin Mead (Boston, 1903).

B. Devere Allen, *The Fight for Peace* (New York, 1930); Peter Brock, *Pacifism in the United States From The Colonial Era to the First World War* (Princeton, NJ, 1968).

Kay Clontz Starnes

CHANNING, William Henry (25 May 1810, Boston, MA—23 December 1884 London). *Education*: B.A., Harvard Coll., 1829; B.D., Harvard Divinity School, 1833. *Career*: edited: *Western Messenger*, 1835–41, *The Present*, 1844, *The Spirit of the Age*, 1849–50; Unitarian clergyman, author, and reformer.

William Henry Channing stood at the crossroads of many mid-nineteenth century reforms—peace, abolitionism, feminism, and transcendentalism. While an active participant in these movements, his struggle for peace and internationalism is characterized by both a messianic and practical impulse.

The Mexican War, 1846–48, was Channing's principal antiwar crusade. While most Unitarian clergymen opposed the shedding of blood on Mexican soil, Channing went far beyond them when he declared that if he were to participate in this "damnable war," it would be with the Mexican army. He attempted to dissuade Americans from volunteering through the circulation of antiwar manifestoes and pledges.

In 1846 at Faneuil Hall in Boston, he denounced all war as a violation of the human spirit. In the same year he attended the annual meeting of the American Anti-Slavery Society and along with *William Lloyd Garrison and Wendell Phillips, excoriated America's role in the war with Mexico as one of "aggression, of invasion, of conquest." He pledged total resistance to the war in refusing to enlist or to pay any wartime taxes.

At the Unitarian ordination of Thomas Wentworth Higginson (1847), Channing delivered a discourse which adumbrated his emerging internationalism. Peace was imbued with godlike qualities; the Law of Love must be substituted for the despotism of force. He demonstrated his concern for world peace by taking an active role in the League of Universal Brotherhood between 1846 and 1852. He served as an officer of the American branch of the League and lectured extensively on League operations, aims, and projects.

Channing's spiritual internationalism was given full expression in his major peace legacy—the Religious Union of Associationists, 1847–50. Under his leadership, members such as George Ripley and Albert Brisbane worked for a universal "reign of love." Goodwill toward all and peace on earth were specific goals of the Religious Union. In an evangelistic manner, Channing sermonized in Bangor, Maine, Cincinnati, Ohio, and New York on "War," "Oppression and Liberty," and "The Omnipotence of Love." *The Spirit of the Age*, under Channing's editorship, disseminated the Religious Union's views of peace class reconciliation, and world community.

In 1849 he was invited to be a delegate to the Paris Peace Convention, but could not attend. Typical of many antebellum peace leaders, Channing supported the Northern cause during the Civil War as if it were a war upon slavery. His fidelity was rewarded with his appointment as Chaplain of the House of Representatives, 1863–64.

During the postwar period in London, Channing rediscovered his antebellum pacifism. In the 1870s he denounced the Franco-Prussian war as a crime against humanity and progressively viewed war as class inspired conflict between capital and labor.

Bibliography:

A. *Discourse at Ordination of T. W. Higginson* (Boston, 1847).

B. Octavius Brooks Frothingham, *Memoir of William Henry Channing* (Cambridge, MA, 1886); T. W. Higginson biography in Samuel A. Eliot, ed *Heralds of a Liberal Faith* (Boston, 1910).

C. William Henry Channing Papers, Houghton Library, Harvard University and Massachusetts Historical Society.

Peter N. Kirstein

CHAPMAN, Maria Weston (25 July 1806, Weymouth, MA—12 July 1885, Weymouth). *Education*: informal, local schools in Weymouth area and in England. *Career*: educator, antislavery activist, author, and editor.

A member of a prominent Massachusetts family, Maria Weston was steeped in the best Yankee traditions and principles. Physically attractive and intellectually gifted, she employed her considerable organizing and executive abilities, as well as her financial resources, to the cause of social justice for all and human liberation. Her marriage in 1830 to Henry Grafton Chapman ended her teaching career at the Ebenezer Bailey's Young Ladies' High School, but launched an active career in the Boston antislavery and nonresistant movements that continued despite her bearing four children. She proved herself a capable leader among New England abolitionists and established herself as an antislavery editor and author.

Like *William Lloyd Garrison, Chapman's abolitionism merged with her radical pacifism. Garrison's stand within the antislavery movement for women's equal participation nurtured the involvement of many women abolitionists in his nonresistance crusade. Influenced by Garrison, Chapman opposed direct participation in the political system and the sectional compromises of the pre-Civil War era. She became recording secretary of Garrison's New England Non-Resistance Society in 1838 and was chosen a member of the American Anti-Slavery Society's executive committee following the exodus from the 1840 convention by male delegates protesting *Abby Kelley Foster's appointment to the business committee. Chapman employed her literary skills tirelessly in the service of the antislavery cause, editing and writing for Garrisonian periodicals, the *Liberator* and the *National Anti-Slavery Standard*. In addition, between 1839 and 1842 she helped edit the *Non-Resistant*, the first pacifist journal in *ante bellum* America. As a nonresistant Chapman shared the conviction that true social reformation could occur only as individual's renounced violence and took up Christ's way to prepare for the millennial establishment of God's kingdom.

Chapman's loyalty to Garrison's radical segment of the antislavery movement in New England and the illness and death of her husband in 1842 eased her out of the mainstream of abolitionism in the 1840s and out of an active role in the antislavery movement by the late 1840s. She took her children abroad for their education in 1848, one year before the New England Non-Resistance Society expired, and returned in 1855, after the tide of nonresistance within the New England antislavery movement had ebbed. Following Garrison's lead during and after the Civil War, Chapman agreed that the Emancipation Proclamation and ratification of the Thirteenth Amendment rendered the prewar antislavery societies obsolete.

In the postwar years, Chapman remained an ardent Garrisonian and defended the principles of nonresistance. Her presence and persona among reform-minded women, such as the *Grimké sisters, served as a role model for all persons of conviction in unpopular causes.

Bibliography:

A. *Right and Wrong in Boston* (Boston, 1832); *Right and Wrong in Massachusetts* (Boston, 1839); *Ten Years of Experience* (Boston, 1842).

B. Peter Brock, *Pacifism in the United States from Colonial Times to the Present* (Princeton, NJ, 1968), Gerda Lerner, *The Grimké Sisters of South Carolina* (Boston, 1967).

C. Maria Weston Chapman Papers can be found in various collections in the Boston Public Library.

Angela Howard Zophy

CHARPENTIER, Armand (24 January 1864, Brest, Finistère, France—19 June 1949, Paris). *Career*: journalist, novelist, and polemicist.

An established writer before 1914, Armand Charpentier became an active pacifist as a result of World War I. Showing early promise as a writer, he entered journalism during the early years of the Third Republic, contributing to various literary reviews. He came under the influence of the Goncourt brothers and Emile Zola and produced several naturalistic novels dealing with the theme of popular love. He also developed political consciousness when, during the Dreyfus Affair, he joined other prominent intellectuals in signing a petition demanding a new trial for the unjustly convicted army captain. His anticlericalism led him to attack the papacy for its "outdated dogmas" and to align himself with the newly-formed Radical party.

After World War I, in which he took no part, Charpentier dedicated himself to the cause of peace. Like many other pacifists, he assailed former president Raymond Poincaré for provoking a war out of his nationalist desire to recover Alsace-Lorraine. For the same reason, Charpentier denounced the nationalism of European states that had led them to the abyss in 1914. He called for "moral disarmament" and a supernational government that could settle disputes. Along with other intellectuals he signed the "Appeal to Consciences" (1926) denouncing the inequities of the Treaty of Versailles and supported the "Appeal to Good

Sense'' (1928) appealing for international disarmament. Charpentier helped found and contributed to the monthly review *Evolution* (1926–33), which presented a forum for writers from all nations to express their abhorence of war and suggest means of preserving peace.

During the 1930s he warned of the perils of aerochemical warfare that might destroy European civilization in a matter of weeks. An early member of the Ligue International des Combattants de la Paix (International League of Fighters for Peace), Charpentier often wrote for its newspaper *La Patrie humaine* until the outbreak of World War II. His articles criticized French nationalism and pleaded for international understanding, especially with Germany.

After the fall of France, Charpentier resumed his journalistic career, writing in newspapers sympathetic to collaboration such as *Les Nouveaux temps* and *L'Union française*. He also contributed to the short-lived *Germinal* (1944), along with other prewar pacifists in an effort to encourage Franco-German rapprochement. After the Liberation, Charpentier's wartime record barred him from pursuing his writing and he died in obscurity.

Bibliography:

A. *Ce que sera la guerre des gaz* (Paris, 1930); *La Guerre et la patrie* (Paris, 1926); *Historique de l'affaire Dreyfus* (Paris, 1933); *Les Responsabilités de M. Poincaré* (Paris, 1924).

B. *Dictionnaire de biographie française*, VIII, 630–31.

James Friguglietti

CHARTIER, Emile-Auguste. See ALAIN.

CH'EN Kung-po (19 October 1892, Kwangtung Province, China—3 June 1946, Soochow, China). *Education*: graduated, Canton Law Coll., 1917; M.A., Columbia Univ., 1924. *Career*: politician.

After a brief period of association with the Chinese Communist party which he helped organize in 1921 and an interlude of study in America, Ch'en Kung-po became politically active in the left wing of China's Nationalist Political party (Kuomintang) in 1925. The Nationalist movement was divided by sharp factional disputes and when Chiang Kai-shek emerged as the leader of the dominant faction within the Kuomintang in the turbulent years from 1926–28, Ch'en found himself an outsider. He rapidly earned recognition as the chief theoretician of the so-called ''Reorganization Faction'' headed by Chiang Kai-shek's archrival, *Wang Ching-wei. Although Ch'en held several important sounding posts in the Nationalist government, he was effectively isolated from positions of genuine power.

The eight-year war that broke out between China and Japan in 1937 welded Chinese of all political persuasions together in a common spirit of resistance to Japan. The decade-old civil war between Communists and Nationalists was declared at an end so that China could face the invading armies of Japan with a ''united front.'' In December 1938, however, a massive crack appeared in the facade of national unity as Ch'en's political mentor and friend, Wang Ching-wei, defected from Chungking, the Kuomintang's wartime capital, in order to lead a peace movement aimed at reconciling Japan and China.

Wang and Ch'en were convinced that neither China nor Japan could achieve a military victory and that a protracted war would cause untold suffering, devastation, and chaos which would ultimately work to the advantage of the Communists. Wang was hopeful that he could use his own considerable prestige as a statesman of unquestioned integrity and his reputation as a friend of Japan to persuade the Japanese that it was in their interest to settle for peace terms which would satisfy patriotic Chinese. Although Ch'en shared Wang's concern about the dire consequences of a long war, Ch'en was clearly more skeptical than Wang about the ability of Wang's peace movement, operating from a position of weakness in Japanese-occupied China, to extract suitable peace terms from the Japanese. In late 1939, after several months of indecision, Ch'en nevertheless decided to join the peace movement. In the months that followed, it was Ch'en and *Chou Fo-hai who were responsible for much of the difficult bargaining with the Japanese preparatory to the establishment of a collaboration regime, the "Reorganized National Government of the Republic of China," in 1940. Ch'en occupied several posts in this government and succeeded Wang Ching-wei as its head in 1944 when Wang died. Ch'en was brought to trial by the Nationalist government after the end of the war and executed as a traitor in 1946.

Bibliography:

A. "The Basis of Sino-Japanese Cooperation," in *Fundamentals of National Salvation*, ed. by T'ang Leang-li (Shanghai, 1942), 273–96.

B. John H. Boyle, *China and Japan at War, 1937–1945: The Politics of Collaboration* (Stanford, 1972); Gerald E. Bunker, *The Peace Conspiracy: Wang Ching-wei and the China War, 1937–1941* (Cambridge, MA., 1972).

John H. Boyle

CHERTKOV, Vladimir Grigoryevich (3 November 1854, St. Petersburg [now Leningrad]—9 November 1936, Moscow). *Education*: at home under tutors. *Career*: cavalryman, editor, publisher, Christian anarchist, and publicist of Leo Tolstoy's ideas.

Born into a wealthy family of Russian aristocrats, Vladimir Chertkov grew up under the strong influence of his deeply religious mother. This family influence, along with his wide reading, particularly of the Gospels and Feodor Dostoevsky's works, finally led young Chertkov in 1881, at the age of 27, to resign his officer's commission in the Horse Guards Regiment as a result of his conviction that true Christianity was incompatible with military service and war. He then settled on one of his family's estates, living a very simple life, and devoted himself to social and educational work among the peasants.

In 1883 he and *Leo Tolstoy each learned through friends about the strikingly similar course of their religious and social thinking, which is perhaps best described as Christian anarchism. Later that year, the two men met each other and began a close association that lasted until Tolstoy's death in 1910. The first fruits of their collaboration appeared in 1884 when Chertkov with Tolstoy's encouragement established ''Posrednik'' (The Intermediary), a publishing enterprise that made good literature, especially of a moral and religious nature, available to the masses in cheap little booklets.

In 1897 Chertkov's activities, along with other followers of Tolstoy, in behalf of the persecuted religious sect of Dukhobors led to his exile abroad. He and his wife lived for nearly eleven years in England, where he devoted his time largely to propagandizing Tolstoy's ideas and publishing uncensored editions of Tolstoy's works in both English and Russian. After the 1905 Revolution his sentence of exile was lifted and he resettled in Russia in 1908. Following the Soviet Revolution of October 1917, Chertkov had an interview with Vladimir Lenin which resulted on January 4, 1919, in a decree by the Council of People's Commissars recognizing conscientious objection to military service on religious grounds and empowering the United Council of Religious Communities and Groups, an organization of religious pacifists representing Tolstoyans, Mennonites, Baptists, and others, with Chertkov as its president, to adjudge the sincerity of objectors to military service. Apparently never officially rescinded, this decree was inconsistently applied and several scores of executions for conscientious objection to military service took place in Russia both during the civil war that followed the 1917 Revolution and during World War II.

A strong-willed, undisciplined man, endowed with many talents but spoiled by his privileged aristocratic upbringing, Chertkov was even more uncompromising in his Christian anarchist convictions than Tolstoy himself. Despite his devotion to the doctrine of nonresistance, however, Chertkov betrayed an all-too-human weakness for power in his relations with Tolstoy and his family and followers. Upon Tolstoy's death, Chertkov gained full control over the great writer's papers (he had persuaded Tolstoy to change his will so as to make him the sole executor of the material) and spent the rest of his life publishing them. In 1928, the 100th-anniversary year of Tolstoy's birth, Chertkov was appointed editor-in-chief of the Jubilee Edition of Tolstoy's complete artistic, philosophical, and religious works, his diaries and notebooks, and his voluminous correspondence, which was completed in 1958 in 90 volumes. Chertkov continued as chief editor until his death in 1936.

Bibliography:

B. Aylmer Maude, *Life of Tolstoy: Later Years* (New York and London, 1931); Ernest J. Simmons, *Leo Tolstoy* (Boston, 1946).

William B. Edgerton

CHILD, Lydia Maria Francis (11 February 1802, Medford, MA —20 October 1880, Boston). *Education*: ''Miss Swan's Seminary'' (one year). *Career*: author, editor, and abolitionist.

Lydia Maria Child was one of America's leading abolitionists and authors in the mid-nineteenth century. Her works revolved around her strong belief in peace and nonresistance. In her early years, she published romantic novels, domestic advice, and served as the editor of *Juvenile Miscellany*, the first periodical for children. In the pages of the magazine, she espoused the cause of nonresistance. The lesson she taught her youthful readers was clear: mutual understanding, rather than violence, would triumph over all injustice.

Child applied the same belief to her own life. She became an active peace advocate, voicing her ideas through the Massachusetts Peace Society, the League of Universal Brotherhood, the New England Non-Resistance Society, and in articles such as "The Beauty of Peace," in *The Advocate of Peace and Universal Brotherhood*. At the same time, she attained national prominence as a leader of the abolitionist movement. Her book, *An Appeal in Favor of that Class of Americans called Africans* (1833), her election to the executive board of the American Anti-Slave Society, and her editorship of the *National Anti-Slave Standard* all marked her as one of the nation's most radical and dedicated reformers.

Child's dual goals of peace and abolitionism were vitally connected. She believed that abolitionist principles and nonresistance were "identical," the former being "a mere unit of the latter." Thus while abolitionists were greeted by threats of death from those who opposed their work, the antislavery leaders such as Child attempted to remain pacifists. Basing their actions on the principles of nonresistance, they met the violence of their enemies with prayers and petitions.

Child's outspoken beliefs often startled polite Bostonian society. Her desire to nurse and pray with John Brown after his capture at Harper's Ferry, for example, brought widespread approbation. Although her offer was rejected by the Governor of Virginia, she earnestly hoped that she could share her dedication to peace with the fiery—and violent—radical. Like many other pre-Civil War peace activists, Child came to view the continuation of slavery as a far greater evil than war. Consequently, she supported the Union cause. Still, she had little doubt that resistance, rather than warfare, was the best course through which to make America an ideal country. In her life and her writings, this was the message that Lydia Maria Child hoped to teach both John Brown and the world.

Bibliography:

A. *An Appeal in Favor of that Class of Americans called Africans* (New York, 1833); *Letters from New York* (New York, 1843); *Letters of Lydia Maria Child* (Boston, 1882).

B. Helene G. Baer, *The Heart is Like Heaven* (Philadelphia, 1964); NAW, I, 330–33.

C. Lydia Maria Child Papers, Cornell University, Ithaca, NY.

Carole Haber

CHOU Fo-hai (1897, Yuan-ling, Hunan, China—February 1948, Nanking, Kiangsu). *Education*: Kyoto Imperial Univ., 1922–24. *Career*: Kuomintang high official, chief architect of the Wang Ching-wei regime, and key leader in occupied China (1940–45).

Chou Fo-hai became a Marxist in his student days in Japan and attended the

First Congress of the Chinese Communist party in Shanghai in 1921. In 1924, he became secretary of the propaganda department of the Kuomintang, then in cooperation with the Communists. He soon left the Communist party and moved closer to Chiang Kai-shek's circles. In 1928, he joined the staff office of Chiang; entrusted with drafting policy papers, he was often in Chiang's entourage. From 1931 to 1937 Chou headed the department of education of Kiangsu province, became a member of the Central Executive Committee and the inner circles of the CC Clique of the Kuomintang, and gained recognition as an authority on Sun Yat-sen's Three People's Principles.

Chou was pessimistic about the outcome of the Sino-Japanese War (July 1937), a view that several prominent government officials and well-known intellectuals shared. Initially, Chou was sent by Chiang Kai-shek to coordinate policy with *Wang Ching-wei, Chiang's long-time political rival and a totally nonmilitary personality. Chou readily agreed with Wang in regarding peace with Japan as a price preferable to continuation of war; they believed that war would only devastate China and benefit the Communists. When Wang defected from Chungking, the wartime capital, to publicize his dissident view, Chou preceded him to Kunming, Hong Kong, and Shanghai, and put into operation the so-called "Chou Fo-hai Line." Chou proposed the organization of a Chinese government under Wang in occupied China to rally all peace workers; should Chungking fail to negotiate with Japan, this Chinese government would parley separately with Japan. As an expert on Japan and having access to Japanese authorities, Chou believed that Japan was anti-Russian and anti-Comintern in orientation and that China could not expect the intervention of Britain and the United States to preserve herself. To form a Chinese government in the Japanese occupied area was to achieve a partial peace, which could be a leverage to induce a total peace between the two nations.

Having brought neither funds nor military forces to the occupied area, Chou nevertheless led the negotiation with the Japanese; relying on the political prestige of Wang, Chou succeeded in persuading the Japanese to let a Chinese national government be "returned" to Nanking, a government which superseded all the existing collaborationist regimes in North and East China. Under the tutelage of a separate Kuomintang with Wang at its head, this Nanking regime collected revenues, maintained internal peace, dispensed justice, distributed food rations, and controlled transportation and communication facilities. It even put together a sizable military force to garrison the Nanking-Shanghai area and beyond. Chou served concurrently as Deputy Premier, Finance Minister, and Governor of the Central Reserve Bank. By interposing layers of personnel between the occupying Japanese forces, who were known for their cruelty, and the large amorphous masses of Chinese people left behind by the Chungking government, Chou was in a position to blunt the blow of the conquerors. These activities were regarded as traitorous by Chungking, and as building a competitive de facto political power in the occupied area by the Communists.

After Pearl Harbor, Chou realized that he had miscalculated international developments and that Japan was doomed. Hoping to assist Chungking's offensive against the Japanese, he stockpiled strategic goods and was in touch with Chungking by radio and through underground agents. However, VJ Day came sooner than expected, even before Chou could put his preparations to test. Chou was the only condemned collaborator whose death sentence was commuted to life imprisonment by Chiang Kai-shek himself. He died in prison in February 1948.

Chou was a peace leader insofar as peace can be considered as cessation of war in the solution of international conflict. It took courage, imagination, and finesse to do what he did. However, Chou's contributions remain controversial. The legitimacy of the peace movement depended on its success. Successful rulers in China write or re-write history and indoctrinate later generations as to what constitutes the legitimate. Chou has been branded a traitor despite many ambiguities of the happenings in 1940–45. The fact that Chou did not eschew the use of force when necessary would not entitle him to esteem accorded to a *Gandhi; moreover, Chou was not impeccable in private life. The motive behind his policy and posture was suspect; his politics of peace could be interpreted as seeking vainglory. Finally, the seeking of peace was inherently entwined in the struggle for power in China. To wage peace, Chou had to contend on three fronts: the Nationalists, the Communists, and the Japanese. In the last analysis, peace-mongering was possible only when there was resistance; had Japan been overwhelmingly victorious in China, it would not have been possible for the Japanese authorities to entertain the idea of a negotiated peace and for Chou to present to them a peaceful alternative. While the peace workers failed to stop the war, they did fill a need in the most populous and richest parts of China under occupation. The usefulness of this political power could be appreciated only by comparing it with the hypothetical case of its absence. The alternative then would have been direct Japanese rule, embellished at best with docile and less able collaborators, and a harsher life for the Chinese people under Japanese occupation.

Bibliography:

A. *Chou Fo-hai jih-chi* (Hong Kong, 1955); *San-min chu-i chih li-lun te t'i-hsi* (Shanghai, 1928); *Wang-i chi* (10th ed., Shanghai, 1944).

B. John H. Boyle, *China and Japan at War, 1937–45: The Politics of Collaboration* (Stanford, 1972); Gerald E. Bunker, *The Peace Conspiracy: Wang Ching-wei and the China War, 1937–41* (Cambridge, MA, 1972); Susan H. Marsh, "Chou Fo-hai: The Making of A Collaborator," in Akira Iriye, ed., *The Chinese and the Japanese* (Princeton, 1980), 304–27.

Susan H. Marsh

CHOWN, Alice (3 February 1866, Kingston, Ontario, Canada—2 March 1949, Toronto, Ontario). *Education*: B.A., Queen's Univ., 1891. *Career*: feminist, pamphleteer, labor and social reformer.

The advent of the First World War drove members of the Women's Christian

Temperance Union and the National Council of Women, who had hitherto been interested in peace programs, into the Red Cross. Only a rump of radicals like Alice Chown remained to call upon the suffragettes to make the world safe for democracy by attacking war profiteers and supporting farmers who resisted conscription.

At the Women's International Congress at The Hague in 1915, Chown contributed to the merging of pacifist and suffragette ideas in a program denouncing militarism, autocracy, secret treaties, and imperialism while calling for a new international order based on compulsory arbitration, universal disarmament, freedom of the seas, and a league of democratic nations. Along with Laura Hughes she established the Women's Peace Organization in Toronto to promote these views, much to the embarrassment of their prominent uncles (Col. Sam Hughes was the minister of militia and defense and S. D. Chown was superintendent of the Methodist Church) who attempted to prevent their interference with recruiting for the armed forces.

After the war, Chown joined with the labor socialists and Quakers in organizing marches and rallies in support of peace. She also worked hard for the League of Nations Society but broke with the parent organization in 1930 to focus on reaching the masses. Through her Women's League of Nations Association she distributed pamphlets, posters, and plays designed to teach the masses how to study international affairs. Through affiliated societies and publications like the *United Church Observer*, they received a wide distribution in North America and the British Commonwealth. In addition to being informative, they stressed that love ought to be the creative motivating force in the world. Nothing so incensed Alice Chown as injustice, callousness, and class smugness. She championed the persecuted whom she believed deserved to live in a more peaceful and just world. She did not hesitate to press her views on the Canadian external office or berate officers of other voluntary organizations who did not take a strong stand on disarmament. Being widely read and traveled, she was too knowledgeable to be ignored but too radical and too prickly for the bureaucrats she attempted to persuade.

Bibliography:

A. *Climbing Life's Stairway* (Boston 1921).

Donald Page

CIMBALI, Eduardo (19 July 1862, Bronte, Sicily, Italy—18 March 1934, Catania, Sicily). *Education*: Univ. of Rome. *Career*: Professor of International Law, Univ. of Macerata and Univ. of Catania.

Eduardo Cimbali was an immensely prolific international law professor with some unusual ideas for a man of his day about how to end war. His early books purported to unveil a new system of international law, based on the equal rights of all peoples. He observed that world peace could never be based on an imperialist status quo. For this reason Cimbali simultaneously denounced imperialism *and* pacifism as the latter was then understood and practiced by Italy's foremost pacifist, *Ernesto Teodoro Moneta. The professor asserted that the members of such high-sounding organizations as the Lombard Union for Peace and Arbitration were unwitting upholders of an imperialist world order and perpetrators of "an ignoble hypocrisy." Cimbali wanted peace, too, but not at the cost of enslaving nine-tenths of the world's population to be the hewers of wood and the drawers of water for the remaining one-tenth.

It was Cimbali's professional misfortune to express these ideas in the crucial beginning years of his academic career, at precisely the high tide of imperialist sentiment in Umbertian Italy. The last thirty years of the nineteenth century witnessed a European rush to colonize and exploit Africa, and the greatest fear of successive Italian governments was exclusion from this scramble. Since the government controlled the university system, it was not surprising that in 1897 an examining committee found Cimbali's academic credentials wanting and the professor himself ineligible for promotion. Professional jealousies seem to have played a role in his downfall as well. For five years Cimbali was deprived of a university position altogether; he could only find work in a small technical institute where he had to teach eight different courses, most of them outside his main field. When Cimbali finally returned to university teaching, at Catania, the normal three-year process of promotion from *straordinario* to *ordinario* took him nine years. He attributed the delay to the unflagging enmity of "the university mafia" and "the merchants in university chairs."

Through all of his university battles Cimbali continued to publish articles and books on the nature of peace, which he insisted would have to be based on a new concept of international law, taking into account the rights of all men, not just Europeans. He was one of the few Italians outside the radical socialist ranks who opposed the Libyan War as an iniquitous imperialist adventure. He was also one of the few people in Italy not to be taken by surprise when Moneta came out in favor of the war. Cimbali had argued all along that organized pacifism amounted to no more than a middle-class exercise in empty rhetoric, and Moneta, with his tortured arguments about how war might be necessary for peace, seemed to confirm the maverick professor's case. It was a little odd and disconcerting for these two to find themselves on the same side of an issue at last, in 1915, when both supported Italy's entry into World War I. No less than Moneta, Cimbali became a fervent supporter of +Woodrow Wilson and solemnly announced, in the characteristic accents of an Italian rhetorician, that the Great War was the war to end all wars because it was the first conflict in history to be fought expressly for principles and not for territorial conquest. Unlike Moneta, Cimbali lived long enough to see this sanguine vision fade away in the violent and totalitarian aftermath of Versailles.

Bibliography:

A. *La Bulgaria e il diritto internazionale* (Rome, 1887); *L'Ipocrisia del presente movimento per l'arbitrato e la pace internazionale* (Rome, 1905); *Per la libertà della scienza e per la morale accademica* (Rome, 1901); *Popoli barbari e popoli civili* (Rome, 1887); *La Società universale degli stati e i problemi della pace, dell' arbitrato e del disarmo* (Campobasso, 1922); *Lo Stato secondo il diritto internazionale universale* (Rome, 1891).

B. Ettore Felix, *Il Pacifismo di T. Moneta e le nuove dottrine di diritto internazionale di Eduardo Cimbali* (Perugia, 1907).

Richard Drake

CLARKSON, John (14 April 1764, Wisbech, England—2 April 1828, Woodbridge, England). *Education*: Wisbech Grammar School. *Career*: naval officer; governor of Sierra Leone; abolitionist; founder and first treasurer, Society for the Promotion of Permanent Peace (London Peace Society), 1816–20; pacifist.

John Clarkson's interest in peace came after a long career as an abolitionist. The death of his father when he was two years old left the family with little money. As a result, when he was only thirteen he left home to become an apprenticed seaman. He spent the next four and a half years on warships, including a long period of fighting the Dutch and French in the West Indies. Commissioned as a lieutenant in the Royal Navy, Clarkson returned to England in 1783.

When the Parliamentary agitation for the abolition of the slave trade began four years later, Clarkson joined his brother *Thomas in the abolitionist movement. Sent to Le Havre in 1788 to investigate the French slave trade, he returned with data that was used as evidence during the Parliamentary investigation. Clarkson's contribution to the abolitionist cause was not confined to work in England and France. In 1792 he went to Nova Scotia and led a group of free blacks back to Africa to the British colony of Sierra Leone. Established with abolitionist support, the colony was created so that runaways and slaves who had been given their freedom could return to Africa. Clarkson was the first governor of Sierra Leone and served for one year before returning to England in 1793. The onset of the French Revolution made all reformers suspect of radical tendencies and Clarkson retired from public life, not to return to the work of reform until the organization of a peace movement in 1816.

John and Thomas Clarkson shared a common concern for just causes. John, however, was more intensely involved in the early years of the Society for the Promotion of Permanent Peace, later renamed the London Peace Society (LPS). He was a founding member when it was organized in 1816 and served as its first treasurer, holding that office until he moved to the country town of Woodbridge in 1820. Although he could no longer attend LPS meetings on a regular basis, he continued to raise money for the organization by selling tracts and recruited members. In 1826 he chaired the tenth anniversary meeting of the Society held in London's Albion Hall. A man of action rather than words, Clarkson did write one tract that explained his pacifist views. Entitled *The Substance of a Letter, Addressed to a Clergyman of the Established Church, on the Subject of War* (1827), it revealed the Christian roots of his commitment to peace. Clarkson shared with the membership of the LPS the Christian idealism that sanctioned no wars, regardless of the provocation. In order to be a perfect

Christian, he believed, an individual must be, among other things, a pacifist, for every soul was precious to God.

After his death in 1828, the London Peace Society in its *Annual Report* paid tribute to him as an exemplary individual, one characterized by "zeal, tempered with Christian meekness."

Bibliography:

A. *The Substance of a Letter, Addressed to the Clergyman of the Established Church, On the Subject of War* (York, England, 1827).

B. Ellen Gibson Wilson, *John Clarkson and the African Adventure* (London, 1980).

C. John Clarkson Papers, British Library, British Museum.

Edith F. Hurwitz

CLARKSON, Thomas (28 March 1760, Wisbeach, England—26 September 1846, Playford, England). *Education*: B.A., St. John's Coll., Cambridge Univ., 1783. *Career*: founder, Society for the Abolition of the Slave Trade, 1787; founder, Society for the Promotion of Permanent and Universal Peace, 1816; abolitionist, historian, antiwar publicist and organizer.

Thomas Clarkson, remembered most for his lifelong dedication to the abolition of slavery and the slave trade, was also a strong supporter of the pacifist views of Friends. His three-volume history of the Society of Friends, *Portraiture of Quakerism*, appeared in 1806. It was highly praised by both Friends and non-Friends alike. It was the first overall, comprehensive study of the historical development of Quaker beliefs. Although not a Quaker himself, Clarkson wrote with empathy and understanding. He deeply respected the Quaker dedication to religious ideals and the commitment to translate principles into deeds of moral worth. This theme again appeared in Clarkson's *Memoirs of the Private and Public Life of William Penn* (1811).

The son of an Anglican clergyman, Clarkson never joined the Society of Friends, but shared their ideals and their moral dedication to just causes. In 1816, along with Friends from the abolitionist movement and his brother *John, Clarkson organized the Society for the Promotion of Permanent and Universal Peace, later known as the London Peace Society (LPS). Believing that peace and freedom were among the greatest goals of Christian humanism, he penned one of the first tracts published by the LPS, *An Essay on the Doctrines and Practice of Early Christians as they Relate to War* (1817). Together with his other pacifist writings, this essay made Clarkson one of the pioneer publicists for the British peace movement.

Bibliography:

A. *An Essay on the Doctrines and Practice of Early Christians as they Relate to War* (Ipswich, 1817); *Memoirs of the Private and Public Life of William Penn* (2 vols., London, 1811); *Portraiture of Quakerism* (London, 1806).

B. A.C.F. Beales, *The History of Peace* (London, 1931); Christina Phelps *The Anglo-*

American Peace Movement in the Mid-Nineteenth Century (New York, 1930); Earl Leslie Griggs, *Thomas Clarkson: Friend of the Slave* (London, 1936); DNB, IV, 454–57.

Edith F. Hurwitz

CLEVELAND, Aaron (3 February 1744, Haddam, CT—21 September 1815, New Haven, CT). *Education*: self-educated. *Career*: Congregationalist clergyman and poet.

Aaron Cleveland's fervent opposition to violence and war was firmly rooted in his religious beliefs. The son of an Anglican clergyman, Cleveland lost both parents by age thirteen and spent the remainder of his youth with family friends. Abandoning his father's church early in life, Cleveland later became a popular Congregationalist minister. In politics he was an outspoken Hamiltonian Federalist and seldom missed an opportunity to excoriate the pernicious doctrines of Thomas Jefferson and his followers.

Greatly influenced by his son-in-law, *David L. Dodge, the New York merchant and outspoken pacifist, Cleveland slowly came around to a nonresistant position. Unfortunately, few of Cleveland's writings have survived, two published sermons and several poems being all that remain. His reputation as a peace leader rests mainly upon his sermon, "The Life of Man Inviolable," delivered at Colchester, Connecticut on March 19, 1815. Throughout this discourse Cleveland relied heavily upon scriptural and religious authority, commmencing with the admonition "Thou shalt not kill." He admitted that in the Old Testament, God sanctioned killing under certain circumstances, but argued that unless divinely ordained, killing was a monstrous sin among the Israelites. The New Testament contained no exceptions, for Jesus Christ clearly denounced all acts of violence.

These arguments would become familiar in later pacifist literature, but in 1815 they were novel and quite uncommon for a Congregationalist minister. The message for modern Christians was clear. They must refuse to bear arms, even in self-defense, and take positive measures to banish the scourge of war forever. The true believer could do nothing less than to put on his spiritual armor and do battle against the sons of Mars.

Bibliography:

A. *The Life of Man Inviolable by the Laws of Christ* (Colchester, CT, 1815; reprinted, New York, 1821).

B. Peter Brock, *Pacifism in the United States: From the Colonial Era to the First World War* (Princeton, NJ, 1968); Charles Everest, ed., *The Poets of Connecticut* (Hartford, CT, 1845).

David R. Contosta

COBDEN, Richard (8 June 1804, Heyshott, Sussex, England—2 April 1865, London). *Education*: several years in private dames' schools in Sussex and Yorkshire. *Career*: commercial clerk in London, 1819–28; London retailer, 1828–31; Manchester manufacturer; alderman for Manchester, 1838–44; leader of Anti-Corn Law League, 1838–46; Member of Parliament, 1841–57, 1859–65.

A no-nonsense man of industry and trade, Richard Cobden sought to use the fulcrum of commerce to move the world towards peace. In a pamphlet entitled *England, Ireland, and America*, published anonymously ("by a Manchester Manufacturer") in 1835, he depicted the youthful United States as England's future great commercial competitor, with England at a disadvantage because of its protectionist trade policies and wasteful military intervention in continental affairs. Eager to overturn those liabilities for three decades Cobden traveled, negotiated, organized, wrote, and spoke for free trade and peace.

He first came to prominence as a Whig leader of the Anti-Corn Law League, a movement to remove protective tariffs on grain. Dating from the reactionary post-Napoleonic era, the Corn Laws represented Tory agricultural interests at the expense of hungry mouths and higher wages according to middleclass industrialists such as Cobden. Armed with illustrative facts and statistics, Cobden often dwelt upon these practical issues, but always in the back of his mind was a principle of free trade. He was a student of Adam Smith, demanding competitive prices on an open international market of manufactured goods as well as food. But necessity, not principle, won the day. In 1846 the prospect of famine in Ireland prompted Robert Peel, the Tory Prime Minister, to lead in the repeal of the Corn Laws.

Cobden optimistically saw the demise of the Corn Laws as "the prelude to a wiser foreign policy." He believed that free international trade would dissolve barriers of nationalistic pride and hostility, and that battles in the future would be for commercial, not military, supremacy. War, he insisted, was never profitable. It consumed wealth and labor in destruction rather than production; it increased taxes and disrupted trade.

In 1848 Cobden represented the Society for the Promotion of Permanent and Universal Peace at an international peace conference in Paris. There he gave a sympathetic ear to disarmament and the submission of international disputes to arbitration. Returning home, he introduced a resolution in the House of Commons for arbitration treaties to be negotiated with foreign nations. The motion failed miserably, by almost a hundred votes.

The bellicose policy of Lord Henry Palmerston, the Foreign Secretary, dominated. In the Don Pacifico affair of 1850, Palmerston sent a British fleet into Athens harbor, seized Greek ships, and established a blockade to extract compensation for a nominal British subject (a former resident of Gibraltar) whose property had been destroyed. Cobden and his friend, *John Bright, opposed the gunboat diplomacy with several convincing arguments for nonintervention in the affairs of foreign nations, but found little support from their old Anti-Corn Law colleagues. Even most merchants and manufacturers, whom Cobden assumed to be peace advocates, jumped on the Palmerstonian bandwagon.

England's readiness to rattle the sabre moved Cobden in 1853 to write a tract for the times on *How Wars Are Got Up in India*, a piece ostensibly about Burma but in fact a thinly disguised message for chauvinistic Britons. In the same year, fears of a French invasion of England inspired yet another pamphlet, *1793 and 1853, in Three Letters*, in which Cobden insisted that war with the new Third French Republic was as unnecessary as was the earlier prolonged conflict with French revolutionary armies. Almost a decade later Cobden would again deal with a supposed French threat in *Three Panics* (1862).

Yet Russia, not France, was the nation most feared by the British public. Years earlier, in 1836, Cobden had produced a pamphlet, *Russia*, in opposition to rampant Russophobia generated largely by the propaganda of David Urquhart. Even then politicians and press threatened to intervene on Turkey's behalf to stop Russian aggression. Cobden countered with every practical and idealistic argument at his disposal, and by 1853 was still doing so. In June 1853 he attended an international peace conference in Manchester, where he devised a program of public lectures and tracts as antidotes to the "poison" of war.

It was all for nought. In 1854 Britain entered the Crimean War on the side of Turkey and France against Russia. Although the war exposed the ineptitude of Britain's diplomatic, political, and military leadership, vocal opponents of the war such as Cobden and Bright became convenient scapegoats of blame. Cobden's prescription for peace, *What Next—and Next*? (1856)—calling for an immediate withdrawal of British troops, a fair settlement with Russia, defensive alliances in Europe, and a general reduction of naval armaments—apparently changed as few minds as did his and Bright's antiwar speeches.

Scarcely had the Peace of Paris ended the Crimean War in March 1856, before Britain again became entangled in distant conflict. In October Chinese authorities boarded a British-registered ship to search for pirates, provoking the British Consul to demand an apology. When none was forthcoming, a British naval squadron bombarded Chinese forts along the Canton River. Palmerston, now England's Prime Minister, supported the action, and was met with a scathing attack from Cobden in the House of Commons. In February 1857 Palmerston narrowly lost a vote of confidence, forcing him to put the question to the nation in a general election. The electorate had its say on Crimean and Chinese-war critics: both Cobden and Bright lost their parliamentary seats.

They soon found new constituencies, and new causes. Returned unopposed for Rochdale in 1859, Cobden immediately began private negotiations with Napoleon III for a free-trade agreement that would reduce French tariffs and completely remove most English duties on French imports. After that Commercial Treaty was signed in January 1860, Cobden negotiated lower postal rates and an abolition of passports between France and England. Behind all these transactions lay the conviction that peace was best served by international commerce, travel, and communication unencumbered by artificial barriers. Often castigated as an isolationist, Richard Cobden was, in the best sense of the term, an "international man."

He was not a pacifist, opposed to all wars. Countering accusations that he wanted "peace at any price" during the Crimean crisis, he declared himself "no

Quaker in the physical force nonresisting sense.'' He admitted the need for a small army and navy to defend his nation, but insisted on ''neutrality and isolation unless attacked.'' Although he publicly supported the Union in the American Civil War and the Danes against the Prussians in 1864, he held out for non-intervention in both cases. Above all, he envisaged Britain as an aggressive commercial, not martial, nation. Unfortunately, his practical, positive voice for peace got smothered in the din of Palmerstonian diplomacy.

Bibliography:

A. *The Political Writings of William Cobden* (2 vols. London, 1867).

B. J. A. Hobson, *Richard Cobden: The International Man* (London, 1919); John Morley, *The Life of Richard Cobden* (London, 1881); Donald Read, *Cobden and Bright: A Victorian Political Partnership* (London, 1967); DNB, XI, 148.

William J. Baker

COFFMAN, Samuel Frederick (11 June 1872, Ruskville, VA—28 June 1954, Vineland, Ontario, Canada). *Education*: Moody Bible Institute, Chicago, 1894–95, 1897–98. *Career*: Mennonite minister, bishop, churchman, 1895–1954; pastor, Moyer Mennonite Church, Vineland, 1901–54; teacher and principal, Ontario Mennonite Bible School, 1907–47.

Bishop Samuel F. Coffman was active in Mennonite and Canadian life, but his most significant contribution came as the result of the leadership he provided to the nonresistant church members during both World War I and World War II. In 1918 he helped organize the Non-Resistant Relief Organization (NRRO), which involved all the Amish, Mennonite, and Brethren in Christ groups then in Ontario. Coffman acted as the primary representative of these peace groups in lobbying the Canadian government for exemption from military service during the First World War. He worked at establishing close relationships between church groups and the government, and made sure that certain Members of Parliament were well informed about the Mennonites and their religious tradition of nonresistance. He received a sympathetic hearing from many public officials largely because of his own judicious attitude and the general trust he put in the government. Part of the NRRO purpose was to raise money to present a memorial of appreciation to the Canadian government, if and when it ruled in favor of Mennonite exemption from military service.

Although Ontario peace groups were unable to gain total exemption from the Conscription Act, Coffman arranged that men be given indefinite ''leaves of absence'' from active duty upon identification of themselves as conscientious objectors. While this provision was being implemented, Coffman assisted in obtaining releases for imprisoned Amish and Brethren in Christ members.

Coffman's activities did not stop with the end of World War I. He continued to be a spokesman for the peace position, writing articles, organizing and addressing peace conferences, and striving to consolidate the Mennonite position of nonresistance. Following the outbreak of World War II, he participated in the creation of the Conference of Historic Peace Churches, an inter-denominational organization that worked with the government to create an alternative service program for conscientious objectors.

Out of his peace conviction grew the belief that the peace churches should assist in the relief of wounds caused by war. Throughout the years 1918–50, Coffman organized, through NRRO, the distribution of relief funds and materials to aid the victims of war. For him, relief work was the social dimension to the peace doctrine of nonresistance. Coffman interpreted the peace position to include not only resistance to war, but also a commitment to acts of love.

Bibliography:

B. Urie A. Bender, *Four Earthen Vessels: Biographical Profiles of Oscar Burkholder, Samuel F. Coffman, Clayton F. Derstine, and Jesse B. Martin* (Scottdale, PA, 1982); Frank H. Epp, *Mennonites in Canada, 1786–1920: The History of a Separate People* (Toronto, 1974); Frank H. Epp, *Mennonites in Canada, 1920–1940: A People's Struggle for Survival* (Toronto, 1982).

Frank H. Epp

COLE, George Douglas Howard (4 September 1889, Cambridge, England—25 January 1959, Oxford). *Education*: St. Paul's School; B.A., Balliol Coll., Oxford Univ., 1910, *literae humaniores*, 1912. *Career*: political philosopher, economist, historian, and novelist; professor and fellow at All Souls Coll.; editor, publicist, author, socialist, and pragmatic pacifist.

Born to a Tory family, G.D.H. Cole became a convert to the idealistic socialism of William Morris in 1905. In his works, Cole concentrated on trying to reform Britain's domestic economy and only occasionally touched on international peace issues. Throughout his life, he worked on three levels: as an Oxford scholar; as a prophet to socialist Britain; and as a propagandist to the larger democratic middle class of the world.

Throughout World War I, Cole remained oblivious to international problems. As a pragmatic pacifist, however, he refused to fight for the British government, viewing the conflict as a product of capitalism and imperialism. He welcomed the Russian Revolution of 1917, but rejected Vladimir Lenin's program as a model for Great Britain. Lenin's revolutionary Bolshevism was the reverse of Cole's revolutionary ideas and reformist means. Instead, Cole promoted "the 2 $^1/_2$ International," an international committee of workers that could somehow reunite the European Social Democrats and the Communists. Throughout the 1920s, Cole denounced the war debts, reparations, tariffs, and capitalist policies which, he believed, would only stimulate another war.

The coming to power of Adolf Hitler in 1933 forced Cole to alter his views on international relations. Until the outbreak of the Spanish Civil War in 1936, he remained unclear whether fascism was worse than traditional liberal capitalism. The Spanish crisis, however, led him to give up pacifism and call for a "grand alliance" of all democratic nations to face the Nazi threat. He remained somewhat ambiguous about supporting the Tory government, but once World

War II started, he reluctantly backed the British war effort and denounced Joseph Stalin for signing a nonaggression pact with Hitler.

The war convinced Cole that nationalism and sovereignty were bigger obstacles to human progress than capitalism. In September 1941 he drafted a plan to reorganize the world into three distinct confederations: the Soviet sphere, the American capitalist sphere, and a West European social democratic sphere. Britain, he argued, should join Europe and avoid ties with a capitalist America. His plan envisioned peaceful coexistence and detente, policies he promoted throughout the post-World War II decade.

During the Korean War, Cole was critical of United States policy and attacked the British government for supporting the American position. He believed that the United States was largely responsible for the continuation of the war and warned about the possibility of an escalation that would bring in China or the Soviet Union. By 1955 Cole was calling for the creation of a new humanist socialist league which would, in part, promote peaceful coexistence. In the late 1950s Cole proved that he was as critical of Soviet imperialism as American imperialism. He condemned the Soviet repression of the Hungarian revolution of 1956, but warned the democratic left not to join in an anti-Soviet crusade.

Cole's primary commitment was to socialism and democracy. During the interwar period he was particularly critical of the capitalist nations, but from the end of World War II to his death, he worked more modestly to promote coexistence and mutual survival.

Bibliography:

A. *The Causes of War*, ed. by Cole and others (New York, 1935); *Europe, Russia and the Future* (London, 1941); *A History of Socialist Thought* (6 vols., London, 1953–60); *Intelligent Man's Guide to Europe Today* (New York, 1933); *World Socialism Restated* (London, 1956).

B. Luther D. Carpenter, *G.D.H. Cole: An Intellectual Biography* (Cambridge, 1973); Margaret Cole, *The Life of G.D.H. Cole* (London, 1971); Gerald Houseman, *G.D.H. Cole* (Boston, 1979); A. W. Wright, *G.D.H. Cole and Social Democracy* (Oxford, 1979).

C. G.D.H. Cole papers, Oxford University.

Robert H. Whealey

COOMANS, Jean-Baptiste Nicolas (6 July 1813, Brussels, Belgium—27 July 1896, Brussels). *Education*: Dr. jur., Univ. of Ghent, 1834. *Career*: artillery officer, 1830; editor and publisher, *Le Journal des Flandres*, 1834–40; *La Revue de Bruxelles*, 1837–42, *Le Messager des sciences historiques*, 1833–40, *Le Journal de Bruxelles*, 1841–53, *Le Courrier d'Anvers*, 1845, *L'Emancipation*, 1853–58, *La Paix*, 1862–80; Catholic communal counsellor and member of the Chamber of Representatives, 1848–96; vice-president, Belgian section of the International Arbitration and Peace Association, 1889; lawyer, writer, and journalist.

Besides numerous historical and philosophical publications, works of fiction, and contributions to various newspapers and journals, Jean-Baptiste Coomans, a man of progressive convictions, founded and edited the weekly *La Paix* which served as a vehicle for his political, economic, and social ideas. A Catholic, Coomans was also an internationalist and free-trader. The columns of *La Paix* welcomed similar viewpoints in the form of contributions from *Edmond Potonié and *Frédéric Passy.

Influenced by the federalism of *Pierre-Joseph Proudhon, Coomans urged federative principles and particularly supported the idea of a United States of Europe. A fierce antimilitarist, he never ceased in his battle against conscription, the increase of armaments, or the growing military expenses which he believed would lead to general bankruptcy. As a pacifist, he opposed all wars—the American Civil War, the Franco-Prussian War, military enterprises in Algeria, the Mexican expedition—but not wars of national defense. A humanitarian, he defended the rights of oppressed peoples, be these Flemish, Arab, American Indian, or Dominican. He also supported movements opposing capital punishment, slavery, prison reform, and the improvement of the conditions of workers.

Bibliography:

A. *De la répression du duel* (Ghent, 1836); *Etude sur les questions d'ordre matériel à l'ordre du jour* (Brussels, 1848); *Histoire de la Belgique* (Ghent, 1836).

B. L. Bertelson, *Dictionnaire des Journalistes-Ecrivains de Belgique* (Brussels, 1960), 26; F. Lehouck, *Het Antimilitarisme in België, 1830–1914* (Antwep, n.d.); *Bibliographie Nationale*, I, 305–6; *Galerie Nationale*, Chambre des Représentants en 1894–95, 263–7; *Les Hommes du Jour*, 25 (1884), 105–8.

Nadine Lubelski-Bernard
Trans. by Sandi E. Cooper

COUDENHOVE-KALERGI, Richard. See *Biographical Dictionary of Internationalists*.

COURTNEY, Leonard Henry, Baron Courtney of Penwith (6 July 1832, Penzance, Cornwall, England—11 May 1918, London). *Education*: St. John's Coll., Cambridge Univ., 1855; Lincoln's Inn, 1858. *Career*: Journalist, *The Times*, 1864–80; Professor of Political Economy, Univ. of London, 1872–75; Member of Parliament (Liskeard), 1876–85 and (Bodmin Division of Cornwall), 1885–1900; Under-Secretary of State for the Home Office, 1880–81 and the Colonial Office, 1881–82; Financial Secretary to the Treasury, 1882–84; chairman, Committees and Deputy Speaker, 1886–92; publicist and statesman.

Few public figures in early twentieth century Britain held convictions so courageously, or paid more dearly for them, as Leonard Courtney. A philosophic radical, nurtured in the Victorian liberal tradition, he had a strong affinity for free trade, religious liberty, and free political institutions. His fervent devotion to peace emerged from a corresponding sense of "little Englandism" and constituted a moderating influence on public opinion in what was otherwise an age of mounting nationalism and militarism.

Inspired by his admiration of John Stuart Mill, Courtney early found his calling in the arena of public opinion formation. As a journalist for *The Times* he wrote about 3,000 articles and was a frequent contributor to other publications, including the *Fortnightly Review*, where he attacked Benjamin Disraeli's imperialist policies and espoused radical viewpoints. During William E. Gladstone's second administration, Courtney was a zealous supporter of proportional representation and rather quixotically resigned office over its omission from the redistribution measure of 1884. His final break with Gladstone occurred over Irish home rule in 1886. As a Liberal Unionist, however, he followed an independent line and strenuously resisted all imperialistic policies in the Sudan and South Africa. Upon the outbreak of the Boer War, Courtney, as the most independent elder statesman in the House of Commons, headed the antiwar movement and set about to mobilize opinion against it as president of the South African Conciliation Committee. For his unpopular views he received many threatening and abusive letters and was forced out of his parliamentary seat in the "khaki election" of 1900. Nevertheless, he continued to plea for an armistice and a negotiated peace and to oppose demands for annexation and retribution.

In the decade prior to 1914, Lord Courtney, by his articles, correspondence, and organizational talents, worked indefatigably for a reduction of armaments and greater international understanding, particularly with Germany. In the summer of 1908, he hosted a meeting of the Universal Peace Congress in London. There he advocated the development of international law and treaties of arbitration as safeguards for peace. Throughout these years Courtney maintained that entangling alliances, such as those which Britain had concluded with Japan, France, and Russia, constituted major threats to peace. Again during the First World War, Courtney assumed a position contrary to his country's course. Although *The Times* refused to print some of his letters, he publicized his views concerning peace by negotiation in the *Manchester Guardian* and in speeches in the House of Lords. Continuance of the war, he argued, would only bring further deadlock and disaster to European civilization.

Lord Courtney was a strong pacifist who, though best remembered as a man of principle, made his greatest contribution by provoking reflection, second thoughts, and even self-criticism in a community governed by opinion.

Bibliography:

B. G. P. Gooch, *Life of Lord Courtney* (London, 1920); DNB, 1912–21, 127–28; LT, May 13, 1918.

C. Courtney of Penwith Papers, British Library of Political and Economic Science, London.

John D. Fair

COUVREUR, Auguste Pierre Louis (24 October 1827, Ghent, Belgium—24 April 1894, Brussels). *Career*: general secretary, Association pour la réforme douanière, 1854–59; secretary, Association internationale pour le progrès des sciences sociales, 1863–68; member, Chamber of Representatives, 1864–84; founding member, Ligue internationale et permanente de la paix, Paris, 1867;

general secretary, l'Association internationale d'hygiène, de sauvetage et d'e-´conomie sociale; founding member and president, International Arbitration and Peace Association (Belgian section), 1889, 1892–94; vice-president, Congrès international sur la législation douanière et le règlementation du travail, 1892; president, La Société d'études coloniales, 1894, Brussels correspondent of *The Time*; politician and internationalist.

Devoted to ideas of the free trade school of economists, Auguste Couvreur inspired the Belgian peace movement in favor of the reduction of trade and tariff barriers. As a liberal politician, he was also a warm partisan of peace and international arbitration, laboring assiduously for close relationships among the diverse Anglo-American and European pacifist societies. Anticipating the Inter-parliamentary Union, Couvreur studied, along with his friends *Frédéric Passy and *Henry Richard, the possible means of assembling a select number of members of parliaments from various countries to plan for common action on behalf of the preservation of peace, arms reductions, and arbitration. Their objective was the creation of an official organization that would permit an elite group of parliamentarians to convene annually and to deliberate in secret on the text of proposals that they would then simultaneously introduce in their own chambers. For that reason, too, he participated with English, American, French, Italian, Swedish, and Dutch colleagues in the campaign to promote arbitration in parliaments.

In 1873 and 1874, Couvreur entered a motion in the Chamber supporting the use of arbitration to resolve international differences, supporting the creation of an international arbitration tribunal, and supporting a code of the rights of men. With the same purpose in mind, he created the Belgian section of the International Federation of Arbitration and Peace in 1889 with *Hodgson Pratt and *Emile de Laveleye.

Couvreur was also a federalist, a supporter of the idea of a United States of Europe. To prepare for the realization of this political transformation and the creation of a European parliament, he established the Society for Social and Political Studies in 1889.

Bibliography:

A. *Annales de l'association internationale pour le progrès des science sociales* (Brussels, 1863; Paris, 1864; Amsterdam, 1864; Berne, 1866); *Congrès international des réformes douanières* (Brussels, 1857); *Congrès international d'hygiène, de sauvetage et d'économie sociale* (Brussels, 1876; Paris, 1877).

B. P. Hymans, "Nécrologie" in *Revue de droit et de législation comparée* (1894), 340–3; *Biographie coloniale Belge*, IV, col. 163; *Bibliographie nationale*, I, 304–5; *Les Hommes du jour*, 38 (1884), 158.

Nadine Lubelski-Bernard
Trans. by Sandi E. Cooper

CREIGHTON, William Black (20 July 1864, Dorchester, Ontario, Canada—30 October 1946, Toronto). *Education*: B.A., Victoria Coll., 1890, D.D.,

1894. *Career*: minister, Methodist and United Church of Canada, 1894–1900; assistant editor, *The Christian Guardian*, 1900–6; editor, *The Christian Guardian*, 1906–25, *The New Outlook*, 1925–37; social reformer and pacifist.

As an editor of the church press for over three decades, W. B. Creighton helped awaken Canadians to a new social consciousness and by the 1920s was particularly instrumental in publicizing the peace movement in Canada.

Born and educated in southern Ontario where he was ordained a Methodist minister by 1894, he developed early in his ministry a lifelong, laryngitis related, health problem which interrupted his career as a preacher and caused him to devote the remainder of his life's work to writing. First as an assistant editor and then as editor of the Methodist journal, *The Christian Guardian*, Creighton emerged as a powerful advocate of the social gospel and its related moral reforms such as temperance and pacifism. Under his pen, the *Guardian* moved into the vanguard of the prewar progressive peace movement.

World War I posed an inescapable dilemma with which he would wrestle for years. Although he hated the physical facts of war, Creighton gradually rationalized that the great moral purpose of the war would ultimately redeem its crimes. Consequently, by 1917 in a cover page editoral he would later regret, he denounced pacifism itself as a vice and claimed there was no room in the Christian Church for those opposed to the war effort. Like many other liberal pacifists, Creighton had come to accept the war as a great cleansing and reforming action that would ensure the beginning of a new social order and peaceful age in international relations.

Once this wartime idealism was replaced by postwar disillusionment, Creighton publicly repented for his sin of supporting the conflict and declared that never again would war have his sanction or blessing. His renewed pacifist conviction, he explained, was a direct result of his wartime experience and consequent realization that war, rather than having any virtue or saving grace, was an utterly unchristian and unforgivable crime. With this personal confession, Creighton launched a lengthy pacifist debate in the *Guardian* and its successor, *The New Outlook*, which continued well after his retirement in 1937. Although aware that some of his readers had grown more than weary of his antiwar campaign, Creighton remained determined to encourage full discussion on the issue and to educate the public mind for peace. Radical pacifists such as *R. Edis Fairbairn were welcomed into the fray, but in his editorials Creighton avoided reference to nonviolent resistance or other forms of pacifist protest and concentrated, instead, on the prevention of war through education and international cooperation. Displaying both force and eloquence, he wrote in a simple but persuasive style that earned him widespread influence over the mass of his readers. To a certain extent, therefore, Creighton's role in the Canadian peace movement mirrored that of his American counterpart, *Charles Clayton Morrison, editor of the *Christian Century*.

Although his career had officially come to an end, Creighton's influence was still felt during World War II since, as editor of one of Canada's most widely read church journals throughout the interwar years, he had been responsible for shaping the attitudes of a generation of Canadians on the issues of war and peace. Many of them, like himself, while never embracing outright absolute pacifism, continued to view war as contrary to the Christian conscience.

Bibliography:

B. Richard Allen, *The Social Passion* (Toronto, 1971); Donald Creighton, "My Father and the United Church," in *The Passionate Observer* (Toronto: 1980).

Thomas P. Socknat

CREMER, William Randal (18 March 1828, Fareham, Hants, England—22 July 1908, London). *Education*: informal; *Career*: shipbuilding apprentice and carpenter; founding member, Amalgamated Society of Carpenters and Joiners; founding member and delegate, International Workingman's Association, 1864–66; founder and permanent secretary, Workmen's Peace Association and International Arbitration League, 1871–1908; Member of Parliament for Haggerston (Shoreditch), 1885–95, 1900–08; founder, Interparliamentary Union, 1889; Nobel Peace Prize, 1903.

Born into a poor, working-class family, Randal Cremer had by the 1860s become not only a prominent figure in the British trades union movement but an internationally known labor leader with an extensive network of contacts on the continent as well. His involvement in the peace movement grew directly out of his conviction that the arbitration procedures successfully utilized by unions and employers in the 1860s to avert domestic strikes would prove useful for the settlement of international disputes that traditional diplomacy was unable to resolve.

Fearful that Britain might be drawn into the Franco-Prussian War, Cremer and a group of trade unionist friends in 1871 established the Workmen's Peace Association and International Arbitration League (IAL), an organization whose policies Cremer, as founder and permanent secretary, would shape and direct for the next forty years. Taking advantage of the enfranchisement of millions of working men by the Reform Acts of 1867 and 1884, Cremer sought to enlist this natural constituency in behalf of the aims of the arbitration movement and to use labor's potential influence to further a program that included the establishment of a "High Court of Nations."

Elected to Commons in 1885 as a Liberal, Cremer became an eloquent spokesman for the trade union and peace movements, often stressing their interrelatedness. Though a frequent critic of imperial adventures, it was as an advocate of permanent treaties of arbitration that Cremer became chiefly known in Commons. Inspired by the settlement of the Alabama claims between Britain and the United States in 1872, he was between 1888 and 1893 the driving force behind the preparation of an Anglo-American Treaty of Arbitration, ultimately enlisting the support of 364 M.P.'s and obtaining the signatures of 7432 officials of British workers' organizations in its favor. His efforts to mobilize legislators on both sides of the Atlantic in support of the Anglo-American Treaty inspired in him the idea of periodically convening members of various European parliaments who favored the extension of the principle of international arbitration. Conferences initially funded by the IAL were held in Paris (1889) and London (1890), where the Interparliamentary Union (IPU) was formally launched, an organization which by 1906 included in its ranks members of twenty-two separate parliaments. The Union surpassed Cremer's most sanguine hopes, its steady growth in membership and prestige serving to refute a widespread if cynical view of arbitration as a "utopian fad." Though Cremer had no direct connection with the Tsar's peace initiative of 1899, it was the draft proposal of a permanent "High Court of Nations," endorsed by the Interparliamentary Union at its Budapest meeting of 1896, which later served as a basis for discussion at the Hague.

Cremer failed to survive the Conservative tide of 1895 by a narrow margin of thirty-one votes. Retirement from Commons predictably led to even greater involvement in the work of both the IPU and the IAL, including personal efforts to lobby both the U. S. Senate and President William McKinley in behalf of the narrowly defeated Arbitration Treaty of 1893. Throughout the period of the Boer War (1899–1902) Cremer participated in numerous public protests and demonstrations. He also sought to rally trade unionists to the antiwar cause. A manifesto which he composed, attributing the war to the greed of South African "capitalists" who sought cheap native labor for their gold mines, was not only widely circulated but secured the endorsement of 140 officials of trade union organizations. Cremer was among the few antiwar Liberals to survive the "Khaki" Election of 1900, regaining his metropolitan Haggerston seat by a slim majority of twenty-four votes.

After the war Cremer became increasingly preoccupied by the state of Anglo-French relations, strained by the Dreyfus case and by the imperial rivalries which had culminated in the Fashoda incident. Seeing in this estrangement a menace to the peace of Europe and a potential source of increased armaments, Cremer used his considerable influence among French Deputies and Senators active in the arbitration movement, such as *Paul Henri d'Estournelles de Constant, to set in motion a process of meetings and consultations which eventually culminated in the conclusion of the Anglo-French Treaty of October 1903, which bound the two governments to arbitrate their differences. Characteristically Cremer worked behind the scenes, preferring to let others enjoy the success which his unique organizational abilities had helped to secure. However the role he had played in convincing a growing public of the utility of arbitration procedures earned him the Nobel Peace Prize in 1903, the first in a series of honors—including a knighthood and the cross of the Legion of Honor—which marked his final years.

Randal Cremer was in large measure the heir to such heroes of earlier peace campaigns as *John Bright, *Richard Cobden, and *Henry Richard. Cremer, however, imparted a distinctively working class cast to a movement which in its origins and leadership had been largely middle class. The participation of trade unionists like Cremer and *Thomas Burt effectively transformed the peace and arbitration movement of the late nineteenth century, broadening its base and enlarging its appeal. Cremer's strong faith in the "industrial class" as a force for peace in the world made of him, early on, a dedicated internationalist, convinced not only of the essential fraternity of all workers but of their mutual interest in establishing a permanent international framework within which the principle of arbitration could be more broadly utilized and applied. Impatient with those who looked upon his goals as visionary or utopian, he strove to bring the question of international arbitration "into the domain of practical politics." The outbreak of the Great War obscured the rising popularity of the principle of arbitration in the decades preceding 1914, the increasing acceptance of its procedures by governments and by the general public, and the numerous successes realized by a movement which Randal Cremer more than any other single individual helped to shape.

Bibliography:

A. "Parliamentary and Interparliamentary Experiences," *The Independent*, 61 (August 30, 1906), 508–13.

B. Hayne Davis, "Cremer and the Interparliamentary Union," *The Independent*, 61 (July 19, 1906), 126–31-; Howard Evans, *Sir Randal Cremer 1828–1908* (London, 1909; reissued, New York, 1973).

Claire Hirschfield

CROSBY, Ernest Howard (4 November 1856, New York—3 January 1907, Baltimore). *Education*: B.A., New York Univ., 1876; LLB., Columbia Univ. Law School, 1878. *Career*: lawyer, legislator, judge, essayist, poet, novelist, co-editor, *The Whim*, 1901–4.

Ernest Howard Crosby's career as a reformer and peace advocate began while serving as a judge on the International Court in Alexandria, Egypt. Following a spiritual crisis in 1894, he chanced to read *Leo Tolstoy's *Life*, which offered solace and at the same time converted him to Tolstoy's doctrine of "love" and "non-resistance to evil." Resigning his post, he journeyed to Russia and spent two fruitful days with the Russian reformer. Upon his return to America, "non-resistance" became his guiding principle, publicized in numerous speeches and articles and summed up in his *Tolstoy and His Message* (1903).

Tolstoy had praised *William Lloyd Garrison as an exemplar of the doctrine of nonresistance to evil; and in 1905, Crosby published *Garrison the Non-Resistant*, a defense of Garrison's behavior during the Civil War. In the book Crosby incorporated his own argument, advanced two years earlier, in "If the South Had Been Allowed to Go," that the Civil War was "unnecessary," doing little for the blacks—who could have been freed without war—and serving only to prepare the nation for the imperialism of 1898.

With war fever mounting after the sinking of the *Maine*, Crosby addressed an appeal "To the Workers of America," countersigned by Bishop C. Potter, William Dean Howells, and other peace advocates. The signers called for arbitration, pointedly questioning the jingoes' call for justice in Cuba while ignoring injustice at home. Crosby's *Peace Echoes* (1898), a collection of pacifist poems, was followed by two more collections containing powerful indictments of war and the warmakers.

As a leading member of the American Peace Society and head of the New York Anti-Imperialist League, Crosby was in great demand as a speaker. After a Boston speech on "The Absurdities of Militarism" (1901), calling for an American Cervantes to ridicule the military profession, he was urged by friends to do the job himself. Composed in six weeks, his one novel, *Captain Jinks, Hero* (1902), the best anti-imperialist novel of the period, was a fanciful tale of the American conquest of the "Cubapines" and the rescue of the missionaries in "Porsslania." Targeting the military mind and all those who support it, including the press and the Christian Church, the novel also ridiculed the exploits of the so-called "heroes" of the war. The novel ended on a ludicruous note with the ostensible hero, "Captain Jinks," happily ensconced in an insane asylum, "a perfectly safe soldier."

With the war continuing in the Philippines, Crosby reiterated his arguments against American policy in a seminar published in *The Independent* (1902). The following year Crosby praised his former friend, President +Theodore Roosevelt, for intervening in the violent coal strike of 1903. Asserting that the operators had incited the violence, he argued that deadlocked labor disputes be arbitrated. The following year, in "Wanted, a New Patriotism," he deplored the popular American propensity always to link patriotism with war, a view exemplified by Roosevelt; and he looked forward to a "new patriotism" based on affection and devoted to all that is best in America.

Attacking what he called "Militarism at Home," in 1904, he warned of the dangers inherent in the amended militia bill centralizing control in Washington. Giving such power to the War Department he branded "military lunacy." In his final peace effort, "A Precedent for Disarmament: A Suggestion to the Peace Conference" (1904), Crosby offered as a model to the delegates to the Second Hague Peace Conference which would convene in 1907, the Rush-Bagot Treaty of 1817, permanently disarming the Great Lakes and insuring Canadian-American peace. He suggested a similar disarmament experiment in the Mediterranean, the Baltic, and the Japan Sea. In time, the principle could embrace the Atlantic and Pacific, ultimately navies and land forces as well. With the Great Lakes precedent at hand, he considered it appropriate that America lead the peace efforts and earn the world's eternal gratitude.

Bibliography:

A. *The Absurdities of Militarism* (Boston, 1901); *Captain Jinks, Hero* (New York, 1902); *Edward Carpenter: Poet and Prophet* (Philadelphia, 1901); *Garrison the Non-Resistant* (Chicago, 1905); *Golden Rule Jones* (Chicago, 1906); *Plain Talk in Psalm and Parable* (Boston, 1899); *Swords and Plowshares* (New York, 1902); *Tolstoy and His Message* (New York, 1904); *Tolstoy as a Schoolmaster* (Chicago, 1903); *War Echoes* (Philadelphia, 1898); *War from the Christian Point of View* (Boston, 1901).

B. Leonard Abbot, *Ernest Crosby: A Valuation and a Tribute* (Westwood, MA, 1907); Peter J. Frederick, *Knights of the Golden Rule: The Intellectual as Christian Social Reformer in the 1890s* (Lexington, KY, 1976); Perry E. Gianakos, "Ernest Howard Crosby: A Forgotten Tolstoyan Antimilitarist and Anti-Imperialist," *Peace Movements in America*, ed. by Charles Chatfield (New York, 1973).

C. Ernest Howard Crosby Papers, Michigan State University, Special Collections.

Perry E. Gianakos

CROZIER, Frank Percy (1879, Ireland?—31 August 1937, Walton-on-Thames, England). *Education*: Wellington Coll. *Career*: soldier, writer, and peace activist.

Frank Crozier was the most improbable leader of the interwar British peace movement. After boyhood in Ireland he followed in the footsteps of his father by opting for a military career. Unable to gain a regular commission because of his poor health, he still managed to serve in South Africa and Nigeria before resigning his commission in 1909. He continued soldiering in one way or another for years to come, and during World War I rose to Brigadier-General in the British Army, receiving the Distinguished Service Order in 1917. His controversial resignation as Commandant of the Auxiliary Division of the Royal Irish Constabulary in 1921 started to transform him from soldier of fortune to outspoken antimilitarist. He later claimed that his resignation had been prompted by his objections to sharing in the Black and Tan atrocities in Ireland, but most observers questioned this.

In the late 1920s Crozier worked briefly as a speaker for the League of Nations Union, and his views appeared to be routinely internationalist. The views he expressed in the colorful muckraking books he began writing with *A Brass Hat in No Man's Land* in 1930 were critical of the conduct of the war but not pacifist. By the mid–1930s he was working with the Peace Army, which Maude Royden and others hoped might avert violent conflict by placing unarmed volunteers between conflicting forces. Although this idea faded after a brief period of publicity during the Manchurian crisis, it brought Crozier into contact with Canon *Dick Sheppard, the founder of the Peace Pledge Union (a British Section of the War Resisters' International). As a result of a conversation between the two men, Dick Sheppard, in 1934, sent his letter to the press asking men to sign a postcard pledging themselves to renounce war. Frank Crozier was on the platform with Dick Sheppard in the Albert Hall, London, at the inaugural meeting of the Peace Pledge Union, and was one of its first sponsors. He spoke many times in support of pacifism at indoor and outdoor meetings.

Bibliography:

A. *Angels on Horseback* (London, 1932); *A Brass Hat in No Man's Land* (London, 1930); *Five Years Hard* (New York, 1932); *Impressions and Recollections* (London, 1930); *The Men I Killed* (London, 1937); *A Word to Gandhi: The Lesson of Ireland* (London, 1931).

B. Martin Ceadel, *Pacifism in Britain 1914–1945: The Defining of a Faith* (Oxford, 1980); LT, September 1, 1937.

Hilda Morris and Donald Birn

CURTIS, Lionel George (7 March 1872, Codlington, Ledbury, England—24 November 1955, Kidlington, Oxford). *Education*: Haileybury; B.A., New Coll., Oxford Univ., 1895; called to the Bar, Inner Temple, 1902. *Career*: town clerk, Johannesburg, South Africa, 1901–3; Assistant Colonial Secretary to the Transvaal for Local Government, 1903–6; Beit Lecturer, Colonial History, Oxford Univ.; Fellow of All Soul's Coll., Oxford Univ.; advisor on Irish Affairs, Colonial Office, 1921–24; co-founder, Round Table Movement, 1909–10; co-founder, Royal Institute of International Affairs, 1920–21; advocate of a world commonwealth.

While in South Africa, Lionel Curtis joined the circle of young intellectuals who gathered around High Commissioner Lord Alfred Milner. Following Milner's lead they argued that the only way to ensure international harmony and to avoid war was to draw together the various nations comprising the British Commonwealth into a single federation. During the winter of 1909–10, Curtis and other members of "Milner's Kindergarten" founded the Round Table Movement to promote the idea of a federation for the entire Empire. From the start, Curtis and Philip Kerr were the Movement's leading spokesmen and together they established *The Round Table Quarterly*, which soon became one of the best journals devoted to British Commonwealth and international affairs. Curtis' commitment to a united Commonwealth based on self-government was total, and over the next ten years, even in the midst of war, he promoted the concept through speeches and in his writings. His early books, *The Problem of the Commonwealth* (1916) and *The Commonwealth of Nations* (1916), emphasized the stabilizing role and the force for good that could be exercised by union.

By the end of World War I Curtis believed that only the creation of an international body representative of all states would ensure that the horrors of 1914–18 would be avoided in the future. He argued strenuously in *The Round Table* and elsewhere in favor of a League of Nations and initiated discussions in Paris in 1920 resulting in the establishment of the Royal Institute of International Affairs. For the rest of his life, Curtis remained a strong advocate of international understanding and international education. He reasoned that mutual understanding would lead to cooperation which in turn would ensure peace and stability.

From 1924 to 1934 he devoted most of his time to writing his book, *Civitas Dei* (1934–37), which was an impassioned plea for the transfer of the tenets of the British Commonwealth as he understood them—democratic institutions and cooperation among diverse peoples—to the world level. Curtis was a devoted and tireless advocate of world unity through federation. He argued forcefully, and often against some of his closest friends, that the nation-state and the nationalism it engendered were pernicious and anachronistic. As long as absolutely sovereign nations existed, he maintained, disputes and war were inevitable.

When war broke out in 1939 Curtis prepared a pamphlet entitled *Decision* (1941) designed to show the practical steps needed to implement a policy of organic union and, thereby, prevent future wars. Other pamphlets and books, largely funded out of Curtis's own pocket, followed on the same theme; *Action* (1942); *Faith and Works* (1943); *The Way to Peace* (1944); *World War; its Cause and Cure* (1945); and *World Revolution in the Cause of Peace* (1949). Curtis constantly urged people to view affairs in a wider context and to abandon the fatalistic assumption that war was inevitable. In his estimation conflicts could be resolved if ''the principle of the Commonwealth'' were adopted on the world stage.

Curtis did not hold public office in his later career, but he remained influential behind-the-scenes and in print. He was often naive, even wrong-headed, but always dedicated to the easing of international friction. His charismatic personality and his passionate commitment left an indelible imprint on all who met him.

Bibliography:

A. *Civitas Dei: The Commonwealth of God* (London 1934–37); *The Commonwealth of Nations* (London 1916); *Dyarchy* (Oxford 1920); *The Problem of the Commonwealth* (London 1916).

B. John Kendle, *The Round Table Movement and Imperial Union* (Toronto 1975); Walter Nimocks, *Milner's Young Men: The ''Kindergarten'' in Edwardian Imperial Affairs* (Durham, N.C. 1968).

C. Lionel Curtis papers, Bodleian Library, Oxford University.

John Kendle

D

DANDURAND, Raoul. See *Biographical Dictionary of Internationalists*.

DARBY, William Evans (10 July 1844, Laugharne, Wales—7 November 1922, Seven Kings, England). *Education*: Tenby; New Coll., Hampstead; Univ. of London; ordained, Congregational minister, 1869. *Career*: Congregational minister, journalist, and author.

William Evans Darby was born in West Wales at a time when the principality was much disturbed by educational and religious debate. He was educated and confirmed in the Church of England, but when he could no longer accept the Thirty-Nine articles he became a Dissenter and went to London to train for the Congregational ministry. His first pastorate was near Chelmsford in 1868 and thereafter he served churches at Chippenham, Bath, Sheffield, Plymouth, and Watford. By the 1880s he was also beginning to be quite well-known as a speaker on peace platforms, and in 1888 he resigned his pastorate at Watford and became secretary of the London Peace Society (established in 1816), succeeding a fellow-Welshman in the post. He served as secretary until 1915, being made a vice-president on his retirement.

As secretary of the London Peace Society, Darby was a frequent lecturer on peace questions in different parts of the British Isles. He made it his special responsibility to try to gain the support and cooperation of the churches on both sides of the Atlantic, using the Arbitration Alliance of the Anglo-American Churches for this purpose. In 1891 he was largely responsible for setting up a committee of the British Churches on Arbitration. Together with a Committee of the Society of Friends it blossomed as the Arbitration Alliance of Great Britain and Ireland in 1893. Darby's chief interest lay in promoting schemes for the peaceful settlement of disputes by arbitration and the use of international tribunals. He was an opponent of the South African War but did not become involved in various "Stop the War" campaigns. His opposition, and that of the London Peace Society, was much influenced by the experience of the Crimean War. It was alleged that there was little to be gained by agitating against war once it had begun. Darby was very active in the organization of the Universal Peace Congresses held in London (1890), Chicago (1893) and Glasgow (1908) and was also a member of the International Peace Bureau at Bern.

In the decade before the First World War, the London Peace Society seemed to be losing impetus. Its leadership was criticized as being insufficiently radical or open to new suggestions. The "new pacifism" of *Norman Angell seemed to some to be a more promising path to peace than the traditional emphasis on "morality" in the work of the London Peace Society. In lectures and writing, Darby reiterated his view that the moral issue was paramount but tried to keep on good terms with those who rejected a religious framework. Nevertheless, some tension remained and the outbreak of war produced sharp divisions of opinion in the London Peace Society. Darby decided to resign within a matter of months. Whatever the future held for the London Peace Society, Darby's tenure of its secretaryship was in a traditional mold of Nonconformist religion and Liberal politics. Darby was also a temperance enthusiast. His writings on international tribunals were frequently referred to in contemporary peace literature.

Bibliography:

A. *The Christ Method of Peace-Making* (London, 1910); *International Tribunals* (London, 1899); *Modern Pacific Settlements Involving the Appreciation of the Principle of International Arbitration* (London, 1904); *Out of the Depths: a Temperance Tale* (London, 1885).

B. A.C.F. Beales, *History of Peace* (London, 1931); G. J. Jones, *Wales and the Quest for Peace* (Cardiff, 1969).

Keith G. Robbins

DAVIES, David. See *Biographical Dictionary of Internationalists*.

DAY, Dorothy (8 November 1897, Bath Beach, Brooklyn, NY—29 November 1980, New York). *Education*: Univ. of Illinois at Urbana, 1914–16. *Career*: reporter, *New York Call*, 1916–17; assistant editor, *The Masses*, 1917; journalist, *The Liberator*, 1918; assistant editor, *The Liberator* (from Chicago), 1923–24; co-founder of the Catholic Worker movement and founder-editor of *The Catholic Worker* newspaper, May 1, 1933–80; free-lance journalist, author, and social activist.

Dorothy Day was born at the end of a century sure of the validity of progress, the believability of evolution. During her student years, Day was drawn to the Naturalist writings of Jack London and Upton Sinclair. Her early passion for these writers fused with her interest in the social-evolutionary theories of Herbert Spencer and William Graham Sumner, providing a firm basis for the type of socialism she endorsed during college. Curiously, though, the pacifism which marked her as a leader began, in the 1920s, to assume a decidedly religious tone.

Day's social consciousness and literary career flowered in the second decade of the twentieth century—first as a student at the University of Illinois and later (1916–23) as a journalist for a variety of Socialist papers under the editorship of *Max and *Crystal Eastman and Floyd Dell. In line with her associates, she publicly opposed World War I as a capitalistic endeavor on the part of the government, waged at the expense of the poor. Meanwhile, Day's involvement in the women's suffrage movement won her both a thirty-day prison sentence and some public notoriety.

Nonetheless her frequent experiences of faith were beginning to impinge on her staunch socialism. Throughout the 1920s her interest in Dostoevsky and her quiet meditations in St. Joseph's Church on Sixth Avenue in New York became the foundations on which she would later build her pacifist life. Thus, May 1, 1933 found Dorothy Day a baptized Catholic and co-founder-editor of *The Catholic Worker* newspaper, which she sold in New York City's Union Square for "a penny a copy."

The distinctive pacifist nature of the Catholic Worker paper and movement were stressed from the first. Using *The Catholic Worker* as a pulpit for her Catholic brand of pacifism, Day was able to disseminate the French Personalists' philosophy to a large Catholic readership. Such a philosophy included her responsibility to point out the madness of war and to relate pacifism to the New Testament notion of peace. Thus, as signs of a new war began to occur in the middle and late 1930s, she took a strong antiwar stand, this time on the basis of the Gospel rather than the socialism of her college days. Though many were eager to take her to task for her stubborn position against the inevitability of World War II, she remained uncompromising. Undaunted by the idea of a "just" war, an idea seemingly endorsed by the Church itself, Day could find in the Gospel no extenuating conditions justifying *any* war. On this point she remained adamant.

Though Day's efforts to resist war were sharply criticized, her resistance encouraged the pre-World War II formation of Catholic Fellowship groups in the United States and a PAX group, chaired by *Eric Gill, in England. As early as October 1933, the *Worker* stated its intention to send "Catholic Pacifism" representatives to the United States Congress to protest America's preparedness for war. Three years later, the *Worker* announced its formation of a peace group. Day's insistence on organizing such a group was primarily to provide a rallying point for those Catholics who were inclined towards conscientious objection to war. Her secondary aim was to disseminate the personalist doctrine of nonviolence, thus providing Catholics with a firmly grounded philosophical alternative to conscription.

In June 1940 the *Worker* featured a "Peace Edition" in which Day reaffirmed her movement's absolute pacifism. The Sermon on the Mount was the cornerstone of her proclamation as well as the Gospel message on which she would continue to preach peace. Catholic conscientious objectors, almost nonexistent before World War II, grew in number during the war under the auspices of Day's Catholic Worker philosophy. Though her pacifism lost some of its sensational value after 1945, Day's antiwar stand continued without remission throughout the remaining four decades of her life, particularly as it applied to atomic warfare and the Vietnam War.

In the early 1960s, Day appointed herself peace ambassador to Cuba traveling to that land in the effort to affect a reconciliation between Cuba and the United States. Her attempt proved fruitless. On the heels of the Bay of Pigs incident, Day's pacifist influence gave renewed impetus to the 1962 formation of an American PAX group chaired by Howard Everngam and James H. Forest. PAX also played an important role during the Vietnam War. For a decade PAX was sponsored by Dorothy Day, providing a forum for conscientious objectors and draft evaders who gained a sizable following and reputation under the title "Catholic Peace Fellowship."

During the last years of her life, Day continued to reassert her peace stand, clarifying again and again that her neutrality was not an expression of indifference in the face of worldly events, nor was her pacifism her attempt to substitute Church sovereignty for national sovereignty. Rather, her pacifism stemmed from her unwavering belief that the moral precepts of the Gospel stood, finally, above everything else. Her Catholic Worker life was her way of imitating Christ's life, and her pacifism a poignant demonstration of her intense belief in Dostoevsky's evocation that "love in practice is a harsh and dreadful thing" [The Brothers Karamazov].

Bibliography:

A. *From Union Square to Rome* (Silver Spring, MD, 1938); *House of Hospitality* (New York and London, 1939); *Loaves and Fishes* (New York, 1963); *The Long Loneliness* (New York, 1952); *On Pilgrimage* (New York, 1948); *Pilgrimage: The Sixties* (New York, 1972).

B. William D. Miller, *Dorothy Day: A Biography* (San Francisco, 1982); William D. Miller, *A Harsh and Dreadful Love: Dorothy Day and the Catholic Worker Movement* (New York, 1973).

C. Dorothy Day Papers, Marquette University archives, Milwaukee, WI.

Sarah Ellen Witte

DE BOSIS, Lauro (9 December 1901, Rome—3 October 1931, over the Tyrrhenean Sea). *Education*: Ph.D., Univ. of Rome. *Career*: poet, translator, lecturer, historian, and political activist.

Lauro De Bosis grew up in a warm, happy intellectual environment provided by his Italian father, Adolpho, who was a poet and translator of Shelley, and his American mother, an educated woman who shared an enthusiasm for Shelley's work. From his background, he absorbed the spirit of American revolutionary independence and Garibaldian Italian national freedom. The young man developed wide ranging interests, was fluent in several languages, loved the classics as well as sciences. He completed a degree in science at the University of Rome, but also wrote poetry. Charles Lindbergh's historic trans-Atlantic flight in 1927 inspired De Bosis' magnificent verse-drama, *Icaro*, for which he was awarded the Olympic prize at Amsterdam.

The theme of *Icaro* is the eternal struggle of Man to achieve liberty through applying scientific thought to the problems of the universe. It is worked out allegorically in the story of Daedalus the inventor who seeks freedom in flight from his master, the tyrant Minos. With the loss of Icarus who represented all that the inventor held most dear, De Bosis demonstrated the dangers of an uncurbed faith in science. Rejecting the view that progress was reflected in material achievement, De Bosis observes that "where there is no vision the people perish."

By 1927 De Bosis had begun to lose his initial feeling that fascism would bring a law-abiding way of life to Italy along with peace and liberty. He perceived the darkness that lay ahead, a darkness compounded by the willful ignorance of people who were willing to ignore Benito Mussolini's increasing despotism. He was equally disturbed by the growing willingness of modern society to accept the materialist worship of science. With a few trusted friends, he created the ''National Alliance,'' an organization that circulated chain letters to Italians that made clear what darkness lay ahead. The society also suggested ways to resist fascism. His adventure into ''politics'' led to his exile. While working as a waiter in Paris, he heard that his mother and comrades had been arrested and imprisoned.

De Bosis resolved to act. With borrowed funds, he bought an airplane which he named ''Pegasus'' and took only five hours of flying lessons. Then, he took off from Marseilles carrying 400,000 leaflets addressed to the king and peoples of Italy. Just before his departure, he mailed a document (in French) entitled ''The Story of My Death,'' which contained a shrewd analysis of fascism as well as a prophetic vision of what would happen were fascism not resisted. The plane arrived over Rome on a beautiful October evening, raining its message of liberty for a half an hour, undisturbed by the much-vaunted Fascist air force. Then the pilot turned west and was last seen in the mists over the Tyrrhenian Sea. He died near his 30th birthday as did Shelley.

Bibliography:

A. *L'Histoire de ma Mort* (Brussels, 1931); *Icaro* (Alpes, 1930, English trans. by Ruth Draper, Oxford, 1933); *Storia della mia morte e ultima scritti di Lauro de Bosis* (Turin, 1948).

B. ''A Man and his Mission,'' in *Listener* (London), October 19, 1981; Neville Rogers, ''Lauro De Bosis, '' in *Rivista* (London), July-September, 1981; Arturo Vivante, ''Lauro de Bosis,'' in *Rivista*, October-December, 1981.

Neville Rogers

DE BROUCKÈRE, Louis Gustave Jean Marie Theodore (31 May 1870, Roulers, Belgium—4 June 1951, Brussels). *Education*: Athénée Bruxelles; studies in physical and mathematical sciences, Univ. of Brussels, 1887–93; studies in law and philosophy, Univ. of Paris. *Career*: member, general council of the Labor party; member, Second International and Executive Committee of the International Socialist Bureau; president, Société générale coopérative; member, Central Committee, International Cooperative Alliance; municipal councillor, Brussels, 1896–1904; Brabant provincial councillor, 1900–6; delegate to League of Nations and Preparatory Commission on Disarmament; senator, 1925–32; minister of state, 1945; founder, New University, Brussels, 1893; professor, Philosophy of Sciences, New University, 1894–1914; professor, University of Brussels, 1919–48; professor, Academy of International Law, The Hague, 1930, 1935; founder of several workers' education projects including the ''écoles socialistes'' and L'Ecole ouvrière supérieure; member and director, l'Académie royale de Belgique; journalist and political editor, *Le Peuple*, 1907–10; politician and educator.

Louis de Brouckère, a courageous and perceptive individual, was not only a preeminent scholar, but also an exceptional teacher and politician. He was one of the great theoreticians of Belgian socialism as well as of international socialism. Propagandist and man of action, he was an enthusiastic militant in the daily struggles of the worker's movement. As an internationalist, the preservation of peace remained his abiding concern.

Before 1914, de Brouckère participated in antimilitarist struggles. In 1896 he was condemned to six months in prison for having signed an article, "Tu ne tueras pas" (Thou Shalt not Kill"). Following the First World War, he threw himself into the struggles in favor of peace and disarmament. As Belgium's delegate to the League of Nations, he was in charge of representing his country's position on the Disarmament Committee. Opposed to any and all agression, he regularly invoked the use of sanctions mentioned in the Versailles Treaty to preserve peace.

De Brouckère opposed Benito Mussolini's Fascism and Adolf Hitler's National Socialism, supporting the socialist effort during the Spanish Civil War. From 1933 he adopted a position in opposition to Belgian neutrality, and in 1940 he left Belgium for France and England where he took up the struggle for a durable peace. In his articles, lectures, and radio broadcasts from London, he battled for the victory of the democratic nations. Until his death, without ever faltering, De Brouckère pursued the ideals of justice and peace.

Bibliography:

A. *L'Affiliation des syndicats au Parti Ouvrier*, with C. Huysmans (Brussels, 1907); "La Belgique stabilisée. La Belgique et le désarmement," *La Revue des Vivants,* II (Paris, 1928) 400–10; *Le "Conscrit" aux assises, Le Procès de L. de Brouckère et Jules Lekeu* (Brussels, 1896); *La grève générale en Belgique, avril 1913*, with L. Vander Smissen and E. Vandervelde (Paris, 1914); *La coopération. Ses origines, sa nature, ses grandes fonctions* (Huy, 1926); "La Naissance difficile de l'Ordre international," *Revue socialiste*, VII (1939), 6–16; *Oeuvres choisies: Le Professeur, le theóricien de l'action ouvrière, Le défenseur de la paix, le journaliste* (4 vols., Brussels, 1954–62); *La Pre-´vention de la guerre* (Paris, 1935); *Les Travaux de la Société des Nations en matieře de désarmement* (Paris, 1929).

B. "Notice sur la vie et les travaux de Louis de Brouckère, professeur honoraire à la Faculté des Sciences sociales, politiques et économiques," Université Libre de Bruxelles, *Rapport sur l'année academique 1950–51*, pp. 161–3; E. Vandervelde, "Erwiderung an De Man und de Brouckère." *Die Neue Zeit* (Stuttgart), April 14, 1911; E. Vandervelde et al, *Louis de Brouckère* (Brussels, 1930).

Nadine Lubelski-Bernard
Trans. by Sandi E. Cooper

DEBS, Eugene Victor (5 November 1855, Terre Haute, IN—20 October 1926, Elmhurst, IL). *Education*: one year of high school; part-time study at Garwin's

Business Coll., 1872–73. *Career*: railroad and warehouse worker, 1870–78; union leader and journalist, 1878–98; Socialist leader, 1898–1924.

Eugene V. Debs was the elder son of immigrants from Alsace who emigrated to the United States in 1849. Educated and middle class, the father was swindled aboard ship and forced to work at unskilled labor until he and wife established a small retail grocery. During Debs' formative years the family lived in rooms over the store.

Against parental protest, Debs quit school at fourteen to work as a paint scraper at 50¢ a day for the Vandalia Railroad; the next year he became a locomotive fireman. He joined the Brotherhood of Locomotive Firemen at age nineteen, and for approximately the next twenty years he devoted his main energies to the railroad labor movement—first as a BLF official and after 1893, as founder and president of the American Railway Union, an industrial organization for all railroad employees. At first highly successful, the ARU suffered utter defeat in 1894 when, to support a strike by workers at the Pullman Car Company, its members refused to work on trains that included Pullman cars. When the ARU ignored a federal injunction, President Grover Cleveland sent soldiers and ordered the prosecution of union leaders. Debs spent six months in jail. The Pullman strike made him a national figure, heroic to some, villainous to others.

A handsome and charming youth, as well as a powerful orator, Debs was elected city clerk of Terre Haute in 1879 as a reform Democrat; he won again in 1881. In 1884 he won a seat in the lower house of the Indiana legislature. When the Senate gutted the worker safety bills he had steered through the House he refused to run again. Upon leaving jail in 1895, he declared himself a socialist, but took only a few tentative steps in that direction. He campaigned for *William Jennings Bryan on the Populist ticket in 1896, having himself declined to have his name placed in nomination. He clearly had become a socialist by 1900, when he first was a candidate for president. He ran again in 1904, 1908, and 1912.

Debs criticized the Spanish-American War and American annexation of the Philippines. His opposition was based not upon pacifist principles—indeed, in the years to come he would make some rather bloody statements in response to violent actions against working men—but upon a deep distrust of capitalism. Though never a sophisticated or even a systematic theorist of society, Debs clearly linked capitalism with imperialism. His public statements on the 1898 war and the Philippines, however, had little effect; most of them were delivered in small midwestern towns. At the time he was concerned mostly with building an effective socialist movement.

Debs and members of the Socialist party generally were appalled when most European Socialists supported war in 1914. The SP dropped its membership in the Second International. In late 1916 Debs spoke out against +President Woodrow Wilson's preparedness campaign. The following March the SP called an emergency convention for April 7 to decide what its position should be if America declared war, which Congress did one day before the convention met in St. Louis. Debs was ill and did not attend. A large majority of the delegates passed a resolution that blamed the war on thirst for profits and pledged the party to "continuous, active, and public opposition to the war, through demonstrations, mass petitions, and all other means within our power." Subsequently, a party referendum overwhelmingly ratified the resolution.

In poor health and frequently bedridden, Debs was relatively quiet for the war's first fifteen months, restricting his public statements to condemnations of gross violations of civil liberty. Regaining some strength by June 1918 and outraged by the imprisonment of other Socialist leaders, he gave several speeches in the Midwest. The most important was a long outdoor address to the Ohio SP convention in Canton. His speech on that occasion compared to some of his earlier statements was mild; its strongest indictment of government policy lay in his assertion that, historically, the working class always fights the battles but the "ruling class" declares the wars.

E. S. Wirtz, United States attorney for northern Ohio, had stenographers at Canton, and he sent a transcript of Debs' speech to the Department of Justice together with a letter stating his belief that Debs had violated the Espionage Act. The Department replied that it was not "strongly convinced" a prosecution was "advisable," but did not forbid one. Wirtz prosecuted, and in September a jury found Debs guilty. Testifying that the transcript was accurate, Debs argued only that the Espionage Act was inconsistent with the First Amendment and that if it "finally stands, then the Constitution of the United States is dead." The judge sentenced him to ten years in prison. In March 1919 the Supreme Court upheld the conviction, with Justice Oliver Wendell Holmes writing the opinion only one week after his enunciation of the "clear and present danger" principle. Debs entered prison the next month.

In 1920 the SP again nominated Debs for the presidency. Federal prisoner 9653 accepted the nomination at Atlanta Penitentiary and quipped that his campaign would be "much less tiresome" than previous ones. That November he received a record number of votes, but not as large a percentage as he had garnered in 1912. During the campaign the usually red-baiting Attorney General, A. Mitchell Palmer, submitted a commutation of sentence to Wilson for his signature. Wilson, however, rejected it. When Warren G. Harding became President, he arranged to have Debs visit him at the White House; Debs traveled alone, without guard, and in street clothes. Harding commuted the sentence December 25, 1921.

Emotionally drained and in fragile health when he returned home, Debs was unable to make more than brief forays into Socialist political action. He was confined to bed much of the time, and beginning in 1922 he had extended stays in the Lindlahr Sanitarium near Chicago. He died there in 1926.

Bibliography:

A. *Walls and Bars* (Chicago, 1927); *Writings and Speeches of Eugene V. Debs* (New York, 1948).

B. Bernard J. Brommel, *Eugene V. Debs: Spokesman for Labor and Socialism* (Chicago, 1978); Ray Ginger, *The Bending Cross: A Biography of Eugene Victor Debs* (New

Brunswick, NJ, 1949); Nick Salvatore, *Eugene V. Debs: Citizen and Socialist* (Urbana, IL, 1982); David A. Shannon, *The Socialist Party of America: A History* (New York, 1955).

David A. Shannon

DE GUBERNATIS, Angelo (4 April 1840, Turin, Italy—27 February 1913, Rome). *Education*: laureate in lettere, Univ. of Turin, 1861; studies in philology, Univ. of Berlin, 1862. *Career*: professor (Sanskrit), Univ. of Florence, 1864–91, (Modern Italian Literature), Univ. of Rome, 1891–1913); editor, author, publisher, scholar, and peace activist.

Prolific as an author, as a publisher of intellectual journals, as a specialist in Asian as well as European literature, and as a political commentator, Angelo de Gubernatis supported and participated in the peace movement initially through his broad cultural interests. He sought to describe mythologies and customs on a cross cultural basis, exploring facets of Oriental culture and seeking the universals shared by West and East. As a founder and editor of five scholarly reviews, he was in touch with a wide ranging network of European scholars, and in several biographical dictionaries of contemporary writers, he further extended his network.

Through his marriage to Sofia Besobrasoff (1865), de Gubernatis became a relative of Michael Bakunin and for a short time thereafter, was attracted to the ideals of the First International. Within two years, he returned to teaching, disenchanted with the violence which radical egalitarianism appeared to demand. Besides teaching, de Gubernatis traveled widely and wrote extensively of the customs he encountered in Russia, Hungary, Transylvania, and France. He lectured abroad extensively, organized numerous international conferences, and generally acted on his presumption that peace would be served best by the widest possible diffusion of culture. His appetite for unique and remarkable social and cultural experiences was insatiable.

With the formation of the French-Italian friendship committee in 1888–89, de Gubernatis lent his name and efforts to the attempt to rebuild the old Franco-Italian Risorgimento relationship and minimize Italy's growing dependence on the Triple Alliance. He shared the views of Italians who rejected Francesco Crispi's militant foreign policy and close liaison with the two Germanic monarchies of Europe. Beyond signing public statements, his form of protest was to arrange a public concert where a mixed chorus of French and Italian singers performed a new composition, a *Hymn to Peace*, which de Gubernatis commissioned. The performance, claimed de Gubernatis, was flung in the face of Crispi and was applauded enthusiastically. A generation earlier, after the Prussian bombardment of Strasbourg in 1870, he had personally organized the shipment of several thousand books to replace many damaged at the University library with a large public fanfare that denounced the barbaric attack on civilization which the Franco-Prussian War unleashed. His vision of peace among civilized nations depended on ever tightening intellectual and cultural relationships, coordinated and led by the elites of the major powers. He also lent his prestigious name and energies to *Ernesto Moneta's peace society in Milan.

In 1910–11, de Gubernatis chaired the committee in Rome which began preparing for a large peace exhibition as well as the 1911 annual meetings of both the Universal Peace Congress and the Interparliamentary Union which were scheduled to occur in conjunction with the celebration of Italy's 50th year as a united nation. Having devoted his energies to making these meetings and the exhibition truly grandiose, de Gubernatis was horrified to hear that Rome was dropped as the site because of Italy's declaration of war against Turkey over Libya. (The Interparliamentary Union leaders preferred to claim it was because of a cholera outbreak.) De Gubernatis, who belonged to the Italian pacifist group which believed in the justness of that war, was infuriated and joined in an immense polemic against the rest of Europe's pacifists and many Italian peace leaders. He took steps to publish a new peace journal and attempted to reorganize the Italian peace movement under a new set of statutes. He also undertook a number of lecture engagements on the theme of patriotic pacifism, arguing that pacifism in no way prevented a state from pursuing its national interests. Further, he insisted as an expert on Oriental cultures, the presuppositions of European internationalism could not be extended to undeveloped or primitive cultures where force ruled. By his death in 1913, de Gubernatis emerged as one of the more forceful exponents of "patriotic pacifism" in Italy.

Bibliography:

A. *Dictionnaire international des écrivains du monde latin*, (Florence, 1905–6); *Dizionario biografico degli scrittori contemporanei* (Florence, 1879); *Fibra: Pagine di Ricordi* (Rome, 1900); *Pacifismo e Patriotismo* (Milan, 1912).

B. Obituaries, *Luce del Pensiero* (Naples), March 20, 1913; *Popolo Romano*, February 28, 1913; *Secolo*, February 28, 1913; *Le Temps*, March 7, 1913.

C. Angelo De Gubernatis Papers, Manuscript room, Biblioteca Nazionale Centrale, Florence.

Sandi E. Cooper

DE LAVELEYE, Émile Louis Victor (5 April 1822, Bruges, Belgium—2 January 1892, Doyon, Belgium). *Education*: Athénée royal de Bruges; Collège Stanislas de Paris; Univ. of Louvain, 1840–42; Dr. jur., Univ. of Ghent, 1844. *Career*: lawyer, economist, professor of Political Economy, Univ. of Liège, 1863; historian, philologist; writer; founder and vice-president, Institute of International Law (Ghent), 1882; secretary-general, International Association for the Reform and Codification of the Rights of Man, 1873; founder and president, Belgian section of the International Arbitration and Peace Association, 1889–92.

Émile de Laveleye, a liberal Catholic who greatly admired British society, had developed a solid international reputation in a variety of areas when he converted to Protestantism in 1878. By then his writings and correspondence had insured his access to eminent persons in a vast network of journalists, literary people, politicians, and economists. Among the many areas he covered, the peace crusade remained central and de Laveleye placed his faith in the hope that an awakened public conscience might be stimulated by his writings to work for the cause of peace.

At the outbreak of each conflict or crisis, de Laveleye burst into print on behalf of justice, humanity and the preservation of peace. During the Alabama claims case between the United States and Great Britain, he campaigned among Western journalists to write sympathetic pieces about the arbitration process and to support the verdict. In 1882–85, he served as a self-appointed international tribune and bombarded the British press with communiqués detailing Turkish atrocities against Bulgarians, conducted with Greek complicity. He labored to make international law a serious area of university study and professional concern by his commitment to the two international associations concerned with developing and spreading precepts of international law.

In *Des causes actuelles de guerre en Europe et de l'arbitrage* (1873), de Laveleye recognized that a multiplicity of causes lay beneath the outbreaks of wars, but he predicted that future wars would largely result from frustrated nationalism. To avoid that probability, he argued for the creation of a "universal" society where free international exchange would build solidarity and interdependence among diverse peoples. The new international social system would have its own code, arbitration tribunal, and executive.

Beyond his writings and activities on behalf of peace, de Laveleye's interests ranged over a vast array of subjects. He wrote on such topics as thc literature and language of the Provence, the relationship between education and the military, Frankish kings, Scandinavian epics, rural economies in numerous parts of Europe, free trade and international commerce, bimetallism, the railway industry, particular political crises, the relationship between social progress and religion, the nature of democracy and socialism, and the opening of Africa. Besides writing over 60 books and lengthy pamphlets, he published articles in more than 25 journals in nearly every European language. His longer works were translated into every major European language as well. Few scholars of his time achieved his stature and reputation in so many fields. Among peace activists, de Laveleye was regarded as a major source of information and inspiration.

Bibliography:

A. *Les Actes de la Conférence de Bruxelles et la participation de la Belgique à la Conférence de Saint-Pétersburg* (Brussels, 1875); *Des causes actuelles de guerre en Europe et de l'arbitrage* (Brussels, 1873); *Essais et Etudes* (3 vols., Paris and Ghent, 1894, 1895, 1897); *The New Tendencies of Political Economy* (New York, 1879); *Du respect de la propriété privée en temps de guerre* (Brussels, 1875).

B. Goblet d'Alviella, *Emile de Laveleye, sa vie et son oeuvre* (Paris & Brussels, 1895); R. Demoulin, "Laveleye et Gladstone," in M. Florkin & L. E. Halkin, eds., *Chronique de l'Université de Liège* (Liège, 1967), I, 335–52; E. Silberner, *La Guerre et la paix dans l'histoires des doctrines economiques* (Paris, 1957), 156–58; *Biographie Coloniale*

Belge, IV, cols. 484–97; *Biographie Nationale*, XXXIV, cols. 528–49; *Notices biographiques et bibliographiques*, 1886, 363–72.

Nadine Lubelski-Bernard
Trans. by Sandi E. Cooper

DE LIGT, Bartolomeus (Bart) (17 July 1883, Schalkwijk, Netherlands—3 September 1938, Nantes, France). *Education*: theology, Univ. of Utrecht, 1903–1909. *Career*: pastor, Nuenen, 1910–15; editor, writer, antiwar activist.

Bart de Ligt trained as a theologian and, for five years, served as a protestant pastor in a small village in the south of Holland. When still in his childhood, his mother had introduced him to the Sermon on the Mount and to the Prophets; ever since, he later wrote, the search for utopia remained a quintessential element in his philosophy of life. His mother also made him aware of the unnatural and unhealthy one-sideness of a male-dominated society, and increasingly he became an advocate of woman's liberation. He read widely and deeply, and was strongly influenced by English libertarian socialists, German idealist philosophers, and such figures as Michael Bakunin and *Leo Tolstoy. His passion for truth and principle soon made him a convinced Christian socialist and antimilitarist. He joined the Bond van Christen-Socialisten (Union of Christian-Socialists) (BvCS) in 1909, becoming its leading member until he left the organization a decade later. His inflammatory antimilitarist manifestos and speeches during World War I led to his expulsion from the southern part of the country (where troops had been concentrated to protect the border, and which had been declared to be in a state of siege) in 1915, and from eastern parts of the country two years later. He was also imprisoned for a few weeks in 1915, and again in 1921 when he organized a general strike to obtain the release of Herman Groenendaal who, as a result, became Holland's most famous conscientious objector. De Ligt's activities to secure freedom of conscience for soldiers contributed significantly to the passing of the first Dutch law on conscientious objection in 1923.

The failure of the churches to oppose World War I, as well as their unquestioned support for the monarchy and the existing social order led to his leaving the church in 1916 and the BvCS in 1919. No longer regarding himself as a Christian, de Ligt went through a period of intellectual and emotional crises during which he studied Greek philosophy and Eastern religions. The end result of this process was that de Ligt was drawn to a more general, cosmic religion. At this time he turned not only against official Christianity, but also against official socialism. He criticized the Second International for having abandoned the socialist struggle at the most crucial moment. Moreover, he regarded the authoritarian approach and rigid structure of socialist parties as being incompatible with the essence of socialism. He also insisted that for the creation of a socialist society a spiritual revolution in the individual was as necessary as a revolution in material and external circumstances. Thus, like *Ferdinand Domela Nieuwenhuis, de Ligt moved from being a Christian to being an anarchist. He considered that the only true revolution was the one in which primitive nature was transformed into the highest form of consciousness. He believed not only that a revolution was needed to overturn society, but that the process had to be uplifting at the same time. The importance that he attached to this spiritual dimension in the revolutionary struggle led him to elaborate the notion of a nonviolent revolution. He maintained that "the more violence, the less revolution; the more revolution, the less violence—since it is simply impossible to enforce social and spiritual freedom, as they can only grow from the bottom upwards." De Ligt was one of the few consistent critics of the use of violence, who at the same time was firmly committed to revolution.

In 1921 he took the initiative in creating the International Anti-Militarist Bureau (IAMB), the successor to Nieuwenhuis's International Anti-Militarist Union. His attempts to coordinate and strengthen the international antimilitarist movement benefitted from his move to Geneva in 1925. There he met such figures as *Albert Einstein, *Jawaharlal Nehru, *Mohandas Gandhi, *Maria Montessori, and *Aldous Huxley, some of whom lent their support to activities which de Ligt organized in his tireless campaign against war and militarism. These included the 1929 Frankfurt Anti-War Congress of Intellectuals, the establishment in 1937 in Paris of the Rassemblement international contre la guerre et le militarisme (International Gathering Against War and Militarism), which created the International Pacifist Association and the creation of the Peace Academy in 1938. De Ligt was uncompromising in his antiwar position. In writings such as his "Open Letter" to Gandhi (1928) and "M. Gandhi's Attitude Toward War" (1932) he criticized the Indian leader for his support of the Boer War and the First World War, and for his identification with the Indian National Congress, thereby compromising his pacifist position.

De Ligt, who from childhood suffered from poor health, nevertheless gave his utmost, both mentally and physically, in everything he undertook, leading to collapse from exhaustion on more than one occasion. Apart from campaigning and organizing, traveling and lecturing all over Europe, he was a very prolific and gifted writer. He edited several journals, most notably, during the last ten years of his life, *Bevrijding* (*Liberation*), wrote hundreds of articles, close to a hundred pamphlets, and a dozen books. Some of these have become the standard works in the literature on peace, including *Vrede als Daad* (*Creative Peace*) (1931–33), an encyclopaedic work on the history of direct action against war and *The Conquest of Violence* (1937), an exposition on the principle of nonviolence in the struggle against war and for a better society. His writing, together with his antiwar activities, made Bart de Ligt one of the most important peace advocates in the Netherlands and in Europe.

Bibliography:

A. *Anarchismus und Revolution* (Berlin, 1922); *De antimilitaristen en hun strijdwijzen* (The Hague, 1921); *Christen-Revolutionair. Over het dramatisch karakter van den godsdienst* (Zwolle, 1915); *The Conquest of Violence: An Essay on War and Revolution* (London, 1937; new ed. New York, 1972); *Erasmus begrepen uit de geest der Renaissance* (Arnhem, 1936); *Introduction to the Science of Peace* (London, 1939); *Kerk, cultuur en *samenleving. Tien jaren strijd* (Arnhem, 1925); *Mobilisatie tegen den oorlog!* (Nieuwe Niedorp. 1934); *Nieuwe vormen van oorlog en hoe die te bestrijden* (Lochem, 1927, Fr. trans., Paris, 1928); *Profeet en Volksfeest* (Amsterdam, 1913); *Vrede als Daad. Beginselen, geschiedenis en strijdmethoden van de direkte aktie tegen oorlog* (2 vols., Arnhem, 1931–33, Fr. trans., Paris, 1934); *Wereldcrisis en wijsbegeerte* (Arnhem, 1928); *Een wereldomvattend vraagstuk. Gandhi en de oorlog* (Utrecht, 1930).

B. *Bart de Ligt, 1883–1938* (Arnhem, 1939); *Bart de Ligt, 1883–1938* (Groningen, 1958); A. R. de Jong, *Bart de Ligt* (Vrij-Religieuse Toespraken, 1938, English trans., *Bart de Ligt, Peacemaker*, London, 1938); C. L. de Ligt-van Rossem, "Biografische Inleiding," *Naar een vrije orde. Bloemlezing uit de werken van Bart de Ligt* (Arnhem, 1951), 7–29; Gernot Jochheim, *Antimilitaristische Aktionstheorie, Soziale Revolution und Soziale Verteidigung* (Assen/ Amsterdam/Frankfurt, 1977); George Lakey, "Introduction," in B. de Ligt, *The Conquest of Violence* (New York, 1972), 5–11; A. Lehning, *Ithaka* (Baarn, 1980); P. Spigt, "Bart de Ligt 1883–1938," *Rekenschap*, (September, 1963); 124–29.

Peter van den Dungen

DE MAN, Hendrik (17 November 1885, Antwerp, Belgium—20 June 1953, Greng, Switzerland). *Education*: Free Univ. of Brussels; Polytechnique Institute of Ghent, 1905; studies in psychology and political economy, universities of Leipzig and Vienna; Doctor of History and Philosophy, Univ. of Leipzig, 1909. *Career*: Socialist politician; editor, *Leipziger Volkszeitung*; founder and secretary, International Federation of Socialist Youth, 1907; member, Second International; secretary, central organization of Workers' Education, 1910; teacher, Akademie der Arbeit, Frankfort, 1922–26; professor, Univ. of Frankfort; director of studies (1934), vice-president (1933), and president (1939–40), Belgian Socialist party; Senator, 1936–44, Minister of Public Works and Unemployment, 1935–36, Minister of Finance, 1936–38, vice-president, Council of Ministers, 1939–40; teacher and politician.

Hendrik de Man became interested in the problems of the working class as a young man. At first influenced by anarchist doctrines and then by Marxism, he belonged to the radical wing of the Socialist party until 1914. After World War I his political convictions were profoundly transformed as a result of the moral and intellectual upheaval which he experienced.

De Man divided his life between teaching—largely in workers' schools—and political labors. In 1933 he developed a labor plan to confront the massive unemployment left by the Depression and his ideas helped fashion socialist doctrine in Belgium. On the international level, he remained a fierce defender of neutrality and his influence on Belgian policy in this regard was considerable.

Given his complex personality and eventful life, de Man's support of peace underwent several changes. In 1914 he initially supported the efforts of the Second International to prevent war. After these failed, his internationalist and antimilitarist faith was badly shaken and he joined the Belgian army. From that moment, de Man wanted to see the total defeat of Germany in order to engender the democratic revolution which German Social Democrats had failed to make in 1914. When the war ended, de Man welcomed President +Woodrow Wilson's Fourteen Points enthusiastically as the basis of a new international order, but he became quickly disillusioned by the Versailles negotiations and the attitudes of the victors.

While ever hoping for a global agreement to reduce arms and create the institutions to organize a durable peace, de Man urged a policy of neutrality on the Belgian government. Tormented with the possibility of war again in 1940, he made a tragic choice. In a Manifesto of June 28, 1940, he expressed his belief that fascism could play a revolutionary role. It could, he argued, destroy those forces which had prevented the realization of social justice and European peace. In 1942 he published *Réflexions sur la paix* which envisioned the supranational organization of Europe and the establishment of a just and lasting peace. In 1946 *Au delà du nationalisme* appeared wherein de Man argued that the atomic bomb totally confounded the international situation and made the creation of a world government essential, if humanity were to be preserved from extinction.

In 1946 de Man received a 20-year prison sentence from a Belgian military tribunal for having served the enemy's purposes. By then, however, he had left Belgium. From 1941 to 1944 he lived in France and from 1944 to 1953 he lived in Switzerland. He died in a car accident.

Bibliography:

A. *Après coup (mémoires)* (Brussels, 1941); *De Catechismus van den Belgischen soldaat* (Ghent, 1903); *Au delà du Nationalisme* (Geneva, 1946); *Gegen den Strom. Memoiren eines europäisichen Sozialisten* (Stuttgart, 1953); *La Leçon de la guerre* (Brussels, 1920); *Une Offensive pour la paix* (Brussels, 1938); *Réflexions sur la paix* (Brussels, 1942); *The Remaking of a Mind: A Soldier's Thoughts on War and Reconstruction* (London, 1920); *Vermassung und Kulturzerfall. Eine Diagnose unserer Zeit* (Bern, 1951).

B. *Actes du Colloque international sur l'oeuvre d'Henri de Man, June, 1973*, Geneva, Faculté de Droit (Geneva, 1974); P. Dodge, *Beyond Marxism: The Faith and Works of Hendrik de Man* (The Hague, 1966); *Hendrik de Man, Persoon en Ideeën* (6 vols., Antwerp, 1974); *Biographie Nationale*, xxxviii, 535–54.

Nadine Lubelski-Bernard
Trans. by Sandi E. Cooper

DEMARTIAL, Georges (28 May 1861, Boulogne-sur-Seine, Seine, France—14 October 1945, Mézy, Seine-et-Oise, France). *Education*: Lycée of Versailles, Collège Stanislas. *Career*: official with the Ministry of Colonies and government commissioner with the Bank of Indochina; freelance writer and polemicist.

Not until the outbreak of World War I did Georges Demartial become an active opponent of war. Scion of a comfortable middle-class family engaged in commerce, he enjoyed a good education and entered the civil service, advancing rapidly through the ranks. His early writings dealt not with peace but with the rights of functionaries within the ministries and the need for administrative reform of the bureaucracy.

The shock and surprise he felt when war erupted in 1914 led him to inquire into its origins. Demartial began to collect documents, to study the diplomatic explanations offered by all the nations involved, and to investigate, as best he could under the circumstances, the responsibilities for the catastrophe. He soon became convinced that Russia rather than either Germany or Austria-Hungary was responsible. Along with other intellectuals, Demartial organized, in January 1916, the Société d'études documentaires et critiques sur la guerre (Society for Documentary and Critical Studies of the War), dedicated to examining the question of responsibility and publishing its findings. Henceforth, Demartial would devote his life almost entirely to the problem of war guilt and the prevention of a future world conflict.

With the end of wartime censorship, he began to publish the results of his findings. Demartial contended that the Allied powers as much as their enemies were responsible for provoking the war and that the Treaty of Versailles represented a harsh and humiliating peace unfairly imposed upon Germany. He attacked his own government for its violations of international law, deceptive propaganda, and use of censorship to conceal its guilt. He called for revision of article 231, which laid exclusive blame on the vanquished. In addition Demartial accused the Quai d'Orsay of distorting and suppressing important diplomatic documents, and he attempted to show that the official French version of how the war started, contained in the *Livre jaune* of 1914, was unreliable and misleading. Demartial contended that President Raymond Poincaré had deliberately misled the people into believing that neither France nor its Russian ally had played any part in starting the conflict.

Demartial's efforts to fix responsibility for the war on the Allies brought violent attacks from the French Right and his suspension from the Legion of Honor for five years. Nonetheless, he continued his crusade, taking an active role in the work of the Ligue internationale des combattants de la paix (International League of Fighters for Peace), organized in 1931 to prevent a new world war. In countless magazine and newspaper articles, he denounced the culprits who had provoked war in 1914 and attacked war as a legitimate means of self-defense. As late as 1939, Demartial condemned his own government for causing World War I.

During World War II, he denounced his own countrymen who had brought on the disaster of 1940 and worked for improved relations with Germany. More than ever before, Demartial regretted that the victors of 1918 had not established an equitable peace that would have prevented a renewed bloodbath. He hoped to establish a league against patriotic lies that would work for international conciliation and peace. Demartial's death at an advanced age prevented him from continuing what had become his work for "peace by means of truth."

Bibliography:

A. *Comment on mobilisa les consciences* (Paris, 1922); *L'Evangile du Quai d'Orsay* (Paris, 1926); La Guerre de l'imposture *(Paris, 1941); La Haine de la vérité* (Paris, 1939); *Le Mythe des guerres de légitime défense* (Paris, 1931).

B. Félicien Challaye, *Georges Demartial, sa vie, son oeuvre* (Paris, 1950).

James Friguglietti

DE MOLINARI, Gustave (3 March 1819, Liége, Belgium—28 January 1912, De Panne, Belgium). *Education*: Collège de Verviers. *Career*: economist, editor, journalist, professor of political economy.

Widely known in his day, Gustave de Molinari's reputation as an economist began in the 1840s as he pioneered the diffusion of the ideas of the free trade school emanating from Manchester onto Belgian and French soil. First as a Parisian journalist writing for the opposition press (1843–51) and then as editor of the prestigious journal, *l'Économiste Belge* (1855–66), de Molinari argued tirelessly for the liberal economic policies of free trade and unrestricted economic development. After 1867 he became editor of the *Journal des Débats* and the *Journal des Économistes* in Paris which further extended his forum. As a professor of Political Economy at Brussels and Antwerp (1852–66), de Molinari introduced the Manchester School to numerous students. Among his close friends were the French economist, *Frédéric Passy, who was equally convinced of the same economic ideology, and the tireless activist, *Edmond Potonié, who founded the Ligue du bien public (League for Public Good) at Antwerp in 1858 to create an international network of European peace reformers. De Molinari belonged to the Ligue.

The problem of war engaged de Molinari's attention more than most other topics. Among political economists, he was in the forefront of examining and reiterating its complex causes and effects. He repeatedly described the relationship between war, peace, and economic development with the undisguised objective of changing contemporary opinion. He argued that while wars may have once served to safeguard civilization and even provided a means for economic growth and profit, in modern times the same aims would be obtained by a system of commercial liberty. De Molinari never maintained that free trade would totally eliminate war, but he did propose that together with a system of collective security it could minimize its occurrence. His view of collective security was that of an association of sovereign states that maintained a joint force prepared to dissuade potential aggressors. A league of small, neutral states should be created to merge the power of their limited military resources into a unified force to aid an attacked nation or dissuade an aggressor. De Molinari hoped that the British would add their enormous naval strength and wealth to the league. Were Europeans to ignore his analysis and persist in the old war system, de Molinari feared, the future of civilization was seriously jeopardized. Despite the wave of protectionism and the growing threats to European peace that appeared with the twentieth century, de Molinari never wavered. Until his death at the age of 93, he insisted on the intimate relationship between civilization, peace, and free trade. His last work, *Ultima Verba* which appeared in 1911, echoed the arguments of 70 years of work.

As an economist, he was prolific. His writings covered the condition of the working classes, the "social question," tariff reform, the general "laws" of political economy, the production and distribution of wealth, Europe's overseas conquests and markets, compulsory education, and public law. His ideas flowed in letters, essays, monograph, and books, including a textbook which became a standard classic on political economy. De Molinari was one of the first and most consistent nineteenth-century analysts who saw that war in the modern world had lost its *raison d'être*.

Bibliography:

A. *L'Abbé de Saint-Pierre, membre exclu de l'académie française. Sa vie et ses oeuvres, précédées d'une appréciation et d'un précis historique sur l'idée de la paix perpétuelle* (Paris, 1857); *Grandeur et décadence de la guerre* (Paris, 1898); "Paix," *Dictionnaire d'économie politique* (Paris, 1873); *Esquisse de l'organisation politique et économique de la société future* (Paris, 1899); *Les problèmes du XXe siècle* (Paris, 1901); *Questions d'économie politiques et de droit public* (2 vols., Brussels, 1861).

B. A. Bieleveld, ed., *Grandes Figures de la Belgique Indpéndante, 1830–1930* (Brussels, 1930), 353–54; E. Silberner, *La querre et la paix dans l'histoire des doctrines économiques* (Paris, 1957), 92–104; *Bibliographie Nationale*, I, 468–69.

Nadine Lubelski-Bernard
Trans. by Sandi E. Cooper

DEN BEER POORTUGAEL, Jacobus Catharinus Cornelis (1 February 1832, Leyden, Netherlands—30 January 1913, Leyden). *Education*: Royal Military Academy, Breda, 1848–52. *Career*: military profession, teacher, author, and diplomat.

In 1869 Den Beer Poortugael, at that time a captain in the Dutch General Staff, became a teacher of strategy and military history at the Military Staff College. Later he became director of the college, governor of the Royal Military Academy, and an inspector of the military teaching institutions. For several months in 1879 he was the Minister of War. In 1891 he retired from his military career, having achieved the rank of major-general; in the following year he was appointed a member of the State Council, a position he retained until his death. The government accorded him the rank of lieutenant-general in 1899.

From 1870 Den Beer Poortugael pursued in effect two related but separate careers. Parallel to his professional military career he started on an intensive study of international law and the law of war, which resulted in many publications. The impetus for this second interest had come from his unexpected appointment, following the mobilization of the Dutch army in 1870, as head of the chancellery section at army headquarters. His new responsibilities led him to read, for the first time, a handbook on international law. This made him realize how deficient the education and training of officers was because of the absence of any instruction on the laws of war. In an attempt to rectify this shortcoming, Den Beer Poortugael wrote a major work on the subject, which was published in 1872. This book was followed by a great number of treatises on such subjects as the laws of war on land, international maritime law, and the rights of neutrals.

Although a soldier and not a professional lawyer, he quickly established a reputation as the foremost Dutch authority on the laws of warfare, and in 1874 received international recognition when he was honored by being appointed "Associate" of the Institute of International Law. He later became a full member.

The Dutch government sent him as an advisor or a delegate to several international conferences, including the Conference on the Laws of War held in Brussels in 1874 and the 1906 Red Cross Conference on the revision of the 1864 Geneva Convention. He made his greatest contribution, however, at the Hague Peace Conferences of 1899 and 1907, when he was a member of the Dutch delegation. Although he was not at its head and represented only a small country, his influence was considerable—largely owing to his unique, dual authority of being both a professional soldier and an expert on and advocate of international law. During both conferences Den Beer Poortugael consistently sided with those who advocated the most humane ideas and proposals. He firmly believed that it was the duty of states to "do as much good" in times of peace and "as little harm as possible to one another" in times of war.

Den Beer Poortugael was not only a great expert on international law but also an ardent advocate of the peaceful settlement of international disputes. After one of his speeches at the first Hague Conference, *Bertha von Suttner exclaimed: "To hear such words spoken by a general!" She regarded him as belonging firmly to the peace camp—a unique compliment indeed.

Bibliography:

A. *1831, De tiendaagse veldtocht* (The Hague, 1906); *Amsterdam in staat van beleg*! (The Hague, 1878); *L'Escaut et la neutralité permanente de la Belgique* (The Hague, 1910); *Le droit des gens en marche vers la paix et la guerre de Tripoli* (The Hague, 1912); *Het internationaal maritiem recht* (Breda, 1888); *Krijgsgebruiken in den oorlog te land* (Breda, 1886); *De militaire jurisdictie* (The Hague, 1881); *Neerland's belang bij de conferentiën te Brussel en St. Petersburg* (Breda, 1875); *Oorlogs—en neutraliteitsrecht* (The Hague, 1900); *Het oorlogsrecht* (Breda, 1872 & 2nd ed., 1882).

B. H. van der Mandere, "Luit.-Gen. Jhr. J.C.C. Den Beer Poortugael," *Grotius Internationaal Jaarboek voor 1913* (The Hague, 1913), 1–18; A. B. van der Vies, "Zijne excellentie Luit.-Gen. Jhr. J.C.C. Den Beer Poortugael," *Vrede door Recht*, 13 (February, 1912), 10–11.

Peter van den Dungen

DERAISMES, Maria (15 August 1828, Paris—6 February 1894, Paris). *Career*: author, political activist, reformer, feminist, and pacifist.

In the career of the wealthy and learned Maria Deraismes, the campaign for peace served less as an immediate objective than as the logical and necessary consequence of a prior political and moral transformation of France. An ardent republican and freethinker, Deraismes engaged in the political struggle that engulfed the late Second Empire (1852–70) and the early Third Republic (1870–1940) by directing a republican salon in Paris and by dominating, especially between 1881 and 1885 when she owned *Le Républicain de Seine-et-Oise*, the republican forces in her home department. She similarly struggled against the

Roman Catholic Church by presiding in 1881 over the first anticlerical congress in France and by assuming in 1885 the honorary presidency of the Fédération française des groupes de la libre-pensée de Seine-et-Oise (French Federation of the Freethinking Groups of Seine-et-Oise). Both struggles in turn drew her toward Freemasonry, a bastion of anticlerical republicanism; but when the Masonic hierarchy refused to rescind its policy against admitting women as fullfledged members and additionally voided, in 1882, her own historic initiation into a lodge at Pecq (Seine-et-Oise), she revolted against the hierarchy by founding Le Droit humain, (Human Right), the first Masonic lodge to practice sex equality.

In her struggle to effect the moral transformation of France, Deraismes inveighed against the novels of Émile Zola and other perveyors of what the called the *Épidémie naturaliste* (1888), played a prominent role in the French section of Josephine Butler's campaign to abolish governmental regulation of prostitution, and sought through participating in two antivivisectionist groups to arrest the moral barbarism caused in her view by experiments on animals. Moral concerns also inspired her to become a leading liberal feminist. In 1870 she helped to found the Société pour l'amélioration du sort de la femme (Society for the Amelioration of Woman's Condition), over which she presided until her death, and in 1878 and again in 1889 she collaborated with Léon Richer in organizing the first two women's rights congresses in France, chairing on each occasion the sessions on morality.

Deraismes' devotion to peace thus represented a direct outgrowth of her interest in moral regeneration through the emancipation of women. This interest expressed itself in Deraismes' close association with *Virginie Griess-Traut, a prominent pacifist who served for nearly three decades as an Amelioration Society vice-president, and in Deraismes' conviction that women, once emancipated, would bring to public life their "beautiful qualities: sagacity, perseverance, abnegation." A war against the enemies of democracy and peace might prove unavoidable in the short run, she acknowledged. For the long run, however, she maintained not only that the "weakening of military prestige is the sign of the advent of woman" but also that woman represented, "by her constitution and by the nature of her mandate, the moral and pacifist agent par excellence" and that the continued "elimination of women from universal suffrage necessarily means the prolongation of the bellicose spirit."

In life Deraismes earned admission into the Société des gens de lettres for writing two major feminist works, *Ève contre Monsieur Dumas fils* (1872) and *Ève dans l'humanité* (1891), as well as numerous political and moral tracts on subjects such as *Nos principes et nos moeurs* (1868) and *France et progrès* (1873). In death she earned an even rarer honor for a woman active in secular causes—a street bearing her name in Paris's 17th arrondissement.

Bibliography:

A. *L'Ancien devant le nouveau* (Pairs, 1869); *Ève countre Monsieur Dumas fils* (Paris, 1872); *Ève dans l'humanité* (Paris, 1891); *France et progrès* (Paris, 1873); *Nos principes et nos moeurs* (Paris, 1868); *Oeuvres complètes de Maria Deraismes*, ed. Anna Féresse-Deraismes (Paris, 1895).

B. Jean-Bernard [Passerieu], "Notice" in *Oeuvres complètes de Maria Deraismes*, ed. Anna Féresse-Deraismes (Paris, 1895), v-iv; Patrick Kay Bidelman, "Maria Deraismes, Léon Richer and the Founding of the French Feminist Movement, 1866–1878." *Third Republic/Troisième République*, Nos. 3–4 (1977), 20–73; Patrick Kay Bidelman, *Pariahs Stand Up! The Founding of the Liberal Feminist Movement in France, 1858–1889*. (Westport, CT, 1982); Gerard Serbanesco, *Histoire de la franc maçonnerie universelle* (4 vols., Paris, 1969), IV, 523–56.

C. Dossier Deraismes, Bibliothèque Marguerite Durand, Paris, France.

Patrick Kay Bidelman

DESCAMPS, Edouard Eugène François (27 August 1847, Beloeil, Belgium—17 January 1933, Brussels). *Education*: doctor of law, Univ. of Louvain, 1869, doctor of political and administrative sciences, 1870; also studies at the Sorbonne and several German universities. *Career*: professor of law, Univ. of Louvain; provincial counsellor, Brabant, 1884–92; senator from Louvain, 1892–93, communal counselor, Louvain, 1895–1907; Minister of Sciences and Arts, 1907–10; vice-president of the Senate, 1922–32; delegate, Hague Peace Conference, 1899; chair, League of Nations Committee for the Permanent Court of International Justice; member, Interparliamentary Union and permanent member, Interparliamentary Union Council; lawyer, university professor, internationalist.

In addition to his university and academic concerns Edouard Eugène Descamps, who was a Catholic statesman, undertook numerous national, colonial and international activities. Jurist and humanitarian, he was a major crusader for peace through law and wanted to substitute law for force in international relations. Thus he tried to develop mechanisms for the peaceful solution of interstate conflict and worked notably in the area of arbitration. He served as a member of the Belgian section of the Fédération internationale de l'arbitrage et de la paix (International Federation of Arbitration and Peace), took an active interest in the International Law Association, and was president of both the Institute of International Law and the International Parliamentary Conference on Commerce.

An active member of the Interparliamentary Union, Descamps worked mainly on the issue of international arbitration and the possibility of establishing a permanent court of arbitration. His ideas for an abritration court were not particularly daring, but they influenced the work of the first Hague Peace Conference in 1899 which produced a convention for the peaceful regulation of international conflicts. As a delegate to the conference, Descamps served as the rapporteur for the Third Committee, charged with discussing the problem of international arbitration. The conference resulted in the establishment of a Permanent Court of Arbitration, and from 1899 Descamps was listed as one of the judges.

Descamps was also the author of a novel idea—the *pacigérat* or peace pact which would work as an international compact among nations contracting to preserve peace. With others from the world of politics and law, he worked for the evolution of the idea of neutrality to a more positive condition. Neutrals would become friends to all nations obliged to intervene to preserve peace when it was threatened. Thus, the nations participating in the *pacigérat* would evolve to a more advanced stage than others.

Bibliography:

A. *Conférence internationale de la paix. Rapport à la conférence sur la convention pour le règlement pacifique des conflits internationaux.* (The Hague, 1900); *Le droit de la paix et la guerre* (Paris, 1898); *Le Droit international nouveau, l'influence de la condamnation de la guerre sur l'évolution juridique internationale* (Paris, 1931); *Essai sur l'organisation de l'arbitrage international. Mémoire aux puissances* (Brussels, 1896); *L'Etat neutre à titre permanent* (Brussels, 1912); *L'Evolution de la neutralité en droit international. Discours* (Brussels, 1898); *La Neutralité de la Belgique au point de vue historique, diplomatique, juridique et politique. Etude sur la constitution des états pacifiques a titre permanent* (Brussels, 1902); *Les Offices internationaux et leur avenir* (Brussels, 1894).

B. *Annuaire de l'Academie royale de Belgique*, CII (1936), 1–35; *Biographie Coloniale Belge*, IV, cols., 219–30; *Biographie Nationale* XLI, cols., 198–247; Van Molle, *Le Parlement Belge 1894–1969* (Grand, 1969), 109–10.

Nadine Lubelski-Bernard
Trans. by Sandi E. Cooper

DETZER, Dorothy (3 December 1893, Fort Wayne, IN—21 January 1981, Monterey, CA). *Education*: Chicago School of Civics and Philanthropy. *Career*: Hull House, Chicago 1916–20; American Friends Service Committee, Vienna, 1920–22, Russia, 1922–24; National Secretary, Women's International League for Peace and Freedom, United States Section, 1924–46; free-lance correspondent, Scripps-Howard Inc., 1956–60.

Dorothy Detzer—pacifist, lobbyist, fund raiser, organizer, and speech maker for the Women's International League for Peace and Freedom (WILPF)—was born and grew up in Fort Wayne, Indiana. She graduated from Fort Wayne High School and for two years attended the Chicago School of Civics and Philanthropy, but never received a college degree. A definite flair for the dramatic and a certain stage presence characterized Detzer's lobbying and speech making and brought her admirers in both the militarist and pacifist camps. Between the world wars, Detzer played a leading role in the movement for internationalism and peace.

When Detzer was twelve years old her mother's friend, *Alice Hamilton, took her to Hull House to meet *Jane Addams. With the beginning of World War I, Detzer went to work at Hull House, joining Jessie Binford in protective work for young women in training camps. After the war she participated in the relief work of the American Friends Service Committee (AFSC) in Vienna, and after two years went to the AFSC relief mission in Russia's Volga famine area. Having observed first hand the suffering the war had brought to children and old people, Detzer returned to the United States in 1924 outraged at the obscenity of armed conflict. Her twin brother, Don, had been fatally poisoned by mustard gas in France; however, it was not Don's fate, but that of Vienna's children, "whose only part in the war had been starvation," that prompted Detzer to question war itself. In Russia she had seen the Quaker's moral stubbornness overome the revolutionary opposition of the local Bolshevik leader. This experience had awakened in Detzer a great faith in human ingenuity by showing her that once the ways of violence and coercion were denied, creative inner resources could be released. Detzer did not become a Quaker. Her pacifism was fundamentally rooted in secular humanism. Conflict, she explained in many of her articles and talks, was basic to human relationships. It was inevitable, and even a necessary aspect of growth. The great human challenge was to resolve conflict without resorting to violence, because violent means could never shape an enduring peace. For Detzer, peace was a humanist value, a human challenge, and specifically, a political challenge.

In 1924 Detzer became the National Secretary for WILPF United States Section and went to work in WILPF's Legislative Office in Washington D.C.. She had wanted to work for an organization that emphasized the important relationship that exists between peace and economic security, and defined war, not as something innate to human nature, but simply as the state's method of dealing with conflict. WILPF's constitution and stated aims accommodated Detzer's views, but nonetheless, she often found herself in conflict with WILPF members who wanted to emphasize peace education. The U.S. Section's National Office in Philadelphia, she believed, should be moved to Washington D.C., where the action was. War, Detzer argued, was no more a part of human nature than the protective tariff. Although peace education was needed, the government made daily decisions that affected peace; therefore, pacifist women were obliged to give Washington their immediate attention.

WILPF agreed that Detzer should concentrate on legislative activities, and during the 1920s she lobbied for U.S. cooperation with the League of Nations and the World Court, for disarmament and the Kellogg-Briand Pact to outlaw war, for the withdrawal of the U.S. Marines from Nicaragua and Haiti, and for liberal immigration laws that would allow U.S. naturalization of conscientious objectors. During the 1930s Detzer actively worked for the enforcement of the League of Nations' Anti-Slavery convention in Kenya, Nigeria, Liberia, and Southern Rhodesia—work which won WILPF an insignia of the Order of African Redemption. She actively lobbied in support of the Wheeler-Howard Indian Bill, the Nye Resolution for a peace division in government and Nye's War Referendum Bill, for the Frazier Amendment to make war unconstitutional, and the Tydings Resolution for a world economic conference. Representing WILPF at numerous Congressional hearings, she urged reciprocal trade treaties and an international munitions investigation.

Working to broaden WILPF's base of support, Detzer often cooperated with other organizations, including the American Civil Liberties Union and the Women's Trade Union League. She lobbied for the Costigan Anti-Lynching Bill in 1933 with the NAACP and was arrested for obstructing the peace when she joined in efforts to integrate Capitol Building restaurants. She made WILPF's legislative office the Washington base for the Southern Tenant Farmer's Union, which awarded Detzer a lifetime membership. For a brief period she worked with Earl Browder, *Roger Baldwin, and J. B. Matthews in establishing an American Branch of the League Against War and Fascism. Often she shared platforms with Norman Thomas. Senator Gerald Nye credited Detzer's lobbying efforts with insuring the passage of the Senate resolution that called for the 1934 investigation of the munitions industries. WILPF's Legislative Office benefited from Detzer's numerous contacts in the press corps, including her friendship with Drew Pearson, which provided important information on up-to-the-minute legislative news and trends.

Detzer resigned as WILPF National Secretary in 1946 with the intention of going to work for the United Nations, having been offered a UN position pending a security clearance. International cooperation through the UN, Detzer believed, was the only path that would lead the world to a peaceful future. But the clearance never came through, possibly because of WILPF's association with socialist and communist organizations. In 1948 Detzer published an account of her work with WILPF, *Appointment on the Hill*, and at the age of 63 married Scripps-Howard editor-in-chief, Ludwell Denny.

Bibliography:

A. *Appointment on the Hill* (New York, 1948).

B. Rosemary Rainbolt, ''Women and War in the United States: The Case of Dorothy Detzer, National Secretary Women's International League for Peace and Freedom,'' *Peace and Change* 4 (Fall, 1977), 18–22.

C. Dorothy Detzer Papers, Swarthmore College Peace Collection, Swarthmore, PA.

Rosemary Rainbolt

DEWEY, John (20 October 1859, Burlington, VT—1 June 1952, New York). *Education*: B.A., Univ. of Vermont, 1879; Ph.D., The Johns Hopkins Univ., 1884. *Career*: educator, Univ. of Michigan, 1884–88, 1889–94, Univ. of Minnesota, 1888–89, Univ. of Chicago, 1894–1904, Columbia Univ., 1905–30, Emeritus, 1930–39; first president, American Association of University Professors, 1915, president, People's Lobby, 1929–36; educational philosopher and social activist.

John Dewey's association with the peace movement began with his disillusionment with the results of World War I. During the war, while teaching at Columbia University, he became America's leading academic spokesman supporting intervention. In numerous articles, appearing mainly in *The New Republic*, he contended that war could not be dissociated from the ends it sought to achieve. But, as noted by his former student, *Randolph Bourne, his excessive optimism led him to overestimate the power of intelligence and underestimate the force of violence and irrationality.

In 1921, returning from a Far Eastern trip and seeking to redress his earlier support for war, Dewey joined *Salmon O. Levinson's American Committee for the Outlawry of War. Searching for an alternative to the League of Nations, which he considered a ''League of governments pure and simple,'' Dewey became the chief theoretician and defender of the outlawry idea. In a pamphlet entitled *Outlawry of War: What It Is and Is Not* (1923), he supported outlawry on the pragmatic assumption that the means proposed to implement this new idea—an educated public opinion which recognizes the need for internationalism and cooperation among nations—was also to function as the means for making the treaty and its enforcement mechanism effective and enduring instruments of international peace. At no time did Dewey contemplate the "chimerical possibility" of successfully outlawing war by a mere juristic declaration or by legal excommunication. In debating +Walter Lippmann, +Raymond L. Buell, +James T. Shotwell, and +Manley O. Hudson before and after the signing of the Kellogg-Briand Pact (1928), he consistently argued that the function and effectiveness of a World Court rested not upon the enforcement of sanctions but upon the educated moral sentiment of humanity.

During the 1920s and 1930s, Dewey joined the Committee on Militarism in Education. He opposed the ROTC program on the grounds that such training represented a threat to academic freedom and democratic individualism. In an introduction to Roswell P. Barnes' *Militarizing Our Youth*, Dewey claimed that militarism in education detracts from the basic goal of education: the promotion of human cooperation and international understanding. In fostering this view he denounced the War Department at the 1932 meeting of the American Association for the Advancement of Science, praised *Jane Addams' pacifism in a 1932 speech before the National Education Association, and wrote numerous articles for *Social Frontier* in the mid-thirties condemning war preparedness and the ROTC. Along with 240 other educators, writers, religious leaders, and businessmen, he signed a pledge, which appeared in the *New York Times* on July 9, 1940, declaring that involuntary military service was undemocratic and "smacks of totalitarianism."

Dewey's concern for the preservation of democratic freedoms also led to his interwar proposal for a transnational education program. In a noted article, "The School as a Means of Developing a Social Consciousness and Social Ideals in Children" (1923), he urged educators to purge all aspects of the glories of war from history texts and to develop a curriculum in history, literature, and geography which transcended national boundaries. The proposed program was geared for elementary school children, whose minds would be opened to counter the poisonous effects of years of patriotic indoctrination.

John Dewey's peace philosophy was based on the premise that there existed a potential goodness in man. It led him to search for new ways in which education could be made to explore and redefine in specific situations the method of nonviolence. Unlike many, if not most, contemporary liberal pacifists, he argued that education is the sole vehicle for bringing about an enlightened public opinion that could work effectively for the creation of a peaceful world order.

Bibliography:

A. *Apostles of War and Peace: S. O. Levinson* (New York, 1929); *Are Sanctions Necessary to International Organization?*, with Raymond Leslie Buell (New York, 1932); *Democracy and Education* (New York, 1916); *Ethics* with James A. Tufts (New York,

1932); *Freedom and Culture* (New York, 1939); *Human Nature and Conduct* (New York, 1922); *Outlawry of War: What It Is and Is Not* (Chicago, 1923); *The Problems of Men* (New York, 1946).

B. George Dykhuizen, *The Life and Mind of John Dewey* (Carbondale, IL, 1973); Charles F. Howlett, *Troubled Philosopher: John Dewey and the Struggle for World Peace* (Port Washington, NY, 1977); Joseph Ratner, ed., *Characters and Events* (2 vols., New York, 1929); Joseph Ratner, *Intelligence in the Modern World* (New York, 1939).

C. John Dewey Papers, Center for Dewey Studies, Southern Illinois University.

Charles F. Howlett

DICKIE, Alfred Matthew (22 June 1903, Melbourne, Australia—30 December 1978, Melbourne). *Education*: trained for ministry, Ormond Coll. Theological Hall, Melbourne; ordained Millicent, South Australia, 1933. *Career*: minister: Millicent, 1933–36, Port Melbourne, 1936–40, Mia Mia, 1940–43, North Essendon, 1943–68; co-founder and chairman, Australian Peace Council, 1949–59; member, World Peace Council, 1950–78; chairman, Democratic Rights Conference, 1950; member, Peace Quest Forum, 1951–68; chairman, Australian and New Zealand Congress for International Cooperation and Disarmament, 1959–63; chairman, Congress for International Cooperation and Disarmament, 1963–72; moderator, Presbyterian Church of Victoria, 1965–66; executive officer, Presbytery of Melbourne, 1968–72.

Apprenticed as a fitter and turner, ''Alf'' Dickie worked at his trade for a number of years before answering a call to the Presbyterian ministry at the age of 30. As a minister he proclaimed the Spirit of Christ to mean more than ceremonial ritual and intellectual acceptance of a belief in God. Christian belief was worthless, he noted, unless man was reconciled to man and ''unless the laws of self-sacrificial service and self-forgetting love'' were made the ''laws of life.'' Applying these principles to his own life, he pursued the Christian truths of peace and social justice with a recognition that his parish extended beyond the congregation that he served.

Influenced by Paul Tillich's sermon, ''The Shaking of the Foundations,'' Dickie argued that although God gave people, through science, ''the power to shake the foundations of the earth,'' they also were given a freedom to decline taking part in shaking further those foundations, which ''if continued will bring doom on God's creation.'' Responsible action for Dickie lay in mobilizing the creativity of ordinary people against the destructive powers of governments. To this end he joined with others, including fellow clergymen *Frank Hartley and Victor James, in the founding of the Australian Peace Council (APC). In his position as chairman of APC and two succeeding peace bodies, he became the central figure in the revival of the post-World War II peace movement.

The period coincided with the most acrimonious years of the Cold War, and since the peace movement virtually stood alone in condemning the consensus view on foreign and defense affairs, its members and particularly its chief spokesperson attracted the main brunt of anticommunist obloquy. Opposition to

German rearmament and to nuclear weapons testing, and proposals for disarmament, a nuclear-free Pacific, disengagement in Central Europe, recognition of China, and withdrawal from Korea were perceived as "pro-communist"—either by design or naîveté. Dickie found himself answering charges of disloyalty among his parishoners as well as in the forums of national debate.

However, due to a willingness to meet his accusers head-on, to present his case firmly but without malice, and to persist calmly whatever the provocations, he gradually gained for himself and the movement widening circles of community respect (if not support). He was acknowledged by the Presbyterian Church with his election as moderator for 1965–66. The press, especially in his later years, accorded him the respect of having his arguments taken seriously. And the peace movement grew, in no small measure because of his efforts. Among his skills of leadership he demonstrated an uncanny ability to presage the policies of the political left. His early objections to a Vietnam commitment helped to place this matter on the public agenda and make it the most important issue of the 1966 federal elections.

Dickie's influence in peace circles extended beyond Australia, and for many years he played a significant role in the World Peace Council. In recognition of his services to peace he received the following international awards: the Joliot Curie Gold Peace Medal, 1959; the Lenin Peace Prize, 1970; and the Jewish Historical Institute, Warsaw, Commemorative Medal on the 30th anniversary of the Warsaw Ghetto uprising. This last award, of which he was particularly proud, was presented to ten recipients: eight Polish Jewish workers and two foreign gentiles.

Bibliography:

A. *Should Such a Faith Offend*? (Melbourne, 1948); *Statement of Common Beliefs* (Melbourne, 1963).

Ralph Summy

DICKINSON, Goldsworthy Lowes. See *Biographical Dictionary of Internationalists*.

DICKINSON, Willoughby Hyett. See *Biographical Dictionary of Internationalists*.

DIEU, Marcel Camille Victor. See HEM DAY.

DIX, Otto (2 December 1891, Untermhaus, Thuringia, Germany—25 July 1969, Singen, Germany). *Education*: painter's apprentice, Gera, 1905–9; Dresden Kunstgewerbeschule, 1909–14. *Career*: taught at Düsseldorf Akademie, 1922–25; professorship at Dresden Kunstakademie, 1927–33; painter of antiwar and social criticism.

The son of a Thuringian foundry worker, Otto Dix emerged from his proletarian childhood by 1920 to become one of the most sophisticated artist-critics in

Weimar, Germany. His experiences between 1915 and 1918 as a German soldier on the Western and Russian fronts molded his sardonic paintings of war and society.

An exponent of the *Neue Sachlichkeit*, he sought a didactic art which would develop a higher consciousness in man. Dix exhibited with most of the German radical artists' groups in the 1920s. Unlike some of his contemporaries, however, Dix remained politically neutral. He never joined the German Communist party nor attached himself to a specific ideology.

Rather than viewing life in the abstract terms of class conflict, Dix invested his art with his personal experiences. For this reason, his main subjects were portraits, self-portraits, war, and urban revolution. Among the latter are such large paintings as *Die Kriegskrüppel* (*The War Cripples*) (1920), *Der Streichholzhändler I* (*The Matchseller I*) (1920), *Der Schützengraben* (*The Trench*) (1920–23), *Der Krieg* (*War*) (1929–32), *Grabenkrieg* (*Trench Warfare*) (1932), and *Flandern* (*Flanders*) (1934–36). Through scale and a realistically detailed style, they stress the brutality of war, the wanton destruction of human life, and the utterly unheroic nature of armed combat.

Dix's realistic mode of representation, inspired by German Renaissance art, intensified his critical outrage. *Der Schützengraben*, for example, was an enormous canvas filled with decomposing bodies, twisted steel posts, and barbed wire. Cartridge belts resembled teeth, and skulls were only partially fleshed. In it, the animate and inanimate coalesced into a representation of organic deterioration. Dix, as an infantryman and machine gunner, had survived such macabre scenes, and his experience would never allow him to romanticize modern warfare. The art dealer, Karl Nierendorf, sent *Der Schützengraben* around Germany as part of an exhibition entitled "No More War." It later became a focal work for the Nazi Exhibition of Degenerate Art and was burned in the spring of 1939. Among Dix's harrowing depictions of war which survived Nazi destruction is the triptych, *Der Krieg*, which reveals an unrelenting pessimism in the face of total destruction.

Dix's paintings became targets for reactionaries. He was tried for obscenity as early as 1923, and in 1930 he was accused of "ethical nihilism" and "cultural bolshevism." He was named an enemy of the German nation along with Bertold Brecht, *Käthe Kollwitz, Erwin Piscator and *George Grosz, and in 1934, Dix was forbidden to exhibit.

Under the twelve years of the Third Reich, Dix turned to landscapes and allegories. But works such as the *Triumph of Death* (1934–35) and *Lot and His Daughters* (1939) demonstrated the continuing intensity of his vision. As a background for the latter work, Dix painted, with uncanny prescience, not an imagined Sodom but a recognizable Dresden engulfed in flames. The power of his critical realism has influenced an entire generation of East German artists since 1945.

Bibliography:

A. *Der Krieg*, 24 *Offsetdruke nach Originalem aus dem Radierwerk* (Berlin, 1924, New York, 1972); *Otto Dix im Selbstbildnis* (Berlin, 1978); *Tod und Auferstehung* (Dresden, 1922).

B. Brigid S. Barton, *Otto Dix and Die Neue Sachlichkeit, 1918–1925* (Ann Arbor, MI, 1981); Florian Karsch, ed., *Otto Dix: Das graphische Werk* (Hannover, 1970); Fritz Löffler, *Otto Dix; Leben und Werk* (Dresden, 1977; 1960); Linda F. McGreevy, *The Life and Works of Otto Dix, German Critical Realist* (Ann Arbor, MI, 1981); NYT, August 2, 1969.

Folke T. Kihlstedt

DODGE, David Low (14 June 1774, Brooklyn, CT—23 April 1852, New York). *Education*: self-taught; *Career*: businessman, peace reformer and organizer.

David Low Dodge was one of the pioneers of the American peace movement. The author of some of the earliest and most effective antiwar literature published in the United States, Dodge also helped organize the first pacifist association in the world and was later instrumental in the establishment of the American Peace Society. During the course of these activities Dodge corresponded and worked closely with *Aaron Cleveland, Samuel Whelpley, *Noah Worcester, *William Ladd, Lyman Beecher, and other men active in the same cause.

Dodge's pacifism was closely linked to his religious fundamentalism. Brought up by strict, Calvinist parents, Dodge remained involved in religious matters all his life. His interest intensified during the 1790s when he attended a number of revivals and married the daughter of Reverend Cleveland. Faced with the responsibility of supporting a family, Dodge entered into trade and, despite his lack of formal education or other advantages, soon prospered as a merchant in New York City.

Dodge's first acquaintance with the costs of war came early in his life, when both his half brothers, soldiers, died during the American Revolution. Two incidents in the early 1800s, however, had a more profound impact upon his thinking. In 1805, while carrying a large amount of money on a business trip, he nearly shot an innkeeper by accident when the man blundered into Dodge's room late at night. Dodge's horror at the possible outcome of this episode convinced him that violent action and deadly weapons were contrary to the Christian principles which he held dear. A few years later, near death as a result of spotted fever, Dodge felt remorseful at having failed to circulate publicly his objections to violence. Upon his recovery Dodge dedicated himself to refining and disseminating his ideas.

In 1809 Dodge anonymously published *The Mediator's Kingdom Not of This World but Spiritual, Heavenly and Divine*. In it he adopted a nonresistant position, rejecting the legitimacy of personal self-defense as well as defensive war. His arguments, leaning heavily upon the Sermon on the Mount, consisted of Biblical injunctions to "love your enemy" and "resist not evil." Dodge pointed out that since God had already reserved to Himself vengeance for misdeeds, true Christians could not infringe upon His prerogative. In the face of violence their only recourse was to trust in the Lord for protection.

Over the next several years Dodge gathered around himself a small circle of like-minded men. In early 1812 they discussed formally organizing a group dedicated to promoting peace through the vehicle of evangelical Christianity. The outbreak of war with England, however, led to postponement of their venture, because they feared that their actions might be misinterpreted. The same reason led Dodge to delay publication of his most ambitious antiwar tract.

The arrival of peace in 1815 was greeted by Dodge's publication of *War Inconsistent with the Religion of Jesus Christ*. Condemning war as "inhuman, unwise and criminal," Dodge bolstered his religious reasoning with practical and humanitarian arguments. Noting that the very concept of warfare was inconsistent with Christian principles of love, mercy, forgiveness, and returning good for evil, he concluded that no true Christian could wage war. War harms everyone, Dodge contended: it oppresses the poor, destroys the property of the rich and inflicts suffering upon man and beast alike. Too often, he claimed, wars create the very problems they are supposed to eliminate, resulting in the corruption of morals and the destruction of personal liberties. Dodge rejected the notion that armed might represented the surest guarantee of peace. Citing historical examples, he demonstrated that military preparations lead inevitably to rivalry and warfare. As in his earlier work, he scoffed at "the pretended distinction" between aggressive and defensive war.

In 1815 Dodge and about three dozen other men established the New York Peace Society, the first such organization in the world. The New York Peace Society preceded by a few months the formation of similar associations in Massachusetts and England. As the Society's first president, Dodge exerted a considerable influence over its direction. Its members reflected him in their beliefs and circumstances: they were, for the most part, middle class, nonresistant, evangelical Christians. The Society remained small; after reaching a peak of perhaps sixty members, it began to decline. The Society's mission, however, was not growth but the circulation of its antiwar message. Dodge furthered that mission by packing pacifist literature in with the merchandise which he sold and shipped.

Dodge played an important part in merging the New York Peace Society with several other groups to create the American Peace Society in 1828. He presided over the organizational meeting, which was held in his home. A year later he chaired the first annual meeting of the American Peace Society. Dodge remained associated with the Society for many years, first as a member of its Board of Directors and later as a life Director, but he played a much less active role than in the past. Uncompromising in his nonresistance, Dodge was disappointed by the reluctance of Worcester, Ladd, and others to condemn defensive war. Pursuing his beliefs to what he believed was their logical conclusion, Dodge throughout his life refused to hold public office or even to vote, since such acts could be construed as supporting a government which relied upon force to exist.

Bibliography:

A. *The Mediator's Kingdom not of this World but Spiritual, Heavenly and Divine* (1809); *Memorial of Mr. David L. Dodge, Consisting of an Autobiography* (Boston, 1854); *Observations on the Kingdom of Peace, Under the Benign Reign of Messiah* (New York, 1816); *War Inconsistent with the Religion of Jesus Christ* (New York, 1815).

B. Peter Brock, *Pacifism in the United States: From the Colonial Era to the First World War* (Princeton, 1968); Edwin D. Mead, ''David Low Dodge: Founder of the First Peace Society,'' *World Unity* (New York, 1933), 11, no. 6, 365–372 and 12, no. 1, 29–36; Edwin D. Mead, ''Introduction,'' in Dodge, *War Inconsistent with the Religion of Jesus Christ* (New York, 1905).

Dale R. Steiner

DOLE, Charles Fletcher (17 May 1845, Brewer, ME—27 November 1927, Jamaica Plain, MA). *Education*: B.A., Harvard Coll., 1868; M.A., 1870; graduate, Andover Theological Seminary, 1872. *Career*: teacher in Noble's school for boys, Boston, MA, and Newport (RI) high school, 1868–69; professor of Greek, Univ. of Vermont, 1873; minister, Plymouth Church, Portland, ME, 1874–76, First Congregational (Unitarian) Church, Jamaica Plain, MA, 1876–1916.

Influenced by lingering transcendentalism, Charles Dole, who was born and raised in rural New England, became a Unitarian minister. He preached a religion which emphasized the practical application of Christian ideals of love and service to others in both the domestic and international realm. He took a special interest in nonwhite peoples and attacked racism in all its forms. Though not a strikingly original thinker or effective speaker, he wrote many books and articles expounding his religious ideals.

During his 40-year ministry in Jamaica Plain, Massachusetts, Dole became acquainted with prominent peace advocates in the Boston area. He was an active member of the American Peace Society for many years. A good friend of +Edwin D. Mead, he succeeded him as president of the Twentieth Century Club, which often sponsored discussions on international questions.

Dole's abhorrence of violence made him an uncompromising pacifist. He opposed the prospect of United States military intervention to reinforce beleaguered Christian missions in Armenia in the 1890s, supported the Olney-Pauncefote arbitration treaty with Great Britain, and resisted American intervention in Cuba. He lobbied against the use of force to acquire the Philippines at the turn of the century. Unlike the pessimistic and backward-looking rhetoric of most anti-imperialists, however, Dole espoused a more affirmative vision of the future. He argued that ''the advancement of the national welfare is not the path of military glory, of territorial aggrandizement, or of arbitrary protectorates over half-civilized peoples. Our real welfare must be . . . finally in creating national happiness that other nations seeing what freedom, law, enlightenment, and peace do for us, shall follow our beneficent lead."

In the twentieth century, Dole attacked the naval arms race that affected the United States as well as Europe. Influenced by evolutionary thought, he remained convinced of the possibilities of man's moral progress while recognizing his occasional lapses into barbarism. The outbreak of World War I profoundly disturbed him but did not shake his underlying idealism. He opposed American involvement in the conflict and criticized the many peace groups which endorsed it. Through his ministry and writings Dole influenced others in the search for peace. His counsel and example helped *Emily Greene Balch to become a dedicated peace activist in the twentieth century.

Bibliography:

A. *The Coming People* (7th ed., New York, 1913); *My Eighty Years* (New York, 1927); "The Navy as a Police Force," *Outlook*, 87 (December 21, 1907), 881; "A Peace Society in War Time," *Advocate of Peace,* 76 (August 1917), 242–43; "The Right and Wrong of the Monroe Doctrine," *World Peace Foundation, Pamphlet Series*, No. 5, Part V (April 1912); "Roosevelt's Naval Policy," *Outlook*, 87 (December 7, 1907), 791–92.

B. DAB, 5, 357; NCAB 20, 355–56; NYT, November 28, 1927.

David S. Patterson

DOLENS, Alma [pseud. Teresita Pasini dei Bonfatti] (18 February 1876, Perugia, Italy—death unknown). *Career*: journalist, feminist, and pacifist activist.

Born into a respected aristocratic family from Umbria, married to a distinguished Milanese lawyer, Teresita Pasini forsook a life of comfort on behalf of causes to further the interest of workers, women, and international peace. Her public debut as an activist began in 1908 when she addressed the National Congress of Peace Societies, following her participation in a women's congress in Rome, arguing in favor of the creation of separate women's peace societies.

Following her own advice, under the name of Alma dolens, she undertook a whirlwind tour of Italian cities, beginning in Umbria and gradually covering the whole peninsula. After two years of traveling and speaking, women's peace societies were created in Vercelli, Asti, Parma, Lodi, Assisi, Cremona, and Palermo. Often the groups took the name of a woman whose fame came from the Risorgimento—such as Anita Garibaldi. Dolens urged the groups not to merely emulate the Red Cross by undertaking work to humanize warfare but to realize that women had a special responsibility to urge governments to adopt arbitration and other legal means for conflict resolution. Women also had to educate their children in the enormously patriotic belief that peace was desirable, right, and the only correct step for the advancement of civilization.

She was recognized as one of the more eminent Italian pacifists, served as delegate to the international and national peace congresses, and was considered a powerful public speaker. In 1910, at a national peace congress, she urged closer links be forged with workers' societies. Shortly after, she addressed a public meeting of workers at the Milanese Camera del Lavoro, from which was organized the Società operaio: pro arbitrato e disarmo (Workers' Society for Arbitration and Disarmament). Unlike other peace societies, this group argued for *obligatory* international arbitration and steps for mutual reduction of arms expenses. It claimed no particular political affiliation, inviting persons of all backgrounds to join, but most of its members were skilled workers. At one point, dolens stated that over 700 people belonged, making this group the largest workers' peace society in pre-1914 Europe.

With the outbreak of the Libyan War (1911), dolens and her society quickly broke ranks with the established pacifist organizations of Milan and Rome, led by *E. T. Moneta and *Angelo de Gubernatis, who found a number of arguments in support of the war. Dolens' group roundly protested the declaration of war. Then, she wrote to the international headquarters of the peace movement in Berne, led by *Albert Gobat, requesting moral and material help in reorganizing the Italian peace movement. In addition, she asked Gobat to try and enlist the good offices of a foreign neutral government to end the war. (Gobat's efforts with the Americans came to nought). The Berne bureau sent a large sum to dolens who distributed it amongst peace groups which took the unpopular course of opposing the war. She used her portion to cover Milan with posters and pamphlets denouncing the war in February, 1912. Throughout, despite hostility and real dangers, dolens continued to deliver antiwar speeches around northern Italy. Along with a few Italian peace activists, such as *Edoardo Giretti in Turin, Domenico Maggiore in Naples, and E. Cimino in Palermo, dolens led the non-socialist Italian peace movement on its antiwar trajectory consistently and despite bitter personal attacks.

Simultaneously, she remained an active participant in women's associations and attended the international meeting in Budapest in 1912 where she became friendly with *Rosika Schwimmer. Her participation in the peace movement diminished after 1913 when the rifts of 1911–12 were superficially healed. No record exists of dolens' position in 1914, when the "official" Italian peace movement slowly moved from its initial position of strict neutrality in World War I to sympathy for intervention on the Allied side. Between 1908 and 1913, however, in the years of her heavy involvement, dolens gained wide recognition as a fervent and successful speaker and organizer among nontraditional peace constituencies.

Bibliography:

B. "La Festa della Pace a Napoli: Alma dolens" in *La Luce del Pensiero* (Naples), February, 1911, p. 9; "Pasini, Teresina [sic] della Pisano nobile Bonfatti" in Alfred Fried, ed., *Handbuch der Friedensbewegung* (Berlin, 1913) II, 386.

Sandi E. Cooper

DORLAND, Arthur Garratt (30 July 1887, Wellington, Ontario, Canada—26 June 1979, Toronto). *Education*: Pickering Coll., 1902–5; B.A., Queen's

Univ., 1910; M.A., Yale Univ., 1911; Ph.D., Univ. of Toronto, 1927. *Career*: school teacher, Pickering Coll., 1911–14; history professor, Queen's Univ., 1916–20, Univ. of Western Ontario, 1920–55; prominent Quaker, historian, and pacifist.

A Quaker by birth and a religious pacifist throughout his life, Arthur Garratt Dorland was a leading internationalist and a prominent figure in the Canadian peace movement for over fifty years.

Descended from a Dutch-American family which emigrated to Canada with the loyalist migrations after the American Revolution, he was instilled with a strong sense of history at an early age. His interest in the progressive peace movement began while a student and later a teacher at Pickering College in Ontario. Although he was enthusiastic about the growing popularity of liberal pacifism at the time, he feared it lacked the moral commitment to withstand the militarism that he believed was slowly developing in Canada. His worst fears were realized after the outbreak of World War I as most liberal pacifists were swept up in war hysteria. Although he was exempted from military service as a religious conscientious objector, his graduate studies at Yale University were interrupted by the war and he was diverted to the study of Canadian history and the task of writing the history of the Society of Friends in Canada.

After the war he attended the first world conference of Friends in London where he was imbued with the new spirit of pacifism as a radical critique of capitalism and a corollary of social and economic justice. Consequently, upon his return to Canada he urged support for postwar relief work in Europe. As the new chairman of the Friends' peace committee in 1922 he emerged as one of the leading Canadian peace activists of the decade and strove to build a broad peace movement that might influence public opinion on international issues. Toward that end, he firmly supported the League of Nations Society and directed a local chapter throughout the interwar years.

By 1926 Dorland overcame initial opposition from certain Protestant denominations to organize a Canadian Council of the World Alliance for Friendship Through the Churches in the hope that religious leaders would convince Canadians of the moral necessity of international cooperation. With the founding of the Canadian Friends Service Committee under his chairmanship in 1931, he devoted himself to the campaign for world disarmament and the search for solutions to the social crisis caused by the depression. His conclusion that the inherent violence of capitalism demanded radical changes led him to become instrumental in founding the Canadian Institute of Economic and International Relations, an annual conference at Lake Couchiching, Ontario, which attracted a wide range of intellectuals and politicians to consider imaginative ways of solving the world's social and economic problems and thereby preserve peace.

Throughout the interwar and World War II years, Dorland exercised commanding leadership in the Canadian peace movement. In cooperation with the Women's International League for Peace and Freedom, he helped lead a concerted campaign against cadet training in Canada's schools as well as against militarism in school textbooks. Dorland also came to realize that the dual quest for social justice and peace placed pacifists in a dilemma. Although he continued to defend the traditional pacifist response, he recognized the revolutionary potential of nonviolent action in the pursuit of social as well as political objectives. In his later years he was a staunch supporter of social democratic politics and he encouraged new outlets for pacifist action.

Bibliography:

A. *Former Days and Quaker Ways* (Belleville, 1972); *The Quakers in Canada: A History* (Toronto, 1968); *The Trail of Life* (Belleville, 1979).

B. Thomas P. Socknat, " 'Witness Against War': Pacifism in Canada, 1900–1945," Ph.D. dissertation, McMaster University, 1981.

C. Arthur G. Dorland Papers, University of Western Ontario Archives.

Thomas P. Socknat

DRAGO, Luís María. See *Biographical Dictionary of Internationalists*.

DRESSER, Amos (12 December 1812, Peru, MA—5 February 1904, Lawrence, KS). *Education*: attended Oneida Institute and Lane Seminary; graduated, Oberlin Seminary, 1839. *Career*: clergyman.

While growing up in a clerical home in Manlius, New York, Amos Dresser came under the sway of religious revivals that shaped his life. At Lane Seminary in 1834 he took part in the famous slavery debates that led the trustees to restrict freedom of discussion, a policy that provoked him and other reform-minded students to withdraw and eventually make their way to Oberlin. Now a zealous abolitionist, he ventured in the summer of 1835 to take antislavery literature into the South. The effort resulted in his trial and whipping by a vigilance committee at Nashville, Tennessee. This well-publicized incident brought Dresser much notoriety and fed the North's swelling antislavery, anti-Southern sentiment.

After graduating from Oberlin in 1839 he and his wife served as missionaries to the blacks in Jamaica until ill health forced their return. In the 1840s when many western abolitionists shifted their efforts from agitation to electoral politics, Dresser subordinated his antislavery activity to work in the cause of peace, especially in Ohio's Western Reserve, where he was an agent of the Universal League of Brotherhood. In 1851 he was a delegate to the International Peace Congress in London and afterward lectured on peace in England and Scotland. For the rest of his long life he held pastorates in various places in Ohio, Michigan, and Nebraska, always the evangelist and the outspoken advocate of reform, especially of abolition, racial justice, and peace.

As sectional tensions heightened in the 1850s, Dresser affiliated with the abolitionist American Missionary Association and again focused most of his reform efforts on the antislavery cause. Despite his fervid condemnation of war, he was not consistently a nonresistant (though he attended the New England Non-Resistance Convention in 1839) and did not shun political action in causes he believed just. Thus during the Civil War he supported the Union and advocated emancipation and other governmental policies aimed at achieving rights for the freedmen.

His signal contribution to peace literature was his tract *The Bible against War* (1849). There he interpreted Biblical texts to demonstrate the immorality of defensive and offensive wars alike. Citing errors in translation as well as shortcomings in the understanding of commentators, he explained away passages that apparently sanctioned the use of force. The Bible, he wrote, often records as a matter of history acts that it by no means sanctions. The Old Testament, he argued, offered types and symbols of the New and thus prefigured a dispensation of peace. In apparent reference to the recently concluded war with Mexico, he scoffed at concepts of ''national honor'' as justification for war. The colonists' resort to force in the American Revolution was the source, he believed, of that despotism and disregard of individual rights which he thought characterized society in his time.

Bibliography:

A. *The Bible against War* (Oberlin, OH, 1849); *The Christian Flag* (Weaton, IL, 1894); *Narrative of Amos Dresser* (New York, 1836).

B. Henry W. Cushman, *A Historical and Biographical Genealogy of the Cushmans* (Boston, 1855), 627–32.

Merton L. Dillon

DU BOIS, William Edward Burghardt (23 February 1868, Great Barrington, MA—27 August 1963, Accra, Ghana). *Education*: B.A., Fisk Univ., 1888; M.A., Harvard Univ., 1891, Ph.D., 1895. *Career*: professor, Wilberforce Univ., 1894–96; assistant instructor in sociology, Univ. of Pennsylvania, 1896–97; professor of economics and history, Atlanta Univ, 1897–1910; professor and chairman, sociology, Atlanta Univ., 1934–1944; editor, *The Moon* (Memphis, TN), 1905–6; *The Horizon* (Washington, DC), 1907–10; *The Crisis*, 1910–34; *The Brownies' Book* (New York), 1920–21; *Phylon*, 1940–44; secretary, First Pan-African Conference, 1900, general secretary, The Niagara Movement, 1905–09; a founder and member of the Executive Board, National Association for the Advancement of Colored People, 1910–34; chief organizer and president, Pan-African Movement, 1919–63; co-chairman (with Paul Robeson), Council on African Affairs, 1948–54; chairman, Peace Information Center, 1950; director, Encyclopedia Africana Project, Ghana, 1961–63; author and social activist.

William Edward Burghardt Du Bois was a founder and leader of the modern movement for full equality of black people in the United States and for the liberation of Africa from colonialism. His main instrumentalities to achieve these goals were the National Association for the Advancement of Colored People, which he guided from 1910 to 1934, and the Pan-African Movement, which he led from 1900 to his death in 1963.

Du Bois was persuaded that racism and colonialism were basic sources of war and that any organization or effort for peace which ignored this reality was bound to fail. One of his most influential and very early essays was ''Credo,'' first published in the New York magazine, *The Independent* (October 6, 1904), and widely reprinted thereafter throughout the world. This short essay denounced war and militarism and urged the establishment of a world of justice, equality, and peace. At the same time, it noted that optimism was required for the endurance needed in a long and difficult struggle. This was essentially the content of his "Last Message," written shortly prior to his death and read at the State funeral given him in Ghana in August, 1963; that "Message" concluded, "Peace will be my applause."

The connection between racism and colonialism—and the making of war—was something hammered upon by W.E.B. Du Bois for 60 years. In the *New York Times* of December 12, 1909 he wrote of his people as "girding themselves to fight in the van of human progress" whose hallmarks would be, he added, "the emancipation of women, universal peace, democratic government, the socialization of wealth, and human brotherhood." His emphasis upon racism and colonialism also appeared in the May 1913 issue of *The Crisis*. In an editorial entitled "Peace," he chided peace societies for confining their subject to peace among European powers, thus ignoring the domination, through force, of the colonial peoples—itself a major source of war. He reiterated this argument in a similarly entitled editorial in *The Crisis* exactly two years later when World War I had already commenced.

His seminal essay, "The African Roots of the War," appeared in May 1915 in the *Atlantic* and developed—before either +John Hobson or V. I. Lenin—the basic connection between the colonial system and the outbreak of global war. This also called attention to the awakening of the peoples of China, India, and Egypt and suggested that Africa could not be far behind.

With considerable hesitation, Du Bois finally was persuaded by President +Woodrow Wilson's rhetoric to support U.S. participation in World War I, although he lived to regret that decision. Throughout the 1920s and 1930s he continued to emphasize the connection between racism, colonialism, and war. He also called for disarmament and urged the recognition of the Soviet Union (which he visited as early as 1926). Du Bois hesitated for some months to support the Allies in the Second World War, especially since he heard no anticolonial statements from either Winston Churchill or +Franklin Delano Roosevelt and felt the anti-Japanese stance partook of racism. (Thus, he excoriated the forcible consignment of Japanese-Americans to concentration camps soon after Pearl Harbor.) But Du Bois did come around to endorsing it, especially after the Hitler-led attack upon the Soviet Union gave the war a fully global dimension and made clear, for Du Bois, its antifascist character.

After World War II Du Bois maintained his antiracist and anticolonial emphases. He was a consultant to the U.S. delegation at the founding of the United Nations and there tried to persuade its members to see the importance of both questions. In the late 1940s and through the 1950s to his death, Du Bois led opposition to rearmament, especially nuclear weaponry. He contributed to mobilizing opinion against the Korean and Vietnam wars. In these years he took the lead in urging recognition of the People's Republic of China, which he visited in 1959.

In 1949–50, Du Bois was the leader of the Peace Information Center, which organized a nationwide campaign against the A-Bomb and succeeded in getting over two million Americans to sign the Stockholm Peace Pledge. As a result, he was indicted in 1950 by the U.S. government as an "unregistered foreign agent" and thus faced imprisonment at the age of 83. His defense was a worldwide one and resulted in acquittal, a notable victory for civil liberties against the national security mania of the early Cold War.

Bibliography:

A. "The African Roots of War," *Atlantic Monthly*, 115 (May, 1915), 707–14; "America and World Peace," *New World Review* (New York), November, 1952, 49–52; *In Battle for Peace*, (New York, 1952); *Color and Democracy: Colonies and Peace* (New York, 1945); "The Realities in Africa: European Profit or Negro Development?" *Foreign Affairs*, 21 (July, 1943), 721–32; "The World Peace Movement," *New World Review* (New York), May, 1955, 9–14.

B. Herbert Aptheker, *Annotated Bibliography of the Published Writings of W.E.B. Du Bois* (Millwood, NY, 1973); Herbert Aptheker, "W.E.B. Du Bois," *American Writers: A Collection of Literary Biographies*, Suppl. II, Part 1, (New York, 1981) 157–89; Herbert Aptheker, ed., *Selected Correspondence of W.E.B. Du Bois* (3 vols., Amherst, MA, 1973–78); Herbert Aptheker, "W.E.B. Du Bois—A Man for Peace," *Political Affairs*, 41 (August, 1982), 31–35; Francis L. Broderick, *W.E.B. Du Bois, Negro Leader in a Time of Crisis* (Stanford, CA, 1959); Arnold Rampersad, *The Art and Imagination of W.E.B. Du Bois* (Cambridge, MA., 1971); Elliott M. Rudwick, *W.E.B. Du Bois: A Study in Minority Group Leadership* (Philadelphia, 1960).

C. W.E.B. Du Bois Papers, The Library University of Massachusetts, Amherst.

Herbert Aptheker

DUCHÊNE, Gabrielle Laforcade (26 February 1878, France?—1954, France?). *Career*: journalist, political activist in feminist organizations and children's welfare and working women's committees; pacifist.

Product of a bourgeois family and married to a prosperous architect, Gabrielle Duchêne early in life transcended her middle class background to involve herself in issues of peace and social justice. In 1905, at the first Congrès international de l'enfant (International Congress of the Child), she introduced a resolution calling for education for social and international peace. Throughout the first three decades of the twentieth century, she also took an active role in children's welfare and working women's committees, particularly the Conseil national des femmes françaises (National Council of French Women), founded in 1901 as the coordinating body for all women's and children's organizations. She strongly supported legislation to regulate sweat shops and favored protection of all working people.

Shortly after the conclusion of the 1915 international women's conference held at The Hague, which later resulted in the establishment of the Women's International League for Peace and Freedom (WILPF) (1919), *Jane Addams and *Aletta Jacobs, its leaders, visited Duchêne and helped her establish a French section. The organization was headed by Duchêne and supported by the *Romain Rolland circle and Avril de Sainte-Croix. They petitioned the French government to give serious consideration to, and to inform the public of, all peace proposals. For her efforts, Duchêne's home was searched and her papers confiscated; other individuals who continued to speak out were imprisoned. As a result, the French section, for the rest of the war, avoided the peace issue and concentrated on women's rights.

In 1919, at the Congress of the WILPF, Duchêne—unable to attend because she could not get a passport—was chosen as one of the representatives to the Versailles Conference, to carry recommendations from WILPF. During the 1920s and 1930s she continued to serve in a leadership role in WILPF, was appointed to the Délégation permanent des sociétés françaises pour la paix (Permanent Delegation of French Peace Societies), and attended virtually every congress of national and international peace organizations.

In 1925 and 1926, contemporaneous with the first League of Nations Disarmament Conference, the French section of WILPF passed a resolution in favor of total disarmament and "radical industrial action." When +Aristide Briand's proposal for a European economic federation of twenty-six states was debated before the Assembly of the League of Nations in October 1930, the WILPF issued a memorandum drafted by Duchêne and Gertrude Baer, which criticized the "political basis of the proposal," and pointed out that it made no provision for limitation of national sovereignty, for allocation of resources, nor for disarmament. Later in 1930, Duchêne organized a national Peace Action Week, with WILPF coordinating the activities of several groups. As preparation for the second Disarmament Conference, WILPF circulated a Disarmament Petition; Duchêne reported in *Pax International* (October 1931) that the petition had 40,000 signatures and that the Comité d'action pour le désarmament (Committee of Action for Disarmament) had the adherence of about forty groups. In November 1931, she presented a declaration from WILPF to +Robert Cecil of the unofficial Disarmament Conference urging that the Disarmament Conference should include representatives of pacifist organizations and exclude anyone with an interest in the preservation of armaments.

After 1933 Duchêne favored more radical action than the WILPF and its French sections were willing to endorse. Arguing that violence might be necessary to attain social justice, she condemned "too much Quakerism" in the international Executive Committee and asserted that capitalism was incompatible with lasting peace. Fascism, she maintained, was merely an extreme manifestation of capitalism. In August 1934 she played a prominent part in organizing the Women's Congress Against War and Fascism. Her action led the Swedish delegation to propose her expulsion from WILPF.

In short, Duchêne became the *enfant terrible* of WILPF. In 1935, at the international conference of the Comité mondial des femmes contre la guerre et le fascisme (Universal Committee of Women Against War and Fascism), she called for all possible sanctions against Italy in regard to the Ethiopian War. In the following year, at the first congress of the Rassemblement universel pour la paix (Universal Assembly for Peace), she demanded the representation of women on all bodies of the League of Nations and in the Rassemblement itself. After Munich, she signed a manifesto in favor of peace but demanding that aggression should "not only be outlawed but made impossible" and denouncing the failure to include the Soviet Union at the Conference. In 1939, with the international situation deteriorating, she called for common action with the Soviet Union to save the peace; the Executive Committee was willing to advocate only "joint international action."

After the German invasion of 1940, Duchêne fled to the Unoccupied Zone, where she was reported to be cultivating her garden and raising poultry. When the war ended, she remained semiretired from her pacifist activities until her death in 1954, emerging only to declare to the WILPF Executive Committee on behalf of the French section that integral pacifism was unrealistic and destructive of real peace.

Bibliography:

A. *Le Droit à la vie et le minimum de salaire* (Villeneuve-St. Georges, 1917); *L'Éducation en vue de la paix* (Geneva, 1925); *La Femme en U.R.S.S.* (Courbevoie, 1934); *Le Progrès de la législation sur le minimum: de salaire* (Paris, 1918); *Le Travail à domicile* (Paris, 1914).

B. Gertrude Bussey and Margaret Tims, *Women's International League for Peace and Freedom* (London, 1965).

C. "Fonds Gabrielle Duchêne," in Bibliothèque du documentation international et contemporaine, Université de Paris, X, Nanterre.

Albert S. Hill

DUCOMMUN, Elié (19 February 1833, Geneva, Switzerland—6 December 1906, Berne). *Education*: Académie de Genève; précepteur in Auerbach, Saxony, 1850–53. *Career*: public school teacher of languages, Geneva, 1853–55; editor, *La Revue de Genève* and *La Nation suisse*, 1855–65, *Le Progrès*, 1865; adjunct-chancellor and chancellor of the canton, 1858–65; member, Grand Council, 1858–65; official translator of the Confederation, 1869–79; founder, Ligue internationale de la paix et de la liberté, 1867; founder, Banque populaire suisse, 1869; secretary-general, Compagnie des chemins de fer du Jura bernois, 1873–91; secretary, Bureau international de la paix, 1891–1906.

Elié Ducommun's father, Jules, was a skilled watchmaker who believed in education for his children in the hope that it would improve their lives. Elié developed a deep love of literature in his childhood and became a teacher of French and German until the liberal politician James Fazy enticed him from the classroom and into public life. Under Fazy's sponsorship, Ducommun became editor of several liberal party papers, a public servant and administrator, and a politician.

Ducommun was devoted to progressive causes throughout his life and this commitment expanded to include pacifism. With Fazy and Pierre Jolissaint, he designed the manifesto for the Ligue internationale de la paix et de la liberté (International League of Peace and Freedom) which held its first meeting in Geneva in 1867 under the presidency of Giuseppe Garibaldi. Ducommun became editor of the French edition of *Les-Etats-Unis d'Europe* and vice-president of the League. But his most important contribution to peace causes was his service as first secretary of the Bureau international de la paix, (International Bureau of Peace) created at the Universal Peace Congress in Rome (1891). For 15 years Ducommun served as the nerve center of the central office of the peace movement during a period of impressive growth. His importance in this role was pivotal. The office began with a budget of about 10 francs in Ducommun's home. At his death, it coordinated activities of peace societies throughout Europe and the United States with a budget in the thousands.

According to the French peace leader, *Jules Prudhommeaux, Ducommun "kept the accounts, classified the archives, filled the dossiers, corresponded with statesmen, edited journals and pamphlets, prepared the annual congresses, gave advice to some and encouragement to others, sustained, coordinated and disciplined the efforts of over 200 societies and thousands of activists dispersed in all corners of the world." Ducommun was the main source of continuity between annual congresses whose mandates he carried out. From 1893–96, the handwritten paper, *Correspondence Bi-mensuelle* came from his pen as the vehicle which informed antiwar groups around the world of peace activities.

In the preparation of agendas for annual meetings, Ducommun was instrumental in finding the necessary compromises to allow delegates from mutually hostile nations to participate with dignity. His personal tact and diplomatic charm prevented confrontations that threatened the smooth working of international conferences particularly in the early years of the movement. In 1902 he shared the Nobel Peace Prize with *Albert Gobat who succeeded him in 1906 at the Bureau. The award properly recognized the labors of a man whose organizational and administrative talents provided the essential cement for the international peace bureau.

Bibliography:

A. *La Fundamentoj de l'pacifism* (Paris, 1906); *L'Inutilité des guerres démontrée par l'histoire* (Stockholm, 1905); *A Key to the Deliberations of the Annual Peace Congresses* (Berne, 1897); *Precis historique du mouvement en faveur de la paix* (Berne, 1899); *The Probable Consequences of a European War* (London, 1906).

C. Elié Ducommun Papers, Archives of the Peace Bureau, United Nations Library, Geneva.

Sandi E. Cooper

DUHAMEL, Georges (30 June 1884, Paris—13 April 1966, Valmondois, France). *Education*: Licence ès Sciences, Univ. of Paris, 1908, Doctorat, Medecin, 1909. *Career*: poet, critic, journalist, physician, essayist, novelist.

Georges Duhamel was trained as a scientist, but made a brilliant career as a writer. He participated in the brief experiment in communal living among several artists at L'Abbaye, in 1906–7, where he shared a home in Créteil on the outskirts of Paris. From 1909 to 1914 Duhamel worked in a Paris laboratory doing biological experiments. His earliest writings were poetry, poetry criticism, and critical studies of Jules Romains and Paul Claudel.

World War I drastically transformed his life and his sensibility. He served for 51 months, stationed close to the front in a mobile surgical unit. The experience of working closely with severely wounded and dying soldiers triggered powerful reactions in the physician/writer—above all, the feelings of disillusionment with the war and rage against the uselessness of all the suffering. Two themes dominated his wartime writings: the senselessness and wickedness of the combat. In two texts, *Vie des Martyrs* (1917) and *Civilisation* (1918), Duhamel wrote with an intensity and empathy for those victimized by the war's brutality. He dwelled on the psychological and physical cruelty of the fighting. His writings revealed shocking accounts of the amputations, the infectious wounds, and the ubiquitousness of death in the trenches. These short stories and sketches were protests against the massive idiocy of the war, attempts to unmask how the war caused apparently civilized men to regress into cave men. Duhamel was able to write about the Great War from the perspective of the traumatized, often doomed, soldiers. His writings created a stir in postwar France, inaugurating a celebrated literary career. He was awarded the prestigious Prix Goncourt in 1918.

Having indirectly criticized the war in his works, it is not surprising that Duhamel would emerge in the postwar period as a pacifist. He equated modern, technological warfare with horror; it went with a devaluation of the individual. He anticipated another world war, sometimes from a viewpoint of anger and frustration, at other times with a sense of pathos and irony. He believed that postwar Europe needed to be regenerated from five years of fratricidal conflict; he tried to reaffirm spiritual, but not religious, values in his works. Duhamel was not an astute political analyst. Nor was he a terribly acute reader of contemporary events. He viewed the Treaty of Versailles not only as weak and ineffective, but as harsh; he predicted that the treaty would lay the groundwork for another collision between France and Germany. During the 1920s he worked for Franco-German rapprochement, mostly through cultural channels—music, literature, and international exchanges. He edited and introduced an anthology of modern French poetry for a German reading public in 1926. Having learned first hand that total war was neither glorious nor legendary, Duhamel had a brief period as an integral pacifist. He opposed international violence unconditionally; he called for disarmament; he defended conscientious objection; and he supported the idea of peace at any price.

Retrospectively, Duhamel saw his absolute pacifist period as a brief Tolstoyan interlude. He tended to underestimate the historical significance and ascendency of international fascism. After the arrival of the National Socialists to power in 1933, he slowly came to see Adolf Hitler as a threat to peace. Nevertheless, he approached the Nazis from a psychological rather than from an historical perspective; he believed that Hitler was a delusional megalomaniac who would never be able to maintain his power. In his *Mémorial de la guerre* (1938), he announced his break with pacifism as a strategy and tactics, as well as an ideology.

Duhamel is best remembered for his novel cycles: his five volume, *Vie et aventures de Salavin* and his ten volume *Chronique des Pasquier*. He belongs to the school of psychological realism, and his best fiction blends intellect and intuition. His chronicles contain perceptive insights into the social and psychological universe of the French bourgeoisie from 1900 to 1940; he also had an eye for generational conflict. Duhamel briefly participated in World War II as a surgeon. After the war he espoused the cause of the United Nations and drifted toward a Gaullist position. He gave numerous public addresses and wrote countless articles voicing his sentimental and chauvinistic loyalty to France. Having relinquished pacifism for nationalism, Duhamel became the model of literary respectability at the end of his career: he was a member of the Academie Française, the Academy of Medicine, he edited the stodgy *Mercure de France*, wrote regularly for *Le Figaro*, was president of the Alliance française, and campaigned for the preservation of the French language and French literature.

Bibliography:

A. *Chronique des Pasquier* (10 vols., Paris, 1933–1944); *Civilisation* (Paris, 1918); *Guerre et littérature* (Paris, 1920); *Les Sept derniers plaies* (Paris, 1928); *Mémorial de la guerre* (Paris, 1938); *Vie des Martyrs*, 1914–1916 (Paris, 1917); *Vie et aventures de Salavin* (5 vols., Paris, 1920–1932).

B. L. Clark Keating, *Critic of Civilization: Georges Duhamel and his Writings* (Lexington, KY, 1965); Pierre-Henri Simon, *Georges Duhamel* (Paris, 1947); Jacques J. Zephir, *Psychologie de Salavin de Georges Duhamel* (Paris, 1970).

David James Fisher

DUMAS, Jacques (13 November 1868, Paris—14 December 1945, Latour, Montbéliard, France). *Education*: Univ. of Montpellier; Docteur en droit, Univ., of Paris, 1893. *Career*: lecturer, Yale Univ., 1900; magistrate in Montpellier, Rethel, Versailles, Paris (Cour de Cassation); founding member and ofiicer, La Paix par le droit; author and professor.

Jacques Dumas' interest in international peace dated from his high school years in Nîmes where he founded the Association des jeunes amis de la paix (Association of Young Friends of Peace) with a half-dozen other lycée students in 1887. This society began as an antimilitarist group which favored disarmament and international arbitration to solve differences among nations. Under the calming tutelage of older French peace activists, notably the venerable *Frédéric Passy, the group gave up its radical antimilitarism and accepted the notion that the most practical path toward international peace was the slow road to be paved by repeated usage of arbitration.

While Dumas and his young associates accepted the legalistic view of peace, they were impatient with the advice that peace activism had to be a low key and noncontroversial form of propaganda. When they changed their name to La Paix par le droit (Peace Through Law) and began publishing a journal with the same name, Dumas, its first editor, established a pattern of controversy and provocatively written articles. Under his leadership, the journal began its long history as one of the best-written and most thoughtful journals of peace activism on the continent. Dumas served as first president and editor from 1893–97. He also began the annual *Almanach de la paix* (*Almanac of Peace*), which he edited from 1891–93. These were attractively written and illustrated yearbooks destined for a popular readership which carried peace propaganda.

Dumas' thesis on English tax practices won him a year abroad in 1895 and on his return, he briefly worked in a government ministry. His published studies on law and land tenure earned him a solid reputation as a scholar and in 1897, having begun his career in the French judiciary, Dumas chose to step down as head of the peace society. (The new president, a young philosophy teacher, +Théodore Ruyssen remained in charge until 1947 when the group and its journal dissolved.) Dumas, however, retained a vice-presidency until his own death.

Following The Hague Peace Conference (1899) and the establishment of the international tribunal, Dumas began to study the entire issue of arbitration awards and the matter of their enforcement. The apparent "conflict" between national sovereignty, which he accepted as an essential right of nations in order to avoid such dangers as posed by potential Bonapartist-style conquerors, and the need to enforce arbitration decisions if international law were to flourish, became an abiding concern of his researches and writings. He considered the problem as early as 1901 in an article which proposed that each government create a post called an "international public minister" to advise on matters of compliance. It later became the subject of his major book, *Les Sanctions de l'arbitrage international* (1906), which established him as a major scholar in the field. Dumas, while becoming a scholar of international law, continued to write for the journal, *La Paix par le droit* and take part in national and international peace congresses. Increasingly, his work became the labor of a scholar who provided peace "ammunition" to the activists.

With World War I, Dumas was mobilized. He believed that France must fight to rid itself of invaders but also that peace activists must continue to struggle with the problems of secret diplomacy and alliances which led to war. He shared the view of his associates in the peace movement that they must work for a better ordered postwar world and was overjoyed with the Wilsonian proposal for a League of Nations. During the war as well, Dumas labored energetically for the creation of "Maisons des enfants" to care for orphaned and abandoned children of all backgrounds who were unwitting victims of the war. In the interwar years, he actively supported the League of Nations as well as other nongovernmental international societies. Until his death, Dumas continued as a vice-president of the peace society, La Paix par le droit.

Bibliography:

A. *Aspects économiques du droit de prise* (Paris, 1924); *Colonisation: essai de doctrine pacifiste* (n.p., 1904); ''De la responsibilité du pouvoir exécutif considerée comme l'une des sanctions de l'arbitrage international,'' *Revue politique et parlementaire*, 29 (Paris, 1901), 312–30; *Les Sanctions de l'arbitrage international* (Paris, 1906); ''La Sauvegarde internationale des droits de l'homme,'' The Hague, Academy of International Law, *Recueil des Cours*, 1937, I, 59 (Paris, 1938), 1–97.

B. ''Jacques Dumas,'' *La Paix par le droit*, 51 (November-December, 1947), 51–53; Jules L. Puech, ''La Paix par le droit (1887–1947),'' *La Paix par le droit*, 51 (November-December, 1947), 33–41.

Sandi E. Cooper

DUNANT, Henry (8 May 1828, Geneva—30 October 1910, Heiden, Switzerland). *Education*: private tutors and Christian academy. *Career*: agent for a North African development company; founder, International Red Cross.

Born into the Genevan patriciate, Jean-Henri Dunant (he changed his first name to Henry as an adult) was given a strict Calvinist upbringing which led him to a profound sense of Christian service to humanity. As a young man, he became interested in the American antislavery movement and joined a group of men who created the parent of the YMCA movement, the l'Union chrétienne de jeunes gens. His work, as an agent for a Swiss company with business interests in North Africa, required several long trips which introduced him to Muslim culture. Dunant's essay, *Notice sur la Régence de Tunis* (1858) was widely read in Europe among those interested in the region.

Business reasons brought him to Italy in the spring of 1859, searching for an audience with Napoleon III who was there with a French army fighting with the Italians against the Austrians. Dunant stumbled onto the battlefield at Solferino littered with dead and wounded and personally began to organize relief to save lives—Austrians, French, Sardinian, and Italian. The horror led to his booklet, *Un Souvenir de Solferino* (1862), which was widely disseminated. In 1862–63 he threw himself into the task of lobbying European governments, particularly the Swiss and Prussian, to hold a meeting that would establish rules for treating wounded soldiers and prisoners of war. In 1864 the meeting held at Geneva produced the famous Geneva Convention, a formal agreement to ''civilize'' warfare by allowing the treatment of wounded. Dunant worked vigorously thereafter to get the bright large red cross on a white field recognized as an international symbol and to create the organization known as the International Red Cross.

Following a disastrous business venture in 1867, Dunant lost his capital as well as his investors. He left Switzerland and spent the next 30 years in obscurity and, frequently, in incredible misery. He lost his position in the Red Cross as well, although during the Franco-Prussian War he continued to use the symbol and his name to aid prisoners and help political targets in Paris flee from the Commune (which he hated). In the late 1890s, he was rediscovered by the leaders of the international peace movement and an embarrassed Swiss government awarded him a small pension. In 1901, together with *Frédéric Passy, he was awarded the Nobel Peace Prize.

To late nineteenth-century peace activists, Dunant became a model of success as an individual who, through personal perseverence, was able to convince skeptical governments to engage in a permanent international arrangement and who inspired others working towards other forms of international collaboration. The creation and success of the International Red Cross remains permanent testimony to the type of activities that private citizens might pursue in the task of minimizing human self-destruction.

Bibliography:

A. *Mémoires*, ed. by Bernard Gagnebin (Geneva, 1970); *Un Souvenir de Solferino* (Geneva, 1862, trans. by N. H. Davis, *A Memory. of Solferino*, Washington, 1939).

B. Alexis François, *Un Grand humanitaire, Henri Dunant, sa vie et ses oeuvres, 1828–1910* (Geneva, 1928); Martin Gumpert, *Dunant, der Roman des Roten Kreuzes* (Stockholm, 1938); Ellen Hart, *Man Born to Live. Life and Work of Henry Dunant* (London, 1953); Daisy C. Mercanton, *Henry Dunant: Essai bio-bibliographique* (Geneva, 1971).

Sandi E. Cooper

DUPIN, Gustave (pseud. Ermenonville) (1861, Paris—17 November 1933, Versailles). *Career*: glassmaker before 1914; polemicist and journalist after World War I.

Prior to World War I Gustave Dupin lived quietly and obscurely, earning his living as a glassmaker at Versailles. Little is known about his early life and he seems not to have participated in politics in an active way. His personal life was shattered, however, when his only son was killed early in the war at Charleroi. So embittered was he by this loss that he spent the rest of his life attacking war and all those he believed were responsible for it.

Dupin was particularly incensed with President Raymond Poincaré who, in August 1914, had issued a proclamation declaring that "mobilization is not war." In 1916 Dupin helped to organize the Société d'études documentaires et critiques sur la guerre (Society for Documentary and Critical Studies of the War), which sought to gather evidence about the origins of the conflict. With peace and the end of censorship, Dupin issued his first work marshaling evidence for Poincaré's responsibility. Using the pseudonym Ermenonville (a tribute to Jean-Jacques Rousseau whom he revered), Dupin reviewed the color books issued by the combatants in 1914, the collections of diplomatic documents published by the various governments, memoirs written by leading participants, historical studies by scholars, and the daily press. He concluded that Russia and France were among the prime culprits in causing the war. Dupin believed that tsarist policy was aimed at expansion into the Balkans. France, to regain its lost province of Alsace-Lorraine, had formed a military alliance with Russia against Germany, then encouraged it to join with Britain in encircling and crushing it in a war that was deliberately provoked. According to Dupin, Poincaré, as prime minister and then as president, encouraged France's Slavic ally because of his own unsatisfied nationalism. He was abetted by the Russian ambassador to Paris, Alexander Izvolsky.

Dupin also blamed the politicians, clergy, journalists, and academicians who had blindly led France into the abyss. Maintaining that a new war had to be prevented by demonstrating the origins of the 1914–18 conflict, Dupin called upon all scholars to expose the falsification of documents and coverup of facts by Allied officials. He established a monthly review, *Vers la Vérité* (1923–24), for this purpose. Dupin severely criticized the French press for its prewar venality, arguing that it had been bought by Russian gold to work against peace and deceive public opinion. Once Frenchmen realized how they had been duped in 1914, he believed, they would strive to prevent a new conflict with Germany. Arguing that a major cause of war was the existence of standing armies, he called for their abolition beginning with the end to compulsory military service.

An individual who opposed capitalism, communism, and fascism, Gustave Dupin never formally joined any pacifist group. Rather, he preferred to express his own ideas free from the constraints imposed by ideology and organization. His numerous publications, based on substantial research and eloquent in tone, brought him prominence among French pacifists and were frequently cited by pacifists during the interwar years.

Bibliography:

A. *Les Chroniques d'Ermenonville* (Paris, 1927); *La Guerre infernale* (Geneva, n.d.); *M. Poincaré et la guerre de 1914 (Etudes sur les responsabilités)* (Paris, 1931); *Le Règne de la bête* (Paris, 1925); *Les Robinsons de la paix* (Paris, 1923).

B. Lucien Roth, "Gustave Dupin," *La Voie de la paix*, April 15, 1961, 1.

James Friguglietti

DURKEE, Charles (10 December 1805, Royalton, VT—14 January 1870, Omaha, NE). *Education*: Burlington Academy. *Career*: merchant and politician.

Charles Durkee was one of those exceptional early nineteenth-century American figures who manifested deep reform commitment while also successfully pursuing a business and political career. His devotion to the cause of peace during the 1840s and 1850s, though considerable, often took second place to what he believed was the more immediately pressing cause of antislavery.

As a youth in Vermont Durkee embarked on a mercantile career which he continued with striking success after settling in 1836 in what became the city of Kenosha, Wisconsin. His active interest in reform, especially in antislavery and temperance, dated from his religious conversion and affiliation with the Methodist Episcopal Church in 1832. Politics soon became his forte. He was elected to Wisconsin's territorial legislature in 1837 and again in 1847. From 1848 to 1853 he served in Congress, where he ranked as a leading member of its small but vocal Free Soil contingent. The next year he was elected to the Senate as a Republican.

In the wake of the War with Mexico, which his antislavery and peace principles led him to oppose, Durkee helped organize a peace society in his home county. He actively supported the League of Universal Brotherhood and organized gatherings in Wisconsin for its founder, *Elihu Burritt. He strongly supported the concept of international peace conferences and attended the 1849 Paris Peace Convention as a member of the American delegation.

Despite an auspicious beginning, peace efforts in Wisconsin developed little momentum in comparison with antislavery and anti-Southernism, of which Durkee was one of that state's earliest political exponents. Thus despite his concern for peace he experienced little difficulty in supporting the Union cause in the Civil War. By his earlier endorsement Durkee, as a respected public figure, helped give the peace movement legitimacy, while at the same time he contributed little to its theory or institutional development.

Bibliography:

B. M. Frank, "Prominent Events in the Life of Hon. Charles Durkee," State Historical Society of Wisconsin, *Report and Collections*, 6 (1872) 123–35; Theodore Clarke Smith, "The Free Soil Party in Wisconsin," State Historical Society of Wisconsin, *Proceedings*, 1894 (1895), 97–162.

Merton L. Dillon

DUTTON, Samuel Train. See *Biographical Dictionary of Internationalists*.

DYMOND, Jonathan (19 December 1796, Exeter, England—6 May 1828, Exeter). *Education*: largely self-taught, although he attended Thomas Davis' Academy, Milverton, Somersetshire, for a short time. *Career*: linen-draper; Quaker moral philosopher.

Jonathan Dymond's exposition of Christian pacifist principles was probably the most influential to appear in the first half of the nineteenth century. His *Inquiry into War* (1823) and his *Essays* (1829) were often reissued, in full or in abridgements, and *John Bright hailed the *Essays* as one of the finest books written on the question of "morals as applied to nations."

Dymond's parents were both "recorded ministers" of the Society of Friends, and he passed most of his life within a somewhat limited Quaker circle in the south-west of England. He worked in the family business, a linen-draper's shop, and was noted for his skill in cutting cloth. But although the social circle was restricted, it was not narrowly sectarian. The habit of light-hearted verse-writing and other literary composition was well established in the family, and he was early accustomed to appreciate felicity of style. In 1819 and subsequent years, the Dymond family and their friends collaborated to produce a manuscript miscellany entitled *The Iscan Budget* (Isca was the Roman name for Exeter), and the *Inquiry into War* originated in some essays contributed there by Jonathan. The essays were revised and expanded, and eventually published in 1823, in an edition of 300 copies. Attracting wide notice, the essays were revised and published several more times.

In May 1825 Dymond attended the ninth annual meeting of the Peace Society and in July of the same year helped to inaugurate an Auxiliary Peace Society in Exeter, serving as one of its secretaries. But his involvement in this work was cut short by increasing ill-health, which in 1826 led to the almost complete loss of his voice and two years later to his death.

In his last years he worked steadily on his *Essays on the Principles of Morality*, in which he argued that war was the most important test of Christian commitment, more important even than the question of slavery. He conceded that his Quaker contemporaries viewed the antislavery campaign as their predominant concern, but he hoped that when slavery was indeed abolished they would direct their energies against war. The leading theme of the *Essays* was that deviations from rectitude were impolitic as well as wrong.

Dymond's views on war and peace were most clearly expressed in *Inquiry into War*. Here he sought to demonstrate the incompatibility of war with Christianity and to meet the arguments that William Paley and others had urged in defense of the opposite position. He took special pains to challenge the contention that Christ's pacific injunctions apply only to the conduct of individuals, and have no direct bearing on the conduct of nations. The obligation, he contended, is the same.

Dymond contributed little directly to the discussion of institutions that might replace war, but in his *Essays* he did propose that arbitration in personal disputes was a wise substitute for expensive lawsuits. His message was that obedience to the Gospel is always the truest wisdom, and that Pennsylvania flourished and Quakers survived the Irish rebellion of 1798 because of such obedience. He shared the belief, widespread in the 1820s, of a great and general moral progress that would lead, eventually, to the abolition of war. For him the question of means was secondary, and his great contribution to the nineteenth-century peace movement lay in his cogent exposition of the basic convictions of the Christian peacemaker.

Bibliography:

A. *Essays on the Principles of Morality and on the Private and Political Rights and Obligations of Mankind* (London, 1829); *An Inquiry into the Accordancy of War with the Principles of Christianity* (London, 1823).

B. C. W. Dymond, *Memoir, Letters and Poems of Jonathan Dymond* (privately printed, 1911).

Geoffrey Carnall

E

EASTMAN, Crystal (25 June 1881, Marlborough, MA—8 July 1928, Erie, PA). *Education*: B.A., Vassar Coll., 1903; M.A., Columbia Univ., 1904. LL.B., New York Univ., 1907. *Career:* participant in the Pittsburgh Survey of Industrial Conditions, 1908; member, N.Y. State Commission on Employers' Liability and Industrial Accidents, 1909–11; author, *Work Accidents and the Law*, 1910; executive director, American Union against Militarism, 1915–17; chair, Woman's Peace Party of New York, 1914–19; co-owner and co-editor of *The Liberator*, 1918–22; attorney, social investigator, feminist, socialist, pacifist.

A committed feminist and socialist, Crystal Eastman became a pacifist because of her belief in human freedom and her conviction that military establishments and wars fought in defense of business interests threatened the very values she most cherished. An active organizer and administrator, she ranked with women like *Jane Addams and *Lillian Wald as one of the founders of the kind of social activist peace organizations which succeeded the more staid, conservative, male-led peace groups of the nineteenth century.

Daughter of two Congregational ministers, Eastman brought an aggressive social conscience to contemporary problems. Developing her feminism early, she soon became an active social reformer and a socialist. As a lawyer, she gained recognition as a leading authority on labor legislation and industrial safety. With the outbreak of World War I and the agitation for "preparedness," Eastman joined Addams, Wald, *Paul Kellogg, *Oswald Garrison Villard and other liberal pacifists to found the American Union against Militarism (AUAM) which decried expansion of the armed forces, proposals for conscription, American expansion into the Caribbean and Latin America, as well as steps leading to U.S. entry into World War I. Viewing war as a threat to social reform caused primarily by commercial interests with imperialist ambitions and suspecting that the profit motive lay behind business proposals for a larger army and navy, Eastman, as executive director of the AUAM, called unsuccessfully for an investigation of the munitions industry and nationalization of the manufacture of armaments. She also worked for mediation of international disputes, taking the lead in creating an unofficial commission of Mexican and American citizens to reduce tensions resulting from the incursion into Mexico of the U.S. punitive expedition against Francisco "Pancho" Villa.

In addition to her role as antimilitarist, Eastman was committed to using the international women's suffrage network as a vehicle for peace and social justice. Together with Jane Addams and others, Eastman founded the national Woman's Peace party (later known as the Women's International League for Peace and

Freedom) in 1915 so that women on both sides of the Atlantic could press their governments to mediate an end to the war. She sought a peace based on non-imperialist terms: no punitive indemnities, no forcible annexations, and self-determination of nationalities. As president of the New York branch of the party, Eastman encouraged more radical confrontational positions than the party's national leaders felt acceptable and they tried to prevent her from attending the Second International Congress of Women in 1919.

Even after the U.S. entered the war in 1917, Eastman continued to oppose what she considered the militarization of America. To defend conscientious objectors against the draft, she, along with *Roger Baldwin and *Norman Thomas, established a bureau in the AUAM which became the forerunner of the American Civil Liberties Union, an action which split the AUAM when its more conservative leaders withdrew. With *Louis Lochner and other wartime pacifists, Eastman also participated in the People's Council, a leftwing antiwar group which was quickly driven out of existence. With her brother, *Max, she established and coedited *The Liberator*, a radical antiwar and social justice magazine which succeeded *The Masses* after it was suppressed by the Wilson Administration. Eastman came to accept revolutionary violence, especially to defend the communist governments of the Soviet Union and Hungary (which she visited in 1919) against the counterrevolutionary military intervention of the Allies.

In the postwar period she advocated an international federation of peoples and democratic control of foreign policy. She was skeptical of the Treaty of Versailles because of its compromises and of the League of Nations, which she viewed as a counter-revolutionary alliance, because of its exclusion of the Soviet Union. From the pages of *The Liberator*, she called for radical social programs in the United States, the release of wartime political prisoners, and universal disarmament. After the Justice Department raided the magazine's offices in 1922, she spent much of the next five years in Europe. Returning to New York, she was denied regular employment because of her radicalism. Her health deteriorated and, at the age of forty-seven, she died of nephritis.

Uncompromising to the end in her condemnation of military institutions, corporate capitalism, and war as destructive of social justice and human liberty, Eastman spent her life pouring her strength, vitality, enthusiasm, and considerable organizational and administrative talent into the fight against them. Equality, freedom, and world peace, she believed, could only be achieved by radical changes in the domestic and international order.

Bibliography:

A. *Crystal Eastman on Women and Revolution*, ed. by Blanche Wiesen Cook (New York, 1978).

B. Blanche Wiesen Cook, ed., *Toward the Great Change: Crystal and Max Eastman on Feminism, Antimilitarism, and Revolution* (New York, 1976); William L. O'Neill, *The Last Romantic: A Life of Max Eastman* (New York, 1978); NAW, I, 543–45.

John Whiteclay Chambers

EASTMAN, Max Forrester (4 January 1883, Canadaigua, NY—25 March 1969, Bridgetown, Barbados). *Education*: B.A., Williams Coll., 1905; Columbia

Univ., 1907–11 (completed all requirements for Ph.D. degree, including dissertation, but chose not to receive it). *Career*: lecturer, Columbia Univ., 1907–11; editor, *The Masses*, 1912–17, *The Liberator*, 1918–21, *Readers' Digest* (roving editor), 1941–69; poet, writer, and lecturer.

During the first half of the twentieth century Max Eastman traveled a familiar path from the far Left to the far Right. One of the best-known and most influential literary radicals prior to World War I—champion of the Bolshevik Revolution and such causes as feminism, birth control, and freedom from Victorian sexual taboos—he became one of the most outspoken critics of communism, going so far as to support Senator Joseph R. McCarthy in his Cold War purges. During his rich and active literary years he wrote more than twenty books on art, poetry, philosophy, science, religion, capitalism, socialism, humor, Soviet culture, German politics, and Marxism. His works include five volumes of poetry, one of fiction, five major translations from Russian, two autobiographies, two volumes of biographical portraits, and a movie. Always an independent thinker, he was one of the first supporters of the Bolshevik Revolution to side with Leon Trotsky in his battles with Joseph Stalin and to condemn the direction of the Soviet state. Later, despite his conservatism and anticommunist preferences, he resigned as editorial advisor to William Buckley Jr.'s *National Review* because it sought to fuse politics and religion.

Eastman was an internationalist before he became a socialist. He rejected the Marxist idea that capitalism necessarily caused war. Instead he argued that the root cause of war was patriotism, which was inherent in humanity. He equated patriotism with nationalism and saw it as the "most banal of stupid human idol-worships." The only way to end war, then, was to subsume nationalism in some kind of international union that would create a larger allegiance, just as American loyalty to separate states had been submerged in a greater loyalty to the United States.

Although he challenged the socialist conception of the causes of war, he joined his fellow radicals in opposing World War I. As editor of *The Masses* he took a strong antiwar position attacking preparedness, the draft, and American intervention. Along with his sister, *Crystal Eastman, he helped create the American Union Against Militarism (originally established in November, 1915 as Anti-Militarism Committee). The American Union, which included *Lillian Wald (chair), *Oswald Garrison Villard, *John Haynes Holmes, and *Rabbi Stephen Wise, sought to coordinate the activities of the various militant peace groups and lobbied Congress against conscription and American intervention.

Eastman's strong and articulate views against the war made him a featured speaker at antiwar rallies in New York, Illinois, and even North Dakota. In Fargo, North Dakota he had to be smuggled out of town when his criticism of the war effort led to the formation of a lynch mob. The government, too, sought to silence him. The June 1917 issue of *The Masses* was excluded from the mails, and in August it lost its second-class mailing privileges for carrying antiwar cartoons and articles. Within a few months *The Masses* folded, but Eastman, together with his sister, replaced it with *The Liberator*, which continued to condemn the war and spoke out forcefully for freedom of speech and the press. Along with John Reed, Floyd Dell, and several other editors and contributors to *The Masses*, Eastman was indicted under the provisions of the Espionage Act of 1917 for conspiring to obstruct recruitment and promoting "insubordination and mutiny in the military and naval forces of the United States." Twice the government tried the case, but each time Eastman and his colleagues were set free by a hung jury.

Eastman's confrontations with mobs and with the government convinced him that continued opposition to the war was futile. Increasingly he turned his attention to the Bolshevik Revolution. Eventually communism became his central concern. After 1918 he measured almost all political issues on the basis of their effect on the Soviet Union, at first supporting those that helped the Soviet Union and later opposing those that benefited Stalin's Russia. Immediately after the outbreak of World War II he favored American neutrality, but quickly came to side with those calling for intervention. Adhering to his earlier internationalist views, he felt that America could not allow events to take their course, for this would not guarantee a decent international order. He supported the idea of a federation of nations that would exercise police power throughout the world, but warned his fellow Americans that the Soviet Union could not be trusted and was not the gallant democratic ally that some made it out to be. After the war Eastman's conservatism and anticommunism became even more pronounced and he became a major critic of the Truman administration for its "appeasement" of the Soviet Union.

Max Eastman was never a pacifist and, in fact, always believed in taking up arms for the right cause. Still, during World War I he spoke out forcefully and bravely for the cause of peace and contributed significantly to the antiwar legacy, even though he eventually abandoned it.

Bibliography:

A. *The Enjoyment of Living* (New York, 1948); *Love and Revolution: My Journey through an Epic* (New York, 1964); "Patriotism, A Primitive Ideal," *International Journal of Ethics* (July, 1906), 472–86; *Understanding Germany* (New York, 1915).

B. Milton Cantor, *Max Eastman* (New York, 1970); John Diggins, *Up From Communism: Conservative Odysseys in American Intellectual History* (New York, 1975); William L. O'Neill, *The Last Romantic: A Life of Max Eastman* (New York, 1978).

C. Max Eastman Papers, Lilly Library, Indiana University.

Harold Josephson

EBY, Benjamin (2 May 1785, Hammer Creek, Lancaster County, PA—28 June 1853, Kitchener, Ontario, Canada). *Career*: minister and bishop, schoolteacher, farmer, author, community leader.

The first half of the nineteenth century saw a steady migration of Mennonites from Pennsylvania to the largely unsettled areas of Upper Canada. Drawn by the offers of good farmland and hopes for freedom to exercise such religious beliefs as nonresistance, these Mennonites discovered that not only was pioneering required on the land, but also with respect to their rights as conscientious objectors. By the mid–1800s the Mennonites, together with the Tunkers and Quakers, had succeeded in petitioning the Canadian government to remove the heavy financial penalties which had hitherto accompanied exemption from militia service.

One of the pioneers of the Mennonite community in Canada and a strong proponent of the nonresistant position was Bishop Benjamin Eby. The founder and leading citizen of Ebytown (now Kitchener), Ontario, Eby was involved in almost every facet of the town's life. He was instrumental in the construction of the first meetinghouse for religious worship in 1813, followed two years later by an annex which served as schoolhouse. Eby can be credited with encouraging the peaceful coexistence of the Mennonites and the rest of the population in the growing community.

Eby was also a man of literary talent, producing a number of published works during his lifetime, including a hymn book, catechism, several school texts, and a church history. The latter publication is clear proof of Eby's emphasis on the nonresistant stance and his belief that war is unacceptable in the Kingdom of God.

Eby promoted reconciliation and unity within the local community as well as on an international scale. He freely opened his church to non-Mennonites and developed warm friendships with local businessmen of different faiths. He donated some of his own land to two men who wished to establish a furniture factory, and gave encouragement and financial aid toward the creation of a printing and publishing business. Hoping to create an international Mennonite fellowship, Eby cultivated a relationship, through correspondence, with church leaders in Europe and America. His rapport with non-Mennonites and his leadership and oratory skills undoubtedly contributed to the gains made by Mennonites in consolidating their peace position in Canada.

Bibliography:

B. J. Boyd Cressman,''Eby, Benjamin,'' *Mennonite Encyclopedia*, II, 138–39; J. Boyd Cressman, ''Bishop Benjamin Eby,'' *Waterloo Historical Society*, 29 (1941), 152–58; Ezra E. Eby and Eldon D. Weber, *A Biographical History of Early Settlers and their Descendants in Waterloo Township* (Waterloo, 1971), 136–37; Frank H. Epp, *Mennonites in Canada, 1786–1920: The History of a Separate People* (Toronto, 1974); Melvin E. Gingerich, ''Mennonite Leaders of North America: Benjamin Eby (1785–1853)'' *Gospel Herald* (March 2, 1965), 178; Ira D. Landis, ''Bishop Peter Eby of Pequea,'' *Mennonite Quarterly Review*. 14 (1940), 41–51.

Frank H. Epp

EDDY, George Sherwood (19 January 1871, Leavenworth, KS—3 March 1963, Jacksonville, IL). *Education*: Phillips Andover Academy; Ph.B., Yale Univ., 1891; additional studies at Union Theological Seminary and Princeton Theological Seminary. *Career*: college secretary of the YMCA in India and traveling secretary, Student Volunteer Movement, in India and Ceylon (1896–1911); YMCA secretary for Asia (1911–14); YMCA work with Allied troops (1914–19); YMCA secretary, founder and director of the Sherwood Eddy Seminar (1921–39); independent author and speaker.

Sherwood Eddy was one of the powerful American leaders in the worldwide Christian evangelism of which the YMCA and Student Volunteer Movement were agents. He earned a degree in civil engineering at Yale but, in the year of his graduation, he was converted to the cause of Christian mission. After theological preparation at Union and Princeton seminaries, he undertook evangelistic work in India, where he learned Tamil. In 1911 he became secretary for evangelism in Asia and, with John R. Mott, conducted campaigns throughout Asia that culminated in China in 1914.

Eddy was impelled by a vibrant, personal Christian commitment. At the same time, he valued the scientific, rational approach and biblical criticism. God is absolute, he believed, but human understanding is relative. So, too, was the Bible; its truth lay in the power which it could elicit in a believing person rather than in its literal exposition. The truth of faith was demonstrated in its impact on a person, not in doctrinal allegiance. Such an approach equipped Eddy for unapologetic evangelism in a religiously and culturally plural world, led him to view religion as constantly expanding revelation, and enabled him to address new issues as a kind of adventure.

With the outbreak of World War I, Eddy led YMCA work with soldiers in Britain. When the United States entered the war, he recruited volunteers for work with Allied troops abroad. The war experience and the influence of his personal secretary, *Kirby Page, broadened Eddy's view of the social dimensions of the gospel and led him to become, for a time, an absolute pacifist. He and Page researched, wrote, and spoke on critical social issues facing the United States in a crusade that carried Eddy into colleges and churches. He helped to found the Fellowship for a Christian Social Order and moved to democratic socialism, weathering conservative attacks on his position with the YMCA, which he served without salary until 1931.

Meanwhile, he and Page were also studying, writing, and speaking on war and international issues. Eddy founded and conducted the Sherwood Eddy Seminar which from 1921 to 1939 took ministers, educators, and lecturers to Europe each summer for firsthand study, utilizing his contacts to gain access to political, economic, scholarly, and religious leaders. In 1926 and after 1929 the Seminar included Russia. Out of this study and world exposure came important widely-read assessments of the contemporary world.

In the crisis before World War II, Eddy shifted from absolute pacifism to a just war position like that of *Reinhold Niebuhr, holding that the absolute ethics of Jesus must be applied to relative situations which might justify warfare. Nonetheless, he remained clear that war must be abolished, especially in a nuclear age, and that internationalism is a fundamental part of Christian responsibility. Throughout his 37 books, many pamphlets, and innumerable speeches ran the theme that the world was in the midst of a revolution which challenged Christianity and American society to respond by embodying their highest social ideals in a changing environment. Familiar with Asia and Europe, including Russia, Sherwood Eddy was a key figure in broadening the social gospel impulse in the YMCA and mainstream American churches to include a worldview and a commitment to peace. In his career he embodied both evangelical experience and social passion.

Bibliography:

A. *The Abolition of War* (with Kirby Page, New York, 1924); *The Challenge of the East* (New York, 1931); *The Challenge of Russia* (New York, 1931).

Charles Chatfield

EFFORD, Lincoln Winstone Arthur (4 August 1907, Christchurch, New Zealand—24 April 1962, Christchurch). *Education*: B.A., Univ. of New Zealand, 1934, M.A., 1935. *Career:* secretary, Workers' Education Association (Canterbury), 1949–62; voluntary social worker and peace activist.

Lincoln Efford first became active in the peace movement as a member of the No More War Movement (NMWM) started in New Zealand in 1928. He was continuously an officeholder from 1929. On the death of *C.R.N. Mackie in 1943 he became Secretary of the National Peace Council. Though he played some part in the Campaign for Nuclear Disarmament, his commitment to the Workers' Educational Association and continued ill-health largely curtailed his peace activities after 1950. His contribution to New Zealand pacifism was mainly as an organizer and publicist, especially during the difficult period of World War II.

Efford's grandfather had been one of the earliest Labour candidates in New Zealand politics, and Efford never departed from the socialist view that modern war had its basic cause in capitalistic greed and exploitation. Education remained his longterm strategy, with political action whenever the opportunity offered. As it happened, the 1930s were increasingly unpropitious for the NMWM: a broad-based peace movement including church groups and trade unions never developed, the Labour government backed rearmament and the Christian Pacifist Society and the Peace Pledge Union were particularly successful in attracting the younger generation of pacifists.

At this stage World War II intervened, and Efford emerged as the pacifist leader who was able to bring most pressure to bear on the Labour government regarding the treatment of conscientious objectors. *Ormond Burton and A.C. Barrington had rather discredited themselves in the government's eyes by their militancy, and Efford had the further advantage of being well-acquainted with many MPs and Labour party leaders. He added to the government's discomfort by developing close links with British pacifists who criticized New Zealand's policy publicly and lobbied visiting New Zealand ministers. In 1943 he twice stood as a peace candidate in parliamentary elections.

During the war Efford made it his first task to monitor carefully the activity of the Appeal Boards which exempted men from military service. By 1943 he had assembled an impressive body of evidence indicating the illiberality and injustice of the government's policy towards conscientious objectors, and initiated a prolonged campaign to obtain a right of appeal from the Appeal Board's decision and the release of men held for the duration of the war in specially established defaulters' camps. Though the government proved unyielding, Efford's campaign did succeed in eliciting considerable public sympathy for the detained objectors. One consequence was that when compulsory military training was reintroduced in 1949—a measure Efford was prominent in opposing—a much fairer system of appeal was instituted.

Efford's concentration on the issue of conscientious objection partly reflected the general contraction of peace activity during a period of war and Cold War. But it also indicated the predicament of the small pacifist community in New Zealand which had to contend with a government whose policy towards conscientious objection was severe in comparison with other Western democracies. Efford, however, continued to hope for a new international order based on justice, equality, and cooperation between peoples.

Bibliography:

A. *Penalties on Conscience: An Examination of the Defaulters' Detention System in New Zealand* (Christchurch, 1945).

C. Papers of Lincoln Efford, Alexander Turnbull Library, Wellington, N.Z.

J. E. Cookson

EGIDY, Christoph Moritz von (27 August 1847, Mainz, Germany—29 December 1898, Potsdam). *Education*: Potsdam Cadet School, 1856–64. *Career*: army officer, 1864–90; co-editor (with Johannes Lehmann-Hohenberg), *Einiges Christenthum Volksschrift zur Förderung der Bestrebungen Moritz von Egidys*, Kiel, 1892–93; editor, *Versöhnung*, Berlin, 1894–99; writer and publicist; speaker; politician.

Christoph Moritz von Egidy was descended from a family of Saxon civil servants ennobled in the seventeenth century. He served in both the Prussian war against Austria and in the Franco-Prussian war, receiving the Iron Cross for bravery. His military experience made him somewhat skeptical concerning war, but did not lead to his rejection of militarism. His superiors considered him an exemplary and capable officer, particularly on account of his training and instructional methods.

Egidy, however, held himself aloof from the customary pleasures and social life of army officers. In reaction to the narrow education he had received in the military academy, he broadened his knowledge and views through self-study. By the age of thirty his attitudes were quite different from those of the average officer. A devout Christian, he became intensely concerned with religious and ecclesiastical issues. Acting on his conviction, he became a member of the Protestant branch of the Johannite Order. As a member of the poor relief board of a working class suburb of Dresden, he strove to ease the oppressive plight of the workers and their families. Siding with those in the church who were sympathetic with social democracy, he published *Ernste Gedanken* (*Serious Thoughts*) in 1890. In this slim volume he charged the church with sacrificing the concept of Christianity to the exercise of power. He reproached the church for failing to nurture the individual to spirituality and to encourage the Christian way of life. He called upon his readers to work within the church for the renewal and preservation of Christianity.

Ernste Gedanken reached a wide audience and triggered an enormous scandal, which made Egidy one of the best known figures in German politics during the 1890s. His views evoked the opposition of established church leaders because they seemed to undercut, at least indirectly, the union of throne and altar which was an axiom of the Prussian-German military state. The opposition was especially vehement because the criticism of the church had come from a respected lieutenant colonel. Although he always remained loyal to his monarchical feelings and denied charges of endangering the throne, Egidy was dismissed from military service in October 1890 after refusing to resign voluntarily. He quickly published additional critiques of the church and invited like-minded friends to a gathering in Berlin on Whit-Tuesday of 1891 to announce their determination to restore Christianity to humanity ''as its blissful possession.'' The two-day conference laid the foundation for a new religiously and ethically based social movement, which became known as the Egidy Movement.

Egidy desired to be neither a theologian, a philosopher, a church reformer, nor a founder of a political party. His objective was to instill in people a deeply felt social consciousness and a serious commitment to social justice. He avoided giving his ideas any firm organizational support or placing himself in the service of one of the already existing left-bourgeois opposition associations, such as *Wilhelm Foerster's Society for Ethical Culture. He likewise rejected offers to join German left Protestantism, the free religious groups, or the German Catholic circles. His efforts for a radical renewal of society based upon a Christian foundation and his differences with the Society for Ethical Culture, heightened Egidy's awareness that the solution to the ''religious question'' was dependent upon surmounting existing political and social problems. He soon came to believe that the preservation of peace was the fundamental condition for the social transformation he sought.

In *Ernstes Wollen* (*Serious Will*) (1891) Egidy was concerned with problems such as the equality of women, the position of the Jewish people in German society, and worker-protection laws. His comments on war and peace, together with his growing concern about clerical support of Prussian militarism, contributed to his formal break with the church. He maintained that the true Christian must reject the concept of ''necessary evil,'' and therefore had to oppose war. The notion that war was necessary for the maintainance of power and the protection of the nation, he believed, was irreconcilably contradictory with the desire for lasting peace. Egidy's opponents reacted strongly against his criticism of war and the Prussian military tradition. From 1891 until his death he was under police surveillance as an exponent of ideas that threatened the existence of the state.

In 1893 Egidy campaigned in an important Berlin electoral district as a nonaligned candidate for the Reichstag. Although he had neither a newspaper nor a party at his disposal, he was a polished speaker and his campaign rallies attracted large numbers of people. Egidy's Christian convictions led him to share the Social Democratic criticism of capitalism and of the undemocratic character of the existing political structure. Despite these beliefs, he refused to become a member of the Social Democratic party, first because he strove for a reconciliation between social classes on a broad ethical basis and second because he saw the party fighting "for a good cause with poor weapons," scoffing and trampling upon "the greatest need of the human soul: the religious." Although he did not succeed in being elected to the Reichstag, he received almost 12 percent of the votes. A second attempt in 1898 to gain a seat as a nonaligned member of Parliament also failed, but his sense of justice and unselfish endeavors in behalf of the poor and exploited gained him the respect of Social Democratic leaders and working class members alike.

In his campaign speeches in 1893, Egidy avoided taking a clear position on increased military spending—a key issue at that time—but later he became increasingly more decisive in his criticism of German militarism and colonialism. Already bound by years of friendship to *Bertha von Suttner, *Wilhelm Foerster, and other peace activists, Egidy supported the goals of pacifism and demanded that youth be educated for peace. The Egidy Associations, founded in several large cities for the dissemination of his ideas, willingly accepted the values of the peace movement, since a number of pacifists, such as *Friedrich Bloh, were themselves leaders in these organizations.

In September 1898, Egidy publicly opposed the popular adoration of Otto von Bismarck by characterizing the late German chancellor as "violent," "tyrannical," and "inhuman (un-Christian)." This further alienated Egidy from the ruling elite and added to suspicions that he was championing ideas that threatened the state. Egidy enthusiastically greeted Czar *Nicholas II's "Message of Peace" which appeared in August 1898. In the following months he spoke in numerous cities in support of the Czar's call for disarmament. His early death was regarded as an immeasurable loss to the peace movement since he seemed predestined to play an important moderating role in the drawing together of the peace and workers movements.

Bibliography:

A. *Beseitigung der Klassengegensätze. Vortrag* (Hannover, 1896); *Das Einige Christentum* (Berlin, 1891); *Ernste Gedanken* (Leipzig, 1890); *Ernstes Wollen* (Berlin, 1891); *Die Friedensbotschaft des Zaren. Vortrag* (Danzig, 1899); *Gedanken über Erziehung* (Bonn, 1897).

B. Geertruida Carelsen, *Christoph M. v. Egidy* (Haarlem, 1899); Heinrich Driesmans, *Moritz v. Egidy* (2 vols., Dresden and Leipzig, 1900); Wilhelm Foerster, "M. von Egidy," *Ethische Kultur*, January 7, 1899; Heinz Herz, *Alleingang wider die Mächtigen. Ein Bild vom Leben und Kämpfen Moritz von Egidys* (Leipzig, 1970).

C. Christoph Moritz von Egidy Papers, Nationale Forschungs—und Gedenkstätte der klassischen Literatur in Weimar (Goethe–und Schiller-Archiv).

Helmut Donat
Trans. by William H. Hopkins

EICHELBERGER, Clark Mell. See *Biographical Dictionary of Internationalists*.

EICKHOFF, Richard (20 October 1854, Moers, Prussia—18 February 1931, Remscheid, Germany). *Education*: studies in classical philology, universities of Leipzig, Heidelberg, Bonn, and Kiel, 1872–81. *Career*: gymnasium (secondary school) teacher, Herford and Remscheid, 1882–98; member, Remscheid City Council, 1898; deputy, German imperial parliament (Reichstag), 1898–1912; deputy, lower house of Prussian state legislature, 1903–18; political writer.

Eickhoff grew up in a Protestant teacher's family, a circumstance which no doubt influenced his choice of teaching as a career before he entered politics. He entered politics as a left-liberal, first as a member of the Progressive People's party and later of the Progressive Liberal People's party. Both parties eventually united with other left-liberal factions into one Progressive party.

In the year 1905, Eickhoff succeeded Max Hirsch as head of the German Section of the Interparlimentary Union. Up to the time he joined the board of directors, the section was dominated by left-liberalism. Eickhoff's ability to compromise allowed him to reorganize the section and attract outside energies into it, especially those from the left-wing of the Center party. As a consequence of his flexibility, he gained the trust of the Imperial government, which made possible holding the Fifteenth conference of the Interparliamentary Union in Berlin in 1908, and soon thereafter the payment of a subsidy to the German section of the Interparliamentary Union. The subsidy, however, led to some loss of the considerable integrity that the German section had enjoyed until then.

Throughout his political career, Eickhoff supported the idea of the peaceful settlement of international disputes through courts of arbitration. It was from this foreign policy position that, on several occasions, he formally questioned the Imperial government on the matter of the German-American Arbitration Treaty and encouraged an arbitration treaty with France. As a co-founder of the Association of International Understanding, Eickhoff was willing, in contrast to other Association members, to collaborate with the pacifists. Like many German left-liberals, however, his antiwar position often was at odds with his support of Germany's aggressive colonial and imperialist policies. Thus he supported expansion of the German navy and the desires of the small and medium-size iron and steel manufactures in Solingen for military contracts to produce bayonets. Eickhoff's positions on German imperialism and naval armaments explain why the German chancellor, Prince Bernhard von Bülow, supported his reelection to the Reichstag in 1907, even enlisting the aid of the Navy League for that purpose.

Despite the discordance between his antiwar position and his support of imperialist policies, Eickhoff remained steadfast in his commitment to a politics of international understanding. During the First World War, he remained aloof from extreme nationalism, and after the war he resumed his activities within the Interparliamentary Union. He frequently attended meetings of the Union and reported about them in the press. As before, he also participated in German pacifist congresses where his positions earned him respect more from the bourgeois moderate side of the German peace movement, than from its younger, radical side.

Bibliography:

A. *Die internationale Schiedsgerichtsbewegung* (Berlin, 1910); *Die Interparlamentarische Union (1889–1914). Der Vorläufer des Völkerbundes* (Berlin 1921); *Politische Profile. Erinnerungen aus vier Jahrzehnten* (Dresden 1927).

B. Roger Chickering, "A Voice of Moderation in Imperial Germany: The 'Verband für internationale Verstämdigung,' 1911–1914," *Journal of Contemporary History* 8 (January 1973), 147–64.

Karl Holl
Trans. by William H. Hopkins

EINSTEIN, Albert (14 March 1879, Ulm, Germany—18 April 1955, Princeton, NJ). *Education*: graduated, Zurich Polytechnic Academy, 1900; Ph.D., Univ. of Zurich, 1905. *Career*: associate professor of physics, Univ. of Zurich, 1909–10; professor of physics, German Univ., Prague, 1910–12 and Polytechnic, Zurich, 1912–14; director, Kaiser Wilhelm Institute for Physics, Berlin, 1914–33; member, Institute for Advanced Study, Princeton, 1933–55; mathematical physicist and peace activist.

Although scientists have contended that Albert Einstein's work in physics is rivaled only by that of Isaac Newton, he also furthered a variety of political causes: civil liberties, democratic socialism, Zionism, and opposition to war.

Analyzing his pacifism, Einstein once claimed that it resulted from his deep antipathy to cruelty and hatred. But scholars have identified other factors as well. Einstein, they observe, saw militarism as a direct threat to intellectual freedom, which he considered the foundation of civilization. Furthermore, he viewed war as an assault upon the natural laws of the universe—laws which he both studied and revered. Finally, Einstein was an internationalist, who despised chauvinism, ethnic hatreds, and national prejudices. In numerous ways, then, Einstein was a typical Enlightenment intellectual, convinced that reason, science, and compassion could usher in a new day for humanity.

Einstein first achieved prominence as a pacifist in 1914, shortly after moving to Berlin to become director of the Institute for Physics of the Kaiser Wilhelm Society for the Development of the Sciences. When the First World War began that summer, he was shocked and horrified. To the French writer and pacifist *Romain Rolland, he posed the question in a letter of March 22, 1915, whether "three centuries of painstaking cultural effort" have "carried us no further than from religious fanaticism to the insanity of nationalism.'' Yet few German intellectuals shared his dismay. An antiwar ''Manifesto to Europeans,'' circulated among the faculty of the University of Berlin, was signed by only four people, one of them Einstein. Given this limited support, the Manifesto was shelved until years later. That November, however, Einstein and a small group of other peace activists organized the Bund Neues Vaterland (New Fatherland League) to press for peace without annexations and the establishment of a supranational organization to make future wars impossible. As a result of its activities the League came under increasing attack by German authorities and, in 1916, was formally suppressed.

The end of the war brought Einstein a new surge of hope. Delighted by the collapse of Imperial Germany, he publicly welcomed the proclamation of a democratic republic and the rise to power of the German Social Democratic party. These stands, together with his prominence as a pacifist, and internationalist, and a Jewish intellectual, made him the object of venomous attacks by Germany's rightwing nationalists. Rather than retreat from the public arena, however, Einstein grew more politically engaged. In 1922 he joined the Committee on Intellectual Cooperation of the League of Nations, through which he hoped to foster global understanding. When, in 1932, he resigned from this body, it was because he thought the committee and its parent organization ineffectual. For some years, in fact, he had been turning toward a more radical break with warfare.

Beginning in 1928 Einstein sought to overcome militarism through promotion of direct war resistance. Drawing upon his immense prestige as a scientist and intellectual, he endorsed and publicized the programs of radical pacifist organizations. War refusal ''is one of the most encouraging developments of our time,'' he announced on November 25, 1928, in a message to the No More War Movement, in London. People ''should assume . . . the solemn and unconditional obligation not to participate in any war, for any reason.'' Einstein signed appeals against conscription, assailed the prosecution of conscientious objectors, made a demonstrative visit to the 1932 world disarmament conference in Geneva, cooperated in efforts to establish an international peace center, and participated in a famous public exchange of letters with Sigmund Freud on the cause and cure of war.

Although the triumph of fascism in Germany confirmed Einstein's distaste for nationalism and militarism, it forced him to come to grips with a new situation. Personally, it meant that it was no longer possible for him to work in Germany. Politically, it undermined his commitment to radical pacifism. By October 1933, when Einstein arrived in America to take up his new duties at the Institute for Advanced Studies at Princeton, he had made a painful transition in his approach to the problem of war. He continued to despise militarism and violence, he informed friends and associates, but now believed that the nations of Western Europe had no alternative except to defend themselves against German aggression. Thus, Einstein became a reluctant proponent of collective security against fascism—a position which eventually led him to call the attention of President +Franklin Roosevelt to the possibility of developing an atomic bomb. Ironically, Einstein had no knowledge of the subsequent Manhattan Project and was thoroughly dismayed by the American government's use of atomic weapons in the final days of the war against Japan.

Indeed, the explosion of atomic bombs at Hiroshima and Nagasaki drew the aging physicist into a new campaign for peace. In repeated public statements, he called for the creation of a world government and argued that, unless the war-making power of the nation-state were curbed, humanity faced the prospect of utter annihilation. To hammer home the threat of atomic holocaust and the concomitant need to develop a transnational authority, Einstein and other prominent Americans organized the Emergency Committee of Atomic Scientists in 1946. Although Einstein's antiwar activities then acquired the intensity of his earlier radical pacifist ventures, they met with only limited success. The deterioration of American-Soviet relations led to a decline in support for his world government proposals and to the collapse of the Emergency Committee in 1948. Even so, Einstein continued his prophetic role, refusing any compromise with the Cold War.

In the early 1950s Einstein remained a towering figure, whose forthright statements challenged the official orthodoxy of the time. Commenting on loyalty investigations of intellectuals by Congressional committees, he publicly championed resistance and individual noncooperation. Although he fell ill in the fall of 1954 and died the following April, in these last months of his life he worked closely with the British mathematician *Bertrand Russell in developing a public appeal by the world's most eminent scientists for the abolition of war. This Einstein-Russell declaration, issued in London on July 9, 1955, was the last document Einstein ever signed and provides a fitting summary of his final concerns. "We are speaking ... not as members of this or that nation, continent or creed, but as human beings ... whose continued existence is in doubt." People "have to learn to think in a new way. We have to learn to ask ourselves, not what steps can be taken to give military victory to whatever groups we prefer, for there no longer are such steps; the question we have to ask ourselves is: What steps can be taken to prevent a military contest of which the issue must be disastrous." Must people "choose death because we cannot forget our quarrels? We appeal, as human beings to human beings: Remember your humanity and forget the rest."

Bibliography:

A. "Atomic War or Peace," *Atlantic Monthly*, 180 (November 1947), 29–32, *The Fight Against War*, Alfred Lief, ed. (New York, 1933); *Why War*? (with Sigmund Freud, London, 1934).

B. Ronald W. Clark, *Einstein: The Life and Times* (New York, 1971), Otto Nathan and Heinz Norden, eds., *Einstein on Peace* (New York, 1960).

C. Einstein Archives, Princeton, NJ; Einstein-Sammlung der Eidgenossiche Technische Hochschule Bibliothek, Zurich.

Lawrence S. Wittner

EISNER, Kurt (14 May 1867, Berlin—21 February 1919, Munich). *Education*: Univ. of Berlin. *Career*: journalist, editor, political commentator, and politician.

Kurt Eisner began his career as a journalist and editor and by 1898 was working solely for the Social-Democratic press. It was the Moroccan crisis of 1905 that convinced Eisner that world war was imminent, and he devoted the years between 1905 and 1914 to alerting Germans to the inevitable outcome of German imperialism. As editor of the *Fränkische Tagepost* (1907–10), the German Social Democratic party (SPD) paper of Nuremberg, Eisner sought to enlighten the working classes about foreign affairs. This set him at odds with his editorial board and party officials. Although reticent about speaking in public, he undertook to do so. He aligned himself with the pacifist minority within the SPD, and during the second Moroccan crisis of 1911, he condemned the party leadership for passively supporting German interests.

Yet on August 4, 1914, Eisner and his pacifist colleagues did not object when the SPD voted to support war appropriations. Eisner viewed the mobilization of 1914 as a defensive response to Russian aggression. By December 1914 he was once again opposing the war; he explained his reversion to pacifism in *Die Mobilmachung als Kriegsursache und Anderes* (*The Mobilization as the Cause of War and Other Writing*). He argued that German militarists had forced the war issue by dishonestly portraying the war as a defensive one, and that the SPD, immediately enthusiastic about the war and quickly abandoning its claims to socialist internationalism, had perpetuated this myth. This position was not popular with the SPD, and Eisner found that his antiwar stance aroused the military censor. The *Münchner Post*, for which Eisner had worked since 1910, dropped his theater reviews and his syndicated column. Finally, the party executive blocked his application to accompany the Bavarian army as a war correspondent.

Eisner found other outlets for his pacifist views as the war continued. With the writer Wilhelm Herzog and the liberal pacifist scholar *Ludwig Quidde, he participated in the Bund Neues Vaterland (New Fatherland League), a pacifist organization. He wrote *Treibende Kräfte* (*Driving Forces*) (1915), in which he attacked the pan-German League and the influential business interests behind German colonial expansion. He urged the SPD to work for a negotiated peace and to return to socialist internationalism. Eisner used a course he taught at Munich's Workers' Education Union as a forum for his antiwar sentiments, arguing that German imperialism was the driving force behind the world war, and that workers had to organize to end the conflict.

Finding no place for himself within the SPD, Eisner took part in the creation of the Independent Social Democratic party (USPD) at Gotha in April 1917. In

Munich, he initiated a weekly antiwar discussion attended by workers, women and students. Dissatisfied with the failure of the Socialists in Bavaria and elsewhere to transform the government and to alter Germany's expansionist war aims, and encouraged by the success of the strikes across the border in Austria, Eisner turned to the proletariat and the weapon of the mass strike. In January 1918, when workers in Munich and other German munitions centers laid down their tools, Eisner spoke out at strike meetings in favor of peace without annexation, self-determination of all nations, democratic reform within Germany, and solidarity with the Bolshevik and Austrian revolutionaries. Eisner believed that, given more time, these working-class antiwar protests would have reached revolutionary proportions. But by the end of January 1918, Eisner and many other strike leaders were in jail, and the SPD had stepped in and ended the strikes, urging moderation upon the workers.

Eisner was released from jail in October 1918, so that he could contest the Reichstag seat formerly held by the retiring leader of the Bavarian SPD. Having concluded that all bourgeois parties were annexationist and therefore incapable of extricating Germany from the war, he used the campaign to propagandize for a revolutionary upheaval in Bavaria. Only a revolution, Eisner argued, could bring immediate and lasting peace. The Bavarian workers and peasants, fearful of the war spilling onto their soil, were prepared to force the hand of the reluctant government, and Eisner took advantage of their readiness to stage an uprising on November 7, 1918.

The Bavarian Republic, with Eisner as its president and foreign minister, worked to achieve a just peace. In his first speech before the Provisional National Council of the Bavarian Republic on November 8, Eisner raised the expectation that a revolutionary government animated by antiwar impulses could win mild peace terms. Eisner appointed pacifists to represent the Republic at Berne and at Berlin, and made repeated appeals to the allies to moderate the cease fire terms in recognition of Germany's new pacifist political stance. His attempts to make personal contact with +Woodrow Wilson and to have an appeal for peace delivered to him were unsuccessful. Eisner favored the creation of an atmosphere conducive to peace negotiations by fully demonstrating Germany's war guilt. This he did by publishing documents on the origins of the war in the *Berliner Tageblatt* and other papers. He again acknowledged Germany's war guilt at the meeting of the Second International in Switzerland near the end of February 1919, thus winning the lasting enmity of many Germans. Shortly after, Eisner was assassinated by Count Arco-Valley, a young right-wing officer. His premature death robbed postwar German pacifism of a forceful leader.

Bibliography:

A. *Die neue zeit* (Munich, 1919); *Sozialismus als Aktion: Ausgew. Aufsätze und Reden* (Frankfurt-am-Main, 1975); *Der Sultan des Weltkrieges* (Dresden, 1906); *Treibende Kräfte* (Berlin, 1915); *Unterdrucktes aus dem Weltkrieg* (Munich, 1919).

B. Freya Eisner, *Kurt Eisner: Die Politik des libertären Sozialismus.* (Frankfurt-am-Main, 1979); Richard Grunberger, *Red Rising in Bavaria* (London, 1973); Allan Mitchell,

Revolution in Bavaria, 1918–1919: the Eisner Regime and the Soviet Republic (Princeton, NJ, 1965); Franz Schade, *Kurt Eisner und die bayerische Sozialdemokratie* (Hannover, 1961); *Neuedeutsche Biographie*, IV, 422–23.

Polly Morris and Michael Dintenfass

ELLIS, Havelock (2 February 1859, Croydon, Surrey, England—8 July 1939, Hintlesham, Ipswich, England). *Education*: L.S.A. (Licentiate in Medicine) in surgery and midwifery in the Society of Apothecaries, St. Thomas Hospital, London, 1889. *Career*: researcher in human sexuality; writer on religion, heredity, intellectual aptitude, psychology, and politics; editor and translator of literary works.

After a wandering youth, Havelock Ellis settled in London as a medical student at St. Thomas Hospital (1881). While a student he attended meetings of the Fellowship of the New Life, a parent of the Fabian Society, and edited literary works of Heinrich Heine and Henrik Ibsen. Upon completion of his medical training, he began his career as a prolific writer, publishing collections of essays, a volume on criminals, and a series of works on sexuality, psychology, and eugenics. His *Study of British Genius* (1904) and *The World of Dreams* (1911) were inspired by the works of Sir Francis Galton and Sigmund Freud, respectively. His later works included essays on literature, art, philosophy, and esthetics.

Although not primarily an activist in the peace movement, Ellis was appalled by World War I and its aftermath. By nature a person who abhorred violence, he believed that love, intelligence, and free will made possible the peaceful resolution of conflicts. War was archaic and counterproductive. In his view war was a consequence of "the ruthless movement of commercial expansion and the reckless movement of the rising birth rate." He was hopeful that the adulation of war, which he believed had reached a climax in the nineteenth century, was in decline and that the carnage of World War I would not be repeated. "The blind and senseless greed of nationalities" which he thought a cause of the war, was less virulent, the birth rate was falling, and the pace of industrial and commercial expansionism was slowing.

Asserting that "there is no world left for war," he argued for the creation of an international police force to preserve peace. He hoped that the human propensity for struggle and heroic action could be channeled into internationalism. The rise of fascism and militarism in the interwar era filled him with alarm, causing him to warn that "another white civil war" would destroy Western civilization. Urging mothers to inculcate in their children a hatred of war, he expressed the hope that the advancement of economic justice and internationalism would prevent future conflicts. Just a few months before Adolf Hitler's invasion of Poland, Ellis wrote in *The London News Chronicle* (1939) that world peace "is our next upward movement" and asked hopefully, "Can we suppose that at this crucial point man will for the first time fail?" He died a few days before the outbreak for World War II in Europe.

Bibliography:

A. *Essays in War-Time* (London, 1916); *The Forces Warring Against War* (Boston, 1913); *My Confessional: Questions of Our Day* (Boston, 1934); *My Life: An Autobiography of Havelock Ellis* (Boston, 1939); *An Open Letter to Biographers* (Berkeley Heights, NJ, 1931); *The Philosophy of Conflict and Other Essays in Wartime* (Boston and New York, 1919); *Unpublished Letters of Havelock Ellis to Joseph Ishill* (Berkeley Heights, NJ, 1954); *What to Do After the War is Over* (Boston, 1915).

B. A. Calder-Marshall, *Havelock Ellis: A Biography* (London, 1959); J. S. Collis, *An Artist of Life* (London, 1959).

John V. Crangle

ELUARD, Paul (pseud. Eugène Grindel) (14 December 1895, Paris—18 November 1952, Paris). *Education*: studies at Ecole primaire supérieure Colbert, 1908–11 (interrupted by lung illness). *Career*: avant-garde poet, cofounder of Dada, 1919; of Surrealism, 1924; Resistance writer, French Communist party member, peace activist, internationalist, and author.

First known as a pacifist writer for his World War I antiwar poetry, Paul Eluard was also a founder of Surrealism and is considered the best Surrealist poet whose love lyrics were inspired by his second wife, Maria Benz (''Nusch''), the great love of his life. The Surrealists vigorously denounced militarism, patriotism, capitalism, imperialism, and organized religion. The first overtly political act of Eluard and his friends was to publish a collective manifesto denouncing the French colonial war with the Riff in Morocco, in 1926, in collaboration with *Clarté*, a left-wing pacifist journal. With four other Surrealists, including *André Breton, Eluard briefly joined the French Communist party in 1927, but their adherence was short-lived. In the 1930s Eluard helped organize the antifascist Maisons de culture. He also joined the Association des écrivains et des artistes révolutionnaires (Association of Revolutionary Writers and Artists) and spoke at the Congrès international des écrivains pour la défense de la culture (International Congress of Writers for the Protection of Culture) in 1935. He broke with the Surrealists because he felt that the poet had a duty to be *engagé* in his work as well as his beliefs and he wrote the political poem, *Guernica*, to commemorate the Popular Front in the Spanish Civil War.

In World War II he became a Resistance leader and joined the underground Communist party in 1942 because he wanted to work with the French people for ''liberty, peace and happiness.'' He was one of the founders of the Comité national des écrivains (National Committee of Writers), an organization of Resistance writers, and he edited a number of clandestine publications: *Les Lettres françaises, Editions de minuit, Bibliothèque française,* and *L'Honneur des poètes,* an anthology of poetry from all the occupied countries of Europe. Copies of his world famous poem, *Liberté*, were dropped by the RAF over occupied France and Eluard was decorated as a hero of the Resistance.

He believed that cultural exchanges between people were a vital element in achieving peace and, after the war, he traveled to Belgium, England, Switzerland,

Czechoslovakia, Italy, Greece, Rumania, Poland, and Russia on peace and cultural missions. He was president of the Comité France-Espagne (Franco-Spanish Committee), vice-president of the Comité français d'aide à Grèce démocratique (French Committee to Aid Democratic Greece), a founder of the Partisans of Peace (1949), and a delegate to the peace congresses of Wroclaw and Mexico. Because he was a member of the Communist party, he was denied a visa to attend the 1949 Cultural and Scientific Conference of World Peace; in New York, instead, he went to Moscow to celebrate the Gogol-Hugo centennial. When he died, just after protesting the death sentences of Ethel and Julius Rosenberg, Picasso dedicated a peace dove drawing to him for his efforts to promote world peace.

Bibliography:

A. *Anthologie des écrits sur l'art* (Paris, 1952); *Capitale de la douleur* (Paris, 1926); *Dignes de vivre* (n.p., 1944); *L'Evidence poétique* (Paris, 1936); *Poèmes politiques* (Paris, 1948); *Oeuvres complètes*, with preface and chronology by Lucien Scheler (Paris, 1968); *Petit dictionnaire illustre de surréalisme* (Paris, 1938); *Poèmes pour la paix* (Paris, 1918); *Poèsie et verité* (n.p., 1942); Ralentir travaux, with André Breton (Paris, 1930).

B. *Europe numéro spécial* juillet-août 1953, supplément, 1962; Maurice Nadeau, *The History of Surrealism* (New York, 1965); Robert Nugent, *Paul Eluard* (New York, 1974); Louis Parrot, *Paul Eluard* (Paris, 1969); Louis Perché, *Paul Eluard* (Paris, 1963); Jean Raymond, *Paul Eluard par lui-même* (Paris, 1968).

Helena Lewis

EMBDEN, David van (22 October 1875, The Hague—14 February 1962, Amsterdam). *Education*: law, Univ. of Amsterdam, 1894–1901, doctorate in political and social science, 1901. *Career*: editor, *Sociaal Weekblad*, 1903–5; professor of economics and statistics, Univ. of Amsterdam, 1905–46; senator, 1918–46.

As a leading member of the small Vrijzinnig-Democratische Bond (VDB), the most radical liberal grouping in Dutch politics in the first half of the twentieth century, David van Embden was one of the country's most eloquent and tireless disarmament advocates in the 1920s and 1930s. In numerous, lengthy speeches in the Senate he argued the case for "national disarmament" with great clarity and conviction. It was part of the VDB's manifesto from 1924 until 1936, although van Embden maintained this position until 1940. The term "national" was meant to indicate both a policy of unilateralism (since international, multilateral disarmament was proving impossible) and an expression of patriotism, which required disarmament to save the country from certain destruction in war.

If you want peace, do *not* prepare for war, he argued ceaselessly. It was not so much that the danger of war created armaments as that the latter heightened that danger and caused war. The development of the means of destruction since 1914 and the prospect of aerial and chemical warfare only reinforced the need for disarmament, as these new factors not only made defense impossible but morally unacceptable. Whether armed (at great expense) or unarmed, the country would be defenseless. As an economist and a social reformer, van Embden was acutely aware of the great burden that armament expenditures imposed on the economy, and these he resented all the more because they did not make the nation any more secure. Not defense but genocide would be their end result. He rejected the argument that Holland had not been attacked in World War I because of its army, calling to his aid military experts who had described the army as virtually worthless. Not armed might but other factors had guaranteed the country's neutrality. He believed that the evolution of weaponry since World War I had made the Dutch army even less of a deterrent. Furthermore, he argued that a policy of neutrality was legally, and even more so, morally and practically, no longer compatible with membership of the League of Nations.

Van Embden was a strong supporter of the League and of upholding and strengthening international organizations and agreements. He also believed that, in a just cause, world public opinion, economic sanctions, and passive resistance would constitute formidable weapons against an aggressor. He accepted military intervention by the League with certain reservations as a final sanction. He emphasized that his advocacy of "national disarmament" was based on technical, objective grounds only and pleaded, unsuccessfully, for a full official inquiry into the subject.

Van Embden's insights into the psychology of deterrence, the dynamics of the arms race, and the possibility of alternative defense have lasting value. He was an active member of the Dutch section of the Interparliamentary Union, as well as of its international council.

Bibliography:

A. *Bezuiniging vlootwet en moraliteit* (Amsterdam, 1923); *De immoraliteit der landsverdediging* (Rotterdam, 1930); *Is er nog kans op neutraliteit*? (Discussion with F. Beelaerts van Blokland, Amsterdam, 1932); *Nationale ontwapening of volksverdelging* (Rotterdam, 1924); *Onze bewapening trekt den oorlog aan*! (Rotterdam, 1928); *De oorlog en het kapitalisme* (Amsterdam, 1914); *De particuliere wapenfabrikanten* (Ammerstol, 1935); *Waarom nationale ontwapening geboden is* (The Hague, 1932).

B. *Biografisch Woordenboek van Nederland* (The Hague, 1979), I, 171–72; *Persoonlijkheden in het Koninkrijk der Nederlanden* (Amsterdam, 1938), 433–34; *Who's Who in the Netherlands 1962/63* (Amsterdam), 212; *Wie is dat*? (The Hague, 1956), 172–73.

Peter van den Dungen

EMERSON, Ralph Waldo (25 May 1803, Boston MA—27 April 1882, Concord, MA). *Education*: B.A., Harvard Coll., 1821. *Career*: Unitarian minister, lecturer, essayist, and poet.

Raised and educated in a family that could boast eight generations of ministerial ancestors, Ralph Waldo Emerson became a leading proponent of liberal religion and social reform in nineteenth-century America. His father, William, was an associate of the reverend *William Ellery Channing as well as a leading literary figure in Boston at the beginning of the nineteenth century. Emerson adopted the liberal principles of Channing and combined them with what were then considered radical ideas from his own eclectic reading in Plato, Swedenborg,

Coleridge, Carlyle, and Wordsworth and created an idealistic philosophy that ultimately influenced the lives and works of many people in the United States and abroad. It is through this influence, then, that Emerson's contribution to peace was made, since the emphasis on individualism in his philosophy coupled with his overdeveloped sense of propriety prohibited Emerson from actively participating in many of the reform movements that are even today closely associated with his name.

Emerson's definitive statement on peace was written during a remarkably productive period in the late 1830s, a period in which he published the most important statements of American Transcendentalism—*Nature* (1836), the "American Scholar" address (1837), and the revolutionary Divinity School address (1838). In March 1838 Emerson addressed the American Peace Society in Boston on the subject of "War." This lecture was later published in Elizabeth Palmer Peabody's *Aesthetic Papers* (1849), in which *Henry David Thoreau's now classic statement on civil disobedience, "Resistance to Civil Government," was also first published. In his essay Emerson suggested that the instinct for war is part of man's nature, but this instinct manifests itself in an evolutionary way—savage races are more warlike than civilized and enlightened races. Since Emerson believed that mankind was constantly evolving toward a higher state of enlightenment and civilization, he saw a concomitant decline in war, and he argued that ultimately war would disappear. However, he also realized that in "difficult and extreme cases" even the most enlightened and civilized of men and nations might revert to war.

Such a crisis was precipitated for Emerson, as well as many other advocates of peace, by the slavery question. There is still some doubt as to when Emerson became sympathetic to and subsequently an active spokesman for the antislavery movement in this country. His sympathy with the cause began early, but his reluctance to become involved with formal movements of any kind stopped him short of being too vocal or visible a supporter of the antislavery cause until after the passage of the Fugitive Slave Law in 1850. After that date, Emerson delivered important addresses in support of the antislavery movement, he defended John Brown and proclaimed him a martyr, and following the lead of many of his antislavery and more radical abolitionist friends, he viewed the Civil War as something of a holy war to remedy a great injustice. In fact in his 1862 address on "American Civilization," Emerson returned to the argument of his 1838 lecture on "War" when he argued that the Southerner enjoys making war because of his "semi-civilized condition," while the more enlightened Northerner, who is unsuited for war, feels compelled to fight for the great principle of emancipation.

Even though Emerson spent the war years offering a philosophical justification for the war, he is remembered today as a man of peace. Emerson's most important contribution to the cause of peace was not, however, any statement or doctrine to which we can point today. His significant contribution was in establishing an atmosphere in which intellectual inquiry and disagreement with and divergence from traditional norms of literature, politics, and religion became an accepted fact.

Bibliography:

A. "War," in Elizabeth P. Peabody, ed., *Aesthetic Papers* (Boston, 1849), rpt. in *Miscellanies* vol. 11 of *The Complete Works of Ralph Waldo Emerson* (Boston, 1904).

B. Gay Wilson Allen, *Waldo Emerson: A Biography* (New York, 1981); William Gilman, *et al.*, eds., *The Journals and Miscellaneous Notebooks of Ralph Waldo Emerson* (16 vols., Cambridge, MA, 1961–82); Ralph L. Rusk, ed., *The Letters of Ralph Waldo Emerson* (6 vols., New York, 1939); Rusk, *The Life of Ralph Waldo Emerson* (New York, 1949); Stephen E. Whicher, *Freedom and Fate: An Inner Life of Ralph Waldo Emerson* (Philadelphia, 1953).

C. Ralph Waldo Emerson Memorial Association Collection, Houghton Library, Harvard University.

Robert E. Burkholder

ENDRES, Franz Carl Niklaus (17 December 1878, Munich—10 March 1954, Muttenz, Switzerland). *Education*: Gymnasium, Munich; cadet, Royal Bavarian Life-Guards Infantry Regiment, 1897–99; War Academy, Munich, 1906–9 *Career*: Bavarian army officer, 1899–1912; teacher, military school for cadets, Munich, 1910-ll; teacher, War Academy, Munich, 1911–12; captain, Bavarian general-staff, 1912; Turkish army officer, 1912–16; professor, Turkish War Academy, Constantinople, 1912–13; Turkish general-staff, 1913; chief of the general staff of the fifth Turkish Army under General Liman von Sanders in the Dardanelles, 1915; journalist, editor, writer, freemason, and pacifist.

Franz Carl Endres, the oldest son of General Karl von Endres, chief of the royal Bavarian general staff, was one of several German officers who became pacifists as a result of their experiences in World War I. Endres' military career came to a sudden end when he fell seriously ill with malaria while on an information gathering trip to Palestine in the spring of 1915. He spent a year in a sanatorium, where his thinking underwent a change and where he recognized that his total night blindness made him unfit for military combat. When he regained his health, he rejected a position in the Bavarian ministry of war, just as he later refused an appointment in the national government as minister of military affairs. The slaughter of the Armenian people by the Turkish government against which he spoke out at the cost of the Turkish government's withdrawing the pension to which he became entitled, the immense misery of the Turkish soldiers, as well as his observations at the German war fronts in 1917 caused him to renounce completely his military profession and adopt a pacifist position.

After his discharge, he became a military analyst for the *Frankfurter Zeitung* (1917) and then for the *Münchner Neueste Nachrichten* (1918). When the latter newspaper was purchased by the industrialist and right-wing politician, Alfred Hugenberg (1919), Endres resigned to become editor of the democratic *Süddeutsche Presse* (1919–21). At the same time, he became editor of *Der Wagenlenker*, the organ of the Reichsbund geistiger Arbeiter (National Association of Intellectual Workers), a left-wing, pro-republican organization which he co-founded during the revolutionary days of November 1918. In 1924 Endres was appointed editorial representative of the *Berliner Tageblattes* first in Constantinople and later in Athens and The Hague. In 1926 he settled in Switzerland where he became a citizen in 1939.

Endres belonged to no political party. Although he was a member of the Deutsche Friedensgesellschaft (German Peace Society) and the Deutsche Liga für Menschenrechte (German League for Human Rights), Endres served the peace movement more as a journalist and a writer than as an organization man or public speaker. He was a prolific and popular writer who published more than sixty books on scientific, travel, ethical, philosophical, religious, social, and pacifist subjects. His most important work for the German peace movement was *Die Tragödie Deutschlands. Im Banne des Machtgedankens bis zum Zusammenbruch des Reiches* (1921). Published anonymously the work went through four editions and had a lasting effect, especially within the pacifist circles. Clearly written and based on solid scholarship, the book revealed the sociological and ideological structure that led to the collapse of the Prussian-German empire. Intentionally, Endres did not tie the concept of militarism to the numerical strength of an army, but defined "true militarism" as a "frame of mind" rooted in rigid and authoritarian social values and relations that developed in the Prussian German empire. Militarism in that sense, Endres warned, still prevailed in the Weimar Republic even though Germany possessed a very small army after 1918. For that reason he considered the benevolent attitude of other countries towards German demands for a general disarmament a fatal error. The latter theme was struck in many articles which he wrote before 1933 as German correspondent for the Swiss newspaper, *Basler Nachrichten*.

To secure a European peace, Endres considered a Franco-German peace to be absolutely necessary. Furthermore, without agreeing entirely with the Pan-European ideas of +Richard Coudenhove-Kalergi, Endres acknowledged the idea of "Fatherland Europe" which included England but not Russia. Russia was excluded because he believed that Bolshevism was leading to its development as an Asian empire that would not only reject, but even be inimical to Western civilization. Endres' internationalism was related in part to his Masonic beliefs. As a member of various lodges in Munich, Vienna, and Paris, and as editor since 1930 of *Die Leuchte*, a monthly periodical for German Freemasons, Endres was active in the supranational endeavors of the Freemasons for international unity and peace. He especially wrote against the dogma, widespread in Germany even after 1918, that war was a naturally inevitable and culturally creative activity. He set out his Masonic philosophy in *Das Geheimnis des Freimaurers* published anonymously in 1920.

Endres' masonic philosophy was only one source of his pacifism. His pacifism also was ethically rooted in religious values. A convinced Christian, but one "not hampered by church membership," Endres was deeply imbued with a sense of the holiness of all living things (a view similar to that held by *Albert

Schweitzer), and with the belief that "there is no happiness at the expense of another." His humanitarian strivings were guided by the conviction that all life was directed toward achieving a harmonious and peaceful condition of existence. At the same time, he rejected the renunciation of all force to the point of self-sacrifice as proposed by *Leo Tolstoy. Instead, he believed that war could be checked or eliminated only by legal arrangements made among nations that were willing to use military force to guarantee peace. For that reason, he demanded that the League of Nations be made a supranational sovereign power stronger than any of its individual member states so that in the future there would exist only wars of the League of Nations against insubordinate member states. These wars, he argued, would increasingly assume the character of purely police actions. In addition, Endres warned against exaggerating conscientious objection and pacifism as means of preventing war. He believed that the effectiveness of all forms of pacifism had been more than countered by the new technology developed during the war. The war of the future, he predicted, would no longer be directed against the armies of the enemy, but first of all against unarmed civilian masses in enemy cities and industrial centers.

In the years before the Second World War, Endres taught at an adult education school in Zurich and was a free-lance writer on political affairs for several Swiss newspapers. His relentless opposition to the Nazi regime in Germany led to attempts by that regime to silence him. During the war Endres was active as a war correspondent. In 1943 he took part in efforts to persuade the population of Bavaria to turn against the Nazi government and the war. He drew up appropriate appeals which were to be scattered in great number all over south Germany. Found guilty of violating Swiss neutrality, he was fined 40 Swiss francs. According to Hans Wehberg, Endres was one of "the best philosophically schooled minds" the German peace movement ever possessed.

Bibliography:

A. *Du bist ich. Träume und Gedanken zur Weltversöhnung* (Leipzig, 1921); *Das Gesicht des Krieges* (Leipzig, 1924); *Gifgaskrieg die grosse Gefahr* (Zurich/Leipzig and Stuttgart, 1928); *Politik und Kriegführung* (Munich, 1917); *Reichswehr und Demokratie* (Munich and Leipzig, 1919); "Soziologische Struktur und ihr entsrechende Ideologien des deutschen Offizierkorps vor dem Weltkriege," *Archiv für Sozialwissenschaft und Sozialpolitik*, 58 (Tübingen, 1927), 282–319; *Die Symbolik des Freimaurers. Von einem Bruder Meister* (Stuttgart, 1920); *Die Tragödie Deutschlands. Im Banne des Machtgedankens bis zum Zusammenbruch des Reiches* (Stuttgart, 1921); "Vom nächsten Krieg," *Archiv für Sozialwissenschaft und Sozialpolitik*, 59 (Tübingen, 1928), 48–74.

B. Hans Hutzelmann, "Pazifisten. Franz Carl Endres," *Die Sonntaqs-Zeitung*, 10, no. 27 (July 7, 1929); Gustav Strohm, Introduction in abbreviated version of 1924 edition of *Die Tragödie Deutschlands* (Stuttgart, 1948), vii-xi.

Helmut Donat
Trans. by Peter Seadle

ERZBERGER, Matthias (20 September 1875, Buttenhausen, Württemberg, Germany—26 August 1921, Bad Griesbach/Schwarzwald, Germany). *Educa-*

tion: teaching training college, Saalgau, 1891–94. *Career*: editor, *Deutsches Volksblatt*, 1891; member of Parliament (Reichstag), 1903–21; minister without portfolio and head of the German armistice commission, October-November, 1918; minister without portfolio for peace negotiations, 1918–19; vice-chancellor and minister of finance, 1919–20.

As a young and self-confident member of parliament, Matthias Erzberger came into conflict with the older politicians of the Catholic-based Center party. They objected to his somewhat brash political style and his support of the recently founded Catholic workers' and trade union movement of which Erzberger was a co-founder in 1899. Before 1914 Erzberger became well known for his attacks on the corruption in the German colonial administration and his advocacy of a militarily strong Germany. Despite the animosity towards him among some of the elders of the Center party, his knowledge of military and financial affairs assured him a leading role within the party. That same knowledge also allowed him to exercise considerable influence over the German chancellor, Theobald von Bethmann-Hollweg. In the early years of World War I, Erzberger was among the most enthusiastic advocates of annexationist war aims. His work as a propagandist for annexations was underwritten financially by the German Foreign Ministry. In connection with this propaganda activity, Erzberger made three trips to Rome to conduct negotiations with *Pope Benedict XV and Italian political leaders aimed at preventing Italy's entry into the war on the side of the Allies.

In 1917 a realistic assessment of the military and political situation of Germany led Erzberger to conclude that Germany had to strive for a negotiated peace without territorial acquisitions obtained by force. He played a major role in the introduction into the Reichstag of the Peace Resolution of July 19, 1917. In a speech at the annual meeting of the Württemberg Center party, Erzberger presented his new policy. He characterized the peace resolution of the Reichstag, the peace note of Pope Benedict XV of mid-August 1917, and the German answer to the papal note as three cornerstones of peace. He defended the peace resolution of the Reichstag on the grounds that a military victory by Germany was unlikely and the weakness of Germany's Austrian ally was obvious. He believed it was necessary to reestablish European-Christian culture on the principles of compromise and reconciliation. Furthermore it was important to strengthen the peace movement in the Entente lands. Erzberger therefore became the only German politician who recognized the peace movement as a political force even if, at times, for tactical and politically calculated reasons.

At the same time that he wanted to strengthen the peace movement in the Entente countries, Erzberger supported the establishment of a Catholic peace movement in Germany in order to provide stronger backing for his policy of compromise. These efforts led to attacks upon him by members of his own party. In the beginning the Catholic peace movement centered around the *Deutsche Kirchenzeitung* (after 1919, *Katholiken-und Kirchenzeitung*) and its editors Josef Kral and Father Praxmarer. Through Kral, the Catholic peace movement had close relations with Max Josef Metzger who founded the Weltfriedensbund vom

Weissen Kreuz (World Peace League of the White Cross) in May 1917, in Graz, Austria. In January 1918 Erzberger, Kral, and Magnus Jocham, a priest also involved in the peace movement, founded the Friedensbundes Deutscher Katholiken (Peace League of German Catholics) (FDK). In August 1919 Erzberger, who had provided much of the financial aid to get the FDK off the ground, became chairman of the organization and a member of the national committee created for propagating the Catholic peace idea.

In October 1918, shortly before the Armistice, Erzberger's book, *Der Völkerbund* appeared. Even earlier, he had concerned himself with the question of an institutional basis for securing peace. He worked in the Anti-Oorlog Raad (Anti-War Committee), founded in the summer of 1914 by the Dutchman *B. de Jong von Beek en Donk, and participated in a conference on the "The Organization of International Relations after the Conclusion of Peace" held in Berne (November 19–22, 1917). In *Der Völkerbund* Erzberger placed special emphasis on the institutionalization of compulsory arbitration of international disputes, thereby associating himself with a central demand of the peace movement. Furthermore, Erzberger demanded far-reaching disarmament and the abolition of universal military conscription. He further developed his conception of a future League of Nations in an "Entwurf der Verfassung des Völkerbundes," which contained forty articles. Implicit in his peace thinking was the idea that the civilized states would organize themselves after the war according to Christian-democratic principles. This idea reflected Erzberger's own religious faith. For Germany, he presumed the introduction of parliamentary democracy, something he had demanded for a long time. Thanks to Erzberger, the national committee of the Center party, on December 30, 1918, approved the introduction of compulsory arbitration, disarmament, and the doing away with secret diplomacy as guidelines for the party. These, however, had little effect on the practical politics of the party.

Political tasks prevented Erzberger from active engagement in the work of the FDK after 1918. He served as an adviser and a provider of contacts. The initiation of contacts between the FDK and the Deutsche Friedensgesellschaft (German Peace Society) made by Jocham was done on the advice of Erzberger and *F. Stratmann. On Erzberger's recommendation, Jocham was able to participate in a conference of Catholic politicians from Germany, Austria, and Switzerland, which was held in Constance in 1921. At the conference, Jocham spoke in favor of establishing contacts with French Catholic political figures such as the social reformer *Marc Sagnier, an idea for which Erzberger unquestionably was responsible. Even before 1914, Erzberger strongly desired an understanding with France and thought highly of Sangnier. At the first congress of the Internationale démocratique, arranged by Sangnier and held in Paris in 1922, Jocham identified himself with Erzberger as representatives of the democratic-pacifist course within the Center party.

Since the Peace Resolution of 1917, and even more since the signing of the Armistice (Erzberger was a member of the armistice commission), Erzberger was one of the most hated and slandered politicians in the Weimar Republic. He was not a pacifist in the strict sense, but he was the only prominent politician in Germany who recognized that the peace movement could suggest alternatives useful to practical politicians trying to master difficult problems. He was shot to death by two members of an extreme right-wing secret league (Organization Consul). Shortly before he was assassinated, Erzberger founded the German branch of the League of Nations Association.

Bibliography:

A. *Christlicher Solidarismus als Weltprinzip* (Mönchen- Gladbach, 1921); *Erlebnisse im Weltkrieg* (Stuttgart, 1920); *Die Kolonialbilanz* (Berlin, 1906); *Millionengeschenke. Die Privilegienwirtschaft in Südafrika* (Berlin, 1910) *Politik und Völkerleben* (Würzburg/ Paderborn 1914); *Der Verständigungsfriede* (Stuttgart, 1917); *Der Völkerbund als Friedensfrage* (Berlin, 1919); *Der Völkerbund. Der Weg zum Weltfrieden* (Berlin, 1918).

B. Klaus Epstein, *Matthias Erzberger and the Dilemma of German Democracy* (Princeton, NJ, 1959); Rudolf Morsey, "Matthias Erzberger," in Rudolf Morsey, ed., *Zeitgeschichte in Lebensbildern* (Mainz, 1973); Dieter Riesenberger, "Der 'Friedensbund Deutscher Katholiken' und der politische Katholizismus in der Weimarer Republic," in Karl Holl and W. Wette, eds., *Pazifismus in der Weimarer Republik* (Paderborn, 1982); Egmont Zechlin, "Die Zentralorganisation für einen dauerndεn Frieden und die Mittelmächte," *Jahrbuch für internationales Recht*, 2 (1962).

Dieter Riesenberger
Trans. by Solomon Wank

ESTOURNELLES DE CONSTANT, Paul Henri d' (22 November 1852, La Flèche, France—15 May 1924, La Flèche). *Education*: diploma, École des Langues Orientales, Paris, c. 1872; licence, École de droit, Paris, 1874. *Career*: French Diplomatic Service, 1876–95; member, Chamber of Deputies, 1895–1904; senator, 1904–24; delegate to The Hague peace conferences, 1899, 1907; founder, Groupe de l'arbitrage, 1903; founder of Conciliation internationale, 1905.

Paul Henri d'Estournelles de Constant began his career in the diplomatic service before turning to politics in the 1890s. After 1894 he served uninterruptedly in the French parliament as a member of the moderate republican Union républicaine. His principal interests, however, remained in the realm of foreign affairs and he soon became a pivotal figure in the movement for international arbitration and arms limitation. An outspoken parliamentary advocate of these reforms, he organized the Groupe de l'arbitrage as the French section of the Interparliamentary Union and served as a delegate to both Hague conferences. His influence extended well beyond his own country. He attempted to build his own broad network of contacts among parliamentarians and scholars in many countries into the foundation of closer relations among France, England, Germany, and the United States. To this end his most concrete achievement was the establishment of Conciliation internationale, an organization dedicated to arbitration and arms reduction that comprised several hundred cultural, political, and business leaders in France, and chapters in Germany and the United States.

D'Estournelles was not only the most important advocate of arbitration in France, but served as the principal contact between the peace movements in continental Europe and the United States. He was a close friend of +Nicholas Murray Butler, and in 1912 he became president of the European Bureau of the Carnegie Endowment for International Peace.

D'Estournelles de Constant was probably the most successful internationalist in Europe in the decade preceding the First World War. He was certainly the most accomplished practitioner of the philosophy that underlay the prewar peace movement, that arbitration and arms limitation were the keys to guaranteeing peace and that the route to these goals was to promote good will and contacts among the cultured elites who were thought to mold public opinion. The outbreak of war in 1914 challenged this philosophy at its foundations and no doubt shortened his life. Like most of this generation of internationalists, D'Estournelles supported the war effort of his country and took consolation in the League of Nations which emerged out of the conflict. In a political atmosphere not conducive to success, he devoted the last years of his life attempting to make something more substantial out of the League and to reestablishing contacts across the Rhine.

Bibliography:

A. *Les Conférences consulaires et le développement économique de la France* (Paris, 1906); *Les États-Unis d'Amérique* (Paris, 1913); *Notre politique extérieure en 1910 et la paix internationale* (Paris, 1910).

B. Roger Chickering, *Imperial Germany and a World Without War: The Peace Movement and German Society, 1892–1914* (Princeton, 1975), 365–75; Adolf Wild, *Baron d'Estournelles de Constant (1852–1924): Das Wirken eines Friedensnobelpreisträgers für die deutsch-französische Verständigung und die europäische Einigung* (Hamburg, 1973).

C. Paul d'Estournelles de Constant Papers, Archives départmentales de la Sarthe, Le Mans.

Roger Chickering

ESTREICHER, Stanislaw (26 November 1869, Cracow, Austrian Poland—28 December 1939, Sachsenhausen-Oranienberg concentration camp, Germany). *Education*: Dr. jur., Jagiellonian Univ., Cracow, 1892; studied at Univ. of Vienna, 1892–93; "Habilitation" in law, Univ. of Berlin, 1894. *Career*: professor of law, Jagiellonian Univ., Cracow, 1895–1939; department head, 1912–39, rector (president), 1919–21; literary editor, *Czas*, from 1889; jurist; writer of political and legal history; educator; translator of German and English poetry; pacifist.

Stanislaw Estreicher was associated from childhood with the Jagiellonian University where his father was director of its Library. As a member of the University's faculty for 45 years, Estreicher was responsible for the institution's transition from its restricted existence under Austria-Hungary to its role of academic leadership in interwar Poland, and for the country's educational reforms in 1920 granting academic and organizational autonomy to institutions of higher education.

Having no official political affiliation, Estreicher leaned toward the Cracow conservatives who advocated moderate domestic and foreign policies. An admirer of the Polish Unitarian tradition of pacifism, he opposed war, the death penalty, anti-Semitism, and discrimination against national minorities. Following World War I, Estreicher appealed to the numerous political factions for moderation and advocated a speedy organization of the newly created Polish state. Having no political ambitions, he turned down offers of political posts, and supported W. J. Rose's effort, in the face of strong Church opposition, to establish the Young Men's Christian Association in Poland. He acted as mentor and protector of the University's Students' Pacifist Association which represented a diversity of political movements, supported the League of Nations, and enjoyed the friendship of +Alexander Skrzyński.

From 1916 Estreicher wrote anonymous political articles in *Czas*. He opposed Joseph Pilsudski's government, criticized the May coup d'état of 1926 which returned Pilsudski to power, and objected strongly to the Breść imprisonment (1930) of some of the Sejm (Polish Parliament) leaders. As the conservatives and *Czas* adapted themselves to the changing political atmosphere, Estreicher broke with them and stopped contributing to the paper (1932).

On March 29, 1939, with the political situation in Europe becoming more bleak, a delegation of academicians and politicians visited the president of Poland in the hope of averting Poland's involvement in what seemed like an inevitable war. Estreicher, as chief spokesman, appealed to the president for a pacific policy in both domestic and foreign matters, for national unification, and for a return of émigré political leaders from abroad. Following the occupation of Poland in the fall of 1939, the Germans approached Estreicher with an offer to form a puppet government. Either seeing this as an opportunity to save Poland from its inevitable fate or not wishing to reject the offer outright, Estreicher made certain demands which the Germans were not about to accept, such as the evacuation of occupying troops, a stop to the requisitioning of property, the release of Polish prisoners-of-war, and the placing of Poles in all civilian and military positions.

That fall, the University Senate, of which Estreicher was a member, decided to start the academic year. On November 6, at a mandatory lecture on the Reich's concept of higher education in occupied territories, the assembled faculty members were informed that their decision to hold classes had violated Reich policy. They were all arrested and deported to Sachsenhausen-Oranienburg outside Berlin. Although offered his freedom, Estreicher refused to leave unless the others were released also. Suffering from prostatism and denied basic medical treatment, the eminent scholar of German law and an opponent of violence and war died an excruciating death in the German concentration camp.

Bibliography:

A. *Historia prawa zachodnio-europejskiego; źródła* (Cracow, 1946); *Kraków i Magdeburg* (Cracow, 19ll); *Kultura prawnicza w Polsce XVI wieku* (Cracow, 1931); *Michał Bobrzyński* (Warsaw, 1936); *Polska literatura polityczna XVI Wieku* (Cracow, 1939); *Rozwój ustroju państw na zachodzie Europy* (Cracow, 1946); *Wł L. Jaworskiego zycie i działalność* (Cracow, 1931).

B. Stanisław *Gawęda, "Universytet Jagielloński w okresie okupacji hitlerowskiej, 1939–1945," Zeszyty naukowe Universytetu Jagiellońskiego, prace historyczne*, 58 (1979), 1–158; Jan Gwiazdomorski, "W sprawie podstępnego uwiiezienia krakowskich profesorów," *Zeszyty naukowe Universytetu Jagiellońskiego, prace historyczne*, no. 19 (1966), 39–44; Adam Kot, "Stanisł*aw Estreicher," Straty kultury polskiej, 1939–1944* (Glasgow, 1945) II, 61–110; Stanisł*aw Kot, "Estreicher, Stanisław" Polski słownik biograficzny* (Cracow, 1948), VI, 312–315.

Zofia Sywak

EVANS, Frederick William (9 June 1808, Leominster, England—6 March 1893, Mount Lebanon, NY). *Education*: self-educated. *Career*: writer, Elder and spokesman for the United Society of Believers (Shakers).

When Frederick W. Evans joined the Shakers in 1830 at the age of twenty-two, he found the perfect metaphysical framework for his social vision. Evans claimed in his autobiography that he had a well-developed socialistic/communistic program including land and educational reform, abolition of slavery, and equal rights for women; he converted the basis of these beliefs from materialism to spiritualism under the Shaker influence. Evans came to the United States when he was twelve with his father and his brother, George Henry Evans. He and his brother lived in Binghamton, New York, and together they developed many agrarian and natural rights reforms. Frederick examined other communal experiments, but joined the Shakers, claiming that the Shaker doctrine of celibacy, which promised to diminish both personal antagonisms and world population, provided the full legitimization for his ideas.

The Shakers had long been associated with pacifism, beginning with Mother Ann Lee's arrest and internment at Poughkeepsie in 1780. Having only recently arrived from England and refusing to support the revolutionary forces, Ann Lee and her early followers were suspected of treason, but the new church members, like the Quakers with whom they had some early association, were dedicated and convincing pacifists. Evans pursued and developed the strain of pacifism. He spoke for the church during the Civil War and negotiated conscientious objector status for Shaker men. Later he attended various conventions for peace.

A limited correspondence between Evans and *Leo Tolstoy adds an interesting dimension to Evans's peace work. Evans tried to convert Tolstoy to Shakerism, believing that Tolstoy could become the leader of the Shaker movement in Russia. Tolstoy, on the other hand, agreed with many Shaker ideas, but could not accept some of its spiritualism. He also questioned how the Shakers could argue against war and still hold property, a factor which Tolstoy found responsible for wars. Evans responded that the Shaker emphasis on the equality of the sexes added to the separation of church and state in America, solved many of the issues causing war, and, therefore, allowed the Shakers to participate in communal land holding.

A proper social order, exemplified by the discipline of celibacy, made possible a life which united belief and practice, science and religion, and constituted the peaceful world in which Evans claimed to live and preach as a Shaker.

Bibliography:

A. *Autobiography Of a Shaker* (Mt. Lebanon, NY., 1869).

B. Henri Desroche, *The American Shakers: From Neo-Christianity to Presocialism*, trans. and ed. by John K. Savacool (Amherst, MA., 1971); Mary Richmond, *Shaker Literature: A Bibliography* (Hanover, NH., 1977) lists over 120 items written by Evans; James M. Upton, "The Shakers as Pacifists in the Period Between 1812 and the Civil War," *The Filson Club History Quarterly*, 47 (July, 1973), 267–83; *DAB* 3, 198–99.

Jane F. Crosthwaite

EWART, William (1 May 1798, Liverpool, England—23 January 1869, Broadleas, England). *Education*: Eton Coll.; B.A., Christ Church, Oxford Univ., 1821; called to the bar at Middle Temple, 1827. *Career*: Member of Parliament (for Bletchingley), 1828–30; (for Liverpool), 1830–37; (for Wigan), 1839–41; (for Dumfries), 1841–68; politician and reformer.

As a leading radical in the mid-nineteenth-century House of Commons, William Ewart made outstanding contributions in the agitation for criminal law reform, free trade, and the development of public libraries. He was also an advocate of peace. His Scottish and middle class origins were akin to those of William Ewart Gladstone who was the godson of his father. The wide assortment of advanced causes Ewart sponsored placed him in the vanguard of the great liberal tradition that dominated the Victorian era. That he never rose to a Cabinet post or any prominent position may be attributed not so much to his radical stance as to his ineffective speaking manner which always betrayed the true strength of his convictions.

Ewart's interest in peace developed as a concomitant to his involvement with the free trade movement in the 1840s. In 1816, following the Napoleonic wars, the Peace Society had been formed, but it attracted little attention until it became linked with the free trade panacea. Although Ewart was not involved at the time of the first British convention in 1843, he attended the first International Peace Congress in Brussels in 1848 as vice president of the British delegation. On that occasion he made a rare impromptu speech that was greeted with loud acclamation. On behalf of the British delegates he signed a four-fold appeal by the congress to abolish war, to include arbitration clauses in international treaties, to devise a congress of nations for the purpose of framing an international code, and to inaugurate disarmament. Later Ewart led a deputation to the Prime Minister, Lord John Russell, and spoke in the House of Commons on behalf of peace, but a motion he seconded favoring a system of arbitration was defeated by 176 to 79. In 1849 Ewart was active at the International Peace Congress at Paris and in 1851 helped to organize a London congress that was held at Exeter

Hall. Peace enthusiasts were encouraged by the large audiences attending this meeting which was held simultaneously with the Great Exhibition. By this time, however, the peace movement was being menaced by Louis Napoleon's coup d'état in France and the approach of the Crimean War.

Despite England's muddled cause and his work in the peace congresses, Ewart subsequently supported the war effort. Unlike *John Bright and *Richard Cobden, he spoke in favor of a vigorous prosecution and speedy end to the conflict. William Ewart's radicalism was comprehensive in nature, but his antiwar sentiment was less than absolute and he succumbed to the war fever of the mid–1850s.

Bibliography:

B. W. A. Munford, *William Ewart, M.P., 1798–1869, Portrait of a Radical* (London, 1960); *DNB*, XVIII, 955–56; LT, January 28, 1869.

John D. Fair

F

FABBRI, Luigi (23 December 1877, Fabriano, Italy—24 June 1935, Montevideo, Uruguay). *Education*: technical schools in Ancona. *Career*: schoolteacher, journalist, editor, and author.

From the late 1890s until the mid–1920s Luigi Fabbri was an increasingly influential figure in the Italian anarchist movement. The turning point in his life occurred in 1896 when he met Italy's paramount anarchist, *Errico Malatesta. Prior to that he had been introduced to anarchism by Virgilio Condulmari and by his late teens had already collaborated on diverse anarchist newspapers, but Malatesta's charismatic force intensified the young man's fervor and galvanized his energies for a lifetime of militant action. This influence never waned, and it is poignantly fitting that Fabbri's last book should have been *Malatesta: Su vida y su pensamiento*, published posthumously in 1945.

Swept up in the dragnet following Milan's violent May Days in 1898, Fabbri spent the next two-and-one-half years in prison, sharing the fate of numerous anarchists and left-wing socialists who had conspired to bring down the government in Italy's *fin de siècle* crisis of liberalism. Upon his release, Fabbri moved to Rome and resumed his journalistic career, eventually founding with Pietro Gori *Il Pensiero* (1903–11), which proved to be one of the most durable anarchist periodicals of the day. At the same time, he contributed to many of the syndicalist publications that Georges Sorel had inspired in Italy, a sign of the developing eclecticism in his thought. Indeed, Fabbri attempted to combine syndicalism, socialism, and anarchism in a practical philosophy that would bring to life a new and ultimately victorious political party in Italy.

Unlike the syndicalists—and many of the socialists and anarchists—Fabbri remained unswervingly faithful to the antimilitarist ideal with which they all had begun their theoretical discussions. A delegate and speaker at numerous congresses on antimilitarism in the pre-World War I period, Fabbri was disheartened by the patriotic fervor of many leftists in 1914, and he heatedly disputed the radical interventionist argument, that the war would serve the cause of revolution. Fabbri retorted that the war could only serve capitalism, and this intransigent antiwar position led to his virtual isolation in Italian politics from 1915 to 1918. After the war he took no pleasure in the triumph of Bolshevism. The Soviet experience proved to Fabbri's complete satisfaction that the fundamental anarchist position was unassailable: any state, even one professing socialist ideals, is intrinsically evil. The triumph of fascism in 1922 seemed to him to complete the catastrophe of Europe, although he would live to see even worse when Adolf Hitler took power in 1933.

Fabbri spent the last nine years of his life being hounded by fascist agents and officials from one place of exile to another, first in France, then in Belgium, and finally in Uruguay. He continued to collaborate on anarchist newspapers all over the world and founded his own monthly journal in Montevideo, *Studi sociali*. Fabbri briefly served as the director of the Italian School in Montevideo, but pressure exerted by the Italian ambassador brought about his dismissal. He continued writing voluminously, attacking capitalism, fascism, and Stalinism—still promoting until the very end his humane vision of free men working in a world at peace.

Bibliography:

A. *Carlo Pisacane: La Vita, le opere, l'azione rivoluzionaria* (Rome-Florence, 1904); *La Contro-rivoluzione preventiva: Riflessioni sul fascismo* (Bologna, 1922); *Dittatura e rivoluzione* (Ancona, 1921); *L'Ideale anarchico* (Bologna, 1911); *Malatesta: L'Uomo e il pensiero* (Napoli, 1951).

B. Armando Borghi, *Mezzo secolo di anarchia (1898–1945)* (Naples, 1954); Ugo Fedeli, *Luigi Fabbri* (Torino, 1948); Carlo Masini, *Storia degli anarchici italiani: da Bakunin a Malatesta (1862–1892)* (Milan, 1969); Enzo Santarelli, *Il Socialismo anarchico in Italia* (Milan, 1973).

Richard Drake

FAIRBAIRN, Robert Edis (17 June 1879, Southampton, England—30 May 1953, St. Marys, Ontario, Canada). *Education*: B.D., Oxford Univ., 1904. *Career*: minister, Methodist and United Church of Canada: England, 1904–14, Bermuda, 1914–17, Nova Scotia and Newfoundland, 1917–25, Ontario, 1925–49; writer and pacifist.

Robert Edis Fairbairn was one of the most vocal and certainly the most contentious pacifist in the United Church of Canada for over three decades.

Originally from England, Fairbairn entered the Wesleyan Methodist Ministry in 1904. He quickly became dissatisfied with what he considered the narrow dogmatism of the Wesleyan Church, however, and by 1914 he emigrated to Canada via Bermuda where he was assigned as an acting chaplain under the British Admiralty during the early years of World War I. Although he had begun to develop pacifist sympathies while a student at Oxford, during his early ministry and through the study and use of Esperanto, it was not until this experience as a navy chaplain, especially his firsthand exposure to the reactions of young men in bayonet drill, that Fairbairn became a committed pacifist.

With the postwar resurgence of pacifism Fairbairn began to voice his convictions and within a decade he emerged as one of the most prolific pacifist writers in Canada (over sixty articles in church journals alone) as well as one of the most radical. His pacifist argument incorporated the socialist analysis of Western capitalism as the "war system," a system which compelled otherwise honorable men to act unscrupulously and which made future war inevitable. Since he saw it as the root cause of conflict between nations as well as between classes, he believed the only alternative was a complete social revolution according to the teachings of Christ.

During the thirties he found support for this view in the Fellowship for a Christian Social Order through which he helped produce the book *Towards the Christian Revolution*. In his chapter, Fairbairn emphasized the revolutionary evangelism of the Christian gospel and argued that one of the primary functions of the Judaeo-Christian faith was to generate opposition to war.

In response to Canada's entry into the Second World War, Fairbairn drafted the "Witness Against War Manifesto," the famous antiwar statement ultimately signed by over 150 United Churchmen. Fairbairn's intention was merely to pressure the church to recognize its moral dilemma and offer an alternative stance for Christians in time of war, but the manifesto received a hostile reception from all quarters and forced Fairbairn from his church. Fairbairn, nevertheless, continued his line of attack throughout the war years. For a time he contributed a regular column to *Reconciliation*, the journal of the Canadian Fellowship of Reconciliation, but his major endeavor was his own newsletter or bulletin entitled "To Maintain Courage by Sharing Conviction." Until well after the war, he distributed several hundred copies monthly at his own expense to an international readership.

By the end of his career, Fairbairn had become the most outspoken radical pacifist in Canada. As long as he felt something needed to be said on the war issue he refused to remain silent, often enraging his readers and stirring a host of critics. He even condemned the entire Christian church as apostate for its failure to oppose escalating violence throughout the world. In his later search for realistic pacifist solutions he came to view Christian cooperative communities as the true revolutionary cells of a new social order, and, in the atomic age, his writing reflected an increasingly strident but hopeless tone.

Bibliography:

A. *Apostate Christendom*, (London: 1948); *The Appeal to Reality* (New York, 1927); *Kingdom of God Evangelism* Toronto, 1935).

B. Thomas P. Socknat, " 'Witness Against War': Pacifism in Canada, 1900–1945." Ph.D. Dissertation, McMaster University, 1981.

Thomas P. Socknat

FALKENBERG, Albert (3 May 1871, Hannover, Germany—7 August 1945, Berlin-Steglitz). *Education*: realschule (non-classical academic high school). *Career*: middle-level and higher administrative positions in the postal service, 1887–1908; editor, *Deutsche Postzeitung*, 1908; editor-in-chief, *Deutsche Nachrichten*; ministerial councillor, Ministry of the Interior, 1919–21; chairman, Allgemeiner Deutscher Beamtenbund (Union of German State Employees), 1922–33; president, Beamten-Internationale (State Employees International Organization), 1930–33; Social Democratic member, Reichstag, 1928–30; pacifist.

After World War I Albert Falkenberg was active as an author, speaker, and organizer in the peace movement; first in the *Deutsche Liga für Volkerbund* (German League for the League of Nations) (DLV), then in the *Deutsche Friedensgesellschaft* (German Peace Society) (DFG) and in the *Deutsche Liga für*

Menschenrechte (German League for Human Rights) (DLM). From 1925–29 he was on the board of the DFG, either as member of the board (1925–26, 1928–29), as vice-chairman (1926–27) or together with *Ludwig Quidde and *Fritz Küster, as co-chairman, in charge of finances (1927–28). In this capacity he succeeded in mediating between the quarreling factions within the DFG, and to lessen internal organizational opposition. At the same time, he presided at the Berlin branch of the DFG, first as vice-president, and from January 1926 as president. From 1926–33 he was co-editor of the *Die Friedenswarte*, and from 1930–33 he belonged to the political executive of the DLM.

Because of his high position in the union movement and his connection to numerous, publicly well-known personalities, Falkenberg was uniquely positioned to increase the membership of the pacifist organization from his circle of acquaintances in the labor movement. He worked actively to direct the unions into closer relations with the pacifist movement and its central office at Geneva, the International Peace Bureau. At the Geneva World Peace Conference in 1926, he played a decisive role in the deliberations on how to activate the working masses for the peace movement, but he later met with considerable resistance from the workers' movement in this regard. It was due to his effort that the Allgemeine Deutsche Beamtenbund (Union of German State Employees), together with other organizations, participated in the demonstrations in favor of conscientious objection to military service in the Rhineland and in Westfalen. Nevertheless, he failed to achieve a broad support for this action from the German Social Democratic party, labor unions, or civil service unions.

In frequent speeches sponsored by the DFG and the DLM, Falkenberg promoted German-Polish reconciliation and warned of the consequences of any future war. His involvement with union and pacifist movements created difficulties for him after 1933, when the Nazis achieved power. He nevertheless decided to remain in Germany. He lost his civil service position and lived in retirement in Berlin until his death in 1945.

Bibliography:

A. ''Gewerkschaften und Friedensbewegung,'' *Das Andere Deutschland*, 6 (July 31, 1926); ''Giftgaskriegsabwehr,'' *Die Friedenswarte*, 33 (February, 1933), 44–48; ''Pazifismus und Sozialdemokratie,'' *Die Friedenswarte* 27 (July, 1927), 199–201; ''Rund um die deutsch-polnische Verstandigung,'' *Die Friedenswarte*, 29 (September, 1929), 257–61.

B. Reinhold Lütgemeier-Davin, *Pazifismus zwischen Kooperation und Konfrontation* (Cologne, 1982); *Die Friedenswarte*, 31 (May 1931), 141–42 and 46 (March 1946), 151–52; *Wer ist's?* (10th ed., Berlin, 1935), 386–87.

Reinhold Lütgemeier-Davin
Trans. by Susan E. Cernyak

FAURE, Sébastien (6 January 1858, Saint-Etienne, France—14 July 1942, Royan, France). *Education*: Collège Saint-Michel, Saint-Etienne; novitiate at the Jesuit seminary, Clermont-Ferrand, 1874–76. *Career*: insurance agent at

Saint-Etienne, 1879–82; candidate of the Parti ouvrier français in the Gironde, 1885; agent, Société des voyages et villégiatures à crédit, 1888; co-founder and editor, *La Libertaire* 1895 to c. 1899; founder and editor, *Journal du Peuple*, February-December, 1899; founder and director of the orphanage "La Ruche," 1904–17; member, Ligue international des combattants pour la paix; journalist and anarchist speaker.

Sébastien Faure found his way to pacifism by a roundabout route. After having left the seminary in order to support his mother and sisters, his reading led him to renounce his faith and adopt socialism. Moving to Bordeaux in 1882, he became the candidate of the Parti ouvrier français of Jules Guesde in 1885, but was defeated. Further reading, particularly in the works of *Peter Kropotkin and Elisée Reclus, and a meeting with the worker-anarchist Joseph Tortelier, (advocate of the general strike), led him to abandon socialism for anarchism, and to his decision to move to Paris in 1888. Anarchism brought him to antimilitarism and pacifism, and—together with his commitment to Freemasonry—to anticlericalism and attachment to the Dreyfusard cause. Influenced by these ideas, and prompted by his remarkable oratorical and literary gifts, he left his employment to devote the rest of his life to writing and giving lectures for their advancement. His *La Douleur universelle*, a summary of his anarchist conceptions, appeared in 1895.

Also in 1895, Faure founded—with Louise Michel—the weekly *La Libertaire*, for the same purpose and became its editor. In the September 4, 1898 issue he declared, over a four-column spread, "Dreyfus is innocent!" He went on to found the daily *Journal du Peuple* in February 1899, joining with Allemane, +Aristide Briand, and others to form the Comité de Coalition Révolutionnaire, and using the *Journal* to disseminate Dreyfusard and anarchist ideas. These had already appeared in his brochure, *Les Anarchistes et l'affaire Dreyfus* (1898).

In 1904 he founded the school and orphanage "La Ruche," near Rambouillet, where boys and girls were educated together in accord with anarchist conceptions; the project collapsed in 1917, because of Faure's inability to derive enough income from lecturing (as a result of the censorship) and because of wartime food shortages.

Faure's speeches and writings led to frequent arrests. In February 1892 he was tried for a speech he had made at Lyon the previous year and sentenced to eighteen months in prison. Released in November 1893, he was again arrested in February 1894, but was acquitted (with several companions, in the famous "Trial of the Thirty") after Faure delivered a stirring defense. Condemned on numerous other occasions—at Paris, Bordeaux, Marseille, Toulouse, Aix, Nimes, and elsewhere—and sentenced to a few months or a few years in prison, he nevertheless continued tirelessly to express his views.

By 1914 Faure's opposition to war and militarism had come to occupy a central place in his thinking, as it did among the syndicalists of the Confédération générale du travail (General Confederation of Labor) (CGT) who had repeatedly advocated sabotage of the mobilization and a general strike in the event of a declaration of war. More moderate and more willing to compromise than many anarchists, his views were tempered with a humanitarian attitude no doubt derived from his early religious background. In January 1915 appeared his manifesto "Vers la paix" ("Towards Peace"), which despite the efforts of the police to suppress it, had a wide distribution all over France and in the trenches. Addressed specifically to "socialists, syndicalistes, revolutionaries and anarchists," it pleaded, in impassioned yet moderate terms, for all peoples to exert pressure for a conference of neutral states to negotiate an immediate peace. One of the earliest of the antiwar statements to appear, "Vers la paix" served to crystallize the pacifist sentiments of the French people.

Subsequently, and under pressure from the Minister of Interior, Faure agreed to renounce his propaganda in favor of peace, but was unable to submit completely. Another manifesto, "La Trêve des peuples" ("The Peoples' Truce") appeared in June 1915, and in April 1916 he began to publish a weekly, *Ce qu'il faut dire*, which appeared with numerous white spaces until it was proscribed by Clemenceau early in 1918. After the war, Faure was an active member of the Ligue internationale des combattants pour la paix (International League of Fighters for Peace), contributing to its organs, *La Patrie Humaine* and *Le Barrage*, through the 1920s and 1930s, and resuming his lecturing career. When the Spanish Civil War erupted in 1936, he again took to the lecture stand, in support of the anarchist Loyalists. He pronounced in favor of the Munich Accord in 1938, in opposition to the stand of the left *paco-bellicistes*, and he remained inalterably opposed to the war which broke out in 1939. When he died in 1942, an unpublished manuscript, "Les Leçons de la guerre," ("The Lessons of War") was found among his papers.

Bibliography:

A. *Les Anarchistes et l'affaire Dreyfus* (Paris, 1898); *La Dictature de la bourgeoisie* (Paris, 1921); *La douleur universelle* (Paris, 1895); *Encyclopédie anarchiste*, with Vsevolod Voline (Paris, 1935); *La Faillité du Christianisme* (1907); *La Philosophie libertaire* (1895); *Nous voulons la paix* (Paris, 1917).

B. F. Alaiz, et al, *La Vie et l'oeuvre de Sébastien Faure* (Paris, 1961); Hem Day, *Sébastien Faure, le pacifiste*, (Paris, 1961); Jeanne Humbert, *Sébastien Faure* (Paris, 1949).

Albert S. Hill

FELDHAUS, Richard (17 August 1856, Neuss on the Rhein, Prussia—28 January 1944, Binningen near Basel, Switzerland). *Education*: gymnasium. *Career*: actor and pacifist.

Deeply moved by the reading of *Bertha von Suttner's *Die Waffen nieder!* (*Lay Down Your Arms!*), Richard Feldhaus dedicated a great part of his life thereafter to spreading the idea of peace. After having given his first pacifist speech in November 1892 in his hometown, he literally traveled from one pacifist speech engagement to another whenever he could get away from his career as an actor of long standing with the city theater in Basel. He thus became the

German peace movement's own wandering speaker, in the words of *Alfred H. Fried, "a second Peter of Amiens." In his speeches, which presented the message of pacifism in a popular form intelligible to all, he read from pacifist poetry and treatises. Frequently, he referred to actual events and underlined visually the horrors of war by means of projected pictures. In that way, he was able to convince many of his listeners that the people themselves must want to have peace, instead of leaving it to governments alone to secure it for them.

As a result of his peace missions, which by 1917 included 700 speeches and which took him not only back and forth across Germany but also into Austro-Hungary, Switzerland, Scandinavia, and to the USA, several local peace organizations were established, such as those in Königsberg, Görlitz, Löwenberg (Silesia), Gera and Kassel in Germany, and Lucern in Switzerland. Participation in a series of national and international peace congresses brought Feldhaus, one of the earliest members of the German Peace Society, into contact with numerous important representatives of the international peace movement, a few with whom he developed close friendships. In one of his few writings *Die Kunst und die Friedensbewegung* (1895), Feldhaus presented his concept of the meaning of art for the peace movement.

From the end of the First World War, the outbreak of which shocked him greatly, he devoted his energies to the protection of animals and to the fight against vivisection.

Bibliography:

A. *Die Kunst und die Friedensbewegung* (n.p., 1895).

B. Hans Wehberg, *Die Führer der deutschen Friedensbewegung* (Leipzig, 1923, reprinted, New York, 1971); Hans Wehberg, "Vier Vorkampfer der Friedensbewegung," *Die Friedenswarte*, 44 (1944), 80–81.

Karl Holl
Trans. by William Hopkins

FERNAU, Hermann (pseud. of Hermann Latt) (born 1884). *Career*: journalist.

Little is known about the private life of Hermann Fernau other than he was born in 1884 and came from a Jewish family that lived in the German city of Breslau. He spent the last nine years before the outbreak of World War I in Paris and greatly admired the political freedom that existed in France. Until his expulsion from France in the spring of 1915, Fernau lived in Paris as the only German permitted to continue his work unhindered during the first few months of the war. In May 1915 he went to Basel and a few months later, in January 1916, his work *Gerade weil ich ein Deutscher bin!* appeared in Zurich. The pamphlet defended *Richard Grelling's *J'accuse* and its strong indictment of Germany for its responsibility in starting the war. French propaganda officials had Fernau's work translated into several languages; a German language version of it was dropped over the German lines.

In *Durch . . . zur Demokratie*, which appeared in Switzerland in 1917, Fernau further developed his views on the world war. Even though he oversimplified the causes of the war as the opposition between democracy (peace-loving) and monarchy (desirous of war), he succeeded in a convincing manner to show German responsibility for the outbreak of the war. In this, and other works, Fernau revealed himself as a convinced pacifist committed to the tradition of the German republicans of 1848. In order to lead Germany to democracy, Fernau pleaded for the military defeat of Germany, for only in that way could the German ruling elite which opposed democracy be dethroned. Beginning in April 1917, Fernau advocated these views in *Die Freie Zeitung*, the newspaper of German democrats in Switzerland. By the end of the year, however, he had separated himself from the paper, probably because of its increasingly one-sided pro-Allied position. Throughout 1917 he also wrote for *Alfred Hermann Fried's antiwar paper, *Die Friedenswarte*.

After 1918 Fernau remained in Switzerland and like many other German emigrés found himself labeled by Germany as a traitor. He continued to present his critique of monarchy and war in brochures and in the periodical *Der Weltbürger* which he began to publish in 1919 but which did not survive beyond the first few issues. During the German revolution of 1918–19, Fernau supported the cause of the "Third Way." He committed himself to a break with the past, for the radical democratization of Germany, and against bolshevization of Germany. This did not prevent him from rejecting the Treaty of Versailles as unfulfillable. In a 1920 issue of *Die Weltbühne* he argued that the German revolution had been bungled by too much compromise by the German Social Democrats and that this made it possible for the reactionary forces to recover from their 1918 defeat.

Although he participated in congresses of the Deutsch Friedensgesellschaft (German Peace Society) during the 1920s, he did not play a leading role in the postwar peace movement and nothing further is known about his fate.

Bibliography:

A. *Durch!... zur Demokratie* (Bern-Bümplitz, 1917); *Die französische Demokratie. Sozialphilosophische Studien aus Frankreichs Kulturwerkstatt* (Munich, 1914); *Gerade weil ich ein Deutscher bin! Eine Klarstellung der in dem Buche "J'accuse" aufgerollten Schuldfrage* (Zurich, 1916); *Das Königtum ist der Krieg* (Bern-Bümplitz, 1918); *Dem neuen Deutschland. Verse eines deutschen Republikaners* (Bern Bümplitz, 1919).

B. Hans Thimme, *Weltkrieg ohne Waffen* (Stuttgart und Berlin 1932).

Lothar Wieland
Trans. by Solomon Wank

FERRER GUARDIA, Francisco (10 January 1859, Alella, Barcelona, Spain—12 October 1909, Barcelona. *Education*: self-educated. *Career*: teacher and educational reformer; editor, *Boletín de la Escuela Moderna*, 1903–9, *L'Ecole Rénovée*, 1908–9; writer: anarchist theorist; Freemason; pacifist.

In addition to original contributions as a reformer of educational institutions and pedagogical styles, Francisco Ferrer Guardia's execution by the Spanish government in 1909—an event notorious in its day—earned him a secure niche as a martyr to antimilitarist agitation in the years before World War I.

From the experience of his own traditional primary education—authoritarian, catechistic, and religion-laden—Ferrer Guardia became an insistent advocate of international educational reform. However, as a young man he had followed the teachings of Ruiz Zorrilla and had been attracted to violent revolution in the 1880s as a means of transforming Spanish society and government. In 1885 he participated in an uprising which forced him to flee to France. There he remained for 15 years, earning a living as a Spanish instructor in Paris and revising his ideas about the utility of violent revolution. He became convinced that a new generation of Spanish children had to be educated for change and that education must follow radical new pedagogical principles. Above all, children had to be protected from "the treacherous teaching" of official schools and from clerical influence.

In 1901 he began to enact his beliefs, aided by a sizeable fortune which one of his wealthy French students left to him. He opened the Modern School in Barcelona where teaching methods emphasizing rationalism, humanitarianism, antimilitarism, and anticlericalism took priority over the usual curriculum. Co-educational classrooms were introduced; the typical system of rewards, punishments, and competition was eliminated. Evening courses in social and political education were given to adults. A number of daughter schools copied the Modern School in Spain and South America and by 1906, to the horror of the clergy, 47 branches existed in Catalonia alone.

While anarchists claimed him as one of their own (a judgment often accepted by scholars), Ferrer Guardia was not comfortable with that appellation. In 1906, accused of complicity in an assassination attempt on the royal family, he commented that he would be pleased to be an anarchist if they adopted his philosophy of love, peace, and humane relations through education.

The trial ended in acquittal, but he was not permitted to reopen the Modern School. He returned to Paris in 1908 to work for an international association for rationalist education and edit its journal, *L'Ecole Rénovée*. The association boasted Anatole France as its president.

His life ended a year later by execution which transformed him into an international martyr. He had been in Barcelona in July 1909 when the Spanish government ordered regular Army as well as Reserve troops to Morocco to crush a Riff uprising. The Reserves, mainly urban workers with family responsibilities, deeply distrusted regular Army officers and felt little inclination to defend mining companies interests in Morocco. There was widespread antimilitarist feeling and a sense that the soldiers were being led to a slaughter. In Barcelona, a stronghold of trade union and radical protest movements, the feeling was transformed into a wave of protests, a general strike (July 26), and, finally, a week of mass rioting and carnage directed mainly against properties of the Catholic Church. The "Tragic Week," as it remains known in Spanish history, ended only with the arrival of loyal Army troops and a military tribunal to prosecute the "guilty."

There is considerable evidence that clerical organizations, particularly the Jesuits, wished Ferrer Guardia to be prosecuted for the insurrection. He was brought before a military court which condemned him to death. Conservatives viewed his Modern School as heavily responsible for the wild anticlericalism of Barcelona's rampaging lower classes in July 1909. His execution was preceded by an international campaign to save his life and when that failed, an international denunciation of the Spanish government from all liberal circles in Europe. His case, a prewar kind of Sacco-Vanzetti affair, produced a ministerial crisis and his death provoked widespread discussion of antimilitarist ideas.

Bibliography:

A. *The Modern School* (New York, 1909); *The Origins and Ideals of the Modern School* (New York, 1913).

B. William Archer, *The Life, Trial and Death of Francisco Ferrer* (London, 1911); Maurice Dommanget, *Francisco Ferrer* (Paris, 1952); Stanlye G. Payne, *Politics and the Military in Modern Spain* (Stanford, CA, 1967); Joan Connelly Ullman, *The Tragic Week, A Study of Anticlericalism in Spain, 1875–1912* (Boston, 1968).

Elda Gentili Zappi

FERRERO, Gugliemo (21 July 1871, Portici, Italy—2 August 1942, Geneva). *Education*: Dr. jur., Univ. of Turin, 1891; Dr. of Philosophy and Letters, Univ. of Bologna, 1893. *Career*: journalist, *Il Secolo* (Milan), 1893–95; lecturer, Collège de France, 1906; lecturer, Harvard Univ., 1908; professor of modern history, Univ. of Geneva, 1930–42; professor of European military history, Institut universitaire des hautes études internationales, Geneva; scholar and author.

Throughout his life, Gugliemo Ferrero concentrated on mankind's major problem—war and peace—in his many books examining the history of Rome, the French Revolution, the Congress of Vienna, and international affairs which established his international reputation as a historical analyst. In 1888, not yet 17, he won a prize for his essay, "Pax Hominibus" in an international competition sponsored by the Societa internazionale per la pace (International Society for Peace) (Milan) under *E. T. Moneta's direction. There he argued that the main impulse towards war arose from the passion for domination and its attendant hatreds which prevailed in the conduct of Europe's middle class societies. Thus, the solution for war had to be found in intellectual progress which Ferrero believed would occur only very slowly.

His thinking on the subject of war matured and found expression in his book *Il Militarismo* (1898) where he offered an analysis of both ancient and modern militarism. Again, he located the basic impetus toward warfare in individual passion and public opinion which often became menacing and led to the creation of military organizations. Continuous and unchecked tendencies toward militarism and nationalism, he argued, would cause the decline of moral order, weaken culture, and destroy religion. The permanent process of making newer and "better" military weapons would result in their eventual use. Nonetheless, Ferrero remained optimistic, concluding that if men were wise, a new age of lasting peace could be inaugurated.

In 1915, with the publication of his study, *Between the Old World and the New*, Ferrero added another dimension to his analysis of the reoccurrence of war. He developed a distinction between "quantitative" and "qualitative" civilizations, arguing that where the former dominate, a menace to progress exists. His books written after World War I dealt with ways in which humanity could move into an age of peace. He believed that the central task of historians was to convince statesmen and politicians of the need to struggle for moral and spiritual values over quantitative forces.

The predilection toward violence in Western civilization (which Ferrero believed increased in the hands of revolutionary over legitimate governments) was a theme which he repeatedly took up. In *Problems of Peace* (1919), he argued that "Occidental civilization has evoked violence in every shape and form from its hiding places in matter and mind." He was inclined to see that violence increased following revolutions and cited the French Revolution as well as the Revolutions of 1848 as examples whereby peace was destroyed. Thus, he argued that revolutionary states or "any state which abuses the principles" of peace should be excluded from the League of Nations and subjected to sanctions. Since he was not convinced that the Treaty of Versailles would avoid a new war, Ferrero proposed the creation of a system resembling the Holy Alliance of 1815 which at least, in his view, managed to preserve peace for most of the nineteenth century. Fundamental to his work was a burning commitment to the preservation of Western civilization which he once described as a grandiose Gothic vault, "soaring sublime toward the sky. One of its arches is Europe; the other, America. If either arch is broken, the other will be endangered."

Ferrero struggled against the rise of Fascism in Italy and National Socialism in Germany. In their belligerent ideologies he recognized a major threat to the fragile peace that followed World War I. His writings for truth and peace brought down the bitter persecution of the Fascist regime which banned his books, forbade his lectures, prohibited his publication in Italy, confined him to his home under constant police surveillance, and finally let him go into exile, to Geneva, in 1930. There, he accepted a teaching position at the University and remained until the end of his life in 1942, not seeing the end of the war or the establishment of a legitimate government in Italy.

Bibliography:

A. *Ancient Rome and Modern America* (New York, 1914); *Between the Old World and the New* (New York, 1915); *Greatness and Decline of Rome* (5 vols., New York, 1909); *Militarism* (London, 1902); *Peace and War* (London, 1933); *Principles of Power* (New York, 1942); *Problems of Peace* (New York, 1919); *The Unity of the World* (New York, 1930); *Words to the Deaf* (New York, 1926).

B. Bogdan Raditsa, *Colloqui con Gugliemo Ferrero* (Lugano, 1939).

C. Casellario, ''Gugliemo FERRERO'' in Archivio dello Stato, Ministero dell'Interno, Rome (EUR); letters to G. Ferrero, Special Collections, Columbia University, New York, NY.

Bogdan Raditsa

FIELD, David Dudley. See *Biographical Dictionary of Internationalists*.

FISCHHOF, Adolf (8 December 1816, Ofen, Hungary—23 March 1893, Emmersdorf, Austria). *Education*: M.D., Univ. of Vienna, 1845. *Career*: physician and political writer.

Active in the 1848 revolution in Austria as a liberal advocate of constitutional reform, Adolf Fischhof was arrested and detained during suppression of the revolution. After his release he returned to the practice of medicine and at the same time became widely respected as a political analyst.

Fischhof's liberal ideas influenced significantly the peace movement in Austria during the latter nineteenth and early twentieth centuries. Though not a pacifist in the strict sense of one who opposes war categorically, Fischhof sought to envisage a political order, domestic and global, in which war would become undesirable and unnecessary. Such an order, he believed, demanded important reforms, both at the national and international levels. At the national level it required transition away from absolutism toward democratic, federated forms of government, and at the international level introduction of a system of adjudicatory arbitration, by which disputes among nations could be resolved without violence.

Applying these ideas to the problems of the Habsburg Monarchy of his own day, Fischhof argued, in his essay *Österreich und die Bürgschaften seines Bestandes* (*Austria and the Guarantees of her Continuance*), published in 1869, that for the Austrian Empire to survive as a strong, centralized state it would, paradoxically, have to decentralize itself by renouncing authoritarian rule from Vienna. By respecting equally each subordinate nationality-group's desire for freedom, cultural autonomy, and meaningful democratic participation in the Imperial government, the Austrian Crown would ensure the political loyalty of these groups and thus the continuance—and the peace—of the Empire. Conversely, to ignore this advice, he believed, would invite internal strife, violent conflict, and the dissolution of the Monarchy.

At the international level of political organization, Fischhof envisaged a similar transition to a peaceful order. In his essay, *Zur Reduktion der continentalen Heere* (*On the Reduction of Continental Armies*), published in 1875, Fischhof urged an end to the escalating European arms race by calling on all nations to recognize the truth (again, seemingly paradoxical) that their security depended on decreased, rather than increased, levels of armaments. Reason and humanitarianism, he averred, summon all governments to vie with one another to disarm, just as they formerly vied with one another to arm. As a practical beginning, Fischhof proposed the invocation of a series of conferences consisting of elected parliamentary representatives and appointed delegates from nonparliamentary countries whose purpose would be to discuss the subject of mutual reductions of national military forces and armaments expenditures. Fischhof's ideas gave impetus to the formation of the Interparliamentary Union as well as the Austrian Peace Society. Both these institutions, whose existence commenced in 1889, sought to secure the basis of a peaceful world order through the establishment of a workable system of disarmament, international arbitration, and world government.

Bibliography:

A. *Österreich und die Bürgschaften seines Bestandes* (Vienna, 1869); *Der österreichische Sprachenzwist* (Vienna, 1888); *Die Sprachenrechte in den Staaten gemischter Nationalität* (Vienna, 1885); *Zur Reduktion der kontinentalen Heere* (Vienna, 1875).

B. Richard Charmatz, *Adolf Fischhof: Das Lebensbild éines österreichischen Politikers* (Stuttgart and Berlin, 1910); Robert A. Kann, *The Multinational Empire: Nationalism and National Reform in the Habsburg Monarchy, 1848–1918* (New York, 1950), II, 143–153; Wilhelm Kosch, *Biographisches Staatshandbuch* (Berne and Munich, 1963), I, 329–330; Obituary, *Neue Freie Presse*, March 24, 1893 (Morgenblatt), pp. 1–2; *Österreichisches biographisches Lexikon 1815–1950* (Graz and Cologne, 1954), I, 325–326; S. Wininger, ed., *Grosse jüdische National-Biographie* (Czernowitz, 1927) II, 260–261.

Richard R. Laurence

FLAMMARION, Sylvie (née Pétiaux-Hugo) (1842, Valenciennes, France—? March 1919, Paris). *Education*: private. *Career*: research assistant to astronomer-husband, Camille Flammarion; pacifist, co-founder of Ligue des femmes pour le désarmement international and founder, La Paix et la désarmement par les femmes; and author.

Sylvie Flammarion, distantly related to *Victor Hugo, on her mother's side, grew up with a love and gift for mathematical precision and measurement which she acquired from her architect father. Married in 1874 to Camille Flammarion, whose popular writings on astronomy were great public successes, the couple took a honeymoon trip up in a balloon which guaranteed their celebrity. Flammarion worked devotedly with her husband, calling herself his secretary in his work at the Paris Observatory, in their own observatory, and in the writing of his many books. The Société astronomique de France eventually recognized her contributions in the form of a medal, and she, in turn, established a medal for women astronomers. The government appointed her an officer of public education.

Besides collaborating with Camille, Sylvie Flammarion became known as a creative writer, publishing successful short stories and novella under the *nom de plume*, Sylvio Hugo. Without much warning, she suddenly became interested in the growing French and European peace movements. In 1896 she attracted considerable attention by publishing an open letter on arms and the arms race. In that year, she joined the Princess *Marie-Gabrielle-Hortense Wiszniewska to create the Ligue des femmes pour le désarmement international (League of Women for International Disarmament), accepting the position of vice-president. In 1899 she founded and led the group, La Paix et le désarmement par les femmes (Women for Peace and Disarmament), which was the first avowedly women-only peace society in France. Flammarion insisted that no distinction of religion, class, or nationality bar membership but members had to be women. Further, she wanted "women of the people" to constitute the majority of the members. These women, she noted, provided the "cannon fodder" in war and only their active involvement in peace labors would suffice to stop the mass murder of their sons.

Accordingly, this quiet and reserved middle class lady approached several women who worked in Les Halles, the central market of Paris, seeking their support. Four women, including one officer of a women's cooperative syndicate in the market, agreed but the recruitment of mass membership was difficult. Flammarion was often greeted with cat-calls and hostile reminders of Alsace-Lorraine. She persisted, however, and her society grew. Her oratorical ability was superb and her short tracts were extremely well written. Often, she was helped by the journalist, *Séverine, in her labors.

Her incessant propaganda on behalf of educating women for peace and on behalf of arms control made her an important figure in the early twentieth-century French peace community. She was appointed to the council of the Délégation permanente des sociétés de la paix, a national council of French peace societies, headed by *Gaston Moch and attended many national and international peace congresses where she distinguished herself by sharp and pithy statements, in contrast to the usual long and wordy speeches. The coming of World War I apparently depressed her greatly and she died shortly after it ended.

Bibliography:

B. *Dictionnaire biographique des philanthropes, des mutualistes*, 89–91; *La Paix par le droit* (1919), 369.

Sandi E. Cooper

FOERSTER, Friedrich Wilhelm (2 June 1869, Berlin—9 January 1966, Zurich). *Education*: Ph.D., Univ. of Freiburg/Breisgau, 1893. *Career*: professor of philosophy, sociology, ethics, and moral pedagogy, Univ. of Zurich and Technical Univ. of Zurich, 1901-ll, Univ. of Vienna, 1913–14, and Univ. of Munich, 1918–19; Bavarian minister to Switzerland, 1918–19; author of numerous works on pedagogy, contemporary history, militarism, and pacifism.

In Berlin, Friedrich W. Foerster came into contact with the anti-Semitic and nationalistic Prussian historian Heinrich von Treitschke. Recognizing the great danger of Treitschke's ideologically conditioned teachings which were bound up with a militant new German nationalism and the growth of Prussian militarism, he battled against Treitschke's doctrines for the rest of his life.

In Freiburg, Foerster founded the Ethical Society and with that laid the foundation for his pedagogy and political ethics. In 1894 he became publisher of the periodical, *Ethical Kultur*, in which he attacked Emperor William II for publicly insulting the German Social Democrats by calling them "rabble without a country." His criticism of the Emperor led to his arrest and imprisonment in 1895. Moreover, it made his appointment to a university professorship in Germany impossible for the next twenty years. Before his imprisonment, Foerster was named general-secretary of the International Ethical League which had its quarters in Berne. After his release from prison, he went to Berne and remained active in the International Ethical League until 1901, when he assumed a university position in Zurich.

Foerster was a very productive scholar. From the time he began his academic career in 1901 until 1913, he published eighteen books, mainly on the subjects of education and political ethics. His political ideas were grounded deeply in a Christian foundation that was not tied to any church. He strongly criticized the nationalism and militarism of Otto von Bismarck and increasingly supported the federalist conceptions of *Constantin Frantz.

After a year at the University of Vienna in 1913, Foerster accepted an appointment at the University of Munich. In the midst of World War I, he clashed with the authorities over his assertions of Germany's war guilt and the refusal of German leaders to open peace initiatives on their own. For this, he was suspended from his professorship for a year. In 1917, as a result of his memorandum, *Das österreichische Problem* (*The Austrian Problem*), he was invited to Vienna by Austrian Emperor Charles I to discuss ways to solve the Austrian problem and to explore possibilities for peace. After that, he lived in Switzerland for a year where he entered into contact with +President Woodrow Wilson's confidante, Professor George D. Herron. Foerster was a strong supporter of Wilson's policies and, upon his return to the University of Munich in 1918, he became the leading spokesman for Wilsonian internationalism. This led to sharp attacks on him and to defamatory references to the "Foerster-Peace."

After the end of the war, Foerster was named by the new Bavarian prime minister, *Kurt Eisner, as Bavarian minister in Berne, a post which he held until the assassination of Eisner in 1919. When, in 1922, he traveled to Germany in order to investigate the newly awakened militant nationalism, he was warned by friends that his fate would be similar to that of the recently assassinated German foreign minister, Walther Rathenau. Not a moment too soon, Foerster fled back to Switzerland and never set foot in Germany again.

From Switzerland he collaborated with *Fritz Küster in the publication of the pacifist-republican newspaper, *Das Andere Deutschland*. In 1926, the same year that Germany joined the League of Nations, Foerster published his pamphlet *Le Réarmement clandestin de L'Allemagne* (*Germany's Clandestine Rearmament*). Although most League delegates were familiar with Foerster's assertions, they chose to believe +Gustav Stresemann when he came before the League Assembly to make his first speech and swore that Germany had disarmed. Ironically, it was Stresemann who received the Nobel Peace Prize in 1926 and not Foerster, who had also been nominated for it. That same year, Foerster settled in Paris. In vain he warned France and England of the threatening dangers of German militarism.

When Adolf Hitler came to power, the dictatorship viewed Foerster as one of its major enemies. As a reward for his earlier efforts to promote Franco-

German understanding, Foerster was granted French citizenship, but in 1940 he had to flee France before the invading German army. He went first to Switzerland, then to Portugal and, finally, to the United States where he continued his work of enlightenment and continued to be slandered. On his ninetieth birthday in 1959, *Pope John XXIII congratulated him as a great scholar and a great pacifist. In 1963 Foerster returned to Switzerland where, with the help of friends, he lived in peace until his death.

Foerster summed up his views in several political-historical works published after World War II: *Erlebte Weltgeschichte* (*Memoirs*) (1953), *Die jüdische Frage* (*The Jewish Question*) (1959), and *Deutsche Geschichte und politische Ethik* (*German History and Political Ethics*) (1961). His psychological-political view of the European, above all the German, question, enabled Foerster to develop a refined analysis of pacifism. Peace was always his chief priority. He saw the danger posed to European federalist ideas by Prussian militarism and the Hitler dictatorship. In the face of the insensitivity of all German governments after 1918 to Germany's responsibility for World War I, Foerster thought through the problem in a comprehensive way. For that he was generally reviled. Not until after World War II, when a new generation of German historians were faced with new and frightful threats of war, did German scholars discover the primary significance of Foerster as a warning voice against the danger of international conflict.

Germany, Foerster maintained, could have learned from the Treaty of Versailles, but it failed to do so, thereby making Hitler and World War II possible. He urged pacifism as a political program. For him, that meant a departure from the sentimental pacifism of "Nie wieder Krieg" ("No More War"), since that kind of pacifism would only stimulate aggressors and cynical neo-nationalists to start new wars. In order to secure peace, he believed, those responsible for the last war had to recognize their guilt instead of immediately placing themselves "in the service of the next war of revenge." Lasting peace required the careful identification of the causes of war and the establishment of European federalism. Real peace had to be based on law and could not rest "on the superstitious belief in the good intention of others." For Foerster, an effective peace strategy required a strong ethical-political orientation. Long before the onset of World War II, Foerster saw clearly "that against the policy of total war a policy of total peace is necessary."

Bibliography:

A. *Angewandte politische Ethik: Bemerkungen zum Verständnis der gegenwärtigen Weltlage* (2 vols., Wiesbaden 1922/1924); *Christus und das menschliche Leben* (Munich, 1952); *Deutsche Geschichte und politische Ethik*, (Nuremberg, 1961); *Die Dominanten der Kriegsschuld* (Berlin, 1932); *Erlebte Weltgeschichte—Memoiren* (Nuremberg, 1953); *Europa und die deutsche Frage* (Lucerne, 1937); *Mein Kampf gegen das nationalistische und militaristische Deutschland: Gesichtspunkte zur deutschen Selbsterkenntnis und zum Aufbau eines neuen Deutschland* (Wiesbaden, 1920); *Politische Ethik und politische Pädagogik. Mit besonderer Berücksichtigung der kommenden deutschen Aufgaben* (Berlin, 1918); *Weltpolitik und Weltgewissen* (Munich, 1919); *Zentralismus und Föderalismus* (Munich, 1922); *Zur Beureteilung der deutschen Kriegführung* (Berlin, 1920).

B. Hans-Henning von der Burg, *Sittengesetz und Sozialorganisation—Wege zur civitas humana. F. W. Foerster und seine politische Ethik* (Freiburg/Br., 1971); Herbert Burger, *Politik und Ethik bei F. W. Foerster* (Bonn, 1969); F. W. Foerster-Gesellschaft, Bonn, ed., *Friedrich Wilhelm Foerster. Das Gewissen einer Generation* (Recklinghausen, 1953); Heinrich Lutz, "Deutscher Krieg und Weltgewissen—Friedrich Wilhelm Foersters politische Publizistik und die Zensurstelle des bayrischen Kriegsministeriums 1915–1918," *Zeitschrift für Bayrische Landesgeschichte*, vol. 25 (Munich, 1962); *Programm einer Lebensarbeit—eine Schrift über F. W. Foerster* (Freiburg/Br., 1961); Harry Pross, "Der Prophet alter Wahrheiten. Ein Versuch über F. W. Foerster," *Neue Zürcher Zeitung*, January 26, 1966; Hans Schwann, ed., *Wer ist Friedrich Wilhelm Foerster? Eine Aufsatzsammlung* (Berlin, 1930); Elise Spahn-Gujer, "Friedrich Wilhelm Foerster—Fragmente aus seinem Leben," *Neue Zürcher Zeitung*. January 15, 1966; *New York Times*, January 22, 1966.

Hans Kühner-Wolfskehl
Trans. by Soloman Wank

FOERSTER, Wilhelm Julius (16 December 1832, Grünberg/Silesia, Germany [now Poland]—18 January 1921, Bornim near Potsdam, Germany). *Education*: Ph.D., Univ. of Bonn, 1854. *Career*: director, Berlin Observatory, 1865–1904; professor of astronomy, Univ. of Berlin, 1863ff; dean, Faculty of Philosophy, Univ. of Berlin, 1881–85; rector, Univ. of Berlin, 1891–92; director, Commission on Weights and Measures, 1869–85; chairman, International Committee for Weights and Measures, 1891ff; privy councilor; scientific writer; author of books and essays on ethics; pacifist.

Wilhelm Foerster, descendant of an old established textile manufacturing family and father of *Friedrich Wilhelm Foerster, was an active participant in the German and international peace movements. At the same time, his reputation as a renowned astronomer, university professor, and expert on weights and measures gained him acceptance in Prussian courtly and aristocratic society. His standing in the peace movement rested on the fact that his advocacy of pacifist ideas was inseparable from the conduct of his own life. In word and deed he rejected all forms of violence.

Foerster's ethically based pacifism was rooted in his happy and harmonious childhood. Both of his parents were bourgeois-liberal in their attitudes and involved in a broad range of intellectual and humanitarian social-reformist activities. In later life, he valued intellectual freedom so highly that, in keeping with his aversion to accepting titles and decorations, he declined an invitation to become a member of the Prussian Academy of Sciences because membership in such a corporate group might inhibit acting on his own inner beliefs. He accepted the title of Privy Councilor upon his retirement as director of the national Commission of Weights and Measures in 1885 only to avoid the impression that his retirement was the result of disciplinary proceedings against him.

Foerster's work as an astronomer played a role in his involvement in the peace movement. The more he engaged in a systematic ordering of the astral world, the more he sensed the narrowness and separateness of the lives of individuals. He considered gazing into the events of the universe and thinking about other worlds and different forms of life as particularly suited for strengthening the sense of earthly community and for advancing a peaceful world order. He considered the most notable task of astronomy to be the advancement of international attitudes and organizations, in order to avoid the cataclysm of war.

Foerster was one of the few German intellectuals to oppose the annexation of Alsace and Lorraine in 1871, believing it to be a contradiction of both the ''higher culture of Germany'' and the ''higher plane of international values.'' Always an opponent of Otto von Bismarck's politics of ''might makes right,'' Foerster believed that the annexation would injure the right of self-determination and would aggravate the future relations between Germans and Slavic peoples, who would join with ''a France continually estranged from us.''

In 1878 Foerster revealed his concern with social and ethical problems by publishing *Geistesfreiheit und Gesittung* (*Intellectual Freedom and Values*), first published anonymously. He concluded that only the cultivation of intellectual depth, of exacting and painstaking thought, and the inner emancipation resulting from that could solve the great social problems confronting mankind. He cautioned, however, that all true advancements also required the cultivation of an understanding and piety for all things from the past that ''still work and are valid.'' Foerster had only limited opportunity as an astronomer to develop these concepts on a broad scale, but in 1891–92 he supported the efforts of the German-American philosopher Felix Adler to spread his ethical culture movement to Europe. Adler's movement, which emphasized the need to look beyond differences of religious opinion, was enthusiastically received in Berlin intellectual circles. A recently enacted school ordinance, which had placed religious supervision at Prussian state schools under increased oversight, had sharpened religious differences, and had unleashed a general protest movement in which the ethical movement instigated by Adler took the lead. In addition to Foerster, *Moritz von Egidy and Georg von Gyzicki became involved as well as a number of other Berlin intellectuals. They prevailed upon Kaiser Wilhelm II to rescind the new school ordinance. On October 18, 1892, Foerster founded the Deutsche Gesellschaft für Ethische Kultur (German Society for Ethical Culture) (GfEK); it soon totalled more than 2,000 members. The following month, Foerster, along with *Bertha von Suttner, *Alfred H. Fried, *Richard Grelling, *Adolf Richter, *Franz Wirth, and others established the Deutsche Friedensgesellschaft (German Peace Society) (DFG).

As president of the GfEK, Foerster promoted the advancement and nurturing of truthfulness, justice, humaneness, and mutual respect, regardless of religious differences and political opinions. Unperturbed by numerous public attacks, especially from the churches, Foerster pressed for an overcoming of class, race, and national hatreds. Through numerous speeches in Germany and abroad he broadened the moral aspirations of the GfEK. In addition, he published several articles in *Ethische Kultur* condemning the arms race and promoting international arbitration. He strongly supported both the German and international peace movements, arguing that peace depended upon the all-pervasiveness of ethics within individuals and society. Rejecting any use of force, he warned German leaders that excessive harshness would only become a new tinder for violence among the lower classes. Believing that a supranational education was an indispensable prerequisite for peace, he and his son, Friedrich Wilhelm, attempted to found an international ethical academy in which the significant men and women of all cultural groups would be represented.

After he had come into contact with *Baron Paul d'Estournelles, Foerster helped disseminate the ideas of the "Conciliation internationale" in Germany. He became its honorary president. In October 1912 he presided, as the chairman of the Berlin local affiliate of the DFG, over the Fifth German Peace Congress in Berlin. Soon thereafter he participated in the Anglo German Rapprochement Conference in London. In addition, he worked on the council of the Carnegie Foundation.

In early October 1914, ninety-three of the most notable German intellectuals and artists issued an "Appeal to the World of Culture," declaring themselves solidly behind Prussian militarism and the war. To counter this document, Foerster, along with *Albert Einstein and Otto Buek signed *Georg Friedrich Nicolai's "Appeal to Europeans." Nicolai's appeal espoused peace and reconciliation between nations, condemned the widespread war enthusiasm, and opposed the fervid nationalism of the "intellectual elite."

After World War I Foerster became especially involved in the German-French Rapprochement. His efforts to organize and maintain peace as well as his commitment to the supranational values of German culture were to become, through his son Friedrich Wilhelm, a rich but neglected legacy for modern Germany.

Bibliography:

A. *Die Anfänge eines neuen sozialen Geistes* (Berlin, 1894); *Die Begründung einer Gesellschaft für Ethische Kultur* (Berlin, 1892); *Die Freude an der Astronomie. Eine kulturgeschichtliche Betrachtung* (Berlin, 1920); *Geistesfreiheit und Gesittung. Ein Beitrag zum sozialen Frieden* (Berlin, 1893); *Himmelskunde und Weissagung* (Berlin, 1901); *Die internationale Wirksamkeit des Judentums in der Vergangenheit und in der Zukunft* (Stuttgart, 1920); *Lebenserinnerungen und Lebenshoffnungen* (1832bis 1910) (Berlin, 1911); *Lebensfragen und Lebensbilder. Sozialethische Betrachtungen* (2 vols., Berlin, 1902); *Sammlung von Vorträgen und Abhandlungen* [Vier Folgen] (Berlin, 1876, 1887, 1890, & 1896); *Zur Ethik des Nationalismus und der Judenfrage* Berlin, 1893).

B. Friedrich Wilhelm Foerster, "Mein Vater. Eine Lebenserinnerung und ein Friedensprogramm," *Die Zeit* 1 (January 5, 1930); 5–6; Willy Jahn, "W. Foerster," *Neue Deutsche Biographie*, 5 (Berlin, 1961); 275–76; "Wilhelm Foersters 80. Geburtstag," *Die Friedenswarte*, 14 (November, 1912), 432.

Helmut Donat
Trans. by William L. Hopkins

FOGELKLOU NORLIND, Emilia Maria (20 July 1878, Simrishamn, Sweden—26 September 1972, Uppsala, Sweden). *Education*: certificate, Higher

Seminary for Women Teachers, 1899, Stockholm; theological degree, Uppsala Univ., 1909. *Career*: teacher, author, and lecturer.

At Uppsala University, Emilia Fogelklou worked with Professor (later Archbishop) +Nathan Söderblom, becoming the first woman in Sweden to receive a theological degree. She taught at Djursholms Samskola, a coeducational secondary school led by the liberal religious pacifist *Natanael Beskow. At The Hague International Congress of Women in April 1915, Fogelklou represented the Swedish Young Women's Christian Association and later became a lifelong member of the Women's International League for Peace and Freedom. For two years (1916–18), she taught at Birkagårdens Folkhögskola, a workers' college in Stockholm and then held a lectureship at the teacher training seminary in Kalmar.

In 1922 Fogelklou married the geographer and Dante-translator Arnold Norlind (1883–1929) and left teaching for writing and lecturing. In 1931 she became one of the first in Sweden to join the Society of Friends. Subsequently, she twice visited the United States and worked for a year at Woodbrooke, the English Quaker study center. During World War II she was involved in humanitarian service: helping emigrants at the Berlin Quaker office, representing British Friends in Finland after the Winter War, helping rehabilitate Polish concentration-camp victims, and working with Swedish volunteers in bombed sections of Hamburg. In addition she participated in the formation of two organizations which prepared young people for service in war-devastated areas.

Fogelklou wrote numerous articles and some thirty books dealing with Biblical interpretation, religious education, mental health, the psychology of religion, literary criticism, and social thought. The early history of women, medieval mysticism, and seventeenth-century Quakerism interested her particularly. In her writing she emphasized the experience of religious reality as the basis for peace and for genuine community transcending lines of nationality, class and sex. Her most lasting literary contribution is her autobiographical trilogy (*Arnold*, *Barhuvad*, *Resfärdig*, 1944–54).

Bibliography:

A. *Birgitta* (Stockholm, 1919); *Förkunnare* (Stockholm, 1915); *Form och strålning* (Stockholm, 1958); *Frans af Assisi* (Stockholm 1907, 1972); *Hat och människomekanisering* (Stockholm, 1943); *James Nayler. The Rebel Saint* (London, 1931); *Medan gräset gror* (Stockholm, 19ll); *William Penn* (Stockholm, 1935).

B. Elisabet Hermondsson, "Om Emilia Fogelklou," *Författarnas literaturhistoria* (Stockholm, 1978) III, 73–83; Erik Hj. Linder, *Resor i rum och tid* (Stockholm, 1956); Howard Lutz, "Emilia Fogelklou: Swedish Mystic and Friend," *Friends Journal*, 24 (July, 1978), 4–6; *Svenska män och kvinnor*, II, 544–45.

C. Emilia Fogelklous Samling, A–1, Women's History Collections, Göteborg University Library.

Howard T. Lutz

FORBECH, Ragnar (23 July 1894, Oslo, Norway—28 December 1975, Oslo). *Education*: Master of Theology, Univ. of Oslo, 1919. *Career*: minister, Vestre

Fredrikstad, 1919–26, Töyen Småkirke (non-conforming), 1926–32, Oslo Cathedral, 1947–64; director, Home for Congregational Sisters, 1932–47; journalist; pacifist.

Born into a middle-class family, Ragnar Forbech began his career as a conservative. While a student, he worked for the Conservative party (Høyre). Later, he became aware of social inequities and, as a minister in his first parish, he started opposing social injustice by writing articles in local and church newspapers. This led very early to his being called a communist, a term that frequently was used against him later. In his next parish, which was in a poor working-class district, he became a socialist and remained one for the rest of his life.

Forbech became a pacifist before World War II, and after the war he initiated his individual campaign for peace and justice. He became a member of the Norwegian branch of the International Fellowship of Reconciliation (IFOR) serving as its chairman from 1951 until 1967. He was deeply influenced by several great peace leaders, especially *Gandhi, *Toyohiko Kagawa, and Stanley Jones, the famous Christian-Indian missionary who became Forbech's close friend. Forbech believed in nonviolent action, and was deeply convinced that war was against the will of God and inconsistent with the life and teaching of Jesus Christ.

Forbech's paramount peace idea was that all mankind was one; all were brothers and sisters having the same Heavenly Father and all should live as one family on earth. The idea of brotherhood formed the basis of his life, and led to a very intensive engagement for peace and friendship with Christians on the other side of the Iron Curtain. As he cared about people in his own country, he also cared about Christians in Eastern Europe. Seven times he visited churches in the Soviet Union as their guest and preached in churches there. He also visited most of the other communist countries in Europe several times, and went to China once as part of a Norwegian peace delegation. In return, and in keeping with his idea of Christian brotherhood and his personal peace campaign, Forbech invited important church leaders from eastern Europe to Norway as his private guests. These included Metropolitan Nicolai of the Russian Orthodox Church in the Soviet Union and Alexander Karev, secretary-general of the Baptist Church in that country. These invitations, together with his own visits to communist countries, were sharply criticized by his fellow Norwegian churchmen. The most sharply criticized invitation was that to Metropolitan Nicolai in February 1956; he was not allowed to speak in Norwegian churches. The University of Oslo at first also refused to allow the Russian churchman to speak on its premises but later relented. The conflict between Forbech and his critics was fueled by the announcement of the award to him of the Lenin Peace Prize in December 1955 (he traveled to Moscow in the spring of 1956 to receive it). Not all reaction to his peace efforts took the form of censure. He received support from people who admired his courage and the philosophy of brotherhood which he exemplified in his own life.

Until his death Forbech took part in many peace and charitable activities. Besides serving as the longtime chairman of IFOR, he edited *Fredsbladet* (*Peace*

Magazine), from 1947 until 1966. For many years he served as vice-chairman of the Norges Kristne Arbeideres Forbund (Christian Workers' League of Norway). Forbech enjoyed preaching his ideas of peace and brotherhood to anyone who would listen. For nearly thirty years he preached almost every Saturday evening in the market place in Oslo. In 1967 he finally published his autobiography under the title *Prest på allfarvei og utenfor*. He also wrote several small booklets on Christians and the problem of peace: *Kristus og krigen* (1967) and *De kristne og krigen* (1968).

Bibliography:

A. *De kristne og krigen* (Oslo, 1968); *Kristus og krigen* (Oslo, 1967); *Prest på allfarvei og utenfor* (Oslo, 1967).

B. *Aschehoug og Gyldendals Store Norske leksikon* (Oslow, 1979), IV, 428; *Media, Cappenlens leksikon* (Oslo, 1977), 238; *Yngvar Ustvedt: Velstand og nye farer; Det skedde i Norge* (Oslo, 1979), II, 510.

Gerd Grønvold Saue

FOREL, Auguste (1 September 1848, Morges, Switzerland—27 July 1931, Yvorne/Vaud, Switzerland). *Education*: M.D., Univ. of Zurich, 1872. *Career*: assistant doctor to Bernhard von Gudden, Munich, 1872–78; professor of psychiatry and director of the university psychiatric clinic, Burghölzli, Zurich, 1879–98; after 1898, private scholar.

Auguste Forel's monistic view of life supposed that the functions of the brain were integrated into a unified whole, i.e. brain and psyche comprised one unit. He believed that all aspects of culture reflected the integrative function of the brain. If there were to be any cultural progress, therefore, the brain would have to be influenced in a way that would destroy the solipsistic impulses in man. In addition to eugenics, Forel advocated using education and enlightenment of the masses to accomplish his goal. He worked unflaggingly for decades, opposing alcoholism, advocating a new sexual morality, and espousing pacifism.

Although Forel did not join the peace movement until 1914, he had always been inclined toward pacifism and had supported peace before World War I within the Internationalen Ordens für Ethik und Kultur (International Order for Ethics and Culture), an organization founded by him in 1908. He announced his problem in a paper entitled "Die Vereinigten Staaten der Erde" ("The United States of the World") and in numerous other papers and newspaper articles during the war years. His program included: a union of all nations of the world, a supranational court of arbitration, disarmament of armies, and—with participation of women, who were to be granted political equality—development of civilian armies-of-peace. As a prerequisite for his program, Forel advocated establishment of a socialist social order consisting of agricultural and industrial cooperatives.

Forel condemned Germany's violation of Belgian neutrality as well as the crimes committed in the German colonies by the countries of the Entente. In

April 1915 he represented the Schweizerisches Komittee zum Studium der Grundlagen eines dauerhafte Friedensvertrages (Swiss Committee on the Study of a Lasting Peace Treaty) at a conference of European pacifists in The Hague. He was also active in the Bund für Menschheitsinteressen und Organisierung des menschlichen Fortschritts (League for the Interests of Mankind and Establishment of Human Progress) and its successor founded in 1917 the Komitee für Vorbereitung des Völkerbundes (Committee for Planning the League of Nations). Forel repeatedly stood up for conscientious objectors and demanded that they be offered alternative civilian service. In contrast to a majority of members of the Sozialdemokratischen Partei (Social Democratic party), of which he had been a member since 1916, Forel supported Switzerland's membership in the League of Nations in spite of many reservations.

Although Forel supported traditional demands of the bourgeois peace movement, including disarmament and a court of arbitration, his views on peace burst the confines of bourgeois pacifism, as can be seen in his position that peace must be secured through a fundamental change in social circumstances and in his support of conscientious objectors.

Bibliography:

A. *Genug zerstört! Wiederaufbauen* (Zurich, 1916); *Kulturbestrebungen der Gegenwart* (Munich 1910); *Ruckblick auf mein Leben* (Zurich, 1935); *Die Vereinigten Staaten der Erde* (Lausanne, 1914).

B. Alex von Muralt, *August Forel* (Zurich and Leipzig, n.d.) (Schweizerköpfe $^{4}/_{5}$); Jean Wagner, *Auguste Forel* (Lausanne, 1918); Hans H. Walser, *Introduction* to *August Forel, Briefe-Correspondance 1864–1927* (Bern, 1968); Annemarie Wettley, *August Forel* (Salzburg, 1953).

Urs Zwahlen
Trans. by Robert C. Reimer

FOSDICK, Harry Emerson (24 March 1878, Buffalo, NY—5 October 1969, Bronxville, NY). *Education:* B.A., Colgate Univ., 1900; B.D., Union Theological Seminary, 1904; M.A., Columbia Univ., 1908. *Career*: ordained minister of the Baptist Church, 1903; pastor of First Baptist Church, Montclair, NJ, 1904–15; associate minister, First Presbyterian Church, New York, 1918–25; pastor of Park Avenue Baptist Church (after 1930 known as the Riverside Church), 1926–46; instructor in homiletics (1908–15); and professor of practical theology (1915–46), Union Theological Seminary; author and speaker.

Harry Emerson Fosdick's significance as a peace leader derives from the fact that, as the most important and popular Protestant preacher of the interwar years, he refused to sanction war on Christian grounds. This was all the more important because he had written a responsible and eloquent defense of World War I. In the *Challenge of the Present Crisis* (1917), Fosdick reiterated the classic just war doctrine: warfare is evil and must be constrained, but under circumstances of social necessity it can be condoned insofar as it is conducted with restraint and toward a just end. The war had been thrust upon the world by German militarism, Fosdick thought, and Christians must accept responsibility for the war, its conduct, and its outcome—the ultimate abolition of warfare.

Fosdick was then an instructor in homiletics at Union Seminary and already had accommodated his mind to the intellectual revolutions of evolution, pragmatism, and biblical criticism. The year after the publication of his book he was appointed to the prestigious First Presbyterian Church of New York where he preached to often overflowing crowds until 1925. While there, he became the protagonist of the so-called modernists in a stormy struggle with fundamentalists. He finally resigned, only to be offered a position with the Park Avenue Baptist Church. The terms of Fosdick's acceptance led to the creation of the Riverside Church, a non-denominational community church adjacent to Union Seminary, which he served for twenty years. Although he was outspoken on social issues, his ministry emphasized pastoral care, worship, and instruction.

In addition to his command of preaching, widely studied and emulated, and his concept of a full-service church, Fosdick's leadership rested on his approach to the Bible, lucidly set forth in *The Modern Use of the Bible* (1924) and *A Guide to Understanding the Bible* (1938). He appropriated the achievements of higher criticism in a way responsible to authentic religious faith. With such a comprehensive base, his leadership in the cause of peace could not be dismissed lightly.

Fosdick, in fact, became increasingly prominent in this area. He supported United States admission to the League and the World Court and, with reservations, the outlawry of war. Moreover, reflection on World War I and the work of *Kirby Page led him to recant his support of war in 1923. He championed numerous peace initiatives and frequently spoke on platforms where he advocated international cooperation and strict neutrality. In 1934 he preached a sermon on "My Account with the Unknown Soldier" in which he vowed never again to support war. The sermon was widely distributed and placed him at the forefront of Christian pacifists. He maintained his position during World War II and retained his pulpit, too, because he recognized the obligation of serving equally those persons who fought, supported the war, or opposed it. He signed *Vera Brittain's attack on obliteration bombing and refused to glorify the war effort.

By World War II Fosdick had reversed his field. Whereas earlier he had argued that Christians must accept responsibility for warfare in order to redeem it, he now held that war could not be sanctioned on Christian grounds even if the society's cause seemed to be just. That a substantial portion of the Protestant churches had moved to this point also was in some significant measure due to his leadership.

Bibliography:

A. *The Challenge of the Present Crisis* (New York, 1916); "My Account with the Unknown Soldier," in *The Secret of Victorious Living: Sermons of Christianity Today* (New York, 1934).

B. Robert D. Clark, "Harry Emerson Fosdick; the Growth of a Great Preacher," in Lionel Crocker, *Harry Emerson Fosdick's Art of Preaching: An Anthology* (Springfield, IL, 1971), 128–85.

Charles Chatfield

FOSTER, Abigail Kelley (15 January 1810, Palham, MA—14 January 1887, Worcester, MA). *Education*: Quaker schools. *Career*: abolitionist and woman's rights lecturer.

Born into a Quaker family where she was imbued with the tenets of pacifism, Abby Kelley was converted to abolitionism in the early 1830s by reading *Willian Lloyd Garrison's *Liberator*. She was among the first to accept Garrison's radical doctrine of nonresistance. By 1838, although she carried on an active correspondence with *William Ladd of the American Peace Society and served as an officer of the Lynn (Massachusetts) Female Peace Society, she found herself becoming increasingly impatient with the moderate aims of the national peace movement, particularly its condemnation of aggressive war only.

At the Peace Convention called by the Garrisonians in September 1838, which led to the formation of the New England Non-Resistance Society, Abby Kelley was made a member of the business committee. *George Beckwith and other moderates from the American Peace Society, realizing that they could not control the meeting, marched out in a body using the pretext that they objected to women being afforded full membership in the convention and its committees.

Abby Kelley subscribed wholeheartedly to the principles of the New England Non-Resistance Society and agreed with Garrison that allegiance to all human government must be renounced. Only strict adherence to nonresistance principles, Kelley believed, would bring a permanent and peaceful end to slavery.

In May 1839 Abby Kelley began her long and tempestuous career as a lecturer and agitator in support of abolition and the cause of woman's rights. In her lectures she disclaimed all allegiance to church and state citing the clergy as the greatest obstacles to nonresistance. In the course of her travels she met and married *Stephen Symonds Foster, a radical abolitionist and active peace reformer, whose views matched her own. After their marriage in 1845 the two often traveled together and lectured as a team.

Stephen and Abby Foster represented the extreme radical wing of the abolitionist movement. By the 1850s they had come to accept the idea of civil war and slave insurrection and were preaching revolution and disunion. In 1856 their demand for an abolitionist third party led to a break with Garrison that never entirely healed.

Although Abby welcomed the approach of Civil War and considered the inevitable "desolation and destruction" which it would bring as a fit punishment for a nation "contaminated by slavery," she herself remained committed to nonresistance. She insisted that she would submit to martyrdom rather than resort to violence.

The Fosters had little hope that the Civil War would bring about lasting freedom for the slaves and insisted that only a constitutional amendment would insure permanent abolition. For the rest of her life Abby Kelley Foster remained personally committed to nonviolence even though she had come reluctantly to accept the necessity of violent means to achieve such desired ends as the abolition of slavery. During the period of Reconstruction, for example, she regarded federal military protection of the freedmen as essential, on the grounds that the government in Washington did not claim to be based on peace principles.

Bibliography:

B. Jane H. Pease, "The Freshness of Fanaticism; Abby Kelley Foster: An Essay in Reform," Ph.d. dissertation, Univ. of Rochester, 1969; NAW 1, 647–50.

C. Foster-Kelley Family Papers, American Antiquarian Society and Worcester Historical Society, both at Worcester, MA.

Deborah P. Clifford

FOSTER, Stephen Symonds (17 November 1809, Canterbury, NH—8 September 1881, Worcester, MA). *Education:* B.A., Dartmouth Coll., 1838; one year at Union Theological Seminary. *Career*: farmer and abolitionist.

Stephen S. Foster was one of the most uncompromising abolitionists and radical pacifists in pre-Civil War America. While a student at Dartmouth, he was jailed for refusing militia duty. In 1838 he became a charter member of the New England Non-Resistance Society, *William Lloyd Garrison's organization dedicated to Jesus Christ's injunction not to return evil for evil. Nonresistants refused to support any government based on force, a conviction to which Foster always remained true.

When Foster left school, he devoted himself to a host of reforms, all of which he subordinated to antislavery. Much of his agitation was directed toward the churches, and his tactics, repugnant even to some of his Garrisonian allies, were those of a martyr. He frequently interrupted religious services, denounced the church for its complicity in slavery, and called on the members to "come-out." Nonresistance was the best defense against the angry mobs he provoked wherever he traveled. He likened himself to St. Paul and took pride in the numerous beatings and jailings he suffered. In 1845 he married kindred spirit *Abby Kelley.

Like other nonresistants, Foster's commitment to abolitionism and radical pacifism gave rise to seemingly contradictory positions. He himself could never commit violence, nor could he support a government that employed violent means, but he often called on those who were not pacifists to strike out against their oppressors. So hostile was he to the Mexican War that he called on friends of justice to fight under the banner of Mexico. In the 1850s he advocated violent resistance to the Fugitive Slave Act, and in his pamphlet, *Revolution the only Remedy for Slavery*, he counseled slaves to rise against their masters. He applauded John Brown's raid, yet he was one of the few abolitionists to condemn the Lincoln Administration and the Civil War. At an antislavery rally in 1863 he expressed his willingness to lead an army into the South, equipped only with the power of God. Most reformers did not regret his retirement in the 1870s. An individual of such resolute convictions is most unsettling to those who are willing to compromise.

Bibliography:

A. *The Brotherhood of Thieves, or A True Picture of the American Church and Clergy* (New London, CT, 1843); *Revolution the Only Remedy for Slavery* (New York, 1855).

B. Joel Bernard, ''Authority, Autonomy, and Radical Commitment: Stephen and Abby Kelley Foster,'' *Proceedings of the American Antiquarian Society* 90 (October 1980), 347–86; Parker Phillsbury, ''Stephen Symonds Foster,'' *Granite Monthly* 5 (1882); Jane H. Pease and William H. Pease, ''The Perfectionist Radical: Stephen Symonds Foster,'' in Pease and Pease, *Bound With Them in Chains: A Bioqraphical History of the Antislavery Movement* (Westport, CT, 1972), 191–217.

C. Foster Papers, American Antiquarian Society, Worcester, Massachusetts and Worcester Historical Society.

Craig Phelan

FOURRIER, Marcel (11 August 1895, Batna, Algeria—23 April 1966, Paris). *Education*: lycée de Constantine, Algeria; studies at École libre des sciences politiques; degree, Faculté de droit de Paris; passed bar, 1927. *Career*: lawyer, journalist, editor, *Clarté*, 1919–28, founder and editor, *Liberté*, *Franc-Tireur*, and editor-in-chief, *Libération*, 1948–64.

Although Marcel Fourrier fought and was decorated in both world wars, he remained an internationalist and antimilitarist throughout his career. As a lawyer, he defended two Surrealists accused of insulting the army (''l'affaire Saint-Cyr''); as a journalist, he was an editor of *Clarté*, founded by *Henri Barbusse, *Romain Rolland, Anatole France and *Paul Vaillant-Couturier. Clarté was also the name of Barbusse's international peace movement which was supported by Maxim Gorky, V. I. Lenin, *Albert Einstein, Upton Sinclair, George Bernard Shaw, and +H. G. Wells, among others, and there were Clarté groups in several countries. The journal consistently condemned the war, the treaty of Brest-Litovsk, the treaty of Versailles, rearmament, Allied intervention in Russia, and France's invasion of the Ruhr. As late as 1927 it was still admonishing its readers never to forget the horrors of the Great War.

Taken over by its younger editors, Fourrier, Jean Bernier, and Georges Altmann, who had all joined the French Communist party, *Clarté*, became Marxist and published Lenin, Mayakovsky, Gorky, and A.V. Lunacharsky. But it never became an official party publication and it always retained its pacifist stance. In 1925, it published a special issue protesting the French colonial war with the Riff in Morocco, *Clarté contre la guerre de Maroc, contre l'impérialisme francais*. The issue also called upon intellectuals to condemn the war, which provoked a counter manifesto signed by much of the establishment and also provoked a threat of legal action. Fourrier and the others then wrote a joint manifesto against the war, *La Révolution d'abord et toujours*, with the Surrealists, the editors of *Philosophies*, a left-wing journal, and the editors of *Correspondance*, a Belgian

Surrealist review. Outside of the French Communist party, this was the only protest against the war in Morocco.

During World War II Fourrier was a Resistance leader and published clandestine newspapers. He also worked with Emmanuel d'Astier, the great Resistance hero who founded *Libération-sud*. After the war, with Georges Altmann, Fourrier became editor of d'Astier's newspaper, *Libération,* and later, d'Astier won the Lenin Peace Prize for *Libération*'s stand against fascism, imperialism, and the Cold War. The ideology of the paper changed when d'Astier became a Gaullist and, because it had been partially subsidized by the Communist party, it was obliged to cease publication in 1964. Fourrier and the rest of the former staff of *Libération* collectively denounced d'Astier's support of Charles de Gaulle in an open letter in *L'Humanité* and, in one of his last articles, Fourrier condemned de Gaulle's and Konrad Adenauer's notion of a federated Europe, saying that first Germany must disarm, then France and the rest of Europe, and then, "we can begin to make peace."

Bibliography:

B. André Breton, *Entretiens 1913–1952 avec André Parinaud* (Paris, 1952); Davis Caute, *Communism and the French Intellectuals* (New York, 1964); Victor Crastre, *Le Drame du surréalisme* (Paris, 1963); Maurice Nadeau, *The History of Surrealism* (New York, 1965); Pierre Naville, *La Révolution et les intellectuels: Que peuvent faire les surréalistes*? (Paris, 1926); Nicole Racine, "The Clarté Movement in France 1919–1921," *Journal of Contemporary History*, 2 (April, 1967), 195–208.

Helena Lewis

FRANK, Leonhard (4 September 1882, Würzburg, Germany—18 April 1961, Munich). *Education*: elementary school; apprenticeship as locksmith. *Career*: novelist and playwright.

Leonhard Frank's first novel, *Die Räuberbande*, published in 1914, reflects the critique of society that led him to socialism and opposition to war. A band of rebellious young men, bent on a revolutionary change of their society, nevertheless finally chooses comfortable bourgeois existence. It had all been merely a game, and only one of them, a poet and their intellectual leader, had taken the game seriously. In despair over the baseness and narrowness of the bourgeois world, he commits suicide. Those responsible for the tragedy are identified and indicted even more strongly in his next work, *Die Ursache*, an attack on repressive educational systems which appeared in 1915. Here a poet has murdered his former teacher, who, through his authority as an educator, supported by the parents and the church, had destroyed his soul. The agonies of the condemned man reveal a spiritless and loveless world of horror and madness. The only hope lies in a socialist revolution. The outbreak of war in 1914 seemed to confirm the views contained in the novels.

Frank's opposition to the war forced him to move to Switzerland. There he joined the circle of pacifists around *René Schickele. Frank's pacifist views found expression in the *Weisse Blätter*, edited by Schickele. But his most effective pacifist statement came with the publication of his next novel in 1917, *Der Mensch ist Gut*. In what is essentially a series of stories, the author shows the dead and living victims of war, of that organized and approved form of murder motivated by a desire for possession, for success, for power, and for authority. But not only the greedy are responsible, even the thoughtless waiter who gave toy guns to his son, even the mother, the bride, the war-widow, who all had believed in the "noble sacrifice on the altar of the fatherland" share the blame. No other novel of that day dealt with the war in an equally moving manner. Before the end of the war, the Socialist party in Germany had reproduced this forbidden book on newspaper stock and sent half a million copies of it to the front. The strange title of the work had been chosen after much thought, and was meant to express a hope rather than a present condition. Man wants to be good, if only he is given the opportunity.

With the end of the war Frank returned to Germany, now fully identified with left-wing socialist thinking and solutions. Yet he was too much of an individualist to become a member of the party or of any other organized political activity. Only briefly did his name become associated with the Group 1925 and the Society of Friends of the New Russia, neither of which presented an effective program of action. His statement in support of the establishment of a socialist society came in another novel, *Der Bürger*, which appeared in 1924. The novel was dedicated to the young generation with the admonition not to follow their elders into bourgeois society.

Frank's name was high on the Hitler regime's list of undesirables, and he had to flee Germany early in 1933. After living in Switzerland, France, and Portugal, Frank eventually found refuge in the United States. Although one of his novels was bought by Hollywood, he preferred to return to Germany after the war (1950) and settled in Munich to take stock of his life in a largely autobiographical novel, *Links wo das Herz ist*, published in 1952. The novel revealed his continued belief in the eventual victory of socialism over capitalism, and his optimism that a future atomic war was unlikely. Such a conflict would not only destroy the capitalist system, but would lead man back to barbarism. Before his death, Frank was honored by both the German Democratic Republic and the German Federal Republic.

Bibliography:

A. *Die Bürger* (Berlin, 1924); *Links wo das Herz ist* (Munich, 1952; Engl. tr., *Heart on the Left*, London, 1954); *Der Mensch ist Gut* (Potsdam, 1916; Eng. tr., *Man is Good*, London, 1930); *Das Ochsenfurther Männerquartett* (Leipzig, 1927; Engl. tr., *The Singers*, London, 1932); *Die Räuberbande* (Munich, 1914., Engl. tr., *The Robber Band*. London, 1928); *Die Ursache* (Leipzig, 1915, Engl. tr., *The Cause of the Crime*, London, 1928).

B. Harold von Hofe, "German Literature in Exile—Leonard Frank," *The German Quarterly*, 20 (March, 1947), 122–28; Therèse C. Mathey, "Das Sozialkritische in den Werken Leonhard Franks," Ph.D. dissertation, University of Southern California, 1968;

Edelgard H. Samorajczyk, "A Bibliography of Leonard Frank's Works," Ph.D. dissertation, University of Southern California, 1974.

Peter S. Seadle

FRANK, Louis (22 January 1864, Brussels, Belgium—25 July 1917, Brussels). *Education*: Athénée de Tournai; Collège communal de Malines; Université libre de Bruxelles; Dr. jur., Univ. of Bologna, 1887; School of Law, Univ. of Paris, 1891; Doctor of Public Law, Univ. of Brussels, 1892. *Career*: lawyer; legal adviser to the (Paris) Rothschild Bank; member, Belgian section of the Fédération internationale de l'arbitrage et de la paix 1889–90; founder and general secretary, Ligue belge du droit des femmes, 1892–93; vice president, Fédération féministe universelle.

Louis Frank, a pioneer of the Belgian feminist movement, argued the case for the absolute equality of the sexes with great courage. Besides struggling for the intellectual, legal, political, economic, and social emancipation of women, he also labored for improved organization of international relations. A partisan of world federation, he believed it was necessary to establish a center, a federal district for such an association, and proposed that Belgium occupy this position. Since Belgium was protected by perpetual neutrality and since it was located conveniently among European powers, he believed that this small nation could aid international relations by becoming the locus of offices of information, research, study and an archival repository—in short, the bureaucratic center—for the United States of the world. Prior to World War I, Belgium was the site of many international activities and approximately one third of the international organizations which existed had headquarters there. Nonetheless, Frank's project received little backing in that period.

Bibliography:

A. *Les Belges et la paix* (Brussels, 1905); *Essai sur la condition politique de femme* (Paris, 1893); *La Paix et le District fédéral du monde. L'Avenir de la Belgique au point du vue international* (Paris, 1910).

B. F. De Bueger Van Lierde, "Louis Frank, pionnier du Mouvement féministe belge" in *Revue Belge d'Histoire contemporaine*, IV, 3–4 (1973), 377–92; *L'Indépendance Belge*, 10 Aug., 1917.

C. Louis Frank Papers, Bibliothèque Royale de Bruxelles.

Nadine Lubelski-Bernard
Trans. by Sandi E. Cooper

FRANK, Ludwig (23 May 1874, Nonnenweier bei Kehl, Germany—3 September 1914, Baccarat, near Lunéville, France). *Education*: studies in law, universities of Freiburg and Berlin. *Career*: lawyer; editor, *Junge Garde*, 1906–8; member, Mannheim City Council, 1904–14, Baden Diet, 1905–14, and German Reichstag, 1907–14.

The son of a small businessman in an indigenous rural Jewish community, Ludwig Frank was moved by an instinctive sense of justice and compassion to identify himself with socialism. Never a systematic thinker, he was rather an inspiring orator and a flexible strategist whose immediate goal was to bring political democracy to Germany. In Baden, Frank was instrumental in creating the socialist-liberal coalition (Great Bloc) which controlled the Diet after 1905. He led the Baden Socialists to support the state budget. Condemned by the party's left and center for the budget vote, Frank, nevertheless, joined with the left in advocating the general strike to secure equal suffrage in Prussia. Accused of inconsistency, he responded that he was always for a "politics of action" and against a "politics of clichés.

His "politics of action" was demonstrated by his 1913 proposal for a conference of French and German parliamentarians. Responding to proposals in both nations for massive expansion of the army, Frank called for a binational conference of parliamentarians to support a one-year moratorium on military expansion. Since he desired neutral parliamentarians to extend the invitation, he contacted *Robert Grimm and other Swiss socialists. A multiparty committee of Swiss parliamentarians eventually extended the invitation, but Frank had to overcome German Socialist reluctance to participate with bourgeois parliamentarians. Then he worked with liberal colleagues, like *Conrad Haussmann, to attain adequate bourgeois representation from Germany. The conference met at Berne on May 10–12, 1913. Frank served on the binational committee which drafted the conference resolutions on arbitration and limitation of armaments.

After the conference Frank helped to organize the standing committee of Reichstag deputies for Franco-German reconciliation, chaired by Haussmann. A member of this committee, Frank attended the second conference at Basel (May 30, 1914). In his speeches of 1913 and 1914 he repeatedly held German military expansion responsible for provoking French military expansion; he argued that parliamentary government in Germany would lead to Franco-German reconciliation and that parliamentary government was therefore a "European necessity."

In July 1914 Frank sharply criticized Austrian policy toward Serbia, but responded with apparent fatalism to the outbreak of war. He advocated Socialist support for war credits. After the party voted support, Frank promptly volunteered for military service, informing friends that the international idea had failed and that "instead of a general strike we fight a war for Prussian suffrage." He fell in battle just inside France; a victim of the war he had attempted to prevent.

Frank's actions in August 1914 were not an aberration; they expressed his emotional commitment to the national community and his political flexibility. His internationalism was not sufficiently grounded in either intellectual analysis or moral principles for him to remain detached. German socialism, however, lost a brilliant leader who had just entered his political prime.

Bibliography:

A. *Aufsätze, Reden und Briefe*, ed. by Hedwig Wachenheim (Berlin, 1924); *Die bürgerlichen Parteien des deutschen Reichstags* (Stuttgart, 1911).

B. Sally Grünebaum, *Ludwig Frank* (Heidelberg, 1924); *Biographisches Lexikon des Sozialismus* (Hanover, 1960); *Neue Deutsche Biographie*, (Berlin, 1961), V, 343.

James C. Hunt

FRANTZ, Gustav Adolf Constantin (12 September 1817, Börnecke near Halberstadt, Kingdom of Prussia—2 May 1891, Blasewitz near Dresden, Germany). *Education*: passed staatsexamen, Univ. of Berlin, 1840; doctorate, Univ. of Jena, 1841. *Career*: free lance writer; Prussian civil servant; political author.

A mathematician by training, Constantin Frantz showed an early interest in the philosophy of German idealism, especially Friedrich Wilhelm Schelling. During the 1840s he took to political writing. His nimble pen and conservative outlook earned him favor with the Prussian government, which offered him a civil service career. Serving briefly, Frantz decided to pursue his goals independently, especially after an exchange of views with Otto von Bismarck in the 1850s revealed divergent opinions about the future of Prussian politics. During the following decade Frantz wrote prolifically and imaginatively in defense of a reformed German confederation. The defeat of Austria in 1866, and more so the founding of the second German Empire under Prussian leadership in 1871, thwarted these hopes, and he became one of the most acerbic and vocal critics of Bismarckian politics during the remainder of his life.

Frantz occasionally tried to join forces with some of the *grossdeutsche* (great-German) or particularist adversaries of Bismarck, but their ideas proved too heterogeneous, and their cause politically too weak, to allow substantial action. Brief acquaintances with pacifists like *Jacques Novicow or Ludwig von Bernuth did not bear any better fruit. The author's popularity gradually waned, and he died impoverished and bitter. After both world wars the search for a new order for Germany awakened a discussion of his proposals, but this interest did not last.

A good deal of the attention Frantz received was due to the apparent attractiveness of his federative plan. Denouncing Bismarck's creation as a militaristic and soulless entity which constituted a breach with the past and commanded no future, he proposed a European federation that would reembody the universality as well as the diversity of the medieval Empire. Europe could only retain its importance, he argued, if the states and nations comprising it ceased quarrelling among themselves. It was the German task, by virtue of historical tradition and geographical location, to function as mediator and link. He envisioned Prussia maintaining her north-eastward thrust by associating with the Baltic countries, Poland, and Scandinavia; Austria federating with the Balkan peoples; the west German states forming their own alignment, to which the Netherlands and Switzerland might adhere. These three major federations would then combine into a stronger whole, which the remaining European nations might wish to join and which could act as a counterpoise to the United States and Russia, the upcoming world powers.

Frantz knowingly advocated German leadership. Association, however, would not come through coercion, but through the voluntary decision of the various members. Historical logic and the obvious advantages of adherence were to be the driving forces. Frantz' scheme may have implied a *pax Germanica*, i.e. German hegemony, but like J. G. Herder he believed in the right of each ethnic group to live according to its own traditions, customs, and insights. It did not occur to him that, in an age of nationalism, his concept must essentially remain a utopian scheme.

Bibliography:

A. *Briefe*, ed. by Udo Sautter and Hans Elmar Onnau (Wiesbaden, 1974); *Der Föderalismus als das leitende Princip* (Mainz, 1879); *Die Weltpolitik unter besonderer Bezugnahme auf Deutschland* (Chemnitz, 1882–83); *Die Wiederherstellung Deutschlands* (Berlin, 1865).

B. P.F.H. Lauxtermann, *Constantin Frantz: Romantik und Realismus im Werk eines politischen Aussenseiters* (Groningen, 1978); Eugen Stamm, *Konstantin Frantz' Schriften und Leben: Erster Teil: 1817–1856* (Heidelberg, [1907]); Eugen Stamm, *Konstantin Frantz 1857–1866. Ein Wort zur deutschen Frage* (Stuttgart, 1930); *Allgemeine Deutsche Biographie*, 48 (1904): 716–720; *Biographisches Wörterbuch zur deutschen Geschichte* (2nd ed., Munich, [1973]) I, 718–19; *Neue Deutsche Biographie* (1961), V, 353.

Udo Sautter

FRIED, Alfred Hermann (11 November 1864, Vienna—5 May 1921, Vienna). *Education*: gymnasium and self-taught. *Career*: book dealer and newspaper correspondent, 1887–1903; editor, *Die Friedenswarte*, 1899–1921; pacifist journalist.

Alfred Fried was, along with *Bertha von Suttner, the leading figure in the central European peace movement in the era before the First World War. He began his career in the movement as the disciple of Suttner, with whom he helped found the Deutsche Friedengesellschaft (German Peace Society) in Berlin in 1892. An irascible and impatient man, Fried was more comfortable, however, in the independence of journalism than as an officer in a peace society. He soon broke with the German Peace Society, and in 1903 he returned to Vienna, where he remained until the war. In 1899 he began to edit his own journal, *Die Friedenswarte*, which soon enjoyed a reputation as one of the most respected peace journals in the world.

Fried's principal contribution to the peace movement was to forge, from disparate intellectual sources, an ideological synthesis which, because it claimed scientific certainty for its conclusions, appealed broadly to pacifists in Germany and Austria until the First World War utterly destroyed its credibility. Fried sought to purge pacifism of its ethical moment, which had been central to his own thinking as well as to that of Bertha von Suttner and most other pacifists in central Europe. He argued that the inexorable evolution of society and technology, the progressive development of commercial and cultural interdependence among the advanced nations of the world, was both making warfare impossible and creating the foundations for an international political order in which all disputes would be peacefully adjudicated. Peace, anchored in a stable international organization, was hence inevitable. Fried's "scientific pacifism" was entirely unoriginal; it betrayed the influence of the Russian sociologist *Jacques Novicow and several other thinkers (including Karl Marx). Fried was nonetheless a skilled and tireless popularizer of the doctrine, which he purveyed in his *Handbuch der Friedensbewegung*, which first appeared in 1905, in countless other books and articles, and in his journal.

The popularity of "scientific pacifism" in central Europe betrayed the difficulties that Fried and other pacifists encountered in the militarized societies in which they tried to promote arbitration and arms limitation. Their many critics attacked them as naive idealists who had failed to recognize the hard realities of international politics and the essential role of warfare in human affairs. Although Fried's theories could not convince most of the peace movement's critics, they at least provided pacifists with a reply and psychological reassurance in the belief that the reforms pacifists advocated were realistic because inevitable. More significantly, Fried's theories did bring the peace movement a measure of respectability in some academic circles. In particular, international lawyers found in "scientific pacifism" a plausible sociological analysis of the advance of their own discipline. It was testimony to Fried's influence that a number of German international lawyers formed the Verbond für international Verständigung (Association for International Understanding) in 1911, in the conviction that the growth of international legal ties could provide a basis for conciliation.

The peace movement remained nonetheless considerably weaker in Germany and Austria than in the western democracies. That pacifism enjoyed even the modicum of influence it did was due in large part to the work of Fried. For his efforts he received the Nobel Peace Prize in 1911 and, in 1913, an even more gratifying award—an honorary doctorate from the university in Leyden, a distinction that seemed to confirm the belief that he, though himself an uneducated man, had created a theory that deserved the status of science. The outbreak of war a year later marked Fried's failure. Although he initially supported the war effort of the Central Powers, he fled Vienna for exile in Zurich, where he continued to publish his Journal during the war. The peace treaties brought further disappointment, for Fried was convinced they were unjust. Nor did the League of Nations fulfill his hopes for an effective and just international organization. A tired and bitter man, he died suddenly in Vienna in May 1921.

Bibliography:

A. *Handbuch der Friedensbewegung*. (Vienna and Leipzig, 1905; 2d ed., 2 vols., Berlin and Leipzig, 1911–13); *Mein Kriegs-Tagebuch* (4 vols., Zurich, 1918–20); *Unter der weissen Fahne: Aus der Mappe eines Friedensjournalisten* (Berlin, 1901).

B. Roger Chickering, *Imperial Germany and a World Without War: The Peace Movement and German Society 1892–1914* (Princeton, 1975); Rudolf Goldscheid, ed., *Alfred H. Fried: Eine Sammlung von Gedenkblättern* (Leipzig, 1922); *Oesterreichisches Biographisches Lexikon, 1850–1950* (1957), I, 361–2; Hans Wehberg, "Alfred Hermann Fried," *Neue deutsche Biographie*, V, 441–42; NYT, May 7, 1921, 11.

C. Papers of Alfred Fried, United Nations Library, Geneva.

Roger Chickering

FRIEDRICH, Ernst (25 February 1894, Breslau, Germany—2 May 1967, Le Perreux sur Marne, France). *Education*: primary school; printer's apprenticeship; drama lessons. *Career*: editor, *Freie Jugend*. 1919–26, *Die Waffen nieder*, 1921–22, *Die Schwarze Fahne*, 1925–29; antimilitarist author, public speaker, activist, and organizer of art exhibitions.

In keeping with his proletarian origins, Ernst Friedrich rose to political consciousness during World War I as a supporter of the Revolutionäre Arbeiterjugend (Young Revolutionary Workers) [later Freie sozialistische Jugend (Free Socialist Youth)] which, unlike the German Social Democratic party, opposed the war and became a revolutionary force in 1918. After the war, Friedrich declared himself a libertarian socialist (anarchist) and founded his own proletarian youth organization, Freie Jugend (Free Youth) (1919–26). In all this, Friedrich showed little theoretical and analytical ability. His strength lay in articulating and organizing the protest of disillusioned youth against the world and wars of their elders.

Friedrich's anarchism was more an expression of personal feeling and a utopian desire for change than the result of rational considerations. Its main components were antimilitarism, a refusal to cooperate with either the state or the leftist parties, anti-authoritarianism (a rejection of all tutelage by the state and church), and anti-materialism. The failure of the political revolution in 1918–19 led Friedrich to seek the origins of authority and militarism in the individual's consciousness and schooling. The reformation of education, therefore, became his goal and the spread of antimilitarist propaganda among young people the central activity of the Freie Jugend. Friedrich edited a reader and a series of nonmilitary adventure stories for children, and advocated nonmilitary toys, and the abolition of corporal punishment in the school.

His pedagogic endeavors led to various propagandistic activities as an orator, organizer of art exhibitions, publisher, and writer. But Friedrich's position of exaggerated moral appeal often weakened his case. The climax of all his educational efforts undoubtedly was the foundation of the first International Anti-War Museum in Berlin (1925), the most striking photographic documents of which he collected in picture books. Translations of these books were widely circulated by the International Federation of Trade Unions. Friedrich thus invented the "weapon" of documentary "shots" which expressed more than words the true and shocking face of modern technical warfare. In 1930 he was proposed as a candidate for the Nobel Peace Prize by the Swedish Peace Society.

With the rise of National Socialism, the limits of Friedrich's methods of enlightenment became all too obvious. He hoped and worked in vain for a united front of all opponents of war, bourgeois and communist alike. The Nazis destroyed his museum (which was already financially ruined as a result of the weakening of pacifist support in Germany in the late 1920s) and almost killed Friedrich himself. The Nazi invasion of Belgium quickly brought an end to the antiwar museum which had been reconstructed in Brussels. Eventually the war turned Friedrich, the antimilitarist, into an activist in uniform with the French resistance. There followed after World War II several futile attempts to resume his old propagandistic activities which left him disillusioned and depressed. Friedrich had outlived his chance of influencing the peace movement, this chance being clearly limited to the early 1920s and the framework of the revolutionary spiritual uprising of the youth movement and the pacifist longings of the proletariat after World War I.

Bibliography:

A. *Das Anti-Kriegsmuseum* (Berlin 1926); *Festung Gollnow* (Berlin, 1932); *Krieg dem Kriege*! (vol. 1, Berlin 1924, vol. 2, Berlin, 1926; reprint vol.1, Frankfurt, 1980); *Nie wieder Krieg*! (Amsterdam, 1929); *Vom Friedens-Museum . . . zur Hitler-Kaserne. Ein Tatschenbericht über das Wirken von Ernst Friedrich und Adolf Hitler* (St. Gallen, Geneva, 1935; reprint, Berlin, 1978).

B. Ulrich Linse: *Die anarchistische und anarcho syndikalistische Jugendbewegung 1919–1933* (Frankfurt 1976); Ulrich Linse, ed.: *Ernst Friedrich zum 10. Todestag* (Berlin, 1977).

Ulrich Linse

FROMM, Erich (23 March 1900, Frankfurt, Germany—18 March 1980, Muralto, Switzerland). *Education*: studies at the Univ. of Munich, Institute of the German Psychoanalytic Society, Psychoanalytic Institute (Berlin), and Univ. of Frankfurt; Ph.D., Univ. of Heidelberg,1922. *Career*: lecturer, social psychology, Institute for Social Research, Frankfurt, 1929–32; lecturer, International Institute for Social Research, Columbia Univ., 1934–39, 1940–41; faculty member, Bennington Coll., 1941–50; lecturer, American Institute of Psychoanalysis, 1941–42, and New School for Social Research, 1946–56; member and chair of faculty William Alanson White Institute for Psychiatry, Psychoanalysis and Psychology, 1945–50; Terry Lecturer, Yale Univ., 1949–50; professor of psychoanalysis, National Univ. of Mexico, 1951–77; professor, Michigan State University, 1957–61, adjunct professor of psychology, New York Univ., 1961–77; director, Mexican Institute for Psychoanalysis, Mexico City, 1962–74; psychoanalyst, educator, social philosopher, and author.

Trained in Germany as a psychoanalyst, Erich Fromm became a leading social critic in mid-twentieth-century America. He blended the insights of Sigmund Freud, Karl Marx, and Eastern religions into a life-affirming alternative to war and destruction.

Born in 1900, Fromm grew up in Frankfurt in an orthodox Jewish middle class family. Through his early religious training, he acquired an exhilarating vision of human redemption—a vision reinforced by his later readings in Marxism and Buddhism. The hysteria and hatred he witnessed during World War I shocked Fromm, and he turned to psychology, at least in part, to better comprehend the hidden motives behind political events. By the late 1920s, he was a practicing Freudian psychoanalyst, a socialist, and a lecturer at Frankfurt's famed Institute for Social Research.

With the Nazi seizure of power in 1933, Fromm emigrated to the United States, more convinced than ever of the need to apply critical intelligence to the problems of humanity. In a flood of widely-read books and articles, he argued that destructive human behavior was not biologically determined; rather, it reflected a pathological character structure. Under healthy conditions, human beings became biophilous (or life-affirming)—loving, compassionate, and creative. Under alienating, life-denying conditions, however, human character became sadistic (emphasizing control) or necrophilic (hating life itself). Both capitalist and communist societies, he contended, were mechanistic, materialistic, and managerial. Herein lay the real cause of the Soviet-American confrontation, for an explosive combination of projection, paranoia, and despair discouraged sane thinking and edged the world toward nuclear holocaust.

In line with this analysis, Fromm helped to organize the National Committee for a SANE Nuclear Policy and, through his writings, outlined concrete steps for dealing with the immediate dangers of the Cold War. He advocated universal, controlled disarmament; mutual recognition of the status quo by the great powers; the development of a neutral bloc; and the strengthening of the United Nations. To redirect human behavior on a deeper level, however, he championed what he called "humanistic communitarian socialism," based upon love, human solidarity, justice, productive work, the unfolding of reason, democratic participation, popular art, and secular ritual.

Bibliography:

A. *The Anatomy of Human Destructiveness* (New York, 1973); *May Man Prevail*? (Garden City, NY, 1961); *The Revolution of Hope* (New York, 1968); *The Sane Society* (New York, 1955).

B. Don Hausdorff, *Erich Fromm* (New York, 1972); Edward S. Tauber and Bernard Landis, "Erich Fromm: Some Biographical Notes," Tauber and Landis, eds., *In the Name of Life* (New York, 1971), x-xiv.

Lawrence S. Wittner

FRY, Anna Ruth (4 September 1878, Highgate, England—26 April 1962, London). *Education*: at home. *Career*: treasurer, Boer Home Industries Commission, 1906; honorable general secretary, Friends Relief Commission, 1914–25; chair, Russian Famine Relief Fund, 1921–25; honorable secretary, National Council for the Prevention of War, 1926–27; treasurer, War Resisters International, 1936–47; author and peace activist.

A. Ruth Fry came from a distinguished Quaker family. Her father, Sir Edward Fry, was a lawyer and judge, who gained an international reputation after his appointment to The Hague Tribunal in 1907 as a skilled negotiator. A. Ruth Fry worked for peace both as an activist and as a writer. Between 1914 and 1924, she was the honorable general secretary of the Friends Relief Commission. She toured the war zones as a traveling commissioner and described relief work in *A Quaker Adventure* (1926). Refugees and others who had suffered the ravages of war were helped by volunteers many of whom were conscientious objectors. American Quakers and members of other denominations also volunteered to work either in the field or at the London offices. The catalyst that brought them together was a committee organized by English Quakers. Their goal was to translate ideals into action by fostering love and understanding even under the most adverse conditions.

In 1921 Fry continued her activist role when she became the first chairperson of the Russian Famine Relief Fund. She also became involved in the women's peace movement, serving as honorable secretary of the National Council for the Prevention of War (1926–27) and treasurer of the London branch of the War Resisters' International (1936–47). The pacifist journal *Reconciliation* appointed her to its editorial board in 1935.

Although in poor health, Fry met the heavy demands of these volunteer positions. She continued to write as well. Her *Memoir of Emily Hobhouse* (1929) revealed Fry's admiration for a good friend who, like herself, lived a life dedicated to the cause of peace. They had become acquainted during the Boer War when Fry was treasurer of the Boer Home Industries Commission and Hobhouse was honorary secretary of the Women's Branch of the South African Conciliation Committee. Knowing her life was an exemplary one, Fry, in telling her story, hoped that others would adopt her ideals. In *Quaker Ways* (1933) she discussed the historical development of Quaker customs and beliefs. Besides her six books, Fry's many tracts brought the message of peace as it related to specific issues. In *Victories Without Violence* (1937) and *More Victories Without Violence* (1938), Fry offered historical examples of international disputes that had been resolved without military action. An alternative to war was found because the parties involved summoned the courage to settle matters peacefully. In *An International Force* (1934), she gave her reasons for not favoring the use of military force or sanctions to keep the peace. The task of the League of Nations, she believed, was to summon the moral judgement of the world to stop the warring nations; they would then cooperate with one another ending wars forever.

Fry's life exemplified the idealistic spirit that is synonymous with the Quaker committment to worthy causes. She continued to write almost to the time of her death, tirelessly explaining why the pacifist position was relevant to the conflicts of the times. In the tradition of her ancestors, hers was a life of testimony dedicated to the ideals of peace and love.

Bibliography:

A. *The Atlantic Charter* (Glasgow, 1941); *Christianity or War* (London, 1931); *The Effect of Disarmament* (London, 1935); *Everyman's Affair: A Plea for a Sane Peace* (London, 1941); *Force or Failure* (Saxmundham, 1938); *An International Force* (London, 1934); *The Laws of* Peace (London, 1935); *More Victories Without Violence* (Suffolk,1938); *A Quaker Adventure: The Story of Nine Years' Relief and Reconstruction* (London, 1926); *Quaker Ways* (London, 1933); *Ruth's Gleanings: An Anthology of Prose and Poetry* (London, 1943); *Sanctions Junction: Change For Peace*. (London, 1936); *An Unarmed World* (London, 1954); *Victories Without Violence* (Saxmundham, 1937); *War: Its Causes and Cure* (York, n.d.); *The Whirlpool of War: Collected Addresses* (London, 1939).

B. *The Friend* (London), May 4, 1962.

C. A. Ruth Fry Papers, Swarthmore College Peace Collection, Swarthmore, PA.

Edith F. Hurwitz

FUČÍK, Julius (23 February 1903, Prague, Bohemia, Austrian Empire [now Czechoslovakia]—8 September 1943, Berlin-Plötzensee Prison, Germany). *Education*: Realschule, Pilsen, 1914–21; studied in the Faculty of Philosophy, Univ. of Prague. *Career*: journalist, literary critic, and political writer.

Julius Fučík's literary activity began in high school. The World War I years in Pilsen, where his father worked in the Škoda armaments works, were hard and exciting times. He and thousands of others had to stand in line for hours for a piece of bread. Hundreds were killed in an explosion of an ammunition dump near Pilsen. Fučík saw hunger riots of workers and soldiers shooting into the crowd. In addition, he witnessed the plundering of stores by the hungry mob and the grief of friends and acquaintances over the loss of a loved one in the war. He heard many stories about the horrors of the war. All of this made a deep and lasting impression, and Fučík was inspired to report the events as he perceived them. In 1919, when he was sixteen years old, he joined the Czechoslovak Social Democratic party. After the establishment of the Czechoslovak Communist party in 1921 he entered its ranks.

In the beginning Fučík wrote reviews for the Communist newspaper in Pilsen and then contributed articles to the student newspaper *Avantgarda* (1925) in Prague. His journalistic career started in earnest when he was called upon to edit the progressive periodical *Kmen* (1927–29). In 1928 he was appointed editor-in-chief of the well-known progressive weekly periodical *Tvorba*, a position which he held with a few interruptions until 1938. In 1929 he started his collaboration with the principal newspaper of the Communist party, *Rudé právo*, and spent the years 1934 to 1936 as its correspondent in the Soviet Union.

As newspaperman and editor, Fučík enlivened his reports with dramatic accounts of every day life, of current political events, and of the tragic effects of the economic crisis of the thirties. He wrote about the threat of war and the dangers of fascism and exhorted the people to care for their fellow man. Toward the end of the thirties and after the Nazi occupation of all of Czechoslovakia in March 1939, he passionately defended the Czech heritage and the Czech people stressing a genuine patriotism that was the opposite of chauvinistic nationalism. Fučík's articles and essays were nonpartisan and free from dogma. He praised moral fortitude, humanism, and peace, and stigmatized the cruelty of man to man. In 1939 Fučík was offered the position of editor of the cultural section of the National Socialist (Nazi) inspired newspaper *Český dělnik*. He refused, noting that what he would write could not be printed and what was supposed to be printed he would not write. Beginning in the summer of 1940 Fučík lived in hiding in Prague. There, despite the fact that the Gestapo was looking for him, he published several illegal communist newspapers. Finally the Germans caught up with him in April 1942 and he was arrested. After having been severely tortured he was transferred, half dead, from the Gestapo headquarters to the Pankrác prison in Prague. He remained there until the summer of 1943 after which he was moved to Berlin-Plötzensee where he was executed after a sham trial.

The year Fučík spent in Pankrác was a time of frequent physical and mental torture and of constant uncertainty whether he would live or die. There, in this most trying stage of his life, he established a monument to moral greatness and human courage and compassion. His *Reportáž psaná na oprátce* (*Notes from the Gallows*) is Fučík's most significant work. Translated into seventy languages, it had an extraordinary echo in the world. It is a dramatic exposé of his encounter with the brutality and tactics of the Gestapo. The *Notes* reveal Fučík's strength of will, optimism, and love of life. In the face of unspeakable horrors, Fučík affirmed the indestructibility and resiliency of life.

Bibliography:

A. *Božena Němcová bojujicí* (Prague, 1940); *Dílo J. Fučíka*, Gusta Fučíkova and Ladislaus Štoll, eds. (12 vols., Prague, 1945–63); *Přijde nám Ruda ármáda na pomoc*? (Prague, 1938); *Reportáž psaná na oprátce* (Prague, 1947) Eng. trans., *Notes from the Gallows*, New York, 1948); *Vyzemi Kde zítra znamená vĉera* (Prague, 1932).

B. Gusta Fučíkova, *Vzpomínky na J. Fučíka* (Prague, 1961); *Československý Svět*, 6 (1963) 3; *Nová Mysl*, 2 (1963); 120–30; *Slovník českých spisovatelů* (Prague, 1964): 107–10; *Slovník českých spisovatelů beletristuaů* (Prague, 1956): 106–10.

Fred Hahn

G

GALTIER-BOISSIÈRE, Jean (26 December 1891, Paris—21 January 1966, Paris). *Education*: École alsacienne; licence ès-lettres and diplôme d'études supérieures, Univ. of Paris. *Career*: artist, journalist, novelist, and editor.

Before World War I, Jean Galtier-Boissière enjoyed the pleasant life of the son of a successful physician and an artistic mother, receiving an excellent education at the best Parisian schools. Although he proved rebellious as a young man and demonstrated literary and artistic ability, nothing indicated that he would later become one of France's most celebrated pacifists. Called up for regular military service in 1911, Galtier-Boissière went to war enthusiastically in the summer of 1914. He took part in the battles of Charleroi and the Marne, quickly discovering the bloodshed and destruction of modern war. Until illness forced him from the front lines to duty in the rear, he served with distinction. Already in August 1915 he founded a newspaper for soldiers entitled *Le Crapouillot*, military slang for a trench mortar. Irreverent in its humor and graphic in its depiction of combat, it was often censored but gained popularity with the troops for its honesty.

With the end of the conflict, Galtier-Boissière undertook to publish *Le Crapouillot* as an illustrated magazine of literary and artistic opinion, with many of his wartime comrades as collaborators. Its attractive format, including drawings by Galtier-Boissière himself, and brisk style established its place on the Parisian scene. But the magazine only attained notoriety with its special issues on the war, using vivid pictures and text to show the true face of a conflict that had taken millions of lives. The success of the number on the ''unknown war'' (which sold 110,000 copies) led him to publish an entire series on the catastrophe of 1914–18 and the fragile postwar peace. In succeeding issues *Le Crapouillot* exposed the economic causes of war and denounced the profiteers who benefited from it at the expense of the common man. Early in 1939 Galtier-Boissière issued a special number on the Czech crisis, criticizing those politicians and journalists who had sought to push France into a new and terrible conflict. The magazine was suspended in September, however, because of the strict censorship imposed by the Edouard Daladier government. Except for a brief stint as columnist on the independent newspaper *Aujourd'hui* in the last months of 1940, Galtier-Boissière remained silent for the duration of the war, tending to his bookstore in the Latin Quarter.

After the Liberation, which he welcomed enthusiastically, Galtier-Boissière published four volumes of the journal he had been keeping since 1940, chronicling the events of the German occupation and the immediate postwar world, which promised only new tensions. In 1948 he resumed publication of *Le Crapouillot*, devoting the first five numbers to World War II and all its cruelty. He continued to publish until the mid–1960s, when age forced him to sell his beloved magazine and retire to his country home. Illness ended his long career soon afterward. By his flamboyant behavior and literary talent, Galtier-Boissière helped to shape French opinion against war during the two decades that followed the Treaty of Versailles.

Bibliography:

A. *La Bonne vie* (Paris, 1927); *La Fleur au fusil* (Paris, 1928); *Un Hiver à Souchez* (Paris, 1917); *Loin de la Rifflette* (Paris, 1921); *Mémoires d'un parisien* (3 vols., Paris, 1960–63); *Mon journal dans la drôle de paix* (Paris, 1946); *Mon journal dans la grande pagaïe* (Paris, 1950); *Mon journal depuis la libération* (Paris, 1945); *Mon journal pendant l'occupation* (Paris, 1944).

B. "Jean Galtier-Boissière," *Le Crapouillot*, no.42 (October, 1958) and no. 66 (May, 1965); *Le Dictionnaire des contemporains*, I, 48–49.

James Friguglietti

GANDHI, Mohandas Karamchand (2 October 1869, Porbandar, India—30 January 1948, New Delhi, India). *Education*: Inner Temple, London, 1888–91. *Career*: lawyer, leader of movement for Indian rights in South Africa, 1893–1914; leader of Indian independence and social justice movements, 1915–48.

The foremost theorist and practitioner of active nonviolence, Mohandas Gandhi was the youngest son of the prime minister of the small coastal state of Porbandar, a Hindu of the Vaishya (Merchant) caste who spoke the Gujarati language. After the death of his father in 1885, Gandhi was sent to London to become a barrister at the Inner Temple, completing his studies in 1891. There he acquired not only legal training and a mastery of the English language, but also acquaintance with Indian nationalists and English theosophists and vegetarian reformers.

After an unsuccessful attempt to establish a legal practice in Bombay and Rajkot, Gandhi accepted the offer of a Porbandar Muslim firm to settle a lawsuit in South Africa. Indians had been recruited for labor in South Africa since 1860, and these had been followed by a small merchant migration, largely from Bombay and Gujarat. Gandhi arrived in South Africa in May 1893, intending to remain for one year, but in fact did not leave permanently until 1914. After settling the lawsuit by compromise, he opened a legal practice in Durban, and being the first Indian lawyer in the colony did very well financially. He formed the Natal Indian Congress as a community organization in 1894 and emerged as a spokesman for the Indian community. His letters and pamphlets on Indian rights made him prominent, and upon his return from India in 1897 he was mobbed by whites and nearly killed. He urged upon the Indians a program of English education, English sanitary habits, and community responsibility. To exemplify the principle of responsibility, he formed an Indian volunteer ambulance corps for the Boer War in 1899, and again in the Zulu Rebellion of 1906. He also did volunteer nursing in a hospital.

After the Boer War, he attempted to settle in India but was recalled due to Lord Alfred Milner's imposition of harsh new restrictions on Indian residence and trading rights in the conquered Transvaal Colony. He established himself in Johannesburg in 1903 and set up a newspaper, *Indian Opinion*. The next year he purchased a farm at Phoenix station, near Durban, as a residence and workshop for the interracial staff, where they could practice "the ideas of Ruskin and Tolstoy combined with strict business principles." Increasing restrictive legislation led on September 11, 1906 to a public mass declaration by Johannesburg Indians of refusal to obey a new registration law, inaugurating the nonviolent civil disobedience for which Gandhi soon invented the name *Satyagraha* (truth-force). He was jailed three times in 1908–9, the last time at hard labor, and, when he attempted a compromise settlement with General J. C. Smuts, he was murderously assaulted by Indians who felt betrayed. The turn to principled lawbreaking came only after years of skilled but unavailing petitions and court challenges which failed to stem the tide of racist legislation.

Becoming more convinced of the power and correctness of nonviolent action, Gandhi debated with Indian terrorists while in London in 1909, and also began a correspondence with *Leo Tolstoy, leading to the publication of his fundamental essay on nonviolent nationalism, *Hind Swaraj, or Indian Home Rule*. He also established a rural base for his *Satyagraha* campaign near Johannesburg in 1910, naming it Tolstoy Farm. There he conducted experiments in education, stressing manual labor, simple food, knowledge of health and natural medicines. Suspending *Satyagraha* in 1911, he moved his family and school to Phoenix, and devoted himself chiefly to work at the settlement. New anti-Indian acts by the government led to the resumption of *Satyagraha* in 1913, resulting in a large-scale strike of Indian sugar and coal workers in Natal, and a march of over 2,000 Indians led by Gandhi into the Transvaal. These events created an international crisis, with intervention by the Viceroy of India and negotiations assisted by the arrival of the Rev. *Charles F. Andrews, concluding in the Indians Relief Act of 1914, after which Gandhi felt free to return to India.

Arriving at Bombay in 1915, Gandhi at the age of 45 was a national hero and was given the popular title Mahatma (Great Soul) by *Rabindranath Tagore. Now an experienced leader with a technique and philosophy of nonviolence which he intended to employ for India, he established an *ashram* (community) at the industrial city of Ahmedabad in his native Gujarat and continued training his core of disciplined workers. His first major confrontation with the government occurred during his systematic documentation of the exploitation of indigo workers in the Champaran district of Bihar in 1917. Then he led a strike of millworkers in Ahmedabad and a peasant strike in the nearby district of Kheda, following which he recruited in the same region for the Indian Army, urging once more that claims for full partnership required assuming the obligations of service.

After World War I, the continuation of wartime anti-terrorist legislation under the Rowlatt Act precipitated Gandhi's emergence into national leadership, in the form of a call for a nationwide one-day work stoppage in April 1919. The disturbances led to a brutal repression in Amritsar, where 379 unarmed civilians were killed. Gandhi was appointed to the investigation committee of the Indian National Congress (INC), and constructed a careful report which contradicted the official explanation of the incident. Soon two newspapers were given over to him, the English *Young India* and the Gujarati *Navajivan*, providing him vehicles for communication throughout the nation.

By 1920 Gandhi had mobilized a new constellation of political groups that gave him significant power within the INC. He used this support to organize a network reaching into the villages and to launch his first mass noncooperation campaign. He called for the boycott of the schools, law courts, polls, legislative councils, and perhaps eventually taxes, as well as the renunciation of foreign goods. The campaign issues were the abolition by the Allies after World War I of the Turkish Caliph, the Amritsar massacre, and "swaraj" or self-rule. Though less than complete in practice, and marred by acts of violence, the movement carried the message of self-reliance in economics and politics throughout India. In 1922, appalled by a murder of police officers, Gandhi suspended the campaign, whereupon he was arrested, tried, and sentenced to six years. His speech at the trial won him many admirers around the world.

Released in 1924 due to ill health, he abstained from politics for the remainder of his term, and devoted himself to his "Constructive Program," including *khadi* (home-spun and home-woven cloth), Hindu-Muslim unity, and the eradication of Untouchability. Moving back into politics, he called for complete independence by the end of 1929, and when it was not forthcoming he secured authorization from the INC to launch civil disobedience again. To begin it, he left his *ashram* on March 12, 1930, to walk the 240 miles to the sea at Dandi, where he broke the salt laws and launched a national wave of protest resulting in the jailing of over 60,000 men and women. Released from prison in 1931, he negotiated the "Gandhi-Irwin Pact" with the Viceroy, ending the protests with a compromise on the salt issue. In September he was in London as the sole INC representative at the Round Table Conference on a new Indian constitution. His efforts to explain the Indian case to the British people were more successful than his interventions in the negotiations.

On returning to Bombay he was immediately jailed by the new Viceroy. In prison he conducted a "fast unto death" against separating Untouchables from caste Hindus on the electoral rolls; he forced B. R. Ambedkar, the Untouchable leader, to accept a compromise. Released in 1933, he moved away from nationalist politics and concentrated on his social and economic programs. For this he began a new weekly paper called *Harijan* (his new name for the Untouchables: "Children of God"), and in 1936 settled in the center of India at a village he named Sevagram (Service Village). Here he demonstrated his belief that service to the poor, through simple technologies, offered the most immediate hope for India's millions.

The coming of war in 1939 precipitated a new involvement in the independence movement. In October 1940 he launched a series of "individual satyagrahas" against Britain's refusal to let Indians make a choice regarding participation in the war. Attempting to force a British decision on Indian freedom, he declared a "Quit India" campaign in August 1942, for which he and other INC leaders were jailed until 1944. In all, he spent 2,338 days in the prisons of India and South Africa.

As independence drew near, renewed Muslim nationalist militance led by M. A. Jinnah threatened the foundations of Indian unity. In 1947 Gandhi walked through many villages in East Bengal to quell Hindu-Muslim violence, and then did the same in Bihar. He halted similar riots in Calcutta with a three-day fast. Failing to prevent the partition of India and Pakistan, he struggled to overcome the fears and violence which had been unleashed, and in the fall of 1947 moved to Delhi, where thousands of refugees were gathering. While trying to bring peace to the city, he was killed on January 30, 1948, by a Hindu nationalist, who resented his concern for Muslims.

Gandhi was the first to demonstrate the strength of nonviolent civil disobedience conducted with mainly untrained volunteers. His career was interwoven with the freedom movement for India, and he was able to explore the power of *Satyagraha* in the protection of minority rights and the overcoming of foreign rule more than in the area of international relations. His successors in India, chiefly *Vinoba Bhave and *J. P. Narayan, have turned the disciplines of *Satyagraha* toward economic issues, developing along lines suggested in Gandhi's Constructive Program. More than any other man in this century he exemplified a dedication to peace and economic justice in his own being.

Bibliography:

A. *An Autobiography: The Story of My Experiment with Truth* (Boston, 1966); *The Collected Works of Mahatma Gandhi* (82 vols., New Delhi, 1958-); *Mohandas Karamchand Gandhi: A Bibliography* (New Delhi, 1974).

B. Erik Erikson, *Gandhi's Truth* (New York, 1969); R. Iyer, *The Moral and Political Thought of Mahatma Gandhi* (New York, 1973); Bal Ram Nanda, *Mahatma Gandhi* (London, 1958); Pyarelal Nayer, *Mahatma Gandhi* (4 vols., Ahmedabad, 1956-); Robert Payne, *The Life and Death of Mahatma Gandhi* (New York, 1969); Paul Power, ed., *The Meanings of Gandhi* (Honolulu, 1971); Gene Sharp, *Gandhi as a Political Strategist* (Boston, 1979); Dinanath C. Tendulkar, *Mohatma, A Life of Mohandas Karamchand Gandhi* (8 vols., Bombay, 1961–63).

James D. Hunt

GARRISON, William Lloyd (10 December 1805, Newburyport, MA—24 May 1879, New York). *Education*: printer's apprentice. *Career*: editor, *The Liberator*, 1831–65; co-founder, American Anti-Slavery Society, 1833, president, 1843–65; founder, New England Non-Resistance Society, 1838; nonviolent abolitionist and feminist.

William Lloyd Garrison was a radical opponent of all violence, going beyond most absolutists of his day in anarchistic noncooperation with government which used force. His pacifism was based on a literal application of the Sermon on the Mount. He was able to quote from memory much of the Bible which he learned from his mother, an itinerant Baptist preacher. His views on peace first appeared while editing his first newspaper, at age 21, recording his favorable impression of the visit of *William Ladd to Newburyport. Patriotism and partial approval of violence mark his early peace views, but his meeting with the abolitionist Quaker Benjamin Lundy in 1828 crystalized his pacifism. He joined Lundy in Baltimore in 1829 to edit his second paper explicitly dedicated to peace and other social reforms. Although never a Quaker, Garrison had close relations with Friends throughout his life, crediting *Lucretia Mott (whom he met in 1830) with having ''liberalized'' his mind from the prejudice of the Old Testament sanction of war.

He publicly adopted ''non-resistance'' in 1829, shortly after paying the fine for conscientious refusal of Massachusetts militia service. He incorporated his nonviolent principles into his Declaration of Sentiments, written for the first national abolitionist organization, the American Anti-Slavery Society, formed in Boston in 1833. The Declaration rejected the use of all carnal weapons for freeing the slaves and called forth, instead, the liberating power of truth and love.

Garrison's going to jail as an ''innocent prisoner'' in Baltimore in 1830 on charges of libel was merely civil obedience. But his refusal to use arms in confrontation with a Boston lynch mob in 1835 can be called true nonresistance, even though he was rescued by the police. Adhering to Quaker principles, he even insisted that his militant speeches, which seemed incendiary and fanatical to his opponents, must be tempered by ''universal love.'' But in 1837 he was deeply influenced by the perfectionist views of *John H. Noyes, whose Christian anarchism he adapted to his own secular and absolute nonviolence. Garrison was already moving toward a ''no-government'' position in reaction to the violence used by the Andrew Jackson administration.

Garrison penned one of the most radical pacifist documents of the nineteenth century when, in 1838, he wrote another ''Declaration of Sentiments,'' this time for the founding of the New England Non-Resistance Society. It opened with the Christian anarchist manifesto: ''We cannot acknowledge allegiance to any human government,'' but only to God. It declared universal loyalty to humanity by repeating the cosmopolitan motto of Garrison's *Liberator*: ''Our country is the world, our countrymen are all mankind.'' Then it set forth an absolute pacifist statement: ''We register our testimony, not only against all wars, whether offensive or defensive, but all preparation for war.'' Arguing that all governments were based on violence, the declaration concluded that ''we cannot hold any office'' nor vote. The signing of the Declaration announced their intention to bring about the Kingdom of God not by violence ''but by the FOOLISHNESS OF PREACHING.''

For almost four years (1839–42) Garrison published the society's bimonthly *Non-Resistant*, the only absolute pacifist paper in America. When it closed, Garrison opened the pages of the *Liberator* for the discussion of nonviolence. Despite his devotion to nonviolence, Garrison was soon preoccupied with the growing struggle against slavery. The Non-Resistance Society languished between annual meetings until 1849, finally disappearing about 1856.

Like other absolute pacifists who believed that slavery had to end almost at all costs, Garrison found it difficult to resolve the contradictions between nonresistance and abolitionism. He never abandoned his nonviolent ideology, and he continued to counsel against slave revolts and armed raids while showing strong sympathy with the oppressed. In his enthusiasm for John Brown's raid he even wished success to slave revolts as "one way to get up to the sublime platform of non-resistance." Even though he continued to see himself as "an ultra-peace man," Garrison once declared that "rather than see men wearing their chains in a cowardly and servile spirit" he would "as an advocate of peace, much rather see them breaking the head of the tyrant with chains." This apparent contradiction anticipated *Gandhi's three level preference for violence over cowardice if nonviolence cannot be practiced.

The final test came with the Civil War which Garrison approved for its destruction of slavery: "Better civil war . . . than for us to crouch in the dust. . . ." Yet he supported conscientious objectors on nonresistant principles as more consistent than religious objectors who had supported military governments in peacetime. Garrison regretted that his eldest son enlisted to fight rather than rise to the "higher plane of moral heroism and nobler method of self-sacrifice" of nonresistance. His other four children carried on his nonviolent leadership in peace and social reform, corresponding with *Leo Tolstoy and founding the Anti-Imperialist League against the Spanish-American War. A grandson, *Oswald Garrison Villard, became a radical opponent of World War I.

Bibliography:

A. *The Abolitionists and their Relations to War* (New York, 1862); *William Lloyd Garrison: The Story of His Life Told By His Children* (4 vols., New York, 1885–89); *Writings and Speeches of William Lloyd Garrison* (Walter M. Merrill and Louis Ruchames, eds., 6 vols., Cambridge, 1971–81).

B. Peter Brock, *Pacifism in the United States* (Princeton, 1968); Ernest Crosby, *Garrison the Non-Resistant* (Chicago, 1905); Fanny G. Villard, *William Lloyd Garrison on Non-Resistance* (New York, 1924).

C. William Lloyd Garrison Papers, Boston Public Library, Harvard University, Massachusetts Historical Society, Smith College, Wichita State University.

James W. Gould

GERIN, René Marius François Léon (3 July 1892 Varennes-les-Nevers, Nièvre, France—20 November 1957, Paris). *Education*: bachelier ès-lettres, Lycée of Nevers, 1909; Lycèe Louis-le-Grand, 1902–12; licence ès-lettres, Univ. of Paris, 1911; agrégation des lettres, Ecole Normale Supérieure, 1919. *Career*: teacher, journalist, and polemicist.

Like so many of his generation who survived the conflict, René Gerin was permanently scarred psychologically by his experiences as a soldier in World War I. The son of a teacher, the young Gerin was a brilliant student who entered the prestigious École normale supérieure in 1913. Called to the colors in the summer of 1914, he served for four years in the front lines, was wounded in combat three times, and rose to the rank of captain. His bravery won him the Legion of Honor. After demobilization, Gerin completed his studies and entered the teaching profession.

Obsessed with the horrors of war that he had seen, Gerin emerged as a prominent figure in the pacifist movement by the 1930s. Devoting considerable research to examining the origins of World War I, he concluded that the Allies, particularly Russia, were as much to blame for starting the war as Germany and Austria-Hungary. Tsarist ambitions to expand into the Balkans as well as the French nationalist desire for revenge against Germany and recovery of Alsace-Lorraine lay at the root of the conflict, he believed. Gerin singled out Raymond Poincaré, claiming that the former president of the republic had encouraged Russia to attack Germany and thereby aid France in regaining her lost provinces.

Soon after it was founded, Gerin became the secretary-general of the Ligue internationale des combattants de la paix (International League of Fighters for Peace) founded by *Victor Méric to promote peace. He published extensively in its newspaper, *La Patrie humaine*, and made speaking tours of France and North Africa to denounce the peril of war. Gerin demanded that the Treaty of Versailles be revised so as to eliminate the injustices imposed on Germany in 1919, especially the war guilt clause. Although an officer in the army reserve, Gerin supported the conscientious objector movement by refusing to participate in military maneuvers. As a result he was expelled from the Legion of Honor and in 1935 briefly imprisoned for his beliefs. These humiliations, far from discouraging him, stimulated him to denounce the military men, industrialists, and politicians he considered responsible for whipping up war hysteria. In 1934 he joined the Comité de vigilance des intellectuels antifascists (Antifascist Intellectuals' Vigilance Committee) which worked to combat fascism at home and the danger of a new war. Even after the opening of hostilities in September, 1939, Gerin signed the manifesto *Paix immédiate*, which called for an immediate end to the fighting.

From 1940 to 1944 during the German occupation, Gerin earned his living as a literary critic for Marcel Déat's newspaper *L'Oeuvre*. He also belonged to the Ligue de la pensée française (League of French Thought) which sought to create understanding between Germany and France. As a result of his journalism, Gerin was arrested soon after the Liberation, tried as a collaborator, and sentenced to prison. Released in 1946, Gerin undertook a strenuous campaign to clear his name, writing endless letters to government officials and publishing brochures to explain his actions. Never able to clear himself entirely of the charges brought against him, he remained an embittered man who believed that he had been unjustly treated when his only crime was the search for peace.

Bibliography:

A. *Les Causes psychologiques de guerre* (Paris, 1935); *Comment fut provoquée la Guerre de 1914* (Paris, 1931); *La Paix auxieuse et obstinée* (Paris, 1938); *Un procès de la Libération* (3rd ed., Paris, 1957); *Les Responsabilités de la guerre* (Paris, 1930); *Si la guerre éclatait, que faire*? (Paris, 1936).

B. Henri Temerson, *Biographies des principales personnalités françaises décédées au cours de l'année 1957* (Paris, 1958); Felicien Challaye, "René Gerin," *Annuaire de l'Association amicale de secours des anciens élèves de l'École Normale Supérieure* (Paris, 1958).

James Friguglietti

GERLACH, Hellmut von (2 February 1866, Mönchmotzelnitz in Silesia, Prussia—1 August, 1935, Paris). *Education*: private tutors; gymnasium (secondary school), Wohlau, Silesia; studied jurisprudence at the universities of Geneva, Strassburg (now Strasbourg), Leipzig, and Berlin. *Career*: official, Prussian civil service, 1887–92; journalist, editor, politician, and pacifist.

Hellmut von Gerlach, the offspring of a Prussian conservative family, pursued a career in the civil service until 1892, when he resigned and underwent a political evolution that took him from right to left. After breaking with the anti-Semitic Prussian Christian conservative movement around Adolf Stoecker, Gerlach associated himself with Friedrich Naumann's National Social Association, winning its only parliamentary seat in the 1903 elections. At the same time Gerlach began his journalistic career first with Stoecker's paper, *Volk*, and then (1896) as editor of the National Social Association organ, *Die Zeit*. In 1898 Gerlach became editor-in-chief and later publisher of *Welt am Montag* (WaM). Remaining with the *WaM* until 1930, Gerlach gave the paper its radical-democratic stamp. He went along with Naumann when the latter joined the National Social Association with the left-liberal Freisinnige Vereinigung (Progressive Alliance) (FV), but then left the party after the election of 1907 (in which he lost his parliamentary seat), because the FV joined the parliamentary bloc (Bülow bloc) opposed to the Social Democratic and Center parties. Together with Theodor Barth and Rudolf Breitscheid, Gerlach founded the Demokratische Vereinigung (Democratic Association) (DV) which he headed after Barth's death in 1909.

A trip to Africa in 1912 acquainted Gerlach with colonial oppression, and while he did not condemn Germany's possession of colonies he developed serious reservations about the government. World War I strengthened his rejection of the Hohenzollern political system and Prussian-German militarism. As a member of the Deutsche Friedensgesellschaft (German Peace Society) (DFG), Gerlach became actively engaged in the peace movement. At the end of 1914, he joined the Bund Neues Vaterland (New Fatherland League) and in 1916 took part in the founding of the Zentralstelle für Völkerrecht (Coordinating Office for International Law). An early opponent of the annexation policy and convinced of Germany's responsibility for the outbreak of the war, Gerlach advocated a quick end to the war and the creation of a new cabinet as a preliminary for a change in the political structure of Germany. These demands placed him close to the radical socialist Unabhängige Sozialdemokratische Partei Deutschlands (Independent German Social Democratic party) (USPD) which he nevertheless did not join. After the war, Gerlach took part in the founding of the pro-republic liberal-bourgeois Deutsche Demokratische Partei (German Democratic party) (DDP), and became a prominent spokesman for the party's left wing.

In early 1919 Gerlach assumed the office of undersecretary of state in the Prussian ministry of the interior where he became head of the Polish department. He pursued a policy of German-Polish understanding and sensible compromise. He resigned from his position in March, after the USPD left the government. Long a target of nationalist attacks, Gerlach narrowly escaped assassination at the beginning of 1920. He left the DDP in 1922, because its policies did not accord with his conceptions of the peace and social policies of a radical-democratic party. Writing for numerous left-liberal and pacifist papers, Gerlach worked for a changed Germany that would gain the confidence of foreign countries by a peaceful foreign policy and a scrupulous fulfillment of the Treaty of Versailles and that would resolutely defend the republic against reactionary chauvinist and militaristic forces. Just as decisively, he supported the western European type of parliamentary system against the radical left.

After World War I, Gerlach carried on a wide range of pacifist activities. Since 1919 he was a member of the Council of the International Peace Bureau; he was a leading member of the Deutsche Liga für Menschenrechte (German League for Human Rights) (DLM); and he appeared as a speaker at numerous pacifist meetings in Germany and abroad. The leitmotiv of his peace activities was his efforts to bring about an understanding with France. The resumption of relations between the German and French peace movements was largely Gerlach's work. Within the DFG, Gerlach, a long time member of the society's directorate, took a position between the left-wing and the pacifist center. He accepted the small Reichswehr (army) both as a defensive army and as a part of a still to be created League of Nations executive, but he demanded the republicanization of the army and condemned Germany's rearmament. He fought against illegal German rearmament, especially against the Schwarze Reichswehr (Black Reichswehr, units of temporary volunteers). In the conflict within the DFG, Gerlach sided with the group around *Ludwig Quidde and took issue with *Fritz Küster and the Westdeutscher Landesverband (West German Regional Association) of the DFG whose pacifist activities alienated the republican parties. In 1929 he broke with Küster and the new DFG national leadership, but remained a member of the local Berlin DFG branch. In 1930 Gerlach, along with Quidde participated in the creation of the unsuccessful Radikaldemokratische Partei (Radical Democratic party).

In the last years of the Weimar republic Gerlach became increasingly more involved in the *Weltbühne*, having given up his work with *WaM* in 1930. In May 1932 Gerlach took over the editorship of the *Weltbühne* when *Carl von Ossietzky was sentenced to prison for high treason, i.e. exposing illegal German rearmament. After Adolf Hitler's accession to power on January 30, 1933, Gerlach fled for his life to exile in France where he founded a relief organization for German refugees, wrote and lectured against the Nationalist Socialist regime in Germany, played a leading role in the campaign to award the Nobel Peace Prize to Ossietzky, and took part in efforts to create a popular anti-Nazi front among German exiles.

Bibliography:

A. *Ein Demokrat kommentiert Weimar. Die Berichte Hellmut von Gerlachs an die Carnegie-Friedensstiftung in New York 1922–1930*, ed. by K. Holl and A. Wild (Bremen, 1973); *Die deutsche Mentalität (1871–1921)* (Ludwigsburg, 1921); *Erinnerungen eines Junkers* (Berlin, 1925); *Die grosse* Zeit der Lüge (Charlottenburg, 1926); *Meine Erlebnisse in der preussischen Verwaltung* (Berlin, 1919); *Von Rechts nach Links*, ed. by E. Ludwig (Zurich, 1937).

B. S. Gilbert, *Hellmut von Gerlach (1866–1935) - Stationene ines deutschen Liberalen vom Kaiserreich zum 'Dritten Reich'* (Freiburg im Breisgau, 1981); R. Greuner, *Wandlungen eines Aufrechten. Lebensbild Hellmut von Gerlachs* (Berlin [East], 1965).

Karl Holl
Trans. by Solomon Wank

GIDE, Charles (29 June 1847, Uzès, France—12 March 1936, Paris). *Education*: Collège communal of Uzès; thèse de doctorat, Univ. of Paris, 1872, agrégé, 1874, *Career*: professor, Faculties of Law of the Universities of Bordeaux, 1874–80, Montpellier, 1880–1906, Paris, 1899–1920, and at the École supérieure des ponts et chaussées, 1900, École supérieure de guerre, 1907, and the collège de France, 1921–30.

Renowned as an economist who challenged laissez-faire doctrines, Charles Gide combined a lengthy teaching career in university faculties of law and special schools with extensive publications and active participation in several reform causes. He spoke out not only for pacifism but also for consumers' cooperatives, feminism, anti-alcoholism, and the campaign against French "depopulation."

Gide was a leading theorist of the "solidarist" school of economists who combined liberalism with social reformism. *Solidarité* was a doctrine framed by French republicans eager to combat the growth of socialism among workers by demonstrating that a democratic regime could produce economic justice and social harmony. Gide and fellow economists founded the *Revue d'economie politique* in 1887 to challenge the apostles of laissez faire then dominant in French political economy. During the 1880s he also entered the consumers' cooperative movement, promoted by the heavily Protestant "Nimes school," and, in turn, in 1895, joined the newly founded International Cooperative Alliance, serving on its central committee for twenty-five years.

Gide readily coupled a quest for international solidarity with his efforts to alleviate conflict within France. He gave hundreds of lectures and speeches for the pacifist cause and wrote numerous articles for *La Paix par le droit*, started in Nimes in 1891. Not only economic doctrine but also Protestant moralism and belief in the benefits of the rule of law were the roots of Gide's impassioned pacifism. Convinced that dangerous economic rivalries could produce wars, he nonetheless disputed the Marxist view that economic causes were primary in the breakdown of peace, for he regarded human passions and moral failings as equally to blame. His attitude toward imperialism was long ambivalent; he deplored the brutality of many colonial conquests but thought that Europeans could peacefully bring many benefits to colonial subjects. He also did not link international cooperation with elimination of the nation-state because he believed that a nation preserved a people's distinctive features.

After World War I Gide warned that harsh economic treatment of Germany boded ill for the future. He criticized the exaction of heavy reparations and opposed the French occupation of the Ruhr in 1923. *Le Bilan pour la guerre pour la France*, co-authored with William Oualid in 1931, showed the high costs of war to victor as well as vanquished and was part of the''Economic and Social History of the World War'' funded by the Carnegie Endowment for International Peace, whose French committee Gide chaired. Viewing international disarmament, not just German disarmament, as vital for world peace, Gide hoped that through the League of Nations international solidarity would triumph over divisive nationalism. At the international conference of cooperatives in Basel in 1921 he pushed through a resolution stating that adoption of the cooperative program and free trade and elimination of the profit motive would reaffirm ''the bonds of international solidarity'' and so reduce the likelihood of future wars. ''Solidarity'' was indeed the key word in both his economic teaching and pacifism.

Bibliography:

A. *La Coopération* (Paris, 1900); *Histoire des doctrines économiques depuis les physiocrates jusqu'à nos jours*, with Charles Rist (Paris, 1909); *Les Institutions de progrès social* (Paris, 1903); *Premières notions d' économie politique* (Paris, 1921); *Principes d' économie politique* (Paris, 1883; 30 French editions and 18 translations).

B. Achille Daudé-Bancel, ''Charles Gide, ''*Revue des études coopératives* 55 (1976), 3–20; *Charles Gide, sa vie et son oeuvre*, special issue of *Revue d' économic politique* 46 (1932); 1681–1837; A. Lavondès, *Un Précurseur de l'Europe unie et de l'O.N.U.: Charles Gide, un apôtre de la coopération entre les hommes* (Uzès, 1953); Charles Rist, ''Charles Gide,'' *Economic Journal* 42 (1932), 333–38; NYT, March 15, 1932.

Linda L. Clark

GIESSWEIN, Sándor (4 February 1856, Tata, Hungary—15 April 1923, Budapest). *Education*: Catholic seminary, Vienna and Budapest; ordination, 1878; Dr. Theol., 1880. *Career*: linguist, theologian, papal prelate, member of Parliament, journalist, author, and pacifist.

For a period of twenty years (1883–1903), Sándor Giesswein performed various functions in the pontifical office of Győr, Hungary. During that time, he wrote several books and articles on ancient Egypt, Assyria, and on comparative linguistics. He was also active in working class organizations and became an early proponent of Christian socialism. In 1903 Giesswein moved to Budapest as the newly chosen vice-president of the Catholic St. Stephen Society. In 1905 he was elected to the Parliament on the ticket of the Catholic People's party.

Christian socialist organization remained Giesswein's primary concern, but he also began to take an active part in pacifist movements as a member of the Hungarian delegation at the 1905, 1906, and 1908 Congresses of the Interparliamentary Union. Giesswein was elected president of the Peace Association of the countries under the Holy Hungarian Crown of St. Stephen in 1909. In his inaugural address, he elaborated on the theme of peace being the necessary outcome of international law rather than a utopian dream. In a parliamentary speech on March 21, 1911, Giesswein demanded the reconvening of the Hague Congress. He also established chapters of the Peace Association in several Hungarian towns and stayed in touch with foreign peace advocates, including *Bertha von Suttner. In 1913 Giesswein published a pamphlet under the title *Keresztènysèg ès Bèkemozgalom* (*Christianity and the Peace Movement*). In it, he pointed out that Catholicism was destined to spread the idea of peace.

During World War I Giesswein continued his work for peace. He traveled to peace conferences held in neutral countries several times and hammered at the need for a lasting and just peace in a number of parliamentary speeches. In a pamphlet, *A Hàborù ès a Tàrsadalomtudomànyok* (*War and the Social Sciences*), published in 1915, Giesswein pointed out that war was not an absolute fact of eternal validity but a phenomenon relative to social changes and bound to last only until other means were found to solve conflicts. In several articles and speeches, Giesswein reiterated his conviction that the future guarantee of a lasting and just peace was to be internationalism which would nevertheless respect and preserve national individuality.

Giesswein believed that the cataclysmic impact of World War I was bound to foster pacifism after the war, a hope he expressed in his pamphlet, *Új Idők Küszöbèn* (*At the Threshold of New Times*), published in 1918. The actual turn of events could not but disillusion him, but Giesswein kept up his work, concentrating on pacifist education as the prerequisite for international understanding and peace. It was in this spirit that he championed the Esperanto cause. He was extremely active in the promotion of pacifist causes up to the time of his sudden death in 1923.

Bibliography:

A. *A Hàborù ès a Tàrsadalomtudomànyok* (Budapest, 1915); *Igazsàgossàg és Bèke* (Budapest, 1917); *Keresztènysèg ès Bèkemozgalom* (Budapest, 1913); *Új Idők Küszöben* (Budapest, 1918).

B. Alfred H. Fried, *Handbuch der Friedensbewegung* (2nd ed., Berlin, 1911–1913, reissued New York, 1972), 353; József Galàntai, *Egyhàz ès Politika* (Budapest, 1960); Giesswein Emlèkkönyv (Memorial Volume) (Budapest, 1925).

Gabor Vermes

GILL, Arthur Eric Rowton (22 February, 1882, Brighton, England—17 November, 1940, Piggots, near High Wycombe, England). *Education*: Chichester Technical and Art School, 1899; Westminister Technical Institute, LCC Central School of Arts and Crafts, 1899–1901. Career: stone-carver, engraver, typographer, lecturer, essayist, author, Tertiary of St. Dominic, founder of PAX.

Eric Gill's advocacy of pacifism during the 1930s represented an historic landmark for English pacifism and Catholicism. Until Gill's founding of PAX in 1936, no Roman Catholic pacifist organization existed in England. Isolated Catholic pacifist advocates apart, the Catholic Church upheld the doctrine of the Just War. In initating PAX and linking it with activities of the Council of Christian Pacifist Groups and the Peace Pledge Union, Gill did not view himself as defying Catholic doctrines. On the contrary, he established his pacifism on the very criteria for Just War enunciated by St. Thomas Acquinas: all modern wars, Gill felt, if judged by Thomistic standards, violated Christian ethics. Aerial bombardment, for example, inevitably transgressed Thomistic insistence on the protection of non-combatants among the enemy population. Since Gill conceded that wars without modern technology might be legitimate, his pacifism was conditional. In this respect he was closer in outlook to secular pacifists of his time, such as *Bertrand Russell, than to the absolutism of most Protestant pacifists.

While Thomistic criteria lent orthodoxy to Gill's pacifism, his primary arguments against war stemmed from a dual Socialist and Christian analysis. A Socialist before he was either a Catholic or a pacifist—in the years before World War I, he was a Fabian and member of the Independent Labour party—Gill viewed modern war as rooted in industrial capitalism. He placed particular emphasis upon the human callousness bred by an economic system that denied workers not only just recompense but their personal dignity and inherent creativity. Further, he felt capitalism necessarily fostered competitive egoism, avarice, and acquisitiveness among individuals and between nations. Though never an industrial laborer, Gill sensed the impact of such labor when he served in the army for four months during World War I. A "monstrous and momentous experience," he recalled, with prison-like discipline and petty officers' crude abuse of authority.

By the 1920s Gill had veered away from the socialism of most of his contemporaries. He regarded communism, Fabianism, labour unions and the Labour party as severely infected with materialism, machine-worship, egoism, and godlessness. Raised in a nonconformist, evangelical family, Gill underwent a sequence of religious stages that led from agnosticism to conversion to Roman Catholicism, in 1913, ultimately to becoming a Tertiary of the Dominican order and establishing in the 1920s with his wife, three children, and friends an experimental community near Ditchling. He envisioned a Christian Guild Socialism in which each local company of workers owned and controlled their enterprise and sought only enough money to satisfy reasonable human needs.

Gill's Christian socialist critique of war intensified during his trip in 1934 to Palestine. He left the Holy Land convinced that British industrial and imperial civilization was deeply responsible for much of the corruption and suffering of twentieth century life. Such a civilization, he concluded, was not worth killing innocent people for.

At the same time that Gill was founding PAX and writing pacifist and Christian socialist essays, he was sculpting bas reliefs for the new League of Nations Assembly Hall at Geneva. Although pessimistic about the viability of the League, he was eager to foster international peace through a medium in which his skills were at their most refined. Gill's artistic accomplishments possessed a precision, grace, and originality often lacking in his otherwise insightful polemical writing.

Bibliography:

A. *Autobiography* (London, 1940); *It All Goes Together* (New York, 1944); *Letters of Eric Gill*, ed. by Walter Shewring (London, 1947); *The Necessity of Belief* (London, 1936).

B. Donald Attwater, ed. *Modern Christian Revolutionaries* (New York, 1947). Robert Speaight, *The Life of Eric Gill* (London, 1966).

C. Eric Gill Papers, William Andrews Clark Library, Los Angeles, CA.

Joyce Avrech Berkman

GINN, Edwin. See *Biographical Dictionary of Internationalists*.

GIONO, Jean (30 March 1895, Manosque, France—8 October 1970, Manosque). *Education*: Collège de Manosque. *Career*: bank clerk, novelist, polemicist, pacifist writer.

Along with the writers *Alain, *Henri Barbusse, Jean Guéhenno, and *Romain Rolland, Jean Giono made pacifism a serious literary subject in France during the years between the two world wars. Giono's social origins were working class. He was born and lived in the south of France, in Provence; his works are suffused with the simplicity, affability, and naiveté of rustic and peasant life. He served at the front during World War I as an infantry private, fighting in major battles, including Verdun. He was demobilized in 1919, after treatment for gas asphyxiation.

Giono was a versatile creative writer. Accomplished at poetry and poetic prose, he became one of the twentieth-century masters of the lyrical novel. His heroes demonstrate a sense of mystery, wonderment, and joy in life. They have an erotic identification with other members of the community and with the earth itself.

Giono was a typical representative of rural anarchism. He exemplified it in a form of open-hearted, invigorating, extreme, and occasionally eccentric individualism. His literary and journalistic works idealize country life, while disparaging the city. Giono hated Paris and resisted living in the French capital. He saw urban living and cosmopolitan consciousness as the basis of France's civilizational malaise. In the city, fear and violence proliferated. Unsurprisingly, Giono's world view was anti-intellectual and anti-progressive; he advocated maintaining local communities at a level of economic under-development in order to preserve local autonomy, simplicity, and individualism. In the 1930s, he attacked capitalism and big business.

Giono's pacifism emerged out of his rural anarchism. His pacifism was of the apolitical and conservative variety, and he never joined any organized group of youth, intellectuals, workers, or conscientious objectors. His writings didactically portray the benefits of peace. He disliked all organizations, all churches, all nationalisms, all regimentation, all dictatorships. Giono briefly joined the Association of Revolutionary Artists and Writers in 1934; he infrequently wrote for pro-Communist and Popular Front journals like *Europe* and *Vendredi*. Yet his pacifism was incompatible with his antifascist stance; he quickly denounced the Popular Front and became anticommunist. He believed that the principles of collective security would lead to a war with Germany. His association with the *Cahiers de Contadour* (1935–39) was more a celebration of the outdoor life, of fresh-air, of free work and craftsmenship, campfires, and the richness of everyday life, than a sustained analysis of war—or of the methods to resist war. Giono's nostalgia for pre-industrial France, for lost habits and straightforwardness, resonated with the less cultivated French reader in the 1930s.

Giono's antiwar stance had a conservative core; he wanted to preserve rather than to transform, to preach rootedness in the land, not social or economic reform. His solutions to the problems of war and peace were poetic. They offered no real program, no incisive analysis of the causes of modern warfare, a mistaken impression of fascism and of the rise of Adolf Hitler, no real political or organizational outlets for antiwar resisters. Giono advocated unilateral disarmament as a moral gesture in the 1930s. He stood for appeasement of Hitler's Germany before and during the Munich crisis. He wanted France to make concessions to Germany to avoid bloodshed at any cost. He felt, erroneously, that France could negotiate in good faith with the National Socialists.

Giono was arrested twice: once in 1939 for three months for unpatriotic utterances before France was invaded by the Germans; and again in 1945 for six months when he was interned for allegedly collaborating with Vichy France. There is no strong evidence of Giono's collaboration with Vichy or of his agreement with extreme right-wing opinions. What is clear is that he was opportunistic during Vichy, that he arrogantly published in pro-Nazi periodicals. But he also sheltered refugees and Jews from the Vichy government, and he was on record to be against the regime's dictatorial policies.

Giono's pacifism was the pacifism of exhortation and self-glorification. He always stood detached, an enraged spectator, an ascetic partisan, a fanatical supporter of the losing side. His pacifism was connected to a lifelong passion for purity. His anarchistic and pastoral pacifism can not be separated from his individualistic temperament and from his poetic sensibility. War, for him, was simply horrific because it shattered human life. War was futile and solved no problems. Giono's antiwar writings, then, tend to be static and ahistorical. They have a fairy-tale quality to them. Even his attractive myth about Provence was an invention; the Provence of his writings only existed in the writer's fantasy. Giono's pacifism was that of a writer who refused to live with or in his time. After 1945 his works became increasingly bitter, full of black humor and cynicism. They mock the present century. They invoke a tone of aristocratic disdain, even insolence. Giono's pacifism was an eloquent but idealistic defense of individual self-sufficiency, of the individual's ability to fuse with nature. Traumatized by his experiences in the trenches, Giono hoped to persuade his public that any course of action was preferable to total warfare.

Bibliography:

A. *Le Chant du monde* (Paris, 1934); *Lettre aux Paysans sur la pauvreté et la paix* (Paris, 1938); *Précisions* (Paris, 1939); *Refus d'obéissance* (Paris, 1937).

B. Lucette Heller-Goldenberg, *Jean Giono et le Contadour* (Nice, 1972); W. D. Redfern, *The Private World of Jean Giono* (Oxford, 1967).

David James Fisher

GIRETTI, Edoardo (10 August 1864, Torre Pellice, Piedmont, Italy—27 December 1940, Bricherasio, Piedmont). *Education*: law, Univ. of Turin. *Career*: industrialist; political economist, member, Chamber of Deputies; peace leader; founder, Società per la pace di Torre Pellice; member, Council of the Bureau international de la paix (Berne); vice-president, national congress of Italian peace societies (Turin, 1904); author, lecturer, and politician.

Edoardo Giretti's major contributions to the Italian and European peace movements before 1914 were just one facet of a busy and productive life. His reputation in Italy was built on his persistent analyses and criticisms of protectionist policies that favored large, inefficient sugar, steel, and grain industries, of government corruption, of misguided government intervention, and of the growth of public bureaucracies. His devotion to liberal ideals derived, in part, from his heritage of stubborn independence forged in the Piedmontese mountains where Waldensianism, a pre-Lutheran form of Protestantism, survived eight centuries of persecution; in part, from his absolute acceptance of liberal economic theories of free trade that he absorbed from the Manchester School, the Cobden Club, and from his friend, *Gustave de Molinari, and in part from his conviction in the superiority of small-and medium-size industry as the best vehicle for Italian economic development. Giretti also admired the Cavourian heritage which he understood as antistatist and adamantly insisted on the separation of church and state.

Outraged at the 1887 treaty signed by Italy, followed by Francese Crispi's militant foreign policy and repeated tariff laws protecting large industries, Giretti launched into a long career of publishing in a variety of journals and newspapers. His carefully documented analyses demonstrated the impact of government policies on industries, on the workers' standard of living, and on Italian development as a whole. After 1900 he was invited to contribute to socialist papers, including *Avanti!* where his ringing defenses of free trade received considerable prominence. His intellectual and moral principles brought him to the young Italian peace movement in the 1890s.

As an organizer of the local peace society in Torre Pellice and of the 1904 meeting in Turin of all Italian societies, Giretti argued vigorously against misguided government efforts to construct an African empire and analyzed, exhaustively, the effects of contemporary military spending on Italy's development. He pleaded for worker and Socialist party support for the essentially middle-class peace movement which he defined as a political movement but not an integrated political party. Therefore, people of all political persuasions could support its objectives. Giretti was one of the few crusaders from the pre–1914 middle class peace movement to labor for a class alliance in the peace camp, despite his own absolute belief in liberal, private economic principles. He insisted that most Italians, whether they be middle class or proletariat, had an overriding interest in preventing the "gangsters" from finance, industry, and government from ruining the nation.

Consistent in his peace position, Giretti did not join the Italian peace leaders (*Ernesto Moneta and *Angelo De Gubernatis) who justified the government declaration of war against Turkey over Libya in 1911. Rather, despite vicious denunciations of his antipatriotism, he stood—with Luigi Einaudi and Gaetano Salvemini—almost as a lone voice predicting that the Libyan invasion would be a military and economic fiasco. He continuously berated the Giolittian government over its expense. Along with *Albert Gobat, secretary of the peace bureau in Berne, Giretti attempted to reorganize the Italian peace movement to remove those who had backed the war. Eventually, by 1913, the rift was patched over but not without severe damage to the movement's credibility.

Again, in 1914–15, Giretti was among the last Italian peace leaders to admit, grudgingly, that Italy had to enter the war on the Entente side. This decision, the most agonizing of his life, came because of the violation of the rights of neutrals, especially Belgium, for he immensely distrusted any reason that the government offered for Italian entry. Almost immediately, he began correspondence with peace leaders in Berne to work out a program for world order after the war that would insure a durable peace. With the end of the war, Giretti was enthusiastic about Wilsonian principles and stood apart from the extremist nationalistic agitation that erupted in Italy as well as in the new Yugoslav state over disputed territory.

The postwar crisis in Italy culminating in Benito Mussolini's appointment (1922) temporarily led Giretti to believe that the Fascists might not be a terrible interim solution to Italy's parliamentary crises. He briefly believed that Mussolini would install a true free trade, liberal economic policy, but that idea was disabused with the corporate state and the disappearance of the liberties which Giretti held so dear. With the exception of one major work published in the 1930s, Giretti retired from most political activity and ran his silk factory as best as he could. There, at least, the ideals he believed could be put into practice. To the end, despite the outbreak of World War II, he never lost his faith in free trade, freedom of exchange of goods and ideas, cooperation, and peace.

Bibliography:

A. *Il Congresso della pace di Ginevra e la calumnia del mio antipatriotismo: Fatti e documenti* (Pinerolo, 1913); *La Guerra per la pace: Lettera al comitato promotore del congresso internazionale per lo studio delle basi di un trattato di pace durevole (Berna,*

14–18 dicembre, 1915), (Pinerolo, 1915); *Il Popolo e la lotta contro il militarismo* (Bologna, 1900); "Spese libiche e spese militare," *Il Secolo*, November 8, 1913; *Le Spese militare* (Rome, 1914).

B. Luigi Einaudi, "Edoardo Giretti," *Rivista di storia economica* (Milan, 1941), 63–66; Antonio Papa, "Edoardo Giretti," *Belfagor*, XXV (1970), 50–70.

C. Correspondence, 1911–12, in Bureau international de la paix, Archives, UN Library, Geneva; correspondence, Fondazoine Luigi Einaudi, Turin.

Sandi E. Cooper

GLASIER, John Bruce (25 March 1859, Glasgow, Scotland—4 June 1920, Levenshulme, England). *Education*: apprenticed architectural draughtsman. *Career*: socialist propagandist and founder of the Independent Labour party (ILP) in Britain; member, ILP National Administrative Council 1897–1909, 1910–20; party chairman, 1900–1903; editor, *Labour Leader*, 1904–9; editor, *The Socialist Review*, 1913–17; poet-artist, author-journalist, and international socialist.

Bruce Glasier did not begin his political career as a pacifist. One of Britain's earliest socialists, Glasier was affiliated in the 1880s first with the Marxist Social Democratic Federation and then with the anarchist-plagued Socialist League. It was not until the late 1890s, after Britain's involvement in the ill-fated Boer War, that Glasier finally rejected violence and anti-parliamentary methods as means of achieving the international socialist state which he envisioned as the hope of the future.

Meantime, in 1893, Glasier helped launch the Independent Labour party (ILP), which was led by the staunch pacifist and Socialist M. P. *Keir Hardie. In time, Glasier became one of the Big Four (with Hardie, +Ramsay MacDonald, and *Philip Snowden) of the ILP, the party which ultimately provided the political leadership and philosophy of the British Labour party. As a member of the ILP, Glasier served on the party's executive, and he succeeded Hardie as chairman of the party in 1900. In 1904 he again followed Hardie, this time as editor of the *Labour Leader*, the party's official newspaper.

While likely influenced by Hardie, Glasier was by temperament and instinct an internationalist, and his pacifist convictions were the natural outgrowth of this predisposition. As both socialists and internationalists, Glasier and his propagandist partner and wife, Katharine, were optimistic and idealistic about human nature, believing that all peoples of the world would live in peace once assured of decent housing and adequate food and clothing. Prior to 1914 Glasier's pacifist sentiments were primarily evident in his pronouncements against the arms race and in his support for the Second International, whose congresses he began attending in 1896. With the outbreak of World War I, Glasier enlisted his pen in the cause of international peace and the survival of the International—goals he sought in vain.

Unlike the Labour party itself, the ILP opposed the Great War, thanks in part to Glasier's efforts, throughout the conflict. Unpopular at first, the ILP's antiwar persistence eventually paid political dividends for the Labour party. In the postwar disillusionment era, such notable British intellectuals as *Bertrand Russell and *Charles Trevelyan assisted the Labourites in ousting the Liberal party as one of Britain's premier political entities.

Bibliography:

A. *Hail Internationalism!: The Advent of the Overthrow of Militarism and War* (London, ?); *The Meaning of Socialism* (Manchester, 1919); *Militarism and Conscription*: Part 1—*Militarism*; Part 2—*The Peril of Conscription* (London, 1915); *The Minstrelsy of Peace: A Collection of Notable Verse in the English Tongue, Relating to Peace and War* (Manchester, 1917?); *Mr. Norman Angell's Dialectic against War* (Manchester, 1913); *Resist the Foreiqn Yoke of Conscription*! (Manchester, ?); *The Religion of Socialism: Two Aspects*, with Katharine Glasier (Manchester, n.d.); *Socialism and Strikes* (N.P., 1893); *William Morris and the Early Days of the Socialist Movement* (London, 1921).

B. Elizabeth Foster, *Bruce Glasier and His Poetry* (privately printed, n.d.); Joan B. Huffman, "John Bruce Glasier," J. O. Baylen and Norbert Gossman, eds., *Dictionary of Modern British Radicals* (Brighton, England, Vol 3 in press); *Memorial* (Manchester, 1920?); Laurence Thompson, *The Enthusiasts* (London, 1971).

C. John and Katharine Bruce Glasier Papers, Sydney Jones Library, University of Liverpool.

Joan B. Huffman

GLUECKLICH, Vilma (9 August 1872, Vágujhely, Hungary—19 August 1927, Vienna). *Education*: teacher training school, Budapest; majored in physics and mathematics as first woman admitted to the Univ. of Budapest, 1896. *Career*: high school teacher, suffragist, feminist, pacifist.

Vilma Gluecklich and *Rosika Schwimmer were joint leaders of the Hungarian woman's movement. Gluecklich was always seen as gentle, serene, modest, patient, tolerant, noble; Schwimmer, as energetic, daring, determined, enterprising, even ruthless. To their associates it was almost unbelievable that these entirely opposite, powerful personalities were able to work in harmony for decades under the most difficult conditions. That the Hungarian Feminist Association, founded by the two women in 1904, was unique in both the international suffrage and peace movements was largely due to their intelligent, unselfish dedication. Gluecklich remained the Association's director to the end of her life; she helped organize the 1913 Budapest Congress of the International Woman Suffrage Alliance. She also was closely associated with the National Association of Women Office Workers.

The impact of the First World War was shattering—she saw "destroyed in an hour all ... our life's labor...." Under her leadership the Association organized immediate relief and employment for the thousands of destitute women and children left without support on mobilization. In September 1914, Gluecklich's was the first loud appeal for peace in Hungary. In April 1915, she led a large Hungarian delegation to The Hague Congress of Women. The Association, unswerving in its support for the Congress resolutions on mediation and world organization, became the Hungarian Section of The Women's International League for Peace and Freedom. Feminist peace meetings were held and peace editorials published in *A Nö* throughout the war. Gluecklich attended the 1919 Zurich Congress of the Women's International League for Peace and Freedom. From 1922–25 she served as the organization's International Secretary in Geneva. Because of her wartime peace activities, she was denied her teacher's pension by the government.

Bibliography:

A. Feminista Ertesitö (Budapest, 1906).

B. Memorial Issue of *A Nö* (Budapest, 1927–28).

C. Schwimmer-Lloyd Collection, New York Public Library; WILPF Papers, Swarthmore Peace Collection; Feminist Association Papers, Hungarian National Archives, Budapest.

Edith Wynner

GOBAT, Albert (2 May 1843, Tramelan, Switzerland—16 March 1914, Berne). Education: universities of Basel, Berne, and Paris; Doctorate of Law, Univ. of Heidelberg, 1867. *Career*: lawyer, Superintendent of Public Instruction, Canton of Berne, 1882–1912; legislator, Grand Council of Berne, 1882–84, Swiss Council of States, 1884–90, Swiss National Council, 1890–1914; president, Canton of Berne, 1886–87; director Interparliamentary Bureau, 1892–1909; secretary-general, Permanent International Peace Bureau, 1906–14; pacifist leader.

Son of a Protestant minister, Albert Gobat received his education in Switzerland, France, and Germany. Although he practiced law until 1882, Gobat thereafter dedicated his energies to education and politics. Throughout most of his adult life, he was simultaneously head of public instruction in Berne and a liberal legislator on either the cantonal or federal level. In 1886, at the age of forty-three, he became President of the Canton of Berne for a two-year term.

A confirmed pacifist, Gobat was a delegate to the first international conference of the Interparliamentary Union, an organization particularly interested in promoting arbitration among nations. In 1892 he presided over the fourth international meeting of the Union which established the Interparliamentary Bureau as the executive arm of the organization with headquarters in Berne. Gobat served for seventeen years as the first director of the Bureau, arranging annual conferences, publishing the minutes of these meetings, editing the Bureau's monthly publication, and supporting the efforts of Union members to promote international harmony. He was particularly successful in increasing the worldwide membership of the Interparliamentary Union. At its meeting in St. Louis in the summer of 1904, the Interparliamentary Union called for a Second Hague Peace Conference. Gobat asked President +Theodore Roosevelt to convene this world meeting. Secretary of State John Hay's attempts in the autumn of 1904 to call a conference were unsuccessful because of the Russo-Japanese War. When The Second Hague Peace Conference met in 1907, it enlarged the machinery for voluntarily settling international disputes, but efforts to limit armaments failed.

On the death of *Elie Ducommun in 1906, Gobat also became secretary-general of the Permanent International Peace Bureau, the administrative organ of the International Union of Peace Societies located in Berne. While the Interparliamentary Union was composed of national associations of legislators, the International Union of Peace Societies brought together a broader spectrum of peace groups organized into national bodies. The Bureau also arranged the annual congresses of the International Union of Peace Societies.

As a liberal legislator, Gobat shared with other pacifist leaders in the years before World War I a firm conviction that democratically elected officials could and should cooperate in guaranteeing international concord. The Interparliamentary Union was founded for that purpose. Accordingly, in his role as secretary-general of the Berne peace bureau, Gobat was instrumental in convening the only meeting of French and German parliamentarians in May 1913. The International Peace Bureau also sought to exert pressure on national governments to submit differences to arbitration and to limit international rivalries through covenants. In a variety of private initiatives, Gobat attempted to influence the foreign policies of European governments. These initiatives included a militant critique of the Italian government in 1911 for its war against Turkey, a devastating attack on Italian pacifists who backed their government, and much pressure on national peace groups to become more militant. Gobat's service to world peace was recognized by his contemporaries. In 1902 he shared the Nobel Peace Prize with his compatriot, Elie Ducommun, the then secretary-general of the International Peace Bureau. In 1910 the Berne peace bureau, which Gobat headed as Ducommun's successor, also received this distinction. Gobat literally died serving the cause of peace. His death occurred at a council meeting of the peace bureau.

Bibliography:

A. *Le Cauchemar de l'Europe* (Strasbourg, 1911); *La Conférence interparlementaire franco-allemande* (Berne, 1913); *Croquis et impressions d'Amérique* (Berne, 1904); *De-´veloppement du bureau international permanent de la paix* (Berne, 1910); *Le Développement des conventions de La Haye* (Berne, 1908); *L'Histoire de la Suisse racontée au peuple* (Neuchâtel, 1900); *Le République de Berne et la France Pendant les guerres de religion.* (Paris, 1891).

B. Frederic W. Haberman, ed., *Nobel Lectures Peace*, I, 39–41; Frederic Passy, "The Recipients of the Nobel Prize of Peace," *The Independent*, 55 (March 5, 1903), 554–57; *Dictionnaire historique et biographique de la Suisse*, III, 472; *Historisch Biographisches Lexikon der Schweiz*, III, 577.

Sabine Jessner

GOBAT, Marguerite (23 February 1870, Delémont, Switzerland—19 June 1937, Macolin, Switzerland). *Education*: public schools, Berne, Switzerland. *Career*: cofounder of the Swiss branch of the Women's International League for Peace and Freedom, 1919; educator, editor, and pacifist leader.

The oldest child of the pacifist leader *Albert Gobat, Marguerite received her formal education in the public schools of Delémont and then Berne after her family moved there in 1882. Involved early in her father's activities, she worked for him in Berne where he headed the Permanent International Peace Bureau, 1906–1914.

Marguerite Gobat's first contributions came in the fields of education and journalism. In 1916 she adopted the infant son of her late sister and began her interest in pacifist education as a teacher at the Fellowship School in Gland (1916–28). In 1928 Gobat founded the Champ du Plane boarding school in Macolin to promote international understanding by bringing together refugees and orphans as well as other children of different nationalities and religions. Simultaneously, she was active as a journalist. First Gobat edited *Aujourd'hui* (1918–24), a magazine dedicated to promoting peace through education, and later she was in charge of "Erzieher" (1924–37), the educational supplement of the women's newspaper *Berna*.

Marguerite Gobat was also important to the peace movement as an activist in Switzerland. She served as secretary of the Union mondiale de la femme pour la concorde internationale (Universal Union of Women for International Harmony) and in 1919 was cofounder of the Swiss branch of the Women's International League for Peace and Freedom (WILPF). An active leader, Gobat helped recruit women to the new Swiss organization and represented her compatriots at WILPF international congresses in the 1920s and 1930s.

Her travels took her to Stockholm, Prague, The Hague, Vienna, and Washington, and she served as an international vice-president of WILPF. But she always returned to her school, overlooking the lake of Bienne, where in harmonious surroundings she was educating the young in the ways of international conciliation. It was there that she died in 1937.

Bibliography:

A. "Albert Gobat," *Historisch Biographisches Lexikon der Schweiz* (Berne, 1926), III, 577.

B. Barbara Traber, "Marguerite Gobat," *Bernerinnen* (Berne, 1980), 109–11. *Der Erzieher*, No. 12, 1937; *La Française*, October 15, 1937; *Pax International*, October 2, 1937.

Sabine Jessner

GOBLET D'ALVIELLA, Eugène Félicien Albert (10 August 1846, Brussels, Belgium—9 September 1925, Brussels). *Education*: Doctor of political and administrative sciences, Univ. libre de Bruxelles, 1868, Dr. jur., 1870. *Career*: provincial counsellor, 1872–78; member, Chamber of Representatives, 1878–84; senator, 1892–94, 1900–25; vice-president, Senate, 1912; minister of state, 1914; minister without portfolio, 1916–18; director, *Revue de Belgique*, 1874–1890; professor, Univ. of Brussels, 1893, rector, 1896–98.

Eugène Goblet d'Alviella, a politician with liberal views including a deep belief in free trade, became interested in the peace movement at a very young age. In 1871 he won the prize essay competition organized by the Paris Ligue internationale et permanent de la paix (International and Permanent League of Peace) and published his work as *Désarmer ou déchoir. Essai sur les relations internationales*. This work urged immediate collective disarmament and further argued that the lowering of tariff barriers, the diffusion of popular education, and the extension of self-government, provided the best objectives for a future of a united humanity. Beyond these recommendations covering economic, social, political, and military spheres, he urged the positive juridical organization of international society.

A warm enthusiast for a United States of Europe, Goblet d'Alviella believed that the immediate creation of a common code of positive laws, a series of tribunals to apply these laws to specific conflicts, and a public force sufficiently powerful to guarantee the execution of sentences must take place. If Europe failed to adopt these routes, he predicted a fatal decline in its status and the concomitant rise of the United States of America which would become the world's center because it was not suffering under the weight of armaments.

Bibliography:

A. *Désarmer ou déchoir. Essai sur les relations internationales* (Brussels, 1872); *Emile de Laveleye, sa vie et son oeuvre* (Brussels, 1895); *Le Vrai et le faux pacifisme* (Paris, 1917).

B. R. Kreglinger, "Le Comte Eugène Goblet d'Alviella" in *Bulletin de la Ligue de l'Enseignement*, 3–4 (1925) 126–31; *Bibliographie Nationale*, II, 148; *Biographie Nationale*, XLI, cols., 359–62. *Dictionnaire des Ecrivains belges*, I, 906–7.

Nadine Lubelski-Bernard
Trans. by Sandi E. Cooper

GODIN, Jean-Baptiste-André (26 January 1817, Esquehéries, Aisne, France—14 January 1888, Guise, Aisne). *Career*: inventor; deputy, 1871–76; founder, Familistère de Guise and the Société de paix et d'arbitrage international; editor, *Le Devoir* and *Le Désarmement*; utopian socialist.

During a half century devoted to practical and theoretical reformism, Jean-Baptiste-André Godin sought international peace as an indispensable precondition for achieving his lifelong goal of overcoming the growing hostility between labor and capital. Struck by the misery of the working class during a youthful Tour de France, Godin, an ironsmith by training, returned to his native village in 1840 determined to improve the lot of the laboring masses. The wealth for translating this determination into practice came from the manufacturing of heating and cooking implements, the processes for which Godin secured through a series of patented inventions. The vision came from Charles Fourier, whose ideas led Godin initially to lose a third of his fortune backing the Texan utopia of Victor Considerant and then to create his own Fourierist community—the Familistère de Guise.

Founded in 1859, the Familistère de Guise embodied Godin's view that "true socialism is not revolutionary, but organizational." Constructed around a central pavilion called the *Palais Social*, the Familistère provided its members with low-cost housing, consumer cooperatives, day-care facilities, a coeducational elementary school, and a library. Whether in residence or not, workers and their families also enjoyed the protection of workmen's compensation, medical insurance, a destitution fund, and a retirement plan. Moreover, consistent with Godin's conviction that capital should be the subordinate partner to labor, a profit-sharing plan guaranteed that the workers, who numbered about 2,000 in 1900, would eventually achieve collective ownership of both the facility at Guise and a smaller facility in the Brussels' suburb of Shaerbeek.

Godin served the cause of peace by personally demanding it, by opening the Familistère's journal to its advocates, and by creating a group to promote it. He argued not only that there could be no human progress without international arbitration of war-threatening disputes, but also that there could never be domestic peace or prosperity until nations stopped wasting their wealth on armaments. Internal as well as external harmony thus depended, he maintained, on the founding of a federation of nations whose collective power, directed by decisions reached at periodic peace congresses, would eliminate war. In *Le Devoir* (1878–1906), the journal through which the Familistère's Comité propagandiste de l'arbitrage et de la paix (Propaganda Committee for Arbitration and Peace) spoke, nearly every one of its 784 issues carried either a peace advocate's appeal or a summary of the status of the international peace movement. Furthermore, in 1885 Godin edited *Le Désarmement européen et l'arbitrage international*, and in 1886, two years before his death, he created his own pacifist group—the Société de paix et d'arbitrage international (Society for Peace and International Arbitration).

Although the July Monarchy (1830–48) tried to undercut Godin's socialist reformism by stripping him of his patents, the Third Republic (1870–1940), which Godin served as a deputy from 1871 to 1876, honored him with the palmes d'officier d'académie and the croix de la Légion d'honneur. Godin's reputation also benefited from the labor of his second wife, Marie A. Moret, who spent the last twenty years of her life compiling his collected works.

Bibliography:

A. *Le Gouvernement, ce qu'il a été, ce qu'il doit être, et le vrai socialisme en action* (Paris, 1883); *Mutualité nationale contre la misère, petition et proposition de loi à la Chambre des députés* (Paris, 1883); *Mutualité sociale et association du capital et du travail* (Paris, 1880); *Oeuvre posthume. La République du travail et la reforme parlementaire* (Paris, 1889); *La Politique du travail et la politique des privilèges* (Paris, 1875); *La Richesse au service du peuple. Le Familistère de Guise* (Paris, 1874); *Les Socialistes et les droits du travail* (Paris, 1874); *Solutions sociales* (Paris, 1871); *La Souveraineté et les droits du peuple* (Paris, 1874).

B. F. Bernardot, *La Familistère de Guise, Association du capital et du travail et son fondateur Jean-Baptiste-André Godin, étude faite an nom de la Société du familistère de Guise* (Guise, 1889); Émile Dallet, *In memoriam. Marie A. Moret: Veuve de J.-B. André Godin* (Nîmes, 1908); D[allet], F[abre], and P[rudhommeaux], *Le Familistère illustré, resultats de vingt ans d'association, 1880–1900* (Paris, n.d. Eng. trans.by Aneunin Williams, *Twenty Years of Co-Partnership at Guise*, London, 1903, 2nd ed., London, 1908); Louis Lestelle, *Étude sur le Familistère de Guise (Son Fondateur: J.-B.-A. Godin)* Paris, 1904); Jean Maitron, ed. *Dictionnaire biographique du mouvement ouvrier français*

(Paris, 1974), XII, 296–97; Alfred Migrenne, *A. Godin, Sa vie, Son oeuvre, 1817–1888* (Saint-Quentin, 1908); Marie Moret, *Documents pour une vie biographie complète de Jean-Baptiste-André Godin, rassemblés par sa veuve, née Marie Moret* (3 vols, Guise, 1897–1910); A. Oyon, *Une Véritable Cité ouvrière: le familistère de Guise* (Paris, 1865); J. Prudhommeaux, *Les expériences sociales de J.-Bte A. Godin* (Paris, 1919); Jeanne Richert, *Das Familienheim zu Guise* (Gross-Lichterfelder, 1910).

Patrick Kay Bidelman

GOEGG, Amand (7 April 1820, Renchen/Baden, Germany—21 July 1897, Renchen/Baden). *Education*: cameralistic studies (political science, national economy, and administration) in Freiburg, Munich, and Heidelberg, 1840–43; state civil service examination, Karlsruhe, 1844. *Career*: government official; minister of finance in the Baden revolutionary government, 1849; manufacturer, factory manager, travel writer, pacifist, political activist, and writer.

After passing the required state examination, Amand Goegg entered the Baden state service. In his political outlook, he was a radical democrat and a socialist who was influenced by early French socialism, above all by *Pierre-Joseph Proudhon. During the later stages of the revolution of 1848–49, Goegg was active as a member of a radical minority that sought to create a democratic republic in Baden. In the winter of 1848–49, Goegg was instrumental in organizing a dense network of democratic associations with a total membership of almost 35,000 members. With the popular rebellion of May 1849, Goegg and his radical political allies appeared to have achieved their goal, but the successful Baden revolution was crushed in July 1849 by the military intervention of Prussia and other German states. Goegg was sentenced to life imprisonment, but evaded prison by escaping to Switzerland. After thirteen years in exile, spent in Switzerland, Paris, London, and the United States, a pardon allowed him to return to Baden in 1862. During his exile in Geneva, Goegg married a native of that city. *Marie Goegg became a well-known feminist and peace advocate in her own right.

In Paris, Goegg became associated with the Sainte alliance des peuples, an organization of democrats from various nations, founded by Giuseppe Mazzini and Auguste Ledru-Rollin. The aim of the organization was to lay the groundwork for a democratic revolution in Europe. Because of his association with the alliance, Goegg was arrested but managed to flee to England where, with other German emigrée revolutionaries, he founded the Comité d'agitation allemand as the German section of the international Comité central démocratique européen. The task of the German committee was to prepare the ground for a revolution in Germany. To this end, Goegg devoted a great deal of energy to propaganda work aimed chiefly at winning the support of journeymen artisans for the revolutionary cause and spreading Utopian socialist writings in Germany. In 1852 he carried his agitation for a revolution in Europe to the United States where he took part in the Congress of European Democrats and founded, in Philadelphia, the American Revolutionary League for Europe.

To support himself, Goegg founded a mirror factory in Geneva in 1857, and after his return to Baden he took over the management of a glass factory. He sharply criticized Otto von Bismarck's military solution to the German question through the Austro-Prussian War (1866). In 1867, together with *Victor Hugo, *Charles Lemmonier, Louis Blanc, Pierre Jolissaint, John Stuart Mill, and Giuseppe Garibaldi, Goegg summoned a "Peace through Freedom" congress in Geneva. At the congress, the Ligue international de la paix et de la liberté (International League for Peace and Freedom) was founded. The League set as its goal the grounding of peace on democracy and freedom, the creation of a cosmopolitan alliance of peoples, the replacement of standing armies by national militias, and the promotion of the welfare of all classes, but especially that of the working class. In 1868 Goegg tried, and failed, to persuade Karl Marx and Friedrich Engels to support the League. In 1869 and 1870, Goegg participated in the International Socialist Congress and the International Peace Congress respectively, both of which were held in Basel.

In the years until 1883, Goegg undertook numerous journeys to Australia, and to North and South America, giving many lectures which won support for his political credo "peace through freedom and social justice." His travel reports, published in 1888 under the title *Uberseeische Reisen*, reveal a European centered outlook and a feeling of superiority towards Latin Americans, Chinese, and Negroes rooted in pride in the colonial and economic achievements of the Germanic peoples (Anglo-Saxon and Germans). Completely in keeping with bourgeois radical democrats of the first half of the nineteenth century, patriotism, national pride, and cosmopolitanism held no contradictions for Goegg. He did not understand that peace was not an automatic consequence of a free and democratic constitution and just internal social circumstances, as his democratic idealism and Utopian socialism assumed, if at the same time a feeling of superiority towards other nationalities and races was present and active among the masses.

Just as Goegg did not give up his early socialist outlook in favor of a Marxian socialist one when, in the last years of his life, he joined the German Social Democratic party, so he did not sacrifice his original bourgeois-democratic constitutional internationalism to Marxist-socialist class internationalism. To the end, Goegg remained a representative of that concept of pacifism that saw in liberal-democratic constitutional arrangements and just social circumstances the fundamental preliminary conditions for international peace.

Bibliography:

A. *Nachträgliche authentische Aufschlusse über die Badische Revolution von 1849, deren Entstehung, politischen und militärischen Verlauf* (Zurich, 1876); *Rückblicke auf die Badische Revolution unter Hinweisung auf die gegenwärtige Lage Deutschlands von einem Mitgliede der badischen konstituierenden Versammlung* (Paris, 1850); *Überseeische Reisen* (Zurich, 1888); *Ein Wort an die natürlichen Vermittler des Völkerbundes zunächst gerichtet an die Elsässer als die Vermittler des Bruderbundes zwischen dem deutschen und französischen Volk* (Colmar, 1851).

B. Alwin Hanschmidt, *Republikanisch-demokratischer Internationalismus im 19. Jahrhundert. Ideen—Formen—Organisierungsversuche* (Husum, 1977); Friedrich Lautenschlager, "Amand Goegg, ein badischer Achtundvierziger. Zur Hundert jahrfeier der deutschen Revolution von 1848/49," *Zeitschrift für die Geschichte des Oberrheins*, 96 (1948), 19–38.

Alwin Hanschmidt
Trans. by Solomon Wank

GOEGG, Marie Pouchoulin (24 May 1826 Geneva—24 March 1899, Geneva). *Education*: public elementary school, self-educated. *Career*: council member and secretary, Ligue international de la paix et de la liberté, 1868–96; founder, Association international des femmes, 1868, (renamed Solidarité in 1870); feminist and pacifist.

Descended from a family of Huguenot refugees who came to Geneva in the eighteenth century, Marie Goegg (born Jeanne-Marie Pouchoulin), daughter of a clockmaker, left school at 13 to work at home and in her father's shop. Under the influence, perhaps, of her maternal uncle, Benjamin Pautex, who was a contributor to the Dictionary of the Academie Française and an author, she was drawn to books and evidently became very well read in history and literature on her own. Her first marriage (1845) at age 19 produced one son and ended in divorce (1856). She then married the Baden revolutionary exile, *Amand Goegg, who adopted her son. Together, they had two more boys. This marriage was never legally dissolved, although Goegg and she appear to have permanently separated in 1874. Not until this second marriage did Marie Goegg ever travel out of Switzerland.

Her well-deserved reputation as a prominent feminist developed directly from her involvement in the democratically oriented Ligue international de la paix et de la liberté (International League of Peace and Freedom), founded in 1867 in Geneva by a circle of European liberals, republicans, socialists and revolutionaries. Giuseppe Garibaldi presided over its famous opening conference which was organized by *Charles Lemmonier, Gustav Vogt, *Victor Hugo, John S. Mill and *Amand Goegg. Marie Goegg became a public figure in her own right through an article which she inserted in the League's organ, *Les Etats-Unis d'Europe* (March, 1868), calling for the creation of a separate international peace society of women. Her proposal was the first ever to appear in Europe and she suggested that while the women's group should coordinate its actions with the League and serve on the League's central committees, it should operate in a separate sphere as well.

Goegg persuaded the League that without the labors of women, their objectives of peace and justice would remain elusive. At the Berne meeting of 1868 she delivered one of the first speeches ever made by a European woman at a public gathering and observed that the men who had made the French Revolution of 1789 had done so with the support of educated eighteenth-century women. In establishing the grand principles of freedom and justice, however, they omitted including wives, mothers, and sisters. The revolutionaries, therefore, produced a new authoritarianism, not unlike the one they were rejecting for themselves. Maintaining that progress required the equality of all its members, Goegg insisted that, given the backward state of women, the League had to embrace a variety of programs for the emancipation of women including education and civil rights. Elected to the council of the League, she then went on to create the first avowedly feminist society in Europe, organized conferences, lectures, meetings, and small social gatherings, and traveled about Switzerland. Her call elicited responses from other nations where corresponding societies of women were established.

The Association international des femmes (International Association of Women) fell victim to the Franco-Prussian War and was reconstituted as a Swiss group, Solidarité. Her agitation for women's rights earned Marie Goegg the sobriquet, ''pétroleuse''—an incendiary—referring to the women who set fires during the Paris Commune. This exaggerated and outrageous label did not stop her and one of her first achievements was the opening of the University of Geneva to women (1872), following the pattern of Zurich which had been the first continental university to admit women. Her crusade for political, educational, and civil rights for women never ended. For the remainder of her life she was also a major force in preserving the Ligue international de la paix et de la liberté by her behind-the-scenes administrative work in her Geneva apartment, her editorial labors on the journal, and her correspondence with members around Europe. Charles Lemmonier served as its president, but Marie Goegg kept the papers flowing. Her services terminated only with her old age and with the move of League headquarters to France when *Emile Arnaud became its president.

Bibliography:

A. *Deux discours* (Paris, 1878).

B. Susanna Woodtli, *Du féminisme a l'égalité politique: Un Siècle de luttes en Suisse, 1868–1971* (Lausanne, 1977); obituaries in *Le Bulletin Continental*, April 1899; *Les Etats-Unis d'Europe*, April/May, 1899; *La Patrie Suisse* (Geneva), April 12, 1899.

C. Scattered letters, Bureau international de la paix, Archives, United Nations Library, Geneva; unpublished genealogy, prepared by W. Zurbuchen, Archives d'État, Geneva.

Sandi E. Cooper

GOLAY, Henri (29 January 1867, Le Sentier, Switzerland—4 October 1950, Geneva.) *Education*: public schools, Le Locle; studies at Univ. of Vienna. *Career*: teacher in Payerne, Le Locle, and St. Gallen; chief of section, Swiss Foreign Office, 1902–11; secretary-general, Permanent International Peace Bureau, 1911–50.

After earning his teaching license in Le Locle in 1883, Henri Golay attended the University of Vienna for a brief time, but did not receive a degree. Golay returned to Switzerland and taught in French first at Payerne and later at a business school in Le Locle. Subsequently the young educator gave classes in German at the commercial academy in St. Gallen. In 1902 he changed both his profession and locale by becoming the head of the French section of the Swiss Foreign

Office in Berne. He began a career in editorial work in 1911 when he was put in charge of the proceedings of the Bernese cantonal legislature. The same year the director of the Permanent International Peace Bureau, *Albert Gobat, appointed him secretary-general of that organization. In accepting this new post, Golay gave up a secure, well-paying position with the Swiss Government to devote himself entirely to peace work. In May 1913 he edited the account of the Franco-German Interparliamentary Conference. For the remainder of his long life, he continued to edit the minutes of international pacifist meetings. On Gobat's death in March 1914, Golay inherited the directorship of the Permanent International Peace Bureau.

Although his career lacked dramatic achievements, Henri Golay's commitment to the ideal of world peace was expressed by toiling behind the scenes as a gifted organizer. From 1914 until his death in 1950, he managed the office of the peace bureau, first in Berne and then in Geneva after 1920. Golay organized twelve international peace congresses from 1912 to 1949 and edited their proceedings. Additionally, he oversaw the *Mouvement pacifiste*, a publication which appeared in German, French, and English. Gifted in languages, Golay translated speeches at international meetings and many articles. His own bibliography consists of a number of pamphlets and pieces in the *Mouvement pacifiste*. By the time he died, Golay had served as both an organizer and an editor for almost four decades.

Bibliography:

A. "An die geistigen Führer aller Nationen!" *Internationales Friedensbureau Bern* (Berne, 1915); "Le Comité directeur du Bureau international de la paix dans les Balkans" (Dǒle-du-Jura, 1929); "Second Addendum," *Notice sur le Bureau international de la paix* (Genève, 1939); "To Peace Societies in all Lands," *International Peace Bureau Berne* (Berne, 1915).

B. Der Bund [Bern] (October 6, 1950); Alfred H. Fried, *Handbuch der Friedensbewegung* (Leipzig, 1911); Das Internationale Friedensbüro, *Geschichte-Ziel-Tätigkeit* (Genf, 1969); Ludwig Quidde, *Der Deutsche Pazifismus während des Weltkrieges, 1914–1918* (Boppard am Rhein, 1979); Hans Wehberg, "Zum Gedenken an Henri Golay, Generalsekretär des Internationalen Friedensbureaus," *Die Friedenswarte*, 50 (1950/1), 266–69; *La Tribune de Genève*, October 6, 1950.

C. Papers of the Universal Peace Congresses, Archive of the United Nations, Geneva.

Sabine Jessner

GOLDMAN, Emma (27 June 1869, Kovno [now Kaunas, Lithuania]—14 May 1940, Toronto, Canada). *Education*: private Jewish school, Königsberg, Prussia; six months schooling, St. Petersburg, Russia; midwifery and nursing course at Allgemeines Krankenhaus, Vienna, 1895–96; largely self-educated. *Career*: migrated to the United States, 1885; factory worker, Rochester, NY and New Haven, CT, 1886–89; editor, *Mother Earth Magazine*, 1906–17; deported from United States, 1919; exile in Soviet Union, Europe, and Canada; anarchist and feminist.

Emma Goldman was arrested in 1917 for her role in the formation of the No-Conscription League in New York. An ardent opponent of war and a prominent advocate of anarchism, she was deported from the United States in 1919. By then, she was a famous public figure, even notorious. A leader in the anarchist movement and uncompromising in her feminist views, Goldman was an early advocate of free speech, birth control, women's equality and independence, libertarian schools, union organization, the eight hour work-day—positions considered quite radical in her time.

Her work against compulsory military service during World War I was motivated both by her belief in the freedom of individuals from governmental coercion and by her commitment to peace. In her early anarchist days, she was associated in the public mind with the anarchist "progaganda of the deed," individual acts of political assassination. In 1892 she was implicated in the assassination attempt upon Henry Frick, head of the Carnegie Steel mills in Pittsburgh by her companion, Alexander Berkman. She was also popularly thought to be involved in Leon Czolgosz's assassination of President William McKinley, though she denied a connection. Later in her career, she reversed her position of approval for Berkman's assassination attempt and other such individual acts of violence. She became an adherent to *Peter Kropotkin's essentially nonviolent vision of anarchism, though she remained a supporter of revolution and the necessary violence that might accompany a just revolution.

Goldman was a remarkable and admired speaker, able to move large audiences—even those that did not share all of her radical commitments. When she turned her eloquence and commitment to anticonscription work during World War I, government authorities labeled her as one of the most dangerous women in America. Early in 1916 she warned that "preparedness means violence and war;... it leads to universal slaughter." She spoke all across the United States against war preparations and conscription; her lecture in mid–1916, "Preparedness, the Road to Universal Slaughter," was later issued as a pamphlet and distributed. She used *Mother Earth Magazine*, the journal she edited for ten years, as a vehicle for expressing her opposition. In March 1917, her essay in that journal, "The Promoters of the War Mania," urged every "liberty-loving person to voice a fiery protest against the participation of this country in the European mass murder." She also counseled youth of draft age to refuse to be ordered to kill and "to hold out determinately against compulsory military service for the murder of your fellow men."

For such admonitions Goldman and Berkman were sentenced on July 8, 1917 to serve two years in prison and to pay fines of $10,000 each on the charge of "conspiracy to defeat military registration under the conscription law." Her work with the No-Conscription League, her chief peace activity in the United States, was so intense that she spent the last moments before entering Missouri State Penitentiary completing a pamphlet denouncing the injustice of the state forcing young men to fight and kill for the benefit of capitalist leaders.

After Goldman served her 18-month prison sentence, the U. S. government deported her to Russia. There her original enthusiasm for the workers' and peasants' revolution was shattered by the bureaucratization and growing authoritarianism of Communist rule. She spoke out against the Bolshevik regime early, when many radical and liberal observers were still praising the Soviet experiment. Eventually, she left for western Europe.

While in exile in Europe, she continued to lecture widely and to write extensively (including her autobiography), staying in touch with all the major political and cultural strands of the period. Speaking out against the rise of fascism, she went to Spain to aid in the fight of the Spanish anarchists against Franco. She worked tirelessly for public support and aid for the thousands of Spanish refugees who fled the fascist regime in Spain after the war.

Goldman longed to return to the United States, but was allowed only a 90-day lecture tour visa in 1934. After her death, she was permitted a final return when she was buried at the Waldheim Cemetery in Chicago, near the graves of the Haymarket Square martyrs whose execution for their anarchist beliefs had been the initial inspiration in the formation of her own anarchist philosophy. Though notorious in her own day, Emma Goldman had an obvious integrity, a willingness to suffer for her principles, and a vision of a world of cooperation of free individuals, with no national interests and no war, that have made her a symbol of the best hopes of humankind.

Bibliography:

A. *Anarchism and Other Essays* (New York, 1911, reprinted 1970); *Living My Life* (2 vols., New York, 1934, reprinted 1970); *Red Emma Speaks: Selected Writings and Speeches by Emma Goldman* (New York, 1972).

B. Richard Drinnon, *Rebel in Paradise* (New York, 1976); Richard and Anna Maria Drinnon, eds., *Nowhere at Home: Letters from Exile by Emma Goldman and Alexander Berkman* (New York, 1975); Candace Falk, *Love, Anarchy and Emma Goldman* (New York, 1983); Alix Kates Shulman, *To the Barricades* (Crowell, NY, 1971).

Candace Falk

GOLDSCHEID, Rudolf (12 August 1870, Vienna—6 October 1931, Vienna). *Education*: gymnasium in Vienna; philosophical studies, Univ. of Berlin, 1889ff. *Career*: editor, *Die Friedenswarte*, 1923–26; founder, Soziologische Gesellschaft (Vienna) and Gesellschaft für Soziologie (Germany); president, Austrian Monistenbund; associate editor, *Annalen für Natur und Kulturphilosophie*; founder, Österreichische Liga für Menschenrechte; writer, scholar, and pacifist.

Rudolf Goldscheid was the son of a wealthy Jewish family from Vienna. His early writings, some under the pseudonym Rudolf Golm, included novels, plays, and philosophic treatises on the problems of social ethics. Attracted to the Austrian peace movement in the first decades of this century, Goldscheid increasingly turned his attention as a writer to the questions of war and peace.

Primarily a liberal in outlook, Goldscheid's thinking at this time proceeded from assumptions which were capitalistic and rationalistic. In *Friedensbewegung und Menschenökonomie* (*Peace Movement and Human Economics*) (1912), he argued, much as *Norman Angell in *The Great Illusion*, that in the context of a highly developed industrial civilization war had become suicidal, hence irrational, and would soon disappear. In Goldscheid's view, war was a "childhood disease of human history" which modern progress would eventually eliminate altogether. International trade, not war, would determine the future of civilization. Respect for private property, which he regarded as the basis of the rule of law, would function among nations, as well as within them, to guarantee peace. Given the modern, strong belief in the sanctity of private property, including even that of enemies, there was nothing to gain from war. War, therefore, had become meaningless, so long as it did not consist of redress for plunder or for ruthless disregard of the rights of others.

The outbreak of World War I sobered the excesses of Goldscheid's prewar optimism. In *Das Verhältnis der äussern Politik zur innern*, published in September 1914, Goldscheid argued that when a nation's foreign policy becomes geared to preparations to fight a major war, military priorities will dominate domestic politics, suppress democracy, and accelerate governmental authoritarianism. No longer contending that an internationally interdependent economy made war impossible, Goldscheid now argued that existence of the prewar arms race itself undermined the trust on which the international economy and world peace rested. Goldscheid's plea, therefore, was for a world unthreatened by the kind of arms race that made World War I possible.

To achieve the goal of a warless world, Goldscheid argued, far-reaching changes in the social and economic structure of society would be required. Increasingly influenced by the ideas of Social Democracy, Goldscheid urged reforms that would reduce social tensions and end exploitation of the working masses. The prewar struggle for armaments control and for world law must go on, he asserted. However, only on the basis of social and economic justice would realization of these aims be possible.

Following the death of *Alfred Hermann Fried, Goldschied assumed the editorship, from 1923 to 1926, of *Die Friedenswarte*, the foremost pacifist journal in the German language. Until his death in 1931 he remained a corresponding editor of that journal, as well as an active author and leading figure in the peace movement in both Austria and Germany.

Bibliography:

A. *Deutschlands grösste Gefahr. Ein Mahnruf* (Berlin, 1915); *Frauen, Freiheit und Friede* (Leipzig, 1921); *Friedensbewegung und Menschenökonomie* (Berlin, 1912); *Sozialisierung oder Staatsbankrott* (Vienna, 1918); *Das Verhältnis der äussern Politik zur innern* (Vienna, 1914).

B. Franz Brümmer, ed., *Lexikon der deutschen Dichter und Prosaisten von Beginn des 19. Jahrhunderts bis zur Gegenwart* (Leipzig, n.d.: circa. 1913), 6th ed., II,397; Gerhard Lüdke, ed., *Kürschners Deutscher Gelehrten-Kalender 1931* (Berlin and Leipzig, 1931), 4th ed., p. 863; *Österreichisches biographisches Lexikon 1815–1950* (Graz and Cologne, 1959), II, 25; S. Wininger, ed., *Grosse jüdische National-Biographie* (Czernowitz, 1925–36), II, 452, and VII (Ergänzungsband), 19–20; *Die Friedenswarte*, 30 (1930), 193–202 and 31 (1931), 342–343.

Richard R. Laurence

GOLDSTEIN, Vida (12 April 1869, Portland, Victoria, Australia—15 August 1949, Melbourne). *Education*: Presbyterian Ladies College, Melbourne, 1884–85; studies at the Univ. of Melbourne. *Career*: editor, *The Women's Sphere*, 1900–5, *The Woman Voter*, 1905–19; feminist and political activist.

Vida Goldstein, (the granddaughter of a Polish-Jewish political refugee who had fled to Ireland, adopted Unitarianism, and passed his religious radicalism on to his Australian descendants), began her political career as a feminist in the 1890s. Later, as editor of *The Women's Sphere* and founder/president of the Women's Political Association (1902), she played a major role in drawing attention to the social conditions of women and the need for the elimination of war. Influenced by the humanitarian ideals of Rev.*Charles Strong, her activism encompassed a broad social spectrum. In 1903 she became the first woman in the English-speaking world to stand as a candidate for a constituted national electorate.

With the beginning of World War I in 1914, Goldstein directed her energies towards peace issues. She was elected chair of the Australian Peace Alliance in 1914 and, in the following year, founded and presided over the Women's Peace Army (WPA). *The Woman Voter*, edited by Goldstein, became the unofficial voice of the WPA, focusing on the publication of antiwar material. Although the WPA shared the same aims as the Sisterhood of International Peace headed by *Eleanor Moore, it was far more militant in its methods, taking a direct action stance.

While Goldstein was interested in alleviating the suffering caused by war and was instrumental in setting up a Women's Unemployment Bureau and a rural cooperative for unemployed women, she was also deeply concerned with eliminating the causes of war. The most significant contribution of Goldstein and the WPA was a highly successful campaign against Australia's conscription referenda of 1916 and 1917. The proconscriptionists based their campaign on a direct appeal to women to selflessly yield up their male progeny to the cause of Empire, "purity of the race, marriage and democracy." The WPA countered by stressing the role of women in nurturing life, exhorting them to exercise their moral superiority in containing male aggressiveness.

Seen against a social milieu of prowar sentimentality and loyalty to the British Empire, it was not surprising that the activities of the WPA became targets of attack by established authority—the press, police, and the military. Meetings were often violently disrupted, threats were made to remove their printing press, and all WPA mail was subject to government censorship.

With the rejection of conscription in the second referendum, Goldstein made her fifth and final attempt to enter the federal parliament, but her advocacy of peace had lost her considerable support. In 1919 she was invited to attend the

International Congress of Women at Zurich as one of the three Australian delegates. The WPA dissolved itself on her departure and shortly after *The Woman Voter* ceased publication. Goldstein herself did not return to Australia for three years and when she did, it was not as a political activist. Imbued with the belief that the social system could avoid destruction only by strengthening its spiritual foundations, she became a practitioner of the Christian Science Church and passed into political obscurity. Her only public political act after 1922 was a statement of support sent to a Melbourne antinuclear meeting in 1946.

Vida Goldstein was a dynamic woman of considerable charm and wit who consistently refused to compromise her principles of peace, justice, and equality. Deeply religious, she felt that good would eventually triumph over evil. While identifying militarism as having its source in commercial interests, she nevertheless remained convinced that women, as the producers of life, were endowed with a unique sensitivity to the concepts of love, justice, and peace—a higher morality not completely attainable by men. She envisaged an international sisterhood dedicated to the higher values and inspired others to work towards this goal.

Bibliography:

B. Pat Gowland, "The Women's Peace Army," E. Windshuttle, ed., *Women, Class and History* (Melbourne, 1980), 216–34; Leslie M. Henderson, *The Goldstein Story*, (Melbourne, 1973); Norman MacKenzie, "Vida Goldstein: The Australian Suffragette," *The Australian Journal of Politics and History*, 6 (November, 1960), 190–204.

C. Vida Goldstein Papers, 1902–19, and Women's Peace Army Papers, State Library of Victoria, Melbourne.

Gay Mason

GOLLANCZ, Victor (9 April 1893, London—8 February 1967, London). *Education*: attended Oxford Univ., 1912–14. *Career*: teacher, Repton School, 1916–18; staff member, Benn Brothers, 1920–28; founder and director, Victor Gollancz Publishing Company, 1928–67; publisher.

Victor Golancz's parents were orthodox Jews. He himself was deeply influenced by Christianity, by the person of Jesus, and by the Christian ethic. In the 1930s he might have become a Christian but felt it wrong to break fellowship with the suffering of the Jews. A friend once said that when his joy in living overflowed he was a Jew, when depressed or in need he turned to the Christian faith. He was in fact an eclectic and a reconciler. In two influential anthologies, *A Year of Grace* (1950) and *From Darkness to Light* (1959), he brought together hand-picked passages from many religious sources all over the world. For him the highest expression of the spiritual life was music, and he used music to shape his anthologies.

Gollancz as a small child had a horror of war and poverty. He recalled at about the age of six identifying himself with a victim of a sabre-charge in a picture of the Crimean War. He recalled his horror a few weeks later at the thought that a bullet could in a second annihilate a man it had taken twenty years to make. The horror of poverty came later, at about 11, with the imaginative realization of the lack of hope that it could ever end. He was educated at St. Paul's School. He went to Oxford and showed himself an able scholar, but chose not to complete his degree. He became dedicated to socialism, freedom, and personal responsibility.

In 1916 Gollancz went to teach at Repton. He was patently a brilliant but unorthodox teacher, and no doubt as great a trial to the headmaster, Geoffrey Fisher, later Archbishop of Canterbury, as Fisher was to him. He was forced to leave because his civics classes were promoting political education, and were deemed to encourage opposition to the war. In fact Gollancz was not in that sense a pacifist. He loathed the idea of causing hurt. He had conceived an intense desire to prevent war. But the war had come, and though he hated much of it, he wanted to go through with it and to win. Only later did he become more radical on the issue of peace.

On leaving Repton he was posted to Singapore, but returned in 1919, and in 1920 joined the publishing firm of Benn Brothers. In 1928 he formed his own company, where he was a benevolent autocrat. With the rise of Nazism he was one of the first to expose its brutality, and in 1936 formed the Left Book Club, which produced a whole series of well-argued books against fascism and in favor of socialism, including John Strachey's *Theory and Practice of Socialism*. These books played an important part in preparing opinion for the Labour landslide of 1945. Through all this he showed a rare combination of business acumen, responsible scholarship, and social conscience.

His greatest contribution to peace was perhaps in the years immediately following World War II, when he started the movement Save Europe Now with a special eye to saving Germany from starvation. His deep concern for the sufferings of the Jews at the hands of the Nazis made his witness doubly effective. He made it through his own authoritative and compassionate pamphlets, through publishing the works of others, and through the eloquence of sincerity in public speaking. The award of the Grand Cross of the German Order of Merit in 1953 meant much to him.

Then in the 1950s and 1960s he became more and more of a public figure in his opposition alike to capital punishment (including opposition to the execution of Adolf Eichmann) and to nuclear war, on both of which he was uncompromising. He was knighted for his services to humanity.

"VG," as he was known, was a complex personality, a bon viveur who rejected indulgence, a man who could identify with persecuted and persecutors, a person of high and detached intellect and deep emotion, friend of many and intimate of few, a politician whose intellectual position was seldom absolute, but whose stands were often stronger than those who professed to be absolute.

Bibliography:

A. *From Darkness to Light* (London, 1959); *More for Timothy* (London, 1953); *My*

Dear Timothy (London, 1952); *Reminiscences of Affection* (London, 1968); *A Year of Grace* (London, 1950).

John Ferguson

GONDRA, Manuel (1 January 1871, Buenos Aires, Argentina—8 March 1927, Asunción, Paraguay). *Education*: Colegio Nacional, Asunción. *Career*: educator, diplomat, President of Paraguay, 1910–11, 1920–21.

Manuel Gondra was a Paraguayan educator, politician, and statesman who was deeply committed to the peaceful resolution of tensions between nations. He was born in Buenos Aires, the son of an Argentine father and a Paraguayan mother. Shortly after his birth his parents returned to Paraguay where he spent his youth in his mother's village of Ypané. He studied at the Colegio nacional in Asunción and remained at that institution for several years teaching grammar, literature, and geography. He also served as secretary of the university, later becoming National Inspector of Schools and one of the leading educators attempting to reform the Paraguayan school system.

After the turn of the century, Gondra focused his attention on political and international affairs. He participated in the 1904 Liberal revolt in Paraguay, served as envoy to Brazil, led the Paraguayan delegation at the Third Inter-American Conference of 1906, became Minister of Foreign Relations in 1908, and in November 1910 was President for a brief period before he was forced to resign by a Colorado party revolt. After serving as Minister of War and reorganizing the Paraguayan army, he returned to diplomatic service as Minister of Foreign Affairs and as Paraguay's representative to the United States.

One of Gondra's major interests was the Chaco boundary question; he played a significant role in defining Paraguay's claims to the disputed area. While he opposed World War I and favored strict neutrality, he urged continental solidarity after the United States and Brazil had entered the conflict. His writings and public addresses reflected a deep commitment to the postwar peace efforts and frequently focused on the need to establish methods to protect the territorial integrity of nations, to further disarmament, and to create a system with coercive powers to enforce international order. He outlined his foreign policy ideals in detail in his presidential address of August 20, 1920 in which he stated that new formulas must be developed for national survival and international cooperation. He believed that a means had to be found to lessen distrust among nations and to settle questions peacefully. He expanded these ideas in a proposal submitted to the delegates at the Fifth Inter-American Conference of 1923 in Santiago, Chile. Leading the Paraguayan delegation to the conference, he introduced the "Treaty to Avoid or Prevent Conflicts Between American States." The Gondra Treaty, as it became known, called for the establishment of a commission of inquiry to investigate disputes between nations. It also called for the suspension of hostilities from the time the commission was formed until six months after the final investigation and report. This "cooling-off" period, which he had acknowledged was based on the earlier Hague Conventions and the *William J. Bryan treaties, was aimed at lessening tensions which would hopefully contribute to the peaceful resolution of problems. The commissions were to mediate disputes until the nations involved established their own commissions of arbitration and conciliation. Although the Treaty was accepted and signed by the representatives at the Santiago conference, it failed to be ratified by many of the participating states. This deeply disappointed the Paraguayan statesman who had worked diligently to enhance the cause of peace in the Americas.

Gondra returned to Paraguay after the conference and spent the remaining years of his life immersed in his books and manuscripts. After his death in 1927, the Pan American Union adopted a resolution recognizing his dedicated service to his nation and to the development of Pan-American ideals.

Bibliography:

A. "El historiador Schmidel ante la crítica del Dr. Domínguez," *La Democracia* (Asunción), July 17, August 9 & 11, 1900; *Hombres y Letrados de America*, (Asunción, Paraguay, 1942); "El idioma guaraní," *Historia Paraguaya* (Asunción), 4–5 (1959–60), 20–30.

B. Justo Pastor Benitez, *Bajo el alero Assunceño*. (Rio de Janeiro, 1955); Arturo Bray, *Hombres y epocas del Paraguay* (Buenos Aires; 1943); Carlos E. Castañeda, "Manuel E. Gondra, Statesman and Scholar," *Calendar of the Gondra Manuscript Collection* (México, 1952); Benigno Riquelme Garcia, *Cumbre en soledad: Vida de Manuel Gondra*. (Buenos Aires, 1951).

C. Manuel Gondra Papers, University of Texas Library, Austin.

Frank Gerome

GOOCH, George Peabody (21 October 1873, London—31 August 1968, Chalfont St. Peter, Bucks, England). *Education*: B.A., Trinity Coll., Cambridge Univ., 1894. *Career*: historian; Liberal Member of Parliament (for Bath), 1906–10; editor, *Contemporary Review*, 1911–60.

G. P. Gooch was a consummate historian of modern Europe focusing on politics, diplomacy, and biography. The South African War (1899–1902) and the two world wars were the salient events in his life. He was concerned with the causes of war, the roles of national leaders, and with international movements for cooperation and conciliation. With the outbreak of the war in South Africa he started a lifelong study of diplomatic events, speaking out against forces which brought on the war. He challenged the imperialism of Cecil Rhodes, Rudyard Kipling, and Joseph Chamberlain. Then and in the First World War, he was more concerned with underlying causes and the means for bringing about negotiated settlements than with condemning the fighting. His book on the causes of the war contributed to public understanding of the Boers.

Active participation in government as a Liberal Member of Parliament from 1906 to 1910 gave Gooch a first-hand knowledge of practical politics. In 1911 he became editor of the *Contemporary Review*, a position he kept until 1960, while continuing to write history prolifically.

Gooch did not protest Britain's entry into World War I, but he objected to his country's ties with the prewar alliance system as compromising its freedom to remain out of European wars. He joined the Union of Democratic Control (UDC), the leading pacifist society in Great Britain, not to condemn the war but to work for a reasonable peace. He supported calls, like that of the Fifth Marquess of Lansdowne in November 1917, for a negotiated peace. Between the wars he continued his historical writing and political activism in the search for international understanding. He supported the League of Nations, kept up his membership in the UDC, and between 1933 and 1936 was president of the National Peace Congress, established in 1904 to organize peace conferences and to coordinate the peace movement.

Gooch's production of historical works was prodigious in the 1920s and 30s. He co-edited the multivolume *British Documents on the Origins of the War, 1898–1914* which went far to illuminate the events that led to the war, and he used the documents to interpret the events and personalities in prewar diplomacy. When Adolf Hitler threatened a new war, Gooch was slow to abandon his trust in negotiated settlements, but he rejected the claim that Britain's honor had been preserved at Munich.

After the Second World War, Gooch wrote a succession of historical studies, biographies, and a brilliant autobiography. In the *Contemporary Review*, he went on supporting efforts to sustain international peace and providing a forum to promote human understanding.

Bibliography:

A. *Before the War: Studies in Diplomacy* (2 vols., London, 1936–38); *British Documents on the Origins of the War, 1898–1914*, ed. with H. Temperley (11 vols., London, 1926–38); *Cambridge History of British Foreign Policy, 1783–1919*, ed. with A. W. Ward, (3 vols., London, 1922–23); *History of Modern Europe, 1878–1919* (London, 1923); *Recent Revelations in European History* (London, 1927); *The Second Empire* (London, 1960); *Studies in German History* (London, 1948); *Under Six Reigns* (London, 1958); *The War and Its Causes* (Westminster, 1900).

B. Cynthia F. Behrman, "Introduction," in G. P. Gooch, *The War and Its Causes* (Garland ed., New York, 1972), 15–18; Herbert Butterfield, "George Peabody Gooch, 1873–1968," *Proceedings of the British Academy*, 55 (1969); 311–38; Frank Eyck, *G. P. Gooch: A Study in History and Politics* (London, 1982); Felix E. Hirsch, "George Peabody Gooch" *Journal of Modern History*, 26 (September 1954): 260–71; Walter Pierce, "George Peabody Gooch: Testament of a Liberal," *Contemporary Review*, 224 (January 1974): 19–26; *DNB,, 1961–1970, 439–41*; LT, September 2, 1968; NYT, September 2, 1968.

Lyle A. McGeoch

GOTHEIN, Georg (15 August 1857, Neumarkt, Silesia—22 March 1940 Berlin). *Education*: studies in law, Univ. of Breslau; Berlin Mining Academy. *Career*: general secretary, Upper Silesian Coal and Steel Association, 1885–87; syndic, Breslau Chamber of Commerce, 1893–1901; left-liberal member of the Prussian Diet, 1893–1903, and German Reichstag, 1901–24; Treasury Minister, 1919.

A convinced free trader, Georg Gothein was a classical liberal in an epoch and nation where liberalism was on the defensive. His internationalism reflected his admiration for liberal Britain as well as his economic interests and convictions.

Gothein entered politics as an advocate for commercial and exporting interests in opposition to the protectionist and conservative bloc of heavy industry and Junker agriculture. Although he accepted the need for tariff protection for nations beginning to industrialize, he tirelessly argued that Germany was now a mature industrial economy and that the mature economies formed each other's best customers. He advocated resolution of tariff issues through multilateral (as against bilateral) treaties and suggested that The Hague court arbitrate conflicts arising out of the treaties. Fully aware of emotional and political causes of international conflict, Gothein did not claim that commercial interdependency would itself lead to peace, but held that it helped maintain peace.

From 1911 on, Gothein, urged by his political friends *Conrad Haussmann and *Ludwig Quidde, became increasingly active in internationalist organizations: the Verband für internationale Verständigung (Association for International Understanding), created by *Otfried Nippold; the committee of Reichstag deputies for Franco-German reconciliation, created by Haussmann, and the Franco-German League, created by Quidde. In a major Reichstag speech Gothein cited Germany's domestic policies—chauvinism, militarism, mistreatment of minorities—as sources of Germany's international isolation; he expressed great confidence in Franco-German reconciliation.

When war came, Gothein, nevertheless, blamed it on Russian and French chauvinism and advocated the limited use of submarines. Yet he and Haussmann labored successfully against great odds to prevent the Progressive party from officially endorsing annexationism or unlimited submarine warfare. Gothein persistently attacked wartime censorship. His own wartime writings concerned restoring commercial relations after the war and creating an independent Poland, for which constitutionally guaranteed minority rights would be protected by the Hague court. In November 1918 Gothein was instrumental in creating the new German Democratic party and in excluding annexationists from leading roles in it.

The Versailles Treaty, however, bitterly disappointed him; like Haussmann and Quidde he voted against signing it. A final bitter blow came when the Third Reich forced the dissolution of the Association for Protection against Anti-Semitism, which Gothein, the baptized son of an assimilated Jew, had chaired since 1909.

An internationalist, Anglophile, friend of pacifists, although not a pacifist himself, Gothein exemplified the liberal virtues of rationality and toleration. His limitations reflected his virtues. A factual, unemotional tone limited his popular appeal. As an issue-oriented economic expert, he never probed the underlying causes of international conflict. His classical liberalism was reflected in laissez-faire positions on social issues which alienated the socialists, the left-liberals' only real ally in the internationalist cause.

Bibliography:

A. *Der deutsche Aussenhandel* (Berlin, 1901). *Deutschlands Handel nach dem Kriege* (Tübingen, 1916). *Das selbständige Polen als Nationalitätenstaat* (Stuttgart and Berlin, 1917).

B. *Biographisches Staatshandbuch* (Bern and Munich, 1963).

C. Georg Gothein Papers, Bundesarchiv, Koblenz.

James C. Hunt

GOUTTENOIRE DE TOURY, Fernand (1876, Châteaudun, Eure-et-Loir, France—1965, Nice, Alpes-Maritimes, France). *Education*: military academy of St. Cyr, 1896–98. *Career*: army officer and polemicist.

Son of an aristocratic family, the young Fernand Gouttenoire de Toury was educated at the prestigious military academy of St. Cyr and seemed destined to spend his life as a career officer. But he quickly grew to dislike the reactionary army officers who hailed the conviction of Captain Alfred Dreyfus. Leaving the military in 1901, he reentered private life. When war erupted in 1914, he returned to active duty as an infantry officer, serving valiantly in the front lines. In October 1915 he lost a leg in an attack on the German lines. His sacrifice won him the Legion of Honor, but it also embittered him permanently against war. Gouttenoire de Toury soon turned his attention to politics, joining the Ligue des droits de l'homme (League for the Rights of Man) and helping to establish the left-wing veterans' organization, the Association républicaine des anciens combattants (Republican Association of Veterans) in 1917, becoming its secretary-general. He also enrolled in the Parti socialiste unifié (Unified Socialist party) and believed that it could reform society and put an end to warfare.

When the Socialists split in 1920 at the Congress of Tours, Gouttenoire de Toury became a member of the Communist party. A militant orator and writer, he spoke out publicly against the war, the policies of the government that had led France into the conflict, the generals who had sacrificed so many lives, and the Treaty of Versailles which imposed a harsh and unjust peace. He blamed former President Raymond Poincaré for helping to provoke the war by his support for Russian imperialism and his own intensely nationalist feelings. The Ligue des droits de l'homme came under fire for its passivity during the conflict and its failure to expose those responsible for it. At the same time, Gouttenoire de Toury showed great sympathy for Germans such as Count von Montgelas, who sought to exculpate their country from charges of having precipitated the war.

Although he broke with the Communist party in 1922 because of its authoritarian nature, Gouttenoire de Toury remained an active pacifist throughout the interwar years. In 1926 he and other intellectuals signed the "Appeal to Consciences" which denounced the inequities of the peace settlement with Germany and demanded its revision. In 1928 he supported the "Appeal to Good Sense" calling for international disarmament to prevent a new war. That same year he angrily resigned from the Legion of Honor after *Georges Demartial was expelled for expressing his strong pacifist views. When the Ligue internationale des combattants de la paix (International League of Fighters for Peace) was formed in 1931, he enthusiastically joined and contributed frequently to its journal, *La Patrie humaine*. Gouttenoire de Toury strongly attacked the courts martial that had wrongly condemned innocent soldiers to death for insubordination and cowardice during the war. A supporter of the Popular Front in 1936, he grew disillusioned with it when Edouard Daladier came to power and began to rearm.

With the outbreak of war in 1939, Gouttenoire de Toury, who had moved to the south of France for reasons of health, withdrew from an active role in the antiwar movement. He did, however, assail the pacifist writer *Jean Giono in 1943 for failing to resist military service as he had pledged. After the Liberation, Gouttenoire de Toury resumed his efforts on behalf of peace. He contributed to the journal *La Voie de la paix* and worked to establish a national referendum on a plan to renounce war to settle international differences.

Bibliography:

A. *Le Front populaire ruiné par ses chefs* (Paris, 1939); *Jaurès et le parti de guerre* (Paris, 1922); *Poincaré a-t-il voulu la guerre*? (Paris, 1920); *La Politique russe de Poincaré* (Paris, 1921); preface to Roger Monclin, *Les Damnés de la guerre. Les Crimes de la justice militaire* (Paris, 1934).

B. *La Voie de la paix*, no. 152, March 1965.

James Friguglietti

GRAHAM, John William (20 July 1859, Preston, England—17 October 1932, Cambridge). *Education*: Ackworth; Stramongate; Flounders Institute, Leeds; B.A., University Coll., London, c. 1881; M.A., King's Coll., Cambridge Univ., c. 1882. *Career:* teacher in Friends' schools until 1886; tutor, Dalton Hall, Manchester, 1886–97; principal, Dalton Hall, 1897–1924; fellow and lecturer, Woodbroke, 1924; Professor of the Principles and History of Quakerism, Haverford, 1925; environmentalist and author.

John W. Graham's role in the British peace movement arose directly from his involvement in the "Quaker Renaissance," a theological rebellion of the late nineteenth century which shaped the modern Society of Friends. In association with men such as John Wilhelm Rowntree and *Edward Grubb, Graham sought to revitalize Quakerism by abandoning biblically centered evangelicalism and embracing the "primitive" ideas and practices of early Friends. One of the most important results of this upheaval was the reaffirmation of Peace Testimony as a central tenet of contemporary Quakerism.

In a series of articles on the theme "Whence Comes Peace?" (*British Friend*, Feb.-April 1896), Graham pointed toward the two most significant aspects of twentieth-century Quaker pacifism. Noting that many Friends seemed satisfied to pay their dues to one or more peace societies without making an effort to actively work for peace, Graham called for a renewed dedication to the *practice* of the Society's historic peace testimony as well as a major effort to coordinate Quaker peace activities with those of other peace advocates, including non-Christians and nonpacifists.

During the Edwardian period Graham helped to lead a resurgent Quaker campaign against the threat of conscription, the military training of youth, and the increasing growth of armaments. Characteristically, his attacks on the enemies of peace were a mixture of Quaker theology and Liberal party dogma. In his most influential book of the period, *Evolution and Empire* (1912), Graham predicted that the application of science to industry, the continuation of free trade, and the growing influence of the working classes would become irresistible forces for peace which would, by an evolutionary process, undermine and eventually destroy imperialism, militarism, and social injustice.

This optimistic view was grievously challenged by the outbreak of war in 1914, but Graham never wavered in his devotion to peace principles nor in his belief in the efficacy of collaborative peace activities. Thus, during the war he was chairman of the Friends' Peace Committee and a ''Quaker chaplain,'' who regularly visited imprisoned conscientious objectors. He also joined such internationalist groups as the Union of Democratic Control and the Peace Negotiations Committee.

At the end of the war, Graham was asked to write a history of the war resistance movement. The resulting book, *Conscription and Conscience* (1922), was for many years the standard work on the subject.

John W. Graham made significant contributions to both Quakerism and to the modern British peace movement, but he was, in many ways, a paradoxical figure never quite at home among twentieth-century radicals. For just as he pioneered in the struggle against air pollution, he also maintained a Victorian abhorrence to the telephone and the automobile. During the 1920s, many younger Friends saw Graham as a conservative force in their society because of his acceptance of armed collective security under the League of Nations and his refusal to support *Gandhi's passive resistance campaign in India. Graham suffered under this criticism, but until his sudden death in October 1932, he never abandoned his tolerant belief that the existence of peace, both inward and outward, was more important than the means by which it was attained.

Bibliography:

A. *Conscription and Conscience* (London, 1922, reprinted New York, 1971); *Evolution and Empire* (London 1912); *War from the Quaker Point of View* (London, 1917).

B. ''Dictionary of Quaker Biography,'' Friends' House Library, London; *The Friend*, October 1932; *Manchester Guardian*, October 19, 1932.

Thomas C. Kennedy

GREGG, Richard (1885, Colorado Springs, CO—27 January 1974, Eugene, OR). *Education*: B.A., Harvard Coll., 1907; LL.B., Harvard Law School, 1911. *Career*: corporate lawyer, Boston; work in industrial relations (labor-management), 1915–25; leading pacifist thinker, writer, and activist.

Throughout the history of the pacifist movement, a common charge against its leaders has been that they have not come to grips with the problem of social conflict. In the name of peace, it has been said, they have refused to confront the fact that conflict of some kind seems to be inevitable. While this charge is only partly valid, there is enough truth in it to give pacifists pause to reexamine their position realistically. This is exactly what Richard Gregg did during his career as a pacifist thinker and activist. In most of his writings, he sought to deal with the problem of conflict rather than to avoid it.

Gregg became interested in the complexities of conflict during the decade of his work in industrial relations. Like the young *Gandhi in South Africa when confronted by conflict between racial groups, Gregg reflected on both the destructive and the constructive possibilities of social struggle. But his observations, unlike those of Gandhi, were within the context of employer-employee relations. He read Gandhi and in 1925 went to India to meet him and learn about his methods. He became personal friends with Gandhi, living at his training school for seven months and remaining in India for nearly four years. He came to view Gandhi's teachings as relevant for all forms of conflict. There was too much sweetness and light in pacifism, he believed. What was needed was a hard-headed analysis of conflict from a pacifist perspective.

This is what Gregg sought to provide in his best-known work, *The Power of Non-Violence* (1934). As *Rufus Jones, the Quaker scholar, pointed out in his introduction to the first edition, the volume was a combination of idealism and realism and it reflected Gregg in several different roles—as historian, psychologist, and lawyer. Before its publication, there had been nothing quite like it in the history of American pacifism. It became a kind of textbook for many of those interested in strategies for nonviolent social change and was influential in the civil rights struggle led by *Martin Luther King, Jr.

In utilizing the term "power" as part of the title for his work, Gregg captured a central theme of all his teaching—that nonviolence was not a reflection of weakness but of strength. Since "power" was usually associated with effectiveness and "practicality," Gregg deliberately used it in connection with his abiding interest in nonviolent conduct. Power was to be seen in the context of nonviolence and not as associated with violence. Indeed, violence militated against effective power.

Gregg illustrated the power of nonviolence in many areas of life—in international affairs, labor relations, treatment of the mentally ill, and criminology. But nonviolence was not merely negative. It represented a positive attitude to human beings, one which began with the assumption that they were to be respected and valued as ends in themselves. Nonviolence as a response to threats was literally "disarming," in the sense that the "enemy" was taken off guard by the nonretaliatory, nonviolent attitude of the pacifist opponent. Gregg likened the "disarming" character of nonviolence to ju jitsu, terming it a kind of "moral ju jitsu." A potentially violent person or group could become open to negotiations and agreement through a thorough exhibition of goodwill and noninjury, combined with firmness. Like traditional Quakerism, Gregg taught that potential opponents might be turned into friends—or at least individuals open to reason—by treating them as persons having "that of God" within them.

Throughout his career, he stressed the importance of voluntary simplicity and of decentralization for the implementation of pacifist ideals. He believed that both simplicity and decentralization were important values for the economy, society, politics, and religion. Gregg was a "realist" as well as an "idealist." He worked out detailed strategies and tactics to be used in nonviolent struggle. To him, as illustrated in such works as a *Pacifist Program in Time of War, Threatened War, or Fascism* (1939), the implications of pacifism were revolutionary, in the sense that, to implement it, many different aspects of society and human personality would have to be transformed. The individual had to be trained and prepared not only for remote goals but also for immediate tasks through nonviolent responses to threats of war, invasion, and tyranny. For example, the pacifist should pledge beforehand not to fight in or help a war and, if war came, the pacifist should carry out the pledge. He or she should work for a new social order; prepare individually and in groups; refuse to cooperate with war preparations; pay all taxes due (Gregg made an important distinction between paying taxes and personal service for war); refuse to demonstrate publicly with communists and fascists; and so on.

Besides being a leading theoretician of American pacifism, Gregg was active in the affairs of such groups as the Fellowship of Reconciliation. He was a quiet and humble person who played a major part in the history of pacifism in the United States. As John Swomley, a pacifist and personal friend remembered him in *Fellowship* (April 1974), Gregg was a "meaningful part of our pilgrimage from a philosophy which honored violence to one in which nonviolence is central."

Bibliography:

A. *Pacifist Program in Time of War, Threatened War, or Fascism* (Wallingford, PA, 1939); *The Power of Non-Violence* (Philadelphia, 1934); *The Value of Voluntary Simplicity* (Wallingford, PA, 1936).

B. John Swomley, "Richard Gregg," *Fellowship* (April 1974), 23.

C. Swarthmore College Peace Collection, Swarthmore, PA.

Mulford Q. and Marjorie H. Sibley

GRELLING, Richard (11 June 1853, Berlin—15 January 1929, Berlin). *Career*: lawyer, writer, dramatist, poet, artist, and pacifist.

As a lawyer in Berlin for the Deutschen Schriftstellerverbandes (German Writers' Association) from 1883 until 1900, Richard Grelling gained an exceptional reputation as a successful defense lawyer in censorship cases. At the beginning of the 1890s, he withdrew from bourgeois left-liberal politics and associated himself with social democracy, believing it closer to pacifism which became central to his political activity. Together with *Alfred H. Fried and *Bertha von Suttner he helped found the Deutsche Friedensgesellschaft (German Peace Society) (DFG). As long as he lived in Berlin he held the post of vice-president of the DFG and ran the day-to-day operation of the organization.

As one of the leading minds of the young pacifist movement, Grelling spoke at numerous meetings about its goals and purpose. He also helped organize local chapters of the DFG in other German cities. In *Quousque tandem: Ein Friedenswort* (1894), the first of his pacifist writings to attract general attention, Grelling warned against continually growing armaments that were threatening peace. He demanded a general halt to the buildup of armaments, called for the creation of an international court of arbitration, and urged the political parties of Europe disposed toward antimilitarism to take up the pacifist cause. By the end of the nineteenth century, however, Grelling withdrew from politics. In 1903 he purchased an estate in Florence and devoted himself to literary and artistic pursuits.

In July 1914 Grelling was suddenly aroused from his idyllic life by the onset of the First World War. He became engrossed in the question of the causes of the war and until his death he sought to enlighten the German people on the events leading up to the conflict. A longtime opponent of Prussian junkerdom and militarism, Grelling recognized from the beginning that Imperial Germany was not conducting a defensive war but rather an aggressive war of conquest. In October 1914 Grelling, who had been living in Germany since August, decided to disclose what he believed was the truth about the origins of the conflict. He returned to Italy and with encouragement from *Eduard Bernstein, *Hugo Haase, and Karl Kautsky, he wrote the book *J'accuse!* (1915) in which he showed that World War I had not been unavoidable, but was brought about essentially by the calculated acts of the German government and the Prussian-German general staff. With the help of *Alfred H. Fried, the book was published in Switzerland anonymously (as were several other pamphlets and articles about the war) in order to save Grelling's substantial Berlin property for his wife and children. Grelling's shattering indictment of Germany became a world success and was quickly translated into sixteen languages, although in Germany the censors immediately banned it. Perhaps as no other before him, Grelling was slandered, hated, and persecuted. German propaganda pronounced him a "paid mercenary writer for the enemy" and as such guilty of "high treason." In May 1918, he was tried in absentia for "treason to the nation." Found guilty, his property was confiscated and he lost more than a million marks.

After Italy's entry into the war in May 1915, Grelling was forced to move to Zurich, where he lived with his family until early 1920 when he returned to his estate in Florence. In Switzerland he became one of the regular contributors to the *Freie Zeitung* that appeared in Berne from 1917 to 1920. It served as the organ of German émigrés in Switzerland who opposed the Imperial, authoritarian German state and supported a republican Germany. In 1918, Grelling, who had been leaning politically toward the views of the Independent Social Democrats, offered his services to the new government, but did not even receive an answer. Although recognized throughout the world as an authority on the war-guilt question, the animus against him led to his rejection as an expert on the very question by the Parliamentary Investigative Commission of the Reichstag.

In the Weimar Republic, Grelling's publications were boycotted by the German book trade and few book retailers were prepared to display his writings. Only pacifist publishers gave him the opportunity to publish small works piercing the deceptive official propaganda and literature of self-justification that maintained the innocence of the Imperial German government for the outbreak of World War I. Grelling could find no German publisher for larger works and had to turn to the French Société de l'histoire de la guerre (Society for the History of the War) for the publication of two major works on the official attempts to whitewash Germany's responsibility for the war. He came to feel that public enlightenment on Germany's responsibility was crucial for the stability of the Weimar Republic and the maintenance of peace. In *Videant Consules . . . oder Die Gefahren der Unschuldskampagne* (1926), he encouraged the republican and antimilitaristic forces in the German republic to demand a halt to propaganda which might plant the seed of new wars. Grelling received a hearing in left-republican and pacifist papers and his views influenced the Weimar peace movement on the warguilt question, but ultimately his efforts were futile. He failed to counteract the strong propaganda campaign waged by the War-Guilt Section of the Foreign Office to convince German's of their innocence for the outbreak of war in 1914, an interpretation supported almost without exception by German historians.

In 1929 Grelling died of complications from a bladder operation. Four years later the Nazis came to power and his main work, *J'accuse!*, was burned in public squares throughout Germany. After World War II, however, many historians, including German scholars, reached the same conclusions as Grelling about the German responsibility for the outbreak of World War I.

Bibliography:

A. *La Campagne innocentiste en Allemagne* (Paris, 1925); *Comment la Wilhelmstrasse écrivait l'Histoire pendant la Guerre* (Paris, 1928); *Die "Enthüllungen" des Prozesses Suchomlinow. Vom Verfasser des Buches "J'accuse"* (Berne 1917); *J'accuse* (Lausanne, 1915, English trans., New York, 1915); *Die Kriegsschuld des deutschen Generalstabs* (Wiesbaden, 1924); *Der Lokalisierungsschwindel. Das Steckenpferd der Unschuldspropaganda* (Olten, 1927); *London—Berlin—Wien—Petersburg. Vom Verfasser des Buches "J'accuse"* (Olten, 1918); *Der Springende Punkt. Von Germanicus* (Zurich, 1916); *Das Verbrechen. Vom Verfasser des Buches "J'accuse"* (3 vols., Lausanne, 1917–18, English trans., *The Crime. By the Author of "J'accuse"*, London, 1917–18); *Videant Consules . . . oder Die Gefahren der Unschuldskampagne* (Hagen, Westphalia, 1926).

B. F. W. Foerster, "Dem 75 jährigen Richard Grelling," *Die Menschheit*, 15 (June 15, 1928); 196 ff.; Fritz Rottcher, "Richard Grelling gestorben," *Die Menschheit*, 16, no. 4 (January 27, 1929), 22ff; R.U. [Rudolf Utsch], "Ein Kämpferleben zum 75 jährigen Geburtstag von Dr. Richard Grelling," *Das Andere Deutschland*, 8 (June 9, 1928).

Helmut Donat
Trans. by William H. Hopkins

GREYERZ, Hans Karl Walter von (7 February 1870, Berne, Switzerland—22 September 1949, Berne). *Education*: gymnasium, Berne, 1879–88; studies in Protestant theology, Basel, 1888–90, Berne, 1890–92, Jena, 1891, Berlin, 1892–93, and Paris, 1893. *Career*: ordination as minister, Berne, 1892; minister,

Bürglen, 1894–1902, Winterthur, 1902–12; Kandersteg, 1912–18, and Berne, 1918–35.

According to his own account, Karl von Greyerz became concerned about the contradiction between the military and the ministry as early as 1890 during his compulsory military education. His concern intensified during his service as military chaplain. The horrors of World War I had a decisive influence on him, making him a lifelong adversary of war.

He encountered the religious-social movement around *Leonhard Ragaz while a minister in the industrial city of Winterthur and through this movement became interested in the religious peace movement. In 1922 he was elected, along with Ragaz, *Pierre Ceresole, and others to the Komite der Zivildienstpetition (Committee on Petition for a Civilian Service Alternative). The group's petition was put before Parliament in 1924 and rejected. In 1922 Greyerz gave an antimilitary lecture in a church in which he demanded alternative civilian service for conscientious objectors and in which he introduced a series of clerical arguments against war and armament. In 1925 he founded, together with *Rudolf Liechtenhan and others, the Vereinigung antimiltaristischer Pfarrer der Schweiz (Union of Antimilitary Ministers in Switzerland), a national organization of ministers dedicated to the elimination of war and its causes. The group's main goal was to enlist the power of the church in the support of peace and in opposition to national militarism. It advocated unilateral total disarmament and the creation of alternative military service. Greyerz's lecture activities made him an important spokesman for the peace organization and also brought him into conflict with the church. He was reprimanded by church authorities in 1925 after he had his Sunday school class perform an antimilitary nativity play. The play, showing that the spirit of Christ was incompatible with war and violence, ended with an angel ordering the soldiers to smash their sabres.

The pacifist crisis in the 1930s and the rise of the Oxford movement, which viewed pacifism primarily as a matter of inner conviction, caused the Union of Antimilitary Ministers to lose membership. In an attempt to counterbalance the loss, the ministers moderated their program, and, under Greyerz's urging, opened the organization to lay members. This expansion led in 1937 to the founding of the Kirchliche Friedensbund der Schweiz (Christian Peace Union of Switzerland) which Greyerz served as president until his death.

Karl von Greyerz distinguished himself by his efforts to unite theory and practice. For his entire life he searched for a way to unite Biblical spirit and contemporary life. He distanced himself from the Pauline theology of Karl Barth; and as a clergyman, teacher, and political speaker, he impressively advocated a Christianity oriented to the Gospels. As a religious pacifist, he emphasized the incompatibility of God, Jesus, and the Gospels with militarism, armaments, and war. His antimilitarism was radical because, in his opinion, duty to God took precedence over nationalism. He was not merely emotionally opposed to war but also actively tried to prevent it through work among his parishioners. He tried to combine criticism of armaments and war with criticism of a liberal economic order. In this regard, however, his efforts remained vague and reveal a weakness of religious antimilitarists, namely, their idealism and the lack of a consistent social theory with which to support their demands.

Bibliography:

A. *Kirche und Antimilitarismus* (Berne, 1929); *Die Kirche und das Friedensproblem*, Flugschrift des KFB (Zurich, 1942); *Das Militärproblem im Lichte des Evangeliums* (Berne, 1924); *Vom Schwert zur Pflugschar* (Winterthur, 1948).

B. Karl von Greyerz, *Ein Vermächtnis*, hrsg vom KFB (Zurich, 1949); Oskar Moppert, *Karl von Greyerz, Briefe* (Berne, 1953).

Andreas Studer
Trans. by Robert C. Reimer

GRIESS-TRAUT, Virginie (1814, Lorraine, France—9 December 1898, Colombes, Hauts-de-Seine, France). *Career*: utopian socialist, anticlerical republican, feminist, and pacifist.

Of the many causes to which Virginie Griess-Traut devoted her life, the campaign to abolish war held for her a status of first among equals. The other causes included utopian socialism, anticlerical republicanism, and feminism. As an utopian socialist, she gave a lifetime of personal service to the ideas of Charles Fourier and, drawing on her considerable wealth, a gift of 50,000 francs to the École sociétaire phalanstérienne. In 1881, as an anticlerical republican, she participated in the first anticlerical congress in France and throughout her career joined with pacifist *Charles Lemonnier, a lifelong friend and colleague, in proclaiming republicanism to be the political form most conducive to peace.

As a feminist, Griess-Traut helped in 1870 to found, along with her husband and Maria Deraismes, the pioneer Société pour l'amélioration du sort de la femme (Society for the Amelioration of Woman's Condition). Later she joined Léon Richer's Ligue française pour le droit des femmes (French League for Women's Rights) as well as Maria Martin and *Eugenie Potonié-Pierre's Société de la solidarité des femmes (Women's Solidarity Society), founded respectively in 1882 and 1891. These groups shared her conviction that, because centuries of pacific socialization had rendered women less bellicose than men, women's emancipation meant peace. She argued, for instance, that coeducation would lead directly to "peace and concord within and without, in the state and in the family" and that women's suffrage would promote "the definitive adoption of arbitration" between nations as well as "the abolition of permanent armies and the vices that they necessitate and engender."

On balance, however, it was less due to feminism than to her "specialty of Peace work," as Elizabeth Cady Stanton acknowledged in *Eighty Years & More* (1898), that Griess-Traut gained international recognition. Her peace proposals ranged from a call for the neutralization of her native Lorraine, rather than a war of revenge, after Germany seized the province in the Franco-Prussian War (1870–71) to a recommendation in 1885 for a permanent arbitration tribunal to oversee an international guarantee of Afghanistan's independence from British and Russian intervention. She also belonged to no less than four mixed peace groups—La Société française d'arbitrage entre nations (The French Society for Arbitration between Nations), La Ligue internationale des travailleurs pour la paix (The International League of Workers for Peace), Les Travailleurs amis de la paix (The Workers' Friends of Peace), and La Ligue internationale de la paix et de la liberté (The International League of Peace and Freedom)—and two women's peace organizations—La Ligue universelle des femmes pour la paix et l'union des peuples (The Universal League of Women for Peace and the Union of Peoples) and L'Union internationale des femmes pour la paix (The International Union of Women for Peace). In part as a result of her influence, women's emancipation became an article of faith among many pacifists, while pacifism became a criterion in general for membership in the French liberal feminist movement and a standard in particular for affiliation with the National Council of French Women, founded three years after Griess-Traut died from injuries caused by a fall.

Bibliography:

A. "Les Écoles Mixtes." *Le Devoir* [Familistère de Guise], 220 (November 26, 1882), 749–50, and 248 (June 10, 1883), 360–62; "Les femmes à l'oeuvre devant le suffrage." *Le Devoir* [Familistère de Guise], 209 (September 10, 1882), 572–73; "Les Femmes et la Guerre." *Le Devoir* [Familistère de Guise], 201 (July 16, 1882), 447; "Toast de Mme Griess-Traut au banquet anniversaire de la naissance de Fourier." *Le Devoir* [Familistère de Guise], 87 (May 9, 1880), 296.

B. Patrick Kay Bidelman, *Pariahs Stand Up! The Founding of the Liberal Feminist Movement in France, 1858–1889* (Westport, CT, 1982); *La Fronde*, December 11, 1898.

C. Dossier Griess-Traut, Bibliothèque Marguerite Durand, Paris.

Patrick Kay Bidelman

GRIMKÉ, Sarah Moore (26 November 1792, Charleston, SC—23 December 1873, Hyde Park, MA). *Education*: private; *Career*: abolitionist and woman's rights pioneer.

Deeply religious and inwardly rebellious, Sarah Grimké early became conscious of the injustices of the slave system in her native South Carolina. While on a visit to Philadelphia with her ailing father, she was introduced to the simple piety of the Quakers, and in 1823, after moving to Philadelphia, she renounced her Episcopalian upbringing and joined the Society of Friends. In 1829 Angelina Grimké (1805–1879), Sarah's younger sister, followed her to Philadelphia and into the Quaker fold.

Both sisters joined the abolitionist crusade in the mid–1830s. Sarah, however, was converted to the cause more slowly than her sister, and never achieved Angelina's skill or notoriety as an antislavery lecturer. Of the two Sarah was the more utopian and introspective.

The death of the sisters' pacifist brother, *Thomas Grimké, in 1834 prompted Sarah to dedicate herself to the cause of peace. By 1837, influenced partly by Thomas' pacifist principles and partly by the nonresistant views of abolitionist

*Henry Wright, Sarah became a supporter of "ultra peace principles." Convinced that slavery was an "offspring of war," she came to the conclusion that nonresistance was the "greatest test" of true abolitionism.

Angelina's marriage in 1838 to Theodore Dwight Weld brought both sisters permanently under the influence of a powerful and dedicated antislavery crusader, but one who had little sympathy with nonresistance.

When *William Lloyd Garrison and others founded the New England Non-Resistance Society in September 1838, Sarah Grimké refused to sign the new society's Declaration of Sentiments which pledged its members to abstain from voting, holding office, and participating in politics. She both feared the effect the issue would have on the growing rift in the antislavery movement and questioned the "no-government" beliefs of the society's adherents.

Although Sarah Grimké continued to support nonviolence throughout the 1840s, she and Angelina were too occupied with domestic cares to have the time or the energy for issues outside the home. By 1854 violence in Kansas had forced Sarah to conclude that slavery could not be abolished peacefully, and, when the war came, she and the Welds reluctantly endorsed it as the only means of ridding the nation of the hated institution.

Bibliography:

A. *An Epistle to the Clergy of the Southern States* (New York, 1836); Gilbert H. Barnes and Dwight L. Dumond, eds., *Letters of Theodore Dwight Weld, Angelina Grimké Weld and Sarah Grimké, 1822–1844*. (2 vols., New York, 1934).

B. Peter Brock, *Pacifism in the United States: From the Colonial Era to the First World War* (Princeton, 1968); Gerda Lerner, *The Grimké Sisters of South Carolina* (Boston, 1967).

C. Weld-Grimké Papers, University of Michigan, Ann Arbor, MI.

Deborah P. Clifford

GRIMKÉ, Thomas Smith (26 September 1786, Charleston, SC—12 October 1834, Columbus, OH). *Education*: B.A., Yale Coll., 1807. *Career*: lawyer, politician, pacifist author, and educational reformer.

Thomas Grimké, a respected lawyer and advocate of various causes from Sunday schools to the rights of Cherokee Indians, became interested in the subject of peace in the late 1820s, when he began a correspondence with *William Ladd and *Samuel J. May, leaders of the American Peace Society. Grimké's conservative background seemed to assure a moderate stance on the peace question. Then in 1832 he was asked to speak before the Connecticut Peace Society. In the course of preparing for this lecture, Grimké was greatly influenced by the radical British Quaker pacifist Jonathan Diamond, whose writings stressed the incompatibility of war with the principles of Christianity. Grimké's *Address on the Truth, Dignity, Power and Beauty of the Principles of Peace*, which he delivered in New Haven on May 6, 1832, created a sensation in the peace circles of the day. Courageously claiming that all wars, including the American Revolution were "utterly indefensible," Grimké maintained that it was the obligation of the Christian to to refuse war service. While the general public greeted Grimké's views with ridicule, his address soon became the center of a debate between moderate and radical pacifists in the pages of the *Calumet*, the organ of the American Peace Society. It was not Grimké's objection to violence or his belief in the futility of war, but rather his insistence that it was unchristian to take up arms for any reason which offended the moderate views of contemporary pacifists, most of whom supported the idea of defensive war.

Meanwhile Grimké became embroiled in the nullification controversy then raging in his native state of South Carolina. In 1832 a state convention passed an ordinance defying the federal tariff acts of 1828 and 1832 and claiming the right of South Carolina to secede from the Union rather than be forced to submit to such measures. Grimké, a staunch Unionist, opposed both the doctrine of nullification and the use of force to protect the ordinance. In *A Letter to the People of South Carolina* he publicly declared that civil contest was ''absolutely and unchangeably antirepublican.'' He made it clear that he was as opposed to the military threats of President Andrew Jackson as he was to those of the South Carolina nullifiers and urged the substitution of the ''law of love'' for the ''law of violence.'' Henry Clay's compromise tariff brought to an end the threat of civil war but not before Grimké had announced his refusal to serve in the state militia. His exemption was denied, and his person and property threatened. By 1834 Thomas Grimké was one of the most hated men in South Carolina.

Grimké's promising career as a pacifist was cut short by his untimely death from cholera while on a visit to Columbus, Ohio in the fall of 1834. By the time of death, his pacifist principles and antiwar commitment had greatly influenced his sisters, *Sarah and Angelina Grimké, who carried on the family's peace crusade. Despite his early death, Thomas Grimké would long be remembered as a powerful and cogent proponent of pacifism who went further than most members of the American Peace Society not only in his opposition to defensive war but also in his objection to capital punishment and other penal codes of the day.

Bibliography:

A. *Address on the Truth, Dignity, Power and Beauty of the Principles of Peace* (Hartford, 1832); *Letter to the Honorable John C. Calhoun, Vice-President of the United States* (Philadelphia, 1832); *A Letter to the People of South-Carolina* (Charleston, 1832); ''Defensive War Part I,'' The *Calumet*, vol. II, no. 1 (Jan.-Feb., 1835); ''Defensive War Part II,'' *Calumet*, vol. II, No. 2 (March-April, 1835).

B. Peter Brock, *Pacifism in the United States*, (Princeton, NJ 1968); *Calumet*, vol. II, no. 5 (Jan & Feb, 1835); Galbraith, C. B., ''Thomas Smith Grimké,'' *Ohio State Archaeological and Historical Quarterly*, 33 (July, 1924), 301–12.

Deborah P. Clifford

GRIMM, Robert (16 April 1881, Wald, Kanton Zurich, Switzerland—8 March 1958, Berne). *Education*: Sekundarschule Wald; printer's apprentice, Zurich. *Career*: editor, *Berner Tagwacht*, 1909–18; member, Berne City Council, 1909–

38, and Swiss Nationalrat, 1911–55; socialist author, historian, parliamentarian, and municipal administrator.

The dominant figure in Swiss socialism for two generations, Robert Grimm played as well an important international role in opposition to war and militarism, immediately before and during World War I. His internationalism may have stemmed from several years as a journeyman printer in France, Germany, and Austria. A class-conscious socialist, Grimm held that the nation was a bourgeois concept, that war was inherent in capitalism, and that the proletarian struggle must be international.

In pursuit of his goals he demonstrated a pragmatic flexibility. Responding to the call of the German Socialist *Ludwig Frank, Grimm helped organize the May 1913 conference in Berne of French and German parliamentarians, both socialist and bourgeois. As the Swiss delegate he participated in the last attempt of the Second International to stave off war: the meeting in Brussels on July 28, 1914. After war broke out, Grimm participated in Swiss and Italian attempts to convene socialists from the neutral nations. When these attempts failed, Grimm organized the Zimmerwald conference of antiwar socialists from both neutral and belligerent states. The conference created the International Socialist Committee to coordinate left-socialist opposition to the war. Grimm was the key figure on the committee and editor of its *Bulletin*. As leader of the "Zimmerwald center," he opposed attempts to turn the movement into an instrument of Bolshevism. In July 1917, however, he was forced to step down; his discussions in Petrograd with the Provisional Government were misinterpreted as favoring the German interest in a separate Eastern peace.

In the spring of 1917 the Swiss Socialists, following Grimm's leadership, adopted a consistently antimilitarist position. They decided to reject all military bills and to organize the working class to oppose participation in war. The antimilitarism had its roots in the growing use of the Swiss army to oppose strikes; it culminated in the general strike of November 1918, which Grimm organized and directed. He had long advocated the general strike as a defensive tactic of workers against repressive measures. The Swiss Socialists maintained their thorough antimilitarism until the late 1930s when the rise of fascism forced a reappraisal. Grimm led the party to accept a position of defending the Swiss nation as a democracy isolated among fascist dictatorships.

As a theoretician and writer, Grimm was concerned with class conflict rather than with international conflict. His specific acts of internationalism reflected a humanitarian revulsion against war, a proletarian condemnation of war and militarism as bourgeois, and a politician's flexible response to the critical issues of the day. He correctly identified the domestic social roots of militarism and saw the ultimate consequences of militarism as the repression of labor, internationally as well as domestically. Neither an advocate nor an opponent of violence, he viewed its use pragmatically, accepting Bolshevik means as necessary for Russia, but opposing attempts to bring Swiss socialism into the communist movement.

Bibliography:

A. *Geschichte der Schweiz in ihren Klassenkämpfen* (Berne, 1920); *Geschichte der sozialistischen Ideen in der Schweiz* (Zurich, 1931); *Der politische Massenstreik* (Basel, 1906).

B. *Robert Grimm: Revolutionär und Staatsmann* (Zurich, 1958); Christian Voigt, *Robert Grimm: Eine politische Biographie* (Berne, 1980); NYT, March 9, 1958, 87.

C. Robert Grimm Papers, International Institute for Social History, Amsterdam.

James C. Hunt

GROSSMANN, Rudolf (pseud.: Pierre Ramus) (1878?, Vienna—1942, place not certain). *Education*: self-educated. *Career*: factory worker, anarchist organizer, agitator, and publicist.

There is little published information on Rudolf Grossmann and to date no scholarly biography or study of him. Born in Vienna, Grossmann emigrated as a youth to the United States, where he found his way into a circle of anarchists residing in New York City. In 1902 he was arrested for leading a strike at a factory in Paterson, New Jersey, and sentenced to five years in prison. While free on bail, Grossmann fled to London, where he joined the noted anarchist community there and came under the personal and intellectual influence of *Peter Kropotkin. Toward the end of 1907, he returned to Vienna and began to agitate among the workers and to publish various pamphlets and books, as well as a newspaper called *Wohlstand für alle!*, a bi-weekly newspaper that appeared from 1908 until 1914.

Grossmann's program was simple and direct, but also revolutionary. It called for the realization of four basic goals: 1) abolition of private property and a radical redistribution of wealth; 2) elimination of political despotism; 3) renunciation of militarism and war; and 4) establishment of a communal society based on voluntary sharing and the absence of coercion. At the 1907 International Anarchist Congress in Amsterdam, Grossmann, a featured speaker on the subject of antimilitarism, declared that an effective campaign against militarism should be the foremost immediate goal of the anarchist movement. The means he believed best suited to attain that goal was the general strike, an idea borrowed from the French syndicalist movement and its much-advocated methods of "direct action." Grossmann eschewed violence, however, as a tactic to achieve his ends, and stressed the importance of nonviolent forms of resistance (what he called "*soziale Gewaltlosigkeit*"). By this he meant refusal of all factory and other work, including military service, that made war possible and perpetuated the present order of society, which he regarded as coercive and unjust.

Though severely constrained during World War I by Austrian police surveillance, Grossmann resumed his labors following the great conflict. His movement, however, including its various revolutionary schemes for the attainment of world peace, never achieved the success he sought because of extensive police infiltration and harrassment, because of the superior power and influence of the

Social Democratic party, which offered a more attractive program to the average Austrian workingman, and because of deep-seated opposition to anarchism by wide sections of the public.

Bibliography:

A. *Das anarchistische Manifest* (Berlin, n.d., revised ed., Vienna, 1922); *Friedenskrieger des Hinterlandes: Der Schicksalsroman eines Anarchisten im Weltkriege* (Mannheim, 1924); *Gegen Militarismus und Monopoleigentum* (Vienna, 1914); *Generalstreik und direkte Aktion im proletarischen Klassenkampfe* (Berlin, 1910); *Die historische Entwicklung der Friedensidee und des Antimilitarismus* (Leipzig, 1908); *Militarismus, Kommunismus und Antimilitarismus* (Uerdingen a. Rhein, n.d.).

B. Gerhard Botz, Gerfried Brandstetter, and Michael Pollack (eds.), *Im Schatten der Arbeiterbewegung: Zur Geschichte des Anarchismus in Österreich und Deutschland* (Vienna, 1977), 29–97; Richard R. Laurence, "Anarchist Antimilitarism in Austria, 1907–1914", *Peace and Change: A Journal of Peace Research,* forthcoming.

C. Police surveillance reports; Allgemeines Verwaltungsarchiv, Vienna; Grossmann's collected works and papers, International Institut voor Sociale Geschiedenis, Amsterdam.

Richard R. Laurence

GROSZ, George (26 July 1893, Berlin—6 July 1959, West Berlin). *Education*: Dresden Kunstakademie, 1909–11; Berlin Kunstgerwerbeschule, 1912; studied in Paris under Colarossi, 1913. *Career*: painter, art teacher, antiwar activist, and social critic.

With biting satire and graphically linear style, George Grosz became the best-known artist-intellectual critic of nationalist and militarist currents in the Weimar Republic. As early as 1915, Grosz met German pacifists such as Wieland Herzfelde in the Berlin studio of Ludwig Meidner; and, beginning with the publication of Herzfelde's *Neue Jugend* in 1916, Grosz regularly began to contribute drawings and articles for pacifist and left-wing journals. Until 1925, he also published sets of lithographs almost exclusively for Herzfelde's Malik Verlag. *Gott mit uns* (*God is with us*), taking its name from the motto on the belt buckles issued to German soldiers, was published in 1920. Its nine lithographs were a scathing depiction of military types. *Das gesicht der herrschenden Klasse* (*The Face of the Ruling Class*) was issued in 1921 as a polemic on the greed of capitalists and the immorality of power politics. This was followed in 1922 or early 1923 by Grosz's famous series, *Ecce Homo*.

Grosz's subjects reveal him clearly as an artist fighting for a humane socialist society and against war. In a plate from *Abrechnung folgt*! (*The Settling of Accounts to Follow*) of 1923 entitled "and the Proletariat Die," in which he simplified and brought into contemporary context Francisco Goya's composition for *May 3, 1808*, Grosz involves the viewer in the massacre of workers by placing soldiers, who fire into the picture space, in the foreground. In this, and all of his art, Grosz adhered to the concept of a *Tendenzkunst*, an art of ideology and political commitment. He denied the validity of pure formalism and the concept of art for art's sake. For him, all art must serve society, and his art sought to arouse people to action against war and social oppression. To this end, he stressed drawing and lithography as media which could be disseminated in quantity. Many of his finest antimilitarist drawings date from the period between 1919–24, by which time he had turned from his solid, academic training to an incisive and almost childlike style under Futurist and Dadaist influences.

Grosz's political and social activities were not limited to publishing essays and folios. After his first discharge as unfit for service in 1915, he and John Heartfield sent political and pacifist messages in the form of collage postcards to soldiers at the front. In 1921 he worked with *Otto Dix and *Kathe Kollwitz designing posters to aid Russian workers. In the same year, he illustrated Richard Huelsenbeck's novel on war profiteers and swindlers, *Dr. Billig am Ende* (*The End of Dr. Billig*); and, in 1927, he worked with Erwin Piscator to produce the antimilitarist play, *Schweik*, for which he made over three hundred drawings which were projected onto screens surrounding the actors. One of these, *The Outpouring of the Holy Spirit*, is typical of Grosz's message. It depicts deadly instruments of war issuing from the mouth of a minister who is addressing his congregation of burghers and industrialists from the pulpit.

The polemical intent and didactic power of Grosz's art was evident to both those who applauded it and those who decried it. *Gott mit uns* was featured in Berlin's First International Dada Fair, held in July and August, 1920. On September 9, 1920, all copies of it were confiscated from the Malik Verlag offices and Grosz was charged with insulting the German army. In 1922, *Ecce Homo* brought similar charges against him. Between December, 1928 and 1930, Grosz was tried for blasphemy and for being a scourge upon society. His acquittal was a short-lived victory, as his works were among those shown at the great Exhibition of Degenerate Art which Hitler and Goebbels personally opened in Munich in 1937. By that time, Grosz was in the United States, having accepted a cabled invitation in 1932 to teach at the Art Students League in New York City.

Grosz's emigration fulfilled an optimistic dream that he had since childhood. He was naturalized in 1928, but soon his optimism was to be clouded by another war. He responded with such cynically desperate paintings as *A Piece of My World* (1939) and *I am Glad I Came Back* (1942). In the latter, a grinning skeleton of Death makes a curtain call, looking into the painting and at humankind, which is once again his audience.

Bibliography:

A. *Abrechnung folgt*! (Berlin, 1923); *Ecce Homo* (Berlin, 1922); *Das Gesicht der herrschenden Klasse* (Berlin, 1919); *Gott mit uns* (Berlin, 1920); *Mit Pinsel und Scheere* (Berlin, 1922); *Das neue Gesicht der Herrschenden Klasse* (Berlin, 1930); *Über alles die Liebe* (Berlin, 1931).

B. Lothar Lang, "George Grosz Bibliographie," *Zeitschrift für Buchkunst und Bibliographie, Pirckheimer Gesellschaft* (July 30, 1968); Beth Irwin Lewis, *George Grosz. Art and Politics in the Weimar Republic* (Madison, WI, 1971); *Neue deutsche Biographie* (1965), VII, 161–2; NYT, July 7, 1959.

Folke T. Kihlstedt

GRUBB, Edward (19 October 1854, Sudbury, Suffolk, England—23 January 1939, Letchworth, England). *Education*: Sidcot School, 1865–68; Bootham

School, 1868–71; Flounders Institute, Ackworth, 1871–72; M.A., University Coll., London, 1880. *Career*: teacher and private tutor, 1872–1901; proprietor-editor, *The British Friend*, 1901–13; secretary, Howard Association, 1901–5; treasurer, No-Conscription Fellowship, 1915–19; author, theologian, social reformer, and Christian pacifist.

Although as a young man Edward Grubb accepted pacifism as a part of his Quaker heritage, his attachment to peace principles was, like that of many of his nineteenth-century co-religionists, largely passive. Only after he became a leading figure in the theological upheaval that has been called the "Quaker Renaissance" did Grubb realize the central importance of peace testimony to the Religious Society of Friends. With men such as John Wilhelm Rowntree and *John W. Graham, Grubb rejected the influence of the Evangelical Movement which had long dominated Quakerism and embraced "primitive" Quaker ideas, especially the concept of the "Inner Light." This egalitarian principle, stressing as it did the Divine Presense in every human being, not only confirmed the sacredness of human life (and forbade inflicting injury on any person), but also freed Quaker pacifism from its Victorian reliance on Scriptural injunctions.

As a regular contributor to both Quaker and radical journals during the late nineteenth century, Grubb was consistently critical of British imperial expansion and the increased arms expenditure it elicited. However, the first hard test of Grubb's pacifist faith came with the outbreak of the Boer War. When many of Britian's leading peace advocates, including some Friends, supported the conflict in South Africa, Grubb concluded that much of what had passed for pacifist activity had been no more the pious, self-indulgent peacetime puffery. As a result of this sobering realization, Grubb assumed a position of absolute pacifism from which he never wavered.

The Boer War briefly caused bitter divisions within the Society of Friends, but its ultimate result was to reaffirm the central importance of Quaker peace testimony and to establish total resistance to war as the norm for twentieth century Friends. As the popular and influential editor of *The British Friend*, Grubb played a leading role in the greatly expanded antimilitarist and anticonscriptionist activities organized by Edwardian Friends. He was also a firm advocate of co-operating with non-Quaker and even nonreligious peace groups in the struggle against militarism and war. Perhaps his most noteworthy contribution to the peace movement during this period was a confrontation with J. St. Loe Strachey, editor of *The Spectator* and supporter of National Service League, a political pressure group which advocated compulsory military service for Britain. In 1909 Strachey's book *A New Way of Life* pleaded the case for universal military training not merely, or even chiefly, as a measure for national defense but as a means of combatting the moral laxity and rampant materialism which were threatening the British way of life. Grubb's reply, entitled *The True Way of Life* (1909), argued that, while organizing citizens for the purpose of killing their fellow men was a time-honored method of evoking support for the national cause, Christian civilization had evolved to the point where most people recognized human brotherhood as superior to the brutality and inhumanity of war. If Grubb underestimated the power of patriotic nationalism, he did provide a prescient warning about the lengths of resistance to which Quaker and other pacifists would go in opposing military service and war.

Because of his passionate belief—greatly influenced by liberal optimism—that humanity had at long last grasped the means to establish permanent peace, Grubb was momentarily shaken and confused by the outbreak of World War I, but he never wavered in his pacifist convictions. Reaffirming his dedication to the struggle against war, Grubb played a prominent role in the conferences and meetings that led to the establishment of the Fellowship of Reconciliation; and, in July 1915, he accepted an invitation to become treasurer of the No-Conscription Fellowship (NCF). Because Grubb was considerably older than most of the young conscientious objectors in the NCF and because his collecting of funds (mainly from wealthy Quakers) provided sustenance for the NCF's war-resistance activities, Fenner Brockway, founder of the Fellowship, called Grubb the "father of the movement." Through the NCF Grubb became acquainted with many of Britain's most influential peace leaders including Brockway, *Clifford Allen, *Catherine Marshall, and *Bertrand Russell, all of whom were deeply impressed by his integrity, his efficiency and his saintliness. For Grubb's part his association with these aggressively secular socialist-pacifists broadened his understanding of the possibilities for "collaborative pacifism" between religious and nonreligious war-resisters. When most of the NCF national committee, including Grubb, were prosecuted for publishing a seditious leaflet, Bertrand Russell remarked upon how Edward Grubb's quiet dignity on the witness stand made many non-pacifists in the audience realize that the trial was more a vindictive persecution of dissenters than an exercise of justice.

Grubb continued as NCF treasurer until the organization dissolved in 1919; and, in the meantime, he fulfilled his concern for a positive peace testimony through his involvement with the Friends War Victims Relief Committee in France. Throughout the 1920s Grubb remained active in Friends' affairs, though not in the mainstream of the peace movement. During his last years ill-health forced him to curtail his activities, but he continued to write as a theologian and peace advocate until his death in 1939.

Edward Grubb's importance in guiding the Society of Friends through the transition from Victorian Evangelicalism to the liberal theology and social activism of the twentieth century cannot be overstated. Among the most significant aspects of his leadership was the emphasis he placed on the central importance of the peace testimony to the historical origins and worldly mission of Friends. Grubb believed that a vital part of that mission was to positively witness for peace by enhancing and saving life in contrast to the life-destroying negation of war. He also stressed the necessity of collaborating with all who similarly chose life, regardless of their religious or political creeds. Thus, his teaching and his example as a peace leader influenced not only his beloved Society but the entire Anglo-American peace movement as well.

Bibliography:

A. *Does War Promote Industry? An Answer to Can We Disarm*? (London, 1899); *The True Way of Life* (London, 1909); "War Resistance," in Julian Bell, ed., *We Did Not Fight, 1914–1918: Experiences of War Resisters* (London, 1935).

B. James Dudley, *The Life of Edward Grubb, 1854–1939* (London, 1946); Mary E. Pumphrey, *Edward Grubb, 1854–1939* (n.p., 1940).

Thomas C. Kennedy

GRUENING, Ernest (6 February 1887, New York—26 June 1974, Washington, DC). *Education*: B.A., Harvard Coll., 1907, M.D., Harvard Medical School, 1912. *Career*: journalist, government official, and politician.

Ernest Gruening was a liberal reformer who came late to public peace activism; but, when he did, he became one of the most influential American opponents of the war in Vietnam. Born in New York City into the family of a prominent ophthalmologist, Gruening was raised in a comfortable and cosmopolitan household that eased his way toward studies at Harvard College and Harvard Medical School.

In 1912, while completing his medical studies, Gruening shifted his career interest toward journalism and public affairs. Between 1912 and 1917, he held several reporting and editorial jobs on various Boston and New York newspapers, quitting only for wartime service on the War Trade Board and in the U. S. Field Artillery. After World War I, he served as managing editor of the liberal periodical, *The Nation*, at the same time as he traveled widely in the Caribbean and developed a lifelong interest in Latin America and in U. S. imperial operations. In 1924 he directed national publicity for Senator *Robert LaFollette's Progressive presidential campaign. Shortly after, he became founding editor of the Portland (Maine) *Evening News*.

An early New Deal supporter, Gruening was named director in 1934 of the Roosevelt administration's newly created Division of Territories and Island Possessions, with responsibility for the management of American holdings from Puerto Rico to the Philippines. In 1939 he accepted a presidential appointment as governor of Alaska, and directed the territory's military defense during World War II and the postwar construction of the "Alcan" highway. In 1953, removed from the governorship by the incoming Eisenhower administration, Gruening began lobbying for Alaskan statehood in a campaign that helped him in 1958 to achieve election to that state's second U. S. Senate seat. Reelected in 1962, he functioned in Washington as a loyal Democratic liberal, backing domestic reform efforts while trying to cut off U. S. aid to various foreign dictatorships.

Except for scattered newspaper reports, Gruening initially knew little of South Vietnam. In March 1964 however, with U. S. military involvement markedly expanding there, Gruening denounced the Johnson administration's decision to support the Saigon regime against a Communist led revolution in the countryside, and called for a UN-supervised cease-fire. Five months later, he and Oregon Senator *Wayne Morse were the only two members of Congress to oppose the

Tonkin Gulf resolution, which gave President Lyndon Johnson extraordinary latitude in waging war in Southeast Asia. In 1965, as U. S. troops poured into South Vietnam, Gruening blasted administration policy as duplicitous, subversive of the 1954 Geneva accords, and provocative of a larger war. He made several appearances at public protests against the war, including the April, 1965, demonstration in Washington sponsored by the Students for a Democratic Society. Together with Morse he tried to block the administration's requests for supplemental funds for the military budget that were earmarked for the Vietnam war effort.

Battling against Johnson's escalation, Gruening argued during 1966–67 for the "planned withdrawal" of U.S. troops to protected urban enclaves, the termination of all U. S. bombing, and the establishment of a reformed Saigon government. Then a shockwave of events in 1968—including the Tet offensive, Johnson's withdrawal from the presidency, and the assassination of Robert F. Kennedy—altered U. S. war strategy, and moved Gruening gradually to support the presidential candidacy of Hubert Humphrey. His expressions of support, however, did little evident good for Humphrey or for himself. That year, Gruening was defeated in his reelection bid by another antiwar Democrat, Mike Gravel.

Yet the loss did not stop Gruening's attacks upon the war. He rejoined *The Nation* as an editorial associate and spoke frequently on college campuses. In 1972 he lent active support to the presidential candidacy of his long-time friend, George McGovern, and was bitterly disappointed when Richard Nixon—a man whom Gruening thought distinguished by his "versatile depravity"—won a resounding reelection victory. Undeterred, Gruening declared his profound skepticism with Nixon's claim in January, 1973, that the Paris agreements had brought peace to Vietnam. And, typically, his skepticism was well founded. The war was still grinding on when he died in Washington in June 1974.

Bibliography:

A. *Many Battles: The Autobiography of Ernest Gruening* (New York, 1973); Ed., *These United States* (New York, 1923–24); *Vietnam Folly,* with Herbert Beaser (Washington, 1968).

Charles DeBenedetti

GUMBEL, Emil Julius (18 July 1891, Munich—10 September 1966, New York). *Education*: Ph.D., Univ. of Munich, 1914; Habilitationsschrift (inaugural dissertation) in statistics, Univ. of Heidelberg, 1922–23. *Career*: lecturer in statistics, Univ. of Heidelberg, 1924–30; associate professor, 1930–32; lecturer, Univ. of Paris, 1932–34; research appointment, Univ. of Lyons, 1934–39; appointments at various universities in the United States, including the New School for Social Research and Columbia Univ., 1940–66; mathematician, statistician, and pacifist author.

The period of Emil Gumbel's most active involvement in the German peace movement coincided with one of the most unsettling periods in Germany's history: the decade following the end of the First World War. Some of the tensions which caused a deep rift in German politics and society in this period were between those who sought revenge for the lost war and those who sought to prevent a repetition of the horrifying wartime experiences. These tensions were well reflected in the relationship between the pacifist Gumbel and some of the extreme rightist students at the University of Heidelberg. Gumbel's lectures were often accompanied by the threat of, and on several occasions actual, physical violence. In 1932, despite his international reputation as a scholar of mathematical statistics, Gumbel was finally dismissed from his post for being undesirable as a pacifist and as a Jew.

Emil Gumbel belonged to the group of left-wing radical pacifists who, in Weimar Germany, gathered in the Deutsche Liga für Menschenrechte (German League for Human Rights). He gained fame and notoriety during the First World War as author of a series of antiwar pamphlets, later published in a volume entitled *Vier Jahre Lüge* (Four Years of Lies) (1919). After the war, he published numerous articles and books which uncovered and documented the secret rearmament efforts by the German Reichswehr as well as the clandestine training of recruits, thus adding proof to the existence of the disputed Black Reichswehr. His most famous work in this series, however, was his extensive documentation of political murder in Weimar Germany by rightist assassination squads. In this connection, he also took to task the German judicial system which often showed astonishing leniency towards rightist criminals.

Gumbel did not contribute to German pacifism through the development of theoretical formulations. For him the task of pacifism in society and politics was one of action, of active involvement in political events and of active struggle against militarism and injustice. He belonged to those pacifist intellectuals in Weimar Germany who set themselves up as watchdogs of the democratic institutions of the Republic. His efforts were concentrated on internal affairs with less emphasis on international relations.

In the history of German pacifism, Gumbel's significance lies in the fact that he was in the forefront of the movement that introduced an element of social activism into the German peace movement. German pacifism was thus transformed into a reform movement with a firm commitment to the betterment of politics and society.

Bibliography:

A. *Verräter verfallen der Feme: Opfer, Mörder, Richter, 1919–1929* (Berlin, 1929); *Vier Jahre Lüge* (Berlin, 1919); *Vier Jahre politischer Mord* (Berlin, 1922); *Vom Fememord zur Reichskanzlei* (Heidelberg, 1962); *Weissbuch über die Schwarze Reichswehr* (Berlin, 1925).

B. *Aufbau*, New York, September 14, 1966.

C. Emil J. Gumbel Papers, University of Chicago Library.

Brigitte M. Goldstein

GURNEY, Eliza Paul Kirkbride (6 April 1801, Philadelphia—8 November 1881, West Hill, NJ). *Education*: Friends School at Westtown, PA. *Career*: Quaker minister.

Eliza Kirkbride worked throughout her life to spread her Quaker beliefs and to further the social reform goals of the Friends. From 1832 through 1837 she traveled as companion to Quaker minister Hannah Backhouse. In 1836 Backhouse's ministry took her to England where she met Joseph John Gurney, a banker and also a Quaker minister. Five years later she married Gurney and together they ministered to congregations in Europe. In France the Gurneys campaigned for prison reform and the abolition of slavery.

John Gurney died in 1847 and Eliza returned to America some years later. Earlier fund raising by the Gurneys led to the founding of Earlham College in Indiana in 1847, and Eliza continued to work on the school's behalf during the 1850s. Simultaneously Eliza Gurney preached pacifism and other Quaker doctrines to congregations of Friends in the East and Midwest.

At the outbreak of the Civil War Gurney confronted a dilemma shared by other Quakers, the conflict between her dedication to pacifism and her abhorrence of slavery. Convinced that Abraham Lincoln had been chosen by God to lead the nation through a cataclysmic transition to a free nation, Gurney continued to urge Quakers to avoid violence, but she avoided any condemnation of the Union cause.

In 1862 Gurney visited the White House in the company of other Friends. In an audience with Lincoln, Gurney assured him of the esteem that Friends held for the President and of their loyalty to the Union, and led the group in prayer. Lincoln wrote Gurney of his appreciation for her prayers and of his hatred of the war. Gurney again expressed her support for Lincoln in an 1863 letter to the President. In his reply Lincoln stated his sympathy with the wartime dilemma of the Quakers and his determination to protect their status as conscientious objectors.

Bibliography:

B. Peter Brock, *Pacifism in the United States: From the Colonial Era to the First World War*. (Princeton, N.J., 1968); NAW, II, 105–6.

C. Gurney Manuscripts, Friends House, London; Quaker Collection, Haverford College Library.

Julia Kirk Blackwelder

GWIS-ADAMI, Rosalia (30 July 1880, Edolo, Italy—1930, Milan). *Career*: editor, *Giovine Europa*, from 1912; founder, Società della gioventù italiana; novelist, journalist, editor, and pacifist.

Born into a family of Risorgimento patriots of comfortable means, Rosalia Gwis-Adami treasured the Mazzinian heritage of her parents throughout her life. When she entered the Italian peace movement in 1908–9, this legacy remained important in shaping her views of patriotic pacifism.

As a young woman, Gwis-Adami gained public attention with the publication of a novel, *Coscienza* (1905). Two later literary works, *Oltre il nido* (1908) and *La Vergine ardente* (1914) established her reputation as a writer gifted in reflecting on the problems facing women in society. A number of short stories and journalistic essays appeared in various north Italian journals, including *La Vita internazionale*, published by *E. T. Moneta, who was head of the Lombard Peace Union and the Nobel Peace Prize winner in 1907.

Gwis-Adami was attracted to Moneta's ideas and from 1909 began a close working association with him and the Milanese based society as well as with the (Berne) International Peace Bureau, attending Universal Peace Congresses as a delegate. This personal association developed further as Moneta, nearing 80, began to lose his eyesight and Gwis-Adami evidently became his devoted assistant, performing secretarial and editorial duties. In February 1909, speaking during a meeting at a Milanese school, she called for the creation of a society of young people and teachers, dedicated to expanding peace ideas among youth. Thus the Società della gioventù italiana was created (its name later changed to the Società delle giovanette italiane, the first meaning the Society of Italian Youth, the second, the Society of Young Italian Women). Her hope was to build a Giovane Europa, a young European society to work for peace as once Giuseppe Mazzini's Young Europe had struggled for national liberation. There was considerable interest in this latter proposal at the 1910 Stockholm conference of the Universal Peace Congress. However, there is no evidence that it remained more than an idea on paper.

The Italian youth association for peace which Gwis-Adami created in 1909 grew to include over 2000 members and published a journal, *Giovine Europa*. It called repeatedly for a realistic approach to peace, maintaining that the desire for "absolute justice" for both individuals and nations could not ignore international realities or the fact that the fragile international system might dissolve into war at any time. Refusing to demand that Italy reduce its military spending while other nations increased theirs, *Giovine Europa* called for a general reduction of arms throughout Europe "to occur simultaneously." Similarly, the organization under Gwis-Adami's firm guidance, never asked Italians to give up what other major powers continued to pursue, namely overseas empire.

In 1911, along with Moneta's group, Gwis-Adami supported the Libyan war, arguing that Italy had the same rights in Africa as France and England and that Italian national interests had been attacked. This position badly divided both the Italian and the international peace movement and Gwis-Adami insisted adamantly that it was correct for peace activists to defend patriotic and national interests. When she went as an Italian delegate to the 1912 Geneva Universal Peace Congress where she confronted the hostility of European peace leaders as well as *Edoardo Giretti (whose Piedmont peace society rejected the Libyan adventure), she wrote in a private letter that the experience was the most difficult and infuriating of her life. She was enraged particularly at Italians who criticized their nation. Gwis-Adami's view of the twin nature of patriotism and pacifism informed her peace labors for the rest of her life.

While European peace leaders criticized her (and Moneta's) patriotic stand in 1911–12, in reality the Lombard group more accurately heralded peace workers' behavior in 1914 than did the principled opposition of 1911–12. Gwis-Adami had claimed that her commitment to the ideas of human fraternity and to a single ideal of European unity were based on the more fundamental principle of the rights of nations and peoples to justice, freedom, and independence. With the outbreak of war in 1914, most Western pacifists in belligerent nations, especially Britain, France, and Belgium quickly adopted that view and insisted that fighting was necessary to destroy the Prussian militarism which could not coexist with a peaceful world.

Italy remained officially neutral at the outbreak of the war. However, by October-November 1914, Gwis-Adami, along with Moneta's group, began to wonder aloud how long neutrality could be kept. By early 1915 she was convinced Italy needed to enter the war on the Entente side, if only to have a seat at the peace table. During the war, she wrote vigorously in support of women's patriotic activities and against the neutralism and pacifism exemplified by *Romain Rolland. Her long pamphlet, *Nella mischia* (*In the Fray*) (1917) denounced the Rolland stance, "above the fray" in Switzerland. There she also called for the postwar recognition by the nation of women's contributions by granting women the vote and absolute civil equality. Again, Gwis-Adami tangled with a leading French peace activist +Théodor Ruyssen, Ruyssen, who attacked Gabriele d' Annunzio's violent Irredentism. Her own vitriolic response was entitled "La Vostra Pace" ("Your Peace") and demonstrated her development into a polemicist of the first order. Her perception that Italian right to Fiume, purchased at the huge blood price of the war, was essential to future European peace contradicted the "Wilsonian" view of many other peace activists but logically followed from the 1911 Libyan stand.

In the last years of her life, Gwis-Adami continued to write for *La Vita internazionale*, supported the League of Nations, and also worked as a translator. In her time, she had been one of the few European women to participate in the largely middle class peace movement and to achieve a position of importance in a major peace society. She has also evolved into a feminist on questions of women's legal and political rights.

Bibliography:

A. *Nella mischia. Riposta di una donna a Romain Rolland* (Rome, 1918).

B. G. Casati, ed., *Dizionario degli Scrittori d' Italia* (Milan, n.d.), p. 260; "Rosalia Gwis-Adami" in *La Luce del Pensiero*, ed. D. Maggiore, IV (Naples, May 18, 1911) 12; T. Rovito, *Letterati e giornalisti italiani contemporanei, Dizionario Bio-Bibliografico* (2nd ed., Naples, 1922); *L'Illustrazione Italiana*, I (1904) 617.

Sandi E. Cooper

H

HAASE, Hugo (29 September 1863, Allenstein, Germany—7 November 1919, Berlin). *Education*: studied law at Univ. of Königsberg. *Career*; attorney, Königsberg, 1890–1911, Berlin, 1912–19; Reichstag Deputy, 1897–1907, 1912–19; co-chairman, Social Democratic party (SPD), 1911–17; cochairman, SPD Reichstag delegation, 1912–15; co-chairman, Sozialdemokratische Arbeitsgemeinschaft 1916–17; co-chairman, Independent Social Democratic party, 1917–19; co-chairman, Council of People's Representatives, November-December 1918.

Even before he achieved national prominence in the Social Democratic party (SPD), Hugo Haase had evinced a deep interest in the peace issue. As a delegate to the congress of the Second International in 1907, he helped to draft the peace resolution which, despite its vagueness, represented the most radical antiwar position ever formally endorsed by the SPD. When he assumed the co-chairmanship of the party in 1911, he became still more deeply involved in the socialist peace movement. Despite his orthodox Marxist view that the imperialist era necessarily brought with it increased dangers of international conflict, he rejected the pessimism of those on the left who insisted that war was inevitable. In major speeches delivered in Germany and abroad, he argued instead that socialists should work to strengthen international ties and thus to counteract the threatening tendencies inherent in imperialism. In May 1913 he led a German delegation which met in Berne with French parliamentarians to discuss ways in which tensions between the two nations could be reduced.

Haase was one of the most determined and consistent opponents of World War I. Although he felt obligated at first to comply with the decision of the Social Democratic Reichstag delegation to support the German war effort, it was not long before he began openly to accuse the German government of aggression and to criticize those in the SPD who refused to recognize that fact. He took the lead at each step in the gradual dissolution of the SPD which culminated in April 1917 in the foundation of a new Independent Social Democratic party which stood squarely against the German war effort.

Although Haase was no doctrinaire pacifist, the focal point of his politics during these years was quite clearly his humanitarian concern to end the war as quickly as possible. In addition to his many speeches, he helped to organize massive antiwar strikes and, as the conflict neared its end, became persuaded that the coming of peace might well bring the triumph of socialism. Refusing to accept the moderate constitutional reforms offered by the government in October 1918, he pressed for the full-scale revolution which finally broke out in November.

As co-chairman of the Council of People's Representatives which succeeded the Kaiser's regime, he assumed special responsibility for foreign affairs. In this new position, however, his efforts to heal the wounds of war proved largely ineffectual. Frustrated by foreign office officials who preferred to obey the moderate leaders of the SPD rather than the Independents and by the victorious Allies' determination to treat Germany as a defeated enemy in spite of the revolution, Haase resigned late in December.

Resuming his role as a critic in the new Reichstag, he spoke out frequently and eloquently against the refusal of the other parties to confront realistically the fact of Germany's defeat. Like so many other progressive leaders of the Weimar Republic, he died the victim of an assassin's bullet.

Bibliography:

A. *Reichstagsreden gegen die deutsche Kriegspolitik* (Berlin, 1919).

B. Kenneth R. Calkins, *Hugo Haase: Democrat and Revolutionary* (Durham, 1979); Ernst Haase, *Hugo Haase: Sein Leben und Wirken* (Berlin, 1929); *Biographisches Lexikon des Sozialismus* (Hannover, 1960), I, 109–11; *Neue deutsche Biographie* (Berlin, 1966), VII, 381–82.

Kenneth R. Calkins

HAILE SELLASSIE I (born Tafari Makonnan) (23 July 1892, Ejarso Goro, Hararghe Province, Ethiopia—27 August 1975, Addis Ababa). *Education*: traditional Ethiopian church primary school; private tutoring in French and modern subjects. *Career*: governor of Selale district, 1906–8; governor of sub-province of southern Sidamo, 1908–10; governor of Hararghe Province, 1910–16; heir apparent and regent of Ethiopia, 1916–28; king and regent of Ethiopia, 1928–30; emperor (king of kings) of Ethiopia, 1930–74.

Throughout his long career, Haile Sellassie sought peace and collective security in order to ensure the survival of Ethiopia as a sovereign and unified state. As a realist, he fully understood the military, economic, and technological weakness of his nation, and tried immediately after World War I to have Ethiopia included in the peace talks in Paris and other places. He sent missions to the Western European Allies and the United States, congratulating them for their victory against the Central Powers, assuring them of Ethiopia's pacific nature and peace-loving intentions, and seeking their recognition of Addis Ababa's sovereignty. When this effort failed, Haile Sellassie, then known as Tafari Makonnan, exercized his considerable diplomatic skills, and Ethiopia finally was admitted to the League of Nations in 1924. Upon entry, Ethiopia promised to work to eradicate its internal slave trade and to introduce other modern reforms, most of which were well underway before the Italians intervened in 1935–36.

Haile Sellassie believed in collective security not only because it offered his poor and weak country a theoretical defense against predatory states, but also because he considered it a mechanism leading to international unity. He also appreciated that collective security could save his country and others millions of dollars that could be expended in worthwhile development projects. His faith in collective security never waned, even if the mechanism failed to assist Ethiopia when attacked by the Fascists in 1935–36. Standing before the League of Nations on June 26, 1936, the first head of state to address the assembly, Haile Sellassie recapitulated his efforts to head off the Italo-Ethiopian War, all of them thwarted by Rome's intransigence. He maintained that Ethiopia's plight was the responsibility of the League's member states: "whether the principle of the equality of nations is to be confirmed or whether the small states will have to accept subjugation to the powerful ones." He warned that Ethiopia's tragedy foreshadowed the world crisis to come, and, while in exile in Europe, he did everything he could to publicize the danger posed by Italy and Germany and the reactionary movements they represented.

When he was finally restored to his throne in 1941 by a combined Commonwealth-Ethiopian force, he joined the Allies, which permitted Ethiopia to become a charter member of the United Nations. When North Korea attacked the South in 1950, and the UN undertook a police action against the regime of Kim il Sung, Haile Sellassie quickly volunteered a battalion for service with the United Nations Command. Ethiopia was the only Afro-Asian country to participate in the largely Western effort, and some 5000 Ethiopians saw action in Korea before the ceasefire of 1953. In an address to the first contingent of troops, the emperor stressed his commitment to collective security more than ten times. He also joined in the peace-keeping effort in Zaire (the ex-Belgian Congo) before he was caught up in the African unity movements of the 1960s.

From the first stirrings of modern African nationalism, Haile Sellassie chose—at first gingerly, then enthusiastically—to cooperate with his African brothers. He was represented at the meeting of the Independent African States in Accra and elsewhere after 1957, and Ethiopia was a party to the Pan-African Movement for East and Central Africa (PAFMECA). He took a leading role in the movement for African unity, so that he could insure the inviolability of colonial frontiers in post-colonial Africa. In May 1963, after much preparation, he convened in Addis Ababa, the inaugural session of the Organization of African Unity (OAU), and presided over the session which confirmed the organization's charter. In becoming a party to the OAU, as with the League of Nations, Haile Sellassie was motivated as much by national interests as by idealistic principles.

Still, as Africa's elder statesman, he used his prestige within the OAU to mediate many disputes, the most important and last of which was the civil war between north and south in Sudan, finally ended by the Addis Ababa Agreements of 1973. This crisis had seemed immune to settlement and had caused upset along Sudan's frontiers for at least a decade. Haile Sellassie's political arrangement was an act of genius, probably his last before he lapsed into senility, and he hoped it would win him the Nobel Peace Prize, which he long had coveted. Unfortunately, however, he had not been able to keep the peace in Ethiopia, and there was insurgency in several of the country's provinces and actual war in Eritrea. The Nobel eluded him as much as did the solutions to his nation's difficult problems, and he was deposed in September 1974, bringing an extraordinary career to an end. Throughout he had stood for peace, even if he himself had not always been able to bring his own country to that happy condition.

Bibliography:

A. *The Autobiography of Emperor Haile Sellassie I, My Life and Ethiopia's Progress, 1892–1937*, trans. by Edward Ullendorff (Oxford, 1976).

B. Christopher Clapham, *Haile Sellassie's Government* (London, 1969); Gontran de Juniac, *Le Dernier Roi des Rois; l'Ethiopie de Haile Sellassie* (Paris, 1979).

Harold G. Marcus

HALLGARTEN, Constanze (12 September 1881, Leipzig, Germany—25 September 1969, Munich). *Career*: pacifist.

Constanze Hallgarten came from a wealthy and cultured family. Her father, a wholesale merchant, played the cello and her mother was a talented painter. In this milieu, she developed a marked aesthetic sensitivity. Her marriage to Robert Hallgarten, son of the philanthropic Jewish banker, Charles Lazarus Hallgarten, brought her to Munich where she came into contact with the pre–1914 innovative art world of that city, and with its leading musicians, artists, and writers.

After the outbreak of war in 1914, Constanze Hallgarten took part in social programs created to help women whose husbands had been called into the army. Following the Women's Peace Congress at the Hague in 1915, she took the lead in founding the Munich branch of the International Women's Committee for a Permanent Peace (IWCPP). After the war, she devoted herself completely to the peace movement. In 1919 she participated in the Zurich congress of the IWCPP which led to the establishment of the Women's International League for Peace and Freedom whose Munich branch she headed from 1919 until 1933. Apart from her involvement with WILPF, Hallgarten belonged to the executive committees of the Munich branches of the Deutsche Friedensgesellschaft (German Peace Society) and the Deutsche Liga für Völkerbund (German League of Nations Union). From its inception in 1922, Hallgarten played a leading role in the Munich Friedenskartell (Peace Cartel), an umbrella organization uniting all peace and antiwar groups. A good speaker, she addressed many public peace demonstrations undeterred by the social proscription she exposed herself to by such activity. Along with *Ludwig Quidde and Karl Gareis, she spoke at the memorial service for *Alfred Hermann Fried in 1922.

Among the high points of her pacifist activity was her tireless work in the organization of a much acclaimed peace exhibition in Munich in 1927, which also was seen in other large German cities. She participated as a speaker at the meeting of German and French youth in Würzburg in 1928, which was arranged by *Marc Sangnier and later protested efforts to make gas warfare acceptable. She also helped establish the German branch of the Ligue internationale des mères et des educatrices (International League of Mothers and [Women] Teachers), the German Mütterliga (Mother's League), one of whose executive committee members was *Elsbeth Bruck.

Hallgarten experienced the rise of Adolf Hitler and National Socialism in Munich, the headquarters of both. Her active opposition to the Nazi movement was carried on in the face of attempts at intimidation and threats of physical violence. Only her precipitate departure to Switzerland on March 14, 1933 saved her from certain persecution by the Nazi regime. Several days before leaving Germany, she helped *Hellmut von Gerlach escape to Austria through Munich. After a short stay in Switzerland, Hallgarten and her son, the later German-American historian, George W. F. Hallgarten, moved to France, and from there to the United States. After World War II she returned to Munich.

Bibliography:

A. *Als Pazifistin in Deutschland. Biographische Skizze* (Stuttgart, 1956).

B. George W. F. Hallgarten, *Als die Schatten fielen. Erinnerungen vom Jahrhundertbeginn bis zur Jahrtausendwende* (Frankfurt am Main, 1969).

Karl Holl
Trans. by Solomon Wank

HAMILTON, Alice (27 February, 1869, New York—22 September 1970, Hadlyme, CT). *Education*: M.D., Univ. Michigan, 1893. *Career*: physician, bacteriologist, and reformer.

After completing the medical course at the University of Michigan and her internship, Alice Hamilton turned to the study of bacteriology that would establish her as a leader in the field of public health. Her studies and investigations brought her international recognition in science and an appointment as the first female faculty member of the Harvard Medical School. In 1897 Hamilton began teaching at the Woman's Medical School of Northwestern University and also began her long association with Hull House. The two activities merged in her writing and activism in the field of occupational safety, which began in 1908 with her appointment to the Illinois Commission on Occupational Diseases and continued through her employment with the U. S. Department of Labor in the 1930s. Hamilton emerged as the authority on occupational health with the publication of *Industrial Poisons in the United States* (1925).

World War I drew Hamilton into an active role in the pacifist movement in which she participated by speaking on the medical consequences of war. Hamilton, *Emily Balch, and *Jane Addams headed the American delegation to the International Congress of Women at The Hague in 1915, a meeting that led to the founding of the Women's International League for Peace and Freedom four years later. The Congress adopted a call for continuous mediation among belligerents by the neutral nations. After the Congress, Hamilton accompanied Addams to the warring nations to press for adoption of the women's peace proposal. Hamilton shared Addams' view that there would be no true victors in the conflict. Upon her return from Europe, Hamilton focused her scientific investigations on weapons being developed secretly in the United States. In 1917 she participated in rallies and petition movements to keep America out of the war, but she withdrew from vocal participation in the peace movement when America entered the war. Like many others, Hamilton remained a pacifist in conscience, but she feared losing her job if her peace activities became too strident.

Hamilton continued in her pacifist beliefs through the 1930s, but German aggression caused her to abandon unqualified pacifism. Her investigations of Nazi abuses and German expansionism convinced her that the United States would have to side unequivocally with the Allies. After World War II, she criticized the American Cold War mentality and the postwar anticommunist crusade. In 1963 she reaffirmed her pacifism when she signed an open letter protesting American military involvement in Vietnam.

Bibliography:

A. "An Inquiry into the Nazi Mind," *New York Times Magazine*, August 6, 1933, 1–2; *Women at the Hague: The International Congress of Women and Its Results*, with Jane Addams and Emily Greene Balch (New York, 1915).

B. NAW, IV, 306–8.

C. Alice Hamilton Papers, Radcliffe College, Cambridge, MA.

Julia Kirk Blackwelder

HAMMARSKJÖLD, Dag Hjalmar Agne Carl. See *Biographical Dictionary of Internationalists*.

HAMMER, Walter (pseud. of Walter Hösterey) (24 May 1888, Elberfeld, Germany—9 December 1966, Hamburg, German Federal Republic). *Education*: attended Höhere Lehranstalt. *Career*: editor and publisher, *Junge Republik*, 1920 ff., *Junge Menschen*, 1920–27, *Junge Gemeinde*, 1923–26; *Der Fackelreiter*, 1928–29; ethical-pacifist writer and historian.

Initally, Walter Hammer was one of the outstanding personalities of the Wandervogel youth movement which developed in Germany around the turn of the century. Sometime later, the growing chauvinism and anti-liberalism of the Wandervogel, led Hammer to play a leading role in the founding of the Freideutschtum (Free German) youth movement which held its first meeting on the Hohe Meissner near Kassel in October 1913. The meeting was intended as a counter-demonstration to the militaristic centenary commemoration of the battle of Leipzig in 1813. Before the outbreak of World War I, he also was the leader of the Elberfeld branch of the Deutsche Vordertruppbund (German Vanguard League) founded in 1911 by *Hermann Popert and dedicated to an ethical reform of life. Through the league he came into contact with *Hans Paasche, co-editor of the League's journal.

After the First World War, in which Hammer served as a soldier from 1915 until 1918, he became active in several pro-republican and antimilitarist organizations. His chief contribution to the antiwar movement, however, was as a writer and editor, supporting ethical-cultural reforms, a democratic youth movement, and peace. Under his guidance, *Junge Menschen*, a periodical which he founded together with Knud Ahlborn and Fritz Klatt, was transformed into a forum "to represent the new will of youth." The periodical contributed decisively to a heightened awareness of progressive ideas and practices. Foremost among Hammer's efforts was resistance to resurgent nationalism and against all veneration of war and false heroism. He called for understanding among nations as well as a far-reaching reform of the world of economics and ethics and, indeed, a reform of the way life was lived. Through his Fackelreiter (Torch Bearer) publishing house, he distributed pro-democratic, ethical reformist, and antimilitarist writings in fifty-three languages. In 1932, at the request of the Social-Democratic government of the state of Prussia, Hammer created a republican propaganda office to counteract the rise of Nazism.

Hammer's writings, journals, and political activities earned him the hatred of the National Socialists and all other reactionary forces. After the Nazis came to power at the end of January 1933, Hammer was arrested and taken to a concentration camp. Released, he emigrated to Amsterdam from where he journeyed throughout Europe to contact like-minded friends in the hope of initiating resistance to the Nazi regime. Together with *Ludwig Quidde, Hammer participated as the only German representative at the World Peace Congress held in Locarno, Switzerland, in the autumn of 1934. In 1938 the Nazis revoked his German citizenship and in 1939 he resettled in Copenhagen. During the occupation of Denmark, Hammer attempted to flee to Sweden but was arrested by the Danish police and handed over to the Nazi authorities who sentenced him to five years imprisonment in the notorious Brandenburg-Göhrden prison. He was liberated by the Russian army on April 27, 1945, but remained in the prison hospital because of an inflammation of the hip joint. While recuperating, Hammer gathered whatever prison records were available, searched for those who were missing, and provided information about the people who had been murdered and those who had survived. He hoped to create there a memorial for all those who had been persecuted for political or religious reasons or who had been murdered. But this humane task came to naught since the German Communist leaders in East Germany, where the prison was situated, rejected Hammer's "objectivism."

In 1950 Hammer fled from the German Democratic Republic to the German Federal Republic and in Hamburg created the Walter-Hammer-Archive which he developed unselfishly into a unique collection of evidence of Nazi barbarism and of the resistance movement. The archive soon became available to historians and the general public. In 1953 he was awarded the Service Cross First Class of the Federal Republic of Germany, and in 1964 he was awarded the Grand Cross for Service. With the help of his wife, Erna Hammer-Hösterey, the collection, after Hammer's death, became part of the Institut für Zeitgeschichte (Institute of Contemporary History) in Munich.

Bibliography:

A. *Das Buch der 236. Infantrie-Division* (Leipzig, 1919); (editor), *Dokumente des Begetarismus* (2 vols., Leipzig, 1912–15); *Die Generalanzeigerpresse als Hort der Korruption* (Leipzig, 1911; *Höhes Haus in Henkers Hand. Rückschau auf die Hitlerzeit, auf*

Leidensweg und Opfergang deutscher Parlamentarier 1933–1945 (Frankfurt am Main, 1956); *Nietzsche als Erzieher* (Leipzig, 1918).

B. Erna Hammer-Hösterey and Hugo Sieker, eds., *Die bleibende Spur. Ein Gedenkbuch fur Walter Hammer* (Hamburg, 1967); Walther G. Oschilewski, *Junge Menschen. Ausgewahlt und mit einer Darstellung zur Biographie Walter Hammers und einer Geschichte der deutschen Jugendbewegung versehen* (Frankfurt am Main, 1981); Gerhart Werner, "Biographie Walter Hammer," *Wuppertaler Biographien* (Wuppertal, 1967), vol. 7.

Walther G. Oschilewski
Trans. by Peter Seadle

HAMON, Frédéric Adolphe Augustin (20 January 1862, Nantes, France—3 December 1945, Port-Blanc-en-Penvénan, Côtes-du-Nord, France). *Education*: Lycée Condorcet, Paris. *Career*: professor, Université Nouvelle, Brussels; Collège libre des sciences sociales, Paris; London School of Economics; author, journalist, editor, socialist, and peace activist.

After a youthful interest in libertarian anarchism, Augustin Hamon's life was largely devoted to activities on behalf of socialism—organizing, lecturing, and writing. Most of his work was done in the west of France where he served as secretary to the Bretagnese federation and as delegate to various national and international Socialist congresses. He was also active in the Freemasons and Freethinkers, edited several socialist journals, including *L'Humanité Nouvelle*, and lectured, occasionally, at nontraditional institutions. During World War I, he lived in London and taught at the School of Economics. Following the war, he suffered ill health but continued to write for journals. In the last year of his life, he served in the Resistance in western France.

Hamon's contribution to the peace cause was mainly through writing. His study, *Psychologie du militaire professionnel* (*Psychology of the Military Professional*), first appeared in 1894 and achieved considerable notoriety which led to translations into many languages. Using sociological and psychological language, Hamon argued that professional soldiers were basically of the same cast of mind as criminals except that soldiering was a legalized version of antisocial, antihuman behavior. Activities which in civilian life might bring imprisonment or execution were viewed by the military and its proponents as the noblest form of patriotism. Traditional sectors of French life were outraged by Hamon's book, and even moderate, middle class peace workers disassociated themselves from his extreme arguments. Nonetheless, this work became part of a major tradition of antimilitarist literature that appeared in pre–1914 Europe and heralded many arguments made in the Dreyfus camp a few years after its publication.

In 1898, following Emile Zola's famous trial and the outbreak of the Spanish-American War which shocked liberal Europeans, Hamon joined with an Italian journalist, G. Ciancabilla, and the Italian peace activist, *E. T. Moneta, to survey several thousand prominent European politicians and intellectuals about their attitudes on war and militarism. Asked to discuss the role of war and militarism in modern life, possible ways of curbing the incidence of war, and the general effects of militarism on society, the responses constituted a rare collection of opinion on the subject. Eventually, Hamon published 138 responses in a special issue of *L'Humanité Nouvelle* which coincided with the opening of the first Hague Peace Conference (May, 1899). The span of views in the publication covered just about every position possible—from Tolstoyan absolutism to militant social Darwinism, but the majority of responses reflected a horror of war and a fear that it was inevitable.

On the matter of disarmament or arms limitation, Hamon examined the economic benefits that would accrue to each major European nation were they to restrict the annual growth of arms but warned peace activists not to fall into the trap of supporting small professional armies, devoid of citizen participation, in the interests of economizing. He argued that any arms control agreement would be meaningless unless accompanied by a system of international arbitration. Thus, Hamon, a socialist, developed a position which came very close to that of the middle class peace movements of his day.

Bibliography:

A. "A propos du désarmament," *L'Humanité Nouvelle*, III (October, 1898), 427–45; "Enquête sur la gûerre et le militarisme," *L'Humanité Nouvelle* (supplement, May, 1899; reprinted New York, 1972); *Leçons de la guerre mondiale* (Paris, 1917); *Patrie et internationalisme* (Paris, 1896); *Psychologie du militaire professionnel* (Brussels, 1894).

B. J. Bossu, "A. Hamon," *L'Idée libre*, March, 1946; *Dictionnaire Biographique du Mouvement ouvrier français*, III, 3rd partie, *1871–1914: De la commune à la grande guerre* (1975), 27–28.

Sandi E. Cooper

HARDIE, James Keir (15 August 1856 Legbrannock, Lanarkshire, Scotland—2 September 1915 Glasgow). *Education*: largely self-educated. *Career*: miner, 1868–78; stationer and journalist, 1878–79; miners' representative (largely unpaid) and journalist, 1879–92; Member of Parliament, (for South West Ham), 1892–95, (for Merthyr Burghs), 1900–15.

Keir Hardie was a Scot to the core, conscious of clan and class. His father was a ship's carpenter, his mother a domestic servant. He worked from the age of seven as messenger boy, shipyard hand, errand boy, and then miner. He went to evening school, joined the temperance movement, was dismissed and blacklisted because he was campaigning for better conditions, and in 1879 married a collier's daughter.

He now turned to journalism, for which he had something of a flair. He supported himself by his writings, at the same time working to organize the miners more effectively, first as correspondence secretary for Hamilton, then as county agent for Lanarkshire, then as county secretary for Ayrshire, and, in 1886, as secretary of the Scottish miners' federation.

During this period he was a Liberal, but in 1888 stood unsuccessfully for Parliament as a Labour candidate. He resisted Liberal attempts to buy him off, and in the same year formed the Scottish Labour party, later a part of the Independent Labour party (ILP). Meantime he had started his own paper *The Miner*. which was succeeded by *The Labour Leader*. This gave him a national position, and in 1892 he was elected Independent Labour member for South West Ham. He refused to compromise with establishment traditions, and his cloth cap and tweed suits roused the fury of his political opponents and were the joy of cartoonists; he was nicknamed the "Member for the Unemployed"—a proud title. He lost his seat in 1895, fought two unsuccessful elections, and was returned for a Welsh constituency in 1900. He was chairman of the ILP from its inception in 1893 to 1900, and again in 1913–14. He led the Parliamentary Labour party from 1906–7.

Keir Hardie believed that capitalism was a primary cause of war, and that working-class organizations should be able to prevent war by using the general strike if necessary. He was active in international working-class cooperation from 1888. He was forthright in opposition to the South African War. The outbreak of World War I broke his heart and his health. He never really recovered and died the following year.

Keir Hardie was much hated and much loved. He created the Labour party, and gave it its distinctive blend of socialism and trades unionism. To this he added pacifism, in which *George Lansbury was his great follower; the ILP remained closer to his vision than the Labour party.

Bibliography:

B. E. Hughes, *Keir Hardie* (London 1936); W. Stewart, *J. Keir Hardie: A Biography* (London 1921).

John Ferguson

HARTLEY, Frank John (11 March 1909, Rutherglen, Victoria, Australia—5 July 1971, Melbourne). *Education*: Licentiate of Theology, Univ. of Melbourne, 1934, B.A., 1937; B.D., Melbourne Coll. of Divinity, 1949. *Career*: chaplain, Australian army, 1940–43; co-founder, Australian Peace Council, 1949, Joint Honorary Secretary, 1949–71; member, World Peace Council, 1951–71; president, Democratic Rights Council, 1950–51; founder and member, Peace Quest Forum, 1951–68; superintendent, Prahran Methodist Mission, 1954–71; foundation member, Australian and New Zealand Congress for International Cooperation and Disarmament, 1959; councillor, Prahran City Council, 1959–71.

Son of a tailor and raised in the coal-mining town of Wonthaggi in Australia, Frank Hartley developed at an early age a strong compassion for the underprivileged and a sharp awareness of the class division in capitalist societies. He felt drawn to a prophetic calling in the Methodist Church, and his strong Christian principles formed the basis of his ministry of social action. As a chaplain during World War II he brought great comfort to his troops, especially to those engaged in the fierce battle for Sananda Road in New Guinea. Of the 420 men who went into action there, only 62 escaped death, serious injury, or grave illness.

One of the survivors was Rev. Hartley, who for his outstanding bravery was mentioned in despatches.

His horrendous wartime experiences led him to the decision to devote the remainder of his life to the cause of peace. Together with *Alfred Dickie and Victor James, he became one of the principal founders and driving forces of the Australian Peace Council. Formed at the height of the Cold War and enjoying the crucial organizational assistance of the Communist Party of Australia, whose influence extended into some of the largest trade unions, this key peace body of the postwar era attracted the anticommunist vilification of many powerful sections of Australian society. Despite the personal abuse he sometimes received, Hartley persisted zealously in his efforts to forge close ties of understanding and peaceful coexistence between the *peoples* of the capitalist and socialist nations. He thought this essential if the world were to survive. He made extensive visits to the Soviet Union, attended many meetings abroad of the World Peace Council, discussed church affairs with religious leaders in the communist countries, and wrote and spoke endlessly of the good will and genuine concern for peace he encountered on all these occasions. On returning home he would spend countless hours addressing factory meetings, debating from the Methodist platform on the Yarra Bank, and preaching the gospel of peace at various church gatherings. A central theme in his peace strategy was the need to weld the Christian Church and the working class in a coalition against the twin evils of war and exploitation. In this spirit he welcomed overseas moves for Christian-Marxist dialogue and arranged such meetings in Australia.

Tolerance for other people's right to express their viewpoint, he argued, was a prerequisite to the creation of a just peace. Thus when the Australian Government took measures to outlaw the Communist party and numerous other devices were introduced to hamper left-wing political activities, such as the conferences and petitions conducted by the peace movement, he responded by taking up the banner of civil liberties. Some notable victories were achieved in this area. Similarly, he could count many instrumental successes in his social welfare work. However, the same success could not be claimed for the main peace policies he espoused—general and complete disarmament, withdrawal from Korea, Australian nonalignment, a nuclear-free Pacific, peace with justice in the Third World countries of Asia, and rapprochement in Europe.

Despite repeated setbacks, he never seemed to waver in his faith in the ultimate triumph of a new world order based on Christian principles. His enthusiasm, warmth, and resolve had an infectious effect on co-workers, and helped greatly to sustain the peace movement during one of its most difficult periods, thereby paving the way for the eventual successes it secured in the anti-Vietnam struggle. Although some of his peace colleagues were highly critical of the way he unswervingly praised the Soviet Union as the greatest force for peace in the world while counterposing U.S. imperialism and other monopoly interests as the greatest threat to peace, no one (not even his arch anticommunist critics) challenged the sincerity of his peace commitment. In recognition of his tireless efforts for peace and humanity, he received numerous international awards including the Comenius Gold Medal, 1956; the Joliot Curie Silver Peace Medal, 1959; the Joliot Curie Gold Peace Medal, 1965; and the Lenin Gold Peace Medal, 1971.

Bibliography:

A. *In Quest of Health* (Melbourne, 1965); *In Quest of Peace* (Melbourne, 1951); *In Quest of Peace II* (Melbourne, 1956); *Sananda Interlude* (Melbourne, 1949).

B. Marion Hartley, *The Truth Shall Prevail* (Melbourne, 1982).

Ralph Summy

HASLAM, Fred (26 May 1897, Middleton, Lancashire, England—16 October 1979, Toronto, Ontario). *Education*: self-educated. *Career*: administrator, Friends Relief Mission, Vienna, 1920–21; secretary-treasurer, Rogers Radio Tube Co., 1924–40; general secretary, Canadian Friends Service Committee, 1931–56; research fellow, Woodbrooke Coll., 1967–68; secretary-treasurer, Canada Yearly Meeting of Friends, 1960–72; social worker; pacifist.

During the First World War Fred Haslam was a British conscientious objector, first at the work center of Wakefield Prison and later in alternative service. Having come from a Congregational church background with little formal education, it was not until this wartime experience that he was attracted to the Society of Friends and the humanitarian and social concerns which came to dominate his life.

Following the war he worked in London with the Friends' Emergency and War Victims Relief Committee and then with the Friends Relief Mission in Vienna before emigrating to Canada in 1921. Once in Toronto, he began a lifelong association with Canadian Friends, including such leading Quakers as *Arthur G. Dorland and Albert S. Rogers. Not only did Haslam accept an administrative appointment in the Rogers family business, a position he maintained until the company changed ownership and began supplying the military with radio parts during the Second World War, but he also assisted Rogers in various humanitarian pursuits during the interwar years: the organization and administration of Canadian funds for Russian Famine Relief, later merged into the Canadian Save The Children Fund; the operation of boys and girls clubs in Toronto; and founding of Camp Neekunis, a youth camp on Georgian Bay. By 1931 Haslam was instrumental in the organization of the Canadian Friends Service Committee, and, as its executive secretary for the next twenty-five years, he was personally responsible for the day-to-day direction of its activities, especially those concerning world peace and the abolition of capital punishment.

Beginning with the disarmament campaign of the early thirties and continuing through the decade, Haslam forged close ties between Friends and other groups in the broader Canadian peace movement such as the Women's International League for Peace and Freedom, the Fellowship of Reconciliation, and the Student Christian Movement. By the outbreak of World War II he turned his attention to the challenge of maintaining a pacifist protest, particularly conscientious objection to military service. In this regard, Canadian Friends joined with Mennonites to form the Conference of Historic Peace Churches, and Haslam assumed a leading role in both its executive and military problems committees. In this position he emerged as a special liaison between sectarian pacifists and those from mainstream Protestant churches. Together they ensured, in negotiations with government authorities, the advancement of the right of all Canadians, regardless of religious affiliation, to conscientious objector status as well as the possibility to perform some type of alternative service, preferably of a humanitarian nature.

Perhaps his greatest achievement during the war was the organization and deployment of a contingent of Canadian conscientious objectors to the Friends Ambulance Unit in China. He also coordinated an effort to assist German Jewish refugees interned in Canada as enemy aliens, and at the same time he became influential in the Robert Owen Foundation and the movement to build model cooperative communities in Canada as an experimental base for a future pacifist society. During the post-World War II years, although he still encouraged and supported traditional pacifist protests, Haslam turned his attention to the search for Christian unity through the ecumenical movement. He became active in the Canadian Council of Churches and the World Council of Churches in the hope of developing an international spiritual basis for world peace and nuclear disarmament.

Bibliography:

A. *1921–1967: A Record of Experiences with Canadian Friends and the Canadian Ecumenical Movement* (Toronto, 1970).

B. Thomas P. Socknat, "The Canadian Contribution to the China Convoy," *Quaker History*, 69 (Autumn, 1980), 69–90; Thomas P. Socknat, " 'Witness Against War' : Pacifism in Canada 1900–1945," Ph.D. dissertation, McMaster University, 1981.

C. Canadian Friends Service Committee Papers, Society of Friends Meeting House, Toronto.

Thomas P. Socknat

HAUSSMANN, Conrad (8 February 1857, Stuttgart, Germany—11 February 1922, Stuttgart). *Education*: studies in law and literature, universities of Zurich, Munich, Berlin, and Tübingen. *Career*: defense lawyer; left-liberal member of the Württemberg Diet, 1889–1922, and German Reichstag, 1890–1922; state secretary without portfolio, 1918; vice-president, Weimar National Assembly, 1919.

Conrad Haussmann, whose father supported the 1848 radical movement in Germany, grew up in a family and community environment that fostered commitment to democracy and internationalism. Conrad and his twin brother Friedrich (member of the Reichstag, 1898–1903) were key figures in the South German Liberal party. This remnant of 1848 radicalism represented a South German rural and small-town protest against Prussian domination and militarism. Within Württemberg, the party led by the Haussmanns and Friedrich Payer secured democratic reforms of the constitution, local government, taxation, and education.

Despite the sudden death of his beloved brother in 1907, Conrad was unshaken in his political optimism. Believing that the democratic gains in Württemberg could be repeated on the national level, Payer and Haussmann fostered the merger of all the left-liberal factions into the Progressive party in 1910. They paid the price for this by abandoning their own perennial opposition to military bills.

At the same time, Haussmann became increasingly active in internationalist endeavors: the Interparliamentary Union, the (unofficial) Anglo-German conciliation conferences, the Verband für internationale Verstandigung (Association for International Understanding). His internationalism was nurtured by family connections with Switzerland, correspondence with politicians and writers of other nations, and a lively intellectual curiosity that ranged from international law to Chinese poetry. Once the first Morocco Crisis triggered his alarm, Haussmann repeatedly branded Germany's diplomatic isolation as a consequence of antidemocratic methods at home and abroad. He called for parliamentary government and parliamentary supervision of foreign policy.

In 1913 the Socialist *Ludwig Frank called for a conference of French and German parliamentarians to support a one-year moratorium on military expansion. The first German liberal to respond, Haussmann labored to attain adequate bourgeois representation from Germany at the conference. Haussmann and the French Socialist *Jean Jaurès played the major roles at the Berne conference both in the resolution committee and as keynote speakers. After the conference Haussmann created a standing committee of Reichstag deputies for Franco-German reconciliation, overcoming the nationalistic reluctance many displayed. The committee met once with its French counterpart at Basel in May 1914.

The assassination of Jaurès and the outbreak of war saddened Haussmann. Yet true to his ideals, he attempted to link up internal reform and a compromise peace. In alliance with *Georg Gothein, Haussmann prevented the Progressives from endorsing annexation and unlimited submarine warfare. He was instrumental in creating the Reichstag majority which passed the Peace Resolution in June 1917 and in forming the Max von Baden government, which attempted a belated democratization in October 1918.

As chairman of the constitutional committee of the Weimar Assembly, Haussmann was instrumental in securing the enactment of Germany's first democratic constitution. Yet stung by the vindictiveness, as he perceived it, of Germany's enemies, he led the party's internationalist wing in rejecting the Versailles Treaty. Committed to the ideal of a League of Nations, he saw the actual League as woefully defective with the absence of the United States, Russia, and Central Europe.

A profound commitment to self-determination at home and abroad lay behind Haussmann's internationalism. His energetic optimism brought partial successes, but may also have caused him to underrate obstacles. His individualistic conception of political action combined with a disinterest in economic and social issues led him to ignore the underlying sources of conflict.

Bibliography:

A. *Aus Conrad Haussmanns politischer Arbeit* (Frankfurt/Main, 1923); *Schlaglichter: Reichstagsbriefe und Aufzeichnungen* (Frankfurt/Main, 1924).

B. James C. Hunt, "Die deutschen Liberalen und ihre Versuche zur französisch-deutschen Verständigung 1913–1914," *Aspekte deutscher Aussenpolitik im 20. Jahrhundert,* Wolfgang Benz and Herman Graml, eds. (Stuttgart, 1976), 28–40; *Biographisches Staatshandbuch* (Bern and Munich, 1963); *Neue Deutsche Biographie*, (Berlin, 1961), VIII, 130–31.

C. Conrad Haussmann Papers, Hauptstaatsarchiv, Stuttgart.

James C. Hunt

HEARD, Henry Fitzgerald (Gerald) (6 October 1889, London—14 August 1971, Santa Monica, CA). *Education*: Sherbourne; B.A., Gonville and Caius Coll., Cambridge Univ., 1913. *Career*: organizer and worker, Agricultural Co-operative Movement, Ireland and England, 1919–27; literary editor, *The Realist*, 1929; science commentator, BBC, 1930–34; council member, Society for Psychical Research (London), 1932–42; author, lecturer, and pacifist.

Gerald Heard's upbringing and education seem properly conventional, but the style in which he lived much of his life most assuredly was not. After leaving Cambridge, he spent some time in the service of a British attorney-general; he then worked for most of a decade with the Agricultural Cooperative Movement. Eventually, however, Heard settled into a career as author and lecturer. By the late 1920s, he was concentrating his efforts on a series of books on the evolution of human consciousness and society, publishing *The Ascent of Humanity* in 1929 and *The Social Substance of Religion* two years later. These books as well as his position as science commentator for the BBC helped to establish Heard's reputation in literary and intellectual circles as one of the most brilliant and perceptive thinkers in England.

Although Heard claimed to be a lifelong pacifist, he became active in the struggle for peace only after the publication of the final volume of his series on human society, *The Source of Civilization* (1935). Heard's work, in general, was too esoteric for the mass reader, but his conclusion that pacifism, with its emphasis on "positive social values," was the "key to harmonious social existence" found a receptive audience. The juxtaposition of this conclusion with the onset of the Abyssinian crisis and the magnetic personality of Reverend *Dick Sheppard brought both Heard and his close friend *Aldous Huxley into the front ranks of the British peace movement as sponsors and members of Sheppard's Peace Pledge Union (PPU). Within a year, however, Heard drifted away from the main body of the PPU and began to preach a singularly radical version of the "New Pacifism." First stated in a public lecture at Friends House in London and later greatly elaborated in *The Third Morality* (1937), Heard's new gospel stressed that the future of effective war resistance lay in the "growth of sensibility," or the resensitizing of human awareness. The means to establish world peace, Heard said, was "mind-body" training of pacifists in the "initiative of social creativeness.'' Small bodies (maximum of twelve) of dedicated, like-minded persons slowly but thoroughly trained in meditation could, by overcoming conflict in the self, provide humanity with the means for overcoming conflict within societies and among nations.

Not surprisingly, Heard's call for the creation of a caste of psychically advanced but politically disinterested ''Neo-Brahmins,'' who would compose an International ''psychological'' Police Force, attracted no mass following. Indeed, many critics tended to dismiss his ideas as muddleheaded mysticism. Still, when Heard traveled to America and established the first of his ''colleges'' for training the new order of peacemakers at Tzabucco (near Laguna Beach) in Southern California, he was visited there by many prominent literary people who continued to revere him as a mentor and sage. Perhaps his influence was most telling on Aldous Huxley, a fellow Californian expatriate, whose novels began to incorporate more and more of Heard's religious mysticism.

During the last three decades of his life, Heard moved further and further away from the mainstream of the peace movement. His activities and publications were largely concerned with religious or esoteric subjects. Eventually Heard, often in the company of Aldous Huxley, experimented with the use of hallucinogenic drugs as a means of heightening consciousness. Despite these latter distractions, Heard's life and work remain a fascinating example of the attempt to integrate nonviolence and pacifism into an all-encompassing way of life.

Bibliography:

A. *Force That Is Not Violence* (n.p., 1940); *Militarism's Post-Mortem* (London, 1946); *Pain, Sex and Time. A New Hypothesis of Evolution* (London, 1939); *Quaker Mutation* (Wallingford, PA [1940]); ''The Significance of the New Pacifism,'' in *Gerald Heard and Aldous Huxley on Pacifism* (London, 1935, reprinted in Gerald K. Hibbert, ed., *The New Pacifism*, London, 1936); *The Source of Civilization* (London, 1935); *The Third Morality* (London, 1937).

B. Martin Ceadel, *Pacifism in Britain, 1914–1945: The Defining of a Faith* (Oxford, 1980).

Thomas C. Kennedy

HEATH, Carl (1 December 1869, Epsom, Surrey, England—4 March 1950, Guildford, England). *Education*: Junior School, Epsom Coll., 1874–80; École Alsacienne, Paris, 1880–86; New Univ., Brussels, 1895. *Career*: teacher and private tutor, 1892–1908; secretary, National Peace Council, 1909–19; chairman and secretary, Council for International Service (later Friends Service Council), 1919–35; chairman, India Conciliation Group, 1935–50.

After teaching for fifteen years, Carl Heath commenced his real life's work in 1909 when he was appointed secretary of the National Peace Council (NPC). The NPC had recently assumed responsibility for coordinating the activities of disparate British peace societies and until 1914 Heath traveled widely in Europe, establishing valuable connections in the peace movement. When the Great War began, the NPC nearly collapsed because two-thirds of its members left the peace movement and embraced the national cause. Those who stayed on to assist Heath in preserving the integrity of the Council were mainly Quakers. This display of steadfastness was undoubtedly a factor in Heath's decision in 1916 to join the Society of Friends, a step that had profound influence on his subsequent career.

Late in the war Heath was called for military service. He claimed conscientious objection and his Quakerism may have persuaded authorities to grant him an exemption on condition of continuing in his present employment. Since the bulk of his work was for the NPC and Friends Emergency Committee—aiding stranded enemy aliens—he accepted the condition and remained at liberty. Though he was free to carry on his pacifist activities, Heath was disturbed by the lack of constructive outlets for peace testimony. This dissatisfaction was the inspiration for his suggestion to a Quaker Conference in 1917 that Friends might perform a positive witness for peace in the postwar era by establishing "Quaker Embassies" in great cities throughout the world "as growing points of the spirit." A few months later Heath elaborated on this concept in a pamphlet depicting Quaker diplomats on "peace service" reporting to a "Friends Foreign Office" in London. Heath's desire to make this vision a reality led to his resignation from the NPC in 1919 to become chairman, then secretary, of the Council for International Service (CIS). Although his grandiose designs were never quite fulfilled, Heath spent the next decade and a half traveling throughout Europe, the Middle East, and the United States administering the activities of Quaker representatives at various peace centers as well as lecturing and writing on the means for attaining international reconciliation. In 1927 the CIS was merged into the Friends Service Council, of which he remained secretary until 1935.

During this same period Heath established a close personal relationship with the Indian leader, *M. K. Gandhi. Their friendship and shared convictions led to the establishment of the India Conciliation Group. As chairman of this body for the last fifteen years of his life, Heath remained deeply committed to the cause of Indian freedom and Anglo-Indian reconciliation.

Heath always defined himself as an "integral pacifist," that is, one whose practical activities on behalf of peace were firmly buttressed by a deep religious faith. He believed that reason and humanitarian idealism were, in themselves, an insufficient basis for maintaining one's commitment to peace under the pressure of modern materialism. Although he worked closely with every sort of secular pacifist and political peace advocate, Carl Heath remained convinced that religious and spiritual values were the necessary foundation for those who would adhere to the pacifist creed. Thus, while the Second World War was a bitter blow to his efforts and hopes, Heath remained confident, right up to his death in 1950, that the international peace movement could design a program to control, and eventually end, violence and war.

Bibliography:

A. *Pacifism in Time of War* (London 1915); *Quaker Embassies* (London 1935); *Towards a Christian Peace* (New York 1944).

B. Horace G. Alexander, *The Growth of the Peace Testimony of the Society of Friends* (London 1956); *The Friend*, March 10, 1950.

C. There is Carl Heath material at Friends House Library, London, and in the National Peace Council Papers in the British Library of Political and Economic Science, London, and the Swarthmore College Peace Collection, Swarthmore, PA.

Thomas C. Kennedy

HEERING, Gerrit Jan (15 March 1879, Pasuruan, Indonesia—18 August 1955, Oegstgeest, Netherlands). *Education*: Dr. of Theology, Univ. of Leyden, 1904. *Career*: minister, Remonstrant Brotherhood, 1904–17; professor, theology, Univ. of Leyden, 1917–49.

Gerrit Heering, son of a Dutch Reformed minister, became a minister himself as well as one of the most outstanding theologians of the liberal religious movement in his country. His two-volume work, *Geloof en openbaring* (*Faith and Revelation*) (1933–37) became a standard of the modernist movement. In addition, during the First World War, Heering, under the influence of the popular peace preacher, Hilbrandt Boschma, became a spokesman for Christian antimilitarism. A speech he delivered in 1921 to the Remonstrant Brotherhood on the church as the conscience of society was transformed into a pamphlet, becoming the basis of antimilitarism in church activity. The society, Kerk en Vrede (Church and Peace) which he helped to create in 1924 and its monthly, *Kerk en Vrede* served as Heering's vehicles for his Christian pacifism.

Heering's increasing insistence on the social and pacifist mission of Christianity aroused considerable opposition which Heering confronted in a 1930 book, *Zondeval van het Christendom* (*The Fall of Christianity*), followed by a lecture tour, in the United States on liberal religious thought. He eventually found more comfortable acceptance in such groups as the International League of Antimilitarist Ministers and Clergy, which met in Zurich in 1931, than among his former friends at home.

Despite much criticism and opposition, Heering continued to build Kerk en Vrede with help from *Johannes Hugenholtz and other associates. Heering remained the theorist of the movement and it survived his retirement in 1935 for reasons of health. He stayed on as a quiet background figure of Christian antimilitarism in The Netherlands, writing and lecturing throughout the difficult years to come.

Bibliography:

A. *Dieu et César, la carence des églises devant le problème de la guerre* (Paris, 1933); *Geloof en openbaring* (2 vols., Arnhem, 1933–7; 2nd ed., 1944); *The Fall of Christianity* (London, 1930); *De kerk als maatschappelijk geweten* (Hillegom, 1921); *Militia Christi* (Arnhem, 1935); *De taak der kerk ten opzichte van de vredesbeweging* (n.p., 1926); *De zedelijke eis tot ontwapening* (Amersfoort, 1924); *De zondeval van het Christendom* (Arnhem, 1929).

B. Walter F. Bense, "Introduction" to Heering, *The Fall of Christianity* (Garland reprint, New York, 1972); *Jaarboek van de Maatschappij der Nederlandse Letterkunde te Leiden*, (Leiden, 1955–1956), 86–94.

J. H. Rombach

HEILBERG, Adolf (14 January 1858, Hirschberg, Silesia, Prussia—17 December 1936, Breslau, Germany). *Education*: studies at the universities of

Leipzig and Berlin. *Career*: lawyer, member, City Council of Breslau, 1887; president, City Council of Breslau, 1915–23; politician and pacifist.

Adolf Heilberg, one of a number of bourgeois liberal Jews inclined toward pacifism, was a lawyer and a longstanding member of the executive committee of the German Bar Association. His great prestige as a lawyer led to numerous honors, including being named Justizrat (Legal Councillor) by the Prussian state, being granted an honorary doctor's degree by the University of Breslau in 1911 and being elected to the leadership of the Breslau Chamber of Attorneys. All of these honors, however, were taken away from him by the National Socialist regime in 1933 because he was a Jew, a pacifist, and a left-liberal politician (he belonged among the leading representatives of the Progressive People's party and later of the German Democratic party in Silesia).

As Heilberg recalled in his memoires, he had been devoted since his youth to the concepts of world peace. He based his position on the immorality and inhumanity of war, and on the restrictions on free will and the rights of personality in war.

Heilberg dated the beginning of his pacifist activities in the winter of 1892–93, when he came to public attention with his successful speech on the idea of international freedom delivered as part of the program of the Breslau Humboldt Society for General Education. Encouraged by +Alfred H. Fried, Heilberg soon joined the leadership of the newly forming Deutsche Friedensgesellschaft (German Peace Society), thus pioneering in the organization of the peace movement in Germany. He proved untiring in the service of pacifism, making numerous speeches and writing for the press. He helped establish several local branches of the German Peace Society in Silesia, including the one in Breslau in 1894. He served as chairman of the Breslau branch, with one short break, until 1933.

On numerous occasions, Heilberg advanced the concept of education for peace as a task for German teachers. He took part in almost all national and international peace congresses, and was widely recognized as a leading antiwar spokesperson. His international acclaim as a commentator on peace movement issues led to his appointment, in 1907, to the Council of the International Peace Bureau in Berne, Switzerland (later Geneva). In his last years he served as an honorary member of the Bureau.

Throughout World War I, Heilberg held fast to the idea of the possibility of peace among nations. Whatever vitality the German Peace Society had during the war was due, in part, to the principles he laid down at the meeting in Erfurt in 1917. Heilberg was, with all of his zeal for the pacifist cause, a sensible, pragmatic, realistic, political thinker, who envisioned the task of the peace movement, above all, to be the strengthening of the concept of justice in international politics. During the Weimar Republic this view led him to oppose the radical pacifists, whose demands for conscientious objection he rejected. He therefore did not go along with the radical course of the German Peace Society at the end of the 1920s, although he did remain in the organization.

Bibliography:

A. *Die Erziehung zum Frieden, eine Aufgabe für die deutsche Lehrerschaft* (1898); *Die Idee des allgemeinen Völkerfriedens* (Breslau, 1893); "Sombart Händler und Helden. Ein Beitrag zum Verständnis des Pazifismus," *Die Friedenswarte*, 15 (1915), 88–92.

B. Hans Wehberg's obituary of Heilberg, *Die Friedenswarte*, 37 (1937), 29–30.

C. Memoirs of Adolf Heilberg, Leo Baeck Institute, New York, NY.

Karl Holl
Trans. by William Hopkins

HEILE, Wilhelm (18 December 1881, Diepholz, Germany—17 August 1969, Harpstedt, Federal Republic of Germany). *Education*: apprenticeship as locksmith and machinist in a shipyard; gymnasium (passed state examination as an external student); engineering studies, Technical Univ. of Hanover. *Career*: political publicist; politician.

Wilhelm Heile became an advocate of a European policy of peace, but never subscribed to pacifist principles. Instead of pacifism, other concerns shaped his political career. Among them was his steadfast devotion to his roots in his lower Saxon homeland where his father worked as a veterinarian and where his forebears had farmed for generations. Also important was his attachment to the Kingdom of Hanover (where the city of his birth was located), which was annexed by Prussia in 1866. This action fueled his aversion to Prussia whose dissolution he demanded at the end of both World War I and World War II. Finally there was his preference for federalist rather than centralist solutions to conflicts between and within states.

As a student, Heile became both a disciple and a co-worker of Friedrich Naumann in the battles for the political direction of the Association of German Students. Renouncing his original engineering interests, he turned to political journalism and in 1912 assumed the editorship of Naumann's publication, *Die Hilfe*. After serving in World War I for two years he returned in 1916, severely wounded, to the editorial offices of *Die Hilfe* and after Naumann's death in 1919 became its co-publisher. Together with Naumann he also founded the Staatsbürgerschule (Citizen's School) in Berlin (1918) which later became the Deutsche Hochschule für Politik.

As deputy of the German Democratic party he was in the German National Assembly in 1919, and in the Reichstag until 1924. Here he advocated the reorganization of the German state and greater European cooperation as the best guarantee of peace. Stimulated by his own experiences at the front and also by Naumann's book *Mitteleuropa*, he favored the establishment of a European customs union that would become the basis for a federally organized United States of Europe, including both Great Britain and the Soviet Union. His activity as secretary of the German section of the Interparliamentary Union and as vice-president of the Entente internationale des partis radicaux et des partis similaires (an organization which united the left-liberal parties in Europe), his work with *Marc Sangnier, and even his position as deputy chairman of the Austrian German Volksbund which was working for the union of Germany and Austria, all aimed at European union. Through his activities furthering European cooperation, Heile harbored the hope of furthering a revision of the Treaty of Versailles to bring about the union of Germany and Austria in accordance with the Greater-German liberal democratic tradition.

Following the preparatory work of *Alfred Nossig, Heile attempted from about 1924 on to bring together in one organization all pro-European forces in Germany. The founding of the Association for European Understanding in 1926 was above all his work. He failed, however, in his attempt at cooperation with +Count Richard Coudenhove-Kalergi, the founder of the Pan-Europa movement, because of differences in their conceptions of European union. Heile was equally unsuccessful in his attempt, in the late 1920s, to have the Association for European Understanding become a powerful and influential European organization with multiple national branches.

The beginning of the National Socialist rule created problems for Heile. After experiencing financial difficulties as a result of his acquisition of a farm in Lower Lusatia, he worked in the Reichsbank in Berlin in a subordinate position where he was exposed to annoyances from the public authorities and mistreatment by the Gestapo.

After the collapse of Germany in 1945, Heile experienced a political comeback. Named as magistrate in Syke (Lower Saxony) by the British occupying forces, he participated in a decisive way in the formation of the Freie Demokratische Partei (Free Democratic Party) (FDP) in the British zone of occupation. He was elected chairman of the party in 1946, but was soon booted out of his position. He left the FDP, among other reasons, because it developed in a direction which he regarded as too unitary. Motivated by his old Hanoverian sympathies, Heile joined the Deutsche Partei, and represented it in the Parliamentary Council which worked out the constitution of the Federal Republic of Germany. His activities in the cause of Europe also were revived when, together with a few like-minded friends, he founded the Europa-Union in late 1946 in his hometown of Syke. On its 25th anniversary in December 1981, former President Walter Scheel came to Syke to honor his memory.

Bibliography:

A. *Nationalstaat und Völkerbund. Gedanken über Deutschlands europäische Sendung* (Halberstadt, 1926).

B. Jürgen C. Hess, "Europagedanke und nationaler Revisionismus. Überlegungen zu ihrer Verknüpfung in der Weimarer Republik am Beispiel Wilhelm Heiles," *Historische Zeitschrift*, 225 (1977), 572–622; Karl Holl, "*Europapolitik im Vorfeld der deutschen Regierungspolitik. Zur Tätigkeit proeuropäischer Organisationen in der Weimarer Republik*," *Historische Zeitschrift*, 219 (1974), 33–94.

C. Wilhelm Heile Papers, Bundesarchiv, Koblenz.

Karl Holl
Trans. by Peter Seadle

HELLER, Vitus (3 May 1882, Tauberrettersheim, Germany—18 October 1956, Würzburg, Federal Republic of Germany). *Education*: volksschule (primary school). *Career*: cultural reformer, editor, pacifist writer, and political activist.

Before World War I, Vitus Heller was actively involved in popular lay Catholic organizations. In 1910 he founded a local branch of the Volksvereins für das katholische Deutschland (the People's Association for Catholic Germany) in Tauberreterrsheim, and in 1911 he established the regional office of the association in Würzburg, of which he became the secretary. His participation in the war as a soldier on the Western front from 1914 until 1917 affected Heller deeply. The war became for him "the great annihilator for all."

Heller approached social, economic, and political questions from a radical-pacifist point of view. He considered the overcoming of the capitalist economic order as a preliminary condition for the realization of a comprehensive order of peace. At the same time, he was part of the Catholic life-reform movement, which stressed that a truly loyal Christian life would make people inwardly free, healthy, and happy. Integral to the movement was the struggle against political lies and war. As a way of actualizing these principles, Heller founded the Christlich-Soziale-Partei-Bayerns (Christian Social Party of Bavaria) in 1921. Four years later he founded a national party, the Christlich-Soziale-Reichspartei (National Christian Social Party) (CSRP), whose program favored reform, socialism, and pacifism. The CSRP was the only party in Weimar Germany to explicitly support a pacifist program. Heller urged the Friedensbund Deutscher Katholiken (Peace League of German Catholics) (FDK) to join his party, but most members of the FDK remained committed to the Catholic Center party and criticized the CSRP for its uncompromising ethical-religious radicalism which prevented the possibility of any political success in conventional terms.

In opposition to the FDK, the CSRP joined German Communists during the late 1920s in taking a strong stand against armaments and militarism. This prompted several members of the FDK, such as *Franziskus Stratmann and J. Antz, as well as members from the Catholic youth movement who were disappointed with the Center party's stand on these matters, to vote for the CSRP in the May 1928 elections. The radicalization of the CSRP drove it increasingly into an anti-parliamentary direction and at times, against the wishes of Heller, into a close association with the German Communist party.

The CSRP experienced difficult times in 1931, when the Würzburg police commissioner repeatedly banned the party's newspaper, *Das Neue Volk*, which Heller had founded in 1918 and for which he wrote almost all of the lead articles. In June 1932 the Bishops of Freiburg, Cologne, Trier, Mainz, and Rottenburg issued a warning against *Das Neue Volk* and accused the CSRP of contravening Catholic religious and moral teachings. Desiring to help the Catholic Center party in the parliamentary elections of 1932, the Bishops made their accusations with little to substantiate them. On March 31, 1933, *Das Neue Volk* was prohibited from publishing by the Nazi government. Heller was arrested several times and was imprisoned for three months in the Dachau concentration camp without, however, being mistreated.

After World War II, Heller supported the establishment of the Christlich-Soziale-Union (Christian Social Union) (CSU) in Unterfranken, and was named by the party as an honorary member of the city council of Würzburg. In the program of the CSU, which called for the socialization of heavy industry, Heller believed that his own ideas had been reactivated. He was soon disappointed, however, and his enthusiasm for the new party waned.

Bibliography:

A. *Das Programm des christlichen Sozialismus* (Würzburg, 1918); *Der Weg zur Rettung* (Würzburg, 1931); *Nie Wieder Krieg* (Würzburg, 1921).

B. Wolfgang Löhr, "Vitus Heller (1882–1956)," in J. Aretz, R. Morsey, & A. Rauscher, eds., *Zeitgeschichte in Lebensbildern* (Mainz, 1980); Dieter Riesenberger, *Die Katholische Friedensbewegung in der Weimarer Republik* (Düsseldorf, 1976).

Dieter Riesenberger
Trans. by Solomon Wank

HEM DAY [pseud. of Marcel Camille Victor Dieu] (30 May 1902, Houdeng-Goegnies, Belgium—4 August 1969, Evere, Belgium). *Education*: accounting. *Career*: founder, Groupe libertaire de Bruxelles and l'Union anarchiste de Belgique; secretary and treasurer, Comité international de défense anarchiste, 1926; member, Belgian section of l'Internationale des résistants a la guerre; director of anarchist publications *Le Combat*, 1926–28, *Le Rebelle* 1927–28, *Ce qu'il faut dire*, *Droit d'Asile*, 1929, *Guerre au fascisme*, 1930, *Pensée et action*, 1930–69; founder, Comité pour les victimes du régime fasciste italien; member, Council of the Internationale des resistants à la guerre, London, 1945; bookseller, writer, lecturer, anarchist, and pacifist.

Marcel Dieu, or Hem Day as he was known in his writings, was an unusual personality, gifted with an originality and Rabelesian temperament. A generous, warm hearted person, he crusaded for nonviolence in numerous conferences and writings. As a young man he was struck by the horrors of the First World War and, particularly, by the sufferings of the working class. From that time on, he threw himself into a struggle against all wars.

In 1922 he was drafted. The call presented him with a dramatic and difficult problem, for he did not want to hurt his family by refusing to serve as much as he did not want to bear arms. Eventually, he succeeded in joining a noncombatant administrative branch of the army. Shortly after, he became an active member of the Belgian section of the Internationale des résistants à la guerre (War Resisters' International).

In February, 1933, along with his friend, Léo Campion, Marcel Dieu sent his military papers to the Minister of National Defense, claiming that his philosophical and social ideas no longer allowed him to recognize any military authority. This gesture signified refusal to participate either directly or indirectly in national defense. He also wished to protest against a proposed law to punish antipatriotic and antimilitarist agitation. On May 3, 1933, as a disciplinary measure, he was called to serve 15 days of military service. Refusing to obey, he was considered a deserter and was arrested on June 16. After a hearing before a military tribunal in July, he received two years in prison, but on August 3 was freed. He quickly threw himself into pacifist propaganda, popularizing the cause of conscientious objectors.

As an anarchist, he also labored to spread libertarian thought in Belgium and abroad. To that end, he organized conferences, gave lectures, and collaborated on many newspapers and journals. Given the realities of European politics in the interwar years, he agitated for the right to asylum and the liberation of political prisoners. In 1937 in Spain, he brought the activities of the Comité international de défense anarchiste (International Anarchist Defense Committee) (CIDA) to Barcelona but left by July for France, convinced of the hopelessness of the situation. He attempted to launch anti-Nazi propaganda in France but was quickly expelled.

The battle against fascism was continued in Belgium. Support for fascist refugees was organized by CIDA in Belgium, but World War II destroyed the pacifist and the anarchist movements. After the war, Marcel Dieu resumed his struggle for the right to be a conscientious objector in Belgium, a right finally won in 1964. While he represented the War Resisters' International in several countries, notably India, Jordan, and Israel, he was against its general policy of indiscriminately supporting any and all war refugees.

Marcel Dieu was a prolific author and many of his articles were translated.

Bibliography:

A. *Alerte, voici les gaz!* (Brussels, 1938); *Ce qu'il faut dire. Contre l'espionnage, contre la guerre, contre le fascisme* (Brussels, 1935–36); *Le Châtiment de Dieu, l'église c'est la guerre* (Brussels, 1934); *Histoire d'une idée. Un rêve se réalise. H. Runham Brown et la résistance à la guerre* (Paris/Brussels, 1950); "Introduction," *Anthologie de l'objection de conscience et de raison* (Paris/Brussels, 1951); "Introduction," *Bible de l'objecteur de conscience* (Enfield, 1957); *Non-violence et action directe* (Brussels/Paris, 1948); *Sébastien Faure, le pacifiste* (Paris/Brussels, 1961); *Souvenirs sur Han Ryner, suivis de pacifisme et violence* (Paris, 1946).

B. *Bibliographie de Hem Day. Quarante ans d'anarchie* (Paris/Brussels, 1964); Léo Campion, *Le Drapeau Noir. L'équerre et le compas*, Montrouge, 1978; "Hommage à Hem Day," *Pensée et Action*, 39–40 (October-November, 1970).

C. Papers of Hem Day, Bibliothèque Royale de Bruxelles.

Nadine Lubelski-Bernard
Trans. by Sandi E. Cooper

HENNACY, Ammon (24 July 1893, Negley, OH—14 July 1970, Salt Lake City, UT). *Education*: attended Hiram Coll., the Univ. of Wisconsin, and Ohio State Univ. *Career*: associate editor, *The Catholic Worker*, 1952–70; anarchist, peace activist, and pacifist author.

Styling himself "the One-Man Revolution in America," Ammon Hennacy was a native American radical born in Ohio and educated for one year each at Hiram College, the University of Wisconsin, and Ohio State University. Leaving the Baptist Church of his birth, he became in turn a socialist, a communist, and a Wobblie. During World War I, he converted to Tolystoyan non-church Christianity, while undergoing a year's solitary confinement in prison for conscientious objection. After the war he entered into a common-law marriage, hiked the contiguous 48 states with his wife, purchased a farm, and worked as a social worker in Milwaukee, where he organized one of the first social workers' unions. Because of his continued radicalism, his wife and two daughters left him in 1940. Between 1942 and 1953, he lived in the Southwest, where he worked as a day-laborer to avoid the withholding of tax from his income.

Strongly influenced by *Dorothy Day and the ideals of her Catholic Worker Movement, Hennacy was baptized a Catholic in 1952. Shortly thereafter he joined the staff of the Catholic Worker House of Hospitality in New York City and became an associate editor of their newspaper. From then until his death in 1970, Hennacy's spirit and personality permeated the Catholic Worker Movement. In 1961 Hennacy moved to Salt Lake City and set up his own House of Hospitality, named in honor of Joe Hill, the IWW songster.

Hennacy's concepts and beliefs were unique. He was philosophically an individualist anarchist committed to Gandhian nonviolence and drawing his ideas from primitive Christianity and the Sermon on the Mount. Blunt and outspoken, he took great pleasure in stirring up people in order to induce in them a rethinking of their positions. He was a thoroughgoing Christian anarchist and believed that the only revolution that was coming was the one that would take place within the individual person. He loved intellectual confrontation and practiced what he termed "moral jiu jitsu," using his adversary's words and ideas to place him at a disadvantage. His basic philosophy, drawn from *Henry David Thoreau, *Leo Tolstoy, and *Gandhi, can be seen in his list of principles: 1) voluntary poverty; 2) the Sermon on the Mount; 3) absolute pacifism (as evidenced in tax refusal); 4) the Mass; 5) work; 6) anarchism; and 7) vegetarianism (including no alcohol, tobacco, or medicine). Hennacy was strict and absolute on all these points and would skip meals in jail rather than eat meat.

Hennacy was very much the rebel. Besides openly refusing to pay federal income tax, he fasted and picketed the Internal Revenue Service office every April 15. He also fasted and picketed beginning each August 6 and continuing as many days as years had elapsed since the 1945 bombing of Hiroshima. He was the prime mover behind the 1950s civil defense drill protests in New York City, where he, Dorothy Day, and others courted jail rather than take cover in a simulated nuclear attack. Yet he was too much of a loner to be an organization person. While he picketed at Omaha and at Groton in the antinuclear actions of the Committee for Non-Violent Action, he never fully participated in this or any other organization.

Hennacy's contributions to peace were not in organizing or in developing a philosophy but in leading a life of total commitment to his personal ideals and giving example. Asked once if he really thought he could change the world, he answered: "I may not change the world, but I'll be damned if it will change me!" It didn't. He died as he had lived, on the way to picket in protest of the impending execution of two convicted murderers. His ashes were strewn on the graves of the Haymarket Martyrs.

Bibliography:

A. *The Autobiography of a Catholic Anarchist* (New York, 1954); *The Book of Ammon* (privately printed, 1965, 1966, 1968, 1970); *The One Man Revolution in America* (Salt Lake City, 1970).

B. Joan Thomas, *The Years of Grief and Laughter: A ''Biography'' of Ammon Hennacy* (Phoenix, AR, 1974).

John L. LeBrun

HERBERS, Heinrich (''Hein'') (2 March 1895, Warendorf, Germany—21 August 1968, Bilthoven, Netherlands). *Education*: studied German language, literature, history, and philosophy, Univ. of Münster. *Career*; secondary school teacher, Warendorf, Herne, Attendorn, Bad Ems, and Kassel, 1922–23, 1928–32; contributor, *Der Pazifist* (Hagen), 1924–25; feuilleton editor, *Das Andere Deutschland* (Hagen/Berlin), 1925–33; teacher and deputy director, ''Werkplaats, Kindergemeenschap Bilthoven,'' 1934–68; pacifist journalist and speaker.

When he was still a secondary school pupil, Hein Herbers was already a member of the Free German Youth Movement, which was formed on the ''Hoher Meissner'' (North Hesse) in October 1913 as a counter demonstration to the dedication of a monument commemorating the Battle of the Nations in Leipzig. The dedication ceremony had been carried out with militaristic pomp, and the counter demonstration sought to set a tone of love of one's native land different from the ''hurrah patriotism'' of the ceremony. Nevertheless, Herbers became caught up in the general war enthusiasm of the early days of World War I and enlisted for military service the following summer. He was badly wounded on the western front in 1917 and discharged from the army.

As a result of his wartime experiences, Herbers became a radical pacifist and socialist. During the revolutionary days of 1918, he joined the Independent German Social-Democratic party and became a member of the Socialist Students' Movement. At the same time, he became a member of several pacifist organizations, including the Deutsche Friedensgesellschaft (German Peace Society), Bund der Kriegsdienstgegner (League of Resisters to Military Service), Deutsche Liga für Völkerbund (German League of Nations Association), Bund Religiöser Sozialisten (League of Religious Socialists), and Deutscher Pazifistischer Studentenbund (German Pacifist Students' Association). Within the youth movement he considered himself to belong to the oppositional pacifist wing.

The bearing and attitude of the west German pacifists during the Ruhr occupation of 1923 led Herbers to commit himself to the cause of peace. Influenced by *Friedrich Wilhelm Foerster, the west German pacifists believed that the German government's previous sabotage of reparations destroyed the moral justification for the passive resistance against the French occupation. Moreover, they considered the resistance movement discredited because of the form in which it was carried out and because of the German government's lack of willingness to negotiate. The events of 1923 strengthened Herbers' conviction that Germany bore the principal responsibility for the outbreak of World War I.

He offered his services as a contributor to *Der Pazifist*, the paper of the west German pacifists and became feuilleton editor of its successor, *Das Andere Deutschland*. In this capacity he commented on current affairs, acted as a propagandist for pacifism, pleaded for German-French reconciliation, criticized Germany's militarization, and eloquently spoke out against the "Hakenkreuz und Stahlhelm" (swastika and steel helmet) at many public meetings. He was the leading member of the west German branch of the German Peace Society.

In 1928 Herbers went back into teaching, but lost his position four years later when he was accused by nationalists of having earlier insulted Field Marshal Paul von Hindenburg, the president of the Reich, in an article published in *Das Andere Deutschland*. Having resigned from the German Social Democratic party in 1931 because of its toleration of Chancellor Heinrich Brüning" and having joined the Socialist Workers' party, he no longer had sufficient political support in his conflicts with nationalistic opponents. Fearing continued persecution for his pacifist views, he emigrated to the Netherlands in 1934 and took a teaching position at the private school of *Kees Boeke. There he became well known as the tutor of Queen Beatrix of the Netherlands.

Bibliography:

A. *Friede durch Gewalt—Friede durch Recht* (Essen,1959); "Schwerer Dienste tägliche Bewährung! " in *Wegweiser in der Zeitenwende*, ed. by Elga Kern (Munich/Basel, 1955), 41–55.

Reinhold Lütgemeier-Davin

HERRIOT, Edouard. See *Biographical Dictionary of Internationalists*.

HERRMANN, Immanuel Gottlob (29 July 1870, Rommelshausen, near Stuttgart, Germany—22 May 1945 Neu-Finkenkrug, near Berlin) *Education*: theological studies, Univ. of Tübingen, 1888–92; mechanical engineering and electrical engineering studies, Stuttgart Institute of Technology, 1894–98. *Career*: associate professor of electrical engineering, Stuttgart Institute of Technology, 1901–28, professor of electrical communication engineering and measurement technology, 1929–33; minister of war, Württemberg government, 1919; pacifist.

Influenced by the works of Ludwig Feuerbach and David Friedrich Strauss and by social democratic publications, Immanuel Herrmann turned away from theological studies and devoted himself to his original interests in mathematics and scientific research. About the same time, in the early 1890s, he became an opponent of war. In 1894 he joined the Stuttgart branch of the German Peace Society which at that time, under the influence of left liberalism, was considered the stronghold of south German pacifism. Despite the fact that he considered himself an opponent of war Herrmann served as a captain in the German army in Flanders between 1914 and 1917. This might be explained in part by the fact that he was an organizational pacifist rather than a radical antimilitarist. In contrast to the radical pacifist efforts to prevent the outbreak of war by a general strike, refusal of military service, and the use of violence, Herrmann's brand of pacifism stressed international law, compulsory arbitration, and disarmament agreements as ways of ensuring a lasting peace. In this sense, organizational pacifism was similar to pacifism based on justice through law (Rechtspazifismus) and the idea of a league of nations (Völkerbundspazifismus).

After his discharge from the army, Herrmann, who earlier had confined his association with the German Peace Society to mere membership, became more actively engaged in the organization's work. As a member of the staff responsible for the daily operations of German Peace Society and as a Socialist deputy in the Württemberg constituent assembly, Herrmann was appointed minister of war in the cabinet of the Social Democratic Württemberg government of Wilhelm Blos. During the time that Herrmann held this politically exposed position—January-June 1919—his powers were restricted. He was mainly concerned with demobilization. Decisions regarding the use of Württemberg troops against the Munich Soviet Republic headed by *Kurt Eisner and against the Sparticists were made by the minister-president or by the entire cabinet. Nevertheless, the fact that the use of military force took place during his term of office led to his being sharply attacked by antimilitarists. Despite that, Herrmann afterwards held a reputable position in the peace movement. He distinguished himself as head of the active Stuttgart branch of the German Peace Society, as president of the society's Württemberg state association, and as a prominent member of the Stuttgart Peace Cartel, the local umbrella organization of peace groups. At the same time he was president of the Stuttgart branch of the German Monist League, and was active in the German Ethical Culture Society, and the Freemasons. He was co-publisher of the freethinking series of pamphlets, *Es werde Licht. Blätter für Humanität, Freiheit und Fortschritt* (*Shedding Light: Papers on Humanity, Freedom and Progress*) published in Leipzig.

During changes in the leadership of the German Peace Society in 1929, Herrmann aligned himself with the west German faction under *Fritz Küster, which leaned toward mass agitation. He supported this direction by aiding in the development of the German Peace Society from an "association of like-minded persons" ("Gesinnungsgemeinschaft") to an "organization for the fight" ("Kampforganization") against fascism and militarism. To be sure, this kind of fight did not signify approval of violence but, rather, a spiritual and intellectual struggle in the tradition of the German Enlightenment. Those pacifists around Küster organized demonstrations against the Nazis and, relying on the power of conviction, they did not shrink from a direct confrontation with the National Socialists for the purpose of unmasking the Nazis' inhuman and warmongering program.

In October 1932 Herrmann was elected a member of the board of directors of the German Peace Society. Shortly after the Nazi take-over of power in January 1933, he was imprisoned for several months and lost his professorship. During the Nazi dictatorship, he went into internal emigration.

Bibliography:

A. "Alte Ziele—neue Wege," *Das Andere Deutschland*, 9 (March 16, 1929); "Freimaurertum und Pazifismus," *Das neue Freimaurertum* (Leipzig, 1923); "Von der Gesinnungsgemein schaft zur Kampforganisation," *Das Andere Deutschland*, 10 (August 1, 1931).

B. Ludwig Ankenbrand, "Immanuel Herrmann," *Die Freigeistige Aktion* 4 (August, 1960), 61; "Aus unserer Kampfzeit. Professor Herrmann, Stuttgart," *Das Andere Deutschland*, 9 (May, 1960); Karl Holl and Helmut Donat, eds., *Der deutsche Pazifismus während des Weltkrieges 1914–1918* (Boppard, 1979); Wilhelm Keil, *Erlebnisse eines Sozialdemokraten* (2 vols., Stuttgart, 1948); *Kürschners Deutscher Gelehrten Kalender 1931* (4th ed., Berlin/Leipzig, 1931), 1136; *Poggendorff's biographisch-literarisches Handwörterbuch für Mathemathik* (Berlin, 1937) VI, 1091–92.

Reinhold Lütgemeier-Davin

HERTZ, Friedrich Otto (26 March 1878, Vienna—21 November 1964, London). *Education*: Ph.D., Univ. of Munich, 1903; studies at the Univ. of Vienna. *Career*: independent author and scholar; secretary Bund Österreichischer Industrieller, 1906; counsellor (Hofrat, Ministerialrat) at the Chancellery and Foreign Ministry of the Austrian Republic; editor, *Reconstruction*, Vienna, 1920–22; professor of sociology and economics, Univ. of Halle, 1930–33.

Friedrich Hertz was one of the leading personalities in the peace movement in Austria and in Europe, especially during the period between the two world wars. He studied economics and political science at the Universities of Vienna and Munich and published several studies of recognized scholarly merit while still in his twenties. Of Jewish descent, Hertz was especially disturbed by the rise of anti-Semitism and its association with aggressive nationalism, in which he saw the seeds of tyranny and war. To counter these tendencies, particularly the racial theories of H. S. Chamberlain, Hertz immersed himself in a lifelong scholarly investigation of the link between racism and nationalism. His most significant publications on the subject are *Moderne Rassentheorien* (*Modern Racial Theories*) (1904), *Rasse und Kultur* (*Race and Culture*) (1915), *Nationalgeist und Politik* (*Nationalism and Politics*) (1937), and *The Development of the German Public Mind* (1957–75). In outlook a liberal, Hertz believed that free trade and parliamentary democracy, uncorrupted by nationalist excesses, offered the best possibilities for a peaceful world order.

As one who opposed the First World War, Hertz urged a compromise settlement from the beginning. However, strict Austrian censorship prevented publication until after the war of important critical studies such as his *Deutschland und England* (1918) and *Die Entstehung des Weltkrieges* (*The Origin of the War*) (1919). In these works Hertz assailed the notion, spread by wartime propaganda in Germany and Austria, that the two powers were fighting primarily a defensive war. Rather, Hertz argued, imperialist motives and aggressive German nationalism played a far greater role in the war than self-defense.

In the chaotic aftermath of the war, Hertz devoted his energy and talent as an economist to the economic recovery of Austria and Central Europe. He regarded this as the essential condition of a stable political order. In Vienna he edited the bi-weekly newspaper, *Reconstruction* (its motto was "Peace, Free Trade, Goodwill amongst Nations"), and he was an important adviser to both the Austrian Federal Chancellery and the Austrian Foreign Ministry. During this period Hertz also served as secretary of the Pan-Europa Union, a society whose goal was the political unification of Europe, and as an associate editor of *Die Friedenswarte*, Europe's leading German-language peace journal. His tenure as professor of sociology and economics at the University of Halle (1930–33) was short-lived, as the advent of the Nazi regime forced Hertz into permanent exile. He spent the remaining years of his life in England, where he devoted his energies largely to his last major work, the three-volume *History of the German Public Mind*. Hertz will be remembered for his efforts to understand the motive forces of modern nationalism, to show the destructive folly of their excesses, and to envisage a humane and peaceful world order.

Bibliography:

A. *Deutschland und England* (Vienna, 1918); *The Development of the German Public Mind* (3 vols., London, 1957–75); *The Economic Problem of the Danubian States* (London, 1947); *Die Entstehung des Weltkrieges* (Vienna, 1919); *Moderne Rassentheorien* (Vienna, 1904); *Nationalgeist und Politik. Beiträge zur Erforschung der tieferen Ursachen des Weltkrieges*, Vol. I: *Staatstradition und Nationalismus* (Zurich, 1937); *Rasse und Kultur* (Leipzig, 1915); *Recht und Unrecht im Boerenkriege* (Berlin, 1902).

B. Frank Eyck, "Foreword" to Frederick Hertz, *The German Public Mind in the Nineteenth Century* (Totowa, NJ, 1975), 5–6; G.P. Gooch, "Obituary: Frederick Hertz," *German Life and Letters: A Quarterly Review,* XVIII, No. 2 (January 1965), 90; S. Wininger, ed., *Grosse jüdische National-Biographie* (Czernowitz, 1925–36), III, 68–69 and VII (Ergänzungsband), 71–72; Obituary, LT, November 25, 1964, p. 17.

Richard R. Laurence

HERVÉ, Gustave (2 January 1871, Brest, Finistère, France—25 October 1944, Paris). *Education*: communal school and Lycée of Brest, 1882–89; license ès-lettres, Lycée Henri IV, 1892, agrégation d'histoire, 1897. *Career*: teacher, journalist, editor, and polemicist.

Few Frenchmen have been as notorious, as much admired or despised for their political views, as Gustave Hervé. The audacity that he showed while still a young man in attacking militarism made him famous and earned him eleven years in prison. Yet, as he grew older, Hervé became an ardent patriot who broke with the left and championed order and authority.

Born into a large, modest Breton Catholic family, Hervé early showed signs of unusual intellectual ability. After studying at schools in Brest and Paris, he entered the teaching profession and taught history at various provincial lycées. While an instructor at Sens, he joined the Federation of Socialist Workers of the Yonne Department and began an active campaign against militarism. His biting columns in local socialist newspapers, written under the pseudonym "Sans patrie," first won him notoriety. The most famous of these, "The Anniversary of Wagram'' (1901), which attacked the idea of military glory, led to his prosecution for attacks on the army and his triumphant acquittal. But suspended from teaching and eventually dismissed, Hervé soon became the ''traveling salesman of socialism,'' who spoke out vigorously against the evils of the military.

His growing celebrity, increased by unsuccessful government efforts to prosecute him, was intensified by his participation in the newly-formed French Socialist party (SFIO). Hervé's advocacy of antimilitarism, combined with his antipatriotism, antiparliamentarism, and call for popular insurrection in case of war, clashed with the moderate position of *Jean Jaurès. In books and his weekly newspaper *La Guerre sociale*, founded in 1906, he sharply attacked governmental policies. Active in the Antimilitarist International Association, Hervé was sentenced to prison in 1905 for calling upon recruits to refuse military service. He spent a total of eleven years behind bars for his violent attacks on the army.

Weary of his long incarceration and sensing a growing mood of nationalism among his countrymen, Hervé shifted from advocating antimilitarism to forcefully defending France as the home of proletarian revolution. Nevertheless, he advocated peaceful solutions to international problems such as Alsace-Lorraine. When war broke out in 1914, Hervé quickly became an ardent patriot who even volunteered for military service despite his age and poor vision. He called for the defeat of Germany in a fight to the bitter end, changing the name of his newspaper to *La Victoire* (1916).

The postwar years saw Hervé demand strong political order and a return to traditional Catholic values such as large families. By the 1930s, however, he also called for a policy of peaceful understanding with Germany, seeking revision of the Treaty of Versailles to avoid a future conflict. Eventually the growing bellicosity of Adolf Hitler drove him to support a strengthened France ruled by an authoritarian leader, namely Marshal Pétain.

When World War II began, Hervé again became an ardent patriot who supported the national war effort. But France's military defeat in 1940 and the German occupation deprived him of his ability to publish and reduced him to silence after so many years of continual uproar. Hervé died in obscurity shortly after the Liberation, forgotten by all but a few followers.

Bibliography:

A. *L'Alsacse-Lorraine* (Paris, 1913); *Après la Marne* (Paris, 1915); *Épitres de Gustave Hervé aux croyants* (Paris, 1949); *France-Allemagne. La Reconciliation ou la guerre* (Paris, 1931); *Jusqu'à la victoire* (Paris, 1916); *Leur patrie* (Paris, 1910); *Mes crimes* (Paris, 1912); *La Muraille* (Paris, 1916); *La Patrie en danger* (Paris, 1915).

B. Victor Méric, *A Travers la jungle politique et littéraire* (Paris, 1930); Michael R. Scher, ''The Antipatriot as Patriot: A Study of the Young Gustave Hervé, 1871–1905,'' Ph.D. dissertation, University of California at Los Angeles, 1972.

James Friguglietti

HEYMANN, Lida Gustava (15 March 1868, Hamburg, Germany—21 July, 1943, Zurich, Switzerland). *Education*: Hamburg girls' school; pension in Dresden; audited courses at the universities of Berlin and Munich. *Career*: feminist activist; co-editor *Die Frau im Staat*, 1919–33.

Lida Gustava Heymann was one of five daughters of a wealthy Hamburg coffee importer and capitalist. Despite conflicts with her father over her desire for independence, she lived at home until his death in 1896. Having helped with his business, she was made executor of his will. Independently wealthy, she could pursue her interest in social reform. Heymann's focus soon shifted from social amelioration through soup kitchens and the like to an attack on regulated prostitution, which embroiled her in conflict with Hamburg's city fathers and alienated her from more "respectable" feminists. In 1902 she and *Anita Augspurg founded Germany's first woman suffrage organization, further identifying her as part of the feminist "left-wing." Heymann and Augspurg became lifelong companions, living in Munich and a series of Bavarian farms, while traveling throughout Germany as feminist lecturers and organizers. Both women were vegetarians and antivivisectionists, as well.

Soon after the outbreak of World War I, Heymann and Augspurg broke with the majority of German feminists, who supported the war effort, and began seeking connections with like-minded women for a peace conference that would bring to bear their sex's opposition to the war. Heymann served as translator at the ensuing Women's Peace Conference at The Hague in April 1915.

After the war, Heymann and Augspurg founded a journal, *Die Frau im Staat*, which furthered peace and international reconciliation as well as women's participation in political matters. After several attempts in the days of the Wilhelmine Empire to win the support of liberal politicians for woman suffrage by campaigning for them, Heymann and Augspurg had given up on "male" parties, so their view was that of the unaffiliated left. Heymann was active in the Women's International League for Peace and Freedom (WILPF), both in Germany and on the international level, where she served as vice-president from 1919 until 1924, and thereafter as honorary chairwoman. However she became somewhat disenchanted with certain developments in WILPF, particularly what she saw as a loss of the old spirit and a declining emphasis on economic justice, which she attributed in part to the increasing influence of Quakers.

Unlike German pacifist and feminist *Helene Stöcker, Heymann and Augspurg had great faith in woman suffrage as an instrument of world peace. Heymann saw war and violence as less a human instinct than a specifically masculine problem, embodied in the male state and economic system. Men ran the states, which then schooled the "butchers of people" known as soldiers. States were grounded in the "masculine" principles of force, authoritarianism, competition for survival, and domination of others. By contrast, Heymann identified as "feminine" the principles of cooperation, kindness, understanding, and compromise. The feminine instinct was, in fact, "identical with pacifism." World War I demonstrated that men could destroy humankind; women must now save it. Heymann urged pacifists to oppose not only war but the general male tendency to resort to force as a solution to problems. Although a few men had somehow attained a "feminine" mentality, and some women had lost their sensibilities through living in the male world, the gender differences upon which Heymann's world-view was based seemed innate.

Heymann and Augspurg were vacationing outside Germany when Hitler became Chancellor in January 1933. Knowing they were in danger if they returned, they emigrated to Zurich.

Bibliography:

A. *Erlebtes—Erschautes: Deutsche Frauen kämpfen für Freiheit, Recht und Frieden, 1850–1940*, with Anita Augspurg, ed. Margrit Twellmann (Meisenheim/Glan, 1972).

B. Gisela Brinker-Gabler, ed., *Frauen gegen den Krieg* (Frankfurt, 1980).

Amy Hackett

HIGGINS, Henry Bournes (30 June 1851, Newtownards, Ireland—13 January 1929, Dromana, Victoria, Australia). *Education*: B.A., Univ. of Melbourne, 1874, M.A., 1875, LL.B., 1875. *Career*: lawyer, 1876–94; member, seat of Geelong, Victorian Legislative Assembly, 1894–99; member, seat of North Melbourne, Commonwealth House of Representatives, 1901–6; federal attorney-general, 1904; justice, High Court of Australia, 1906–29; president, Commonwealth Court of Conciliation and Arbitration, 1906–22.

Australian historians have usually drawn attention to Henry Bournes Higgins as the president of the Commonwealth Court of Conciliation and Arbitration, in which capacity he delivered the famous "Harvester Judgement," In 1907 this established the doctrine of the basic wage, one which would at that time support an unskilled laborer and his family in Melbourne in frugal comfort. Besides arbitration, Higgins' other principal interests were Ireland, the Australian constitution, and world peace.

In 1899 Higgins was one of the few members of the Victorian Legislative Assembly to oppose the sending of colonial soldiers to assist the British against the Boers in South Africa. While several members opposed it for reasons of expediency or finance. Higgins declared the war to be "unnecessary and unjust," a position which led to criticism from both his constituents and many associates. His forthright condemnation of British and colonial intervention in South Africa was also decisive in costing him his seat at the elections in November 1899. Undeterred, Higgins became a staunch supporter of the Peace and Humanity Society, established in Melbourne in July 1900 to oppose the war. After being elected to the first federal parliament Higgins continued to oppose the war from the floor of the House of Representatives and was one of only five members to vote against the sending of the first Commonwealth contingent to South Africa.

Higgins frequently found himself in the minority. In 1901 he led the fight against the federal government's first Defence Bill, introduced to provide for a military force of permanent, volunteer citizen-soldiers, and to authorize compulsory military training. He feared that Australia would establish a military caste similar to those which existed in England and Europe. Accepting the inevitable, however, he sought to make provision for conscientious objectors to military service, to ensure that conscription would not occur in the event of an ill-defined national "emergency," and to limit service beyond Australia to volunteers. Higgins' specific objections were heeded and were incorporated in the Act of 1903.

In 1906 Higgins became vice-president of the newly formed Melbourne Peace Society, a group designed to be a local branch of the London Peace Society established in 1816. He rejected absolute pacifism, and when war broke out in 1914 Higgins argued that the Empire could not keep out of the conflict. In 1916 his son and only child was killed in action. After the war Higgins resumed his support for the peace movement in Australia. In 1921 he rejected the federal government's proposal to spend £200,000 on a war memorial and endorsed instead the proposal of the Australian Peace Alliance conference in Melbourne to spend the money on a system of traveling scholarships to further international goodwill. In July 1928 the Victorian branch of the World Disarmament Movement was formed at a meeting in the Melbourne Town Hall and Higgins became its president. He had served only six months in this capacity before he died suddenly in January 1929.

A quiet and revered man, Henry Bournes Higgins was little involved in the organizational side of the peace movement. Nor did he contribute much writing; his principal works were concerned with problems other than the attainment of world peace. Nevertheless, he spoke frequently on peace platforms in public and served as a spearhead for the peace movement in both the Victorian and Commonwealth houses of Parliament. Widely regarded as a man of great integrity, he drew attention and gave hope and respectability to the tiny and embattled peace movement in Australia during the first three decades of the twentieth century.

Bibliography:

B. Nettie Palmer, "Henry Bournes Higgins," *Australian Quarterly* (June 1929), 30–37; Nettie Palmer, *Henry Bournes Higgins; A Memoir*, (London, 1931); G. V. Portus, "Henry Bournes Higgins," *Meanjin Quarterly*, X (Summer, 1951), 359–63; Russell Staiff, "Henry Bournes Higgins: His Attitudes to the Boer War, Australian defence and Empire," unpublished Bachelor of Arts thesis, Flinders University of South Australia, 1972; John Uhr, "H. B. Higgins: Policies and and Politics of an Australian 'Independent Liberal,' " unpublished Bachelor of Arts thesis, University of Queensland, 1972.

Malcolm James Saunders

HILLER, Kurt (17 August 1885, Berlin—1 October 1972, Hamburg). *Education*: Dr. jur., Univ. of Heidelberg, 1907. *Career*: political journalist, freelance writer, and pacifist organizer.

Kurt Hiller, born into a Jewish family of manufacturers, had a genius for caustic polemic which almost invariably aroused either extreme rejection or admiration. A wholly independent spirit, his relentless criticism feared nothing and no one, though he himself could tolerate any honest publicistic attack by an opponent. As a Berlin writer, he published in left-oriented bourgeois and socialist newspapers, magazines, and periodicals of the avant-garde. He spoke publicly and organized, gave his firm support to expressionist literature, founded the Neue Club in 1909, and soon after that the literary cabaret, The Gnu, all this in the service of a new intellectual movement called Aktivismus (Activism), which from 1915 to 1924 even had its own public voice called *Das Ziel*, devoted to the realization of his pretentious ''logocratic'' ideas.

In the course of the German November revolution of 1918, Hiller assumed the leadership of the newly founded Politischer Rates Geistiger Arbeiter (Political Council of Intellectual Workers) in Berlin. In 1920, he joined the Deutsche Friedensgesellschaft (German Peace Society) in which he occupied a radical pacifist position on the left wing, often cooperating with *Helene Stöcker. His harsh attacks on his opponents within the peace society frequently were the cause for irritations and conflicts.

Through the Group of Revolutionary Pacifists, which Hiller founded in 1926, he tried to create both a platform and a following for himself within the German Peace Society and the German Peace Cartel. However, his criticism of the West German Regional Association within the German Peace Society, and his constant arguments with *Fritz Küster and *Friedrich Wilhelm Foerster over differences concerning both the domestic and the foreign political stand to be followed by the peace movement, weakened both the Peace Society and the Peace Cartel. Hiller did not share the general West German orientation on foreign policy, was skeptical about the League of Nations, and encouraged unity of action among pacifists, Socialists, and Communists. His repeated accusation in the 1920s that the leaders of the West German Alliance had been corrupted by accepting French, Polish, and Czechoslovakian monies—an accusation that the right-wing was only too happy to seize upon—contributed significantly to the erosion of German pacifism.

After Adolf Hitler became German Chancellor on January 30, 1933, Hiller suffered severely. In March of that year he was arrested and, after terrible mistreatment by the Nazi SS, taken to the Oranienburg concentration camp from where he was released in April 1934. He avoided a second arrest by fleeing to Prague in September 1934. There, as a contributor to the *Neue Weltbühne*, he eked out a meagre existence. In 1938, just prior to the German invasion of Czechoslovakia, Hiller again fled, this time to England. In London, from 1939 to 1946, he was president of the Gruppe unabhängiger Autoren (Group of Independent Writers) and founded the Freiheitsbund Deutscher Sozialisten (Freedom League of German Socialists).

After the war, Hiller returned to Germany for an occasional visit and then settled permanently in Hamburg in 1955. He remained there until his death. In 1956 he founded the Neusozialistischer Bund (New Socialist League), but it remained without any appreciable influence. Throughout his life, Hiller regarded himself as a socialist, but at the same time rejected a doctrinare socialism of the Marxist stripe.

Bibliography:

A. *Der Aufbruch zum Paradies* (Munich, 1922, new ed., Munich, 1952); *Geist Werde Herr* (Berlin, 1920); *Ist Genf der Friede*? (Berlin, 1927); *Köpfe und Tröpfe* (Hamburg and Stuttgart, 1950); *Leben gegen die Zeit: Eros* (Hamburg, 1973); *Leben gegen die Zeit: Logos* (Hamburg, 1969); Profile (Paris, 1938); *Ratioaktiv. Reden 1914–64. Ein Buch der Rechenschaft* (Wiesbaden, 1967); *Das Recht auf sich selbst* (Heidelberg, 1908); *Rote Ritter* (Gelsenkirchen, 1951); *Selbstkritik links* (Leipzig, 1932); *Der Sprung ins Helle* (Leipzig, 1932); *Die Weisheit der Langenweile* (2 vols., Leipzig, 1913); *Das Ziel: die rote Einheit* (Leipzig, 1931).

B. Reinhold Lütgemeier-Davin, *Pazifismus zwischen Kooperation und Konfrontation. Das Deutsche Friedenskartell in der Weimarer Republik* (Cologne, 1982); Lewis D. Wurgart, *The Activists. Kurt Hiller and the Politics of Action on the German Left 1914–1933* (Philadelphia, 1977).

Karl Holl
Trans. by Peter Seadle

HILLQUIT, Morris (1 August 1869, Riga, Latvia—7 October 1933, New York). *Education*: Riga Gymnasium, 1881–86; LL.B., Univ. Law School, New York, 1893. *Career*: Socialist candidate for mayor, New York City, 1917, 1932; National Chair of Socialist party; Socialist author and historian.

A founder and leader of the American Socialist party, Morris Hillquit's focus prior to World War I was on the trade union movement, Socialist political campaigns, and internal party matters. His writings on international relations were brief; he attributed war to the international economic rivalries of "the profit-seeking capitalist classes." At this stage, Hillquit's activities reflected little interest in the peace movement, and his remarks on the peace societies reflected the prevailing socialist analysis that capitalist-led peace societies were futile.

When World War I broke out, however, Hillquit played a prominent role in the antiwar movement. In May 1915 the American Socialist party adopted a peace manifesto prepared by Hillquit. It called for no annexations, no indemnities, the right of political self-determination, disarmament, and an international parliament. To help implement this program, Hillquit and *Eugene V. Debs led a Socialist party delegation to President +Woodrow Wilson to ask him to call a conference of neutral nations to mediate the end of the war. In 1916 Hillquit again led a Socialist delegation to Wilson to repeat the request. As prowar sentiment grew in response to the German U-boat attacks, the Socialist party issued a proclamation moved by Hillquit. Denouncing war, the proclamation ended with a warning that if the United States were drawn into war, the lives of American workers would be sacrificed on "the altar of capitalist greed." Within weeks the United States had entered the war. With help from Algernon Lee and Charles Ruthenberg, Hillquit authored the St. Louis Manifesto, the Socialist party's official position on the conflict. It clearly condemned the war as a crime against the American people and the nations of the world, interpreted the conflict as an imperialist war, and called for a wide variety of antiwar activities. Some have interpreted Hillquit's authorship as a political move necessitated by the growth of the left wing within the Socialist party. In reality, however, the St. Louis Manifesto reflected Hillquit's own position on the war—a position which combined moral indignation and the Socialist economic interpretation. In 1915, two years before the St. Louis Manifesto, Hillquit had written of the "ghastly carnage" and "cold-blooded butchery." And he had, at that time, analyzed it in terms of the desire for economic advantage and power by all "warring nations."

During the war years, Hillquit reached the height of his antiwar activities and the most militant phase of his socialism. In 1917 he took a leading role in organizing the People's Council for Democracy and Peace. The People's Council was a bold attempt to bring together Socialists, peace activists, and unionists to form a political structure that would more genuinely represent the American people. It urged a democratic peace and sought to combat conscription and government violations of civil liberties. Its most audacious proposal called for the creation of a permanent, alternative political structure to Congress. Modeled roughly after the Council of Workmen's and Soldier's Delegates in Russia, the plan collapsed in the face of governmental harrassment at all levels and by the weakening of union support. Ironically, another of Hillquit's antiwar activities played a role in its demise; his 1917 mayoralty race in New York City. Conducting a vigorous antiwar campaign despite attacks upon his patriotism, Hillquit ran a strong third, increasing the Socialist vote almost five-fold. The campaign, however, diverted attention from the People's Council.

When the Wilson administration moved to silence opposition to the war, Hillquit, as a leading Socialist lawyer, participated in many defense campaigns, including the defense of the *Masses*. In the middle of handling three cases (*Eugene Debs, *Victor Berger, and Scott Nearing) Hillquit was discovered to have tuberculosis and was forced to withdraw from public activity for two years. When he returned to the public scene, the war was over, the Communist split had occurred, and radicalism was facing the strong conservative forces of the 1920s. Hillquit's main efforts in his last years once again became domestic—the union movement, the 1924 LaFollette campaign, trying to rebuild the Socialist party.

Without World War I, Hillquit would probably never have played a central role as a peace leader. His whole background was rooted in the trade union movement and in the domestic reforms which he felt would lead to socialism. Accordingly, he showed little interest in peace activities until World War I propelled him into action. His economic analysis alone would not have led him to condemn the war so strongly and to play so prominent a role in organizing opposition to it. It was also the sensitivity to suffering that had originally brought him to socialism that made him a champion of peace.

Bibliography:

A. *From Marx to Lenin* (New York, 1923); *History of Socialism in the United States* (New York, 1903); *Loose Leaves from a Busy Life* (New York, 1934); *Socialism in Theory and Practice* (New York, 1909); *Socialism Promise or Menace*? with John A. Ryan, (New York, 1914); *Socialism Summed Up* (New York, 1912).

B. C. Roland Marchand, *The American Peace Movement and Social Reform, 1898–1918*, (Princeton, NJ, 1972).

C. Morris Hillquit Papers, Wisconsin Historical Society and Tamiment Library, New York University.

Frank A. Warren

HIRST, Francis Wrigley (10 June 1873, Huddersfield, England—22 February 1953, Sussex, England). *Education*: B.A., Wadham Coll., Oxford Univ., 1896. *Career*: journalist, editor, *The Economist*, 1907–16.

Francis Hirst came from Yorkshire stock with strong nonconformist connections. A classical scholar at Oxford, he was also active in Liberal circles, contributing to *Essays in Liberalism* (1897). He later assisted John Morley in compiling material for his *Life of Gladstone*. It was the outbreak of the Boer War in 1899 which confirmed his opposition to imperialism. He played a part in forming the League against Imperialism and Militarism and was a frequent contributor to the periodical press. He was not an absolute pacifist, however, and with the conclusion of the Boer War he turned his attention to other political issues, notably the defense of free trade.

Hirst's opposition to war was chiefly from an economic standpoint—a position he expounded, anonymously, in *Arbiter in Council* (1906). As editor of *The Economist* after 1907 he wrote leading articles that were frequently critical of the foreign policy of Sir +Edward Grey and British attitudes toward Germany. He was, however, emphatically a mid-nineteenth century radical in outlook rather than a "New Liberal." His criticism of British involvement in World War I did not align him with other opponents of war, although he did attempt to work with the Union of Democratic Control, believing that Great Britain was in danger of becoming a military despotism which would bring with it "conscription, protection and a substitution of martial law for trial by judge and jury." In 1916 he felt obliged to resign as editor of *The Economist* and instead became editor of a new journal, *Common Sense*, which more closely represented his viewpoint.

After the war, Hirst continued to write occasional journalism and books, but was more concerned with eminent Liberals and economic issues than war and peace. He failed in his efforts to enter the House of Commons as a Liberal M.P. and his influence waned as the Liberal party declined. Keynesianism left him quite unimpressed. He wrote an introduction to Morley's posthumously published memorandum on his resignation from the British Cabinet in 1914. In public life he found it increasingly difficult to identify with any organized or official strand of political opinion. He supported the Munich agreement of 1938 and reluctantly acquiesced in the necessity of fighting Nazi Germany in 1939. After the Second

World War he ceased to play any significant part in public affairs. Perhaps his most important assessment of twentieth-century war was his *The Consequences of the War to Great Britain* (1934), a volume which may be taken as a classical statement by a representative of the political and economic tradition to which he belonged. Hirst cannot be described as primarily a pacifist or someone who played a major part in British peace groups, but he was a significant controversialist whose opposition to some wars was vigorously expressed.

Bibliography:

A. *Early Life and Letters of John Morley* (London, 1927); *In the Golden Days: Autobiography* (London, 1947); *Liberty and Tyranny* (London, 1935); *The Political Economy of War* (London, 1916).

B. *The Economist 1843–1943, A Centenary Volume* (London, 1943); *F.W. Hirst* by his friends (London, 1958).

C. Some Papers are at Wadham College, Oxford but they are not at present open for research.

Keith G. Robbins

HIRST, Margaret Esther (1882, Huddersfield, England—25 August 1954, England). *Education*: Newnham Coll., Cambridge Univ. *Career*: lecturer in Greek and Latin, Univ. of Birmingham, 1920–47 author.

Margaret Hirst had many intellectual interests. With her brother *Francis Hirst, who was a well-known author of books on economic and political subjects and the editor of *The Economist* from 1907 to 1916, she shared many interests including history and peace. She began her writing career with a biography of the German free trade advocate *Frederick List* (1909), and this was followed by her second book, *The Story of the Trusts*. (1913).

Margaret Hirst joined the Society of Friends as an adult. She began her comprehensive study of Friends' attitudes toward peace and war before the outbreak of World War I, but did not complete it until 1923 when *Quakers in Peace and War* was published. It appeared at a timely moment in history, for Quakers were in the forefront of the British peace movement that emerged after the Great War.

Hirst's study was a scholarly one and traced the historical development of Quaker antiwar attitudes from the seventeenth century through the end of World War I. Using a method of exposition familiar to Friends, she allowed historical characters to give testimony about the evils of war. She provided lengthy excerpts from the works of early Quakers, including Robert Barclay, William Penn, and John Bellers. Rejecting the nineteenth-century belief that Quaker pacifism came from New Testament scriptural pronouncements, she argued that the basis of Friends' pacifist beliefs was the conception of the "inward light, the divine soul . . . that lighteth every man that cometh into the world. . .! *Quaker in Peace and War* explored the subsequent development of Friends' testimony against war not only in England but on the continent and in the United States and the West Indies as well.

When the book came out in 1923, it followed in the wake of several new studies of the Society of Friends. Most of these books were part of a series organized by *Rufus M. Jones of Haverford College, Pennsylvania, and John Wilhelm Rowntree, the Yorkshire industrialist who died at a young age. Known as the Rowntree Series in his honor, seven books appeared between 1909–21. Hirst's book was not specifically written for the series, but Rufus Jones considered it on a par with any of those published. He wrote the introduction to the book, declaring that it illustrated the history of the Society of Friends as a "peace society that has never adjourned."

Margaret Hirst settled into the life of a university lecturer at Birmingham and remained there until 1947 when she retired. Her only other book after *Quakers in Peace and War* was a short biography of *John Bright published in 1945. Hirst respected Bright and considered him to be the greatest statesman ever to emerge from the Society of Friends. She admired Bright for his consistent and successful battle against the discriminatory practices leveled against Friends and other nonconformist sects by the state and the established Anglican Church. Bright also helped the workingman whose political rights and economic position he sought to uplift.

Margaret Hirst's personality, according to an obituary that appeared in *The Friend* (September 10, 1954), was severe yet tempered by "the warmth of loyalty and affection." Her prose and the subjects she chose to write on reflect these characteristics. She brought discipline and dedication to her writing and conveyed an infectious love of subject. She remained devoted to the ideals of her adopted faith, always ready to give testimony of faith.

Bibliography:

A. *John Bright: A Study* (London, 1945); *Quakers in Peace and War: An Account of their Peace Principles and Practice* (New York, 1923).

B. Edwin B. Bonner, "Introduction" to *Quakers in Peace and War* (Garland reprint, New York, 1972); *The Friend*, September 10, 1954, 908.

Edith F. Hurwitz

HOBSON, John Atkinson. See *Biographical Dictionary of Internationalists*.

HOBZA, Antonin (6 January 1876, Rokytnice, Bohemia, Austria [now Czechoslovakia]—6 September 1954, Prague, Czechoslovakia). *Education*: J.U.D., Charles Univ., Prague, 1902; Ph.D., Univ. of Brno, 1904. *Career*: clerk, Bohemian Land Council, 1904–11; professor of canonical and international law, Charles Univ., 1911–47, dean of the law faculty, 1923–24; legal counsel to the post-World War I Czechoslovak government; member, Permanent Court of International Arbitration; member, Institut de droit international; member, Czechoslovak Academy of Sciences.

The crisis that engulfed Europe in the years preceding the start of World War I revealed the fragility of the legal foundations on which the international equilibrium had been based. Antonin Hobza saw the war as a cataclysmic event reminding mankind of the need for a new principle of collective security to replace the old idea of balance of power. In his book, *Právem mezinárodním ku právu světovému* (*From International Law to World Law*) (1915), he advocated many of the reforms which later were realized in the League of Nations and the United Nations.

In the wake of World War I, his interest was directed primarily to strengthening the system of international justice. In his writings and lectures, as well as in his expert opinions +Eduard Beneš, the Czechoslovak Minister of Foreign Affairs and the League of Nations Rapporteur for disarmament and collective security, Hobza pleaded for the extension of the World Court's jurisdiction to include all disputes arising out of the postwar peace settlement.

The rise of fascism exposed Europe to an ideological influence openly contemptuous of the notions of international law and order. Hobza perceived the danger of fascism, and in an essay on "International Crime" (1933) he forewarned potential transgressors that any act regarded by international law as morally repugnant and, by analogy requiring punishment by domestic penal law, would be subject to international criminal liability. Hobza had thus anticipated the development of a principle which—twelve years later—became the cornerstone of the Nuremberg Trials.

The Munich "settlement" of 1938, which resulted in the dismemberment of Czechoslovakia, dealt a severe blow to everything Hobza stood for. Shortly before the German occupation authorities shut down the University of Prague. Hobza, in one of his last lectures, stated that the notion of war was irreconcilable with the idea of law. Common sense suggested that there was no distinction between individual murder and collective murder as it occurred in war. At the same time, no distinction in principle existed between the right to self-defense against individual assault and a defensive war. It was impermissible, he concluded, to practice one morality at the domestic level and another in international life.

Bibliography:

A. *Právem mezinárodním ku právu světovému* (Prague, 1915); *Právo mezinárodní* (2 vols., Prague, 1915); *Trestání válečných zločinců* (Prague, 1946); *Úvod do mezinárodního práva mírového* (Prague, 1933).

B. Vladimír Kopal, "O životě a díle akademika Antonína Hobzy," *Právník*, no. 115 (Prague, 1976) 461–65.

Vratislav Pechota

HODGKIN, Henry T. (21 April 1877, Darlington, England—26 March 1933, Dublin, Ireland). *Education*: Bootham; Leighton Park; B.A., King's Coll., Cambridge Univ., 1902; M.B., St. Thomas' Hospital, 1902. *Career*: traveling secretary, Student Christian Movement, 1902–5; medical missionary, China, 1905–10, 1920–22; secretary, Friends Foreign Mission Association, 1910–20; founder, Fellowship of Reconciliation, 1914; chairman, Fellowship of Reconciliation,

1914–20; secretary, National Christian Council of China, 1922–29; director of studies, Pendle Hill Center for Religious and Social Studies, 1929–32.

Although Henry Hodgkin fully embraced the Quaker peace testimony from an early age, he became a leader in the British peace movement only after the outbreak of the First World War. During the summer of 1914, Hodgkin, in his capacity as clerk of the London Yearly Meeting of Friends, attended an international conference of the Church Peace Union in Constance. When the impending political crisis forced a suspension of this meeting, Hodgkin's horrified realization that many of the peace-loving delegates at Constance were officially his "enemies" galvanized him into action.

During the first days of the war, Hodgkin supervised the drawing up of a "Quaker Message to Men and Women of Goodwill" which condemned the war as unchristian. In September 1914 he used the occasion of a Friends' conference at Llandudno to call for a united Christian effort to reestablish the foundations of peace. As a result of his call, over one hundred Christian pacifists, including *Richard Roberts, Maude Royden, *George Lansbury and *Leyton Richards, met at Cambridge in December to form the Fellowship of Reconciliation (FOR), a nonsectarian body of individuals dedicated to promoting a spirit of Christian reconciliation. The original members of the FOR recognized Hodgkin as the moving spirit of their fellowship by acclaiming him chairman. And the spirit Hodgkin brought to the FOR emphasized positive, constructive Christian action for international reconciliation rather than negative protest and war resistance. In the autumn of 1915, Hodgkin undertook a speaking tour in the United States, one result of which was the founding of the still-existing American branch of the FOR.

Despite his emphasis on reconciliation, Hodgkin remained absolute in his opposition to the war. As a conscientious objector he demanded and received complete exemption from all wartime services except peace work. As a leader of the Society of Friends, he urged that Quakers make no compromise with the government nor cooperate in any way with the prosecution of the war. At the same time, however, he refused to accept the view of many younger Friends that no efforts should be made to relieve the punishments suffered by conscientious objectors and other war-resisters because he believed that imprisoning men for refusing to fight was a species of religious persecution that should not be tolerated.

After the Great War, Hodgkin continued his work of reconciliation until he returned to China in 1920. Because of his work with the National Christian Council of China until 1929 and the increasingly delicate state of his health thereafter, Henry Hodgkin was not prominent in the interwar peace movement, but the founder and first leader of the Fellowship of Reconciliation remained a convinced and practicing Christian pacifist and one of the most beloved and influential British Friends until his sudden death in 1933.

Bibliography:

A. *The Christian Revolution* (London, 1925); *Lay Religion* (London, 1918); *Personality and Progress* (London, 1929).

B. Vera Brittain, *The Rebel Passion: A Short History of Some Pioneer Peacemakers* (London, 1964); *The Friend* (London), March 31 and April 7, 1933; Herbert G. Wood, *Henry T. Hodgkin: A Memoir* (London, 1937).

Thomas C. Kennedy

HOFFMAN, Isidor B. (4 August 1898, Philadelphia, PA—27 January 1981, Danbury, CT). *Education*: B.A., Columbia Coll., 1920; M.H.L. and Rabbinical Ordination, The Jewish Theological Seminary of America, 1924. *Career*: rabbi and counselor to students at Cornell Univ. and Columbia Univ.; co-founder, Jewish Peace Fellowship; co-founder, American Jewish Society for Service; pacifist.

Rabbi Isidor B. Hoffman, the Jewish chaplain to students at Columbia University from 1934 to 1967 was the preeminent American Jewish pacifist. His lifelong commitment to nonviolence sprang from his belief that peace was the highest value in Judaism and that the Biblical injunction "Not By Might, Nor By Power But By My Spirit Saith The Lord" was an eminently practical guide to relations between individuals and nations.

Following a stay at the American School of Oriental Research in 1924–25 in Jerusalem and study at the Hebrew University in that city in 1925, Hoffman added a new dimension to his belief in the value of the Judaic prophetic teachings—bi-nationalism. He participated in the early conversations among Palestinian Jewish Zionist intellectuals—Ernst Simon, Martin Buber, and Arthur Ruppin—who were beginning to advance the notion that peace and harmony in that turbulent corner of the Middle East could only be advanced by Jews and Arabs sharing authority.

Thus, in the 1930s, he became an American member of Ichud (Union). Under the leadership of *Rabbi Judah L. Magnes, president of the Hebrew University, Ichud actively backed the formation of a bi-national state. But with the destruction of six million Jewish people during the Holocaust, Hoffman became a supporter, if at times mildly critical, of the State of Israel.

In the 1970s, although he advocated reconciliation between Israelis and Arabs, he was troubled by both the absence of Arab peacemakers and by those in the Middle East who sought to turn their nations into military bases for the Great Powers.

Hoffman's career—in the words of Jane Evans, a co-founder of the Jewish Peace Fellowship (JPF)—was a "remarkable life of thought, sensitivity, service and action." Certainly his major achievement was the JPF. In 1941 he, Evans, and Rabbi Abraham Cronbach of the Hebrew Union College in Cincinnati, Ohio founded the pacifist fellowship. All of them saw Jewish tradition, Hoffman wrote, "as a continual calling toward peace, justice and compassion." With the outbreak of war in Europe, Hoffman, Evans, and Cronbach were deeply disturbed that Jews who chose to be pacifists and found support in Judaic tenets for their religious opposition to the draft and war were compelled to turn to the Quakers and other Christian peace churches, or to rely on secular political organizations for support and help. Thus, the JPF came into existence, with Hoffman as its moving spirit.

Over the next forty years, he argued the case of conscientious objection and peace before Jewish and governmental bodies, visited Civilian Public Service camps (during World War II) laden with parcels and literature, and counseled thousands of young men on questions of war and peace. During the Vietnam War, Hoffman's office became a mecca for those who chose to oppose the conflict on the grounds of conscience derived from Jewish tradition. At the time of his death the JPF had become a widely recognized Jewish representative to the worldwide peace movement.

Hoffman, who was a member of both the (Reform) Central Conference of American Rabbis and (Conservative) Rabbinical Assembly, was welcomed by the two rabbinical groups and made chairman of their social justice and conscientious objector commissions and coordinator of the Alternate Service Committee of the Synagogue Council of America, an umbrella group representing virtually all branches of religious Judaism. In addition, he co-founded the American Jewish Society for Service, an organization dedicated to harnessing the idealism of young Jewish men and women for constructive and peaceful projects. He was also active in the pacifist Fellowship of Reconciliation, SANE, and the National Interreligious Board for Conscientious Objectors.

Just before he died of a heart attack in 1981, he organized a dozen elderly residents of his retirement village in Connecticut into a peace group which protested the building of a Trident nuclear submarine in nearby Groton. A frequent speaker in local high schools, he remained an active pacifist until the end of his life.

Bibliography:

A. "JPF's 40th Birthday," *Shalom* (Autumn-Winter 1980–81), 1; "Notes for a History of the JPF," *Shalom* (Winter 1968), 5.

B. "Rabbi Isidor B. Hoffman, 1898–1981," *Shalom*, 14 (Spring-Summer 1981), 4–8; Michael Young, "Facing A Test of Faith: Jewish Pacifists During the Second World War," *Peace and Change*, 3 (Summer-Fall 1975), 34–39.

C. Isidor Hoffman Papers, Jewish Peace Fellowship Archives, American Jewish Historical Society, Brandeis University, Waltham, Massachusetts.

Murray Polner

HOHENLOHE-SCHILLINGSFÜRST, Alexander von (6 August 1862, Lindau, Württemberg, Germany—17 May 1924, Badenweiler, Germany). *Education*: gymnasium (high school); studied jurisprudence, universities of Graz, Vienna, Paris, Leipzig, Strasbourg, and Göttingen. *Career*: member, lower house of the imperial German parliament (Reichstag), 1893–1903; councillor of legation in the German foreign office and private secretary to his father, 1895; district president of Upper-Alsace in Colmar, 1898–1906; writer, journalist, and pacifist.

The cultured and enlightened Prince Alexander von Hohenlohe-Schillingsfürst came from an old and prominent South German aristocratic family. His heritage permitted him to lead an independent and elegant life, enriched by the various high offices held by his father, Prince Chlodwig zu Hohenlohe-Schillingsfürst (Ambassador in Paris, 1874–85; Governor of Alsace-Lorraine, 1885–94; German Chancellor, Foreign Minister, and Prime Minister of Prussia, 1894–1900). As confidant and close collaborator of his father, Alexander von Hohenlohe had the opportunity to get to know life at the court in Berlin, the character and attitudes of both Otto von Bismarck and the Emperor William II, and to observe the mentality of the prominent German politicians of his day. Quickly the critically inclined Prince saw through the brittleness, emptiness, and futility of the power structure of the German empire and court life. He came to view the Prussian officer corps as narrow-minded and anachronistic, a baleful influence on Prussian and German politics. He recognized that German foreign policy categorically rejected any understanding with France and believed a peaceful settlement of conflicting interests with England to be impossible. From 1899 on, he followed with great concern the "dilletantism" and the "unbelievable incompetence" of German diplomacy. He was surprised that the policies of the German Foreign Office did not lead to a world war prior to 1914.

For the most part Hohenlohe did not concern himself with trying to prevent the coming war. Before 1914 he adhered to the view that wars were an unavoidable evil and that nothing could be done to avoid violent conflict between nations beyond the pursuing of a peaceful and rational foreign policy. However, since he did not consider the resolution of conflict by force desirable, he sought to defuse the conflict over the Alsace-Lorraine question by reconciling the population of the provinces to the conditions that had resulted from the annexation in 1871—initially as personal assistant to his father during the latter's governorship of Alsace-Lorraine, then as a high official in the administration of the annexed provinces—by a sympathetic and just administration which respected their feelings, memories, and peculiarities. As a member of Parliament from the Alsatian district of Weissenburg-Hagenau, Hohenlohe saw his hopes of winning the confidence of the inhabitants of Alsace-Lorraine disappointed through lack of understanding, national resentments, and militaristic encroachments. Although he briefly sided with the Conservatives in Parliament, Hohenlohe became an independent delegate who, by opposing laws such as the one introduced by his father curtailing the freedom of association of German workers, gained him both the reputation and the stigma of a "red Democrat."

Hohenlohe's political career ended in 1906 when he had his father's memoirs published. The publication earned him the displeasure of the emperor, for he included in the text the conversations of his father with Emperor William II and the Grand Duke of Baden concerning the dismissal of Bismarck. From 1906 until 1914 he lived in Paris as a private person. After the outbreak of World

War I (he was now paralyzed and tied to his bed and wheelchair), he elected to go into exile in Switzerland, preferring to observe the further course of events impartially from a neutral land. The battle of the Marne revealed to him the brutality of an extended war and he set his hopes upon an early negotiated peace without victor or vanquished. The inflexibility of the German military and civilian leadership, however, convinced him that Germany was on a ruinous course that offered no possibility of peace. Increasingly he spoke out for a negotiated peace, denounced Germany's prolongation of the war, and condemned the press and intellectuals who urged upon the German people new sacrifices.

Writing for newspapers in neutral nations, especially for the *Neue Züricher Zeitung*, Hohenlohe became one of the most significant critics of Bismarckian and Prussian statesmenship without conscience.'' He traced the will to fight World War I to the ''moral and intellectual decline in Germany'' evoked by Bismarck's policy of might before right and strengthened even further by the rule of William II. He argued that from Bismarck the German people had learned the belief in the exclusive authority of force and the depreciation of moral values, and thus changed from a ''nation of thinkers'' to ''obedient, disciplined subjects'' and finally into ''Byzantines.''

Even though he never belonged to a pacifist association, and up until 1914 knew little about the German peace movement, Hohenlohe's way to pacifism was accelerated rather than caused by the war. It was above all his aristocratic spirit of opposition, unbroken by Prussianism, and his experiences and observations as his father's aide, as well as his regard for the freedom of the individual which he defended against any and all attempts to subjugate it, that predestined him to see pacifism as an historical alternative to Prussian-German militarism.

After World War I, Hohenlohe acknowledged both a ''supranational human nature'' and pacifism. He wrote for a number of pacifist publications and strongly supported a federalistically organized Germany that would do away with Prussian domination and guarantee peace in Europe. He demanded a German foreign policy that broke with the past and recognized both the forces and the personalities responsible for Germany's fateful history since 1871. He believed that if Germany did not turn away from the systematic falsification of history concerning the deeper causes of the collapse of 1918, it would face an even greater disaster.

The maintenance of peace and of European civilization, according to Hohenlohe, required an agreement between and reconciliation of the European nations. Consequently, he called for a ''League of Nations'' and for the establishment of a ''United States of Europe'' to include England and, if at all possible, the United States. He believed that all associations of nations were doomed to failure as long as the notion of the ''unavoidability of war'' continued to shape the thinking of nations. He also thought that future wars would be caused by the systematic fostering of a warlike spirit in the nation by parents, schools, universities, the press, and the church. He, therefore, challenged the idea of the deterring effect of arms stockpiling, called for a new education that would promote peace, and attacked the nationalist press for its role in war agitation.

Hohenlohe was one of a minority of German pacifists whose "vain warnings" sought to avoid the conditions that led to the Second World War. Destitute as a result of his self exile during World War I, he died in abject poverty. +Hans Wehberg characterized him as "one of the most striking personalities and intelligent minds of pacifism matured by the experience of war."

Bibliography:

A. *Aus meinem Leben* (Frankfurt am Main, 1925); *Vergebliche Warnungen* (Munich, 1919).

B. [Friedrich Wilhelm Foerster] "Prinz Alexander Hohenlohe." *Die Menschheit*, 11 (May 23, 1924), 75; Annette Kolb, "Alexander von Hohenlohe," *Die Weltbühne*, 20 (June 19, 1924), 834–38; Emil Ludwig, "Erinnerung an Hohenlohe," *Neue Zürcher Zeitung* May 21, 1924, Zweites Abendblatt; René Schickele, "Matratzengruft," *Neue Zürcher Zeitung*, June 15, 1924, Siebtes Blatt.

C. Prince Alexander von Hohenlohe-Schillingsfürst Papers, Bundesarchiv Koblenz.

Helmut Donat
Trans. by Irene Seadle

HOLCOMBE, Henry (22 September 1762, Prince Edward County VA —22 May 1824, Philadelphia, PA). *Education:* largely self-taught; D.D., Coll. of Rhode Island (Brown Univ.), 1800. *Career*: Baptist minister and writer.

From the age of twenty-two until his death four decades later Henry Holcombe devoted his life to the ministry. Beginning as a Presbyterian, he early converted to the Baptist faith, secured a license to preach, and filled several pulpits in the South before taking up his last assignment in Philadelphia in 1812. Like many other clergymen during the first years of the romantic nineteenth century, Holcombe believed that Christians must strive to transform the world into a heavenly city. Accordingly, he launched a number of crusades against contemporary evils, ranging from illiteracy and deism to poverty and harsh criminal codes. Opposed to the theological bias of many Baptists, he founded the Mount Enon Academy near Augusta, Georgia.

It was during his pastorate at the First Baptist Church in Philadelphia that Holcombe took up the cause of peace. He became a moving force in the Pennsylvania Peace Society and carried on an active correspondence with other peace leaders, including *Noah Worcester, *William Ladd, and *David L. Dodge. In 1823 the Pennsylvania Peace Society published his most important peace tract, *The Martial Christian's Manual*. Admitting that Scripture was replete with scenes of conquest and war, Holcombe insisted that God had sanctioned such violence only in the Old Testament. Christ had offered a new dispensation of righteousness and peace; nowhere did Jesus condone physical force. He charged his followers to forgive their enemies and to "turn the other cheek." The true Christian, according to Holcombe, had a duty to live Christ's teachings to the letter and this meant abandoning all violence and force.

Unfortunately, few Christian nations had emulated the Prince of Peace. Late Roman emperors had transformed Christ into a God of battle and their barbarian successors had often embraced the cross as an excuse for conquest. Popes and Protestant reformers alike had defiled Christianity in the name of doctrinal purity, and secular rulers were all too willing to connive with them for worldly treasures. Modern leaders also had left a sorry legacy as they sent their armies forth to mete out death and destruction to their Christian neighbors.

Despite the bloody past, Holcombe saw signs of a new age of peace. Missionaries, Bible societies, and Sunday schools were spreading the Gospel to the four corners of the earth. It was now up to the true "martial Christian" to buckle on his spiritual armor and to hasten the day of justice and peace.

Bibliography:

A. *First Fruits* (Philadelphia, 1812); *The Martial Christian's Manual* (Philadelphia, 1823).

B. DAB, 9, 133–34.

David R. Contosta

HOLMES, John Haynes (29 November 1879, Philadelphia, PA—3 April 1964, New York). *Education*: B.A., Harvard Univ., 1902; S.T.B., Harvard Divinity School, 1904. *Career*: clergyman; editor, *Unity*; pacifist writer and speaker.

John Haynes Holmes was a man of many causes. A formidable writer and preacher, he played a catalytic role in a host of reform activities in the United States from the turn-of-the-century to the 1960s. He participated in the formation of the National Association for the Advancement of Colored People (1909), the American Civil Liberties Union (1917–20), and in the first protests against U. S. involvement in Vietnam (1963). At the core, however, Holmes was a radical religious pacifist. He worked to overcome the sin of war and the evil of force through the gospel of love and the righteousness of human brotherhood.

Born in Philadelphia in 1879, Holmes was heir to the liberal dissenting tradition of Boston-area Unitarianism. Raised in the Boston suburb of Malden, he attended Harvard College and Harvard Divinity School, where he received a Bachelor's of Sacred Theology in 1904, the same year as he was ordained a Unitarian minister and assumed his first pastorate at the Third Religious Society of Dorchester. Three years later, he accepted the associate pastorship at New York's Church of the Messiah. He became full pastor there in 1912.

Early in his career, Holmes preached a faith blended from the optimistic evolutionism of John Fiske and Herbert Spencer and the Christian reform teachings of *Theodore Parker and Walter Rauschenbusch. Shucking some youthful conservatism, Holmes claimed a spiritual affinity for Christian socialism shortly after his arrival in New York; but he declined to promote any specific socialist agenda. Instead, he backed a range of reform efforts, confident that right reason and the law of progress were advancing humankind toward a blissful new era.

The outbreak of World War I worked a transforming effect upon him. Horrified by the mass violence, Holmes retreated for the first time into serious contemplation of the relationship of Christianity and war. Reflecting upon the teachings of Jesus, various Quakers, the French novelist *Romain Rolland, and the Russian writer *Leo Tolstoy, Holmes adopted a pacifist stance that he enunciated most convincingly in *New Wars for Old* (1916). Holmes' tract argued that a loving but militant nonviolence must displace force as the most effective and redeeming way of resisting evildoers while advancing good. The book eventually went through thirteen printings and established Holmes as one of the most important voices of Western pacifism.

World War I also led Holmes toward peace activism. He participated in the formation of the American branch of the Fellowship of Reconciliation, joined in the anti-preparedness battles of the American Union Against Militarism, and, after U.S. intervention, defended conscientious objection to the draft through the nascent American Civil Liberties Union. Holmes' vigorous antiwar position brought him under vicious attack, and completed his estrangement from Unitarianism. In 1919, after cutting his Unitarian ministerial connections, he presided over the transformation of the Church of the Messiah into The Community Church of New York, committed to building an undenominational, non-covenanted congregation that stood for the oneness of the human spirit and the necessity of religion to serve people in their broadest needs.

Also during 1918–20, Holmes became absorbed in pacifist literary endeavours. He began a 26-year term as editor of *Unity*, a weekly publication issued by the Abraham Lincoln Center, a Chicago church settlement. He contributed articles to the *Nation*, *The New Republic*, and *The World Tomorrow*. Most importantly, he discovered *Gandhi. Impressed by an article about Gandhi's nonviolent struggle against South African racism, Holmes undertook an inquiry into Gandhi's life and teachings that soon made him the Mahatma's main champion in America. According to Holmes, Gandhi's unquenchable determination to mobilize the oppressed masses for nonviolent action against systematic social injustice—from South African brutality to British imperialism—marked him as one of the greatest figures of the ages. He stood with Lao-Tse and Jesus in the small pantheon of history's nonviolent heroes.

In the 1920s Holmes was an outspoken critic of the Versailles Treaty and the League of Nations, condemning both as unjust new instruments of great power imperialism. More positively, he supported the Outlawry of War campagin, sponsored by the Chicago lawyer *Salmon O. Levinson, that aimed to delegitimize war and replace it as an international institution for the settlement of disputes with a new world court and code of world law. In the 1920s Holmes also boosted prohibition, defended the teaching of Darwinism in Tennessee, and asserted the innocence of the Italian anarchists Sacco and Vanzetti in Massachusetts.

In 1929 Holmes accepted the chairmanship of the six-year-old War Resisters League. In the same year, he visited Palestine in an attempt to live out more firmly his long-held Zionist sympathies and also joined his longtime friend and reform associate, Rabbi *Stephen S. Wise, in a City Affairs Committee which waged a nine-year crusade to free New York politics from well-organized corruption managed by Mayor Jimmie Walker.

Meanwhile, the international crisis bounded violently forward. With Germany, Italy, and Japan on the offensive, Holmes argued for American neutrality and reiterated his pacifist opposition to war in any form. He denounced Stalinism for its internal oppression, condemned Hitlerism, and assailed the fascist attack upon the Spanish Republic. At the same time, he resolutely opposed all hints of U.S. military action abroad. Grimly, Holmes viewed the crisis of the late thirties as a vindication of his arguments that World War I, the Versailles Treaty, and the League of Nations would only breed more bitterness and strife. Yet he found little comfort in a sense of right when the world was so clearly going wrong.

In 1940 Holmes began a ten-year term as chairman of the board of directors of the American Civil Liberties Union. One year later, following U. S. intervention in World War II, he repeated his pacifist commitment from the pulpit of The Community Church and reiterated his refusal to support the war effort in any way. With other progressive-neutralists, Holmes found a wartime audience for his views in magazines like *Fellowship* and *The Progressive*. But his continuing contempt for great power imperialism and his suspicion of the proposed United Nations as a new imperialist combine kept him apart from the internationalist crusade that swept up the great majority of prowar liberals.

During 1947–48, Holmes visited India on an extended tour that included a hurried meeting with Gandhi. In 1949, when Holmes was discovered to be suffering from Parkinson's disease, he decided to retire from his fulltime ministry. While preaching intermittently in the 1950s, he re-affiliated with the Unitarian ministerial fellowship, convinced that the Unitarian position on world peace had finally caught up to his own. He died in New York City in 1964, at the age of 84.

As his autobiography contends, John Haynes Holmes always spoke for himself. A serious-minded individualist, he had a passion for righteousness and a commitment to make real the oneness of humankind. Holmes was a churchman and writer, preacher and energizer, who believed that patriotism was no more than universal religion rightly lived. He was a fearless battler for justice who discovered for himself that pacifism was not passivism but ''moral militancy, spiritual chivalry, the knighthood of the Kingdom,'' and the most profound expression of love. He strove to live according to its commands.

Bibliography:

A. *I Speak for Myself: The Autobiography of John Haynes Holmes* (New York, 1959); *My Gandhi* (New York, 1953); *New Wars for Old* (New York, 1916); *Patriotism Is Not Enough* (New York, 1925).

B. Carl Herman Voss, *Rabbi and Minister: The Friendship of Stephen S. Wise and John Haynes Holmes* (Cleveland, 1964); Carl Herman Voss, ed., *A Summons Unto Men: An Anthology of the Writings of John Haynes Holmes* (New York, 1970).

C. John Haynes Holmes Papers, Manuscript Division, Library of Congress.

Charles DeBenedetti

HOLT, Hamilton. See *Biographical Dictionary of Internationalists*.

HOPF, Heinrich Wilhelm Leonhard (12 October 1842, Wippershain/Hersfeld, Hesse-Kassel, Germany—16 March 1921, Melsungen, Germany). *Education*: Lutheran theological studies, universities of Leipzig and Marburg (passed pastor's examination in Marburg, 1866). *Career*: pastor, teacher, editor, *Hessische Blätter* Melsungen, 1872–1921, *Hessisches Volksblat*, Melsungen, 1909–11.

Committed to the independence of Hesse-Kassel within the German confederation, Wilhelm Hopf, the son of a Lutheran pastor, became a leader in the anti-Prussian opposition movement. The Prussian invasion of electoral Hesse in the summer of 1866, its annexation by Prussia, and the destruction of the legal order of the German confederation were the decisive events that molded Hopf's political career. Influenced by the conservative views of his uncle, the theologian August Vilmar, Hopf embodied an ethically and religiously grounded monarchism which was oriented toward anti-Prussianism.

Organized in the Hessian Conservative party, Hopf and his colleagues strove to reinstate the Electoral Prince and regain the political independence of the state of Hesse-Kassel within a federalistic Germany. In this regard, Hopf and his followers identified themselves with the political ideas of *Constantin Frantz. In 1872 Hopf began editing the periodical *Hessische Blätter* which was to become the journalistic mouthpiece in the struggle for federalism and legitimacy. In the constant altercations with Prussian authorities, Hopf often found himself in serious difficulty. In 1873 his name was struck from the official list of pastoral candidates and in the following year he was imprisoned for four months for violating the press law. In 1895, Hopf published his most important work, *Die Deutsche Krisis des Jahres 1866* (*The German Crisis of 1866*), in which he sought to counter the attempt by German historians to equate the Prussian destruction of the confederacy with the idea of a "German mission." Hopf's rich sourcebook based on rare documents ran through three editions by 1906, but it was ignored by most German historians because of its strong anti-Prussian tendencies.

Hopf saw World War I as lineally connected with the Austro-Prussian war of 1866 and the Franco-Prussian war of 1871. Shortly after the outbreak of war in 1914, Hopf argued that Germany and Austria-Hungary bore the chief responsibility for the conflict. He, therefore, supported pacifist aims which many readers of his *Hessische Blätter* took amiss. Because of his attacks on German war aims and the war euphoria of large portions of the German people, Hopf's periodical was placed under pre-publication censorship. In 1916, Hopf became an active supporter of the Zentralstelle für Völkerrecht (Central Coordinating Office for International Law). This brought him into contact with *Friedrich W. Foerster, *Fritz Küster, and other pacifists. After 1918 Hopf, although a lifelong monarchist, advocated a federalistic new order for Germany within the framework of the Weimar Republic.

Bibliography:

A. *August Vilmar. Ein Lebens—und Zeitbild* (Marburg, 1913); *Die Deutsche Krisis des Jahres 1866* (Melsungen, 1896); *Kurhessens Deutsche Politik im Jahre 1850. Ein Beitrag zur Geschichte der deutschen Verfassungskämpfe* (Hannover, 1920).

B. Enno Knobel, ''Die Hessische Rechtspartei. Konservative Opposition gegen das Bismarckreich'' (Ph.D. dissertation, University of Marburg, 1975).

C. Wilhelm Hopf papers, State Archive of Marburg.

Lothar Wieland
Trans. by Solomon Wank

HORRICKS, Henry Magee (4 May 1883, near Thessalon, Ontario, Canada—17 November 1968, Calgary, Alberta). *Education*: B.A., Univ. of Toronto; B.D., Victoria Univ., Toronto, 1913. *Career*: minister, Methodist Church (later United Church of Canada), 1913–58; founder and president, Alberta School of Religion, 1924–58.

Reverend Henry Horricks founded the Alberta School of Religion in 1924 in order to provide a refresher course of a week to ten days during the summer for ministers and their families. During the years between the two world wars, the school became a center for Canada's western Christian radicals and provided the core support for an interwar peace movement before the organization of a Canadian branch of the Fellowship of Reconciliation on a national basis.

At first the Alberta School was affiliated with the United Church of Canada, but in 1935 it affiliated with the Fellowship for a Christian Social Order, which believed that the existing economic system denied the spirit of human community and which called for the social ownership of the means of production. The decision of the Alberta School to affiliate with the Fellowship for a Christian Social Order coincided with a change in locale. Until 1935 the school had resided at St. Stephen's United Church College in Edmonton, Alberta. Apparently, the board of governors of St. Stephen's thought the program was getting too radical and objected to the presence of *J. S. Woodsworth, the prominent Canadian socialist and pacifist, at one of the summer sessions. In 1936 the school moved to the Indian Industrial School in Morley, Alberta and then, in 1938, to Camp Fairweather, a church camp on the Bow River about twelve miles west of Calgary, Alberta. With the decline of the Fellowship for a Christian Social Order during World War II, the Alberta School of Religion affiliated with the Fellowship of Reconciliation.

Under Horricks' leadership the Alberta School sought to assist in breaking down the barriers of nationalism and race prejudice separating peoples of different countries. Among the subjects explored at the school were the armaments race and its probable outcome, the viewpoints of labor, farmers, and the dispossessed classes, and the relationship between the social system and human values. Through the school, Horricks popularized the peace movement in western Canada and those who joined the ''Horricks Fellowship'' took a pacifist pledge declaring: ''I will endeavor as far as my influence goes to discourage the use of violence as a method of settling disputes among nations but will rely on love and good will as the most powerful force in all life.'' Through the years, Horricks attracted an impressive roster of lecturers to the school, including Bishop Paul Jones, H.

Richard Niebuhr, *A. J. Muste, Harry F. Ward, *Sherwood Eddy, Elmore Philpott, Paul A. Schilpp, Scott Nearing, Jerome Davis, and many others.

In 1958 Horricks suffered a severe illness that forced him to discontinue his work with the Alberta School of Religion. Nonetheless, for thirty-five years he gave leadership to a vital center of radical and pacifist intellectual activity on the Canadian prairies.

Bibliography:

A. "A Place to Stand," *The United Church Observer*, February 15, 1948.

C. Henry Magee Horricks Papers, Saskatchewan Archives Board.

James M. Pitsula

HÖSTEREY, Walter. See Hammer, Walter.

HOSTOS, Eugenio María de. See *Biographical Dictionary of Internationalists*.

HOUZEAU DE LEHAIE, Charles Auguste Benjamin Hippolyte (28 July 1832, Mons, Belgium—22 May 1922, Mons). *Education*: Collège Rollin, Paris; Collège communal, Mons; Univ. Libre de Bruxelles, 1850–51. *Career*: professor of political economy and geography, l'École des mines de Mons, 1870; communal counsellor, 1867–84, 1894–96; burgomaster, 1867–78; 1896; member, Chamber of Representatives, 1882–94; senator (liberal), 1897–1900, (Parti Ouvrier Belge), 1900–22; founder and officer, Société de géographie de Belgique, 1867–1903; member, Ligue internationale de la paix et de la liberté, Geneva; member and president, Interparliamentary Union, 1893–1914; member, Belgian section of the Fédération internationale de l' arbitrage et de la paix; president, Universal Peace Congress, Anvers, 1894; president, organizing committee of First National Belgian Peace Congress, 1913; member, I'Institut international de la paix, Monaco and Paris; politician and peace activist.

First as a liberal and then as a socialist politician, Charles Houzeau de Lehaie gave of his time freely in the crusade to improve workers' education and devoted his life to spreading the humanitarian ideals in which he believed. In parliament, he fought protectionism and supported public education, the regulation of female and child labor, universal suffrage, and the maintenance of peace. After the Franco-Prussian War, he was horrified by the anguish of the victims of the battle of Sedan and decided then to struggle against all such disasters. Recognizing the importance of studying the causes of conflicts before eliminating them, he nonetheless saw the value of interim means to reduce the chances of the outbreak of war. Arbitration, to Houzeau de Lehaie, offered the best existing means to diminish belligerent explosions. Therefore, he devoted his maximum energies to popularizing and refining the techniques of international arbitration. As a participant in a number of private peace societies, he also was a leading figure in the Interparliamentary Union. At its 1895 meeting in Brussels, he offered a plan for the creation of a permanent court of arbitration which was adopted by the Union.

Bibliography:
B. *Biographie Coloniale Belge*, III, cols. 458–9; Van Molle, *Le Parlement Belge, 1894–1969*, 182–3; De Seyn, *Dictionnaire Biographique des Sciences, des Lettres, et des Arts de Belgique*, II, 577.

Nadine Lubelski-Bernard
Trans. by Sandi E. Cooper

HOWE, Julia Ward (27 May 1819, New York—17 October 1910, Portsmouth, RI). *Education*: private; *Career*: poet, lecturer and reformer.

Julia Ward Howe, author of the "Battle Hymn of the Republic," became interested in the cause of world peace in 1870 when she was 51. Appalled by the outbreak of the Franco-Prussian War, which she attributed to senseless greed on both sides, the idea came to her that the mothers of mankind might do something to prevent such barbaric conflicts and she proceeded on her own to organize a woman's peace movement.

Mrs. Howe began her efforts for peace by publishing and distributing *An Appeal to Womanhood Throughout the World* (1870), a short pamphlet which she hoped would encourage women all over the globe to support the cause. She also organized a meeting in New York that December to discuss her plan for convening a world congress of women on behalf of international peace. This was followed by one in Boston in the spring of 1871 at which an American branch of the Women's International Peace Association was formed, with Julia Ward Howe as president. For the next two years she labored incessantly to organize her international congress, which she hoped would be held in London in 1872.

Julia Ward Howe's tireless efforts on behalf of peace were largely abortive. Such later pacifists as +Edwin D. Mead gave her credit for initiating the postwar peace movement, but in fact she was able to interest very few in her cause and those few were mainly Quakers. She did go to London in the spring of 1872, but her dream of a woman's international peace congress never materialized.

In the end Howe had more success with her peace idea at home than abroad. Upon returning from England in 1872 she conceived of a plan to hold annual Mothers' Peace Day festivals in various parts of the United States and abroad. On June 2, 1873, the first of these festivals was celebrated in a number of places, including London, Geneva, Constantinople, and Boston. In Boston the occasion was well attended and Howe was gratified by the interest shown in the festival. The following year, however, she could not arouse the same enthusiasm. Yet she and a group of faithful friends and followers continued, for the next decade or so, to hold a yearly Mothers' Peace Day festival in Boston on the second of June.

For the remainder of her life, Julia Ward Howe continued to support the cause of peace. As late as 1904, when she was 85, she addressed a Peace Congress in Boston. Yet beginning in the 1890s a martial note had begun to creep into many of her writings. She regarded the Boxer Rebellion in China, the Cuban

Civil War, the revolutionary uprisings in Russia, and finally the struggles of the Americans against the Turks as symptoms of a worldwide struggle of backward people to rise up against oppression. They were just wars and Julia Ward Howe, the author of the Battle Hymn had always been a believer in just wars.

Bibliography:

A. Julia Ward Howe, *Reminiscences* (Boston, 1899).

B. Deborah Pickman Clifford, *Mine Eyes Have Seen the Glory; A Biography of Julia Ward Howe* (Boston, 1979); Edwin D. Mead, *Julia Ward Howe's Peace Crusade* (World Peace Foundation Pamphlet, 1914); Laura E. Richards and Maud Howe Elliott, *Julia Ward Howe, 1819–1910*. (Boston, 1916).

Deborah P. Clifford

HROMÁDKA, Josef Lukl (8 June 1889, Hodslavice, Austria [now Czechoslovakia]—26 December 1969, Prague). *Education*: Protestant theological studies in Vienna, Basel, Heidelberg, and Aberdeen (Scotland), 1907–11; Ph.D., Univ. of Prague, 1917. *Career*: Lutheran pastor, author of books on theology and Christian social philosophy; organizer of Christian peace groups.

After his ordination as a Lutheran minister in 1912, Josef Hromádka served as pastor for several churches in Bohemia and Moravia and, in 1918, as a chaplain in the Austro-Hungarian army. In 1920 he was appointed to the Protestant Hus Faculty in Prague where he remained until forced to flee from the Nazis in 1939.

Hromádka's philosophy has often been described as a theology of crisis. He examined the traditional protestant authoritarian church in the critical spirit of *Thomas G. Masaryk's liberal-humanistic rationalism. Hromádka did not look at Catholicism with total disapproval, since Catholicism is a major component of Christian world ecumene. He appreciated the profound piety and the devotion to fellow beings which characterized the early Christian orthodoxy. As a theologian, originally molded by Lutheranism, Hromádka took a favorable stand towards the union of the Lutheran and Reformed churches because he hoped that the quasi-democratic organization of the Reformed church might exercise a moderating influence on hierarchical ecclesiastical structures. He, therefore, actively assisted in the formation of the general synod of the Lutheran and Reformed churches of Bohemia (December 1918) which led to the foundation of the united Protestant Church of the Czech (Bohemian) Brethren.

In cooperation with *Friedrich Siegmund-Schultze, Hromádka helped organize the ecumenical disarmament congress of the International Federation of Friendship Work in Prague in 1928. As co-founder of the academic Young Men's Christian Association (1927), which was incorporated into the Federation of Christian Students (1928), Hromádka often participated in ecumenical conferences and thus got to know the founders of the later World Council of Churches (WCC). From 1927 onward, Hromádka was co-editor of the *Christian Review*, a theological magazine. In 1936 he helped organize assistance to victims of the Spanish Falange and German-Italian fascist intervention in Spain. After the Nazi takeover of all of Czechoslovakia in 1939, Hromádka and his family managed to flee to Geneva, and from there to the United States where he was appointed professor of Christian ethics at the Princeton Theological Seminary.

Hromádka returned to Prague in 1947 and visited the Soviet Union for the first time in the same year. In 1948 he participated in the founding of the WCC in Amsterdam, where he opposed +John Foster Dulles' call for a crusade against communism. Hromádka was convinced that true Christianity was equal to the then thirty-year old challenge of communism and that Christianity must not be interpreted as an expression of feudal or bourgeois social structures. In 1959 he was appointed dean of the newly founded Protestant Comenius faculty in Prague. From 1954 to 1968, he was a member of the Executive Committee of the WCC and, for part of that time, vice-president of the World Federation of Reformed Churches.

Hromádka played a major part in the foundation of the Christian Peace Conference (CPC) in Prague (1958), whose president he was from 1961 until shortly before his death in 1969. In 1958 he was awarded the Lenin Peace Prize. With the incorporation of the International Federation of Friendship Work into the WCC there no longer was any organizational basis for ecumenical Christian peace activity during the Cold War. The CPC filled that void. It united Christian and church representatives from East and West and, to an increasing extent, representatives of the Third World who sought a dialogue beyond borders and blocs. Hromádka fostered the dialogue with Marxists in and out of power by his openness, his undogmatic theological position, and his readiness to learn, which was informed by a profound historical awareness. He regarded the Soviet invasion of Czechoslovakia, in August 1968, as a breach of the basis of this dialogue and wrote a note of protest to the Soviet ambassador. In April 1969, six months after the ouster of the reformist Czech Communist party leader, Alexander Dubček, Hromádka resigned as president of the CPC.

Bibliography:

A. *Křesťanstvi v Myšleni a životě* (Prague, 1931).

B. Josef Smolik and Heinz Kloppenburg, eds., *Von Amsterdam nach Prag;. eine ökumenisch Freundesgabe an Professor D. Josef L. Hromádka* (Hamburg, 1969); Gunter Wirth, *Josef L. Hromádka* (Berlin, 1977); NYT, December 29, 1969.

Klaus Ehrler

HUBER, Max. See *Biographical Dictionary of Internationalists*.

HUGENHOLTZ, Johannes Bernardus Theodorus (14 May 1888, Kattendijke, Netherlands—25 December 1973, Renkum. *Education:* theological studies, Univ. of Utrecht, 1907–13. *Career*: minister, Dutch Reformed Church, Vledder, 1913–18, Purmerend, 1918–21, Ammerstol, 1924–54.

In 1912, when still a student of theology, Johannes Hugenholtz came into contact with the Bond van Christen-Socialisten (Union of Christian Socialists) (BvCS) through meeting its leading figures, J. W. Kruyt and *B. de Ligt. The BvCS held that the teachings of Jesus Christ called for a moral and spiritual revolution in the individual, and for a society free of the twin evils of capitalism and militarism. The churches and Christianity at large were condemned for not having taken this message seriously. This criticism was reinforced by the outbreak of war in 1914. Hugenholtz, with other BvCS members, was disappointed and angered when the Church did not forcefully condemn it. For the next forty years his whole life was devoted to the cause of radical Christian pacifism and he became one of its leading organizers and propagandists.

Toward the end of 1914 he established a local branch of the Nederlandse Anti-Oorlogs Raad (Dutch Anti-War Council) (NAOR), but when it envisaged the creation of a just international order without taking a principled stand against war and military preparations, Hugenholtz was disappointed. During the war years his own antimilitarist conviction, which he frequently expounded in writings and sermons, brought him before the courts on charges of incitement. Hugenholtz felt more at home in *K. Boeke's Christian Fellowship than in the NAOR (which stopped its activities early in 1919). He became, in that year, a co-founder of the International Fellowship of Reconciliation which grew out of Boeke's Fellowship.

In 1924 he was called to the small village of Ammerstol where he was to remain as minister until his retirement, thirty years later, and where he devoted most of his energies to organizing the Christian opposition to war. This campaign started within days of his arrival, when he became gripped by a "feverish indignation" upon hearing that the Minister of War was commemorating the mobilization of ten years earlier. He organized a meeting which was well-attended in his new parish, and sent an open letter to 5,000 clergymen urging them to end their silence and connivance and join him in an antimilitarist campaign. With *G. J. Heering, who held similar ideas, he called a meeting of like-minded colleagues, which was held in Utrecht and which resulted in the formation of a Church Anti-War Group. The following year this radical pacifist union of ministers and church members changed its name to Kerk en Vrede (Church and Peace). Hugenholtz was its general secretary and also responsible for editing its influential monthly journal of the same name until 1941 when, with other members, he was sent to a concentration camp. By 1933, 100 branches with 9,000 members (400 of them ministers) had been established; today it is still very active in the Dutch peace movement. He also founded the International Union of Antimilitarist Ministers and Clergymen (IUAMC) in 1928 which held four international conferences in the next ten years.

When in 1924 the Dutch branch of Women's International League for Peace and Freedom established the Nooit Meer Oorlog Federatie (No More War Federation) (NMOF) to unite all peace forces in the country, Hugenholtz became its general secretary. The Federation established in 1927–28 an International Committee for Frontier Meetings, which consisted of Belgian (Flemish & Walloon), Dutch and, later, German peace groups which met in border towns of the three countries (Maastricht, Aachen, and Liège), because the organizers believed that it was especially important to work for peace among the people living in these areas. Hugenholtz also created an ad hoc committee to support, mainly via the distribution of literature, the peace and disarmament parties participating in the parliamentary elections of July 1925. Recognizing the need to continue this work, he founded a Nationale Vredes-Actie (National Peace Action) Bureau in 1925. It secured the cooperation of hundreds of correspondents and, for the next ten years, engaged in a great variety of educational and propagandistic activities, some very imaginative.

Hugenholtz represented Dutch peace organizations in the International Peace Bureau and attended its conferences from 1925 until 1939. He was the first antimilitarist to be elected to its Council in 1928, retaining this function until 1947. When in March 1946 Hein van Wijk initiated the Algemene Nederlands Vredes Actie (General Dutch Peace Action) (ANVA), which became the Dutch section of the War Resisters' International, Hugenholtz acted as its chairman and also edited its journal until 1954. He was a co-founder of the Nederlandse Organisatie voor Internationale Bijstand (Netherlands Organization for International Assistance) (NOVIB) and in the early 1960s took a keen interest in the emergence of peace research. In half a century of incessant peace work he had ensured that churches and Christians were no longer silent on the subject of war but, on the contrary, had moved to the forefront in the struggle against it.

Bibliography:

A. *Gij zult niet doodslaan*! (Schiedam, 1915); *Handboek voor de vredesbeweging in Nederland* (Gouda, 1932); *Kerk en Vrede* (Ammerstol, 1931); *'Kerk en Vrede' en haar strijd* (Ammerstol, 1939); *Open Brief aan alle predikanten* . . . (Rotterdam, 1924); *De vredesbeweging* (Ammerstol, 1929); *Het vredeswerk in Nederland* (Ammerstol?, 1925); *Het werk van de Stichting 'Nationale Vredes-Actie'* (Ammerstol, 1930); *Hoe werken wij voor een duurzame vrede* (Ammerstol?, 1946); *Wij mogen niet!. Bezwaren inzake het oorlogsvraagstuk weerlegd* (Assen, 1935).

B. J.B.Th. Hugenholtz, *Memorandum vredeswerk 1914–1964* (n.p., 1967); *Militia Christi* (March 23, 1963), 42–43; *Who's who in the Netherlands 1962/1963* (Amsterdam), 344.

Peter van den Dungen

HUGHAN, Jessie Wallace (25 December 1875, Brooklyn, NY—10 April 1955, New York). *Education*: B.A., Barnard Coll., 1898, M.A., Columbia Univ., 1899, Ph.D., 1910. *Career*: public school teacher, 1899–1945; pacifist, socialist, organizer, and author.

Jessie Wallace Hughan was both a socialist and a pacifist by the time of World War I. Her socialism grew out of graduate research at Columbia University where her doctoral advisor suggested that she attend socialist meetings to deepen her understanding of socialism, the topic of her dissertation. In 1907 she joined the Socialist party. She served in several party offices and became its candidate for New York alderman in 1915, secretary of state in 1918, lieutenant governor in 1920, and U. S. senator in 1924. She preached pacifism to her socialist friends and socialism to her pacifist friends. To her, capitalism contained the roots of modern war, but she did not insist that antiwar activity must be based on socialism.

It was during World War I that Jessie Wallace Hughan undertook her lifelong mission to make more pacifists and to provide an organization for those war resisters who had no traditionally religious basis for their pacifism. In 1915 she took the initiative to organize the Anti-Enlistment League with headquarters in her home. The League enrolled 3500 people who signed a declaration against any military enlistment, but differences among the members and government harassment, including seizure of the files, led to its disbanding. Hughan continued to publicly encourage objectors to military service and after the war she led the campaign to organize an active war resistance movement in the United States.

Hughan, an active Unitarian, was also a charter member of the religious Fellowship of Reconciliation. She persistently urged the FOR to set up a pacifist recruitment committee, raising the issue at several annual conferences. Her proposal was approved in 1923 and after meeting with several others to hammer out details she got FOR, the Women's Peace Society, and the Women's Peace Union to endorse the idea and the pledge which the committee had produced. From this activity came the War Resisters League (WRL), an American affiliate of the War Resisters International which, in its early years, was in part an enrollment agency for those who declared: "War is a crime against humanity. I therefore am determined not to support any kind of war, international or civil, and to strive for the removal of all causes of war."

For years Jessie Wallace Hughan spearheaded the WRL, again with headquarters in her apartment. She kept all the records, and when the organization finally engaged a halftime staff person, she and her sister, Evelyn West Hughan, paid his salary. During the 1920s she continued to sign up prospective war resisters, made numerous speeches, and wrote pamphlets and tracts explaining the role of war resistance as a method of eliminating war. She also organized various public protests to war and militarism, including several New York "No More War" parades.

She worked to defeat the 1940 conscription bill and when it passed she protested the conscientious objectors provision, which limited C.O. status to religious objectors who registered for the draft and which ruled out wages for those who accepted civilian conscript labor. She persuaded the WRL to support all objectors, regardless of the position they took concerning the draft. She continued to head the League as secretary until 1945, when she became honorary secretary.

Along with her political and organizational contributions, Jessie Wallace Hughan took a personal stand against war. When the witch-hunting Lusk Committee of the New York Legislature called her to testify, she refused to back down. She was denied that committee's Certificate of Character and Loyalty because she added to the teacher's loyalty oath the words: "This obedience being qualified always by dictates of conscience." During World War I she was threatened with dismissal from public school teaching because of her pacifism. When New York teachers were requested to register young men for the World War II draft, she refused and helped organize others who took a similar stand in the Pacifist Teachers League.

Her writings on socialism and pacifism made substantial contributions to the theories underlying both movements. Her doctoral thesis, *The Present Status of Socialism in America* (1911), also published as *American Socialism of the Present Day* (1911), described a socialism which drew on the Christian social gospel as well as from Marx. *Three Decades of War Resistance* (1942) summarized the war resistance movement between the world wars, and her pamphlet, *If We Should Be Invaded: Facing a Fantastic Hypothesis* (1940), is a major statement of the possibilities for the use of active nonviolence by a highly organized population to defeat the objectives of any outside power that might attempt to invade the United States and control its people. Her ideas were later drawn on and amplified by other scholars of nonviolent action.

Jessie Wallace Hughan was a major figure in the war resistance movement. More than anyone else, she was responsible for the birth and early years of the WRL, and for a number of public demonstrations against war. Her ability to work with diverse groups along with her emphasis on a personal declaration to refuse participation in war made numerous antiwar actions possible. Her writings spread the message and contributed new and important concepts to the antiwar movement. Above all, her personal example of highly competent, dedicated service to the peace movement over a period of forty years provided inspiration to thousands of the World War II generation of resisters.

Bibliography:

A. *The Challenge of Mars and Other Verses* (New York, 1932); *If We Should Be Invaded: Facing a Fantastic Hypothesis* (New York, 1940); *New Leagues for Old: Blueprints or Foundations*? (New York, 1947); *A Study of International Government* (New York, 1923); *Three Decades of War Resistance* (New York, 1942).

B. Michael David Young, " 'Wars Will Cease When Men Refuse to Fight': The War Resisters League, 1925–1950," B.A. Honors Thesis, Brown Univ., 1975; NAW, 4, 345–55.

Larry Gara

HUGO, Victor (26 February 1802, Besançon, France—22 May 1885, Paris). *Education*: Lycée Louis-le-Grand; studies in law, Univ. of Paris. *Career*: poet, playwright, novelist, essayist, politician (member, Constituent and Legislative Assemblies, 1848–51, National Assembly, 1871, Senator, 1872–85).

World famous for his literary productivity and creativity, Victor Hugo played an important role in at least two continental peace congresses, largely by lending his name and his magical oratory. He agreed to chair a peace assembly in August 1849 in Paris which was organized by Anglo-American activists in cooperation with French liberals, mainly political economists. There, Hugo's presidential addresses provided peace activists with language quoted down to 1914 and beyond. Hugo made famous the phrase, "the United States of Europe," which actually had been used a year earlier in an Italian book title by *Carlo Cattaneo.

In his presidential address Hugo pointed to the history of France, once a collection of warring provinces and now a unity which preserved cultural diversity within, as a model for all Europe. He predicted that the nations of Europe, without losing their "distinctive qualities" or their "glorious individuality," would one day "be blended into a superior unity and constitute a European fraternity, just as Normandy, Brittany, Burgundy, Lorraine, [and] Alsace have been blended into France." Hugo foresaw a day when this unity would eliminate the horrendous arms race and constant threat of war, when competition of ideas and markets would replace struggles over territory. In one short speech, he encapsulated the vision of secular pacifism which inspired five more decades of peace thinking and activism. His speech was also a turning point in the nineteenth-century movement insofar as it was couched in the progressive language of secular analysis and not the religious homilies of the earlier, Anglo-American pacifists.

From 1852–70, Hugo endured his famous exile, refusing to recognize the illegal regime of Louis Napoleon, whom he labeled "Napoleon the Little" in an enduring epithet. In 1869 Hugo agreed to travel to Lausanne to preside over a peace congress of the Ligue international de la paix et de la liberté (International League of Peace and Freedom) which had been formed two years earlier under the honorary presidency of Hugo's dear friend, Giuseppe Garibaldi. At Lausanne, Hugo's speeches revealed how much more radical his politics had become. He connected the cause of peace with that of republicanism, socialism, women's and children's rights, and social justice. In addition, he called for class collaboration. Clearly, he welcomed wars and struggles of liberation as legitimate and agreed with the League's philosophy that no peace was possible in a world of absolute monarchs and police-state emperors. He practically called for the overthrow of Napoleon III, to the gasps and delight of the audience (but not the police spy). Hugo connected the need to cut arms spending with human needs, another move that peace activists were to espouse in ensuing years.

While obviously Hugo's participation in the nineteenth-century peace movement in Europe constituted a minor sideshow in his life, it was a major contribution for a movement seeking legitimacy. Because of Hugo's participation at the 1849 meeting in Paris, the established press did not treat the peace congress with sarcastic ridicule. His importance as a star should not be underestimated. In 1872 the League again invited him to preside, but this time Hugo declined. Depressed by the Franco-Prussian War, he wrote of a "sinister environment which jeopardizes civilization itself" and felt it was the wrong time to talk of organizing peace. Hugo believed that the achievement of peace for Europe would perhaps be delayed until the twentieth century. As a gesture symbolizing this distant hope, he planted an oak tree in front of his exile home in Guernsey which might live to see that day. It was dedicated to "the United States of Europe."

Bibliography:

A. *Oeuvres Complètes* (46 vols., Paris, 1880–1885), especially vol. 37, *Avant l'exil 1841–1851*; vol. 38, *Pendant l'exil 1852–1870*; and vol. 39, *Depuis l'exile 1870–1876*.

B. Pierre Angrand, *Victor Hugo, raconté par les papiers d'état* (Paris, 1961); J. B.

Barrere, *Hugo: l'homme et l'oeuvre* (7th ed., Paris, 1969); Elliott M. Grant, *The Career of Victor Hugo* (Cambridge, MA, 1945); Elliott M. Grant, *Victor Hugo During the Second Republic* (Northampton, MA, 1938); André Maurois, *Victor Hugo* (Eng. trans., New York, 1956); Michel Revon, "Hugo et la Paix," *Les Etats-Unis d'Europe*, 67 (April-July, 1935), 393–97.

C. Victor Hugo Papers, Bibliothèque Nationale, Paris.

Sandi E. Cooper

HUHTALA, Kyösti (3 April 1871, Lapua, Finland—23 July 1913, Mustasaari, Finland). *Education*: teacher's certificate, Jyväsakylä Teachers' Coll., 1894. *Career*: teacher, 1894–1913; journalist, *Väinämöinen*, 1905–7, 1910–11; author, lecturer, and pacifist.

Kyösti Huhtala's family upbringing in Ostrabothnia provided him with a religious background which emphasized peace and love. After qualifying as a teacher in 1894, he took a position in Tampere and there became acquainted with the pioneers of the Finnish peace movement, *Aaku Mäki and *Juho Mäkinen. Under their influence he became active in the pacifist cause.

Beginning in 1901 Huhtala started publishing pedagogical essays in many Finnish publications. He was among the founders of Finland's Peace Union in 1907, serving on its board and becoming its president after Mäki resigned in 1911. He remained president until his death two years later, when the Union went out of existence. Huhtala's writings often created a good deal of excitment. In 1903 he published *Sotakertomuksia* (*War Stories*), which contained a realistic description of the Russo-Japanese War. In 1907 he edited *Murha on Murha* (*Murder is Murder*), which contained antiwar writings from many countries translated into Finnish for the first time.

Huhtala wanted to apply pacifism to his own life, to resist the presence of violence in his own circle, and to make it known in his public work. He believed that pacifism developed more from inner growth than from social or political activity. He resisted all armed activity, as well as national liberation movements, and refused to participate in the anti-Russian movement at the beginning of the twentieth century. Permanent peace, he believed, could be obtained only by increasing peace education in homes and schools. He wanted to root out from education and upbringing all competition and literature supporting aggression and war. Believing that national ideals had often led to war, Huhtala sought to promote improved international relations and cooperation between states.

As a teacher and educator, Kyösti Huhtala worked industriously for pacifism. Positive results from such work cannot be statistically demonstrated, but it became the ideological basis on which the Finnish peace movement developed.

Bibliography:

A. *Murha on murha* (Tampere, 1907); *Sota ja rauhanatte kristinopin valossa* (Tampere, 1908); *Sotakertomuksia* (Tampere, 1903).

B. Waldemar Rantoja, "Kyösti Huhtala," *Eteläpohjalaisia elämäkertoja* (Vaasa, 1963).

Kalevi Kalemaa

Trans. by Oliver and Rita Whitehead

HUMBERT-DROZ, Jules (September 1891, La Chaux-de-Fonds, Switzerland—16 October 1971, La Chaux-de-Fonds). *Education*: Faculty of Theology, Univ. of Neuchâtel. *Career*: ordained pastor, Swiss Evangelical Church; pacifist, socialist, communist, author.

Jules Humbert-Droz had an extraordinary career. His origins and background help to explain its apparently contradictory aspects. He was born in the Jura, a French-speaking region of Switzerland well known for its nonconformance. Anarchism and a radical form of socialism was well entrenched there in the early years of this century. Humbert-Droz's grandfather had fought on the liberal side in the Swiss civil war of 1847, and his father, a highly skilled watchmaker, was well known as a defender of labor's cause.

Since the Jura was also a bulwark of evangelical Protestantism, it is not surprising that the young Humbert-Droz was attracted to Christian socialism. But his was a peculiar combination of the two doctrines. He was convinced that Marxian socialism offered the solution to the social and economic questions of the day but did not provide answers for problems in his "personal and moral life." On this basis he began his preparation for the ministry but with a singular reservation: he did not believe in penance and the redemption of sins through faith in the sacrifice of Jesus Christ. Nevertheless, Humbert-Droz completed his theological studies (his thesis was on "Christianity and Socialism") and was ordained as a pastor in September, 1914.

In 1912–13 theological studies had led him to sojourn in Paris and Berlin. In the former, he observed the belligerent chauvinism of the nationalist revival that was taking place in France at that time; in the latter, he became strongly influenced by the philosophical works of *Leo Tolstoy, the "Neue Wege" ("New Way") of *Leonhard Ragaz (a Swiss theologian and leader of a social-religious and pacifist movement) and the Christian socialism of Elie Gounelle. These convictions deepened his antimilitarist convictions, made him more aware of the threat to peace posed by exclusive nationalism, and shaped his career during World War I in ways that had little to do with the pastoral. In the fall of 1914, Humbert-Droz was sent to London as pastor of the French Reformed Evangelical Church of Bayswater. It was there that he began his active career as a pacifist and antimilitarist. On Friday evenings, he gave a series of lectures as both a pastor and a Swiss socialist on the causes of war. His audience consisted mostly of French anarchists (along with a few Germans) who had fled to London after refusing to bear arms. Soon he was in trouble with the authorities of both his Church and the British government. Thus by 1916, he was back in Switzerland, this time as a reporter for *La Sentinelle*, a left socialist newspaper. That same year he gave a series of antimilitarist lectures, including one at a meeting in

Berne against the imprisonment by the German government of the antiwar Socialist, Karl Liebknecht.

In the summer of 1916, he was subjected to his first arrest occasioned by his refusal to undergo a medical examination for the Swiss army. He remained in prison until January 24, 1917. His prison experience seemed only to have hardened his will and convictions. While there, he wrote and published his first successful pamphlet, *Guerre à la Guerre! A bas l'Armée!* (*War against War! Down with the Army!*). While the work received the enthusiastic approval of *Romain Rolland, its Tolstoyan ideas were not entirely appreciated by the Swiss Young Socialists who under the influence of Lenin, encouraged young men to infiltrate the army and prepare for the revolution.

Like so many others of the generation of the 1890s, Humbert-Droz's life was profoundly marked by the Russian Revolution. By the summer of 1917, he had become a fervent supporter of Lenin, a position to which he remained faithful for the rest of his life. True enough, his Leninism (later Bukharinism) was rooted in his own ethical worldview based on pacifism, antimilitarism, and a deep identification with the fate of the working class. Humbert-Droz's relationship with the communist movement internationally and in Switzerland was long and complex. He helped create the Swiss Communist party in 1921 and remained a member until his expulsion in 1943 for, among other things, his anti-Stalinism. From 1920 until 1929, Humbert-Droz played an important political role in the Communist International as one of its three secretaries. After Stalin's triumph over Bukharin, Humbert-Droz, who was personally and politically very close to Nikolai Bukharin, was removed from his secretary's post and sent to South America as a representative of the Communist International. Returning to Switzerland in 1931, Humbert-Droz worked for the Swiss Communist party (he was its secretary for several years) until his expulsion in 1943, with the exception of several years in Spain during the civil war.

The last phase of Humbert-Droz's life began with his readmission to the old Swiss Socialist party in July 1943. Not only was he not required to apologize for his Communist past (his anti-Stalinism was well known), but even more remarkable was the election in September 1947 of this former secretary of the Communist International to the post of secretary-general of the Swiss Socialist party.

In addition to the writing of his invaluable memoirs, Humbert-Droz devoted a good part of his last years to three questions: 1) the struggle for the political unity of the Swiss working class; 2) the furtherance of worker self-government in industry (he found Yugoslavia most interesting in this respect); and 3) the struggle for world peace and disarmament. His activities in this third area were, in fact, a return to his earliest ethical and political interests. In September 1950 Humbert-Droz was a principal promoter of Action pour la paix, a union of several Swiss pacifist organizations. He announced that its program would include the interdiction of atomic arms, the rapid convocation of a world conference for immediate disarmament, the creation of a federative Union of Europe, and the commencement of talks between East and West toward the development of mutual confidence. This organization brought a new vitality to the older Conseil suisse des associations pour la paix (Swiss Council of Peace Associations), which had been founded in 1945 and of which Humbert-Droz was the president from 1953 to 1964.

Others may regard Humbert-Droz's career as contradictory and circular, but he himself did not so regard it. In his memoirs, he proudly asserted that he had remained faithful to the philosophy of struggle for the betterment of man and society. Adherence to socialism, freedom, and peace were inseparable in his concept of a better world. The Church, labor, socialist, communist, and pacifist movements were to him none other than means by which he might reach "a higher level which goes beyond them all."

Bibliography:

A. *Memoires de Jules Humbert-Droz* (4 vols., Neufehâtel, 1969–73).

B. Siegfried Bahne, ed., *Archives de Jules Humbert-Droz. I. Origines et Débuts des Partis Communistes des Pays Latins* (1919–1923) (Dordrecht, 1970).

C. Jules Humbert-Droz Archives, La Chaux-de-Fonds, Neuchatel, Switzerland.

John M. Cammett

HUXLEY, Aldous Leonard (26 July 1894, Laleham, near Godalming, England—22 November 1963, Los Angeles, CA). *Education*: Eton; B.Litt., Balliol Col., Oxford Univ., 1916. *Career*: man of letters.

Within Aldous Huxley's prodigious, multifaceted career, the period of pacifist activism, limited to the mid 1930s, is brief. Yet Huxley's writings, public lectures, and radio interviews during these few years were instrumental to the unprecedented growth and appeal of 1930s British pacifism. As an early founder and sponsor of the Peace Pledge Union, which coordinated the varied secular pacifist groups of the time, and especially as one of England's most distinguished novelists, Huxley attracted a wide reading public for his numerous pacifist publications. Among these works, *What Are You Going To Do About It? The Case for Constructive Pacifism* (1936), *An Encyclopedia of Pacifism* (1937), and *Ends and Means* (1937) were invariably listed by pacifist organizations as essential reading for pacifist recruits. *Ends and Means* endures as a classic statement of one principle mode of pacifist reasoning.

Although Huxley's social activist phase was brief, his pacifist convictions long preceded his public advocacy and persisted until his death. They began to form during World War I when Huxley, initially disappointed that his feeble eyesight disqualified him from fighting, soon lost his patriotic idealism. Decisive to his antiwar conversion were his several months of farm work at Garsington Manor (the home of pacifists Phillip and *Ottoline Morrell) where he became part of a seminal coterie of writers, artists, and public figures who were either pacifists or, even if supporting the British government's entrance into the war, sharply critical of that government's war methods and aims. With a fervent commitment to rigorous, rational, and scientific inquiry befitting the descendant of Thomas

Henry Huxley, Matthew Arnold, and Thomas Arnold of Rugby, he treated sentimental rationalizations for individual and communal destructive behavior with acid wit.

During the 1920s, traveling through parts of Europe, the Far East, the West Indies, and Mexico, with his wife and their only child, Huxley found his hostility deepening toward the many forms of cultural and political nationalism basic to war. By the end of the 1920s, he was on a quest for a philsophical framework, an alternative system of spiritual values to Christianity (which he thought the war had proven bankrupt), to encompass the political attitudes he had come to hold, principally, pacifism, social decentralism and political libertarianism.

His quest took on greater urgency in the early 1930s with acutely deteriorating world affairs: the depression, the rise of fascism, the demise of the League of Nations, and the increasing destructiveness of military and scientific technology. By 1932, the year he published *Brave New World*, Huxley took his first plunge into political involvement, issuing an antiwar piece, ''Notes on the Way'' in *Time and Tide*. In 1934 he joined the roster of the Federation of Progressive Societies and Individuals, formed in December 1933 by *C.E.M. Joad, with the declared aims of unilateral disarmament, world government, and radical social change. A year later Huxley helped the charismatic minister, *H.R.L. Sheppard, launch the Peace Pledge Union and became one of its foremost lecturers.

During the peak of his political activity in the mid 1930s, Huxley underwent a profound intellectual change. Like many other interwar pacifists who could no longer find moral authority in western religious traditions, Huxley rooted his pacifism in eastern modes of transcendental philosophy. His conversion to mysticism and neo-Buddhism, partly inspired by his therapy with F. M. Alexander and his friendship with fellow pacifist *Gerald Heard, reached fullest expression in *The Perennial Philosophy* (1945) but was prefigured in his novel, *Eyeless in Gaza* (1936) and permeated his pacifist exposition in *Ends and Means* (1937). The universe, in Huxley's view, was fundamentally harmonic and moral as in the Buddhist concept of Ahimsa. Whereas ''evil'' acts promoted social and cosmic fragmentation, ''good'' acts were always nonviolent and strengthened social and cosmic unity. Huxley pursued the traditional Buddhist goal of non-attachment. This goal consisted neither of Christian ascetism nor secular altruism, but, instead, demanded strenuous cultivation of rational and intuitive consciousness, keen awareness of behavioral consequences and of the self as a participant within an intricate web of social and cosmic relations. Such belief, Huxley claimed, provided the ''best metaphysical environment for pacifism.''

The appeal of Oriental thought for Huxley and for other pacifists fastened, too, on *Gandhi's nonviolent campaigns in South Africa and India. In his pacifist treatises, Huxley urged adoption of Gandhi's techniques, advocating rigorous training of small bands of pacifists in psychological self-reliance and nonviolent tactics. Even in his fictional writing, such as *After Many A Summer Dies the Swan* (1939), he proposed the formation of small pacifist communities, nucleii of an alternative society, which, if unable to prevent war, would nourish civilized values during wartime.

Huxley shared the widespread pacifist fear that the military defense of English democracy would inevitably turn England into a fascist state. Citing historical evidence, rational inference, and emotional intuition to bolster his metaphysical convictions, Huxley argued that "good" ends could be realized only through "good" means, since violent means, even in the service of peace, spurred further hatred, revenge, and warfare. Although he did not expect nonviolent tactics to avert another world war, he believed that the consequences of fascist occupation of England, no matter how ruthless the invaders, were less politically, morally, and psychologically destructive in the long run than violent resistance.

Ultimately, Huxley did not witness firsthand the impact of England's military involvement in World War II. In early 1937 he began an extended visit to America, where in 1938 he decided to settle (while never becoming an American citizen since the oath of citizenship was repugnant to his pacifism). Although Huxley's politically activist phase ended then, his pacifism remained vigorous in his personal life and writings. In *Science, Liberty and Peace* (1946), written for the Fellowship of Reconciliation, he lambasted scientists' support of patriotic and capitalistic war-making interests. *Ape and Essence* (1947) dramatized nuclear catastrophe, and *Themes and Variation* (1950) indicted the modern state as an idolatrous entity, worship of which unleashed collective greed, bestiality, and war. In his final novel, *Island* (1962), Huxley depicted a beguiling utopia, the island of Pala, where Mahayanist Buddhism influenced by Tantric practices guided the islanders in nonaggressive, peaceful, life-affirming activities. Mind and body, intuition and reason, science and religion were at one. On Pala there was no army, political and economic organizations were decentralized, residents enjoyed rough economic parity, and conservation and population controls kept needed resources in balance. Realistically, the novel concluded with Palanese surrender to external attack, but the resolute Palanese pacifism sustained its integrity to the end.

Critical opinion on Huxley's pacifist writing is widely divergent, usually reflecting the critic's own position on nonviolence. But even Huxley's harshest detractors acknowledge his intellectual breadth, penetration, and bravery, his clarity and concision, and his historically significant and persuasive role as a premier pacifist spokesperson of the 1930s.

Bibliography:

A. *Collected Essays* (New York, 1959); *An Encyclopedia of Pacifism* (London, 1937); *Ends and Means: An Enquiry into the Nature of Ideals and into the Methods Employed for their Realization* (London, 1937); *Eyeless in Gaza* (London, 1936); *Island* (New York, 1962); *The Olive Tree and Other Essays* (London, 1936); *The Perennial Philosophy* (New York, 1945); *Science, Liberty and Peace* (New York and London, 1946); *What Are You Going To Do About It? The Case for Constructive Pacifism* (London, 1936).

B. E. E. Bass, *Aldous Huxley: An Annotated Bibliography* (New York, 1981); Sybille Bedford, *Aldous Huxley: A Biography* (2 vols., New York, 1973–74); Milton Birnbaum,

Aldous Huxley's Quest for Values (Knoxville, TN, 1971); Thomas D. Clareson and Carolyn S. Andrews, "Aldous Huxley: A Bibliography, 1960–1964" *Extrapolation*, VI, 2–21 (Department of English, College of Wooster, Wooster, Ohio); Ronlad W. Clark, *The Huxleys* (New York, and Toronto, 1968); Claire John Eschelbach and Joyce Lee Shober, *Aldous Huxley: A Bibliography 1916–1959* (Berkeley, CA, 1961); Charles M. Holmes, *Aldous Huxley and The Way to Reality* (Bloomington, IN and London, 1970); George Woodcock, *Dawn and the Darkest Hour: A Study of Aldous Huxley* (New York, 1972).

C. Aldous Huxley Collection, University of California, Los Angeles; Aldous Huxley Papers, University of Texas and Yale University; Huxley Family Papers, Imperial College of Science and Technology, London.

Joyce Avrech Berkman

HUYSMANS, Camille Jean Joseph (26 May 1871, Bilzen, Belgium—25 February 1968, Antwerp). *Education*: Athenée de Tongeren, 1882–86; doctorate in philology, Univ. of Liège, 1895. *Career*: secretary, Second International, 1905–22; founder, International Socialist Workers Association, 1923, president, 1940–44; member, Chambre des représentants, 1910–65, president, 1936–39, 1954–58; communal councillor, Brussels, 1908–21, Antwerp, 1921–33; mayor, Antwerp, 1933–40, 1944–46; Minister of Science and Arts, 1924–27; Minister of State, 1945, Prime Minister, 1946–47; Minister of Public Education, 1947–49; philologist, professor, writer, journalist, socialist politician, and pacifist.

From 1887 when he joined the Belgian Labor party until the end of his life, Camille Huysmans devoted himself to political struggles on the domestic and international levels. Appointed secretary of the Socialist International in 1905, his responsibilities and efforts to develop and maintain international unity among disparate socialist parties required the utmost tact and negotiation skill. On many occasions, Huysmans' gifts as a mediator were responsible for preserving a socialist front.

Prior to 1914, Huysmans warned of the possible outbreak of a war in Europe and urged socialists to collaborate in order to prevent governments from declaring war. He hoped that, in the event of war, a call for a general strike would win support from all major socialist parties. Whenever a crisis appeared, he worked diligently to defuse it.

The Moroccan crisis of 1911 provided a major test of socialist unity and Huysmans' skills as an intermediary. He found himself pressed between French socialist demands for an international meeting (urged by *Paul Vaillant-Couturier and *Jean Jaurès) and German socialist unwillingness (led by *August Bebel) to take up an issue involving colonial policy. The problem was further complicated by private overtures to the international socialist headquarters made by German diplomats who sought a peaceful resolution of the crisis. Eventually, Huymans was able to persuade all parties to attend a closed-door meeting in Zurich to establish a unified socialist policy.

Mediating socialist differences was even more difficult in 1914. Huysmans' overriding desire to organize unified socialist opposition to the impending world war led him to Paris and a meeting with a representative of the German Social Democratic party just days before the conflict ensued. When war broke out and Belgium was invaded, he took the archives of the International and moved to the Netherlands for the duration. From there he did what he could to promote the cessation of hostilities and to continue the work of the office. His calls for a negotiated settlement found favor with neither the French nor German socialists, but he promoted the Stockholm Conference of 1917 and did what he could to preserve the international tradition of the socialist movement. It was a difficult and thankless task.

Following the Russian Revolution, his task became complicated even further by the division among socialists over the "war or revolution" question. Still, he labored to preserve elements of socialist unity from 1919 to 1922 by organizing meetings among representatives of the new Communist parties and older socialist parties. Finally, he turned to parliamentary socialism at home for most of the interwar years, never giving up his struggle for peace which merged with an antifascist struggle as the thirties wore on. During World War II he fled to London where he worked with the government in exile as well as the socialist International in exile. In recognition of his lifetime of struggle, he was made head of a coalition government after the war and then a minister in +Paul-Henri Spaak's government. Huysmans served in public office to his 87th year and in the remaining decade of his life continued to speak out for the preservation of peace.

Bibliography:

A. *Camille Huysmans. Ses discours prononcés en Hollande du 9 au 31 janvier, 1916* (Belgium, 1916); *Camille Huysmans geschriften en Documenten*, ed. by D. De Weerdt & W. Geldolf (6 vols., Antwerp and Amsterdam, 1974–76); *Correspondance entre Lénine et Camille Huysmans (1905–1914)*, ed. by Georges Haupt (Paris, 1963); *The Policy of the International. A Speech and Interview with the Secretary of the International* (London, 1916).

B. H. Balthazar, D. De Weerdt, W. Geldolf, J. Gotovitch, et al, *Bijdragen tot het Camille Huysmansonderzoek. Etudes de la personalité de Camille Huysmans* (Antwerp, 1971); J. Kuypers, *Het werk van Kamiel Huysmans*, (Brussels, 1928); R. Roemans & H. Van Assche, *Camille Huysmans. Een levensbeeld gevestigd op persoonlijke getuigenissen en eigen werk*, (Hasselt, 1961); A. Van Laar, *Camille Huysmans, zi jn leven, zi jn streven*, (n.p., 1937–38); P. Van Molle, *Le Parlement Belge, 1894–1969*, 186–8; A. Zevaes, "Les Manoeuvres du Kamarade Huysmans," *Republicain socialiste*, (June, 1916), 1–16.

C. Camille Huysmans Papers, Stichting Camille Huysmans, Antwerp.

Nadine Lubelski-Bernard
Trans. by Sandi E. Cooper

I

IGLESIAS, Pablo (18 October 1850, El Ferrol, Spain—9 December 1925, Madrid). *Education*: printer's apprenticeship. *Career*: printer, journalist, political organizer, union leader, politician, and member of parliament.

Born into a family of modest means, Pablo Iglesias became apprenticed at a young age to a printer in Madrid. Following the proclamation of a Spanish republic in 1873, Iglesias joined the Nueva Federación Madrilêna (New Madrid Federation), a small socialistic group that opposed both the official republicanism of the bourgeoisie and the violence of the Bakuninist anarchists of the day. Elected to lead the prestigious Asociación del arte d' imprimir (Association of Printing Arts) in 1874, Iglesias then emerged as the leader of the new Partido socialista obrero español (Spanish Socialist Working-Class Party) (PSOE) and its organ *El Socialista* in 1879. From that position, Iglesias and the PSOE occupied the political ground between anarchists, on the one hand, and the "opportunistic" socialists and their bourgeois democratic allies, on the other. Further, in 1888, Iglesias led the formation of the Union Generale del Trabajo (General Workers' Union) (UGT), which drew its initial support from skilled craftsmen in Castila and from Basque ironworkers.

From such positions of influence, Iglesias resolutely opposed the recourse to violence, whether international or intranational in character and scope. While not officially a pacifist, Iglesias opposed the use of violence for political ends. He gained a larger forum for the expression of these views through his election to the Madrid city government in 1905 and to the Cortes (parliament) in 1909. He opposed Spanish policies in Cuba which helped to lead to war with the United States in 1898; Iglesias condemned as well the Spanish colonial war in Morocco which began prior to World War I. In 1911, following a massive uprising against the war in 1909, the PSOE and its Republican coalition allies launched a nationwide campaign in opposition to the continued Moroccan conflict. Iglesias, exhausted at the end of a parliamentary session, nevertheless contributed to the movement by means of a rigorous speaking tour. In 1914 the PSOE also advocated Spain's nonparticipation in World War I, but it refused to condemn the war and displayed an open preference for the Allies during the conflict.

Iglesias continued to espouse the peaceful road toward social change in his last years. In 1921, amid strikes and lockouts and violence from almost all quarters, his *El Socialista* condemned the use of force unequivocally. Violence, Iglesias's journal warned, is "essentially reactionary" in the context of Spanish political culture, whether it is utilized by the left or by the government and the Right. "The saving formula," *El Socialist* concluded, "is liberty and justice.

There is no other.'' Iglesias's inability to prevent a pro-French reaction within the PSOE in 1914–18 and to stem the tide of violence which emanated from that war did not diminish his conviction that the true road to power for the Spanish working class lay in the direction of an evolutionary process and incremental gains. To that end and to that process, Pablo Iglesias held firm.

Bibliography:

A. *Exhortaciones a los trabajadores* (Madrid, 1926).

B. Juan José, Morato, *Pablo Iglesias Posse: Educador de muchedumbres* (2nd ed; Barcelona, 1968); Julian Zugazagoitia, *Pablo Iglesias* (Netzahualcoyotl, Mexico, 1965).

James A. Young

INNES, Kathleen Elizabeth Royds (15 January 1883, Reading, Berkshire, England—27 March 1967, St. Mary Bourne, Hampshire, England). *Education*: B.A., Univ. of London, 1912. *Career*: writer, internationalist, and peace activist.

Before the First World War Kathleen Royds became a lecturer in English literature for the London County Council. In 1915 she went to Salonika with a unit of the Scottish Women's Hospital, and thence accompanied a flood of refugees to Corsica; for this work she was awarded the Order of St. Sava. On returning to England, Kathleen joined the British committee of the International Committee of Women for Permanent Peace which had been formed at the Hague Congress of Women in 1915; by the end of the war the British committee had 4,000 members and 50 branches. She attended the postwar Congress at Zurich in 1919, when the International Committee was consolidated as the Women's International League for Peace and Freedom (WILPF), and remained dedicated to the work of the League throughout her long life. She was elected an international co-chairman of the League, along with Gertrud Baer and Clara Ragaz, in 1937 and in 1946 became an international vice-president.

Kathleen Royds married George Innes in 1921, the start of a lifelong partnership in international work. Both were deeply concerned with the League of Nations: George was organizer for the London Federation of the League of Nations Union (1924–37), while Kathleen devoted herself to lecturing and writing. She joined her husband as a member of the Society of Friends in the 1920s and served as secretary of the Friends Peace Committee in London from 1926 to 1936.

Kathleen Innes wrote to *The Friend* magazine in 1933 that her hobby was literature but she was ''driven by war into politics.'' She did not believe, however, that a change in the social and economic order would necessarily bring peace. She expressed this view at a WILPF Congress in Geneva in 1934: ''I want to emphasize that peace is a *method* and not a *state* and that under every system there will be causes for clash unless we remove the psychological causes.'' Her first priority was the eradication of violence. At the same time, her democratic and antifascist principles urged strong support for oil sanctions against Mussolini's aggression in Ethiopia and opposition to the ''vested interests'' that sabotaged this policy.

Kathleen and George Innes retired to St. Mary Bourne in Hampshire in 1938. During World War II the office of the British section of the WILPF was evacuated from London to her home at St. Mary Bourne and she acted as honorary secretary of the section. Throughout her life she remained committed to internationalism and peace.

Bibliography:

A. The *League of Nations* (London, 1936); *The League of Nations and the World's Workers* (London, 1927); *Peace Hath her Victories* (London, 1929); *The Prevention of War* (London, 1932); *The Reign of Law* (London, 1929); *The Romance of the Health Work of the League of Nations* (Andover, 1938); *The Story of Nansen and the League of Nations* (London, 1931).

B. Gertrude Bussey & Margaret Tims, *Pioneers for Peace: WILPF 1915–1965* (London, 1965, reprinted with new material, London, 1980); "Dictionary of Quaker Biography (typescript)," Friends House Library, London; *The Friend*, May 12, 1967.

Margaret Tims

IVENS, William (28 June 1878, Baford, England—20 June 1957, Chula Vista, CA). *Education*: B.A., B.D., Wesley Coll., Winnipeg. *Career*: Methodist Ministry, 1909–18; editor, *Western Labor News*. 1918–19; member, Legislative Assembly, Manitoba, 1920–36.

Heavily influenced at Wesley College by the major Canadian exponent of the social gospel, Salem Bland, William Ivens went beyond his mentor in becoming a pacifist during World War I, working closely with a notable group of Winnipeg pacifists who included *J. S. Woodsworth, Fred Dixon, Vernon Thomas, and Francis Marion Beynon. With the imminence of conscription threatening conscientious objectors after mid–1916, Ivens went public with his pacifism, writing in the local labor press and going on speaking tours in the prairie provinces.

Congregational reaction in 1918 forced Ivens from his church, whereupon he initiated a Labour Church movement, allying social gospellers, labor reformers, and socialists, and became editor of the *Western Labor News*. In both arenas he did much to foster critical debate on the war and on an economic system he considered a major root of international violence. Arrested, tried, and imprisoned as a leader of the Winnipeg General Sympathetic Strike in 1919, he viewed the strike as a means of nonviolent economic action for social change and did much to keep strikers on that course through the special strike edition of his paper.

While in prison, Ivens was elected to the Manitoba legislature in 1920. An able and colorful representative until 1936, he was one of the primary founders of the Canadian socialist party, the Cooperative Commonwealth Federation in 1933. Increasingly secular after the demise of his Labour Churches, his pacifism was absorbed into a socialist analysis of the roots of war. He continued an outspoken foe of international violence, but little record remains to document any significant response by Ivens to World War II or international issues thereafter.

Bibliography:

B. Richard Allen, *The Social Passion* (Toronto, 1971); Kenneth McNaught, *A Prophet in Politics* (Toronto, 1959); D. F. Pratt, "William Ivens and the Winnipeg Labour Church" (B.D. Thesis, St. Andrew's College, Saskatoon, 1958); Thomas Paul Socknat,

" 'Witness Against War': Pacifism in Canada, 1900–1945," Ph.D. dissertation, McMaster University, 1981.

C. William Ivens Papers, Manitoba Archives.

Richard Allen

IVERSEN, Felix (22 September 1887, Lübeck, Germany—31 July 1973, Helsinki, Finland). *Education*: B.A., Univ of Helsinki, 1909, M.A., 1914, Ph.D., 1914. *Career*: lecturer in mathematics, Univ. of Helsinki, 1920–54; editor; peace organizer and publicist.

Felix Iversen, one of Finland's most important peace activists, was a significant academic and mathematician. He took an active role in the Peace Union of Finland from its inception in 1920 and edited its journal *Rauhaa Kohti* from 1925 until 1967, when it joined forces with *Ydin*, published by the Committee of One Hundred. Together with Matilda Wrede, he also founded the Finnish section of Towards Christian International (later Fellowship of Reconciliation).

In 1926 Iversen became chairman of the Peace Union and helped make it Finland's most significant antiwar organization until the outbreak of World War II. He served in that post until 1967. His knowledge of Finnish, Swedish, Danish, German, French, and Russian enabled Iversen to establish extensive contacts with European peace leaders. He participated (mainly at his own expense) in numerous peace congresses throughout Europe, acting often in the capacity of secretary or chairman. He corresponded with, among others, *Bertrand Russell, *Albert Einstein, and *Albert Schweitzer. Besides the Peace Union of Finalnd, Iversen served as secretary of the Union of Reconciliation, as chairman of the Scandinavian Teachers Peace Union, on the board of directors of the Scandinavian Peace Union, and as a member of the Committee Fighting against War, the Union of Human Rights, and the Committee Fighting against Capital Punishment. In 1932, he helped found the Joint Committee of Peacework and acted as its chairman. He won great esteem in European peace circles and gained membership in the Council of the International Peace Union (1936–39) and in the World Peace Council (1950–73). He was also appointed to the post of vice-president of the World Union of the United Nations Association (1951–54).

During the interwar period the Finnish peace movement was often referred to an "Iversenian," in recognition of the central position Felix Iversen played in founding, organizing, and directing most of Finland's central antiwar organizations. He devoted his time and money to the cause of peace and often had to combat economic difficulties, political pressure, indifference, prejudice, hate, and scorn. The problems he faced were often exacerbated by his own attitudes and personality. He considered it important to expand the peace movement as much as possible, but he alienated many by his autocratic behavior in the organizations he directed. He emphasized cooperation between peace organizations, but he preferred to do almost everything alone. Not without reason, he was often called the most "Iversenian" of all.

Iversen sought to keep the peace movement outside party politics. He resisted political extremes, because in his opinion they tended to weaken democracy and the political balance. He called for peace education in schools and emphasized international cooperation. After World War II, he worked actively in the anti-nuclear weapons movement, supporting the work of the World Peace Council and, in 1949, helping to found its Finnish section called Rauhanpuolustajat (Peace Defenders or Peace Committee). For his achievements in the peace movement, Iversen received in 1954 the Lenin Peace Prize.

As a peace fighter Felix Iversen was independent and brave. He was a typical ''one idea'' man. Just before he died he stated that he would probably have gone further as a mathematician, but he preferred peace work to a personal career. His commitment to peace and his antiwar activities have become well known in Finland.

Bibliography:

A. *Rauhanaate ja rauhantyö* (Helsinki, 1934).

B. Kalevi Kalemma, *Suomalaisen rauhanliikkeen juurisa* (Vaasa, 1981); Deryck Sivén, ''Felix Iversen in memoriam,'' *Fredsposten*, 5 (1973), 3–4; Deryck Sivén, ''Felix Iversen 70 vuotias,'' *Rauhaa Kohti*, 10 (1957), 61; Ilkka Taipale, ''Sitoutumattomuns iversen-iläisen rauhanliikkeen persussävy,'' *Sanomat* (Helsinki), October 25, 1980.

C. Felix Iversen and Peace Union of Finland Papers, State Archives, Helsinki.

Kalevi Kalemaa
Trans. by Oliver & Rita Whitehead

IVERSEN, Toini Elizabeth Hjelt (13 December 1894, Helsinki, Finland—10 August 1973, Helsinki). *Education*: teacher's certificate, Helsinki Handicraft Seminary. *Career*: teacher, Helsinki Handicraft Seminary; teacher, continuation classes of Finnish-and Swedish-speaking elementary school, Helsinki, 1920–23; peace activist.

Toini Iversen's father, August Hjelt, was a senator and one of the leaders of the labor movement. He also participated in the Finnish resistance movement and opposed the illegal military conscription organized by the Russian government in Finland. From her home background, then, Toini Iversen inherited an interest in social and political questions.

She joined the peace movement in the immediate aftermath of World War I. With her future husband, the well known peace activist, *Felix Iversen, she participated in the organization of Towards Christian International (later Fellowship of Reconciliation), established by Mathilda Wrede. In 1920 she attended the meeting which founded Finland's Peace Union and after marrying Felix Iversen in 1923, she started to participate actively in peace organizations. She belonged to the central board of Finland's Peace Union and the Swedish Peace Friends, which operated in Helsinki. From 1926 to 1928 she served as secretary of the Peace Union, and from 1929 to 1930 she served as treasurer.

Toini Iversen helped tie the feminist movement to the organized peace effort. She helped establish the Finnish section of the Women's International League for Peace and Freedom (WILPF) and argued forcefully that women as procreators and child rearers must fight war more actively than their male counterparts. She believed that the maintenace of peace for a woman was a deeply personal matter, but that men often approach the issue as a political game.

Iversen's antiwar activities were not limited to the Peace Union or the WILPF. She helped found Finland's Teachers' Peace Union and devoted both her time and energy to developing it. She represented Finland on the central board of the Nordic Teachers' Peace Union. With her husband, she participated in many European peace meetings throughout the interwar period. During World War II she cooperated in a committee which supported Jewish refugees. The Helsinki home of Felix and Toini Iversen became known as a meeting place for international refugees and for traveling peace friends in Finland.

Although overshadowed by her well-known husband and although subjected to prejudices which denigrated the role of women in political and social activities, Toini Iversen laid the groundwork for the active participation of women in the post-World War II peace movement.

Bibliography:

B. Bertha Olsoni, "Toini Iversen," *Fredsposten* 6 (1973); Deryck Siven, "Toini Iversen on poissa," *Fredsposten*, 5 (1973).

Kalevi Kalemaa
Trans. by Oliver & Rita Whitehead

J

JACOB, Berthold [pseud. of Berthold Salomon] (12 December 1898, Berlin—26 February 1944, Berlin). *Career*: freelance journalist for various newspapers of the democratic left; antimilitarist.

In 1916 Berthold Salomon (later known by his pseudonym Berthold Jacob) volunteered for the artillery and fought on the Western front. A victim of gas poisoning, he returned home in 1918 an absolute opponent of war and an advocate of conscientious objection as a means of preventing war. He joined a circle of writers associated with the bourgeois-democratic *Berliner Volkszeitung* (BVZ). On October 2, 1919, this group, which included Karl Vetter and *Carl von Ossietzky, founded the Friedensbund der Kriegsteilnehmer (Veterans' Peace Union), an antimilitary organization of former soldiers. In the early years of the Weimar Republic the Peace Union issued proclamations calling for the elimination of war. Jacob was also a leader in the short-lived Republikanische Partei Deutschlands (German Republican Party), an organization formed by members of the Peace Union, which had collapsed soon after its founding, and former members of the Deutsche Demokratische Partei (German Democratic Party).

Recognizing in postwar Germany both a growth in militarism and a deep resentment at having lost the war, Jacob began writing about war guilt and armaments. Under the influence of *Emil Julius Gumbel, he became a knowledgeable military journalist, helping to uncover proof of secret German armaments. Defying accusations of high treason, Jacob continued to publish his findings and in 1925 co-authored a white paper on secret German rearmament (Schwarze Reichswehr). The document was widely read and stimulated numerous debates within the Weimar Reichstag. Refusing to be intimidated, he exposed, in *Das Anderes Deutschland* the recruitment of ''volunteers'' into the military in violation of the Versailles Treaty. In 1928 he and *Fritz Küster, the paper's publisher, were sentenced in a sensational trial to nine months in prison for undermining the republic. Their sentence was later canceled by a general amnesty.

As a well-qualified military journalist, Jacob supported the Deutsche Liga für Menschenrechte (German League for Human Rights) (DLM) in its fight against militarism, rearmament, and war. Greatly in demand, he wrote for numerous left-democratic publications, including *Weltbühne*, *Das Anderes Deutschland*, *Die Menschheit*, and *Friedenswarte*. In all his articles, Jacob attacked critical issues such as secret armaments, political assassinations, state supported coups, and the military policies of the Weimar government.

Because of his pacifist writings, Jacob moved to Strasbourg and was high on the National Socialist list of citizens to be expatriated. In the spring of 1933, he started publishing the German/French dual language news information service "Unabhängiger Zeitungsdienst"/"Service de presse indépendant" ("Independent Newspaper Information Service"). From France he sharply criticized German rearmament under Adolf Hitler and helped destroy the legend that had built up around Paul von Hindenburg. After the summer of 1933, Jacob directed the Strasbourg branch of the DLM. In 1935 he was involuntarily taken from Switzerland to Germany by German agents and released only after extensive diplomatic activity of the Swiss government. Afterwards he lived in Paris and was interned in the spring of 1940 in Camp Vernet. In 1941 he fled via Madrid to Libson, where he was again abducted by German secret agents and later was murdered after a long imprisonment in a concentration camp.

Bibliography:

A. *Das neue deutsche Heer und seine Führer* (Paris, 1936); *Weissbuch über die Schwarze Reichswehr. Deutschlands geheime Rüstungen*? with E. J. Gumbel, F. A. Lange, Paul von Schoenaich, O. Lehmann-Russbüldt, and L. Persius (Berlin, 1925); *Weltbürger Ossietzky* (Paris, 1937).

B. Heinz Cawill, *Der Fall Jacob* (Zurich 1935); Ruth Greuner, *Gegenspieler. Profile linksburgerlicher Publizisten aus Kaiserreich und Weimarer Republic* (Berlin, 1969); Heinrich Hannover and Elisabeth Hannover-Drück, *Politische Justiz 1918–1933* (Frankfurt/Main, 1966); Reinhold Lütgemeier-Davin, *Pazifismus zwischen Kooperation und Konfrontation* (Köln, 1982); Jost Nikolaus Willi; *Der Fall Jacob-Wesemann (1935–36). Ein Beitrag zur Geschichte der Schweiz in der Zwischen-Kriegszeit* (Bern/Frankfurt a.M., 1972).

Reinhold Lütgemeier-Davin
Trans. by Robert C. Reimer

JACOBS, Aletta Henriëtte (9 February 1854, Sappemeer, Netherlands—10 August 1929, Baarn, Netherlands). *Education*: studied medical sciences, Univ. of Gröningen, 1871–76; Univ. of Utrecht, 1878; M.D., Univ. of Gröningen, 1879. *Career*: physician, Amsterdam, 1879–1903; president, Dutch Suffragette Society, 1903–19.

Aletta Jacobs led a rich and unconventional life. She was the first woman admitted to a Dutch university and was also the first woman doctor in the Netherlands. Following her graduation, she traveled to London and there met many of the leading radicals and reformers, including Charles Bradlaugh, Annie Besant, and Millicent Fawcett. She also took a great interest in the Fabian Society and the suffragette movement. These contacts reinforced her own, deeply felt convictions about social injustices. The miseries they led to were daily brought home to her in her medical practice, which she had established upon her return from England. Appalled by the degree of misery and ignorance, she offered, for fourteen years, twice weekly free help and advice to every woman in need.

A small and frail woman, of great intelligence and with qualities that made her a natural leader, she fought with energy and immense dedication against the bad working and housing conditions that severely affected the health of working-class women and children. In her advocacy of birth control and family planning she was confronted with widespread opposition and hostility with some of the most severe attacks coming from her own profession. She was deeply concerned with prostitution and frequently addressed the issue of its elimination. It was only natural that before long she became convinced that the position of women in society would only improve if their inferior position in law was reversed. By 1882 she became involved in a campaign for suffrage, a struggle she pursued over the next forty years.

Aletta Jacobs was not only a prominent social reformer and a great feminist leader; with the onset of World War I she became a combative pacifist as well. Her name is largely associated with the International Congress of Women that met in The Hague during April-May, 1915. When the International Suffrage Alliance decided not to go ahead with a planned conference because of the war, Jacobs, president of the Dutch Suffrage Society, disagreed and argued that an international meeting of women was now needed more than ever. Since the Alliance (as well as the Dutch Society) opposed the idea, she decided to call the congress independently of any organization, assisted by some able and equally determined collaborators. Despite wartime difficulties and official opposition in many countries, women from twelve countries representing both neutral and belligerent states gathered for the congress, which took place under the presidency of *Jane Addams. It had been agreed that participants would not discuss the origins of the present war or the way in which it was conducted but solely the nature of the future peace. The resolutions adopted foreshadowed +Woodrow Wilson's Fourteen Points; in order to give them wide publicity and to enhance the possibility of their being adopted, the Congress instructed Addams and Jacobs to personally present the resolutions to heads of government of a number of states. This they did in May and June, traveling all over Europe in an exhausting but instructive and much-discussed journey. The Congress also decided to establish an "International League for Permanent Peace," of which Addams was elected chairman and Jacobs first vice-chairman. Its central office was located in Amsterdam, and Jacobs served as its secretary, with Rosa Manus as assistant secretary. Their main task was to maintain contact between the women pacifists in the various countries during the war. [At a conference in Zurich in 1919 the League changed its name to Women's International League for Peace and Freedom (WILPF).] In August-September 1915, Jacobs was in the United States, where she and *Carrie Chapman Catt, *Emily Balch, and Jane Addams discussed the idea of a "League of Neutral Countries" as a mediating force with Secretary of State +Robert Lansing, Colonel +Edward M. House, and President Wilson himself, reporting her findings to the Dutch prime minister upon her return. Noteworthy, too, was a study tour through Germany in the summer of 1919, in the company of Addams and several English Quaker women. Deeply affected by seeing the consequences of the war and of the food blockade on the German population, and also by the discovery that half a million German POWs were still captive in Siberia, she took the initiative in setting up an action committee whose work would, eventually, be taken over by the International Committee of the Red Cross. Physical exhaustion forced her to abandon her initial work for a revision of the Versailles Peace Treaty, which was expounded at the International Congress of the WILPF in Vienna in 1921.

Bibliography:

A. *Herinneringen van Dr. Alletta H. Jacobs* (Amsterdam, 1924); *De vrouw en de vredesbeweging in verband met het vrouwenkiesrecht* (The Hague, 1917).

B. Gertrude Bussey Margaret Tims, *Women's International League for Peace and Freedom* (London, 1965), 17–26; O. Noordenbos & P. Spigt, *Atheisme en vrijdenken in Nederland* (Nimwegen, 1976), 206–9; W. H. Posthumus-van der Goot, *Vrouwen vochten voor de vrede* (Arnhem, 1961), 150–56; *Biografisch Woordenboek van Nederland* (The Hague, 1979), I, 271–74; *Winkler Prins Encyclopaedie* (Amsterdam/Brussels, 1951), XI, 428.

Peter van den Dungen

JACOBSOHN, Siegfried (28 January 1881, Berlin—3 December 1926, Berlin). *Education*: uncompleted studies at a Berlin gymnasium and the Univ. of Berlin. *Career*: theater critic, *Die Welt am Montag*, 1901–4; publisher and editor, *Die Schaubühne*, 1905–18, and *Die Weltbühne*, 1918–26; theater critic, political writer, and editor.

One of Germany's best-known theater critics and founding editor of the famous left-wing intellectual journal, *Die Weltbühne* (originally called *Die Schaubühne*), Siegfried Jacobsohn was the son of a cultured Jewish merchant family in Berlin. He left school in order to devote himself to the theater, and he was already a well-experienced journalist and critic when, at 24, he founded *Die Schaubühne* in Berlin. Although primarily an avantgarde aestheticist, he also believed that the theater could serve as a vehicle for the reconciliation of the bourgeoisie with the working class. Yet, inspired by a group of young contributors in the years just prior to World War I (among them *Kurt Tucholsky), he became increasingly involved with political and social issues. This trend away from the aesthetic toward the political was highlighted when, in April 1918, Jacobsohn changed the name of his journal from *Die Schaubühne* (*A Glimpse of the Stage*) to *Die Weltbühne* (*The World Stage*).

In 1914 Jacobsohn had been an enthusiastic supporter of the war, but now he endorsed peace, socialism, universal disarmament, and a dominant role for intellectuals in Germany. Under Jacobsohn's direction, *Die Weltbühne* became one of the most progressive, outspoken journals of the Weimar period—a haven for such left-wing intellectuals as Lion Feuchtwanger, Egon Friedell, Arthur Koestler, *Heinrich Mann, *Ludwig Quidde, *Helene Stöcker, *Ernst Toller, Arnold Zweig, and Leon Trotsky. *Die Weltbühne* firmly endorsed republicanism, antimilitarism, democratic socialism, and reconciliation with France, but under the editorship of Jacobsohn, unlike later under *Carl von Ossietzky, it never veered close to communism. Nor did it ever break with the Social Democratic party.

Jacobsohn and his *Weltbühne* were self-appointed watchdogs of the Reichswehr. In 1925 he published a series of 16 articles uncovering the existence of the "Black Reichswehr," a secret force trained, equipped, and financed by the regular Reichswehr, in violation of the Versailles Treaty. Jacobsohn's writers proved, at some risk to their own lives, that the "Black Reichswehr" was not only illegal but counter-revolutionary and terroristic.

Jacobsohn's foreign policy orientation was decidedly pro-Western. His primary goal was for the German people to accept the consequences of the Versailles Treaty and to understand the need to work with France. In this way, the writers of the *Weltbühne* hoped, the French could be persuaded to limit their own armament efforts. Jacobsohn strongly opposed Soviet-German cooperation, especially in military matters, because it hindered reconciliation with the West and strengthened the military establishment in Germany. A passionate man of enormous editorial talents, winning ways, and a profound commitment to democracy, Jacobsohn died suddenly in 1926.

Bibliography:

A. *Der Fall Jacobsohn* (Charlottenburg, 1905); *Das Jahr der Bühne*, (10 vols., Berlin, 1911–21); *Max Reinhardt* (Berlin, 1910); *Das Theater der Reichshauptstadt* (Berlin, 1904).

B. Istvan Deak, *Weimar Germany's Left-wing Intellectuals. A Political History of the "Weltbühne" and its Circle* (Berkeley and Los Angeles, 1968); *Neue Deutsche Biographie* (Berlin, 1974), X, 425–6.

Istvan Deak and Monica Scorcia

JAEGERSTAETTER, Franz (20 May 1907, St. Radegund, Austria—9 August 1943, Berlin). *Education*: volkschule. *Career*: farmer.

In the strictest sense it is strange to think of Franz Jaegerstaetter as a "peace leader." He did not found, nor was he even aware of, any German or Austrian peace movement during his lifetime. He lived in obscurity and went to his death convinced no one outside of his family and the few others immediately involved would ever know of him or the sacrifice he felt called upon to make. It is remarkable that this simple peasant from a remote little village would provide inspiration and moral strength to an untold number of witnesses for peace or would one day be presented to the Catholic bishops gathered in solemn conclave at the Second Vatican Council as a model to guide them in their deliberations.

Born in a tiny village in Upper Austria, Jaegerstaetter spent his entire life there, except for a brief period of exile as a young man and the last few months spent in prisons awaiting his execution. The "exile" was the result of a conflict he had as a rambunctious young man. Both he and his opponent were sent away for a time to keep peace in the community. When Jaegerstaetter returned, he had changed from a young ruffian into a devoted churchgoer and a daily communicant. He ultimately assumed the responsibilities of sacristan for the village church. Dissuaded by his pastor from entering a religious order, he took over the family farm, married, and became the father of three daughters.

There was nothing to distinguish his life from that of the other peasants of

St. Radegund. Nothing, that is, except the intensity of his religious commitment and his equally intense opposition to National Socialism. In his mind the two were inseparably linked: he rejected Adolf Hitler and his Thousand Year Reich because he believed they were incompatible with his devotion to the teachings and practices of Christianity. In the plebiscite called to approve the annexation of Austria as part of the Greater Third Reich, Jaegerstaetter was the only one in his village who refused to vote yes.

Outspoken in his opposition to the Nazi regime, he might have been ignored as the village eccentric except for the challenge he posed to the Nazi regime in the Spring of 1943. Upon receiving his orders to report for induction into the armed forces, he announced his refusal to serve. Arrested at once, he was shortly thereafter sent to Berlin where, after a trial before the Supreme Military Tribunal, he was condemned to death and beheaded on August 9, 1943.

For almost twenty years Jaegerstaetter was forgotten. However, following upon the publication of a biography in 1964, this modern martyr began to receive the attention he deserved. Sermons extolling his sacrifice were preached in Austria, Great Britain, the United States, and elsewhere in the world; pilgrimages began to visit the grave in the St. Radegund churchyard where his ashes had been given ceremonial burial after the war; Austrian television prepared a prize-winning film for prime-time showing. In short, this man who lived and died in almost total obscurity is now recognized as a national hero and, as Archbishop Roberts declared in that Vatican II intervention referred to earlier, a hero to his Church as well.

No one would have been more surprised by this attention than Jaegerstaetter himself. He went to his death knowing that his fellow villagers regarded him as mentally unbalanced by religious fanaticism; none of the priests he had consulted gave him any encouragement in his stand. Even his bishop, in a face-to-face meeting, told him he had no right to judge the justice or injustice of the war. So he would have been surprised—though not necessarily too impressed. After all, as he saw it, what others thought of him and his decision made little difference. It was a matter between him and his conscience, between him and his God.

What would please him though (and it is here that we find justification for honoring him as a peace leader) is the extent to which his prison letters and other occasional writings have given inspiration and support to others in their opposition to war and military service. During the tragic Vietnam years, peace activists in the United States, including such prominent figures as Daniel and Philip Berrigan and Daniel Ellsberg, acknowledged the influence his story had had upon them. Other young people, faced with a call to service in a war they believed immoral and unjust, drew moral strength from the heroic example of this simple Austrian peasant as they, too, chose prison over compliance with evil.

Bibliography:

B. Gordon C. Zahn, *In Solitary Witness: The Life and Death of Franz Jaegerstaetter* (New York, 1964).

Gordon C. Zahn

JAKSCH, Wenzel (25 September 1896, Langstrobnitz, Bohemia, Austrian Empire [now Czechoslovakia] 27 November 1966, Wiesbaden, Federal Republic of Germany). *Education*: elementary school and self-educated. *Career*: Social Democratic politician and writer.

Wenzel Jaksch was the son of a poor Bohemian-German mason and after a rudimentary education he pursued his father's occupation. In 1913 he joined the socialist youth movement. After serving in the Austrian army in the years 1917–18 he returned to Southern Bohemia where, in 1919, he joined the German Social Democratic party in the new Czechoslovak Republic. Here his rapid rise to prominence started. His goal was to work for the well-being of the underprivileged, to achieve equality between the nationalities of Czechoslovakia, and thus bring peace and prosperity to the large German minority and the whole country. The party provided the ambitious Jaksch with a platform, first as editor of several social democratic newspapers and then from 1929 to 1938 as a deputy of the German Social Democratic party in the Czechoslovak parliament.

The world economic crisis of the 1930s hit the industrialized northern regions of Bohemia hard. At that time the very serious social and economic problems of the German worker also assumed a grave national dimension under the impact of both the rabid nationalistic propaganda of the Hitler inspired and guided Sudeten German party and the mistakes of the Czech nationality policy. In this situation Jaksch concluded that the German Social Democratic party in Czechoslovakia needed a more national and less Marxist direction. He desired to counter the Hitler inspired propaganda and to prevent the drifting of the desperate workers into the Sudeten German party. Under the influence of Otto Strasser—a former follower of Adolf Hitler, who had to flee Germany in July 1934—Jaksch wrote a book *Volk und Arbeiter* (*People and Worker*) in 1936, in which he revealed his ideas for a reorganization of the party. Declaring that Marxist theory did not always reflect reality, he tried to introduce a popularized version of socialism (*Volkssozialismus*) with some nationalistic coloring by replacing the term class by nation. He argued further that the military armaments race was the road to disaster. Jaksch supported close cooperation with the Czech government in order to solve the Sudeten question. In a speech in December 1937, he maintained that it would be wrong to create the impression that all Czechs wanted to push the Germans to the wall and that all Germans had taken an oath to destroy the Czech state. Looking at the world situation, Jaksch again attacked the armaments race which he called a mistaken investment of national wealth, and he advocated trade with the Soviet Union for economic reasons and in the interest of peace.

At the end of March 1938, Jaksch was elected chairman of the German Social

Democratic party with the moral support of President +Eduard Beneš and against the protest of the orthodox wing of the party and the unions. Before his election Jaksch had written in an article that a German-Czech peace could be achieved only by political and linguistic equality for both nations and the recognition of the Germans as the second people of state (Das zweite Staatsvolk). His efforts along these lines were cut short by the Munich Agreement of September 29, 1938, which gave the predominantly German part of Czechoslovakia to Nazi Germany and led to the dissolution of the German Social Democratic party of Czechoslovakia. Jaksch was instrumental in organizing the emigration of more than 3,000 party members thereby saving them from potential persecution by Nazis.

The occupation of Prague in March 1939 caught Jaksch by surprise, and he fled across Poland and Sweden to England. There he published in September 1939 a pamphlet *Was kommt nach Hitler?* (*What comes after Hitler*?). In it he developed a program for the remnants of the party. He demanded the right of self-determination for the Germans in Czechoslovakia and federalization of the country within a federalized Central Europe with Germany as a member. The Germans in the new Czechoslovakia should have their own administration, government, and parliament. The most controversial part of Jaksch's ideas was the proposal to solve the Czech-German minority question by a transfer and exchange of population. Many people reproached Jaksch for having been the first one to originate the idea of the transfer—i.e. expulsion of the Sudeten Germans—which was carried out in 1945 by the Czechs.

The years from 1939 to 1945 were the most tragic, disappointing, and controversial years of Jaksch's life. His combination of idealism and nationalism alienated many friends while his inflexible adherence to his preconceived goals and his methods of action led to a split in the Social Democratic party and to the break with Beneš. All his dreams for postwar Czechoslovakia not only came to naught, but the Germans were expelled from their homeland.

After the war, the allies at the instigation of the Czechoslovak government did not allow Jaksch to move to Germany. Only in 1949 did he succeed in settling in Wiesbaden in the German Federal Republic. In 1950 he was elected to the Executive Committee of the German Social Democratic party. He turned his attention once again to the ideas of peace and better relations between nations. In 1953 he was elected to the parliament of the Federal Republic of Germany and remained a member until his death in 1966. He was preoccupied chiefly with foreign affairs, especially with relations with Eastern Europe. In 1961 he recommended the establishment of better relations with the East advocating especially economic cooperation with them. Jaksch's role as the president of several expellee organizations was used by the East European countries to accuse him of revanchism. His publications and especially his book, *Europe's Road to Potsdam*, prove this charge false. Jaksch strove to be a mediator between nations and he believed that federalization of Central Europe and of the Danube Basin would be the best way to peace and security.

Bibliography:

A. *Benesch war gewarnt* (Munich, 1949); *Can Industrial People be Transferred? The Future of the Sudeten Population* (London, 1943); *Europe's Road to Potsdam* (New York, 1964); *Sozialistische Möglichkeiten in unserer zeit* (London, 1944); *Volk und Arbeiter* (Bratislava, 1936); *Was kommt nach Hitler*? (London, 1939) *Westeuropa-Osteuropa-Sowjetunion* (Bonn, 1965).

B. Martin Bachstein, *Wenzel Jaksch und die Sudetendeutsche Sozialdemokratie* (Munich, 1974); Edmund Jauerning, *Sozialdemokratie und Revanchismus* (Berlin [East] 1968); Seliger Gemeinde Stuttgart, *Wenzel Jaksch, Sucher und Künder* (Munich, 1967); Seliger Gemeinde Stuttgart, *Wenzel Jaksch, Patriot und Europaer* (Munich, 1967); *Neue Deutsche Biographie*, X (Berlin, 1974): 326–7.

Fred Hahn

JAMIESON, Laura Emma (29 December 1888, Park Head, Ontario, Canada—3 July 1964, Vancouver, British Columbia). *Education*: B.A., Univ. of Toronto, 1908. *Career*: journalist, feminist, judge, and provincial and municipal politician.

During the First World War, Laura Jamieson was associated with a small group of disgruntled feminists and pacifists in Vancouver. When this group became the Vancouver branch of the Women's International League for Peace and Freedom (WILPF) in 1921, she became its president and later national secretary for the Canadian Section she helped organize. Through her writings for WILPF publications, the *Western Producer* and reprints of her pacifist poetry, she inspired other branches in Toronto and Saskatoon.

Jamieson rejected most of the contemporary notions of peace being achieved through the League of Nations, arbitration, or disarmament. For her, peace was not merely the cessation of war, but a way of life built on cooperative human relationships that allowed for the peaceful release of emotions and exchange of ideas. She looked to women as the advocates of peace, arguing that child bearers were more likely to understand the inhumanity of war. They had developed a cooperative spirit during the industrial revolution and subsequently used it in winning the franchise and promoting moral and social reforms. By developing cooperative enterprises the aggressive spirit and selfish nationalism of the capitalistic economic system could be destroyed. She hoped that once Canadians showed the way, the WILPF could spread the message throughout the world. In 1926 she became a juvenile court judge and this gave an added prestige to her ideas.

Experiences in the depression made her take a more radical socialist position which few of her readers appreciated. In 1938 she resigned from the bench to sit as a socialist member of the provincial legislative assembly and later as a municipal alderman. Her crusading spirit for justice and decency, and cooperative, peaceful living remained, but her perspective was much more parochial.

Bibliography:

B. Vancouver *Province*, July 4, 1964; Vancouver *Sun*, July 3, 1964.

C. Laura Jamieson Papers, Provincial Archives of British Columbia, Victoria, B.C.

Donald M. Page

JANNASCH, Lilli (1872?, Germany). *Career*: journalist, author, publisher, and graphologist.

Apart from the fact that she was the daughter of a German professor and half French, little else is known about the details of Lilli Jannasch's life. The perceptiveness of her diagnosis of German militarism, however, distinguished her from many other female representatives of the German peace movement. She became associated with organized pacifism via the Deutsche Gesellschaft für ethische Kultur (German Society for Ethical Culture), which *Wilhelm J. Foerster had founded, and of which she had been a member since the beginning of this century. A contributor to the journal *Ethische Kultur* since 1903, she took part in the founding of the Deutsche Liga für weltliche Schule und Moralunterricht (German League for Secular and Moral Education) in November 1906, serving as secretary in the League's directorate.

In October 1914 Jannasch founded the Bund Neues Vaterland (New Fatherland League) (BNV), in cooperation with *Albert Einstein, *Otto Lehmann-Russbuldt, *Kurt von Tepper-Laski, and others. One month previously, in Berlin, she founded the Neues Vaterland publishing house, which published Lehmann-Russbüldt's *Die Schöpfung der Vereinigten Statten von Europa* (*The Creation of the United States of Europe*). As the administrative director of the BNV she opposed—at great personal sacrifice—the German annexation policy, and supported a speedily negotiated peace and a democratic reorganization of domestic political life. She was arrested at the end of March 1916 and, without a trial, imprisoned for four months on suspicion of "treason." She owed her release to the efforts of her family and influential friends such as *Hugo Haase. Although forbidden by the military authorities to engage in any kind of political activity for the duration of the war, she continued her pacifist work.

Her expectation that the November Revolution (1918) would bring about a new orientation in German politics quickly gave way to a more realistic assessment. In 1918 she sharply criticized the churches for refusing to support pacifist policies. She denounced the prowar stance of the church and the alliance of "altar and throne" in the First World War, and called for a "mass exit from the churches." Within the framework of the German branch of the Women's International League for Peace and Freedom, she supported "vigorous antimilitarist propaganda among the masses" and the concept of conscientious objection to military service. As a member of the Internationaler Sekretariat für Erziehung im Geiste des Pazifismus (International Secretariat for Education in the Spirit of Pacifism), she worked for peace education and international reconciliation. In her many articles in pacifist journals she advocated a federal solution of the German question, dealt critically with the nationalistic tendencies of the large women's organizations, and called for a spiritual and moral revolution in Germany.

Franco-German rapprochement became the focus of her postwar efforts for peace. She castigated the "soul destroying power of Prussian militarism" and the "mendacious propaganda of German Nationalist circles." In "Crimes of Prussian-German Militarism in Occupied France and Belgium" (1924), she documented German breaches of international law, annexations plans, and inhuman treatment of civilians in occupied Belgium and Northern France during World War I. Her influence, however, was restricted to pacifist groups. She passionately refuted the racialist propaganda of German nationalism about the so-called "black shame"—i.e. the presence of African colonial troops in the French occupation forces in Germany after the war. In 1923 Jannasch initiated the "fund for reconciliation with the French and Belgian people" as atonement for the destruction and devastation wreaked by German troops as they withdrew from France and Belgium. At the Third International Democratic Congress in Freiburg/Breisgau, a considerable sum of money was handed over to the French left-Catholic pacifist, *Marc Sangnier. Later money was collected in France to alleviate human suffering and distress in the industrial Ruhr in 1923.

In the occupied zone of Germany Jannasch organized numerous lecture tours, one of which featured the Generals *Paul von Schoenaich (German) and Verraux (French) in ten large Rhenish cities. In order to combat the anti-French agitation and the lies in the German press about French atrocities in the Rhineland, she published information about German-French pacifist initiatives. She also founded the Rhenish group of the Deutsche Liga für Menschenrechte (German League for Human Rights) and, in cooperation with French members of the same organization, she initiated the Franco-German League in the Rhineland.

In 1927–28 Jannasch came to the conclusion that "every creative, revolutionary spirit" was doomed to failure in the face of the superior force of the nationalist agitation in Germany. Therefore, she ceased all political activity in order not to create the false impression abroad that German pacifism was a force to be reckoned with. After her withdrawal from politics, she worked as a graphologist, first in Wiesbaden, then in Frankfurt/Main. In the spring of 1933, after the Nazi seizure of power, her house was searched and she was interrogated in the Frankfurt Police Headquarters. She fled to France to escape imprisonment. She settled in Strasbourg where she once again established herself as a graphologist. Nothing more is known of her fate.

Bibliography:

A. *Schwarze Schmach und schwarz-weiss-rote Schande* (Flugschriften des BNV, Nos. 18/21, Berlin, 1921); *Untaten des preussisch-deutschen Militarismus im besetzten Frankreich und Belgien* (Wiesbaden 1924).

Helmut Donat
Trans. by William J. Hopkins

JÄRNEFELT, Arvid (16 November 1861, Pulkova, Finland—27 December 1932, Lohja, Finland). *Education*: B. A., Helsinki Univ., 1885, Master of Law, 1890. *Career*: journalist, shoemaker, farmer, and author.

Arvid Järnefelt was born into a Finnish-Russian family. From his father, a Finnish-born general, he adopted Finnish nationalism and through his Russian-born mother, he adopted an intellectual liberalism and artistic creativity. Järnefelt was expected to have a brilliant career as a lawyer and politician, but, after familiarizing himself with the doctrines and action of *Leo Tolstoy, he gave up the pursuit of a social career and became a freelance author. In his articles of faith called *Heräämiseni* (*My Awakening*) (1894), he gave an account of his attitude towards sexual morals, Christianity, war, and social questions. Like his master, Tolstoy, he also questioned the action of the state and the church. He felt that the church had turned into a mere tool of exploitation, that Christianity would be best fulfilled in everyday work and life, and that it did not need support from any irrational belief or separate institution.

Järnefelt bought a small farm in Vieremä, Lohja, and began to put into practice the life style of his master. Within a couple of years his farm became Finland's "Jasnaja Poljana," where Finnish Tolstoians, theosophists, social utopians and representatives of the peace movement visited him. Like Tolstoy, Järnefelt considered war as one of mankind's worst plagues. In his novel *Helena* (1902) he wrote that the most useless of all professions was that of a soldier. He found it impossible to find anything good in war; all it created was grief and bloodshed. According to Järnefelt it was better to refuse to kill even at the expense of one's own life, than to kill and lose one's human dignity.

Järnefelt was quite radical in his social thinking. He demanded social reforms and wrote and spoke on behalf of farm laborers and small tenant farmers in particular. He approved of the aims of the labor movement, but was not a socialist himself. The basis of his social program was Tolstoyism plus the idea of an agrarian reform put forward by Henry George, an American. In 1917 he tried to conciliate the social contradictions which he quite rightly saw leading up to a bloody civil war. He gave a series of speeches in the churches of Helsinki, in which he specified his resistance towards church, state, welfare, and social injustice.

Järnefelt condemned outright all wars and violence, yet he joined no peace organization. In his opinion peace and Christianity had to become central to the daily lives of human beings. Peace and Christianity would come about through practice, not through institutions or organizations.

Järnefelt's literary works were largely forgotten after his death, but his actions and thoughts about church, state, rights and responsibilities, war, and militarism continued to have influence. In many of the mass movements following the Second World War, "Järnefeltician" attitudes were still visible.

Bibliography:

A. *Helena* (Helsinki, 1902); *Heräämiseni* (Helsinki, 1894); *Maa kuuluu kaikille* (Helsinki, 1907).

B. Pekka Häkli, *Arvid Järnefelt ja hänen maailmansa* (Porvoo, 1955); Pekka Lounela,

Ken talonsa jättää, Järnefelt (Helsinki, 1977); Armo Nokkala, *Tolstoilaisuus Arvid Suomessa* (Helsinki, 1958).

Kalevi Kalemaa
Trans. by Oliver and Rita Whitehead

JAURÈS, Jean Léon (3 September 1859, Castres, France—31 July 1914, Paris). *Education*: Lycée Sainte-Barbe, Paris, 1876–78; agrégé, École Normale Supérieure, 1881; Ph.D., Univ. of Paris, 1892. *Career*: professor of philosophy, Univ. of Toulouse, 1883–85, 1889–92; member, Chamber of Deputies (from Tarn), 1885–89, 1893–98, 1902–14; editor, *L'Humanité*, 1904–14.

Jean Jaurès, a central figure in French socialism, a founder of one of France's most important newspapers, and an important socialist scholar, emerged in the years before World War I as a leading French pacifist.

The nature and importance of Jaurès' efforts for peace are reflected in his background. Born to a rural middle-class family, Jaurès quickly exhibited the intellectual talents that would make him one of the most renowned orators and respected socialist writers in France. After teaching and completing his doctoral dissertation in the 1880s, he integrated his concern for the working class and his interest in politics in a career as a socialist member of the Chamber of Deputies. With the exception of a defeat in 1898 caused by his pro-Dreyfusard stand, Jaurès was elected to the Chamber from 1892 until his death in 1914.

Jaurès was a neo-Marxist, moderate socialist. While accepting much of Marx's theory of the class struggle and economic determinism, he also believed in idealism, the possibility of socialism by evolution, and the uniqueness of France's historical experience. Jaurès, therefore, was willing to work with the middle class and its leaders in government and to accept some elements of nationalism.

Such views brought Jaurès into prominence and into conflict with other socialists. He became one of the leaders of the French socialists during the first years of the twentieth century, but also became involved in factional disputes—in part over his willingness to work with nonsocialist governments. Yet he maintained a position of leadership and increased his influence by helping other leading socialists to found *L'Humanité*, which was to become the major organ of French socialism.

During the final ten years of his life, Jaurès became increasingly concerned with the problem of war. He, like other socialists, analyzed war as a product of capitalism, something which held nothing of benefit for workers of any country. He argued that France was wasting her resources in military preparations and imperialist efforts, thus deterring economic and especially industrial growth. Increasingly he saw imperialism as a primary cause of war. He thought that war was a constant probability between Russia and Austria over the Balkans, between England and Germany over commercial and naval rivalry, and between France and Germany over Morocco. Moreover, he argued that European imperialism would inevitably give way to nationalism and revolution in the newly established colonies.

His growing concerns with the possibility of war with Germany led him in 1907 to embark upon a project which resulted in a book, *L'Organisation socialiste de la France: L'Armée nouvelle*, in which he developed his ideas for institutionalizing steps toward pacifism. The book culminated in a legislative proposal, which he placed before the Chamber of Deputies in 1910. With this proposal, Jaurès hoped to establish a working formula for peace, or at least the minimization of warfare. He argued that the new army should be effective as a defensive force, but ineffective when it came to offense. Its strength would make it a good deterrent to potential foreign aggressors; its weakness a restraint to French governmental and military officials harboring dreams of aggressive military action. Second, he argued that by infusing the ranks and especially the officer corps with working-class people, the army would be dominated by people who were inherently pacific. Third, Jaurès sought to incorporate the principles of pacifism and the use of arbitration into his proposal; making a declaration of war without previous public efforts toward arbitration a cause for rallying against an aggressive government rather than rallying behind it.

Jaurès felt that his proposed reorganization of the military would lead toward the socialization of France. In the years before World War I, European socialism seemed more robust every day. The working classes throughout Europe were growing in numbers, consciousness, and sophistication, as were the socialist parties. To Jaurès and other socialists, the forces of history seemed to be with socialism, whether by evolution or revolution. A reorganization of European society along socialistic lines was not just a utopian dream; it was sufficiently foreseeable to enable Jaurès to propose a socialistic arrangement of France's army with some hope of success. Once the army became democratized and socialized as he proposed, other institutions would be more easily transformed. In turn, any victory for socialism was seen as a victory for pacifism. Jaurès believed that the establishment of a socialist society would eliminate most if not all causes for war, and he hoped that his proposal would be an important step in that direction.

Nevertheless, that proposal never came up for vote or discussion. Most army officers, political leaders, and newspaper editors viewed it as naive fantasy. As World War I approached, Jaurès continued to argue that a peaceful solution was possible until the end. This stand won him and his followers ridicule and accusations of treason. Jaurès was finally stopped by the bullet of an emotionally disturbed assassin only a few days before the outbreak of the Great War. The subsequent quick about-face by French and German socialists made Jaurès' campaign for reconciliation and pacifism look vain and unrealistic. On August 4, the French socialist deputies voted for all measures of national defense proposed by the government. Socialists failed or were unable to place their loyalty to the international working class above the nation. Nevertheless, in the years following World War I, Jaurès' stature as a socialist and pacifist grew. Today he is regarded as one of the most honored figures of French history.

Bibliography:

A. *Discours parlementaires* (Paris, 1904); *Études socialistes* (Paris, 1902); *Histoire socialiste de la revolution française* (8 vols., Paris, 1901–8); *L'Organisation socialiste de la France: L'Armée nouvelle* (Paris, 1911).

B. Samuel Bernstein, "Jaurès and War," *Science and Society*, 4 (Summer, 1940), 127–64; Harvey Goldberg, *The Life of Jean Jaurès* (Madison, 1962); Charles Rapport, *Jean Jaurès* (Paris, 1915); Roland N. Stromberg, "La Patrie en Danger: Socialism and War in 1914," *Midwest Quarterly*, 18 (1977), 268–85; Harold R. Weinstein, *Jean Jaurès: A Study of Patriotism in the French Socialist Movement* (New York, 1936).

Dennis M. Sherman

JAY, William (16 June 1789, New York—14 October 1858, Bedford, NY). *Education*: B.A., Yale Coll., 1807, private law study, Albany. *Career*: founder and supporter of Bible and temperance societies, county judge, abolitionist, and antiwar writer.

William Jay publicly committed himself to the cause of peace in the biography of his father, Chief Justice John Jay (1833) by vigorously defending his success in avoiding war with Great Britain through the negotiated settlement of thorny disputes in mixed commissions.

War and Peace (1842) brought its author to the forefront of the American peace movement. Hailed by *The Advocate of Peace* as a "work of great beauty" by "one of the best writers in the land," the book amplified familiar arguments with new emphases. It became at once a major primer of peace principles and objectives. In this short, forceful treatise and elsewhere Jay appealed to common sense in spelling out the economic costs of war and preparation for it, contending that both robbed the public purse at the expense of worthy civilian needs.

In appealing to history Jay offered plausible as well as questionable examples. He accepted the use of force to keep domestic order and suppress piracy and banditry and even conceded that it might as a last resort be employed in national self-defense. But no war, he claimed, had ever been fought that negotiation might not have prevented. He refuted the self-defense argument with reference to the American Revolution and other wars. Citing examples, he concluded that more wars had resulted in suppressing than in winning freedom. Against the argument that preparedness was the best safeguard for preventing war, Jay recalled the failure of Napoleon's formidable armies to prevent bloodshed. Nor did experience support war in defense of national honor. Great Britain's scandalous justification of the Opium War against China by appeals to national honor was only one historical example. Further, both the Napoleonic wars and the Crimean War showed the misleading nature of "the balance of power" theory—"a Devil's trap." Again, the historical record showed that unexpected contingencies often defeated the rational expectations held when a war was begun.

Jay broke new ground in his appeals to human nature. His view of the relation between human nature on the one hand and war and peace on the other was shaped by Federalist doctrine, the Episcopal Church's reconciliation of determinism and free will, and his own reading of the Bible. War did indeed result from man's deep-seated, ineradicable lust. But, since man to some extent was a free agent, he could limit or even abolish it. Recognizing the emotional aspect of human nature, Jay appealed to compassion in his graphic pictures of the brutal horrors of the battlefield and the effect of the toll on families. Another example of Jay's use of the human nature argument was his reminder that violence, cruelty, and death hardened the heart and depraved the mind. An understanding of human nature further showed that having the power to commit aggression made it all the easier to do so and that military strength excited fear, jealousy, and hostility among other peoples.

Jay did not stop with his effort to influence public opinion by all these appeals to history and human nature, though he regarded this effort as the first necessary step toward a peaceful world. Building on his father's commitment to negotiation, he proposed the incorporation in the next treaty between the United States and France of a clause stipulating that when diplomacy failed to resolve future disputes, each government would accept the outcome of the negotiation of a friendly nation to whom the dispute had been submitted. Jay held that such a promising experiment would provide a model for similar provisions in treaties every government might make with another. In his view the practicality of his proposal lay in its "extreme simplicity."

Though public opinion was not yet ready for a Congress of Nations, Jay saw no reason why such an institution might not ultimately be established. The plan found favor in peace circles on both sides of the Atlantic. *Joseph Sturge, president of the London Peace Society, made it possible for every member of Parliament to receive a copy of *War and Peace*. In the House of Commons *Richard Cobden introduced a resolution embodying the main features of the Jay plan. Though immediate success was not at hand, the idea was later embodied in several treaties, notably those that Secretary of State *William Jennings Bryan negotiated in +Woodrow Wilson's first administration.

In attributing the origin of slavery to war Jay saw a close connection between the two institutions. His full-fledged involvement in the anti-Garrison wing of the abolition cause resulted in a good deal of writing in which connections between war and slavery were made explicit. In *The Creole Case* (1841) he argued that black fugitive slaves had the same right as masters to defend themselves even if this involved killing. However deeply felt Jay's commitment to preserving peace by compromise, he harshly rebuked northern members of Congress for their concessions to secession-threatening Southerners in the Compromise of 1850. After much weighing of his conscience he had decided to resign his judgeship if and when he was required to have any part in the return of a fugitive slave. Had he lived longer he would have been faced by a conflict between his oppostion to war and his commitment to the slave's freedom.

As president of the American Peace Society for a decade before his death, Jay supported its activities with undiminished engagement. His role was welcomed, especially by conservatives in the movement. His testimony was valued because of his reputation for benevolence in the early organization of temperance and Bible societies, the prestige, wealth, and social position of his family, and his courage in openly rebuking those bishops in his beloved Episcopal Church who frowned on peace societies and who favored slavery. Experience in law and as a judge gave added importance to his systematic and acute analysis of motives for war as did his precise and conservatively practical plan for its limitation.

Bibliography:

A. *An Address delivered before the American Peace Society* (Boston, 1845); *The Eastern War; An Argument for the Cause of Peace* (Boston, 1855); *The Life of John Jay; with Selections from his Correspondence* (2 v., New York, 1833); *A Review of the Causes and Consequences of the Mexican War* (Boston, 1849, New York, 1969); *War and Peace: The Evils of the First and a Plan for Preserving the Last* (New York, 1842, 1919).

B. Franklin Bowditch Dexter, *Biographical Sketches of the Graduates of Yale College, Sept. 1805-Sept. 1815* (New Haven, 1912); William M. Wiecek, "The Problem of Unjust Laws . . . ", in Lewis Perry and Michael Fellman, eds. *Antislavery Reconsidered: New Perspectives on the Abolitionists* (Baton Rouge, LA, 1975).

Merle Curti

JEANSON, Henri (6 March 1900, Paris—6 November 1970, Honfleur, Calvados, France). *Education*: communal school, Lycée Henri IV. *Career*: journalist, dramatist, screen writer, and polemicist.

Wit and satire were the weapons that Henri Jeanson used in his long struggle against war. The son of a professor of economics, he enjoyed a comfortable middle class childhood. But he early developed a rebelliousness and disregard for authority that would mark his entire adult life. After completing his education, Jeanson tried a variety of careers, eventually becoming an actor who played minor parts in small productions. Although he eventually abandoned the stage, Jeanson never lost his taste for the theatrical. During World War I, in which he was too young to serve, he turned his hand to journalism. Jeanson demonstrated his skill when he wrote a column on military affairs for *La Bataille syndicaliste* under the pseudonym of "General N."

After the conflict, Jeanson authored several plays and film scripts that displayed his talent for clever dialogue. But his sympathies for the left and the cause of peace became increasingly important in his work. He contributed regularly to the satirical and pacifist reviews *Le Canard enchaìné* and *Le Crapouillot* (edited by his friend *Jean Galtier-Boissière) as well as to the antiwar daily *La Flèche*. As the threat of war grew stronger, the columnist turned his fire against his own government, which he believed was pushing France into a conflict that would repeat the mistakes of 1914–18. Particularly during the premiership of Edouard Daladier, Jeanson found much to attack in matters of foreign and domestic policy.

In November 1938 he went so far as to condone the assassination of the German embassy secretary von Rath by the young Jewish refugee Grynszpan. This led the goverment to prosecute him for the offense to a foreign power.

In 1938–39 Jeanson contributed frequently to the anarchist and pacifist weekly *Solidarité internationale antifasciste*. One of his columns, entitled "Live Free and Not Die," declared that his body was his own and was not subject to use by the military in the event of war. A month later, Jeanson signed the manifesto *Paix immédiate*, which called for an end to the war in Europe. Nonetheless, Jeanson obeyed his summons to military duty and served without incident until he was suddenly arrested and imprisoned in November for "incitement to disobedience." He spent some eight months in prison, being released shortly before the fall of France. During the German occupation, the undaunted Jeanson founded *Aujourd'hui*, a daily newspaper that attempted to adhere to an independent position. It frequently criticized the actions of Marshal Pétain and called for the release of those pacifists who had been imprisoned under Daladier. Because of his forthrightness, Jeanson was removed as editor after two months and soon imprisoned by the German authorities when they learned of his earlier article praising Grynszpan. Released in 1942, Jeanson joined the Resistance and remained underground for the rest of the year.

After the Liberation, Jeanson returned to his work as screen writer and free-thinking columnist, but he took no further role in the pacifist movement. At his death, he was one of France's leading writers and satirists.

Bibliography:

A. *Soixante-dix ans d'adolescence* (Paris, 1971).

B. "Henri Jeanson," *Dictionnaire biographique français contemporaine* (2nd ed., Paris, 1954), 350–51; *Le Monde*, November 8–9, 1970.

James Friguglietti

JOAD, Cyril Edwin Mitchinson (12 August 1891, Durham, England—9 April 1953, Hempstead, England). *Education*: Blundell's, Tiverton; M.A., Bailliol Coll., Oxford Univ., 1915; D.Litt., Univ. of London, 1936. *Career*: civil servant, 1914–30; head, Dept. of Philosophy, Birkbeck Coll., Univ. of London, 1930–53.

C.E.M. Joad, popular philosopher of the 1930s and the 1940s, belonged to that generation indelibly marked by the experience of World War I, although he did not himself see actual combat. After leaving Oxford, where he had been John Locke Scholar in Moral Philosophy, Joad entered the Home Civil Service. He received an appointment as a junior official in the Labour Exchange Department of the Board of Trade. At this stage in his career, Joad's political allegiance was to the revolutionary Socialist Independent Labour party.

While a civil servant Joad embarked on his prolific career as an author of popular philosophical and political works. Eventually he published forty-seven volumes on various topics. In 1930 Joad left the Ministry of Labour to become head of the Philosophy Department at Birkbeck College, University of London.

This move sparked by frustration at his lack of advancement in his career as a government official as well as dissatisfaction with the narrowness of the scope for positive reform offered by the civil service. Joad retained his position at Birkbeck College until his death in 1953.

During the interwar period Joad elaborated his views as both a pacifist and an agnostic. His pacifism was of a "utilitarian" nature, as he explained in his 1939 publication *Why War*? For Joad, as for so many of his contemporaries, the uselessness and waste of World War I led him to doubt the efficacy of any war. Joad tirelessly propounded his views in print and in public forums. In 1933 he was present as a guest speaker when the Oxford Union debated and approved the famous motion "That this house will in no circumstance fight for King and Country." He became a sponsor of the Peace Pledge Union after its formation in 1936 and was also chairman of the National Peace Council in 1938.

Joad's commitment to pacifism, severely shaken by the rise of Adolf Hitler, did not survive the outbreak of World War II. He first resigned his sponsorship of the Peace Pledge Union, and then lent his prestige to the war effort by conducting a series of talks on philosophical topics for the BBC. His disenchantment with pacifism paralleled an increasing religiosity. In Joad's view the existence of evil in the world entailed an obligation to struggle against evil utilizing all available weapons, including force. Fascism was of course the particular evil Joad had in mind. He recorded the evolution of his views in the autobiographical *The Recovery of Belief* (1952).

Joad's pacifism reflected rather than shaped British opinion. As a popular writer and teacher, he articulated and reinforced the sentiments of a generation disillusioned with war. The contrast between his views in 1933, when he spoke in support of the peace motion put before the Oxford Union, and the views he expressed in his talks for the BBC during the war years, aptly symbolizes the development of those who found themselves, despite previous affirmations to the contrary, taking up arms in yet another European war during the 1940s.

Bibliography:

A. *The Book of Joad* (London, 1935); *The Recovery of Belief* (London, 1952); *Why War*? (London, 1939).

B. Martin Ceadel, *Pacifism in Britain 1914–1945: The Defining of a Faith* (Oxford, 1980); LT, April 10, 1953.

Gail L. Savage

JOHN XXIII [Born Angelo Giuseppe Roncalli] (25 November 1881, Bergamo, Italy—3 June 1963, Rome). *Education*: studied for the priesthood at the Seminario Romano; ordained, August 10, 1910. *Career*: professor of theology and secretary to the Bishop of Bergamo, 1905–15; sergeant, then lieutenant, Italian Army, 1915–18; president, Sacred Society for the Propagation of the Faith, 1921–24; Archbishop of Aeropolis and Apostolic Visitor to Bulgaria, 1925–33; Papal Legate to Turkey and Greece, 1931–44; Papal Nuncio to Paris, 1944–52; Cardinal Patriarch of Venice, 1952–58; Pope, 1958–63.

Until he was elected as a "caretaker" Pope in 1958, there was little in Angelo Roncalli's career which distinguished him as a modern peace leader. He was born into a peasant family of sharecroppers, the eldest of thirteen children. His early calling to the priesthood was interrupted by voluntary service in the Italian army (1901–2) of which he wrote "I dislike this life intensely." After his ordination in 1904, Roncalli taught in the seminary and served his local Bishop until he was called back into the army in 1915. He served for one year as a sergeant in the Medical Corps and for three years as a lieutenant-chaplain.

After 1918 he held a series of diplomatic posts which were distinguished by his piety and aloofness from political concerns. He was reported to be an excellent diplomat and conciliator and demonstrated a constant concern for the poor. His foreign service in Bulgaria, Turkey, Greece, and France made him acutely aware of the problems of international peace, and during World War II he helped relieve the victims of war in Greece and prevented the Turkish government from returning to Germany over one hundred Jewish children who had escaped from the Nazis. If anything characterized Roncalli's career prior to the papacy it was his compassion for the poor, his active involvement in ecumenical affairs, and his lack of notoriety.

After the death of Pope Pius XII in 1958, Angelo Roncalli was elected to the papacy and it was thought that this "compromise" pope would merely serve in a "provisional" and "transitional" capacity. But John XXIII was to shock both the church and world by calling for renewal in the church through announcing the Second Vatican Council and through issuing his two historic social encyclicals *Mater et Magistra* (1961) and *Pacem in Terris* (1963). Through these and other publications and actions, John XXIII sought to counter the *mentalité maginot* of so many in the church and world who refused to face the challenges of justice and peace on an international level. Both Pope John's humble origins and his experience of depression and war were undoubted influences in his publication of *Mater et Magistra*, in which he called for social and economic justice at an international level and repeated his predecessors' concern that there could be no peace without justice as its basis.

But it was with the publication of *Pacem in Terris* that John radically challenged the thinking of so many in regard to international peace, the threat of nuclear weapons, and the need for an international juridical system which could outlaw war and promote justice. It is reliably reported that the recklessness of the Cuban missile crisis had a profound effect on the pope, but his own personal experiences with war also led him to call for not only an end to nuclear weapons but to war itself. While his predecessors as far back as Pope Leo XIII evidenced great concern over war (especially *Benedict XV), the unique contribution of John in *Pacem in Terris* was to galvanize the fears and hopes of so many outside the Catholic church (including the communist world) concerning the possibilities of nuclear holocaust and the necessity for disarmament. Within the Catholic church John's encyclical caused many—from Cardinal to layperson—to reexamine the church's fifteen-century-old acceptance of war, even if it be of the ''just'' variety. His words: ''In this age which boasts of its atomic power, it no longer makes sense to maintain that war is a fit instrument with which to repair the violation of justice'' undoubtedly directly led the world's bishops at Vatican II to ''evaluate war with an entirely new attitude.'' These same bishops issued the only condemnation at Vatican II declaring that ''Any act of war aimed indiscriminately at the destruction of entire cities or of extensive areas along with their population is a crime against God and man himself. It merits unequivocal and unhesitating condemnation.''

Clearly, *Pacem in Terris* is the *Rerum Novarum* of the twentieth century. Where *Rerum Novarum* opened the church to the plight of the working classes, *Pacem in Terris* challenged both church and world to alter radically the thousands of years of history in which war was held to be an acceptable method of settling disputes. The theme of peace dominated John XXIII's papacy. It has chartered the church on a course of rejecting its centuries old justification of war along with a return to the nonviolent quest for peace which dominated the first three centuries of Christianity. John XXIII's jovial personality, his personal warmth and humor, and his profound identification with the poor gave credibility to his words on peace and his papacy will long be remembered as one that fully opened the church to truly human concerns and to the advancement of human survival. Certainly the church, and perhaps the world, will not be the same because the humble peasant, Angelo Roncalli, accepted peacemaking as the essential ministry of a religious leader.

Bibliography:

A. *Discorsi, sessaggi, colloqui del Santo Padre Giovanni XXIII* (5 vol., Vatican City, 1961–64); *Encyclicals of Pope John XXIII* (Washington, 1965); *Journey of a Soul* (New York, 1980); *Mater et Magistra* (Rome, 1961); *Pacem in Terris* (Rome, 1963).

B. L. Algisi' *John the Twenty-Third.* (Westminster, Md., 1963); U. Groppi and S. Lombardi, *Above All a Shepherd: Pope John XXIII*, (New York, 1959); E. E. Hales, *Pope John and His Revolution*, (London, 1965); Alden Hatch, *A Man Named John*, (New York, 1965); ''Le Mysteré Roncalli,'' *Études*, 318 (1963); F. X. Murphy, *John XXIII Comes to the Vatican*, (New York, 1959).

Joseph J. Fahey

JOHNSON, Reverdy (21 May 1796, Annapolis, MD—10 February 1876, Annapolis, MD). *Education*: B.A., St. John's Coll., Annapolis, 1811. *Career*: lawyer; U.S. Senator from Maryland, 1845–49, 1863–68; U.S. Attorney-General, 1849–50; Minister to Great Britain, 1868–69.

As a border state politician committed to preservation of the Union, Reverdy Johnson was a member of the unsuccessful Washington Peace Conference of 1861 and fully supported its proposals to save the Union. During the Civil War he supported the Union and helped prevent the secession of Maryland. Emerging after the war as a friend of the embattled President Andrew Johnson, he was sent as Minister to Great Britain in 1868.

A firm proponent of Anglo-American friendship, he confronted three disputes between the two nations. They concerned the citizenship of naturalized Irish-Americans, particularly the Fenian nationalists arrested for agitation in Ireland; the international boundary through the San Juan islands in Puget Sound; and the American claims for damages inflicted by the British-built Confederate ships during the Civil War, especially the *Alabama*. Johnson secured a preliminary settlement of the naturalization question, although final agreement was delayed until the Motley-Clarendon Convention of 1870. He also obtained agreement for arbitration of the San Juan dispute and in his greatest diplomatic achievement, the Johnson-Clarendon Convention of 1869, a claims commission to settle all outstanding claims by either nation for the period after 1853.

The U. S. Senate promptly rejected the Johnson-Clarendon Convention as too pro-British, deploring its lack of specific mention of the *Alabama* claims or of a British statement of regret. After renewed negotiation the Treaty of Washington (1871) included specific mention of the *Alabama* claims and a British apology along with a system of arbitration to settle the claims as well as the San Juan dispute, which had been delayed.

Johnson's diplomatic efforts were unpopular during a wave of Anglophobia that swept the North after the Civil War. His own somewhat ostentatious expressions of friendship for Britain, including even a cordial greeting for John Laird, builder of the *Alabama*, did not suit the mood of the times. However, his efforts to seek peaceful reconciliation of Anglo-American tensions presaged the general direction of relations between the two countries in the late nineteenth and early twentieth centuries.

Bibliography:

B. Adrian Cook, *The Alabama Claims: American Politics and Anglo-American Relations: 1865–1872* (Ithaca, 1975); R. G. Gunderson, *Old Gentlemen's Convention: The Washington Peace Conference of 1861* (Madison, 1961); B. C. Steiner, *Life of Reverdy Johnson* (Baltimore, 1914); DAB, V, 112–14.

C. Reverdy Johnson Papers, Library of Congress.

John B. Weaver

JOLIOT-CURIE, Frédéric (19 March 1900, Paris—14 August 1958, Paris). *Education*: engineering degree, École de physique et de chimie industrielle, Paris, 1924. *Career*: physicist.

Frédéric Joliot-Curie had a commitment to peace that was deliberate, expressed in his decision to be "a Communist as a Frenchman, as a scientist and as a citizen." As a child, he heard stories of the Franco-Prussian War of 1870–71, of the encirclement of Paris, of his grandmother's death in Siege, and of family sufferings in that terrible period. His brother, moreover, was killed in the First World War.

When he began as a student in 1920 at the École de physique et de chimie industrielle (EPCI) in Paris, he came under the influence of Pierre Langevin, a distinguished physicist and a progressive in politics. Through him, in 1924, Joliot was interviewed by Marie Curie, and was engaged to work as her assistant.

Her laboratory was one of the very few, and most distinguished, world centers in the study of radioactivity. There he met and married her daughter, Irène, in 1926. Because they worked so well together, they adopted the name of Joliot-Curie. In 1933 they made their unique discovery of artificial radioactivity for which they received a Nobel prize.

In his speech at the award ceremony in Stockholm, Joliot predicted that in the near future scientists would be able to build up and break down the elements at will and that they would develop "transmutations of an explosive character, like chemical chain reactions, one transmutation provoking many others." He further predicted that such transmutations in matter would release enormous amounts of useful energy. His statement was a vision and a warning. Within three years his vision of nuclear fission was realized. Within ten years Hiroshima and Nagasaki were destroyed by atom bombs.

When the Germans occupied Paris in 1940, Joliot stayed in Paris to look after his laboratory and became one of the Resistance leaders. It was only after the war that he learned the atom bomb had been made and used. The effect on him was highly traumatic. He regarded such use of atomic fission as a great betrayal of science and of mankind. He had always considered science as a positive factor in human progress. After Hiroshima, he felt it had become a negative factor, a change that was largely the result of his own scientific work.

From then until his early death he engaged in peace activities. In April 1949 he declared open the World Congress of the Partisans of Peace in the Salle Pleyel in Paris. In 1950, in Stockholm, he stated that the main aim of the organization was to abolish nuclear weapons. That idea took form as the Stockholm Appeal, the true beginning of the world movement against atomic weapons. The Appeal to the people of the world read: "We demand the absolute banning of atomic weapons which are weapons of terror and of the mass destruction of whole populations." It also called for "rigorous international control" of atomic energy and sought international condemnation of any government resorting to the first use of atomic weapons. At the Second World Congress of the Partisans of Peace in Warsaw, 2,065 delegates from 80 countries set up the World Peace Council. Joliot was elected unanimously president of the organization, a position he held until his death.

Frédéric Joliot-Curie always believed in the widest possible approach to the problems of peace. He initiated negotiations through the World Federation of Scientific Workers, of which he was the first president, with such leaders as *Albert Einstein and *Bertrand Russell for international conferences of scientists. From this initiative came the Pugwash Movement, although its origins can be traced to a number of different sources. He was never able to take part in a Pugwash meeting. By the time they began his health was already poor. In March 1956 his wife died of leukemia; two years later he too died, probably a victim of radioactivity, but certainly exhausted from his peace activities.

Bibliography:

B. Pierre Biquard, *Frédéric Joliot-Curie et l'energie atomique* (Paris, 1961); Pierre Biquard, *Frédéric Joliot-Curie, the man and his theories* (London, 1965); Maurice Goldsmith, *Frédéric Joliot-Curie* (London, 1976); Michel Rouzé, *Frédéric Joliot-Curie* (Paris, 1950).

Maurice Goldsmith

JONES, Rufus Matthew (25 January 1863, South China, ME—16 June 1948, Haverford, PA). *Education*: B.A., Haverford Coll., 1885, M.A., 1886; studies at the Univ. of Heidelberg, 1887, and Univ. of Pennsylvania, 1893–95; M.A., Harvard Univ., 1901. *Career*: professor of philosophy; leading exponent of mysticism, Quaker leader and activist; first chairman, American Friends Service Committee, 1917.

Rufus Jones, reared in a Quaker family and educated in Friends' schools, accepted the peace testimony of the sect early in life and became a leading advocate of pacifism in the United States. In his first editorial in the *American Friend*, the national magazine he created by combining the *Friends Review* and the *Christian Worker* in 1894, he called for loyalty to the traditional peace testimony. He was a prominent figure in the first national peace conference of Friends in Philadelphia in 1901, and he worked for peace, along with his other concerns, in the years before the beginning of World War I. He rallied American support for the work of the Friends' Ambulance Unit and the Friends' War Victims Relief Committee in Britain, and shared in founding the Fellowship of Reconciliation in 1915.

When the American Friends Service Committee (AFSC) was formed in April, 1917, within the month after the United States entered World War I, Jones was asked to chair it. He headed the training program at Haverford College to prepare young men to do relief work overseas, interceded in Washington to obtain recognition of alternative service for pacifists, and later traveled overseas to observe the relief and reconstruction work of Quakers and others in the aftermath of hostilities. In *A Service of Love in Wartime* (1920), he told the story of this period. He chaired the AFSC until 1928, and again from 1935–1944, and was honorary chair when the AFSC, along with the Friends Service Council in Britain, won the Nobel Peace Prize in 1947.

Late in 1919, Jones received a letter from +Herbert Hoover asking that the AFSC undertake a massive child feeding program in Germany, which was suffering from the allied blockade. Quakers responded to this call, and in 1922 cooperated with Hoover and the American Relief Administration in famine relief in Soviet Russia. One of the high points of Jones' work for peace was his visit in 1938, with two younger Quakers, to Gestapo headquarters in Berlin to intercede on behalf of the Jews who were suffering dreadful persecution in Nazi Germany.

Stimulated by a research project as an undergraduate at Haverford, Jones delved deeply into the field of Christian mysticism during his entire career. His published works in this area included *Studies in Mystical Religion* (1909); *The Church's Debt to Heretics*, (1924); *New Studies in Mystical Religion* (1927);

and *The Flowering of Mysticism* (1939). His fifty published volumes also included several scholarly works on Quaker history and thought.

Rufus Jones was even better known as a lecturer than as an author. His deep faith, evident sincerity, and marvelous sense of humor made him a popular speaker on college campuses and before all sorts of audiences. He was awarded numerous honorary degrees on both sides of the Atlantic, and was warmly welcomed in all parts of the world as he traveled to share his message of hope.

Bibliography:

A. *The Church's Debt to Heretics* (New York, 1924); *The Later Periods of Quakerism* (2 vol., London, 1921); *The Nature and Authority of Conscience* (London, 1920); *The Quakers in the American Colonies* (London, 1911); A *Service of Love in War Time* (New York, 1920); *Social Law in the Spiritual World* (Philadelphia, 1904); *Spiritual Reformers in the Sixteenth and Seventeenth Centuries* (London, 1914); "A Rufus M. Jones Bibliography (1887–1948)," typescript in the Quaker Collection, Haverford College.

B. Harry Emerson Fosdick, ed., *Rufus Jones Speaks to our Time* (New York, 1951); Elizabeth Gray Vining, *Friend of Life, the Biography of Rufus M. Jones* (Philadelphia, 1958); DAB, Suppl. 4, 441–43.

C. Rufus M. Jones Papers, Quaker Collection, Haverford College.

Edwin B. Bronner

JONG, Albert de (29 April 1891, Amsterdam, Netherlands—27 July 1970, Heemstede, Netherlands). *Education*: Rijkskweekschool (teacher training college), Haarlem, 1906–10. *Career*: teacher, Amsterdam, 1911–16; independent stenographer, 1916–70.

Albert de Jong grew up in a working-class family of Frisian origin with strong libertarian socialist and free-thinking ideas. In 1914 he established personal contact with *Ferdinand Domela Nieuwenhuis, the most important advocate of these ideas in Holland during the late nineteenth and early twentieth centuries, and throughout World War I they appeared together at numerous antimilitarist gatherings. After the death of Nieuwenhuis in 1919, de Jong, a great orator and agitator, and a prolific and gifted writer, became Holland's most important propagandist of the libertarian socialist and revolutionary antimilitarist movement.

During the First World War de Jong was already involved, with Nieuwenhuis, *Bart de Ligt, and Jos Giesen in preparations to internationalize the struggle against war by reviving the International Anti-Militarist Union (IAMV), which had organized conferences in Amsterdam in 1904 and 1907. As a result, a third International Anti-Militarist Congress took place in The Hague in 1921, when it was also decided to establish a permanent International Anti-Militarist Bureau against War and Reaction (IAMB). In the struggle against the threat of a new world war, growing fascism, and the suppression of liberation movements in the colonies, the IAMV/IAMB played a leading role, especially in Holland.

In 1926, shortly after de Jong had succeeded Giesen as its secretary, the IAMB entered into formal cooperation with the Internationale Arbeiter Assoziation (International Working Men's Association) (IAA), the so-called Berlin International, which grouped syndicalists and other revolutionary trade unionists who, in 1922, had rejected the Moscow-dominated Comintern. Together IAMB and IAA created the International Anti-Militarist Commission (IAK). Its two secretaries, Arthur Lehning (for the IAA) and Albert de Jong (for the IAMB), were also joint editors of the IAK Press Service, set up to distribute antimilitarist articles and commentaries, in four and sometimes more languages, to some 750 journals and individuals worldwide. In the turbulent period 1928–38 this monthly service was widely acclaimed and used in antimilitarist circles. Conflicts between those who accepted and those who rejected violence in the antifascist struggle in the Spanish Civil War led to a rupture in the IAMB/IAMV, resulting in the demise of the IAMB and the IAK in 1938. The IAMV, however, survived until the Second World War.

In searching for ways to defend social revolutions against the background of attempts to crush the Bolshevik Revolution and the rise of the Red army, de Jong, and others in the anarcho-syndicalist and antimilitarist movement during the interwar period, helped develop a theory of nonviolent conflict resolution. In numerous speeches and writings de Jong argued that the most important task of the working class was to fight all varieties of militarism, not only capitalist militarism but the communist variety as well. He pointed out that by its very nature militarism was always an instrument for the suppression of the masses by an elite (who wants to maintain power and to continue exploitation), and was thus the implacable enemy of freedom. Military means, he maintained, could not be truly liberating and the workers' movement had to resist it by use of direct, economic action and by refusing conscription. De Jong believed that the adoption of such a strategy was dictated, moreover, by the modern techniques of war; pragmatic considerations rather than a rigid doctrine of nonviolence based on ethics or morality prescribed the means for achieving (and defending) a social revolution.

Organizationally de Jong was active not only in the antimilitarist movement, but equally in the anarcho-syndicalist one, both being inextricably linked in his life, his work, and his vision of a world without war or exploitation. He played an important role in the Nederlands Syndicalistisch Vakverbond (Netherlands Syndicalist Union) (NSV), which he represented in the IAA, and he became chairman of the NSV's anarcho-syndicalist faction (GSV) when it was established in 1926. In 1933 de Jong became editor of the NSV's weekly, *De Syndicalist*, and turned it into a militant, revolutionary organ of anarcho-syndicalism. Earlier from 1926 to 1931, he had been editor of *De Wapens Neder*, the organ of the IAMV. After the Second World War he edited *De Persdienst* and later *Buiten de Perken* (1961–64), journals which stimulated renewed interest in anarchism. After an active lifetime in this field, it was very appropriate that de Jong in his last years returned to the figure of Domela Nieuwenhuis, becoming his biographer.

Bibliography:

A. *Domela Nieuwenhuis* (The Hague, 1966); "Fragmenten uit mijn leven," *Buiten de Perken* (n.p., 1961–64); "Het revolutionnaire anti-militarisme in Nederland," in J. de Graaf et al., eds., *Handboek voor de vredesbeweging* (The Hague, 1954), 202–22; "*Onze*

Vloot" ontmaskerd! (Nieuwe Niedorp, 1935); *Oorlog tegen Hitler-Duitschland* (The Hague, 1933); *Over de verdediging van de revolutie* (n.p., 1930); *De praktijk van het anti-militarisme* (The Hague, 1921); *Toch weer? De SDAP en de oorlog. Neen nooit* (Haarlem, 1934); *25 Jaar oorlog aan den oorlog* (n.p., 1929).

B. "Albert de Jong in memoriam," *Vredesactie* (June-August, 1970), 1; Gernot Jochheim, *Antimilitaristische Aktions-theorie, Soziale Revolution und Soziale Verteidigung* (Assen/Amsterdam/ Frankfurt, 1977); Gernot Jochheim, "Een discussie over de verdediging van de revolutie," in Maria Hunink et al., eds., *Voor Arthur Lehning* (Baarn, 1979); R. de Jong, "Over mijn vader Albert Andries de Jong," *Mededelingenblad*, 39 (1971), 16–62; Arthur Lehning, *Ithaka* (Baarn, 1980), 133–39; Hans Ramaer, *De piramide der tirannie. Anarchisten in Nederland* (Amsterdam, 1977).

Peter van den Dungen

JONG VAN BEEK EN DONK, Benjamin de (29 March 1881, Gorinchem, Netherlands—31 January 1948, Geneva). *Education*: LL.D., Univ. of Leyden, 1909. *Career*: civil servant, Ministry of Justice, The Hague, 1907–16; peace activist.

Benjamin de Jong van Beek en Donk's interest in social reform first showed itself in his concern for the improvement of housing legislation. It was the subject of both his doctoral dissertation and of his work in the Ministry of Justice. The initial impetus for his interest in peace had come from Professor *C. van Vollenhoven, who had asked him to prepare a study on the concept of an international police force. In the course of this study, completed in 1911, de Jong van Been en Donk's curiosity in the wider subject of peace was stimulated, leading him a few years afterwards to give up a promising career to devote all his efforts to the peace movement.

During World War I he became involved in one of Holland's most active antiwar organizations. He served as secretary of the Nederlandsche Anti-Oorlog Raad (Netherlands Anti-War Council) (NAOR), established in October 1914 to coordinate the efforts of all peace forces in the country and to maintain contacts with similar groups abroad, especially those in the belligerent states. Adopting the motto "If you want peace, prepare for peace," the NAOR recognized the necessity of going beyond pious utterances of a general wish for peace, and moved to specify concrete reforms which would reduce the likelihood of future war. It developed a "Minimum Programme" of five points; (a) no annexation or transfer of territory without approval of the population; (b) liberalization of colonial trade; (c) development of the work of the Hague Conferences; (d) reduction of armaments; and (e) parliamentary control of foreign policy.

On the initiative of the NAOR an international meeting was organized in The Hague in April 1915. It was successful beyond expectation and led to the foundation, in the same city, of a Central Organization for a Durable Peace (CODP), which sought to coordinate the various national organizations working for peace. Adopting the NAOR's "Minimum Programme," CODP was less interested in working to end the conflict than in establishing guidelines for a durable peace once the fighting ceased. De Jong van Beek en Donk believed that the program of the CODP was superior to that drawn up, a month later, by the League to Enforce Peace. He argued that a promise to arbitrate and machinery to enforce this promise between states was not the universal remedy against war. If the coming treaty were to create new wrongs or to consolidate existing ones, he warned, then even the best-planned league of nations would be unable to maintain a permanent peace. Eventually those who were wronged or who were oppressed would challenge the existing order. Only if a peace was organized along the lines suggested in the "Minimum Programme" would future wars be avoided.

De Jong van Beek en Donk contributed to *De Toekomstige Vrede*, the fortnightly review of the NAOR, and to *Holland News*, its international edition. He was not only one of NAOR's strongest activists, but also served as one of the Dutch members of the International Council of the CODP. The CODP had members in 26 countries, including all the belligerent ones; outside Holland its success was especially notable in Scandinavia and in such countries as Switzerland, Spain, Brazil, and the USA. It organized several national and international commissions to study in detail aspects of the Minimum Programme; de Jong van Beek en Donk took a leading part in the organization of these commissions.

He had also played a prominent role in the leading pre–1914 Dutch peace organization, Vrede door Recht (Peace through Justice), and he was editor-in-chief of its journal from 1912 to 1915. After the war, both the NAOR and Vrede door Recht were disbanded and a new organization was created in their place, the Vereniging voor Volkenbond en Vrede (League of Nations and Peace Society). De Jong van Beek en Donk was a regular contributor to its monthly journal, *De Volkenbond*, from 1925 to 1939, reporting from Geneva, where he had gone to live, on the successes and failures of the League of Nations.

Bibliography:

A. *History of the Peace Movement in the Netherlands* (The Hague, 1915, reprinted in Sandi E. Cooper, ed., *Peace Activities in Belgium and the Netherlands*, New York, 1972); *In 't zicht der Derde Vredesconferentie* (Dordrecht, 1911); *Het nationaliteitenvraagstuk. De betekenis van het Minimum-Programma, punt 1* (The Hague, 1918); *Neutral Europe and the League of Nations* (The Hague, 1917); "De ontwikkeling der vredesbeweging," Nico van Suchtelen et al., *Wereld welvaart, wereldrecht, wereldvrede* (Amsterdam, 1913), 121–69; "Quelques aspects des conférences internationales dans l'organisation du monde d'après-guerre," *Bibliotheca Visseriana* (Leyden, 1926), VI, 113–30; *De vredesbeweging* (The Hague, 1914).

B. "Karakterschets," *De Hollandische Revue*, 22 (1917), 598–600, 653–66; *Nederland's Adelsboek 1943–1948*, 41, 82; *Nederland's Adelsboek 1975*, 67, 297; Hans Wehberg, "B. de Jong van Beek en Donk 60 Jahre alt," *Die Friedenswarte* 41 (1941), 36–38.

Peter van den Dungen

JORDAN, David Starr (19 January, 1851, Gainesville, NY—19 September, 1931, Stanford, CA). *Education*: M.S., Cornell Univ., 1872, M.D. Indiana Medical Coll., 1875. *Career*: professor of natural history, Northwestern Christian Univ. (now Butler Univ.), 1875–79; professor and later president Indiana

Univ., 1879–91; first president Stanford Univ., 1891–1913; later chancellor; director, World Peace Foundation, 1910–15; naturalist, botanist, vertebrate zoologist, ichthyologist, author, lecturer, and explorer.

A noted scientist and educator, David Starr Jordan brought the prestige of the natural sciences to the peace movement and for nearly two decades in the early twentieth century was one of America's leading spokesmen against militarism and war. He sought to link scientific teachings with the cause of peace by popularizing the theory that war killed or maimed the strongest and healthiest individuals, those most suitable to propagate the human race, while sparing the ones declared unfit for military service. Writing during an era that widely accepted Social Darwinism, racial theories, and an emphasis on hereditary characteristics, Jordan challenged the pervasive view that military prowess and conflict among nations constituted a parallel to the evolutionary process of natural selection. Moreover, he was an activist as well as a theorist. Unlike many pre–1914 peace advocates, Jordan persisted in his strong anti-militarist position following the outbreak of World War I and spoke out against American involvement down to the very declaration of U.S. belligerency.

Possessed of a strong Puritan conscience, Jordan could still remember in the last decade of his life how he had been profoundly stirred at the age of eight by an Abolitionist sermon. As a youngster, Jordan was deeply affected by the death of his older brother, who had enlisted in the Union army. For a time his studies in the natural sciences overshadowed his interest in public affairs, but it was not long before he became concerned with issues such as free trade, currency stability, and civil service reform. In 1896 his reputation as a naturalist led President Grover Cleveland to appoint him as head of the American division of a Joint High Commission on the Fur Seal Problem in the Bering Sea. The Commission's success made Jordan a strong advocate of this method of settling international disputes.

The Spanish-American War focused Jordan's attention on foreign policy questions, and after that time a major portion of his activities was devoted to promoting arbitration and peace. While in strong sympathy with the Cuban rebels against the excesses of Spanish rule, he believed that the final concessions made by Spain should have sufficed to keep the United States from going to war. Jordan refrained from criticizing the conduct of the war, but he denounced efforts to annex the Philippines, arguing that the United States should seek no territory it did not intend to make co-equal with the other states. The road to empire, Jordan believed, would eventually turn the United States away from democracy and toward militarism. Accordingly, he served as one of the vice-presidents of the Anti-Imperialist League. When American troops fought the Philippine insurgents, he criticized U.S. atrocities and during the 1900 presidential campaign urged the Democratic nominee, *William Jennings Bryan, to jettison the free silver issue and make anti-imperialism the centerpiece of his campaign.

Following the Spanish-American War Jordan undertook a study of war's impact upon human evolution. In 1907 he published *The Human Harvest* in which he attacked the idea that "martial virtues" were inherent in war. Displays of heroism and self sacrifice were products of peace that somehow survived amid the clash of arms. Jordan was no less critical of the view that war was ingrained in human nature, rather finding it an acquired vice foisted upon peoples by their rulers.

Jordan's address to the National Peace Congress in 1909 so impressed the wealthy textbook publisher Edwin Ginn that he offered Jordan the directorship of his newly established World Peace Foundation. Jordan toured Japan in 1911 and during the Balkan wars visited that troubled area on the Foundation's behalf. In 1914 and again in 1916, he sought to avert conflict between the United States and Mexico.

Despite his concern about the armaments race in Europe, Jordan, like many Americans, underestimated the likelihood of a conflict involving the major powers. The outbreak of war in 1914 and then Germany's invasion of Belgium shocked him; nevertheless he staunchly opposed American involvement. From 1914 to 1917 Jordan supported all attempts to end the war by mediation. When these failed and relations with Germany approached a crisis, he accepted the chairmanship of the Emergency Peace Federation, a hastily assembled coalition that sought to check the drift to war. In early 1917 he addressed a series of antiwar meetings from Boston to Baltimore arguing that war would inflict greater damage on American democracy than any of the evils it was supposed to cure. The interventionists bitterly denounced him, and, when a mob stormed a Baltimore meeting he was addressing, Jordan barely managed to escape its wrath. Once war was declared, however, he accepted the Wilsonian crusade while consoling himself with the hope that a more just world would emerge from the shambles. But the Versailles Treaty and the League of Nations left him disappointed. The latter, he believed, resembled a league of victors. This disillusionment, combined with declining health, led him to curtail his peace-related activities. Jordan continued to write, nevertheless, and in 1921 he completed his impressive autobiography, *The Days of a Man*. In December 1924 Jordan was awarded the Raphael Herman prize of $25,000 for the best plan to create and maintain international peace.

Jordan's critique of turn-of-the century American imperialism has stood the test of time. This cannot be said of his racial theories that associated certain desirable character traits with Anglo-Saxon heredity. More significantly, perhaps, he never shrank from criticizing his own government when, in his judgment, it risked plunging the United States into bloody conflict without sufficient cause.

Bibliography:

A. *The Days of a Man* (Yonkers, NY, 1922); *The Human Harvest* (Boston, 1907); *Imperial Democracy* (New York, 1899); *War and Waste* (Garden City, NY, 1914); *War's Aftermath* (Boston, 1914).

B. Edward McNall Burns, *David Starr Jordan: Prophet of Freedom* (Stanford, CA, 1953).

C. David Starr Jordan Papers, Hoover Institution on War, Revolution and Peace, Stanford Univ., Stanford, CA.

Michael A. Lutzker

JOUHAUX, Léon. See *Biographical Dictionary of Internationalists*.

JOUVE, Andrée (1884, Boulogne-sur-Mer, France—5 August 1972, Paris). *Education*: agrégée, in history, Univ. of Paris. *Career*: History teacher in French schools; member and later vice-president, Women's International League for Peace and Freedom (WILPF); WILPF's international representative to UNESCO, 1948–66.

As a major force in the Women's International League for Peace and Freedom (WILPF), Andrée Jouve worked closely with many of the world's leading pacifists following World War I. Her most remarkable and original activity was the creation of WILPF's "summer schools" for peace education which began in 1922. Eminent peace activists, including *Jawaharlal Nehru, *Romain Rolland, *Albert Schweitzer, and *Bertrand Russell, as well as Jouve offered lectures and courses around special themes. Among the themes discussed were "The International Idea and Civilization"(1922), "International Economic Cooperation" (1925), "Cooperation among Races" (1927), and "Peaceful Means to Combat Oppression"(1932). Her circuit as a lecturer included the United States. She was powerfully committed to education in the peace cause.

During World War II, remaining in occupied France, Jouve risked her life to save several young women from deportation.When the war ended, she resumed the work of her summer schools and picked up the threads of peace education. From 1948 unti11966 she represented the WILPF at sessions of UNESCO. She was among the earliest critics to object to the use of space exploration for military purposes. She dedicated her life "to do everything in order to avoid the rule of injustice and violence and to reconcile all human beings to each other."

Bibliography:

B. Gertrude Bussey & Margaret Tims, *Women's International League for Peace and Freedom* (London, 1965).

Yvonne Sée

JUDD, Sylvester (23 July 1813, Westhampton, MA—26 January 1853, Augusta, ME). *Education*: B.A., Yale Coll., 1836; B.D., Harvard Divinity School, 1840. *Career*: Unitarian clergyman and author.

A convert from Congregationalism to Unitarianism in 1831, Sylvester Judd reflected the heavy Unitarian clerical presence in the American Peace Society. His interest in a birthright church, a concept he pushed vigorously among Unitarians, and his social ethics bridged Quakerism and Unitarianism to inform his peace work.

At Harvard Divinity School Judd had been strongly influenced by the social ethics of Henry Ware, Jr., and took an interest in social reform, expressing special concern for the reformation of criminals, temperance, abolitionism, and pacifism. As early as 1832, he had written essays on pacifism and during his Harvard days he developed his Christian pacifist principles in letters to his family. Privately, he deplored even the militia system which he considered an invitation to barbarism, but he made no public statement of his absolute pacifism until his ordination in 1840 as pastor of the Unitarian church in Augusta, Maine, a pulpit he held until his death. At the church Judd inaugurated a series of Sunday-night lectures on social issues. On March 13, 1842, as part of the series, Judd presented "a moral review of the Revolutionary war," an address intended to show the bane of all war by pointing to the evils that attended even "the holiest war on record." Judd argued that the causes of the American Revolutionary War did not justify the use of violence. American violence, he continued, provoked the British to respond in kind, thereby escalating the political dispute into a needless war. Judd reproved the American patriots for their corruption and atrocities committed during the War, and he pointed to military conflict as a cause of liberty's suppression in parts of America. Judd offered no alternative to war that would have settled the differences between the colonists and the crown, save for his belief in mediation. His purpose, however, had not been historical but political. He wanted to stir Americans from their smugness and apathy regarding war by demonstrating that even the "holiest war" violated Christian morality.

Judd succeeded admirably in awakening public interest with his sermon. Until his "moral review," the American peace movement had declined to condemn the American Revolutionary War. To do so insured public outrage, for the conflict had assumed mythic proportions in the American public mind as a God-ordained event beyond criticism. Judd felt the sting of public rebuke immediately. The Maine legislature dismissed him from his position as honorary chaplain to that body, and several members of his congregation stalked out of his church to protest his sermon. As the Judd case attracted national attention, the American Peace Society made Judd's cause its own and published his lecture under the title of *A Moral Review of the Revolutionary War* (1842). Judd agreed to publish his lecture hoping to dispel charges that his attack on all war was meant to disparage the founding fathers. Circulated widely, the pamphlet caused the furor in Maine to subside and also contributed significantly to ending the tendency of pacifists to exonerate the Revolutionary War.

Within the peace movement Judd strongly supported *Elihu Burritt's peace conventions and sought to discourage continued cooperation by pacifists with apologists for defensive war. During the Mexican War he worked with Burritt's League of Universal Brotherhood, giving dozens of lectures on the aims and objectives of the organization. In 1847 he organized a statewide branch of the League in Maine and served as its corresponding secretary. He also endorsed Burritt's idea of sending peace missionaries to Europe to hold peace congresses and promoted heavy American representation to the international conferences Burritt successfully staged in Brussels, Paris, Frankfurt, and London in the late 1840s and early 1850s.

In 1847 Judd launched his own unique protest against the Mexican War. He dispensed with the governor's Thanksgiving pronouncement and made the day a time of fasting. He also read the entire Book of Lamentations to his congregation. As one legislator observed, Judd was "death against war." Judd added to his pacifist witness between 1845 and 1847 by writing lengthy discourses to quiet anti-British feelings relating to the boundary disputes in Oregon and Maine. Interestingly, he warned that Russia, not Great Britain, was America's greatest potential antagonist. Judd made pacifism a regular part of his preaching and his Sunday night lecture series and converted Augusta into the center of Maine peace activity. In 1850 Judd sponsored a major peace convention there which included addresses by Elihu Burritt.

Judd's principal claim to fame came as a writer and lecturer. He produced essays on temperance, politics, religion, and war, among other works. His most important work, the novel *Margaret* (1845), which received considerable critical attention for its New England flavor, manifested Judd's religious and social views, but it added nothing to his pacifist arguments. However, he did weave pacifism into his novel, *Richard Edney and the Governor's Family* (1850), and into his didactic poem, *Philo, an Evangeliad* (1850). In the 1850s Judd's active pacifism gave way to his literary efforts and to a growing interest in the birthright church.

Bibliography:

A. *A Young Man's Account of His Conversion from Calvinism* (Boston, 1838); *A Moral Review of the Revolutionary War or Some of the Evils of that Event Considered* (Hallowell, 1842); *Margaret. A Tale of the Real and Ideal, Blight and Bloom* (Boston, 1845); *Philo, an Evangeliad* (Boston, 1850); *Richard Edney and the Governor's Family* (Boston, 1850); *The Church: In a Series of Discourses* (Boston, 1854).

B. Francis B. Dedmond, *Sylvester Judd* (Boston, 1980); Arethusa Hall, comp., *Life and Character of the Rev. Sylvester Judd* (Boston, 1857); Richard D. Hathaway, *Sylvester Judd's New England* (University Park, PA, 1981).

Randall M. Miller

K

KAGAWA Toyohiko (10 July 1888, Kobe, Japan—23 April 1960, Tokyo). *Education*: graduated, Kōbe Shingakkō (Kōbe Theological Coll.), 1911; B.D., Princeton Theological Seminary, 1916. *Career*: author, preacher, and leader of various social movements.

Kagawa Toyohiko was a legend in himself. He authored numerous books on Christian themes such as *Kami ni yoru shinsei* (*New Birth through God*) (1929). He penned many popular novels including *Shisen o koete* (*Across the Deathline*) (1920), one of the greatest bestsellers in modern Japan. He wrote *Hinmin shinri no kenkyū* (*Psychology of the Poor*) (1915), a classical study of poor people in Japan. He was one of the top leaders of the labor movement in Japan shortly after World War I. He led a farmers' movement in the early 1920s. He was Japan's most successful mass preacher. The list of what he accomplished seems endless.

Kagawa, exceptionally versatile and multi-faceted, was, perhaps, Japan's leading pacifist in the twentieth century. Beginning with his adolescent work "Sekai heiwa ron" ("On World Peace") (1906), he published quite a few articles that dealt directly with the question of peace. "Heiwa no michi" ("The Way of Peace") (1919), "Gunbi no teppai serareru made" ("Until Armaments Are Abolished") (1922), and "Sensō wa bōshi-shi-uru ka" ("Can We Prevent Wars?") (1935) were other examples of his pacifist writings. Equally important were persistent, though often fragmentary, expressions of pacifist sentiments found in the periodicals such as *Kumo no hashira* (*Pillar of Clouds*), *Friends of Jesus*, and *Kagawa Fellowship Bulletin*, which served as vehicles of communication between Kagawa and his supporters. These writings reveal that even in the period after the Manchurian Incident (1931) Kagawa continued to stress the importance of being internationally minded. In addition to publishing pacifist statements, Kagawa helped organize like-minded Japanese. Under his auspices the National Anti-War League of Japan was formed in 1928. That Kagawa was later accused of wartime cooperation with the militarists and was nearly "purged" by the occupation authorities after World War II indicates the tremendous difficulties a Japanese pacifist had to face, especially when his pacifism was not strictly apolitical.

Before the outbreak of war with the United States, Kagawa visited America several times (1914–17, 1924–25, 1931, 1935–36, and 1941). As the most famous Japanese in the eyes of many Americans, he was a person ideally suited to act as a bridge between the two countries in the critical decade before the Pacific War. However, to act in concrete terms during as complex a time as this in U.S.-Japan relations meant to risk moral ambiguity. To promote peace Kagawa sought to create sympathetic understanding among Americans for Japan, but these efforts were sometimes little distinguishable from acts of whitewashing Japan and her policies.

Kagawa, who renounced his pacifist position in 1943, resumed his pacifist activities with great vigor as soon as the war had ended. He staunchly defended the ideal of a peaceful state as embodied in the 1946 constitution with his talks and pen until the very end of his life.

Kagawa's importance as a pacifist leader should not be denigrated because of his alleged wartime cooperation with the militarists. He chose the difficult path of full commitment to Japanese reality, instead of withdrawal to preserve the integrity of his pacifist position. Kagawa also directed his efforts toward devising concrete programs for the realization of world peace. Hence came his emphasis on the cooperative movement from the 1930s. He stressed realistic pacifism and emphasized that moral and emotional antiwar ideals had to be buttressed by considerations of world politics and international economics. However, as a Christian, he also stressed the spirit of Christ's redemptive love as a spiritual basis for international economic cooperation.

Bibliography:

A. *Kagawa Toyohiko zenshū* (Kagawa Toyohiko Zenshū Kankō Kai, ed., Tokyo, 1962–64).

B. Yokoyama Haruichi, *Kagawa Toyohiko den* (2nd rev. and enl. ed., Tokyo, 1959); Yuzo Ota, "Kagawa Toyohiko: A Pacifist?", Nobuya Bamba and John F. Howes, eds., *Pacifism in Japan: The Christian and Socialist Tradition* (Vancouver, 1978), 169–97.

Yuzo Ota

KALISCH, Arnold (22 January 1882, Berlin—?). *Education*: study of law and philology, universities of Berlin, Freiburg, and Copenhagen, 1903–10; Dr. jur., Univ. of Leipzig, 1914. *Career*: lawyer, language teacher, editor, journalist, freelance writer, and pacifist.

Arnold Kalisch practiced law for only a short time. Based on his studies of modern languages—he was fluent in six languages—Kalisch worked as a language teacher and freelance writer in Berlin. In 1909–10 his appreciation of Scandinavian culture led him to criticize in various German and Danish newspapers the harsh Prussian policies against the Danish minority in north Schleswig. During the next four years he lived in Copenhagen, and many trips through Sweden and Norway confirmed his view that knowledge and appreciation of foreign cultures helped to counteract nationalistic prejudices and chauvinistic tendencies.

After World War I, in which he served first as a soldier on the Western front and then as an interpreter at the War Press Office, Kalisch joined the peace movement and became one of the most active German pacifists in the Weimar Republic. In Berlin, he organized large public demonstrations with the Friedensbund der Kriegsteilnehmer (Peace League of War Veterans). He also got the Arbeite Jugend (Young Workers) to participate in the annual Nie Wieder Krieg! (Never Again War!) demonstrations in Berlin. Among his other activities, he co-founded the Gewerkschaft Deutscher Geistesarbeiter (Union of German Intellectuals), served as a board member of the Berlin local of the Deutsche Friedensgesellschaft (German Peace Society) (DFG), and contributed to many periodicals, including *Arbeiter-Jugend*, *Kulturwehr*, *Die Friedenswarte*, *Deutsche Zukunft*, and *Das Andere Deutschland*. He also was the representative of the Bund der Kriegsdienstgegner (War Resisters League) (BdK) in the Deutschen Friedenskartell (German Peace Cartel).

The BdK owed the publication of its bi-weekly magazine *Die Friedensfront* to Kalisch's active involvement in the movement of conscientious objectors as well as his connections with *Johann Ohrtmann and the North-German pacifists, who were proposing a German-Danish reconciliation. As editor of *Die Friedensfront* from 1929–33, Kalisch protested against the contemptuous treatment of pacifists and war resisters by German government circles. He also called for recognition and just treatment for conscientious objectors in other countries. Objecting to the militaristic spirit spreading in Germany, he sought to strengthen the concept of conscientious objection as a moral, ethical, and political decision for peace and disarmament. He was vigorous in stressing the international aspects of the war resisters movement and succeeded in convincing many of those in the War Resisters' International to contribute to *Die Friedensfront*. Among the German contributors to the paper were Ohrtmann, *Otto Lehmann-Rüssbuldt, *Magnus Schwantje, Baron Paul von Schoenaich, *Oskar Stillich, *Theodor Lessing, *Frantz Keller, *Siegfried Kawerau, *Auguste Kirchhoff,*Hans Schwann, and *Helene Stöcker.''

Kalisch, who had serious doubts about the foreign policy of +Gustav Stresemann, wrote most of the articles in *Die Friedensfront* which criticized German policy, especially the harrassment of Poland and the nonacceptance by Germany of its eastern border. Kalisch was a very energetic champion of the rights of national minorities in Europe and of peaceful solutions to conflicts between states arising out of disputes over minorities. Just as strongly, he propagated the idea of racial equality, even devoting one issue of *Die Friedensfront* to contributions exclusively by North American blacks.

Kalisch sharply condemned the ''unconstitutional existence'' of paramilitary organizations in the Weimar Republic, and he condemned the campaign to challenge Germany's responsibility for the outbreak of World War I. He also spoke against the movement to revise the Treaty of Versailles. He saw the treaty as the ''first attempt toward constitutional organization of the world.'' To him the Sozialdemokratische Partei Deutschlands (German Social Democratic Party) (SPD) was the ''problem child'' of the pacifists. The SPD, which during the regime of Emperor William II had opposed every military budget, now approved all arms requests. In Kalisch's view the SPD had become a ''military party.'' Still, as the differences between the fascist and anti-fascist forces in Germany became clearer, Kalisch put his trust in the SPD as being the only political party capable of halting the fascist tide. He accused the communists, who opposed conscientious objection, of transforming war into civil war rather than preventing it. He further maintained that nowhere in the world were war resisters "as shamefully" suppressed as in the Soviet Union.

Kalisch specifically demanded the disarmament of the Weimar Republic as an indispensable prerequisite for worldwide disarmament and for the success of the Geneva Disarmament Conference (1933). During the controversy concerning the course of the organized German peace movement, Kalisch favored the position of *Friedrich Wilhelm Foerster by printing a number of his articles from the *Zeit* (Berlin, 1930–33) in *Die Friedensfront*.

Kalisch escaped persecution by the Nazi regime by fleeing to Denmark in February or March, 1933, where he and his wife ran a small language school until 1943. When the Nazis tightened their occupation of Denmark, Kalisch was arrested, but after eight months detention he managed to escape to Sweden sometime in 1943 or 1944. After that, nothing more is known about him.

Bibliography:

A. *Durch sechs Länder. Bericht über die Reise zum Kongress der Kriegsdienstgegner in Lyon 1931* (Heide in Holstein, 1931); *Die Landtage und die Instruierung der Bundesratsbevollmächtigten. Beiträge zur Lehre vom Bundesstaat* (Abhandlungen aus dem Staats—und Verwaltungsrecht mit Einschluss des Kolonialrechts und des Völkerrechts, 32. Heft) (Breslau, 1913).

B. J. O. [Johann Ohrtmann], "Arnold Kalisch—22. January 1932–50 Jahre alt," *Deutsche Zukunft*, (February 1, 1932); Hans Wehberg, *Dr. Arnold Kalisch–50 Jahre alt. Die Friedenswarte*, 32 (1932), 20.

Helmut Donat
Trans. by Karl M. Gabriel

KALLINEN, Yrjö (15 June 1886, Oulunjoki, Finland—1 January 1976, Helsinki). *Education*: elementary school; *Career*: book printer; railway worker, lecturer; Member of Parliament, 1943–48; Minister of Defense, 1946–48; pacifist.

In 1899, after elementary school, Yrjö Kallinen went to work in a printing shop and learned about theosophy. He was attracted to the inner side of the doctrine: the feeling of brotherhood towards everything organic, the feeling of cosmic identity which is experienced in the depths of one's being. Besides theosophic literature, Kallinen started reading Marxist literature, economics and social sciences, comparative science of religion, astronomy, and philosophy. He was convinced that the universe is a coherent unit, a harmonious organization where on its deepest level peaceful coexistence prevails. Because war and violence disrupt harmony, they have to be opposed.

From the year 1905 Kallinen participated in the activities of the labor movement and in 1907 became a member of the Social Democratic party. He approved of the central aims of the labor and trade union movements, but not of the violent methods used to realize them. In 1917 he challenged his local union when it promoted rifle training for railway workers. During the civil war in 1918, he tried to bring about reconciliation in Oulu between the fighting factions by acting as a peace negotiator and conciliator. In spite of this, the white victors condemned him to death, but later reduced the sentence to a prison term, which he served from 1918 until 1921.

Between the world wars Kallinen was active in the cooperative movement and gained a reputation as a charismatic speechmaker, who with charm and immense knowledge was able to "capture" his audience in any situation. Kallinen often gave speeches at the meetings of Finland's Peace Union. In the 1930s he joined Finland's Antimilitaristic Union, but soon resigned when he was told that the antimilitarists in France and Germany had supported World War I for nationalistic reasons. Before the Second World War he worked unremittingly to increase the desire for peace, especially in the Social Democratic party and the cooperation movement. During the war he joined those resisting the extradition of Jewish refugees, and took part in Ryhmä 33 (Group 33), the antiwar opposition organization founded by well known politicians and scientists. In 1943 he was elected to Parliament and did what he could to promote peace. Following the war he was elected an honorary member of Finland's Antimilitaristic Union. As Minister of Defense (1946–48) he sought to hold down the growth and cost of armaments. He proposed that Finland take the lead in disarming, thereby becoming an example for the rest of the world.

Yrjö Kallinen believed in social radicalism and intellectual idealism. He approved of the social aims of the labor and peace movements, but maintained his distance, claiming that their doctrines and practices were too often in contradiction. Regarded as an abolute pacifist, he never became a member of a peace organization. As a socialist he was independent and relied more on individual thinking and personal solutions than on institutions or organizations. Through his efforts to restrain violence and promote pacifism he set an excellent example for the Finnish peace movement.

Bibliography:

A. *Elämmekö unessa* (Helsinki, 1971); *Hälinää ja hiljaisuutta* (Helsinki, 1958); *Tässä ja nyt* (Helsinki, 1965).

B. Saul Nieminen, *Mies äänen takana* (Helsinki, 1978); *Parempaa Etsimässä, Yrjö Kallinen juhlakirja* (Helsinki, 1966); Teuvo Rasku, *Yrjö Kallinen-legenda jo eläessään* (Porvoo, 1979).

C. Yrjö Kallinen Papers, Workers' Archives, Helsinki; Yrjö Kallinen Papers, Archives of the Central Union of Consumers, Helsinki.

Kalevi Kalemaa
Trans. by Oliver and Rita Whitehead

KANNER, Heinrich (1846, born either in Vienna or Galatz, Principality of Moldavia [now Romania]—1930, Vienna). *Education*: gymnasium; Univ. of Vienna. *Career*: newspaper correspondent in Vienna; founder (with Isidor Singer and Hermann Bahr) and chief editor, *Die Zeit*, 1894–1917; journalist and author.

As publisher and editor of the liberal, social reformist newspaper, *Die Zeit*,

Heinrich Kanner opposed the imperialistic foreign policies of Austria-Hungary and Germany long before the outbreak of World War I. Because of their opposition to the war, Kanner and Isidor Singer, one of the founders of *Die Zeit*, found themselves under a great deal of pressure from the German military command. They finally had to sell the paper in 1917. Thereafter, Kanner lived as a free-lance journalist and writer, devoting much of his time and effort to the war-guilt question. He published brochures, essays, and the well-known book *Kaiserliche Katastropenpolitik* (*The Catastrophic Imperial Policy*), published in 1922. In a monthly journal, *Der Krieg*, which Kanner founded in 1928 and for which he wrote most of the articles, he fought against German propaganda which sought to exonerate the Central Powers of any responsibility for the outbreak of World War I.

Kanner's journalistic essays, based on a considerable amount of investigation, were sharply critical of the war policy of the Central Powers and of the ideology and mentality of the German military cast which led to the outbreak of war in 1914. Unfortunately, his ideas on preserving peace through the creation of a central European confederation of European states, presented in several articles during the 1920s, were not clearly thought out or tightly argued. Kanner's significance, consequently, lies more in his opposition to war, especially World War I, than to any active participation in the organized peace effort or to the promotion of ideas that would insure continued peace.

Bibliography:

A. *Ist Wilhelm II. strafbar* (Ludwigsburg, 1923); *Kaiserliche Katastrophenpolitik. Ein Stück zeitgenössischer Geschichte* (Leipzig, 1922); *Der mitteleuropäische Staatenbund. Ein Vorschlag zum Frieden* (Vienna, 1925); *Die neueste Geschichtslüge* (Vienna, 1921); *Der Rechtsweg zur Revision des Friedensvertrages* (Ludwigsburg, 1922); *Der Schlüssel zur Kriegsschuldfrage* (Munich, 1926); *Das Weltstrafgericht. Ein neuer Vorschlag zur Verhinderung von Kriegen* (Wiesbaden, 1924); *Wilhelms II. Abschiedsbrief an das deutsche Volk* (Berlin, 1919).

B. Robert A. Kann, *Kaiser Franz Joseph und der Ausbruch des Weltkriegs* (Sitzungsberichte der Öster. Akademie d. Wissenschaften, v. 274, 3. Abhandlung, Vienna, 1971); Johann Nagl, Jakob Zeidler, Eduard Castle, eds., *Deutsch-österreichische Literaturgeschichte* (Vienna, 1937); IV, 1708–9; Fritz Rebhann, "*Die Zeit*," Ph.D. dissertation, University of Vienna, 1948; Ilse Tielsch, "Die Wochenschrift '*Die Zeit*' als Spiegel literarischen und kulturellen Lebens in Wien um die Jahrhundertwende," Ph.D. dissertation, University of Vienna, 1952.

Fritz Fellner
Trans. by Solomon Wank

KASHIWAGI Gien (30 March 1860, Yoita, Niigata Prefecture, Japan—8 January 1938, Anaka). *Education*: B.A., Dōshisha Univ., 1889. *Career*: Christian minister for Annaka Church; essayist and publisher of monthly *Jōmō kyōkai geppō;* pioneer pacifist thinker in Japan.

Kashiwagi Gien used his pulpit at Annaka Christian Church (Gumma prefecture) and the church sponsored monthly tabloid, *Jōmō kyōkai geppō*, to condemn war and promote peace during the first four decades of the twentieth century. The eldest son of a Buddhist priest, Kashiwagi studied in Gumma prefecture where he came under the influence of Niijima Jō, the founder of the Annaka church. This church and geographical area, noted for their involvement in popular rights, women's education, anti-prostitution, and other social movements, deeply influenced the young Kashiwagi. At Dōshisha University, he read widely from *Leo Tolstoy, *Kitamura Tōkoku, *Kinoshita Naoe, and *Uchimura Kanzō and counted classmates Tokutomi Rōka and *Abe Isō among his close friends.

Kashiwagi's chief organ was the tabloid *Jōmō kyōkai geppō*. He edited, published, and wrote for this journal from 1898 until 1936. Through 459 issues, he treated affairs of the Congregational Church, introduced the writings of progressive thinkers, supported social and humanitarian causes, and championed pacifism. The tabloid's foreword stated, "We hope to spread the idea of international peace and thus be able to realize a world without war." In the monthly, Kashiwagi opposed the Russo-Japanese War for the suffering it brought upon people, criticized General Nogi's suicide as a feudal relic, opposed the expansion of armaments, attacked imperialism, criticized the Manchurian Incident and its military expansionism, and admonished Christian churches to avoid supporting war. During its long existence, Kashiwagi published over thirty antiwar articles in the journal and helped set the theoretical tone of Japanese pacifism.

Kashiwagi's first antiwar essay, "Anti-war Arguments, National Policy Arguments," appeared in 1903 during the troublesome times when Japan and Russia glared at each other. For the next thirty-five years Kashiwagi regularly penned essays which, with unbending principle, condemned war. His antiwar arguments were never clouded with extremist views but presented calm and moderate reasons for supporting an unyielding pacifism. With measured criticism, Kashiwagi spoke out in Tokyo at the Reinanzaka Church in 1933 saying that peace is the greatest problem facing humanity and that it was inconsistent to attempt to maintain peace by force. All parties are losers in war. He questioned Japan's actions in Manchuria and urged the military to adopt a peaceful solution. The military should be controlled by the state, but unfortunately, charged Kashiwagi, it has taken charge of the state. For Kashiwagi, consistent, penetrating arguments, not emotional, bombastic outbursts, characterized his antiwar writings. His moderate style, his age, his position of social leadership, and the type of media he employed all rendered him less likely to be silenced by government officials. Yet the authorities occasionally suppressed issues of his monthly and finally pressured him to end his steady rain of criticism in 1936.

Kashiwagi was unusually consistent and tenacious in his antiwar spirit. Yet certain questions or problems remained. His was a theoretical pacifism. Theory and practice were not developed together. Although regularly pressured, he was not personally tested as to his stance. Among members of his congregation, community, and Christian circles he exerted considerable personal influence but did not arouse a commensurate response among them for his antiwar efforts.

His arguments were not backed by any decisive actions or major campaigns. It is difficult to cite any historical succession for his ideas. Kashiwagi, the advocate pacifist, died before the Pacific War was able to test the integrity of his beliefs.

Bibliography:

A. *Kashiwagi Gien shū* ed. by Itani Ryūichi (4 vols., Tokyo, 1970–79).

B. Horikawa Kan'ichi, *Kenshinroku - Heiwa no shito Kashiwagi Gien*, (Tokyo, 1954); Itani Ryūichi, *Hisen no shisō, Dochaku Kirisutosha Kashiwagi Gien* (Tokyo, 1967).

William D. Hoover

KÄSTNER, Erich (23 February 1899, Dresden, Germany—29 July 1974, Munich). *Education*: studies at the universities of Leipzig, Rostock, and Berlin, 1920–22; Ph.D., Univ. of Leipzig, 1925. *Career*: journalist, correspondent, free-lance writer in Leipzig to 1928, Berlin, 1928–45, Munich, 1945–74; cultural editor, *Die Neue Zeitung* Munich, 1945–47; president, Deutsches PEN-Zentrum der Bundesrepublik, 1952–62; pacifist author and poet; literary critic.

As a 19-year-old German recruit in World War I, Erich Kästner wrote his first antiwar poems, thus beginning a lifelong commitment to pacifism. Although he was to use every literary genre, Kästner established himself with the publication of four books of poetry (1928–32), which he characterized as *Gebrauchslyrik* or practical poetry for use in the treatment of ills of modern society. Its satirical pleas for rationality justified Kästner's claim to being a "great-grandchild of the Enlightenment" and brought him wide popularity as one of a small group of social critics including Bertolt Brecht, Walter Mehring, and *Kurt Tucholsky, whose poems echoed through cabarets, radio, newspapers, and periodicals of the Weimar Republic.

Many of Kästner's poems condemned the society which had expended his generation physically and spiritually in war ("Jahrgang 1899" ["Generation of 1899"], "Misstrauensvotum" ["Vote of No-Confidence"]), levied trenchant charges against continuing militarism ("Kennst Du das Land, wo die Kanonen blühen?" ["Do you Know the Land Where the Cannons Boom?"]), and raised an even worse specter in "Die andre Möglichkeit" ("The Other Possibility"): what if Germany had won the war? "Fortunately, we didn't win it," this poem concluded. Unlike many colleagues in the *Weltbühne* circle (a popular periodical of the literary left), Kästner did not join organized pacifist movements of the 1920s. A true representative of the homeless left, he supported no party or social class, directing his real commitment to the coming generation. Consequently, he devoted immense literary energy to writing widely-acclaimed children's books which sought to cultivate the values of peace and social harmony. However, the apocalyptic visions of violence he revealed in several poems and his novel *Fabian* (1931) were soon borne out.

Although his books were burned and his writings banned, Kästner chose to remain in Germany during the Third Reich to act as witness to the events it brought. He saw the German defeat of 1945 as a call to action for building a democratic Germany and a true peace. Through an editorship on the *Neue Zeitung* in Munich, the publication of a new children's magazine, and the founding of a cabaret, he hoped to help Germans understand what had happened in order that it might never happen again. Exemplary of his optimism was the children's book, *Die Konferenz der Tiere* (1949), whose utopian convocation of animals was able to overcome the obstacles to peace that humans had built.

During the 1950s, Kästner's dedication to the coming generation produced more children's books, and his commitment to pacifism led to prominent participation in *Bertrand Russell's Committee against Nuclear Armament, but amidst new conflicts, alliances, and weaponry his hopefulness waned. When even his friends lambasted his bleak cabaret skits of nuclear devastation, and when his drama portraying totalitarianism, "Die Schule der Diktatoren" (The School of Dictators") (1956), achieved little notice, his satirical pen dried up. Kästner's literary exhaustion derived in no small part from Cold War struggles within the literary left of the divided Germany, but to children and non-children, to Germans and non-Germans, the self-proclaimed schoolmaster and moralist left a rich legacy of protest against violence in all its forms.

Bibliography:

A. *Gesammelte Schriften* (7 vols., Zurich, 1959); *Let's Face It* (London, 1963).

B. Renate Benson, *Erich Kästner, Studien zu seinem Werk* (Bonn, 1973); Luiselotte Enderle, *Erich Kästner in Selbstzeugnissen und Bilddokumenten* (Reinbek b. Hamburg, 1966); R. W. Last, *Erich Kästner* (London, 1974); Dirk Walter, *Zeitkritik und Idyllensucht. Erich Kästners Frühwerk (1928–1933) als Beispiel linksbürgerlicher Literatur in der Weimarer Republik* (Heidelberg, 1977); NYT, July 30, 1974; *Neue Deutsche Biographie*, X, 737–40.

Katherine Larson Roper

KATSCHER, Leopold (30 August 1853, Csákova, County Temes, Hungary—25 February 1939, Lucerne, Switzerland). *Education*: commercial academies in Budapest and Vienna. *Career*: writer, translator, reformer, feminist, internationalist, and pacifist.

Leopold Katscher, uncle of *Rosika Schwimmer, was a prolific writer in German on a broad range of subjects. His articles were distributed through some ten syndicates and published in hundreds of European newspapers. He also wrote in English, French, and Hungarian, as well as translating from German into English and French, and from the latter into German. Zealous in publicizing reform movements in which he believed, Katscher was especially diligent in promoting peace and women's rights. His association with Baroness *Bertha von Suttner began with his finding a German publisher willing to take her antiwar novel *Die Waffen Nieder* (*Lay Down Your Arms*) and continued with his involvement in organizing the Austrian Society of Friends of Peace (1891) and the German Peace Society (1892). Then, with Suttner's assistance, he organized the Hungarian Peace Society (1895). During World War I he was a member of the Swiss Committee for the Preparation of the League of Nations, taking part in the drafting of its Constitution for a Universal League of Nations (1918).

Katscher was a true cosmopolitan, residing in London, Berlin, Budapest, Baden (Austria), and in various cities in Switzerland. In 1933 he was honored to learn that his name was included in the Nazi Press Boycott list as a "notorious pacifist, feminist, internationalist, and atheist." He was a gentle and kindly person, always willing to help place books and articles for European authors, or finding support—even employment—for refugees from Tzarist, and later, Soviet Russia and Nazi Germany.

Bibliography:

A. *Bertha von Suttner, Die "Schwärmerin" für Güte* (Dresden, 1903); *Frieden! Frieden! Frieden!* (Dresden, 1890); *Friedensstimmen: eine Anthologie* (Leipzig, 1894); *Kleine Völkerbund-Anthologie* (Zurich, 1919); *Krieg und Frieden* (Suttnersammlung) (Berlin, 1895); *Geschichte des Völkerbundgedankens* (Zurich, 1920).

C. Schwimmer-Lloyd Collection, New York Public Library.

Edith Wynner

KAWAI Michi (29 July 1877, Ise Yamada, Japan—11 February 1953, Tokyo). *Education*: graduated, Hokusei Jogakkō (Sapporo), 1895; B.A., Bryn Mawr Coll., 1904. *Career*: educator and founder of Keisen Jogakuen, active member of two Japanese peace organizations, and secretary-general of the Japanese YWCA, 1916–25.

Kawai Michi dedicated her life to the advancement of women's education, the promotion of world peace, and the betterment of Japan's international relations. Although born into an Ise Shinto priest family, she moved to Hokkaidō in 1886 with her family where an uncle, a Christian minister, strongly influenced her Christian education. In 1898 she went to the United States where she attended prep school in Philadelphia. Upon graduation from Bryn Mawr College, she returned to Japan and taught for more than a decade at Tsuda Juku and other schools. Kawai helped organize the Japanese YWCA in 1912 and became its full time secretary-general in 1916. For a decade she led the YWCA in its efforts to correct social problems. Strongly confident in the efficacy of education, Kawai founded Keisen Jogakuen, a school for young women which stressed Christian religious experience, horticulture, and internationalism.

Kawai's efforts on behalf of peace were not spectacular, but were long-range and consistent with her culture and time. She visited the United States and Europe eight times and Asian countries several times. There she quietly advocated a pacifist-internationalist approach to world issues. In Kawai's mind, pacifism was inextricably linked with Christianity. At Keisen Jogakuen she taught "internationalism," weekly sessions examining foreign cultures and introducing foreign speakers. Kawai and the guests led general discussions of current events to broaden the students' minds and give them an "international spirit."

From 1931 to 1933, Kawai served as president of the Women's Peace Society. She led a Society delegation to the Army and Educational Departments to express concern over events in Manchuria. Under her leadership, the Society collected signatures endorsing the 1932 Geneva disarmament conference and carried these to Prime Minister Inukai Tsuyoshi. Kawai was also a member of the Japan branch of the Fellowship of Reconciliation. In the summer of 1934, she visited the United States as a messenger of Japanese-American friendship. There, she gave some two hundred short speeches and even made a fifteen minute national radio broadcast on behalf of peaceful international relations. In 1941 Kawai and eight other Japanese Christians, the so-called "Riverside group," traveled to the United States in an attempt to clarify positions and thereby avoid hostilities.

Kawai recognized that the times were not particularly receptive to her message of peace. For her, the goal was to build, educate, and convert until a future day when people of the world would live in peace. In particular, she emphasized that women of the world had a special responsibility to cooperate in order to make the world peace movement a success. Kawai took her stand on behalf of peace and good international relations at no small personal risk. Authorities in Kyoto questioned her about a speech calling for peace in August 1941 and dismissed her only after a stern warning. In Tokyo, the police interrogated her about her views, her international activities and associations, and her Christian school. Kawai Michi distinguished herself in Japan as a Christian educator and an advocate of peaceful international exchange. Her pacifism was deeply rooted in her religious and international experience.

Bibliography:

A. *My Lantern* (*Watashi no rantaan*) (Tokyo, 1939; 3rd ed. 1949); *Sliding Doors* (Tokyo, 1950).

B. Sekine Bunnosuke, *Kawai Michi no shōgai* (Tokyo, 1954, 1967); Isshiki Yoshiko, *Ai no hito Kawai Michiko sensei* (Tokyo, 1953); *Kawai Michi - teikō ni ikiru hibi* (Tokyo, 1975).

William D. Hoover

KAWERAU, Georg Siegfried (8 December 1886, Berlin—16 December 1936, Berlin). *Education*: Ph.D., Univ. of Königsberg, 1910; secondary school teaching certificate. *Career*: teacher, realschule in Bucharest, 1911–12; teacher, gymnasium in Landsberg on the Warthe, 1913–19; head-master of Kollnisch Gymnasium, and Kaemphrealschule in Berlin, 1927–33; city councillor of Greater Berlin; school reformer and pacifist.

Georg Siegfried Kawerau volunteered for military duty in 1914 and served on the Western Front. In 1915, at Verdun, he was injured in battle and subsequently discharged from the military. He then entered into teaching. In spite of having lost his enthusiasm for war, Kawerau advocated continuing the war effort until Germany was victorious, a position supported by most traditional political parties. He hoped for a form of government which he referred to as "social empire." In 1918 he volunteered for teaching duty in the German marches.

Kawerau's political transformation took place after the monarchy was discredited by Germany's defeat in the war. In 1919 he became a member of the Sozialdemokratische Partei Deutschlands (German Social Democratic Party) (SPD) and helped found the Bund Entscheidener Schulreformer (Association of Determined School Reformers) (BES), a group of "militant pacifists" which he helped lead until 1925. Between 1920 and 1923 he was co-editor of *Neue Erziehung*, a BES publication that reported on school reform as well as on the peace movement.

Kawerau was politically active in the Bund der Kriegsdienstgegner (War Resisters League) and the Deutsch Liga für Menschenrechte (League for Human Rights). As their speaker he advocated conscientious objection, universal disarmament, international understanding, and acceptance of German war guilt. His brave support of radical pacifism during the Weimar period earned him attacks from National Socialist (Nazi) newspapers. Kawerau was a teacher and school reformer who strongly believed that education could create a "new man." His activities in the area of education and school reform were directed at furthering international understanding. In school he endeavored to uphold republican views and to expose the biased accounts of World War I, defeat, revolution, and the Weimar constitution found in history text books. He further represented the cause of school reform—as headmaster, school inspector, and member of several educational delegations—before the Prussian cultural minister. He organized the Internationale Geschichtstagung (International History Conference) in 1924. The conclusions reached at that conference also appear, sometimes verbatim, in the proceedings of the Berliner Weltfriedenkongress (Berlin World Peace Congress). Kawerau repeatedly came into conflict with so-called "patriotic clubs," the reactionary press, and the Verband deutscher Geschichtslehrer (Association of German Teachers of History) for his efforts in exposing historical myths, especially those which obscured Germany's war guilt. His attempts at serving peace and disseminating historical truth earned him the hatred of the National Socialists. Shortly after their rise to power they imprisoned him for several months and officially removed him from school service on September 1, 1933. Three years later he died in prison.

Bibliography:

A. *Alter und neuer Geschichtsunterricht* (Leipzig, 1924); *Denskschrift über die deutschen Geschichts—und Lesebücher* (Berlin, 1927); *Die Geschichte des Bundes Entschiedener Schulreformer* (Leipzig, 1923); *Selbstbildnis* (Leipzig, 1928); *Soziologische Pädagogik* (Leipzig, 1921); *Soziologischer Ausbau des Geschichtsunterrichts* (Berlin, 1921); *Das Weissbuch der Schulreform* (Berlin, 1920).

B. Jochen Huhn, "Georg Siegfried Kawerau," *Deutsche Geschichtsdidaktiker*, des 19. und 20. Jahrhunderts, ed. by Siegfried Quandt (Paderborn, 1978), 280–303; *Neue Deutsche Biographie* (Berlin, 1977), XI, 378–79.

Reinhold Lütgemeier-Davin
Trans. by Robert C. Reimer

KAYSER, Friedrich (5 March 1894, Schwerte on the Ruhr/Westphalia, Germany—12 March 1945, Dortmund, Germany). *Career*: teacher, journalist, and editor.

The son of a shoe cobbler, Friedrich Kayser served in the German army on the Eastern Front from 1914 until 1918. His experiences in the First World War, in which he was wounded and decorated, turned him into an opponent of war and a propagandist for conscientious objection. In November 1918 his regiment elected him chairman of the Soldiers' Council. Returning to Germany in 1919, he freed himself from the Wilhelminian tradition. Convinced of the goal to overcome the Prussian military spirit that threatened peace and the Republic, Kayser, as a member of the peace movement, pressed for intense activities within the local groups and meetings, and took it upon himself to win the working masses for pacifism. Already chairman of the Schwerte branch of the Deutsche Friedensgesellschaft (German Peace Society) (DFG), he became a member of the executive committee and the secretary of the South Westphalian branch of the DFG, which rejected Otto von Bismarck's "might before right politics" and called for a "politics of law and justice." Kayser's lively exchange of ideas with *Fritz Küster led to a political and personal friendship that had great importance for the dissemination of pacifist concepts in the Rhenish-Westphalian industrial area.

During the French occupation of the Ruhr, sparked by Germany's failure to meet its reparation payments in 1923, Kayser joined the leading pacifists in western Germany who spoke out against the extreme nationalistic call for passive resistance and who called for a solution to the reparations problem based on negotiations. Throughout the rest of the decade he traveled almost every afternoon after teaching school from Schwerte to Hagen, in order to take up his editorial responsibilities on *Das Andere Deutschland*, the organ of the Westdeutscher Landesverband (West-German Regional Association) (WLV) of the German Peace Society. Kayser played a leading role in developing *Das Andere Deutschland* into one of the most influential journals of postwar German pacifism. Writing numerous articles himself, almost always unsigned, Kayser, next to Fritz Küster, was most important in determining the direction of *Das Andere Deutschland* and the WLV. At the same time, he took care of the business of the WLV, whose chairmanship he accepted in 1929.

When the Sozialdemokratische Partei Deutschlands (German Social Democratic Party) (SPD) declared in 1931 that simultaneous membership in the DFG was incompatible with the aims of the party, Kayser withdrew from the SPD. With friends of like mind, he untiringly warned of the threat of fascism and appealed to the SPD and the Kommunistische Partei Deutschlands (German Communist Party) (KPD) alike, to give up their feud and to unite in a broadly based antifascist front.

Even after 1933, Kayser remained true to his political principles. His fearlessness commanded respect even from his political enemies. The high regard children, parents, and colleagues had for him—he was considered the best teacher in his district—may also have contributed to the fact that Kayser was released from prison by the Nazis after three or four weeks. After his release he immediately began—illegally—to work against the Nazi regime. He was successful in persuading Nazi authorities to free imprisoned pacifists and he helped Jews to flee Germany. He traveled around untiringly in order to keep the spirit of resistance alive and took part in the different actions of the larger antifascist resistance organizations. Kayser lost his life during an air attack on Dortmund.

Bibliography:

B. Hein Herbers, "Friedrich Kayser (1894–1945). Ein Pazifist und Vorkämpfer der deutschen Widerstandsbewegung," *Die Friedenswarte*, 46 (1946), 230–32; F. K. [Fritz Küster], "Aus unserer Kampfzeit. Friedrich Kayser," *Das Andere Deutschland*, 8 (April, 1960), 8, and 9 (May, 1960), 8.

Helmut Donat
Trans. by Ruthann Richards

KELLER, Franz (24 July 1873, Karlsruhe, Germany—6 June 1944, Freiburg/Breisgau, Germany). *Education*: theological studies, Univ. of Freiburg (ordained as Catholic priest in 1896); Doctor of Political Science, Univ. of Freiburg, 1903, Doctor of Theology, 1905. *Career*: lecturer in moral ethics, Univ. of Freiburg, 1912–23, professor, 1924–34; editor, *Jahrbuch für Caritas Wissenschaft*, 1927–38; Catholic priest, editor, and pacifist writer.

Franz Keller was convinced that modern war was neither theologically nor morally justifiable. In 1932 he was a contributor to "Theologischen Gutachtens über die sittliche Erlaubtheit des Krieges" ("Theological Opinion on the Moral Permissibility of War"), which was published in *Der Friedenskämpfer* (*The Peace Fighter*). Others who participated in drawing up the statement were: Professor F. Charrières, Bishop of Lausanne-Geneva-Freiburg since 1945, Professor P. Delos of Lille, Professor de Solages of Toulouse, and *Franziskus Stratmann. Keller recognized the fundamental right of individuals and states to defend themselves. However, in view of technological development, he considered the use of war as a means of defense unjustified on three grounds: 1) because of the manipulation of public opinion it was virtually impossible to objectively confirm a case of real defense; 2) the consequences of modern warfare were so unforeseeable that they could not be justified by the right to defense; and 3) modern wars were so destructive that victory was meaningless. Consequently, traditional concepts of defense had to be abandoned and new techniques such as passive resistance and boycotts had to be developed.

Based on these beliefs Keller supported the refusal to perform obligatory military service. Furthermore, he contested the right of the state to compel its citizens to perform military service. This compulsion, according to Keller, involved a fundamental infringement on an individual's freedom of conscience, since freedom of conscience meant the right and the responsibility to decide freely. By making military service a legal obligation, the state, according to Keller, robbed the individual of the possibility of making a free decision. Keller mistrusted the state, for it ignored personal moral values and recognized only its own political interests. To him, the modern state in its godless hunger for power, was the "Leviathan." He also criticized the Church for having formed too close an association with the state.

Against the power politics of the state and its brutal egoism, Keller set the international binding force of solidarity and Christian "Caritas"—i.e. Christian love and service. His alternative to power politics was national security through international assistance based on the idea of Caritas. He hoped for the growth of international reconciliation and understanding through active love. In 1925 Keller, together with the Deutschen Caritasverband (German Caritas Association), established the Institut für Caritaswissenschaft (Institute for Scientific Study of Caritas). From 1927 until 1938, Keller edited the institute's journal, *Jahrbuch für Caritaswissenschaft*. In keeping with his ideas about the international role of Caritas, Keller supported the founding, in 1928, of Caritas catholica which brought together Caritas associations from twenty-two countries. Keller saw the most important task of Caritas catholica as that of bringing people together through common action in common crises and overcoming prejudice and hatred.

Besides writing for the Caritas *Jahrbuch*, he published essays in several other pacifist journals, including *Die Friedenswarte*. His criticism of the existing social and economic order and of militarism was often severe and radical, making him part of the left-wing of the pacifist movement. His subsequent avowal of National Socialism in May 1933, therefore, dismayed and confounded his friends. Most likely motivated by ambition, Keller's support of Hitler's Germany had its limits. Although he supported National Socialism in general, he opposed specific Nazi policies, such as the killing of racially "worthless" individuals and euthanasia. Despite his general accommodation, these reservations led to his dismissal from the University of Freiburg in 1934, although he continued to edit the *Jahrbuch für Caritaswissenschaft* until 1938. On the other hand, Keller came into conflict with the Archibishop of Freiburg because of his pro-Nazi attitudes and the Caritas association distanced itself from him. He lived in relative isolation during the last years of his life.

Bibliography:

A. *Bevölkerungspolitik und christliche Moral* (Freiburg,1905); *Caritaswissenschaft* (Freiburg, 1925); *Grundzüge der Dorfcaritas* (Freiburg, 1924); *Kriegsächtung und Friedensrüstung* (Freiburg, 1929).

B. Beate Höfling, *Katholische Friedensbewegung zwischen zwei Kriegen* (Waldkirch, 1979); Dieter Riesenberger, *Die katholische Friedensbewegung in der Weimarer Republik* (Düsseldorf, 1977); Richard Vökl", "Franz Keller," *Neue Deutsche Biographie*, 11 (Berlin, 1977) 435.

Dieter Riesenberger
Trans. by Solomon Wank

KELLOGG, Paul Underwood (30 September 1879, Kalamazoo, MI—1 November 1958, New York). *Education*: studies at Columbia Univ., 1901–2 and part-time for several years thereafter. *Career*: editor, *Charities*, 1902–9 and its successor, *Survey: The Magazine of Social Work*, 1909–52; director, Pittsburgh Survey of Industrial Conditions, 1908; journalist, social reformer, and pacifist-internationalist.

A member of a group of liberal pacifists and social reformers in New York City and Chicago, Paul U. Kellogg played an important role in espousing world peace in the first half of the twentieth century. An activist and publicist rather than a profound thinker, Kellogg worked for peace through a few organizations and primarily through his magazine, the *Survey*, which he made a forum for ideas about peace as well as social work.

Viewing war and the preparation for war as destructive to the spirit and resources of movements for better living and working conditions, Kellogg joined with a number of social justice progressives—*Jane Addams, *Lillian Wald, *Crystal Eastman, *Oswald Garrison Villard, *Stephen A. Wise, and J. Hollingsworth Wood—to found the American Union against Militarism (AUAM) in 1915. Unable to prevent expansion of the American armed forces in 1916, the AUAM, nevertheless, played a pivotal role in averting war between the United States and Mexico. Kellogg served on an unofficial joint commission of Mexican and American citizens which helped to reduce tensions resulting from the incursion of United States Army forces in pursuit of Francisco "Pancho" Villa. Two months before the U. S. entered World War I, Kellogg published a personal statement in the *Survey* warning that belligerent status would cost the nation its position as a mediator and might militarize society.

Many of the *Survey*'s major supporters sharply criticized Kellogg and, when the United States entered the war, the editor chose not to support the AUAM's "anti-war agitation." Instead, Kellogg aided refugees in Europe through the Red Cross and worked to influence the postwar peace towards a reformed international order that would eliminate the political and economic conditions leading to war. In defense of what he held to be the true Wilsonian principles—equal economic opportunity for all nations, self-determination of nations, and collective security—Kellogg organized the League of Free Nations Association (later the Foreign Policy Association) in the winter of 1918–19 and supported the Treaty of Versailles and the League of Nations.

In the interwar period, Kellogg and others committed to political activism eventually resigned from the Foreign Policy Association when the dominant faction chose to pursue educational goals. Kellogg personally worked on behalf of international disarmament conferences and the Nye Senate Committee investigation of munitions makers and international bankers. A supporter of the Soviet Union's social planning and antifascism, Kellogg became concerned about Russian bureaucracy and the threats to individual liberty during a visit to the USSR in 1936. During the Spanish Civil War he was an active member of the American Friends of Spanish Democracy.

As World War II approached, Kellogg hoped the United States could pursue a middle path, a great neutral democracy wielding power for international justice and welfare. But the middle way proved elusive and, after 1939, Kellogg advocated modifying neutrality legislation, sought to rescue and resettle refugees, and by 1941 argued for military aid to the Allies. After the Japanese attack upon Pearl Harbor, he supported the war effort and subsequently the United Nations and postwar refugee and famine relief. In ill health, he retired from public life in 1952, closing down the *Survey* and ending four decades as a centrist spokesman for liberal pacifism and internationalism.

Bibliography:

A. *British Labor and the War*, with Arthur Gleason (New York, 1919).

B. Clarke A. Chambers, *Paul U. Kellogg and the "Survey"* (Minneapolis, 1971); DAB, Supp. 6, 329–30.

C. Paul U. Kellogg Papers and the *Survey* Associates Papers, University of Minnesota.

John Whiteclay Chambers

KEMÉNY, Ferenc (17 July 1860, Nagykikinda, Hungary—21 November 1944, Budapest). *Education*: Hungarian equivalent of B.Sc. in physics and mathematics, Univ. of Budapest, 1883, B.A., 1888; studies at the Univ. of Paris. *Career*: educator; author; active in pacifist movements.

Ferenc Kemény started his career teaching mathematics and languages in high school, first in Kőszeg, then in Brassó and Eger. He was transferred to Budapest in 1894, where he taught until his retirement in 1920. During this period, he was appointed titular regional superintendent of schools.

Kemény was instrumental in the establishment of the Hungarian Peace Association in 1895. Around the same time, in 1894, he became a founding member of the International Olympic Committee, retaining his membership in that committee until 1916. Subsequently, Kemény attended several international pacifist conferences, where he became known for his repeated emphasis on the need of inculcating the idea of a lasting peace in schools. He wrote a regular column on pacifist education in the pedagogical journal *Minerva*, and became a correspondent of the Carnegie Endowment's European Bureau.

Kemény's proposal for a world academy, published first in French in 1900, then in German and Hungarian, was nominated for a Nobel prize in literature. This idea was the forerunner of international cooperation in education which came to be realized only after World War I and World War II as the International Pedagogical Institute and UNESCO respectively. Kemény fell victim to the fascist Arrowcross terror in November, 1944.

Bibliography:

A. A Békenap Jelene és Jovője (Budapest, 1914); A Békeprobléma Megoldásának Egyik Módja (Budapest, 1900); A Békemozgalom Pedagógiai Jelentősége és a Békenap (Budapest, 1907); Világakadémia (Budapest, 1902); A Világbéke (Budapest, 1911).

B. Alfred H. Fried, *Handbuch der Friedensbewegung* (2nd. ed., Berlin, 1911–13, reissued New York, 1972), 362.

Gabor Vermes

KESSLER, Harry Klemens Ulrich. See *Biographical Dictionary of Internationalists*.

KEY, Ellen (11 December 1849, Västervik, Sweden—25 April 1926, Alvastra, Sweden). *Education*: Miss Rossander's Course for Adult Women, Stockholm,

1868–72. *Career*: teacher, Anna Whitlock's Coeducational School, Stockholm, 1880–99; Workers' Institute, Stockholm, 1883–1903; prolific essayist.

When Emil Key went to the Swedish Parliament in 1868 to represent a new liberal party, his eldest daughter went along as housekeeper and secretary. Ellen Key used this assignment as a political apprenticeship, despite being unenfranchised. In the defense debate of the 1870s, she shared her father's moderate position between the extremes of militarism and unilateral disarmament and joined the Friends of Conscription (Värnpliktens Vänner), liberals who sought compulsory military service for all men in the name of democracy.

When her father lost his seat in 1883, Ellen Key launched her own career and declared her independence from partisan politics. She lectured weekly at the Workers' Institute, the Social Democratic party's educational arm, but never joined the party. In 1899, after fifteen years of magazine essays, she published her first book and entered a national controversy with a pamphlet criticizing the liberals for their weak stand against censorship. That bold act, coupled with the enormous popularity of her lectures, established her as a major opinion maker on a wide range of issues.

Her first public statement on peace was a lecture in Stockholm in 1897 supporting Norwegian efforts to dissolve the union with Sweden and form an alliance for cultural exchange and mutual defense. Charged with being unpatriotic, she redefined patriotism, borrowing *Rudolph Goldscheid's concept, ''Kulturpatriotismus'' (''Cultural Patriotism''). Love of country did not mean allegiance to a political state, an ''incomplete form for a people's joint development of power,'' but to a geographical district, a language, a folk culture. Key was a National Romantic to the core. In the Swedish context this meant opposition to the conservative patriotism that equated Swedish grandeur with military might. She believed that patriotism in the sense of a strong love of homeland was a prerequisite for international cooperation.

The ''union crisis'' was a formative event for Key, and she saw its peaceful resolution as a model for settling other international disputes. She attributed her particular views on war and peace to the influence of *Bertha von Suttner's *Die Waffen nieder* (*Lay Down Your Arms*) (1889) and other continental writings. Peace would be best assured, she thought, by courts of arbitration, arms limitations, abolition of secret diplomacy, parliamentary control of foreign policy, and recognition of the right to self-determination. She opposed unilateral disarmament as a strategy for achieving peace because she thought the risk to domestic security too great and,therefore, a naive self-sacrifice. She did, however, support disarmament agreements that resulted from international negotiations.

Key's pacifism was deeply rooted in her monist moral philosophy. Her mission was to reconcile polarities, to help steer social development on a natural evolutionary course toward harmony. Like cannibalism and slavery, war would be rejected as an atavism by an increasingly civilized humanity. To succeed in the struggle for food and space, nations would have to join together to overcome ''international anarchy''. She offered this ''scientific pacifism'' as an alternative to Christian pacifists' ideal of self-abnegation, which she thought contrary to human nature.

The most distinctive feature of Key's pacifism was her hope that women's growing public influence would bring an end to war. She believed that war would turn an innate maternal compassion into pacifism. Women who lost fiancés would not willingly bear sons for cannon fodder. Women who nursed the wounded would ask why the wounds were necessary. Just as women, who work for social betterment in times of peace, are often led to the idea of social reorganization, so the care of the sick during war would force women to consider political reorganization. Once women stopped allowing their "power to renew what war has destroyed" to be exploited, war would cease. Echoing *Fredrika Bremer's call for an international peace union in 1854, she urged women to unite in a "holy revolt against war," a "solicitude for motherhood." Key saw herself as a "spiritual influence" rather than an activist and was quickly frustrated by organizational discipline. She encouraged the formation of the Swedish Women's Peace Union but kept herself on the sidelines. Rather than attend the Women's Peace Congress in The Hague in April 1915, she sent a lengthy letter of encouragement.

Key's writings on peace are not the best evidence of her stature as a peace leader. A better measure is to be found in the many contemporary homages to her energy, charisma, and inspiration. Feeling vilified in Sweden for her views on feminism and sexual morality, she was welcomed into progressive circles throughout Europe while living abroad from 1903 to 1909. During World War I she was generous in helping displaced intellectuals resettle. On her seventieth birthday, *Romain Rolland wrote to her that all who benefited from her good will constituted a spiritual family around her.

Friends saw Key giving in to an uncharacteristic pessimism during the war. Germany, the home of her intellectual forebears, had succumbed to militarism. Key avoided denouncing Germany, insisting that the only proper pacifist stance was neutrality, and she led a campaign of reconciliation after the war, believing that compassion would prevent further aggression. Most demoralizing of all, women in the warring countries did not revolt, and the leading feminist and established women's organizations in France and Germany balked at sending delegates to The Hague to support a peace movement initiated by women. Nevertheless, she maintained her "otherwise helpless and hopeless trust in women," declaring that she did not know "where salvation would come from" if outraged feelings of motherhood did not lead to a mass uprising. As the war dragged on, her pessimism about the possibility of ending war in general grew deeper. In that mood, she declined an invitation to join the Ford Expedition, explaining that she lacked faith in its success, and without that faith she could not act.

Key's participation in a campaign for weapons shipments to the Whites in Finland in the 1917–19 war has puzzled some scholars. Her internationalism, however, was never truly international, but European. Europe was the cradle of civilization and had evolved beyond "the prevailing barbarism of the East, where might is right." She saw the Finnish war neither as a civil war nor a socialist revolution, but as a justifiable defense against an inferior invader. In the end, her evolutionism and a traditional Swedish distrust of Russia proved firmer than her pacifism.

Bibliography:

A. *Allsegraren I* (Stockholm, 1918); *En djupare syn på kriget* (Stockholm, 1916); *Kriget, freden, och framtiden* (Stockholm, 1914, English translation *War, Peace, and the Future*, New York, 1916); *Själarnas neutralitet* Stockholm, 1916); *Tva föregångskvinnor i kriget, mot kriget* (Stockholm, 1918); *The Younger Generation* (New York, 1913).

B. Ronny Ambjörnsson, *Hemmets århundrade* (Stockholm, 1976); Mia Leche-Löfgren, *Ellen Key, hennes liv och verk* (Stockholm, 1930); Louise Hamilton Nyström, *Ellen Key, en livsbild* (Stockholm, 1904, English translation *Ellen Key: Her Life and Work*, New York, 1913); Cheri Register, "Motherhood at Centre: Ellen Key's Social Vision," *Women's Studies International Forum*, 5:6 (1982), 599–610; Ulf Wittrock, *Ellen Keys väg från kristendom till livstro* (Stockholm, 1953); NYT, April 26, 1926.

C. Ellen Key Collection, Royal Library (Kungliga Biblioteket), Stockholm.

Cheri Register

KING, Martin Luther, Jr. (15 January 1929, Atlanta, GA—4 April 1968, Memphis, TN). *Education*: B.A., Morehouse Coll., 1948; B.D. Crozer Theological Seminary, 1951; Ph.D., Boston Univ., 1955. *Career*: pastor, Dexter Avenue Baptist Church, Montgomery, AL, 1954–60, co-pastor, Ebenezer Baptist Church, Atlanta, GA, 1960–68; president, Montgomery Improvement Association, 1955–60, president, Southern Christian Leadership Conference, 1957–68; civil rights leader and proponent of nonviolent protest; outspoken opponent of American militarism and the Vietnam War.

Martin Luther King, Jr.'s quick rise to national and international prominence as leader of the American civil rights movement began with the advent of the Montgomery, Alabama, bus boycott in December, 1955, and with the selection of King as primary spokesman for the black protest organization. With a strong family heritage in the Baptist church, and superb educational training in philosophy and theology, the young minister brought both excellent oratorical skills and a familiarity with intellectual arguments for peace and social justice to his new role.

Counseled by both Bayard Rustin of the War Resisters League and Glenn Smiley of the Fellowship of Reconciliation in the early weeks of the Montgomery protest, King melded their exposition of nonviolent resistance with his religious commitment to the Christian ethic of love and forgiveness to produce a powerful new statement of black Americans' desire to free themselves from racial oppression and discrimination by peaceful but aggressive efforts.

Influenced by the writings of Walter Rauschenbusch and *Reinhold Niebuhr more so than by *Henry David Thoreau or *Gandhi, King moved forward in the wake of the success of the Montgomery protest to found the Southern Christian Leadership Conference (SCLC), dedicated to pursuing the struggle against racial segregation on a wider basis. Arguing in his many writings and public addresses that black Americans and their white allies could combat the evils of racism, poverty, and militarism more successfully through mass action than through the slower and more elite-oriented channels of legal redress favored by the National Association for the Advancement of Colored People, King symbolized a new stage in the black freedom struggle. When the student sit-in movement burst forth across the South in the spring of 1960, signaling a renewed effort to end legalized segregation through nonviolent means, the American press focused upon King as the spokesman and symbol of the black struggle in the South.

Disappointed by the reluctance of the Kennedy administration to act on civil rights issues, and distressed by the lack of success in a major SCLC-assisted black protest movement in Albany, Georgia, in 1961–62, King decided early in 1963 to launch a major and uncompromising assault on one of the south's most rigidly segregated cities, Birmingham, Alabama. The effort was aimed not only at forcing changes in Birmingham, but also at prodding the federal government to pass legislation eliminating legalized segregation and racial discrimination throughout the United States. When peaceful black protest marchers were met by policemen using snarling dogs and high-powered fire hoses, King's anti-segregation effort made headlines throughout the world and impelled the Kennedy administration to put forward a major civil rights bill that later would emerge as the Civil Rights Act of 1964. The national outrage also forced concessions upon the segregationists of Birmingham.

The worldwide attention given King's effort was magnified by his cogent "Letter From a Birmingham Jail," (1963) a powerful statement about both the goals of the "Negro revolution" and King's commitment to pursue them in a nonviolent but persistent fashion. Three months later King's "I Have a Dream" oration at the March on Washington was heard by millions of Americans and brought more white support to the black cause while also further increasing his worldwide prominence. Late in 1963 *Time* magazine chose King its "Man of the Year," and eight months later King was awarded the Nobel Peace Prize for his nonviolent leadership of the American civil rights struggle.

Receipt of the Nobel Prize accelerated a broadening of King's vision and goals that had been underway since at least 1958. King's initial focus upon the evil of bus segregation during the Montgomery protest had been expanded into both a broader and more aggressive assault upon all manifestations of American racism and into areas beyond race. Racism was only one of several pressing evils in the world, and nonviolent protest could be used to combat these other scourges as well. Poverty and economic injustice could destroy human spirit much as racial oppression could, and King believed that thoroughgoing changes were needed both in American society and in the international economic order. King had spoken out against colonialism as early as 1956, and over time he increasingly coupled such attacks with denunciations of any sort of war as a means of resolving conflict and with warnings about the growing danger of nuclear annihilation.

The year 1965 brought King's most successful civil rights campaign, an effort designed to win federal legislation guaranteeing southern blacks' constitutional right to register and vote. SCLC-sponsored demonstrations in Selma, Alabama, evoked a violent police response much like that in Birmingham two years earlier, and led to swift congressional approval of the Voting Rights Act of 1965. With that effort behind him, King increasingly turned his attention, and his voice, to the issues of economic injustice in America and the United States' militaristic foreign policies.

King confronted the economic issue by launching SCLC's first major effort outside the South, a "war against slums" in Chicago. When SCLC staffers experienced only modest success in organizing poor ghetto residents, King shifted the focus to open-housing marches in all-white neighborhoods of the city. An inconclusive agreement with city authorities led most observers to judge King's first foray into this new area less than a success.

Beginning as early as the summer of 1965, King spoke out explicitly against the United States' military involvement in Vietnam. He amplified and strengthened his critique in the spring of 1967, and drew harsh criticism from many who previously supported his civil rights initiatives. Many whites, plus some notable black leaders, asserted that King had no expertise in the foreign policy arena, that his advocacy of nonviolence in the international realm was foolish, and that his outspokenness on Vietnam was costing the civil rights movement much of its support. King responded that he had a moral and prophetic responsibility to preach the truth as he saw it, regardless of short-term political consequences.

In the last year of his life, prior to his assassination in Memphis, Tennessee, on April 4, 1968, King's beliefs about American society became increasingly radical. Early in his public career he had been very much an optimist, believing that great racial progress could be obtained in several years' time, and that most significant ills in American society could be cured through political reform. As he matured, King increasingly realized not only the tenacity of racism but the depth and breadth of changes that American society needed to undergo before social justice would prevail. This growing realism, coupled with a judgment that nonviolent tactics would have to become more obstructive, was manifest in King's plans for a massive "Poor People's Campaign" in Washington, an effort that did not come to fruition until after his death.

King and the civil rights movement transformed the American South, and forever altered American race relations. Though at the end of his life he was pessimistic about securing his additional goals of economic justice and the elimination of war, King's commitment and message continue to represent a living challenge.

Bibliography:

A. *Strength to Love* (New York, 1963); *Stride Toward Freedom* (New York, 1958); *Where Do We Go From Here: Chaos or Community*? (New York, 1967); *Why We Can't Wait* (New York, 1964).

B. Lerone Bennett, Jr., *What Manner of Man* (4th rev. ed., Chicago, 1976); David J. Garrow, *Protest at Selma: Martin Luther King, Jr., and the Voting Rights Act of 1965* (New Haven, 1978); David J. Garrow, *The FBI and Martin Luther King, Jr.: From 'Solo' to Memphis* (New York, 1981); David L. Lewis, *King: A Biography* (2nd ed. Urbana, IL, 1978); Stephen B. Oates, *Let the Trumpet Sound* (New York, 1982); Lawrence D. Reddick, *Crusader Without Violence* (New York, 1959); Kenneth L. Smith and Ira G. Zepp, Jr., *Search for the Beloved Community: The Thinking of Martin Luther King, Jr.* (Valley Forge, PA, 1974).

C. Martin Luther King, Jr. Papers, Special Collections Department, Mugar Library, Boston University; Martin Luther King, Jr. Papers, and the Southern Christian Leadership Conference Papers, Martin Luther King, Jr. Center for Nonviolent Social Change, Atlanta, Ga.

David J. Garrow

KINOSHITA Naoe (12 October 1869, Matsumoto, Japan—5 November 1937, Tokyo). *Education*: B.A., Tokyo Semmon Gakkō (Waseda University), 1888. *Career*: editor-in-chief, *Shinano Nippō*, *Shin kigen*; pacifist author and journalist.

After graduation from the Tokyo Semmon Gakkō in 1888, Kinoshita Naoe became interested in Christian lay activities, the Yasuhara Virtue Society, and the Matsumoto Prohibition Society. He participated in the anti-prostitution campaign. At the age of twenty-four he was baptized. In 1897 he became a member of a social problems study group and led the universal suffrage movement. As a reporter for the *Mainichi*, one of the largest newspapers in Japan, he tackled the Ashio Mine copper pollution problem in 1900. In the following year, Kinoshita joined the Socialist Alliance and helped form the Shakai Minshutō, the first socialist party in Japan. The party was immediately banned by the government. By this time, he enjoyed a reputation as a Christian socialist reformer.

In the flourish of nationalism during the Russo-Japanese War (1904–5) Kinoshita wrote two antiwar novels, *Hi no hashira* (*The Pillar of Fire*) and *Otto no jihaku* (*The Husband's Confession*). The former is a story of a Christian socialist, Shinoda Chooji, who fights against Yamagi Gōzō, an avaricious capitalist. Yamagi forces his daughter, Umeko, to marry Captain Matsushima who is expected to become Naval Minister, while Umeko is in a platonic relationship with Shinoda. By attacking the corrupt collusion of a capitalist and a military officer, Kinoshita advocates socialism and peace. The central theme of the latter novel is antifeudalism. Kinoshita asserted that free love between man and woman should be admitted and that land should be given to those who cultivate it by abolishing the landlord system. In both works, Kinoshita's concern was with casting off the constraints of "semi-humanity" and restructuring a "whole man."

He valued above all else the "independent person," a self-aware human capable of autonomous action.

Kinoshita's pacifism was based upon the same conviction. War is wrong in itself, but it is also the greatest crime against humanity. War is often justified for the preservation of national sovereignty. For Kinoshita, however, the nation was only an instrument to realize the ideals of mankind, peace founded on the mutual love of human beings. As a Christian, he asserted that Japan's mission, ordained by God, was to act as the prime mover for world peace. In order to realize this goal, he recommended the reduction and abolition of armaments. When individuals transcended the idea of national sovereignty and thought in terms of all mankind, Kinoshita believed they would see how shortsighted was a peace based on the balance of terror resulting from armament rivalry. Consequently, the individual Japanese should do two things: reject the domestic "military government," which is permeated with "paternalistic despotism" and, in external relations, seek to realize international peaceful coexistence. This practical manifesto was surprisingly similar to the pacifist principles incorporated into the post-World War II Japanese constitution.

After the Russo-Japanese War, Kinoshita, once active in political movements, entered into a life of "religious seclusion," because though he was convinced that peace meant fulfilment of love, yet within himself he found only envy and hunger for power and reputation. He believed that war originated in the mind of people, and therefore a "human revolution" rather than a social revolution was essential for world peace. One finds similar ideas in the UNESCO Charter about half a century later.

Bibliography:

A. *Kinoshita Naoe Chosaku-shū* (15 vols, Tokyo, 1968–73); *Meiji Bungaku Zenshū* (vol. 45, *Kinoshita Naoe Shū*, Tokyo, 1965).

B. Takeshi Nishida, "Kinoshita Naoe: Pacifism and Religious Withdrawal," Bamba Nobuya and John F Howes, eds. *Pacifism in Japan: The Christian and Socialist Tradition* (Vancouver, 1978), 67–89; Takeda Kiyoko, *Seitō to Itan no Aida* (Tokyo, 1976).

Takeshi Nishida and Nobuya Bamba

KIRCHHOFF, Auguste Christine Louise Zimmermann (23 June 1867, Asbach, Germany—12 September 1940, Bremen, Germany). *Career*: social reformer, feminist, and pacifist.

Independence with regard to social conventions and prejudices apparently was instilled into Auguste Kirchhoff in her parents' Rhenish home. Her father was a liberal-minded Catholic lawyer who renounced his ties with the church. His daughter followed suit, only to return to Roman Catholicism in her later years. Kirchhoff had artistic talents and inclinations; she worked as a singer and voice teacher. Not only her artistic and literary inclinations, but her political convictions as well, were shared and supported by her husband, Gerhard Heinrich Kirchhoff, a liberal lawyer, jurist, member of the Bremen City Council, and Senator of the City of Bremen. Despite the care of a large family, the responsibilities of entertaining frequently, and her artistic interests, Kirchhoff became extremely active in the areas of social reform, feminism, and peace, both as a writer and lecturer.

Kirchhoff was prominent in the Deutsche Verband für Frauenstimmrecht (German Association for Women's Suffrage) which demanded universal, equal, secret, and direct voting rights for women. When this organization appeared to betray its old principles, she joined the more radical Deutschen Bund für Frauenstimmrecht (German Women's Suffrage League). Repeatedly, she took part in national and international congresses on women's rights where she came into contact with *Jane Addams. With similar energy, she, along with her friend *Helene Stöcker, fought for the protection of motherhood. In numerous articles in Stöcker's periodical, *Die Neue Generation*, she attacked the hypocritical social morality of Europeans towards prostitution, unmarried mothers, and children born out of wedlock. At the same time, she appealed to the sense of responsibility and self-respect of unwed mothers, promoted birth control, and called for the improvement of life for the less fortunate.

Kirchhoff demonstrated as much energy and passion in her support for the peace movement as she did for feminism. Above all, she appealed to German mothers—even during World War I—to educate their children in the spirit of peace. She participated in numerous international meetings of pacifist women, including the 1915 international women's Peace Congress held at The Hague. She was one of the leading members of the German branch of the Women's International League for Peace and Freedom (WILPF), whose local Bremen branch she founded and led until 1933. She participated in WILPF congresses in Zurich (1919), Vienna (1921), and The Hague (1922), as well as in the German conference of WILPF in Bremen in 1922, which she organized. Her peace work brought her into contact with the Quakers and with the Deutsche Friedensgesellschaft (German Peace Society) of which she became a member, and with whose presidents, first *Ludwig Quidde and then *Baron Paul von Schoenaich, she was in close touch.

Unconcerned about the opinions of her contemporaries and without sparing her health, this determined foe of nationalism and anti-Semitism continued her public activities, often bound up with exhausting travels in Europe and the United States, until 1933. Her last years were made more difficult not only by the actions of the Nazi regime, but also by the loss of her husband and a lingering illness.

Bibliography:

B. *Bremische Biographie 1912–1962* (Bremen 1969), 271–73.

Karl Holl
Trans. by Solomon Wank

KIRCHWEY, George Washington (3 July 1855, Detroit, MI—3 March 1942, New York). *Education*: B.A., Yale Coll., 1879; law studies, Yale School of Law and Albany Law School. *Career*: dean, Albany Law School, 1889–91;

professor, Columbia University School of Law, 1891–1916, dean, 1901–10; Commission on Prison Reform, New York State, 1913–14; warden, Sing Sing Prison, 1915–16; head, Department of Criminology, New York School of Social Work, 1917–32; law educator, criminologist, penologist, and internationalist; president, American Peace Society, 1915–17.

A student of international law and a strong advocate of peace, George Kirchwey became dissatisfied with his thriving law practice and accepted positions first at the Albany Law School and then at the School of Law at Columbia University. He became increasingly involved in social welfare activities and an outspoken critic of the administration of justice in the United States. Believing that specific proposals and not mere sentiments were required to guarantee peace, he called for the codification of international law and advancement of the Hague Peace Conferences. He helped found the American Society of International Law and served as its director from 1906 to 1921.

In 1906 Kirchwey also helped establish the New York Peace Society. Complaining that the Society lacked a working class membership, attracting only educational, ecclesiastical, and legal elites, Kirchwey worked diligently to alter the organization's composition. He failed, however, to bring labor into the peace movement. In 1912 he served as a delegate to the International Peace Congress in Geneva and from 1915 to 1917 he served as president of the American Peace Society.

Prior to American entry into World War I, Kirchwey strongly supported the concept of a league of nations. Believing that the United States was safe from attack, he insisted that the nation maintain its tradition of peace and reject the path of militarism. He favored close alliance with other neutral countries for the protection of their mutual interests and called for the creation of a league of peace amongst the American states to which other peacefully inclined states might later join.

As president of the American Peace Society, Kirchwey strongly opposed United States involvement in World War I, but he failed to suggest any specific policies that would guarantee American neutrality. He was severely criticized by officials of the Carnegie Endowment for International Peace, which financially supported the American Peace Society, for his reluctance to recommend a clear-cut course of action. When, however, in 1917, as President +Woodrow Wilson took the United States closer to the brink of war, Kirchwey recommended the creation of a world court and periodic congresses to settle international disputes, Carnegie Endowment officials again criticized him for offering too little too late.

Under pressure from the Endowment, Kirchwey resigned from the presidency of the American Peace Society shortly after America's entrance into the war. He turned his attention away from the peace movement and concentrated his efforts on the criminal justice system. Until his death in 1942, he played an important role in establishing the study of criminology as a scientific discipline in the United States and in fighting for methods of penal treatment based on rehabilitative care rather than deterrence. Both his ideas on penal reform and on peace were strongly influenced by his optimism, compassion, and Unitarian religious views.

Bibliography:

A. "How America May Contribute to the Permanent Peace of the World," *The Annals of the American Academy of Political and Social Science*, 61 (September, 1915), 230–34.

B. DAB, Suppl. 3, 1941–45, 420–21; NCAB, Current Volume B, 466–67; NYT, March 5, 1942.

Sherylle Petty

KIRYŪ Yūyū (20 May 1873, Kanazawa, Japan—10 September 1941, Nagoya, Japan). *Education*: B.A., Tokyo Imperial Univ., 1899. *Career*: journalist, editor, and publisher.

Kiryū Yūyū was an antiwar journalist who staunchly opposed war for nearly forty years. A precocious young man, he published essays, novels, and a book while still an undergraduate. During the decade following his graduation, he worked as an editor and writer for three different newspapers, where he developed a free, tough journalistic spirit that surrendered neither to power nor money.

In 1909 Kiryū became editor-in-chief of the *Shinano Mainichi shimbun*, but was forced to resign when he criticized the ritual suicide of General Nogi in 1912. Kiryū's resistance to military matters and his independent, indomitable spirit would cause him to lose editorial positions on several occasions. In 1924 he ran for membership in the House of Representatives, but was overwhelmingly defeated when the people of Nagoya rejected his uncompromising idealism. He also started a daily newspaper, *Chūkyō Asahi*, but was not successful with this venture.

In 1928 Kiryū again became editor-in-chief of the *Shinano Mainichi shimbun*. His editorials consistently opposed the militarists in Japan for their arbitrary adventures and openly attacked their actions. His essays such as "The Ominous Cloud of the Japan-America War," "The Coming Fate of the Japanese-Chinese Direct Negotiations," "The Great Lessons of the Ketsumeidan Incident," and "A Look at the Coming Difficulties for Japan" aroused the ire of military authorities and brought pressure from the special police. Finally, Kiryū's editorial, "Laughing at the Kanto Air Defense Exercises," forced his removal from the newspaper in 1933.

Kiryū then founded a private journal of ideas and contemporary criticism, *Tazan no ishi*, through which he eagerly wielded "the axe of a praying mantis" against the military and the bureaucracy. During his last eight years, he published 176 issues of *Tazan no ishi*. His columns regularly lashed out at the military and their war efforts as he uncompromisingly argued that "if the pen does not kill the sword, then the sword will kill the pen." His stinging criticisms caused the government authorities frequently to cancel publication of his journal. At the time of the Minobe Incident of 1935, Kiryū insisted on opposition to war.

He urged not only armament reduction but also military abolishment. During the critical 1936–37 period, Kiryū published articles praising *Saitō Takao's House speeches which attacked the military, criticized the folly of the Japan-China War, complained of undue emphasis on nationalism and defense, derided the lack of economic sense of war, and argued that he who advocated pacifism could be a patriot. In 1939 Kiryū condemned the "military diplomacy" and denied the existence of a "holy war." He called for a world controlled by "love" and urged people to fear "modern war." In 1940 he criticized the Japanese expansionistic concept of "eight corners of the earth under one roof," strongly supported political democracy as represented by the Diet system, and spoke of his anxiety against the long war. In 1941 he advised his decreasing readership that Japan should avoid war with the United States and advocated the principle of "moral nationalism." Fittingly, the government banned the last issue of *Tazan no ishi* shortly before Kiryū's death.

Kiryū Yūyū died of pneumonia on September 10, 1941, thus ending the journalism career of a man who staunchly resisted war throughout his life. Although operating only on a small scale and suffering the frequent censureship and prohibitions of the government authorities, Kiryū maintained a steady stream of caustic criticism toward military fascism in Japan.

Bibliography:

A. *Kiryū Yūyū hangun ronshū*, edited by Ōta Masao (Tokyo, 1969); *Kiryū Yūyū Jiden*, (Tokyo, 1973); Kiryū Masaji, *Chikushōdō no chikyū - Kiryū Yūyū* (Tokyo, 1952).

B. Maeda Yūji, *Pen wa shinazu - Kiryū Yūyū no shōgai* (Tokyo, 1962); Ōta Masao, *Kiryū Yūyū Aru hansen jyānarisuto no shōgai* (Tokyo, 1970).

William D. Hoover

KITAMURA Tōkoku (10 February 1869, Odawara, Japan—16 May 1894, Tokyo). *Education*: attended Tokyo Semmon Gakkō (now Waseda Univ.). *Career*: editor-in-chief, *Heiwa* (*Peace*); founder, Nihon Heiwa-kai (Japan's first peace society), 1889; author, poet, and pacifist thinker.

By the autumn of 1883 when Kitamura Tōkoku, at the age of fourteen, entered the Department of Political Economy at Tokyo Semmon Gakkō, he had already been an active member of the Popular Rights Movement, which called for the establishment of a popular assembly. Ready to "sacrifice" himself for the "cause of freedom," he soon became disgusted by the corruption and internal schisms in the Movement and decided to become a writer like *Victor Hugo "who propounded his political ideals through the power of the pen."

Through the influence of Ishizaka Mina, a pious Christian who subsequently became his wife, Kitamura was baptized at the age of nineteen. With extreme sensitivity and burning passion, he struggled to explore the world of the inner life—self, ego, and love. Through these literary themes he sought to explore individual freedom. He fought against every form of external restriction including the Imperial Rescript on Education (1890) with its emphasis on loyalty to the state as a means to achieve national strength.

Kitamura was greatly influenced by William Jones, an active member of the British Peace Society, who visited Japan in August, 1889 and gave a lecture on the goals of his organization. Giving a vivid account of his experience in the Franco-Prussian War of 1870, Jones portrayed the cruelty and misery of war. He warned that future wars would be more cruel and might even invite the total destruction of mankind. Jones's sermon shocked all the Japanese at the meeting, including Kitamura and Katō Kazuharu (1861–1932), Kitamura's friend, for they had never experienced a modern international war. The year of 1889, when Jones visited Japan, was a memorable year for world peace movements: in this year the Second International opposing war was organized and the Universal Peace Congress in Paris attracted various peace organizations from many countries. Amid such world currents, and stimulated by Jones's preachings, Kitamura, together with Katō organized Nihon Heiwa-kai, the first peace society in Japan. About two years later, Kitamura began to publish the Society's journal, *Heiwa*. In the first issue (March 15, 1892), he wrote: "The word 'Peace' is still novel in Japan, and it is even more so to our non-Christian population. Nevertheless, we believe that to establish 'Peace' must be our most fundamental and lofty aspiration. Following Christian teachings, which support the truth that all peoples of the four seas are brothers, I believe that to break this great law and to fight among countries is the greatest shame of mankind."

Kitamura's pacifism was based upon Christianity, especially Quakerism, but it was broad enough to include other religions as well. Kitamura asserted that peace was the ultimate ideal for mankind, and that it could be achieved only through the union of conscience by all people in the world. While most Japanese were immersed in militant nationalism, he warned them that a military build-up could never exalt national prestige. On the contrary, it would eventually destroy the nation. Those who kill others are doomed to be killed. He foresaw a horrible destiny for mankind if modern wars continued with ever more sophisticated weapons.

For Kitamura, the problem of war and peace was essentially the problem of the free individual's conscience which man shared with his fellow men. To attain peace, according to Kitamura, man must, first and above all, secure the independence of the inner world by emancipating himself from the imprisonment of the external world. In the inner world, there is a "secret world," the core of which is Mind. He called it *seishin*, literally meaning "the just mind." Hence, in Kitamura's thinking, only when every individual in the world succeeds in attaining his Inner Freedom, and thereby in securing his conscience, can peace be established. And, because the just mind is a special quality given to each individual by nature, it is inalienable. Nobody, no power, and no system should deprive the individual of this treasure. Man at the same time has to value it above all else. He must constantly cleanse it and purify it. Then, says Kitamura, the greatest crimes and the greatest evils will disappear, and instead, the greatest love and the greatest good will emanate from the secret world. And this real Man, the true Man, can communicate with Heaven by transcending time and space. He is blessed with eternal Life, eternal Freedom, and eternal Peace. In short, Kitamura's idea of world peace was fundamentally interconnected with his belief in the universality of the free individual's conscience unbound by the particulars of race, state, or international system.

In Meiji Japan (1868–1912), amid feudalistic remnants, autocratic power, and overwhelming patriotism, Kitamura's search for an "inner life" and spiritual freedom was a lonely and painful path that finally ended in suicide. Although he lived for only twenty-five years, as a leader of neoteric writers, as a modernizer, and as a precursor of the pacifist movement, Kitamura's influence was enormous. The important literary figure Shimazaki Tōson (1872–1943) believed that "he was a true genius." *Kinoshita Naoe recollected in his later years that Kitamura together with Fukuzawa Yukichi (1835–1901), a giant among Meiji intellectual leaders, were the two "great benefactors" of his thought.

Bibliography:

A. *Tōkoku Zenshū* (3 vols., Tokyo, 1950–55).

B. Nobuya Bamba, "Kitamura Tōkoku: His Pursuit of Freedom and World Peace," Nobuya Bamba and John F. Howes, eds., *Pacifism in Japan* (Vancouver, 1978), 35–66; Hiraoka Toshio, *Kitamura Tōkoku Kenkyū* (Tokyo, 1967).

Nobuya Bamba

KLEINEIBST, Richard (30 March 1886, Weilburg on the Lahn, Germany—27 April 1976, Kilchberg near Zurich, Switzerland). *Education*: Ph.D., Univ. of Strassburg [now Univ. of Strasbourg], 1915. *Career*: editor, publisher, journalist, writer, and pacifist.

Richard Kleineibst, son of a Jewish family, served in the German army on the Western Front from 1915 until 1918. During the revolutionary period of 1918-19, he was chairman of the Soldiers' and Workers' Council of Freiburg im Breisgau. The experience of the First World War caused him to give up his philosophical-literary ambitions, join the Sozialdemokratische Partei Deutschlands (German Social Democratic Party) (SPD) and become a political journalist. From 1919, as editor-in-chief of and contributor to several left-opposition newspapers as well as the *Sozialistische Monatshefte*, Kleineibst adopted a critical stance toward Weimar Germany's domestic development and foreign policy as well as toward the foreign policies of other European states. The nationalism whipped up in response to the Franco-Belgian invasion of the Ruhr resulting from Germany's default on reparations payments in 1923, strengthened Kleineibst's view that the "Wilhelmine imperialist bacillus" lived on in Germany after 1918, nourishing a growing "will to war." To counter this pernicious development, Kleineibst supported the course of the Westdeutsche Landesverband (West German Regional Association) (WLV) of the Deutschen Friedensgesellschaft (German Peace Society) (DFG), which gave priority in its peace strategy to extirpating the Prussian military tradition.

Among others, Kleineibst fought against the secret and illegal rearmament of Germany and propaganda alleging that France and Poland were threats to Germany. He also challenged the official line maintaining the innocence of the imperial German government in the unleashing of World War I; and the efforts to undermine the Treaty of Versailles. He condemned the policies of all of the center-left political parties including the SPD and the Kommunistische Partei Deutschlands (German Communist Party) (KPD) for supporting policies weakening the republic and favoring the rise of the Nazis. In view of the increasing militarization of politics he was very critical of the SPD's continuing justification of German defensive measures, especially the funding for building a pocket battleship in 1928. In European international relations, Kleineibst reproached the British government for failing to see that its support of German desires for far-reaching revisions of the Treaty of Versailles only served to isolate France and that its pursuit of balance of power politics was being exploited by nationalist German military and political circles to restore Germany's position as a great power. Kleineibst believed that England hindered a Franco-German understanding which he felt was crucial for future peace.

Kleineibst wrote for both *Fritz Röttcher's *Menschheit* and *Friedrich W. Foerster's *Die Zeit*. As one of the most important contributors to *Fritz Küster's *Das Andere Deutschland*, Kleineibst became embroiled in conflict with the SPD when Küster and the more radical WLV took over the leadership of the DFG in 1929. Kleineibst left the SPD in 1931 and took part in the founding of the Sozialistiche Arbeiterpartei Deutschlands (German Socialist Workers Party) (SAP), becoming editor-in-chief of the party's newspaper, *Sozialistische Arbeiterzeiting*, in November 1931. Within the SAP, Kleineibst was a representative of the radical pacifist minority around *Heinrich Ströbel and *Anna Siemsen which wanted to make a pacifist policy the chief plank of the party's program. The majority opposed this and Kleineibst was removed from his editorial position. In May 1932 Kleineibst moved to Switzerland, but returned to Berlin in October to become chairman of the Berlin chapter of the DFG and *Heinz Kraschutzki's successor as editor-in-chief of *Das Andere Deutschland*.

Seeing the threat to peace coming from developments in Germany, Kleineibst appealed to the SPD and KPD to bury their differences and concentrate on preventing a fascist take-over of power. He urged the two parties to break with their past policies and to use the "economic weapon" of the workers to preserve democracy in Germany. After the Nazi accession to power in January 1933, Kleineibst and his wife, a well known novelist under her French Huguenot maiden name of Claude Lepère, fled to Switzerland where they settled in a worker's district on the edge of Zurich. Through Siemsen and Ströbel, Kleineibst came into contact with the Religious-Social Association under *Leonhard Ragaz. Under various pseudonyms, Kleineibst continued his journalistic struggle against the danger of war represented by Germany, publishing in various European papers. He continued to attack England for yielding to German desires at the cost of French security and even charged the British in 1938 with abetting "criminality, barbarism and the destruction of civilization and culture." France, however, did not escape his criticism. He pilloried France's "policy of suicide" and urged France to throw off its fatalism "and give priority to collective security." In June 1939 the Nazi regime deprived Kleineibst of his German citizenship, and he chose to remain in Switzerland after the Second World War.

Bibliography:

A. *Englands Schatten über Europa. 300 Jahre englischer Aussenpolitik* (under the pseudonym of Klaus Bühler) (Paris, 1938); *Georg Christoph Lichtenbergs Stellung zur deutschen Literatur* (Strassburg, 1915).

B. H. Drechsler, *Die Sozialistische Arbeiterpartei Deutschlands. Ein Beitrag zuer Geschichte der deutschen Arbeiterbewegung am Ende der Weimarer Republik* (Meisenheim am Glan, 1965); P. Trauvetter, "Dr. Richard Kleineibst aum 70. Geburtstag," *Der Aufbau*, 15 (Zurich, 6 April 1956).

Helmut Donat
Trans. by Solomon Wank

KOLLONTAI, Aleksandra Mikhailovna Domontovich (31 March 1872, St. Petersburg, Russia—9 March 1952, Moscow). *Education*: private tutors. *Career*: Marxist revolutionary and feminist; Commissar of Social Welfare, first communist government of Soviet Russia, 1917-18; head, Woman's Bureau of the Communist party of the Soviet Union, 1920-22; diplomat, 1922-45; author.

Aleksandra Kollontai was first a Marxist revolutionary, dedicated to the destruction of the established order in Europe, and only secondarily a peace advocate. She was not a pacifist; she was quite willing to support wars which she considered just, as during the Russian Civil War (1918-20), but she did feel deeply the horrors of war and she did devote herself wholeheartedly to opposition to World War I and to making peace between the Soviet Union and Finland during World War II.

During World War I, Kollontai supported V. I. Lenin's call for the troops at the front to turn their guns against their officers, then march home to begin an assault on the ruling classes. This mutiny, Lenin wrote, would usher in the international revolution which would sweep capitalism from Europe. Kollontai promoted Lenin's views in Scandinavia and in the United States, which she visited in 1915 and 1916. She also wrote a pamphlet, *Komu nuzhna voina*? (*Who Needs the War*?) (1916) which was smuggled to the front lines. Kollontai's work as Lenin's lieutenant had few results, however, since most socialists who opposed the war would not accept Lenin's theories or his leadership.

Far more productive were Kollontai's efforts to end the war between Finland and the Soviet Union during World War II. Kollontai was serving as Soviet ambassador to Sweden when word came of the Soviet attack on Finland on November 30, 1939. There was a special sadness in this news for Kollontai, for she had spent her childhood summers in Finland and her maternal grandfather had been a Finn. As the ensuing negotiations between Helsinki and Moscow flowed through her embassy and the Swedish Foreign Ministry, Kollontai took the risk of softening Soviet ultimata from time to time in order to persuade the Finns to make peace. She also continually reassured V. I. Molotov, Soviet

Foreign Minister, of the Finns' good faith, and at least once suppressed a communiqué from Helsinki certain to anger Molotov. Although the terms agreed to in March 1940 were draconian, Kollontai's work may have shortened the war.

In 1943 and 1944 Kollontai played the role of intermediary again. This time the process was more difficult and protracted, because of the presence of substantial German forces on Finnish territory. Again Kollontai used every means at her disposal to keep the negotiations from breaking down. Again her objective was to save Finnish and Soviet lives, but she also feared a Soviet occupation of Finland. A harsh peace was finally signed in September 1944. Swedish diplomats involved in the negotiations believed that Kollontai's gentle but zealous diplomacy had won easier terms for Finland than might have been imposed otherwise. For her work in ending both wars she was nominated for the Nobel Peace Prize in 1946.

Bibliography:

A. *The Autobiography of a Sexually Emancipated Communist Woman* (New York, 1971); *Komu nuzhna voina*? (Bern, 1916); *Love of Worker Bees* (Chicago, 1978); *Selected Writings of Alexandra Kollontai* (Westport, CT, 1977).

B. Barbara Evans Clements, *Bolshevik Feminist, the Life of Aleksandra Kollontai* (Bloomington, IN, 1979); Beatrice Farnsworth, *Alexandra Kollontai* (Stanford, CA, 1980).

Barbara Evans Clements

KOLLWITZ, Käthe Schmidt (8 July 1867, Königsberg, East Prussia, Germany—22 April 1945, Moritzburg, German Democratic Republic). *Education*: Zeichen-und-Malschule des Vereins der Kunstlerinnen (Women's School of Drawing and Painting), Berlin, 1885-86, Munich, 1888-89. *Career*: graphic artist and sculptor, 1899-1943; professor, Graphic Arts, Akademie der Künste, 1919-33; feminist and pacifist.

By the time Käthe Kollwitz became a peace leader in the mid-1920s, her reputation as one of Europe's outstanding graphic artists was firmly established. In 1899 she had been the first woman to receive the Gold Medal for artistic excellence; in 1907 she had been granted the Villa Romana Prize, a year's sabbatical in Florence, Italy, by the German Historical Commission. In addition to these honors, Kollowitz was well known because of the intense popularity of her works.

A personal tragedy during World War I created a turning point in Kollowitz's political principles and practices. Prior to 1914, personally and through her graphic work, Kollwitz was a revolutionary advocating violent means of societal change. But in October 1914, the death of her eighteen-year-old son, one of the first draftees of World War I, permanently changed her political vision and stance from that of revolutionary Marxist to pacifist.

By profession and temperament Kollwitz was independent, though she did ally herself, from its founding in 1915, with the Women's International League for Peace and Freedom (WILPF). To this group she contributed many works, created specially commissioned posters, and was a primary signatory for all its antiwar policies and legislation. A phrase from German folk custom and literary tradition, ''seedcorn for planting must not be ground,'' was the moral cornerstone of Kollwitz' pacifist stance. She used this almost archaic reference to a farming practice employed in preparation of the soil as a metaphor applied to the waste, especially of youth, in war. From the period of shattering grief and self-searching during World War I to her death in 1945, the phrase became her written standard bearer against war. It titled not only a major, influential article against the draft, published in October 1918 in the dailies, *Vorwärts* and *Vossiche Zeitung*, but also titled drawings of important antiwar works and her last great lithograph, done in 1942.

The decade of the 1920s, in addition to being the most prolific period in Kollwitz's worklife, was also the period in which her influence as a peace leader became widespread throughout western and eastern Europe. Her contribution to the cause of peace was as original as her artistic genius. She had an incomparable power to move people to pacifist sentiment and action. During the 1920s Kollwitz created more antiwar works of art than any other artist in the twentieth century. One of these, ''The Volunteers,'' equals Picasso's, ''Guernica'' as the century's most eloquent visual expression against war. In addition to creating works for the WILPF, Kollwitz produced art for the International Trade Union Congress (Amsterdam and Brussels), the International Workers' Relief Organization (Vienna), and Nie Wieder Krieg! (Never Again War!) (Leipzig). For Nie Wieder Krieg!, founded in 1919 to introduce German youth to pacifist sentiment among soldiers and workers, Kollwitz produced one of the world's most stirring antiwar works, ''Nie Wieder Krieg!'' a composition of a youth, arm high, beside him Nie Wieder Krieg! writ large and broad.

In addition to ''The Volunteers'' and ''Nie Wieder Krieg!'' ''Brot!'' ''Brotherhood,'' and ''The Mothers,'' were monumental works used and widely reproduced to draw pacifist support. The public effect of these was enormous, for all were posters, or poster-like in scale, passionate and unequivocal in their protest against war. Kollwitz thus became a peace leader due to the eloquence of her artistic genius, in which she combined exquisite craft with the subject matter of personal suffering and the perspective of a moral vision applied to politics. By 1929 she was the most famous and highly regarded artist of antiwar art.

In 1933, with the rise of Adolf Hitler and National Socialism to political power, Kollwitz, with many other artists, was forced into a decline. She was dismissed from her professorship at the Berlin Academy of Art, where she had been the first woman to teach the Master Class in Graphic Art. With artists *Georg Grosz, Max Lieberman, Ernst Barlach, and Otto Nagel, Kollwitz was labeled ''degenerate,'' and banned from exhibiting works publicly. Despite the hostile political climate, Kollwitz created as many powerful and inspiring works of antiwar art in the 1930s as she had the decade prior this time in a new medium, sculpture. A pair of works, ''The Mother,'' and ''The Father,'' resembling Käthe and her doctor-husband Karl, are lifesize, mourning parents, universal monuments to war-created grief. Other bronze sculptures, antiwar in theme and exquisite in artistry, were "Picta" and "Tower of the Mothers."

Although threatened by the Gestapo with removal to a concentration camp, Kollwitz and her husband remained in their north Berlin home. Her husband was prohibited from practicing medicine because he "did not have enough Aryan blood in him," but Kollwitz supported both of them through the private sale of antiwar works. In 1940 her husband died and the following year Kollwitz left Berlin, her home in ruins from air-raid bombings.

Her last work, a lithograph, visualizing the creed she had embraced throughout her lifework, "Seedcorn for planting must not be ground," was done in Moritzburg, a country village close enough for her to hear the bombing of Dresden. In 1945, her final year, Kollwitz wrote prolifically about pacifism, broadening her basic moral position to include philosophy. She died affirming the hope that pacifism would revolutionize the world. "Some day," she wrote, "a new ideal will arise, and there will be an end to all wars."

Bibliography:

A. *The Diary and Letters of Kaethe Kollwitz*, ed. by Hans Kollwitz, trans. by Richard and Clara Winston (Chicago, 1955).

B. Martha Kearns, *Käthe Kollwitz: Woman and Artist* (New York, 1977).

C. Tagebuchblätter [Diaries] 1909-1943, Käthe Kollwitz Archiv., Akademie der Künste, West Berlin.

Martha Kearns

KŌTOKU Shūsui (pseud. of Kōtoku Denjirō) (5 November 1871, Nakamura, Kōchi prefecture, Japan—24 January 1911, Tokyo). *Education*: irregular formal schooling through the fourth grade of the middle school, but studied Chinese classics and English outside the official school system. *Career*: journalist, author and revolutionary.

Kōtoku Shūsui was an exceptionally bright child, but he was unable to finish even middle school due to financial difficulties and extensive political involvement. It was fortunate for him that in 1888 he became a servant-student in the house of Nakae Chōmin, a famous scholar-journalist. Kōtoku received a tremendous influence from this rather eccentric "Rousseau of the Orient" who was not only a teacher but also a kind of father figure for Kōtoku whose father had died earlier.

Kōtoku started his career as a journalist in 1893. After working for two newspaper companies, in 1898 he joined the staff of the *Yorozu chōhō*, a newspaper which attracted many leading intellectuals as editorial writers. In the same year he became a member of the Society for the Study of Socialism, a pioneer group for the study of socialism in Japan.

His exposure to socialist ideas may have attracted him to pacifism. Kōtoku published his first pacifist articles at the time of the Boxer Rebellion (1900) in which Japan became involved by joining the international relief expedition to China. The platform of the ephemeral Social Democratic party (Shakai minshu tō), which Kōtoku founded with five other people in 1901, also advocated complete disarmament in order to realize world peace.

Kōtoku's opposition to war was much more conspicuous at the time of the Russo-Japanese War (1904-5). In October 1903 Kōtoku, together with two other colleagues, resigned from the *Yorozu chōhō* because they could not endorse its decision to support the coming war with Russia. In the socialist weekly *Heimin shimbun*, which he created with his comrades, Kōtoku continued to voice his opposition to the war. Unlike *Uchimura Kanzō, Kōtoku did not soften the tone of his denunciation of the war even after its actual outbreak in February 1904.

Kōtoku's pacifist stand inevitably brought him to a headlong collision with state power. Increasingly intense government interference with his activities transformed him into an anarchist. Kōtoku was executed in 1911 as the alleged chief conspirator of a plot to assassinate the Meiji Emperor.

Kōtoku was one of the very first people in modern Japanese history who took a conscious antimilitaristic stand as a matter of principle. Kōtoku disagreed with *Leo Tolstoy and believed that economic competition, rather than moral depravation of individuals, was at the root of war. Thus he advocated a socialist transformation of the existing capitalistic system as a real remedy for wars. However, his pacifist writings are not without strong ethical notes of their own, a condition which might be connected with his early exposure to confucian classics. At any rate, their appeal is not confined to socialist readers. It was Uchimura Kanzō, a nonsocialist, who wrote the recommendatory foreword to Kōtoku's first book, *Nijusseiki no kaibutsu: teikokushugi* (*Imperialism: The Spectre of the Twentieth Century*) (1901). This book was a vigorous denunciation of the so-called patriotism and militarism behind imperialistic policies. In it Kōtoku pointed out that wars could be profitable only to a small minority and that they would bring misery to the majority. Despite his violent end, incongruent with the usual image of a pacifist, Kōtoku's antimilitarism was very consistent and was surprisingly central to all his activities.

Bibliography:

A. *Kōtoku Shūsui* (Itō Sei, ed., Tokyo, 1970); *Kōtoku Shūsui Shū*, Asukai Masamichi, ed., (Tokyo, 1975).

B. Asukai Masamichi, *Kōtoku Shūsui: Chojusetsu kōdō ron no genryū* (Tokyo, 1969); F. G. Notehelfer, *Kōtoku Shūsui: A Portrait of a Japanese Radical* (Cambridge, 1971); Ōhara Satoshi, *Kōtoku Shūsui no shisō to taigyaku jiken* (Tokyo, 1977); Tanaka Sōgorō, *Kōtoku Shūsui: Ichi kakumeika no shisō to shōgai* (Tokyo, 1971).

Yuzo Ota

KRASCHUTZKI, Heinz (20 August 1891, Danzig, Germany [now Gdańsk, Poland]—27 October 1982, Füssen/Allgäu, Federal Republic of Germany). *Education*: gymnasium (secondary school), passed school-leaving examination (Abitur), 1910. *Career*: officer, Imperial German Navy, 1910-19; director, Norddeutschen Netzwerke (North German Net Factory in Itzehoe), 1919-22; manager Hochsee-Netzwerke (High-Sea Net Factory in Itzehoe), 1922-26; editor, *Das*

Andere Deutschland 1926-32; founder and director of a factory in Spain, 1932-36; lecturer in history and teacher education, Potsdam, 1946-48; prison official, first as head of the educational program at the prison for juveniles in Berlin-Plötzensee and then chief welfare officer in the Berlin penitentiary, 1948-56; writer, journalist, and pacifist.

Heinz Kraschutzki, the son of a military physician (who was more military than physician), followed tradition by becoming an officer. As a counter-balance to the mindless militaristic spirit of the German empire the young naval officer turned to the youth and life-reform movements whose aims were attractive to him because he was both a vegetarian and teetotaler. His first doubts about his military career led him to consider a future in private shipping, but he gave up those plans in August 1914 and enthusiastically followed the call to arms. His enthusiasm began to wane near the end of 1916 when he realized that Germany was heading for defeat and revolution. He turned completely against the war when he read forbidden literature supplied him by *Hans Paasche which revealed the guilt of the imperial regime for unleashing World War I. In the revolutionary upheaval of November 1918, Kraschutzki, a lieutenant-commander and captain of a minesweeper, was elected by revolting sailors to represent them in the Bremershaven Workers and Soldiers Council.

Convinced of the senselessness of militarism, Kraschutzki became increasingly involved in the German peace movement. He joined the Deutsche Friedensgesellschaft (German Peace Society) (DFG) and the Deutsche Liga für Menschenrechte (German League for Human Rights) (DLF). He founded the Itzehoe branch of the DFG and served as its chairman until October 1926. In June 1925 he was elected as vice-chairman of the Arbeitsgemeinschaft Schleswig-Holstein (Schleswig-Holstein Study Group) of the DFG and was a member of its steering committee until 1927. Aside from his interest in German-Danish, German-French, and German-Belgian reconciliation, Kraschutzki, who in 1925 joined the War Resisters' International, demanded the abandonment of the Prussian-German spirit of aggression which he saw as responsible for the world war. In addition to his activity in various organizations, Kraschutzki wrote for the monthly *Junge Menschen*, the organ of the republican-pacifist wing of the youth movement published by *Walter Hammer, and for *Deutsche Zukunft*, the publication of the North German Branch of the DFG.

In 1926 Kraschutzki associated himself with the more radical West German wing of the DFG which held that a peaceful Germany and Europe was impossible without German acknowledgment of the pre-1914 imperial government's responsibility for the outbreak of World War I and the rooting out of the Prussian military tradition which continued to exist in the Reichswehr (army) and elsewhere in the Weimar state. Initially, he became a speaker for the Westdeutsche Landesverband (West German Regional Association) (WLV) of the DFG and, a short time thereafter, editor of the weekly *Das Andere Deutschland* published by *Fritz Küster. In addition to his peace activities, Kraschutzki opposed the death penalty and propaganda for German-Austrian Anschluss. Specifically charged with reporting about the situation in Poland for *Das Andere Deutschland*, Kraschutzki advocated the recognition of the eastern borders and the Polish Corridor.

Having been a member of the Sozialdemokratische Partei Deutschlands (German Social Democratic Party) (SPD) from 1925, he left the party in 1928 after its elected representatives approved funds for the construction of a pocket battleship. From then on he remained free from any party affiliation. Accused of "treason" because he had helped to reveal the illegal German rearmament efforts, he avoided arrest in May 1932 by emigrating to Spain with his wife and four children. In March 1934, he was deprived of his German citizenship by the Nazi government. A few days after the outbreak of the Spanish Civil War in July 1936, he was arrested upon the instigation of the Nazi regime and sentenced to life imprisonment.

He returned to Berlin in 1946. There he worked for the American occupation authorities and once again became an important collaborator for *Das Andere Deutschland*, which Fritz Küster had resumed publishing in 1947. He spoke out against rearming Germany and demanded the recognition of the Oder-Neisse border as a necessary condition for German-Polish reconciliation. As a member of the council of the War Resisters' International from 1947 to 1962, he made use of his international contacts to support an East-West policy of detente. His activity as a prison official was characterized by his belief in rehabilitation and the humane treatment of prisoners. In 1968 he was appointed to a federal commission to reform the prison system.

Up to the very moment of his death, Kraschutzki, blind since his eightieth year but imbued with a deep religiosity that was tied to no dogma and no institution, directed his energies toward the preservation of a peaceful world. In the last years of his life he became concerned about man's destruction of nature and of the environment. Shortly before his death he wrote to numerous politicians of the Federal Republic to convince them of the necessity of continuing a policy of detente.

Bibliography:

A. "Meine Wandlung: Fort von Militarismus! Ein Kapitanleutnant a.D. erinnert sich an Hans Paasche," in H. Donat, ed., *Auf der Flucht erschossen . . . Schriften und Beiträge von und über Hans Paasche* (Bremen/Zeven, 1981), 49-52; *Ost und West* (issued by the Internationale der Kriegsdienstgegner, Deutscher Zweig, Hamburg, 1949); ed., *Staatsgefährdung? Ein dokumentarischer Bericht über den Düsseldorfer Prozess gegen Angehörige des Friedenskomitees der Bundesrepublik Deutschland* (Hannover, 1961); *Die Untaten der Gerechtigkeit. Vom Übel der Vergeltungsstrafe, dargestellt an lll Fällen aus der Urteils- und Vollzugspraxis unserer Tage* (Munich, 1966; 2nd abridged ed., *Die Gerechtigkeitsmaschine. Erfahrungen mit Strafen und Strafvollzug* (Karlsruhe, 1970); *Die verborgene Geschichte des Korea-Krieges* (Hannover, 1957).

B. Helmut Donat, "Erinnerung an einen vergessenen Veteran der deutschen Friedensbewegung: Heinz Kraschutzki," in H. Donat and Johann P. Tammen, eds., *Frie-*

denszeichen Lebenszeichen. Pazifismus zwischen Verächtlichmachung und Rehabilitierung. Ein Lesebuch zur Friedenserziehung (Bremerhaven, 1982), 174-84.

Helmut Donat
Trans. by Peter Seadle

KRAUS, Karl (28 April 1874, Jičin, Bohemia, Austria-Hungary [now Czechoslovakia]—12 June 1936, Vienna). *Education*: gymnasium (high school) diploma, 1892; studies in law and philosophy, Univ., of Vienna, 1893-96. *Career*: satirist, poet, aphorist, lecturer, cultural critic; founder, publisher, editor, and, from 1909, sole contributor, *Die Fackel*, 1899-1936.

Karl Kraus was one of the few German-Austrians and members of the educated upper classes who was not swept along by the tide of chauvinism at the outbreak of World War I. He was the only Austrian writer of rank who from the beginning openly challenged the war. Kraus' pacifism and antiwar stance appear surprising in the light of his prewar conservative political and social views, but they were consistent with the ethical vision underlying his pre-war cultural criticism.

Before 1914 Kraus, the son of a wealthy Jewish businessman, was a scathing critic of what he saw as the dehumanizing forces of laissez-faire capitalism, commercialization of culture, mass-democracy, and technology. The daily press and journalistic language, as the chief instruments of the trivialization and mechanization of life, were, for Kraus, the incarnation of all of these evils. He assigned to language a primary role in human affairs; culture was constructed out of language and existed only in language. Therefore the corruption of language—i.e. its loss of meaning through a rift between what was being said and what was being done—was synonymous with the corruption of morality, culture, and politics. Kraus associated the corruption of language in his time with the press which he saw as an offshoot of the cultural relativism and marketplace values of Liberalism. As a consequence, his crusade to preserve authentic values and restore meaning to language led to his extolling the conservative forces in Austria—church, army, aristocracy—as representatives of absolute value and standards apart from the marketplace. Kraus later admitted that his trust in the moral fibre of Austrian conservatism had been misplaced and that he had idealized those very forces which had plunged Austria-Hungary into a destructive war. In any event, the sources of Kraus' ethical vision lay elsewhere than in idealized conservative values. His ethical vision of a more perfect form of community based on the potential for goodness residing in man's imaginative and creative faculties was similar to the vision of a nonviolent transformation of human values held up by the idealist strain of anarchism represented by *Leo Tolstoy and *Peter Kropotkin with which Kraus sympathized but never identified himself. It was this positive, pacifist ethical vision, underlying his pessimistic satirical writings, that broke through the thin veneer of his prewar conservatism and makes comprehensible his becoming an unconditional pacifist rejecting all violence—opposition to Adolf Hitler later becoming the only exception.

Kraus waged a lonely war on war in the years 1914-18. He never joined any of the more explicitly political antiwar circles such as those around +Heinrich Lammasch and *Julius Meinl. His weapons were the same ones he used in his prewar cultural battles—his pen and his voice. Lonely though his struggle against the war may have been, his courage and penetrating wit planted the seeds of opposition to war in others. "In dieser grossen Zeit" ("In This Great Time"), a public lecture delivered in November 1914 and published in the December issue of *Die Fackel*, was characteristic of Kraus' wartime writings. With mordant satire and irony, he deflated the inspiring platitudes mouthed by every politician, military leader, and educator in wartime. He revealed the incongruity of words and deeds, the collusion of commerce with the military, and the mendacity of the press. All of these themes were enlarged to gigantic proportions in his extremely satirical *Die letzten Tage der Menschheit* (*The Last Days of Mankind*), parts of which were published in *Die Fackel* beginning in 1915.

Die letzen Tage der Menschheit portrayed World War I in all of its lurid detail. About half of the text consisted of newspaper reports and documents of all kinds, such as reports from the front, editorials, government decrees, court judgments, business advertisements, and letters. In hundreds of "pictures" Kraus depicted the misery, murder, and destruction of the war. Many of the "pictures" depicted in a farcically "comic" way, the frightful stupidity, cruelty, hypocrisy, and venality of the avid supporters of the war, especially those in the upper crust of society and in certain professions. The epilogue, which presented an apocalyptic vision of the destruction of mankind by war and militarism, is even more relevant today than it was in Kraus' lifetime.

Bibliography:

A. *Die Dritte Walpurgisnacht* (Munich, 1952); *Half-Truths & One-and-a-Half Truths: Karl Kraus, Selected Aphorisms*, ed. by Harry Zohn (Montreal, 1976); *In These Great Times: A Karl Kraus Reader*, ed. by Harry Zohn (Montreal, 1976); *Die letzten Tage der Menschheit* (Vienna, 1922 new edition, Munich, 1964; English trans., New York, 1976); *Weltgericht* (2 vols., Leipzig, 1919); *Werke*, ed. by Heinrich Fischer (14 vols., Munich, 1952-1967).

B. Frank Field, *The Last Days of Mankind: Karl Kraus and His Vienna* (New York, 1968); Wilma A. Iggers, *Karl Kraus: A Viennese Critic of the Twentieth Century* (The Hague, 1967); Alfred Pfabigan, *Karl Kraus und der Sozialismus: Eine politische Biographie* (Vienna, 1976); Mary Snell, "Karl Kraus's Die Letzten Tage Der Menschheit: An Analysis," *Forum For Modern Language Studies*, 4(1968), 234-247; Frederick Ungar, ed., *Handbook of Austrian Literature* (New York), 153-8; Harry Zohn, *Karl Kraus* (New York, 1972); *Neue Osterreichische Biographie Ab 1815*, 16 (Vienna, 1965), 153-169; *Osterreichisches Biographisches Lexikon 1815-1950*, 4 (Vienna, 1969), 130-2.

Solomon Wank

KRIPALANI, Jeewatram Bhagwandas (1888, Hyderabad, Sind, Pakistan—19 March 1982, Ahmedabad, India). *Education*: M.A., Wilson Coll., Bombay; Fergusson Coll., Poona. *Career*: professor, Benaras Hindu Univ., 1919-20;

principal, Gujarat Vidyapith, Ahmedabad, 1922-27; editor, *Vigil*, 1950-62; prominent Indian politician and leader.

Throughout his career as a politician, J. B. Kripalani upheld Gandhian values in private and public life and came to be regarded as one of the best exponents of Gandhian thought and the philosophy of nonviolent political action. During the formative years, when *Gandhi started his constructive program, with its stress on rural uplift, village industry, national education, and removal of untouchability, Kripalani was chosen by him to be principal of Gujarat Vidyapith, which was to impart education and training on Gandhian lines. As a member of the Working Committee of the Indian National Congress (1934-46), Kripalani devoted himself wholeheartedly to the cause of national liberation. Later, in 1946, he was elected President of the Indian National Congress. Despite the high positions he occupied in India's premier political organization, Kripalani remained a lonely man. He wielded a powerful pen and wrote numerous articles, pamphlets, and books expounding Gandhi's philosophy and on the Indian National Congress.

After India achieved independence, he broke away from the Indian National Congress and started a new party known as Krishak Mazdoor Praja party, which subsequently merged with the Praja Socialist party. Although held in high esteem, Kripalani was intensely individualistic and was somewhat of a misfit as a party man. He was a member of the Indian Parliament for two decades, and displayed flashes of brilliance in oratory and wit, but his bitter denunciations of the government for having departed from Gandhian principles and policies, as he saw them, was seldom well received. After 1971 he lived in political retirement, although as an elder statesman who continued to offer advice to those who sought it.

In 1977 he, along with *Jayaprakash Narayan, persuaded the several political parties opposed to the Indian National Congress led by Indira Gandhi, to come closer. The result was the Janata party, which eventually won the general election held in March 1977. The euphoria generated by the victory of the Janata party was short-lived, however, and the party soon disintegrated. The Indian National Congress, led by Indira Gandhi, was returned to power in 1980 with a triumphant majority.

Disillusioned and frustrated, Kripalani died in 1982. He was one of the few politicians of the Gandhian era, who sought to uphold moral values in politics, and the philosophy of nonviolent political action as conceived and propounded by Gandhi.

Bibliography:

A. *Gandhi: His Life & Thought* (Delhi, 1970); *Gandhian Thought* (Delhi, 1961); *The Gandhian Way* (Bombay, 1938); *The Indian National Congress* (Bombay, 1946); *The Nightmare & After* (Bombay, 1980).

D. N. Panigrahi

KROPOTKIN, Peter Alekseevich (27 November 1842, Moscow—8 February 1921, Dmitrov, USSR). *Education*: Corps of Pages, St. Petersburg. *Career*: geographer, revolutionary, and anarchist thinker.

Born into an old Russian aristocratic family, Kropotkin was educated at home and at the Corps of Pages in St. Petersburg. Military service in Siberia (1862-67) enabled him to engage in geographical exploration and to collect evidence for his sociological theories. Growing disillusionment with the tsarist system of government induced him to abandon his military career in 1867. On his return to St. Petersburg, he produced several important works, establishing his reputation as a geographer. He was also deeply involved in revolutionary activities. Arrested in 1874, he escaped abroad in 1876 and spent over forty years in Switzerland, France, and England. After the downfall of tsarism, he returned to Russia in 1917.

Already by the late 1880s, Kropotkin was the leading theoretician of "anarchist communism" or "libertarian communism," and a persuasive advocate of a stateless, classless, wageless, decentralized society in which basic human needs would be fulfilled through various forms of cooperation and exchange of goods. Opponents of this type of society were bitterly denounced regardless of whether they were conservatives, laissez-faire liberals, or Marxists. They were accused of using violence to perpetuate or impose their rule. Strikes, demonstrations, popular revolts, revolution, and "propaganda by deed" by individual anarchists were justified on the ground that those who wielded political and economic power allowed no other effective form of protest and means of changing what Kropotkin considered to be a wasteful, unjust, and violent society.

War, according to Kropotkin, was a tool used to perpetuate the rule of a small minority of exploiters. In 1896 he wrote that "war always comes from above," that "workers have nothing to win at wars," and that wars "provide a new lease . . . to the upper classes for living upon the fruit of the labour of proletarians." Workers will "have to establish tranquility, which will remain a mere sarcasm so long as the state organization will give to the few the means to drive millions of men against each other for mutual extermination."

In line with these sentiments Kropotkin repeatedly attacked militarism and war in the last quarter of the nineteenth century and at the beginning of the twentieth. The growing power of imperial Germany, however, induced him to shift his ground after 1905. Like other revolutionaries of his generation, he considered republican France as the embodiment of liberty, progress, and revolution, a country to be defended against Prussian militarism. To the dismay of many anarchists, he supported the Western Allies in World War I, urging his compatriots to fight Germany and to resist the lure of Bolshevism. During the Russian Civil War he opposed Allied intervention on Russian soil and was an uncompromising critic of V. I. Lenin's methods of government, which he equated with the worst aspects of Jacobin rule during the French Revolution. Although Kropotkin was not associated with the organized peace movement or with any pacifist organizations, several of his ideas, especially his idea of mutual aid, influenced pacifists and sections of the peace movement.

Bibliography:

A. *Appeal to the Young* (London, 1885); *The Conquest of Bread* (London, 1906); *Ethics* (London, 1925); *Fields, Factories and Workshops* (London, 1898); *Law and Authority* (London, 1886); *Memoirs of a Revolutionist* (London, 1899); *Mutual Aid* (London, 1899); *The State* (London, 1903).

B. Martin A. Miller, *Kropotkin* (Chicago, 1976); George Woodcock, *Anarchism* (Cleveland, 1962); George Woodcock and Ivan Avakumovic, *The Anarchist Prince—A Biographical Study of Peter Kropotkin* (London, 1950).

Ivan Avakumovic

KULISCIOFF, Anna (9 January 1854, Moskaya, Kherson, Russia—29 December 1925, Milan, Italy). *Education*: studied engineering, Univ. of Zurich, 1871-72; studied medicine, Univ. of Berne, 1882-84; degree in medicine, Univ. of Naples, 1886. *Career*: practiced medicine in Milan, 1887-c.1891; co-founder and administrator, Critica Sociale 1891-c.1910; editor, *La Difesa delle lavoratrici*, 1911-12.

The letters of advice which the Italian Socialist Anna Kuliscioff exchanged daily with her political partner of 35 years, *Filippo Turati, while he was a Socialist deputy in parliament in Rome and she remained in Milan, testify to the strong nexus between European socialism and the peace movement before the First World War. Those letters reveal Kuliscioff's two-fold concern about peace from a socialist standpoint. First, she trusted that the Second International could weld such tight bonds of proletarian solidarity among the workers of all nations so as to obviate future wars. Second, she encouraged the Socialists in the Italian Parliament in their effort to trim the military budget to the minimum necessary for defense. Further, Kuliscioff's letters to Turati, the private expression of her political reasoning and sentiments, revealed some of the doubts which assailed so many socialists on the eve of the First World War—doubts which led most to abandon the International in 1914 and to support their respective national war efforts. Kuliscioff, although sharing privately in this agony of doubt, was among the few who came through the experience with her antiwar principles intact. She thus publicly supported the Italian Socialist party's policy of passive opposition to the war, summed up in her party's wartime slogan, "neither support nor sabotage".

In common with her generation of European socialists, Kuliscioff had an intense "faith" in the "scientific" validity of Marxism which convinced her that the Second International could become the embodiment of more than token proletarian unity. Once European workers understood that the working class was united by strong bonds of mutual self-interest against the world's capitalists, it would no longer be possible for bourgeois governments to use nationalism to turn workers into soldiers. Without soldiers there could be no war.

On the national level, Kuliscioff's political advice to Turati revealed the extent to which the success of the program of their Reformist faction of the Italian

Socialist party depended on peace. In the period 1900-14, when the liberal Prime Minister Giovanni Giolitti practiced a policy of attempting to neutralize all political forces in the nation by co-opting parts of their programs, serious social legislation seemed possible in Italy for the first time. Socialists in parliament adopted a two-pronged strategy aimed first at convincing the Giolittian majority to pass the major portion of their reform programs and second at cutting the military budget in order to free funds for these social programs. Kuliscioff differed from Turati only in her conviction that the Socialists could increase their parliamentary leverage if they worked less exclusively in parliament and more with the rank and file membership.

Kuliscioff's fleeting vacillation on the question of war and peace in the tense days after the Sarajevo assassination was motivated by socialist, not nationalist, considerations. Reasoning that the Marxist revolution was a two-step process—first the bourgeois, liberal revolution and then the proletarian, socialist revolution—and believing that the first revolution had succeeded everywhere in Europe except Germany, Kuliscioff wondered whether the socialists of Europe could afford to sit back and allow German militarism to triumph. Nationalism only led Kuliscioff to urge Turati to support the Italian war effort, when—near the end of the war—there was a genuine question of national defense, following the Austrian breakthrough at Caporetto.

Bibliography:

A. Anna Kuliscioff and Filippo Turati, *Carteggio 1898-1925* (6 vols. Turin, 1977).

B. Franco Damiani and Fabio Rodriguez, eds., *Anna Kuliscioff: Immagini, scritti, testimonianze* (Milan, 1978); Alessandro Schiavi, *Anna Kuliscioff* (Rome, 1955).

Claire LaVigna

KUO Sung-t'ao (1818, Hsiang-yin, Hunan, China—1891, Hsiang-yin, Hunan). *Education*: Yüeh-lu Academy, Shan-huo, Hunan; *Chü-jen* (state administered degree), 1837; *Chin-shih* (highest state administered degree), 1847. *Career*: Hanlin academician, 1847; assistant to Tseng Kuo-fan, 1850, and to Prince Seng-ko-lin-ch'in, 1858; acting governor, Kwangtung, 1863; ambassador to Great Britain, 1876-78; civil servant and government official.

Kuo Sung-t'ao came into contact with the encroaching forces of the West while in Kwantung. As a follower of the Ch'ing philosopher, Wang Fu-chih (1619-92), he advocated intellectual flexibility in a rapidly changing world and believed that China had to evolve a new strategy for dealing with the Western invaders. Paradoxically, it may have been his own extensive military experience that convinced him of the folly of trying to defeat the West by force of arms. He had helped Tseng Kuo-fan organize the Hsiang army against the Taipings and built up the defenses of Taku against the Anglo-French attack. It was then that he became persuaded that negotiations, not war, constituted the only effective way of stemming the tide of the Western invasion, arguing that the foreigners wanted trade, not war.

Kuo's first clash with the military faction led to his resignation from office and subsequent demotion. Nevertheless, he refused to swerve from his pacifist position, even though the Anglo-French forces were at the gates of Peking (1860). Instead he continued to insist that the "barbarian problem" could not be solved by war but only by diplomacy, though to put forward such views was highly dangerous. The small but vociferous peace party, of which Kuo was perhaps the most outspoken member, found itself ostracized, for the officials of the time were virulently anti-Western and belligerent. It was such futile bellicosity that led to one humiliating defeat after another for China from 1860 to the downfall of the Ch'ing dynasty in 1911.

In the teeth of persecution and vilification, Kuo argued for peace, insisting that throughout most of her history China's attitude to her neighbors had been governed by morality and protocol. Only since the Southern Sung dynasty (1127-1279) had a reckless militarism prevailed. The real enemies of the state were irresponsible officials who "considered it disgraceful to draw up peace treaties but excellent to wage war." What was needed, Kuo argued, was good faith and sincerity in relations with the West, which would eventually lead to mutual trust. Failure to understand the West and to realize that China was not the only civilization in the world would lead to inevitable disaster. Furthermore, China was so far behind the West technologically that military solutions were doomed to disaster.

Kuo's advocacy of peace was upheld at great cost to his reputation and career. In his insight, his honesty, and his mature wisdom he towered above most of his contemporaries. Yet even to this day, thanks to his pacifism, his true worth and brilliance have never been recognized in China.

Bibliography:

A. *Yang-chih shu-wu yi-chi* (Peking, 1882); *Yü-ch'ih lao-jen tzu-hsü* (Peking, 1883); *Shih hsi chi-ch'eng*, in *Hsia-fang-hu-chai yü-ti ts'ung-chao*, XI (Peking, 1891-97).

B. J. D. Frodsham, *The First Chinese Embassy to the West* (Oxford, 1974).

J. D. Frodsham

KÜSTER, Friedrich (Fritz) Heinrich Christoph (11 December 1889, Ober-Einzingen, Germany—13 April 1966, Hanover). *Education*: elementary school (Volksschule) in Dorfmark, 1896-1904; secondary school, 1904-7; after an apprenticeship as a bricklayer, Royal Prussian Technical College, Buxtehude near Hamburg, 1909-12; *Career*: technician, German state railroad, Elberfeld, 1913-23; construction engineer and manager with a railroad construction company, Hanover, 1938-45; editor, *Das Andere Deutschland*, 1921-33, 1947-63; construction engineer, political journalist, and publisher.

As a member of the Deutsch Hannoversche Partei (German Hanoverian Party) (DHP), founded after the annexation of the Kingdom of Hanover by Prussia (1866), Friedrich Küster, saw the "rape" of Belgium and the First World War as a result of Prussian militarism. An employee of the German state railroad, he incurred the wrath of his superiors by refusing to buy the first war bonds. He unsuccessfully demanded of the leadership of the DHP that it oppose German war policies. After the war he worked in journalism for, among others, the *Freie Zeitung*, originally the organ of German emigrés in Switzerland during the war, and the *Hessische Blätter*, edited by *Wilhelm Hopf.

Küster's early disputes with the German historian Hans Delbruck over German responsibility for the outbreak of World War revealed to him the significance that question would have in the Weimar Republic. From then on Küster worked for public acceptance of the reality of the Treaty of Versailles and for recognition of the responsibility of the government of Wilhelmine Germany for the First World War, convinced that it would be impossible to end the "might makes right" policies of Prussian militarism without punishing the guilty parties. In May 1920 Küster left the DHP and joined the Deutsche Demokratische Partei (DDP), which he in turn left in November 1920, because of a parliamentary speech by a DDP deputy (Bernhard Dernburg) condemning the Treaty of Versailles as a "Magna Charta of rape, intimidation and destruction" and demanding its "immediate revision." He joined the Sozialdemokratische Partei Deutschlands (German Social Democratic Party) (SPD) in 1921, but did little political work within the party because of what he saw as its lack of political will to fight reactionary forces and its participation in the nationalist campaign against the Treaty of Versailles.

In 1919 Küster founded a local branch of the Deutsche Friedensgesellschaft (German Peace Society) (DFG) in Hagen, the first one in the Ruhr, and in 1921 he created the Arbeitsgemeinschaft der südwestfalischen Ortsgruppen (Association of South Westphalian Branches) of the DFG. He condemned the passive resistance to the French in the Ruhr in 1923 as part of the opposition of German nationalists to the Treaty of Versailles. As a result of that, and his democratic and pacifist activity in general, he lost his position with the German state railroads in 1923, after which he devoted himself to pacifist agitation and journalism. In 1924 Küster established the Westdeutscher Landesverband (West German Regional Association) (WLV) of the DFG. In a short time the WLV became the most influential of the DFG regional associations, comprising 300 local branches in 1926. Its goals and methods were soon adopted by other DFG regional associations.

Küster's weekly newspaper, *Das Andere Deutschland* (*AD*, previously named *Der Pazifist*), at first the organ of the WLV, and, after 1928, one of the papers of the DFG, became within a few years the most important peace publication within the Weimar Republic. The *AD* was an expression of Küster's activist pacifism that built upon working people and aimed at establishing a mass organization. Numerous politicians, writers, and journalists such as *Heinrich Ströbel, *Friedrich W. Foerster, *Kurt Tucholsky, *Paul von Schoenaich, *Richard Grelling and *Friedrich Kayser, as well as many other little known peace activists contributed to the distinctive profile of the *AD* and to its ability to infuse pacifist ideas into day-to-day politics. In his publishing house, Das Andere Deutschland, he published works explaining pacifism, some of which appeared in printings of 80,000 to 200,000 copies.

In the *AD*, Küster tirelessly promoted an awareness of the imperial German government's responsibility for World War I and the acceptance of the realities created by the Treaty of Versailles. He condemned the propaganda against the Treaty of Versailles, which was financially backed by the organs of the state, because he believed it bound the German people ideologically to a state of war and prepared them for a new war. He criticized the baleful influence of Prussian militarism on German politics and propagated the concept of understanding among nations, particularly the reconciliation of Germany with France and Poland. The paper stood for a "politics of law and justice" as well as for a synthesis of socialist and pacifist ideas which were part of the French and German Enlightenment. These ideas would free the Weimar Republic from the post-1918 Prussian visions of militarism and imperial grandeur and would protect Europe against another war. Like F. W. Foerster, he was convinced that the threat of a war still emanated from Germany, and Küster used the pages of the *AD* to expose secret and illegal German rearmament measures. For that he was convicted, along with *Berthold Jacob, of treason and sentenced to nine months in jail in 1928, but later was granted amnesty.

From 1924 to 1929 Küster served as president of the WLV and from 1929-33 as head of the DFG. He brought to the national policies of the DFG and WLV emphasis on German militarism and nationalism as the greatest threats to peace. This emphasis led to conflict within the DFG between Küster on the one hand and, on the other, *Ludwig Quidde and *Hellmut von Gerlach. Constantly engaged in trying to build a united front of all democratic and antiwar elements, Küster appealed to the SPD and the Kommunistische Partei Deutschlands (German Communist Party) (KPD) to end their differences in the name of the fight against fascism. Resigning from the SPD in 1931 because of its support for the construction of pocket battleships, Küster took part in the organization of a new socialist party, the Sozialistische Arbeiter Partei Deutschlands (Socialist Workers' Party of Germany), which he soon left because the new party gave priority to the battle against capitalism over the battle against militarism and fascism. On March 6, 1933, three days after the *AD* was banned by the Nazi regime, Küster was arrested and sent to several concentration camps, lastly to Buchenwald, from which he was released in 1938 as a result of the efforts of, among others, *Runham Brown, the secretary of the War Resisters' International.

After the war, Küster, supported by Schoenaich, reestablished the DFG. As chairman of the DFG in 1945-46, Küster worked to denazify and democratize Germany. To assist these efforts, he resumed publication of the *AD* in 1947, which played a prominent part in the protest movement, Ohne mich! ("Without me!") against the rearming of Germany in 1950-51. Küster resigned from the DFG in 1954, when it failed to take a strong stand against German rearmament, after which he conducted his peace politics completely through the *AD*. The paper called for German recognition of the Oder-Neisse border with Poland and reconciliation with the east European countries. The *AD* supported several antiwar movements; the Paulskirchen Bewegung (St. Paul's Church Movement), a wave of demonstrations and rallies initiated by the German Trade Union Association and the SPD against the ratification by the German parliament of agreements for the rearmament of the Federal Republic, i.e. the Paris Accords; The ''Kampf dem Atomtod'' (''War Against Atomic Death'') campaign against the German parliament's decision in 1958 to equip the German army with atomic weapons; and the 1960/70 Ostermarsch Bewegung/Kampagne für Demokratie und Abrüstung (Easter March Movement/Campaign for Democracy and Disarmament), a movement of independent antiwar groups which mobilized and educated on the grass roots level. In 1969, three years after Küster's death, the *AD* was discontinued for financial reasons; opposition to the Vietnam war was one of its last campaigns.

Bibliography:

A. *Die Hintermänner der Nazis, Von Papen bis Deterding* (Hanover, 1946); *Vernunft der Ketten* (Hanover, 1946).

B. Helmut Donat and Lothar Wieland, *Das Andere Deutschland. Eine Auswahl (1925-1933)* (Königstein/Taunus, 1980); Hein Herbers, ''F.K. [F. Küster]—seine Zeit und seine Streit,'' *Das Andere Deutschland* (July, 1966), 9; Ingeborg Küster, *Politik—haben SIE das denn notig? Autobiographie einer Pazifistin* (Hamburg, 1983); Lothar Wieland, '' 'Hakenkreuz und Stahlhelm'. Prognosen zu Deutschlands Zukunft in der pazifistischen Zeitung *Der Andere Deutschland*,'' in Thomas Koebner, ed., *Das Ende von Weimar. Prognosen und Diagnosen in der deutschen literatur und politischen Publiziztik 1930-1933* (Frankfurt/Main, 1982), 80-102.

Helmut Donat
Trans. by William L. Hopkins

L

LACAZE-DUTHIERS, Gérard de (26 January 1876, Bordeaux, Gironde, France—3 May 1958, Paris). *Education*: Collège Saint-Elme, Arcachon; Lycée Rollin, Paris; Univ. of Paris. *Career*: teacher, aesthetician, anarchist, and journalist.

Born into a noble family from southwestern France, the son of an historian turned museum curator, Gérard de Lacaze-Duthiers would become an aristocratic anarchist and pacifist. As a young man he received an excellent education in provincial and Parisian schools before taking advanced degrees in law and philosophy. Beginning in 1900 he taught at a variety of schools, notably the prestigious lycée Henri IV.

Before World War I broke out, his strong interest in philosophy had led him into both the study of art and anarchism. Throughout his life, Lacaze-Duthiers remained a strong believer in individual freedom and self-expression, particularly in art and literature, and an opponent of war and militarism which would destroy them.

Despite his pacifism, Lacaze-Duthiers was mobilized in May 1916 and served for more than a year as a secretary to the General Staff. When released from service the next year because of age, he resumed his teaching. He also returned to his anarchist activities, motivated by the long and bloody conflict then raging. Lacaze-Duthiers contributed to the libertarian and pacifist review, *Les Humbles*, founded by Maurice Wullens, and to an anarchist newspaper published by E. Armand. In addition, he ardently defended the views of *Romain Rolland, whose *Au-dessus de la mêlée* provided a beacon for many pacifists during the war. In speeches he attacked nationalist writers who sought a war to the bitter end against Germany. All these activities brought him under the watchful eyes of the police, but he escaped punishment because he never called for violence or disobedience.

After the war, Lacaze-Duthiers published numerous brochures on anarchism, esthetics, and sexual freedom. In 1926 he signed the manifesto "Appeal to Consciences" drafted by *Victor Margueritte and protesting against the inequities of the Treaty of Versailles. Two years later he adhered to the "Appeal to Good Sense" which called for general disarmament to safeguard the peace of Europe. Lacaze-Duthiers was an early member of the Ligue internationale des combattants de la paix (International League of Fighters for Peace), organized by *Victor Meric in 1931 and contributed to the pacifist review *Le Barrage* until its suppression in 1939. Associated with the anarchist journal *L'En dehors*, he published his brochure *Un Individualiste devant la mêlée* in 1934 to attack the dangers of fascism and dictatorship in France. In it he reformulated his philosophy of "leading one's own life, obeying one's own conscience, harming no one, living the life of a free man," "an internal life of nobility and beauty."

During the Second World War, the elderly philosopher took no part in either collaboration or resistance. He did write for the short-lived socialist newspaper *Germinal*, which sought to encourage understanding between Frenchmen and Germans. After the Liberation he again returned to his writings on esthetics and literature. In the final years of his life, he contributed to the journals *Défense de l'homme* and *La Voie nouvelle*, both devoted to opposing war and promoting international cooperation. In 1951 Lacaze-Duthiers helped to establish a committee concerned with initiating a referendum to require popular approval for any French involvement in a war.

A gentle man who never married and lived quietly in a world of art and literature, Lacaze-Duthiers remained a theoretician of violence who succeeded in living by his ideals.

Bibliography:

A. *L'Art et la vie. La liberté de pensée* (Paris, 1911); *Un Individualiste devant la mêlée. Jours d'emeute (février, 1934)* (Paris, n.d. [1934]); *Le Pacifisme avant l'histoire* (Paris, 1937).

B. *Défense de l'homme*, no. 115, May, 1958; *Dictionnaire biographique française contemporain*, vol. 2 (Paris, 1954).

James Friguglietti

LADD, William (10 May 1778), Exeter, NH—9 April 1841), Portsmouth, NH). *Education*: B.A., Harvard Coll., 1797. *Career*: sea captain; merchant; planter; founder and official, American Peace Society, 1828-41; peace leader and publicist.

The son of a sea captain and shipbuilder, William Ladd spent most of the years between his graduation from Harvard College in 1797 and 1814 at sea. He gave up the life of a sea captain for a time in 1800, when he became a merchant in Savannah, Georgia, and then a cotton planter in Florida, but returned to the sea in 1806 and made many voyages until the outbreak of the War of 1812. In 1814 he moved to a farm near Minot, Maine. The farm was to be his home for the remainder of his life and headquarters for the struggle against war which he began in the early 1820s.

Ladd's interest in the peace movement began in 1817 when he read *Noah Worcester's famous essay *A Solemn Review of the Custom of War*. In 1824 Ladd joined the Massachusetts Peace Society and became one of its leaders, organizing six branches of the society. He organized a peace society in Minot and, in 1826, reorganized the Maine Peace Society. Believing that the various peace societies should coordinate their efforts in a national organization, Ladd became the principal mover in the founding of the American Peace Society (APS) in New York on May 8, 1828. He served the society as secretary, treasurer, director, and general agent. From 1837 to 1841 he was president. He also edited the organization's first periodicals, the *Harbinger of Peace* and the *Calumet*. Although he first established APS headquarters in Hartford, Connecticut, in 1837 he moved it to Boston.

Ladd traveled widely, addressing many peace meetings, and published his views in the society's periodicals and in the *Christian Mirror*, a Portland, Maine newspaper in which he developed his understanding of war and the Christian response to it. In one essay he said that "love of power, lust of praise, thirst for gold, and desire of revenge" were the principal causes of war. In other articles, he emphasized the desire for territory and the love of military glory as prime causes. Ladd was long uncertain whether all war was wrong for a Christian, but he eventually came to believe that for followers of Christ all wars, offensive or defensive, were morally wrong. He resisted, however, attempts to restrict membership in APS to only those Christians who believed as he did. Consequently, the organization included individuals with very different peace views and seemed to the more radical nonresisters as far too equivocal in its programs.

Ladd believed that a primary mission of peace societies was to persuade civilized, Christian governments to found institutions to resolve international disputes peaceably. Upon his initiative the American Peace Society sponsored a contest for the best essay on the subject and in 1840, Ladd published the five best essays, adding one of his own, *An Essay on a Congress of Nations*. Melding elements from the other essays with some of his own ideas, he proposed a world organization divided into two parts: a congress of ambassadors from "all those Christian and civilized nations who should choose to send them" and a court of nations "to arbitrate or judge such cases as should be brought before it, by the mutual consent of two or more contending nations." He proposed that the congress, which was to meet only occasionally, be charged with the placing of international law on a regular, treaty basis. All decisions of the congress were to be unanimous. The international code of law expected from its labors was to be binding on both belligerents and neutrals.

During the late nineteenth and early twentieth centuries, Ladd's project was probably even more important than in its own time, for it inspired American supporters of The Hague Peace Conference (1899 and 1907) and the ideas of arbitral justice associated with them. During World War I and the making of peace after that war internationalists who could not accept the concept of collective security in the Covenant of the League of Nations found support for their views in Ladd's proposals.

Bibliography:

A. *An Essay on a Congress of Nations For the Adjustment of International Disputes Without Resort to Arms* (Boston, 1840, reprinted New York, 1916); *The Essays of Philanthropos on Peace and War* (Exeter, NH, 1827, reprinted New York, 1971).

B. Peter Brock, *Pacifism in the United States from the Colonial Era to the First World War* (Princeton, NJ, 1968); Merle Curti, *The American Peace Crusade: 1815-1860* (Durham, NC, 1929); W. Freeman Galpin, *Pioneering for Peace: A Study of American Peace Efforts to 1846* (Syracuse, NY, 1933); John Hemmenway, *The Apostle of Peace: Memoir of William Ladd* (Boston, 1872); Edson L. Whitney, *The American Peace Society: A Centennial History* (Washington, 1928); DAB, X, 527-28.

C. American Peace Society and William Ladd Collections, Swarthmore Peace Collection, Swarthmore College.

Calvin D. Davis

LA FOLLETTE, Robert Marion (14 June 1855, Primrose Township, WI—18 June 1925, Washington). *Education*: B.S., Univ. of Wisconsin, 1879. *Career*: Dane County District Attorney, 1881-84; U.S. Representative, 1885-91; attorney 1891-1900; Governor of Wisconsin, 1901-5; U.S. Senator, 1906-25; editor and publisher, *La Follette's Magazine*, 1909-14 (weekly), 1914-25 (monthly); progressive and antiwar political leader.

Robert M. La Follette developed his position as a leading critic of United States expansionist foreign policy by adapting his progressive interpretation of domestic events to the revolutions of the early twentieth century. As a Republican Congressman in the 1880s, La Follette supported his party's emphasis on promoting U.S. markets for farm and factory products abroad. But by the early twentieth century, he saw history as a democratic struggle by majorities of people to gain control over their lives from the special interests that exploited them. La Follette believed that, by electing him governor and convincing the legislature to enact laws taxing and regulating railroad companies and giving to voters themselves the power to nominate political candidates that had previously rested with political leaders, the people of Wisconsin were achieving democracy. "The will of the people shall be the law of the land" was his lifelong motto, emblazoned on the magazine that he edited after 1909.

La Follette viewed the abortive Russian revolution of 1905-6 and the crusade for independence by the Filipinos as somewhat similar to Wisconsin campaigns for popular control. But it was the Mexican Revolution that led La Follette to develop the analogy between revolutionaries abroad and progressives at home, and led him to fear that the very corporations that exploited American farmers, workers, and consumers did the same in underdeveloped countries. La Follette believed that the most realistic way that he could aid the Mexican revolutionaries was by trying to prevent the United States from intervening in Mexican affairs. Fearing that American meddling would be used to protect American property interests abroad, he strongly opposed +Woodrow Wilson's military interventions in Mexico in 1914 and 1916.

By the outbreak of World War I, La Follette believed that wealthy American investment bankers, manufacturers, and other businessmen were leading the Wilson Administration increasingly to a military buildup at home that meant higher prices and taxes for Americans and the strong probability that the U. S. would abandon its neutrality and come to the support of Britain and France. As a believer in popular rule, he proposed that any U. S. military participation in war be contingent upon a majority vote of the American people. The Hearst newspapers and ex-Secretary of State *William Jennings Bryan joined him in promoting the war referendum bill in the months before the U.S. entered World War I in 1917. La Follette's final step in trying to restrain U.S. participation was his organization of a Senate filibuster to block Wilson's bill to arm merchant ships. The filibuster killed the bill, but Wilson armed merchant ships by executive order. On April 4, 1917, La Follette joined five other senators in voting against the war declaration.

Convinced that most Americans believed the war had been imposed against their will by powerful interests, La Follette insisted that the burdens of war be borne by its supporters. Joining many labor unions in opposition, he fought the draft which he saw as the only way the wealthy war supporters could raise enough soldiers to field armies. He favored financing the war by taxing the war profits of individuals and businesses. He defended the rights of freedom of speech, assembly, and the press in the face of the Wilson Administration's massive suppression of civil liberties. In all of these areas he was overwhelmingly outvoted by a coalition of Wilson Democrats and conservative Republicans. At the same time, he was supported by progressive farm groups, labor unions, and Socialists. Prowar conservatives, led by superpatriotic Minnesotans, tried to get the Senate to expel La Follette for his antiwar views, but the Senate committee charged with this decision simply delayed the expulsion resolution until the war and its passions had ended.

Although a believer in international cooperation, La Follette bitterly fought Wilson's Versailles Treaty, which he saw as a conservative scheme to forestall movements for popular democracy that were erupting as a result of the unpopular war in Ireland, India, China, Egypt, Germany, Hungary, and, most spectacularly, Russia. He introduced six reservations to the Versailles Treaty that insisted that all signatories insure the right of revolution, an end to the draft, an advisory popular vote before war, an 80 percent reduction in arms spending, and prohibitions of annexing further territory and on exploitation of natural resources of weaker countries. When his reservations were soundly defeated, La Follette voted against the Versailles Treaty both as Wilson had proposed it and as conservative Republican leader +Henry Cabot Lodge had tried to amend it. In championing the right of peoples to choose their governments, La Follette worked with groups like the American Association for the Recognition of the Irish Republic, the India Home Rule League, and the Chinese Defense League. He also opposed the postwar U.S. invasion of the Soviet Union.

La Follette was an eloquent champion of the idea that the best way for Americans, makers of the first modern revolution, to assist the democratic aspirations of other peoples was by turning the Declaration of Independence into a reality at home, a model for others. The basic way to end war, he concluded, was to take the profit out of preparing for war by severing the partnership between big corporations and government. And the way to do that was to create a more democratic America, in which consumers, workers, and farmers would exercise the political power then wielded by the large corporations.

Bibliography:

A. *La Follette' Autobiography: A Personal Narrative of Political Experiences* (Madison, 1913); *The Political Philosophy of Robert M. La Follette*, Ellen Torelle, ed. (Madison, 1920).

B. Belle Case and Fola La Follette, *Robert M. La Follette* (2 vols., New York, 1953); Padraic C. Kennedy, "La Follette's Foreign Policy: From Imperalism to Anti-Imperialism," *Wisconsin Magazine of History*, 46 (Summer 1963), 287-93; David P. Thelen, *Robert M. La Follette and the Insurgent Spirit* (Boston, 1976).

C. Robert M. La Follette Papers, State Historical Society of Wisconsin (1879-1906) and Manuscripts Division, Library of Congress (1906-1925).

David P. Thelen

LA FONTAINE, Henri Marie (22 April 1854, Brussels, Belgium—14 May 1943, Brussels). *Education*: Dr. jur., Univ. Libre de Bruxelles, 1877. *Career*: lawyer, professor, and lecturer; socialist politician; senator, 1895-98, 1900-32, 1935-36; vice-president of the Senate, 1919-32; communal counsellor, Brussels, 1904-8; Belgian delegate to the League of Nations, 1920-21; founder and general secretary, Belgian section of the International Arbitration and Peace Association, 1889-1914; organizer, Universal Peace Congress at Antwerp, 1894, and first National Belgian Peace Congress, Brussels, 1913; council officer, Interparliamentary Union and International Peace Bureau; president, International Peace Bureau, 1907-43; founder and general secretary, Union of International Associations.

The long and unflagging lifetime of labor which Henri La Fontaine gave to the cause of peace began in 1883 when he entered the peace movement, inspired by *Hodgson Pratt who founded the International Arbitration and Peace Association. La Fontaine helped establish its Belgian section in 1889 and from that time, never suspended his struggle for peace both in Belgium and internationally. After organizing the 1894 Universal Peace Congress in Antwerp, La Fontaine's reputation in European peace circles grew so that he became a major force in the Berne Peace Bureau as well as in the Interparliamentary Union. In response to the movement's need for systematic educational materials, La Fontaine produced a comprehensive and scholarly bibliography on peace and international arbitration which remains useful today.

An advocate of the use of arbitration and the creation of a world tribunal, a defender of disarmament, and an articulate spokesman for the extension of international law, La Fontaine was unique in his participation both in the middle class peace internationals as well as in the socialist movement. In Belgium, he helped organize nearly every peace meeting that was held. In his capacity as senator, he never lost an opportunity to challenge the government on its foreign policy or its positions on free trade. Beyond working for the extension of officially sponsored pacific initiatives and institutions, La Fontaine worked to create private and informal networks among peoples and private organizations which he saw as necessary to construct the interdependence of peoples. Thus he helped found and sustain an incredible number of offices, unions, and societies in fields of professional concern—education, bibliographical cataloging, labor and industry, commerce, immigration, statistics, and monetary standards. With +Paul Otlet he established the Union of International Associations, still in existence. The

International Institute of Bibliography which he established with Otlet in 1895 exists in modern form through the general bibliographical services provided by UNESCO. In working to establish a standardized center collating major scientific work in every language, La Fontaine acted on his firm belief in the need to institutionalize international culture and achievement. Similarly, he worked to establish a periodic assembly of official government delegates to create a worldwide administrative system.

With the outbreak of World War I, La Fontaine published an article examining what pacifists must work for as well as what they had done. He insisted that all nations be represented at a peace congress when the conflict ended in order to adopt an international charter. He further developed his ideas on postwar organization while in the United States during the war where he published *The Great Solution, Magnissima Charta* (1916), an effort to influence Anglo-American thinking in the direction of a permanent society of nations. In La Fontaine's view, what was needed was a federal constitution among states that provided for international courts. These courts would be empowered to use armed force if needed to oversee the execution of their judgments.

Awarded the Nobel Peace Prize in 1913, La Fontaine's reputation led to his official appointment as a technical advisor to the 1919 Peace Conference and then as a Belgian delegate to the newly formed League. This official recognition did not preclude his continued service to the Carnegie Endowment for International Peace, the Interparliamentary Union, and the International Peace Bureau in Geneva. He continued through 1938 to attend and participate in meetings, despite advanced age. When he died at 89 years of age, his beloved Belgium and Europe remained in the hands of the conqueror from Germany.

Bibliography:

A. "Ce que les pacifistes auraient à dire," *Le Mouvement Pacifiste*, #812 (Berne, August-December, 1914) 375-82; *La Conférence de la paix* (Brussels, 1908); *Essai de bibliographie de la paix et de l'arbitrage international* (Brussels, 1904); "The Existing Elements of a Constitution of the United States of the World," *International Conciliation* (October, 1911) 1-13; *The Great Solution. Magnissima Charta* (Boston, 1916); "The Neutralization of States in the Scheme of International Organization," *American Society of International Law* (1917), 1-7; *Pasicrisie internationale. Histoire documentaire des arbitrages internationaux, 1794-1900* (Berne, 1902).

B. J. Baugniet, "Deux pionniers de la coopération internationale et de la paix universelle: Henri La Fontaine et Paul Otlet," *Textes et Documents*, #260 (June, 1970, Brussels); *Henri La Fontaine (1854-1943), Paul Otlet (1868-1944)* (Brussels, 1954); De Seyn, *Dictionnaire des Ecrivains Belges* (Bruges, 1930), II, 1122; *Biographie Nationale*, 38, cols. 213-221; "Biography", F. W. Haberman, ed., *Nobel Lectures, Peace* (1972), I, 271-76.

C. Henri La Fontaine Papers, Mundaneum, Brussels.

Nadine Lubelski-Bernard
Trans. by Sandi E. Cooper

LAMMASCH, Heinrich. See *Biographical Dictionary of Internationalists*.

LAMSZUS, Wilhelm (13 July 1881, Altona, Germany—18 January 1965, Hamburg, Germany). *Education*: Teacher's College, Hamburg. *Career*: primary school teacher, Hamburg; teacher, experimental school, Hamburg-Barmbek, 1918-33; educational reformer, antiwar writer, and journalist.

Wilhelm Lamszus, whose father was a shoemaker from East Prussia, had already gained a reputation as an educational critic and reformer before becoming famous through the publication of his book, *Das Menschenschlachthaus. Bilder vom kommenden Krieg* (*The Human Slaughterhouse: Scenes from the Coming War*), which appeared in 1912. The novel, which made him hated in military circles and led to calls for dismissal from his teaching post, predicted the approaching world war in graphic detail. He described the operation of technologically highly developed war machines (automatic machine guns, trench mortars, and air war) and their horrible consequences for human beings. He also anticipated the new characteristics of the coming war—the battle for resources and static (trench) warfare. The hero of the novel, who responds to mobilization orders out of a vague love of fatherland and who regards the war as inevitable, experiences all of the horrors of modern battle until his final disillusionment at the time of his death. Through his controversial novel, Lamszus succeeded in unmasking the numerous war-glorifying myths of Imperial Germany.

Although Lamszus did not clearly analyze the economic and political causes of the coming war, he did make clear enough that it had to do with an imperialist war of conquest fostered by an insatiable lust for power. Most German literary critics dismissed the book as tendentious and it was banned in 1915. However, it enjoyed great success abroad and was translated into English, Danish, and French. In 1919 Lamszus published *Das Irrenhaus* (*The Insane Asylum*), which was a continuation of his first book and contained a foreword by *Carl von Ossietzky. Both books were published in a one-volume edition in 1923, and by 1928 80,000 copies were sold. In 1921, Lamszus brought out his third antiwar publication, a volume of poems entitled *Der Leichenhügel* (*The Hill of Corpses*).

Until 1918 Lamszus, who served in the army in 1915-16, tried to get a hearing for peace-political ideas from the German Social Democratic party, above all from the Social Democratic teacher's association (Sozialwissenschaftliche Vereinigung). In 1919 he joined the German Communist party, remaining a member until 1927. Throughout the Weimar period, he published numerous articles in pacifist newspapers and journals such as *Die Friedenswarte*, *Das Andere Deutschland*, *Deutsche Zukunft*, and *Der Pionier*. After the Nazis assumed power at the end of January 1933, Lamszus was forbidden to write and forced to retire from his teaching post with a reduced pension. He was also denied a pending appointment as professor of pedagogy at Brunswick. His book on the coming of another war, written before the Nazis assumed power, could find no publisher. His penetrating predictions about the nature of the Second World War were nearly equal to those he made earlier about World War I. Among other things, he foresaw that World War II would be substantially a war of bombs. The book appeared in 1946 under the title, *Der grosse Totentanz. Geschichte und Gedichte vom Krieg* (*The Great Dance of Death: Stories and Poems of the War*).

After 1945 Lamszus, who did not return to teaching, worked as a journalist for several years and wrote essays for *Das Andere Deutschland*. He did not, however, regain the wide audience of his earlier years. His significance lies in his having been the first German author who, in visionary, strikingly pictorial language, combined elements of Naturalism and Expressionism, warned of the coming of terribly destructive wars, and called, thereby, for their prevention. For German literature, *Das Menschenschlachthaus* was the beginning of a long chain of pacifist and antimilitarist literary works which appeared between 1913 and 1933; these included, among others, works by *René Schickele, Andreas Latzko, *Leonhard Frank, *Armin T. Wegner, *Karl Kraus, *Ernst Toller, *Erich Maria Remarque, Ludwig Renn, Adam Scharrer, Edlef Köppen, and Arnold Zweig.

Bibliography:

A. *Fluch den Waffen. Photos, Gedichte, Reden und Aufsätze von Danton, Ernst Friedrich, Wilhelm Lamszus, Leo Tolstoi* (Berlin, 1923); *Der grosse Totentanz. Geschichte und Gedichte vom Krieg* (Hamburg, 1946); *Das Irrenhaus. Visionen vom Krieg, II. Teil* (Hamburg, 1919); *Der Leichenhügel. Gedichte während des Krieges* (Leipzig, 1921); *Das Menschenschlachthaus. Bilder vom kommenden Krieg* (Hamburg, 1912; new edition, Munich, 1980; Eng. trans., *Human Slaughterhouse: Scenes from the War That Is Sure to Come*, New York, and London, 1913); *Der verlorene Sohn. Eine Geschichte aus der Fremdenlegion* (Hamburg, 1914).

B. Willi Bredel, "Ein Hamburger Schullehrer," *Neue Deutsche Literatur* 3 (1955), no. 9, 150ff; Marieluise Christadler, *Kriegserziehung im Jugendbuch* (Frankfurt, 1978), 306-16; Wolfgang Emmerich, "Wilhelm Lamszus," *Neue Deutsche Biographie*, 13 (1982), 472ff; Bernhard Gleim, "Wilhelm Lamszus," *Jahrbuch für Lehrer* 5 (1980), 372-83; Appendix to *Das Menschenschlachthaus* (Munich, 1980), 121-214.

Wolfgang Emmerich
Trans. by Solomon Wank

LÅNGBACKA, Runar (23 February 1905, Teerijärvi, Finland—4 November 1970, Närpiö). *Education*: teaching certificate, Uusikaarlepyy Teacher's Coll., 1927. *Career*: teacher, municipal politician, librarian and pacifist writer.

After qualifying as a teacher in 1927, Runar Långbacka took several positions in elementary, comprehensive, and grammar schools in Finnby, Närpiö, and other places. Throughout his teaching career he promoted peace education. During the 1930s, when ultranationalism and fascism were on the rise, he became more of an activist in the peace movement and openly resisted the militarization of the public schools. Following World War II, he participated in the activities of Närpiö's Peace Friends and acted as chairman of the organization from 1952 until his death. He was also active in Finland's Peace Union, which he had joined in the 1920s, and served on its central board during the last years of his life. He maintained good relations with the northern peace movements and cooperated with the Swedish peace movement.

Långbacka was an active man, full of ideas, a tireless organizer, and an excellent speaker who was capable of transmitting his enthusiasm to his audience. As a poet and writer he impressed his readers with the depth of his knowledge and his commitment to pacifism. He was an industrious assistant to the Finnish-Swedish peace journal, *Fredsposten*, and frequently wrote for the magazine. Many of his articles, speeches, and poems were assembled into a collection called *Idealist och fredsvän* (*Idealist and Peace Friend*) (1974).

Långbacka considered Christianity as one of the foundations of his own peace work, but he often questioned the activity of the state church. Claiming that the church had moved away from original Christian principles, he attacked it for supporting hate and violence during the two world wars. Besides his peace activism, Långbacka took an interest in social and political questions. Believing that differing social values often caused tension and violent outbursts, he sought to reduce these contradictions as a municiple politician and as a social activist. He used his position as a librarian in Finnby to make peace and humanistic literature available to the general public. He believed that libraries had an important educational task and that every librarian was a significant educator.

As a teacher, as a librarian, and as a municipal politician, Runar Långbacka left his imprint on Finnish life and promoted pacifist ideals.

Bibliography:

A. *Idealist och fredsvän* (Vaasa, 1974).

Kalevi Kalemaa
Trans. by Oliver and Rita Whitehead

LANGE, Christian Louis. See *Biographical Dictionary of Internationalists*.

LANGE, Oskar Ryszard (27 July 1904, Tomaszów Mazowiecki, Poland—2 October 1965, London). *Education*: Ph.D., Jagiellonian Univ., Cracow, 1928. *Career*: lecturer in statistics and economics, Jagiellonian Univ., 1927-37; lecturer in economics at the universities of Michigan (1936), California (Berkeley, 1937), and Stanford (1937-38); lecturer in economics (later professor), Univ. of Chicago, 1938-45; professor of statistics, Main School of Planning and Statistics, Warsaw, 1949-55; professor of economics, Warsaw Univ., 1956-65; Polish ambassador to the USA and representative in the UN Security Council, 1945-46; member, Polish parliament, 1947-65; member and deputy chairman, Council of State, 1957-65.

Oskar Lange gained worldwide recognition for his pioneering work on the economic theory of socialism (as author of the so-called "competitive solution"), for refining neoclassical and Keynesian tools of economic analysis, and for attempting a synthesis of Marxian and Western (Anglo-American) economics.

Lange's attitude toward war oscillated between pacifism and revolutionary Marxism. In his early youth, as a student, he belonged to the Academic Union of Pacifists in Cracow. He argued in favor of peaceful cooperation among all nations in all areas of social life, and criticized economic protectionism and nationalism. The years of the Great Depression, and particularly the concurrent fascist victories, radicalized Lange's views. He considered the fascist advances in Germany to be the result of capitalist retrogression caused by the ever increasing power of large corporations. Lange differentiated two phases of capitalist imperialism: first, the peaceful penetration of the world by capitalist countries cooperating in the colonization of noncapitalist regions; next, the capitalist countries' imperialistic rivalry over territories suitable for exploitation (chiefly those rich in raw materials). Lange foresaw a threat to peace in massive unemployment, which could serve as the basis for "people's imperialism" (i.e., the policy of full-employment through military expansionism). He hoped for the elimination of war through a system grounded in social equality and democracy. The drive for democracy and peace, he argued, required that the economic stranglehold of the state as well as of private monopolistic interests be broken through the division of the ownership of capital and land, the decentralization of economic and political decisionmaking, and the separation of economic administration from the political apparatus.

During and after World War II, Lange agitated for a world organization and Soviet-American rapprochement. Faced with the dangers of atomic warfare, he demanded the elimination of war from the arsenal of political means and defended the idea of peaceful competition between differing social systems. He considered the maintenance of peace "the central problem of our era." As an expert to the UN he presented a programmatic outline for disarmament linked with economic assistance to the Third World. For many years, Lange was one of the leaders of the Soviet-backed World Peace Movement.

Bibliography:

A. *Economic Development, Planning and International Cooperation* (New York, 1963); *Essays on Economic Planning* (Bombay, 1963); "*Pozbrojenie a rozwoj gospodarczy swiata*," *Dziela* (Warsaw, 1973), I, 902ff.

B. *International Encyclopaedia of Social Sciences*, VIII, 581-3; *On Political Economy and Econometrics: Essays in Honour of Oskar Lange* (Warsaw, 1964); NYT, October 4, 1965.

Tadeusz Kowalik

LANSBURY, George (21 February 1859, Halesworth, Suffolk, England—7 May 1940, London). *Education*: elementary school. *Career*: Labour Member of Parliament (Bow and Bromley 1910-12, 1922-40; editor, *Daily Herald*, 1914-22; First Commissioner of Works in Labor government, 1929-31; labor leader, politician, and Christian pacifist.

George Lansbury entered local politics in 1885 as a radical Liberal in London's East End. During the 1890s, he became a leading member of the Marxist Social Democratic Federation (SDF). Although the SDF sharpened his opposition to capitalism, Lansbury rejected its emphasis upon the violent overthrow of existing society and advocated instead political change through peaceful means. In the 1900 General Election, which took place during the Boer War (1899-1902),

Lansbury ran unsuccessfully as an antiwar candidate. He emerged, however, as one of London's leading pacifists, opposing the war as being both capitalist and imperialist. He also opposed the conflict on the pacifist grounds that war itself was wrong. In the early 1900s, a resurgence in Lansbury's former Christian faith caused him to leave the atheist dominated SDF. An Anglican, his Christian beliefs were from this time a pervading influence in his political outlook. He remained a Christian socialist for the rest of his life. Although unoriginal intellectually, his personal sincerity and moral force made him one of the most effective of the pioneer socialist speakers.

In 1903 Lansbury joined the emergent Labour party and during 1910-12 was a Labour Member of Parliament. In 1914 he became editor of the socialist *Daily Herald*, thereby gaining a national prominence he had previously lacked. After the outbreak of war in 1914 the *Herald* (now a weekly) became the most important antiwar newspaper in Britain. In May 1918 it achieved a great journalistic success in publishing the text of the secret wartime Allied treaties. After the war, Lansbury waged a vigorous press campaign through the *Daily Herald* opposing the Allied war of intervention against Soviet Russia.

In 1922 Lansbury reentered Parliament as Labour member for the London constituency of Bow, a seat he held for the rest of his life. By now a major figure of the Labour Left, he was elected to the Executive of the Parliamentary party in 1922 and to the Chairmanship of the party in 1928. Following Labour's 1929 election victory, Lansbury became a member of the Cabinet, but in the modest office of First Commissioner of Public Works. Following Labour's massive defeat in the 1931 General Election in which all the former members of the Labour Cabinet lost their seats, except Lansbury, he was elected as party leader. He now became the leading advocate of pacifism in the Labour party, a tradition of long standing as an expression of the party's idealism and its belief in human brotherhood. This pacifist feeling had been revived by the disillusionment of the postwar years, although in a new form. Except for a few, like Lansbury, the earlier idealist pacifism had disappeared. Most of the party had also discarded the syndicalist belief that the working classes could prevent war by industrial action. These earlier ideas had been replaced by a belief in the League of Nations as an international body which could outlaw war by peaceful means. But the implications of supporting the League of Nations, especially the issue of military sanctions, had not been fully debated within the party. Lansbury was the leader of a small minority who adhered to the earlier tradition of socialist pacifism, whereas the great majority now favored an effective League of Nations able to enforce collective security. The rise of fascism brought the two groups into open confrontation at the 1935 Annual Party Conference. The Italian invasion of Ethiopia in that year ensured that the party had to face squarely the possibility that support for collective security might involve going to war and not merely an attempt to remove the causes of war. Although Lansbury was at odds with the majority of the party, he put the pacifist case to the Party Conference with great emotion, identifying himself with the pacifism of the early Christians. But a fierce attack upon his pacifist position by the trades union leader Ernest Bevin led to the adoption by an overwhelming vote of a resolution supporting sanctions, with the clear understanding that sanctions might mean war. Lansbury then resigned as party leader.

In the last four years of his life, Lansbury devoted himself to the preservation of international peace by a personal crusade to spread Christian socialist pacifism, calling for a "Truce of God." He had personal meetings with many world leaders, including Adolf Hitler, in a vain attempt to avert war. After the outbreak of the Second World War Lansbury was the spokesman for the pacifist cause in the House of Commons before his death in 1940.

Two aspects of Lansbury's pacifist beliefs stand out. As a Christian, he believed that if the Christian tradition in Western civilization could be properly tapped then war between the Western powers, and hence world war, could be averted. As a socialist, he strongly urged the solidarity of the international working class as a means of breaking the war-producing capacity of national states. He advocated his cause with unsurpassed moral force, but his career illustrates the difficulty of combining pacifism with the leadership of a major political party in a country which is a Great Power.

Bibliography:

A. *Looking Backwards and Forwards* (London, 1935); *My Life* (London, 1928); *My Quest for Peace* (London, 1938).

B. Raymond Postgate, *The Life of George Lansbury* (London, 1951); DNB, 1931-40, 524-26.

C. George Lansbury Papers, London School of Economics and Political Science.

Geoffrey Matthews

LATT, Hermann. See FERNAU, Hermann.

LAURENDEAU, André (21 March 1912, Montreal, Quebec, Canada—1 June 1968, Ottawa, Ontario). *Education*: B.A., Coll., Sainte-Marie, Montreal, 1931; further studies in philosophy and literature at the Université de Montreal, 1933-35, and at Sorbonne, the collège de France, and the Institut catholique in Paris, 1935-37. *Career*: editor, *L'Action Nationale*, 1937-1942, 1948-1954, editor-in-chief, *Le Devoir*, 1947-1968, *Le Magazine Maclean*, co-chairman of the Royal Commission on Bilingualism and Biculturalism, 1963-68.

André Laurendeau came to prominence during the Second World War as a highly articulate anti-imperialist and anticonscriptionist spokesman. In the Spring of 1942 he helped organize and then became secretary-general for the League for the Defence of Canada, a public pressure group created to convince Canadians to vote "No" in the April 1942 plebiscite asking Canadians to release the Liberal government from its publicly-stated promise not to impose conscription for overseas service. English speaking Canada voted 80 percent "Yes," while French-speaking Canadians voted nearly 90 percent "No". Hoping to keep the pressure on the Liberal government Laurendeau joined other French-Canadian nationalists in the Bloc Populaire Canadien, founded in September, 1942, to fight the growing eventuality of conscription, to limit the war effort, and to push for a reconstruction program which included significant socio-economic reforms. The movement elected four members to the Quebec legislature, including its leader Laurendeau, in the 1944 provincial election, but fell apart shortly after the end of the War.

Like *Henri Bourassa and canon Lionel Groulx, his French-Canadian Catholic mentors, Laurendeau strongly rejected all forms of imperialism, especially military imperialism. In the 1930s Laurendeau became a strong advocate of a liberal social catholicism as articulated by Jacques Maritain, Etienne Gilson, and Emmanuel Mounier. His French-Canadian nationalism was tempered by a deep concern for the rights of individuals as well as a sensitivity and tolerance for the views and values of all religious and ethnic groups. For Laurendeau, the moralist and the humanist, imperialists were racists who desired the integration and eventual assimilation of ethnic and religious minorities. The effect of British imperialism in Canada had been to create hostility, tension, and even hatred between French-speaking and English-speaking Canadians thereby preventing the country from achieving an autonomous and mature foreign policy.

Canada's continued ties with the British Commonwealth meant that a policy of neutrality, a policy that would have been more in tune with Canada's geopolitical position as a small North-American nation, was out of the question. French Canada agreed to participate on a voluntary basis in what was proclaimed as a "limited" war. But when the "limited" war effort turned into a "total" war effort, the imposition of conscription became a foregone conclusion. When conscription for overseas service was implemented, late in 1944, Laurendeau declared that Quebec had been betrayed by the Liberal government and its French-Canadian representatives. Furthermore, Confederation, a compact of two nationalities as well as provinces, had been violated because the expressed wishes of the French-Canadian minority had been overruled by an aggressive and intolerant English-speaking majority. Pluralistic societies such as Canada could only survive, according to Laurendeau, if a keen sense of justice tempered the rule of majoritarian democracy.

Following the war Laurendeau spent his career as journalist, writer, and television commentator trying to ensure a peaceful and harmonious existence between Canada's French-speaking minority and English-speaking majority. In the early 1960s he clearly foresaw the growing crisis facing Canada's two linguistic communities. As co-chairmain of the Royal Commission of Bilingualism and Biculturalism, he and his colleagues dissected the nature of the sociopolitical crisis and proposed various solutions which would allow Canada's two linguistic communities to coexist and flourish as distinct groups under shared political and economic institutions.

Bibliography:

A. *La Crise de la conscription* (Montreal, 1962).

B. Ramsay Cook and Michael Behiels, "Introduction," Cook and Behiels, eds., *The Essential Laurendeau*, (Toronto, 1976).

C. André Laurendeau Papers, Institut Lionel Groulx, Montreal.

Michael D. Behiels

LAWSON, Wilfred (4 September 1829, Brayton, Cumberland, England—1 July 1906, London). *Education*: tutored at home and self-educated. *Career*: Liberal Member of Parliament (Carlisle), 1859-65, 1868-85, (Cockermouth), 1886-1900, 1906, (Camborne), 1903-06.

A baronet who claimed *Richard Cobden and *John Bright as his mentors, Sir Wilfred Lawson was throughout his lengthy career in Commons faithful to the tenets of "advanced Liberalism." Though he strongly supported the whole of the Radical agenda of the late nineteenth century, the issues which most roused his moral passion were temperance reform and peace. Scornful of domestic "fire-eaters" and "jingoes" whom he described as "irresponsible, impulsive, ignorant shouter[s] for war," he was an uncompromising advocate of neutralism, writing, for example, in 1878 that he would not "give the bones of one British soldier to help the Turks keep Russia out of Constantinople."

An instinctive "little Englander" even before the term itself was much in use, he was the purest of Radicals in his insistence that colonial expansion be curbed and the army and navy reduced in size. In 1875 he introduced a motion to reduce the British Army, which won 61 votes but was defeated. He was especially critical of efforts to impose British control upon Afghans, Zulus, and Egyptians whom he felt should be left alone to govern themselves. It was during the Boer War (1899-1901) that the aged Lawson reached the climax of a long career as antiwar moralist. Recalling the earlier campaign of Cobden against the Crimean War, which history had so clearly validated, Lawson was among the first in Commons to oppose Chamberlain's South African policies on the premise that "we had no earthly right to interfere in the Transvaal." During the first year of the conflict Lawson was a frequent speaker at protest rallies and antiwar demonstrations despite the risk of mob violence, as on one occasion in March of 1900 when he barely escaped the blows of "patriotic roughs" who invaded a meeting at Exeter Hall. In Commons Lawson was numbered among the most extreme of pro-Boers because of his consistent votes against further supplies of money and men to prosecute the "iniquitious war" in the Transvaal. Many antiwar Liberals preferred to sidestep the supply issue through abstentions, and Lawson ascribed the loss of his Cockermouth seat in 1900 by 240 votes to his refusal to follow suit. Despite his loss he later characterized the four thousand votes cast in his behalf by a largely working class constituency as "the most . . . satisfactory poll . . . ever cast for me," and as a heartening "vote for Peace" at a time when the nation seemed "wholly given up to the worship of Baal."

Through a career spanning five decades Sir Wilfred Lawson never deviated from the belief that war was a "useless sacrifice of men and money," inhibiting domestic reform, and that the "military madness" which "ever and anon attacks the nation" must be resisted, no matter the personal cost. The lonely resistance which he often mounted made him a "nuisance," as much to the "Respectables" of his own party as to the Conservatives. He remained, however, the authentic voice of an unyielding morality and of an honorable tradition of Radical dissent.

Bibliography:

A. Sir Wilfred Lawson, *A Memoir*, ed. by Geo. W. Erskine (London, 1909).

B. G. H. Dyer, *Sir Wilfred Lawson, His Life, His Humour, and His Mission* (London, 1877); William B. Luke, *Sir Wilfred Lawson* (London, 1900); DNB, 1901-1911 Supp., II, 428-31.

C. Lawson Estate Records, The Record Office, The Castle, Carlisle.

Claire Hirschfield

LEAVITT, Joshua (8 September 1794, Heath, MA—16 January 1873, New York). *Education*: B.A. Yale Coll., 1814; B.D. Yale Theological Seminary, 1824. *Career*: editor, *New York Evangelist*, 1831-37, *Emancipator*, 1837-48; author and reform activist.

Throughout his career as a reform activist, Joshua Leavitt worked for world peace. Best known as an abolitionist and editor of the antislavery paper, the *Emancipator*, Leavitt's strong evangelical commitment led him to take an active role in the peace struggle. Like *William Lloyd Garrison, he believed that Christian America should free its slaves for the sake of Christ and the salvation of the country. He viewed slavery as an inherently violent system whose destruction would help preserve peace between the North and South as well as among nations. Yet Leavitt did not share Garrison's absolute pacifism and became a leader of the political anti-Garrisonian wing of the abolitionist movement. He rejected nonresistance and criticized those peace advocates who had come to oppose defensive wars. He feared that any denial of a nation's or an individual's right of self-defense would weaken civil government, which he considered a vital instrument for the eradication of slavery.

During the 1840s he continued to view the issues of slavery and war as intertwined. He sought to prevent American annexation of Texas—and thus war with Mexico and perhaps Great Britain—by attempting to persuade the British Government to induce Texans to give up slavery and maintain an independent republic. When war with Mexico developed, he denounced it bitterly in the columns of the *Emancipator*. Throughout the conflict he urged Congress to end appropriations for the war effort on the grounds that America was an aggressor nation waging an unjust war in order to strengthen the slave system.

Leavitt was an outspoken supporter of *Elihu Burritt's League of Universal Brotherhood in the 1840s. Never a pacifist, he chose to interpret the League's pledge to work for the abolition of war not as a denial of the right of self-defense, but rather as a protest against war and all forms of oppression. Although he supported the international peace congresses, Leavitt believed that the cause of world peace could best be advanced by increasing contact among nations through trade and communication rather than by creating a formal international organization. From 1840 until the Civil War, he played a leading role in the free trade and cheap postage movements. In editorials and pamphlets, as a lobbyist in Washington, and as a prominent spokesman for the Anti-Corn Law League and president of the Boston Cheap Postage Association, Leavitt argued that drastic reductions in tariff duties and international postage rates would facilitate trade and enhance the prospect of peace.

Bibliography:

A. *Memorial of Joshua Leavitt, Praying the Adoption of Measures to Secure an Equitable Market for American Wheat* (Washington, D.C., 1841); *The Moral and Social Benefits of Cheap Postage* (New York, 1849).

B. Joshua Leavitt Papers, Library of Congress.

Hugh Davis

LECOIN, Louis (30 September 1888, St. Amand-Montrond, Cher, France—23 June 1971, Pavillons-sous-Bois, Seine, France). *Education*: primary school. *Career*: manual laborer, anarchist, and writer.

Few individuals in the history of French pacifism have endured as much for their cause as did Louis Lecoin. He spent some twelve years in prison because of his ceaseless struggle against the evils of war and capitalism. The reasons for his lifelong campaign against social injustice are to be found in the unhappy circumstances of his early years. One of seven children born to a poor agricultural worker, Lecoin knew poverty and insecurity from childhood. After receiving the rudiments of an education, he went to work to help meet family expenses, finding employment as a printer's apprentice, gardener, and groundskeeper. His naturally rebellious temperament, which caused him problems with his employers, as well as his distaste for rural life led him to migrate to Paris by 1907. There he lived by doing odd jobs and sleeping wherever he could for want of money. Lecoin was soon attracted by anarchist ideas and he participated in several demonstrations against the government.

His first brush with militarism took place in 1910 when he was called up for service in the army. He displayed insubordination when he refused to help guard railway lines during a general strike, and was sentenced to six months in prison. After his release, Lecoin joined and became the secretary of an anarchist organization that called upon young conscripts to refuse to serve and upon soldiers to desert. Arrested and brought to trial in 1913, he was jailed for five years. Prison meant loneliness, poor treatment, and inadequate food, but Lecoin's iron will enabled him to survive.

While he was serving his sentence, World War I broke out. From prison Lecoin and a fellow inmate, Pierre Ruff, drafted a tract declaring: "Enough barbarism! Enough blood! Let us demand peace. Let us impose peace," and calling upon young men to refuse to take part in the conflict. Released in 1917, he was quickly rearrested for failure to report for military service and returned to prison, where he remained until 1920.

During the interwar years, Lecoin engaged in anarchist and antimilitarist activity. Most notably he worked to save the condemned American prisoners Nicola

Sacco and Bartolomeo Vanzetti, organizing numerous meetings and petitions on their behalf. He strongly condemned fascism in Italy and sought to bar its advance in Spain during the 1930s. He created a Committee for a Free Spain and later organized Solidarité internationale antifasciste to combat Franco and assist Spanish republican refugees in France. At the time of the Czech crisis of 1938, he organized appeals for a peaceful settlement that would avert war.

When World War II erupted in September 1939, Lecoin defied the Edouard Daladier government by issuing a manifesto that called for "immediate peace." He painfully gathered signatures of leading intellectuals on a leaflet that he personally circulated in a hasty trip across France. For his efforts, Lecoin was arrested and sentenced by a military tribunal to detention, first in a prison camp in southern France, then in Algeria. He suffered seriously from ill treatment and malnourishment before he was released late in 1941. For the remainder of the war he stayed in seclusion.

After the Liberation, Lecoin resumed his campaign for peace. In 1948 he founded the monthly review, *Défense de l'homme*, which attacked militarism, rearmament, and colonialism. He argued for an amnesty of political prisoners regardless of their beliefs. Lecoin appealed for an end to the bloody Algerian war and undertook a campaign on behalf of conscientious objectors. Demanding a statute that would recognize their right not to participate in war, Lecoin began a long hunger strike in 1962 that was rewarded with a law recognizing conscientious objection. Increasingly frail, Lecoin nonetheless continued to work against the threat of war until shortly before his death. His long career of protest against injustice and his willingness to endure personal suffering remain remarkable testimony to the strength of his convictions.

Bibliography:

A. *Le Cours d'une vie* (Paris, 1965).

B. NYT, June 24, 1971, 42; *France-Soir*, June 25, 1971, 3.

James Friguglietti

LEDEBOUR, Georg (7 March 1850, Hannover, Prussia—31 March 1947, Berne, Switzerland). *Education*: business training in realschule, Hannover. *Career*: pursued variety of occupations in Hannover and England; journalist and organizer for Hirsch Duncker trade unions, 1882-85; editor, *Demokratische Blätter* (Berlin), 1885-87; political editor, *Volkszeitung* (Berlin), 1889-90; active as journalist and lecturer for Social Democratic party from 1891; editor, *Sächsische Arbeiter-Zeitung* (Dresden), 1898-1900; Reichstag deputy, 1900-24; co-chairman, Sozialdemokratische Arbeits-gemeinschaft (Dissident Reichstag delegation), 1916-17; co-chairman, Independent Social Democratic party, 1917-18, 1920-22; founder and leader of Socialist League 1924-31; active in Socialist Workers party, 1931-33.

Georg Ledebour began his long and stormy political career as a radical democrat. By 1891, however, he had moved beyond liberalism to socialism and, indeed, soon assumed a leading position on the left wing of Sozialdemokratische

Partei Deutschlands (German Social Democratic Party) (SPD). By the turn of the century he had emerged as one of the most highly regarded and intransigent opponents of imperialism within the party. During the final years before the outbreak of World War I he was an articulate advocate of disarmament and of German reconciliation with England and France. Although he had consistently maintained that every state must be prepared to defend itself against attack, he rejected the argument of the majority of his Social Democratic colleagues in August 1914 that Germany faced such a situation and opposed the German war effort. By mid-1915 Ledebour had become one of the most important spokesmen for the antiwar minority within the SPD. He participated in the international conferences of dissident socialists held in Zimmerwald in September 1915 and Stockholm in September 1917 and was a leader of the opposition deputies who broke away from the SPD Reichstag delegation in March 1916 as well as of the Unabhängige Sozialdemokratishe Partei Deutschlands (German Independent Social Democratic Party) that was founded just over a year later. By January 1918 he had become associated with the Revolutionary Shop Stewards, a group which engaged in active preparations for a revolution to end the war and overthrow the capitalist order.

After playing a central role in the revolutionary events of November 1918–January 1919, he again became a frequent and eloquent speaker on international affairs in the Reichstag, advocating international arbitration and the creation of a world parliament. When he refused to join the majority of his colleagues in returning to the SPD in 1922, however, he became increasingly isolated and soon found himself relegated to the periphery of German political life.

Bibliography:

A. *Die Deutsche Kolonialpolitik* (Berlin, 1907); *Der Ledebour-Prozess* (Berlin, 1919); *Ledebour vor den Geschworenen* (Berlin, 1919).

B. Minna Ledebour, ed., *Georg Ledebour: Mensch und Kämpfer* (Zurich, 1954); Ursula Ratz, *Georg Ledebour* (Berlin, 1969); *Biographisches Lexikon des Sozialismus* (Berlin, 1960), I, 183-84; *Biographisches Wörterbuch zur deutschen Geschichte* (Munich, 1974), II, 1600-1.

Kenneth R. Calkins

LEFEBVRE, Raymond (4 April 1891, Paris—October, 1920, drowned at sea near Normandy). *Education*: Lycée Janson de Sailly, Paris; diplôme, L'Ecole libre des sciences politiques, 1913; studies at the Univ. of Paris. *Career*: writer, journalist, and political activist.

As a young man of 17, Lefebvre defined himself as a "passionate Christian" as well as a "spirited monarchist and socialist," but by the eve of World War I, he had broken with the conservative milieu of his upbringing and associated himself with revolutionary syndicalists. With the outbreak of the war, he became a convinced pacifist and made contact with *Romain Rolland and the British Union of Democratic Control. Drafted, he demanded to be sent to the front in order "to sabotage 'glory' with all the prestige of one who has been there." He joined Charles Longuet's group of the Socialist party after Verdun (1916), where he was wounded, but also supported the vision of +Woodrow Wilson and the socialist Zimmerwald movement at the same time. His "ecumenical" approach to political change was characterized by his admiration of the Russian Revolution from the viewpoint of a "left Wilsonianism."

Tuberculosis, contracted at the front, forced him to leave Paris in April, 1918 for the countryside where he wrote a brochure, *L'Ancien Soldat*, as well as a number of political articles. He argued for the creation of an international republic in which the separate nations would be given autonomy and hoped that veterans would become the spearhead of such a movement. This hope, plus his disillusionment with the Versailles Peace Conference, moved him toward communism and the creation of the International Association of Veterans. In his writings, particularly in a second brochure, *L'Ancien Soldat*, Lefebvre demonstrated that he had become a pacifist communist, rejecting all forms of bourgeois pacifism, denouncing the intervention into the Russian Revolution, and celebrating the Black Sea Mutiny of Entente soldiers who refused to fight against the Bolsheviks. Finally, in August 1919, he came out in favor of the Third International.

The failure of the general strike in July 1919 further convinced him of the hopelessness of naive leftist democracy; Lefebvre moved closer toward embracing an iron revolutionary discipline and turned his attention to the role of the intellectual elite. Returning to Paris in October 1919, he founded the Clarté group with *Henri Barbusse and *Paul Vaillant-Couturier which became the literary soul of revolutionary pacifism. He contributed numerous articles to a wide variety of dailies and journals, including *Le Populaire*, *La Verité*, *Le Journal du Peuple*, *L'Humanité*, *Le Combattant*, *La Vague*, and *Bulletin communiste*. In the remaining months of his life, he was enormously active in propagating his Communist views. Among French revolutionary youth, his was the most original and creative mind, endowed with literary gifts and a wide cultural knowledge. His work helped make the Association révolutionnaire des anciens combattants (Revolutionary Association of Veterans) one of the major forces in the French Communist movement. Many veterans followed him from pacifism to communism and he was regarded as a great future leader of the party. In July 1920 he left for Moscow as a delegate to the second Comintern congress and on his return trip, he was drowned.

Bibliography:

A. *L'Ancien soldat* (Paris, 1918); *La guerre des soldats*, with P. Vaillant-Couturier (Paris, 1919).

B. Shaul Ginsburg, "Raymond Lefebvre et le Mouvement clarté," *Le Mouvement social*, 60 (1974), 47-76; Shaul Ginsburg, *Raymond Lefebvre et les origines du communisme francais* (Paris, 1975); Annie Kriegel, *Aux Origines du communisme francais, 1914-1920* (Paris, 1964); Robert Wohl, *French Communism in the Making, 1914-1924* (Stanford, CA, 1966).

Shaul Ginsburg
Trans. by Sandi E. Cooper

LE FOYER, Lucien (29 June 1872, Paris—6 October 1952, Paris?). *Career*: lawyer; member, Chamber of Deputies; member, secretary, vice-president, member of Executive Committee, Radical party; honorary secretary, Groupe parlementaire française pour l'arbitrage; member, Bureau International de la Paix; vice-president, Association de la paix par le droit; co-editor (with *Jules Prudhommeaux), *Le Paix par le Droit*.

Prominent as a Mason, Lucien Le Foyer, along with *Gaston Moch, +Léon Bourgeois, and others, was instrumental in getting the lodges to introduce and to support a successful resolution at the National Peace Congress (Rouen, 1903) calling for reduction in armament and the strengthening of international law. Two years later, both the Grand-Orient and the Grande-Loge passed a resolution calling for a Fédération des patries to prevent war. In 1925 Le Foyer was president of the Parisian lodge Cosmos, and from 1928 to 1930 he served as Grand Master of the Grande-Loge de France.

His leadership in the Masonic order served as a platform for advancing his pacifist views in the Ligue des droits de l'homme (League for the Rights of Man) (LDH) and in the Radical party, as well as elsewhere. In 1917 Le Foyer was a co-founder—with *Mathias Morhardt, *Georges Demartial, and others—of the Société des études documentaires et critiques sur la guerre (Society for the Documentary and Critical Study of the War). As such, he came under police surveillance and was the subject of two police reports. The first reported that in November 1917 the Congress of the LDH adopted a motion to press for a League of Nations without waiting for the end of the war. Le Foyer also supported a call for immediate arbitration, but it did not pass.

In 1920 Le Foyer, with Georges Demartial and others, founded the Union populaire pour la paix universelle (Popular Union for Universal Peace) (UPPU), affiliated with the Union of Democratic Control. Its objective was to establish democratic control of foreign policy and to establish a genuine federation of peoples. In the following year, Le Foyer addressed a meeting (sponsored by the LDH, the Association républicaine des anciens combattants, and the Parti socialiste) of 10,000 persons, calling for amnesty for the mutineers of 1917 and others, and for the elimination of *Conseils de guerre* and *Cours martiales*. At the National Congress of Peace in 1926, he pronounced himself in favor of a law permitting conscientious objection but opposed disobedience, and revealed that, during the war, he adopted a position midway between *guerre à l'outrance* and *paix à tout prix*. In 1928 he was one of the principal members of the newly founded Association pacifiste internationale des journalistes (International Association of Pacifist Journalists).

Le Foyer believed that, in order to be more effective, the authority of the League of Nations needed to be expanded, by making it more democratic, by establishing an international police, and by working towards a United States of Europe. These views were expressed before meetings of the LDH and other groups in 1930, 1931, and 1932. As one of the founders of the Comité d'action pour la paix en Espagne (Action Committee for Peace in Spain) in 1937, he advocated mediation by the League of Nations and a plebiscite.

With the onset of the Czechoslovakian crisis, Le Foyer took a strong antiwar position, opposing hostilities with Germany. After Munich, the Délégation permanent des sociétés françaises pour la paix (Permanent Delegation of French Peace Societies) (DPSP), with Le Foyer serving as president, declared that it "joyfully associates" with the people saved, and applauded the "victory of peace over war;" no problem now exists, it said, between France and Germany, and it saluted a peace made "prior to a war."

Le Foyer was a leading figure in most of French antiwar organizations during the 1920s and 1930s, serving as secretary-general, vice-president, or president of the DPSFP, the UPPU, and the International Peace Bureau. He was a delegate from these or other organizations to the annual National Congresses of Peace and to the Universal Congresses of Peace. His commitment to pacifism remained right up to the outbreak of the war.

Bibliography:

A. *Les alliances et les engagements de la France* (Paris, 1938); *La guerre et la paix par les chiffres* (Paris, 1901); *Lettre a Mm. les membres de la Conférence de la paix à la Haye: le droit des peuples* (Paris, 1899); *Le minimum de salaire en Belgique* (Paris, 1897); *Patriotisme et civisme* (Nimes, 1903); *Rapport sur de désarmement* (Geneva, 1927); *Le suffrage international* (Paris, 1924).

B. Alfred Fried, "Le Foyer, Lucien," *Handbuch der Friedensbewegung* (Leipzig, 1911-13), II, 371-2.

Albert S. Hill

LEHMANN, Max (19 May 1845, Berlin—8 October 1929, Göttingen, Germany). *Education*: Ph.D., Univ. of Berlin, 1867. *Career*: gymnasium teacher, 1868-75; historian with the Prussian state archives, 1875-78; professor of history, Univ. of Marburg, 1888-93, Univ. of Leipzig, 1893, Univ. of Göttingen, 1894-1929; editor, *Historische Zeitschrift*, 1875-93.

As a historian committed to nineteenth-century liberalism, Max Lehmann gained a reputation as a young man for his attack on the Hohenzollern legend. His writings, in which he revealed himself as an opponent of the Small-German (*kleindeutsch*) historical interpretation, unleashed a scandalous hate campaign against him. Even before World War I, Lehmann belonged to the critics of Germany's "World Policy," in whose unbridled expansionist strivings he saw a threat to peace. From ethical-moral motives he spoke against Pan-Germanism and militarism. His debates with the representatives of national chauvinism reached a high point during World War I. Although he was caught up in the wave of nationalism that swept Germany in the first months of the war, he soon turned against German war policy. This led to violent clashes with his nationalist colleagues at the University of Göttingen.

Lehmann took a strong stand against the so-called Professors' Memorandum of June 20, 1915, in which over 1,000 German professors supported a policy of extensive annexations. He signed the memorandum written by Hans Delbrück and sent to the German imperial chancellor on July 9, 1915, criticizing an expansionist policy. In the same year, he gave his support to the restoration of the Polish state. He moved closer to pacifism and became a member of the Bund

Neues Vaterland (New Fatherland League) and the Deutsche Friedensgesellschaft (German Peace Society). In 1916 he supported the effort to establish the Zentralstelle für Völkerrecht (Central Coordinating Office for International Law).

Although Lehmann greeted the German revolution of 1918 with skepticism, he had advocated the introduction of parliamentary democracy since the summer of 1917. Together with Hans Delbrück and Friedrich Meinecke, he publicly demanded the reform of the franchise in Prussia. Directly after the cabinet of Prince Max von Baden took over the reins of government in October 1918, Lehmann, together with Arthur Holitscher, *Kurt von Tepper-Laski, and Count *Georg von Arco, submitted a petition to the new imperial chancellor requesting the release of all persons imprisoned for their peace activities.

In the 1920s Lehmann sympathized with the right-wing of the Sozialdemokratische Partei Deutschlands (German Social Democratic Party) (SPD). After 1918 he was one of the few German historians who publicly supported the Weimar Republic. In the Spring of 1919 he signed *Romain Rolland's "Declaration for the Independence of the Mind (Spirit)," which enlisted prominent personalities in support of the reconciliation of European peoples.

Bibliography:

A. *Aus der Zeit des Waffenstillstands von 1813* (Munich and Leipzig, 1888); *Bismarck. Eine Charakteristik*, Gertrud Lehmann, ed. (Berlin, 1948); *Die Erhebung von 1813* (Göttingen, 1913); *Freiherr vom Stein* (3 vols., Leipzig, 1902-5); *Friedrich der Grosse und der Ursprung des Siebenjährigen Krieges* (Leipzig, 1894); *Historische Aufsätze und Reden* (Leipzig, 1911); *Knesebeck und Schön: Beiträge zur Geschichte der Freiheitskriege* (Leipzig, 1875); *Die preussische Reform von 1808 und die französische Revolution* (Berlin, 1908); *Stein, Scharnhorst und Schön: eine Schutzschrift* (Leipzig, 1877).

B. "Max Lehmann (autobiographisch)," *Die Geschichtswissenschaft der Gegenwart in Selbstdarstellungen*, Sigfried Steinberg, ed. (Leipzig, 1925), I, 207ff; Waltraut Reichel, *Studien zur Wandlung von Max Lehmanns preussisch-deutschem Geschichtsbild* (Göttingen-Berlin-Frankfurt, 1963); Gunter Vogler, "Max Lehmann," *Studien über die deutsche Geschichtswissenschaft*, Joachim Streisand, ed. (Berlin/DDR, 1965), II, 57ff.

Lothar Wieland
Trans. by Solomon Wank

LEHMANN-RUSSBÜLDT, Otto (1 January 1873, Berlin—7 October 1964, Berlin). *Education*: realschule; self-educated. *Career*: bookseller, journalist, political journalist, and peace activist.

Following an apprenticeship as a bookseller, Otto Lehmann-Russbüldt advanced to a position as a reporter for a parliamentary press agency before the turn of the century. Shortly after 1900 he joined the Giordano Bruno Bund and a short time later the Deutsche Monistenbund (German Monist League). His interest in social-philosophical questions led to his first publications and to involvement in the movement to promote the withdrawal from church membership. In addition, he operated a mail-order house for monistic writings.

On November 16, 1914 he founded, together with *Kurt von Tepper-Laski, the Bund Neues Vaterland (New Fatherland League). He became general secretary of the League and throughout the war advocated a negotiated peace. In the fall of 1914, even before the founding of the League, he published the essay "Die Schöpfung der Vereinigten Staaten von Europe" ("The Creation of the United States of Europe"), which opposed the German drive for annexations and spoke for the united Europe. In April 1915 Lehmann-Russbüldt participated as a delegate of the League in the founding of the Zentralorganisation für einen dauernden Freiden (Coordinating Organization for a Permanent Peace) in The Hague.

Lehmann-Russbüldt was the type of left-oriented independent intellectual who, although sympathetic towards the left wing of the German Social Democratic party, participated actively in Communist organizations. Still, as a pacifist, he represented the view that a lasting peace could be attained even under the rule of capitalism.

After the war, Lehmann-Russbüldt devoted himself above all to rapprochement with France and Poland, to propagandistic activity in the cause of Germany's entrance into the League of Nations, and to opposition to the strengthening of the German army in violation of the terms of the Treaty of Versailles. He sought to counter the influence of Prussian-German militarism and published in left-wing and pacifist journals such as *Die Weltbühne* and *Das Andere Deutschland.* His work *Die blutige International der Rustungsindustrie* (*The Bloody International of the Armament Industry*) (1929) gained international recognition and reached 40,000 copies by 1933. In 1927 he wrote the history of the New Fatherland League and immediately before the coming to power of the Nazis in January 1933 he supported the Sozialistische Arbeiterpartei (Socialist Workers party).

On February 28, 1933, one day after the Reichstag fire, Lehmann-Russbüldt was arrested. He managed to escape from prison the following month with the help of two clergymen and fled to Holland. From there he went to England, where, together with Rudolf Olden and *Ernst Toller, he represented the DLM in exile. While in London he wrote a great deal and participated in the Deutsche Volksfront (German Popular Front) constituted in Paris. From 1941 to 1948 he published the "Rundbriefe des Flüchtlings" ("Circular of the Emigré"), in which he called for the "deprussianizing" of a future Germany and for the creation of a decentralized public administration. In 1951 he returned to Berlin and was appointed honorary president of the DLM, but he broke with the organization in 1954 as a protest against the organization's support of the communist-led German Democratic Republic.

Bibliography:

A. *Aggression. The Origin of Germany's War Machine* (London, 1942); *Die Brücke über den Abgrund* (Berlin, 1925); *Europa den Europäern*, with Alexander Hirsch (Hamburg, 1948); *Germany's Air Force* (London, 1935); *Hitler's Wings of Death* (New York, 1936); *Der Krieg als Geschäft* (Zurich, 1938); *Landesverteidigung ohne Profit* (London, 1936); *Landesverteidigung. Vortrag vor deutschen Kriegsgefangenen in England* (Hamburg, 1947); *Neues Deutschtum* (Paris, 1939); *Reiter durch Jahrhunderte. Jugendphan-*

tasien eines Revolutionssoldaten (Dusseldorf, 1947); *Should and Could the Jews Return to Germany*? (London, 1944); *Weissbuch über die Schwarze Reichswehr* (Berlin, 1925); *Wer rettet Europe? Die Aufgabe der Kleinen Staaten* (Zurich, 1936).

B. Werner Röder and Herbert A. Strauss, eds., *Biographisches Handbuch der deutschsprachigen Emigration nach 1933* (Munich-New York-London-Paris, 1980), I, 425; Jakob Stöcker, *Männer des deutschen Schicksals. Von Wilhelm II. bis Adolf Hitler. Geschichte in Porträts* (Berlin, 1949); Hans Wehberg, "Otto Lehmann-Russbüldt 75 Jahre alt," *Die Friedenswarte*, 6 (1947), 365-68.

Lothar Wieland
Trans. by Peter Seadle

LEMONNIER, Charles (1806, Beauvais, Oise, France—3 December 1891, Paris). *Education*: degree in law. *Career*: professor of philosophy, Collège de Sorèze; lawyer; journalist, *La Phare de la Loire*; legal officer, Chemins de fer du nord; secretary general, Crédit mobilier; St. Simonian activist; a founder, Ligue internationale de la paix et de la liberté, Geneva, 1867; editor, *Les Etats-Unis d'Europe* (from 1868).

In September 1867, after the government of the Second French Empire (1852-70) denied him the use of Paris, Charles Lemonnier cooperated with *Elie Ducommun, *Marie Goegg, *Émile Arnaud, Jollisaint, and others in organizing an international peace conference at Geneva. Geneva thus emerged, alongside London and Paris, as a third major center of peace activism in Europe. From the congress itself, moreover, issued the Ligue internationale de la paix et de la liberté (International League of Peace and Freedom) and its journal, *Les Etats-Unis d'Europe*). Both remained under Lemonnier's control until his death in 1891.

As the word "freedom" in the name of his league implied, Lemonnier emphasized political reform as the precondition for peace. In conjunction with his support for universal suffrage, separation of church and state, and Goegg's campaign for women's rights, this emphasis on political reform reflected a youthful enthusiasm for the utopian socialism of Henri de Saint-Simon as well as a lifelong commitment to republicanism. Typically, his Saint-Simonianism, coupled with his training in law and finance, led him initially under the Second Empire to assume the post of claims chief at the Crédit mobilier and the editorship of the *Journal des tribunaux de commerce*. His republicanism, however, eventually led him not only to oppose the Second Empire but also to politicize the campaign for peace. Indeed, he proclaimed, "to abolish royalty, this would be, virtually, to abolish war; to establish the Republic, this would be, virtually, to establish peace and freedom."

Lemonnier's emphasis on republican liberty provoked objections from others within the international peace movement, notably *Frédéric Passy of the Paris-based Ligue de la paix (League of Peace), Ferdinand Santallier of the Le Havre-based Union de la paix (Union of Peace), and *Henry Richard of the London-based Peace Society. In part they feared that Lemonnier's open association with radical republicans such as Giuseppe Garibaldi, who attended the league's founding conference, would tarnish the peace movement's public image. Beyond this, however, they feared that his espousal of "liberty" would provide a pretext for war and that his plan for a multinational peace-keeping army would, if implemented, result in a reinforcement of the martial spirit. They further objected to his revival of the call for a United States of Europe, initially and widely popularized in 1849 by the republican poet *Victor Hugo, fearing in particular that it would inevitably arouse nationalistic opposition to the peace campaign. Consequently, although they cooperated with Lemonnier in organizing international events such as the Paris peace conferences of 1878 and 1889, their aversion to his political emphasis impeded the emergence of a permanent international peace coalition.

Bibliography:

A. *De l'arbitrage international et de sa procédure, mémoire présenté à l'Assemblée générale de la paix et de la liberté, le 8 september 1873* (Geneva, 1873); *Commentaire sur les principales polices d'assurance maritime usitées en France* (2 vols., Paris, 1843); *Élisa Lemonnier, fondatrice de la Société pour l'enseignement professionnel des femmes* (Saint-Germain, 1866); *Les États-Unis d'Europe* (Paris, 1872); *Présent et avenir, brochure politique* (Toulouse, 1834); *La Question sociale, rapport présenté au congrès de Lausanne, le 27 septembre 1871* (Paris, 1871); *La Vérité sur le congrès de Genève* (Berne and Geneva, 1867).

B. A.C.F. Beales, *The History of Peace: A Short Account of the Organised Movements for International Peace* (New York, 1971); "Lemonnier, Charles," in Jean Maitron, ed., *Dictionnaire biographique du mouvement ouvrier français*, Première partie: 1789-1864, II, 490-91; L. de Montluc, "La Vie de Charles Lemonnier," in *Les États-Unis d'Europe*, July & October, 1924, January, 1925; Jules Puech, "Charles Lemonnier et notre temps," in *Les États-Unis d'Europe*, October, 1930; Jules L. Puech, *La Tradition socialiste en France et la Société des nations* (Paris, 1921); *Le Devoir* (Familistère de Guise), December, 1891; *Le Droit des femmes*, December 20, 1891.

Patrick Kay Bidelman

LESSING, Theodor (8 February 1872, Hannover, Germany—31 August 1933, Mariánské Lázně (Marienbad), Czechoslovakia). *Education*: Ph.D., Univ. of Erlangen, 1899; medical and philosophical studies, Universities of Freiburg (1892-93), Bonn (1893-94, 1898-99), Munich, (1894-96). *Career*: professor of philosophy, Technical University, Hanover, 1907-26; teacher, philosopher, journalist.

Theodor Lessing had a difficult childhood because of the strained relations between his parents. His father was a Jewish doctor and his mother was the daughter of a prosperous and influential Düsseldorf banker. This contributed to his becoming a social, political, and philosophical outsider and a sharp critic of established authority in social, political, and philosophical questions. As a teacher and journalist, his aggressive critical tendency often embroiled him in controversy. Before 1914 he resolutely devoted himself to social problems and became a member of the German Social Democratic party. He supported women's emancipation, opposed official regulation of prostitution, advocated alcoholic abstinence, and urged international understanding.

After the outbreak of World War I, Lessing unsuccessfully appealed to prominent contemporaries to oppose the war. The war, in which he served first in the medical corps and then as an assistant instructor at schools in Hanover, caused his pacifistic convictions to mature. From that time on, he professed his pacifistic convictions with decisiveness as, for example, in articles he contributed to magazines and newspapers like the liberal Dortmund *Generalanzeiger*, which was edited in the 1920s by *Jakob Stöcker. His pacifist views as well as his socio-political criticism of various German institutions made him a controversial figure. In 1925 his published views on Field-Marshal Paul von Hindenburg and the latter's candidacy for the presidency of the Weimar Republic caused an unprecedented sensation. In a character study set in the form of a psychograph, Lessing warned of the dangers of electing the old and politically naive field-marshal. A storm of indignation erupted immediately, fueled by extreme nationalist and reactionary circles who believed that their idol had been slandered. These right-wing forces initiated a militant and anti-Semitic campaign against Lessing which forced him to resign his philosophy professorship at the Hanover Technical University in 1926. As a result of the controversy, Lessing lived with the threat of physical danger, but he did not leave Germany until March 1933, when Adolf Hitler, who had become chancellor two months earlier, was granted dictatorial power. Lessing's hope of finding safety for himself and his family in exile remained unfulfilled. Five months after arriving in Czechoslovakia, Lessing was shot down by Nazi assassins sent from Germany.

Bibliography:

A. *Deutschland und seine Juden* (Prague, 1933); *Einmal und nie wieder. Lebenserinnerungen* (Prague, 1935; Hanover, 1969); *Geschichte als Sinngebung des Sinnlosen* (Munich, 1921); *Der judische Selbsthass* (Berlin, 1930); *Untergang der Erde am Geist—Europa und Asien* (Hanover, 1924).

B. Ekkehard Hieronimus, *Theodor Lessing. Otto Mayerhof. Leonard Nelson. Bedeutende Juden in Niedersachen* (Hanover, 1964); Ekkehard Hieronimus, *Theodor Lessing* (Hanover, 1972); Hans Mayer, "Theodor Lessing. Bericht über ein politisches Trauma," in Hans Mayer, *Der Repräsentant und der Märtyrer* (Frankfurt am Main, 1971).

Karl Holl

Trans. by Ruthann Richards

LESTER, Muriel (1883, London?—11 February 1968, Loughton, Essex, England). *Education*: St. Leonard's School, St. Andrew's, Scotland. *Career*: cofounder of Kingsley Hall, East London; alderman, Poplar Borough, London; roving ambassador and international secretary, International Fellowship of Reconciliation, 1934-64; Christian social worker, pastor, author, and lecturer.

Muriel Lester was born into a London business family which was devoutly Anglican, believing that "God is Love." Reading *Leo Tolstoy's *The Kingdom of God Is Within You* made her a Christian pacifist, while a chance visit to

London's poverty-stricken East End led her to found a Christian social center (Kingsley Hall) there. She became a Christian socialist and adopted a life of voluntary poverty. In 1914 she helped form the Fellowship of Reconciliation (FOR); and from 1934 to 1964 she served as a roving ambassador for the International FOR. In the late 1930s and early 1940s, she was one of its international secretaries.

Muriel Lester belonged to many Christian, pacifist, women's, and humanitarian organizations and participated in humanitarian movements around the world. Beginning in the 1920s, she became an international traveler and speaker. Most important were her visits to India, where she became a friend and disciple of *Gandhi. Briefly interned by the British government in 1941, she continued thereafter to speak out for the pacifist cause. After 1945 she pursued her commitment to speak and write for the cause of pacifism, especially for the FOR. As a by-product of her concerns, she wrote a number of small books and pamphlets presenting the Christian and pacifist viewpoints. She believed also in taking direct action by public demonstrations and meetings and by directly contacting leading public figures. She did not seek to be a philosopher of pacifism; rather, she sought to be a spokeswoman for the Christian truth as she understood it.

Bibliography:

A. *Dare You Face Facts?* (New York, 1940); *Entertaining Gandhi* (London, 1932); *It Occurred to Me* (London, 1937); *It So Happened* (London, 1947); *Kill or Cure*? (Nashville, 1937); *Ways of Praying* (Nashville, 1931).

DeWitt C. Ellinwood

LEVINSON, Salmon Oliver (29 December 1865, Noblesville, IN—2 February 1941, Chicago, IL). *Education*: Univ. of Chicago, 1883-86; B.A., Yale Univ., 1888; LL.B., Chicago Coll. of Law, 1891. *Career*: lawyer; peace publicist.

Prior to the outbreak of World War I, Salmon O. Levinson showed little interest in foreign policy or the problems of war and peace. He built a successful legal practice and amassed a fortune, specializing in the financial reorganization of business corporations. The outbreak of war in 1914, however, shocked him and led to his consideration of a plan to prevent future armed conflicts. He eventually developed a proposal that was simple, direct, and comprehensive. Since international law recognized war as legal, the best way to eliminate international armed conflicts was to brand them as unlawful. He urged nations to outlaw war and then to agree upon sanctions for those disobeying the decrees of an international court established to adjudicate disputes. Just as courts of law had replaced dueling as an acceptable method for settling disputes between individuals, an international court would replace wars for settling disputes between nations. Wars might still occur, just as individual acts of violence occurred, but under Levinson's scheme they would be branded as criminal and those guilty of the crime would have to face the combined force of the world.

At first Levinson supported President +Woodrow Wilson's plan for a League of Nations, but when he discovered that the League Covenant failed to embody his principle, he denounced it bitterly. During the early 1920s he refined and developed the idea for the ''Outlawry of War.'' In 1921, while the Washington Naval Disarmament Conference was in session, he called for the nations of the world to follow a three-step process. He urged them to make the institution of war illegal, to codify international law, and finally to establish an effective world court. He envisioned a court independent of the League of Nations and modeled on the United States Supreme Court, with compulsory jurisdiction over all international disputes. Hoping to win support from anti-League Congressmen and Senators, he no longer emphasized international sanctions to back up outlawry. Instead he called for enforcement based upon good faith, public opinion, nonrecognition of changes made by the use of armed force, punishment by each state of its own war fomenters, and the use of whatever means necessary, including force, to put down a ''mad-dog state.''

By sanctioning the use of force Levinson alienated many pacifists in the peace movement. Similarly, his condemnation of the League of Nations angered advocates of the new world organization. Still, his plan for the outlawry of war won broader support from the multifarious peace movement than any other specific proposal made during the 1920s. Levinson promoted his idea with indefatigable energy and gained the support of a diverse group of individuals, including anti-League Senators Philander Knox and William E. Borah, the reformer, Raymond Robins, the philosopher, *John Dewey, the progressive preacher, *John Haynes Holmes, and the editor of the *Christian Century*, *Charles Clayton Morrison. In February 1923 Senator Borah introduced a resolution in Congress calling upon nations to outlaw war ''as an institution and means for the settlement of international conflicts.'' That same year Levinson hired a publicist to spread his views in Europe. Two years later he worked out a ''Harmony Plan'' with the pro-League faction of the peace movement. In 1927, however, he gained his greatest success when +Aristide Briand, the French Foreign Minister, used the term ''outlawing war'' (although not the full concept) in suggesting a bilateral treaty between the United States and France. Levinson worked diligently and helped rally public opinion behind what became the multilateral Kellogg-Briand Peace Pact. Signed by most of the nations of the world in an elaborate ceremony in Paris in 1928, the treaty was ratified by the United States the following year. Levinson attended the White House ceremony launching the Pact as the only invited guest of President +Herbert Hoover.

Lacking enforcement machinery, the Kellogg-Briand Pact was ignored during the 1930s and the outlawry of war idea lost favor with most peace groups. The combined onslaughts of Germany, Italy, and Japan, moreover, buried hopes for almost all antiwar proposals. Still, the outlawry campaign was one of the most extraordinary attempts in the 1920s to rally conservative and progressive antiwar advocates behind a specific proposal. Without significant political backing or organized support, it won adherence from a broad and significant segment of the peace movement. Salmon O. Levinson deserved most of the credit for this success.

Bibliography:

A. "Aggression, International," *Encyclopaedia of the Social Sciences* (New York, 1930), vols. 1-2, pp. 485-86; "The Legal Status of War," *New Republic*, 14 (March 9, 1918), 171-73; *A Plan to Outlaw War* (Chicago, 1921).

B. Charles DeBenedetti, *Origins of the Modern American Peace Movement, 1915-1929* (Millwood, N.Y., 1978); Robert H. Ferrell, *Peace in Their Time: The Origins of the Kellogg-Briand Pact* (New Haven, Conn., 1952); John E. Stoner, *S. O. Levinson and the Pact of Paris: A Study in the Techniques of Influence* (Chicago, 1943).

C. Salmon O. Levinson Papers, Regenstein Library, University of Chicago.

Harold Josephson

LIBBY, Frederick Joseph (24 November 1874, Richmond, ME—26 June 1970, Washington). *Education*: B.A., Bowdoin Coll., 1894; studied at universities of Berlin, Heidelberg, Marburg, and Oxford; S.T.B., Andover Theological Seminary, 1902. *Career*: minister, Union Congregational Church, Magnolia, MA, 1905-11; faculty, Phillips Exeter Academy, 1912-15, 1919-20; relief work with the American Friends Service Committee (AFSC) in France, 1918-19; AFSC official, 1920-21; executive secretary, National Council for Prevention of War, 1921-70; peace society executive.

The name of Frederick J. Libby is closely linked to the National Council for Prevention of War (NCPW), an organization he founded in 1921 to serve as clearing house for disarmament efforts. Born just in time to promote the Washington Disarmament Conference, this peace society reached the height of its power during the 1930s, when it fostered the neutrality acts and the Ludlow war-referendum amendment. No peace organization, before or since, has equalled the number of paid workers, pieces of literature distributed (two million in 1931), or educational impact that the NCPW possessed in the early 1930s. Modeled on the Anti-Saloon League, the NCPW supplied speech writing, publicity, and informal congressional liaison to a degree shunned by such absolutist pacifist groups as the Fellowship of Reconciliation and the War Resisters League. If the NCPW was nonpartisan, it was hardly nonpolitical. Unlike many pacifists, Libby had strong Republican leanings and made no secret of his admiration for such figures as Colonel Charles A. Lindbergh, Senator Robert A. Taft, and Wall Street lawyer +John Foster Dulles. A short and wiry man, Libby was a particularly gifted speaker, writer, and fundraiser.

Born in south Maine, Libby graduated from Bowdoin College with distinction and studied theology in Europe. After serving a Congregationalist parish and teaching Bible at Phillips Exeter, he engaged in relief work overseas with the newly organized American Friends Service Committee. His activities in France turned him into a Quaker while reinforcing his pacifist leanings.

Finding the Versailles settlement "brutal" and fearing future United States interventions, Libby launched his peace lobby in the hopes that war could be eliminated. His group was originally founded in 1921 as the National Council for the Limitation of Armaments and was headed by Christiana Merriman, executive secretary of the Foreign Policy Association. By November, however, Libby, with the backing of some eastern Friends, had become its leader. He called for progressive world organization, worldwide reduction of armaments by international agreement, and worldwide education for peace. The NCPW listed many prominent religious and civic organizations among its sponsors.

During the twenties, the NCPW promoted peace pamphlets in grammar schools, sought to eliminate nationalistic distortions from textbooks, and pushed ratification of the Kellogg-Briand Peace Pact and the World Court. Although Libby at first opposed American membership in the League of Nations, viewing it as too linked to the Versailles treaty, he decided in 1924 that the League was an essential institution of world order and hence deserving of support. He never gave up his opposition to Articles X and XVI of the League Covenant, however, and he wanted the United States to avoid any obligation to participate in coercive measures.

The rise of dictatorships increased Libby's fears of American intervention, and in the 1930s he frequently voiced his apprehension. During the Manchuria crisis, Libby endorsed the Stimson Doctrine. He opposed the levying of sanctions upon Japan, fearing that such action would lead to war. Within several years, he was saying that any Pacific war would be fought over American trade and investment in China, that such a conflict would turn the United States fascist and all Asia communist, and that stopping Japan's advance was less important than halting the economic aggression of the richer states. Although he advocated discretionary embargoes as late as 1934, he opposed giving President +Franklin Roosevelt such powers and supported mandatory neutrality legislation. In addition, he urged a war referendum, fought the War Department's mobilization plan, endorsed the Munich agreement, and sought a military policy based on defense only.

In 1936 the NCPW was at the peak of its influence. Thereafter, it continually lost ground to Roosevelt's interventionist policies and a host of affiliated organizations withdrew. In October 1939, with the war begun in Europe, Libby made the first of his frequent calls for a truce to be negotiated by a mediation commission established by sixty neutral nations. Unlike some other pacifists and isolationists, Libby did not want Roosevelt as mediator, for he found the president less neutral than Benito Mussolini or Joseph Stalin. During the debates of 1940 and 1941, Libby lent his staff to the America First Committee, presided over business meetings of the Keep America Out of War Congress (which he had helped to organize in 1938), and testified in Congress against the sending of convoys to Europe.

Japan's attack on Pearl Harbor, Libby claimed, was prompted by Roosevelt's provocative economic war. During World War II, Libby continually called for a negotiated peace; to him the doctrine of unconditional surrender was anathema. He claimed that the Yalta Conference ensured the enslavement of Germany and the Russian domination of Poland. He criticized the United Nations Charter for relying upon force to preserve a victor's peace, although he praised such UN bodies as the General Assembly and the Economic and Social Council.

At the outset of the Cold War, Libby helped launch the Foundation for Foreign Affairs, a group designed to counter the influence of such interventionist groups as the Foreign Policy Association. He was particularly concerned with the rehabilitation of Germany and promoted it in a number of ways: pushing for food shipments, opposing the dismantling of factories, calling for the termination of war crimes trials, and seeking restitution of confiscated property. The Truman Doctrine and the Atlantic Pact both met with his opposition, for he found the measures far too belligerent. During the Korean War, he continually called for negotiation and during the Indochina crisis of 1954, he opposed American intervention so strongly that he called for the resignation of his former backer John Foster Dulles as Secretary of State.

Bibliography:

A. *To End War: The Story of the National Council for the Prevention of War* (Nyack, NY, 1969).

B. Peter Marabell, ''Frederick Libby and The American Peace Movement, 1921-1941,'' Ph.D. dissertation, Michigan State University, 1975.

C. National Council for Prevention of War Papers, Swarthmore College Peace Collection.

Justus D. Doenecke

LIE, Trygve Halvdan. See *Biographical Dictionary of Internationalists*.

LIECHTENHAN, Rudolf (6 December 1875, Basel, Switzerland—29 November 1947, Basel). *Education*: theological studies, universities of Basel, Marburg, and Berlin; theological degree, Zurich, 1901. *Career*: Protestant minister, Basel, 1909-35; lecturer in New Testament, Department of Theology, Univ. of Basel, 1921-47 (unsalaried until 1935); Christian pacifist organizer and writer.

Rudolf Liechtenhan initially supported the political center of the Protestant church. At the beginning of the twentieth century he joined the religious-social movement of *Leonhard Ragaz and in 1906 co-founded the periodical *Neue Wege*, remaining its editor-in-chief until 1911. He continued to contribute regularly to the periodical until 1917. Believing that the gospel was more than merely a ''solace for man's sins and a slave for his suffering'' he tried to make religion a part of all aspects of life, even economics and politics. His religious-social orientation led him to become an antimilitarist.

In 1925 Liechtenhan helped found the Vereinigung antimilitaristischer Pfarrer der Schweiz (Union of Antimilitary Ministers in Switzerland). He served for ten years as the group's president and represented it at international conferences. In 1937 the Union expanded into the Kirchlichen Friedensbund der Schweiz (Christian Peace Union of Switzerland) in order to attract nontheologians into the peace movement. Liechtenhan served on the governing body of this organization until his death. Unfortunately, his antimilitarism soon hindered his academic career. In 1928 the Protestant faculty at the University of Berne unanimously recommended his appointment as professor, but the Bernese government refused to make the appointment solely because of his pacifist convictions, choosing instead a man who later was to become a National Socialist (Swiss Nazi).

Liechtenhan's scholarly activity made him a significant theoretician of religious antimilitarism in Switzerland. Advancing the thesis that "true disciples of Christ" could never be reconciled with a system of armaments and war, he frequently used scripture to support radical antimilitarism. His antiwar ideas were most clearly articulated in 1927 in a paper commissioned by a group of antiwar ministers entitled *Ist Abrustung Christenpflict?* (*Is Disarmament a Christian Duty?*).

He published numerous other papers dealing with a wide variety of subjects, including ethical problems in the New Testament and the relationship of biblical commandments for the contemporary world. He published a new translation of Erasmus's *Klage des Friedens* (*Lament of Peace*); and as late as 1945, he defended Christian involvement in the peace movement against attacks by Professor E. Brunner, warning against leaving the question of peace solely in the hands of politicians.

Rudolf Liechtenhan, who seemed to many of his contemporaries to be a quiet scholar and who was supposed to have had difficulties in his association with others, displayed a remarkable, thoughtful objectivity in his dispassionate writings.

Bibliography:

A. *Erasmus von Rotterdams Klage des Friendens*, trans. and introduction by Rudolf Liechtenhan (Berlin/Leipzig, 1934); *Gottes Gebot im Neuen Testament sein ursprünglicher Sinn und seine bleibende Bedeutung* (Basel, 1942); *Ist Abrüstung Christenpflicht?* (Bern, 1927); *Völkerfriede, eine Illusion oder eine Aufgabe für die Christenheit*?, Flugschrift des KFB (Zurich, 1945).

Andreas Studer
Trans. by Robert C. Reimer

LINDHAGEN, Anna Jacobina Johanna (7 April 1870, Stockholm—15 May 1941, Stockholm). *Education*: secondary schooling in Stockholm followed by nurse's training; Red Cross certificate, 1890. *Career*: office worker with publishing firm, 1892-1902; child welfare inspector, 1902-28; member, Stockholm Welfare Commission, 1902-30, member, Stockholm City Council, 1911-23; member, Stockholm City Planning Commission, 1921-40; editor, *Morgonbris*, 1911-16; social worker, writer, and humanitarian.

Coming from a family prominent in public service (*Carl Lindhagen was her brother), Anna Lindhagen was appointed to the Stockholm Welfare Commission and worked many years as an inspector of child care. She was a leading proponent of low-cost public housing and played an important role in obtaining legislation assuring humane treatment of children, particularly those of unwed mothers. A campaigner for voting rights for women, she held office in Stockholm's foremost suffrage organization (1902-16). In 1909 she joined the Social Democratic party and soon became editor of its women's journal, *Morgonbris*. She was elected to the Stockholm City Council in 1911. She introduced Sweden's first allotment gardens and was instrumental in setting up special commissions to preserve Stockholm's natural beauty and historic neighborhoods.

Lindhagen became active in the peace movement in the 1890s. She was secretary of Sveriges Kvinnliga fredsförening (Sweden's Women's Peace Society) 1898-1902. She was a delegate to the International Congress of Women held at The Hague in 1915 and helped organize the Swedish branch of the Women's International League for Peace and Freedom, serving on its executive committee from 1919. During and after World War I, she took a leading part in relief operations for war victims and refugees. She was an officer in the Swedish campaign to aid Belgian children (1914-18). In Rädda barnen (Save the Children) she held leadership positions after 1919 and in 1923 went under its auspices to work in the Ruhr. Russian, Baltic, Polish, Czech and, after 1933, German refugees were among the many beneficiaries of her efforts. With broad practical experience in local and international affairs, Lindhagen was a devoted advocate of the neglected and the oppressed, as well as an effective promoter of general community welfare.

Bibliography:

A. *Nationalitstsfrågan* (Stockholm, 1917); *Vad vi tänkte: Minnen* (Stockholm, 1941).

B. H. Flood, *Den socialdemokratiska kvinnorörelsen i Sverige* (Stockholm, 1960); H. Lindberg, *Svensk flyktingpolitik under internationellt tryck 1936-1941* (Stockholm, 1973); C. Lindhagen, *Memoarer* (Stockholm, 1936-1939); L. Wahlström, *Den svenska kvinnorörelsen* (Stockholm, 1933).

C. Anna Lindhagens Collection, Stockholm City Archives.

Howard T. Lutz

LINDHAGEN, Carl Albert (17 December 1860, Stockholm—11 March 1946, Stockholm). *Education*: law degrees, Uppsala Univ., 1879, 1883. *Career*: member, lower house of the Swedish parliament, 1897-1917, upper house, 1919-40; member, Stockholm City Council 1903-42; mayor of Stockholm, 1903-30; editor, *Folkets Dagblad Politiken*, 1917-1918; editor, *Sol och Jord* 1920-23; social reformer and author.

Carl Albert Lindhagen entered government administration in Stockholm, eventually becoming mayor of the city. As legal advisor to the *Alfred Nobel estate, he drafted the Nobel Foundation charter in 1899. On election to Parliament in 1897, he became the champion of small farmers and voting rights for women. In 1909 he changed party affiliation from the Liberals to the Social Democrats, but remained a political maverick. Twice he proposed bills to make Sweden a republic. He supported the socialist ''defense nihilists'' in opposing Swedish military build-up in 1914. When the Social Democratic party split in 1917, Lindhagen went with the more revolutionary Left-Socialists, becoming their parliamentary leader and editor of their journal. After the Left-Socialists joined the Third International, he rejected their authoritarianism and in 1923 returned to the Social Democrats.

Lindhagen's pacifism was rooted in ethical and humanistic principles. He worked for peace as a speaker, writer, organizer, and participant in international conferences. When, in 1915-16, it was hoped that the war might be stopped by intervention of neutral powers, Lindhagen arranged meetings and demonstrations and hosted the Ford Peace Expedition in Stockholm. Believing in what he called "maximist" peace-making, he put little faith in arms reduction and instead stressed removing the causes of war. Thus he agitated on behalf of oppressed racial and national groups, among them the Lapps, the Danes in Schleswig, and the Lithuanians. Colonial peoples in Africa and Asia also claimed his attention. In January 1918 he was sent on a trade mission to Petrograd and shortly afterward became involved in attempts to mediate the civil war in Finland.

A leader in several peace organizations, Lindhagen was most closely associated with Svenska freds- och skiljedomsföreningen (Swedish Peace and Arbitration Society). He founded the short-lived Förbundet för humanistisk politik (League for Humanistic Policy) (1919-23) and edited its monthly. He energetically promoted the League of Nations, the use of Esperanto, and relief for persecuted minorities, as well as domestic social reform. He helped organize the Swedish People's Parliament for Disarmament in 1932 and worked in such international peace movements as Nordiska fredsförbundet (Nordic Peace League). Lindhagen won both popularity and condemnation for his outspokenness on controversial topics and for his persistence in causes he thought essential for a humane worldwide community.

Bibliography:

A. *Alla folks frihet, hela världens fred* (Stockholm, 1943); *Kampen mot krigen och deras orsaker* (Stockholm, 1929); *Krigsväsendets avrustning och folkförbundets fulländning* (Stockholm, 1924); *La paix mondiale. Choix de discours* (Stockholm, 1939).

B. R. Edenman, *Socialdemocratiska riksdagsgruppen 1903-1920* (Uppsala, 1946); J. Lehman, *Carl Lindhagen* (Coppenhagen, 1950).

C. Carl Lindhagen Collection, Stockholm City Archives.

Howard T. Lutz

LISZT, Franz von (2 March 1851, Vienna—21 June 1919, Seeheim an der Bergstrasse, Germany). *Education*: Dr. jur., Univ. of Vienna. *Career*: professor of criminal law, Univ. of Giessen, 1879-82, Univ. of Marburg, 1882-89, Univ. of Halle, 1889-99, Univ. of Berlin, 1899-1916; Progressive party member of the Prussian Diet, 1908-18, and German Reichstag, 1912-18.

Scion of a family of Austrian jurists and godson of the composer, Franz von Liszt developed his concern for the resolution of conflict from criminal law to international law to parliamentary activism. He pioneered in the sociological interpretation of crime and advocated reform of criminal law to foster the re-socialization of the criminal. In his field of criminal law he played a transnational role: his textbook was translated into most European languages; he studied criminal law on the transnational comparative basis, and founded in 1889 the Internationale Kriminalistische Vereinigung (International Criminology Organization) with the help of the Dutch and Belgian jurists G. A. van Hamel and G. A. Prins.

The emerging international community of criminologists was to Liszt one example of a growing network of international ties. He was one of a mere handful of German jurists who seriously studied international law prior to 1914. Explicitly to encourage its study by university students, he wrote a textbook of international law, which itself was translated into a half-dozen languages. His views reflected the positivist and nationalist conceptions of the nineteenth century while advancing beyond them. While rejecting natural law as a source of international law, Liszt considered the ultimate source to be the "dominant legal convictions of the civilized nations." Although these convictions were expressed mainly in custom or treaty, even unratified treaties (e.g., certain of The Hague agreements) exercised influence by the "power of their intrinsic attraction." A lengthy section entitled "The Community of Interests of the International State System" thoroughly and favorably evaluated the emerging international courts and functional agencies. Eternal peace was a utopian idea, Liszt asserted, but war was being progressively limited by codification of the law of war and the development of courts of arbitration.

An advocate of unifying the shattered liberal parties of Germany, Liszt entered politics after 1900 when this goal appeared on the brink of realization. He was most active politically in the last few years prior to World War I and in the cause of international conciliation: as a member of the executive committee of the Verband für internationale Verständigung (League for International Understanding), created by *Otfried Nippold; as a member of the committee of Reichstag deputies for Franco-German reconciliation, created by *Conrad Haussmann; as a member of the Franco-German League, created by *Ludwig Quidde; and as Progressive Reichstag spokesman during the Zabern Alsace affair of 1913. During World War I Liszt opposed the extreme annexationists. While advocating the liberal imperialists' goal of a unified *Mitteleuropa*, he envisioned it and the Pan-American Union as steps to reduce international anarchy by reducing the number of competitive actors.

As professor of law and parliamentarian, Liszt remained aloof from the small German pacifist movement. But he sought to define specific and practical means of conciliation and to make them respectable within a largely hostile university and political environment.

Bibliography:

A. *Ein mitteleuropäischer Staatenverband* (Leipzig, 1914); *Das Völkerrecht systematisch dargestellt* (Berlin, 1898).

B. Arthur Kaufmann, "Franz von Liszt," *Staatslexikon*, (Freiburg, 1960), V, 404-7; *Österreichisches Biographisches Lexikon*, 1850-1950, V (1972), 248-9.

James C. Hunt

LITVINOV, Maksim Maksimovich. See *Biographical Dictionary of Internationalists*.

LOCHNER, Louis Paul (22 February 1887, Springfield, IL—8 January 1975, Wiesbaden, German Federal Republic). *Education*: B.A., Univ. of Wisconsin, 1909. *Career*: general society, Univ. of Wisconsin Alumni Association; secretary, Chicago Peace Society, 1914-15; general secretary, Ford Peace Expedition, 1915-16; director, Neutral Conference for Continuous Mediation, 1916; journalist (Berlin bureau chief after 1928), Associated Press, 1924-41; 1944-46; radio commentator, 1944-46; peace worker, journalist, and free-lance writer.

Louis Lochner's lifelong interest "in the possibilities of international friendship" began at the University of Wisconsin where he founded a national association of Cosmopolitan Clubs, which he served as first president. After he graduated, and while he was employed by the university's alumni association, he became a leader of Corda fratres, an international student association. As a lecturer, journalist, secretary of the Chicago Peace Society, and director of the American Peace Society's Central West Department, Lochner worked with many of the leading peace activists of Europe and the United States.

After the outbreak of World War I in 1914, Lochner helped organize the nationwide Emergency Peace Federation to promote the idea of a lasting and durable peace and to encourage President +Woodrow Wilson to mediate between the warring nations. On these two goals, Lochner focused all his considerable energies for the next two years, attending peace conferences and organizing demonstrations.

When President Wilson refused to mediate, Henry Ford sponsored a peace expedition in December 1915 that visited the Scandinavian countries and Holland. Lochner served as general secretary of Ford's peace expedition and also assumed managerial control of the six-nation Neutral Conference for Continuous Mediation, organized in Stockholm in February 1916. In the summer, Ford cut the funding and the conference adjourned, but Lochner remained in Europe to practice personal diplomacy between the two main warring powers, as Ford's representative. In January 1917 Lochner told Wilson he had assurances that the Allies and Central Powers would welcome the President's intervention to end the war. After reporting Wilson's encouraging reception to Ford, Lochner was stunned to learn that the quixotic automaker was ending his peace effort and that he was summarily dismissed.

Lochner's career as a professional peaceworker was not yet over. After the United States broke diplomatic relations with Germany, he joined other activists in organizing mass demonstrations protesting United States participation in the war. Until 1919 he served as executive secretary of the People's Council for Democracy and Terms of Peace.

In the early 1920s Lochner went to Germany as a foreign correspondent. From 1924 through 1941 he worked in the Berlin bureau of the Associated Press, becoming bureau chief in 1928 and winning a Pulitzer Prize for distinguished foreign reporting in 1939. He returned to the United States after the Second World War began. Retiring from the Associated Press, he wrote several books and undertook short-term assignments for the U.S. Department of State, the United Nations, and the Lutheran Church.

Although Lochner's service as a peace leader ended after the First World War, he never ceased to believe in the philosophy of internationalism that had first led him into the peace movement. He always distinguished between the people and their political and economic leaders who favored arms increases and who used war as an instrument of national policy. World peace could be maintained, he believed, through education, especially the exchange of foreign-born students and through the application of law and reason.

Armaments, Lochner said in 1914, are "not guarantors of peace but provocations for war," resulting in "inevitable conflict" with no nation the victor. Rather than arm their countries, he argued, world leaders should extend the principles that govern cities and nations to international federations and world government. Our heroes, he wrote, should be those who make the world a better place to live in through inventions, technology, and ideas. Pacifism, he declared, had to become "aggressive" to overcome the public view of the military expert as the speaker of fact and the pacifist as the unrealistic visionary.

Bibliography:

A. *Always the Unexpected: A Book of Reminiscences* (New York, 1956); *America's Don Quixote: Henry Ford's Attempt to Save Europe* (London, 1924); *What About Germany*? (New York, 1942).

B. Barbara S. Kraft, *The Peace Ship: Henry Ford's Pacifist Adventure in the First World War* (New York, 1978).

C. Louis P. Lochner Papers, State Historical Society of Wisconsin.

Barbara S. Kraft

LOCKWOOD, Belva Ann Bennett (24 October 1830, Royalton, NY—19 May 1917, Washington). *Education*: B.A., Genessee Coll. (later Syracuse Univ.), 1857; B.L., National University Law School, 1873. *Career*: principal and teacher in schools in upper New York State, 1846-48, 1857-66; teacher, Washington, 1866-67; head of her own private school, Washington 1868-71; lawyer.

Belva Lockwood's work for peace evolved out of her previous professional and reform interests. Widowed at the age of twenty-two and without independent income, she became a school teacher and principal in her native upstate New York to support herself and her young daughter. She also managed to complete her high school education and went on to receive her college degree.

Following the American Civil War, she moved to Washington, DC and in 1868 married Ezekial Lockwood, a dentist and minister. Her marriage allowed her to pursue more ambitious career goals. She obtained a law degree and developed a successful law practice. Because many of her clients sought government pensions, she learned how to lobby in Congress. When she found that women were barred from arguing law cases before federal courts, she lobbied extensively until Congress changed the law in 1879 to give women this right. Shortly thereafter, she became the first woman to argue a case before the Supreme

Court. An ardent feminist, she became active in the suffrage movement and was the presidential candidate of the Equal Rights party in 1884 and 1888.

Increasingly thereafter, she turned her attention to the peace movement. Her main contribution to peace reform was her talent for publicity. Though her writings and speeches were well reasoned arguments on the advantages and desirability of international cooperation, she understood the importance of dramatizing reform causes to call public attention to them. She had found that direct appeals and lobbying to redress injustices to her sex had often succeeded, and she utilized these tactics in the peace movement.

She was elected secretary of the International Peace Bureau, an international clearing house for peace proposals after its founding in 1893, and she published lists of arbitration treaties. Drawing on her knowledge of the workings of Congress, she lobbied for the Olney-Pauncefote arbitration treaty with Great Britain which the Senate rejected in early 1897. She often cooperated with *Alfred H. Love in the Universal Peace Union and helped to edit its journal. Deploring the rising jingoism in the nation, she, like Love, lobbied against American military intervention against Spain in Cuba. She wrote to Presidents Grover Cleveland and William McKinley urging nonintervention and tried to use the International Peace Bureau to promote European mediation of the Cuban problem. When the United States went to war with Spain in 1898, Lockwood believed it was futile to continue the antiwar protest. While opposing American imperialism, she reemphasized international arbitration. She promoted the Hague Peace Conference of 1899 and publicized its creation of a Permanent Court of Arbitration which allowed nations voluntarily to submit their disputes to a panel of arbitrators for peaceful settlement.

Though a septuagenarian, Belva Lockwood continued her peace efforts into the twentieth century. She complained about the failure of The Second Hague Peace Conference of 1907 to improve the procedures for arbitration and mediation but promoted United States efforts to create a court of justice for five Central American nations. She viewed the establishment of this court, which the United States did not join, as a prototype world court which was created shortly after her death.

Bibliography

A. *The Central American Peace Congress and an International Arbitration Court for the Five Central American Republics* (Washington, DC, 1908); "The Growth of Peace Principles and the Methods of Propagating Them," *American Magazine of Civics*, 6 (May 1895), 504-15; "International Arbitration, Venezuela, Cuba, and the National Conference at Washington," *American Magazine of Civics*, 9 (July 1898), 15-26; *Peace and the Outlook* (Washington, DC, 1899).

B. Mary Virginia Fox, *Lady for the Defense: A Biography of Belva Lockwood* (New York, 1975); Julia Hull Winner, *Belva A. Lockwood* (Lockport, NY, 1969); DAB, 11, 341; NAW, 2, 413-16.

David S. Patterson

LOEBE, Paul Gustav Emil. See *Biographical Dictionary of Internationalists*.

LOEWENTHAL, Eduard (12 March 1836, Ernsbach, Württemberg, Germany—26 March 1917, Berlin). *Education*: studies in law and philsophy, Univ. of Tübingen, 1855-58; Ph.D., Univ. of Freiburg, 1859. *Career*: journalist, editor, philosopher, writer, and pacifist.

Eduard Loewenthal belongs to those nineteenth-century prophets of peace who have yet to receive due recognition for their pioneering work. His myriad attempts at launching a peace movement in Imperial Germany were dismissed as the ventures of an eccentric by his contemporaries as well as by later historians. For decades he carried on a lone crusade which sought to popularize such ideas as the necessity for the creation of a European league of states, disarmament, reform of international law, as well as the introduction of obligatory arbitration of disputes among nations through an international system of "peace justice." All of these points were eventually to become the pillars of German pacifist thought.

As early as 1869, Loewenthal sought to advance these ideas through the founding of the Europaeischer Unionsverein (Association of European Union) in Dresden. After the Franco-Prussian War sent him temporarily into exile in Brussels, he returned to Berlin and in 1874 revived the organization and renamed it Deutscher Unionsverein fuer internationale Friedenspropaganda (Association for International Peace Propaganda). During this same period he began to publish some of the earliest pacifist journals in Germany which he used to elaborate his program for permanent peace. He always put his work as a journalist for various newspapers in the service of the cause of peace.

Perhaps his greatest achievement and contribution to the development of modern pacifism was his work for the creation of the Interparliamentary Union. As early as 1874, he prepared a pamphlet which he sent to all European peace societies in which he suggested the convening of regular meetings between elected officials from all European countries. Subsequently, while living in exile in France during the 1880s, he became instrumental, in cooperation with *Frédéric Passy, in setting up what came to be called the Interparliamentary Union.

In Germany, Loewenthal's influence on the burgeoning peace movement in the 1890s was less direct. Denied recognition by his fellow pacifists for his pioneering work for peace, he set up yet another pacifist organization in Berlin in 1895, the Deutscher Unionsverein fuer Friedenspropaganda (German Association for Peace Propaganda). However, this organization like all the others drew only a very small following. Nevertheless, he continued his organizational and journalistic activities until his death.

Loewenthal's significance in the history of German pacifism lies in the fact that he early perceived the need for political and social reforms if the goals of pacifism were to be achieved. His attempts to integrate his ideas of social, political, and economic reform into a comprehensive religious system based on scientific knowledge may indeed confirm his reputation as an eccentric. This eccentricism, however, should not deny Loewenthal due recognition as one of the first pacifists to connect the various strands of the reform movements of the nineteenth century with modern pacifism.

Bibliography:

A. "Aufruf zur Einberufung eines Weltparlaments," *Die Geissel* (Paris) September 19, 1875; *Eine Religion ohne Bekenntnis* (Berlin, 1865); *Geschichte der Friedensbewegung*, (Berlin, 1907); *Grundzüge zur Reform und Codification des Völkerrechts* (Berlin, 1874); *Mein Lebenswerk auf sozialpolitischem, neureligioesem, philosophischem und naturwissenschaftlichem Gebiet. Memoiren* (Berlin, 1910); *Neues System der Soziologie*, (Berlin, 1908) *Die soziale und geistige Reformation des 19. Jahrhunderts* (Frankfurt/Main, 1859); *System und Geschichte des Naturalismus* (Frankfurt/Main, 1861).

Brigitte M. Goldstein

LOGAN, George (9 September 1753, Germantown, PA—9 April 1821, Germantown, PA). *Education*: M.D., Univ. of Edinburgh, 1779. *Career*: physician, farmer, legislator, and self-appointed peace envoy during the "quasi" war with France in 1798 and again during the prelude to the War of 1812.

Although born into a strict Quaker family (his father was a leader of conscientious objectors), George Logan did not become a prominent peace proponent until he was nearly 45 years old. He received his early education in England, and then—despite his desire to study medicine—succumbed to his father's insistence that he follow in the Logan family tradition of prosperous Philadelphia merchants.

During his apprenticeship in the counting house, however, Logan managed to find time to read medical books and in 1779 graduated with a degree in medicine from the University of Edinburgh. But when he returned to Philadelphia in 1780, he found that his parents and brother had died and that he had inherited the family's war-ruined estate, "Stenton."

He thereupon turned his interests from medicine to agriculture, and he became a well-known advocate of scientific farming. Beginning in 1785 he was elected several times to the Pennsylvania Assembly, where he backed measures encouraging agriculture, education, and development of domestic industries.

Although a Quaker, Logan did not take exception to all war, believing instead that the Christian proscription against war did not include conflicts "strictly of a defensive kind." In fact, he joined the Pennsylvania militia and refused to heed the advice of several prominent Philadelphia Friends who urged him to withdraw. Despite the influence of his family, Logan was separated from the Quaker fold in 1791. Perhaps motivated by his conflict with the Society of Friends, Logan launched a one-man peace initiative forever associated with his name when, in the late 1790s, war fever heightened and many Federalists urged a formal declaration of war against France. Raising money by selling some of his land, he set sail for Europe and arrived in Paris on August 7, 1798. He visited numerous French officials and discussed the situation with Talleyrand. As a consequence of these discussions, France agreed to reduce its attacks on American ships, free some captured American seamen, and welcome an official U.S. envoy.

Despite the success of his mission, Logan was greeted with official contempt upon his return. On January 30, 1799, Congress passed the Logan Act, making it illegal for a private citizen to conduct diplomatic negotiations without prior authorization from the U.S. government. But Logan's initiative encouraged President John Adams to persist in seeking a peaceful resolution of the crisis, and war between the United States and France—much to the disappointment of the High Federalists—was averted.

A hero in his home state, Logan was elected to the U.S. Senate in 1801, but declined reelection after one term. In 1810—disregarding the Logan Act—he went to England in another attempt to stop the drift toward war through direct talks with British leaders. But this time he was unsuccessful, and relations worsened until the United States and Great Britain declared war on each other in 1812.

Logan retired to his Pennsylvania estate where, at the age of 67, he died.

Bibliography

B. Frederick B. Tolles, *George Logan of Philadelphia* (New York, 1953).

Jerold L. Kellman

LONGUET, Frédéric Jean Laurent (10 May 1876, London—11 September 1938, Aix-les-Bains, Savoie, France). *Education*: Lycée Condorcet, Caen, c.1894; degree, Faculté de Droit, Sorbonne, c.1899. *Career*: lawyer and journalist, to 1914; deputy (Seine), 1914-19, 1932-36; law practice, 1919-32; mayor, Chatenay-Malabry, 1925; conseiller-général, Seine, 1929-38.

The son of Charles Longuet, exiled Communard, and of Karl Marx's daughter Jenny, Jean Longuet was influenced from childhood toward socialism. A militant from 1894, he joined the Parti Ouvrier Français (French Worker's Party) of Jules Guesde, founded the review *Le Mouvement Socialiste* soon thereafter, and in 1897 became secretary of the Groupe des etudiants collectivistes (Group of Collectivist Students). Forsaking Guesdism in 1901, he joined *Jean Jaurès as a contributor to *La Petite République* and with him founded *l'Humanité* in 1904, becoming its editor for international affairs. He headed the left wing of the unified Socialist party (SFIO), won election to the central committee of the SFIO, then to the executive committee of the Second International, where he endorsed sabotage of mobilization in the event of war.

As deputy during the war years, Longuet served on several important committees (including Foreign Affairs, where he was involved in the debate on the peace treaties) and sponsored several proposals for social reform. For the first two years of the war he supported the government's position, though with some reservations; as late as December 1916, he recommended to the Socialist Federation of the Seine that the war be continued until Germany agreed to minimal conditions. However, in April 1916, he adopted the position of *Alphonse Merrheim of the Federation of Metalworkers calling for "peace without annexations or indemnities," a view affirmed at a meeting of the Section of Sceaux where he also announced the founding of *Le Populaire*, a new organ of the pacifist Socialists. Longuet thus emerged as a leader of the "minority" Socialists, a group which sought an immediate and unconditional end to the war—a position he maintained until peace came. Earlier, in November 1915, he undertook the defense of *Louise Saumoneau, who (according to a police report) expressed "Germanophile and pacifist views" for having distributed copies of *Clara Zetkin's Peace Appeal.

As a result of the nationalist victory in 1919, Longuet lost his seat in the Chamber and returned to private law practice. With *Paul Faure, he supported the Third International, though with reservations, and when the schism came at the Congress of Tours in 1920 he remained with the Socialist party, becoming again a member of the Permanent Administrative Committee.

Longuet's pacifism rested firmly on his left Socialist views. In January 1926 he signed an "Appeal to Conscience" which appeared in *Evolution*, calling for repeal of the war guilt clause and abolition of reparations as a form of moral disarmament which must precede disarmament. As deputy from 1932 to 1936 he served on the Committee on Foreign Affairs and the Committee of Inquiry into the Events of February 6, 1934, involving himself in numerous debates on internal and external fascism and on the Franco-Soviet Pact. With the coming to power of Adolf Hitler, Longuet's antifascist and pacifist activities were intensified; as a member of the Ligue internationale des combattants pour la paix (International League of Fighters for Peace), he joined *René Gerin in a speaking tour of France and Algeria advocating peace and conscientious objection. In 1936 he was an important figure in the Comité international pour la défense du peuple ethiopien et de la paix (International Committee for Ethiopian People and Peace) and in the World Committee Against War and Fascism, but with the outbreak of the Spanish Civil War, he opposed Léon Blum and the "majority" wing of the party, declaring that the "abominable comedy" of nonintervention must end and that he would never accept the "domination of German militarism" in the world. He proposed decisive action against Germany on the issues of Spain and Czechoslovakia and subscribed to the idea that French socialism must oppose fascism by force if necessary. He was killed in an automobile accident in September 1938.

Bibliography:

A. *L'évolution du mouvement socialiste en France* (Paris?, 1906); *Le mouvement socialiste international*, vol. 8 of *Encyclopedie socialiste, syndicale et cooperative de l'Internationale ouvrière* (Paris, 1913); *Les socialistes allemandes contre la guerre et le militarisme* (Paris, 1913).

Albert S. Hill

LORD, John (27 December 1810, Portsmouth, NH—15 December 1894, Stamford, CT). *Education*: B.A., Dartmouth Coll. 1833. B.D., Andover Theological Seminary, 1837; *Career*: lecturer, American Peace Society, 1837-39; historical lecturer and writer.

John Lord's interest in pacifism grew out of the influence of his maternal uncle, *William Ladd, founder of the American Peace Society, and the peace societies at Dartmouth College and Andover Seminary, where he attended school. He was also influenced by the "theocratic" vision of his uncle, Nathan Lord, president of Dartmouth College. Lord's gifts as a lecturer persuaded Ladd to enlist him as an agent for the American Peace Society after Lord's graduation from Andover Seminary in 1837. Lord proved a vigorous and vivid lecturer, traveling extensively in New York and New England and delivering 143 lectures in the year 1839 alone. In his lectures Lord endorsed Ladd's call for a congress of nations to resolve international disputes, but otherwise adopted no extraordinary arguments. His work in Maine and Vermont helped to cool the "Canadian fever" concerning boundary disputes. In Vermont Lord responded to Thomas A. Merrill's plea for the revitalization of the Vermont Peace Society by becoming the Society's principal speaker for almost a year. Lord complained of the poor financial support he received from the Vermont farmers and moved to New York, where he reported greater success in garnering money and crowds. In 1839 Lord resigned his position with the American Peace Society because of differences over policy and because of his difficulties in earning a living from peace work.

During his peace ministry Lord argued that reliance on general Christian conversion of society was not enough to end war and other social evils. He advocated specific reform activities to eradicate each social evil. He also observed that martial values were deeply imbedded in the national character of all peoples. As he stated in his address to the annual meeting of the American Peace Society in 1838, military enthusiasm was everywhere "synonymous with patriotism" as each country lavished praise on its warrior heroes in its histories. Oddly, Lord contributed to the martial spirit in America after his retirement from the peace movement by lecturing on and writing about military chieftains. Among his many works were sympathetic treatments of Frederick the Great, Napoleon, Robert E. Lee, and Otto von Bismarck.

Lord aligned himself with the nonpacifist critics of *George C. Beckwith's "Peace and Government" philosophy which made a distinction between war and domestic law enforcement. In 1839 he broke with the Society on the issue of defensive war. In his address before the peace society of Amherst College on July 4, 1839, Lord pointed up the contradiction between condemning even defensive war while sanctioning a government's right to suppress piracy, murder, and insurrection. Lord criticized the Society for trying to deny the nonresistance logic of its official position and Beckwith for confusing the issue with his intellectual legerdemain regarding law enforcement. Lord questioned whether there was a difference "in the grand principle" between domestic and foreign robbers and murders.

Lord abandoned the Society to grapple with the question without his counsel. He devoted the remainder of his life to historical lecturing and writing, earning fame and fortune as one of nineteenth-century America's most popular historians. Although he spoke and wrote on a wide variety of subjects, pacifism hardly informed his later work and the subjects of his historical writings bore little imprint of his early pacifist connections.

Bibliography:

A. *An Address Delivered Before the Peace Society of Amherst College* (Amherst, 1839); *A Modern History from the Time of Luther to the Fall of Napoleon* (New York, 1849).

B. Alexander S. Twombly, "The Life of John Lord," in John Lord, *Beacon Lights of History* (8 vols., New York, 1896), VIII; DAB 11, 408-09.

Randall M. Miller

LORIA, Achille (2 March 1857, Mantua, Italy—6 November 1943, Luserna San Giovanni, Piedmont, Italy). *Education*: Dr. jur., Univ. of Bologna, 1877. *Career*: professor of economics, Univ. of Siena, 1881-91; Univ. of Padua, 1891-1903; Univ. of Turin, 1903-32; appointed to the Italian Senate, 1919.

A prolific writer, economist, and socialist sympathizer, Achille Loria was best known for his theory relating free land to the successive stages of society. He elaborated this comprehensive view from many sources and applied it empirically by studying the evolution of colonial areas such as the United States where abundant free land had recently existed. Loria's research influenced Frederick Jackson Turner and Charles Beard.

Loria explained economic and social development as passing through three stages. In the first, free land abounds and population density is relatively low. Any man can appropriate unoccupied tracts and make a living by working the soil with simple tools. Since no man will work for another while such conditions persist, slavery is introduced. Later, serfdom replaces slavery because greater efficiency is required to offset the land's declining productivity. In the next stage, characterized by greater population density, diminishing soil fertility, and the scarcity of free land, wages are reduced to a degree which prevents savings and the price of land increases beyond the capacity of workers to buy it. Workers are transformed into wage earners in factories and the capitalist era begins. Finally, free land disappears and wages are reduced to a minimum.

Loria applied his general views to international law and to war. As the economies of different societies become more complex, they give rise to interrelationships which produce international law and institutions, a development which Loria meticulously traced. As the revenues of societies decrease, as they must according to Loria's system, as there is no way of increasing profits, societies appropriate the revenues of other societies by war. By analyzing the causes of numerous wars Loria demonstrated that war was only a "diversion" where sufficient unoccupied fertile lands kept profits high but always resulted from declining revenues caused by the disappearance of free land, an increase in population, declining soil productivity, and the forced association of labor (which lowers productivity). Thus for Loria, war was the main route by which great capitalists increased declining profits.

With improvements in the methods of production through industrialization, productivity increased and appropriation of the products of other societies became less urgent. Furthermore, economic interrelationships built on commerce restored international law and the increasing costs and destructiveness of war, along with its diminished advantages, produced international institutions for the prevention of armed conflicts.

While Loria believed that these developments reduced the frequency of wars, he did not believe that they would eliminate them. Indeed, the rarity of wars only increased their ferocity. Loria interpreted World War I in this vein. The great capitalists of England, France, and Germany, the large landowners of central and eastern Europe, and the declining economic position of Great Britain vis-à-vis Germany produced the greatest conflagration in history after forty-three years of continental peace.

Although Loria modified some of the details of his interpretation after World War I, he reinforced its general validity. He demonstrated the economic origins of the war and defended the pacific institutions designed to prevent it, although they had failed the test. On the surface this position led him into a dilemma, for peacekeeping institutions accelerated capitalist wealth and hastened the decline in revenue, which led to wars. Hence Loria's insistence that viable peace institutions required a profound internal transformation of the individual states. He meant the elimination of the existing "artificial" democracies based upon restricted ruling castes and their replacement by actual governments of the people, "true" democracies based upon the free association of labor. Until then, Loria believed, "all projects for perpetual peace will be unrealizable utopias."

Bibliography:

A. *Analisi della proprietà capitalistica* (2 vols., Turin, 1889); *Aspetti sociali ed economici della guerra mondiale* (Milan, 1921); *La costituzione economica odierna* (Turin, 1899); *La dinamica economica* (Turin, 1935); *The Economic Causes of War* (Chicago, 1918, first published in French in 1912); *Marx e la sua dottrina* (Milan, 1902); *La rendita fondiaria e la sua elisione naturale* (Milan, 1880); *Ricordi di uno studente settuagenario* (Bologna, 1927); *Studi sul valore della moneta* (Turin, 1891); *La terra ed il sistema sociale* (Verona and Padua, 1892).

B. Luigi Einaudi, "Bibliografia di Achille Loria," *Riforma Sociale*, 43, No. 5 (1932) (Supplement); Luigi Einaudi, "Achille Loria (1857-1943)," *The Economic Journal*, 56 (March 1946), 147-50; G. Scaglia, *Il materialismo storico e il socialismo: Raffronti critici tra Carlo Marx e Achille Loria* (Milan, 1920).

Spencer M. Di Scala

LOUS-MOHR, Marie (19 February 1892, Mandal, Norway—25 November 1973, Oslo). *Education*: teacher's certificate, 1914; studies at the Quaker Coll., Woodbrooke, England, 1921; studies in French literature, Sorbonne, Paris. *Career*: teacher, 1916-66; peace activist.

The time that Marie Lous-Mohr spent in Germany during World War I and at the Quaker center in Woodbrooke, England, after the war were decisive in shaping her views on war and peace. What she learned in Germany and England made her a fervent opponent of war and violence. In 1934 she spent some time in Switzerland after having received a grant for studying the work of the League of Nations. That same year she was elected chairman of the Norwegian section of the Women's International League for Peace and Freedom (WILPF), where she continued to work until the WILPF office was closed and its activities banned by the Nazi occupiers in 1940. Lous-Mohr spent more than two years in the concentration camp at Grini for having refused to follow Nazi orders in her teaching. In 1945 she resumed her work with WILPF, and was elected international president of the League in 1952. She resigned from her post as international president in 1956 and resumed the leadership of the Norwegian section which she held until her death.

Marie Lous-Mohr was an excellent speaker in her own country and, because she also spoke English, French, and German, was effective elsewhere in Europe. In addition, she aroused interest for the cause of peace in the United States, China, and India. She wrote numerous articles in WILPF publications, including *Pax et Libertas* and the Norwegian *Fred og Frihet*. Lous-Mohr influenced many people by the deep conviction with which she communicated her belief that it was possible to establish a world where people can live in mutual understanding and cooperation.

Bibliography:

B. Margareta Larsson, "Kvinnoföreningar i Sverige med fred på sitt program," Ph.D. dissertation, Univ. of Stockholm, 1970.

Elisabeth Ståhle

LOVE, Alfred Henry (7 September 1830, Philadelphia, PA—23 June 1913, Philadelphia, PA). *Education*: diploma, Central High School, Philadelphia, 1847. *Career*: founder, American Literary Union, 1845, president and honorary president, 1875-1913; package woolen commission merchant, 1853-1913; vice-president, Pennsylvania Abolition Society; founder and president, Universal Peace Union, 1866-1913, and editor of its journals, *Bond of Peace*, 1868-74, *Voice of Peace*, 1874-82, and *Peacemaker and Court of Arbitration*, 1882-1913; vice-president, Pennsylvania Prison Society; co-editor, *Journal of Prison Discipline and Philanthropy*.

Alfred Love's commitment to peace derived from his Quaker upbringing and the influence of *William Lloyd Garrison's ideas of peaceful nonresistance. The widening debate over slavery forced peace-loving individuals in the North to choose between pacifism and acquiescence in the use of force to obtain freedom for blacks. As the Civil War approached, most chose to support the Northern cause with varying degrees of enthusiasm as the most practical alternative for attaining the abolition of slavery. Love, however, was one of a small minority of reformers who remained steadfast in opposition to the war. His Quaker faith and Garrisonian nonresistance mutually reinforced his pacifism.

In June 1862 Love published *An Appeal in Vindication of Peace Principles and Against Resistance by Force of Arms*, which forcefully elaborated his opposition to the war and his defense of nonviolence in resolving injustices in society. This tract clearly revealed the profound humanistic faith underlying Love's radical pacifism. Support of the war, he argued, was un-Christian and inhumane, and he warned against "becoming absorbed in the enthusiasm of the hour" and being caught up "on the swelling tide, forgetful that popular movements always should be watched, often even doubted."

When Love was drafted in 1863, he refused to serve in the Union army or to find a substitute. He also did not allow his woolen commission business to sell goods in support of the war effort. In consequence, his business suffered, and he also had to endure personal abuse from those who endorsed the war and found his absolutist pacifist viewpoint too uncompromising. His intellectual mentor, William Lloyd Garrison, wrote Love that he could pay money instead of serving in the military without compromising his pacifist principles, but Love refused to alter his strict position. Love remained a radical pacifist for the rest of his life.

Because many peace organizations, including the American Peace Society, had supported the Civil War, Love and several other nonresistants believed a new peace group reflecting their pacifist position was needed. The result was the formation in 1866 of the Universal Peace Society, soon renamed the Universal Peace Union with headquarters in Philadelphia. Love served as president of the society until his death. He also edited its periodicals, *The Bond of Peace* (1868-74), *The Voice of Peace* (1874-82), and *The Peacemaker and Court of Arbitration* (1882-1913).

Love's writings in these journals reveal his position on a number of war and peace issues. His philosophical commitment to the pacifist tradition shines through the pages of these journals. Love believed the word "peace" had meaning not only for foreign relations but also for the home, family, local community, and business life. Peace, he maintained, meant individual moral perfection. It involved the development of a peace-loving personality molded by the parents, family, and community. He thus maintained that the true pacifist had to be vitally interested in the entire social fabric, and he emphasized the importance of a wholesome home, and a religious and an educational environment. He championed a number of reforms, including temperance, women's rights, social purity, justice to American Indians, arbitration of labor-capital disputes, prison reform, and abolition of capital punishment. He also promoted free trade. He argued that the free exchange of goods in the world community would result in the victory of internationalism, anti-imperialism, anticolonialism, humanitarianism, and peace over nationalism, imperialism, colonialism, protectionism, and war, and he often cited with approval the British free trade theorist *John Bright.

Love vigorously campaigned against American military intervention in the Cuban crisis. He urged calm after the sinking of the United States battleship *Maine* in Havana harbor and sent several letters and cables to Steward Woodford, the American minister in Madrid, urging acceptance of third party mediation of the conflict. When the United States nonetheless went to war against Spain in 1898, Love became a victim of the virulent nationalistic and patriotic fervor which swept the nation. A jingoistic crowd entered the Universal Peace Union's office, tore down some of its pictures and banners, and hung Love in effigy.

Love continued to oppose the war and also spoke out against the McKinley administration's decision to annex the Philippines and its subsequent military conquest of the Filipinos.

Despite Love's wholehearted commitment to the Universal Peace Union, its membership declined steadily after 1900. A major reason for this decline was Love's radical leadership. Other peace groups, such as the American Peace Society, downgraded peace-at-any-price and endorsed more "practical" solutions, including the creation of new international institutions such as the Permanent Court of Arbitration and other permanent bodies. The message of the Universal Peace Union, however, remained too simplistic in an age of increasing involvement of the United States in world affairs. Love also continued to prefer voluntary and personal relationships to the institutional and professional ones that were becoming increasingly a part of American life after about 1900. Thus when Love died, the Universal Peace Union died with him.

Bibliography:

A. *Address before the Peace Convention, held in Boston, March 14 & 15, 1866* (Hopedale, MA, 1866); *An Appeal in Vindication of Peace Principles and Against Resistance by Force of Arms* (Philadelphia, 1862).

B. Peter Brock, *Pacifism in the United States: From the Colonial Era to the First World War* (Princeton, 1968); James H. Doherty, "Alfred H. Love and the Universal Peace Union," Ph.D. dissertation, Univ. of Pennsylvania, 1962; David S. Patterson, *Toward a Warless World: The Travail of the American Peace Movement, 1887-1914* (Bloomington, IN, 1976); David S. Patterson, introduction to microfiche reproduction of *The Peacemaker and Court of Arbitration* (New York, 1982), 1-12; DAB, 11, 431-32; NYT, June 30, 1913.

C. Alfred Love, manuscript diary, Swarthmore College Peace Collection, Swarthmore, PA.

David S. Patterson

LOWELL, James Russell (22 February 1819, Cambridge, MA—12 August 1891, Cambridge, MA). *Education*: B.A., Harvard Coll., 1838, LLB, Harvard Law School, 1840. *Career*: editor, *The Pioneer*, 1843, and *The Atlantic Monthly*, 1857-1961; Smith Professor of Modern Languages and Literature, Harvard College, 1856-72 and 1874-78; United States ambassador to Spain 1877-80 and to England 1880-85; poet and essayist.

James Russell Lowell was a poet, essayist, and critic whose antiwar feelings were intimately related to his oppostion to slavery. Lowell's abolitionism, inherited from his father and amplified by his first wife, was evidenced by numerous contributions to a variety of antislavery journals. Like many of his fellow Northerners he regarded the outbreak of war with Mexico in 1846 as a thinly-disguised Southern plot to add more slave states to the union, a view which prompted him immediately to criticize America's role in the conflict.

Lowell's vehicle for opposing the war was a series of satiric poems titled *The Biglow Papers*. Regarded by contemporaries and later critics alike as his greatest work, *The Biglow Papers* hurled barbs at apologists of the war who hid behind rationalizations like manifest destiny and racial superiority. Lowell also derided former peace advocates who got caught up in the war fever, but reserved his sharpest gibes for politicians, particularly Whigs.

The threat of civil war in 1861 demonstrated the conditional (if not confused) nature of Lowell's antiwar feelings. Initially he urged a policy of "firmness" toward the South as a means of averting actual conflict. Next Lowell advocated "coercion" while renouncing "violence"—without, however, drawing any useful distinction between them. When fighting finally erupted, he pronounced himself in favor of the Northern war effort, declaring that peace would be preserved only under terms "vastly more disastrous" than the bloodshed itself.

Lowell's career was long and varied, encompassing not only literary pursuits but a professorship at Harvard and appointments as ambassador to Spain and England. But it was with his pen that he made his mark, literally and figuratively. Lowell's political essays helped shape public opinion, especially on the slavery issue; his poetry attracted a considerable following and as an editor and critic Lowell influenced literary perceptions and style. Although his writings focused only briefly upon the problem of war and American society, Lowell's *Biglow Papers* scored a direct hit and proved effective as a rallying point for opponents of the Mexican War.

Bibliography:

A. *The Writings of James Russell Lowell* (10 vols. Cambridge, MA, 1891).

B. Martin Duberman, *James Russell Lowell* (Boston, 1966); Thomas Wortham, ed., *James Russell Lowell's The Biglow Papers: A Critical Edition* (De Kalb, IL, 1977).

Dale R. Steiner

LUTHULI, Albert John (1898, Southern Rhodesia [now Zimbabwe]—21 July 1967, Stanger, Natal South Africa). *Education*: Teacher's Certificate, Adams Coll., 1921. *Career*: teacher, Adams Coll., 1918-36; chief of Umvoti Mission Reserve, 1936-52; president-general, African National Congress of South Africa, 1953-67.

Chief Albert Luthuli, a champion of African rights and nonracial democracy in white-run South Africa, was a devout Christian, a firm adherent of Gandhian principles of nonviolence, and the first African to receive the Nobel Peace Prize. The grandson of a Zulu chief, Luthuli attended mission school and graduated from Adams College, a boarding secondary school run by American Protestants in Natal. He remained at Adams as a teacher until he was elected chief of the Umvoti Mission Reserve, a Zulu area at Groutville, Natal, in 1936.

As chief, Luthuli acted as a magistrate with civil jurisdiction over the African population of Groutville. He also worked for the welfare of African sugar cane farmers and laborers on European sugar estates. A member of the Durban Joint Council of Europeans and Africans and the Institute of Race Relations, he served as a Natal delegate in the interracial South African Christian Council until 1952. In 1938, Luthuli was one of the four African Christian Council delegates to the International Missionary Conference held in Madras, India. Ten years later he undertook a lecture tour of the United States under the joint aegis of the American Board and the North American Missionary Conference to discuss missions in South Africa.

Chief Luthuli was elected the acting-chairman of the African National Congress (ANC) for Natal province in 1946 and became chairman and a member of the National Executive of the African National Congress in 1951. He was an architect of the ANC's Program of Action, which in April 1952 led to a nonviolent campaign of civil defiance against the white minority government's oppressive laws. As a result, the government removed him from his chieftainship, but Luthuli intensified his work with the ANC, and in December 1952 the National Conference of the ANC elected him president-general of the Congress. His election was a turning point in the Black struggle for freedom in South Africa, for it meant a tremendously intensified passive resistance campaign against the government's apartheid policies. Under Luthuli's leadership, the ANC led nonviolent campaigns in the cities, extended the campaign to the countryside, and finally undertook countrywide mass demonstrations, including industrial action.

In mid-1953 the government banned Luthuli from entering large centers and cities of South Africa for one year. A few months after his first ban had expired, the government banned him again, this time for two years. On December 5, 1956 Luthuli was arrested in his home in Groutville and with many other leaders charged with high treason. In 1959, while the treason trial was still going on, he was banned for a third time, silenced, and confined to his home in Groutville for five years. Nevertheless, on March 28, 1960 he led a peaceful demonstration for a national day of mourning for the Sharpeville killings by burning his pass.

In 1960, while under virtual house arrest, Luthuli was awarded the Nobel Peace Prize. In its announcement, the Prize Committee cited his long peaceful fight against racial discrimination by nonviolent means. The South African government denounced the award, but nevertheless granted Luthuli and his wife permission to travel to Oslo, Norway to accept the Prize. By then, the ANC and other groups had been outlawed and some opponents of apartheid were turning to violence. Luthuli deplored the turn away from passive resistance, but his critics argued that nonviolence had failed to achieve racial justice. Luthuli, still harrassed by the government, died in a railway accident on July 21, 1967.

Bibliography:

A. *Let My People Go* (Johannesburg, 1962).

B. Mary Benson, *Chief Albert Luthuli of South Africa* (London, 1963); Edward Callan, *Albert John Luthuli and South Africa Race Conflict* (Kalamazoo, MI, 1965); NYT, July 22, 1967.

C. Albert Luthuli Papers (on microfilm), Center for Research Libraries, Chicago.

'Layiwola Abegunrin

LYNCH, Frederick Henry. See *Biographical Dictionary of Internationalists*.

M

MACAULAY, Emilie Rose (1 August 1881, Rugby, England—30 October 1958, London). *Education*: Oxford High School; B.A., Somerville Coll., Oxford Univ. 1903. *Career*: writer.

One of the most celebrated "converts" to pacifism in the late 1930s, Rose Macaulay was a schoolmaster's daughter and a collateral of the historian Lord Macaulay. Her childhood was spent in Italy; Oxford gave her an enthusiasm for history and an independence of outlook, and helped her to overcome an ingrained shyness. Of independent means, she became a writer, living first in Wales, then near Cambridge, and finally in London. Her first novel, *Abbots Verney* appeared in 1906; six more appeared in the next eight years. During World War I she was engaged in war work of different kinds. It was the war which helped to bring out in her a keen vein of satire which appeared first in *What Not* (1918). During the 1920s she wrote her most popular novels, including *Dangerous Ages* (1921) and *Crewe Train* (1926).

An internationalist and supporter of League sanctions against Italy in 1936, she became a sponsor of the Peace Pledge Union. On one memorable occasion, when she was supporting *Dick Sheppard's candidature as Rector of Glasgow University, she was narrowly rescued from kidnapping by the Scottish Nationalists. In the pacifist movement her learning was regarded with awe. Her kindness and sense of humor, however, made her a favorite with peace activists. She resigned from the Peace Pledge Union with the outbreak of World War II, in which she served as a voluntary part-time ambulance driver, but she remained a pacifist until 1940. During the war she lost all her possessions in a bombing raid and she wrote little, but her postwar novels show a rich compassion and human understanding. She was created a Dame of the British Empire (DBE) in 1958 and died suddenly the same year.

Bibliography:

A. *Non-combatants and Others* (London, New York, and Toronto, 1916).

John Ferguson

MACDONALD, James Alexander (22 January 1862, East Williams, Ontario, Canada—13 May 1923, Toronto). *Education*: B.A., Edinburgh Univ., 1884; B.D., Knox Coll., 1887. *Career*: Presbyterian minister; editor, *Knox College Monthly*, 1886-91, *The Westminister*, 1896-1902, *Globe* (Toronto), 1902-15; preacher, public lecturer, and author.

In the decade preceeding the First World War, James A. Macdonald was well known as the editor of the prestigious Toronto *Globe* and a widely traveled orator. Together with Oliver Howland, an Ontario legislator, *Mackenzie King, Canada's Minister of Labour, and Justice William R. Riddell he presented what became known as the "North American idea" at the annual Lake Mohonk Conference on International Arbitration. Each extolled the value of the Canadian-American experience in the peaceful resolution of disputes. Macdonald blended it with his Christian convictions.

As basic as the law of gravity, maintained Macdonald, was the law of the world's goodwill which had existed since mankind dwealt together and found its early expression in the Levitical code for loving thy neighbor as thyself. With pen and speech Macdonald lashed out at the bigoted, intolerant, petty, or selfish nationalist who gave no service to mankind. When Europe bowed to the forces of militarism, Canada and the United States remained as the world's trustees for liberty, democracy, and international goodwill. Monuments to past heroes of Anglo-American conflicts became memorials to the undefended border and symbols of their common allegiance to finding an alternative to war in settling disputes.

When poor health forced his retirement from the *Globe* in 1916, Macdonald summoned his remaining strength to convince Americans that their neutrality was destroying the Anglo-American bond needed to advance his ideal. His lectures at United States universities were published as *The North American Idea* (1917). Japanese audiences would also hear the message before further illness quenched his fiery eloquence. While his critics had branded him as unpatriotic in mixing talk of peace with the forceful destruction of German militarism, Macdonald sought to plant his ideal. Canadian statesmen would take his arguments to imperial conferences and the League of Nations only to find the way blocked. The United States rejected the partnership needed for its prosecution and subsequent events gave it a hollow ring in Europe. But on both sides of the border it became the touchstone of too much self-indulgent oratory on Canadian-American friendship.

Bibliography:

A. *Democracy and the Nation; A Canadian View* (Toronto, 1915); *The North American Idea* (Toronto 1917).

B. Donald Page, "Canada as the Exponent of North American Idealism," *The American Review of Canadian Studies* (Autumn, 1973), 30-46.

Donald M. Page

MACGREGOR, George Hogarth Carnaby (Garth) (26 November 1892, Aberdeen, Scotland—3 July 1963, Glasgow, Scotland). *Education*: B.A., Gonville and Caius Coll., Cambridge Univ., 1914; M.A., Cambridge Univ., 1922, B.D., 1929, D. Litt., Univ. of Glasgow, 1929. *Career*: Hosmer Professor of New Testament Exegesis, Hartford Theological Seminary, Connecticut, USA, 1929-33; professor, Univ. of Glasgow, 1933-63.

Garth Macgregor was a distinguished New Testament scholar, writer, and teacher, whose principal position was the Professorship of Divinity and Biblical

Criticism at the University of Glasgow. He believed that the essential message of the New Testament had to find practical application in contemporary life, and that this application involved a pacifist position.

His volume, *The New Testament Basis of Pacifism* (1936) was a scholarly, thorough, and lucid attempt to discover the specifically Christian way of overcoming evil, in light of the teaching, life, and death of Jesus Christ. His argument was theological, not political, emphasizing the centrality of love and reconciliation, an attitude that involved the refusal to fight. Widely regarded as the best Christian defense of pacifism published in the interwar period, Macgregor's work influenced a generation of theological students and others. Many were sufficiently convinced to undertake a long-term commitment to pacifism, others who could not accept the pacifist position found a new respect for it.

During World War II, Macgregor challenged critics of pacifism with *The Relevance of the Impossible; A Reply to Reinhold Niebuhr* (1941). This book recognised *Reinhold Niebuhr's stature as a Christian thinker but challenged him for not defining the distinctively Christian way of overcoming evil. In an article on "The Christian's Dilemma" (1943) in *The Christian Pacifist*, Macgregor rejected the defense of several British Christian leaders that the Christian could defend the heavy bombing of German cities as the lesser of two evils; the Christian, he argued, should be prepared to accept "the way of the Cross," not because it would produce any particular desired effect, but because it was Christ's way.

After the Second World War Macgregor, while continuing with his theological teaching and writing, played an important role in the Fellowship of Reconciliation. He was vice-chairman (1945-58), chairman of the International Fellowship of Reconciliation Council (1955-59), and president of the Scottish FOR.

Above all he was a committed Christian scholar, with the gift of expressing his beliefs with clarity, commitment, and courtesy.

Bibliography:

A. *The New Testament Basis of Pacifism* (London, 1936, 2nd ed., London 1953); *The Relevance of the Impossible: A Reply to Reinhold Niebuhr* (London, 1941).

B. Hugh Anderson and William Barclay, eds., *The New Testament in Historical and Contemporary Perspectives: Essays in Memory of G.H.C. Macgregor* (Oxford, 1965).

Elaine Kaye

MACKIE, Charles Robert Norris (30 April 1869, Christchurch, New Zealand—15 October 1943, Christchurch). *Education*: self-taught. *Career*: voluntary social worker and peace activist.

Charles Mackie was born into a wealthy South Island runholding family. A man of private means, he was able to devote himself fulltime to peace work and other interests like the Workers' Educational Association, the Society for the Protection of Women and Children (which he helped found), and the Howard League for Penal Reform.

Mackie lived in England between 1884 and 1901. On his return to New Zealand he became a prominent Baptist layman, representing New Zealand at a number of inter-church conventions while overseas in 1910. His long involvement with the peace movement began the following year when he and others established the National Peace Council to oppose the compulsory military training of boys which had just been introduced. Mackie was to remain the Council's Secretary and leading figure until shortly before his death.

In 1912-14, backed by English Quaker money, Mackie led a vigorous campaign for the abolition of "boy conscription," collecting a significant amount of support among the churches and trade unions. Some modification of the scheme, particularly with regard to the exemption of religious objectors and the punishment of defaulters, can be attributed to his efforts. It was claimed that the NPC distributed nearly 1,000,000 leaflets and other propaganda. But this was the heyday of the Council's existence. During World War I it was greatly weakened by hostile public opinion, wartime regulations, lack of finance, and its single issue platform. After the war it continued to be handicapped by the very slow revival of organized pacifism and the failure to develop a broadly based movement. Apart from the pacifist societies, the affiliated organizations included only the Society of Friends, the WEA in Christchurch, and several local trade unions.

But while Mackie never succeeded in restoring the NPC to its former effectiveness, he dedicated himself completely to the task. For a short time (1919-24) the NPC was affiliated with the Labour party, and this association strengthened the link between the peace movement and a rising political force that took over the government in 1935. Mackie also moved the NPC away from its old preoccupation with conscription and militarism (though "boy conscription" lasted until 1930) toward the idea of a new international order founded on arbitration and economic and social justice. His response to the failure of disarmament by international agreement in the early 1930s was excitingly novel—a proposal to have New Zealand and its Pacific region declared a demilitarized zone by the League of Nations. To some extent the development of a more internationalistic view within the country's peace movement may be related to Mackie's great work in establishing and maintaining contact with the worldwide movement. He understood better than most the importance of the international connection, both for the morale of a small, remote, pacifist community and for the quality of its educational effort, to which he always gave priority. This achievement might well be regarded as his most significant.

Bibliography:

C. Papers of C.R.N. Mackie, Canterbury Museum, Christchurch, New Zealand.

J. E. Cookson

MACLEOD, Alexander Albert (2 April 1902, Black Rock, Nova Scotia—13 March 1970, Toronto). *Education*: Kings' Coll., Windsor, Nova Scotia; Halifax Business School. *Career*: YMCA secretary, 1920s; business manager and executive editor, *The World Tomorrow, 1929-34*; chairman, Canadian League

Against War and Fascism (League for Peace and Democracy), 1934-39; council member, International Peace Campaign, 1936-37; politician.

Alexander Albert MacLeod, born and raised near the coal fields of Nova Scotia, was exposed as a youth to working class protests and a social gospel rhetoric which helped launch him on the road to radical social and political activism. During the twenties he served as a YMCA secretary in Halifax and Chicago before joining the staff of *The World Tomorrow* in 1929, first as business manager and later becoming executive editor. In association with *Devere Allen, *Reinhold Niebuhr and *Kirby Page, MacLeod promoted the journal's call for a militant pacifism as the best way to achieve a just socialized state.

In the early 1930s, he organized over one hundred and fifty peace meetings throughout Canada and the United States. Then in 1933, he visited his native Nova Scotia to assist and organize idle miners through the establishment of a worker's school. The following year, reflecting an increasingly politicized outlook, he resigned from *The World Tomorrow* to assume the chairmanship of the Canadian League Against War and Fascism, the new Communist wing of the Canadian peace movement, later renamed the Canadian League for Peace and Democracy.

MacLeod hoped to steer the peace movement away from dogmatic pacifism and towards the view of peace as realizable through radical change and socialist solidarity. He was successful in attracting a wide range of supporters and the League often cooperated with the Fellowship of Reconciliation and the Women's International League for Peace and Freedom in staging peace rallies and sponsoring such speakers as André Malraux, Thomas Mann, and Harry Ward.

In 1936 MacLeod headed a fifteen man Canadian delegation to the First World Peace Congress in Brussels where he was elected to the General Council of the International Peace Campaign inspired by *Lord Robert Cecil. MacLeod was also asked to personally assess the newly erupted armed conflict in Spain, thus becoming the first North American to witness the Spanish Civil War. He became a strong advocate of the Republican cause and later accompanied a Spanish diplomatic delegation on tour of Canada and the United States in an effort to build support for Spanish democracy. Back in Spain the following year, he officially presented the Republicans with the famous Canadian Blood Transfusion Unit, under the direction of Dr. Norman Bethune, as a gift from Canadian sympathizers. Shortly afterward, as part of a delegation to the League of Nations Council, he urged League action to end German and Italian intervention. At home in 1938, he successfully secured large contributions of grain from the western wheat pools for the first Canadian food ship to Spain. Then, shortly before Franco's victory, MacLeod arrived in Barcelona to expedite the safe return home of Canadian volunteers in the Mackenzie-Papineau Battalion. Throughout the Spanish conflict, MacLeod actively searched for ways to halt hostilities and relieve the suffering civilian population.

While in Prague during the Munich crisis, MacLeod also became instrumental in the emigration of Czech intellectuals and during the Second World War he remained active in the Canadian National Committee on Refugees and Victims of Political Persecution. Following the war, although he helped found the Canadian Peace Congress under the leadership of James G. Endicott in 1948, MacLeod became almost totally absorbed in the political activities of the Communist Party of Canada, leaving behind a legacy of humanitarian efforts and an antiwar campaign which reflected his belief that peace could only be attained through the establishment of social justice.

Bibliography:

B. Thomas P. Socknat, " 'Witness Against War:' Pacifism in Canada, 1900-1945," Ph.D. dissertation, McMaster University, 1981.

Thomas P. Socknat

MACPHAIL, Agnes (24 March 1890, Grey County, Ontario, Canada—13 February 1954, Toronto). *Education*: teacher's certificate, Stratford Normal School, 1910. *Career*: school teacher, 1910-21; Member of Parliament, 1921-40; columnist, Toronto *Globe and Mail*, 1941-42; member, Ontario Legislature, 1943-45; 1948-51; politician, lecturer, and journalist.

Agnes Macphail was the first woman elected to the Canadian House of Commons. Initially she sat for the riding of South-East Grey (later called Grey-Bruce) as a representative of the United Farmers of Ontario, which was part of a broader national farm coalition called the Progressive party. Later when the Progressive party disintegrated, she sat as an Independent and in the 1940s represented East York for the social democratic Co-operative Commonwealth Federation (CCF) in the Ontario provincial legislature. In addition to her political activities, she undertook a number of extensive lecture tours in Canada and the United States and wrote a regular column for the local newspapers in her constituency and briefly for the Toronto *Globe and Mail*. Throughout her career, Macphail's four compelling interests were farm issues, women, prison reform, and peace.

Macphail's pacifist convictions seem to have sprung initially from her work with farm organizations opposed to conscription during World War I. As she gradually became more involved with the women's movement she also began to argue for peace as a natural concern of women as the nurturers of life. Macphail was a member of the Women's International League for Peace and Freedom (ultimately honorary president of the Canadian Section) and attended several international peace conferences in the 1920s. Although never a member of a party in power and thus unable to help formulate legislation, she nevertheless used every opportunity to argue for peace and disarmament in Parliament. Frequently she led or supported motions to sharply reduce the Canadian defense budget. Her special concerns, not surprisingly given her background as a rural school teacher, were with youth and education. She criticized school texts which glorified war and she consistently opposed government-funded cadet training in the schools because it helped instill the military mentality in the minds of young boys. The creation of a "peace psychology" in the minds of Canadian youth was, for her, the key to the future. She also urged the Canadian government to set up a Department of Peace, which would finance lectures, pamphlets and scholarships to teach Canadians about international friendship.

Macphail was a firm supporter of the League of Nations in the 1920s. She was the first female member of a Canadian delegation when she attended the tenth Assembly in 1929 and the first woman member of the Disarmament Committee. In the 1930s her belief in collectivism was gradually undermined by the failure of the League. She became increasingly isolationist, stressing that Canada must avoid again being dragged by loyalty to Britain into European conflicts that were of no concern to North Americans. In the unlikely event that Canada should ever come under attack, she said, it should rely on its continental ally the United States for protection.

Although not formally a member of the CCF, Macphail attended CCF caucus meetings in the 1930s. With the rest of that party, except leader *J. S. Woodsworth, she accepted the compromise of limited Canadian participation in a war to stop Hitler in early 1939 and in September she supported the Canadian declaration of war against Germany. During the war she returned to collectivism, advocating a more effective postwar international organization than the League had been, one with some sovereign powers and its own strong police force.

Agnes Macphail began her political career as a representative of rural interests, but her concerns broadened over the years to encompass many social reform issues. Throughout, world peace remained one of her highest priorities, and she strove not only to educate ordinary Canadians about issues of peace and internationalism but to involve them.

Bibliography:

B. Doris French, "Agnes Macphail," in M.Q. Innis, ed., *The Clear Spirit* (Toronto, 1966); Margaret Stewart and Doris French, *Ask No Quarter* (Toronto, 1959).

C. Agnes Macphail Papers, Public Archives of Canada.

Mary Vipond

MADARIAGA Y ROJO, Salvador de. See *Biographical Dictionary of Internationalists*.

MAGALHÃES LIMA, Sebastião (30 May 1851, Rio de Janeiro, Brazil — 7 December 1928, Lisbon, Portugal). *Education*: Doctor of Laws, Univ. of Coimbra (Portugal), 1875. *Career*: editor, *Espectro de Juvenal*, 1872-76, *Comercio do Portugal*, 1880, *O Seculo*, 1880-81, *Folha do Povo*, 1881-1907; lawyer, author, journalist, Freemason (Grand Master, Portugal, 1907), political activist, and pacifist.

From his student days, through writing, oratory, and political activity, Sebastião Magalhães Lima strove to transform the Portuguese monarchy into a socialist republic. His humanitarian and rationalist approach to social and political issues was shaped by the ideas of *Pierre-Joseph Jules Proudhon, Jules Michelet, Edgar Quinet, and *Victor Hugo. His republicanism was a creed which he held to be valid for all nations, much in the manner of Giuseppe Mazzini, and he labored for a peaceful confederation of free peoples throughout the world. No social system or political order would be just or justified in his view without the emancipation of women, children, and workers as well as an end to overseas oppression. In his conception of the ideal state, the weak and elderly would be protected; the vestiges of divine right government (as in Portugal) would be abolished; a rational system of universal education would be instituted; all papal influence and clerical fanaticism would be eradicated; and militarism would be replaced by the organization of peace among sovereign, republican nations.

In Portugal he crusaded in print and in person against royal domestic and foreign policies, leading the republican criticism of the monarchy. During the decades of the 1880s and 1890s, he made much of the government's incompetence by focusing on its inability to protect its colonial authority against British inroads in the zone between Angola and Mozambique. In January 1890, when violent protests broke out in Portugal against the government's acquiescence to British demands, he was held responsible and was forced to flee. During his ensuing exile, he delivered lectures all through Europe denouncing both British policy and the Portuguese government.

He returned to Lisbon but was again forced into exile after an insurrection in 1906 which was aimed against the repressive measures of the royally appointed dictator, João Franco. Magalhães Lima had been active on the barricades this time and went to Paris to escape a sedition trial. Finally, in 1910, Portugal did become a republic but its shape and form hardly resembled that which Magalhaẽs Lima had struggled for and he continued his battles for the transformation of state and society.

In addition to his unremitting concern for a just Portugal, Magalhaẽs Lima took an active part in the organized international peace movement whose headquarters were in Berne after 1891 (Bureau international de la paix). He participated in almost every annual congress convened up to 1913 by the Universal Peace Congress, serving as the main representative from his nation on many committees and commissions. He also collaborated closely with the newer peace societies organized by women, particularly *Princess Wiszniewska's Paris-based Alliance universelle des femmes pour la paix par l'education (Universal Alliance of Women for Peace through Education). True to his commitments, he backed Emile Zola during the Dreyfus Affair and organized Portuguese protests in defense of *Francisco Ferrer Guardia in 1909. He was frequently invited to lecture on European federalism and internationalism, offering a course at the Free University in Brussels in 1898 as well as before international conventions of Free Thinkers and Masons. In Lisbon, he served as head of the small peace society but was not able to increase its membership to any sizeable degree.

With the coming of World War I, Magalhães Lima adopted an interventionist position similar to that of the Italian peace leader, *E. T. Moneta—arguing that a crusade against German militarism was essential in order for the rest of Europe to organize a peaceful congress of nations. In 1916 he spoke out in favor of Portuguese intervention in the war.

In his capacity as a journalist and editor, he defended peace and international arbitration at meetings of the International Press Bureau both before and after the war. In 1927, before his death, he was elected as its president.

Bibliography:

A. *L'Effort portugais et l'union occidentale* (Auxerre, 1918); *Episodios da Minha Vida* (Lisbon, 1927); *Os Estados Unidos do Europa* (Lisbon, 1874); *A Federacão Ibeŕica* (Lisbon, 1895); *O Livro da Paz* (Lisbon, 1895); *A Obra Internacional* (Lisbon, 1895); *L'Oeuvre internationale* (Paris, 1897); *O Socialismo na Europa* (Lisbon, 1892).

B. Antonio Iraizoz, *El Apóstol de la democracia portuguesa. Dr. Sebastián de Magalhaes Lima* (Havana, 1929); Alvaro Néves, ed. *A vida dum a póstolo, Sebastião de Magalhães Lima* (3 vols., Lisbon, 1930-31).

Elda Gentili Zappi

MAGNES, Judah Leon (5 July 1877, Oakland, CA—27 October 1948, New York). *Education*: B.H.L., Hebrew Union Coll. 1898; Ph.D., Heidelberg Univ., 1902. *Career*: rabbi; chancellor and first president of the Hebrew Univ., Jerusalem, Israel; pacifist and Zionist.

Profoundly influenced by the American experience and the freedom it afforded Jewish immigrants, Judah Magnes was nonetheless an inveterate dissenter. As a young man, for example, he criticized the Spanish-American War and prowar Christian ministers, but he particularly attacked rabbis who classified themselves among the "fighting parsons." Although once described as "a splendid type of Jewish Quaker," Magnes was most likely inspired by the ethical and religious message of Judaism's prophetic tradition as well as by Ahad Ha'am's writings about spiritual Zionism.

By 1914, the year of the outbreak of the war in Europe, Magnes was already well known. He had served as rabbi of a small synagogue in working-class Brownsville in Brooklyn and later of the elegant Temple Emanu-El on New York's Fifth Avenue. As the war dragged on, his Jewish sympathies and pacifist sentiments led him to become actively involved in sending relief supplies to suffering Jews in Eastern Europe and Palestine. And with the U.S. entry into the war, in 1917, his pacifism became even more important to him. He had always thought the right of Jews to defend themselves in pogroms necessary and proper, but war, he believed, was quite a different matter. In 1917 he joined such pacifists and antiwar activists as *Roger Baldwin, *Eugene Victor Debs, and *Norman Thomas in Madison Square Garden to excoriate the warmakers. Afterwards, he appeared in other cities to reiterate his opposition to the war. Despite the fact that many non-socialist American Jews were appalled at his views—fearing that their patriotism would be questioned because of his outspoken opinions — Magnes neither apologized nor compromised. "Do spiritual ideals have no validity in times of war?" he asked.

His antiwar efforts brought him into contact with British pacifist leaders +Ramsay MacDonald, *Philip Snowden, and *Norman Angell and his work in the United States helped lead to the establishment in 1918 of the Civil Liberties

Bureau (a forerunner of the American Civil Liberties Union) and later, the Bureau of Legal Advice for Conscientious Objectors. Although harassed and investigated by the government, he refused to desist. In a series of articles published in the *New York Evening Post* between November 1917 and February 1918 and signed "Observer," he condemned the resort to war and called for the negotiation of a fair peace treaty.

In the early 1920s, he moved to Palestine and in 1925 was named chancellor of the Hebrew University in Jerusalem. Ten years later he became its initial president. From that vantage point, he continued to press his pacifist views. He became the moving spirit — along with Martin Buber, Henrietta Szold, and Ernst Simon — in organizing Ichud (Union) which sought to plant the seeds for a binational state in the Palestine Mandate, one that would emphasize reconciliation between Arab and Jew and shared governance instead of unitary sovereignty of one over the other. Other alternatives, he believed, might bring conflict and more war.

His pacifism remained absolute until the rise to power of Adolf Hitler and the worldwide Nazi attack against Jewish life. In 1939 he declared that Nazism was a greater evil than war; thus reluctantly — indeed, very reluctantly — he endorsed World War II. Even so, he added his hope that out of the ashes of war would emerge a vanguard of religious conscientious objectors who might lead yet another antiwar movement.

As a rabbi and pacifist, as a believing Jew, Zionist and universalist, as one opposed to violence in principle and practice, Judah Magnes was not without his supporters and critics. Yet he was a man of respected moral principles, as even his critics conceded. As for his admirers, one of them, Lea Ben Dor, wrote in the *Jerusalem Post* on the centenary of his birth: "The lonely road he walked is once more worth thought and study."

Bibliography:

A. *Arab-Jewish Unity: Testimony before the Anglo American Inquiry Commission for the Ichud (Unity) Association. Judah L. Magnes and Martin Buber* (London, 1947); *The Bond, Two Letters to Gandhi from Martin Buber and J.L. Magnes* (Jerusalem, 1939); *Dissenter in Zion: From Writings of Judah L. Magnes*, ed., Arthur A. Goren (Cambridge, MA, 1982); *"The People Do Not Want War" — Address Delivered At Madison Square Garden, March 24, 1917* (New York, 1917); *"The Spirit of Peace and the Spirit of Man," World Fellowship Through Religion* (London, 1936); "Toward Peace in Palestine," *Foreign Affairs*, 21 (January, 1943), 239-49; *Towards Union in Palestine: Essays on Zionism and Jewish Arab Cooperation* (Jerusalem, 1947).

B. Norman Bentwich, *For Zion's Sake: A Biography of Judah L. Magnes* (Philadelphia, 1954).

C. Judah L. Magnes Papers, Hebrew University, Jerusalem, Israel.

Murray Polner

MAKAROFF, Peter George (15 May 1894, Kars, Russia — 5 December 1970, Saskatoon, Saskatchewan, Canada). *Education*: LL.B., Univ. of Saskatchewan,

1918. *Career*: school teacher, 1911-15; lawyer, 1918-70; politician, peace activist, World Federalist.

Peter George Makaroff was born into an obscure community of illiterate but passionately religious peasants who came to be known derisively as Doukhobors (spirit wrestlers) much as the members of the seventeenth-century English Society of Friends were called Quakers. Because of their renunciation of war and resistance to military conscription, the Doukhobors were cruelly persecuted by the Tsar's soliders. Their plight came to the attention of *Leo Tolstoy, who enlisted the aid of the Society of Friends to find them a haven in the New World. The Friends negotiated with the Government of Canada for the emigration of the Doukhobors from Russia to the unbroken prairie of western Canada in 1898-99; and so the young Peter Makaroff came with his family to share the hardships and the grinding toil of pioneer farmers on the banks of the North Saskatchewan River.

The Friends, who made regular visitations to the new community, spotted a bright boy and helped Peter to a high school education, first in Philadelphia and later (1911) at the Rosthern Academy, fifty miles north of Saskatoon. He became a school teacher, and then with money saved from teaching and farm work he was able to attend the University of Saskatchewan and obtain a Bachelor of Laws degree. He thus became the first Doukhobor in the world to get an education, to receive a university degree, and to enter a profession.

After graduation from university in 1918, he established a law practice in Saskatoon which he continued to the end of his life. For his success as a barrister he was made a King's Counsel in 1932. His most notable case, which at the time attracted international attention, was his successful defense of Peter Veregin, Jr., spiritual leader of the Doukhobors, from deportation to the Soviet Union in February 1933. He also defended the unemployed men arrested in connection with the Regina Riot of July 1, 1935.

Makaroff was a close friend of *J. S. Woodsworth, founder of the social democratic Co-operative Commonwealth Federation (CCF), whose socialist and pacifist convictions he shared. He was twice an unsuccessful candidate for the CCF, first in the Saskatchewan provincial election of 1934 in the constituency of Shellbrook, and again in the Canadian federal election of 1940 in the constituency of Rosthern. In 1940 he campaigned in support of Woodsworth's stand, in the Canadian Parliament, of opposition to Canada's entry into World War II. A committed pacifist, Makaroff was a long-time member of the Fellowship of Reconciliation, and the Saskatoon chapter often met in his law office. He was especially dedicated to the peaceful resolution of domestic tensions and from the early fifties to 1964 he served as Chairman of the Saskatchewan Labor Relations Board, mediating disputes between employers and trade unions.

In his later years he was active in the World Federalist movement. He came to believe that, after the atom bomb, the best hope for peace was in the rule of law under a world federation of nation states. Accordingly, he endowed the World Federalist Prize "for the best annual essay relating to world peace through world law" and urged everyone he knew to join the movement.

Bibliography:

B. W.H. McConnell, *Prairie Justice* (1980).

C. Peter G. Makaroff Papers, Saskatchewan Archives Board, Saskatoon.

Carlyle King

MÄKI, Aaku (1 April 1865, Tampere, Finland — 15 May 1948; Paimio, Finland). *Education*: Jyväskylä Teachers Coll. *Career*: primary school teacher; journalist; editor and publisher, *Väinämöinen*, 1896-1907, 1909-10; pacifist publicist, bookseller; director of Paimio nature healing center.

After being certified as a teacher at Jyväskylä Teachers College, Aaku Mäki taught at Tampere for several years. Among all the new currents of thought which reached Finland at the turn of the century, he took greatest interest in the peace movement. He read pacifist literature and began to write about peace issues for the newspaper *Tampereen Sanomat*. Unfortunately, tight control of Finnish newspapers and censorship by the Russian government caused many of the large newspapers in Finland to take a negative attitude towards pacifism. To promote his new found interest in the antiwar movement, Mäki, together with G. R. Grundstrom, an industrialist, founded a paper called *Väinämöinen*. Mäki served as editor and also began to publish Christian, temperance, and pacifist literature. He encouraged the translation into Finnish of some of the better known peace writers, including *Leo Tolstoy, *Alfred H. Fried, and *Klas Arnoldson. He published works by Finnish peace pioneers *Kyösti Huhtala and *Juho Mäkinen. Through a bookshop established by the Väinämöinen Cooperative, he displayed and distributed peace literature.

Mäki's publishing efforts helped promote the establishment of an organized peace movement in Finland. In 1907 the Peace Union of Finland, the nation's first antiwar organization, was founded and Mäki was elected to its top position. Made up predominantly of cultured, middle class people from the countryside, the Peace Union articulated the Christian doctrine of love and sought to promote peace by strengthening the individual will. Never attracting many members, the Union's influence remained small and insignificant.

In 1911 Mäki resigned from the presidency of the Union and began to publish a paper called *Luonnon Parantaja* (later renamed *Parantaja*), which stressed natural ways of living. Mäki began putting his theories into practice after becoming the head of the Nature Healing Centre of Paimio. He became so engrossed with the new movement that he changed his name to Sampsa Luonnonmaa (Nature Country), largely ignoring other political and social issues.

Mäki's contribution to the peace movement was as a pioneer. He began his peace work at a very difficult period in Finnish history — at a time of Russian oppression and revolutionary stirring. He laid the groundwork for an organized antiwar movement and through his publishing ventures brought to the Finnish people some of the best writings on the subject from around the world.

Bibliography:

B. Juho Makinen, *Piirkita Suomen rauhanliikkeesta* (Tampere, 1919).

Kalevi Kalemaa
Trans. by Oliver and Rita Whitehead

MÄKINEN, Juho Aatto (12 May 1872, Ähtäri, Finland — 10 March 1949, Seinäjoki, Finland). *Education*: Tampere Business Coll., 1891-93. *Career*: journalist, *Tampereen Sanomat*, 1894-96, *Väinämöinen*, 1909-11; bank clerk; pacifist author and social reformer.

From his elementary school teacher, Emil Sjöberg, Juho Mäkinen adopted humanistic, antiwar, and nonviolent ideals. In 1894, after qualifying at the Business College, he took a job as a journalist with a nationally vigilant newspaper called *Tamereen Sanomat*. He served on the paper at the very time that the government of Tsar *Nicholas II sought to repress Finland's national right of self-determination. As a result a national resistance movement gained strength and also gained support from the awakening peace movement. Mäkinen began to publish articles about peace in *Tampereen Sanomat*. He also began to write for the antiwar paper *Väinämöinen*, which began in Tampere in 1896. He became a journalist for the paper in 1909. His peace activism also spread to organizational work. He helped found the original Finnish Peace Union in 1907 and served on its board until 1913 when the Union was abolished.

Through self-education Mäkinen attained a wide knowledge of fiction and learned ten foreign languages. He was one of the first Esperantists in Finland and believed that Esperanto brought nations closer to each other and increased mutual understanding. Consequently, he considered studying Esperanto as essential to international peace. Because of his knowledge of languages, Mäkinen helped maintain foreign contacts for the Finnish Peace Union. In later years he worked as a bank clerk in Ähtäri and studied and wrote articles on peace, several of which were published in Swedish, French, Swiss, German, and American antiwar publications. He also published three major works on the peace movement.

Mäkinen was one of the pioneers in the Finnish peace movement. Although not a very dynamic writer nor a charismatic personality, his antiwar activities prepared the way for pacifist ideas in Finland. Besides pacifism, Mäkinen was interested in temperance and youth club work, but he viewed these as a way to spread his antiwar message. Although he participated in peace organizations, he viewed the writing and dissemination of peace literature more important. He was elected an honorary member of Finland's Peace Union in 1928.

Bibliography:

A. *Piirteitä rauhanliikkeestä* (Tampere, 1905); *Piirteitä Suomen rauhanliikkeestä* (Tampere, 1919); *Pikapiirtoja Suomen rauhanliikkeestä* (Helsinki, 1932).

B. Waldemar Rantaoja, "Mäkinen, Juho Aatto," in *Eteläpohjalaisia Elämäkertoja, M-Ö* (Vaasa, 1965), 510.

Kalevi Kalemaa
Trans. by Oliver and Rita Whitehead

MALATESTA, Errico (14 December 1853, Santa Maria Capua Vetere, Caserta, Italy — 22 July 1932, Rome). *Education*: Liceo dei Padri Scolopi, Naples; medical studies, Univ. of Naples, 1868-70. *Career*: electrician, journalist, revolutionary organizer, and anarchist theoretician.

By the end of his life, Errico Malatesta's fame as an anarchist thinker and international revolutionary was so widespread that Benito Mussolini kept him under surveillance and house arrest but did not imprison or exile him. His entire adult life was devoted to the cause of anarcho-socialism. As a young man, Malatesta had initially been an ardent republican while in medical school. When he became interested in the revolutionary message of anarcho-socialism, he left medical school, eventually gave away his inheritance, earned his living as an electrician, and entered a life of false papers, secret identities, prison terms, and occasional exile in Europe and the Americas. As a gifted polemicist, he produced critiques of all hierarchically structured authority, both capitalist and socialist.

Organized international peace as conceived by the European peace movement was decidedly not on Malatesta's agenda, and yet he admired the voluntarist element that produced the private societies of peace activists. His vision of a just future contained a powerful measure of peace, brotherhood, and a universal association of humanity, but it would be achieved only by the complete destruction of all existing order, including government and economic institutions. The peace movement hardly subscribed to such views.

No pacifist, Malatesta nonetheless detested the use of violence for its own sake, for the sake of consciousness-raising, or for its "exhilarating" effect as might be defended by "terrorist" groups. He saw how counter-productive such capricious applications of violence could be. In his estimation, however, selectively applied sabotage, strikes, class warfare, and insurrection would most likely be needed to achieve freedom.

With the coming of World War I, he remained faithful to his principles, ridiculing comrades who went off to fight German militarism. "Would a world dominated by a victorious combination of English capitalism and Russian autocracy be any worse than one run by Prussian militarists?" he asked. In 1914 he anticipated that the war would end in a long, exhausting draw between the two sides. Malatesta spent the war years in London, refuting all justifications for class collaboration. Only a war on behalf of true socialism would be justified. His advice to his countrymen was to refuse service. If the nation were to be invaded, workers should fight to protect what is theirs and not to defend bourgeois property or the state.

After the war, he returned to Italy. In 1919-20, anarchism experienced a brief resurgence before its total suppression under the Fascists. Malatesta remained stubbornly attached to his vision of true revolution, denouncing organized socialism, the Bolsheviks, and the capitalist state.

Bibliography:

A. *Anarchy* (London, 1891); *Il Nostro Programma* (New York and Patterson, NJ, 1903-5); *Programma Anarchico* (Bologna, 1922); *Scritti*, L. Fabbri, ed., (3 vols., Geneva, Brussels, 1934-36); *Scritti Scelti*, G. Berneri and C. Zaccaria, eds., (2 vols., Naples, 1947-54); *Scritti scelti*, G. Cerrito, ed., (Rome, 1970).

B. G. M. Bravo, "Errico Malatesta," in F. Andreucci and T. Detti, eds., *Il Movimento operaio italiano* (1977), III, 246-55; L. Fabbri, *La vida y el pensamiento de Errico Malatesta* (2 vols., Barcelona, 1935); M. Nettlau, *Errico Malatesta* (Berlin, 1922); V. Richards, ed., *Errico Malatesta, His Life and Ideas* (London, 1965); G. Woodcock, *Anarchism* (Cleveland, OH, 1962).

C. Casellario politico centrale, (police file), Archivio centrale dello Stato.

Sandi E. Cooper

MANDERE, Henri Charles Glaude Jacob van der (17 March 1883, Amsterdam, — 6 March 1959, The Hague). *Education*: grammar school. *Career*: secretary, Nederlandse Cooperatieve Bond, 1908; secretary, Koninklijke Nederlandse Edelmetaalbedrijven, 1919; secretary, Beniso (Confederation of Dutch-Indonesian Sugar Industries), 1920-29; director, Haagse Volksuniversiteit 1928; author, journalist, and editor.

From an early age, Henri van der Mandere was closely associated with the "official," respectable peace movement in the Netherlands and became its dominant figure for forty years. The propagation of peace and international cooperation, the strengthening and implementation of treaties of arbitration, and support for other articles of the Hague Conventions were the central tasks of his life to which he devoted his considerable literary and organizational talents.

At the relatively young age of 24 he had published a lengthy study on the Hague agreements concerning the peaceful settlement of international disputes and the Permanent Court of Arbitration. Apparently fearing not to be taken seriously because of his age, he wrote under the pseudonym Edgar de Melville. He also adopted this name for a number of other books, including a follow-up study on the work of The Hague Conferences which appeared in 1924, as well as for his biographies of T.M.C. Asser (1910) and Frederic von Martens (1912). The latter two were part of a series of popular biographies of "Men and Women of Importance" of which he was the general editor and for which he also wrote volumes on *Bertha von Suttner (1909), Prince Albert of Monaco (1911), +David Lloyd George (1918) and +Woodrow Wilson (1919). Many of his forty or so other books dealt with international institutions and agreements (Hague Conferences, League of Nations, United Nations) or the history of contemporary world politics. These works, as well as countless articles in journals, were largely written for a general audience; for several years the author was also a popular commentator on foreign politics for Dutch radio and a lecturer in adult education institutions on the same subject. Whereas financial difficulties had prevented him from attending university, his own activities thus greatly helped to increase public knowledge and awareness of these important issues.

Van der Mandere was not only one of the first chroniclers of the peace movement in the Netherlands but also one of its pivotal figures. From the turn of the century onwards he played a leading role in a number of important peace organizations. In 1911 he became secretary of the Algemene Nederlandse Bond "Vrede door Recht" (General Dutch League "Peace Through Justice") which emerged in 1901 as a result of the fusion of the two main existing peace organizations in the country. Its activities and its journal (of which he was editor-in-chief) greatly contributed to the revival of the peace movement in the period lasting up to the War. When, in 1914, many of the groups working for peace in Holland formed the Nederlandse Anti-Oorlog Raad (Dutch Anti-War Council), van der Mandere became its secretary. Both organizations were dissolved in 1919 and replaced by the Vereniging voor Volkenbond en Vrede (League of Nations and Peace Society) whose general secretary he became until 1939. This organization was increasingly identified with support for the League. In 1945 it became the Vereniging voor Internationale Rechtsorde (Society for International Order and Justice) with van der Mandere again serving as secretary until 1949. In all these organizations he was very actively involved, as both a founder and activist.

He maintained contacts with local committees and represented the organizations at international conferences, such as the 1913 World Peace Congress and the 1928 conference of the League of Nations Unions, both held at The Hague. His role in the convocation of these meetings was crucial. Among his notable achievements were several exhibitions which he organized and which attracted widespread publicity and support. The first of these was held in 1925 to commemorate the tricentenary of the publication of Grotius's famous work; the success of this exhibition prompted van der Mandere to organize a "Peace and League of Nations Exhibition" in The Hague in 1930. Encouraged again by its success, he opened, a few years afterwards, a permanent museum which bore the same name as the exhibition.

He was directly involved in the international political arena on a few occasions only, as secretary at the Opium Conferences before 1914, in the plebiscite in the Saar in 1934-35, and in similar work for the League of Nations in the Middle East in 1937-38.

Bibliography:

A. *Achtergronden van de wereldpolitiek (1900-heden)* (Rotterdam, 1954); *Dertig jaar wereldstrijd (1914-1945)* (Assen, 1947); *Geschiedenis van het Nederlandsche Roode Kruis* (1867-1917) (Amsterdam, 1917); *Kleine geschiedenis van den grooten oorlog (1939-1945)* (Leyden, 1945); *Neurenberg en Tokio* (Leyden, 1946); *L'oeuvre de La Haye (1871-1921)* (Leyden, 1924); *Vijftien jaren arbeid van den Volkenbond (1919-1935)* (Hilversum, 1935); *De Volkenbond in woord en beeld* (Utrecht, 1930); *De vredesbeweging en hare geschiedenis* (Leyden, 1928).

B. *Levensberichten van leden der Maatschappij der Nederlandsche Letterkunde te Leiden* (Leyden, 1959-60) 97-100. *Wie is dat*? (The Hague, 1956) 398-9.

Peter van den Dungen

MANN, Heinrich (27 March 1871, Lübeck, Germany — 12 March 1950, Santa Monica, CA). *Education:* self-educated. *Career*: novelist, essayist, lecturer, internationalist, and antimilitarist.

Heinrich Mann's ideal of a rational and humane society owed a great deal to French literary and intellectual currents in which he saw that ideal embodied. In his view, German writers and intellectuals had to end their isolation from society and become active voices in shaping ideals comparable to those developed by their French counterparts. The first task was to bring German society to a recognition of its true self. Following the example of Emile Zola, Mann set out to provide a mirror of Imperial Germany in a series of novels that exposed the arrogance of authority and the subservience of common people. The first of these, *Im Schlaraffenland* (1900), portrayed the decadence of the haute-bourgeoisie in Berlin in the 1890s. It was followed in 1905 by the more famous *Professor Unrat* (best known through its film version, *The Blue Angel*), a look at the petit-bourgeois world in a North German town. In *Die Kleine Stadt* (1909), artistically his best novel, he described an ideal world in Italy and a model for democratic values. But the sharpest and most satirical indictment of Imperial Germany was *Der Untertan*, which began to appear in weekly installments that were then cancelled with the outbreak of World War I and could not be published in book form until 1918.

As a Francophile and humanist, Mann was horrified, but hardly surprised, by the outbreak of the war in 1914. His own attitude had changed drastically since his early articles for *Das Zwanzigste Jahrhundert*, a periodical he had edited in 1895. Gone now was the sympathy he had then expressed for a constant state of preparedness for war and his scepticism towards peace movements as an effective instrument to prevent war. Now, in a thinly veiled essay about Zola, (published first in *Die Weissen Blätter* in 1915) he called on intellectuals to join him in opposing the war and to expose the military as an essentially self-serving caste deriving its power from equally self-serving politicians and millionaires. What he proposed was an intellectual revolution whose weapons were to be words that would educate and enlighten. After a May Day rally for peace, led by a leading radical Social Democrat, Karl Liebknecht, during which the police fired into the crowd, Mann felt that he too must risk public opposition to the war. At another peace rally, he delivered a speech, "To the 20-year-olds of 1936," which warned the coming generation that future historians would lie to them about the present conflict, would pretend that the nation had fought for liberty and justice, and had acted in the interest of humanity. He reminded them that war neither cleanses nor civilizes, but rather creates an indifference towards others. In his analysis, the arrogant and decadent prewar wielders of "Imperial

Power'' were carrying on their self-interested machinations under the guise of defense of the ''Fatherland.''

Mann, along with others, recognized that the end of the war and the beginning of the Weimar Republic brought no real change in German social and political life. Consequently, he immediately formed a Council of Intellectual Workers whose task would be to help towards bringing about a meaningful change. In a series of essays and speeches over the next few years, Mann pleaded the cause of a Social-Democratic Germany, rapprochement with France, and the establishment of an effective European Federation of States. But he recognized that again power had hidden its identity, this time under the name of ''Economics,'' and in an open letter to Chancellor +Gustav Stresemann, *Diktatur der Vernunft* (1923), he warned against a world dominated by industrialists. But the warnings were in vain and the republic drifted more and more to the right. As president of the literary section of the Prussian Academy, Mann co-authored a new history text to be used in the schools; a history not of battles, warriors, or nobles, but of the works of the people. It was never adopted. When in 1932 the liberal journal *Die Weltbühne* urged him to become a candidate for the presidency of the republic, he declined out of despair and an unwillingness to split the liberal ranks any further. In a last desperate public act before he had to flee Germany in 1933, Mann signed an appeal, along with *Albert Einstein and *Käthe Kollwitz, that called on Social-Democrats and Communists to unite against Adolf Hitler.

Mann's work to unite the various factions opposed to Nazism continued in France. His reputation made it possible for him to publish in French newspapers and in the many refugee publications, and he even addressed the League of Nations as a representative of a culture in exile. The newly formed ''Volksfront'' (popular front) elected him as its president and he had much hope for its future. The ''Volksfront'' had organized both unaffiliated and politically committed exiles hoping to oppose Nazism by informing those in and out of Germany of its true face. It also sought to demonstrate that German culture was still alive, albeit in temporary banishment. But, unhappily, the Weimar experience was repeated once more; intellectuals spoke to each other while no one listened, and such challenges as the call to German workers to refuse to produce arms for the war in Spain went unheard. Within the organization, a power struggle developed which led to its early death. In spite of all his political activity, Mann continued his literary work, publishing a major novel about the French King, Henry IV, whom he praised for his rationale and humane use of power. With the fall of France, Mann had to flee again as his name was at the top of the Vichy list of undesirables.

Mann's years in the United States were hard and frustrating essentially ending his active antimilitarist role. Still, he remained optimistic and even believed in an eventual fulfillment of his dreams. When in 1949 an invitation came from East Germany for him to return, he hesitated, sensing that he might be used by the new regime. Death spared him a final decision.

Bibliography:

A. *Henri Quartre, King of France* (London, 1938); *Die Kleine Stadt* (Leipzig, 1909; Eng. trans., *The Little Town*, New York, 1962); *Politische Essays* (Frankfurt am Main, 1968); *Professor Unrat; oder, Das Ende eines Tyrannen* (Munich, 1905, Eng. trans., *The Blue Angel*, New York, 1976); *Im Schlaraffenland* (Leipzig, 1900; Eng. trans., *In the Land of Cockaigne*, New York, 1929); *Der Untertan* (Leipzig, 1918, Eng. trans., *Man of Straw*, London, 1947); *Ein Zeitalter wird besichtigt* (Berlin, 1945).

B. David Gross, *The Writer and Society — Heinrich Mann and Literary Politics in Germany, 1890-1940* (Atlantic City, NJ, 1980); Nigel Hamilton, *The Brothers Mann* (New Haven, CT, 1979).

Peter S. Seadle

MANN, Horace (4 May 1796, Franklin, MA — 2 August 1859, Yellow Springs, OH). *Education*: B.A., Brown Univ., 1819; Litchfield Law School. *Career*: law practice, 1823-37; member, Massachusetts State Legislature, (House), 1827-33, (Senate), 1833-37; secretary, Massachusetts State Board of Education, 1837-48; member, U.S. House of Representatives, 1848-53; president, Antioch Coll., 1853-59; lawyer, educator, reformer, and politician.

Although never a major peace leader, Horace Mann devoted considerable attention to the problem of war and became a pioneer advocate of what later came to be called peace studies. In 1837 education became Mann's primary concern when he was named secretary to the Massachusetts State Board of Education. Yet reform had a much broader range of interests in the early nineteenth century and when Mann was elected to Congress he temporarily put aside education for antislavery. He also advocated temperance, federal aid to the indigent insane, prison reform, and world peace.

Mann was not an absolute pacifist and remained convinced that in some cases war might be justified. Yet, his belief in the "Idea of Progress" — a progress that would come through education — led him to the view that war was destined to disappear from human experience. As a phrenologist he hoped that educators would develop in their students a talent for philanthropy and brotherhood. School children, said Mann, should not be taught that wars are heroic, and school histories should be rewritten to emphasize the heroes of peace. He once advised his wife not to take their children to visit a battlefield, for he believed that young people should not be subjected to the history of "the wrongs and wickedness of men." In his lectures and essays he condemned war and bemoaned huge military expenditures.

Some of his views of war were included in a speech he made to the graduates of West Point when, as a congressman, he was on its Board of Visitors. He confided to his wife that his nature rebelled against what he saw at the Academy, but that he meant to gather materials so that he could "make war on war." Mann told the cadets that prophecy, the growth of world trade, more enlightened humans, and advanced technology all pointed to the demise of war. He predicted the end of war when "some great invention" capable of destroying two opposing armies "in an hour" was introduced onto the battlefield. He told the cadets to prepare themselves to accept the coming day when war would inevitably be a thing of the past.

Although peace was a secondary concern with Horace Mann, he frequently referred to it and because of his influence among educators he made an important contribution to the movement. In pointing out the need for deemphasizing military values and assumptions in the schools, he foreshadowed a concern of many later educators regarding education and its relationship to war.

Bibliography:

A. *Slavery: Letters and Speeches* (Boston, 1851).

B. Mary Peabody Mann, *Life of Horace Mann* (Boston, 1865); Jonathan Messerli, *Horace Mann* (New York, 1972).

C. Horace Mann Papers, Massachusetts Historical Society.

Larry Gara

MARCOARTÚ Y MORALES, Arturo de. See *Bibliographical Dictionary of Internationalists*.

MARGUERITTE, Victor (1 December 1866, Blida, Algeria — 23 March 1942, Monestier, Isère, France). *Education*: Lyceé Henri IV, Paris; Cavalry School of Saumur. *Career*: military officer, novelist, and polemicist.

One of the most ardent and prolific pacifists of the interwar period, Victor Margueritte was, ironically, the son of an heroic officer who perished in a cavalry charge against the enemy during the Franco-Prussian War. Always devoted to his father's memory, Margueritte wrote an elegiac biography of him in 1930, when he had become one of the most outspoken critics of war. But the young Margueritte first sought to emulate his father, enlisting in the cavalry and serving in his native Algeria. After more than five years of active duty, he resigned his commission to devote himself exclusively to writing.

In collaboration with his older brother Paul, Victor Margueritte published some twenty volumes, including four historical novels devoted to the period 1870-71. Going his own way in 1906, he turned to novels dealing with social problems such as the condition of women and financial speculation. By 1914 he had established his reputation as a highly successful and wordly novelist, but there was little hint of his career as an opponent of war.

With the outbreak of World War I, Margueritte returned to military service as a captain with the General Staff, assigned to the office of the military governor of Paris. Later attached to the press bureau, he founded a propaganda organ, *L'Information universelle* intended to promote France's cause in Latin America. Retiring from the army in 1916, Margueritte published his novel *La Terre natale* the next year. In it he expressed his hatred of war with all its death and destruction, and called for a league of nations that would maintain peace once the conflict had ended. After 1918 he devoted himself largely to the cause of peace, using his skill as a writer to bring the question before the general public.

In 1919 Margueritte published his study *Au Bord du gouffre*. It sharply attacked the politicians whose stupidity took France into the conflict and the generals whose incompetence caused the death of so many soldiers. When Margueritte put aside the theme of pacifism to return to that of women's rights, he raised a storm of controversy with his daring novel *La Garçonne* in 1922. Its frank sexuality sold many thousands of copies; it also created such a scandal that the Legion of Honor expelled him from its ranks.

Undaunted, he wrote *Les Criminels* (1925), a scathing account of European diplomacy from 1870 to 1914. Margueritte excoriated the political and diplomatic leaders of all countries for having brought on the disaster of world war. Heavily documented and unsympathetic to Allied claims that Germany alone was responsible for having provoked it, the book added weight to pacifists' arguments for disarmament and reconciliation.

Along with *Armand Charpentier, he founded *Évolution*, a monthly journal devoted to questions of international relations and understanding among peoples. It explored issues such as the causes of World War I and problems that threatened world peace. Margueritte used it pages to launch an "Appeal to Consciences" (1926), signed by 103 prominent intellectuals, which denounced the injustices of the Versailles settlement, and an "Appeal to Good Sense" (1928), that called for worldwide disarmament to guarantee peace.

During the 1930s Margueritte produced a long succession of works promoting pacifism. *La Patrie humaine* (1931) called for good will among all the peoples of Europe and prompted *Victor Méric to found a newspaper with the same name to advance the antiwar effort; *Non! un roman d'une conscience* (1931) extolled conscientious objection; *Aristide Briand* (1932) praised the foreign minister's efforts on behalf of peace and reconciliation with Germany; and *Debout les vivants!* (1932) appealed to all Europeans to demand a referendum that would decide the question of peace or war. By the mid-1930s, however, Margueritte's confidence in a peaceful world began to crumble. The Japanese invasion of Manchuria and particularly the Italian conquest of Ethiopia destroyed his faith in the League of Nations. In two bitter studies he mourned the growing inability of the organization to maintain peace, calling it a "rouged corpse." Still he continued to voice his hopes for international understanding. The author's anguish was heightened by his advancing blindness, which became total by 1939, and the death of his beloved wife. Apart from a volume of poetry devoted to her memory, he virtually ceased to write.

When a new war erupted in 1939, Margueritte did not hesitate to sign the manifesto *Paix immédiate* which the anarchist *Louis Lecoin brought to him. Although it called only for an immediate ceasefire, the tract so angered the government of Eduard Daladier that it took vigorous measures against all those who had adhered to it. Threatened with prosecution by a military court, the old man admitted that he had signed the document, but claimed that Lecoin had deceived him by adding inflammatory passages to the text afterwards. In letters sent to the press, he denounced the tract as an act of treason. Margueritte died during the German occupation, his efforts on behalf of peace largely forgotten, his scandalous novels still vividly recalled.

Bibliography:

A. *Aristide Briand* (Paris, 1932); *Avortement de la S. D. N. (1920-1936)* (Paris, 1936); *Au Bord du gouffre* (Paris, 1919); *Le Cadavre maguillé. La S. D. N. (mars-septembre 1936)* (Paris, 1936); *Les Criminels* (Paris, 1925); *Debout les vivants!* (Paris, 1932); *Marchés de dupe? Dix-sept ans de politique extérieure française* (Paris, n.d. [1937]); *Non! roman d'une conscience* (Paris, 1931); *La Patrie humaine* (Paris, 1931).

B. Jean Guirec, *Victor Margueritte. L'Homme et l' écrivain* (Paris, 1927); Louis Lecoin, *Le Cours d'une vie* (Paris, 1965); NYT, March 24, 1942.

James Friguglietti

MARSHALL, Catherine E. (29 April 1880, Harrow, England — 30(?) March 1961, London). *Education*: privately and at St. Leonard's School, St. Andrews, Scotland. *Career*: various offices, notably parliamentary secretary, National Union of Women's Suffrage Societies, 1908-14; founding member, Women's International League for Peace and Freedom, 1915; associate and honorary secretary, No-Conscription Fellowship, 1916-19; various offices in Women's International League for Peace and Freedom (international section) and Women's International League (British section), 1919 to c. 1941; Czech Refugee Committee, 1938-43; pacifist and nonviolent political organizer.

Catherine Marshall's first significant political work was for the National Union of Women's Suffrage Societies (NUWSS). In 1908 she formed a local branch in Cumberland (then her home), and two years later promoted more democratic and effective regional structures. Moving to NUWSS headquarters in London, Marshall (working with Kathleen Courtney) developed an exceptional talent as a political organizer; the extraordinary network of detailed information, personal contact, and political pressure which was woven by 1912 touched every level of government, party, and public. Organized working-class support was drawn increasingly towards the nonviolent wing of the movement, which, in spite of disappointments, had a strong forward strategy by 1914.

When World War I came, Marshall found herself with an integrated philosophy of nonviolence, developed in response to the antisuffrage "argument from physical force" and to the increasingly autocratic and violent campaign conducted by Emmeline and Christabel Pankhurst (Women's Social and Political Union). Marshall and a substantial number of suffrage leaders throughout the world transferred to the international sphere the doctrine of a prewar manifesto against militancy; "We . . . believe that physical force can produce no permanent settlement of any political issue." Militarism was seen as antithetical to women's political equality.

Despite considerable support, Marshall was unable to commit the NUWSS as a body to work for a new postwar international order. Resigning from the executive, she was one of a handful of women who met in Holland in February

1915 to plan, with care and brilliance, the International Conference at The Hague (April 1915) from which sprang the Women's International League for Peace and Freedom (WILPF).

From 1916 to early 1918, Marshall worked fulltime for the No-Conscription Fellowship, sharing with *Bertrand Russell major responsibility for its survival after the younger leaders (notably *Clifford Allen and Fenner Brockway) went to jail. By 1918 her never very robust health gave way and she had the first of a series of incapacitating illnesses. After the war, Marshall served the International Section of WILPF at Geneva, concerning herself particularly with the League of Nations, treaty revision, economic reconstruction, and the Irish situation.

In the late 1930s Marshall assisted Jewish refugees from Czechoslovakia. Her concerns about the rise of fascism led her to renounce the absolute pacifist position, and she temporarily withdrew from active participation in WILPF. Until her death, Catherine Marshall retained an active interest in the Labour party, the Union of Democratic Control, the United Nations Organization, and a number of other bodies concerned with peace and human rights, conducting a lively correspondence of which little has survived. When she died, her crucial leadership roles in the women's suffrage movement and during the First World War had already been almost forgotten.

Bibliography:

B. Gertrude Bussey and Margaret Tims, *Women's International League for Peace and Freedom* (London, 1965); Jo Vellacott Newberry, "Anti-War Suffragists," *History*, 62 (October, 1977), 411-25; Jo Vellacott, *Bertrand Russell and the Pacifists in the First World War* (Brighton, 1980).

C. Catherine E. Marshall Papers, Cumbria Record Office, Carlisle.

Jo Vellacott

MARTENS, Frederic Frommhold de. See *Biographical Dictionary of Internationalists*.

MARTIN, Jesse Bauman (22 December 1897, St. Jacobs, Ontario, Canada — 4 March 1974, Waterloo, Ontario). *Education*: Hesston Coll., Kansas, 1923-24; Goshen Coll., 1924. *Career*: pastor, Erb Street Mennonite Church, Waterloo, 1929-64; teacher, Ontario Mennonite Bible School and Institute, 1932-65; church worker, administrator, and committeeman with various Mennonite organizations.

When Canada entered World War II and began to seek young men for the armed forces, the government of +Mackenzie King was faced with the dilemma of the many conscientious objectors who, for mostly religious reasons, were exempt from military service. Jesse B. Martin, a simple Mennonite bishop, played a key role in the creation and operation of an alternative service plan for Canadian conscientious objectors (COs).

He was influential in the formation in Ontario in 1940 of the Conference of Historic Peace Churches, a coalition of Mennonite, Brethren in Christ, and Quaker groups, all of them with an historic stance on peace and nonresistance.

Martin became its most active member and spokesman, as chairman of the Military Problems Committee.

He possessed the type of tolerant, even personality, that was necessary to promote negotiations with a government uncertain about its policies with respect to COs when the country was at war and also to establish a unified working relationship amongst the various peace churches, each having its own view on what position to take. Martin's many trips to Ottawa and endless committee meetings contributed to the beginnings of an Alternative Service program in the summer of 1941. As camps were established, he traveled across Canada to organize, encourage, and provide spiritual leadership to men who were far away from their homes.

Martin's involvement in wartime negotiations with the government was inspired not only by a sudden interest in the peace effort, but also by a lifelong belief in reconciliation and unity. Pervading his work as pastor, teacher, and committee member, both inside the Mennonite community and beyond, was a desire to promote cooperation and resolve conflict, peacefully and justly.

Bibliography:

B. Urie A. Bender, *Four Earthen Vessels: Biogaphical Profiles of Oscar Burkholder, Samuel F. Coffman, Clayton F. Derstine, and Jesse B. Martin* (Scottdale, PA, 1982).

Frank H. Epp

MARTIN DU GARD, Roger (23 March 1881, Paris — 22 August 1958, Bellême, France). *Education*: diploma, École des chartes. *Career*: pacifist novelist.

Roger Martin du Gard's first important novel, *Jean Barois* (1913), dealt with the Dreyfus Affair. It was humanitarian and progressive though not overtly pacifist in tone. However, Martin du Gard's pacifism was illustrated in private correspondence as early as 1911. He was distressed over the Second Moroccan Crisis of that year, and appalled at the intoxication of bellicose nationalism, which he feared had invaded the majority of the French population. During the early summer of 1914, he and an Alsatian friend laid plans to write a book on the myopia of French policy toward Germany. They hoped that Franco-German rivalries could be settled peacefully.

Both Martin du Gard's promising career as a novelist and his desire for peace were dashed by the events of July and August, 1914, and he reluctantly accepted mobilization as a noncomissioned officer in a motorized supply group. He was not discharged from the French army until February 1919. His letters during the war revealed his bitter discouragement over the violence and barbarism he saw everywhere. A ray of hope came in 1915 when he obtained a copy of *Romain Rolland's famous antiwar pamphlet, *Au-dessus de la mêlée*. In a burst of enthusiasm he wrote Rolland, indicating that he once again desired to "experience the future."

The war was a nightmare for Martin du Gard, a brutal and senseless interruption, which he believed would be followed by a return to the peaceful Europe of the nineteenth century, with increasing social justice. His instincts were always to the left, though he never actually joined the French Communist party.

In 1920 Martin du Gard began work on a major novel series, *Les Thibault*, which was to be his principal occupation for the next two decades. He dedicated the volumes to the memory of a close friend who died in a military hospital in 1918. The early segments of the vast novel, which was eventually published in eight parts, demonstrate primarily psychological and sociological concerns. They concentrate on personal struggles within bourgeois families. In 1920 Martin du Gard was so certain that the political future of Europe would be stable that he mapped out the destinies of his principal characters through 1935!

By 1931 six parts were published, each of which added to Martin du Gard's growing reputation as a writer. With the seventh volume nearly completed, Martin du Gard suffered a serious automobile accident, and while convalescing developed grave doubts about the future of his novel. These doubts were inextricably linked with the developing crisis in Europe. Finally, he decided to throw the entire manuscript into the fire and begin again, this time enormously expanding his treatment of the principal characters' encounter with the First World War, and changing the plot so that the war snuffed out the lives of his heroes.

The result of five years of grueling effort was *L'Eté 1914*, which was immediately recognized as one of the greatest pacifist novels of all time. The central character, Jacques Thibault, dies in agony after attempting to fly from Switzerland over the Franco-German battle lines with a planeload of pacifist leaflets. For this novel Martin du Gard was awarded the Nobel Prize for Literature in 1937.

During the 1930s Martin du Gard signed many antiwar manifestoes with Rolland, André Gide, and others, and his private correspondence reflects horror at the prospect of a new world conflict. Martin du Gard was an extremely shy and reticent man, and hesitated to speak to reporters. Just after the announcement of his Nobel Prize (significantly on Armistice Day, 1937), he did grant an interview in which he admitted a "secret hope" that the award would help the distribution of *L'Eté 1914*, in which he had tried to "work for peace" by bringing to life the days of anguish which had preceded the mobilization of August 1914.

His Nobel Prize address also contained a fervent statement of his pacifism. He saw that the sound of arms was once again threatening, and hoped that his work would help in the struggle against the "disastrous contagion" of the forces of war. He feared at the end of 1937 that there was a return to that "cowardly fatalism" which allows wars to begin. He wished that the old who had forgotten and the young who were ignorant would read *L'Eté 1914*, to become aware of the "pathetic lessons of the past."

Sometime before September 1939, Martin du Gard came to believe that absolute pacifism was no longer appropriate, and during the Nazi occupation, he was active enough in helping refugees to be placed on a list of suspects by the Germans. He managed to escape arrest, and after the war lived quietly, occasionally speaking out for pacifist and humanitarian causes. His last public action occurred in April 1958, a few months before his death, when he joined a protest against the use of torture by the French army during the Algerian War. This document was also signed by François Mauriac, André Malraux, and Jean-Paul Sartre.

Bibliography:

A. *Jean Barois* (Paris, 1913, English trans., New York, 1949); *Les Thibault* (Paris, 1922-40, English trans., New York, 1937, 1941); Nobel Prize Speech, in *Les Prix Nobel en 1937* (Stockholm, 1938).

B. Rafic Jouejati, *The Quest for Total Peace: The Political Thought of Roger Martin du Gard* (London, 1979); David L. Schalk, *Roger Martin du Gard; The Novelist and History* (Ithaca, 1967).

David L. Schalk

MASARYK, Jan. See *Biographical Dictionary of Internationalists*.

MASARYK, Thomas Garrigue (7 March 1850, Hodonin, Moravia, Austria [now Czechoslovakia] — 14 September 1937, Lány, Czechoslovakia). *Education*: Ph.D., Univ. of Vienna, 1876. *Career*: lecturer, Univ. of Vienna, 1878-82; professor of philosophy, Charles Univ., Prague, 1882-1914; member, Austrian parliament, 1891-93, 1907-14; chairman, Czechoslovak National Council in exile, 1914-18; first president of the Czechoslovak Republic, 1918-35; philosopher, educator, and statesman.

All powerful nations of Europe at the end of the nineteenth century were aggressively nationalistic and drifting toward oppression of peoples within their orbit. This was true in the Habsburg empire where German and Magyar ideas of national superiority did much to exacerbate the national feelings of Czechs and other Slavs throughout Central and Eastern Europe. For a young, brilliant, and dynamic intellectual such as Thomas Masaryk who, at the same time, was passionately devoted to the ideals of democracy and justice, it became virtually impossible not to get involved in the political struggles of the time.

Masaryk was first and foremost a philosopher. Philosophy, especially Plato's ideas of truth and justice, provided him with a set of propositions that he brought to bear in his public life. Dedicated to the principle of truthfulness in public life, he never hesitated to point out injustices such as the use by the Hungarian and Austrian governments of forged documents against their political adversaries in the famed Zagreb treason (1908) and Friedjung libel (1909) trials respectively. Similarly, in the notorious ritual murder case of Leopold Hilsner (1899), whose trial revived the medieval myth of Jewish ritual sacrifice, Masaryk did not hesitate to denounce the anti-Semitism fanned by influential circles in the monarchy. His zealousness in pursuit of the truth did not spare his co-nationals. He caused a sensation by denouncing as fakes several historical literary documents on which certain Czech nationalists based their nationalist claims.

Masaryk interpreted nationalism and the idea of the state in a democratic and nonaggressive spirit which recognized the right of other nations to an independent existence. Before 1914 Masaryk strove to save the multinational Austro-

Hungarian Empire by advocating its reorganization into a democratic federation of autonomous national societies in which the Slavic, Rumanian, and other peoples in the Habsburg Empire would be able to realize their national aspirations. He believed that such a reorganization held out hope for stability and peace in the region. When those efforts failed and after the outbreak of World War I, Masaryk turned to the idea of creating an independent Czechoslovakia that would subsequently enter a union of independent Central European republics. A declaration adopted in Philadelphia by a congress of national representatives on Masaryk's initiative in October 1918, proclaimed the desirability of such a union as a contribution "to the peace and welfare of the world."

After the collapse of the monarchy and the creation of a democratic Czechoslovak republic, Masaryk, as the first president of the country, advocated national reconciliation and international cooperation among the states of Central Europe. He tried to dissociate himself and his country from the squabbles of the various factions in European politics and to build, step by step, the union he envisaged in the Philadelphia declaration. But the advent of fascism with the concomitant spread of extreme nationalism preempted the plan.

In the universal realm, Masaryk, who was both an idealist and a practical politician, advocated a humane, liberal, and realistic approach to world problems based on support for the League of Nations. Together with his wartime companion and foreign minister in his government, +Eduard Beneš, Masaryk strove to make the League of Nations an effective instrument in promoting peace, collective security, and international justice.

Bibliography:

A. *Humanistic Ideals* (Lewisburg, PA, 1971); *The Making of a State: Memories and Observations 1914-1918* (New York, 1969); *The Meaning of Czech History* (Chapel Hill, NC, 1974); *The New Europe* (Lewisburg, PA, 1972).

B. A. van den Beld, *Humanity: The Political and Social Philosophy of Thomas G. Masaryk* (The Hague, 1976); Karel Čapek, *President Masaryk Tells His Story* (New York, 1935); Edward W. P. Newman, *Masaryk* (London, 1960); Paul Selver, *Masaryk: A Biography* (London, 1940); W. Preston Warren, *Masaryk's Democracy: A Philosophy of Scientific and Moral Culture* (Chapel Hill, NC, 1941); Petr Zenkl, *T. G. Masaryk and the Idea of European and World Federation* (Chicago, 1955); NYT, September 14, 1937; *Österreichisches Biographisches Lexikon, 1815-1850*, 6 (1975), 123-24.

Vratislav Pechota

MAURIN, Peter Aristide (9 May 1877, Oultet, France—15 May 1949, Newburgh, NY). *Education*: Licentiate, St. Joseph's Scholasticate, Paris, 1895. *Career*: teaching brother, Christian Brothers, 1895-1903; founder and editor, *The Catholic Worker*, 1933-49; lecturer and essayist.

Peter Maurin, of French peasant stock, was a reactionary social Catholic. Joining forces with an ardent crusading journalist and convert to Catholicism, *Dorothy Day, he founded the Catholic Worker movement. Since 1933, this movement has consistently inspired American Catholic social activists and pacifists.

Maurin, while a Christian Brother, joined both the Oeuvre des Cercles Catholiques, the French social Catholic movement founded by Albert de Mun and René de la Tour du Pin, and the Christian democratic Sillon of *Marc Sangnier. He emigrated to Saskatchewan in 1909 and later became an itinerant laborer wandering throughout much of eastern Canada and the United States. By the late 1920s, he had experienced a religious conversion which provided the ideological basis for the Catholic Worker movement. Communities were quickly established in major cities and rural locations throughout the United States and Canada. Until his death in 1949, Maurin remained associated with the movement, living at its rural and urban houses of hospitality, speaking throughout the United States, and preparing free verse ''Easy Essays'' for the movement's monthly newspaper, *The Catholic Worker*.

The Catholic Worker became the major force for Catholic pacifism in the United States. Condemning violence in all forms, the movement antagonized leading Catholic officials with its outright condemnation of both sides during the Spanish Civil War. Many who had been attracted to the movement by its demand for a cooperative and communitarian alternative to industrial capitalism left the Worker because of its condemnation of American participation in World War II. During that war, the Catholic Worker urged draft resistance and published many theological treatises exploring conscientious objection in the light of the Catholic Just War tradition. The movement administered a civilian alternative service camp for Catholic conscientious objectors at Stafford, New Hampshire. An uncompromising condemnation of the American nuclear bombing of Hiroshima and Nagasaki was published in its newspaper.

Maurin saw war as but one manifestation of the social disorder inevitably symptomatic and resulting from industrial capitalism. While participation in, or support of, war was never justifiable, war would be eliminated only with the total transformation of society into a free association of communities based on voluntary poverty and practicing ''cult, culture and cultivation.'' Maurin's Green Revolution was a variant of Christian anarchism, drawing not only from the traditions of French social Catholicism and English Distributism, but also from the writings of the communitarian anarchists *Pierre-Joseph Proudhon and *Peter Kropotkin.

After Maurin's death in 1949, Catholic Workers looked to his ''Easy Essays'' as the foundation for their movement, even as they cooperated more closely with the secular American Left. They drew from his writings the basis for their opposition to the Korean conflict, the arms race, civil defense drills and, most notably, the Vietnam War. During that conflict, several Catholic Workers founded the Catholic Peace Fellowship and Pax Christi. Others led in the formation of the New Catholic Left, especially active in draft and tax resistance, mass demonstrations, draft board raids, and direct action at induction stations and military industries. Though Maurin considered pacifism subordinate to and a result of Christian social transformation, his Catholic Worker has remained in the forefront of the American peace movement.

Bibliography:

A. *The Green Revolution: Easy Essays on Catholic Radicalism* (Fresno, CA, 1949).

B. Marc H. Ellis, *Peter Maurin: Prophet in the Twentieth Century* (New York and Ramsey, 1981); Anthony W. Novitsky, ''The Ideological Development of Peter Maurin's Green Revolution,'' Ph.D. Dissertation, State University of New York at Buffalo, 1976; Anthony W. Novitsky, ''Peter Maurin's Green Revolution: The Radical Implications of Reactionary Social Catholicism,'' *Review of Politics*, 37 (January, 1975), 83-103; Arthur Sheehan, *Peter Maurin: The Gay Believer* (Garden City, 1959); DAB, Supp. 4, 561-62.

C. Dorothy Day, Catholic Worker Collection, Archives, Marquette University Memorial Library, Milwaukee, WI.

Anthony W. Novitsky

MAY, Samuel Joseph (12 September 1797, Boston, MA—1 July 1871, Syracuse, NY). *Education*: B.A., Harvard Coll., 1817. *Career*: organizer, Windham County Connecticut Peace Society, 1826, New England Non-Resistance Society, 1838; Unitarian clergyman and peace lecturer.

Samuel Joseph May, a Unitarian minister and an educator, temperance advocate, and radical abolitionist, was also a leader in the antebellum peace crusade. Active in New England and New York state reform circles, May organized antiwar associations, lectured indefatigably on nonviolence, and used pacifist principles as the foundation of his varied benevolent activities. Throughout the pre-Civil War era the gentle and forgiving May was one of pacifism's most revered advocates.

By the mid-1820s, May had developed a fully articulated ideology of pacifism. Like his mentor *William Ellery Channing, May believed all men possessed a spark of divinity—a spark he wished to ignite. Pacifism, he was convinced, would help realize the kingdom of heaven on earth. In Brooklyn, Connecticut May helped organize the Windham County Peace Society which became a center of Connecticut's peace movement. After working with *William Lloyd Garrison, May broadened his pacifist activities by becoming an active member of the American Peace Society. Although he worked closely with the organization's moderates, May was dissatisfied with their unwillingness to condemn all violence and war. With Garrison and *Henry Clarke Wright he helped found the New England Non-Resistance Society in 1838. May supported the radicals because he believed the New Testament made all wars immoral; nonviolence was part of the new dispensation that had superseded the Mosaic code. But May remained on good terms with the moderates and worked actively on behalf of *Elihu Burritt's League of Universal Brotherhood. In a movement racked by ideological disputes, factionalism, and personal rancor, May shunned bickering in order to make his peace beliefs serviceable to all men.

After 1845 May transferred his benevolent activities to Syracuse, New York where he continued to labor for radical pacifism and abolitionism. May had always believed it was immoral and ineffectual to try ending slavery by violent means. But after the passage of the Fugitive Slave Law in 1851, May became more defiant and openly advocated disobeying the law. At local conventions May pledged to aid fugitive slaves in retaining their freedom. His house in Syracuse became a station on the underground railroad and May told his parishioners it was their moral duty to resist the new statute.

With the outbreak of civil war in 1861, May, like many other Garrisonians, condemned its violence but wanted to turn it into a war of liberation. Even though he eventually came to support the Union cause, he was deeply shaken by the carnage the conflict created. During Reconstruction May championed the Radical Republicans and fought to end segregation in New York state public schools.

May was one of the most likable and respected pacifists in antebellum America. *Theodore Parker aptly described him as a "philanthropist without cant" and a "Christian without bigotry." His advocacy of nonviolence centered around the simple belief in the transcendental divinity of all men. Throughout his fifty year reform career May was always motivated by the pacifist principles of love and reconciliation.

Bibliography:

A. *An Address delivered before the American Peace Society* (Boston, 1860); *Liberty or Slavery, the Only Question* (Syracuse, 1856).

B. Peter Brock, *Pacifism in the United States: From the Colonial Era to the First World War* (Princeton, 1968); Jane H. Pease and William H. Pease, *Bound with Them in Chains* (Westport, CT, 1972); DAB 6, 447-48.

C. Antislavery Collection, Boston Public Library.

Jayme A. Sokolow

MAYOUX, François (24 June 1882, Beaulieu-sur-Sonnette, Charente, France—21 July 1967, La Ciotat, Bouches du Rhône): **MAYOUX, Marie** (24 April 1878, Lesterps, Charente, France—16 June 1969, La Ciotat, Bouches du Rhône). *Careers*: schoolteachers; leaders in the schoolteachers' union (Fedération des syndicats d'instituteurs); pacifists.

The federation of schoolteachers' unions was among a very small number of French labor unions to take an early and unequivocal stand against World War I and, in particular, against the participation of working-class organizations in the war effort. While unionized schoolteachers represented a small minority of the profession, the French government's resistance to their union activity had accustomed them to an adversarial relationship with public authorities. Since schoolteachers such as the Mayoux considered themselves part of the organized working class, their pacifism had developed in the context of prewar syndicalist struggles against the state.

As early as June 1915, when pacifist sentiment in France had yet to find public expression, Marie Mayoux convened the remaining leaders of the federation of schoolteachers' unions in Tours for the purpose of taking a public stand against the war. On July 1, 1915, they issued a manifesto entitled "Assez de Sang verse" ("Enough Spilled Blood"), calling on the Allied countries to take the lead in bringing about a negotiated end to the war. At the first wartime meeting of the Confédération Générale du Travail (CGT) in Paris on August 15, 1915, representatives of unionized schoolteachers joined the metal workers' union (led by *Alphonse Merrheim) and the union of barrel-makers (led by *Albert Bourderon) in forging the antiwar minority within the French syndicalist movement.

Throughout the war, the illegal pamphleteering of the Mayoux couple contributed to the wide dissemination of pacifist views—views which were suppressed not only by the government but by the leadership of the Socialist party and of the labor confederation. Both Marie and François Mayoux also wrote for the frequently-censored weekly of the schoolteachers' federation, *L'École Emancipée* (1910-15) and its successor, *L'École de la Fédération* (1915-19) as well as for the anarchist journal *Ce Qu'Il Faut Dire* (1916–17), published by *Sébastien Fauré. In late 1915 François Mayoux joined the Comité pour la reprise des relations internationales (Committee for the Restoration of International Relations), the important pressure group born of the Zimmerwald Conference, whose pacifist internationalism threatened the official leadership of both the Confédération générale du travail and the Socialist party. By 1917 striking evidence of war-weariness in France led the government to try to silence militant pacifists such as the Mayoux. In their pamphlet, *Les Instituteurs syndicalistes et la guerre*, (May 1917), they welcomed the physical hardships of prolonged warfare as harbingers of an early peace. In July 1917 the Mayoux were indicted for pacifist activity and suspended from teaching. Both were tried for "defeatist" propaganda, found guilty, and sentenced to six months in prison. On appeal, the sentence was increased to two years. Though released in the amnesty of April 1919, they were not allowed to resume teaching until October 1924.

Repelled by the reformist tendency of the Socialist party, the Mayoux couple resigned their membership in November 1919. Their refusal to countenance class collaboration at the dawn of a revolutionary era led them to a newly-formed Communist party, from which they were expelled in 1922. In the immediate postwar years the Mayoux were highly critical of the CGT leaders' willingness to seek reforms in anticipation of an economic recovery. François Mayoux promoted the break-up of the CGT into reformist and revolutionary branches. When this schism was realized in December 1921, the Mayoux joined the more radical wing, from which they were excluded in 1929. Thereafter, they devoted their efforts to the creation of an independent schoolteachers' union.

Bibliography:

A. *Les Instituteurs syndicalistes et la Guerre* (Dignac, 1917); *Nôtre Affaire* (Epône, 1918).

B. Robert Brécy, *Le Mouvement syndical en France, 1871-1921* (Paris, 1963); Max Ferré, *Histoire du Mouvement syndicaliste révolutionnaire chez les Instituteurs* (Paris, 1955); Jean Maitron, ed., *Dictionnaire biographique du Mouvement ouvrier français* (vol. 14, Paris, 1976); Alfred Rosmer, *Le Mouvement ouvrier pendant la première Guerre mondiale* (vol. 2, Paris, 1959).

Ioannis Sinanoglou

MAYREDER, Rosa Obermayer (30 November 1858, Vienna—19 January 1938, Vienna). *Education*: self-taught. *Career*: feminist organizer, writer, painter, and pacifist.

With the publication of *A Survey of the Woman Problem* (1905) and *Sex and Culture* (1923), Rosa Mayreder established herself as the leading theorist of the Austrian independent bourgeois women's movement. An active feminist, she helped organize, in 1893, the General Austrian Women's Society and served as its vice-president until 1903. From 1899-1900 she was co-editor and co-founder of the Austrian journal entitled *Documente der Frauen*, which postulated radical legal, economic, and social reforms for women of all social classes.

In 1894 Mayreder, along with *Bertha von Suttner, belonged to the Vienna Ethical Society, which advocated the promulgation of humane ethics based on scientific findings and the idea of peace and international rapprochement. Beginning in 1915, Mayreder lectured and wrote against war and in support of internationalism. She became a member of the Austrian Peace Society, founded by Suttner in 1891, and the Women's International League for Peace and Freedom (WILPF), founded in 1919. After World War I she served as vice-president of the Austrian section of the WILPF as well as a member of the International Executive of the organization.

In her article "Women and War" (1915), she criticized the nationalism of women in warring countries that ultimately led to a split within the women's movement at the International Congress of Women at The Hague in April, 1915. In organizing women internationally, Mayreder hoped to develop a political force for the realization of peace. In her lecture "Women and Internationalism" (written in 1916 but prohibited from publication until after World War I), she expressed the view that the female principle of preservation of life was opposed to the inherent laws of war and that the prevention of armed conflict must be the task of women who found themselves in a world created by men.

Between the wars, Mayreder continued her pacifist endeavors. In 1921 she participated in the organization of an international peace congress in Vienna. Three years later her WILPF branch, in cooperation with the New Women's Club, organized an exhibition of antimilitarist toys. In 1928 she spoke before the Vienna Peace Society on the topic of "Man and Humanity," refuting the idea, popular in chauvinistic circles at the time, that pacifism was a sign of decline in an effeminate and dying culture. In 1936 she was one of the last women openly to oppose militarism.

Rosa Mayreder continued the tradition of Austrian pacifism after the death of Bertha von Suttner in 1914. Her criticism of military conflicts and her pacifist efforts were the consequence of her analysis of patriarchal domination. By pointing out the connections between individual psychological and social mechanisms, she explained war as the final consequence of aggressive competition of a "primitive and dominating masculinity." Indebted to John Stuart Mill's liberalism and to ideas of evolution and humanism, she considered the emancipation of both sexes and the creative influence of women in all aspects of society a precondition for a peaceful evolution.

Bibliography:

A. *Die Frau und der Internationalismus* (Vienna, 1921); *Geschlecht und Kultur* (Jena, 1923); *Zur Kritik der Weiblichkeit* (Jena, 1905, Engl. trans., *A Survey of the Woman Problem* (London, 1912).

B. Hanna Schnedl, ''Rosa Mayreder—Eine Sympathisantin des Lebendigen,'' in Hanna Schnedl, ed., *Rosa Mayreder Zur Kritik der Weiblichkeit* (Munich, 1982), 9-32; Hanna Schnedle-Bubeniček, ''Grenzgängerin der Moderne. Studien zur Emanzipation in Texten von Rosa Mayreder,'' in *Das ewige Klischee* (Autorinnengruppe Uni Wien, ed., Vienna, 1981), 179-205.

Hanna Schnedl-Bubeniček

MAZZOLENI, Angelo (13 June 1838, Milan, Italy—18 September 1894, Milan). *Education*: Univ. of Pavia. *Career*: member, Chamber of Deputies, co-founder, Unione Lombarda per la pace, 1887-88; lawyer and peace activist.

Angelo Mazzoleni, trained in law, grew to adulthood in the exciting years when the movement for Italian unification achieved its goals. Mazzoleni participated actively and enthusiastically as a volunteer in two of Giuseppe Garibaldi's expeditions to Sicily (1860) as well as in the intellectual ferment as a follower of *Carlo Cattaneo and Giuseppe Ferrari. Politically his sympathies were republican; but accepting the realities of a constitutional monarchy, Mazzoleni committed his pen to studying issues which would produce a morally and socially healthy new Italy. He published on a wide range of topics—the relationship between individual and family, public education, civil marriage, the quality of Italian life, tariff policies, and the complex problem of church-state relations. Twice he was elected to the Chamber of Deputies (1874 and 1888) from Milan representing the Radical platform, but his essentially philosophical personality was not well adapted to the sinuous political manipulations of Chamber hallways. His distaste for political games did not prevent him from attacking the expansionist policies of Francesco Crispi who became a bitter enemy. Mazzoleni raged against foreign adventures by a country that had so many unfilled domestic needs.

With Professor Francesco Vigano he created the Unione Lombarda per la pace in 1887-88, a Milanese group that began life by active participation in local and regional elections, lobbying for candidates who opposed foreign expansion. Most of his remaining years were devoted to the Italian and European peace movements. He published long pamphlets, organized and participated in congresses in Italy, proselytized among Italian intellectuals, helped establish the International Peace Bureau (Berne), and joined the labors of the Interparliamentary Union. He remained firm in his convictions that arbitration and legal relationships among states could be substituted for war and that the current European state system could be molded into a permanent peace keeping organization to reduce the size and cost of standing armies. To Mazzoleni, the time had come to organize the peace of Europe predicted by Giuseppe Mazzini once the wars of national liberation were completed.

His death in 1894 was a shock to his friends and associates, and to them and all peace activists, he left an enormous collection of pamphlets and books on peace, donated to the Risorgimento Museum in Milan.

Bibliography:

A. *La famiglia nei rapporti coll'individuo e colla società* (Milan, 1870); *Giuseppe Ferrari, i suoi tempi e le sue opere* (Milan 1877); *La guerre; est-elle necessaire*? (Berne,

1892); *Il popolo Italiano; studi politici* (Milan, 1873); *L'Italia nel movimento per la pace* (Milan, 1891).

B. *Libertas, Justitia Pax* (Milan, 1895).

Sandi E. Cooper

MCNAUGHTON, Violet (11 November 1879, Borden, England—3 February 1968, Saskatoon, Saskatchewan, Canada). *Career*: founding member and first president, Women's Grain Growers Association (Saskatchewan), and Women's Section of the Canadian Council of Agriculture; journalist; political and women's rights activist.

As a wartime suffragette, Violet McNaughton sought to reconcile the pacifist program of the Women's International League for Peace and Freedom (WILPF) with the cooperative spirit she was promoting in western Canadian society. After World War I, Harris Turner, a disabled veteran who tried to use his *Western Producer* to instruct farmers about the ''real'' motives guiding militarists and diplomats, invited her to use the women's page to create a grass roots movement for peace.

Inspired by the writings of the WILPF and *Laura Jamieson, McNaughton argued that the masses must develop a will to peace through the adoption of the same cooperative spirit that was required for successful living on the desolate prairies. On her page she publicized hopeful international signs like the Kellogg-Briand Peace Pact and serialized books denouncing the horrors of war. School textbooks, movies, and pictures which purportedly stressed the events more than the follies of war were resolutely condemned. Equally objectionable were imperial vestiges like Empire Day and Rule Britannia. However, her most sustained attack was on the cadet movement. Although she managed to persuade a number of schools to abolish military uniforms and rifle shooting, the cadet corps remained as an inexpensive means of physical education. She also organized one-day peace conferences at which speakers denounced defense expenditures and advanced schemes for teaching people to live in the spirit of cooperative internationalism.

By 1930 McNaughton had a large readership and following. About 10,000 farmers had been persuaded to subscribe to the WILPF's *Pax International*. She personally organized the collection of 17,917 of the half a million signatures on a petition supporting the World Disarmament Conference in 1932. When the conference failed and the realities of the Manchurian crisis became apparent, the movement faltered. In times of depression few farmers could afford a subscription and fewer still seemed interested in continuing the fight against militarism in the schools. As World War II approached, the discouraged McNaughton focused more on her first love, the rights and opportunities for farmer's wives, although she remained a committed pacifist. She had, in the end, at least caused many to question and challenge the Canadian symbols of militarism.

Bibliography:

B. Donald Page, ''The Development of a Western Canadian Peace Movement'' in S. M. Trofimenkoff ed., *The Twenties in Western Canada* (Ottawa, 1972), 75-106.

C. Violet McNaughton Papers, Saskatchewan Archives Board, Saskatoon.

Donald M. Page

MEAD, Edwin Doak. See *Biographical Dictionary of Internationalists.*

MEAD, Lucia True Ames. See *Biographical Dictionary of Internationalists.*

MECHELIN, Leopold (Leo) (24 November 1839, Hamina, Finland—26 January 1914, Helsinki). *Education*: B.A. Helsinki Univ., 1860, Dr. jur., 1873. *Career*: professor of law, Helsinki Univ., 1874-81; senator, writer, human rights advocate, and peace movement organizer.

In 1873 Leo Mechelin published his dissertation, *Om stats förbund och statsunioner (On Unions of States*), in which he argued that the concept of "humanizing wars" was absurd, because all wars were inhuman. He argued that no international problem had been solved by war and that every war left political and economic contradictions which contained the seeds of new and larger wars. The best guarantee for world peace, he believed, was independent states and the expansion of democracy. In his work "Om en internationall domstol" (On an International Court of Law), which also attracted attention in 1873, he proposed that an international court of law be founded for peacefully solving disputes between states.

Leo Mechelin was one of the most well-known and influential Finns of the early twentieth century. He wanted to combine the aims of the national fight for justice with those of the peace movement. At the eighteenth World Peace Congress in Stockholm in 1910, he succeeded in placing Finland's battle for independence on the agenda. After returning from Stockholm, he helped establish a peace union, Fredsvannerna i Helsingfors (Swedish Friends of Peace in Helsinki). He also represented Finland at the Geneva Peace Congress of 1912 and convinced the delegates to establish an international committee to investigate the causes of wars since 1815. He made a strong plea at the congress that international law and the principles of international justice be applied equally to all nations. The following year, he helped chair the Moscow Peace Congress. In recognition of his peace work, Mechelin was made a member of the Institut international de la paix (International Institute of Peace), established by the monarch of Monaco in 1913.

Mechelin was not a pacifist in the true meaning of the word. In his opinion total disarmament was not possible until the creation of an international legal system which guaranteed all states and peoples basic security. He recognized that peace and international security could not be guaranteed simply by international contracts; as long as ultra-nationalism and militarism dominated some nations, international war was a possibility. Mechelin examined the questions of war and peace as a politician and a lawyer. He saw the peace movement as one part of Finland's legal battle for independence. The peace organization he led neither aimed at getting a large number of members nor at influencing crowds of people. It sought to study war, educate, and promote specific social and political goals. Long after his death in 1914, Leo Mechelin continued to hold a central place in Finnish peace research. His work has also found a sympathetic response and many successors in modern peace research.

Bibliography:

A. *Om statsförbund och statsunioner* (Helsinki, 1873).

B. Tekla Hultin, *Leo Mechelin* (Helsinki, 1900); T. Rein, *Leo Mechelin* (Helsinki, 1915).

Kalevi Kalemaa
Trans. by Oliver and Rita Whitehead

Meijer-Wichmann, Clara Gertrud (17 August 1885, Hamburg, Germany—15 February 1922, The Hague). *Education*: doctorate in law, Univ. of Utrecht, 1912. *Career*: solicitor, Utrecht, 1913; assistant director, School for Social Work, Amsterdam, 1913-14; Central Bureau of Statistics (Juridical-statistical division), The Hague, 1914-22.

Clara Meijer-Wichmann was the daughter of a German professor of geology at the University of Utrecht. She was a very sensitive and precocious child, fascinated by history and philosophy and driven by a desire for greatness. Even as a teenager she had begun to consider a multitude of social, religious, and philosophical questions. The same passion for understanding and for discovering the truth, without ever being dogmatic, also characterized her later work, which consisted of a great number of essays and journalistic writings.

Throughout her short life she was aware of a tension between reflection and action. Philosophical scepticism always tempered her idealistic outlook. She became a social activist only gradually (in addition to being a social philosopher) and she choose—with some hesitation—law over history for a university education and professional career. She already had ten years of activism behind her, mainly in the women's movement but increasingly also in the socialist and syndicalist movements, when, in 1919, she helped to found the Committee on Crime and Punishment, and wrote its first manifesto. The Committee agitated not for mere prison reform (most of its seven members, including her husband J.B. Meijer, had first-hand experience of prison life as a result of their antimilitarist convictions), but for a radical rethinking of the very notions of crime and punishment and a complete overhaul of the penal system which would have to go with it. In place of the traditional doctrine that evil had to be met with evil and that punishment was necessary for purposes of retribution, deterrence, or improvement of the individual, she urged the adoption of a principle which attempted to combat evil with compassion and understanding. Her pathbreaking, authoritative work on criminal law made her, even in the eyes of established scholars, Holland's most original thinker on the subject.

Clara Meijer-Wichmann's deep insights into the root causes of social problems and concern over the relationship between means and ends were also applied to war. In her address to the National Congress of the Dutch Committee of Women for a Durable Peace at The Hague in 1917, she stressed the fallacy of much conventional wisdom on war, the need to struggle with more refined and spiritual tools than brute force, and, above all, the need for a spiritual revolution in the individual and society at large, before meaningful social reform could take place.

In the same year she first met *Bart de Ligt, on whom she had a profound influence. She joined the Bond van Christen-Socialisten (Union of Christian Socialists) (BvCS), which was actively involved in social struggle, especially against militarism and violence. Although not a Christian, she was attracted by the BvCS's insistence that revolution was required not only in social and political institutions, but also in the spiritual life of the individual. She became a member of the executive committee of the International Anti-Militarist Bureau as well, when this was founded in 1920. Her discussion with *Henriëtte Roland Holst in 1921 on the role of violence and coercion in revolution became famous as a classic exposé of the nonviolent position.

Clara Meijer-Wichmann concluded from her study of history and felt intuitively that actions undertaken in the pursuit of an objective must be in accordance with that objective, otherwise it would remain elusive. Bad means will not achieve good ends. She applied this general principle of human and social life to the numerous reforms she advocated. She refused, however, to accept nonviolence as an absolute dogma. In advocating spiritual resistance (very much akin to *Gandhi's concept of soul-force) and nonviolent means of struggle, she was concerned about pushing back as far as possible the moment when violence had to be used and demonstrating that alternatives were available and had to be systematically investigated.

With all her brilliance and prominence Clara Meijer-Wichmann remained a very modest person, the softness of her character and her timid appearance reflecting her dislike of force and violence. Yet she became, involuntarily, the center of everything she involved herself in, and she deeply affected all who met her. Bart de Ligt called her one of the most gifted women of her time.

Bibliography:

A. *Anti-Militarismus und Gewalt* (Vienna, 1922); *Bevrijdingo Opstellen* (Arnhem, 1924); *Inleiding tot de philosophie der samenleving* (Haarlem, 1917); *Mensch en maatschappij* (Arnhem, 1923, includes bibliography of her writings); *Misdaad, straf en maatschappij* (Utrecht, 1931); "Soziale Revolution und Gewalt. Ein Briefwechsel (with Henriëtte Roland-Holst)," in Franz Kobler, ed., *Gewalt und Gewaltlosigkeit* (Zurich, 1928, reprinted, New York, 1971), 129-39; *Tegen de heerschende opvattingen omtrent misdaad en straf* (Amsterdam, 1919); *Vrouw en maatschappij* (Utrecht, 1936); *De vrouw en de vredesbeweging i.v.m. de ontwikkeling der wereldbeschouwing* (The Hague, 1917).

B. Thom Holterman Hans Ramaer, eds., *Bevrijding, Een Keuze uit het werk van Clara Meijer-Wichmann* (Amsterdam, 1979); Maria Hunink et al., eds. *Voor Arthur Lehning* (Baarn, 1979), 137-62; Gernot Jochheim, *Antimilitaristische Aktionstheorie, Soziale Revolution und Soziale Verteidigung* (Assen/Amsterdam/Frankfurt, 1977), 211-20; Bart de Ligt, "Clara Meijer-Wichmann," *Kerk, cultuur en samenleving* (Arnhem, 1925), 336-39; Bart de Ligt, "Clara Meijer-Wichmann als verdedigster der menschelijkheid," *Bevrijding* (June, 1931), 4 pp.; J.B. Meijer, "Biografie," in Clara Meijer-Wichmann,

Inleiding tot de philosophie der samenleving (2nd ed., Haarlem, 1925), 5-76; H. Roland Holst-van der Schalk, ''Clara Meijer-Wichmann herdacht,'' in Clara Meijer-Wichmann, *Vrouw en maatschappij* (Utrecht, 1936), 11-54.

Peter van den Dungen

MEINL, Julius (18 January 1869, Vienna—16 May 1944, Alt-Prerau, Austria). *Education*: Vienna Commercial Academy. *Career*: businessman.

At the age of twenty, Julius Meinl went to work in his father's food store in Vienna. By 1914 he had transformed the business into the largest food store chain in Austria and one of the largest in central Europe. As part of his business education, he spent some time as a young man working in grocery firms in England where he made many friends and acquaintances. Perhaps his positive English experience played a role in turning him into an opponent of World War I from its beginning. More important, in fueling his opposition to the war, however, was his experience in providing food for the population and for the Austro-Hungarian army.

Beginning in 1915, Meinl actively advocated an anti-war policy. In that same year, he founded the Österreichische Politische Gesellschaft (Austrian Political Association) as a forum for discussing an Austrian peace policy. In the society, he worked together with +Heinrich Lammasch, Joseph Redlich, and *Friedrich W. Foerster. After the accession to the Habsburg throne of Emperor Charles in 1916, Meinl intensified his activities. These reached their high point in June and July 1917, when his efforts to build a peace cabinet narrowly failed. Meinl used his economic connections to make contact with foreign pacifists, above all *Bide Jong van Beek en Donk, *Wilhelm Mühlon and Foerster. Through George D. Herron he sought contact with American political figures and wrote numerous memoranda in which he presented his ideas on a separate Austrian peace treaty. These ideas came to nothing. After the end of the First World War, Meinl, on behalf of the Austrian government, was influential in obtaining foreign help in providing the Austrian population with food. In his later years, Meinl no longer took an active interest in politics.

Bibliography:

B. Heinrich Benedikt, *Die Friedensaktion der Meinlgruppe 1917/1918* (Graz, 1961); *Neue österreichische Biographie*, XVI, 140-52; *Österreichisches Biographicsches Lexikon, 1815-1950* VI, 196; NYT, August 30, 1944, 17.

Fritz Fellner
Trans. by Solomon Wank

MELLO FRANCO, Afranio de. See *Biographical Dictionary of Internationalists*.

MÉRIC, Victor (10 May 1876, Marseilles, Bouches-du-Rhône, France—10 October 1933, Paris). *Education*: Coll. of Toulon. *Career*: journalist, novelist, anarchist, socialist, and communist.

All his life, Victor Méric remained a rebel with a cause. His family background was no doubt responsible: his grandfather Charles had been sent to prison in 1851 by the government of Louis Napoleon because of his ardent republicanism, and his father, Victor Sylvain, had served as a Radical-Socialist senator from the Var Department and opponent of Georges Clemenceau. As a youngster, Méric showed signs of literary ability and a lively imagination. But the three years he spent in the army as a young man gave him a permanent dislike of the discipline and conformity of military life so that he was led towards anarchism and antimilitarism. The Dreyfus Affair only added to his intense dislike of the army as an institution. Drifting to Paris in the 1890s, he lived a bohemian life in the company of dissolute poets and made a bare living as a proof reader and petty thief. But his literary talents and unruly temperament soon brought him into contact with anarchists such as *Sébastien Faure, editor of *Le Libertaire*, to which Méric contributed frequently.

When the Association internationale antimilitariste was founded in 1904, Méric took an active role in spreading its propaganda against war by making an extensive speaking tour of France. Méric soon joined *Gustave Hervé to found the irreverent weekly *La Guerre sociale* (1906) and with Henri Fabre to establish the iconoclastic magazine **Les Hommes du jour* (1907). Méric's pungent columns attacking leading political and military figures cost him more than a year in prison, but this only intensified his disrespect for established authority. An active member of the French Socialist party (SFIO) after 1906, Méric attended several party congresses where he supported Hervé's call for a general strike in the event of war.

Nonetheless, when war did break out in 1914, Méric reluctantly went on active duty and spent more than four years in the trenches as a military engineer. His first-hand experience with death and destruction reaffirmed his antimilitarist sentiments, so that after 1918 he worked harder than ever in the cause of peace. Infatuated with Bolshevism and Lenin, Méric supported the cause of the Third International at the SFIO Congress at Tours in 1920, quickly rising to power in the new French Communist party. He wrote regularly for its newspaper and twice ran unsuccessfully for office under its banner. Méric's writings lashed out at the Bloc National, its militarism and hard-line policy towards Germany.

Méric's inability to accept discipline, however, drove him from the party by 1923 and he returned to the socialist fold. During the 1920s he pursued his career in journalism, contributing to the nonconformist *Le Merle blanc* and the SFIO monthly *La Nouvelle Revue socialiste*. He grew increasingly concerned that a new world war, born of the injustices of the Versailles settlement, was looming. Méric feared that a second world war would prove even more disastrous than the first because modern airplanes could destroy civilian targets with bombs and poison gas. Using his novels and the pages of the Parisian daily *Le Soir*, Méric campaigned against the threat of aerochemical warfare, describing in hideous detail the horrors that it would produce. In 1930 he organized the Ligue internationale des combattants de la paix (International League of Fighters for Peace) to fight against war and founded a newspaper, *La Patrie humaine*, to spread his message. Through countless meetings and demonstrations, the league repeated the warning that war meant the total devastation of Europe and that all means, especially disarmament and revision of the Versailles Treaty, were necessary to forestall it. Méric's strenuous lecture tours and prolific literary output undermined his health and eventually killed him. Despite factionalism and quarrels over strategy, his organization and ideals survived into the 1930s, only to be crushed by the outbreak of World War II, which he had striven so hard to prevent.

Bibliography:

A. *Coulisses et tréteaux* (Paris, 1931); *Le Crime des vieux* (Paris, 1927); *La ''Der des der''* (Paris, 1929); *Fraîche et gazeuse: La guerre qui revient* (Paris, 1932); *Lettre à un conscrit* (Paris, 1905); *A Travers la jungle politique et littéraire* (Paris, 1930).

B. *Victor Méric, sa vie, son oeuvre, par ses amis* (Paris, 1934); James Friguglietti, ''Victor Méric: The Evolution of a Pacifist,'' in *France and North America. L'Entre Deux Guerres. The State of Democracy. Proceedings of the Fourth Symposium of French-American Studies. April 7-11, 1975* (Lafayette, LA, 1980), 99-110.

James Friguglietti

MERRHEIM, Alphonse Adolphe (7 May 1871, La Madeleine, Nord, France—22 October 1925, Paris). *Education*: primary school. *Career*: coppersmith, secretary, Federation of Metalworkers, 1904-23; author, revolutionary syndicalist leader, and antimilitarist.

Alphonse Merrheim, the son of a coppersmith, was born near the industrial center of Lille and trained in his father's trade. Very early, he became involved in the workers' movement in the Nord, first as a Guesdist socialist and then as a revolutionary syndicalist. In 1904 he became secretary of the Federation of Metalworkers and moved to Paris to direct the union. Like so many syndicalists, Merrheim resented the army and war. The army, he believed, attempted to inculcate patriotism in working class recruits and then forced them to defend the interests of the liberal capitalist state. Moreover, the army frequently broke up strikes.

Active in the Confédération générale du travail (General Confederation of Labor) (CGT), whose leadership shared his antimilitarism, Merrheim introduced a resolution at the 1908 Congress of Marseilles which became the organization's official statement on war. The resolution proclaimed that ''workers will respond to a declaration of war with a declaration of the revolutionary general strike.'' In addition, Merrheim was the first revolutionary syndicalist leader to warn that the European nations were heading towards a general war. In 1909, and especially in 1911 he studied the European arms race and military budgets, and predicted, in a famous series of articles, ''L'Approche de la guerre,'' in *La Vie Ouvrière*, that England and Germany would fight each other and drag the other European nations into the conflict. He urged workers to prepare themselves to oppose mobilization and he called for a general strike as their response.

When war did come in August 1914, however, neither Merrheim nor the CGT called for a general strike. For +Léon Jouhaux, secretary-general of the labor confederation, and a majority of the CGT leaders, fear of government repression against the organized workers was an important factor in their actions. So, too, was their Jacobin tradition and hostility to German monarchism. Merrheim was too stunned, too isolated, too long involved in trade unionism, and, initially too fearful to counsel a general strike. He could not remain silent long, however, and gradually disassociated himself from his nation's war effort and broke with most members of the CGT Executive Committee. Early in the war, he emerged as the leading spokesman in the CGT for an antimilitarist and pacifist program.

In September, when Jouhaux formally joined France's *union sacrée* against the German attack, Merrheim criticised the decision and temporarily took control of the CGT, since the secretary-general's actions were personal and could not, as Merrheim argued, officially involve or implicate the entire labor confederation. Throughout the first year of the war Merrheim continued his criticism of the *union sacrée* policy of the CGT's Executive Committee. He was especially angry that the committee refused even to respond to an invitation from Scandinavian socialists to attend a meeting of neutral socialists in Copenhagen. *Pierre Monatte, Merrheim's close friend and fellow peace advocate, resigned from the Executive Committee over this issue. Merrheim remained on the Committee, however, because he preferred to exercise his influence and leverage from within the labor confederation. He became an important member of a band of peace advocates which gathered at the offices of Monatte's review, *La Vie Ouvrière*; at the same time, he was able to attend the February 1915 London Conference of socialists from the Allied nations. He attended the meeting in order to present the "minority" position against the war.

On May 1, 1915, Merrheim outlined his peace program in a special pacifist issue of the Federation of Metalworkers' official journal, *L'Union des Métaux*. In the lead article he demanded "not a militarist peace with forced annexations, not a peace with imperialist conquests, but a peace based upon the following principles: no annexations; political and economic independence for all nations; disarmament; obligatory arbitration [of international disputes]." "This is enough!" he concluded, "This war is not our war."

Although Merrheim could not move Jouhaux or the CGT's Executive Committee from their prowar position, his pacifist campaign attracted other labor federations to his side. Among them were those representing teachers, leather and hide workers, ceramic workers, hatters, and brewery workers.

Merrheim also linked his pacifist efforts in France with an international antiwar movement. Along with *Albert Bourderon, who represented French socialists, Merrheim attended in September 5-8, 1915, the Zimmerwald Conference. The conference pointed up the important limits to his pacifism. At Zimmerwald, Vladimir Lenin challenged Merrheim and the entire conference to break with the Second International and establish a new, revolutionary Third International. Lenin also argued that the Zimmerwald meeting should call for an immediate general strike of the masses against the war. Merrheim answered Lenin privately that he was at Zimmerwald not to start a new international or a social revolution but merely to utter "the cry of my tortured conscience to the workers of all countries, so that they could direct themselves in a common action against the war." At the conference, therefore, Merrheim supported the majority pacifist, nonrevolutionary resolutions which urged an end to the war and called upon workers to reorganize and "begin the struggle for peace." The conference left the specific tactics to be worked out in individual countries.

Merrheim did not argue for peace at any price or a unilateral French surrender. Germany, he argued, should evacuate the invaded territories; England, too, should abandon the German colonies it had seized. He opposed any attempt to organize a revolutionary general strike during the war, for he did not believe that workers were ready for such an action. Throughout the rest of the war, Merrheim urged an end to hostilities based on these principles. Ironically, he believed that the Russian Revolution and a separate Russian peace would only prolong the conflict since German troops would now be free to concentrate on the western front. He rejected the Russian Revolution also for ideological reasons—as a revolutionary syndicalist he did not want labor unions subordinated to any political party—and found +Woodrow Willson's Fourteen Point program for peace more to his liking. Merrheim's antirevolutionary pacifism was a significant factor in guiding many French workers to a nonrevolutionary left position during and after the war.

Bibliography:

A. *Amsterdam ou Moscou* (Paris, 1921); *La Leçon des faits* (Paris, 1918); *L'Organisation patronale* (Paris, n.d.); *La Metallurgie: son origin et son development* (Paris, 1913); *La Revolution economique* (Paris, 1919).

B. Nicholas Papayanis, "Collaboration and Pacifism in France During World War I," *Francia*, Band 5 (1977), 425-51.

C. Alphonse Merrheim Letters, Marx-Lenin Institute, Moscow.

Nicholas Papayanis

MERTENS, Carl (9 March 1902, Kassel, Germany—17 October 1932, between Fontainebleau and Paris, France). *Education*: grammar school; education as a book retailer. *Career*: novelist, poet, journalist, and pacifist.

The youthful prejudices of Carl Mertens, the son of a Prussian soldier and police commissioner, led him into several rightist paramilitary and violently antirepublican organizations that flourished in Germany after the defeat in World War I. Imbued with the brutal spirit fostered by these nationalist organizations, he even beat up an Upper Silesian teacher who was suspected of having friendly ties with Poland. Yet in the mid-1920s, after returning to Germany from two years abroad as a reporter in Italy and Switzerland, Mertens found his way into the peace movement. His efforts to expose Germany's secret rearmament and preparations for war caused him to be ostracized as a "traitor to his country" and to be the subject of thousands of defamatory articles.

Following the election of Paul von Hindenburg to the presidency of the Weimar

Republic in 1925, an event that Mertens considered an expression of the growing power of reactionary forces in Germany, and shocked by the experiences of his own previous political activities, Mertens published, at great danger to his own life, a series of sensational articles in *Weltbühne*. The articles exposed assassinations of "traitors" by extreme nationalist groups, the existence of the secret army (Schwarze Reichswehr), and the goals and organization of the patriotic associations Vaterländische Verbände. Appearing in book form under the title *Verschwörer und Fememörder* (1926), these reports and other disclosures by Mertens about the anticonstitutional machinations of the paramilitary organizations led to lively parliamentary debates, to investigations by the Reichstag, and to a series of Vehmic murder trials.

Just prior to Germany's entrance into the League of Nations in 1926, Mertens further alienated the right-wing forces by contributing to *Die deutsche Militärpolitik seit 1918*. The book contained documents about Germany's illegal rearmament, about the close ties between the army and right-wing associations, about the plans of the army command for an attack on Poland and Czechoslovakia, and about the internal political threat posed by the militaristic groups. Mertens also succeeded in infiltrating several highly secret meetings in which leaders of the extremely nationalistic veteran's organization, Stahlhelm, representatives of the army, and executives from the airplane industry not only reached agreement on the military-political basis for a war against Poland, but also worked out a long term strategy to bring about the fall of the Republic and the conquest of Europe. Mertens disclosed these plans in *Menschheit*, published in July, 1927, and concluded that the army should be disbanded because it contributed to the ever-present danger of civil war and obstructed the efforts towards worldwide disarmament.

Fearing judicial and political persecution because of his revelations, Mertens went into exile, living at different times in Austria, Switzerland, and France. In Paris he became one of the important co-workers of *Friedrich W. Foerster, for whom he served as secretary for a while. In September 1927 Mertens and Foerster submitted to the meeting of the League of Nations in Geneva a pamphlet entitled *Le Réarmement clandestin de l'Allemagne*, which documented the discrepancy between German Foreign Minister +Gustav Stresemann's statements about Germany's disarmament and the actual facts. Stresemann, who received the Nobel Peace Prize in 1926, denied the charges of secret rearmament and called Foerster and Mertens "liars and rogues."

During the late 1920s, Mertens continued to examine the military-political and industrial-technical preparations Germany was making for war while it was concurrently demanding disarmament by France and other nations. He urged his fellow Germans to oppose aggression and to resist the government-sponsored propaganda which portrayed Germany as threatened by France and Poland. In the *Zeit*, published by Foerster since 1930, Mertens emphasized the growing foreign mistrust concerning the secret rearmament efforts and challenged the government's arguments that its military expenditures were strictly for defensive purposes. Mertens met an early and untimely end in an auto accident on a dark road from Fontainebleau to Paris.

Bibliography:

A. *Die deutsche Militärpolitik seit 1918*, with Otto Lehmann-Rüssbüldt and Konrad Widerhold (Berlin, 1926); *Ein Dokument zur Reichswehr—und Stahlhelmpolitik* (Wiesbaden, 1927); *Der Kommende Krieg* (Genf, 1927); *La Préparation de la guerre en Allemagne: Faits, chiffres, commentaires, conclusion*, with F.W. Foerster (Paris, 1927); *Reichswehr oder Landesverteidigung? Ein Beitrag zu den Wehrmachtsproblemen Deutschlands* (Wiesbaden, 1927); *Verschwörer und Fememörder* (Berlin, 1926)

B. M.M. Gehrke, "Vaterländische Verbände," *Die Weltbühne*, 28 no. 43 (October, 25, 1932), 630-31; F.W. Foerster and H. Schwann, "Carl Mertens," *Die Zeit. Organ für grundsätzliche Orientierung*, 3, no. 20 (October 20, 1932), 711; Hubert Frank, "Carl Mertens tot," *Das Andere Deutschland*, 11, no. 43 (October, 22, 1932); O. Lehmann-Russbüldt, "Carl Mertens," *Dortmunder General—Anzeiger*, 45, no. 292 (October 22, 1932); Arthur Seehof, "Carl Mertens ist tot," *Chronik der Menschheit*, 18, no. 121 (October 25, 1932), 841-42; H. Wehberg, "Carl Mertens," *Die Friedenswarte*, 32, no. 12 (December, 1932), 371-72.

Helmut Donat and R. Lütgemeier-Davin
Trans. by William H. Hopkins

MERTON, Thomas (31 January 1915, Prades, France—10 December 1968, Bangkok, Thailand). *Education*: Lycée de Montauban, France, 1926-28; Oakham School, England, 1929-32; Clare Coll., Cambridge Univ., 1933-34; B.A., Columbia Univ., 1938, M.A., 1939. *Career*: instructor in English, Columbia Univ. Extension Division, 1938-39, St. Bonaventure Univ., 1939-41; book reviewer, *New York Times* and *New York Herald-Tribune*, 1938-39; entered Abbey of Gethsemani (became Trappist monk), 1941, took solemn vows, 1947, ordained priest, 1949 (religious name: Father M. Louis), master of scholastics, 1951-55, master of novices, 1955-56, complete monastic life, 1965-68; religious writer and poet.

Thomas Merton is perhaps best known for the range and intensity of his spiritual writings. His studies of the lives and works of the early church fathers, his explorations into the nature and practice of monastic contemplation, and the bridges of understanding he built between the religions of West and East preceded and contributed to his contributions in the area of peace and nonviolence. Though there were some who considered it "unseemly" for a Trappist monk to involve himself in such worldly controversies, he persisted in his efforts to awaken Christians to a fuller awareness of the moral implications of modern war. Even when silenced on the subject for a brief period, he continued to find permissible outlets for his views in private correspondence with a worldwide circle of friends and admirers.

In the extravagantly successful account of his personal journey to Catholicism and the contemplative life (*The Seven Storey Mountain*, 1948) he revealed that he had thought of limited service conscientious objection in World War II, a decision he was spared when he entered the Gethsemani monastery in Kentucky. Even so, he repeatedly insisted that he was not a pacifist, for he was unwilling to abandon the traditional Catholic teachings concerning the ''just war.'' At the same time, however, he made it clear that while he accepted the possibility *in theory* of such a war, he did not believe it could be achieved in fact. His articles dealing with nuclear weapons, modern war, and nonviolence—especially those dating from the later years of his tragically shortened life—reveal Merton to be more of a pacifist than he was aware or ready to admit.

Certainly his admiration for *Dorothy Day and the Catholic Worker, dating back to his student days at Columbia University, testifies to an interest in, and sympathetic attitude toward, that movement's pacifism. Other personal associations through the years of World War II and the ensuing Cold War kept that interest alive and active. It was not until the early 1960s, however, that he began to address the issues of war and peace in his published writings. Those earliest essays concentrated on questions related to the morality of nuclear weapons and tests, but there was an important shift of emphasis and a greater sense of urgency in his writings during years of the Vietnam War. Indeed, in May 1964, he conducted a retreat on ''The Spiritual Roots of Protest'' which, some would hold, marked the beginning of ''the great Catholic peace conspiracy.'' Almost all of the participants went on to activist protests and subsequent imprisonment!

Another major peace concern, and the one which may prove to be his most lasting contribution, was his strong advocacy of nonviolence as the Christian alternative to war.

In addition to a steady stream of his essays and books devoted in whole or part to peace issues, Merton provided personal moral support and encouragement to individual war resisters as well as to the emerging Catholic peace movement. He lent his name to such groups as the Catholic Peace Fellowship and the American Pax Society, the forerunner of Pax Christi USA. His final word on the issue of peace and nonviolence was a message addressed to the latter group at its 1968 meeting on the eve of his departure on the Asian journey which would end tragically with his death, by accidental electrocution, in Bangkok.

Bibliography:

A. *Breakthrough to Peace* (New York, 1962); *Gandhi on Non-Violence* (New York, 1965); *Faith and Violence* (Notre Dame, IN, 1968); *The Nonviolent Alternative,* ed. by Gordon C. Zahn (New York, 1980; revised ed. of *Thomas Merton on Peace* New York, 1971); *Raids on the Unspeakable* (New York, 1964); *Seeds of Destruction* (New York, 1965); *New Seeds of Contemplation* (London, 1962).

B. Marquita Breit, *Thomas Merton: A Bibliography* (Metuchen, NJ, 1974); James Forest, *Thomas Merton: A Pictorial Biography* (New York, 1980); Gerald Twomey, *Thomas Merton: Prophet in the Belly of a Paradox* (New York, 1978); Gordon C. Zahn, ''Introduction,'' to *The Nonviolent Alternative* (New York, 1980).

C. Thomas Merton Collection, Bellarmine College, Louisville, KY.

Gordon C. Zahn

MEULEN, Jacob ter (3 December 1884, The Hague—12 August 1962, The

Hague). *Education*: Univ. of Amsterdam, 1906-9; law, Univ. of Zurich, 1910-13, doctorate, 1914. *Career*: teacher, 1915-16; assistant librarian, University Library, Utrecht, 1917-21; librarian, Neth. School of Economics, Rotterdam, 1922-23; director, Peace Palace Library, The Hague, 1924-52).

Among students and advocates of peace whose main concern is the literary history of peace, Jacob ter Meulen occupies a preeminent position. Several factors contributed to make this possible. Having been impressed by the scientific reputation and the practical activities of Max Huber at the Second Hague Peace Conference (1907), he decided to go to Zurich and study, under Huber, the history of the idea of international organization. The third and final volume of his truly encyclopedic work on this subject was published only at the outbreak of the Second World War. Meanwhile ter Meulen acquired considerable library experience, and was appointed director of the Library of the Peace Palace in The Hague, which contains one of the best collections of peace literature in existence. With the help of others, he published two supplements to the printed catalogue of the Library (in 1929 and 1937 respectively). In the *Grotius Annuaire International*, of which he was co-founder and editor, he reported on developments in the Library. Two voluminous bibliographies concerning the writings of Hugo Grotius are also among his notable and lasting achievements.

His interest and professional expertise included, besides international law and international organization, pacifism and the peace movement. When the International Committee of Historical Sciences at its 1932 meeting in The Hague decided to create a "Sub-Committee for the bibliography of the peace movement in history," ter Meulen became its secretary. Most of the work of the subcommittee, which also numbered +Christian Lange, Merle Curti, +Hans Wehberg, and Rafael Altamira as its members, was undertaken by him. Two provisional lists, still of great value today, were issued in subsequent years. Ter Meulen's exhaustive bibliographical investigations may be regarded as his own contribution to the scientific study and practice of peace. In what appears to be his first published article, written in 1912, he showed the significance of *Alfred Fried for the peace movement, stressing the importance of Fried's attempts to provide it with a scientific basis.

Gradually, ter Meulen's personal interest and involvement in the peace movements of his own day increased. He was particularly interested in the Christian values that inspired antimilitarism. Whereas in 1914 he had returned from Zurich to fulfill his military service, by the 1930s his association with the Mennonites made future participation in war anathema to him. He was instrumental in setting up a "Mennonite working-group against conscription," of which he was the secretary, in 1932. Four years later, its international contacts led to the creation of an International Mennonite Peace Committee at a meeting in Holland. Again ter Meulen became the secretary, with *Harold Bender as the chairman. It was felt that a vigorous witness for peace and a reaffirmation in the power of nonviolence were now more than ever necessary. The scholar of peace had also become an activist, speaking out increasingly against war and preparations for it.

Bibliography:

A. *Beitrag zur Geschichte der Internationalen Organisation 1300-1700. Inaugural-dissertation* (The Hague, 1916); *Bibliographie des écrits imprimés de Hugo Grotius*, with P.J.J. Diermanse, (The Hague, 1950); *Bibliographie des écrits sur Hugo Grotius imprimés au XVIIe siècle*, with P.J.J. Diermanse (The Hague, 1961); *Bibliography of the Peace Movement before 1899* (2 vols., The Hague, 1934-36); *Concise Bibliography of Hugo Grotius* (Leyden, 1925); *Der Gedanke der Internationalen Organisation in seiner Entwicklung* (3 vols., The Hague, 1917-40); *Samenkomst van Doopsgezinden* (The Hague, 1937); *De wederopleving van het militarisme* (n.p. 1930); *Wij willen goede burgers zijn, maar de wapenen zullen wij niet dragen* (The Hague, 1932).

B. *The American Journal of International Law*, 57 (1963), 391-93; *Persoonlijkheden in het Koninkrijk der Nederlanden* (Amsterdam, 1938), 1005; Hans Wehberg, "Die Entwicklung des Gedankens der internationalen Organisation. Zur Vollendung des grossen Werkes von Jacob ter Meulen," *Die Friedenswarte*, 41 (1941), 217-36.

Peter van den Dungen

MIALL, Edward (8 May 1809, London—29 April 1881, Sevenoaks, England). *Education*: Wymondley Coll., 1828-31. *Career*: editor, *Nonconformist*, 1841-81; member of Parliament (Rochdale), 1852-57, (Bradford), 1869-73; founder of the Liberation Society; author and social reformer.

Though best-known as a campaigner for religious equality and a leader of the Liberation Society, Edward Miall became involved in a broad spectrum of reforming causes, associating with leading radicals and nonconformists. In foreign affairs he was in the mainstream of the radical tradition but, despite his friendship with men such as *Joseph Sturge and *Henry Richard, Miall constantly stressed that he was not a member of the Peace Society. War, he reluctantly conceded, was justifiable in certain circumstances, but he was critical of most aspects of British foreign policy.

There is no single explanation of his general dislike of war. Partly it rested on a liberationist conviction that a "State Church" and an aristocratic establishment were inherently bellicose and unduly disposed to interfere in the internal affairs of other nations: Britain had no right to behave as the "policeman of Europe." It sprang also from a belief that military intervention in Europe was unlikely to assist causes dear to radicals, such as liberalism or nationalism. Miall's sympathies were with European liberalism, but he opposed suggestions that Britain should aid Polish or Hungarian liberals or the forces of Italian unification. He consistently condemned colonial wars, and his support for *Richard Cobden's censure of the government over the Canton incident contributed to his electoral defeat in 1857.

Miall's stance during the Crimean War best exemplifies his attitude. He regretted that the dispute had not been settled peacefully, but since war had broken out, it should be pursued vigorously and effectively; Tsarist aggression merited punishment. With Cobden, he believed that most disputes could be settled by arbitration, that war interrupted commerce and absorbed energies and resources that could better be used for domestic purposes, that trade was the supreme agency of peace. But Miall's abhorrence of war was not wholly pragmatic; if he could not accept all the ideals of the Peace Society, he gave it general support in the *Non-conformist* and spoke at international conferences in Paris (1849) and Frankfort (1850). Though not a pacifist, Miall deployed his influence in the cause of peace and free trade, regarding war as an evil, if sometimes a necessary evil.

Bibliography:

A. *The British Churches in Relation to the British People* (London, 1849); *The Non-conformist's Sketch-Book* (London, 1845); *The Politics of Christianity* (London, 1863); *Views of the Voluntary Principle* (London, 1845).

B. Arthur Miall, *Life of Edward Miall, formerly Member of Parliament for Rochdale and Bradford* (London, 1884); J. S. Newton, "The Political Career of Edward Miall, Editor of the *Nonconformist* and founder of the Liberation Society," Ph.D. dissertation, University of Durham, 1975.

J. S. Newton

MIAO Pin (1899, Wasih, Kiangsu, China—21 May 1946, Soochow, Kiangsu, China). *Education*: electrical engineering degree, Nanyang Univ. (later Chiao-tung Univ.), Shanghai, 1923. *Career*: organizer and vice-president, Hsin-min-hui, 1937-40; businessman, government official.

When Japan encroached upon north China in the mid-1930s and an anti-Japanese movement broke out as a result, Miao Pin became apprehensive about the future of Japan-China relations and appealed in the pamphlet, *Serious Reflection on the Anti-Japanese Crisis*, to the leaders of the two nations to work for a peaceful solution of the crisis. Anxious to return to political life from the business world in order to restore peace between Japan and China in 1937, Miao Pin left Shanghai for Beijing, where he became associated with the East Asian League, an organization founded by General Ishiwara Kanji to promote the latter's ideal of liberating Asia and constructing a new order in Asia in cooperation with Japan, China, and Manchukuo based on genuine equality and brotherhood. He also organized the Hsin-min-hui (New People's Society) funded by the Japanese and became its vice-president. He frequently told his friends of the need for Japan-China cooperation as they were brothers who did not appreciate mutual brotherly love until they found themselves in difficulty. He also confided his feelings to his Japanese friends that he loved Japan as much as he loved his own country. Miao became pessimistic about the outcome of the war, predicting that Japanese aggression would be defeated and Japan would be destroyed morally if she continued invading. Thus, he urged his Japanese friends to conclude peace with China.

Disappointed with the increasing Japanese influence in the Hsin-min-hui and feeling his life would be in danger if he remained in Beijing, Miao fled to

Nanking in 1940. He joined the government of *Wang Ching-wei, who appointed him vice-chairman of the Legislative Yuan and later vice-director of the cultural committee of the East Asian League. Miao tried, at a Japanese embassy official's request, to communicate with General Ho Ying-Ch'in in Chungking for Japan-China peace negotiations. This unauthorized attempt angered Wang and disgraced Miao. He was demoted to a sinecure forcing him to semi-retirement in Shanghai.

Sometime in the fall of 1943, Miao became involved in a peace maneuver as a result of his attempt to assist in the rescue of the family of Ch'en Chang-feng, head of KMT intelligence operations in Shanghai, from the Japanese gendarme. He and Tamura Shinsaku, a former *Asahi* reporter, tried to bring Ch'en and Colonel Tsuji Masanobu, and influential staff officer, together to establish communication with Tai Li, chief of KMT intelligence operations. This did not materialize because Tsuji was transferred to Burma.

In late 1944, Miao learned that Prime Minister Koiso Kuniaki was seeking peace with the KMT government. He was convinced that now was the last chance for Japan to conclude peace with Chungking in order to save her from a total annihilation and also Japan and China from Sino-Soviet communism. Koiso invited Miao to Tokyo, where he arrived alone on March 16, 1945, as an emissary to sound out Japan's response to Chungking's alleged "peace proposals." The mission failed as the Japanese Supreme War Council opposed Koiso's effort on the grounds of Miao's doubtful credentials and ill reputation. The Koiso cabinet dissolved as a result on April 7.

After the war the KMT government arrested Miao and placed him under protective custody until March 24, 1946, when Tai Li and Ch'en Chiang-feng died in an airplane accident. Three days later, the KMT government brought him to trial and sentenced him to death. He was executed on May 21 without appeal.

To this day, it remains a mystery whether Miao was a sincere peace seeker or a "peace broker." Opponents insist that he was a fake because of his dubious political career; friends maintain that Miao was a genuine humanist seeking peace between Japan and China, and that he became the victim of bureaucratic politics and political rivalry within the Tokyo and Chungking governments. History's final verdict is yet to be rendered on Miao.

Bibliography:

B. Yoji Akasi, "A Botched Peace Effort: The Miao Pin *Kosaku* 1944-1945," *China and Japan: A Search for Balance Since World War I*, Alvin D. Coox and Hilary Conroy, eds. (Santa Barbara, CA, 1978) 267-88; *Biographical Dictionary of Republican China* (1970), III, 36-37.

Yoji Akashi

MICHALTSCHEFF, Theodor (born Baklaroff) (20 April 1899, Gabarewo, Bulgaria—29 April 1968, Sofia). *Education*: Ph.D., Univ. of Hamburg, 1936. *Career*: editor, *Die Friedensrundschau*, 1947-66; chairman, Internationale der Kriegsdienstgegner, 1947-55, 1958-59, secretary general, 1956-66.

In his youth, Theodor Michaltscheff Baklaroff devoted much time to propagating that line of revolutionary anarchism which approved of violence as a means of changing an unjust society. As a conscientious objector, he was imprisoned for one and a half years in 1920. The killing of a policeman who came to arrest Michaltscheff and some of his comrades turned Michaltscheff into an absolute pacifist in 1923. He fled from Bulgaria and went finally to Hamburg, where he changed his name.

During World War II, Michaltscheff recognized that conscientious objection required organization if it was to become effective. In 1947 he helped establish the Internationale der Kriegsdienstgegner (War Resisters' International) (IdK). The IdK served as the German section of the War Resisters' International (WRI) and propagated a program of absolute nonviolence and radical objection to active service. In order to devote himself entirely to the cause of peace, Michaltscheff gave up his scientific work (linguistics), although this meant a life of material want and privation. He edited the *Friedensrundschau* and did most of the organizational work for the IdK, serving as its only theoretician. During the mid-1950s, his influence decreased when the IdK (7,800 members at its height), became increasingly interested in current political matters. Still, Michaltscheff continued to play an important role as a symbol of absolute pacifism and as a mediator among the different currents which had developed inside the IdK.

Michaltscheff, a vegetarian and Esperantist, defined pacifism as a strategy of active nonviolence which not only resisted military service, but which also sought nonviolent forms of resolving conflicts and which tried to establish a radical, democratic society free from state authority. First and foremost, however, Michaltscheff was a theoretician. He used the pages of the *Friedensrundschau* to discuss the theory of nonviolence, but generally avoided developing strategies for nonviolent actions. This failure, and the lack of the periodical's concern with current politics, forced Michaltscheff to suspend publication in 1966. The following year, he returned to Bulgaria. Despite the shortcomings of his peace work, Michaltscheff helped spread the idea of conscientious objection in the Federal Republic of Germany.

Bibliography:

A. *Gewissen vor dem Prüfungsausschuss* (Hamburg, 1961); *20 Jahre Friedensrundschau und IdK. Persönliche Erinnerungen* (Hamburg, 1966).

B. Guido Grünewald, *Die Internationale der Kriegsdienstgegner (IdK). Ihre Geschichte 1945 bis 1968* (Köln, 1982).

Guido Grünewald

MICHON, Georges (6 October 1882, Cormenon, Loir-et-Cher, France—23 July 1945, Paris). *Education*: École Alsacienne, Paris, 1893-96; Coll. Sainte-Barbe, 1896-98; licence ès-lettres and diplôme d'études supèrieures, Univ. of Paris, 1909, Dr. in Law (economic sciences), Faculty of Law, Univ. of Paris, 1913; Dr. in History, Univ. of Paris, 1924. *Career*: administrator of maritime companies, historian, and journalist.

It was as an historian and journalist that Georges Michon served the cause of peace during the interwar years. Before World War I, however, there was little in his background that foreshadowed his later career. The son of a prosperous public works contractor, Michon enjoyed the benefits of education at the best Parisian schools. Earning a doctorate in economics for a dissertation on English navigation companies, he seemed destined to enter a career in business. During the World War, when so many of his generation fought in the trenches, Michon entered government service to help organize merchant marine lines between France and North America, thereby assuring adequate supplies for the war effort.

Yet the four years of the conflict effectively radicalized him. His hostility to war was expressed through his strong interest in history, which he had studied as an undergraduate at the University of Paris. Michon was drawn into association with Albert Mathiez, the well-known specialist in the French Revolution and president of the Societé des études robespierristes (Society for Robespierre Studies). Joining this society in 1920, Michon soon was elected its treasurer, then its secretary-general. He frequently presented papers to it on topics dealing with military history. His research led him to conclude that France had foolishly gone to war in 1792 because of intrigues by the court of Louis XVI and agitation by self-seeking politicians. Only the farsighted Robespierre opposed France's entry into what became a near disastrous conflict. In a series of studies on the armies of the Revolution, Michon demonstrated how greatly military justice had changed between the 1790s and 1914-18. Whereas during the Revolution ordinary soldiers were treated fairly and dishonest and incompetent officers rigorously punished, in contrast the enlisted men of the World War suffered harsh sentences from courts-martial while officers were handled leniently. Pacifists frequently cited such disparities in their attack on militarism during the postwar period.

Michon pursued his career in history, receiving his doctorate in 1924. But he soon turned from the Revolution to investigate the burning question of the origins of the World War. Using both his historical knowledge and business expertise, Michon sought to expose the men who had precipitated the conflict. In his work on the Franco-Russian Alliance, he concluded that the military ties forged between the Third Republic and tsarist Russia in the 1890s had been selfishly promoted by French commercial and financial interests. As a result, France placed herself in the service of a corrupt regime whose territorial ambitions in the Balkans would draw Frenchmen into the "most awful cataclysm of modern times."

A second study, dealing with the Three Year Law of 1913, traced the legislation that extended military service in France from two to three years. Michon declared that the law served to strengthen the power of the army as well as benefit powerful financial and industrial concerns, promote the forces of nationalism, and aid tsarist Russia. He concluded that it helped prepare the country psychologically and militarily for a war with Germany.

During the 1930s Michon pressed his campaign against war through his active membership in the Ligue des droit de l'homme (League for the Rights of Man).

He also used the columns of the syndicalist journal *La Révolution prolétarienne* and the pacifist newspaper *La Patrie humaine* to denounce the dangers of war being stirred by fascism and predatory capitalism. He blamed the riots of February 6, 1934, which saw right-wing mobs threaten the safety of Parliament, on the sinister forces of high finance and large industry that aimed to overthrow democracy and the republic. To combat the growing threat from the right, Michon joined the Comité de vigilance des intellectuels antifascistes (Vigilance Committee of Antifascist Intellectuals) organized in March, 1934. The organization worked to combat war and fascism as well as to form a viable political alliance among the parties of the left—what later became the Popular Front. The electoral victory of the Popular Front in 1936 seemed to justify Michon's hopes. The Vigilance Committee continued to campaign against armaments and for peace during the period of increasing tension with Germany in the late 1930s. Michon, who accepted the Munich Pact of 1938, assailed "war mongering" by the French press at the time of the Czech crisis.

With the outbreak of hostilities in 1939, the antiwar press was effectively closed down, leaving Michon without a forum for his ideas. During the German occupation of 1940-44, he remained in Paris but did not collaborate or take an active role in politics. Instead, he retreated into historical scholarship, resuming his studies on the Revolution. Suffering from poor health for many years, he died shortly after the defeat of Germany.

Michon's greatest contribution to pacifism took the form of historical polemic. His experience in the world of business combined with his knowledge of the past enabled him to fight against those interests whose selfish desire for gain, he believed, threatened the safety of France and the peace of Europe.

Bibliography:

A. *L'Alliance franco-russe* (Paris, 1927); *La Préparation à la guerre. La lei de trois (1910-1914)* (Paris, 1935); *Les Puissances d'argent et l'émeute du 6 février* (Paris, n.d. [1934]).

B. Gustave Laurent, "Georges Michon," *Annales historiques de la Révolution française*, 19 (1947) 264-67; Nicole Racine-Furlaud, "Le Comité de Vigilance des Intellectuels Antifascistes (1934-1939). Antifascisme et pacifisme," *Le Mouvement social*, 101 (October-December, 1977), 87-113.

James Friguglietti

MIGLIOLI, Guido (18 May 1879, Cremona, Italy—24 October 1954, Milan). *Education*: laureata in literature and in law, Univ. of Parma. *Career*: politician; editor, *Nuova Terra* and *L'Azione*; author.

A politician and a life long advocate of the peasant and working classes, Guido Miglioli was born in Cremona, Italy in 1879. Active in the Catholic youth movement before World War I, Miglioli organized the peasants of Cremona into "white unions," became their spokesman in the Provincial Council in 1907, and was elected to the Chamber of Deputies in 1913. After the war, he joined the newly formed Partito Popolare Italiano (Italian Popular Party) (PPI) of *Don

Luigi Sturzo, serving as a deputy until 1923. Miglioli's work among the peasants, especially his role in the Cremona dairy strike of 1922, drew the fire of the Fascists who numbered him among their most bitter foes. Within the PPI, he became a major figure on the Left, advocating firm opposition to Benito Mussolini and conciliation with the Socialists.

With the collapse of democracy in Italy, Miglioli was forced into exile where he drew closer to communism and remained a leader of the "fuorusciti," exiled opponents of Fascism. Participating in the resistance in Northern Italy, Miglioli reentered political life with the establishment of the Republic. In 1945, with Ruggero Grieco, he founded the "Movimento cristiano per la pace", reflecting his continual desire to organize a viable Leftist Christian movement in Italy.

The "Movimento cristiano per la pace" included former members of the Christian Democratic party and of the defunct Sinistra Christiana, as well as Catholic socialists. Miglioli and Grieco hoped to remain independent of both the Christian Democrats and the Catholics within the Socialist and Communist parties. In a manifesto announcing the formation of the movement, Miglioli attacked the hatred generated by wars and pointed out that it was always the poor, the workers, the peasants, and the uneducated who suffered most when peace was disrupted. In his journal *Nuova Terra*, Miglioli was critical of the Christian Democrats for alienating Catholic workers from socialist and communist ones and for betraying the traditions of the Partito Popolare. For both Miglioli and Grieco, genuine peace was not possible as long as the peasants and workers continued to suffer at the hands of others.

During the early years of the new Republic, Miglioli in his writings and political activity attempted to nurture a peace predicated upon social justice and equality. Although accused by his enemies of being an "emissary of Moscow", Miglioli always believed himself to be a true Christian and Catholic.

Bibliography:

A. *La Collectivisation des Compagnes soviétiques* (Paris, 1934); *Con Roma e con Mosca* (Milan, 1945); *Un dibattito inedito sul contadino della Val Padana*, with R. Grieco (Florence, 1958).

B. Antonio Fappani, *Guido Miglioli e il movimento contadino* (Rome, 1964); Franco Leonari, *No guerra, ma terra! Guido Miglioli: una vita per i contadini* (Milan, 1969).

Richard J. Wolff

MILIUKOV, Pavel Nikolaevich (28 January 1859 Moscow—31 March 1943 Aix-le-belle, France). *Education*: M.A., Moscow Univ., 1892. *Career*: leader of the Constitutional Democratic (Kadet) party; member of the Third and Fourth Dumas (parliaments); member, Carnegie Endowment for International Peace, International Investigatory Commission on the Balkan Wars; Minister of Foreign Affairs, Russian Provisional Government, March-May, 1917; editor, *Rech'*, 1906-17, *Posledniia novosti*, 1921-40; historian; publicist.

The outstanding representative of Russian liberalism, Pavel Nikolaevich Miliukov embodied all the contradictory views on peace, nationalism, and revolutionary change that brought moderates to grief in 1917. As a leader in the Liberation Movement (1900-5) and the Union of Unions during the first Russian revolution, Miliukov promoted an alliance of liberals and revolutionaries. In the midst of 1905, fearing the spontaneity of the masses, Miliukov retreated to a purely parliamentary strategy in which the Constitutional-Democratic (Kadet) party that he helped to create would represent everyone interested in peaceful, evolutionary approaches to change.

A lifelong opponent of terrorism, Miliukov proclaimed himself a pacifist in the years following the 1905 revolution, became a member and vice-chairman of the Parliamentarian Union of Peace (headed by Lord Werdel and +Christian Lange) as well as the St. Petersburg branch of the Moscow Peace Society.

*Norman Angell's famous *The Great Illusion* significantly influenced Miliukov's thinking about peace. Adopting its analysis as his own, he undertook a nationwide lecture tour in 1909-10, in which he argued that wars should stop for the simple reason that they were not profitable. He contended that conquerors and the conquered lose equally, and that no acquisitions whatsoever, neither material nor territorial, could bring profits. Miliukov called this kind of pacifism "revolutionary" because it set out to alter basic attitudes about the utility of war. He contrasted it snidely with the pacifism of "disarmament fanatics" who feared the creations of man. Believing in the perfectability of man, Miliukov put his faith in international law and compulsory arbitration as new ways of solving conflicts between nations. Miliukov codified his views in *Vooruzhennyi mir i ogranichenie vooruzhenii (The Armed World and the Limitation of Armaments)* (1911).

Carnegie Commission chairman *Baron d'Estournelles de Constant selected Miliukov as a member of the group investigating the Balkan Wars and he wrote four chapters of *Report of the International Commission to Inquire into the Causes and Conduct of the Balkan Wars* (1914). Subsequently, Miliukov claimed that his observations of cruelty and rampant nationalism shook his pacifist beliefs.

Miliukov clung to his pacifist ideals until the outbreak of World War I, when as a leader in the fourth Duma he helped form a *union sacré* dedicated to supporting the national cause. In February 1917 Miliukov became the key figure in the first Provisional Government as minister of foreign affairs. Instead of pursuing a peace policy, Miliukov aggressively continued the war effort, honored all the tsarist treaties, and pushed for seizure of the Dardanelles.

Miliukov's imperialist aims, his rejection of the call of the Socialist Zimmerwald Conference for "peace without annexations," and his outspoken commitment to the Allies provoked furious attacks from the Soviet of Workers Deputies and the left parties. The object of massive street demonstrations that threatened the Provisional Government, Miliukov resigned his post in early May. He spent the rest of 1917 as an outside advisor to the dwindling number of Kadets in the faltering coalition governments. After the October Revolution, he joined the counter-revolutionary White forces in South Russia. Following their defeat, he emigrated to France where he resumed a career as an historian and publicist. A vehement enemy of Bolshevism, Miliukov's militant and emotional Great-Russian nationalism which had earlier undercut his shallow-rooted pacifism made him a vocal supporter of the Soviet state against the Nazis in the last years of his life.

Bibliography:

A. *Russia and its Crisis* (Chicago, 1905); *Russia Today and Tomorrow* (New York, 1921); *Vooruzhennyi mir i ogranichenie vooruzhenni* (Moscow, 1911); *Vospominaniia* (2 vols., New York, 1955; condensed Engl. version, ed. by Arthur P. Mendel, *Paul Miliukov Political Memoirs, 1905-1917* (Ann Arbor, MI, 1967).

B. Thomas Riha, *A Russian European, Paul Miliukov in Russian Politics* (Notre Dame, IN, 1969); W.G. Rosenberg, *Liberals in the Russian Revolution* (Princeton, NJ, 1974); B. S. Smirnov et al., eds., *P.N. Miliukov: Sbornik materialov po chestvovaniiu ego semidesiatiletiia, 1859-1929* (Paris, 1929).

C. P.N. Miliukov Archive, in the Bakhmeteff Archive of Russian and East European History and Culture, Columbia University, New York City; P.N. Miliukov archive (f. 579), Tsentral'nyi gosudarstvennyi arkhiv oktiabr'skoi revoliutsii, Moscow.

Jonathan Sanders

MILLER, Orie Otis (7 July 1892, Middlebury, IN—10 January 1977, Lititz, PA). *Education*: short courses at Purdue Univ.; B.A., Goshen Coll., 1915. *Career*: shoe manufacturer; lay churchman; peace, service, and mission advocate and administrator.

Orie O. Miller was president of Miller-Hess Shoe Company, but spent much of his time building up Christian mission, service, and peace-advocacy institutions, mainly in Mennonite and historic peace church circles. Son of a northern Indiana Mennonite farmer-bishop and church leader, Miller imbibed the Mennonites' very biblically-based pacifism. His peacemaking style was businesslike; he was practical, careful of administration, highly institutional, and rather autocratic.

Miller wanted Mennonite peace testimony to be positive, and in 1919 he went to the Near East with one of his church's first service units. Soon he was Red Cross director in Beirut. In 1920 he headed efforts to aid Mennonites suffering in revolutionary Russia. From that came the Mennonite Central Committee (MCC), thereafter North American Mennonites' chief peace, relief, and service agency. From 1935 to 1958, Miller was the MCC's Executive Secretary-Treasurer, establishing its headquarters at Akron, Pennsylvania, and shaping it very much around his own straightforward style. He held many other such posts, often peace-related: member of the MCC's Peace Section, 1942-58; vice-president, then secretary, of the Eastern Mennonite Board of Missions and Charities, 1925-58; financial agent of the Mennonite Board of Education, 1922-55; and president of Mennonite Mutual Aid from its founding in 1945 until 1962. The MCC, however, was his main base for peace activity.

As MCC head, and member of his church's Peace Problems Committee from 1925 to 1963, Miller worked with other historic peace church leaders to negotiate alternative service programs for conscientious objectors: World War II's Civilian

Public Service and the later I-W program. Miller also helped found the National Service Board for Religious Objectors (NSBRO) and helped administer Mennonite CPS camps. Although seeing some of alternative service's dilemmas, Miller, like his church, accepted it as a way of being obedient to government. In 1948 he became NSBRO's acting chairman, just when others organized another committee more oriented toward noncooperation. He helped form Mennonite Voluntary Service in 1944-45 and Pax Service in 1951. Such institutions embodied Miller's approach—neither the quietism of his Mennonite ancestors, nor radical confrontation.

Bibliography:

A. *Feeding the Hungry: Russia Famine, 1919-1925. American Mennonite Relief Operations Under the Auspices of Mennonite Central Committee*, with P.C. Hiebert (Scottdale, PA, 1929).

B. Paul Erb, *Orie O. Miller: The Story of a Man and an Era* (Scottdale, PA, 1969); Melvin Gingerich, *Service for Peace: A History of Mennonite Civilian Public Service* (Akron, PA, 1949); [Philip Jacob], *The Origins of Civilian Public Service* (Washington, D.C., [1941?]); Albert Keim, "Service or Resistance? The Mennonite Response to Conscription in World War II," *The Mennonite Quarterly Review*, 52 (April 11, 1978), 141-55; Mulford Sibley and Philip Jacob, *Conscription of Conscience: the American State and the Conscientious Objector, 1940-47* (Ithaca, NY, 1952); Nelson P. Springer and A.J. Klassen, *Mennonite Bibliography, 1631-1961* (Scottdale, PA, 1977).

C. Orie O. Miller Papers, Archives of the Mennonite Church, Goshen College, Goshen, IN.

Theron F. Schlabach

MILLS, Charles Wright (28 August 1916, Waco, TX—20 March 1962, Nyack, NY). *Education*: B.A., Univ. of Texas, 1938, M.A., 1939; Ph.D., Univ. of Wisconsin, 1942. *Career*: Associate Professor of Sociology, Univ. of Maryland, 1941-45; Associate Professor and Professor of Sociology, Columbia Univ., 1945-62; director, Labor Research Division, Bureau of Applied Social Research, Columbia Univ. 1945-48; sociologist, research consultant, teacher, and author.

C. Wright Mills began his academic career as a sociologist during World War II and came to intellectual maturity during its Cold War aftermath. Academically based at Columbia University throughout the most productive years of his career, he came to be a major figure among a small but diverse group of radical intellectuals who struggled to sustain critical social inquiry as the politics and culture of the Cold War descended upon America in the decade following World War II. Although of independent and dissenting temperament, Mills was not a political activist and defined himself as a scholar and intellectual. Nevertheless, he insisted that the social sciences must address themselves to the central issues of their time. Among these were the rise of a new "power elite" in the United States, the integral position of the military within it, and the use of a "military metaphysic" as the prevailing definition of reality among the power elite as a whole.

Mills' sociological work rejected the tenets of both traditional liberal social theory and orthodox Marxism. Instead, drawing upon the anti-Utopian tendencies of such European sociologists as Max Weber, he developed an interpretation of

America as an emerging "mass society." This interpretation suggested that an increasingly bureaucratized social world generated political (and cultural) passivity at the middle and lower social levels, that informed and organized publics played a decreasing role in the decision-making process at the national level, and that a "power elite" had developed in which the exercise of power was ever more concentrated, conscious, and unaccountable. Corporate wealth and power, the objective interests of the political directorate and the military establishment were all served, Mills argued in *The Causes of World War III* (1958), by a permanent war economy, in which "to a considerable extent, militarism has become an end in itself and economic policy a means of it."

The publication of this book marked a new phase in Mills' writing. Strongly committed to democratic and humanist values, he reacted against the bleakness of the political and human condition portrayed in his earlier work, as well as against the mounting tensions of the Cold War, by adopting a more overtly polemical and activist tone, addressing himself primarily to the problem of peace. He was not a pacifist on principle, but believed that with the advent of the thermonuclear age, war had lost any claim it may once have had as a rational instrument of foreign policy. "We are at the very end of the military road," he wrote, "It leads nowhere but to death .... War has become total. And war has become absurd." In this book Mills set forth a series of "guidelines" for the reorientation of American (and Soviet) foreign policy in the direction of coexistence, negotiation, and disarmament. In *Listen, Yankee* (1960), he developed analogous proposals with respect to American policy toward social revolution in the Third World. With these books, Mills emerged as one of the foremost academic critics of the Cold War and the social theory, liberal or Marxist, which legitimated it.

During his lifetime, Mills' heightened politicization led to some degree of professional and intellectual isolation. Yet he became one of the most widely read American sociologists, both in the United States and abroad, and after his premature death, in 1962, his ideas, like those of several other radical intellectuals of the older generation, had a catalytic effect on the emerging New Left and the growing antiwar movement.

Mills' work was marked by a tension between analysis and polemic, programmatic weakness, and a mood ranging from stoic despair to outrage and acerbic belligerence. Yet his vision of a social science serving the cause of enlightenment, freedom, and humane values assures his place in the tradition of American radical dissent.

Bibliography:

A. *The Causes of World War III* (New York, 1958); *Listen, Yankee* (New York, 1969); *The Power Elite* (New York, 1956); *Power, Politics, and People: The Collected Essays of C. Wright Mills*, ed. by Irving Louis Horowitz (New York, 1963).

L. Paul Metzger

MILNE, Alan Alexander (18 January 1882, London—31 January 1956, Hartfield, Sussex, England). *Education*: Westminster; B.A., Trinity Coll., Cambridge Univ., 1903. *Career*: assistant editor, *Punch*; signalling officer, Royal Warwickshire Regiment (World War I); author, playwright, and peace advocate.

A. A. Milne became well-known as a humorist and as the author of plays, novels, essays, and short stories. During the 1920s he became interested in children's literature, publishing in poetic form *When We Were Very Young* (1924), dedicated to his only son Christopher Robin, and in prose form *Winnie-the-Pooh* (1926), his best selling work. These writings attracted much attention on both sides of the Atlantic. His last work, *Year In, Year Out* (1952) was a collection of diverse essays on various themes.

On the subject of international relations Milne published *Peace With Honour: An Enquiry into the War Convention* (1934), in which he asserted that the national prestige of a state should be based on nonviolent actions and the renunciation of force in international affairs. Declaring himself a pacifist, he maintained that modern warfare had become organized brutality. He sharply criticized that system of values whereby governments could declare war seemingly on impulse and yet remain secure in the knowledge that the average citizen had been adequately brainwashed and would support war measures without much dissent. Milne further asserted that the renunciation of aggression was in itself not enough. He believed that governments must also renounce defense.

After the coming of World War II, Milne, like many other European antiwar advocates, came to see the defeat of Nazi Germany as more important than maintaining his former pacifist principles. In two hastily published pamphlets, *War with Honour* (1940) and *War Aims Unlimited* (1941), he modified his earlier views. Denouncing the militaristic actions of Adolf Hitler, he warned that German political ambitions must be stopped. He claimed that he was still a pacifist in theory, but observed that the time to work for peace was between wars and not during a bitter conflict whose frightfulness shocked the senses.

In 1952 Milne underwent a brain operation which left him an invalid. He spent his last years in retirement at his home in Hartfield, Sussex. Although his professional career as a writer was now over, admirers throughout the world remembered Milne for his plays and his books for children which had brought enjoyment to so many. Pacifist leaders remembered him for his carefully written cultural critique on the causes of war which had attracted much attention when it first appeared in 1934.

Bibliography:

A. *It's Too Late Now: The Autobiography of a Writer* (London, 1939); *Peace with Honour: An Enquiry into the War Convention* (London, 1934); *War Aims Unlimited* (London, 1941); *War with Honour* (London, 1940).

B. Martin Ceadel, *Pacifism in Britain, 1914-1945: The Defining of a Faith* (Oxford, 1980); Thomas Burnett Swann, *A. A. Milne* (New York, 1971).

Bernerd C. Weber

MISIANO, Francesco (26 June 1884, Ardore, Reggio Calabria, Italy—16 August 1936, Moscow). *Education*: Franciscan Brothers school; Univ. of Naples.

Career: employee, Italian State Railways; journalist; editor and collaborator, *L'Avvenire del lavoratore* (Zurich), *Arbeiter Illustrierte Zeitung* (Berlin); director, International Workers Relief (Berlin), 1922-33; pacifist.

Born and raised in modest circumstances, Francesco Misiano worked on the National railways in Naples as a young man. There he married a teacher, Maria Conti, and became involved in workers' movements and socialism. An early interest in socialist organization led him to examine means by which the two large federations of Italian labor, the Confederazione generale de lavore (General Confederation of Labor) and the Unione sindacale italiana (Italian Syndicalist Union) could collaborate more closely.

With the coming of World War I, Misiano undertook active propaganda in favor of peace and Italian neutrality, not only because of his opposition to violence but because he believed that Italy could negotiate its continued neutrality for the Austrian controlled areas, the Trentino, and Trieste. Moreover, Misiano shared the view of most Italian socialists in leadership positions—that the war was an imperialist venture and not a war of liberation. Aware that the Central Powers were ruled by retrograde, absolutist monarchs, he believed that the democratic and socialist forces there would eventually come to power by their own efforts. A long war would probably engender fury everywhere, reinforce reactionary forces, fuel revenge both in defeated and victorious nations, and set back socialist movements by inflaming anti-worker sentiments.

When called to serve, Misiano requested permission to attend officer candidate school, but the authorities rejected his application. Regarded as a dangerous antimonarchist and antimilitarist, the government feared his oratorical prowess and influence over soldiers. A trap was set to catch him. One night a rumor was spread in his barracks that the troops would be moved to the front on the next morning. With 36 others, Misiano left to say goodbye to his wife and children who were in a nearby town. On their return, a few hours later, only Misiano was arrested and charged with desertion. To avoid execution, he fled to Switzerland where he joined a group of immigrant Italian workers and began his collaboration on the journal, *L'Avvenire del lavoratore*, edited by Angelica Balabanoff. When she returned to Italy in 1916, Misiano became editor.

In the journal Misiano disclosed the profitable business deals that industrialists from the belligerent nations were conducting with each other in neutral Switzerland while, on the front, the young died. He campaigned for an immediate peace treaty and for the revival of socialist forces throughout Europe. In Zurich, he met V. I. Lenin and the "left" of the Zimmerwald Manifesto group.

The postwar period was a decided turning point in Misiano's life. He joined the newly created Italian Communist party in 1921, but ruthless persecution by the Fascists drove him and his family to seek exile in the Soviet Union to avoid being murdered. A trial was held in his absence, where the eminent socialist lawyer G. E. Modigliani compared Misiano's persecution to Giuseppe Mazzini's who had been denounced, too, as an enemy of the people.

In the Soviet Union, he engaged in the humanitarian efforts to assist children who were victims of the postwar ravages. From about 1922 to 1933, along with the Swiss, W. Munzenberg in Berlin, he was director of the International Workers Relief and edited the review *Arbeiter Illustrierte Zeitung*. He also performed important services in disseminating the best of the new Soviet cultural productions, including the film, "Battleship Potemkin" in the West.

From 1927 Misiano became very active in the League Against Imperialism, attending its peace congresses in Amsterdam and Paris. This group included socialists, social democrats, and antifascist Catholics. He managed to engage support from the Englishman, Stafford Cripps, and the American defender of Sacco and Vanzetti, John Garfield. His last years were lonely and sad. Despite the esteem which Italian exile leaders held for him, Misiano was persecuted and falsely charged until his death.

Bibliography:

B. G. Arfè, "Per la storia del socialismo nappoletano. Atti della Sezione del PSI di Napoli dal 1908 al 1911," *Movimento Operaio* (1953), 2; Raffaele Colapietra, *Napoli tra dopoguerra e fascismo* (Milan, 1962); Michele Fatica, *Origini del comunismo e del fascismo a Napoli* (Firenze, 1971); Helmut König, *Lenin und der italienische Sozialismus 1915-1921* (Cologne, 1967); Franca Pieroni Bortolotti, *Francesco Misiano. Vita di un internazionalista* (Rome, 1972).

Franca Pieroni Bortolotti
Trans. by Sandi E. Cooper and John M. Cammet

MISTRAL, Gabriela (pseud. of Lucila Godoy Alcayaga) (7 April 1889, Vicuña, Chile—10 January 1957, Hempstead, New York). *Education*: public schools in the Province of Coquimbo, Chile. *Career*: educator, poet, and diplomat.

The first Latin American poet to have received the Nobel Prize (1945) Gabriela Mistral, whose real name was Lucila Godoy Alcayaga, is remembered not only for the universal themes of her poetry and prose, but also because of her dedication to the causes of social justice and world peace. Mistral typified the Latin American intellectual; she had a capacity for multiple self expression revealed in her diverse roles.

The diplomatic phase of her life began in 1922, when she left Chile to accept an invitation from the Mexican government to take part in the educational reforms President Alvaro Obregón promoted. During two years in Mexico, she worked with José Vasconcelos to reorganize the school system and integrate Indians into national life.

Mistral first went to the United States in 1924. The Pan American Union honored her in Washington for her dedication to the welfare of humanity. During this time, she became a contributor to the magazine *Nueva Democracia* (New York), in which she published many articles dedicated to improving the relationships between nations and peoples.

In 1926 the Chilean government appointed her to the International Committee on Intellectual Cooperation, a part of the League of Nations, located in Paris. Mistral was South American affairs advisor. Later in the 1920s, she represented the Teachers' Association of Chile at the Congress of Educators in Italy and attended the Congress of Children's Welfare held at the League of Nations center in Geneva. Throughout the decade, she continued to write and promoted, through translations, the works of Latin American writers. The common thread in all her activities was the promotion of better understanding of the New World and the improvement of the Latin American self-image.

Another phase of her life began when she accepted the post of Chilean consul in Madrid in 1933. She expressed concern for Spain during the era of its civil war with the generous act of turning over the proceeds of her book, *Tala*, for the benefit of children left homeless by the conflict. In 1935, by special law, the Chilean government appointed Mistral consul-for-life. This situation allowed her to live in any city she chose and the salary permitted her to become an indefatigible traveler in Europe, Latin America and the United States. Two years later in Brazil she was made an honorary member of the local Pan American Society for her contribution to the cause of inter-American brotherhood and peace. Again in Brazil, at the onset of World War II, she took an active part in fighting against fascism, prejudice, and oppression. She remained constant in her struggle to forge a closer relationship between Portuguese-speaking Brazil and Spanish America, stressing the unity of Ibero-American culture and values.

With the creation of the United Nations, Mistral became the Chilean delegate to the Commission on the Status of Women. She went to Mexico in 1948 at the invitation of the Director General of UNESCO; two years later, she worked as an advisor to UNESCO in Italy. Offered the directorship for South America of the United Nations International Children's Emergency Fund (UNICEF)—an organization she helped found—she declined the post due to failing health. She accepted, however, the appointment as Chilean delegate to the U.N. Commission of the Status of women gathering in New York in 1953-54.

At the end of 1956, while in New York, she learned that she had cancer. When she died in January 1957, the General Assembly of the United Nations interrupted debate to honor her memory. Spokespersons from more than twenty nations offered eulogies.

Bibliography:

A. *Desolación* (New York, 1922); *Lagar*, (Santiago, 1954); *Tala* (Buenos Aires, 1938); *Tenura* (Madrid, 1924).

B. Fernando Alegría, *Genio y figura de Gabriela Mistral* (Buenos Aires 1966); Margot Arce de Vázquez, *Gabriela Mistral: The Poet and Her Work*, trans. by Helene Anderson (New York, 1964); Marie-Lise Gazarian-Gautier, *Gabriela Mistral: The Teacher from the Valley of Elqui* (Chicago, 1975); Matilde Ladrón de Guevara, *Gabriela Mistral: Rebelde magnífica* (Santiago, 1957); Efraím Szmulewicz, *Gabriela Mistral: Biografía emotiva* (5th ed., Santiago, 1974).

Mal Bochner

MOCH, Gaston (6 March 1859, Saint-Cyr-l'Ecole, France—3 July 1935, Paris). *Education*: École polytechnique; École d'artillerie at Fontainebleu. *Career*: artillery captain to 1893; president, l'Institut international de la paix; president, Delégation permanente des Sociétés françaises de la paix; council member, International Peace Bureau; army officer, author, and journalist.

Following the tradition of his Alsatian forebears, Gaston Moch planned a career in the French Army and became an artillery officer as well as the author of articles in the *Revue d'Artillerie* on technical subjects. Between 1887-93, he was closely associated with a group of young officers who were to become an important corps of engineers.

During his military service, however Moch met a number of pacifists whose point of view impressed him. He resigned from the army in 1893 to join the peace movement, offering his talents as an orator and writer. Moch was first active in the Ligue internationale de la paix et de la liberté (International League of Peace and Freedom) over which *Emile Arnaud presided following the death of *Charles Lemonnier. Moch gave up the pseudonym "Patiens," under which he had written his first books while still in the military, and went on to publish over 30 books on artillery, the military craft, the history and organization of states, linguistics, international politics, translations into Esperanto, and the relationship between democracy and militarism. Under the pseudonym "Patiens" he wrote one of the most important peace-oriented works of the 1890s—a study of the Alsace-Lorraine problem which offered a political rather than a military solution. His realistic and solid technical knowledge gave the peace movement an important set of skills. His editing of *L'Indépendance Belge* provided the movement with a reliable newspaper organ. Called on by Albert, Prince of Monaco, to serve as head of his cabinet, Moch convinced that ruler to fund an International Institute of Peace which became a source of research and publication for the European movement.

The furor created by the Dreyfus case led Moch to think seriously about the army as a social and political institution. He concluded that France needed a citizen army for defensive purposes, structured on the Swiss militia model and not on the professional military caste which sapped the national treasury and harbored antirepublican officers. The fruits of his thinking appeared in *L'Armée d'une democratie* (1899), *La Réforme militaire: vive la milice* (1900) and *L'Ere sans violence* (with the German colonel, *Moritz von Egidy, 1901). Much of Moch's position in these works was adopted, without attribution, by *Jean Jaurès in his celebrated *L'Armée Nouvelle* (1910). Regarding Dreyfus personally, Moch was convinced of his innocence and so testified at the Rennes hearing (1906).

Active both in the French and international peace movements, Moch established the headquarters of the French movement, corresponded with *Elie Ducommun and *Albert Gobat of the Berne International Peace Bureau, and presided over the 1902 Monaco international congress. He lectured widely at popular universities and the École des hautes études sociales and worked closely with German pacifists. Moch saw little hope that treaties would bring about arms limitation. Instead he believed that arms reductions would evolve as the logical fulfillment of an international order governed by law that would increase security and lessen the need for weapons. Lacking a rule of law, arms limitation struck Moch as a utopian fantasy for peace activists to pursue.

When a militant and even subversive variety of antimilitarism developed at the turn of the century, preaching sabotage, mutiny, nonresistance, and, eventually, conscientious objection, Moch was absolutely unsympathetic. He believed in the need for defense and the right to fight a just war. With the outbreak of World War I, he rejoined the army, serving first on the General Staff of the Army of Paris and then as secretary to the Bureau of Inventions of the War Ministry. At the close of the war, he was appointed an officer of the Legion of Honor.

During the 1920s Moch rejoined his surviving colleagues from the prewar movement as well as new people who supported the League of Nations and disarmament in an effort to promote internationalism and peace. The rise of fascism in Europe distressed Moch, but he lived to see the defeat of the fascist initiative in France in February 1934.

Bibliography:

A. *L' Alsace-Lorraine devant l'Europe: essai de politique positive* (Paris, 1895; reprint, New York, 1972); *L ' Armée d'une démocratie* (Paris, 1900); *Autour de la Conference interparlémentaire* (Paris, 1895); *L'Ere sans violence*, with Moritz von Egidy (Paris, 1901); *L 'Initiation aux théories d'Einstein* (Paris, 1922); *La Question de la legion etrangère* (Paris, 1914); *La Relativité des phénomènes* (Paris, 1921); *Sur le Désarmement: chimères et réalitiés* (Paris, 1906); *Vers la Fédération d'Occident: Désarmons les Alpes* (Paris, 1905).

B. Obituaries, *La Paix par le droit* (1935), 377; *Les Etats-Unis d'Europe* (1935), 406-8.

[Material for this entry was provided by Jules Moch]

Sandi E. Cooper

MOENIUS, Georg (19 October 1890, Adelsdorf, Franconia, Germany—2 July 1953, Munich). *Education*: theological studies, Univ. of Würzburg, 1911-15; ordained as a Roman Catholic priest, 1915; Ph.D., Univ. of Erlangen, 1919. *Career*: priest, Archdiocese of Bamberg, 1915-24; editor, publisher, author, cultural philosopher, and pacifist writer.

Because of growing disagreements with the episcopal administration in Bamberg, Georg Moenius asked for a leave from his office as priest in 1924 and went to Munich. Here Moenius, who had studied history and art history at the universities of Marburg and Erlangen, won a considerable circle of readers as a cultural philosopher and historian through his publications *Italienische Reise* (1925) and *Paris, Frankreichs Herz* (1926). In both works he sought to formulate a cultural philosophy of Europe. Equating Europe with "Western culture," he argued for a return to its Roman-Mediterranean and Christian essence and attacked all political and philosophical views that departed from this traditional heritage. For Moenius, Prussian militarism had deviated from "Western culture," and, therefore, had to be eliminated.

In the hope of reaching an even larger audience, Moenius turned to journalism after 1925. In 1928 he acquired part ownership in *Die Allgemeine Rundschau*, a newspaper which up until that time followed a conservative-federalist course. Under Moenius' influence the *Allgemeine Rundschau* became open to pacifist opinions. In the columns of the paper, Moenius fought a vigorous anti-Prussian and antimilitaristic battle. His strong antiwar stance led to severe criticism from reactionary Catholic clerics, veterans' organizations, and conservative scholars. They particularly disliked his criticism of German foreign policy towards Belgium and Poland. Moenius's efforts at paving the way for an honest accommodation with these countries brought him little but ingratitude, hatred, and persecution. When he published a special issue on Belgium dealing with former war crimes, even the Foreign Office and the Ministry of Defense joined in the campaign to discredit him. Moenius found himself in serious difficulty when he spoke out against the participation of Catholic student associations in celebrations honoring the anniversary of the execution for sabotage of Leo Schageter, a right-wing supporter, by the French during their occupation of the Ruhr in March 1923. His statements prompted the academic senate of the University of Munich to vote unanimously to exclude him "from the community of Germans."

After January 30, 1933, the *Allgemeine Rundschau* was no longer permitted to publish. Moenius escaped arrest in April for his inflammatory writings in the paper only by fleeing Germany. He went to Austria where he began writing for the periodical *Der Christliche Ständestaat*. He also spent some time in Rome. In the spring of 1937 he became a member of the Christliche Reichsbund für deutsche Freiheit (Christian National Association for German Freedom) founded in Vienna. After the occupation of Austria he went to Paris and then, in the summer of 1940, he fled to the United States. There he served as a priest in Seattle, Washington, and in Hollywood, California, returning to Germany in 1945 as an American citizen. He remained in Germany until his death, devoting himself to charitable work.

Bibliography:

A. *Kardinal Faulhaber* (Vienna, 1933); *Karl Kraus, der Zeitkämpfer* (Vienna, 1937); *Der neue Weltmonarch* (Augsburg, 1948); *Ein römisches Jahr* (Innsbruck, 1936).

B. Peter Jakob Kock, "Mit spitzer Feder gegen Hitler. George Moenius - ein streitbarer Publizist und Priester," in *Unser Bayern, Heimatbeilage der Bayerischen Staatszeitung*, 10 (October, 1980), 75ff; Dieter Riesenberger, *Die Katholische Friedensbewegung in der Weimarer Republik* (Düsseldorf, 1976); Werner Röder and Herbert A. Strauss, eds., *Biographisches Handbuch der deutschsprachigen Emigration nach 1933* (Munich/New York/London/Paris, 1980), I, 505.

Lothar Wieland
Trans. by Peter Seadle

MØLLER, Diderike (Dikka) Annette Anker (18 June 1838, Østfold, Norway—26 November 1912, Christiania [now Oslo]). *Career*: peace activist.

Dikka Møller became a peace activist after the death of her husband in 1885. Dedicated to the cause of peace, she was largely influenced by her strong Christian education and feelings, and by her friendship with the pacifist author, *Bjørnstjerne Bjørnson. It was largely as a result of her efforts that the Norges Fredsforening (Norwegian Peace Association) was founded in 1895. She became one of the association's most active members and, in 1898, its head. Overcoming extreme shyness, she became an effective speaker and peace propagandist. In addition, she wrote articles for *Det Norske Fredsblad* (*The Norwegian Peace Journal*). As leader of the Norwegian Peace Association, Møller was instrumental in gaining support in Norway for the statement of support which the association sent to the Hague Peace Conference in 1899. She took the initiative in founding a Norwegian section of Alliance universelle des femmes pour la paix (Universal Alliance of Women for Peace), and was for a time president of its Norwegian section and later its honorary president. She also was elected Norwegian representative to the peace section of the International Committee of Women.

Møller contributed greatly to the peace movement, both morally and economically, and her extensive correspondence with her fellow countrywomen meant much to them for the encouragement and guidance which she provided. Her correspondence with the Swedish peace leader *Emila Broomé contributed significantly to the peaceful separation of Norway from Sweden in 1905 and to Sweden's recognition of Norway as an independent nation. At the time of her death, Møller was venerated by all as ''Peace Mother.''

Bibliography:

B. Margareta Larson, ''Kvinnoföreningar i Sverige med fred på sitt program,'' Ph.D., dissertation, Univ. of Stockholm, 1970; *Norsk Biografisk Lexikon*.

Elisabeth Ståhle

MONATTE, Pierre (15 January 1881, Monlet, Haute-Loire, France—27 June 1960, Paris). *Education*: baccalauréat, Coll. de Brioude. *Career*: editor, *La Vie Ouvrière*, 1909-14, 1919-22; editor, *La Révolution Prolétarienne*, 1925-39, 1947-51; member, Executive Committee, Confédération générale du travail, 1904-14; proof-reader, revolutionary syndicalist, and internationalist.

Pierre Monatte was born in Monlet in the Haute-Loire. Profoundly influenced by *Victor Hugo's *Les Miserables* and the many anarchist publications he read as a young man, he moved to Paris in 1902 and there worked for or collaborated with the journals *Pages Libres, Temps Nouveaux*, and *Libertaire*. In Paris, he met *Alphonse Merrheim, secretary in 1904 of the Federation of Metalworkers and a leading antimilitarist, and Emile Pouget, assistant secretary-general of the Confédération Générale de Travail (General Confederation of Labor) (CGT) from 1902-8. In 1904 Monatte took up the trade that he would exercise for the rest of his working life, that of proof-reader. That same year, he became a member of the CGT's Executive Committee and in 1909, founded *La Vie Ouvrière*, a revolutionary syndicalist review devoted to providing CGT leaders with intellectual and factual support for their activities. Among its contributors were Merrheim, *Alfred Rosmer, *Georges Yvetot, Victor Griffuelhes, and Georges Dumoulin.

Shortly after the start of World War I, Monatte, who was a committed internationalist, converted the editorial offices of *La Vie Ouvrière* into an informal center of opposition to patriotism and the war fever sweeping the CGT leadership. Syndicalist activists like Rosmer, Dumoulin, and Merrheim met there to work out a strategy of resistance to the war. The review, however, suspended publication during the conflict.

Monatte also protested the war by publicly resigning, in December 1914, from the CGT's Executive Committee. He took this action because the Executive Committee refused to implement its prewar antimilitarist stand and, more specifically, to demonstrate against the CGT's refusal to attend an international socialist conference sponsored by the Scandinavian socialists. In his letter of resignation, which Monatte printed and circulated among the CGT's directors, he charged that some syndicalist leaders had used "a language worthy of pure nationalists." He concluded that "to speak of peace, in these tragic hours, is the duty which falls upon all workers' organizations conscious of their role." Shortly after Monatte's resignation, the government drafted him. Although he could no longer take such public stands, he kept in close private contact with the antiwar group that had gathered around *La Vie Ouvrière*. He was demobilized in March 1919 and immediately resumed his syndicalist activities.

Following World War I, Monatte set two priorities for himself: to support the Russian Revolution and to push the CGT in a revolutionary direction. He lined up with the minority opposition within the CGT and attacked the Confederation's Executive Committee for supporting the wartime *union sacrée* and for not being sufficiently enthusiastic about the Russian Revolution. When the CGT split into reformist and communist wings—something Monatte regretted—Monatte sided with the communists. In March 1922 he began to write for *L' Humanité*, and in May 1923 he joined the French Communist party. Soon after, however, he began to attack the increasing bureaucratization of the party. In April 1922 he resigned from *L'Humanité*. Two years later the party expelled him because of his persistant criticisms. In January 1925 he founded *La Révolution Prolétarienne*, a monthly review committed to a syndicalist-communist position. Monatte continued to simultaneously criticize and battle against reformism on the one hand and, on the other, against rigidity and especially Stalinism within the Communist movement.

During World War II, Monatte, always faithful to his internationalism, opposed war and fascism alike. After 1939 he suspended publication of *La Révolution Prolétarienne* because of government censorship. He took no public stand during the conflict, but was extremely hostile to the German occupation of France and maintained contact with the syndicalist resistance movement. His basic position was that one should struggle against the occupation but not be swept up by nationalism or the *union sacrée* mentality.

Bibliography:

A. *Syndicalism revolutionnaire et communisme: les archives de Pierre Monatte*, ed. by Jean Maitron and Colette Chambelland (Paris, 1968); *Trois Scissions Syndicales* (Paris, 1958); *La lutte syndicale*, ed. by Colette Chambelland (Paris, 1976).

B. Jean Maitron, ed., *Dictionnaire Biographique du Mouvement Ouvrier Français* (Paris, 1976), pt. 3, XIV, 117-23.

C. Pierre Monatte Archives, Institut français d' Histoire Sociale, Paris.

Nicholas Papayanis

MONETA, Ernesto Teodoro (20 September 1833, Milan, Italy—10 February 1918, Milan). *Education*: Liceo di Brera, Scuola Militare di Ivrea. *Career*: editor, *Il Secolo* (Milan), 1867-96; editor, *La vita internazionale* (Milan), 1898-1918; journalist and pacifist.

Pacifism became important to Ernesto Teodoro Moneta as a result of his wartime experiences in the Risorgimento. A Mazzinian and a combatant in all the peninsular wars from 1848 to 1866, Italy's pioneering pacifist was always immensely proud of having been with Giuseppe Garibaldi in Sicily. After unification he joined the national army of King Vittorio Emanuele II and remained in the South where he fought against the brigands. However, Italy's crushing defeat at Custoza in 1866 ended his military career and intitiated the dramatic transformation of his thinking about war.

Moneta certainly did not become a pacifist in 1866, but rather left the army with the vague idea of waging a journalistic campaign for military reform, as well as for other reforms that would strengthen the country. He joined the staff of Milan's *Secolo* in 1866 and the next year became editor, a position he would hold until 1896. From this powerful editorial base, Moneta sought to influence public opinion in favor of the progressive ideas of the day—disarmament, international arbitration, European federalism—and it was in association with other progressive thinkers that pacifism gradually became an important issue with him. Under Moneta's direction the paper never ceased to be vibrantly patriotic and nationalistic, but it was a patriotism and a nationalism of the older Mazzinian vintage, with the nation serving as an instrument for world peace.

Increasingly influenced by the ideas of *Hodgson Pratt and *Frédéric Passy, Moneta took the lead in organizing the Italian pacifist movement. In 1878 he helped to establish the League of Liberty, Brotherhood, and Peace in Milan. Ten years later Moneta was heavily involved in establishing the Lombard Union for Peace and Arbitration, and throughout the Umbertian period he opposed Italy's expansionist designs in Africa while simultaneously working to reduce the threat of war with France and Austria. Pacifists the world over cheered in 1907 when he received the Nobel Peace Prize in recognition of these services, as well as for his principal role in nearly all the major European peace conferences during a thirty-year period.

In 1911, however, most of these well-wishers turned on the now blind old man in a fury of vindictiveness over his perceived betrayal of the peace movement. The cause of Moneta's fall from their favor was his refusal to condemn the Italian war against the Turks in Libya. In the editorial columns of *La vita internazionale*, a journal he had founded in 1898 and which had become the main literary vehicle of Italian pacifism, he even defended Italy's military policies in Africa. Moneta justified them on orthodox Mazzinian grounds, that internationalism would only be possible with a full flowering of nationalism, which in practical terms meant that world peace would come only after his nation got what it needed to fulfill its destiny. Thus, under the pressure of twentieth century events Mazzinian nationalism proved to be no different than any other form of nationalism. That Moneta should have become an ardent supporter of the Italian war effort in 1915 was perfectly logical in the context of what he had been writing since 1911 and what he had believed since the 1860s. To the old Risorgimento veteran, Italy was still the highest immediate good, and he died at the age of eighty-four, near the end of World War I, pronouncing a patriotic benediction to his uniformed son, Luigi.

Bibliography:

A. *Le Guerre, le insurrezioni e la pace nel secolo xix* (4 vols., Milan, 1903-10); *L'Italia e la conferenza dell' Aja* (Milano, 1911); *La Pace ed il diritto nella tradizione italiana* (Nobel Peace Prize acceptance speech) (Milan, 1909); *Patria e umanità: orrori dell'invasione delle truppe alleate in Cina* (Milan, 1900).

B. Sandi E. Cooper, ed., *Internationalism in Nineteenth Century Europe: the Crisis of Ideas and Purpose* (New York and London, 1976); Christian Louis Lange, *Histoire de l'internationalisme*, vol. 3 (New York, 1963); Filippo Meda, "Teodoro Moneta," *Nuova antologia*, April 16, 1918.

Richard Drake

MONNET, Jean Omer Marie Gabriel. See *Biographical Dictionary of Internationalists*.

MONTESSORI, Maria (31 August 1870, Chiaravalle, Ancona, Italy—6 May 1952, Noordwijk aan Zee, Netherlands). *Education*: graduate, Regia Scuola Tecnica Michelangelo Buonarroti, 1886; graduate, Regia istituto tecnico Leonardo da Vinci, 1890; Diploma di licenza, Univ. of Rome, 1892, M.D., 1896; additional studies in psychology, pedagogy, and anthropology, Univ. of Rome, 1898-99, 1901-3. *Career*: practicing physician, 1896-1910; lecturer in hygiene and anthropology, Regio istituto superiore di Magistero Femminile, 1899-1906, 1911-16; co-director, Scuola magistrale Ortofrenica, 1900-1; lecturer in pedagogical anthropology, Univ. of Rome, 1904-8; director, Casa dei Bambini, Rome, 1907-10; government inspector of schools, Italy, 1922; president Association Montessori internationale, 1929-52; author, lecturer, and educator.

Maria Montessori was the first woman admitted to the Medical School at the University of Rome, and the first woman in Italy to receive an M.D. degree. Early in her career she became involved in the treatment of mentally retarded children, who until that time had been given only custodial care in institutions for the mentally ill. Her discovery that they were educable led to the development of an educational method which she then applied to normal children in nursery schools (Children's Houses) for children of the poor in Rome. The key elements of her system were "self education" (letting children find out things for themselves), training the sensory faculties by handwork before moving on to intellectual training, self-restraint on the part of parents and teachers so as not to impose their own personalities on children, abolition of rewards, marks, and punishments from the educational process, and discipline that was entirely free and self-imposed. Results of this system were so remarkable in contrast to the traditional authoritarian approaches that, from 1907 on, educators from all over the world flocked to learn her system and to establish Montessori schools in their own countries.

In addition to numerous honors as one of the leading educational innovators of the twentieth century, Montessori was nominated for the Nobel Peace Prize in three successive years—1949, 1950, and 1951. Having expressed opposition to war and militarism throughout her career, her main contribution to the peace movement came during the last two decades of her life. She developed her views on the relation between education and peace through numerous lectures given at meetings of the League of Nations, the International Bureau of Education, the International Peace Congress (Brussels, 1936), the International School of Philosophy, the World Fellowship of Faiths, the Theosophical Society, UNESCO, and many other groups. Two of the nine International Montessori Congresses which she called were devoted to peace and education (the sixth, at Copenhagen in 1937, and the eighth, at San Remo, Italy in 1949). Some of her lectures, given at various places in Europe from 1932 to 1939, were published together in 1949 under the title *Educazione e pace*. Jaime Torres Bodet, UNESCO's Director General, introduced her to the June 1950 UNESCO conference in Florence as "someone who has become a symbol of our great expectations for education and world peace."

Anticipating the recent discussions of "positive peace," Montessori conceived of peace as much more than the absence of war; she envisioned a condition of social health in which justice, love, and harmony would prevail. To build such a world, content-oriented efforts at peace education would not suffice. The only way to establish a lasting peace, she argued, is by a radical reform of the entire process of education, beginning at birth, so that education no longer stifles the normal development of individuals but rather fosters the spiritual liberation of humanity. Montessori proposed her own educational theory and method as a starting point, but was also an early proponent of a science of peace. Such a science would investigate the essential social and psychological conditions of human development that could establish peace as a permanent way of life for all human beings.

As leader of the international educational movement which bore her name, Montessori traveled widely and spent many years outside Italy lecturing, giving courses, and establishing schools, especially in Spain, England, the Netherlands, and India (where she was interned during World War II as an Italian national). While a definitive assessment of her role in the development of peace education and research remains to be made, she appears to have had a formative influence in urging the development of a science of peace, fostering ideas of positive peace and of education for liberation, and emphasizing the essential connections between peace and education at all levels.

Bibliography:

A. *The Absorbent Mind* (Adyar, Madras, 1949); "Disarmament in Education," *New Era*, 13 (September, 1932), 257-59, also in *American Childhood* 18 (January, 1933), 14; *Education for a New World* (Adyar, Madras, 1946); *Educazione e Pace* (Milan, 1949, translated by Helen R. Lane as *Education and Peace*, Chicago, 1972); *Peace and Education* (Geneva, 1932); *Peace and Education* (Adyar, Madras, 1943); *The Reform of Education During and After Adolescence* (Amsterdam, 1939); *The Secret of Childhood* (London, 1936); *To Educate the Human Potential* (Adyar, Madras, 1948).

B. J. N. Burstyn, "Maria Montessori," *History of Education Quarterly*, 19 (Spring 1979), 143-49; Gilbert E. Donahue, *Dr. Maria Montessori and the Montessori Movement: A General Bibliography of Materials in the English Language, 1909-1961* (Detroit, 1962); *The Education of Man for a Peaceful World Community: Congress Report of the XIIIth International Montessori Congress, Amsterdam-Holland, April 1-4, 1964* (Amsterdam, 1964); A. M. Joosten and R. K. Gupta, eds., *Maria Montessori's Contribution to Educational Thought and Practice* (New Delhi, 1970); Rita Kramer, *Maria Montessori: A Biography* (New York, 1976); Anna Maccheroni, *True Romance: Dr. Maria Montessori as I Knew Her* (Edinburgh, 1947); Marziola Pignatari, ed., *Maria Montessori: Cittadina del mondo* (Rome, 1967); Maria Remiddi, "Vision of Mankind Transformed: Maria Montessori and Education for Peace," *UNESCO Courier*, 17 (April, 1964), 16-20; E. M. Standing, *Maria Montessori: Her Life and Work* (London, 1957); U. S. Bureau of Education, Library Division, *List of References on Maria Montessori and Her Methods* (Washington, DC, 1913, 1914).

Clinton F. Fink

MONTLUC, Léon de (9 July 1847, Châtillon-en-Vendelais, Ille-et-Vilaine, France—10 December 1933, Havre). *Education*: Lycée Bonaparte and Lycée Louis-le-Grand, Paris; Licencié ès Lettres and Docteur en Droit, Univ. of Paris, 1867. *Career*: private secretary to Jules Favre; officer, French Army, 1870-71; sub-prefect, Brest; prefect, Morbihan; counseiller, cours de Grenoble, Angers, Douai; author and peace activist.

Descended from one of France's most fearsome warriors, Blaise de Montluc, as well as from a member of the National Convention in the French Revolution, Léon de Montluc was an avowed supporter of the French Republic. After a brilliant career as a student (his doctoral dissertation won the gold medal at Paris), he became an important member of the judiciary as well as a respected legal scholar on a wide variety of topics. His rise in the judiciary was remarkable for a young man, going from 1877 at Grenoble to become president of the court at Douai (1889) and then honorary counsellor. At the same time, he published some of his most important works—a study of the Mexican criminal code, of the Mexican leader, Benito Jaurez, a comparative study of British and French legal procedure, and an important refutation of the right of conquest argued by the German scholar Holtzendorf.

De Montluc's reputation brought him an invitation to join the Institut de droit international (Institute of International Law) and he became an active participant at meetings and through his contributions to the journal. He also became interested in workers' cooperatives, helping to stimulate their establishment in Fougères where he also served as mayor and a member of the town council. At 37, de Montluc was awarded the rank of officer in the Legion of Honor.

As a young man de Montluc joined the Ligue internationale de la paix et de la liberté (International League of Peace and Freedom). De Montluc remained one of the most reliable members of the League, faithful to its mixture of republican ideals and progressive social views as well as its objective, an organized international peace. On behalf of the League, he spoke widely around northern and western France, creating sub-sections of the society including an important group at Lille. De Montluc never wavered from his view that international law and arbitration were patriotically respectable positions to support. In his own town, Fougères, he established a peace journal, *Paix et Travail*, which merged peace and issues of concern to the cooperatives that he backed.

Along with other members of the League, de Montluc always believed that defensive war was justified and thus, with a sad heart, supported the French cause in 1914. Following World War I and the death of *Emile Arnaud, head of the League, de Montluc became president of the organization from 1921-28. Besides running its affairs, including the journal, *Les Etats-Unis d'Europe*, de Montluc undertook to preserve much of the history of the peace society before 1914 through long articles in the journal on the lives and works of its founders.

Bibliography:

A. *Correspondance de Juarez* (Paris, 1885); *Droit de Conquête* (Ghent, 1871-2); *Procédure criminelle britannique et française comparée* (Paris, 1910).

B. J. Pr. [Jules Prudhommeaux], "Léon de Montluc," *La Paix par le droit* 44, 12 (December, 1934), 495-96; Michel Revon, "Léon de Montluc," *Les Etats-Unis d'Europe*, 66th year (Paris, 1934).

Sandi E. Cooper

MONTÚFAR Y RIVERA MAESTRE, Lorenzo (11 March 1823, Guatemala City, Guatemala—21 May 1898, Guatemala City). *Education*: Bachiller en Leyes, Univ. de San Carlos Borromeo, 1845; Doctor en Leyes, Univ. de Santo Tomás, 1865. *Career*: lawyer, judge, jurist, legislator, university professor and administrator, politician, diplomat, and historian.

Lorenzo Montúfar published his final work, an international law text, in 1893. By that time, he had been foreign minister in Costa Rica and in Guatemala and he had represented those two states, as well as El Salvador, in Europe, the United States, and Peru. He had introduced international law courses in Costa Rica and Guatemala in the 1880s. Montúfar's book sought to explain normal diplomatic practice in peace time, explored the causes of war and the means of averting hostilities like arbitration, embargoes, and troop mobilizations, and outlined the rules of warfare, the rights of neutral nations, and the procedures for ceasing hostilities. It was an impressive monument to his many active years as politician, statesman, and historian.

Earlier, as a diplomat, Montúfar had worked toward the peaceful settlement of international disputes. In the 1870s, through negotiations, he pressed Costa Rica's claims to Colombian territory, based upon the evidence of historic documents rather than force. His insistence that this could also be done in Guatemala's controversy with Mexico over control of Chiapas led to his resignation from the Justo Rufino Barrios cabinet in 1882. Later, he sought documents in the Seville archive to support Guatemalan sovereignty over Belice.

Within Central America, he also attempted to negotiate the peaceful resolution of two quarrels. He argued that Costa Ricans had free access to the San Juan River under international law, despite Nicaraguan claims. Likewise, he presided over a meeting of plenipotentiaries at Amapala in 1871 to resolve a conflict between El Salvador and Honduras. Although none of these disputes were finally resolved in Montúfar's lifetime, he devoted unceasing efforts to rebuilding Central America unity. He believed that the division of the Isthmus into five states had invited British territorial expansion and the filibuster expedition of William Walker. Reunification was the theme of his major historical work, *Reseña histórica de Centro-América* (*Brief History of Central America*) (1878-88). In addition, he encouraged the development of railroads, telegraph lines, and an interoceanic canal as economic bases for political unity.

Montúfar opposed provincialism. He visited Europe five times and the United States five times over a thirty-year period. He promoted immigration, even to the extent of authorizing cemeteries and places of worship for non-Catholic foreigners in Costa Rica. He was a consistent free trade advocate and he was one of the first Latin Americans to contribute to the *Royal Spanish Dictionary*.

Upholding the ideal of civilian supremacy over the military, Montúfar argued that standing armies disrupted the labor supply and consumed goods without producing anything. Nevertheless, he saw universal conscription as an instrument for education and a deterrent to personal armies. As Costa Rican war minister, he averted a coup through negotiations and discouraged exiles from operations against El Salvador and Guatemala. His theory of government respected human rights and he believed equally in a strong judiciary and the abolition of capital punishment.

Certain imperfections marred Montúfar's stand for peace. He participated in the military coup that brought Tomás Guardia to power in Costa Rica and he supported the military dictatorship of Barrios in Guatemala. He lived, however, in an unsettled era. Three of the eight presidents he served met violent deaths. One of his sons, General José Montúfar, died in battle. On the other hand, another son, Rafael, was a founding member of the Guatemalan Red Cross.

Bibliography:

A. *Memorias autobiográficas* (Guatemala, 1898); *Nociones de derecho de gentes y leyes de la guerra para los ejércitos centroamericanos* (Guatemala, 1893); *Reseña histórica de Centro-américa* (7 vols.; Guatemala, 1878-1888).

B. Robert H. Claxton, "Lorenzo Montúfar, Central American Liberal," Ph.D. dissertation, Tulane University, 1970.

Robert H. Claxton

MOORE, Eleanor May (10 March 1875, Lancefield, Victoria, Australia—1 October 1949, Melbourne). *Education*: Malvern Road State School; Presbyterian Ladies' Coll. *Career*: reporter, secretary, and peace activist.

Eleanor Moore devoted most of her adult life to the cause of peace and to the involvement of women in the peace movement. As a young woman she studied stenography and, at age 20, was only the second woman to qualify as a shorthand reporter in the law courts, a position she was never allowed to take up because of her sex. In her early adulthood she had several jobs including one as a reporter for *Hansard* and another for eight years as a secretary for a large stock and station agency, Dalgety and Company, in Melbourne. In later life she supplemented her income by working as a freelance reporter. She never married, but inherited the family house in Toorak, Melbourne where she lived with her younger sister, Daisy. Her constant employment and frugal lifestyle enabled her, in 1904, to travel to Europe. Although skeptical about religion, she was a member of the congregation of *Charles Strong's Australian Church and worked in several of the church societies and other social welfare bodies with which he was associated. Like him, too, she was an absolute and uncompromising pacifist, and in later life was very scathing toward those peaceworkers who abandoned pacifism as they grew older, more affluent, and more influential.

Moore's involvement in the peace movement dates from the First World War. In March 1915 she became a foundation member and international secretary of the Sisterhood of International Peace, a group which in 1920 became the Australian section of the Women's International League for Peace and Freedom (WILPF). Principal among its aims was the substitution of arbitration for war. In 1928 she became general-secretary of the group, a post she held until her death. Although WILPF could never boast more than a few hundred members throughout Australia, the work it achieved was impressive and it became the most enduring group in the Australian peace movement. The dedicated and indefatigable Moore was its central figure. She personified WILPF, whose self-appointed role was to educate the public about the causes and effects of war. It favored persuasion over provocation and its activities and efforts were characterized by decorum, restraint, and persistence. Naturally enough much emphasis was devoted to describing the impact of war on women and children. Constant attempts were made to persuade the Education Department of Victoria to have less jingoistic songs sung and less militaristic books read by children in the classroom.

During World War I Moore became one of six women members of the executive of the Australian Peace Alliance, a composite organization formed in October 1914 to advocate negotiated peace, general disarmament, the abandonment of secret diplomacy, and the civil liberties of antiwar activists. Moore took part in the campaigns of 1916 and 1917 against the government's attempts to introduce conscription for overseas military service. She addressed countless meetings and wrote several pamphlets on the subject. During this period she was expelled from the National Council of Women, a group which favored a vigorous prosecution of the war. In May 1919 she was the sole representative of the Sisterhood of International Peace at the International Women's Congress in Zurich. There she met the veteran American peaceworker and international president of WILPF, *Jane Addams, a woman for whom Moore had an intense admiration and later described as "a patron saint." Later that year she addressed many meetings in England. Returning to Australia in February 1920, she became part-time secretary of the Australian Peace Alliance but the group folded two years later. During the postwar years, Moore and WILPF pressed for the revision of the Treaty of Versailles and the cancellation of reparations from the defeated nations.

During the interwar years Moore was in great demand as a speaker not only in Melbourne but also in Sydney. In 1928 she became a vice-president of the Melbourne section of the World Disarmament Movement, a group which lasted five years and attracted much wider support than the Australian Peace Alliance. That year, and again in 1930, she represented WILPF at the Pan Pacific Women's Union Conference in Honolulu, lecturing in New Zealand before returning to Australia. Between 1936 and 1938, as a representative of the Australian Pan Pacific Women's Conference and on the invitation of the Country Women's Association of Victoria, she undertook a series of lecturing tours in Victoria and southern New South Wales. But the approach of the Second World War posed many problems. Disbelieving that the principal causes of war were economic, WILPF and Moore found it difficult to cooperate with other peaceworkers, particularly the socialists and communists. While WILPF advocated the establishment of a Ministry for Peace, other groups sought to build up an alliance against Nazi Germany. During the 1930s WILPF severed connections with both the International Peace Campaign, because it appeared to sanction joint military action, and the Movement Against War and Fascism, because its promoters were very sympathetic with the Soviet Union.

During the war years, WILPF suffered decline and several branches fell apart. Especially after Russia joined the Allies in June 1941, communism not pacifism attracted new adherents. That WILPF did not completely dissolve in Australia must be attributed to Moore and a tiny core of members. Old age and the debilitating effects of Parkinson's disease did not deter her. In August 1945, two days before the bombing of Hiroshima, she spoke at a public meeting against the further manufacture and use of atomic bombs, and over the next three years she attended as many interstate conferences organized by the Federal Pacifist Council. She completed nearly a lifetime of service to the peace movement with her semi-autobiographical history of the movement in Melbourne, a book finished only a few months before her death.

Bibliography:

A. *The Quest for Peace: As I Have Known It in Australia*, (Melbourne, 1949).

B. Mary Colligan, "Brothers and Sisters in Peace: The Peace Movement in Melbourne, 1900-18," Bachelor of Arts thesis, Monash University, 1973; *Peacemaker*, November 1949.

C. Eleanor Moore Papers; Mitchell Library, Sidney.

Malcolm Saunders

MOORE, John Bassett. See *Biographical Dictionary of Internationalists.*

MOREL, Edmund Dene (15 July 1873, Paris—12 November 1924, Dartmoor, England). *Education*: student, Bedford Modern School, 1886-88. *Career*: shipping clerk, Elder Dempster Company, Liverpool, 1890-1901; subeditor, *West Africa*, 1901-3; editor, *West African Mail*, 1903-16; honorary secretary, Congo Reform Association, 1904-13; honorary secretary, Union of Democratic Control, 1914-24; editor, *Foreign Affairs*, 1919-24; Member of Parliament (for Dundee), 1922-24.

Born Georges Edmund Morel de Ville, the son of a French father and an English mother, Morel received an English education and returned to live permanently in England at the age of seventeen. A post as a clerk in a shipping firm engaged in the African trade gave him access to news of African developments that provided him with material for a part-time career in journalism which he pursued under the name "E. D. Morel." At first merely a spokesman for the Liverpool shipping interests, Morel gradually developed a critical attitude toward much European activity in Africa, deploring its effect on African culture of which, under the tutelage of the anthropologist Mary Kingsley he had become a great admirer.

In 1900 Morel published the first of his numerous exposés of conditions in King Leopold's Congo where natives were forced, by various brutal methods, to collect rubber without receiving payment in return. Four years later, with the assistance of Roger Casement, Morel founded the Congo Reform Association with the purpose of bringing pressure on the British Foreign Office to use its influence to force the Belgian king to relinquish the territory. Morel served as honorary secretary of the organization, and he proved to be a superb organizer and propagandist, welding missionaries, humanitarians, and businessmen into an effective pressure group.

Although British diplomatic efforts finally led to the annexation of King Leopold's Congo by the Belgian Parliament and to the subsequent reform of the infamous rubber system, Morel had, in the course of the campaign, become critical both of the British Foreign Office and of the Anglo-French entente. These views led him, in 1914, to oppose Britain's participation in World War I. He was the leading figure in the antiwar Union of Democratic Control, a group formed to expose the "secret diplomacy" that he was convinced had led to the war. Utilizing the organizational and propaganda techniques he had perfected during the Congo campaign, Morel succeeded in building a significant movement that received an increasingly sympathetic hearing on the Left in the final years of the conflict.

Although Morel had been a prospective Liberal candidate for Parliament on the outbreak of the war, his critical view of the Liberal Government's foreign policy led him in 1918 to join the Independent Labour party, a small antiwar socialist group affiliated with the Labour party. Between 1919 and 1924 he was a major influence in the shaping of the Labour party's foreign policy, and he used that influence to enlist the party in the crusade for revision of the Treaty of Versailles. Elected to the House of Commons in 1922, he was not included in the Labour Government of 1924 and devoted the final months of his life to efforts, usually unsuccessful, to hold the Labour party to the extreme revisionist position it had earlier adopted at his urging.

Bibliography:

A. *E. D. Morel's History of the Congo Reform Movement*, ed. by William Roger Louis and Jean Stengers (Oxford, 1968); *Great Britain and the Congo* (London, 1909); *King Leopold's Rule in Africa* (London, 1904); *Morocco in Diplomacy* (London, 1912, e.g. reissued as *Ten Years of Secret Diplomacy*, London, 1915); *Truth and the War* (London, 1916).

B. Catherine A. Cline, *E.D. Morel, 1873-1924: The Strategies of Protest* (Belfast, 1981); F. Seymour Cocks, *E. D. Morel: The Man and His Work* (London, 1920); Marvin Schwartz, *The Union of Democratic Control in British Politics during the First World War* (Oxford, 1971).

Catherine Ann Cline

MORGAN, Laura Puffer. See *Biographical Dictionary of Internationalists*.

MORHARDT, Mathias (1863, France?—1939, France?). *Career*: general-secretary, Société d'études documentaires et critiques sur la guerre, 1916-39; antiwar activist.

Little is known about Mathias Morhardt's private life or his career. He received a good deal of public attention, however, because of his pacifist work which was largely accomplished through his activity in the Société d'études documentaires et critiques sur la guerre (Society for the Documentary and Critical Studies of the War) (SEDC). Established on January 23, 1916, the SEDC was organized principally by Morhardt and *Georges Demartial, but among the forty individuals who attended the initial meeting were such notable figures as *Charles Gide, *Victor Basch, and Charles Seignobos.

At the outbreak of World War I in 1914, Demartial, an official in the Ministry of Colonies, was assigned to Bordeaux as liaison with the Banque d'Indochine. Repelled by what he observed, he resigned within the week to undertake a study of the diplomatic documents leading to the war. Shortly thereafter, he and Morhardt, who was then secretary-general of the Ligue des droits de l'homme (League for the Rights of Man), resigned from the Central Committee and from the League itself, in protest against the chauvinist majority on the Committee.

The initial meetings of the SEDC became the subjects of police reports. At an October meeting, Morhardt announced that the journal *Demain* printed in Switzerland but proscribed in France, would serve as the unofficial organ of the organization. The objectives of the SEDC were in the main, to expose the diplomatic background of the war and to reveal the blatant propaganda of the French government. Morhardt became general-secretary and devoted his remaining years to promoting these ends. He chose to live the semi-reclusive life of a scholar, seldom attending congresses of the peace organizations and generally avoiding public appearances. Instead, he assumed that meticulous research exposing France's share in the responsibility for the war and the government's role in deceiving the masses would convince all that war was unjustified.

In 1919 Morhardt signed the Villeneuve Declaration, protesting the thesis, included into the Treaty of Versailles, that Germany and her allies were solely responsible for the war. Again, in 1925, he joined with about one hundred others, including Gide, Jules Romain, *Victor Margueritte, and *Romain Rolland, demanding the abrogation of those articles in the treaty proclaiming Germany's war guilt (Article 231) and imposing sanctions on Germany (Articles 227-230). When the War Resisters' International circulated an anticonscription manifesto in 1926, calling for the abolition of military conscription in all countries, Morhardt was one of the earliest signers; this manifesto was adopted by the National Peace Congress (Valence,1926) and the International Peace Congress (Geneva, 1926). The following year, in an article in *L'Europe*, Morhardt asserted his opposition to the new Military Service Law, extending the period of service for conscripts, and in 1928, he endorsed Victor Margueritte's concept of *la patrie humaine*. Until his death in 1939, Morhardt served as head of the SEDC and contributed articles on antimilitaristic topics to numerous journals, including *Le Barrage*, *La Patrie Humaine*, *l'Humanité*, and *Vers la Verité*.

Bibliography:

A. *Les Preuves* (Paris, 1921, 1924).

B. Felicien Challaye, *Georges Demartial* (Paris, 1950); *La Patrie Humaine*, April 28, 1938.

C. Police reports F7-13086 & F7-13372, Archives National, Paris.

Albert S. Hill

MORRELL, Ottoline Bentinck (16 June 1873, London—21 April 1938, Tunbridge Wells, England). *Education*: private. *Career*: society hostess and art patron.

Ottoline Bentinck was born into the English aristocracy, into a family which was noted for its eccentrics. Throughout her adult life, she flouted convention in dress and in morals, both of which gained her notoriety. After her marriage in 1902 to the solicitor Philip Morrell, she established a salon in Bloomsbury, London and a country residence at Garsington outside Oxford which attracted many of the leading artists, poets, writers, and thinkers of Britain. She became the mistress of Augustus John, Henry Lamb, and *Bertrand Russell, and the friend of *Lytton Strachey, *Aldous Huxley, Virginia Woolf, T. S. Eliot, +John Maynard Keynes, D. H. Lawrence, Stanley Spencer, and *Siegfried Sassoon. Her independent means enabled her to be generous in support of them when they were struggling and this involved her in their quarrels and problems. They based characters on her in their novels and she resented their caricature portrayals; they resented their dependence on her generosity, but, despite everything, friendships continued and the gossip and legend grew.

Philip Morrell entered politics as a Liberal—to the consternation of his family and hers which were both staunchly Conservative—and Ottoline was vigorous in support, campaigning for him and active in his constituency after he had been elected. Both of them belonged to the section of the Liberal party opposed to the First World War and Philip Morrell made a speech in the House of Commons on August 3, 1914 condemning Britain's participation. Ottoline herself opposed the war as a Liberal, a woman, and a Christian.

After Britain entered the war, the Morrells, were a rallying point for the pacifist cause. Philip's courageous speech eventually cost him his seat in Parliament, but despite this setback to their hopes neither Philip nor Ottoline wavered in their opposition to the war. Ottoline was appalled at the upsurge in anti-German feeling, fomented by the press, and her immediate concern was to relieve the suffering and distress of interned aliens. She remained active in antiwar activities, in helping Belgian refugees, but outwardly her life as a society hostess was resumed.

In 1916 conscription was introduced in Britain. Philip Morrell voted in the House of Commons against its introduction and subsequently appeared as a solicitor on behalf of conscientious objectors at their tribunal hearings. Many of those who were granted exemption from military service by the tribunals were bound to undertake alternative service and many of these worked on Ottoline Morrell's country estate at Garsington, where they were condemned by the patriotic local people for their idleness and proved to be ineffective farmers. The Morrells, however, continued to strongly support the conscientious objectors' cause.

Ottoline Morrell never had a prominent position in public life in Britain and after the war she remained an unconventional and controversial figure in fashionable and intellectual society. Her importance as a peace leader was of two kinds—her courageous and outspoken opposition to the war at a time of patriotic war fever, and her generous and constant support of the war's opponents, such as Bertrand Russell, who had a much more prominent position of influence.

Bibliography:

A. *Ottoline*: vol. 1. *The Early Memoirs 1873-1915*, ed. by Robert Gathorne-Hardy (London, 1963); vol. 2, *Ottoline at Garsington 1915-1918*, ed. by Robert Gathorne-Hardy (London, 1974); *Ottoline, The Early Memoirs of Lady Ottoline Morrell*, ed. by Robert Gathorne-Hardy (New York, 1946).

B. Sandra Jobson Darroch, *Ottoline, The Life of Lady Ottoline Morrell* (New York, 1975).

C. Morrell Papers, Humanities Research Center, Austin, Texas.

Elnora Ferguson

MORRIS, Stuart (13 August 1890, London—1 November 1967, Gt. Henny, Sudbury, Suffolk, England). *Education*: Cranleigh; M.A., Corpus Christi Coll., Cambridge Univ. *Career*: ordained into Anglican Church; general secretary, Peace Pledge Union, 1937-43, 1947-64; pacifist lecturer and organizer.

After being ordained into the Anglican Church shortly before the outbreak of World War I, Stuart Morris became a canon and vicar at a church in Birmingham. During the war he served as a chaplain in the Fleet Air Arm, but was asked to resign from that office because of his pacifist sermons. His major service in the antiwar cause, however, did not start until 1934, when he responded to the Reverend *Dick Sheppard's appeal in the press for men to sign the pledge, "I renounce war and will never support or sanction another." Receiving thousands of replies, Sheppard founded the Peace Pledge Union (PPU) and Morris became its traveling secretary. When Sheppard died in 1937, Morris assumed the position of general secretary of the PPU, a position he held, with a short interruption of some four years, until his retirement in 1964. At the start of his full-time work for the PPU, and as his pacifist convictions grew stronger, Morris felt it necessary to resign his canonry and to renounce his Anglican Orders.

Morris's short separation from the PPU came about as the result of difficulties with British authorities. In 1943, after speaking in London's Hyde Park, he was approached by someone who claimed to work at the India Office. The unknown man offered to give him some confidential papers dealing with, among other issues, the government's intentions with regard to *Gandhi. Perhaps unwisely, Morris accepted the offer, although he never made use of the documents. Still, British officials came to know about the exchange of documents and arrested Morris under the Official Secrets Act. Tried and convicted, he was sentenced to nine months in prison. Following his release, he did a variety of work and three years later was reappointed general secretary of the PPU.

Morris had a flair for organization and administration, and he had a talent for mediating disputes amongst his pacifist colleagues and for creating consensus. In addition, he was an exceptional public speaker and was constantly in demand by PPU groups and other organizations throughout England. He also traveled widely in Europe and the United States, although American officials saw fit to intern him for several weeks on Ellis Island before allowing him to present his pacifist views. Apart from his work for the PPU, Morris served, for many years, as a member of the International Council of the War Resisters' International. He visited the Soviet Union and the German Democratic Republic as a member of peace delegations, and Yugoslavia on a fact-finding tour in connection with a border conflict between that country and Bulgaria.

Morris' pacifism was closely tied to his Christian faith. He believed that the essence of God was love, and his whole attitude to life and all aspects of pacifism rested on that conviction. "Not peace at any price but love at all costs" was one of his often repeated phrases. The true Christian, he felt, was not indifferent to evil, but resisted evil by overcoming it with good. For Morris, pacifism rested on the principle that the way to eliminate evil was to let good win out over what is bad and allow love to convert hatred and fear. He shared this idea with many other Christian pacifists, including Gandhi and *Martin Luther King.

Bibliography:

B. Sybil Morrison, *I Renounce War; The Story of the Peace Pledge Union* (London, 1962); Sybil Morrison, *The Life and Work of Stuart Morris* (London; [1968]).

Hilda Morris

MORRISON, Charles Clayton (4 December 1874, Harrison, OH—2 March 1966, Chicago, IL). *Education*: B.A., Drake Univ., 1898; fellow in philosophy, Univ. of Chicago, 1902-5. *Career*: ordained minister, Disciples of Christ, 1892; pastorates in Clarinda and Perry, IO, Chicago and Springfield, IL, 1892-1906; founder and editor, *Christian Century*, 1908-47; founder and editor, *Christendom* 1935-39; founder and editor, *Pulpit* 1929-47; editor of religious journals.

As editor of the *Christian Century*, Charles Clayton Morrison turned a broken-down denominational weekly into what was undoubtedly the most important Protestant journal in the world. From 1908, when he bought the magazine at a sheriff's sale, until he retired as editor in 1947, Morrison vigorously advanced the causes of social reform, liberal theology, and church union. Among his most famous crusades was the outlawry of war; indeed, Morrison was one of the initiators of the Kellogg-Briand Peace Pact.

Before World War I, Morrison claimed that technology and international morality were so advanced that war was unthinkable. When, in 1917, +Woodrow Wilson asked Congress for a declaration of war, Morrison supported the president. Wilson, he said, had no choice. Similarly, in 1920, Morrison called for entry into the League of Nations. By 1931, however, he considered the Great War a tragic mistake and denied that war was compatible with Christianity.

In his classic work, *The Outlawry of War* (1927), Morrison outlined the political cause closest to his heart. Dedicated to *Salmon O. Levinson, the Chicago attorney whose proposals Morrison backed, and possessing a laudatory forward by *John Dewey, the book called for isolating the renunciation of war from all other peace proposals. Morrison found the League of Nations and the Geneva Protocol of 1924 foolishly using "the war system" itself to curb a warring nation, the World Court a mere arbitration tribunal, and compulsory arbitration susceptible to manipulation by an offending power. Morrison endorsed Senator William Borah's resolution of February 1923, which would make war a public crime under the law of nations and would establish an international court empowered to decide pressing controversies. Indeed, to Morrison, war could not be fully outlawed until the nations had (1) codified the laws of peace and (2) set up a permanent international court, staffed it with the world's most competent jurors, and given it jurisdiction to summon an offending nation to the bar. Morrison opposed enforcement by economic and military sanctions, saying that "the plighted word of the nations," backed by the "united public opinion of the world," was the only compulsion necessary.

Critics claimed that the book revealed an ignorance of international politics, placed too much trust in the world's masses, dangerously bypassed existing international agencies, and reflected a tone of haughty superiority towards Europe. Praise came, however, from such figures as *Norman Thomas and Senator Borah. Morrison remained so active in the outlawry movement that he was invited to witness the final signing of the Kellogg-Briand Pact on August 27, 1928. "Today," he said, "international war was banished from civilization."

During the 1920s and 1930s, Morrison opposed rearmament and endorsed the Neutrality Acts. In 1933 he called for a boycott of German goods, and in the ensuing years he condemned German anti-Semitism and supported the anti-Nazi Confessional Church. Once World War II broke out in Europe, Morrison opposed all of +Franklin Roosevelt's interventionist moves. Repeatedly predicting that stalemate was imminent, he called for a negotiated peace. He even went as far as to serve as a sponsor of the Chicago chapter of the isolationist America First Committee and to testify before Congress against the president's proposals.

In a series of editorials written in 1941, Morrison outlined his ideal international order. It would include: general reduction of tariffs, with the ultimate goal of world free trade; an end to "monopolistic exploitation of empires;" general disarmament; freedom of the seas; a unified Europe; a world court with jurisdiction to administer a codified body of international law; the gradual abolition of all colonial empires; demilitarization of the Pacific; restoration of all occupied nations; plebiscites over disputed areas in Europe; and full sovereignty for China.

Once the Japanese attacked Pearl Harbor, Morrison called American entry into the war "an unnecessary necessity." While maintaining that the United States could have avoided war with Japan by more conciliatory policies, he found no way out but "the bloody war of slaughter and immeasurable sacrifice." In a series of much publicized editorials, put in book form in 1942, Morrison warned war backers against preaching a holy crusade and pacifists against arrogantly claiming to be above the conflict. War, he said in a most provocative passage, was neither righteous nor unrighteous, for it transcended all ethical categories. It was not sin but tragedy in its starkest form, the results of sin that preceded it. Indeed, it was God's judgment—a penality that people in their sinful blindness had brought upon themselves.

Yet Morrison did not remain silent, either during the war or afterwards. In October 1943 he sought a negotiated peace based upon an allied statement of war aims. In January 1945 he feared that the new United Nations charter, launched at Dumbarton Oaks, would simply mask the inevitable scramble for empire bound to follow the war. That August Morrison attacked what he called "America's atomic atrocity." Opposing such Cold War measures as the Truman Doctrine and the Atlantic Pact, he charged that they would bring about the very confrontation they were designed to avert.

Bibliography:

A. *The Outlawry of War: A Constructive Policy for World Peace* (Chicago, 1927); *The Christian and the War* (Chicago and New York, 1942).

B. "Apostle in Print," *Christian Century*, 83 (March 16, 1966), 323-25; "Voice of the Century," *Newsweek*, 29 (June 23, 1947), 72; NYT, March 4, 1966.

C. Charles Clayton Morrison papers and *Christian Century* archives, Morrison Library, Southern Illinois University, Carbondale, IL.

Justus D. Doenecke

MORROW, William Robert (22 October 1888, Rockhampton, Queensland, Australia—12 July 1980, Sydney). *Career*: railwayman and union official in North Queensland, 1898-1925; various jobs and businesses, 1925-35; secretary, Tasmanian branch, Australian Railways Union (ARU), 1936-46; member, national council, ARU, 1936-47; senior vice-president, ARU, 1937-42; vice-president and later president, Tasmanian Trades Union Council, 1943-46; member, Tasmanian Executive Australian Labor party (ALP), 1944-53; Federal Senator from Tasmania, 1947-53; member, Australian Peace Council, 1950-63; elected to Bureau of World Peace Council, 1953; secretary, New South Wales Peace Council, 1955-60; joint secretary, NSW Peace Committee for International Cooperation and Disarmament, 1960-63; foundation member, Australia China Society (ACS) and president of Queensland ACS; union official and peace activist.

Leaving school at the age of 10 to become "waterjoey" to a railway construction gang, Bill Morrow spent the next 27 years at various railway-related jobs. He eventually qualified as an engine driver, but his involvement in union affairs led to his election in 1920 to the position of full-time secretary of the North Queensland branch of the Australian Railways Union (ARU). At about the same time he joined the Communist party, only to resign a year later in disillusionment over its internal manipulations. However, throughout his long life he remained staunchly loyal to the cause of the workingman and outspoken in his espousal of radical socialism. His concept of an enduring class struggle carried over to a Leninist interpretation of the imperialist nature of modern wars.

Morrow had joined the Australian Labor party (ALP) in 1908, and during the First World War took an active part in the party's internal struggle over the issue of conscription for overseas service. When he and his fellow anticonscriptionists triumphed, thereby precipitating an alliance between the party's proconscriptionist national leadership and the parliamentary Opposition, he campaigned tirelessly to help defeat the newly formed Government's two conscription referenda. In future years his opposition to conscription never wavered. In 1938 he was expelled from the ALP over openly refusing to endorse its policy of universal military training, and in 1951, as a member of Federal Parliament, he led the debate against the National Service Bill in the Senate.

Although twice nominated by the ALP to stand for Federal Senate, winning on both occasions (1946 and 1951), Morrow's political career was marked by an unusually high degree of controversy, both within and outside the party. In an atmosphere of rabid anticommunism he was the only member of Federal Parliament to oppose the sending of Australian troops to Korea. Claiming, "we are creating an act of aggression in Korea," he advocated the withdrawal of United Nations forces to the 38th parallel and a conference to solve the conflict without further bloodshed. He took a host of other unpopular stands: he was the ALP's most outspoken critic of the Communist Party Dissolution Bill 1950; he charged the Australian Government, in 1950, with preparing for a war in Malaya; he defended his association with the Australian Peace Council and its sponsorship of the Stockholm Peace Petition as part of "the greatest force for peace in the world today;" he asserted that Australian whites were perpetrating on Aborigines a tragedy greater than any ever inflicted by the Japanese on the Chinese; and he aroused the ire of almost every established public figure in Australia by becoming the focal point of a call for the recognition of the People's Republic of China and its admission to the United Nations.

Failing to win a Senate seat in 1953, he turned his attention to full-time peace work with the World Council of Peace and its affiliates. He attended numerous conferences abroad, visiting enroute many of the communist and nonaligned nations. Although labelled a "pro-communist," the genuineness of his dedication to the cause of better understanding with the noncapitalist world was seldom questioned. Morrow's peace commitment was expressed in long hours of administrative work as well as endless rounds of public speaking. In recognition of these efforts he received the Joliot Curie Gold Medal and the International Lenin Peace Prize for 1960. However, his close relationship with the World Peace Council became strained as the gulf widened between the Soviet Union and China. Since he adhered to a strong Maoist position, he found it difficult to work with most of the political and religious components of the organized peace movement.

In 1963 Morrow retired from the secretaryship of the NSW Peace Committee and returned to Queensland. He spent the remainder of his life promoting Australian-Chinese friendship.

Bibliography:

B. Audrey Ferguson, *Biography of William Morrow* (forthcoming).

C. W. R. Morrow Collection, Fryer Memorial Library, University of Queensland.

Ralph Summy

MORSE, Wayne Lyman (20 October 1900, Madison, WI—22 July 1974, Portland, OR). *Education*: B.A., Univ. of Wisconsin, 1923, M.A., 1924; LL.B., Univ. of Minnesota, 1928; J.D., Columbia Univ., 1932. *Career*: teacher; university administrator; U.S. Senator, 1944-68.

Wayne Morse made a career of independent thinking and feisty politicking. Equipped with a sharp mind, a fast tongue, and a U.S. Senate seat, Morse operated during the 1960s as a prominent opponent of American intervention in Vietnam. Between 1964-68, he issued the critical attacks that epitomized liberal opposition to Washington's war in Indochina.

Morse always seemed to be on the attack. Born in Madison, Wisconsin in 1900, he was raised in a middle-income farm family that encouraged his competitive commitment to public speaking and debate. While teaching argumentation at the University of Minnesota, he earned a law degree and in 1929 began teaching law at the University of Oregon. Within three years, he rose to the deanship of the University's law school. During the 1930s Morse won a national reputation as an authority on criminal justice and as an industrial-labor negotiator. The latter achievement led to his service during World War II on the National War Labor Board. In 1944 Morse successfully ran as Oregon Republican candidate for the U.S. Senate. In Washington, he attached himself to the internationalist wing of the Republican party, supporting the United Nations Charter, the North Atlantic Treaty Organization, and President Truman's decision to intervene in Korea. In 1952, opposed to the party's retrograde platform, he backed Adlai Stevenson for the presidency and declared himself an Independent. Three years later, he officially registered as a Democrat.

Atlhough an extraordinary debater and floor speaker, Morse was a rather ordinary liberal senator in the 1950s—critical of U.S. Cold War tactics but tolerant of the anticommunist hysteria generated by Joseph R. McCarthy and his Senate colleagues. In 1960 Morse made an abortive run for the Democratic presidential nomination. Then, following John F. Kennedy's assassination in 1963, he became a warm supporter of Lyndon Johnson and his plans to build a Great Society. He showed less enthusiasm, however, for Johnson's willingness to wage a war in support of an anticommunist government in South Vietnam.

Early in 1964, Morse became (along with Alaskan Democrat *Ernest Gruening) one of the few vociferous Senate critics of U.S. involvement in Vietnam. Worried about Chinese intervention and concerned about America's counterrevolutionary image in the Third World, Morse attacked the foolhardiness of U.S. policy and the corruption of the Saigon regime. In August, 1964, following U.S. military escalation after the Tonkin Gulf incident, Morse blasted the Johnson administration for initiating an illegal war against North Vietnam in defiance of UN principles. He also attacked U.S.intervention as fundamentally immoral, arguing that the enormous harm inflicted upon Vietnamese civilians far exceeded in importance Washington's declared war aims.

During 1965-66, Morse repeatedly warned that the war might escalate into a nuclear conflict and protested Vietnam's cost to the Great Society. In speeches and appearances, the Oregon Democrat took an early and leading role in the proliferating antiwar opposition. His high position, apparent access to inside information, and professional if combative style all added credibility and fuller political legitimacy to antiwar dissent.

Morse's preferred alternatives, however, bared the limitations of liberal antiwar opposition. Rejecting the demand for immediate U.S. withdrawal from Vietnam, Morse backed the idea of an American troop reconcentration into protected coastal enclaves, the cessation of U.S. bombing of North Vietnam, and a negotiated settlement through international or third-party offices. At home, he opposed antiwar exercises in civil disobedience as harmful to reasoned debate. Furthermore he maintained that, if the Congress properly declared war in Vietnam, he would support the U.S. effort as firmly as he had the American cause in World War II and Korea.

The forcefulness of Morse's antiwar attacks ebbed in 1968, after the Tet offensive exposed the bankruptcy of Johnson's policies and as the Senator geared up for a tough reelection fight. After defeating a prowar Democrat in a bitter primary battle, Morse lost his reelection bid in November to Republican candidate Robert Packwood. Retreating into retirement, Morse returned in 1972 to lose another Senate contest against incumbent Republican Mark Hatfield. Two years later, while preparing to challenge Packwood, he died suddenly in Portland.

Wayne Morse offered some of the most incisive, inspiring, and widely circulated criticism of the U.S. war in Vietnam. A longtime political loner, he could provide no organizational support to the antiwar forces. Rather, he enhanced the visibility, credibility, and respectability of internal dissent.

Bibliography:

B. William Patrick Neal, "Senator Wayne L. Morse and the Quagmire of Vietnam, 1964-1968," Ph.D. dissertation, Univ. of Oregon, 1979); A. Robert Smith, *The Tiger in the Senate: The Biography of Wayne Morse* (New York, 1962).

C. Wayne L. Morse Papers, Special Collections, University of Oregon.

Charles DeBenedetti

MOSCHELES, Felix Stone (8 February 1833, London—22 December 1917, Tunbridge Wells, England). *Education*: King's Coll.; studies in Hamburg, Leipzig, Paris, and Antwerp. *Career*: portrait painter, pacifist activist, and author.

The son of the distinguished pianist-composer, Ignaz Moscheles, Felix Moscheles' childhood was spent in a circle of literary and artistic celebrities. Following some exciting experiences in the Central European Revolutions of 1848-49, Moscheles pursued his artistic studies in Paris and witnessed the coup d'etat of Louis Napoleon. In Paris his life was a fortunate blend of the best Parisian society and residence in the Bohemian Latin Quarter. It was as a student in the Atelier Gleyre that Moscheles began his career as an outstanding portrait painter. Following further study in Antwerp, he established a studio in London which attracted a variety of writers and artists including Du Maurier, Whistler, Dickens, Wilkie Collins, the Rossettis, Arthur Sullivan, Ellen Terry, and Margarete Sobernheim ("Grete," whom he married in 1875).

As a result of his experiences in the upheavals of 1848-50 and in Paris during the Franco-Prussian War and the Paris Commune in 1870-71, Moscheles became convinced that modern warfare was the curse of mankind. Thus, from 1870 onwards, he became (under the tutelage of *Hodgson Pratt) one of the most active workers in the international peace movement. Moscheles brought a new dimension to the British peace movement which was uniquely his own. While Pratt, *Henry Richard, *Richard Cobden, and *John Bright were staunchly English in outlook and distinguishable from Continental pacifists by their ardent political, economic, and religious bourgeois Liberalism, Moscheles was cosmopolitan and attracted to political refugees, radicals, trade unionists, and socialists. His studio in Chelsea was always the gathering place of foreign politicians of all creeds, revolutionaries, musicians, poets, eccentrics, and handsome women, enjoying the hospitality of the "Grelix", as Felix and Grete were known.

The fragmentation of the British and Continental peace movements into small sectional and sectarian groups, with a multiplicity of political, juridical, religious, and economic views, was an anathema to Moscheles. Hence he persistently advocated a more catholic and practical approach and especially the necessity for a unified peace movement. Thus in 1880, he assisted Pratt in establishing the International Arbitration and Peace Association of Great Britain and Ireland, with Pratt as president, and for three decades served as its chairman. Like such British pacifists as Pratt, *Evans Darby, and *Randal Cremer, who journeyed to the United States as "peace evangelists" during the 1880s and 1890s, Moscheles came to America in 1893. During his stay he painted the portrait of Grover Cleveland, while preaching to him international arbitration as a means of limiting war. In 1889 Moscheles told *Bertha von Suttner that his great mission was "propagandizing" the objectives of the Association wherever he traveled. With her assistance, he established a branch of the organization in Italy. Later, in 1892, they collaborated at the Fourth World Peace Congress and the Interparliamentary Conference in Berne and during 1896 Suttner assisted Moscheles in the establishment of a "Peace Day" on February 22 (later altered to May 18, to celebrate the opening date of the First Hague Conference) as an annual demonstration of the solidarity of the international peace movement.

During the "Peace Crusade," which preceded the First Hague Conference, Moscheles joined Darby, Cremer, Pratt, and +W. T. Stead in traversing Britain and in flooding the nation with peace literature to evoke support of the conference. He was a member of the deputation that communicated the results of the campaign to the Russian ambassador in London and subsequently went to The Hague to lobby delegates at the conference. Ever the optimist and encouraged by the limited success of the conference, Moscheles intensified his efforts on behalf of the peace movement. Following the outbreak of the Boer War in 1899, he joined British antiwar elements in denouncing the conflict and in demanding a cessation of hostilities. Neither verbal abuse nor physical vilification deterred Moscheles from his purpose until the end of the war in 1902.

Moscheles was also a friend and disciple of Dr. Ludovic Zamenhof, the inventor of Esperanto, and was the long-time president of the London Esperanto Club. By the early 1900s, Moscheles was a familiar figure at the annual International Peace Conferences and meetings of the Standing Committee of the Peace Movement in Berne where he was revered for his generous sympathies and "indomitable gaitey." He continued to be a leading light in the International Association, writing indefatigably for its organ, *Concord*. In 1911, after long service as chairman, Moscheles was elected president of the Association and served in this post until his death in 1917.

During the last decade of his life, Moscheles faithfully supported the Second Hague Conference, but viewed with great concern the armaments race and the growth of Anglo-German antagonism. He bitterly condemned "the costly luxury of preparing for war with Germany" and urged Anglo-German rapprochement, ardently advocated an Anglo-American arbitration treaty, denounced the Italian invasion of Libya, and persisted in predicting that the enemies of militarism and patriotism would triumph over "Caesarism and national egotism." The outbreak of the First World War was "a smashing blow from which he could not recover." Nevertheless, until his death at the age of eight-four, he continued to condemn the war as supreme folly. On his death, Moscheles was mourned by friends and associates as "the dean and beloved veteran" of the British peace movement.

Bibliography:

A. *Boy Scouts . . .* (London, 1909); *The Folly of It All* (London, 1915); *Fragments of an Autobiography* (London, 1899); *Patriotism as an Incentive to Warfare* (London, c. 1909); *Patriotism Challenged* (London, c. 1909).

B. Obituaries: LT, December 24, 1917, p. 9; *Manchester Guardian*, December 26, 1917, p. 6; *Advocate of Peace*, 79-80 (February 1918), 42; *Review of Reviews*, 57 (January 1918), 14.

J.O. Baylen

MOTT, James (20 June 1788, North Hemstead, Long Island—26 January 1868, Brooklyn, NY). *Education*: Society of Friends boarding school at Nine Partners, NY. *Career*: Quaker pacifist, abolitionist, and feminist.

James Mott's pacifism was greatly influenced by his maternal grandfather, James Mott (1742-1823). The elder Mott was a preeminent Christian pacifist who wrote *The Lawfulness of War for Christians, Examined* (1814), a seminal work in the history of American pacifism. This Quaker tract, inspired by the War of 1812, declared that love of God is incompatible with war and that God's law denies the practice of war. In this work, Mott advocated universal resistance to militarism, denounced the concept of self-defense, excoriated war to attain glory or wealth, compared war to murder, and attacked the concept of the war hero. The elder Mott's work represents one of the earlier nineteenth century calls for internationalism and remains a classic statement of theological rejection of nationalism. During the war of 1812, Mott engaged in acts of resistance; he would not purchase imported goods when duties were imposed as a war tax and he refused to pay postage when the rates were increased to finance the war.

During the 1820s, his grandson of the same name continued the family's pacifist witness. He engaged in direct resistance to mandatory military service and joined the Quaker resistance to compulsory militia training. Fined for refusing military duty, James Mott would not pay his fine and was jailed for two days in Philadelphia. His civil disobedience was representative of his lifelong pacifist courage and activism.

Mott's reforming impulse included abolitionism and women's rights. He attended the World Anti-Slavery Convention in London in 1840 and chaired the

Seneca Falls Woman's Rights Convention in 1848, which his wife, *Lucretia Coffin Mott, had helped to organize. But the issue of peace remained a prominent concern throughout his life. During the 1840s and 1850s, James and Lucretia Mott were strong supporters of *Elihu Burritt's League of Universal Brotherhood and his international peace congresses.

Mott analyzed war and violence as a social and cultural disease which was inculcated in children. His last public address in Abington, Pennsylvania (1867), was an affirmation of his major thesis that war can be eradicated through the teaching and rearing of children. He denounced corporal punishment as a relic of barbarism that vitiates "love, gentleness, and kindness." Mott advocated the implanting of community and compassion in children through emphasizing peace and love in the home and the school. He bemoaned global militarism and the persistence of war throughout history. At the time of his death in 1868, he was president of the Pennsylvania Peace Society and prominent in the Society's work for universal peace.

Like his grandfather, James Mott contributed through word and deed to the dissemination of peace and the practice of interfering with state-supported bellicosity.

Bibliography:

B. Thomas C. Cornell, *Adam and Anne Mott: Their Ancestors and Their Descendants* (Poughkeepsie, NY, 1890); A. D. Hollowell, ed., *James and Lucretia Mott: Life and Letters* (Boston, 1884); DAB, 7, 288.

C. James Mott Papers, Friends Historical Library, Swarthmore College.

Peter N. Kirstein

MOTT, Lucretia Coffin (3 January 1793, Nantucket, MA—11 November 1880, Roadside, PA). *Education*: Society of Friends boarding school at Nine Partners, NY, 1806-8. *Career*: teacher, Quaker minister, abolitionist, feminist, and peace advocate.

One tenet of the Quaker faith that Lucretia Mott never forgot was the Testimony of Peace, an explicit repudiation of violence and war. The second daughter of a well-established Nantucket Island family, Mott dedicated her life to the abolitionist, peace, and women's rights movements. As a young woman she taught school, raised a family of five, and served as a Quaker minister. In 1833 she and her husband were present at the founding convention of the American Anti-Slavery Society. Since no women were as yet allowed to join the society, she helped set up the Philadelphia Female Anti-Slavery Society. One year after it was established in 1838, Mott became a member of the New England Non-Resistance Society, an organization that rejected not only war but force and all government based on force. She made the opening and closing addresses at the 1848 Seneca Falls Woman's Rights Convention, which was chaired by her husband, *James Mott. Although she supported all twelve of the convention's resolutions, she was never outspoken on the issue of female suffrage.

Mott's nonresistance convinced her that no person should participate in a government that employed coercion and the sword. She even tried to act as peacemaker between the various factions within the abolitionist and women's movements. Although she agreed with the Garrisonians on most issues, she tried, unsuccessfully, to persuade them to temper their stridency, which she believed alienated others. In 1869 she attempted, again without result, to heal the breach between the radical National Woman Suffrage Association and the more moderate American Woman Suffrage Association.

As the Civil War drew near, Mott's attitude toward peace and nonresistance became somewhat ambivalent. She praised John Brown as a hero and martyr, but she could not sanction his actions. During the summer of 1861, a Boston newspaper interpreted a sermon she gave as support for the war. She denied the charge, but then explained that the war was a righteous cause and hoped it would end slavery. At the end of the war, the Motts and *Alfred Love established the Universal Peace Union and the Pennsylvania Peace Society. Lucretia Mott became vice-president of the Union, and in 1870 she was elected president of the Society, a post she held until her death. As president she agitated for the removal of military training from the public school curriculum. Throughout her life, Lucretia Mott promoted the peace movement by offering her prestige as a reformer, her organizational talent, and her boundless energy.

Bibliography:

A. *Discourse on Woman* (Philadelphia, 1850).

B. Margaret Hope Bacon, *Valiant Friend: The Life of Lucretia Mott* (New York, 1980); Otelia Cromwell, *Lucretia Mott* (Cambridge, MA, 1958).

C. Mott Manuscripts, Friends Historical Library, Swarthmore College; Garrison Papers, Sophia Smith Collection, Smith College.

Craig Phelan

MUEHLON, Johann Wilhelm (31 October 1878, Karlstadt/Main, Germany—5 February 1944, Klosters-Serneus, Graübünden, Switzerland. *Education*: Dr. jur., Univ. of Würzburg, 1904. *Career*: lawyer, 1906-7, Foreign Office preparatory training for Consular Service, 1907-8, assistant to Krupp Board of Directors, 1908, deputy director, 1911, director of Krupp War Materials Department, 1913-15, pacifist author.

By the outbreak of World War I, Wilhelm Muehlon already had an unparalleled career behind him. Only 35 years old in 1913, he was made director of the Krupp War Materials Department. Repulsed by business methods in the international armaments trade, he voluntarily resigned from the firm at the end of 1914. Because of his friendly relations with the Romanian prime minister, the Foreign Office in 1915 appointed him "Special Commissar for Imperial Matters in the Balkan States" to negotiate deliveries of wheat and oil to Germany. In order to maintain his independence, Muehlon refused both the position of German Minister to Rumania and to officially represent the 1916 German peace proposals in Bucharest because he could not guarantee German promises.

A democrat and a liberal, although a member of no party, Muehlon maintained a critical attitude toward the annexationist war aims of the German Empire. However, he stood ready to serve Germany as long as he perceived a willingness to negotiate and believed in the chances of +Woodrow Wilson's attempt to mediate peace. In the Fall of 1916, he moved to Switzerland where he worked unofficially with the German legation in Berne. After the declaration of unlimited submarine warfare, Muehlon broke all connections with official German agencies. In a letter of early May 1917 to Imperial Chancellor Bethmann-Hollweg he openly condemned German war aims, unrestricted submarine war, the deportations from Belgium, the systematic destruction in France, and the torpedoing of English hospital ships.

In August 1917 he composed a confidential memorandum on the July 1914 Crisis meant only for German parliamentarians, but it was leaked to the press and became a sensation. In the memorandum, Muehlon reported conversations with Karl Helfferich and Gustav Krupp von Bohlen und Halbach from which it was clear that the German government had indicated to Austria-Hungary a willingness for war even before the ultimatum to Serbia. Outside of Germany the memorandum was seen as evidence of German war guilt.

In March 1918 Muehlon was defamed in the Reichstag and in the German press as being pathological. In response he decided to publish his diary covering the first months of the war. Under the title, *Die Verheerung Europas*, it appeared in Zurich in the Spring of 1918 and was soon translated into French, English, and several other languages. In the book, Muehlon stated that all of his German readers "who rejected trickery and violence and strive for Truth and Justice" had to agree with his condemnation of the German government. The effect in Germany was limited, but abroad the author became known as "the first European in Germany."

In Switzerland, Muehlon stood in the center of a circle of German pacifists, republicans, and democrats such as *Alfred H. Fried, *Friedrich W. Foerster, and H. Staudinger. He also was connected with *Eduard Bernstein and *Ludwig Quidde, as with writers such as L. Frank, A. Kolb, R. M. Rilke, H. Hesse, and *René Schickele. In the hopes of bringing about a compromise peace, Muehlon and Austrians such as *Julius Meinl maintained contact with the American George D. Herron who was in Switzerland spreading Woodrow Wilson's ideas.

Only after the war did Muehlon's moral appeal, his "truth offensive," find resonance in a minority of Germans. After the murder of *Kurt Eisner in February 1919, he received an offer to become minister-president of Bavaria. However, Muehlon rejected all offers to return to active political life; he remained in Switzerland withdrawn from politics and public activities until his death.

Bibliography:

A. *L'Europe dévastée* (Lausanne, 1918); *Dr. Muehlon's Diary* (London, 1918); *Die Verheerung Europas* (Zurich, 1918).

B. Wolfgang Benz, " 'Der Fall Muehlon'. Bürgerliche Opposition im Obrigkeitsstaat während des Ersten Weltkriegs," in *Vierteljahrshefte für Zeitgeschichte* (1970), 343-65.

C. Wilhelm Muehlon Papers, Institut für Zeitgeschichte, Munich, Germany.

Wolfgang Benz

MÜHSAM, Erich (6 April 1878, Berlin—16 (?) July 1934, Oranienburg, Germany). *Education*: elementary and partial secondary education; self-educated. *Career*: author; editor and publisher, *Kain*, 1911-14 and *Fanal*, 1926-31; anarchist writer and political activist.

Erich Mühsam had already begun to speak out against war in the first decade of the twentieth century, and he remained a committed opponent of war until his death in 1934. Dismissed from gymnasium for socialist activities, Mühsam remained in Berlin and became an apothecary's assistant and then a writer. Introduced to anarchism by Gustav Landauer, Mühsam spent the years prior to 1908 as an anarchist journalist and speaker, attacking both Wilhelmine militarism and the Social Democratic Party (SDP) proposal for a popular militia. He was active in the Zurich Anti-Militarism League, founded in 1905 by Fritz Brupbacher, and spoke at the Second International Anti-Militarism Congress in Amsterdam in 1907. Mühsam called for antiwar agitation among workers, soldiers, and students during peace time and argued for direct action against war should it be declared.

In the years immediately before World War I, Mühsam moved to Munich where he attempted to undertake the revolutionary instruction and organization of the *lumpenproletariat*. He used his journal, *Kain* (1911-14), to elaborate a socialist account of the origins of war, stressing that war was necessary to the successful functioning of the capitalist state. War was not only good business, expanding markets and uncovering new sources of raw materials, it was an effective agent of social control, subjecting the working classes to army discipline.

The outbreak of World War I marked a puzzling hiatus in Mühsam's pacifist activities. On August 2, 1914, he brought out a special edition of *Kain* explaining that it would cease publication for the duration of the war because continued opposition to the conflict might endanger his personal security under the conditions imposed by martial law. In a second statement a few days later, Mühsam expressed his solidarity with the German people and wished them success in keeping out the "foreign hordes." He then attempted, unsuccessfully, to volunteer for noncombattant medical work. This sudden repudiation of his pacifism horrified Mühsam's political colleagues, who unanimously condemned him as a chauvinist. According to Mühsam, he became profoundly depressed when war was declared and in his disorientation succumbed to the prevailing war hysteria. Whatever the explanation, Mühsam's behavior seriously hampered his future antiwar efforts.

When Mühsam resumed his antiwar activities later in 1914, he did so on three fronts: the organization of mass agitation; the attempt to create a united pacifist front; and the production of antiwar poems, which were published after the war, and an unpublished antiwar novel, *Abrechnung*. Mühsam organized street demonstrations in order to bring the inarticulate longing for peace of the apolitical masses to the attention of the government and to channel popular concern over material conditions into opposition to their cause, war. When Mühsam was not organizing the masses, he traveled throughout Germany urging cooperation among the many pacifist groups, the antiwar anarchists, and the Socialists. His mission failed because the antiwar faction within the SPD rejected an alliance with bourgeois pacifists, and because of widespread suspicion of his early support of the war. This failure confirmed Mühsam's belief that only the direct revolutionary action of working people, in refusing to fight, to produce weapons, and initiating a general strike, could end the war. In January 1918, when munitions workers in Munich and other cities went on strike to press for a negotiated peace, Mühsam joined *Kurt Eisner in addressing mass meetings and encouraging the agitation. The authorities were sufficiently aroused to ban Mühsam's public activities and to imprison him in April 1918 when he violated this ban.

Mühsam was released from prison in October 1918, in time to participate in the Bavarian Revolution of 1918-19. With the collapse of the revolution in 1919, he was again imprisoned for committing high treason, but was released from his fifteen-year term in 1924 by a general amnesty. After his release, he continued his anarchist and socialist activities, both political and literary. His journal, *Fanal* (1926-31), articulated Mühsam's fully developed socialist critique of war and continued to advance the view, formulated before 1914 and forged in the crucible of World War I, that only revolution promised enduring peace. Agitation against war, because it undermined the main support of capitalism, was necessarily revolutionary agitation, with the transformation of society as its goal. Mühsam's views proved as unpalatable to the Nazis as they had to the Wilhelmine authorities and to the SPD opponents of the Munich Soviet Republic. Arrested the day after the Reichstag fire in 1933, Mühsam was ultimately sent to the concentration camp at Oranienburg, where he was murdered in 1934.

Bibliography:

A. *Auswahl: Gedichte, Drama, Prosa* (Düsseldorf, 1961); *Die Befreiung der Gesellschaft vom Staat* (Berlin, 1933); *Namen und Menschen, unpolitische Erinnerungen* (Leipzig, 1962); *Von Eisner bis Levine, die Enstehung der bayerischen Räterepublik* (Berlin, 1929).

B. Heinz Hug, *Erich Mühsam: Untersuchungen zu Leben und Werk* (Glashütten im Taurus, 1974).

Polly Morris and Michael Dintenfass

MURO, Céline Renooz. See RENOOZ, Céline.

MURRAY, George Gilbert Aimé. See *Biographical Dictionary of Internationalists*.

MURRY, John Middleton (6 August 1889, Peckham, London—13 March 1957, Bury St. Edmunds, England). *Education*: B.A., Oxford Univ., 1912.

Career: free-lance journalist; War Office 1916-19; editor, *The Athenaeum*, 1919-21. *The Adelphi*, 1923-48, *Peace News*, 1940-46; literary and social critic.

Raised in a poverty-stricken family, Middleton Murry won his education by scholarships. From then on his career was marked out as a critic of outstanding gifts. Murry was a stormy, in some ways tragic figure, whose personality could never match his gifted ability. His home life was full of tension. He lived with, and later married, the writer Katherine Mansfield, the first of his four wives. His relations with D. H. Lawrence were intimate and stormy. He believed in community and formed a farming community, but his own blend of autocracy and ineffectualness led it to break up.

As a literary critic he showed a quite extraordinary sensitivity, from his first full-length study of Dostoevsky onwards. His approach and idiom were unfashionable, and it is a tribute to him that his reputation stood so high. His work on D. H. Lawrence was marred by his inability to distance himself from his own involvement, but his writings on Shakespeare, Swift, Keats, and Blake showed an astonishing and original perceptivity.

Murry was not a pacifist during World War I, but developed an aversion to it and was one of *Lady Ottoline Morrell's protégés. He worked in the War Office and shared the belief that a whole generation had been sacrificed to "profits and possessions and revenge." In the period between the wars he passed from religious individualism to religious socialism. He often attacked pacifism vehemently, but his friend *Max Plowman's book *The Faith Called Pacifism*, published in 1936, persuaded him and he joined *Dick Sheppard in the Peace Pledge Union. Now he became one of the movement's leading publicists. He spoke widely, wrote articles, pamphlets, and books, notably *The Necessity of Pacifism* (1937) and *The Pledge of Peace* (1938).

In 1939 Murry had a breakdown and the onset of war brought despair. However, he reasserted his view that pacifism's task was not just to prevent war but to witness against the dehumanization of humanity. He wrote the influential *Betrayal of Christ by the Churches* (1940) and *Christocracy* (1942). He became editor of *Peace News*, though he was too good a writer to be a good editor. But his own position became increasingly ambivalent. Before the war was over he felt that the ordinary citizen was incapable of nonviolent resistance and that totalitarianism was capable of permanent tyranny. He doubted whether pacifism had any answer to totalitarianism. Murry eventually called for a supernational authority that would force its power on the Soviet Union by the atomic bomb. In 1946 he resigned as editor of *Peace News* and in 1950 debated pacifism with Donald Soper.

Murry lived on till 1957, having at last found a personal love, but no longer with anything to offer the peace movement. Still for ten years he had been the leading pacifist writer in Great Britain.

Bibliography:

A. *The Betrayal of Christ by the Churches* (London, 1940); *The Brotherhood of Peace* (London, 1940); *Christocracy* (London, 1942); *The Economics of Peace* (London, 1943); *The Necessity of Pacifism* (London, 1937); *The Pledge of Peace* (London, 1938).

B. F. A. Lea, *The Life of John Middleton Murry* (London, 1959); Mary Middleton Murry, *To Keep Faith* (London, 1959).

John Ferguson

MUSTE, Abraham John (8 January 1885, Zierikzee, the Netherlands—11 February 1967, New York). *Education*: B.A., Hope Coll., 1905; B.D., New Brunswick Theological Seminary, 1909; B.D., Union Theological Seminary, 1913. *Career*: ordained minister, Dutch Reformed Church of America, 1909-14; ordained minister, Congregational Church, 1914-18; recorded minister, Society of Friends, 1918-26; executive secretary, Amalgamated Textile Workers, 1919-21; director, Brookwood Labor Coll., 1921-33; executive secretary, Conference for Progressive Labor Action, 1929-33; executive secretary, American Workers party, 1933-35; executive secretary, Workers Party of the United States, 1935-36; director, Labor Temple, 1937-40; executive secretary, Fellowship of Reconciliation, 1940-53; labor leader, pacifist, and editor.

A. J. Muste exerted an influence on most of the major social movements in twentieth century America. These included the labor movement, movements by minorities to achieve civil rights and economic justice, campaigns by dissenters for civil liberties, and the search by advocates of peace for alternatives to violence, war, and the international arms race.

Born Abraham Johannes in Zierikzee, the Netherlands in 1885, his parents moved the family to Grand Rapids, Michigan, in 1891. Educated in Dutch Reformed Schools, Muste became an ordained minister in 1909. He was married in the same year to Anna Huizenga and assumed the position as pastor of Fort Washington Collegiate Church in New York City. Increasing exposure to currents of social reform and further study at Union Theological Seminary led Muste to an "agonizing reappràisal" of his religious and political beliefs. In 1914, he resigned from the Dutch Reformed pastorate and from January 1915 to March 1918, he served as minister to the Central Congregational Church in Newtonville, Massachusetts.

During World War I Muste became involved with the antiwar movement. His work with the Fellowship of Reconciliation (FOR) and other pacifist groups was ill-received at Central Church. In April 1918 he moved his family to Rhode Island, where the Providence Friends Meeting (Quakers) provided shelter and subsistence pay in exchange for Muste's services as their Recorded Minister. The family returned to Boston in the fall of 1918 and lived in a communal household of Boston members of the FOR calling themselves "the comradeship." Three members of the comradeship—Muste, Harold Rotzel and Cedric Long—became involved in supporting striking textile workers in Lawrence, Massachusetts. From February to May 1919 Muste led the strike, which ended in a victory for the workers and established him as the Executive Secretary of a newly created Amalgamated Textile Workers Union. After two years Muste accepted an invitation to become Director of Brookwood Labor College in Katonah, New York.

At Brookwood, Muste helped to train a body of "Musteite" labor activists and shape an outlook of "progressive labor action" which foreshadowed the industrial union campaigns of the late nineteen thirties. But attacks on Brookwood by the American Federation of Labor and a factional split within the college resulted in the departure of Muste and his followers in the spring of 1933.

Their Conference for Progressive Labor Action (CPLA) maintained an active presence in the mining, steel, and textile industries, established unemployed leagues, and adopted a vocabulary of revolution. In December 1933 the CPLA became the American Workers party (AWP) and was instrumental in achieving victories for strikers at the Auto Lite and Chevrolet plants in Toledo, Ohio, in 1934 and 1935. The AWP then merged with the Communist League of America (Trotskyists) to become the Workers Party of the United States. As executive secretary of that party, Muste became a full-fledged Marxist revolutionary. However, when he and Anna returned from a European trip in the summer of 1936, which included a visit with Leon Trotsky, he was once again a Christian pacifist.

The change arose from a culminating experience in a series of mystical events which had marked each of the major transitions in his life. Resting in St. Sulpice Church in Paris, he had been overcome by a sense of not belonging among secular revolutionaries. "I must lead a religious life," he concluded.

As industrial secretary of the FOR from October 1936 to May 1937 and then as Director of the Presbyterian Labor Temple in New York City until 1940, Muste called on workers to forego violent ideologies and adopt approaches of nonviolence. When World War II erupted, he became executive secretary of the FOR. He maintained that military action against fascism only fed the very forces of brutality that had created it and advocated instead redistribution of the world's resources. While supporting draft resistance and conscientious objection, he also pleaded for U.S. assistance to the victims of persecution in Europe.

After U.S. atomic bombs were dropped in Japan in 1945, Muste insisted that Americans take unilateral initiatives for disarmament and nonviolent resolution of world conflicts. The methods he used became increasingly radical, and he adopted new commitments in the War Resisters League and the Committee for Nonviolent Action. He faced jail and prosecution for refusing to pay income taxes, defying civil defense laws, encouraging attempts to halt atomic testing, and trespassing on federal property in order to protest construction of nuclear missiles.

Working to enlist the support of scientists, academicians, and churchmen in the cause of peace, Muste helped to organize and sustain the Society for Social Responsibility in Science, the Council for Correspondence, and the Church Peace Mission. The outreach of the Church Peace Mission to religious leaders in Western Europe and the Soviet bloc demonstrated the transnational nature of many of Muste's efforts. He also worked in Asia and Africa as co-chair (with Englishman Michael Scott and Gandhian *Jayaprakash Narayan) of the World Peace Brigade and participated in three major transnational walks for peace—

the San Francisco to Moscow Peace Walk of 1960-61, the Quebec to Guantanamo Walk of 1963, and the New Delhi-Peking Friendship March of 1963-64.

Perceiving an intimate connection between aggression and imperialism in foreign policy, and racism and injustice in domestic actions, Muste also championed civil liberties and civil rights. Rallying support for dissidents whose First Amendment rights were abrogated in the era of the Cold War, he was himself a target of investigations by government witch-hunters. In an effort to rally the factionalized political left in the United States, Muste organized the American Forum for Socialist Education in 1956.

In the area of civil rights, Muste encouraged the organization of the Congress of Racial Equality (CORE) under the auspices of the Fellowship of Reconciliation. Three FOR secretaries, James Farmer, George Houser, and Bayard Rustin, all lent their talents to the new organization. Mentor for all of them, and especially for Rustin, Muste influenced their experiments with nonviolent direct action against segregation and racial violence. When *Martin Luther King Jr. emerged as chief spokesman for nonviolence, Muste and the FOR provided important guidance and support. Through James Lawson, yet another FOR secretary who acknowledged Muste as a ''major teacher,'' Muste's influence reached a new generation of student activists in the nineteen sixties.

As the war in Vietnam intensified, Muste appealed to these activists to join forces with the peace movement. The increasing involvement in antiwar activities of young blacks was influenced by Muste, as was the deepening of Martin Luther King Jr.'s own resistance to the war.

In his last years Muste pushed himself relentlessly to find ways to end the slaughter in Vietnam. Helping to organize national demonstrations, encouraging draft resisters, and championing military defectors, he also urged understanding and respect for those who immolated themselves in protest against the war. With a team of American pacifists, he visited South Vietnam in April 1966. Nine months later he journeyed to North Vietnam with Rabbi Abraham Feinberg and Anglican bishop Ambrose Reeves. From a personal meeting with North Vietnamese Premier Ho Chi Minh, the clergymen returned with an invitation to U.S. President Lyndon Johnson to visit North Vietnam to talk about peace.

Less than three weeks later, Muste developed an aneurism and, on February 11, 1967, died in St. Lukes Hospital in New York City. Mourned by comrades from the many movements and causes to which he had devoted his life, Muste would have especially approved the death notice published in the antiwar newsletter, *The Mobilizer*: ''In lieu of flowers, friends are requested to get out and work—for peace, for human rights, for a better world.''

Bibliography:

A. *The Essays of A. J. Muste*, ed. by Nat Hentoff (New York, 1967); *Nonviolence in an Aggressive World* (New York, 1940); *Not By Might* (New York, 1947, Garland reprint, New York, 1971).

B. Nat Hentoff, *Peace Agitator, The Story of A. J. Muste* (New York, 1963); Jo Ann O. Robinson, *Abraham Went Out: A Biography of A. J. Muste* (Philadelphia, 1982).

C. A. J. Muste Papers, Swarthmore College Peace Collection.

Jo Ann O. Robinson

MYGATT, Tracy Dickinson (12 March 1885, Brooklyn, NY—22 November 1973, Philadelphia). *Education*: B.A., Bryn Mawr Coll., 1908. *Career*: founder, Chelsea Day Nursery, Bureau of Legal Advice, and Campaign for World Government; organizer, War Resisters League, pacifist writer and activist.

Proud of her colonial forebears who came from England in 1633, Tracy Mygatt was a deeply religious and passionate pacifist. She wrote books, plays, and articles that celebrated first century Christians and explored themes of violence and morality. Unlike her spiritual ancestors, she wrote, she was committed to radical social change in specific political terms. Mygatt determined to devote her life to the struggle for the eradication of social evils, such as child labor and unemployment, emphasizing always the quest for world peace and the establishment of international unity based on world government and a democratic socialist economy.

After graduation from Bryn Mawr in 1908, she became involved in the settlement house movement and founded the long-lasting Chelsea Day Nursery, a day care center for the children of working mothers, in 1910. A Christian socialist in the tradition of *Dorothy Day and the activists of the poor church, she demanded that the Episcopal church create food and shelter programs for the hundreds of homeless unemployed in New York City in 1913. With her lifetime companion and colleague *Frances Witherspoon, she organized a Socialist Suffrage Brigade within the Christian Socialist League. On May Day 1915 their banners proclaimed: "Votes for Women/ For Socialism and Peace."

World War I was a turning point in Mygatt's life. She regarded the war as a "betrayal and crucifixication of humanity." She became an "aggressive pacifist" associated with the militant members of the New York-based antiwar movement, notably the Woman's Peace party, the People's Council, the American Union Against Militarism, the Fellowship of Reconciliation and, in particular, those early organizations that merged into the War Resisters League in 1923. In 1915, with *Jessie Wallace Hughan, Mygatt, Witherspoon, and others founded the Anti-Enlistment League to provide free legal services for poor conscientious objectors. In 1917 it became the Bureau of Legal Advice. Militant and uncompromising, the Bureau was partially funded by, the Civil Liberties Bureau created several months later by *Roger Baldwin, *Crystal Eastman and *Norman Thomas. In 1923 the Civil Liberties Bureau became the American Civil Liberties Union and absorbed the legal service aspect of the Bureau of Legal Advice. Mygatt and her co-workers called for the absolute renunciation of war and that became the central focus of the War Resisters League.

The War Resisters League was a forerunner of Britain's Peace Pledge Union and called on its members to renounce all wars, offensive and defensive. Mygatt insisted that "all wars—no matter how offensive—are always called defensive, and we wanted to be perfectly clear about that." After World War I, Mygatt worked also for the Women's Peace Union and embraced the principle of nonviolent resistance to war. In the 1930s she worked with Senator Lynn Frazier of North Dakota for a constitutional amendment to disarm the United States and outlaw war.

After World War II, Mygatt was one of the founders, and until her death east coast secretary of the Campaign for World Government. As a representative to the United Nations from that nongovernmental organization, she worked to transform the UN into "an instrument of universal democracy and world federation." To those who thought this goal unattainable, she responded: "Of course it is difficult! But . . . we dare not forget that nuclear destruction for all lurks in the dark, lawless shadows." Throughout the 1950s and 1960s, she wrote letters, organized activities, and remained active on behalf of racial integration, clean water, social justice, and opposition to the war in Vietnam. At her death on Thanksgiving Day, 1973, her colleagues in the Campaign for World Government wrote that Tracy Mygatt was a "dedicated, valiant worker for peace and equal rights for all human beings." She was consistent and courageous. As she wrote in 1939: "We pacifists are stubborn people. We still believe that our world can be saved."

Bibliography:

A. *Children of Israel* (New York, 1922); *Good Friday* (New York, 1919); "A Plea for War Resistance," *The Churchman*, May 28, 1932; "Toward a New Earth," *Unity*, June 19, 1939.

B. Ann Morrissett Davidon, "Founding Mothers: Tracy Mygatt and Frances Witherspoon," *WIN*, 9 (July 1973), 10; Ann Morrissett Davidon, "The Lives of Tracy D. Mygatt and Frances Witherspoon," *War Resisters League News* (January-February, 1974), 6; Nancy Manahan, "Future Old Maids and Pacifist Agitators: The Story of Tracy Mygatt and Frances Witherspoon," *Women's Studies Quarterly*, 10 (Spring 1982), 10-13.

C. Tracy Mygatt-Frances Witherspoon Papers, Swarthmore College Peace Collection.

Blanche Wiesen Cook

N

NANSEN, Fridtjof. See *Biographical Dictionary of Internationalists*.

NARAYAN, Jayaprakash (11 October 1902, Sarah district of Bihar, India—8 October 1979, New Delhi). *Education*: studied political science and economics at Univ. of California at Berkeley, Univ. of Wisconsin, and several other U.S. universities; M.A., Ohio State Univ., 1929. *Career*: acting general secretary (1932) and member, Working Committee, Indian National Congress, 1936, 1946-47; organizing secretary (1934-36) and general secretary, Congress Socialist party, 1936-53; leader, Praja Socialist party, 1953-54; leader, Sarvodaya Movement, 1954-79.

During the struggle for India's freedom from British rule, J.P., as Jayaprakash Narayan was popularly called, had advocated the use of violent means when necessary, particularly during 1942-43 and 1946-47. After the achievement of independence in 1947, however, he became a strong champion of peaceful methods in the movement for ushering in socialism. Even before the achievement of independence, he argued in an article entitled "Transition to Socialism" (1947), that the transition to socialism in India must be a peaceful, democratic process. The following year, he went a step further and, in his report to the Socialist party's annual conference, lauded *Gandhi's teaching that "evil means can never lead to good ends and that fair ends require fair means."

In June 1952, during a self-purificatory fast, lasting twenty-one days, J.P. finally realized that he no longer believed in dialectical materialism, which he had accepted ever since his student days at the University of Wisconsin during the mid-twenties. In an article entitled "Incentives to Goodness," written shortly after the fast, he affirmed that man must move beyond the material in order to find the incentives to goodness.

The break with dialectical materialism cleared the way for a fuller understanding and adoption of Gandhi's teaching. In his address to the foundation conference of the Praja Socialist party (1953) he pointed out that both communism and socialism (as practised in the West) were unsuccessful. While communism had ended up in state capitalism and dictatorship, socialism had become a parliamentary or legalistic creed. Gandhi offered a third and attractive alternative, that of "revolution by non-violent mass action." The goals of socialism did not require any modification, but those goals were more likely to be reached by following Gandhi's methods.

Behind such an assertion lay J.P.'s fascination for the *Bhoodan*, or land-gift movement, which had been carried on in India since 1951, under the leadership of *Vinoba Bhave, who was widely acclaimed as the spiritual heir of Gandhi. J.P. considered it not only a movement for the redistribution of land, but also the beginning of a great human and social revolution. Here was, he thought, "revolution by non-violent mass action" and he soon plunged into it. In 1957 he withdrew from politics in order to devote all his time to the movement.

After having worked in the *Bhoodan* movement for more than a decade, J.P. realized that Vinoba had committed a mistake by emphasizing only one side of the Gandhian technique, namely, persuasion. He thought it was necessary also to emphasize the other side of that technique, nonviolent struggle, and to put up a fight against the widespread corruption in public life and the growing trend towards authoritarianism. This was J.P.'s singular contribution to the Gandhian movement, and although the socio-economic goals of that movement remained as distant as ever, the struggle against authoritarianism led by him between 1974 and 1977 is regarded by many as India's second liberation, ensuring its continuation as a democracy. When Prime Minister Indira Gandhi declared an "emergency" in 1975 that suspended many constitutional freedoms, including a free press and free speech, J.P. was one of the first imprisoned. He was accused of fomenting agitation against the government and remained in prison several months.

Throughout his public career, J.P. consistently worked for the creation of an atmosphere conducive to the maintenance of communal harmony and peace in India. After the achievement of independence he pleaded for the adoption of a peaceful approach to the solution of the problem of national integration in areas like Kashmir and Nagaland. He worked for conciliation between the government of India and the local populations, emphasizing the need to respect the popular sentiments and aspirations of the latter. Above all, he advocated a policy based on understanding and goodwill towards all of India's neighbors, including Pakistan and China. In 1962 he founded the Pakistan Conciliation Group and the following year sought to organize a Friendship March to Peking. At the same time, he remained a champion of freedom and democracy everywhere. He raised his voice against Soviet intervention in Hungary in 1956 and in Czechoslovakia in 1968. He equally condemned Chinese repression in Tibet in 1959-60. In 1971 he undertook a world tour in order to mobilize opinion in favor of the struggle for freedom in Bangladesh and pleaded for early recognition of its independence.

Bibliography:

A. *Communitarian Society and Panchayati Raj*, ed. by Brahmanand (Varanasi, 1970); *Nation Building in India*, ed. by Brahmanand (Varanasi, 1974); *A Revolutionary's Quest: Selected Writings*, ed. by Bimal Prasad (Delhi, 1980); *Socialism, Sarvodaya and Democracy*, ed. by Bimal Prasad (Bombay, 1964); *Towards Struggle*, ed. by Yusuf Meherally (Bombay, 1946); *Towards Total Revolution*, ed. by Brahmanand (4 vols., Bombay, 1978).

B. Ajit Bhattacharya, *Jayaprakash Narayan: A Political Biography* (Delhi, 1975); Lakshmi Narayan Lal, *Jayaprakash: Rebel Extraordinary* (New Delhi, 1975); Minoo Masani, *J.P.'s Mission Partly Accomplished* (New Delhi, 1977); Minoo Masani, *Is J.P. the Answer*? (New Delhi, 1975); Allan Scarfe and Wendy Scarfe, *J.P.: His Biography* (New Delhi, 1975).

C. Jayaprakash Narayan Papers, Nehru Memorial Museum and Library, New Delhi.

Bimal Prasad

NEHRU, Jawaharlal (14 November, 1889, Allahabad, India—27 May 1964, New Delhi). *Education*: Harrow, 1905-7; B.A., Trinity Coll., Cambridge Univ., 1910; studied law, Inner Temple, 1910-12, called to the bar, 1912. *Career*: president, Indian National Congress, 1930-36, 1947, 1951-54; Vice-President, Governor-General's Executive Council and Minister of External Affairs and Commonwealth Relations, 1946-47; Prime Minister and Minister of External Affairs, 1947-64; politician, author, and historian.

Jawaharlal Nehru adopted *Gandhi's idea of the nonviolent struggle for freeing India from British rule. Like Gandhi he believed that only the right means could produce right ends and once declared that "It is only in the minds of men that you can build the defences of peace." Nehru was also influenced by the teachings of Gautama Buddha, who had emphasized the virtues of truth, compassion, and reverence for life. In addition, he greatly admired Asoka, the Indian Emperor (269-232 B.C.), who propagated Buddha's law of duty or piety through his edicts and foreign missions.

In February 1927 Nehru attended the International Congress of Oppressed Nationalities against Imperialism. During this visit he began to form his ideas about world peace. By 1939 he was attracted to the scheme of World Federation, consisting of large autonomous units under a socialized economy and functioning more independently than the League of Nations whose effectiveness, he felt, had been weakened by some European states. Nehru strongly opposed fascism from the outset.

As Prime Minister, Nehru was the architect of India's policy of nonalignment in international politics. He saw the world divided into two antagonistic blocs committed to mutual confrontation and leading towards a third world war. He viewed nonalignment as a positive and dynamic concept. Seeking peaceful solutions to international problems, he developed the *Panchsheel* (known as the Five Principles of Peace) which was enumerated in the preamble to the Sino-Indian Agreement on Trade with Tibet in April 1954. It formed a part of the joint statement issued by Nehru and the Chinese Prime Minister *Zhou Enlai when the latter visited India in June of that year. Included in the Five Principles were 1) mutual respect for each other's territorial integrity and sovereignty; 2) nonaggression; 3) noninterference in each other's internal affairs; 4) equality and mutual advantage; and 5) peaceful coexistence and economic cooperation. In April 1955, at the Bandung Conference, the Five Principles, though not specifically mentioned, were incorporated into the final draft of the peace declaration and Nehru urged Zhou Enlai to settle the Formosa question peacefully.

Nehru hoped to improve the operation of the international system. By India's decision as a republic to remain in the Commonwealth of Nations in 1948-49, Nehru intended to bridge the racial gap and to forge new and friendly relations with Great Britain. He offered mediation in the international conflicts in Korea

(1950-53), Indo-China (1954), and Suez (1956). During the Korean conflict, Nehru urged Zhou Enlai to localize the conflict. Initially India had voted for the American resolution in the United Nations branding North Korea as an aggressor, but later challenged the U.S. decision to cross the 38th parallel. Nehru helped initiate the Prisoner of War Agreement signed between the United States and China, stating that with the agreement the world was faced with the "outbreak of peace."

Nehru's special appeal for a cease-fire in Indo-China on February 27, 1954, helped create a suitable atmosphere for the Geneva conference which ended the war. The final terms of the Geneva accord reflected Nehru's earlier six-point proposal. Similarly, he offered Indian mediation in the Suez crisis of 1956 and took a strong stand against the violent excesses of the Mau Mau movement in Kenya, but did not disguise his sympathy for their fight against racism.

Nehru sought to strengthen the United Nations by making it serve the purposes for which it had been founded. Consequently, he insisted on recognition of Communist China and pressed for its membership in the U.N. He also challenged Soviet objections to the admission of some eighteen countries to the world organization and succeeded in getting Soviet leaders to agree to the entry of Japan and Mongolia in 1955. Recognizing Nehru's passionate concern for peace and his commitment to the United Nations, +Dag Hammarskjöld, secretary-general of the organization, invited him in 1955 to participate in the tenth anniversary celebration.

At the Belgrade Summit meeting of nonaligned countries in September 1961, Nehru called for a suspension of nuclear testing and following the meeting journeyed to Moscow with a message of peace. He consistently advocated the use of atomic energy for peaceful purposes. He realized that the world as constituted could not banish the use of force in international politics, but he believed that force ought to be used only for self-defense and for national self-protection when no peaceful alternatives were available. He once said that he would have liked to be a pacifist, but regretted that prevailing circumstances precluded that option. Instead of opposing war as a matter of principle, he sought to localize areas of conflict and thereby create a climate of opinion that would enhance negotiations and mutual cooperation for resolving international disputes.

Bibliography:

A. *An Autobiography* (London, 1936); *The Discovery of India* (New York, 1960); *Selected Works of Jawaharlal Nehru*, ed. by S. Gopal (New Delhi, 1976-); *Toward Freedom* (New York, 1941).

B. Michael Brecher, *Nehru, A Political Biography* (London, 1959); S. Gopal, *Jawaharlal Nehru: A Biography* (2 vols., Delhi, 1976-79); B. N. Pandey, *Nehru* (London, 1976).

V. N. Datta

NELSON, Leonard (11 June 1882, Berlin—29 October 1927, Landerziehungsheim Walkemühle near Melsungen, Germany). *Education*: studies in mathematics, philosophy, and psychology at universities of Berlin, Göttingen, and Heidelberg, 1901-4; Dr. Phil., Univ. of Göttingen, 1904. *Career*: professor of philosophy, Univ. of Göttingen, 1919-27; writer, ethical socialist, and pacifist.

Leonard Nelson was a writer and educator who emphasized the function of reason and will in the approach to socialism. He proclaimed an absolute belief in the creative and law-giving power of reason and hoped to realize a social condition "in which no illegal acts occur." Nelson believed that the root causes of immorality lay in economic and social relations, and constantly searched for a way between socialism and communism. He viewed the abolition of private property as the chief means for changing society.

Shortly after the outbreak of World War I, Nelson announced the idea of an international peace society, but was unable to bring it into existence. He was more successful, however, in 1917-18, when he organized the International Jugend-Bund (International Youth League) to give structure to his philosophical and political principles. The League's mission was to promote both his philosophical and political principles, and Nelson hoped to accomplish this mission by indoctrinating a small group of elite youth. The total concept of his political system involved an idealistic theory of personality, which he hoped to inculcate through pedagogical measures. In 1924 he established a school near Melsungen to promote his principles among his followers and later he established a second school for children. In both institutions the avowal of pacifism was an important principle.

In the years after the founding of the International Jugend-Bund, Nelson and the members of his league associated themselves with the Social Democratic Party (SPD) and worked in several of its organizations. He recommended a politics of culture oriented towards the needs of workers. In 1925 the league was expelled from the SPD as a result of its revolutionary and anticlerical doctrines. In 1926 the International Sozialistischer Kampf-Bund (International Socialist Combat League) (ISK) was created under Nelson's influence as an independent party to realize his political goals.

Until his death, Nelson devoted a considerable amount of his energy to fighting against what he saw as the pernicious influence of traditional religion in the public schools. Nelson's anticlericalism also found expression in the formation of the Sozialistisch-dissidentischen Lehrer-Kampf-Bund (Socialist Dissident Teachers' Combat League) (LKB). This organization, founded in 1924 by those of Nelson's followers who were teachers, fought primarily against religious lessons in public schools. The LKB also joined the campaign to persuade people to resign from churches and collaborated with the Verein für Freidenker und Feuerbestattung (Society for Free Thinkers and Cremation). In the last years of his life, Nelson and his followers, while rejecting fascism absolutely, turned against the SPD for what they perceived as the party's growing nationalism.

Bibliography:

A. *Gesammelte Schriften*, ed. Paul Bernays (9 vols., Hamburg, 1971ff.); *Vernunft, Erkenntnis, Sittlichkeit*, ed. Peter Schroeder (Hamburg, 1979); *Vom Selbstvertrauen der Vernunft*, ed. Grete Henry-Hermann (Hamburg, 1975).

B. Werner Link, *Die Geschichte des Internationalen Jugend-Bundes (IJB) und des Internationalien Sozialistischen Kampf-Bundes (ISK)* (Meisenheim am Glan, 1964); Juergen Ziechmann, *Theorie und Praxis der Pädagogik bei Leonard Nelson und seinem Bund* (Bad Heilbrunn/Obb., 1970).

Juergen Ziechmann

NEUFVILLE, Eduard de (29 January 1857, Frankfurt am Main, Germany—7 September 1942 Blonay/Vevey, Switzerland). *Career*: pacifist.

Cosmopolitan humaneness and a Christian motivated love of peace were characteristics, which Eduard de Neufville possessed by virtue of his birth into an old Huguenot family with German and English lines. The prosperity of the family—his father was the Frankfurt banker Robert De Neufville—allowed him to live unencumbered, so that he was never forced to take up a profession. Instead, he placed all his energies in the service of peace and also supported the idea of peace as a generous patron. Among other things, he made regular contributions to the Deutsche Friedensgesellschaft (German Peace Society) (DFG) in Stuttgart and to the International Peace Bureau in Berne. In 1903 he financed a lecture tour of *Richard Feldhaus in the Frankfurt area.

As a young man de Neufville spent some time in the Netherlands on commercial business. After his marriage and return to Frankfurt in 1890, he became a member and later vice-president of the long-standing local peace association. From that time on he regularly visited national and international peace congresses. At the World Peace Conference of Rouen in 1903, he met *Bertha von Suttner, who, through de Neufville's generosity, was able to attend the Second International Peace Conference in The Hague (1907).

During the meetings of the Second Hague Peace Conference, de Neufville presided over the recently founded International Club. Encouraged by Joseph Allen Baker and by a memorandum from English and American pastors, which Baker relayed to the Conference president, de Neufville founded, together with Baker in 1908, the Kirchliches Komitee zur Pflege freundschaftlicher Beziehungen zwischen Grossbrittannien und Deutschland (Church Committee for the Maintainance of Friendly Relations Between Great Britain and Germany). Its founding owed much to the energies of de Neufville who in 1905 had organized the Deutsch-englisches Verständigungskomitee (German-English Committee of Understanding), and had become its vice-president. His efforts toward a rapprochement between Great Britain and Germany were guided by his deep religious convictions. The outbreak of the war in 1914 hindered him, and others of like mind, from realizing the goal of expanding the work of German-English cooperation of churches into a world organization.

De Neufville not only sought to promote Anglo-German cooperation, he also sought to develop understanding between other nations as well. He made numerous trips abroad to further this end. Besides extensive travels in Europe, he visited the United States in 1904 and again in 1912, the latter of which he undertook to participate in the Lake Mohonk Conference on International Arbitration. As the war approached, he worked diligently to promote a German-French rapprochement.

Between 1907 and 1922, de Neufville served as one of the German members of the Council of the International Peace Bureau in Berne (later at Geneva). When he moved to Switzerland in 1922, he was made an honorary member of the Council, an indication of his reliability and loyalty to the organization. The high respect that de Neufville had earned for himself through his personal modesty, his readiness to help by quiet and diplomatic activity, and his financial support of the aims of the peace movement, were further emphasized when he became one of the five friends of peace to be invited to the dedication of the Palace of Peace in The Hague in 1913.

Bibliography:

B. Hans Wehberg, "Eduard de Neufville," *Die Friedenswarte*, 37 (1937), 28-9; Hans Wehberg, "Nachruf," *Die Friedenswarte*, 42 (1942), 182-3.

Karl Holl
Trans. by William H. Hopkins

NIBOYET, Eugénie Mouchon (11 September 1796, Montpellier, France—6 January 1883, Paris). *Education*: tutored at home. *Career*: editor, *Conseiller des femmes*, 1833-34, *La Paix des deux mondes*, February-October, 1844, *L'Avenir*, October, 1844-April, 1845, *La Voix des femmes*, 1848; author, translator, feminist, social reformer, and pacifist.

Eugénie Mouchon was the daughter of a doctor from Montpellier and the granddaughter of a Swiss pastor. Both of her parents were of liberal persuasion and Protestant faith. Her childhood was spent in the cult of equality and Bonapartist glory which followed the revolution. While she was studying at home her brothers gained many honors in the Grande Armée. At the age of twenty she married Niboyet, a Protestant lawyer from an influential family.

After her marriage, Eugénie Niboyet became interested in prison reform and published her first book in 1836 calling for the abolition of the death penalty. She was equally interested in improving education for all children, writing *Des Aveugles et de leur education (The Blind and Their Education)* in 1837. Niboyet viewed her work as part of the moral obligation of good Christians. In Paris, she became the secretary-general of the Société de la morale chrétienne (Society for Christian Morals), presided over by La Rouchefoucauld-Liancourt.

She was also attracted by some of the ideas of Saint-Simonians who appointed her the chief of their chapter in the fourth arrondissement of Paris. She adopted some of the Saint-Simonian principles about women, especially the idea that women far from being blamed with original sin, should be man's moral guide through life. In 1833, when she accompanied her husband back to Lyon, she started a feminist journal, *Le Conseiller des femmes*, dedicated to the advancement of all women. Niboyet believed that women's position in society must be improved so that they would be able to exercise a salutary influence on men.

Eugénie Niboyet was also influenced by another Saint-Simonian belief, that progress did not require guns, nor war, but only industry. In 1844, following an international peace congress in London (which she probably attended), Niboyet helped establish a French peace society and launched a pacifist journal, *La Paix des deux mondes*. She collaborated in her pacifist work with Emile Souvestre, Michel Chevalier, de St.-Aignan, and the Countess Oleskewitch. The goal of the thirty-two men and twenty women who made up her organization was to attract the well-educated and intellectual leaders of society to pacifism. To that end they sponsored essay writing contests, such as: ''On the possibility of universal and permanent peace, and of the influence of peace on the happiness of mankind and on the means to realize peace.'' The journal was shortlived but was the first Continental effort at a peace organ, not again attempted until 30 years later.

In 1863, Eugénie Niboyet summed up her philosophy in *Le Vrai Livre des femmes*. In it she approved of a division of labor, with men caring for politics and commerce, while women reigned over morals and the family. The good mother would engrave her lessons on the hearts of her children and thus improve the world. Her final participation in the peace cause occurred in 1878 when she convinced the (Paris) Congrès des amis de la paix (Congress of Friends of Peace) to support the creation of specifically women's peace societies for the advancement of the cause.

Bibliography:

A. *Le Vrai Livre des femmes* (Paris, 1863).

Laura S. Strumingher

NICHOLAS II (6 May 1868, St. Petersburg—16 July 1918, Ekaterinburg, Russia). *Education*: tutored privately, received military training as officer of Preobrazhensky Regiment. *Career*: last member of Romanov dynasty to rule Tsarist Russia, 1894-1917.

The name of Nicholas II is forever associated with The First Hague Peace Conference of May-July 1899. The praise lavished on Nicholas at the time by the pacifist movement and large sections of the European and American public, if not all government circles, was certainly not undeserved. In a formal sense, the initiative was his, and without it The Hague Peace Conference might never have taken place.

Unlike his father Alexander III, however, Nicholas II did not become known as Tzar-Peacemaker. Though he did not actively seek the costly war with Japan (1904-5), he accepted it with his customary fatalism and rejected any arbitration attempts as outside interference. Similarly, except for a fleeting suggestion that the Serbo-Austrian conflict be submitted for arbitration, he did little to arrest Russia's rush into World War I that would spell the end of his reign and the tzarist regime.

The same considerations of Realpolitik that limited the Hague Conference's accomplishments were responsible for its inception in the first place. Concerned about the prohibitive cost of matching the Western powers in introducing rapid-fire artillery and rifles, the Russian Minister of War Alexei Kuropatkin originally suggested an agreement with Austria-Hungary to refrain from such an expensive measure for a minimum of ten years. Under the influence of the Ministers of Finance and Foreign Affairs, *Sergei Witte and Michael Muraviev, who wanted to avoid the impression of weakness that a bilateral agreement might create, Kuropatkin's original proposal grew into a plan for an international conference on limiting or reducing armaments worldwide. This idea eventually met with Nicholas's approval, reportedly after he had read a six-volume study on *The Future of War* and talked extensively with its author, *Jean de Bloch. With the publication of the conference proposal in August 1898, the tzarist government hoped to portray Russia as a champion of peace at a time of rising international tensions. In particular, it sought to head off a rumored agreement between England and Germany that would isolate Russia, and to pacify British public opinion which was becoming inflamed over Russia's recent advances in the Far East and conflicting claims for spheres of influence. At the same time, the Russian government assured its nervous French ally that the proposed conference would not touch on bilateral treaties or political issues and that disarmament, contrary to public impressions, was out of the question. Only socialists, Jews, and hysterical old maids could seriously entertain such harebrained ideas, Nicholas told Muraviev. Without belittling the agreements that were reached, it is clear that the ostensible reason for the conference—the all-important problem of establishing ceilings on personnel, existing and new weapons, as well as expenditures—had become moot even before the meeting was convened. Doomed, too, was the obligatory arbitration of international disputes.

Nicholas was neither a pacifist nor was his initiative for the peace conference motivated by genuine idealism, though he did nothing to disabuse the world of that impression. At best, he might have wished to extend the tzar's traditional domestic arbiter role to the international arena, without sacrificing Russia's interests, however. Belying his pacific personal traits, Nicholas considered himself first and foremost a soldier. Incapable of internalizing a coherent and consistent conception of the autocrat's role and alienated from its onerous duties, he sought refuge in the soldier's world to the point of wanting to join his troops in the Far-Eastern theater in 1904 and personally taking command in 1915. The limitations of Nicholas's peace policy were best expressed in the resolution with which he approved the peace conference: "Peace is more important than anything, if honor is not affected." Tragically, considerations of honor, however hollow or self-serving, intervened time and again.

Bibliography:

B. Jost Duelffer, *Regeln gegen den Krieg? Die Haager Friedenskonferenzen von 1899 und 1907 in der internationalen Politik* (Frankfurt, 1981); Dan L. Morrill, "Nicholas II and the Call for The First Hague Conference," *Journal of Modern History*, 46 (1974): 296-313; S. S. Oldenburg, *Last Tsar. Nicholas II, His Reign and His Russia* (3 vols., Gulf Breeze, Florida, 1975-6); L. Teleshev, "Kistorii Gaagskoi konferentsii 1899 g.,"

Krasnyi Arkhiv, 50-51 (1932), 64-96; L. Teleshev, "Novye materialy o Gaagskoi mirnoi konferentsii 1899 g.," *Krasnyi Arkhiv*, 54-55 (1932), 49-79.

Andrew M. Verner

NICOLAI, Georg Friedrich (6 February 1874, Berlin—8 October 1964, Santiago, Chile). *Education*: studies at the universities of Königsberg, Berlin, Paris, and Heidelberg; M.D., Univ. of Leipzig, 1901. *Career*: instructor, later professor of physiology and medicine, Univ. of Berlin, 1904-22, Univ. of Cordoba, Argentina, 1922-27, Univ. of Rosario (chair of sociology), 1928-30, Univ. of Chile, 1936-54; scientist, militant pacifist, author, and humanist.

Georg Friedrich Nicolai, a renowned physician and scientist, was the only German academic who publicly opposed World War I from the outset. In his "Appeal to the Europeans," written in October 1914 (in response to a prowar manifesto by 93 eminent German scholars and artists) and co-signed by *Albert Einstein and *Wilhelm Foerster, he deplored the rupture of cultural ties, predicted that there would be no victors, only losers at the end of the war, and called for a peace that would not become the source of future wars. Banished to a West Prussian fortress in 1915, he wrote *Die Biologie des Krieges* (*The Biology of War*) (1917), a far ranging examination of modern warfare from the viewpoint of a natural scientist, refuting the prevailing pseudo-Darwinist view of war as a means of natural selection. For him war was an atavism, the persistence of aggressive instincts which had ceased to be useful to the species and needed to be controlled in favor of man's social instincts if mankind was to survive and continue to progress. He equated nationalism with chauvinism, called for the abolition of national sovereignties in which he saw the fundamental danger to peace, and—anticipating Oswald Spengler and Arnold Toynbee—recognized not nations but civilizations as the units of history.

As a conscientious objector Nicolai was forcibly inducted into the German army as an orderly in the Medical Corps. His book was suppressed in wartime Germany, but the manuscript was smuggled into Switzerland, where it was published in 1917. Nicolai was thereupon courtmartialed, but *The Biology of War* became one of the most influential pacifist documents of World War I and was translated into nine languages, though it was boycotted in Germany even after the war. In 1918 Nicolai was threatened with imprisonment because of his refusal to bear arms and fled to Denmark, where he founded (with the participation of *Romain Rolland, *Ellen Key, +Fridtjof Nansen, and others an international pacifist magazine, *Das werdende Europa*. Rejecting the offer of Soviet citizenship, he returned to Germany after the Armistice, joined the pacifist Bund Neues Vaterland (New Fatherland League), was elected to the presidium of the German Peace Society, and proposed the creation and organization of a "Peace Party" which should be active not only in politics but in church, school, university, and communal life. He played a major role in the early attempts to have Germany admitted to the League of Nations and to promote Franco-German reconciliation.

As a target of vicious nationalist attacks Nicolai was prevented in 1920 from resuming his medical lectures at the University of Berlin by rioting students and expelled from the faculty by the Academic Senate as "unfit to be a teacher of German youth." After two years of futile efforts to obtain redress, he left Germany to become professor of physiology at the University of Córdoba, then governed by a progressive administration. Forced out by the return of the conservatives, he went to Rosario, where the students insisted on his appointment as professor of sociology, but here too he became the victim of university politics. After serving temporarily on the faculty of the Colegio Libre de Estudios Superiores in Buenos Aires, of which he was a co-founder, he led a nomadic existence in Argentina, Uruguay, Soviet Russia, and Spain, until in 1933 he found lasting asylum in Chile.

Nicolai was an original thinker whose pacifism was part of a larger philosophical concept. He envisaged a universal moral law based not on the "subjective," or intuitive morality of the great religious leaders and philosophers, but on "objective" principles derived from the study of man's continuing biological and cultural evolution. "It is an error to view ethics and science as separate spheres," he declared. Moral systems evolve because they serve the vital interests of a close-knit group. Formerly that group was the tribe or the nation, but, according to Nicolai, the only viable group was humanity as a whole, and tribal or national moralities had become inadequate.

Nicolai's influence as a thinker, teacher, and author extended throughout Latin America. A Sociedad de amigos de la ciencia (Society of Friends of Sciences) with branches in many countries was founded in his honor in Lanus, Argentina, in 1954.

Bibliography:

A. *Die Biologie des Krieges* (Zürich, 1917, English trans., *The Biology of War*, New York, 1919); *El Mundo físico y moral* (Buenos Aires, 1931).

B. Wolf W. Zuelzer, *Der Fall Nicolai* (Frankfurt, 1981, English trans., *The Nicolai Case*, Detroit, 1982).

Wolf W. Zuelzer

NIEBUHR, Reinhold (21 June 1892, Wright City, MO—1 June 1971, Stockbridge, MA). *Education*: attended Elmhurst Coll., 1910, Eden Theological Seminary, 1913; B.D., Yale Univ., 1914, M.A., 1915. *Career*: ordained minister of the Evangelical Synod of North America, 1915; pastor, Bethel Evangelical Church, Detroit, Michigan, 1915-28; associate professor of ethics and theology, Union Theological Seminary, New York, 1928-60; author, editor, and lecturer.

Reinhold Niebuhr was the preeminent American theologian of his time, and his influence extended to political leaders and analysts. His intellectual career spanned the history of modern liberalism, and he fashioned an ethics of Christian realism which both sharpened the social ethics of pacifism and gave new scope and thrust to just war thought.

Niebuhr gave conventional support to World War I. His subsequent disillusionment with it coincided with his social awakening in Detroit. The resulting social consciousness, coupled with his effectiveness as an author and speaker, brought him to the attention of reformist pacifists such as *John Nevin Sayre, *Kirby Page, and *Sherwood Eddy. Initially paying his salary, they arranged for him to go to New York to teach at Union Theological Seminary and to co-edit the radical and pacifist journal, *The World Tomorrow*. With them Niebuhr became an active supporter of Socialist leader *Norman Thomas.

Meanwhile, the young theologian rethought the underlying assumptions of Christian liberalism and the Social Gospel, first in *Does Civilization Need Religion*? (1927) and most fully in *Moral Man and Immoral Society* (1932). He also was developing the language of paradox and irony which became characteristic of his thought. Grappling with the relativism of understanding, the indeterminacy of choice, and the pervasiveness of sin and fallibility in human and social nature, Niebuhr distinguished between individual and social ethics. He granted the validity of *a priori* ideals for the individual, and even their importance as social standards. But he insisted that social and political choices require realistic assessment of consequences and of the role of power in human affairs. For the individual the ultimate value might be love; for society it must be justice in at least the sense of an equitable distribution of power.

Niebuhr applied distinctions such as these to political issues in a stream of books and articles and in his editing of *Christianity and Crisis*. In the mid-1930s he broke with the Thomas faction of the Socialist party on the question of nonviolence in the social struggle, and he challenged that doctrine in the Fellowship of Reconciliation. He insisted that nonviolence could be justified as a social strategy only in relative political terms and not on absolute religious grounds. His challenge contributed to the sharper analysis of *Gandhi in the United States and to the development of nonviolent resistance theory.

Meanwhile, after 1936 he criticized pacifists with increasing sharpness, advocating aid to the Allies in opposition to Nazi Germany and, finally, war. His judgment of the twin failures of liberal naiveté and totalitarian maliciousness appears in *The Children of Light and the Children of Darkness* (1944). About the same time he deepened the theological basis of his ethics in studies which culminated in *The Nature and Destiny of Man* (1941, 1943).

From Niebuhr's point of view the struggle against totalitarianism and inequitable power was continued in the Cold War, and his trenchent analyses of issues and underlying philosophy informed the writings of important decision-makers and analysts such as George F. Kennan, Dean Acheson, Arthur Schlesinger, Jr., and +Hans Morgenthau. Niebuhr's adaptation of just war pragmatism to a world of relative understanding and contingent situations was a two-edged sword, however, and the same Christian realism that was used to support containment in the 1950s was turned against the war in Vietnam and the nuclear arms race. Reinhold Niebuhr exerted a strong influence on the development of both the Christian realism he espoused and the social pacifism he critiqued.

Bibliography:

A. *The Children of Light and the Children of Darkness: A Vindication of Democracy and a Critique of Its Traditional Defense* (New York, 1944); *Christian Realism and Political Problems* (New York, 1953); *The Irony of American History* (New York, 1952); *Moral Man and Immoral Society: A Study in Ethics and Politics* (New York, 1932).

B. June Bingham, *Courage to Change* (New York, 1961); Gordon Hanland, *The Thought of Reinhold Niebuhr* (New York, 1960); Ronald Stone, *Reinhold Niebuhr: Prophet to Politicians* (Nashville, TN, 1971).

C. Reinhold Niebuhr Papers, Manuscript Division, Library of Congress, Washington, D.C.

Charles Chatfield

NIEUWENHUIS, Ferdinand Domela (31 December 1846, Amsterdam—22 November 1919, Hilversum, Netherlands). *Education*: Amsterdam gymnasium, 1858-64; theological studies, universities of Utrecht and Amsterdam, 1864-69; licensed as clergyman, 1869. *Career*: editor, *Recht voor Allen*, 1879-98; delegate, Dutch parliament, 1888-91; labor leader, anarchist, and reformer.

Ferdinand Domela Nieuwenhuis, Dutch antimilitarist, was the son of a Lutheran clergyman and was himself ordained in the Lutheran ministry. In 1878, dismayed with the institutional church, Nieuwenhuis resigned from his fashionable parish in The Hague and spent the rest of his life in labor-organizing, writing, and public speaking. As a writer and a leading political reformer in the Netherlands, Nieuwenhuis advocated a broad inclusive socialist vision which was internationalist and humanitarian in scope, a determined opposition to militarism, and a staunch anticolonial position.

Nieuwenhuis served as a socialist delegate in the Dutch parliament from 1888 to 1891. His prominence in the workers' movement as well as the notoriety of his eight month imprisonment for lese majesty in 1887 made him a forceful voice for workers' rights. His parliamentary experience, however, left him a convinced opponent of legislative channels as adequate means of social change. Nieuwenhuis' opposition to parliamentarianism signaled his growing sympathy with anarcho-syndicalist thought and the usefulness of direct action by workers to achieve social change. Similarly, in 1891 at the Brussels congress of the Second International, Nieuwenhuis called for a general strike by all workers if war should be declared in Europe. In Nieuwenhuis' view workers needed to recognize their opportunity for control of their own industries and their potential for halting war through individual noncooperation and collective general strikes.

Following the expulsion of the anarchists from the Second International, Nieuwenhuis founded the anarchist organization, Free Socialists, in 1898. In 1903 Dutch anarchists suffered a severe setback when a general strike, which they had supported, failed to succeed. Although Nieuwenhuis's influence in the Netherlands waned after this defeat, he remained active in the European peace movement and was named to the executive board of the International Antimilitarist Association in 1904. Throughout the rest of his life (including World War I in which the Netherlands remained officially neutral) Nieuwenhuis continued to campaign against militarism, reiterating the themes of conscription refusal and the viability of a general strike to paralyze the war machine. His blend of religious humanitarianism and fervent opposition to war motivated his peace and labor movement activities and fashioned his vision of a free and just society.

Bibliography:

A. *De geschiedenis van het socialisme*, (Amsterdam, 1901-2); *Krieg dem Krieg*, (Berlin, 1907); *Mijn afscheid van de kerk*, (Amsterdam, 1879); *Socialisme libertaire et socialisme autoritaire*, (Paris, 1890); *Van Christen tot anarchist*, (Amsterdam, 1910).

B. Albert de Jong, *Domela Nieuwenhuis*, (The Hague, 1966); Evert Zandstra, *Vrijheid: het leven van F. Domela Nieuwenhuis*, (Amsterdam, 1968).

C. Ferdinand Domela Nieuwenhuis Papers, International Instituut voor Sociale Geschiedenis, Amsterdam.

Walter H. Conser, Jr.

NIGHTINGALE, Florence (12 May 1820, Florence, Italy—13 August 1910, London). *Education*: at home instruction and self-educated. *Career*: pioneer of nursing, hospital, and sanitation reform.

Florence Nightingale, the Lady with the Lamp, the Ministering Angel of Scutari Barracks Hospital in the Crimean War, did not question war as such, but she did challenge unnecessary death on the battlefield and devoted her life to improving the army medical services and to creating a home and hospital nursing profession.

Six months after Great Britain and France declared war on Russia in March 1854, the British Army in the Crimea was involved in suffering on an appalling scale, with no adequate army medical service. Such battlefield conditions were not new; what was new was the presence of a war correspondent. Telegraphy, a recent innovation, enabled the reports of William Howard Russell to reach *The Times* of London within hours of the events and their publication caused a public outcry for action. At the time nursing as a profession was nonexistent. Hospitals were places to be avoided by the genteel, and most nurses were drunken prostitutes, untrained, uneducated, unacceptable in society. Desiring to act quickly before the situation was made worse by well-meaning, but ill-equipped personnel going to the front as volunteers, the government turned to Florence Nightingale. Born into a well-to-do English family, Nightingale had defied established custom and her family's opposition by studying nursing techniques. Unwilling to be simply an adornment at home until she found a husband and adorned his home, she decided that her vocation lay with the sick, not in marriage. With the assistance of sympathetic family friends, she visited hospitals in France and spent a brief period with the Kaiserwerth Institution in Germany. She also studied the Blue Books on Health and Sanitation that governments were publishing during the 1840s as urban problems multiplied. In 1853 her family reluctantly agreed to her becoming Superintendent of the Institution for Sick Gentlewomen in Distressed Circumstances in London. There she discovered her organizing capacities and a sympathy with her charges. Meager as this training was by modern standards, Nightingale was better equipped than anyone else to organize the Scutari Barracks Hospital.

Reaching Scutari in November 1854, she was surrounded by opposition, incompetence, inefficiency, vested interests in the status quo, bureaucratic indifference, inadequately prepared assistants, nonexistent food and medical supplies, a vast building lacking essential equipment, and wounded men arriving by the thousand from the frontline. Her long years of fighting family opposition taught her patience, subtlety, diplomacy, and firmness in the achievement of her ends. These traits were invaluable in achieving some order, system, and medical care in this chaos. Her habit of rising very early to study in secret had accustomed her to enormously long days, which she endured without break for twenty months. The task was impossible, and the mission, by most criteria, a failure. On a visit to the frontlines, Nightingale herself contracted Crimean fever and was an invalid for the rest of her life. The mortality rate in the Scutari Barracks Hospital was enormous, due to the unsanitary conditions of the building's construction. Three things, however, were gained. Until that time, the common soldier had been regarded as a drunken brute and the scum of the earth. Nightingale demonstrated that he was drunk only because the army provided no recreational facilities and no efficient means of relaying money home. She taught officers and officials to treat the soldier with human dignity. Second, Nightingale developed an unquenchable determination for reform and to this she devoted the rest of her life. Third, the reports that soldiers took home of the loving care they had received created a legend and the legend gave her power: no politician, however reluctant, could completely ignore her reforming zeal.

Her first concern was reform of the Army Medical Service. She collected statistics and presented her facts by pictorial charts (she believed that she had invented the method), showing among other things that mortality in army barracks was double that in civilian life. After much hard work and in the face of official apathy, Nightingale finally succeeded in convincing the government to set up a Royal Commission to investigate sanitary conditions in the army. Through the Nightingale Fund she sought to establish a trained nursing profession, and in 1860, she helped organize a Training School for Nurses, in St. Thomas' Hospital in London. She also wrote two highly influential books, *Notes on Hospitals* (1859), which led people from all over Europe and the United States to seek her advice, and *Notes on Nursing* (1860) which remained for over a century a sound primer on home nursing.

Although Florence Nightingale did not challenge war directly, she did help to lessen its terrible consequences and to encourage other private citizens to commit themselves to the task of minimizing human self-destruction. In 1872, in an address in London, *Henry Dunant, the founder of the International Red Cross and the originator of the Convention of Geneva (1864), which ''civilized'' warfare by allowing for the treatment of wounded, credited Nightingale's work in the Crimea as his main inspiration.

Bibliography:

A. *A Contribution to the Sanitary History of the British Army during the Late War with Russia* (London, 1859); *Notes on Hospitals* (London, 1859); *Notes on Matters Affecting the Health, Efficiency and Hospital Administration of the British Army* (London, 1858); *Notes on Nursing: What It Is, and What It Is Not* (London, 1860).

B. Nancy Boyd, *Three Victorian Women Who Changed Their World: Josephine Butler, Octavia Hill, Florence Nightingale* (New York and Oxford, 1982); Edward Cook, *The Life of Florence Nightingale* (2 vols., London, 1913); Sarah A. Tooley, *The Life of Florence Nightingale* (London, 1910); Cecil Woodham-Smith, *Florence Nightingale, 1820-1910* (New York, 1951).

C. Florence Nightingale Papers, British Museum, London.

Elnora Ferguson

NIPPOLD, Otfried (21 May 1864, Wiesbaden, Germany—27 July 1938, Thun, Switzerland). *Education*: Dr. jur., Univ. of Jena, 1887. *Career*: lawyer, teacher of international law, and author.

In 1871 Otfried Nippold moved to Switzerland where his father had accepted an appointment as professor of Protestant church history in Berne. He went to school there, eventually becoming a Swiss citizen. After university studies in Germany and a brief period as a teacher in Tokyo (around 1890), Nippold entered the German foreign office in Berlin. He remained in the German foreign service for only two years. From 1898 until 1909, he earned a living as a lawyer and as a Privatdozent (lecturer) for international law at the University of Berne. He became known to the public through the publication of a standard work on the problems of international arbitration in which he evaluated in detail the accomplishments of The First Hague Peace Conference of 1899 and its impact on the second conference of 1907.

In 1909 Nippold moved to Frankfurt am Main, became a contributor to the *Frankfurter Zeitung* and, in 1911, founded the Verband für internationale Verständigung (Association for International Understanding), whose meetings in Heidelberg (1912) and Nuremberg (1913) attracted a great deal of interest and attention. As a result of this activity Nippold made close contacts with the pacifist movement and with its leaders such as *Alfred H. Fried, +Walther Schücking and +Hans Wehberg. These contacts, however, were not without friction. Nippold did not reject all war or consider himself to be primarily a pacifist. Rather, through the further development of international law and the process of international arbitration, he wanted to reach a point where it would be possible to distinguish clearly between a justifiable defensive war and a willful war of aggression. It was from this perspective that he castigated the German delegates at The Hague peace conferences for sabotaging efforts to create an effective system of international arbitration.

As a concerned and perceptive critic of his times, Nippold, in a penetrating essay in 1913, pilloried the increasingly unbridled "German chauvinism" and pointed to the Prussian military cult as the most dangerous of all threats to world peace. Immediately after the outbreak of the First World War, he returned to

Switzerland where he carried on a tireless campaign as a political writer against German imperialism, whose defeat he considered to be the fundamental preliminary condition for a peaceful world order. From 1920-34, Nippold held the post of president of the supreme court in the League of Nations administered Saar region. After leaving that post, he refrained from involvement in politics.

Bibliography:

A. *Der deutsche Chauvinismus* (Stuttgart, 1913); *Deutschland und das Völkerrecht* (2 vols., Zurich, 1920); *Durch Wahrheit zum Recht. Gesammelte Kriegsaufsatze* (Berne, 1919); *Die Fortbildung des Verfahrens in völkerrechtlichen Streitigkeiten* (Leipzig, 1907); *Meine Erlebnisse in Deutschland vor dem Weltkrieg (1909-1914)* (Berne, 1918).

B. Roger Chickering, "A Voice of Moderation in Imperial Germany: The 'Verband fur internationale Verstandigung,' 1911-1914," *Journal of Contemporary History*, 8, 1 (January, 1973), 147-64; Hans Wehberg, "Otfried Nippold (1864-1934)," *Die Friedenswarte*, 38, 5 (1938), 235-43.

Adolf Gasser
Trans. by Solomon Wank

NITHACK-STAHN, Walter (23 October 1866, Berlin—22 December 1942, Berlin). *Education*: theological studies, universities of Berlin, Tübingen, Leipzig, Greifswald, and Halle; passed examinations in theology and teaching (neither required a university degree at the time) 1888. *Career*: Lutheran pastor, teacher, author, and pacifist.

Nithack-Stahn was descended from a long line of theologians. He spent his youth in Eisleben where his father was a pastor. After passing his theological and teaching examinations and sojourning in Italy for several months, Nithack-Stahn became both a vicar and a teacher in Grossbeeren. Following that, he was appointed to the faculty of a Lutheran theological seminary in Plötzensee. Concurrently, he served as teacher and adjunct pastor at the military orphanage in Potsdam. The two-fold activity betrays Nithack-Stahn's vacillation between the vocations of teaching and the ministry before he finally decided on the latter. He served as vicar in Görlitz from 1897 until 1907 and the Kaiser Wilhelm Memorial Church in Berlin from 1906 until 1929. At the same time he gained a reputation as a writer of dramas and novels as well as of theological and literary historical works.

Nithack-Stahn's significance for the German peace movement lies in the fact that he was one of the few German theologians who broached peace themes in his sermons and in published pamphlets and journal articles. Several of his articles appeared in *Martin Rade's *Christliche Welt*. The pacifistic theme running through his published works was the belief that the promoting of peace constituted the unique mission of Christianity. In response to the defense bill introduced into the German Reichstag in 1913, Nithack-Stahn, together with *Otto Umfrid and Hans Francke, signed a statement calling for international peace. This document was sent to three thousand ecclesiastics, members of university Protestant theological faculties, and pastors, and it was published in *Ethische Rundschau* in May 1913.

Bibliography:

A. *Barbareien* (Berlin, 1913); *An Alle. Eine Sorge aus unseren Tagen* (Leipzig, 1922); "Das Evangelium und der Krieg," *Christliche Welt*, 24 (1910), 674-76, 709-11, 724-27, 747-52, 776-77.

Karl Holl
Trans. by Solomon Wank

NKRUMAH, Kwame (21 September 1909, Nkroful, Ghana—27 April 1972, Conakry, Guinea). *Education*: teacher's certificate, Achimota Coll., Accra, 1930; B.A., Lincoln Univ., 1939, Bachelor of Theology, 1942; M.S., Univ. of Pennsylvania, 1942, M.A., 1943. *Career*: editor, *African Interpreter*, 1942-43, *New Africa*, 1946-48, *Accra Evening News*, 1949-50; publisher, *Morning Telegraph*, 1949-51; *Daily Mail*, 1949-51; political activist, Pan Africanist, and author.

Kwame Nkrumah will long be remembered as the most widely known and the most controversial African leader in the first decade of independence. A member of the Nzima tribe in South Western Ghana, he started life under some very difficult circumstances. With determination and dedication, he obtained primary and secondary education in his homeland before moving out into the wider world. He daringly left Ghana for America instead of the traditional Britain where previously almost all students from the colonies in Africa flocked. His American education and his association with a wide range of groups and movements in the United States together prepared him for the challenges of human organization he met upon his return to Ghana.

Though Nkrumah never wrote a treatise specifically addressing the peace question, his politics and his activism, while in and out of office in Ghana, leave one with the strong impression that he cared and strove for peace. He embraced the principles of nonviolent civil disobedience developed by *Gandhi and applied them more specifically to the colonial conditions of Ghana. His "positive action" drive, which later paid dividends to him and his movement, apparently attracted the attention of other Africans fighting against colonial rule. Though Kwame Nkrumah later changed his attitude towards the use of violence in the political process, his early attitudes and activities provided an African mirror of Gandhi, and others like Kenneth Kaunda of Zambia joined this Ghanaian bandwagon to wrest power from the hands of colonial settlers.

Nkrumah's numerous writings were filled with appeals for peaceful resolution of international problems. His loud expression of outrage at France's bold testing of the atom bomb in the African Sahara was a message much appreciated by the peace groups in the West and many Western peace groups echoed his call. Although his associations with the world peace movement were never direct or institutional, he demonstrated his love and hope for world peace by banding together with *Nehru of India and others concerned about the state of the Cold War. They institutionalized their feelings of insecurity in a nuclear age by forming the Non-Aligned Movement, a group that initially sought to mediate between the United States and the Soviet Union. Kwame Nkrumah made his most remarkable bid for a world leadership role and peacemaker when he decided to pay a visit to Hanoi, specifically to mediate between the United States and North Vietnam. Though his efforts resulted in his disgraceful overthrow, his supporters in Africa and elsewhere still see this act of courage on the part of a Third World leader as irrefutable evidence of his sincerity and commitment to the nonaligned concept, world peace, and security.

Bibliography:

A. *Africa Must Unite* (London 1963); *Ghana: The Autobiography of Kwame Nkrumah* (New York, 1957).

B. Basil Davidson, *Black Star: A View of Life and Times of Kwame Nkrumah* (New York-Washington, 1973); *Dictionary of African Biography* (New York, 1977), I, 272-77.

Sulayman S. Nyang

NOBEL, Alfred Bernard (21 October 1833, Stockholm, Sweden—10 December 1896, San Remo, Italy). *Education*: tutors, father's laboratories, private studies, and occasional courses with scientists. *Career*: inventor and businessman.

Alfred Nobel's remarkable last will and testament which endowed five prizes for outstanding work in physics, chemistry, medicine or physiology, literature, and peace enshrined the name of this self-made millionaire in the popular consciousness. The first prizes were awarded in 1901, after years of litigation and debate over the proper groups to administer his fortune and distribute the prizes.

Much of Nobel's childhood was spent in St. Petersburg where his father had opened a factory to manufacture war products for the Russian government. A frail boy, he was tutored at home and studied chemistry in his father's atelier. Following the Crimean War, his father went bankrupt, leaving the St. Petersburg business to his elder sons and returning to Sweden to begin again. Young Alfred left to travel in western Europe and the United States where he learned English and French. From a Russian professor, he learned about nitroglycerine and then in 1863, returned to Sweden to begin his experiments which eventually led to the discovery of dynamite. By the end of his life, he held 129 patents in five countries and was a millionaire. The Nobel brothers who remained in Russia built another fortune developing the Baku oilfields.

The more famous he became, the more reclusive and suspicious he became. Nobel never married and was often disappointed with his laboratory and business associates who often became unscrupulous thieves of his ideas. Political hostility drove him from France to Italy in 1891. Nobel found his solace in literature, particularly Percy Bysshe Shelley and *Bjørnstjerne Bjørnsen, and in poems and plays which he wrote for himself. Very little in his life points to the surprising will which designated a sum to "...the person who shall have done the most or best work for fraternity among nations, for the abolition or reduction of standing armies and for the holding and promotion of peace congresses." The one connection he had to the late nineteenth-century peace movement was his brief friendship (mainly correspondence) with Baroness *Bertha von Suttner who was well known as a peace activist. He frequently wrote to her, however, that he doubted the efficacy of the peace movement and evidently mused that he might have made a better contribution to peace through his awesome technical inventions. Nobel developed an early form of the "balance of terror" theory, arguing that governments might begin to consider collective security as an approach to international affairs when war machines became too terrible to use.

Nobel's will was the work of a skeptic who hoped humanity might save itself by learning to follow the best instincts of its elites. There is no evidence that it was the product of a guilt-ridden man. Nobel loved humanity but disliked people. He worshipped higher civilization and his will reflected that passion.

Bibliography:

B. Hilaire Cuny, *Nobel de la dynamite et les prix nobel* (Paris, 1970); Oscar J. Falnes, *Norway and the Nobel Peace Prize* (N.Y., 1938); Ragnvild Moe, *Le Prix nobel de la paix et l'Institut nobel norvégien* (Oslo, 1932); H. Schück and R. Sohlman, *Nobel, Dynamite and Peace* (London, 1929); H. Schück, R. Sohlman, et al, *Nobel, The Man and His Prizes* (U. of Oklahoma and the Nobel Inst. 1951).

Sandi E. Cooper

NOEL-BAKER, Philip John [Baron Noel-Baker of the City of Derby] (1 November 1889, England—9 October 1982, London). *Education*: Bootham School, York; Haverford Coll.; M.A., Kings Coll., Cambridge Univ., 1912. *Career*: vice principal, Ruskin Coll., 1914; ambulance units, 1914-18; member, British Delegation to the Peace Conference, 1919; League of Nations Secretariat, 1920-22; Cassel Professor of International Relations, Univ. of London, 1924-29; Member of Parliament (for Coventry), 1929-31; principal assistant to the president of the World Disarmament Conference, Geneva, 1932-33; Dodge Lecturer, Yale Univ., 1934; Member of Parliament (for Derby), 1936-50; parliamentary secretary, Minister of War Transport, 1942-45; Minister of State, Foreign Office, 1945-46; Secretary of State for Air, 1946-47; Secretary of State for Commonwealth Relations, 1947-50; Member of Parliament (for Derby South), 1950-70; Minister of Fuel and Power, 1950-51; chairman, Foreign Affairs Group, Parliamentary Labour party, 1964-70; House of Lords, 1977-82; politician, scholar, and internationalist.

Philip Noel-Baker's long and varied career won him many honors. As an Olympic athlete, he captained the British team and won a silver medal for the 1,500 meter run in 1920. As a scholar, he wrote several outstanding books on peace and disarmament, one of which *The Arms Race* (1958), received the Albert Schweitzer Book Prize for 1961. As a Labourite politician, he held cabinet office and ended his career as a life peer. As a lifelong crusader for peace who had done relief work during the Russian famine of the early 1920s and supported the League of Nations and disarmament, he was awarded the Nobel Peace Prize in 1959.

Philip Baker (he took the additional surname of Noel from his wife in 1921) was born into a family prominent in Liberal politics. His father was Joseph Allen

Baker, "the fighting Quaker," a Member of Parliament who helped develop the London tramway system. While an honors student at Cambridge University in economics, Baker became the first person to serve as both the president of the Union and of the University Athletic Club. When the war came he was a noncombatant, quickly volunteering to serve in the Friends' Ambulance Unit. By the end of the war he had won several honors for his courage in action.

When a public movement arose at the end of the war to create a world organization and realize disarmament, Baker found his mission in life. He assisted Lord +Robert Cecil as a member of the League of Nations Section of the British delegation at the Paris Peace Conference and then worked in the League Secretariat as the principal assistant to Sir +Eric Drummond, the first secretary-general of the organization. Although Cecil was a Conservative and Baker joined the Labour party, the two worked together closely for many years and Baker became the most important Labourite leader of the League of Nations Union, which Cecil headed. This group, and its successor organization, the United Nations Association, were the largest and most influential in the British peace movement. They included many pacifist supporters, but their outlook—and his—were internationalist and accepted the necessity for using force in some situations.

Appointed to a professorship at the University of London in 1924, Noel-Baker wrote several books which established him as a leading authority on international affairs. These included *The Geneva Protocol* (1925), *Disarmament* (1926) and *The Coolidge Conference* (1927). His scholarly career was interrupted in 1929 by his election to parliament and appointment to serve as the Parliamentary Private Secretary to the Foreign Secretary, +Arthur Henderson. When both lost office in 1931, Henderson kept Noel-Baker as his principal assistant when he became the president of the World Disarmament Conference which met in Geneva from 1932 on. During these years Noel-Baker continued to study the armaments situation, and in 1937 his monumental study, *The Private Manufacture of Armaments*, appeared. Arms makers, the "merchants of death," had been the target of many popular works in the interwar years. He now carried the discussion of them away from individuals towards an analysis of why the system of producing weapons for private profit was open to abuse and should be ended. He examined the way the arms industry manipulated the news media, legislatures, and public opinion.

Returned to parliament in 1936, Noel-Baker moved ahead of most of the Labour party into outspoken opposition to the National Government's policies of nonintervention in the Spanish Civil War and appeasement of the dictators. His formidable intellectual gifts and energy won him attention, and in 1942, Winston Churchill made him Joint Parliamentary Secretary to the Ministry of War Transport. When the Clement Attlee Government was formed in 1945 he held a variety of offices, winning particular distinction as Commonwealth Relations Secretary from 1947-50. He also represented Britain at the General Assembly of the United Nations and chaired the Labour party in 1946 and 1947.

Out of office in the 1950s, he remained in the Labour shadow cabinet and continued his writing and campaigning for disarmament. He made it clear that he had no sympathy for the unilateral renunciation of arms, and headed the Socialist Campaign for Multilateral Disarmament which opposed unilateralism. When he retired from the Commons in 1970, he announced "while I have health and strength, I shall give all my time to the work of breaking the dogmatic sleep of those who allow the nuclear, chemical, biological and conventional arms race to go on." He did this, and more. As president of the British Vietnam Committee he campaigned against American intervention in Vietnam. As an elder statesman of the Labour party, he continued to attend party conferences and offer counsel to its members. When he died at the age of 92, the *Guardian* said in its obituary that he had kept the conscience of the House of Commons.

Bibliography:

A. *The Arms Race* (1958); *Disarmament* (London, 1926); *The Private Manufacture of Armaments* (London, 1937).

B. *Guardian* (London), October 9, 1982; LT, October 9, 1982.

Donald S. Birn

NOSSIG, Alfred (18 April 1864, Lemberg, Galicia, Austria [now Lwów, Poland]—22 February 1943, Warsaw). *Education*: university studies in philosophy, medicine and law. *Career*: writer, poet, playwright, sculptor, musician, and political publicist.

From the beginning, the paradoxical and erratic behavior of the extraordinarily versatile and talented Alfred Nossig appeared puzzling to many people. As a young man he not only played a considerable role in the artistic life of his native city, but he also emerged politically as a member of the Polish Socialist party in Galicia. At first a proponent of the policy of assimiliation for Polish Jews, he shifted to Zionism in 1887 and wrote several books and essays on Jewish national problems which strongly influenced Jewish intellectuals, especially in Galicia. Nossig's collaboration with Theodore Herzl failed because of Nossig's refusal to subordinate himself to Herzl. Moving to Berlin in 1899, Nossig laid the foundation for the empirical study of Jewish statistics by publishing several works on the subject. These works led to the establishment in 1902 of the Verein für Statistik der Juden (Association for Jewish Statistics) and encouraged the establishment of the Jüdisches Statistisches und Demographisches Institut (Jewish Statistical and Demographic Institute).

His numerous activities and negotiations with German and Polish officials concerning the improvement of conditions for Jews in Poland led to suspicions that Nossig was unreliable. These suspicions were strengthened when, at the end of World War I as a Polish citizen, but operating from Berlin, he turned to plans for the unification of Europe and for a system of world order to ensure peace. As a figure who operated constantly between the fronts, he could well have appeared in a dubious light and be distrusted by the Germans, Poles, and Jews as an agent for the other side.

Together with the German left-liberal politician *Wilhelm Heile, Nossig, in competition with Count +Richard Coudenhove-Kalergi, pushed in the early 1920s for a European Peace Union. This union, based on close cooperation between Germany, France, England, and Poland, would serve according to Nossig, as a complement to the League of Nations. It would do this particularly through provisions securing the territorial integrity of the signators, banning war absolutely, making arbitration of disputes obligatory, and creating a joint military force. The Verband für europäische Verständigung (Association of European Understanding) came out of these efforts in 1926. Nossig acted as the general secretary of the association and it was mostly as a result of his efforts that sections were established in, among others, France and Poland. However the association failed at the end of the 1920s because of internal and external political as well as personal strains. Independent of the Association, Nossig founded a Jewish section of the Freidensbund der Religionen (Peace Unions of Religions).

Driven out of Germany after the National Socialist seizure of power in January 1933, Nossig returned to Poland where he continued his often fantastic appearing peace activities. Thus he planned the erection of a monumental statue, "Der heilige Berg" ("The Holy Mountain") on Mount Carmel as a symbol of world peace and of a national homeland for the Jews in Palestine. Soon after the takeover of Poland by German troops, Nossig appeared in Warsaw and took over leadership of the Emigration Committee of the Warsaw Jewish Council (Judenrat). He held this position with the agreement of the Germans, to whom he had outlined plans for the emigration of the Jewish population of Poland. The distrust of Nossig that arose among the Jews in the Warsaw Ghetto probably grew when, under German pressure, he became a member of the Jewish Council and chairman of its department of art and culture. At the beginning of 1943, Nossig was charged by a Jewish underground court in the Warsaw Ghetto with traitorous collaboration with the Germans (the validity of the charge remains unclear) and sentenced to death. He was shot by members of the Jewish military organization.

Bibliography:

B. Karl Holl, "Europapolitik im Vorfeld der deutschen Regierungspolitik. Zur Tätigkeit proeuropäischer Organisationen in der Weimarer Republik," *Historische Zeitschrift*, 219 (1974), 33-94; Michael Zylberberg, "The Trial of Alfred Nossig. Traitor or Victim," *The Wiener Library Bulletin*, 23 (1969), 41-45.

Karl Holl
Trans. by Solomon Wank

NOVICOW, Jacques (29 September 1849, Constantinople [now Istanbul], Turkey—21 March 1912, Odessa, Russia). *Education*: studies at the universities of Odessa, Florence, and Naples. *Career*: founder and vice-president, International Institute of Sociology; member, International Peace Bureau, 1896-1912; scholar, author, and sociologist.

Jacques Novicow, son of a Greek mother and Russian father, inherited a comfortable legacy from his father's manufacturing business which allowed him to pursue the life of a private scholar. As a young man he gave up the Orthodox faith in which he was raised and became a free thinker and admirer of Western liberal culture. His lengthy studies on the role of war in society published between 1886 and 1899 established his reputation as a sociologist. With René Worms, he founded the Institut International de Sociologie in Paris. By the time he died, he published 13 major works examining social structures, war, possibilities for peaceful organization among nations, the nature of associations, women's emancipation, poverty, and Social Darwinism. After the 1896 Universal Peace Congress in Budapest, he became a major voice in its annual proceedings and an influential chair of study commissions for the International Peace Bureau.

Novicow's major contributions to sociological thought centered on the roles of elites, which he termed "social sensoria," in societies. He insisted on an organic conception of social structures, articulated most completely in *Conscience et volonté sociales* (1897), a minor classic in its day. In addition, he was an early and persistent critic of the modish Social Darwinism of the late nineteenth century. What concerned him most were the wellsprings of progress and social improvement which he hoped would come from enlightened liberal leadership. As he grew older, Novicow apparently began to despair of liberal circles and increasingly admired, and sometimes supported, groups such as the well organized German Social Democratic party and women's rights organizations. In 1910 he helped sponsor a special meeting on the women's question at the annual international meeting of sociologists in Paris.

As a leading participant in the international peace movement, Novicow worked to broaden its essentially legalistic thrust to encompass a wider view of European federation. Impatient with the slow pace of the movement, he urged that peace activists imitate the success of the international socialist movement by organizing political activities directly. His main antiwar activities, however, were his books and articles. Novicow denied that violence offered the mainspring to progress. In *Les Luttes entre sociétés humaines et leurs phases successives* (1886), he offered a sweeping, historical portrait of the types and purposes of wars carried out since pre-history, demonstrating that struggle tended to become increasingly less physical and more intellectually competitive with modernization. In modern civilization, the survival of ancient forms of violence—notably warfare and territorial expansion—utterly contradicted the productive forces in society and tended to obliterate the cultural advances. Modern norms of progress transcended national boundaries and class lines. To writers and politicians who exalted the nation-state as the highest form of social organization, Novicow pointed out that there were no natural limits to human association and the likelihood was very great that a federation of states would evolve in the future. He argued continuously with the Polish sociologist Ludwig Gumplowicz, who insisted that wars of racial confrontation were laws of nature. To the growing voices demanding protectionist tariffs in Europe, Novicow equally insisted that these were backward measures.

His particular affection for Italian history and culture inspired, in part, his hopes for European federation. This new nation was, merely four centuries earlier, a collection of hostile sovereign principalities. In Novicow's lifetime, it became a single state—albeit troubled—based on struggles conducted by all its social classes against common enemies. The Italian experience, in Novicow's estimation, was by far a more fruitful model to study than the Bismarckian creation which remained far too mired in its feudal traditions and militarist mentalities, for Novicow's taste.

A Russian outsider to European culture, Novicow became in the words of the French pacifist *Charles Richet, "an internationalist among internationalists." His favorite self-description was "a European." His writings stood at the intersection of imaginative propaganda, social science, and historical analysis, permeated throughout with a plea against the insanity of war for advanced civilization.

Bibliography:

A. *L'Affranchissement de la femme* (Paris, 1903); *L'Alsace-Lorraine: obstacle à l'expansion allemande* (Paris, 1913); *Conscience et volonté sociales* (Paris, 1897); *La Critique du Darwinisme sociale* (Paris, 1910); *La Fédération de l'Europe* (Paris, 1901); *Les Gaspillages des sociétés modernes* (2nd ed., Paris, 1899); *La Guerre et ses prétendus bienfaits* (Paris, 1894); *La Justice et l'expansion de la vie* (Paris, 1905); *Les Luttes entre sociétés et leurs phases successives* (2nd ed., Paris, 1886); *La Missione dell'Italia* (Milan, 1903); *La Politique internationale* (Paris, 1886); *Le Problème de la misère* (Paris, 1908); *La Théorie organique des sociétés* (Paris, 1899).

B. Harry E. Barnes, "A Sociological Criticism of War and Militarism: An Analysis of the Doctrines of Jacques Novicow," *Journal of International Relations*, 12 (1921), 238-65; Sandi E. Cooper, ed., *Peace and Civilization: Selections from the Writings of Jacques Novicow* (New York, 1975).

Sandi E. Cooper

NOYES, John Humphrey (3 September 1811, Brattleboro, VT—13 April 1886, Niagara Falls, Canada). *Education*: B.A., Dartmouth Coll., 1830; attended Theological Seminary at Andover, 1831-32, and Yale Theological Department, 1832-34. *Career*: social reformer and founder of Oneida Community.

John Humphrey Noyes was best known as the founder of Oneida, a utopian community based on the principles of perfectionism, complex marriage, and communalism. Converted to perfectionism in 1833, Noyes became convinced that, with a strong belief in God, man could rid himself of all sin, desire, and jealousness and attain unity with Christ. In 1834, in fact, Noyes announced that he had reached the state of complete sinlessness and was ready to lead his followers to the creation of a perfect society. Establishing his community first in Putney, Vermont, and later in 1848 in Oneida, New York, he devised a world in which monogamy and private property no longer existed. The members of the community shared "spiritual mates" through a process of mutual agreement and criticism.

Noyes' belief in perfectionism led him to create his own distinctive notion of pacifism. According to Noyes, wars begun by men without the authority of God had to be resisted. Whether offensive or defensive in nature, they were merely ''lawless and private brawls.'' In contrast, Noyes believed that there were just wars, begun by God, that deserved the support of all individuals. This philosophy permitted Noyes to support the Union's army during the Civil War without the conflict of spirit often experienced by other pacifists. For Noyes, the struggle to free the slaves represented a true ''holy war'' devised by divine authority. Thus, while he kept the members of Oneida out of war, he gave the North his continued encouragement and support.

Noyes' unique notion of pacifism also caused him to refuse membership in any peace society. Existing groups, he believed, wrongly attempted to convince people of the horrors of war. Instead, he believed that the only way to attain peace was to establish a perfect society, justified by ''the direct authority and inspiration of God.'' This, he argued, he had done in western New York. For Noyes, Oneida had come to represent the world's best example of God's ''peace on earth.''

Bibliography:

A. ''Bible Principles of Peace and War,'' *Circular*, 1 n.s. (August 29, 1864), 185-86; ''Our Belligerent Principles,'' *Perfectionist and Theocratic Watchman*, 5 (March 22, 1845), 3; ''Peace and War,'' *Perfectionist*, 3 (January 15, 1844), 89; ''Peace Principles,'' *The Berean*, pp. 446-51; ''Philosophy of Non-Resistance, no. 3,'' *Free Church Circular* (June 20, 1851), 234.

B. Robert A. Parker, *A Yankee Saint: John Humphrey Noyes and the Oneida Community* (New York, 1935); Robert David Thomas, *The Man Who Would Be Perfect* (Philadelphia, 1977).

Carole Haber

OESTREICH, Paul Hermann August (30 March 1878, Kolberg, Germany—28 February 1959, Berlin, German Democratic Republic). *Education*: realgymnasium, Kolberg, 1888-96; study of mathematics and natural sciences, universities of Berlin and Greifswald, 1897-1900. *Career*: secondary school teacher, Berlin-Schöneberg, 1905-33; city council member, Berlin 1906-8, 1919-21; cultural and educational reformer, writer, editor, and pacifist.

Like *Hellmut von Gerlach, Paul Oestreich went through a development leading from Friedrich Naumann's imperialistically oriented Nationalsozialer Verein (National Social Union), to which Oestreich belonged from 1897 until 1903, to the Demokratische Vereinigung (Democratic Alliance), of which he was a member from 1908 until 1912. This latter organization, demanding arms limitations and international arbitration, adopted the key points of the pre-1914 bourgeois liberal-democratic pacifist movement. Rejected for active military duty in World War I because of poor health, Oestreich became active in the pacifist movement in 1915 as a member of the anti-annexationist Bund Neues Vaterland (New Fatherland League, renamed in 1922 Deutsche Liga für Menschenrechte [League for Human Rights]), and then in the Zentralstelle für Völkerrecht (Coordinating Office for International Law) and the Deutsche Freidensgesellschaft (German Peace Society) (DFG). He served on the executive board of the DFG from 1921 until 1926.

The greater part of Oestreich's work was devoted to the Bund Entschiedener Schulreformer (Association of Determined School Reformers) (BES), which he founded in 1919 and which he directed as president until its demise in 1933. The BES, which was politically neutral in the sense of not being affiliated with any political party, was dedicated to cultural and political aims with a pacifist orientation. The BES held school reform to be synonymous with lifestyle reform and advocated an education instilling humaneness. Oestreich believed firmly in the "universal constructive power of a pacifism that united the peoples of the earth." He believed in combatting chauvinism and revanchism (the desire for revenge after 1919), by a moral reeducation of people.

The BES belonged to the Deutsches Friedenskartell (German Peace Cartel) (DFK), the association of all pacifist and progressive cultural and political societies in Germany. Oestreich represented the interests of the BES in the DFK. As a recognized expert in the field of peace education, Oestreich maintained a high visibility in the DFK when it came to educational matters, and he also spoke out on the question of safeguarding parliamentary democracy in Germany. A frequent lecturer on peace education themes, Oestreich saw himself as a ''combative pacifist'' who wrote aggressively on the idea educating youth in the spirit of international conciliation, peace, and democracy.

Oestreich recognized that an enduring peace had to be socially secured. He therefore supported the referendum for the expropriation of the princely German houses without compensation (1926), worked for Franco-German reconciliation, and, after Germany joined the League of Nations, strongly rejected the growing trend to neocolonialism which had taken the form of demands for the transfer of colonial mandates to Germany. The establishment of the National Socialist dictatorship in 1933 ended Oestreich's peace and education work. He was arrested and held in ''protective custody'' for two months and dismissed from his teaching position. During the Nazi period Oestreich chose ''inner emigration.'' He was active in the resistance movement in the Kreisau and Leuschner Circles. Immediately after the liberation of Germany from fascism, Oestreich joined the Kommunistische Partei Deutschlands (German Communist party) and became a school board member in West Berlin. The rise and spread of strong anticommunist forces in West Germany soon induced him to transfer his activities to the German Democratic Republic (East Germany) where he joined the Communist Sozialistische Einheitspartei Deutschlands (Socialist Unity Party of Germany).

Bibliography:

A. *Aus dem Leben eines politischen Pädagogen* (Berlin, Leipzig, 1947-48); *Die elastische Einheitsschule* (Berlin, 1921); *Die Pädagogik der Gegenwart in Selbstdarstellungen* (Leipzig, 1925); *Unabhängige Kulturpolitik* (Leipzig, Vienna, 1924).

B. Winfried Böhm, *Kulturpolitik und Pädagogik Paul Oestreichs* (Bad Heilbrunn, 1973); Manfred Radtke, ''Paul Oestreichs Kampf für die Demokratisierung des deutschen Schulwesens,'' Habiltationsschrift, Univ. of Greifswald, 1961; Bernhard Reintges, *Paul Oestreich und der Bund Entschiedener Schulreformer* (Rheinstetten, 1975).

C. Paul Oestreich Papers, Pedagogical Seminar, Univ. of Würzburg.

Reinhold Lütgemeier-Davin
Trans. by Susan E. Cernyak

OHRTMANN, Johann Ingwert Knut (18 March 1898, Flensburg, Germany—27 May 1978, Kiel, Federal Republic of Germany). *Education*: Royal-Prussian Teachers' College (Präperandenanstalt), Apenrade [now Denmark], 1913; Teachers' College (Lehrerseminar), Tondern, 1915-16; passed examination for elementary school teachers (Volksschullehrer), Rendsburg, 1919. *Career*: elementary school teacher, Flensburg, 1920-24, Vollstedt near Husum, 1924-29, Lägerdorf near Itzehoe, 1930-33; government councillor and school inspector, Schleswig-Holstein state government, 1945-63; editor, *Deutsche Zukunft*, 1927-33; educational reformer, writer, journalist, and pacifist.

At the outbreak of World War I, Johann Ohrtmann, son of a coachman and garderner's helper, indulged in youthful dreams of ''night attacks'' and ''heroic death.'' Doubts about militarism began to arise after his entry into the army in 1916, when he had to endure the harassments and sadisms of his superior officer during recruit training. On the battlefield before Verdun he finally recognized how he had been imbued in school and through the press with the idea of the necessity of the war and with a heightened nationalism. From that time Ohrtmann resolved to fight against war and to enlighten mankind about the devastating effects of militaristic thinking.

In 1920 Ohrtmann, who returned to Germany in 1919 after nearly two years in a French prisoner of war camp, became co-founder and member of the board of the Flensburg branch of the Deutsche Friedensgesellschaft (German Peace Society) (DFG). That same year he also became a member of the Sozialdemokratische Partei Deutschlands (German Social Democratic Party) (SPD). As a member of the Flensburg SPD directorate, Ohrtmann had charge of the local youth organization. As a consequence of his pacifist and socialist activities and his educational reform ideas, most notably the development of Arbeitsschule (Work Schools), he was transferred, in 1924, to a one-room school in a remote village in Schleswig-Holstein. Following his suggestion, the Flensburg DFG, in 1924, began to publish a periodical called *Die Brücke*, as a way of closing the gap between Danes and Germans in Schleswig-Holstein and furthering of the cultural, economic, and political relations between the two nationalities. The publication appeared from 1925 until 1933 under the title of *Deutsche Zukunft* (*DZ*). Apart from an analysis of political events in the Weimar Republic from a pacifist point of view, this publication spoke most especially for a German-Danish rapprochement as a model for a general rapprochement among all nations.

Although Ohrtmann was not the official editor of the *DZ* until February 1932, he was the moving force behind it and its real editor since 1927. Under his guidance the *DZ* achieved a more than regional significance and became one of the official organs of the DFG. Its work in support of a German-Danish rapprochement managed to attract the attention of the Weimar peace movement at the same time that it won the condemnation of German nationalist Irredentists. Ohrtmann provided space for some of Germany's leading pacifists, including *Friedrich Bloh, *Franz Carl Endres, *Friedrich W. Foerster, *Otto Lehmann-Russbüldt, *Carl Mertens, *Ludwig Quidde, and *Hans Schwann.

Ohrtmann published hundreds of articles in the *DZ* under his own name and under several pseudonyms. In his political editorials he denounced the attempts to make gas warfare seem a harmless undertaking and the illegal rearmament of Germany sponsored by the army. He pointed to the dangers of militarism and nationalism and warned of the rise of fascism. He condemned the nationalist attempt to exonerate Germany from responsibility for World War I, urging the abandonment of the persisting "psychosis of the vanquished" and the near hypnotic fixation on the Treaty of Versailles. Instead of dwelling on the past, he urged his fellow Germans to cooperate in "the reconstruction of a better and more peaceful world, and of a united Europe."

Although he condemned the SPD's approval of the construction of a pocket-battleship in 1928, he held fast to the utopian ideal of a socialism that rejected war and militarism. He continued to cling to the SPD as an ally of the peace movement and longed for its return to the "straight road to peace." He rejected, however, the view that peace would have to follow the establishment of a socialist or communist society. He urged the concentration of all efforts to prevent the next war and to oppose the spirit of force aggressively. He rejected a general strike, sabotage against the war effort, and a refusal to serve in the military as a way of preventing an armed conflict already underway by arguing that no cannon starts to shoot by itself. A future war, he maintained, was unthinkable unless people had previously been systematically prepared by incitement. Only when the peaceful resolution of international conflicts became a matter of course morally could peace be guaranteed. Until that time, he sought to convince his readers that war was not some future possibility, but an ever-present danger. He called for the ''disarmament of the mind'' and a massive educational effort to limit the chances of future wars.

Concerned about both the lack of interest in the peace movement by German citizens and the direction of the Weimar Republic policies, Ohrtmann worked unceasingly from 1927 to 1933. In addition to his almost single-handed work as editor of the *DZ*, he lectured publicly, organized two German-Danish meetings to consider border questions, founded a branch of the DFG in the small Schleswig city of Bredstedt, and served as secretary of the Norddeutsche Arbeitsgemeinschaft (North German Study Group) of the DFG. In 1933 Ohrtmann became a member of the national executive committee of the Bund der Kriegsdienstgegner (War Registers League) (BdK). He also gave support to the *Die Friedensfront* edited by *Arnold Kalisch as the organ of the BdK.

Ohrtmann was one of the few contemporary German pedagogues who recognized the importance of education for peace. In his *Jugendlicherbüchlein Völkerversöhnung* (1929-30), he espoused an ''educational pacifism,'' which was designed not to teach but to awaken in children the spirit of the League of Nations and the notion of reconciliation among nations. Consisting of two small volumes, the work combined writings by Ohrtmann with short stories, poems, and biographies about peace movement pioneers such as *Albert Schweitzer and *Leo Tolstoy. Ohrtmann's volumes attracted considerable attention in both the pedagogic and pacifist press.

After the Nazis came to power, Ohrtmann was imprisoned for a short time in April 1933 and then dismissed from his teaching post. He spent the years 1933-39 as a private tutor and teacher in private schools. From 1939 until 1945, he was a bookkeeper for a ship-building company in Kiel. After the war he was a leader in the formation of a democratically oriented teacher training program in Schleswig-Holstein. The notion of a reconciliation among nations continued to be one of the leitmotivs of his life along with his dedication to pedagogy. His efforts in the cause of German-Danish understanding resulted in a number of contributions to *Grenzfriedenheften*, the organ of the Grenzfriedensbundes (Border Peace League) which was established after 1945 to carry on Ohrtmann's pioneering work for a peaceful ''bridge'' between Germany and the North.

Bibliography:

A. *Die Bewegung der Kriegsdienstgegner. Ein schlichter Bericht von Schlichtem Heldentum* (Heide in Holstein, 1932); "Erinnerungen Grenzfriedensbestrebungen in der Weimarer Zeit," *Grenzfriedenshefte* (1971), 231-38; *Ist organisatorischer Pazifismus möglich*? (Heide in Holstein [1932]); *Jugendbüchlein Völkerversöhnung* (2 vols., Heide in Holstein, 1929-30); "So fern liegt das alles .... Erinnerungen eines Deutschen an die Volksabstimmung 1920," *Grenzfriedenshefte* (1970), 25-30.

B. Gerhard Beier, "Johann Ohrtmann (1898-1978)," *Grenzfriedenshefte*, 3/4 (December, 1978), 208ff; Helmut Donat, "Johann Ohrtmann (1898-1978). Die historische Friedensbewegung im öffentlichen Bewusstein," *Grenzfriedenshefte* (1983), 90-102; Fritz Ohrtmann, "Johann Ohrtmann 80 Jahre alt," *Kieler Nachrichten*, March 18, 1978.

Helmut Donat
Trans. by Peter Seadle

ORCHARD, William Edwin (20 November 1877, Linslade, Bedfordshire, England—12 June 1955, Brownshill, Glos., England). *Education*: Westminster Coll., Cambridge Univ., 1904; B.D., Univ. of London, 1905, D.D., 1909. *Career*: minister, St. Paul's Presbyterian Church, Enfield, Middlesex, 1904-14, King's Weigh House Church, London, 1914-32; Roman Catholic priest, 1935-55.

William E. Orchard trained for the Presbyterian ministry at Westminster College, Cambridge, and was ordained in 1904. After a successful ten year ministry at Enfield, he began in October 1914 what proved to be a notable and influential eighteen year ministry at the King's Weigh House, a historic Congregational church in Mayfair, London.

From the beginning of World War I he was a convinced pacifist. His reading of *Leo Tolstoy and his study of Old Testament prophets and the Gospels had already persuaded him that a Christian could not support war, but must always seek reconciliation. The events of 1914 compelled him to think out and expound the Christian faith afresh. An outstanding preacher, witty, courageous and compelling, his church was full throughout the war, despite the suspicion that his views often aroused in official quarters. He became part of a small group which gathered with *Henry Hodgkin and *Richard Roberts to explore a Christian response to the war and which founded the Fellowship of Reconciliation. He spoke all over the country for the Fellowship, acted as chaplain to conscientious objectors in Wormwood Scrubs prison, and took part in rallies calling for peace. When the war was over, Orchard became an outspoken critic of the terms of the peace treaty.

During the 1920s Orchard was a leading member of the Society of Free Catholics. He appropriated more and more of Catholic ritual and Catholic doctrine, and it was no great surprise to his friends when he resigned from the Weigh House and joined the Roman Catholic Church in the summer of 1932. He was ordained priest in 1935.

He never again enjoyed a public position, though he led missions and continued to preach and write. Early in the Second World War he wrote a book (which was never published) on "War and the Will of God," reiterating his pacifist beliefs. In 1943-44, he played a leading part in "Pax," the Roman Catholic peace society, until his superior told him to resign. He died in 1955.

Bibliography:

A. *From Faith to Faith: An Autobiography of Religious Development* (London, 1933); *The Outlook for Religion* (London, 1917); "Some Implications for Pacifism," Hugh Martin, ed., *The Ministry of Reconciliation* (London, 1916).

B. Elaine Kaye and Ross MacKenzie, *W.E. Orchard* (Bogno Regis, England, 1984).

Elaine Kaye

OSSIETZKY, Carl von (3 October 1889, Hamburg, Germany—4 May 1938, Berlin). *Education*: uncompleted studies at a Realschule. *Career*: contributor to *Das Freie Volk*, and other liberal periodicals, 1913-19; secretary, German Peace Association, 1919-20; staff member, *Die Berliner Volks-Zeitung*, 1920-24, and of various pacifist periodicals; editor, *Das Tage-Buch*, 1924-26; editor-in-chief, *Die Weltbühne*, 1927-32; pacifist journalist.

An inmate of the Nazi concentration camps and recipient of the 1935 Nobel Peace Prize, Carl von Ossietzky was a lifelong antimilitarist. He made his most significant contributions to peace as editor of the famed left-wing journal, *Die Weltbühne*.

Neither his petty noble origin nor the poverty of his family would have predisposed Ossietzky to intellectual activity and militant pacifism. And yet even before World War I, as an office clerk, he published antiwar articles in the journals of the Democratic Alliance, the German Peace Society, and the German Monist League, all of which shared the goals of social justice, international disarmament, and anticlericalism. Because of ill-health, Ossietzky was drafted only in 1916, serving in a construction unit on the Western front. The experience deepened his antimilitarism. In 1919 he became secretary of *Ludwig Quidde's German Peace Association, but tired of the pacifists' "bellicose squabbles," he soon resigned his post. He sought more active ways to express his commitment to peace, and between 1920 and 1922, he joined the more radical Peace League of War Veterans and its "No More War" campaign, editing *Nie Wieder Krieg*, the organization's journal. The League soon disbanded due to a lack of political party support, a reflection of the fundamental weakness of the organized peace movement in Weimar Germany.

In 1924 Ossietzky ran for a Reichstag seat as a candidate of the newly formed Republican Party of Germany, which combined socialist, radical, youth-oriented, and nationalist slogans. The party, however, suffered utter defeat at the polls and soon disbanded. Ossietzky's political career had thus far been a complete failure, but by then he had become an established Berlin journalist, contributing to such democratic papers as the *Berliner Volks-Zeitung* and *Das Tage-Buch*. His writings in the mid-1920s betrayed a growing impatience with the Republic for its failure to curb the right-wing and militarist forces. He began to advocate extra-parliamentary methods to combat the right-wing antirepublican threat, which inevitably brought him closer to the Communists.

In 1927 Ossietzky became editor-in-chief of the *Weltbühne*, which, under his guidance was to become Germany's most celebrated and most hated antimilitarist journal. In 1928 a higher court fined him for having offended the Reichswehr (the Army), but the more famous case involving him came in 1931 when, in the so-called *Weltbühne* trial, he and a fellow journalist, Walter Kreiser, were tried for treason. Two years earlier, Ossietzky had published a series of articles by Kreiser which, among other things, exposed the Reichswehr's secret rearmament program in the Soviet Union. Even though Soviet-German military collaboration was quite well known and German law forbade secret rearmament, the court sentenced both defendants to 18 months in prison. The trial had been held in secret and the accused were given the opportunity to flee abroad, but only Kreiser did so. Ossietzky's case became an international issue and did much to discredit the Republic which was, in any case, in its death-throes. Although released in December 1932, during a Christmas amnesty, Ossietzky was rearrested by the Nazis in February, 1933. He spent the remaining five years of his life in various concentration camps and hospitals. His torture by the Nazis brought him the Nobel Prize of 1935, awarded in 1936, but a special German decree prohibited him from accepting the award in person. His works were burned by the Nazis and he died of tuberculosis at Nordend hospital in April, 1938.

Carl von Ossietzky was a superb political journalist with a deep sympathy for human suffering. His political position was and has remained controversial: a committed republican, he incessantly and ruthlessly criticized the Weimar Republic's chief supporters, the Social Democrats, and although rather contemptuous of the Communists, he ended up consistently endorsing Communist presidential candidates. Like so many of his contemporaries, Ossietzky underestimated the Nazis, even after Adolf Hitler's assumption of power, at least until he himself was sent to a concentration camp.

Bibliography:

A. *Der Anmarsch der neuen Reformation* (Hamburg, 1919), *Carl von Ossietzky: Schriften*, ed. by Bruno Frei and Hans Leonard, (2 vols., [East] Berlin, 1966).

B. Istvan Deak, *Weimar Germany's Left-wing Intellectuals. A Political History of the "Weltbühne" and Its Circle* (Berkeley and Los Angeles, 1968); Kurt Grossmann, *Ossietzky. Ein deutscher Patriot* (Munich, 1963); NYT, May 5, 1938.

Istvan Deak

OTLET, Paul (23 August 1868, Brussels—10 December 1944, Brussels). *Education*: Collège Saint-Michel, Brussels; studies at the universities of Louvain and Brussels; Docteur en Droit, Univ. of Paris, 1890. *Career*: editor, *La Vie Internationale*; editor, *Bulletin de l'Institut international de Bibliographie*; general secretary, Union of International Associations, 1910; professor, l'Institut des Hautes Études de Belgique and l'École centrale de Service Social de Bruxelles; lawyer, librarian, bibliographer, and archivist; sociologist, internationalist, and pacifist.

From young adulthood, Paul Otlet's life was inspired by his devotion to all things international and universal—education and information for all peoples, improvement of mutual understanding among peoples, and systematically organized international relations among states. His meeting with *Henri La Fontaine gave a decisive turn to his career, and in 1892 they began a collaboration that lasted a lifetime. Otlet gave up the bar and family business affairs to devote himself entirely to the organization of selected areas of international life. A diary entry summed up his commitment: "I care nothing for money. I want the universal good of all people."

The fruits of Otlet's collaboration with La Fontaine included the preparation of a universal library classification system based on a modification of the Dewey decimal system. They also organized an international bibliographers association (1895) and held the first international conference of bibliographers in Brussels. This was followed by the foundation of a book museum (1906), an international press museum (1907), and an international museum (1910) where the styles of diverse civilizations were displayed. In 1910 they established the Union of International Associations (still in existence) which attempted to serve as a clearing house for numerous interest groups. Otlet also became interested in the creation of an international city to serve as a permanent headquarters for all supranational organizations, an idea proposed by H. C. Andersen who suggested Brussels, Antwerp, or Geneva for this role. The heart of the network of political, economic, social, and intellectual organizations in the "world city" would be the "Mundaneum" or a world intellectual center. Then came World War I.

From the outset of the war, Otlet threw himself into the work of proselytizing for a league of nations through pamphlets and books published in the Netherlands, Paris, Geneva, and London. *Les problèmes internationaux et la guerre* (1916) specifically laid forth proposals for a set of worldwide executive organs. In Paris, he worked with proponents of the "Ligue pour une société des nations" which hoped for an international constitution. His work, *La Constitution mondiale de la Société des nations, le nouveau droit des gens* (1917), offered finely detailed proposals for the various sections of such an international social contract. In addition to the political, economic, and legal aspects of internationalism, Otlet was convinced that the central institution had to be an intellectual one. Indeed, his whole vision of internationalism revolved around the universal interests of intellectual groups.

In November 1920, with La Fontaine, Otlet proposed a plan for the organization of an office coordinating intellectual work, affiliated with the League of Nations. The Committee on Intellectual Cooperation was formed. In March 1923 it met at the Palais mondial in Brussels (Mundaneum) which had been placed in the Palais du Cinquantenaire (1920). Thus, it appeared as if Otlet's dream of a "world city" might be realized.

The work of building a world civic center was severely hampered by lack of resources during the interwar years and during the Second World War, the occupation of Belgium by Germany led to the destruction of 63 tons of archives, periodicals, and reviews.

At his death in 1944, Otlet did not see the end of the war which he had given his life and fortune to prevent. On his tomb, he asked for the inscription: "Paul Otlet, he was nothing if not an internationalist."

Bibliography:

A. *Une constitution internationale. Project présénté à la Ligue Résumé* (Paris, 1916); *La Constitution mondiale de la Société des nations. Le nouveau droit des gens* (Geneva and Paris, 1917); *Introduction aux travaux de la Commission de coopération intellectuelle de la Société des nations* (Brussels, 1922); *L'Organisation internationale et les Associations internationales* (Brussels, 1910); *Plan d'Organisation internationale du travail intellectuel au sein de la Société des nations* (Geneva and Paris, 1917); *Les Problèmes internationaux et la guerre. Tableau des conditions et solutions nouvelles de l'économie, du droit et de la politique*, (Geneva and Paris, 1916); *Sur la création d'une université internationale* (Report to the Union of International Associations, Brussels, 1920); *Traité de paix générale basé sur une charte mondiale déclarant les droits de l'humanité et organisant la confédération des Etats*, (Brussels and The Hague, 1914); *La Vie internationale et l'effort pour son organisation*, with E. Vandevelde (Brussels, 1912).

B. J. Baugniet, "Deux Pionniers de la coopération internationale et de la paix universelle: Henri La Fontaine et Paul Otlet," *60e anniversaire de la Fondation en Belgigue de l'U.A.I.*, Textes et Documents (Brussels, June, 1970), #260, 53-59; *Biographie Nationale*, XXXII, col. 545-558; *Henri La Fontaine, 1854-1943; Paul Otlet, 1868-1944* (Brussels, 1954).

C. Paul Otlet Papers, Mundaneum, Brussels.

Nadine Lubelski-Bernard
Trans. by Sandi E. Cooper

OUTRATA, Vladimir (19 April 1909, Čáslav, Bohemia, Austria [now Czechoslovakia]—9 July 1970, Prague, Czechoslovakia). *Education*: J.U.D., Charles Univ., Prague, 1933; law degree, Univ. of Paris, 1935; postgraduate studies, Oxford Univ. *Career*: Czechoslovak diplomatic service, 1935-46; professor of law, School of International Politics, Prague, 1946-48; Czechoslovak Ambassador to the United States, 1948-51; professor of international law, Charles Univ., 1951-70; diplomat and scholar.

The years of the Second World War, which Vladimir Outrata spent partly in London, partly in Moscow, afforded him a unique opportunity to observe and analyze the uneasy alliance between the West and the East. His main interest, however, was in the future of the European nations temporarily occupied by Nazi Germany. The Atlantic Charter of 1941, to which all the allies had adhered, proclaimed the "right of all peoples to choose the form of government under which they will live." Peace and self-determination, in Outrata's view, were not simply desirable goals but twin principles of the modern international legal order. He saw in their consistent application a cornerstone of a system of collective security in postwar Europe—a theme to which he continually returned throughout his academic career.

While still in London, Outrata began work on the question of the federalization of Central Europe. His study was never published because, as it turned out, the subject became an anathema to the Soviet Union. In it, Outrata maintained that the peaceful future of Europe depended on the creation of a zone of peace and military disengagement comprising Poland, Czechoslovakia, and possibly other Central European countries, which would become not only a buffer between traditional adversaries but, more importantly, a solid component of the system of postwar security and cooperation spanning the Western and the Eastern parts of the continent.

In his postwar studies, Outrata had to take into account the fact of the division of Europe; he advocated a *modus vivendi* which would be both just and realistic. He envisioned the possibility of evolving a flexible system of security and cooperation in Europe in which smaller nations would be given full opportunity to realize their aspirations and which would progressively obviate the need for the continued existence of antagonistic military blocs and the attendant armaments race. His intellectual and academic preoccupation with the question of human rights and fundamental freedoms resulted in several legal studies in which he convincingly argued that social progress and individual freedom were fully compatible and indeed complementary.

Bibliography:

A. "Mezinárodně právní ochrana bezpečnosti státu," *Studie z mezinárodního práva*, 1 (Prague, 1955), 23-60; *Mazinárodní právo věrejné* (Prague, 1960).

B. R. Bystrický, "Introduction: to the collection of essays honoring Vladimir Outrata," in *Časopis pro mezinárodní právo*, 13 (Prague, 1969), 97-99; obituary, *Časopis pro mezinárodní právo*, 14 (Prague, 1970), 285-87.

Vratislav Pechota

OWEN, Wilfred Edwards Salter (18 March 1893, Oswestry, England—4 November 1918, Sambre Canal, France). *Education*: Birkenhead Institute; Shrewsbury Technical School. *Career*: teacher, 1913-15; soldier, 1915-18; poet.

Wilfred Owen's father was a railway clerk. The boy had a good education but did not attend university. What interested him was writing poetry. He had a brief period as a pupil-teacher, and as an assistant to the Vicar of Dunsden, near Reading. In 1913 he moved to Bordeaux as a teacher of English. Despite World War I he stayed until 1915, when he returned to Britain to join the army.

Late in 1916 Owen crossed to France as a 2nd Lieutenant. He fought on the Somme and the experience was traumatic, leading him to proclaim the basic principles of Christian pacifism. He now wrote that one of Christ's essential commands was "passivity at any price." "Be bullied, be outraged, be killed," he now pronounced, "but do not kill." Christ was "literally in no man's land," and Owen found himself in the midst of a bloody conflict.

The combination of strain and trench fever caused him to be sent to Craiglockhart in Scotland for rest and rehabilitation. While there he met *Siegfried Sassoon, showed him some of his poems, and received his friendship and critical encouragement. In the late summer of 1918, Owen returned to France and was awarded the Military Cross for conspicuous gallantry. A month later, just seven days before the Armistice, he was killed.

Owen lives in his poetry. In assonance or half-rhyme, he found a new medium to express the disharmony around him. His poems remain a searing critique of war. The great opening line of "Anthem for Doomed Youth" is "What passing-bells for these who die as cattle?" One of his most memorable lines comes in "Strange Meeting"—"I am the enemy you killed, my friend." His introduction to his poetry summed up his approach: "My subject is war, and the pity of war. The Poetry is in the pity. Yet these elegies are to this generation in no sense consolatory. They may be to the next. All the poet can do is to warn. That is why true poets must be truthful."

Bibliography:

A. *Collected Poems* (London, 1963); *Collected Letters* (Oxford, 1968).

B. A. Orrmont, *Requiem for War* (New York, 1972); H. Owen, *Journey from Obscurity* (Oxford, 1963); J. Stallworthy, *Wilfred Owen* (Oxford, 1974).

John Ferguson

P

PAASCHE, Hans (3 April 1881, Rostock, Germany—21 May 1920, on the estate "Waldfrieden" near Hochzeit in the Neumark [now Poland]). *Education*: Joachimsthaler Gymnasium, Berlin; naval cadet, Imperial German Navy. *Career*: naval and colonial officer; co-editor, *Der Vortrupp — Halbmonatsschrift für das Deutschtum unserer Zeit*, 1912-17; hunter, writer, reformer, and pacifist.

When Hans Paasche, the son of the National-Liberal vice-president of the German Reichstag, Hermann Paasche, received orders as First Officer of the cruiser SMS *Bussard* to put down uprisings of the native population in German East Africa (1905), he began to doubt the professional honor and status of German naval and colonial officers. In 1908 he applied for separation from the service even though the previous year he had been promoted to the rank of naval lieutenant-commander for his bravery and courage in the African bush-war. Intending to help with the dissemination of pacifist principles, he began contacting members of the peace movement. In 1912 he became a member of the Gesellschaft zur Förderung des Tierschutzes und verwandter Bestrebungen (Society for the Protection of Animals and Related Endeavors) founded by *Magnus Schwantje, which after World War I adopted the name Bund für radikale Ethik (Society for Radical Ethics). In addition, Paasche took an interest in the German youth movement and the Wandervögel (Scouts), whose politically socialist oriented wing he represented prior to the outbreak of World War I.

In an effort to stimulate the search for new values, Paasche published in the reform-oriented periodical *Der Vortrupp* his "Briefe des Negers Lukanga Mukara" ("Letters of the Negro Lukanga Mukara") (1912-13). In these fictional reports about "an exploratory journey into innermost Germany," Paasche lets an African untouched by European civilization but endowed with common sense and practical wisdom, criticize the social and political conditions in Germany in an ironically humorous manner that shows sympathy for the sufferings of the whites. Implicitly, the letters opposed Germany's imperialist and colonial endeavors. During World War I, censorship prohibited the publication in book form of "Lukanga Mukara," but it appeared after the end of the war and by 1929 had become one of the most widely read books of the German youth movement.

Paasche's ethically founded pacifism combined with support of numerous political and social reform movements. As a "Friend of Africa," he demanded, before 1914, a policy of developmental aid which was to be based on the interests and needs of the natives. He supported women's suffrage, wrote and drew up appeals against the "Feather-fashion" (1911), which exterminated entire species of birds, spoke for a drastic lowering of the quotas for the catching of seals, demanded the protection of the environment, promoted temperance, and advocated the creation of a peaceful life in harmony with nature for both men and animals.

Initially convinced that Germany was not responsible for unleashing World War I, Paasche reenlisted in the Imperial German Navy in 1914. Only a few months later, however, he began to doubt the innocence of the Prussian-German empire. Refusing to deny his pacifist, ethical, and antimilitary convictions, he was discharged from the imperial navy at the end of 1916. Already much influenced by the ideas of Arthur Schopenhauer, the former naval lieutenant now occupied himself with the writings of *Leo Tolstoy, Feodor Dostoevsky, Leonid Andreev, Maxim Gorki, *Peter Kropotkin, and Michael Bakunin, all of whom provided him with an even more solid foundation for his opposition to war. In the summer of 1916, Paasche helped found the pacifist alliance Zentralstelle Völkerrecht (Coordinating Office for International Law) which advocated a rapid negotiated peace with the Entente.

Paasche, married to the oldest daughter of *Richard Witting, disappeared into the political underground after his discharge from the navy. He disseminated radical pacifist appeals and other writings prohibited by the official censorship, such as *Richard Grelling's *J'accuse*! and Count Lichnowsky's memorandum *My Mission to London 1912-1914*. In October 1917 Paasche was arrested and accused of incitement to treason. After many months in prison, the case was dropped with the explanation that Paasche had committed the criminal acts of which he had been accused in "a state of mental illness." He was then placed in protective custody in a sanatorium in Berlin-Grunewald, from where he was freed by rebellious sailors on November 9, 1918. Immediately, he was elected to the executive committee of the Workers and Soldiers Councils, but his efforts to have those guilty for the war arrested and tried were in vain. Paasche was quick to realize that the German revolution did not put an end to the Prussian-German drive for power. Thus he demanded even more fervently in his pamphlets *Meine Mitschuld am Weltkrieg* (*My Complicity in the World War*) (1919) and *Das verlorene Afrika* (*The Lost Africa*) (1919), as well as in several other appeals, that the German people must settle accounts with that part of their history which had been stamped by the military traditions of Prussia. As a member of the steering committee of Bund Neues Vaterland (New Fatherland League), Paasche stood for Franco-German reconciliation and for a state organized along antimilitarist principles.

Even though he had withdrawn in disillusionment from all political activity, Paasche was denounced in May 1920 for having hidden a cache of weapons on his estate for a communist uprising. During the search of his house, Hans Paasche was shot "trying to escape" by soldiers of the German army. There was, in fact, no document authorizing his arrest, nor were any weapons ever found on his estate. The murder remained unpunished and the investigation of the crime was dropped in late 1920 without any tangible result.

Bibliography:

A. *Die Forschungsreise des Afrikaners Lukanga Mukara ins innerste Deutschland* (Hamburg, 1921, new ed., Berlin, 1980); *Fremdenlegionar Kirsch. Eine abenteuerliche Fahrt von Kamerun in den deutschen Schützengraben in den Kriegsjahren 1914/1915* (Berlin, 1916); *Im Morgenlicht. Kriegs-, Jadg- und Reise-Erlebnisse in Ostafrika* (Berlin, 1907); *Neudruck* (Berlin, 1980).

B. Helmut Donat, ed., *"Auf der Flucht" erschossen . . . Schriften und Beiträge von und über Hans Paasche* (Bremen/Zeven, 1981); Magnus Schwantje, *Hans Paasche. Sein Leben und Wirken* (Berlin, 1921); Otto Wanderer (pseud. of Marinegeneraloberarzt a.D. Otto Buchinger), *Paasche Buch* (Hamburg, 1921).

Helmut Donat
Trans. by Peter Seadle

PAASIKIVI, Juho Kusti (27 November, 1870, Tampere, Finland—14 December 1956, Helsinki). *Education*: B.A., Univ. of Helsinki, 1892, Master of Law, 1897, Doctor of Law, 1901. *Career*: lecturer, Univ. of Helsinki, 1899-1903; bank director; diplomat; president of Finland, 1946-56.

While studying at the University of Helsinki, Juho Kusti Paasikivi adopted from a well-known Finnish patriot, Yrjö Sakari Yrjö-Koskinen, the political view that the proximity of Finland to Russia was a reality which should dictate Finnish foreign policy. Throughout his political career, this central principle guided Paasikivi's actions. As a young politician he sought to improve the conditions of land ownership and to extend democracy. After the general strike of 1905, he worked towards reforming Parliament and helped convince Finnish party opinions in favor of a unicameral legislature. He strongly believed that an expansion of democracy would reduce the danger of social revolution. In the Finnish fight against Russian repression, he supported a policy of submissiveness in order to avoid greater repression and sought compromise with the Russian government.

Paasikivi's career as a peace politician started after the conclusion of World War I. In 1920 he led the Finnish delegation to Tarto in order to negotiate a settlement with the Soviet Union. It was mainly due to Paasikivi that a mutual and satisfying peace was reached. In 1934-36, he acted as chairman of the Coalition party delegation and helped separate the Coalition party from the National Movement (IKL) which continued the fascist Lapua movement tradition.

In 1939, when the Soviet Union demanded military bases on the Karelian Isthmus, Paasikivi was asked to negotiate for Finland. Despite his skills as a statesman, no agreement was reached and war broke out between the two countries. Throughout the war Paasikivi searched for opportunities to bring about Finland's withdrawal from the conflict. However, he was loyal to the official policy of his country and did not join any of the antiwar opposition activities. In 1944 he was asked by the president of Finland to form a new government. He agreed and succeeded in including in his administration the first Communist minister in a Finnish government.

Seeking to improve relations with the Soviet Union, Paasikivi called for an end to traditional Russophobia and concluded a treaty in 1948 calling for friendship, cooperation, and assistance between the two nations. It was the first friendship agreement, emphasizing mutual equality, negotiated between a capitalist and a socialist state. It remained the basis for Finnish foreign policy and a testimony to President Paasikivi's leadership. The policy of peace and neutrality was followed by President Urho Kekkonen, leading to calls for a nuclear-free north and a series of European security conferences. The first such conference was held in Helsinki in 1975.

Bibliography:

A. *Muistelmia Sortovuosilta I-II*, (Porvoo, 1957); *Paasikiven Linja I-II* (Porvoo, 1956); *Toiminatani Moskovassa Ja Suomessa, 1939-41 I-II* (Porvoo, 1958).

B. Toivo Heikkilä, *Paasikivi Perāsimessa* (Keuruu, 1965); Kauko Kare, ed., *J. K. Paasikivi* (Hämeenlinna, 1956); Urko Kekkonen, *J.K. Paasikivi: Rauhantekija-Presidentti* (Porvoo, 1960).

C. Juho Kusti Paasikivi Papers, State Archives, Helsinki.

Kalevi Kalemaa
Trans. by Oliver and Rita Whitehead

PAGE, Kirby (7 August 1890, Fred, TX—16 December 1957, LaHabra, CA). *Education*: B.A., Drake Univ., 1915; postgraduate study, Univ. of Chicago, 1915-16, and Columbia Univ., 1918-20. *Career*: ordained minister of the Disciples of Christ and pastor in Brooklyn, 1919-21; personal secretary for YMCA Secretary, *Sherwood Eddy, 1916-19, 1921-22; editor *The World Tomorrow*, 1926-34; independent author, speaker, and organizer.

Kirby Page emerged from World War I as a social evangelist who related religion comprehensively to issues of social equity, international peace, and personal living. A powerful exponent of the Social Gospel between the world wars, he edited a journal, edited or authored some twenty-five books and thirty-five pamphlets, and published articles in at least seventy-eight periodicals. He was a popular speaker and an effective fund-raiser for social justice and peace movements. Intellectually, he extended the Social Gospel tradition of Walter Rauschenbusch, and organizationally he contributed to the rise of a politically active, reformist pacifism.

World War I was the catalyst of Page's thought and career. Prior to it he had attended Drake University to prepare for the ministry. Studies in contemporary social issues and an attraction to the Social Gospel led him to take postgraduate work at the University of Chicago. Active in the YMCA and Student Volunteer Movement, he felt called to the overseas mission field. But, instead, he accepted a position as personal secretary to the YMCA evangelism secretary, *Sherwood Eddy, whom he followed to Europe when war broke out. With a handful of young YMCA workers who were providing services to German prisoners of war, Page worked toward a pacifist position.

A two-fold indictment of war both on essentially religious and instrumental grounds became characteristic of Page's writing. On biblical and religious lines, he concluded, war is altogether wrong and is prohibited to Christians. Moreover, in social and historical terms, modern war is an atrocious method which is unjustified by its results. It is the instrument of injustice and violence, a means which necessarily yields further injustice and violence. The abolition of war requires the development of alternative methods of settling disputes. Accordingly, seeking alternatives to war and not merely refusing to sanction it is both a Christian and a civic responsibility.

This point was drawn in *The Sword and the Cross* which Page composed during the war. It was elaborated in *War* (1923), *The Abolition of War* (with Eddy, 1924), *National Defense* (1931), *Must We Go To War?* (1937), and *Now Is the Time to Prevent the Third World War* (1946). In each case, Page related his central theme to the contemporary international scene, drawing fully upon revisionist history and empirical data. Because many of his books and pamphlets were sold inexpensively or given away, they had a wide circulation—a million copies in his estimation. Some of them were translated into at least nine languages.

Following World War I, Page turned his attention to problems of social inequity. At Ridgewood Heights Church of Christ in Brooklyn he implemented typical Social Gospel programs for the neighborhood. Leaving the ministry with Eddy's backing, he began to explore the systematic roots of social injustice, writing on labor problems and taking social issues to college campuses and churches. With Eddy he helped to found in 1921 what became the Fellowship for a Christian Social Order. Increasingly, Page moved closer to democratic socialism, and he was one of a coterie of reformist pacifists around *Norman Thomas. His social views are expressed in his editing of *The World Tomorrow* and his writing in the *Christian Century*, and are summed up in *Individualism and Socialism* (1933).

Page pressed the case for alternatives to war, even as he concentrated on social issues. He cautiously supported U.S. admission to the League of Nations. He was active in a futile attempt to unite the peace movement, divided as it was between outlawry of war and accession to the World Court. With the collapse of international order in the thirties, Page became increasingly active in the peace movement—writing, speaking, organizing, and raising funds for it. He had a central role in initiating, financing, and running the half-million dollar Emergency Peace Campaign of 1936-37 which was designed to reorient American foreign policy to international cooperation, mediation between European powers, and strict neutrality. Page's last significant writings on international affairs were produced in 1946 and 1950, and his analysis of the emerging Cold War restated established patterns of thought.

From 1932 to 1950 he published a series of religious devotionals that reached thousands of people with the message that salvation is corporate as well as personal and that provided programs of mediation through which personal devotion was focused on social issues. Increasingly confined to the pen, Page remained the social evangelist.

Although much of Page's writing was cluttered with derivative ideas and information, there was also originality to his thought. The latter was found in the totality of his insight, the consistency of his message in various contexts, and the pervasiveness of his distinctions—between war as an ideal and as method, between coercion and violence, between working in a broad peace coalition and maintaining a strict pacifist witness, and between the idealism of spiritual resources and the realism with which they must be applied. It was his legacy to couple trenchant analysis with religious motives in the service of public action.

Bibliography:

A. *War: Its Causes, Consequences, and Cure* (New York, 1924); *Imperialism and Nationalism* (New York, 1925); *Must We Go to War?* (New York, 1937); *Now Is the Time to Prevent a Third World War* (LaHabra, CA, 1950).

B. Charles Chatfield and Charles DeBenedetti, eds., *Kirby Page and the Social Gospel: An Anthology* (New York, 1976).

C. Kirby Page Papers, School of Theology at Claremont, Claremont, CA.

Charles Chatfield

PAPANASTASIOU, Alexander (8 July 1879, Arcadia, Greece—17 November 1936, Athens). *Education*: Doctorate in Law, Univ. of Athens; studies in sociology and political science, universities of Heidelberg, Berlin, London, and Paris. *Career*: politician and reformer.

Throughout his life Alexander Papanastasiou associated peace with social justice and international cooperation. A founding member of the socialist Sociological Society, he was first elected to parliament in 1910 as a representative from Arcadia. His Sociological party was eventually absorbed by Eleftherios Venizelos' liberal movement, but it remained the source of reformist influence within the larger Liberal party. Papanastasiou became prime minister and held several ministerial offices, but his political career was associated with the Ministry of Agriculture and his efforts to improve the lot of the peasants. An avowed republican, he was instrumental as prime minister in the expulsion of the Monarchy through a plebiscite and in the establishment of the first modern Greek republic in 1924. Although his Democratic Union party and Peasant-Workers party never secured more than 6.7 percent of the popular vote, his integrity and parliamentary stature won him a reputation that far exceeded his electoral gains.

In October 1929 Papanastasiou was elected chairman of the 27th International Peace Conference which met in Athens. During the conference he put forth his plan for European unity as the only credible deterrent against war and later he proposed that the experiment begin with the unification of the Balkans. He subscribed to an eventual federation of European nations but was opposed to any forced restriction of national sovereignty. He believed that national differences would naturally disappear within a larger community governed by principles of justice and equality and that national identity would yield to an identification with the interests of the federation. Although he supported the League of Nations, he pointed out that international disputes were usually settled in accordance with political considerations which preserved inequalities among nations.

Between 1930 and 1934, he gained an international reputation as an exponent of peaceful cooperation and repeatedly urged the European powers to bury their emnities. In 1939 he took an active part in the 26th International Peace Conference in London and was elected president of the Committee for a Balkan meeting. During the same year he presided over the first Balkan meeting in Thessaloniki. A year later, he participated in the International Peace Conference in Brussels and in the second Balkan meeting in Ankara. Throughout the following Balkan meetings he strove towards a comprehensive treaty among Balkan states that would cover economic as well as security issues. As a safeguard to peace, the 1934 Balkan Entente between Turkey, Greece, Rumania, and Yugoslavia fell short of his expectations because it invited conflicts and great power involvement in southeast Europe. Bulgaria, with its revisionist policies against the treaties of World War I, and Albania, an Italian dependency, were left out of the company of Balkan nations. Italy was convinced that the Entente was set up to the serve French and British interests.

At home, Papanastasiou was faced with the erosion of the Republic and parliamentary politics. In October 1935 he denounced the plebiscite which reinstated the monarchy in Greece as fraudulent. Nine months after his reinstatement, King George II of the Hellenes established the Metaxas dictatorship. Papanastasiou died shortly thereafter having witnessed the collapse of his ideals in both domestic and international politics.

Bibliography:

A. *Alexandrou Papanastasiou meletes, logoi, arthra* (Athens, 1957).

B. Pericles Argyropoulos, "Alexander Papanastasiou," *Les Balkans, Revue Mensuelle* (December, 1936), 129-44; Nikos Kastrinos, *Al. Papanastasiou, ho anamorphōtēs kai hē dēmokratia* (Athens, 1975); NYT, November 18, 1936.

Thanos Veremis

PARANHOS, José Maria de Silva, Jr. See *Biographical Dictionary of Internationalists*.

PARK, Alice Locke (3 February 1861, Boston, MA—17 October 1961, Palo Alto, CA). *Education*: teaching credential, Rhode Island Normal School, 1879. *Career*: author of the California Bird and Arbor Day Law, 1909, and the California Equal Child Guardianship Law, 1913; international correspondent for the Federated Syndicate [Labor] Press, 1913-33; journalist, reformer, and pacifist.

An absolutist in her pacifism, Alice Park first joined an organized peace movement in 1898 to protest the Spanish-American War. Her belief in the power of organization to exert moral suasion grew out of her work within the women's suffrage movement; her convictions were shaped by her Unitarian-Quaker heritage and encyclopedic reading; and her near-century of activism was fired by her remarkable intellectual and physical stamina.

In the years between 1884 and 1901, she moved from Denver to El Paso to Helena to San Diego with her husband Dean, a mining engineer, and their two children, finally settling in Palo Alto in 1906. In each community she helped to organize suffrage groups, and used the forums of the Women's Christian Temperance Union and Unitarian discussion circles to espouse her feminist and pacifist ideas.

Her most significant contribution to the international peace movement was her role as a disseminator of information, as a speaker, author, and distributor of peace literature. Between 1906 and 1933, she traveled widely as a delegate and spokesperson for the Women's Peace Society, of which she was a member of the Advisory Board, and for the Women's International League for Peace and Freedom, on whose board of directors she served. She attended the International Peace Congresses at The Hague (1913), Washington, D.C. (1924), Dublin (1926), Duisberg (1927), and York (1927). In 1915 she joined the Ford Peace Expedition, and in 1928 attended the Pan American Congress in Havana. Never affluent, her travels were supported by philanthropists (notably Mrs. J. Sargeant Cram of the Peace House, New York City), and by subsidies from various organizations. Her home in Palo Alto became a clearinghouse for the distribution of news stories, pamphlets, copies of speeches, and articles which supported pacifism and women's rights; for nearly seven decades she mailed out these materials as well as her own articles to some 550 newspaper and journal editors in the English-speaking world.

In 1917 she joined the Socialist party and renounced her membership in the Unitarian Church in protest against the church leadership's failure to oppose United States entry into World War I. Alongside her son Carlton she spoke at West Coast demonstrations supporting the rights of conscientious objectors. Out of her work with conscientious objectors she became involved with prison reform and organized a state-wide network for prisoner relief work in California.

Consistent with her pacifist beliefs was Alice Park's leadership in the American Humane Society, whose purpose was to educate young children in the ways of kindness and peace. She wrote many broadsides against the practice of whipping school children and the exploitation of child labor. Her most widely published piece, written in 1914, was titled "Disarm Christmas." It decried the custom of giving children weapons as gifts.

Bibliography:

B. Una R. Winter, ed., *Alice Park of California: Worker for Woman Suffrage and for Children's Rights* (Upland, CA., 1948).

C. Alice Park Collection, Hoover Institution on War, Revolution and Peace, Stanford University.

Francesca Miller

PARKER, Theodore (24 August, 1810, Lexington, MA—10 May 1860, Florence, Italy). *Education*: attended Harvard Coll., 1830-34; graduated, Harvard

Divinity School, 1836. *Career*: Unitarian clergyman, theologian, author, lecturer, and reformer.

A militant spokesman for every kind of social reform, Theodore Parker advocated a philosophy of peace based on the transcendental ethic. Peace, he maintained, could not be achieved through force or by obedience to formal law or convention. True peace would only occur when society conformed to the universal moral laws which resonated within the hearts of all men. Therefore, peace was essentially a matter of conscience, which he considered an infallible and perfect moral guide.

The son of a Yankee farmer, Parker passed the entrance examination for Harvard College in 1830 and attended classes for four years. Unable to pay the required fees, however, he did not receive a Bachelor of Arts degree, although he was awarded an honorary Masters of Arts degree in 1840. In 1834 he enrolled in the Harvard Divinity School and graduated two years later. Parker took his first church, the Spring Street Church in West Roxbury, Massachusetts, in 1837 and soon became one of Boston's most prominent and controversial Unitarian ministers. Inspired by *Ralph Waldo Emerson and George Ripley, he set out to correct the ''truncated supernaturalism'' of Unitarian theology with the insights of Transcendentalism and radical German philosophy. Attacking Unitarian orthodoxy, he maintained that the great truths of morality and religion were perceived intuitively and by instinct, not on the basis of external law (Bible), or authority (the Church), or supernatural occurrences (miracles). Parker's heretical beliefs, sharp tongue, and contentious spirit brought condemnation and ostracism from most of his colleagues. In 1845 a group of Boston gentlemen, aware of Parker's alienation, decided his views deserved to be heard. The result was the organization of the Twenty-eighth Congregational Society which became Parker's stronghold until 1859.

Believing it to be his mission to reflect on everything of national and social concern, Parker threw himself into every reform movement. Assisted by Emerson and Elliot Cabot, Parker founded and edited *The Massachusetts Quarterly Review* (1847-50), a journal which combined scholarship with issues of social reform. He was an organizer of the Anti-Sabbath Convention, campaigned against crime, capital punishment, and prostitution, worked for prison reform, and supported women's rights and temperance reform. Of all reformers, he had the most accurate statistics on violence and corruption in America. He joined Dorothea Dix to help the mentally ill. Influenced by Charles Fourier, he opposed private property, favored Brook Farm, and credited the Shakers for solving the problem of industrialism. Of all his reform efforts, however, Parker's most notable achievement was his effective leadership in the antislavery movement.

Parker was neither a pacifist nor a Garrisonian nonresistant. He did sign, however, *Elihu Burritt's Peace Pledge declaring war ''inconsistent with the Spirit of Christianity and destructive to the best interests of mankind.'' He took a very strong stand against the Mexican War, arguing that it was a ''national infidelity,'' and nothing less than ''a denial of Christianity and of God.'' He urged his fellow citizens not to participate in the conflict.

Parker's commitment to peace and his militant opposition to slavery came into conflict during the last decade before the Civil War. He hailed the nonviolent opposition to the Fugitive Slave Act, but by 1856 he joined Henry Ward Beecher in sending ''Sharp's rifles'' to the antislavery settlers in Kansas. A few years later, he supported John Brown financially, becoming involved in the conspiracy that led to Brown's raid on Harper's Ferry. Like many other abolitionists who once held strong peace principles, Parker came to believe that the end of slavery was a more important objective than the avoidance of violence.

Bibliography:

A. *Sermons on War* (Garland ed., New York, 1973); *The Works of Theodore Parker* (15 vols., Boston, 1907-11).

B. Robert C. Albrecht, *Theodore Parker* (New York, 1971); John White Chadwick, *Theodore Parker, Preacher and Reformer* (Boston and New York, 1900); Henry Steele Commager, *Theodore Parker* (Boston, 1936); John Weiss, *Life and Correspondence of Theodore Parker* (New York, 1969); Conrad Wright, ed., *Three Prophets of Religious Liberalism* (Boston, 1961); DAB, VII, 238-41.

C. Theodore Parker Papers, Boston Public Library and Massachusetts Historical Society.

John T. Grayson

PASINI DEI BONFATTI, Teresita. See dolens, Alma.

PASSY, Frédéric (20 May 1822, Paris—12 June 1912, Neuilly-sur-Seine, France). *Education*: Lycée Louis-le-Grand; Lycée Bourbon; studies in philosophy, law, and economics, Univ. of Paris, 1843-46. *Career*: public servant, Council of State, 1847-49; member, Chamber of Deputies, 1881-89; founder, Ligue internationale et permanente de la paix (later Société française des amis de la paix and société française pour l'arbitrage entre nations), 1867; co-winner (with *Henry Dunant), first Nobel Peace Prize, 1901; author, lecturer, and specialist in political economy.

At his death at 90 years of age, Frédéric Passy was universally regarded as the ''dean'' of European pacifists. This title justly resulted from over a half-century of efforts to propagate the ideas of an organized peace among European nations which Passy sustained, frequently alone and by his own private means.

Born into a propertied family, nephew of the well known economist and public official, Hippolyte Passy, young Frédéric's public career ended with the revolution of 1848. Attracted to the writings of the then new school of liberal economics, Passy turned to economic studies, writings, and lecturing. His early work was published by Michel Chevalier in the influential *Journal des Economistes*. During the Napoleonic Second Empire, Passy was offered a government position, but his refusal to swear the oath of loyalty to a regime he disliked closed that door. He supported himself and his large family by small private rental incomes and public lectures. Most of his early fame as a lecturer spread in southern France where he took his family each winter because of his own poor health. By the end of the Empire, he had a reputation as a stout defender of free trade and a vigorous antiprotectionist crusader.

The war scare known as the Luxembourg crisis in 1867 prompted him to send a letter to *Le Temps* in which he attacked the growing war fever in the country. Passy was astonished at the deluge of mail that he received in support of his position and along with several influential religious and business leaders, created the Ligue international et permanente de la paix (International and Permanent League of Peace). The group faced hostile government officials who stopped its mails and made meetings difficult. With the Franco-Prussian War of 1870—which it vigorously protested—the group was temporarily disbanded. Passy, however, did not give up and after the war the organization reappeared despite a very hostile climate. At the 1878 Paris Exposition, Passy was able to gather together a meeting of pacifists from various countries and during the next decade, he began to work with English pacifists, notably *William Randall-Cremer to produce a permanent organization of members of parliaments who were interested in pushing international organization schemes and arbitration treaties on their governments. The Interparliamentary Union was born in 1889 at the Paris Exposition. At the same time, Passy helped assemble a group of citizens from various nations to create the Universal Peace Congress. From 1889 until his death in 1912, through increasingly poor health and numerous family tragedies, Passy devoted himself, his pen, and his name to the struggle to prevent a major catastrophe in Europe.

During his two terms as a member of the Chamber of Deputies (1881 and 1885), Passy demonstrated his remarkable independence from all party lines. His was almost a lone voice attacking the colonial policies of Jules Ferry which ended in the French occupation of Annam (Vietnam) on the grounds that such European control violated the most basic rights of a people to its own land and culture.

Philosophically, Passy was a conservative peace advocate. His assessment of European realities led him to argue in favor of legal means, notably arbitration, among existent governments. Only when governments felt secure in the operation of peaceful means to resolve their disputes, Passy argued, would they undertake the difficult process of arms limitation and disarmament. This moderate position never prevented him from arguing vigorously against the social and economic costs of militarism which he viewed as the prime cause of social friction and the main reason for the success of Socialist parties (whose philosophy he hated). Passy believed that peace activism must be undertaken on the elite levels of policymaking (such as through the Interparlimentary Union) and on the popular levels of education. It was not furthered, he believed, by dramatic acts such as urging young men to flee conscription and sabotage the military. Passy's legalistic approach to proper international pacifist labors also led him to question those demanding support for national liberation—such as Poles, young Turks, and Armenians who occasionally demanded support from the Universal Peace Congress. Similarly he opposed the Congress taking a stand on Alsace-Lorraine or the Trentino, for he feared this would drive out German, Austrian, Italian, and French delegates.

While he greatly admired English pacifists such as *Henry Richard, Passy never became an absolute pacifist. He never spoke out against the right of self defense or in favor of absolute nonresistance. Although he argued all the classical positions of the nineteenth century liberal school of laissez-faire economics, he insisted on the responsibility of the state to interfere in one area—that of education. He became a staunch crusader for free, compulsory education and a close associate of *Jules Simon who designed the French system. As he grew older, Passy moved away from the Catholicism of his childhood and became a close supporter of social, evangelical Protestantism. In part this movement resulted from the fierce Catholic hostility to his peace societies which gathered together liberal Catholic, Jewish, and Protestant ministers at the same podium.

His death in 1912 spared Passy the horror of seeing the great war of 1914 wherein most of his prophecies were fulfilled.

Bibliography:

A. *Armements de l'avenir* (Paris, 1895); *L'Education Pacifique* (Paris, 1902); *Leçons d'économie politique* (Montpellier, 1861); *Mélanges économiques* (Paris, 1857); *La Guerre et la paix* (Paris, 1867); *La Paix internationale et la paix sociale* (Paris, 1892); *Pour la paix: notes et documents* (Paris, 1909, reprint, New York, 1973); *La Question de la paix* (Paris, 1891).

B. Institut internationale de bibliographie, *Répertoire bibliographique universel: Bibliographie des écrits de Frédéric Passy* (Brussels, 1900); Notices biographiques, Academie des Sciences (Paris, I, 1892, 114-18; 1906-7, 107-12); Jean Lagny, "Un conseilleur général de Saint-Germain, premier prix Nobel de la paix, Frédéric Passy (1822-1912)" in *Histoire et archéologie dans les Yvelines* (Supplément à *Connaitre les Yvelines*, no. 4 (1979) 21-30; Paul Passy, *Un Apôtre de la paix: La Vie de Frédéric Passy* (Paris, 1927); Jules L. Puech, "Frédéric Passy," *The Interparliamentary Union from 1889-1939* (Geneva, 1939), 153-57; A. Robert, E. Bourloton, & G. Cougny, eds., *Dictionnaire des parlementaires français* (Paris, 1891), 558; *Les Droits de l'homme*, June 2, 1912.

C. Letters, Archive, Bureau international de la paix, UN Library, Geneva; Archive, Library, Peace Palace, The Hague.

Sandi E. Cooper

PEABODY, George Foster (27 July 1852, Columbus, GA—4 March 1938, Warm Springs, GA). *Education*: private schools until the age of fourteen. *Career*: investment banker, philanthropist, and peace activist.

George Foster Peabody was somewhat of a paradox as a businessman. Not only did he accumulate a huge fortune and attempt to give most of it away to worthy causes, but he energetically supported such capitalist anathemas as the single tax movement and the government ownership of railroads. Peabody had a long standing reputation as an orthodox pacifist and his name was well known in American and international peace circles. A strong supporter of the Lake Mohonk Conferences on International Arbitration, he also served as vice-president of the American Peace Society and an energetic member of the New York Peace Society and the International Committee on a Durable Peace.

Peabody's pacifism was rooted in the destruction of his hometown, Columbus, Georgia, by Union troops during the Civil War. The war impoverished his father and left an indelible mark on his character. Devastated by financial hardship, the family moved to Brooklyn, New York, where Peabody educated himself in the library of the Brooklyn Young Men's Christian Association and took a job as an errand boy for a Brooklyn dry goods firm. Peabody seemed graced with a natural acumen for business and his rise to Wall Street prominence was nothing short of meteoric. In 1906 he was able to retire from business, having amassed a fortune investing in such diverse enterprises from railroads in Mexico to sugar beets in Nebraska. Serving an executor of his own trust fund, he devoted the rest of his life to contributing his wealth to humanitarian enterprises, notably equal educational opportunity for blacks in the South. Influential in Democratic politics, he acted as the treasurer of the Democratic National Committee (1904-5) and in 1914, President +Woodrow Wilson appointed him as first Deputy Chairman of the New York Federal Reserve Bank, a post he held for eight years. In his later years, Peabody vigorously supported +Franklin Roosevelt's New Deal programs and was instrumental in the planning of the Tennessee Valley Authority.

Perhaps haunted by the spectre of his own Civil War experiences, Peabody became an avowed pacifist and throughout his life proved to be one of the most enterprising propagandists for the cause of peace. A devout Episcopalian who called himself a "thorough believer in non-resistance," he firmly trusted that the life of Jesus Christ exemplified true statesmanship to the world. Wars would end, he suggested, when men learned to turn the other cheek and follow the saving dictates of the Sermon on the Mount. Peabody held life more important than property and blamed the Machiavellian-like imperialism of the rising nation states for promoting the wanton destruction of human life in the name of peace and prosperity. War, he believed, was not only inhuman but inherently undemocratic.

Peabody's pacifism blossomed into full public view during the Spanish-American War, which he condemned as a "wicked" war and a tawdry excuse for insatiable, imperialistic greed. In 1902 he attended the Eighth Lake Mohonk International Conference on Arbitration and preached the need to propagandize the horrible results and enormous costs of war to the public at large. He became a devoted Lake Mohonker. In 1905 he funneled thousands of dollars into the American Peace Society, of which he was a vice-president, in order to have the poems and pamphlets of two of his fellow pacifists, Katrina Trask and the radical Episcopal clergyman, Algernon Crapsey, printed and distributed throughout the country. This type of expenditure for the cause of peace was not at all unusual for Peabody. He even informed *Benjamin Trueblood, secretary of the American Peace Society, that he desired to have one of Crapsey's pacifist sermons translated into six languages—including Russian and Japanese.

In the presidential campaign of 1912, Peabody threw his considerable support behind Woodrow Wilson. He strongly supported the president's noninterventionist policy in Mexico's revolutionary turmoil, even though he had considerable business holdings there and other influential tycoons, like William R. Hearst, clamored for Wilson to declare war. True to his pacifist ideals, Peabody criticized Wilson's ill-fated Vera Cruz expedition in 1914 and General John J. Pershing's pursuit of Pancho Villa into Mexico the following year.

After the outbreak of World War I, Peabody took a strong stand against the preparedness movement in the United States, arguing that "true preparedness" was following the Sermon on the Mount. In January 1917, just three months before the United States entered the war, Peabody was elected chairman of the American Neutral Conference Committee. He strongly supported Wilson's policy of neutrality in the face of war, but when the United States entered the conflict in April, Peabody anguished over the need to choose between his staunch antiwar principles and his loyalty to Wilson and the democratic republic. He chose the latter and surrendered his pacifist ideals for Wilson's promised war to end all war. With the same energy he had promoted peace, he now supported the campaign against "Prussian militarism," withdrawing his support from the Emergency Peace Federation, a union of peace forces which he had helped organize. He now argued that if a democratic nation declared war, even pacifists should remain loyal to the republic in order to safeguard democracy in its time of crisis.

At the close of World War I, Peabody devoted his time, influence, and money in support of Wilson's quixotic campaign for America's entry into the League of Nations. Perhaps he felt that universal peace could now arise like the phoenix from the meaningless ashes of war or that his conscience would somehow be exonerated from his earlier breach of faith with pacifism. When Peabody died at the age of eighty-six in March 1938, war once again loomed as a hideous spectre on the horizon in spite of all his work and earnest hope for a peaceful world.

Bibliography:

B. Louise Ware, *George Foster Peabody: Banker, Philanthropist, Publicist* (Athens, GA, 1951); DAB, Supp. 2, 520-21.

C. George Foster Peabody Papers, Library of Congress.

Frederick J. Stefon

PEARSON, Lester Bowles. See *Biographical Dictionary of Internationalists*.

PEASE, Joseph Whitwell (23 June 1828, Darlington, England—23 June 1903, Falmouth, England). *Education*: private tutoring. *Career*: industrialist, chairman of Pease and Partners Ltd. and of North-Eastern Railway Company; Liberal Member of Parliament (for South Durham), 1865-85, (for Barnard Castle), 1885-1903; president, Peace Society to 1903.

Joseph Whitwell Pease was born into great wealth and influence. His grandfather, Edward Pease, known in the north of England as the "Father of the Railway," had founded the family fortune. His father, Joseph Pease, extended family holdings to include collieries, dock facilities, mills, and limestone quarries. In spite of its swiftly accumulating wealth, the Pease family remained imbued with the precepts of an austere Quaker faith, and Joseph Whitwell, the eldest son, was reared in a tradition stressing philanthropy and service. His great-grandfather had been the first Quaker Member of Parliament, and his father had represented South Durham in Commons since 1832. In 1865 Joseph Whitwell succeeded to his father's seat, thus inaugurating a career of thirty-eight uninterrupted years as a Liberal M.P.

A close associate and admirer of *John Bright during his early years in Commons, Pease generally subscribed to the Gladstonian agenda of "peace, retrenchment, and reform," although on such issues as Home Rule for Ireland, he was not afraid to distance himself from the party leadership. Over the years he lent support to a variety of causes in Commons. He was an advocate of free trade; he favored extension of the franchise (but not to women); and he voted consistently for the expansion of civil and religious liberties. He was a vigorous opponent of the death penalty, insisting in formal debate that "capital punishment is no deterrent to murder," and declaring that human life must be recognized as "a thing too sacred to be sacrificed even by the law." He was equally articulate on the subject of the opium trade, speaking out strongly in Commons on the need to suppress the cultivation of poppies in India and the sale of opium to the reluctant Chinese. Despite a conspicuous lack of support from William E. Gladstone on this issue, Pease did not hesitate to "obey the voice of religion" and to denounce the infamous traffic.

A staunch advocate of reduced military expenditures, Pease voted for the contraction of the army at every opportunity. He opposed imperial expansion and the "horrid" little wars it engendered such as those against the Chinese, Afghans, and Zulus. The Boer War of 1899-1902 found him firmly ranged against the policies of the Conservative Unionists. Though never identified with the more extreme antiwar activists, Pease voted with a bloc of forty-five Liberal "pro-Boers" on all important war-related divisions in Parliament. Ironically the Peace Society, which he had served as president for many years, took a nonpartisan stand in 1899, refusing to assign blame or responsibility to either side and restricting its rhetoric to a somewhat general denunciation of militarism.

Pease and his family provided the Peace society with three presidents between 1872 and 1911. The Society, founded by Quakers in 1816 as the Society for the Promotion of Permanent and Universal Peace, was the oldest of British peace organizations. In 1881, during the first Anglo-Boer War, the Society had, under the dynamic aegis of *Henry Richard, been very active in behalf of the Transvaal Boers. In contrast it refused in 1899 to open its platform to partisan speakers, lest the expression of controversial views "contribute to the continuance of strife." Such passivity was doubtless indicative of the senescence of the Peace Society. It was also reflective of the weak leadership of an aging Pease who was preoccupied by a troublesome law suit at the very moment when the principles he had espoused all his life—conciliation, arbitration, anti-imperialism—were under sustained attack. The adverse judgment of the Court in the Portsmouth Case and the loss of his personal fortune cast a final shadow over what had been a long and honorable career.

Bibliography:

A. *Speech in Favor of the Immediate Abolition of Capital Punishment Reprinted after Revision from the Report in the South Durham and Cleveland Mercury* (London, 1877); *Traffic Between India and China: the Debate in the House of Commons on Mr. J. W. Pease's Motion* (London, 1880).

B. Amy Charlotte Menzies, "Sir Joseph Whitwell Pease," *Modern Men of Mark* (London, 1921), 217-52.

Claire Hirschfield

PECKOVER, Priscilla Hannah (27 October 1833, Wisbech, England—8 September 1931, Wisbech). *Education*: private tutors, briefly attended school in Brighton. *Career*: founder, Women's Local Peace Association, 1879; founder, Wisbech Local Peace Association, 1881; editor, *Peace and Goodwill*, 1882-1931; Christian pacifist, linguist, and temperance worker.

Priscilla Hannah Peckover was born to a wealthy and prominent Cambridgeshire Quaker family. Although nearly all of her education was private, it was extensive enough for her to develop a remarkable linguistic facility and to master several European languages.

Because she devoted her youth and early middle age to raising the three daughters of her widowed brother Alexander (later Lord Peckover), Priscilla Peckover was nearly fifty years old before she became seriously involved in peace work. She later remembered that the call to active service on behalf of peace came at a Friends' meeting in 1878 where the question was asked: "Are you faithful in bearing your Christian testimony against all war?" Her response to that call was to enlist in the Women's Auxiliary of the Peace Society, but upon joining she was shocked to learn that only two hundred women in all of Britain had similarly enrolled. Convinced that there were many more persons devoted to peace than was reflected in the membership of any existing peace group, Peckover began a personal appeal to women in and around her native town of Wisbech. By May 1879 she had found nearly 150 women willing to pay a minimum subscription of one penny a year and to sign a declaration stating: "I believe all war to be contrary to the mind of Christ . . . and am desirous to do what I can to further the cause of Peace." These early subscribers became the first members of the founding branch of the Women's Local Peace Association (WLPA) movement, which eventually had over thirty branches and 15,000 members in Britain as well as affiliated groups in thirty-one foreign countries. In 1881 a Wisbech men's peace committee joined with local women to form the Wisbech Local Peace Association.

As a means of maintaining communications among Local Peace Association branches, Peckover began, in the spring of 1882, to edit and publish a quarterly journal called *Peace and Goodwill*. Thereafter, the journal was published continuously for nearly fifty years; indeed, Priscilla Hannah Peckover worked on the final edition of the journal on the day she died in 1931. In addition to publishing *Peace and Goodwill*, the Wisbech Local Peace Association also established a "depot" which stocked large quantities of peace literature for distribution to branches throughout the British Isles and the continent. Because of Peckover's linguistic ability, she often translated English language tracts into various foreign tongues and paid the cost of printing and transporting these materials to places where they might be read.

The principles and objectives of the Local Peace Association movement, as set out in the first edition of *Peace and Goodwill*, were simple and straightforward: to advocate settlement of all international disputes through the arbitration of an internationally sanctioned High Court of Nations; to inform fellow citizens of the danger, immorality, and cost of military establishments; and to urge members of Parliament that Britain should, in the interest of civilization and humanity, propose a mutual and simultaneous reduction of armaments as the first step to their eventual abolition.

When she began her career as a peace activist, Peckover believed that the Christian churches, especially in their female membership, were the most fertile ground for sowing peace propaganda. Thus, much of the early work within the Local Peace Association was limited to the Christian community. Soon, however, she recognized that many individuals and groups who did not hold Christian or any other religious views might still be earnest and dedicated workers for peace. Thereafter, while she always remained a staunch Christian pacifist, Priscilla Hannah Peckover was also one of the earliest advocates of cooperation between religious and secular peace groups. She strongly supported the collaborative pacifism that became a central feature to the twentieth century British peace movement.

One cooperative effort in which the Local Peace Association movement took the initiative was the establishment of a yearly Peace Sunday, the celebration of which became a major activity of various British peace groups. Peckover was also an early leader in the long-standing campaign against any attempt to impose compulsory military service in Britain. She strongly condemned the development of semi-military youth movements such as the Boys' Brigade which, she believed, were sowing the seeds of militarism from which the nation could only reap a bloody harvest.

Throughout the 1890s and early years of the twentieth century, Priscilla Peckover and her Local Peace Association colleagues, such as *Ellen Robinson, were among the most active and persistent voices against war and militarism. During those years, the Wisbech Local Peace Association continued to grow steadily, reaching a total of over 8,000 members by 1914. The coming of World War I, however, struck a severe blow to Peckover's organization. By the end of the war, WLPA membership had been reduced by one-half, and although there was a brief revival in the immediate aftermath of the conflict, adherents continued to fall away during the 1920s. Despite these setbacks, Peckover maintained her international correspondence with peace leaders and continued regular publication of *Peace and Goodwill*; but neither the journal nor the WLPA survived her death in 1931.

A pioneer of the modern British peace movement, the life and career of Priscilla Hannah Peckover have been virtually ignored, Perhaps her refusal to seek the limelight and her rather traditional views on religion and temperance have helped to keep her in the shadows. But both prior to and after World War I, she was one of Britain's leading voices calling for peace and international goodwill.

Bibliography:

B. *Dictionary of Quaker Biography*, Friends Library, Friends House; *The Friend* (London), September 18, 1931, 851-853; LT, September 10, 1931.

C. The records of the Wisbech Local Peace Association, including the personal correspondence of Priscilla Hannah Peckover and the entire run of *Peace and Goodwill*, are housed in the Swarthmore College Peace Collection, Swarthmore, PA.

Thomas C. Kennedy

PEKURINEN, Arndt (14 Feburary 1905, Tuusula, Finland—5 November 1941, Finland). *Education*: elementary school. *Career*: lorry driver; chairman, Antimilitaristic Union, 1923-41.

Arndt Pekurinen joined Finland's Peace Union after moving to Helsinki early in the 1920s. Together with *Aarne Selinheimo, he founded the Antimilitaristic Union of Finland in 1923 and served as its chairman until his death in 1941. Pekurinen was the most well known and consistent conscientious objector of his time, whose steadfastness brought about a change in attitudes towards those who refused military service.

When Pekurinen was conscripted into the army in 1929, he refused to put on the military uniform. As a result, he was moved from prison to prison, subjected to mental examinations, as well as being tortured and punished. A religious conviction was finally accepted as a reason to refuse to perform military service, but Pekurinen's ethical reason was rejected. Pekurinen started a hunger strike and when news of this was publicized by the press, it sparked a nation-wide discussion of his beliefs and his treatment. As a consequence of the debate, Pekurinen's prison sentences, which were of different lengths, were fused into one two-year sentence. By the time this decision was arrived at, however, Pekurinen had served nearly that length of time without ever having been formally sentenced.

With the help of Selinheimo, Pekurinen's refusal to join the army received international attention. +H. G. Wells and *Henri Barbusse, along with nine other well-known representatives of the European peace movement, sent a letter to the Finnish government demanding an investigation of the Pekurinen case. Furthermore, a great deal of attention was given to the correspondence between *Albert Einstein and Juho Niukkanen, the Minister of Foreign Affairs. Einstein maintained that Pekurinen was a member of the War Registers' International since 1927, and could not, therefore, support any military activity.

In 1931, due to the persistence of Pekurinen and other antiwar activists, the Finnish parliament passed a new law defining conscientious objection and a second law prohibiting the arbitrary imprisonment and sentencing of conscientious objectors. Throughout the 1930s, Pekurinen and the Antimilitaristic Union were the objects of fascist pressure and threats. When the so-called Winter War started on the last day of November, 1939, Pekurinen was called into military service, but he refused to take up a gun. Since the 1931 law applied only to religious conscientious objectors and Pekurinen refused military service for ethical reasons, he was tried in military court, sentenced to two years in prison, and not permitted to see his next of kin. In June 1941, when the so-called Continuing War began, Pekurinen was again taken to the front and again he refused to perform military service. A few months later he was brutally murdered.

The Antimilitaristic Union led by Pekurinen was small in numbers, but it attracted widespread public interest in the cause of conscientious objection. Pekurinen was not an inspiring public speaker nor an impressive writer. His main contribution to the cause of peace was his brave and consistent refusal to perform military service and, thereby, heightening public awareness of the plight of conscientious objectors. By his life and concrete activity, he committed himself to the cause of peace.

Bibliography:

B. Kalevi Kalemaa, *Suomalaisen rauhanliikkeen juuria* (Vaasa, 1981); Toivi Vare, "Aseistakieltaytyjan elama tuhottiin," *Kansan Uutiset*, November 25, 1979.

Kalevi Kalemaa

Trans. by Oliver and Rita Whitehead

PELLETIER, Anne-Madeleine (18 May 1874, Paris—29 December 1939, Perray-Vaucluse, France). *Education*: Baccalauréat, Univ. of Paris, M.D., 1899, licenciée ès science, c. 1917. *Career*: physician, first woman on staff of Assistance Publique (1889), first woman resident, Paris mental hospital, 1903; author of over forty books and brochures; founder-editor, *La Suffragist*, 1907-14, 1919; contributor, *La Guerre Sociale*, 1907-10, *Le Voix des Femmes*, 1917-37; co-leader, Solidarité des femmes, 1906-14; member, Commission Administrative Permanente, French Socialist party, 1909-11.

Madeleine Pelletier considered war a capitalist device to make profits at the expense of working class lives and to divert workers' attention from legitimate grievances and possible revolution. She also linked war with antifeminism, calling it the basis of men's power over women. As an example, she pointed to nationalists who told women to salute the flag by bearing more male babies. They, in turn, labeled her as unpatriotic and an enemy of the family for insisting that women be released from their biological bondage and arguing that depopulation was in women's interest.

Pelletier believed that war was a learned behavior: if boys were not given wooden rifles, they would not dream of becoming soldiers. Because women were not prepared for war, women's suffrage represented a powerful means of combatting militarism.

Feminism became the highest priority of Pelletier's career. She identified with revolutionary socialists and anarchists, yet she broke with both over women's suffrage. The same was true of her commitment to peace. An ardent pacifist, Pelletier was one of only two French suffragists to use violence to dramatize their cause. Although she denounced rearmament and the Berry-Millerand draft law, she advocated conscription of women to obtain the vote.

In 1914 Pelletier felt betrayed by socialists who rallied to the war. Yet she declined to join in the protests of socialist women at Berne the next year. Instead, she tried to join the medical corps, then volunteered with the Red Cross. Stationed near the front, she treated the wounded of both sides, to the horror of socialist comrades. In 1915 she was questioned as a spy for attempting to speak out on feminist issues.

Pelletier, an internationalist, hailed the Russian Revolution, voted for the Third International at Tours, and made a clandestine pilgrimage to Russia. By 1925 she was disillusioned with collective action. She spent the rest of her life practicing medicine among poor women, including performing abortions, a crime for which she was confined to an asylum at age 64 where she died six months later.

Bibliography:

A. *Dépopulation et civilisation* (Paris, n.d.); *La Femme en lutte pour ses droits* (Paris, 1908); *La Guerre est-elle naturelle* (Paris, n.d.); *Justice social?* (Paris, 1913); *Mon Voyage aventureux en Russie communiste* (Paris, 1922); *Philosophie sociale* (Paris, 1912); *La Question du vote des femmes* (Paris, 1909).

B. Marilyn A. Boxer, "Socialism Faces Feminism in France, 1897-1913," Ph.D., dissertation, University of California at Riverside, 1975; Marilyn A. Boxer and Jean H. Quataert, *Socialist Women* (New York, 1978); Claude Maignien, introduction, M. Pelletier, *L'Education féministe des filles* (Paris, 1978); Charles Sowerwine, *Les Femmes et le socialisme* (Paris, 1978).

Anne R. Kenney

PERCIN, Alexandre (4 July 1846, Nancy, Meurthe-et-Moselle, France—12 October 1928, Paris). *Education*: Lycée of Nancy; École Polytechnique, 1865-67. *Career*: military service, 1867-1911, 1914.

Alexandre Percin became that greatest of rareties—a professional soldier who was also a pacifist. Nothing in a long military career that spanned more than forty years foreshadowed that he would advocate pacifism during the post-World War I period. The son of a mathematics teacher, he entered the École Polytechnique because he was impressed by the fine uniforms that its students wore. Percin enjoyed a distinguished career from his service as an artillery officer in the Franco-Prussian War of 1870-71, when he was twice wounded in combat, to his membership in the Conseil Supérieur de la Guerre in 1908-11, when he helped to shape French military policy. Throughout his career as an officer, he argued for a greater role for long-range guns and closer ties between infantry and artillery formations.

It was only after his retirement from active service that he began to express doubts about France's military establishment. He came to believe that the high command was ignoring the danger of a massive German attack through neutral Belgium and neglecting the use of a strong ready reserve and heavy artillery units. Percin's antagonism towards the high command intensified when it gave strong support to the Three Year Law of 1913 which extended military service from two to three years. He considered such legislation both unnecessary and even harmful because it failed to make effective use of existing manpower resources. Like *Jean Jaurès, he saw the Swiss military system of a citizen army as the proper model for France. His numerous articles in the press against the law and his candidacy for the Chamber of Deputies on the Radical-Socialist ticket in the elections of 1914 show just how far he had moved from traditional military positions.

But Percin's sense of outrage was most aroused when he was named commander of the First Region on the endangered northern frontier during the opening days of World War I, then summarily relieved of his command after the fall of Lille. Percin argued that the town was indefensible for lack of adequate artillery and that he had ordered his forces to withdraw after pleas from local officials who feared the town's destruction. He spent the remainder of the war seeking to justify his actions and bitterly attacking the high command for what he considered shabby treatment.

After 1919 Percin waged a relentless campaign against France's military leadership. He assailed it for not adequately providing for the country's defense, for poor planning (especially in artillery), and for squandering countless lives in senseless trench warfare. As his resentment against the high command grew, Percin was increasingly drawn into the pacifist movement. His personal knowledge of the inner workings of the military and his distinguished career made him a valuable ally of the antiwar forces. Percin supported the League of Nations and called for "moral disarmament," the end to international distrust and hatred, as a precondition to world peace. He feared that a renewed conflict would inevitably cause France heavy losses, worse than those of 1914-18. His numerous books and articles were read by many and may have influenced French planning for a defensive strategy in the event of a new war.

Bibliography:

A. *Cinq années d'inspection* (Paris, 1912); *Le Désarmement moral* (Paris, 1925); *Guerre à la guerre* (Paris,1927); *La Guerre et l'armée de demain* (Paris, 1917); *Le Massacre de notre infanterie, 1914-1918* (Paris, 1921); *1914: Les Erreurs du Haut Commandement* (Paris, 1919).

B. Robert Nanteuil, "Le General Percin," *Les Hommes du jour*, July 5, 1913, 1-3; *Qui êtes-vous?* (Paris, 1924), 595.

James Friguglietti

PÉRICAT, Raymond Louis (23 January 1873, Gretz, Seine-et-Marne, France —13 July 1957, Paris). *Education*: primary school. *Career*: plasterer, 1885-91; soldier in Algeria, 1891-95; building trade worker and trade union organizer, 1895-1908; secretary, Federation of Building Workers, 1908-10, general secretary, 1910-12; member, Confederal Committee (CCN) of the General Confederation of Labor (CGT), 1913?-20; founder, Committee for the Resumption of International Relations (CRRI), 1916; general secretary, Committee for Syndicalist Defense (CDS), 1917-18; founder, Communist Party, the French Section of the International, 1919; affiliated with the Unity CGT (CGTU), 1921-24; concierge, 1926-29; trade union organizer.

Raymond Péricat gave of himself unsparingly to all forms of trade union activity. In 1910, at the Eleventh Congress of the French national confederation of trade unions, his proposal was accepted to create a fund for conscripts which aimed at preserving links between worker draftees and the trade union movement. Péricat believed that soldiers should be reminded of their working class origins which included an obligation not to shoot their brothers. As a revolutionary syndicalist, he held the usual view that war benefited the oppressors of the working class and therefore should be opposed.

Péricat's antiwar commitment was far from perfunctory. On July 31, 1914, when the Confederal Committee (CCN) of the General Confederation of Labor (CGT) met, Péricat along with only one other member, urged that the CGT organize some effective action against the war. The next day when the order for general mobilization was posted, members of the CCN met again and drew up a text indicating their acceptance of the war. Péricat was the only one who remained faithful to the antiwar declarations of the prewar CGT congresses. His own immediate mobilization, even though he was no longer a young man, was probably due to his stand that day.

Péricat sought out those few other socialists and particularly the syndicalists who opposed the war. They became known as *minoritaires* and assembled together, first in the Committee for International Action and then in the Committee for the Resumption of International Relations (CRRI). By the autumn of 1916, most of the syndicalists had separated from the CRRI to form the Committee for Syndicalist Defense (CDS). The CDS soon became the center of the syndicalist, *minoritaire* movement and Péricat, as secretary general, became its leader. The CDS organized speaking tours and published leaflets and brochures. It attempted, despite censorship and surveillance, to coordinate *minoritaire* activities. On May 19-20, 1918, Péricat and the CDS organized a *minoritaire* conference. Péricat was arrested despite the fact that the general strike (which its organizers had desired) did not materialize. He was released in November only after the armistice.

On May 8, 1919, the CRRI, in a joint meeting with the CDS, decided to become the Committee for the Third International. Péricat became one of its secretaries. Impatient, he resigned from this position and formed his own Communist party. This small group soon split into tiny, warring factions and disintegrated. In 1921 Péricat became prominent in the new, procommunist Unity CGT (CGTU) and remained affiliated with it until 1924. After 1924 he ceased to play a major role in trade union activities, or in politics.

Péricat's consistent adherence to antiwar principles, even in 1914, and his leadership of the CDS attested to his sincere commitment to the working class antimilitarist position developed over a lifetime of struggle.

Bibliography:

A. *Etre un homme* (Courbevoie, n.d.); *Maitres et valets* (Paris, [1917]).

B. R. Brécy, *Le Mouvement syndical en France* (Paris, 1963); H. Dubief, *Le Syndicalisme révolutionaire* (Paris, 1969); A. Kriegel, *Aux Origines du Communisme français* (Paris, 1964); J. Maitron, ed., *Dictionnaire Biographique du Mouvement Ouvrier Français, 1871–1914*, XIV, 236–37; Robert Wohl, *French Communism in the Making, 1914-1924* (Stanford, CA, 1966).

C. Raymond Péricat Archives, Institut français d'histoire sociale, Paris.

Jane Bond-Howard

PEROUTKA, Ferdinand (6 February 1895, Prague, Bohemia, Austrian Empire [now Czechoslovakia]—20 April 1978, New York). *Education*: gymnasium in Prague. *Career*: editor, *Tribuna*, 1919-24; editor-in-chief, *Přitomnost*, 1924-39; political editor, *Lidové Noviny*, 1924-39; editor-in-chief, *Svobodné Noviny*, and *Dnešek*; director, Czechoslovak section of Radio Free Europe, 1948-60; journalist, literary critic, and political writer.

Throughout his career Ferdinand Peroutka, a man of great culture who characterized himself as a liberal, fought for understanding and for peace among nations. In the hate-filled atmosphere after World War I, he urged reconciliation between European peoples based on an irrepressible and undeniable community of interests. Peroutka's articles attracted the attention of President *Thomas G. Masaryk. A lifelong friendship developed between the 29 year old Peroutka and the 74-year old philosopher and Czech president. With the moral and financial support of Masaryk, Peroutka established in 1924 the *Přitomnost* (*The Present*) which became the most respected periodical in Czechoslovakia and was published until 1939.

In *Přitomnost*, Peroutka called for reconciliation among the nations in order to preserve the fragile peace. He wrote objectively about the nationality problem in Czechoslovakia and warned of the destructive force of nationalism to internal and external peace and to the existence of the republic. He recognized that the Czechs wished to have a nation state — "their state" — while the Germans in the Czech republic wanted a nationality state — a state composed of several nationalities. However, he argued that if the Czechs wished to continue to live in peace within the historic and strategic borders for which they had fought, instead of within the ethnographic borders which they had rejected, they had to accept the reality that Czechoslovakia was a nationality state and the Germans a part of it. He agreed with Masaryk that cooperation was absolutely necessary among the nations and states as a precondition for peace and progress. In the trying days of September 1938, he supported the surrender of President +Eduard Beneš to the dictate of Munich. Like Beneš, he was opposed to military resistance without foreign support. Use of the army to resist the invasion would be irrational, he argued, and would cause great bloodshed. It would be senseless because resistance could not succeed and it would be irresponsible to lead the nation into suicide.

Together with Milena Jesenká, Peroutka continued to publish *Přitomnost* for a few months even after the German occupation of all of Czechoslovakia in March 1939. But despite a changed and subdued publication policy, the Nazi regime prohibited the periodical in the summer of 1939; Peroutka was arrested shortly afterwards. He spent the war years in the concentration camp at Buchenwald. In May 1946, after his liberation, he returned to Prague. Everywhere he noticed a mood of depression and apprehension about the future and distrust of the Communists. In this period of uncertainty, insecure democracy, and constant discussions with the Communists, Peroutka's new newspapers, *Svododné Noviny* and *Dnešek*, had a precarious existence. After the Communists took over the government in February 1948, Petroutka was excluded from the syndicate of Czech writers. He emigrated soon thereafter. As director of the Czechoslovak section of Radio Free Europe and also after his retirement from that post, he wrote extensively on literary and foreign policy topics. In these writings, as in those before the war, he showed himself to be a man of peace.

Bibliography:

A. *Boje o Dnešek* (Prague, 1925); *Budovaní Státu* (New York, 1974); *Byl Eduard Beneš Vinen?* (London, 1949); *Demokratický Manifest* (New York, 1959); *Oblak A Valčik* (Toronto, 1976); "Příjezd do Prahy," *Proměny*, 18, no. 1 (Washington, D.C., 1981), 49-54; *Projevy K Domovu* (Toronto, 1976); T.G.M. *Představuje Plukovnika Cunninghama* (Zurich, 1977).

B. Václav Holešovský, "Peroutka-Setkavání a Stretávaní," *Proměny*, 18, no. 1 (Washington, D.C., 1981), 49-54; *České Slovo* (Munich), May, 1978, 1-2; *Slovnik Českých Spisovatelů* (Toronto, 1982), 365-67.

Fred Hahn

PERRIS, George Herbert (29 January 1866, Liverpool, England—23 December 1920, London). *Education*: self-educated. *Career*: political journalist, editor, and peace activist.

Raised in modest circumstances in a clergyman's family, George H. Perris began his journalistic career at 17 years of age writing for *The Speaker* and the *Hull Express*, whose editor he became in 1885. He began his association with the peace movement as editor of *Concord*, the journal of *Hodgson Pratt's

International Arbitration and Peace Association, serving in that capacity from 1898-1906. Simultaneously, he was secretary of the Cobden Club in London. Perris' skills as a journalist made *Concord* into one of the finest pacifist papers in the pre-1914 years. Besides its excellent coverage of pacifist activities, the journal regularly exposed war-mongering in both the English and European press, printing balanced accounts of alleged crises and one-sided nationalistic news stories.

With +W. T. Stead and *Felix Moscheles, Perris produced a popularly written and succinct history of the first Hague Peace Conference, based in part on personal, first-hand impressions. Shortly after the Conference ended, the Boer War broke out and Perris led the criticism of his own government for its unwillingness to use the arbitration machinery which it had helped design at The Hague.

A regular participant at Universal Peace Congresses beginning in 1898 at Turin, Perris became close friends with most continental pacifists and wholly supportive of the ideas of the international peace movement — organized international arbitration laying the groundwork for gradual arms control and then disarmament, immediate reductions in military spending, cultural exchanges among European nations, extensive peace education, opposition to violent imperialism, and the slow extension of democratic rights to all the world's peoples. He publicized every effort to bring about those ideals, writing about topics as disparate as *Leo Tolstoy, the Near East crises, the Luzern War/Peace Museum, the 1905 Russian Revolution, the labors of pacifist leaders, and the history of industrialization.

With the conclusion of the Anglo-French Entente in 1904, Perris set about to create an Anglo-German Friendship Society (1905) and an Anglo-Russian Friendship Society (1906) in an effort to promote British neutrality toward all European powers. When he was appointed as foreign editor of *The Tribune* in 1906, he privately promised European peace leaders that he would work to influence its editorial policy in a pro-German direction and to counter the growing conservative mood in England towards a permanent policy of hostility toward Germany. *The Tribune*, a liberal paper, did not last more than a year, but Perris then became foreign editor of the *Daily News* (to 1910) where he attempted to continue that commitment. He was one of the few highly placed career journalists before World War I who was publicly identified with pacifism.

Besides his peace activism which included frequent lecture tours (including one of the United States in 1902), participation in international and national peace congresses, and membership on the British National Peace Council, Perris was a prolific author of books on political topics and a chronicler of the peace movement. During the First World War, he worked on the western front as a correspondent for the *Daily Chronicle* and wrote several books about the military campaigns. At the end of the war, he was awarded the C.B.E. of the British Empire and made a Chevalier in the Legion d' Honneur.

Bibliography:

A. *Arbitration or War?* (London, 1899); *The Battle of the Marne* (London, 1920); *The Campaign in France and Belgium* (London, 1915); *For an Arrest of Armaments* (Westminister, S.W., 1906); *Germany and the German Emperor* (London, 1912); *Hands Across the Sea; Labour's Plea for International Peace* (Manchester, [1909?]); *A History of the Peace Conference at the Hague*, with F. Moscheles and W. T. Stead (London, 1899); *Jean de Bloch and the Museum of War and Peace at Lucerne* (London, 1902); *The Life and Teaching of Leo Tolstoy* (London, 1901); *A Short History of War and Peace* (New York and London, 1911); *What Is the Peace Movement* (London, 1908).

B. "Perris, Georges Herbert," in Alfred Fried, *Handbuch der Friedensbewegung* (Garland reprint, New York, 1972), II, 388-89.

C. Miscellaneous letters in Archives, Bureau international de la paix, United Nations Library, Geneva.

Sandi E. Cooper

PERSIUS, Lothar (19 April 1864, Kyritz, Ost-Prignitz, Prussia [now German Democratic Republic]—1944, Ascona, Switzerland). *Education*: naval cadet, 1883-86; commissioned, Leutnant zur See (ensign), Imperial German Navy, 1886. *Career*: naval officer, journalist, and writer.

The son of a Prussian public official, Lothar Persius developed his pacifist ideas slowly, believing that Germany's naval and colonial policies were harmful and provocative. Trained as a naval officer, he experienced the Spanish American War in the area of the Phillipines. Early in 1900 he was put in command of a cruiser assigned to the Far East. At first he supported Germany's arms buildup and belonged to the Flottenverein (Naval League) which lobbied for an increase in German naval armaments. While in the Far East, however, he published articles under a pseudonym which criticized Germany's colonial policy towards China. When the true author was discovered, he was recalled to Germany. In 1908 he gave up active service as a naval captain and initially wrote for conservative newspapers about naval affairs. Viewing Germany's naval program as inadequate, he called for the construction of submarines as *defensive* weapons rather than the construction of battleships. By 1912 he had become a member of the editorial staff of the democratic *Berliner Tageblatt* and also wrote for other liberal publications.

Writing with authority, he warned of the pernicious side-effects of the policy of naval construction and predicted the consequences of German arms policy and the growing alienation of Germany and England. Persius' pacifism grew as he contemplated the terrible consequences of Germany's arms buildup. He strongly supported Winston Churchill's proposal to declare 1913 as a year free from an increase in naval power. At the same time, *Alfred H. Fried persuaded him to become a contributor to *Die Friedenswarte*, one of Germany's leading pacifist journals.

Shortly before the outbreak of World War I, Persius wrote, under the sponsorship of the Carnegie Endowment for International Peace, *Rüstungsrivalität und die Möglichkeit ihrer Ausschaltung* (*Armament Rivalry and the Possibility* *of Its Elimination*). Once the war began, his activity as a journalist was curtailed because he was placed under general censorship. In 1918, however, he became a contributor to the *Weltbühne*, where he published articles critical of the navy. Here, and in the pacifist publication, *Die Menschheit*, for which *Friedrich W. Foerster wrote a weekly editorial, Persius called for the clarification of the war-guilt question as a presupposition for the democratization of Germany and for the elimination of militarism. Since Germany would have to free itself from Prussian militarism, he demanded the formation of a federal court which would try German war criminals.

During the interwar period Persius was a member of the Deutsche Liga für Menschenrechte (League for Human Rights) and supported the League's campaign to publicize the activities of conservative and nationalistic paramilitary organizations. In 1926, however, he withdrew from the League after accusations were published that it had received financial support from French sources. In the late 1920s he continued to promote a pacifist line and strongly opposed the construction of pocket battleships. Although not much information exists about his last years, it is likely that he left Germany prior to the coming to power of Adolf Hitler, for his last article appeared in the *Weltbühne* in 1930.

Bibliography:

A. *Graf Ernst zu Reventlow* (Berlin, 1918); *Menschen und Schiffe in der kaiserlichen Flotte* (Berlin, 1925); *Schlachtschiff und Unterseeboot* (Leipzig, 1914); *Der Seekrieg* (Charlottenburg, 1919); *Tirpitz, der Totengräber der deutschen Flotte* (Berlin, 1918); *Die Tirpitz-legende* (Berlin, 1918); *Warum die Flotte versagte* (Leipzig, 1925); ''*Wie es kam*,'' *dass der Anstoss zur Revolution von der Flotte ausging* (Berlin, 1919).

B. Johannes Fischart (Ernst Dombrowski), ''Lothar Persius,'' *Die Weltbühne*, July 4, 1918.

Lothar Wieland
Trans. by Peter Seadle

PFEMFERT, Franz (20 November 1879, Lötzen, Germany [now Poland]—26 May 1954, Mexico City). *Education*: training as a photographer; self educated in literature and politics. *Career*: journalist and writer.

Coming from a petty-bourgeois background, Franz Pfemfert was active as a journalist. Writing primarily for left-wing radical and anarchistic literary newspapers, he took anticlerical and socially critical positions. He also wrote for the left-liberal press, and in 1910 became editor of the left-liberal weekly paper, *Der Demokrat*. Pfemfert developed into a critic and analyst of bourgeois institutions, aesthetic views, and moral concepts. After a short time, he had a run-in with Georg Zepler, the publisher of *Der Demokrat*. In February 1911, Pfemfert started his own periodical, *Die Aktion. Zeitschift für freiheitliche Politik und Literatur*, which he published and edited until 1932. In the journal, whose antimilitarist and anticlerical character was determined largely by Pfemfert, he especially criticized the revisionism of the Sozialdemokratische Partei Deutschlands (German Social Democratic Party) (SPD). Before World War I, *Die Aktion* became the most important forum for German Expressionism, and Pfemfert moved from being a radical democrat to a champion of those humanitarian-pacifist views that were related to anarchism.

In order not to fall victim to the military censors, Pfemfert took no political positions after the beginning of World War I. He expressed his opposition to the war by printing questionable excerpts from right-wing publications and speeches of prominent political figures who favored the war. In addition, he attempted to counter the internal German hate campaigns against enemy states by publishing special issues on the nations at war with Germany. Together with his collaborators on *Die Aktion*, Pfemfert, in 1915, founded the Antinationale Sozialisten-Partei (Antinational Socialist Party), which stood close to the Spartacus League and which later was absorbed by the Kommunistische Partei Deutschlands (German Communist Party) (KPD).

As a member of the Deutsche Friedensgesellschaft (German Peace Society) (DFG), Pfemfert, together with *Georg F. Nicolai, represented the radical opposition to the moderate position taken by the Society's executive committee. His demand for sharper action by the DFG led to violent arguments with the DFG's president, *Ludwig Quidde. After the German revolution of 1918, Pfemfert supported the idea of a Council or Soviet form of political organization advocated by the KPD. In October 1919, however, he was expelled from the KPD together with the left opposition. In the following years, Pfemfert and the *Aktion* took increasingly radical positions which led to the journal's loss of literary significance. Pfemfert escaped the Nazis by fleeing to Carlsbad, Czechoslovakia, on March 1, 1933. From there he went to Paris in 1936. Forced to leave France in 1940, after its defeat by Germany, Pfemfert spent the remainder of his life — except for one year in the United States — in Mexico.

Bibliography:

A. *Das AKTIONS-Buch* (Berlin, 1917); *Die Parteidiktatur der III. Internationale* (Berlin, 1920); *Die Sozialdemokratie bis zum August 1914* (Berlin, 1918); *Uber die Märzkatastrophe des deutschen Proletariats (mit anderen Autoren)* (Berlin, n.d.).

B. Manfred George, "Ein Berliner in Mexiko. In memoriam Franz Pfemfert," *Deutsche Rundschau*, 80 (1954); Lothar Peter, *Literarische Intelligenz und Klassenkampf. "Die Aktion" 1911-1932* (Cologne, 1972); Paul Raabe, *Ich schneide die Zeit aus. Expressionismus und Politik in Franz Pfemferts Aktion* (Munich, 1964).

Lothar Wieland
Trans. by Solomon Wank

PICKETT, Clarence Evan (19 October 1884, Cissna Park, IL—17 March 1965, Boise, ID). *Education*: B.A., Penn Coll., Oscaloosa, IA, 1910; B.D., Hartford Theological Seminary, 1913; studied at Harvard Divinity School, 1922-23. *Career*: pastor, Toronto Friends Meeting, 1913-17; pastor, Oscaloosa Friends Meeting, 1917-19; secretary, Young Friends Organization of America, 1919-22; professor of Biblical literature, Earlham College, Richmond, IN, 1922-29; executive secretary, American Friends Service Committee, 1929-50; honorary executive secretary, 1950-55; executive secretary emeritus, 1955-65; co-chairman, Committee for a Sane Nuclear Policy, 1957-63.

After 1929 Clarence Pickett's life was inseparable from the American Friends Service Committee (AFSC). The AFSC had been established in Philadelphia in 1917 by *Rufus Jones and other Quakers to undertake wartime relief and reconstruction work overseas. Pickett was its staff head for 22 years during the depression, World War II, and its aftermath.

Pickett's family moved to Glen Elder, Kansas, when he, the youngest of nine children, was two. They were Quakers farming in a Quaker community. He early developed a tender social conscience. One summer was spent working in the Spring Street settlement in New York. As Friends pastor at Oscaloosa in 1917-18, he counseled young men on conscientious objection, seeking their understanding of all alternatives; opponents of his pacifism painted yellow crosses on his house. Later, at Earlham College, his most popular course was "Modern Social Problems in the Light of the Teachings of Jesus."

When Pickett succeeded Wilbur Thomas in 1929 as executive secretary of the AFSC, it was a small organization with an annual budget of some $100,000, working principally on social service projects, interracial questions, and peace education in the United States. Until 1936 the emphasis continued to be domestic. Pickett was immediately involved in organizing food and clothing relief for striking textile workers in Marion, N.C., and then in organizing the feeding of destitute miners in the Appalachian coal fields. The latter project developed into retraining the jobless, teaching handicrafts, and facilitating subsistence homesteads. The AFSC experience led President +Franklin Roosevelt to appoint Pickett assistant director of a Federal subsistence homestead project in 1933-34. In 1936-39 the AFSC developed its own homesteading project, Penn-Craft, for 50 miner families. Pickett visited Europe's Quaker centers in 1930 and added Russia to his itinerary; thereafter he sought ways to improve American-Russian relations. He chaired the Emergency Peace Committee in 1931, coordinating the work of many American organizations for disarmament and other causes. Another European trip in 1934, with his wife Lilly, provided him with an insight into the mounting problem of refugees from Nazism.

After 1936 international concerns pushed to the fore. Clarence Pickett served on the executive committee of the Emergency Peace Campaign in 1936-37. The AFSC began relief feeding in 1937 on both sides in the Spanish Civil War. As Spanish refugees poured into France, the AFSC began retraining and rehabilitation programs for them there. Late in 1938 it created a refugee division to help especially in getting Jews out of Nazi Europe; a Quaker mission to Berlin won from the Gestapo an oral promise of freedom of action, but no practical facilities. Yet many refugees were aided — by 1950 over 50,000 — with personal services, centers, and hostels. With the war, projected feeding of refugees and children in Nazi-occupied Europe was thwarted by British blockade measures, but the AFSC continued relief in Vichy France until late 1942, when eight Quaker workers were interned. AFSC activity in China during the war and after, to 1950, focused on medical and sanitation assistance.

At home, meanwhile, the AFSC worked with Mennonite and Brethren agencies to get the broadest possible provisions for conscientious objectors (COs) into the 1940 Draft Act. Thereafter it cooperated with the federal government in establishing and operating alternative service camps for COs. The AFSC also tried to alleviate the distress of the thousands of Japanese forcibly removed from the west coast to ''relocation centers''; among those helped were about 4,000 students, released to colleges inland.

Relief work increased as war ended. By 1947 the AFSC had some 200 workers abroad in feeding, clothing, and refugee aid projects in Europe and Asia. Its annual foreign service expenditure reached $7,000,000. The AFSC also lent a team to UNRRA. International work camps, earlier established in Mexico, were extended to Europe in 1947. When Britain was leaving the Palestine mandate in May 1948, Pickett was asked by the United Nations to become a kind of interim mayor of Jerusalem; he declined in favor of Harold Evans, another Friend. The AFSC did assist the UN in 1949-50 with 50 workers responsible for Arab refugee relief in the Gaza strip. In 1947 the AFSC was awarded the Nobel Peace Prize, sharing it with the Friends Service Council of London.

Despite his semiretirement in 1950, Clarence Pickett continued to be active. From 1950 to 1955 he was a member of the Quaker team at UN Assembly meetings. He worked on race relations and the fair employment practices law in Philadelphia, served President Harry Truman in 1952 as a member of the Commission on Immigration, and helped organize SANE in 1957 with Norman Cousins. He served President John F. Kennedy on the Peace Corps National Advisory Council after 1961. In 1962 he picketed Kennedy's White House one morning, demonstrating against the nuclear arms race, and the same evening was received, in white tie, by the president, along with other Nobel laureates. Traveling, three years later, he died at Boise.

Clarence Pickett participated in the many AFSC programs in various ways — as organizer, facilitator, fund-raiser, negotiator, administrator, and leader through consensus. He was gentle, realistic, patient, persistent, happy to work whenever possible with government—at once its ''critic and friend,'' as he put it. He was at home with the great, consulted by four presidents, but represented the humble. He believed mass action to be sometimes necessary, but usually shallow; consequently, he preferred individual or small-scale action that reached deeper. He practiced doing the possible. His best known lecture, entitled (after Ephesians) ''And having done all, to stand,'' emphasized the need for *doing* to the utmost before *standing*. Clarence Pickett's whole life was a ministry of doing.

Bibliography:

A. *And Having Done All, To Stand* (Philadelphia, 1951); *For More Than Bread* (Boston, 1953).

B. Mary Hoxie Jones, *Swords into Ploughshares* (New York, 1937); Walter Kahoe, *Clarence Pickett: A Memoir* (Moylan, PA, privately printed, 1966); Harold E. Snyder,

"Clarence E. Pickett: Statesman for Humanity," *Saturday Review*, 48 (April 24, 1965), 25+.

C. Friends Service Committee Archives, Philadelphia, Pa.

Roderic H. Davison

PIECZYNSKA-REICHENBACH, Emma (19 April 1854, Paris—10 February 1927, Berne, Switzerland). *Education*: private schools, Geneva, 1861-70; maturitätsprüfung (school certificate examination), 1887; medical studies, universities of Geneva and Berne, 1887-91 (studies broken off for reasons of health). *Career*: political writer and lecturer.

From 1874 until 1885, Emma Reichenbach Pieczynska lived in Poland as the wife of Count Pieczynski. After her divorce in 1885, she returned to Geneva where she assumed the name Pieczynska-Reichenbach and became, together with her friend Helene von Mülinen, a leader in the first Swiss women's movement. The feminism which she represented was philanthropic in nature and stemmed from a religiously motivated social involvement. In addition she was closely associated with the Christian Social movement around *Leonhard Ragaz, with whom she had a close relationship. Through her work as collaborator on various Christian Social publications, she enjoyed close contact with a circle of intellectuals who thoroughly examined the question of war and peace.

Pieczynska-Reichenbach's involvement with pacifism was primarily theoretical. She played only a minimal role in pacifist organizations. Although she and Helene von Mülinen were members of the Bernese Friedensverein (Peace Association) in 1896, they never held leading positions. As far as her lecture activities were concerned, however, Pieczynska-Reichenbach dealt repeatedly with the subject of peace. In 1915, for example, she gave a talk to the Women's Club in Morges entitled "Nous femmes, la patrie suisse et l'oeuvre de la paix" ("We Women, the Swiss Fatherland and the Work of Peace"). Her lecture "l'Education pour la paix" (Education for Peace), delivered in Aarau in 1916 at the 20th Christian Student Conference, became famous. In this lecture she supported the conviction that the causes of war lay in man's instinctual nature. For this reason, laws and international agreements were without effect because they did not recognize the deeper causes of war. Peace was constantly being threatened by innate human instinct, i.e. the lust for power and wealth. These instincts could not be controlled by laws because laws merely suppressed rather than destroyed men's drives. According to Pieczynska-Reichenbach, the only possibility for a true pacifism lay in educating men toward peace. This could be accomplished by overcoming the instinctual nature of man which in turn could be accomplished only through acceptance of the Christian ideals of self-denial, readiness to serve, and renunciation of wealth. Although these Christian ideals had existed solely in the asceticism and seclusion of the monastery, she believed they could now play an effective role in society. The first task was to implant these ideals in the minds of educators, so that they, in turn, could serve as examples to the rest of society. Educators would not be in a position to instill peace in others until they themselves had accepted the Christian spirit of self-denial.

Pieczynska-Reichenbach represented a form of pacifism deeply influenced by Christian ideals. It was based on Christian notions of man's sinful nature which, however, could be overcome by following the teachings of Christ. Peace, according to this view, becomes, above all, a problem of educating mankind. Politics, consequently, recedes into the background.

Bibliography:

A. *L'Education pour la paix, Vortag vor der 20. christlichen Studentenkonferenz in Aarau 1916* (Berne, 1916).

B. Elie Gounelle, ed., *Madame E. Pieczynska, Ses Lettres* (Neuchatel and Paris, 1929); Naomi Regard, *Madam E. Pieczynska Sa Vie* (Neuchatel and Paris, 1933); E. Serment, "Emma Pieczynska née Reichenbach, dans ses oeuvres," *Jahrbuch der Schweizerfrauen*, 13 (1927), 113-143.

Brigitte Schnegg
Trans. by Robert C. Reimer

PIERRE, Eugénie. See POTONIÉ-PIERRE, Eugénie.

PIOCH, Georges (9 October 1873, Paris—27 March 1953, Nice, Alpes-Maritimes, France). *Education*: Lycée Chaptal, Paris; attended Sorbonne and Coll. de France. *Career*: poet, journalist, and polemicist.

Born to a modest family, the son of a lead and zinc worker and a seamstress, Georges Pioch nonetheless received a lycée education and attended classes at the Sorbonne and Collège de France, without taking degrees there. After spending a year as a bank employee, he became a proof reader for various newspapers, using his spare time to compose verse and short stories. His literary talents and ability to produce quantities of prose quickly enabled him to join the staffs of such musical and literary reviews as *Musica*, *Comœdia*, and *Gil Blas*. Politically, Pioch allied himself with the anarchist, antimilitarist movement, contributing to *Le Libertaire* and *Temps nouveaux*, as well as to the satirical weekly *Les Hommes du jour*. A great admirer of the Socialist leader *Jean Jaurès, Pioch was profoundly shocked by his assassination and composed many poems in his honor.

With the outbreak of World War I, he was called to the colors but did not see combat because of his weak health and was soon demobilized. Pioch returned to journalism, crusading tirelessly against the war. Many of his articles in *Le Journal du peuple* (which he founded with *Marcelle Capy) and *La Vague* were deleted by the censor. He defended the pacifism of *Romain Rolland and the conferences held at Zimmerwald and Kienthal.

Elected secretary of the Socialist Federation of the Seine in 1920, Pioch enthusiastically joined the newly-founded French Communist party later that year. His numerous articles in *L'Humanité* and *L'Internationale* and his many fiery speeches made him a prominent figure in the party. But by the end of 1922 he broke with it over questions of discipline, forming a "committee of resistance" that publicly attacked its authoritarian organization. Pioch joined other dissidents to form the Parti Communiste Unitaire (Unitary Communist party), but after 1924 adhered to the Socialist party (SFIO). He signed the "Appeal to Consciences" (1926) criticizing the harshness of the Treaty of Versailles and the "Appeal to Good Sense" (1928) calling for international disarmament to prevent war.

During the 1930s Pioch continued his dramatic and political writing for pacifist newspapers such as *La Flèche*, *La Vague*, and *Vendredi*. He joined the Ligue Internationale des combattants de la paix (International League of Fighters for Peace) in 1931, becoming its president by 1938 and speaking his mind in its journal *La Patrie humaine*. A member of the Ligue des droits de l'homme (League for the Rights of Man), Pioch resigned in protest in 1937 because it supported French intervention in the Spanish Civil War and refused to denounce the Moscow purge trials. During the Czech crisis of 1938, he spoke out vigorously on behalf of a peaceful settlement to the problem. After war broke out in September 1939, Pioch signed the manifesto "Paix immédiate," which called for an immediate halt to the conflict. But when threatened with arrest and imprisonment, Pioch broke under the pressure and claimed that he had been duped into signing.

During the early months of the German occupation, Pioch contributed to Marcel Deat's newspaper *L'Oeuvre*. By the end of 1940, however, he was forced from the staff because of his lack of enthusiasm for Nazism. Deprived of a means of expression, he remained passive until the Liberation. After the war he moved to the south of France and resumed his career as a journalist, but he never regained his prewar stature as a spokesman for peace.

Bibliography:

A. *La Paix inconnue et dolente* (Paris, 1929); *Les Résponsables* (Paris, 1916); *Les Victimes* (Paris, 1917).

B. *Nice-Matin*, March 28, 1953.

James Friguglietti

PIRE, Dominique-Georges (10 February 1910, Dinant, Belgium—30 January 1969, Louvain, Belgium). *Education*: Collège de Bellevue, Dinant; studies in philosophy, Couvent de la Sarte, Huy, 1928-32; Doctorate in Theology, Univ. Angelicum, Rome, 1936; studies in social and political sciences, Univ. of Louvain, 1937. *Career*: ordained priest, 1934; teacher of moral philosophy and sociology, Couvent de la Sarte, 1938-48; pacifist and humanitarian.

Father Dominique-Georges Pire's life was devoted to teaching and to providing a wide range of humane and social services to the poor, the displaced, and the disinherited. From 1938, when he established a mutual aid society for poor families (Service d'Entraide familiale), through 1945, when his fresh-air camps for children (Stations de plein air) had served as home for thousands of children from bombed out Belgian towns and from Paris, Lyon, and Cluny, his commitment to charitable work was solidly established. During the war and the occupation, Pire was a chaplain to the underground secret army and an agent of the Services de renseignements et d'action, a communications sector of the Resistance. A visit to a displaced persons camp in 1949 led him to establish L'Aide aux personnes déplacées, which provided services to alleviate the miseries of refugees. These included over 18,000 sponsors who sent mail and packets and the opening of four homes in Belgium and seven villages (in Germany, Austria, and Belgium) to receive refugees and help search for their families. Simultaneously, he launched a European wide movement, L'Europe du coeur, to unite persons of good will across national, social, religious, and linguistic barriers and help fund his activities.

After receiving the Nobel Peace Prize in 1958, Pire moved to extend his labors on behalf of interpersonal communication to a worldwide scale. Le Coeur ouvert sur le monde, founded 1959, promoted a "fraternal dialogue" amongst peoples of greatly differing background. One fruit of this new effort was the establishment of a Peace University in 1960 at Tihange-lez-Huy (now in Namur) which offered short courses in peace activism to men, women, and youth, from all nations. A second initiative was Amitiés mondiales which encouraged friendly exchanges between individuals of widely different backgrounds. A third outcome was Parrainages mondiaux, a system of concrete aid and sponsorship for Asian and African refugees. And finally, he launched the Iles de paix which sought to provide poor, rural Third World communities with aid to develop themselves along autonomous lines in order to reduce their dependence on outside assistance. The first Ile de paix was established in Bangladesh in 1962 and the second in Kalakad, south India in 1968.

For his remarkable devotion to the poor, to war victims, and to the encouragement of understanding among diverse peoples, Pire won — besides the Nobel Peace Prize — the Sonning Prize, awarded in 1968 in Copenhagen in recognition of his services to European culture.

Bibliography:

A. *Bâtir la paix* (Verviers, 1966); "Brotherly Love: Foundation of Peace," in F. W. Haberman, ed., *Nobel Lectures, Peace*, 1972, III, 157-68; *Vivre ou mourir ensemble*, with R. Vander Elst (Brussels, 1969).

B. *Dominique Pire 1958-1978* (Huy, Organizing Committee for the XXth Anniversary of the Dominique Pire Nobel Peace Prize, 1978); Victor Houart, *The Open Heart*, London, 1959; Hugues Vehenne, *Souvenirs et entretiens du R. P. Pire, prix Nobel de la paix* (Brussels, 1959); Franz Weyergans, Le père et l'Europe du coeur (Brussels, 1958).

Nadine Lubelski-Bernard
Trans. by Sandi E. Cooper

PIVERT, Marceau (2 October 1895, Montmachoux, Seine-et-Marne, France —1958, France?). *Education*: diploma, École Normale d'Instituteurs de la Seine, 1914; École Normale Supérieur de Saint Cloud, 1919-21. *Career*: army service, 1915-17; teacher, 1917-19; professor, mathematics and physics, École Primaire Supèrieure, Sens, l'Yonne, 1921; adjunct to office of premier, director of cinema and radio information services, 1926; editor, *Le Drapeau rouge*, 1936-39; professor, lycée Jean-Baptiste Say, Paris, 1946; Socialist party activist.

Marceau Pivert was by vocation an educator; politics was for him a sideline, but one which he pursued with passion. Attracted to socialism while a student at Saint Cloud, upon his appointment at Sens he joined the local section of the Fédération Nationale des Instituteurs (National Federation of Teachers) and the Federation of the Yonne of the French Socialist party, where he was strongly influenced by the antimilitarist ideas of *Gustave Hervé. After the schism of 1920, Pivert remained with the Socialist party, though on the extreme left; he was too much of a rationalist and too much of a democrat to accept the discipline of the Third International. In 1924 he joined the Federation of the Seine, eventually becoming secretary. In 1933 he was elected to the Permanent Administrative Committee of the French Socialist party.

Previously known as an effective propagandist, Pivert began in 1934 the period of his greatest activity as an organizer, especially by founding a Socialist self-defense and antifascist group known as Toujours Prêt Pour Servie (Always Ready to Serve) (TPPS). He utilized the TPPS to organize demonstrations in 1934, 1935, and 1936 in support of the Popular Front movement. Also in 1934, he established a Socialist motion-picture service (Service Cinématographique), which helped record and preserve many activities of workers during the 1930s. In 1936 he served as adjunct to the premier, directing information services by cinema and radio, a post from which he resigned in 1937 as a result of differences with +Léon Blum over the Spanish Civil War.

A member of the left wing of the Socialist party, Pivert joined Jean Zyromski in the Bataille Socialiste, opposing armaments and advocating that the workers refuse to join with bourgeois nationalists in the event of war. When the Franco-Soviet Pact was signed in 1935, however, Zyromski endorsed it as the most effective way of combatting fascism and Nazi Germany. For Pivert, on the other hand, adherence to the pact seemed to be nothing more than a revival of the prewar Triple Entente; support for the alliance would involve workers in the rivalry between bourgeois governments, and thus would be contrary to the class interests of the proletariat. He advocated instead "revolutionary defeatism" — a program of economic boycott, general strike, and revolutionary seizure of power — which he outlined in the pamphlet *Révolution d'abord*. He continued to oppose French rearmament, on the ground that national defense was meaningless under a capitalist regime; in case of war the French proletariat should attack imperialism at home and call upon their German "brothers" to do the same. Only through such a policy could socialism and the Soviet Union be effectively defended.

The result was that in 1935 Pivert broke from the Bataille Socialiste to form another Socialist party group, Gauche Révolutionnaire. His disagreement with Zyromski was matched by his opposition to Blum over the latter's policy of "non-intervention" in the Spanish Civil War. He advocated a policy of full support for the Loyalists, to include arms instead of "tons of string beans," and formed with Zyromski the Comité d'action socialiste pour l'Espagne (Socialist Action Committee for Spain).

In 1937, with the fall of the Blum government, Pivert agreed, in the interest of party unity, to dissolve the Gauche Révolutionnaire, but his intransigent attitude remained. In 1938, after the Anschluss, he distributed an inflammatory tract, "Alerte: le parti est en danger," the result of which led to his exclusion from the French Socialist party. He thereupon founded the Parti Socialiste Ouvrier et Paysan (Socialist Worker and Peasant Party) (PSOP), through which he continued support for the Loyalists and (after the fall of Barcelona) relief for Spanish refugees.

Even after Munich and the Prague occupation, Pivert and the PSOP remained steadfast in opposition to war and in favor of revolutionary action. When war was declared in September 1939, Pivert signed the manifesto "Paix immédiate," drafted by *Louis Lecoin and Nicolas Faucier. Shortly thereafter the PSOP was dissolved and its leaders — lumped with the Communists — arrested, but Pivert was in the United States, having been invited to address union leaders. When France fell, he sent a letter to General Charles de Gaulle in London; dated June 25, 1940, it asked de Gaulle to distribute some "political dynamite" in the form of a recently published manifesto of the Front ouvrier international contre la guerre (to be distributed by airplanes), calling on German soldiers to choose between a hollow national victory and "world revolution." The general declined.

Only in March 1946 was Pivert permitted to return to France, rejoining the Socialist party and again becoming secretary of the Federation of the Seine, and head of the Service Cinématographique. In the following year, he founded the Mouvement démocratique socialiste pour les Etats-Unis de l'Europe, and, in 1948, the Congrès des peuples, made up of residents of the former colonies. In the 1950s Pivert returned to teaching and was active in teaching organizations. Through it all, Pivert remained devoted to his teaching, to the socialist world revolution, and to international peace.

Bibliography:

B. L. Bodin and J. Touchard, *Front populaire 1936* (Paris, 1961); Daniel Guérin, *Front populaire, révolution manquée* (Paris, 1970); Etienne Weill-Raynal, *Marceau Pivert* (Arras, 1958).

Albert S. Hill

PLANCK, Karl Christian (17 January 1819, Stuttgart, Germany—7 June 1880, Winnental, near Stuttgart). *Education*: theological studies, Univ. of Tübingen, 1836-40, Ph.D., 1841. *Career*: instructor, Univ. of Tübingen, 1846-55; secondary school teacher, Ulm, 1855-69; teacher, Protestant Theological Seminary, Blaubeuren, 1869-79; rector, Maulbronn Seminary, 1879; author and philosopher.

Karl Christian Planck, a cousin of the physicist Max Planck, was one of the most productive and versatile thinkers of the nineteenth century. His creative work never received sufficient public acclaim even though or perhaps because his writings were so prophetic. As one of the last universal philosophers he worked in almost all disciplines with the exception of mathematics and medicine. Although a scholar who did not become prominent in the political arguments of his time, Planck, along with *Constantin Frantz, was one of the theoreticians of federalism and provided the political model for several German pacifist groups, whose members included *Otto Umfrid and *Friedrich Wilhelm Foerster.

Planck, who lived in Württemberg, was influenced by south German liberalism. His later philosophical views could already be seen in his dissertation entitled ''Die Völker der neueren Zeit'' (''The Peoples of Modern Time'') in which he attempted to portray the racial character of the ethnic groups surrounding Germany in order to determine the true mission of the German people. In his essay *Katechismus des Rechts* (*Catechism of Law*), published at his own cost in 1852, Planck advanced the idea of a world government, a view not widely held at the time. In this respect Planck saw German unification as a preliminary step to an international confederation.

Planck differentiated between the concepts of morality and law, arguing that the state embodied a moral order only when it was based on a system of law. As long as nations were characterized by arbitrary action and egotism, the relationship between nations would be governed by competition, envy, and finally war. Planck was convinced that the Christian spirit of genuine community would develop only when individuals and nations were members of an overlapping universal order. In order to achieve this genuine community social conflicts had to be reduced. At a time when the capitalist economic system began to evolve in Germany, Planck advocated cooperation between entrepreneurs and workers. He condemned class hatreds and argued that all citizens were entitled to a vocational education and to career advancement. Supporting the right to private property, he also advocated a system of international economic planning that would regulate capitalism.

Planck's philosophical theories achieved importance after 1871 when the supporters of a federated Germany, including Austria, used them in their struggles against the centralized state of Otto von Bismarck. Planck himself rejected any unification of Germany through ''blood and iron.'' He proclaimed in 1866 that Prussia could win the sympathy of the German people only with a policy rooted in the national soil and thus, without war, overcome Austria's opposition to unification under Prussia. Bismarck's policy, on the other hand, forced unity on the people. The result of the ''civil war'' of 1866, according to Planck, was that Austria was excluded from Germany, and the new Klein-Deutschland (Small-Germany) had to abandon the idea of a supernational Christian empire. Instead of accepting its role as mediator between East and West for which it was suited because of its geographic location, Klein-Deutschland, under Prussia's leadership, engaged in selfish national behavior which he felt would give rise to new wars. Planck prophesied, in his main work *Testament eines Deutschen* (*Testament of a German*), published in 1881 after his death, that these terrible future wars finally would make Germany recognize that it was its destiny to create an order of justice and therefore of peace in Europe.

After Planck's death his children promoted his philosophical teachings. His youngest daughter, Mathilde Planck, who was later to become a writer, was particularly active in behalf of her father's legacy and published a comprehensive assessment of his contribution.

Bibliography:

A. *Jean Pauls Dichtung im Lichte unserer nationalen Entwicklung* (Berlin, 1867); *Katechismus des Rechts oder Grundzüge einer Neubildung der Gesellschaft und des States* (Tübingen, 1852); *Süddeutschland und der deutsche Nationalstaat* (Stuttgart, 1868); *Testament eines Deutschen* (Tübingen, 1881); *Wahrheit und Flachheit des Darwinismus, ein Beitrag zur Geschichte heutiger deutscher Wissenschaft* (Nördlingen, 1872); *Die Weltalter*: vol. I, *System des reinen Realismus* (Tübingen, 1850), Vol. II, *Das Reich des Idealismus oder zur Philosophie der Geschichte* (Tübingen, 1871).

B. Mathilde Planck, Karl Christian Planck. Leben und Werk (Stuttgart, 1950); Annemarie Rayhrer, "Karl Christian Planck," *Lebensbilder aus Schwaben und Franken*, 11 (Stuttgart, 1969), 263ff; Otto Umfrid, *Karl Christian Planck* (Tübingen, 1881).

C. Karl Christian Planck Papers, Württemberg State Library, Stuttgart.

Lothar Wieland
Trans. by Robert C. Reimer

PLENER, Ernst von (18 October 1841, Eger, Bohemia, Austria [now Czechoslovakia]—30 April 1923, Vienna). *Education*: Dr. jur., Univ. of Vienna, 1863. *Career*: Austrian diplomat; member, lower house (Reichsrat) of Austrian parliament, 1873-1900; Austrian Finance Minister, 1893-95; member of the Austrian House of Lords (Herrenhaus), 1900-1918; member and (from 1906) chairman, the Austrian delegation to the Interparliamentary Union for International Arbitration, 1889-1914; member, Hague Court, 1899-1914; patent of nobility, 1907.

Ernst von Plener, for half a century a major figure in Austrian parliamentary and public life, shared the ambivalent involvement with the peace movement characteristic of Austrian liberalism and the upper-bourgeois constituency of ethnic Germans of the Habsburg Empire, for whom he was the leading political spokesman. Plener thus supported the Austrian system of universal male conscription, and he believed that for Austria-Hungary the best guarantee of international peace was a strong national military force coupled with close and unswerving support of the Triple Alliance. A leader of the liberal German faction in the Austrian parliament, Plener was an enthusiastic admirer of the Bismarckian system in Germany and argued that only an assertive policy of strength would contain the aggressive tendencies of the Russian Empire and of France, and thus preserve the general peace of Europe. If you want peace, in short, prepare for war. As for the domestic peace of Austria-Hungary, Plener believed that the Habsburg Monarchy should remain firmly controlled by its traditional German ruling elite, even at the expense of suppressing the aspirations of the non-German nationalities. He opposed the introduction of universal suffrage, insisting it would undermine the German hegemony in the Monarchy and open the state to political chaos.

Despite these "hard-line" or imperialistic positions, Plener also believed, as did many liberals of his day, that development of a system of international arbitration administered through duly constituted international tribunals (such as The Hague Court, established in 1899) offered a method better than war for settling those disputes among nations which could not be resolved by the usual processes of diplomacy and which did not threaten a nation's vital interests, sovereignty, or honor. If these last-named were threatened, no nation, Plener held, would surrender its right to go to war in self-defense. The agenda for the peace movement, therefore, Plener urged at the 1906 conference of the Inter-parliamentary Union, was to establish a network of treaties and international conventions by which nations would pledge themselves to submit their future disputes to some form of binding arbitration without raising — at least at the outset — those reservations about vital interests, sovereignty, or national honor. These hopes were all but dashed at the 1907 Hague Conference, when Germany and Austria-Hungary adamantly refused to consider any form of obligatory arbitration — a policy that Plener regarded as shortsighted and mistaken. From 1907 to 1914, Plener worked to find ways to overcome the diplomatic impasse on the arbitration issue, but the outbreak of World War I deprived these efforts of any practical significance.

During the war Plener supported loyally the cause of the Central Powers, regarding Tsarist Russia as the principal enemy. He thus encouraged the pan-German policy of military annexations aimed at creating a German-dominated Central Europe, or "Mitteleuropa," carved principally out of former Russian territories. The defeat of the Central Powers, however, frustrated all such ambitions. After the war, Plener denounced the League of Nations as an organization imposed by the victorious Allied powers to their advantage against the will of the defeated nations. As such, he asserted, the League made a mockery of the basic principles of the Hague Conferences and the spirit of international cooperation manifested in the peace movement before the Great War.

Bibliography:

A. *Erinnerungen von Ernst Plener* (3 vols., Stuttgart and Leipzig, 1921); *Reden von Dr. Ernst Freiherrn von Plener 1873-1911* (Stuttgart and Leipzig, 1911).

B. Albert Fuchs, *Geistige Strömungen in Österreich* (Vienna, 1949), 14-17; *Neue österreichische Biographie 1815-1918*, (Vienna and Leipzig, 1925) 164-85; *Österreichisches biographisches Lexikon 1815-1950*, 8 (Vienna, 1980), 122-23; Hellmuth Rössler and Günther Franz, eds., *Biographisches Worterbuch zur Deutschen Geschichte* (Munich, 1953), 681-82.

Richard R. Laurence

PLOWMAN, Mark (Max) (1 September 1883, London—3 June 1941, London). *Education*: attended several minor private schools until the age of sixteen. *Career*: employed in his father's brick factory at Edmonton; free-lance writer in London after World War I; general secretary, Peace Pledge Union, 1937-38; editor and pacifist author.

Max Plowman's efforts to establish himself in a literary career in London were suddenly interrupted by the outbreak of war in 1914. He volunteered for ambulance service in November of that year and a few months later he received a commission in an infantry regiment. In August 1916 he was sent to the front in France. Early the following year he suffered severe injuries from an exploding shell and was brought back to England. During a long period of convalescence Plowman gradually came to the conclusion that he was really a pacifist. Accordingly, he resigned his commission in January 1918, stating his definite opposition to all forms of organized warfare.

Plowman elaborated upon his antiwar views in a work entitled *War and the Creative Impulse* (1919). Subsequently he related his military experiences in a book published in 1927 under the pseudonym of Mark VII, *A Subaltern on the Somme in 1916*. During the postwar years Plowman gave serious attention to his literary interests. He published a book on William Blake, one of his favorite authors, and produced four books of verse. He also made contributions to *Adelphi*, one of the smaller literary magazines of the time. On two separate occasions he served as an editor of this magazine, the last time being from October 1938 to May 1941.

Plowman remained an unwavering pacifist following World War I. His most important writing concerning the peace movement in Great Britain was *The Faith called Pacifism*, published in London in 1936. Beginning in March 1937 he held for one year the post of general secretary of the Peace Pledge Union, an important antiwar organization that had been founded in May 1936 under the sponsorship of *Dick Sheppard, *George Lansbury, and others. Plowman clearly demonstrated his loyalty to the pacifist cause by devoting to it much time, energy, and talent.

Bibliography:

A. *Bridge into the Future, Letters of Max Plowman*, ed. by D.L.P.[Dorothy Lloyd Plowman] (London, 1944); *The Faith Called Pacifism* (London, 1936); *The Meaning of Rearmament* (London, 1937); *War and the Creative Impulse* (London, 1919).

B. Martin Ceadel, *Pacifism in Britain 1914-1945: The Defining of a Faith* (Oxford, 1980).

C. Max Plowman Papers, University College, London.

Bernerd C. Weber

POLITIS, Nicholas Socrate. See *Biographical Dictionary of Internationalists*.

PONSONBY, Arthur Augustus William Henry; Ponsonby of Shulbrede, First Baron (16 February 1871, Windsor Castle, England—23 March 1946, Hindhead, Sussex, England). *Education*: Eton; attended Balliol Coll, Oxford Univ., 1890-92. *Career*: diplomatic service, 1894-1902; Member of Parliament (Stirling Burghs), 1908-18, (Brightside, Sheffield), 1922-30; Under-Secretary of State for Foreign Affairs, 1924; Parliamentary Under-Secretary for Dominions, 1929; parliamentary secretary, Ministry of Transport, 1929-31; Chancellor of Duchy of Lancaster, 1931; leader of the opposition, House of Lords, 1931-35; politician and antiwar leader.

Arthur Ponsonby, the third son of Sir Henry Ponsonby, private secretary to Queen Victoria, attended Eton and Balliol College, Oxford and then entered the diplomatic service. After holding several posts abroad and in London, Ponsonby resigned in 1902 in order to enter politics. Defeated for a parliamentary seat in 1906, he became the private secretary to Liberal Prime Minister Sir Henry Campbell-Bannerman, and when Campbell-Bannerman died in 1908, Ponsonby took his seat in the House of Commons. By this time he had accepted the tenets of socialism, although he remained a member of the Liberal party. Abhorring the arms race and proposing instead a reduction in armaments, Ponsonby openly criticized the foreign policy of *Sir Edward Grey. When the Liberal party led England into World War I, Ponsonby expressed his opposition on the floor of the House of Commons and became involved in the formation of the Union of Democratic Control. Organized in September 1914, by members of the Liberal and Labour parties who had opposed Britain's entry into the war, the UDC advocated a negotiated settlement of the conflict, free, open, and democratic conduct of diplomacy, international organization of states, and disarmament.

Ponsonby's antiwar activities alienated him from both his colleagues and his constituents. He joined the Independent Labour party and then the Labour party itself, in 1922 regaining a seat in Commons as a member for Labour. He served the first and second Labour governments in numerous capacities and in 1930 entered the House of Lords as Baron Ponsonby of Shulbrede. Upon the formation of the National Government in 1931, Ponsonby became the Labour opposition leader in the House of Lords. He held that position until 1935 when he resigned because of his disagreements with party policy on sanctions and other matters of foreign policy. He then proceeded to devote his time to writing, restricting his political activities to work in support of the Peace Pledge Union. He resigned from the Labour party in May, 1940, when Labour joined the Conservatives in a national coalition to wage war against Germany.

Ponsonby's commitment to peace remained strong throughout the interwar period. In October 1925 he wrote an open letter—the so-called Peace Letter—calling for a public declaration of resistance to war. He received more than 40,000 responses by the following December. Inspired by this evidence of support, he organized the next year a large rally at Albert Hall where many eminent speakers declared their allegiance to pacifism. In December 1927 he was able to present to Prime Minister Stanley Baldwin a petition containing 128,770 signatures. Ponsonby's work as a sponsor of the Peace Pledge Union in the 1930s grew naturally out of his organizing efforts in the 1920s.

In addition to Ponsonby's activities as a politician, a speaker, and an organizer, he contributed to the antiwar effort through his writings. In 1925 he published *Now Is the Time: An Appeal for Peace*, in which he argued that the costs of war invariably outweigh any benefits that waging war might produce. Three years later he published the results of a massive research project on the use of propaganda in World War I. *Falsehood in Wartime* discredited many of the atrocity stories widely circulated by the British government during the war and generated a lasting skepticism of governmental propaganda efforts in wartime.

Arthur Ponsonby outlived the surge of popular pacifism and found himself one of very few in his opposition to the British declaration of war in 1939. One of the most important pacifist leaders during the interwar period, his work with the Union of Democratic Control and his *Falsehood in Wartime* had a strong impact upon British public opinion. He died in 1946.

Bibliography:

A. Martin Ceadel, *Pacifism in Britain 1914-1945: The Defining of a Faith* (Oxford, 1980); Marvin Swartz *The Union of Democratic Control in British Politics during the First World War* (Oxford, 1971); LT, March 25, 1946.

B. *Falsehood in Wartime* (London, 1928); *Now Is the Time; An Appeal for Peace* (London, 1925).

C. Arthur Ponsonby Papers, Bodleian Library, Oxford University.

Gail L. Savage

POPERT, Hermann Martin (12 November 1871, Hamburg, Germany—5 February 1932, Hamburg). *Education*: Dr. jur., Univ. of Leipzig, 1892. *Career*: lawyer; county and district court judge; member, Hamburg City Council, 1907-10; writer and journalist.

Before World War I, Hermann Popert was a Liberal member of the Hamburg city council and active in the abstinence movement. In 1910 he published the novel, *Helmut Harringa*, the theme of which was the struggle against alcoholism. Together with *Hans Paasche, Popert founded *Der Vortrupp. Deutsche Zeitschrift für Menschentum* (*Vanguard. German Journal for Humanity*), which dedicated itself to the search for new values and principles of life.

During World War I, Popert turned his attention to the issue of peace. He differed with pacifists such as *Hellmut von Gerlach and *Alfred H. Fried over the war-guilt question. Although he supported Fried's scientific pacifism and demanded the laying aside of the international anarchy and its replacement by an international legal order, he became convinced, unlike Fried, that France and Russia were chiefly responsible for the war and that Germany bore no responsibility at all. He even considered the attack on Belgium as an act of defense on Germany's part. These views made Popert, who served as an army captain until 1916, representative of a form of German pacifism which sought to fuse patriotism with an abstract commitment to peace. Popert's views led him to support the policy of the German chancellor, Theodor von Bethmann-Hollweg, whom he defended against the chauvinistic agitation of the Pan-Germans. In essays published in the *Vortrupp*, under the pseudonym of Fidelis, Popert justified unrestricted submarine warfare and the peace treaties of Brest-Litovsk and Bucharest.

Taking the view that the Reichstag's Peace Resolution of June 19, 1917, had made pacifism part of the German policy Popert disapproved of the revolution of 1918. With equal vehemence, he spoke out against the Treaty of Versailles. Never becoming part of the organized pacifist movement in Germany, Popert frequently engaged in sharp exchanges with other pacifists such as *Georg F. Nicolai, *Hans Paasche, Fried, and Gerlach. Unlike them he rejected the position that the new Germany had to lay bare the responsibility of Imperial Germany for the outbreak of World War I in order to begin a new democratic existence. Instead he favored an internationalist approach and during the 1920s, he played a leading role in the Deutsche Liga für Völkerbund (German League of Nations Association).

Bibliography:

A. *Tagebuch eines Sehenden 1914-1919* (Hamburg, 1920).

B. Alfred H. Fried, "Deutscher Pazifismus," *Die Friedenswarte*, 19 (1919), 60ff; "Nachruf," *Die Friedenswarte*, 32 (1932), 88; Hans Paasche, "Nationalistische Pazifisten," *Die Friedenswarte*, 20 (1920), 67ff.

C. Hermann Popert Papers, Zentrales Staatsarchiv, Potsdam, German Democratic Republic.

Lothar Wieland
Trans. by Solomon Wank

POTONIÉ-PIERRE, Edmond (21 August 1829, Paris — 22 August 1902, Fonteney-sous-Bois, France). *Career*: language teacher, business representative, journalist, and editor.

In his seventy-three years, Edmond Potonié (he added Pierre to his name after 1879 when he and *Eugénie Pierre established a home together) lived through the birth, decline, and revival of the major continental European peace movements. Born into a comfortable family, his father's circle included *Victor Hugo, *Frédéric Bastiat, Francisque Bouvet, and other liberals who founded the journal *Le Libre Echange* (1846), supported the Revolution of 1848, and helped organize the Paris Peace Congress of 1849. Potonié became an advocate of *Richard Cobden's ideas relating free trade and peace.

As the younger son, Potonié was sent to represent his father's business abroad and made many acquaintances among the liberal elites of Europe. He launched several small newspapers and journals in Belgium and Berlin and in 1858-59, called for the organization of a Ligue du bien public (League for Public Good). Potonié envisioned the League as the successor of the peace congresses which ended in 1853. It stood for an end to standing armies, indirect taxes, and monopolies as well as separation of church and state, guarantees of civil liberties, public education, sexual equality, abolition of the death penalty, and mandatory international arbitration of disputes. Potonié edited and distributed the League's journal, *Le Cosmopolité*, which was disseminated in the Germanies, Italies, England, Belgium, and France when the police of the Second Empire did not confiscate it. During the 1860s while living largely in Berlin, Potonié carried on his peace activities but also began moving in the direction of a vague form of cooperative socialism which was nonviolent and democratic. In 1869 he returned to Paris following serious business setbacks and worked as a salesman there when the Franco-Prussian War broke out.

Potonié was offended when the Ligue internationale de la paix et de la liberté (International League of Peace and Freedom), created in Geneva in 1867 under the presidency of Giuseppe Garibaldi, called its first congress without giving him any recognition for his long years of labors. He eventually overcame his disappointment and merged *Le Cosmopolité* with *Les Etats-Unis d'Europe*, the Genevan league's journal. He was also suspicious of *Frédéric Passy's Paris based Ligue internationale et permanente de la paix (International and Permanent League of Peace), also organized in 1867, because it had obtained permission from the Imperial police to hold meetings, and, therefore in Potonié's estimation, could not be seriously committed to the cause. His jealousies and suspicions prevented him from actively working for these organizations even though they were committed to the same ends. Potonié preferred to work outside their aegis, and during the 1870-71 war, he attempted to organize a balloon brigade to leaflet German soldiers and remind them of their obligation not to kill French workers. The project never materialized but Potonié himself fell under suspicion during the Commune and was nearly arrested.

From 1873-78, Potonié returned to Berlin where he attempted to revive the failing family business as well as busy himself with a variety of publications, including various peace pamphlets and irregularly published journals. On his return to Paris in 1879 he became editor of *Le Travailleur* (later *Le Travailleur des Villes et Campagnes*) and met the young Eugénie Pierre who had just moved to the city and become active in Leon Richer's women's rights movement. They shared the rest of their lives together, refusing legal marriage on principle and each taking the other's name. Despite limited income and a frugal life style which included language lessons for income, they both gave generously of their small resources and immense energies to social and political causes. Both shared a commitment to cooperative socialism, feminism, pacifism, and human rights.

Potonié-Pierre's commitment to peace activities remained alive through the 1880s and 1890s mainly in the form of writing and editing. He published *Petits Plaidoyers contre la guerre* (*Small Arguments Against War*), a newsletter which appeared irregularly and was sent all over Europe. In *Un Peu plus tard* (*A Little Later*) (1893), a utopian novel probably written by Potonié and his wife, he chronicled the peace movement and fantasized a mid-twentieth century where armaments did not exist and a regime of international law governed world relationships. In 1899 he issued his *Histoire du mouvement pacifiste* (*History of the Peace Movement*), an important source of nineteenth-century peace activities. While he was in touch with the International Peace Bureau in Berne, he took no part in the organized national or international congresses that revived after 1889 and viewed them as too timid and conservative. Until his death, Potonié-Pierre considered the cause of peace as indissolubly linked to issues of social justice and criticized the international movement for not addressing this interconnection. In many ways, Potonié-Pierre's pacifism was the most radical of the entire century.

Bibliography:

A. *Histoire du mouvement pacifiste* (Paris, 1899); *Un Peu Plus Tard* (Paris, 1893).

B. Jean Maitron, ed., *Dictionnaire Biographique du Mouvement Ouvrier Français, 1864-71* (Paris, 1970), VIII, 230.

C. Dossier B[A]/1.224 in Préfecture de Police, Seine; Correspondence in Bureau international de la paix, The Archives, Library of the United Nations (Geneva).

Sandi E. Cooper

POTONIÉ-PIERRE, Eugénie (5 November 1844, L'Orient, Morbihan, France — 12 June 1898, Paris). *Career*: founder, La Solidarité des femmes, 1891; founder (with *Ellen Robinson), L'Union internationale des femmes pour la paix, 1895; teacher, labor organizer, journalist, editor, and feminist.

From 1878 when she moved to Paris until her death 20 years later, Eugénie Potonié-Pierre devoted her entire energy to causes for social justice, equality, and peace. She was one of the first feminists in France to move away from the purely legalistic and cultural demands of the movement for equality to struggle for political rights and equality of pay. A tireless organizer and speaker, she first attracted police notice when she circulated a petition at a teacher's meeting protesting social injustice and attended a private meeting where universal suffrage was urged (1881).

In 1879-80 she and *Edmond Potonié met and became lifelong companions, sharing each others names and political concerns but refusing on principle to join in legal marriage. They crusaded for cooperatives, amnesty for condemned Communards, free and secular public education, sexual equality, and international peace. Eugénie Potonié-Pierre did not shy from unconventional tactics. On one occasion, she persuaded a feminist group in Paris to question candidates for the National Assembly despite the fact that the women could not vote. Though a convinced socialist, she never refrained from criticizing Jules Guesde and leading French socialists for footdragging on women's issues. She also conducted an acerbic public exchange with French officials on conditions of employment for women in public services such as the post office and took on Cesare Lombroso, the famous Italian sociologist, for his views of what constituted a normal woman.

Among nineteenth-century feminists, Eugénie Potonié-Pierre was one of the first to see the connection between women's status and the international system. She wrote numerous pieces to publicize the work of peace organizations and in the official peace movement circles, she endeavored to make women's equality a central concern. During the 1890s, with *Ellen Robinson and several others, she launched the appeal to create an international network of feminists and women peace activists which became L'Union internationale des femmes pour la paix

(International Union of Women for Peace). Such an organization had been proposed in 1868 by *Marie Goegg and a call had gone out to establish it, but the results of that early initiative were largely confined to Switzerland. The new group established its task as coordinating the work of women in the United States, Britain, France, Italy, and Germany.

While the official peace movement during the 1890s cautiously confined itself to calling for ways to establish international legal arrangements, Eugénie Potonié-Pierre called directly for disarmament (arms limitations) to be initiated at once by a conference of powers. Her view was simple and direct — the cost of maintaining armaments was the cause of social misery and a major reason for women's oppression. The weapons of one year could fund all the needed day-care centers in France to help women go to work. In the utopian novel written by "E. Potonié-Pierre" (which appears to be a collaboration) entitled *Un Peu plus tard* (*A Little Later*) (1893), a twentieth century world of international peace (achieved through law), armies that perform the work of labor brigades, and social justice was portrayed. This fantasy, merging feminism, socialism, and pacifism, was what the future could be like were the principles of these three great movements merged. Eugénie Potonié-Pierre was directly responsible for injecting a feminist vision into *Un Peu plus tard*, but her consort, Edmond, was its official author.

Bibliography:

B. Jean Maitron, ed., *Dictionnaire Biographique du Mouvement Ouvrier Francais, 1871-1914* (Paris, 1976), XIV, 298.

C. Scattered letters in Bibliothèque Marguerite Durand, Paris; and the Bureau international de la paix, Archives, Library of the United Nations, Geneva.

Sandi E. Cooper

POTVIN, Charles (2 December 1818, Mons, Belgium — 2 March 1902, Brussels). *Education*: law, Univ. of Louvain. *Career*: founder, *La Belgique démocratique*, 1849; founder and editor, *La Revue de Belgique*, 1869-93; editor, *Le Nation*; director, Musée Wiertz, 1883-1902; member, Association internationale des amis de la paix, 1867; author, poet, literary critic, journalist, and pacifist.

After a youth troubled by personal difficulties — which coincided with the conflicts of newly independent Belgium — Charles Potvin emerged as a spokesman for liberal ideas. His political writings revealed a commitment to equality, progress, and peace. He was an adversary of religious fanaticism and clerical chicaneries; he defended the destitute and attacked French annexationist designs on Belgium. The means by which nations could achieve peace were, for him, a constant preoccupation.

With the outbreak of the Franco-Prussian War in 1870, Potvin urged the Brussels Loge des amis philanthropes to send an address to both German and French lodges to mobilize on behalf of a quick and peaceful solution. The Germans were asked not to use race, nationality, and the argument of national security as a pretext for extending their frontiers. The French were asked to work for a true peace, including disarmament and not a peace that was the usual interlude between warfare or an invitation for reprisals. Both nations were asked to sign a preliminary protocol to initiate a union and a lasting peace.

Later, in 1872, Potvin presented the same Lodge with a report on peace prepared by a committee of Masons. This study summarized every imaginable method of preventing armed conflict that had ever been devised, but noted that no previously proposed plan had examined the deep-seated causes of war or the social necessities which it served. Potvin concluded that only ''science'' — meaning study and increased knowledge — would eventually be able to eliminate war. The science of peace, he wrote, is ''the most essential requirement of modern civilization, the only hopeful haven for the freedom of nations.''

Bibliography:

A. *Adressé à tous les maçons de France et d'Allemagne* (Brussels, September 15, 1870); *L'Appel à l'Europe, réponse aux limites de la France par un Belge* (Brussels, 1853); *1852 ou la paix en Belgique* (Brussels, 1851); *Le génie de la paix en Belgique, écrivains, diplomates, utopistes, professeurs et pamphlétaires. Esquisse historique* (Brussels, 1871); *Du gouvernement de soi-même*, vol. VI of *Les Nations, droit international, la paix et la guerre* (Verviers, 1877); *Rapport sur la question de la paix*, with P. Tempels and E. Feron, in *La Chaîne d'union de Paris, Journal de la Maçonnerie Universelle*, 9 (August 1, 1872), 463-67.

B. Charles Conrardy, *Essai sur Charles Potvin, 1818-1902* (Brussels, 1925); E. De Seyn, *Dictionnaire des Ecrivains Belges* (Bruges, 1931), II, 1483; M. Wilmotte, ''Charles Potvin'' in *Revue de Belgique*, 100 (1902), 203-13; Académie Royale de Belgique, *Notices biographiques*, 1896, p. 573; *Bibliographie Nationale*, III, 1897, 178-83; *Biographie Nationale*, 34, cols. 664-70.

Nadine Lubelski-Bernard
Trans. by Sandi E. Cooper

PRATT, Hodgson (10 January 1824, Bath, England — 26 February 1907, Le Pecq, Seine et Oise, France). *Education*: Haileybury Coll. (near Coventry, England), 1844-46. *Career*: employee, East India Co.; public official, government of Bengal; author, editor, and peace advocate.

After serving in India for fourteen years where he was employed by the East India Company and the government of Bengal as an under-secretary and inspector of public instruction, Hodgson Pratt returned to England in 1861. He remained interested in Indian affairs, but also became active in the workingmen's improvement movement. He supported the industrial cooperative movement, serving on the council of the Working Men's Club and Institute Union and acting as its president (1885-1902), initiating trade classes for working men in London, and promoting international understanding among the working classes.

Pratt was a major figure in the British and European peace movements, primarily as a leading advocate of the theory of international arbitration as a substitute for war. He deplored the Franco-Prussian War (1870) which he thought could have been resolved by negotiations and came out against Britain's many wars of imperial expansion which plagued the Empire from Benjamin Disraeli's second ministry forward. In 1877 he joined in the founding of the International Arbitration and Peace Association (IAPA) of the United Kingdom and Ireland, serving on the executive committee; and in 1884, he founded and edited the Association's publication. On behalf of the Association he visited the Continent helping in the foundation and promotion of peace and arbitration organizations in the major countries of Europe. He also attended numerous international peace congresses.

The IAPA stood for the prevention and suppression of war through agitation, lobbying, pressure tactics, electoral politics, and publication campaigns. Advocating arbitration and disarmament, the IAPA favored the inclusion of an arbitration clause in the Treaty of Berlin (1878), petitioned Otto von Bismarck to support arbitration, and issued peace declarations during the Eastern crisis. Linked to the Peace Society with which it shared many members and ideals, the IAPA was also tied to the Trades Unions Congress, the Workmen's Peace Association, and the pacifist wing of the Liberal party, especially the Radical element. Pratt headed the British delegation at the 1882 Brussels Peace Congress, organized by *Henry Richard and sponsored by the IAPA. Attended by over five hundred delegates from various countries, the congress promoted arbitration, disarmament, international law, and international tribunals. Two years later, as chairman of the IAPA Executive Committee, Pratt visited France in an effort to settle the crisis in Egypt by compromise and to establish an international peace federation.

The British imperialist adventures in Egypt divided the IAPA. The membership hotly debated the issue of ''just'' wars and the sending of troops up the Nile River. The 1885 war scare involving Russia and Britain also divided the IAPA, as the Russophobe faction, led by Dr. Karl Blind, a member of the executive Committee, thought arbitration with Russia was impossible because of the barbaric and despotic nature of the country. Pratt worked hard to disavow Blind's views.

Toward the end of his life Pratt's peace work expanded. Not only did he continue to attend many international peace meetings, but he also undertook the IAPA sponsored translations of *Elie Ducommun's *The Programme of the Peace Movement* (1896) and *Edouard Descamp's *The Organization of International Arbitration* (1897). His supporters recommended him for a Nobel Peace Prize in 1906, the year in which +Theodore Roosevelt received the reward.

Pratt's retiring disposition and his failing eyes combined with his inclination to the role of facilitator prevented him from acquiring great prominence or fame. He provided stable, moderate, and energetic services as a member and chairman of the Executive Council of the IAPA leaving the roles of politician, prophet, and preacher to more charismatic and more aggressive members of the peace movement.

Bibliography:

A. *Address by the President of the International Arbitration and Peace Association at its Seventeenth Annual Meeting* (London, 1898); *A Peacemaker in Germany* (London, 1887); *A Selection of Articles and Letters on Various Indian Questions* (London, 1857); *University Education in England for Natives of India* (London, 1860).

B. DNB, 1901-11, 132-33; Lt, March 5, 1907.

John V. Crangle

PROUDHON, Pierre-Joseph (15 February, 1809, Besançon, France — 19 January 1865, Paris). *Education*: self-educated. *Career*: newspaper editor, parliamentary representative during Revolution of 1848; leading socialist theoretician and propagandist.

Pierre-Joseph Proudhon's views were greatly influenced by the character of the times in which he lived. The development of capitalist industry in France after the Napoleonic Wars and the generally peaceful character of international relations formed the background to his activity.

Like many others, Proudhon was struck by the apparent disorganization and anarchy of production. His early writings attacked private property and the state as the sources of social conflict, and he argued that everyone should be able to satisfy basic needs. His desire to ensure peace led him to equivocate during the Revolution of 1848, and he turned toward the theory of "mutualism" after 1852 in an effort to promote harmony, justice, and peace.

The free exchange of equivalents, guaranteed by the preservation of different centers of production, was the basis of the "mutualist" economic order and its federalist political form. The increased production which would result from the liberation of market forces would guarantee social peace as the arbitrary state was absorbed back into society and free association replaced force as the cement of society. Social peace would result from the balancing of autonomous centers of production.

Proudhon began thinking about war after Louis-Napoleon's Italian adventure of 1859, and the result was *La Guerre et la Paix* (1861). It was his only systematic analysis of war, and he did the same thing for the "principle of war" that he had done earlier for the economic categories: he tried to isolate war from other "social categories" and analyze its internal contradictions. His effort was to identify the "good" and "bad" aspects of war and figure out how its ennobling, purifying side could be separated from its destructive and degrading side. His conclusion was familiar: the positive aspects of war could be developed only if the economy was organized along "mutualist" lines. The way he had structured his argument made it appear that he was defending war—which was certainly not his intention.

Proudhon believed that injustice and social disorganization was the cause of war and conflict. Violence could not be eliminated until inequality was ended and society reconstructed along "rational" lines. The reign of political economy would be the reign of peace. Social equilibrium and harmony would come with the organization of work and the protection of small property.

Bibliography:

A. *Oeuvres complètes* (Paris, 1923); *Correspondence* (Paris, 1875).

B. Robert L. Hoffman, *Revolutionary Justice: The Social and Political Theory of P.-J. Proudhon* (Urbana, IL, 1972); Karl Marx, *The Poverty of Philosophy* (New York,

1963); Allen Ritter, *The Political Thought of Pierre-Joseph Proudhon* (Princeton, 1969); George Woodcock, *Pierre-Joseph Proudhon* (London, 1956).

C. Proudhon Papers, Bibliothèque Nationale, Paris, France.

John Ehrenberg

PRUDHOMMEAUX, Jules Jean (2 November 1869, Chevennes, Aisne, France — sometime after 1945, France). *Career*: university professor; founding member, Association de la paix par le droit; editor (with *Lucien Le Foyer), *La Paix par le Droit*; director, European Center of the Carnegie Endowment for International Peace.

Jules Prudhommeaux was an indefatigable worker in the cause of peace. In 1887, at the age of eighteen, he became a founding member of the Association de la paix par le droit (Association of Peace Through Law) (APD), which merged in 1912 with the Société pour l'arbitrage entre les nations (Society for International Arbitration). In 1922 the APD formed a close association, although not a merger, with the Association française pour la société des nations (French League of Nations Association), Prudhommeaux was its president in 1932, as well as secretary-general of the Fédération des associations françaises pour la société des nations (Federation of French Associations for the League of Nations). From 1911, when it was founded, Prudhommeaux was director of the European Center for the Carnegie Endowment for International Peace. As a delegate from one or more of the above organizations he was a member of the Délégation permanente des sociétés françaises pour la paix (Permanent Delegation of French Peace Societies) and, in that capacity, attended virtually every national and international peace congress between the two World Wars, as well as several before 1914. In these organizations he was closely associated with *Théodore Ruyssen, *Frédéric Passy, and *Charles Richet.

Prudhommeaux's pacifism was that of a bourgeois intellectual, placing strong emphasis on the rule of law and great faith in the role of education. He lectured tirelessly before any group that would hear him, making use of the large collection of lantern slides in the library of the APD. Moreover, he was the author of several hundred articles for pacifist journals—more than 200 prior to 1911. Disavowing the more militant forms of pacifist action, he avoided association with such groups as the Ligue des réfractaires (League of Insubordinates) or the Ligue des objecteurs de conscience (League of Conscientious Objectors). He was not a socialist.

Yet, Prudhommeaux recognized the need for involving the masses. In 1905, at the Congrès internationale de la paix (Lucerne), he noted that the pacifist movement had been largely the work of intellectuals and the middle class, and called for promoting it among the workers. To this end, he proposed to the Carnegie Foundation in 1921 an inquiry into schoolbooks, especially history texts, for the purpose of eliminating chauvinist and bellicose interpretations. The culmination was the publication in 1923 of the *Enquête sur les livres scolaire d'après guerre* by the Foundation, a study of the textbooks of the principal belligerents; a second volume, on sixteen other countries and rather less forceful, was published in 1927. As a result, the French teachers' unions—as well as those of other nations—launched a campaign to purge schoolbooks of the offending material.

In 1931 the APD, with Prudhommeaux as secretary-general, arranged exchanges of correspondence between nearly 10,000 French and German schoolchildren, and during several years organized an international summer school for teachers. In the same year, Prudhommeaux was a member of the Quaker Peace Action Committee, participated in the organization of the informal Disarmament Conference, and attended the national conference of the Association française pour la paix par l'éducation (French Association of Peace Through Education).

Prudhommeaux was one of the principal figures in the formation of the Cartels de la paix in 1932; these were local and departmental committees that coordinated the activities of the various peace groups and that sponsored peace caravans of antiwar films and speeches. When the Spanish Civil War erupted, Prudhommeaux was one of the founders of the Comité d'action pour la paix en Espagne (Action Committee for Peace in Spain), serving as a vice-president until the end of the hostilities and beyond. The group advocated mediation by the League of Nations and a plebiscite.

With the outbreak of the war in 1939 Prudhommeaux was forced to suspend open action in defense of peace, as did so many others. In 1945 he was again involved in APD, but not as active as in previous years. His peace work had spanned more than half a century.

Bibliography:

A. *Les causes économiques des guerres moderne* (Lyons, 1901); *Le Centre Européen de la Dotation Carnegie pour la paix internationale, 1911-1921* (Paris, 1921); *Cooperation et pacification* (Paris, 1904); *France et Allemagne: la cours à l'abime* (Nimes, 1913); "La Litterature scolaire d'apres guerre en France et en Belgique," in *Enquêtes sur les livres scolaire d'apres guerre* (Paris, 1923), *Pour la paix par l'école* (Nimes, 1924); *Les Rapports du pacifisme et du mouvement ouvrier* (Nimes, 1905).

B. Alfred Fried, "Jules Prudhommeaux," in *Handbuch der Friedensbewegung* (Leipzig, 1911-13), II, 392.

Albert S. Hill

Q

QUESADA, Vincente Gregorio (5 April 1830, Buenos Aires, Argentina—19 September 1913, Buenos Aires). *Education*: Dr. jur., Univ. of Buenos Aires, 1855. *Career*: diplomat, politician, author, and historian.

Vincente Quesada served the cause of peace both as a deputy to the Argentine Congress and as a government official. In 1856, his first year in Congress, he spoke out vigorously for national unity while Buenos Aires and the provinces of the interior continued their divisive battles. He had witnessed first-hand the damage caused by these on-going hostilities, for in 1852, when he was returning from a diplomatic mission to Bolivia, he had traversed the interior and had encountered severe violence in the Argentine provinces. He returned to Buenos Aires where he completed his studies in law at the University of Buenos Aires and became involved in both politics and journalism (writing for *El Comercio* and *El Nacional Argentino*). In his speeches as well as his writings he defended the cause of Argentine confederacy.

In 1858, the year of Argentina's unification, Quesada again served as a deputy in Congress and then left politics to pursue a career in publishing. In the ensuing years he was offered numerous government positions which he refused. He did, however, accept the directorship of the Buenos Aires public library and two years later, in 1873, a commission to acquire manuscripts about colonial history from Spain. Eventually, in 1877, he accepted appointment as Minister of Government for the province of Buenos Aires. His return to politics came at a crucial time in Argentine history, for in 1877 rivalries between Bartolome Mitré and Alfonso Alsina threatened Argentina with civil war once more. Quesada's moderation and prudence proved essential to the reconciliation of the rival factions.

After being elected and serving a term in Congress in 1878, Quesada left politics once more and continued his pursuit of historical studies. In 1881 he published a paper entitled "El Virreinato del Rio de la Plata, 1773-1810" ("The Viceroyalty of Rio de la Plata, 1773-1810"), which provided the fundamentals for the peaceful resolution of the Andean boundary question between Argentina and Chile. Two years after the publication of this treatise, Quesada returned to his role of diplomat abandoned more than three decades before.

Quesada was first assigned Brazil's Imperial court where he worked to eliminate boundary problems that troubled the two countries. After serving two years in Brazil, he was appointed to the United States in 1885. He served six years in Washington before going on to his next assignment in Mexico. Quesada's initial mission in the U.S. was to present the Argentine government's claims against the Americans for their role in the British takeover of the Malvinas

Islands earlier in the nineteenth century. His service in Washington and later in Mexico impressed his hosts in such a way that in 1897 both governments agreed to name him sole arbitrator in one claims dispute. Before finishing his diplomatic career in 1904, Quesada also served in Madrid and Rome. His three-volume diplomatic history of Latin America, published posthumously, was a pioneering work in that field.

Throughout his lifetime Quesada continued with his writing, published numerous works, at times under pseudonyms such as Víctor Gálvez and Domingo de Pantoya. He was also president of the Argentine Academy of the Faculty of Philosophy and Letters and corresponding member of Spain's Royal Academy of Language and History.

Bibliography:

A. *Los Estados Unidos y La América del sur: Los Yankees pintados por si mismos* (pseud. Domingo de Pantoya, Buenos Aires, 1893); *Historia diplomática Latino-Americana* (3 vols., Buenos Aires, 1919-20); *Memorias de un viejo: Escenas de costumbres de la República Argentina* (pseud. Victor Galvez, Buenos Aires, 1912); *Memorias Diplomáticas: Misión ante el gobierno del Brasil* (Buenos Aires, 1907); *Recuerdos de mi vida diplomática: Misión en México*, 1981 (Buenos Aires, 1904).

Abelardo A. Arias

QUIDDE, Ludwig (23 March 1858, Bremen, Germany—5 March 1941, Geneva). *Education*: Ph.D., Univ. of Göttingen, 1881. *Career*: member, Historical Commission of the Bavarian Academy of Sciences, 1897; professor and first secretary of the Prussian Historical Institute in Rome, 1890; editor, *Deutsche Reichstagsakten* (ältere Reihe), *Deutsche Zeitschrift für Geschichtswissenschaft*; pacifist, historian, and politician.

Coming from an upper-middle class merchant family, Ludwig Quidde early adopted a democratic great-German and anti-Prussian position towards the politics of Otto von Bismarck and, later, towards the Wilhelmine system. His political orientation manifested itself in his joining the Deutsche Volkspartei (German People's Party) in 1893, in his essay "Der Militarismus in heutigen Deutschen Reich" ("Militarism in the German Empire of Today") (1893), and above all in the satirical essay "Caligula" (1894), which was directed against Emperor Wilhelm II. The latter essay unleashed a scholarly row which ranged the academic establishment against Quidde and destroyed his university career.

Living in Munich since 1890, Quidde's political and parliamentary activity was determined from then on by the south German middle-class democratic milieu of the city. As a member of the left-liberal German People's party and then of the Fortschrittliche Volkspartei (Progressive People's Party), he belonged to the Munich Community Council from 1902 until 1911, and to the Bavarian state legislature from 1907 until 1918. As a member of the newly founded Deutsche Demokratische Partei (German Democratic Party) he serve in the provisional Bavarian National Council in 1918-19, and in the German Constituent

National Assembly in 1919. After 1920 Quidde no longer held a parliamentary mandate.

Quidde's pacifistic activity began in the context of the Peace Association in Munich. His agitation for an end to the Boer War led to his becoming known in pacifist circles far beyond the boundaries of Munich. As a result, he became entrusted with leadership tasks within the German peace movement. From 1901 on, he led the German delegation at World Peace Congresses, and he contributed greatly to the success of the 1907 World Peace Congress held in Munich. In addition, he belonged to the International Peace Bureau as the German representative and, at the same time, to the executive council of the Deutsche Friedensgesellschaft (German Peace Society) since 1902. From 1902, he was a member of the German group of the Interparliamentary Union. His organizational talent and his willingness to compromise were helpful at the meetings of the German and French parliamentarians in Berne (1913) and Basel (1914), at which new possibilities of reconciliation between the two countries were discussed. On the eve of World War I, Quidde became the head of the German Peace Society.

The war put his organizational talent to a hard test in view of the oppressive measures of the military authorities. Quidde was the author of numerous petitions to the Reichstag in which the German peace movement took positions on important political events. At the same time, Quidde faced difficulties within the peace movement. His conviction that the Central Powers were not solely responsible for the outbreak of the war found opposition in peace movement ranks; among peace advocates abroad, Quidde's attitude towards the government during the war was regarded as too compromising. His leadership, based more on educated middle-class supporters rather than on the proletarian masses, was criticized as out of date. His negative attitude towards the peace treaty of Versailles, which he expressed publicly for the first time in the Constituent National Assembly in May 1919, was not unanimously shared within the German peace movement.

Although criticism of Quidde within his own ranks could not be silenced after 1919, he was, even if under discouraging conditions, repeatedly confirmed as head of the German Peace Society and he also headed the German Peace Cartel, an umbrella organization that brought together all of the new pacifist organizations founded after the war. His paramount organizational aim remained the preservation of the unity of the German peace movement and its closest possible connection with the political parties of the Weimar coalition which identified with the republic and provided governments for it. The attainment of this aim became increasingly more difficult because of the rightward movement of Quidde's own German Democratic party, and because of the increasing radicalization of German pacifism.

At the beginning of 1924, Quidde was imprisoned by the Bavarian authorities for exposing the illegal rearming of the German army contrary to the Versailles peace treaty. His release and the suppression of treason charges followed a strong démarche by the English government. To the displeasure of other German pacifists, Quidde was inclined in the future to take official German assertions about the nonexistence of illegal German armaments at face value. Together with *Ferdinand Buisson, Quidde received the Nobel Peace Prize in 1927. Two years later he was pushed out of the presidency of the German Peace Society by the more radical wing around *Fritz Küster and *Baron Paul von Schoenaich. Resignedly, Quidde withdrew from the organization without, however, giving up his international activities, above all his position with the International Peace Bureau.

In 1930 Quidde lost his political home when he refused to go along with the fusion of the German Democratic party and the antipacifist and latently anti-Semitic Jungdeutschen Orden (Young German Order) to form the Deutsche Staatspartei (German State Party). With little conviction, he took part in the creation of the unsuccessful Radikaldemokratischen Partei (Radical Democratic Party). Quidde escaped arrest by the Nazis and probable internment in a concentration camp by fleeing to Switzerland in the spring of 1933. There he lived in straitened financial circumstances until his death, supported largely by grants from the Nobel committee of the Norwegian parliament in return for writing his (uncompleted and posthumously published) work on German pacifism in the First World War.

Quidde's pacifist activity, which he continued in exile, extended to his participation in the work of the International Peace Bureau, attendance at World Peace Congresses and at national peace conferences in Switzerland and France, as well as to the formation of an organization to aid émigré German pacifists. His statements in favor of the ostensible peace policy of Hitler, by which Quidde perhaps sought to protect from persecution his half-Jewish wife who had remained behind in Munich, aroused the strong displeasure of other émigré pacifists. In any event, he was deprived of his German citizenship only after the death of his wife in June 1940.

Quidde was a prominent representative of liberal German pacifism who, grounded in the ethical rigorism of Immanuel Kant, comprehended the will to peace essentially as an expression of individual insight, effort, and conviction. Consequently, he could neither negotiate between organized pacifism and modern mass democracy, nor could he maintain organized pacifism in the face of the ethical nihilism of fascism. However, his failure in this regard is, at the same time, an expression of the failure of political democracy and its political value system in the Weimar Republic.

Bibliography:

A. *Der deutsche Pazifismus während des Weltkrieges 1914-1918. Aus dem Nachlass Ludwig Quidde*, ed. by Karl Holl (Boppard, 1979).

B. Karl Holl, "Ludwig Quidde. Das Leben eines Deutschen Pazifisten," in *Der deutsche Pazifismus während des Weltkrieges 1914-1918. Aus dem Nachlass Ludwig Quidde*, ed. by Karl Holl (Boppard, 1979); Utz-Friedebert Taube, *Ludwig Quidde. Ein Beitrag zur Geschichte des demokratischen Gedankens in Deutschland* (Kallmünz, 1963); NYT, March 8, 1941, 19.

C. Nachlass Ludwig Quidde, Bindesarchiv, Coblenz; Fonds Quidde, Archives de la Société des nations, Geneva; Quidde Papers, Swarthmore College Peace Collection; Nachlass Margarethe Quidde, Handschriftensammlung der Stadtbibliothek München.

Karl Holl
Trans. by Solomon Wank

QUINCY, Edmund (1 February 1808, Boston, MA.—17 May 1877, Dedham, MA). *Education*: B.A., Harvard Coll., 1827, M.A., 1830. *Career*: editor, *The Non-Resistant*, 1839-42, *The National Anti-Slavery Standard*, 1844-65; pacifist and reformer.

Educated at the Phillips Academy in Andover, Massachusetts, and a member of the Harvard College class of 1827, Edmund Quincy opened a law office in 1830 but never seriously considered the law his true profession. For ten years following graduation, he drifted aimlessly between Beacon Hill salons, the theatre, and a promising literary career, unsure of his calling yet deeply troubled by his lack of decision.

By 1837 parental pressure, his marriage to Lucilla Pinckney Parker, the burden of his family name—his grandfather was a Revolutionary era hero, his father a congressman, mayor of Boston, and president of Harvard College, and his brother a railroad director and rising figure in the Whig party—together with attendance at the soul-prodding sermons of *William Ellery Channing, awakened Quincy to the need for action. Earlier, in 1835, he had witnessed the anti-abolition riot against *William Lloyd Garrison, outspoken editor of the Boston *Liberator*, which incited him to a detailed study of the slavery question. The next year conversations with Harvard friend Richard Hildreth, recently returned from a Florida plantation, the congressional gagging of cousin John Quincy Adams for introducing antislavery petitions on the floor of the House, and most importantly, the November 1837 murder of Elijah Parish Lovejoy by another anti-abolition mob in Alton, Illinois, convinced Quincy that the antislavery movement represented a Christian crusade and the completion of the work begun by his revolutionary forebears.

At the *Liberator* office, Boston headquarters of the Garrisonian abolitionists, Quincy met other reformers and early in 1838 he participated in a series of discussions on pacifism with Garrison, *George Beckwith, *Joshua P. Blanchard, *William Ladd, *Samuel J. May, and *Henry Clarke Wright. Quincy was at first hesitant to accept the doctrines of absolute pacifism and nonresistance to authority, but by September he had not only helped organize a peace convention but also helped found the New England Non-Resistance Society and shortly thereafter accepted the editorship of its journal, *The Non-Resistant*.

Between 1839 and 1842, during which time he edited *The Non-Resistant* and served as a member of the Executive Board of the Non-Resistance Society, Quincy remained one of the most outspoken pacifists in ante-bellum America. Through *The Non-Resistant* he advocated love of enemies, self-sacrifice, and forgiveness of injuries. In addition, unlike the American Peace Society and other pacifist groups that recognized the beneficial aspects of civil government, he believed all agencies of the state incompatible with true pacifist principles. Since any state that participated in wars, executed criminals, or supported slavery was beyond regeneration, he reasoned, moral suasion and personal regeneration rather than political reforms should be employed.

Quincy not only advocated these principles, he lived them, As a practicing nonresistant, he renounced allegiance to all governments and all recourse to physical force. He opposed not only all wars, offensive or defensive, but all preparations for war. Applying these beliefs to his private life, Quincy resigned his commission as Justice of the Peace, withdrew from all organized religion, and for more than twenty-five years refused to vote, explaining that he could not in good conscience obey the directives of any institution that employed, supported, or sanctioned force.

When financial difficulties forced an end to *The Non-Resistant* in June 1842, Quincy continued his active involvement in the peace movement through the Non-Resistance Society. The annexation of Texas, the election of James K. Polk, and the growing antislavery sentiment in the North, however, soon commanded his full attention and he decided to accept the editorship of the New York *National Anti-Slavery Standard*. Through the antislavery press Quincy remained faithful to his pacifist principles. He denounced the Mexican War as a proslavery conspiracy, as bloody, wasteful, and immoral. At the outbreak of the Civil War he favored peaceful secession of the South, thinking it would save lives and eventually lead to the nonviolent abolition of slavery.

After the war, with emancipation accomplished and the triumph of the Radical Republicans assured, Quincy retired from active life and rather surprisingly returned to the cavalier style of earlier days. He spent the last decade of his life writing a biography of his father and articles for the New York *Independent*, reopening old friendships which politics and reform had soured, and supervising affairs on his Dedham estate. He died suddenly on May 17, 1877.

Bibliography:

A. *Wensley: A Story Without a Moral* (Boston, 1854); *Where Will It End? A View of Slavery in the United States in Its Aggressions and Results*. (Providence, 1863).

B. Mark A. DeWolfe Howe, "Biographer's Bait: A Reminder of Edmund Quincy," *Proceedings of the Massachusetts Historical Society*, 68 (Boston, 1952), 377-391; Robert V. Sparks, "Abolition in Silver Slippers: The Life of Edmund Quincy," Ph.D. dissertation, Boston College, 1978.

C. Edmund Quincy Papers, Massachusetts Historical Society, Boston, MA.

Robert V. Sparks

R

RADE, Paul Martin (4 April 1857, Rennersdorf, Saxony—9 April 1940, Frankfurt am Main, Germany). *Education*: theological license, Univ. of Leipzig, 1881. *Career*: Lutheran pastor, 1882-92; instructor, systematic theology and history of religion, Univ. of Marburg, 1900-1904, associate professor, 1904-21, professor, 1921-; founder and editor, *Christliche Welt*, 1887-1940; pacifist.

Martin Rade was one of the few Protestant theologians of note in Wilhelmian Germany to become a member of the Deutsche Friedensgesellschaft (German Peace Society) and to remain loyal to pacifism. He had a thoroughly irenic nature and, as indicated by the intelligent and understanding position he took towards Catholicism and Judaism, he recognized in everything the binding characteristics more than those that divide. Yet, he never denied his own convictions but, rather, maintained them against attack with determination and courage.

The piety Rade acquired from his Lutheran pastoral upbringing in Saxony, which was later influenced by the study of modern theology under Adolf Harnack, combined with a practical interest in the problems of the external world. His unfailing sense of justice, his active tolerance, his involved humaneness, all found expression in the influential journal *Christliche Welt*. He used the columns of the journal to address a variety of issues: the genocide of the Armenians; the horrors of colonial rule in the Congo; the social political battles in his own land; the condition of workers; the ecclesiastical political questions concerning the Lutheran faith and of its ecclesiastical organization; and the treatment of ethnic minorities like Poles and Danes in Germany. He also opened the columns of the *Christliche Welt* to antiwar advocates, such as *Otto Umfrid, and internationalists, such as +Walther Schücking.

Through his marriage to Dora Naumann, Rade accompanied his brother-in-law, Friedrich Naumann, in their mutual political path toward the establishment of the Nationalsozialen Verein (National-Social Association), then to left-liberalism as a member of the Freisinnige Vereinigung (Progressive Alliance), the Fortschrittliche Volkspartei (Progressive Liberal People's Party), and, finally, after World War I, the Deutsche Demokratische Partei (German Democratic Party). In 1919 he attended the Prussian Constitutional Convention and played a role in reorganizing the structure of Prussian Church institutions. In 1930 Rade joined the newly founded Deutsche Staatspartei (German State Party), but he resolutely disapproved of the behavior of the party's Reichstag members during the vote concerning the Enabling Act in March 1933, which gave dictatorial power to Adolf Hitler.

His conviction that Christianity was a religion of peace which had a growing responsibility to promote peace among nations, led Rade into the antiwar movement. In 1908, at the German Peace Congress in Jena, he publicly avowed his commitment to peace principles in a speech entitled "Authoritarian State, Constitutional State, Civilized State." In the same year, he accompanied other German church representatives on a peace tour of England, working thereafter within the Ecclesiastical Committee for the cultivation of peaceful relations between Great Britain and Germany. Through association with the Committee he also became actively involved with the World Union for International Friendship Cooperation of Churches, and at its 1928 Prague Congress he addressed the issue of "Moral Disarmament: An Urgent Necessity." In 1911 he helped found the Association for International Understanding and spoke at its first meeting in Heidelberg (1912) on the contribution of the Christian churches to international understanding.

Martin Rade remained true to himself even during the convulsions of national hatred in the First World War. The fact that he only briefly belonged to the Bund Neues Vaterland (New Fatherland League) does not diminish the earnestness of his pacifist convictions. His prayers published in the *Christliche Welt* at the beginning of World War I and his statements on political events in the Weimar Republic attest to his continued commitment to Christian pacifism.

Bibliography:

B. Jörn-Peter Leppien, *Martin Rade und die deutschdänischen Beziehungen 1909-1929* (Neumünster, 1981); Rudolf Liechtenhan "Zu Martin Rades 80. Geburtstag," *Die Friedenswarte*, 37 (1937), 60-64; Hermann Mulert, ed., *Vierzig Jahre Christliche Welt—Festgabe für Martin Rade um 70. Geburtstag* (Gotha, 1927); Johannes Rathje, *Die Welt des freien Protestantismus. Ein Beitrag zur deutsch-evangelischen Geistesgeschichte. Dargestellt am Leben und Werk von Martin Rade* (Stuttgart, 1952); Christoph Schwöbel, ed., *Karl Barth-Martin Rade: Briefwechsel* (Gütersloh, 1982); Christoph Schwöbel, *Martin Rade Das Verhältnis von Geschichte, Religion und Moral als Grundproblem seiner Theologie* (Gütersloh, 1980).

C. Martin Rade Papers, Manuscript Division, University of Marburg Library.

Karl Holl
Trans. by William Hopkins

RADHAKRISHNAN, Sarvepalli (5 September 1889, Tiruttani near Madras, Chittor district, Madras Presidency, India—17 April 1975, Madras). *Education*: M.A., Madras Christian Coll., 1909. *Career*: educator, taught at Presidency Coll., Calcutta Univ., Oxford Univ., and Univ. of Chicago, among others; headed India's delegation to United Nations Educational, Scientific and Cultural Organization, 1946-49 (chair, 1948-49); ambassador to the Soviet Union, 1949-52; vice-president of India, 1952-62; president, 1962-67; scholar, statesman, and author.

Sarvepalli Radhakrishnan is best known for his scholarly career and as an international figure in the years immediately following Indian independence. Although he was not conspicuously active in the nationalist movement, having during that period held three university chairs in philosophy, two vice-chancellorships, and a chancellorship, his status as a patriot and man of culture and vision was such that many high offices came his way in free India. His lectures in Great Britain, the United States, and China showed him to be not only an able interpreter of the Indian philosophical heritage but a man who could think beyond frontiers.

He was a member of the Constituent Assembly which framed the Constitution of India. A leader of the Indian delegation to the United Nations Educational, Scientific and Cultural Organization (UNESCO) from 1946-52, he was elected chairman of its executive board for the year 1948-49. From 1949-52 he was India's ambassador to the Soviet Union. In 1952 he became vice-president of the Republic of India and then in May, 1962, was elected president, subsequently being awarded the Bharata Ratna, the highest honor given by the Indian Government.

Radhakrishnan's work as a peace leader is to be identified through his public utterances in favor of total disarmament, his pleas for intercultural cooperation, and in his prolific writings which strove to articulate a philosophical framework for peace in modern society. Belonging to a people whose greatest thinkers had always advocated nonviolence, Radhakrishnan was particularly aware of India's responsibility both to foster a conflict-free community within her own borders and to defuse potential areas of friction abroad. Friendly relations should be maintained with close neighbors and the policy of noninvolvement in military blocs along with the settlement of international disputes through negotiations should be followed. When he spoke, as he so often did, of "the human family" and "the family of nations," he had in mind a spiritual view of the universe which had at its center the cultivation of inner harmony in each individual. As an educator he believed that men needed to be educated to a common conception of human destiny, to the goal of one world. In conceiving peace-making in these terms Radhakrishnan's thinking to some extent synthesized the approaches of *Mohandas K. Gandhi and *Jawaharlal Nehru. He had absorbed something of the Gandhian belief in soul-force as an effective check on the exploitative potential of nation states. In the post-independence era, his grasp of India's philosophical tradition gave an intellectual foundation and a more positive content to what came to be known as the policy of nonalignment.

Radhakrishnan began his philosophical career at a time when the label "idealist" had not yet acquired a pejorative sense. Trained in missionary institutions, he became aware of the teachings of the New Testament and at the same time reacted against the unsympathetic attitude of many Christians in the India of his day towards Hinduism. Along with Swami Vivekananda, whom he much admired, Radhakrishnan helped open Western eyes to the message of the Vedanta and the Hindu way of life. His philosophical writings presented an ethical dimension in Hinduism with which foreign critics had not been readily willing to credit it. He furthermore emphasized its rationality where others had tended to stress its intuitive character. In the 1920s he published his monumental two volume study of Indian philosophy, which long remained an authoritative work on the subject. In *The Future of Civilisation* (1929), based on an address given at Harvard University, Radhakrishnan warned of the dangers inherent in scientific advance unaccompanied by discipline and cultivation of the living spirit. He argued that the reign of law and justice was intended to enable the soul to gain "inward peace" and that civilization was "an act of spirit," not of mind or body.

Like Sri Aurobindo, Radhakrishnan was attracted by the idea of integration and looked forward to the time when the interrelationships between peoples which were being brought about by economic and political factors would be matched by the birth of the world's "yet unborn soul." Radhakrishnan believed that it was possible to cultivate a "world perspective" in philosophy. It was in these terms that he envisaged the task of the philosopher as one that could contribute to peace.

While he was equally critical of the notion of mechanistic progress in history and of the notion which sees history as a series of conflicts, his own insight favored a model of dynamic interplay operative amidst ideas and cultures. He drew on the Indian sense of kinship with all living things, including human beings, and wanted this part of the Indian heritage to become a living reality in his own country and beyond its boundaries.

Radhakrishnan identified the enemies of peace as anarchic individualism, the economic interpretation of history, and the materialistic view of life. Although this diagnosis of the world's ills was ideational rather than one which centered on political realities, it recognized the risk of regarding the institutional apparatus for peacemaking as an end in itself. Radhakrishnan's plea for the cultivation of a world outlook was an important one. As an ambassador of a newly independent country, he yet projected an internationalist image rather than a nationalist one. As a statesman when the world seemed to be split into rival camps, he envisaged the horizon of peacemaking as something which went beyond the idea of neutral coexistence to what he described as "mutual educative coexistence." His own contribution in this educative process made him one of India's most important peace leaders.

Bibliography:

A. *Education, Politics and War* (Poona, 1944); *The Hindu View of Life* (London, 1926); *Kalki or the Future of Civilization* (London, 1929); *Radhakrishnan Reader*, ed. by P. Nagaraja Rao, K. Gopalaswami, and S. Ramakrishnan (Bombay, 1969); *Religion in a Changing World* (London, 1967).

B. P. A. Schilpp, ed., *The Philosophy of Sarvepalli Radhakrishnan* (New York, 1952); NYT, April 17, 1975.

Margaret Chatterjee

RAEMAEKERS, Louis (6 April 1869, Roermond, Netherlands—26 July 1956, Scheveningen, Netherlands). *Education*: Rijksnormaalschool and Kunstnijverheidsschool (grammar school and industrial arts school), Amsterdam, 1891-93;

Arts academy, Brussels and Paris. *Career*: teacher, Arts & Crafts school, Tilburg, 1894; director, Burgeravondschool, Wageningen, 1895; illustrator, *Het Algemeen Handelsblad*, 1907-9; illustrator, *De Telegraaf*, 1909-40.

Louis Raemaekers started his career as a painter of landscapes and portraits, and as a writer and illustrator of children's stories. His first political cartoons appeared in 1907 in the newspaper *Het Algemeen Handelsblad*. In 1909 he joined the Amsterdam *De Telegraaf*, and he was to remain with this paper until the end of his working life. On August 1, 1914, in this newspaper, appeared his drawing "Humanity after twenty centuries of Christendom," which showed a bowed and weeping figure crouching under the sword and lash. This was the beginning of an impressive and often moving series of cartoons, which depicted the horrors of the war, especially the barbaric nature of Prussian militarism and the inhumane effects of new devilish weapons and methods of warfare. The effects of land and sea mines, gas warfare, aerial bombardments, submarine warfare, trenches and barbed wire, the senseless burnings and devastations as well as the horrors inflicted on women and children—all were realistically and movingly portrayed. His drawings were meant not only to provide a permanent record of man's inhumanity to man, but also to appeal to all people to struggle against it.

To ascertain the truth of the rumors concerning atrocities in Belgium, Raemaekers, whose own mother was German, left his neutral Holland at great risk to find out for himself. He discovered "a hell. . . terror unspeakable," which he depicted with great intensity and directness. Only towards the end of the following year, in Christmas week 1915, as a result of an exhibition of his drawings in a prominent London art gallery, did his fame spread outside Holland. Following highly successful exhibitions in the rest of the country, as well as in Paris, he gained universal recognition as the supreme cartoonist of the war. The German authorities, anxious to suppress his work, managed to have Raemaekers charged in the Dutch courts with endangering the neutrality of his country, but he was acquitted.

His drawings soon appeared in a great number of papers and periodicals both in Europe and the United States. Raemaekers was very productive, about 1200 of his drawings having been published during the war, for an average of almost one a day. He exhibited them in allied and neutral countries, and they were also published in collections, which appeared in eighteen different languages, In addition several million postcard editions of his cartoons were sold. Often his exhibitions and sales were in support of the French or English Red Cross, or for charities concerned with war victims. In order to be able to supply the allied press more easily, he went to live in England for a few years after 1916; at various times he also lived in Paris, Brussels, and the United States. The University of Glasgow awarded him an honorary doctorate in 1924 for his work during the war. During the Second World War, Raemaekers, now in his seventies, continued to work as a cartoonist, again attacking Germany. "But," as a recent commentator of his cartoons wrote, "beneath their hatred of the Germans there was an even more fundamental hatred...of war itself" (Frank E. Huggett, *Cartoonists at War*, Leicester, 1981, p. 144).

Bibliography:

A. *America in the War* (New York, 1918), *Dessins d'un neutre* (2 vols., Amsterdam, c. 1916); *La guerre; dessins exécutés pendant l'année 1916* (Paris, 1917); *The Great War, A Neutral's Indictment* (London, 1916); *Ha! ha! ha! ha! Alweer een vredesconferentie* (Amsterdam, 1907); *Het toppunt der beschaving* (7 series, Amsterdam, 1914-17); *Hun rekening opgemaakt* (Rotterdam, 1918); *The "Land & Water" Edition of Raemaekers' Cartoons* (2 vols., London, 1916-17); *Raemaekers' Cartoon History of the War*, comp. by J. Murray Allison (3 vols., New York, 1918-19); *"There will be no war—said Europe"; an exhibition of drawings and cartoons* (New York, 1941).

B. Cynthia F. Behrman, ed., *Raemaekers' Cartoons* (New York, 1971); *Grote Winkler Prins Encyclopedie* (Amsterdam/ Brussels, 1973), XVI, 92; *Persoonliijkheden in het Koninkrijk der Nederlanden* (Amsterdam, 1938), 1196; Pieter A. Scheen, *Lexicon Nederlandse beeldende kunstenaars 1750-1950* (The Hague, 1970), 210.

Peter van den Dungen

RAFFIN-DUGENS, Jean-Pierre (3 December 1861, Saint-Pierre d'Allevard, Isère, France—26 March 1946, Eybens, Isère). *Education*: teaching certificate, École normale, Grenoble, 1882. *Career*: schoolteacher, 1882-1910; active in the socialist movement, 1898-1920; Socialist deputy from the Isère, 1910-19; active in the Communist party, 1920-25.

Like many militant pacifists during the First World War, Raffin-Dugens had been a leader in the prewar syndicalist and socialist movements. He had joined Jules Guesde's Parti Ouvrier Français, one of the predecessors of the French Socialist party, in 1898; had begun writing for the Socialist daily *Le Droit du Peuple* (Grenoble) in 1903; and he had organized the first schoolteachers' union in the Isère in 1911. An ardent publicist, Raffin-Dugens conducted his first antimilitarist campaign among schoolteachers in 1905 with the help of two other union members, *Alexandre Blanc and *Pierre Brizon. As Socialist deputies all three men played leading roles in the genesis of an antiwar movement in France during the First World War.

In the patriotic exaltation of 1914-15, Raffin-Dugens was one of the few precursors of a move to dissassociate the Socialist party from the war effort. He voted against the Socialists' participation in wartime governments as early as May 1915, more than two years before this became the prevalent view within the party. Both the origins and the conduct of the war troubled Raffin-Dugens. He doubted that Germany was solely responsible for the outbreak of the war. Long before the French Army mutinies of spring 1917, Raffin-Dugens warned the government that soldiers increasingly were convinced that they were being sacrificed on the field of battle by incompetent and uncaring commanders.

With Alexandre Blanc and Pierre Brizon, Raffin-Dugens took part in the Kienthal Conference (April 24-30, 1916), the second wartime meeting in Switzerland of antiwar socialists from across Europe. When the Socialist party called the three "Kienthalians" to account for defying party policy, Raffin-Dugens appeared before the party's administrative commission to accuse party officials of violating the decisions of prewar international Socialist conferences.

The Bolsheviks' call for an immediate armistice in November 1917 made Raffin-Dugens a steadfast defender of the Russian Revolution. In 1919 he took up the cause of French sailors who mutinied against their country's counterrevolutionary intervention in the Black Sea region. Raffin-Dugens provided an assessment of the war in a long speech at the Socialist party's congress in Tours (December 1920)—the congress which formally ratified a schism engendered by the war and saw the founding of the Communist party. Blaming his fellow-Socialists for not having opposed the war from its very inception, Raffin-Dugens made clear that the party's wartime conduct had convinced him that parliament was not the appropriate arena in which to struggle for the liberation of the proletariat. Accordingly, he urged the congress to repudiate the party's reformist past by voting to join the Third International.

Throughout the war, Raffin-Dugens used the newspaper which he edited in Grenoble, *Le Droit du Peuple*, to oppose both the war itself and the reformist tendencies which it nurtured among Socialist politicians. In 1920 he joined the Communist party and became first secretary of the Communist federation of the Isère. He was purged from the party in 1925.

Bibliography:

B. Pierre Broué and Jean Machu, "Le Mouvement ouvrier dans l'Isère et à Grenoble de 1914 à 1921," *Cahiers d'Histoire*, 22 (Lyon, 1977), 203-8; Jean Charles *et al.*, eds., *Le Congrès de Tours* (critical edition, Paris, 1980); Jean Maitron, ed., *Dictionnaire biographique du Mouvement ouvrier français* (Paris, 1976), vol. 14. Alfred Rosmèr, *Le Mouvement ouvrier pendant la première Guerre mondiale* (Paris, 1959), vol. 2.

Ioannis Sinanoglou

RAGAZ, Leonhard (28 July 1868, Tamins, Graubünden, Switzerland—6 December 1945, Zurich). *Education*: study of protestant theology, universities of Basel, Jena, and Berlin; passed pastor's examination, Graubünden, 1890. *Career*: pastor, Flerden (Graubünden), 1890-93; Chur, 1895-1902; head church of Basel, 1902-6; gymnasium (secondary school) teacher, Chur, 1893-95; professor of systematic and practical theology, Univ. of Zurich, 1908-21; adult education teacher, Zurich, 1921-45; editor and publisher, *Neue Wege*, 1906-45; theologian, writer, pacifist, and socialist.

As a young man Leonhard Ragaz, the son of a mountain peasant, was a cadet-officer and military field chaplain. Through his wife, Clara Ragaz-Nadig, he became acquainted early with the work of *Bertha von Suttner and before the outbreak of World War I became a convinced pacifist. In August 1914 Ragaz took a solemn vow "to dedicate the rest of my life to the fight against war." He participated in the peace efforts of the Socialists during the war, but turned against the Leninist concept of peace and wrote *Sozialismus und Gewalt (Socialism and Violence)* (1919).

Ragaz was one of the first to work for alternative service for conscientious objectors. In the interwar years the Religious-Social Union of German Switzerland served as a branch of the International Fellowship of Reconciliation (IFOR). Ragaz participated in IFOR conferences in Nyborg (1923) and Bad Boll (1924) in which he asserted that Christian Socialists should acknowledge Christ and take a consistent attitude toward private property and violence. During a trial blackout shortly before the Second World War, Ragaz left his window illuminated as a protest against the attitude of war-fatalism. For a long time he was the most-hated pacifist in Switzerland. In 1941 the censorship authorities, which were subordinated to the military, imposed pre-censorship on the *Neue Wege*. Ragaz refused to comply with the order and published the periodical as a private publication until 1945.

Ragaz was one of the staunchest supporters of the League of Nations idea and of President +Woodrow Wilson in Switzerland. Nevertheless, despite his sympathy for the Entente in World War I, Ragaz decisively rejected the Treaty of Versailles. After the victory of National Socialism in Germany and the outbreak of war as a result of Adolf Hitler's policies, Ragaz did not hold firm to his position of integral pacifism. Basing himself on *Gandhi's use of the word ''cowardice'' to explain his (Gandhi's) own temporary deviation from the principle of nonviolence at the outbreak of World War I, Ragaz, in the face of the evil of Nazism, chose—temporarily—the ''defensive power'' of the cowardly surrender of the truth. Toward the end of World War II, Ragaz published numerous essays on the future order of peace as spokesman for the Weltaktion für den Frieden (World Action for Peace).

Ragaz's earlier pacifism was based on the concept of brotherhood and of all human beings as children of God. Later, his pacifism increasingly became rooted in an eschatological comprehension of history: war and violence are a form of the demonic against which Christians are enjoined to do battle in the name of the Kingdom of God until war and violence are definitively conquered by the second coming of Christ.

Bibliography:

A. *Die Abrüstung als Mission der Schweiz* (Zurich, 1924); *Dienstverweigerung und Zivildienst* (Zurich, 1923); *Dient das Milizheer dem Frieden*? (Zurich, 1932); *Das Programm des Friedens* (Zurich, 1939); *Die Schweiz im Kampf um den Frieden* (Zurich, 1945); *Sozialismus und Gewalt* (Olten, 1919); *Sozialismus und Völkerbund* (Zurich, 1920).

B. H. U. Jäger, *Ethik und Eschatologie bei Leonhard Ragaz* (Zurich, 1971); M. Mattmüller, *Leonhard Ragaz und der religiöse Sozialismus* (2 vols., Zurich, 1957 and 1968); A. Lindt, *Leonhard Ragaz* (Zollikon, 1957).

Markus Mattmüller
Trans. by Solomon Wank

RAJAGOPALACHARI, Chakravati (10 December 1879, Salem District, India—25 December 1972, Madras, India). *Education*: B.A., Presidency Coll., Madras, 1910. *Career*: independence leader; politician; lawyer; author; editor, *Young India*, 1922, *Vimochanam*, 1925-29, *Prohibition*, 1925-29.

C. R. Rajagopalachari, known in India as Rajaji, was a member of the Indian National Congress as early as 1905. Following a meeting with *Mohandas K. Gandhi in 1919, he exchanged his career as a lawyer for that of a full-time worker and later a leader in the Indian Congress party. He became as well an advocate for religious and social reform especially with regards to untouchables and women, for village self-sufficiency, and for prohibition. Rajaji advocated nonviolent civil disobedience as the only possible way to bring about a united and peaceful independent India. Later in his life, Rajaji became an antinuclear advocate. Intellectually, he was influenced by the *Mahabharata*, the *Baghavad Gita*, and as well the works of *Leo Tolstoy and *Henry David Thoreau.

Between 1905-7 he supported the "extremist" position of B. G. Tilak. As with Tilak, Rajaji was forced from an active role in National Congress politics following the 1907 Surat session of the Congress. In 1908 he began to advocate the use of nonviolent civil disobedience as a means of bringing change in the politics of the Government of India. He urged Congress to follow the example of Gandhi in South Africa. Rajaji remained inactive in National Congress affairs until 1919. However, events in India following World War I, most particularly the Amritsar Massacre and passage of the Rowlatt Act, led him to join the Gandhi wing of the Congress. He became general secretary of the Congress during 1921-22 and was chosen by Gandhi to be the editor of *Young India* while the former was in prison in 1922.

Rajaji founded an *ashram* in South India in 1925. Here he spent much effort encouraging the use of *khadi*, hand spun cotton. He believed the hand spinning was important for two reasons. First, it lessened village dependence on costly manufactured cloth either foreign or domestic. Second, and more importantly, hand spinning symbolized the importance Gandhi had placed on obtaining the support of all levels of Indian society for the independence movement. Rajaji also taught villagers about sanitation, the need for prohibition, and the need for an end to untouchability. Rajaji became the leader of the civil disobedience movement in South India and led a salt march to Vedarayam in 1930 which resulted in his arrest and nine months imprisonment.

In 1937 he became chief minister of Madras for the Congress party. He was successful in obtaining passage of Prohibition (1937) and the Madras Temple Entry Act (1939) as part of his program for religious and social reform. Rajaji resigned his office in 1939 in support of the Congress party's decision to withdraw from government and to practice noncooperation with respect to British war policy.

During World War II he sought to find a way to overcome the refusal of Muslim League leaders to present a united front of nationalist leaders to the Government of India. Rajaji was convinced that some arrangement for the geographical division of India based on religious affiliation was inevitable. At his urging in April 1942 the Congress members of the Madras legislature passed a resolution calling for the National Congress to agree to acknowledge the Muslim League's claim for a separate state if the League should still wish such at the time of independence. The Congress leadership was unhappy with this resolution and repudiated it. In 1943 and 1944 he suggested that the League join Congress in its demands for independence in exchange for a promise that after independence Muslim majority areas would be allowed to vote on the issues of retaining membership in the Indian State or forming a separate country. The plan was rejected by the Muslim League.

Soon after this, Rajaji broke with Gandhi over the issue of support to the British war effort. Rajaji believed that noncooperation against the British at this time or against the Japanese should they successfully invade India represented at best neutrality towards the fascists. He believed that peaceful and democratic government would best be served by forming a National Government which supported the war aims of the allies.

In 1946 he joined the Government of India and served as a member of the Governor-General's Executive Council. After independence in 1947, Rajaji became the first Indian Governor-General, a post he retained until the Republic was founded in 1950. In 1952 he was called from retirement to lead the Congress party in Madras and served as chief minister in Madras from 1952-54.

During the 1950s Rajaji became increasingly concerned by *Jawaharlal Nehru's success in gaining Congress' acceptance for development programs which relied on central planning and which stressed industrialization and, where necessary, nationalization. Rajaji believed Nehru had abandoned the Gandhian goal of *panchayat raj* or village self-sufficiency and village self-rule. The policies of Nehru, Rajaji stated, would lead to mass migrations to the cities and would totally dislocate the village economy. The "Nagpur Resolution" of the Congress in 1958 on "joint co-operation farming" was seen by Rajaji as an attempt to collectivize rural India on the model of China and Russia. He joined with M. R. Mansani, Sir Homy P. Mody, K. M. Munshi, and N. G. Ranga to form the Swantartra party in 1959 to oppose the "statism" of the Congress party.

Rajaji espoused the cause of pacifism in the later years of his life. He was a member of the Gandhi Peace Foundation mission to Washington in 1962 to urge an end to nuclear testing. He spoke directly with John F. Kennedy about the matter and later contacted Nikita Khruschev on the same topic. He saw peaceful coexistence as the only reasonable choice for India.

Throughout his career Rajaji urged nonviolent opposition to those things he considered evil, but he opposed compulsion as a means of securing the good. For these reasons he opposed Gandhi over the issue of a separate Muslim State and Nehru over the issue of national economic and social reform. Rajaji argued that the state could not compel reform in religious and social structure of a society. Rather, the state must limit itself to making such change possible by removing "unjust" laws and replacing them with "permissive" laws. Rajaji was not opposed to change, however. He resisted change which was imported and favored instead change that came from what was good in the internal spiritual values and culture of a society.

Bibliography:

A. *Defense of India* (Madras, n.d.); *Our Culture* (Bombay, 1963); *Our Democracy* (Madras, 1956); *Rajaji's Speeches* (Bombay, 1950).

B. Howard Erdman, *The Swantartra Party and Indian Conservatism* (Cambridge, 1976); R. K. Murthi, *Rajaji, Life and Work* (New Delhi, 1979); Masti Venkatesa, *Rajaji* (Bangalore, 1975).

John C. Hume, Jr.

RANDOLPH, Asa Philip (15 April 1889, Crescent City, FL—16 May 1979, New York). *Education*: studies at City Coll. of New York. *Career*: co-editor and editor, *The Messenger*, 1917-28; labor organizer and trade union leader, The Brotherhood of Sleeping Car Porters, 1925-68; member of the Executive Council and a vice-president, AFL-CIO, from 1955; president, Negro American Labor Council, 1960-64; president, National Negro Congress, 1936-40; director, March on Washington Movement, 1941-47; co-chair, Committee Against Jim Crow in Military Service, 1947; head of the League for Nonviolent Civil Disobedience Against Military Segregation, 1948; national director and planner of the March on Washington, 1963; civil rights leader.

In an active public career spanning the half-century from 1917 to 1968, A. Philip Randolph was in the forefront of numerous campaigns for both civil rights and economic justice. As an antiwar socialist during World War I, a labor organizer during the 1920s and 1930s, a leader in and elder statesman of the civil rights movement from the mid 1930s to the mid 1960s, and as a ranking member of the AFL-CIO hierarchy during the late 1950s, and 1960s, Randolph actively involved himself in crusades to eliminate racial discrimination and to improve economic opportunities available to black workers.

During World War I in the pages of the *Messenger* and in public speeches, Randolph argued against both American and Afro-American participation in a war he deemed imperialist. Reflecting a branch of the emergent postwar "New Negro" leadership, Randolph espoused support for trade unionism as the most viable means by which blacks could attain civil rights and economic justice. From 1925 until 1937, Randolph led the protracted but successful struggle against the Pullman Railroad Company over that company's refusal to recognize the newly formed Brotherhood of Sleeping Car Porters as a legitimate bargaining agent.

Always one to view the interrelatedness of campaigns for social and economic change, Randolph served from 1936 to 1940 as president of the National Negro Congress (NNC), a coalition of diverse black organizations interested in civil rights and economic opportunity. Resigning from the NNC in 1940 due to policy differences with Communist party members and sympathizers within the organization, Randolph concerned himself with the problems of racial discrimination in employment in defense industries and in government agencies, as well as discrimination and segregation in the armed services. In 1941 Randolph issued a call for a proposed March on Washington by thousands of black demonstrators unless President +Franklin D. Roosevelt issued an executive order barring racial discrimination in government and defense industry employment. To monitor the government's enforcement activities and to galvanize his followers during World War II, Randolph established and headed the March on Washington Movement. Like other peace-oriented advocates of social change in the United States during the 1930s and 1940s, Randolph came to admire and to emulate the philosophy and tactics of Mohandas K. Gandhi.

Supportive of individual resisters to World War II, Randolph later focused his attention upon the unresolved issues of racial segregation and discrimination in the military. By proposing that black and white youths refuse induction in a segregated military, Randolph was able to get President +Harry Truman to issue the 1948 executive order barring racial discrimination in the armed forces.

Throughout the 1950s and early 1960s, Randolph, the ranking black trade unionist, sought to combat racial discrimination within the member unions of the AFL-CIO. Although not always successful in getting more conservative craft unions to end discriminatory and exclusionary policies, Randolph helped sway the labor hierarchy to support federal civil rights and social welfare legislation. By the early 1960s, Randolph was no longer a dominating figure in the fight for racial equality. However, as a respected elder statesman and as a planner for the 1963 March on Washington, he was able to influence the course of the civil rights movement throughout most of the decade.

Over the course of a public career spanning five decades, A. Philip Randolph worked unceasingly and tirelessly in campaigns for social change. Ever conscious of the problems of class and caste in modern America, Randolph continually pursued strategies and developed approaches to eliminate racial discrimination, to eradicate poverty, and to secure economic justice. Influenced by his African Methodist Church upbringing, by his friendships and associations with *Eugene V. Debs, *Norman Thomas, *A. J. Muste, and Bayard Rustin, and by his readings of Gandhi, Randolph turned to nonviolent resistance as the best means to bring about social and economic change. While not a theoretician of nonviolence, Randolph, as a trade union and civil rights leader, exemplified how nonviolent, mass-based protest could overcome oppression and proscription.

Bibliography:

B. Jervis Anderson, *A. Philip Randolph: Biographic Portrait* (New York, 1973); Herbert Garfinkel, *When Negroes March*, (rev. ed., New York, 1973); Benjamin Quarles, ''A. Philip Randolph: Labor Leader at Large,'' in *Black Leaders of the Twentieth Century*, ed. by John Hope Franklin and August Meier (Urbana, IL., 1982); NYT, May 18, 1979.

Gerald R. Gill

RANKIN, Jeannette (11 June 1880, Montana Territory near Missoula—18 May 1973, Carmel, CA). *Education*: B.S., Univ. of Montana, 1902. *Career*: suffragist; U.S. Representative, 1917-19, 1941-43; field secretary and board member, Women's International League for Peace and Freedom, 1920-25; founder, Georgia Peace Society, 1928; lobbyist, Women's Peace Union, 1929; Washington lobbyist and field organizer, National Council for the Prevention of War, 1929-39.

Jeannette Rankin's pacifism originated in connection with her suffragist activities in the states of Washington and Montana. In particular, her association with a transplanted eastern pacifist, Minne J. Reynolds, convinced Rankin by 1910 that the quest for peace should be incorporated into the suffrage. Like so many of her female contemporaries, Rankin's participation in the social justice wing of the Progressive movement reinforced her pacifistic views. Finally, books by the English sociologist Benjamin Kidd led her to the singular and powerful conclusion that women were the primary source of "power" for all future peace activities in the United States and the world.

After helping win the vote for women in Montana in 1914, Rankin became the first woman elected to the House of Representatives, in 1916. Within four days after assuming her seat in Congress, she voted along with 56 others against United States entrance in World War I. Later, in 1941, while serving a second term in the House, she became the only Congressional opponent of entry into World War II. In the intervening years she continued her pacifist activities in a variety of official capacities. As early as 1915 Rankin joined the Woman's Peace party. She subsequently belonged to the National Committee on the Cause and Cure of War, the Women's Peace Union, the Women's International League for Peace and Freedom (WILPF), and finally the National Council for Prevention of War (NCPW). With the exception of the Georgia Peace Society, which she founded in 1928, none of these organizations subsequently lived up to Rankin's idealistic or organizational standards.

Often she opposed their political tactics or they refused to finance her grassroots plans for organizing. For example, Rankin left her position as field secretary with the WILPF in 1925 after it proved impossible to finance her elaborate plans for gaining western members. In 1929 she resigned as a lobbyist for the Women's Peace Union, whose sole purpose was to outlaw war through a constitutional amendment, in a dispute over tactics. Similarly, after a ten-year association with the NCPW, Rankin ended this affiliation in 1939 primarily because she had become much more critical than the National Council of the international policies of both Secretary of State +Cordell Hull and President +Franklin D. Roosevelt.

Rankin's difficulties with the NCPW were due, in part, to her particular foreign policy views. In the interwar years she remained a "nationalist," or one who supported very limited American commitments around the world. She was not, however, an isolationist. She did not support isolation from European affairs while accepting the use of force in the Far East or Latin America like most isolationists in the 1920s and 1930s. Instead, Rankin remained true to her pacifist ideals: she objected to the use of American military force anywhere in the world, except for the defense of the continental United States. Consequently, she supported international cooperation, but opposed American interventionism.

Economic views conditioned Rankin's brand of pacifism between the two world wars. As America became an urban and consumer nation, those who first experienced mass consumerism in the 1920s tended to be more interventionist than those who did not. Rankin increasingly turned away from the consumer society and led a spartan life outside Athens, Georgia, without a telephone or electricity or running water until after 1943. Although she continued to vote and own property in Montana, Georgia became her "home" and the Georgia Peace Society remained her base for pacifist activities from the late 1920s until its demise on the eve of World War II. From Georgia she pursued a lifestyle without modern conveniences, organized "sunshine" Clubs for local boys and girls to teach them "peace habits," established a foreign policy study group for adults, and transformed the Georgia Peace Society into one of the first peace action groups in the country with perennial attempts to defeat the naval appropriations bills of Congressman Carl Vinson. The Atlanta American Legion Post labeled Rankin a "communist" for these efforts and prevented Brenau College in Gainesville from establishing a "Chair of Peace" for her.

Senator Gerald Nye's investigation from 1934 to 1936 of the role played by the munitions industry in America's entrance into World War I confirmed Rankin's worst suspicions about the economic origins of modern warfare. After World War II, her economic argument became an attack on the military industrial complex and its relationship to the monetary system. Accordingly, she revived an idea she had espoused during both World Wars which called for the creation of special "profit removing" currency in time of military hostilities. She also championed other domestic reforms she thought would correct the defects she saw in the American capitalist system.

Although she never lived to see any of her peace reforms enacted, she was a consistent critic of the Cold War, including the Korean and the Vietnam conflicts. Increasingly she associated American expansionism with deficiencies in the country's political economy and with the power of a conspiratorial military-industrial complex. As the war in Indochina escalated, she gave serious consideration, at the age of eighty-eight, to running for the House of Representatives a third time. Although she had been out of the national limelight for over two decades, the Vietnamese conflict revitalized both her spirits and her career. Her final protest against war would not be as a Congresswoman, however, but as an antiwar demonstrator and titular head of the Jeannette Rankin Brigade, organized in 1967. Thus her long pacifist career ended as it had begun, amidst a flurry of travel, public appearances, and exhortations against war.

Bibliography:

A. "Beware of Holy Wars," *World Outlook*, November, 1938; "I Would Vote 'No' Again," *Christian Science Monitor*, April 1, 1936; "Two Votes Against War," *Liberation*, March, 1958.

B. Kevin Giles, *Flight of the Dove* (Beavertown, OR, 1980); Joan Hoff-Wilson, "Peace Is a Woman's Job. . .' Jeannette Rankin's Foreign Policy," *Montana: The Magazine of Western History*, 30 (January, 1980), 28-41, 30 (April, 1980), 38-53; Hannah Josephson, *First Lady in Congress: Jeannette Rankin* (Indianapolis, 1974).

C. Jeannette Rankin Papers, Schlesinger Library, Radcliffe College and Swarthmore

College Peace Collection; ''Activist for World Peace, Women's Rights, and Democratic Government,'' 1974 Regional Oral History Project, Bancroft Library, University of California, Berkeley.

Joan Hoff-Wilson

RAPPARD, William Emmanuel. See *Biographical Dictionary of Internationalists*.

RAUZE, Marianne [pseud. of Marie-Anne-Rose Gaillarde] (20 September 1875, Paris—23 October 1964, Perpignan, France). *Career*: author, publicist, feminist, and pacifist.

Daughter of a family which, for several generations, had produced career military officers, Marie Gaillarde married army Captain Léon Comignan, adopting the pseudonym Marianne Rauze, in order to protect her husband's career from the effects of her political activity. From 1900 to 1905, while Comignan was stationed in Brittany, she was charmed by Breton myths and wrote poetry in the Celtic. But after 1906, when they were posted to Paris, she began to interest herself in feminism.

In 1907 Rauze made the acquaintance of the neo-Malthusian feminist, Nelly Roussel, and was briefly associated with *La Française*, a conservative feminist journal. Shortly thereafter, under the influence of Paul and Laura Lafargue, she became a socialist, but remained on the central committee of the Ligue française pour le droit des femmes (French League for the Rights of Women). In 1912 Rauze joined the French Socialist party (SFIO), and on the following January 5, she—with *Louise Saumoneau, Elisabeth Renaud, and others—called on women to attend the organizational meeting of the Groupe des femmes socialistes (Group of Socialist Women), established as a sub-group of the SFIO.

In February 1913 Rauze founded *l'Equité*, whose pages were open to bourgeois feminists as well as socialists. In its pages, a polemic divided Rauze from other socialist feminists such as Saumoneau and *Hélène Brion on the issue of whether class or gender should be considered primary and whether bourgeois and socialist feminists had anything in common. Rauze wanted to include all positions.

Rauze and Saumoneau clashed, too, on the question of responsibility for the war. Whereas Saumoneau, in January 1915, undertook the distribution of the *Appeal* of *Clara Zetkin opposing the war, Rauze, in *l'Equité*, attacked ''Prussian feudalism'' and ''the ferocious autocracy which rules through brutality.'' But with the death of her husband in September 1916 from wounds received a year earlier, Rauze, in *Le Populaire*, November 27, 1916, declared herself a pacifist, and in the December Congress of the SFIO she interrupted a speech supporting the war by crying out ''Enough killing.''

Thereafter Rauze directed her attention equally to pacifism, feminism, and socialism. She worked tirelessly in support of the Stockholm Conference in 1917, and in November 1918 she advocated ''social revolution,'' the hour for which she saw as near. At the Congress of Tours she went with the majority, giving lectures at the École Marxiste communiste on Engel's theories concerning women and their role. But by 1923 Rauze became disillusioned with the Red Army, which she saw as a professional army, and adopted a form of pacifism so absolute as to alarm even *Romain Rolland; it was a pacifism almost mystical, in which she spoke of forming a "*syndicat* of defense against death."

This uncompromising antimilitarism culminated in the publication of *l'Anti-Guerre (The Anti-War)* (1923). It was further expressed in Rauze's membership in peace organizations and her activism for pacifist causes. She was leader of the French Section of the War Resisters' International (WRI), attending its triennial conference in 1925. In the same year an article on "The Pacifism of the French Peasant" appeared in *Réconciliation* (she had made a circuit of twenty *départementes* of the Center and the South). A police report of January 1926 cited her for antiwar and antiviolence speeches in Meurthe-et-Moselle, and in 1926 and succeeding years she was denied a passport by the French government. In the same year, she disclosed her editorship of *Les Libérés de toutes les guerres*, published in Lyon. From 1925 to 1927 she was the French representative on the International Council of the WRI. She was associated with *Madeleine Vernet in *Les Amis de la Mère Educatrice* and in *La Volonté de Paix*, and in that role she took the lead in forming a committee to oppose the military conscription bill of 1927.

Rauze was one of the endorsers of *Victor Margueritte's appeal, "La Patrie humaine," published in *Évolution*, December 1928. She contributed as well to the *Anthologie des écrivains pacifistes* (*Anthology of Pacifist Writers*), edited by Jean Souvenance and René de Sanzy (Paris, 1932). Continuing her active engagement in pacifist and feminist causes, she served on the Commission Nationale Féminine until 1958, the year before her death.

Bibliography:

A. *L'Anti-guerre: Essai d'une doctrine et d'une philosophie de l'anti-militarisme* (Niort, 1923); *L'École de la paix* (Niort, 1923); *Nanon, Nanette* (Saumur, 1927); *La propagande socialiste révolutionnaire* (Paris, 1919).

B. Jean Maitron, ed., *Dictionnaire Biographique du Mouvement Ouvrier français, 1871-1914*, XV (Paris, 1977) 8-9; Charles Sowerine, *Les Femmes et le socialisme* (Paris, 1978); Charles Sowerine, *Sisters or Citizens? Women and Socialism in France since 1876* (Cambridge, 1982).

C. Fonds Marianne Rauze, Bibliothèque historique de la Ville de Paris.

Albert S. Hill

RAVEN, Charles Earle (4 July 1885 Paddington, London—8 July 1964 Cambridge, England). *Education*: B.A., Gonville and Caius Coll., Cambridge Univ., 1908. *Career*: assistant secretary, Education, Liverpool, 1908-9; fellow and dean, Emmanuel Coll., Cambridge, 1910-15; assistant master, Tonbridge School, 1915-17; army chaplain, 1917-18; rector, Bletchingley, 1919-23; canon, Liverpool Cathedral, 1924-32; Regius Professor of Divinity, Cambridge, 1932-50, vice-chancellor, 1947-49; master, Christ's Coll., 1939-50; warden, Madingley Hall, 1950-54; theologian and scientist.

Charles Raven's father was a barrister and his mother's father a business man. He attended boarding-school at Uppingham. From his youth he was a brilliant scholar, obtaining first-class honours in Part I of the Classical Tripos, first-class honours with distinction in Part II of the Theological Tripos, and at the same time developing his expertise in the biological sciences.

In the first half of his life three experiences especially moulded him. Experience of boys' clubs in a working-class area challenged his presuppositions and showed him a fellowship transcending class and upbringing. Experience as a chaplain in the front line in 1917-18 intensified this and gave him a great respect for the courage and comradeship of ordinary people in danger. His work after the war in Liverpool convinced him that, given vision and organization on the part of Christians, Jesus could transform both individuals and society.

Raven was joint-secretary of the Conference of Christian Politics, Economics and Citizenship (COPEC), where he worked closely with William Temple in bringing the Christian gospel to bear on social issues. Slowly in the 1920s Raven, unlike Temple, came to adopt the pacifist position as the only one faithful to the New Testament. In 1932 he became Chairman of the Fellowship of Reconciliation and was its national leader till his death. In 1934 he was one of the sponsors of the Peace Pledge Union. When the Second World War came his friendship with Temple saved the Church from splitting over pacifism. Raven served the peace movement by statesmanlike leadership. He wrote well, and *Jesus and the Gospel of Love* (1931), *Is War Obsolete*? (1935), *War and the Christian* (1938), and *The Cross and the Crisis* (1939) remain classic expositions.

Raven was deeply concerned about the reconciliation of science and religion and wrote and spoke widely on this subject. He was an outstanding vice-chancellor, who secured the admission of women to full University status, and helped to choose J. C. Smuts as chancellor, the friendship between the field-marshal and the pacifist arose from profound mutual respect. Above all he was one of the greatest preachers and public speakers of this century, with his magnificent presence, his sonorous organ-voice, his brilliant eyes, and a nervous restlessness which was the mark of his depth of feeling.

Bibliography:

A. *The Cross and the Crisis* (London, 1939); *Is War Obsolete*? (London, 1935); *Jesus and the Gospel of Love* (Cambridge, 1931); *Musings and Memories* (Cambridge, 1931); *War and the Christian* (London, 1938).

B. F. W. Dillistone, *Charles Raven* (London, 1975); DNB, 1961-70, 868-70.

John Ferguson

READ, Herbert Edward (4 December 1893, Kirbymoorside, Yorkshire, England—12 June 1968 Stonegrave, Yorkshire). *Education*: attended, Leeds Univ. 1912-14. *Career*: assistant keeper, Victoria and Albert Museum, 1922-31; Watson Gordon Professor of Fine Art, Univ. of Edinburgh, 1931-33; editor, *Burlington Magazine* 1933-39; poet and art critic.

Herbert Read came of farming stock and was proud of it. He loved his native

North Yorkshire, was frustrated when he moved away, and returned there in his late fifties.

When the First World War broke out in 1914 Read joined the famous Green Howards. He served with outstanding courage and distinction as an officer, being mentioned in dispatches and being awarded the Military Cross and DSO. As with *Siegfried Sassoon, his distinguished record as a soldier added power to his later pacifist witness.

Read had a visual imagination, and was a less distinguished poet than his friend, T. S. Eliot. He is rather classified with another friend, T. E. Hulme, as an Imagist. As such he used free verse to convey closely focussed pictures and emotions. He reflected his experience of war in "Kneeshaw Goes to War," in the six short pieces which make up "The Scene of War," in the poignant "My Company," and a longer dramatic poem "The End of the War." Read wrote comparatively little verse, and his next serious poetry also was on the theme of war, relating to the Spanish Civil War and the Second World War; the finest of these, and perhaps the finest of all his poems, is "To a Conscript of 1940."

Between the wars Read established himself as one of the leading art critics in Britain, giving his critique a strong social dimension. He wrote three books of exceptional influence, *Art Now* (1931), *Art and Industry* (1934), *Art and Society* (1937). He was avant-garde and defended the Surrealists at the time of the 1936 Surrealist exhibition. Had it not been for the outbreak of war in 1939 he would have become director of a new Museum of Modern Art in London. After the war he joined with Roland Penrose in forming the Institute of Contemporary Arts (1947).

Read's social philosophy was anarchist, though it might be truer to say that he believed in the creative tensions between tradition and innovation, order and anarchy. He became a passionate defender of individual freedom. His pacifism was rooted in his anarchism (his mentors were *Leo Tolstoy and Edward Carpenter). In 1914 he had declared himself a political but not an ethical pacifist, and went to war. In 1938 he wrote "Anarchism naturally implies pacifism" but supported Britain's declaration of war. After the war he espoused the pacifist cause, but was reluctant to expound this in writing; his *Education for Peace*, while attacking war, is largely on art in education. He was an unsystematic thinker and a pacifist in general philosophy rather than in political commitment, though he was ready to join *Bertrand Russell in active protest against the shadow of nuclear destruction.

Read was knighted posthumously (to the dismay of some of his friends) in 1973.

Bibliography:

A. *Art and Society* (London, 1937); *Collected Poems* (London, 1946); *The Contrary Experience* (London, 1963); *Education for Peace* (London, 1950); *The Green Cloud* (London, 1935); *Poetry and Anarchism* (London, 1938).

B. C. Woodcock *Herbert Read: The Stream and the Source* (London, 1972).

John Ferguson

REICHENBACH, Emma Pieczynska. See PIECZYNSKA-REICHENBACH, Emma.

REMARQUE, Erich Maria [pseud. of Erich Paul Remark] (22 June 1898, Osnabrück, Germany—25 September 1970, Ascona, Switzerland). *Education*: Teachers Training Coll., Osnabrück. *Career*: elementary school teacher, organist, salesman, journalist, and numerous other jobs, 1919-28; pacifist novelist, 1929-70.

In 1929 Erich Maria Remarque achieved immediate renown with the publication of his portrayal of trench warfare in *Im Westen nichts Neues (All Quiet on the Western Front)*. Although the book's epigraph claimed the novel was neither an accusation nor a credo, Remarque's powerful depiction of the mechanized violence that consumed virtually every member of a high school class of conscripts was a vehement denunciation of modern war. The novel has been translated into thirty-two languages, and, as indicated by its sustained popularity, Remarque's German recruits have come to symbolize the agony of twentieth-century Everyman.

Remarque's pacifism was rooted in his own experience in serving in World War I and of returning to a homeland beset by political violence. Unhappy with petty demands of his chosen career as teacher, he spent most of the 1920s wandering from job to job until he found catharsis in the writing of *Im Westen*. In subsequent novels, *Der Weg zurück (The Road Back*) (1931) and *Drei Kameraden (Three Comrades*) (1937), he continued to develop the theme of the war as the explanation for the aimlessness and disillusionment of his generation. Remarque portrayed the surviving members of this generation as passive victims of a mindless civilian patriotism, of a brutal military establishment, and of a peace that proved to be an extension of war. His use of fiction as a means of confronting the devastating effects of World War I placed him in the company of others of his generation like Theodor Plievier, Ludwig Renn, Georg von der Vring, and Arnold Zweig. Some pacifist reviewers accused Remarque of sentimentality or even commercial opportunism in his portrayals of war and its aftermath, while others criticized his generalized opposition to violence as an inadequate call to action. Most, however, lauded him for his ability to reach millions of readers who were far removed from pacifist advocacy.

Violent tactics by Nazi agitators led to the banning of the film version of *Im Westen* in 1930 and to Remarque's decision to leave Germany. After the Nazis assumed power, they publicly burned his books and stripped him of his German citizenship because of his "literary betrayal of the German soldier." In exile, Remarque became an American citizen and ultimately settled near Ascona, Switzerland. His numerous novels of these years probe the possibilities of human relationships in the upheaval wrought by Nazism and World War II and, like his earlier novels, rest upon a resounding condemnation of the destructive forces of modern civilization. Despite mixed critical response, the World War II novels were widely translated, and several were transformed into successful films.

In a 1962 interview Remarque described himself as a militant pacifist whose opposition to military and political violence had never wavered. His pacifist critics continue to be divided into those who believe this opposition failed to provide a basis for radical commitment to the cause of nonviolence and those who believe that *Im Westen nichts Neues*, with its stark portrayal of the cataclysm of modern warfare, still represents the greatest antiwar novel of the century.

Bibliography:

A. *Arc de Triomphe* (Zurich, 1946, Eng. trans., *Arch of Triumph*, New York, 1945); *Drei Kameraden* (Amsterdam, 1937, Eng. trans., *Three Comrades*, Boston, 1937); *Der Funke Leben* (Cologne, 1952), Eng. trans., *The Spark of Life*, New York, 1952); *Im Westen nichts Neues* (Berlin, 1929, Eng. trans., *All Quiet on the Western Front*, Boston, 1929); *Der Schwarze Obelisk* (Cologne, 1956, Eng. trans., *The Black Obelisk*, New York, 1957); *Der Weg Zuruck* (Berlin, 1931, Eng. trans., *The Road Back*, Boston, 1931); *Zeit Zu leben und Zeit zu sterben* (Cologne, 1954, Eng. trans., *A Time to Live and a Time to Die*, New York, 1954).

B. Alfred Antkowiak and Pawel Toper, *Ludwig Renn. Erich Maria Remarque* (Berlin, 1965); A. F. Bance, "*Im Westen nichts Neues*: A Bestseller in Context," *Modern Language Review*, 72 (1977), 359-73; Christine Barker and R. W. Last, *Erich Maria Remarque* (London, 1979); Modris Eksteins, "*All Quiet on the Western Front* and the Fate of a War," *Journal of Contemporary History*, 15 (April 1980), 345-66; Brian A. Rowley, "Journalism into Fiction: *Im Westen nichts Neues*," in Holger Klein, ed., *The First World War in Fiction* (London, 1976), 101-11; NYT, September 26, 1970.

C. Remarque-Sammlung, Niedersächsisches Staatsarchiv in Osnabrück.

Katherine Larson Roper

RÉMY, Caroline. See SÉVERINE

RENNER, Karl (4 December 1870, Unter-Tannowitz, Moravia, Austria [now Czechoslovakia]—31 December 1950, Vienna). *Education*: Dr. jur, Univ. of Vienna, 1896. *Career*: Social Democratic party member of the Austrian parliament, 1907-34; chancellor, first Austrian republic, 1918-20; chancellor and president of the second Austrian republic, 1945-50; statesman, sociologist, political economist, lecturer, and author.

All of his life, Karl Renner was a suporter of a supranational concept of law and its institutionalization which, he believed, would put an end to the rule of force on an international level. As a leading Social Democratic party writer on the Austro-Hungarian nationality problem and member of Austrian parliament since 1907, Renner strove for a peaceful and evolutionary solution to social and national questions. The objective behind all of his political reform ideas was the transformation of Austria-Hungary into a democratic federal state based on the nationalities living within its borders.

Despite his internationalist ideas and his call for peaceful change, Renner supported the prowar policy of the Social Democratic party's executive committee after the outbreak of World War I. His position reflected the conviction that internationalism could only triumph over nationalism and war through effective international organization and sanctions and not through a one-sided and idealistic rejection of the logic of national defense. Therefore, on the one hand, he was a supporter of the idea of a domestic armistice between social classes for the duration of the war and, on the other, a determined advocate of democratic reform within the supranational framework of the old Austrian state.

Upon the collapse of the Habsburg empire and the proclamation of the first Austrian republic on November 12, 1918, Renner became the chancellor and head of a coalition government that included the Social Democrats and Christian Socialists, the two leading Austrian political parties. As head of the Austrian peace delegation to the conference of St. Germain, Renner strove, unsuccessfully, to prevent substantial losses of territory by appealing to Wilsonian principles of self-determination. Despite prevailing tensions, Renner tried to establish good relations between Austria and those states formed wholly, or in part, out of territories formerly included within the Austro-Hungarian monarchy, especially Czechoslovakia. He even proposed a "little entente" between Austria, Czechoslovakia, and Rumania. All of these efforts came to nought in the confused postwar situation in central Europe. By 1920 the coalition broke up, electoral results made the Social Democratic party an opposition party, and Renner no longer was in the political forefront.

In the 1920s Renner devoted himself to his tasks as chairman of the workers' cooperative movement and president of the Workers' Bank. At the same time, he futilely called for domestic peace and warned against the radicalization and polarization of politics. Renner returned to active politics in April 1931, when he was elected president of the National Council, the lower house of the Austrian parliament. He resigned the position in March 1933, in order to be able to vote with the Social Democrats on issues before the parliament. After the conservative-clerical coup d'état in 1934, which turned Austria into a corporate-authoritarian state, Renner lived in self-imposed withdrawal first in Vienna and then from 1938-45 in his home in Gloggnitz. Despite his opposition to National Socialism, Renner, in a controversial public statement, supported the Anschluss of Austria to Hitler's Third Reich on the ground that the attachment of Austria to Germany had been a Social Democratic goal since 1918. He comforted himself with the thought that states and nations last for centuries while regimes change and parties last only for generations.

With the collapse of the Third Reich, Renner again became chancellor. He was entrusted by the Russian occupation forces with the task of forming a provisional government for Austria. In December 1945, following the national elections the previous month, he was elected the first president of the second Austrian republic, a position he held until his death. As president, Renner fought for a policy of neutrality for the Austrian republic. This policy found formal expression in the Austrian State Treaty of 1955. Renner saw his policy of neutrality as part of a European peace policy which would lead to the realization of his supranational concept of law and the elimination of force in international relations. This concept underlies his posthumously published work, *Die Nation: Mythos und Wirklichkeit (The Nation: Myth and Reality)* (1964).

Bibliography:

A. *An der Wende zweier Zeiten.* Lebenserinnerung (Vienna, 1946); *Der Anschluss Österreichs und Deutschland als Europäisches Problem* (Berlin, 1926); *Deutschland, Österreich und die Völker des Ostens* (Berlin, 1922); *Der Kampf der Österreichischen Nationen um der Staat*, (published under the pseud. Rudolf Springer) (Leipzig and Vienna, 1902); *Marxismus, Krieg und Internationale* (Stuttgart, 1917); *Die Menschenrechte: Zwei Vorträge* (Vienna, 1948); *Die Nation als Rechtsidee und die Internationale* (Vienna, 1914); *Wege der Verwirklichung* (Vienna, 1929).

B. Jacques Hannak, *Karl Renner: Versuch eine Biographie* (Vienna, 1965); Norbert Leser, "Karl Renner als Gesellschaftsdenker" in *Zwischen Reformismus und Bolschewismus* (Vienna, 1968); Hans Schroth, *Karl Renner: Eine Bibliographie* (Vienna, 1970); *Neue Österreichische Biographie ab 1815* (1956), 9-30; NYT, December 31, 1950.

Norbert Leser

RENOOZ, Céline [Muro] (7 January 1840, Liège, Belgium—28 February 1928, Paris). *Career*: author and lecturer.

Céline Renooz was born in Liège of French and Belgian parents. Her father, Emmanuel Nicolas Renoz, was a prominent attorney and political figure. Her mother was Parisian. Céline Renooz married a Spanish engineer, heir to a banking fortune, and resided in Spain until 1876, when she took her four children to Paris for their education. Thereafter she made Paris her home.

Though without formal university education, Renooz entered rapidly into the intellectual life of Paris. In 1878 she conceived the inspiration for a series of scientific and historical works that appeared in subsequent years, and began her career as writer, salonnière, and lecturer. In 1883 her first published book, *L'Origine des animaux*, proposed a theory of natural evolution countering that of Charles Darwin, whom she characterized as her precursor. Her impressive erudition and lucid, persuasive style won her invitations to lecture at the Sorbonne and at international professional meetings in the field of physiology, zoology, and other sciences, but her extraordinary ideas and outspoken attacks on Darwin and other leading authorities soon led to ostracism by the organized scientific community.

In 1888 Renooz founded and edited *La Revue scientifique des femmes*, published in Paris from May 1888 to May 1889. In 1890 she founded the Société néosophique which published the *Bulletin Mensuel de la Société néosophique*. Renooz strongly supported women's suffrage and the peace movement. At the Sixth International Peace Congress held in 1894 at Anvers, Belgium, she was a delegate representing the Union internationale des sciences et des arts. Renooz' published writings included articles, pamphlets, periodical contributions, and books. The latter were eventually brought together in two multi-volume works, *La Nouvelle Science* (1883-98) and *L'Ère de vérité* (1921-28).

In 1917 Renooz published a pamphlet entitled *La Paix glorieuse*, setting forth her analysis of war as a manifestation of patriarchal culture and her vision of peace as founded on matriarchal principles of reason, truth, and political decentralization. Her matriarchalist views were further developed in the six volumes of *L'Ère de vérité*, in which Renooz foreshadowed contemporary radical feminism in some of its sharpest attacks on male-created culture, knowledge, religion, language, science, and institutions. Renooz identified the female spirit with reason, truth, creative intelligence, and natural science. She regarded these as essential to order, harmony, peace, and progress in human affairs. She argued that there had existed at first in the human past a "period of light and peace" under the guidance of female rationality. This was succeeded by a struggle ending in the subordination of women and the victory of masculine power through lies and force. The culmination of this process in Roman androcracy was founded on glorification of patriotism, war, and conquest. The entire history of religion and civilization under masculine rule, Renooz maintained, was based upon falsifications and atrocities compiled by men to justify and enforce their illegitimate assumption of power, authority, and privilege.

In *La Paix glorieuse*, Renooz differentiated between the principles of nationality and patriotism. Nationality, she argued, was rooted in the place of birth, the "ancient *Matrie*, country of the mother." Patriotism, to the contrary, was "the principle of the Roman Empire . . . founded on despotism, imperial power, militarism and a code of laws giving the male rights of life and death over females, children, and slaves." To achieve peace, Renooz argued, it was necessary to restore the dignity and authority of the female sex, restore the nations (as opposed to the imperial *Patries*), and establish a decentralized federation of peoples ruled by reason and the female spirit.

Renooz won attention from the press in her own time, and praise in some quarters for her courage, clarity, and logic. She drew around her a small but devoted following in the Société néosophique. Her writings, astounding in their range and daring, were often so deviant from existing canons, so denunciatory, and so deeply challenging to male intellectual authority, that she was largely isolated in later life and her works reduced to obscurity after her death. They stand nonetheless as monumental contributions in the tradition of matriarchalist pacifism.

Bibliography:

A. *L'Ère de vérité* (6 vols., Paris, 1921-28); *La Nouvelle Science*, 4 volumes, including: *L'Origine des animaux* (Paris, 1883); *La Force* (Paris, 1890); *Le Principe générateur de la vie* (Paris, 1890); and *Psychologie comparée de l'homme et de la femme* (Paris, 1898); *La Paix glorieuse* (Paris, 1917).

B. *Dictionnaire biographique International des Écrivains, Artistes, Membres des Sociétés Savantes*, XVI (Paris, 1907), 5-7.

C. Bibliothèque Marguerite Durand, Paris, France (holdings include publications, typescript biography by Marguerite Guépet, clippings, and other material).

Berenice A. Carroll

REVON, Michel (24 March 1867, Geneva—10 January 1947, Chauconin, France). *Education*: Lycée Annecy; Doctor of Law, Univ. of Grenoble, 1888.

Career: professor (first chair of International Law), Univ. of Tokyo, 1892-99, Univ. of Paris, 1900-40; council member and president, Ligue internationale de la paix et de la liberté; council member, La paix par le droit; author and peace activist.

Michel Revon's initial participation in the French peace movement began in 1887 when, as a student, he established a branch of the Ligue internationale de la paix et de la liberté (International League of Peace and Freedom) in Grenoble. Five years later, the publication of his study on the history and prospects of international arbitration was honored with a prize from the Institut de France and became one of the most influential works within the peace movement in France. Recognized as a brilliant young scholar of international law, Revon was urged by the Minister of Public Education to accept an appointment to fill the first chair of international law at the University of Tokyo. There he taught international law and delivered a series of open lectures on the illegality of war as a violation of international precepts—all through the Sino-Japanese War of 1894-95. A second major book studying the philosophy and roots of war came out in 1896, partly inspired by the lectures.

Revon preserved his contacts with the peace movement while abroad. Before returning home to fill a chair in Japanese studies—a subject on which he had become expert—he traveled through the United States, visiting Washington to lobby for a standing treaty of arbitration between France and the United States. Such a project had been a favorite idea of the Interparliamentary Union and the Universal Peace Congress of 1893 (Chicago) and Revon supported it as feasible and useful, a view not shared by the U.S. Senate. Indeed, it exemplified the sort of specific action which Revon's views of international organization supported. He was cautious and realistic, insisting that the peace movement not urge impossible ideals on a world of naked national sovereignty and power politics. His study of arbitration examined in close detail those cases where it worked, such as the famous *Alabama* settlement between Great Britain and the United States. Revon wanted pressure put to bear by peace activists in favor of extending arbitration treaties where they had a chance of working and thus could become part of a growing tradition of positive success.

As a professor at the Sorbonne, he became noted for his studies of Japanese literature and culture, and also for his work with peace societies. To foster better relations between highly disparate cultures, he established a center in Paris to welcome Japanese students. Throughout the interwar years, Revon persisted in working for organized international institutions, writing for *Les Etats-Unis d'Europe* and heading monthly meetings of the Ligue internationale de la paix et de la liberté. Old age and the Second World War ended a lifetime of commitment and scholarship.

Bibliography:

A. *L'Arbitrage internationale, son passé, son présent, son avenir* (Paris 1892); *Le Droit de la guerre sous la République romaine* (Paris 1891); *Philosophie de la guerre* (Paris 1896).

B. Paul Combe, "Michel Revon" in *La Paix par le droit* (May, 1848), 130-31; "Revon, Michel" in A. H. Fried, ed., *Handbuch der Friedensbewegung*, (1911-13, reprint NY, 1972) II, 396-7.

Sandi E. Cooper

RICHARD, Henry (3 April 1812, Tregaron, Cardiganshire, Wales—20 August 1888, Treborth, Wales). *Education*: Highbury Coll. (Portsmouth, England), 1830-34. *Career*: Congregational minister, 1835-50, Member of Parliament (Merthyr boroughs), 1868-88; writer, speaker, reformer, and peace advocate.

Inclined to the ministry by his father, a Calvinistic Methodist minister, Henry Richard was ordained as the Congregational pastor of Marlborough Chapel, London in 1835. During the 1840s, however, his interest in politics and the peace movement grew to such an extent that he relinquished the ministry in 1850 and devoted himself completely to pacifism, reform causes, and politics. Richard became famous as "the Apostle of Peace," an outspoken champion of the concept of international arbitration, an energetic participant in numerous international peace congresses, and a vigorous antiwar journalist and author. He attached himself to many reform causes, including that of the Liberation Society, a nonconformist disestablishmentarian group, the cause of more democratic parliamentary representation for Wales, and, later in his career, the successful promotion of the improvement of intermediate and higher education in Wales. His twenty-year career in the House of Commons gave him a forum in which to agitate for the amelioration of conditions in his native Wales, a principality plagued by poverty, injustice, and neglect.

In 1848 Richard was appointed secretary of the Peace Society, a position he held for thirty-seven years. As secretary he became involved with the publication of the Society's monthly organ, *The Herald of Peace*, and with the management of the *Morning Star* and the *Evening Star*, two dailies that strongly supported an antiwar position. Following *Richard Cobden's first motion in the House of Commons on behalf of arbitration in 1849, Richard helped to organize an international peace congress at Paris in the same year, sharing the presidency with the author *Victor Hugo and the American pacifist *Elihu Burritt. He promoted a series of congresses at Frankfurt (1850), London (1851), Manchester (1853), and Edinburgh (1853). The outbreak of the Crimean War provoked him to write the antiwar study *A History of the Origin of the War with Russia* (1855); and the conclusion of the conflict brought him to the Paris peace conference where, with the assistance of *Joseph Sturge and Charles Hindley, he was able to secure the inclusion in the peace treaty of Protocol 23, a declaration in favor of arbitration of international controversies.

Maintaining his pacifist convictions, Richard refused to support the nationalist revolutions and liberation struggles that won endorsement from many British humanitarians, radicals, and reformers. Divisions within the British peace movement created by these conflicts were made sharper by the defeat of *John Bright and Cobden in the general elections of 1857 and by the Indian Mutiny. Reacting to this series of antiwar reversals, Richard published his *The Present and Future of India under British Rule* (1858) in which he denounced British imperial conquest, annexation, militarism, and exploitation in Asia and Africa. In the 1860s he denounced the second Opium War in China, the New Zealanders' decimation of the Maoris, and the attack on Kagoshima, Japan. The peace movement itself was again divided by the American Civil War: many pacifists favored the Union and emancipation, but Richard argued that partisanship would only prolong the war, urging instead British neutrality, recognition of the Confederacy, and the idea of a negotiated end to the war.

In 1869, the year following his election to Parliament, Richard undertook a mission to continental Europe on behalf of international disarmament. His travels were accompanied by the introduction of disarmament motions in a number of European legislatures. Although the outbreak of the Franco-Prussian War in 1870 shattered burgeoning hopes for arms reductions, the idea of international arbitration was resuscitated by the successful arbitration of the *Alabama* claims, defusing tensions between the United States and Britain. Richard's introduction of a motion urging both disarmament and arbitration in the Commons in 1873 mustered encouraging support; and the legislatures of Italy, Belgium, Holland, Denmark, Canada, and the United States followed by passing arbitration resolutions. Despite these encouraging signs, his leadership of a pacifist delegation to the Congress of Berlin (1878) brought no concrete results, his 1880 motion in favor of gradual disarmament provoked a parliamentary debate but without a vote, and the outbreak of expansionist wars in Afghanistan, Zululand, Egypt, and the Sudan constituted further setbacks for the movement. Nevertheless, Richard pushed forward, joining in the founding of the Anti-Aggression League in 1882 which supported the creation of ad hoc peace committees to deal with new outbreaks of armed conflict and publishing his *Papers on the Reasonableness of International Arbitration* (1887), based on his addresses to conferences of the Association for the Reform and Codification of the Law of Nations.

Richard's crusade for peace was as protracted, energetic, and unwavering as it was frustrating, disappointing, and controversial. His doctrinaire adherence to his peculiarly personal notions of pacifism seemed at times morally myopic: he opposed wars of national liberation and the cause of the Union in the American Civil War as much as he opposed brazen wars of imperialism; he favored disarmament and arbitration even while both schemes seemed more than a trifle simplistic and naive; and he never presented a comprehensive analytical study of the causes of war and a comprehensive strategy of peace. Nevertheless, his voice was raised repeatedly against war for nearly a half century and every British ministry which made war had to reckon with the certain criticism of Richard, a nonconformist whose personal morals always informed his views on international and national matters.

Bibliography:

A. *Defensive War* (New Vienna, OH, 1872); *The Destruction of Kagoshima and Our Intercourse with Japan* (London, 1863); *Evidence of Turkish Misrule* (London, 1877); *The Gradual Triumph of Law over Brute Force* (London, 1874); *A History of the Origin of the War with Russia* (London, 1855); *Memoirs of Joseph Sturge* (London, 1864).

B. Lewis Appleton, *Memoirs of Henry Richard, M.P.* (London, 1889); Rhys T. Davies, *The Story of Henry Richard* (Wrexham, 1925); C. S. Miall, *Henry Richard, M.P.* (London, 1889); *Biographical Dictionary of Modern British Radicals*, II, 1832-1870 (London, 1983); DNB, XVI, 1094-96; LT, August 22, 1888.

John V. Crangle

RICHARDS, Leyton Price (12 March 1879, Sheffield, England—22 August 1948, Mortimer Common near Reading, England). *Education*: studies at Gordons Coll., Aberdeen; M.A., Univ. of Glasgow, 1903; theological degree, Mansfield Coll., Oxford, 1906. *Career*: minister and pacifist.

Because he came from a relatively poor family Leyton Richards did not at first intend to pursue university training. The direction of his life changed through the influence of Dr. Ambrose Sheperd, a Congregational minister, who persuaded young Richards to prepare himself for the ministry. In June 1906 Richards was ordained as a minister in the Congregational Church and in August of that same year he married Edith, the oldest daughter of the Reverend Samuel Pearson, himself a Congregational minister. Richards' first appointment as a full time minister took him to Peterhead, a small Scottish town in Aberdeenshire, where he remained until the end of the year 1910. Subsequently he held ministerial appointments in Australia and England.

While preaching at the Bowdon Downs Congregational Church in Cheshire, he clashed sharply with the civil authorities because of his public denunciations of the Conscription Act of 1916. He was tried in a London court, along with several other defendants, and fined. World War I galvanized Richards' pacifism. From 1920 onward he participated in a number of lecturing and preaching tours of the United States and Canada. He also played an active role in the "Christ and Peace" program which had beern launched in the Fall of 1929 to awaken churches to the necessity of condemning modern warfare. During the years 1940 to 1944 he served as warden at Woodbrooke, an important Quaker International College on the outskirts of Birmingham. Here he drew closer to Quaker principles and in 1946 joined the Society of Friends.

Leyton Richards took the time to write extensively on the subject of Christian pacifism. Through these writings and by his distinction in effective preaching and teaching he became well-known as one of the leading Christian pacifists in twentieth-century England.

Bibliography:

A. *The Christian Foundation of Peace* (London, 1938); *Christian Pacifism after Two World Wars. A Critical and Constructive Approach to Problems of World Peace* (London, 1948); *The Christian's Alternative to War. An Examination of Christian Pacifism* (London, 1929); *The Christian's Contribution to Peace. A Constructive Approach to International Relationships* (London, 1935).

B. Martin Ceadel, *Pacifism in Britain, 1914-1945: The Defining of a Faith* (Oxford, 1980); Edith Ryley Richards: *Private View of a Public Man; The Life of Leyton Richards* (London, 1950).

Bernerd C. Weber

RICHARDSON, Lewis Fry (11 October 1881, Newcastle-upon-Tyne, England—30 September 1953, Kilmun, Argyllshire, Scotland). *Education*: Durham

Coll. of Science, Newcastle, 1898-1900; B.A. King's Coll., Cambridge Univ., 1903; D.Sc. (physics), Univ. of London, 1926; B.Sc. (Psychology), Univ. College, London, 1929. *Career*: variety of jobs in industry and teaching, 1903-13; Superintendent of Eskdalemuir Observatory, Meteorological Office, 1913-16; Met. Office, 1919-20; head, Physics Dept., Westminster Training Coll., 1920-29; principal, Paisley Technical Coll., 1929-40; Fellow of the Royal Society, 1926.

Lewis F. Richardson was born into a Quaker family with a distinguished background. One of his main passions was meteorology, in which field he made important contributions, culminating in the publication in 1922 of *Weather Prediction by Numerical Process*, a book which only after his death would be recognized as "a pioneer work of great vision." His strong pacifist convictions made it impossible for him to remain in the Meteorological Office when this was incorporated into the Air Ministry in 1920, and he resigned to take up a career in education. He continued, however, his research and writings in meteorology for several years, and returned to it again briefly towards the end of his life.

From 1916 until 1919 Richardson, a conscientious objector, served with the Friends' Ambulance Unit in France. The experience deeply affected him and was to propel him into his second passion, the pursuit of the intellectual understanding of war. While still in France, he completed an essay on "The Mathematical Psychology of War." Unwilling to send "so unconventional a work" to a learned society, he made 300 copies by multigraph and distributed them among his friends. This work was little noticed, and he took up some of the same ideas in a paper published in 1935, when he had transferred his main spare-time occupation from the study of weather to that of war. In order to devote all his time to this, he decided, shortly after the outbreak of the Second World War, to retire early on a very modest pension. At this time also he was offered a professorship, something he had longed for all his life but which according to his wife, his pacifist convictions had prevented him from securing. Now, with great regret, he refused the invitation because of his commitment to research on war and peace.

Whereas his Quaker background and his experiences in the First World War undoubtedly accounted for his concern with and interest in war, the specific Richardsonian approach adopted in its study directly derived from his scientific training. He applied objective mathematical techniques in the belief that to the extent that wars are governed by quasi-mechanical and quantifiable processes, they can be predicted.

In the ten years following his retirement extensive empirical investigations resulted in his two most important studies, *Arms and Insecurity* (1947) and *Statistics of Deadly Quarrels* (1950). Unable to find a publisher, he produced both books in microfilm. In the early fifties they came to the attention of scholars such as Kenneth Boulding and Anatol Rapoport, who were greatly excited by them. Boulding has referred to those who read Richardson in microfilm as the

''Early Church'' of the peace research movement. Indeed, Richardson laid the groundwork for this movement which started in earnest within a few years after his death. When both studies were published posthumously in 1960, they were widely reviewed and helped establish Richardson as the pioneer of peace research. He was one of the very first to put into practice the maxim,''If you want peace, understand war.'' By doing so Richardson inspired a whole generation. In 1969 a ''Richardson Institute for Conflict and Peace Research'' was founded in London and is now based at the University of Lancaster.

Bibliography:

A. *Arms and Insecurity: A Mathematical Study of the Causes of War*, Nicholas Rashevsky and Ernesto Trucco, eds. (Pittsburgh, 1960); ''Could an Arms-Race End without Fighting?'' *Nature*, 168 (September 29, 1951), 567; ''The Distribution of Wars in Time,'' *Journal of the Royal Statistical Society*, 107 (1945), 242-50; *Generalized Foreign Politics* (Cambridge, 1939); ''Mathematical Psychology of War,'' *Nature*, 135 (May 18, 1935), 830-31; *Statistics of Deadly Quarrels*, Quincy Wright and C. C. Lienau, eds. (Pittsburgh, 1960); ''The Submissiveness of Nations,'' *British Journal of Statistical Psychology*, 6 (November, 1953), 77-90; ''War Moods,'' *Psychometrika*, 13 (1948), 147-74, 197-232. See also ''A Bibliography of Lewis Fry Richardson's Studies of the Causation of Wars with a View to Their Avoidance,'' *Journal of Conflict Resolution*, 1 (September, 1957), 305-7.

B.Oliver M. Ashford,''Mathematics of Weather and War,'' *The Friend*, October 9, 1981, 1281-84; Anatol Rapoport, ''Lewis Fry Richardson's Mathematical Theory of War,'' *Journal of Conflict Resolution*, 1 (September, 1957), 249-99; Stephen A. Richardson, ''Lewis Fry Richardson: A Personal Biography,'' *Journal of Conflict Resolution*, 1 (September, 1957), 300-4; David Wilkinson, *Deadly Quarrels: Lewis Fry Richardson and the Statistical Study of War* (Berkeley, 1980); DNB, 1951-1960, 837-39.

Peter van den Dungen

RICHET, Charles (26 August 1850, Paris—4 December 1935, Paris). *Education*: Lycée Bonaparte; Docteur ès sciences, Faculty of Medicine, Univ. of Paris, 1877. *Career*: professor, Faculty of Medicine, Collège de France, Univ. of Paris, 1877-1927; founder and editor, *Annales des sciences physiques*; founder and president, Institut Metaphysique International; president, Academie des Sciences, 1933; president, Société française pour l'arbitrage entre nations, council member Délégation permanente françaises des sociétés de la paix; director and editor, *L'Independance Belge*; scientist, novelist, poet, and peace leader.

One of the most active and respected members of the French and European peace movements prior to World War I, Charles Richet first made his reputation as a scientific researcher whose work on anaphylaxis led to the Nobel prize in medicine (1913). His researches covered a huge range of scientific areas including studies in poisons, stomach acids, epilepsy, tuberculosis, animal temperatures, psychology, and parapsychology. Some of his unsuccessful work led others to the discoveries of serums for tetanus and diphtheria. For the challenge of it, he and a friend built an airplane in 1888 which was ridiculed as were his later studies in parapsychology. Between 1877 and 1929, he published over a dozen full-length books in the sciences including one that became the standard physiology text in several universities. He was immensely active in the world of scientific publishing and present at most major society meetings.

His interest in other areas led to books of poetry and fiction as well as to the peace movement. Richet was infuriated by the vast sums spent in Europe for military preparations which he viewed as wasted funds that could better be used supporting scientific research and cultural activities, the real mainsprings of progress. He joined *Frédéric Passy's Société française pour l'arbitrage entre nations (French Society for International Arbitration) and eventually became its president. He attended national and international peace conferences, served on numerous study committees, was elected to the national council of the central organization of French peace societies, and worked with the Carnegie Endowment for International Peace and the International Peace Bureau. He presided over the 1900 Universal Peace Congress in Paris, regarded as one of the most successful meetings of that group. In addition, his books, *Guerres et paix* (*Wars and Peace*) (1899) and *Le Passé de la guerre et l'avenir de la paix* (*The End of War and the Future of Peace*) (1909) ranked among the more important such works of the period.

Richet cleverly detailed the increasing sums which the major powers had spent on arms from the 1870s to the opening of the century. Once he pointed out that approximately 80 million European families paid an annual average of 240 francs for military upkeep. In 1913 he observed that the annual percentage increases across the continent for military expenditures were escalating geometrically every decade and by 1930, were this to continue, the percentages would be 100 fold what they were in 1910. Comparing these figures to the relatively static amounts spent on basic research as well as to the growing difficulties of the poor and working class in Europe, Richet predicted disaster. His writings and speeches also attacked the extreme nationalists and the so-called realists who insisted that military expenditure assured security. His pen attacked false patriotism and twisted social Darwinism.

Richet's sense of the European military madness led him to predict that a potential war between France and Germany would produce hundreds of thousands of casualties within the first days as well as the eventual unravelling of civil society through unbearable hardships on the home front. He was not one who imagined there would be a quick victory as in 1870-71, but rather a long tortuous war. When it came, he served at a hospital on the front, developing transfusion techniques that saved lives and watching, first hand, his fears come to pass. His book at the end of the war, *L'Homme Stupide* (*Stupid Man*) (1919), summarized his response to that vast bloodletting. He continued to struggle for the acceptance of international organization after the war though with a considerably chastened set of expectations.

Charles Richet was truly an internationalist, an individual who understood what the true needs of humanity were, despite the blinding light of the current idols of the tribe.

Bibliography:

A. *Guerres et paix* (Paris, 1899); *L'Homme Impuissant* (Paris, 1927); *L'Homme stupide* (Paris, 1919); *Le Passé de la guerre et l'avenir de la paix* (Paris, 1907); *Le Savant* (Paris, 1923).

B. "Richet, Charles," in P. Augé, ed., *Larousse Mensuel Illustré*, 10 (Paris, 1935-37), 38, 678-79.

Sandi E. Cooper

RICHTER, Adolf (1 February 1839, Wiesbaden, Germany—13 August 1914, Pforzheim, Germany). *Career*: member, Ligue internationale de la paix et de la liberté, 1879-1914; delegate to International Peace Bureau, 1892-1914; president, German Peace Society, 1899-1914; chemist, industrialist, pacifist.

Like *Franz Wirth, Adolf Richter was one of the central figures in the early history of the German peace movement, a south German dignitary who gave of both his energies and his money to the cause in the 1890s. Richter made a modest fortune in gold and silver processing in Pforzheim in Baden. His contacts among Germany's democratic politicians were extensive. He was a cousin to Eugen Richter and served on the executive committee of the Süddeutsche Volkspartei (South German People's Party) in Pforzheim.

Richter was for many years the only man in Germany to belong to a peace society. The lone German in *Charles Lemonnier's Ligue internationale de la paix et de la liberté (International League of Peace and Freedom), he was also conspicuous in his solitude at the first Universal Peace Congress in 1889. When the Deutsche Friedensgesellschaft (German Peace Society) finally did take shape in the 1890s, Richter was at the forefront in exploiting his network of political friends to found chapters in south Germany. When in 1899 the headquarters of the German Peace Society were transferred from Berlin to Stuttgart, Richter became president of the organization.

Richter's role in the German peace movement was principally diplomatic. At home he served as mediator among its frequently bickering factions; abroad he was its representative at international conferences, long the most well known and respected of the German pacifists. After the turn of the century, however, he became increasingly a figurehead. As his health deteriorated, he left the administration of the German Peace Society to *Otto Umfrid and the role of representative abroad to *Ludwig Quidde, who succeded him as president of the German Peace Society in May 1914. Richter died shortly after the outbreak of World War I.

Bibliography:

A. *Die wichtigsten Einwendungen gegen die Friedensbewegung* (Esslingen, 1902); "33 Jahre im Dienste des Weltfriedens," in Georg Grosch, ed., *Deutsche Pazifisten: Eine Sammlung von Vorkämpfern der Friedensbewegung in Deutschland* (Stuttgart, 1920), 8-16.

B. Roger Chickering, *Imperial Germany and a World Without War: The Peace Move-*

ment and German Society, 1892-1914 (Princeton, 1975); Ludwig Quidde, "Zum Gedächntis Dr. Adolf Richters," *Der Völker-Friede*, 16 (March 1915), 25-26.

Roger Chickering

ROBERTS, Richard (31 May 1874, Blaenau Festiniog, North Wales—10 April 1945, New York). *Education*: Liverpool Institute, 1887-91; University Coll. of Wales, 1891-94; B.D., Bala Theological Coll., North Wales, 1896. *Career*: evangelist, Forward Movement, Wales, 1896-97; minister, Presbyterian and United Church of Canada, England, 1897-1915, New York City, 1917-20, Canada, 1921-39; assistant principal, Bala Theological Coll., 1898-1900; secretary, Fellowship of Reconciliation, 1915-17; editor, *The Venturer*, 1915-17, *The World Tomorrow*, 1917-20; moderator, United Church of Canada, 1934-36; lecturer, Pine Hill Divinity Coll., Halifax, 1939; writer and pacifist.

An internationally acclaimed radical Christian theologian and author of over thirty books and pamphlets expounding the social responsibilities of the Christian conscience, Richard Roberts was one of the most influential pacifists in Canada during the interwar years.

He was first attracted to socialism in the 1890s while a student evangelist with the Forward Movement preaching the social gospel in the coal fields of South Wales. With the outbreak of the First World War, Roberts embraced pacifism as a natural extension of radical religion and joined with *Henry Hodgkin in an effort to preserve a Christian pacifist front by founding the Fellowship of Reconciliation. After being forced to resign from Crouch Hill Presbyterian Church, London, because of his pacifism, Roberts served a secretary of the new pacifist organization as well as editor of its journal, *The Venturer*, until 1917 when he emigrated to New York City, in part, to help with the fledgling American branch. While in the United States he joined *Reinhold Niebuhr and *Kirby Page on the editorial board of *The World Tomorrow* and acted as a liaison between American and British pacifists for the duration of the war.

In 1922 Roberts emigrated to Montreal's American Presbyterian Church and thereafter provided a vocabulary of ideological depth to the resurgent peace movement in Canada. By mid-decade he joined W. A. Gifford and others in the Protestant Ministerial Association of Montreal to produce *The Christian and War* (1926), the definitive Canadian pacifist statement of the period. Shortly afterward he moved on to the Sherbourne United Church in Toronto where he helped establish a local chapter of the Fellowship of Reconciliation and then led it during the early 1930s in a campaign in defense of civil liberties and in support of disarmament.

Although Roberts drafted the United Church of Canada's endorsement of the International Disarmament Conference in Geneva, he criticized the talks as doomed to failure because they concentrated on traditional arms and strategies while largely ignoring the airplane and its terrifying ability to unleash the brunt of future war upon urban civilian populations. In vain, he appealed to the Canadian government to take the lead in organizing a new disarmament conference that would confront the frightening reality of aerial warfare.

As moderator of the United Church of Canada during the depth of the depression, Roberts endorsed the radical quest for social and economic justice and, although definitely not a Marxist, he lent his influential support to the Fellowship for a Christian Social Order and other groups working in that direction. He also called upon the United Church to register its uncompromising opposition to all future wars, the same goal he promoted as the leading Canadian delegate to the 1937 Oxford Conference of the Universal Council for Life and Work representing all major Protestant denominations. The Conference statement on war, drafted jointly by Roberts and Canon *Charles Raven, recognized three possible positions for Christians in time of war, including the pacifist rejection of all wars. Roberts was pleased with this official recognition of absolute pacifism as a legitimate Christian stand, but he was ultimately disappointed by the response of Canada's churches during the Second World War. Consequently, Roberts publicly reasserted his pacifism by signing the "Witness Against War Manifesto," the defiant pacifist statement circulated among United Churchmen by *R. Edis Fairbairn.

In the spring of 1945 Roberts' distinguished career as a pacifist spokesman came to a close. For over three decades he had nurtured the growth of the Fellowship of Reconciliation, in three countries, as a spearhead of social and moral reform and consistently articulated an intelligent theological case for pacifism. His lasts major contribution to that end was his open wartime dialogue with Reinhold Niebuhr in which he criticized Niebuhr's "moral relativism" as the first step towards the wholesale abandonment of Christian principles. In Roberts' final analysis, pacifism remained the only alternative to the evil of war perpetuating itself throughout society.

Bibliography:

A. *The Christian and War*, with W. A. Gifford, et. al. (Toronto, 1926).

B. Thomas P. Socknat, " 'Witness Against War': Pacifism in Canada, 1900-1945," Ph.D. dissertation, McMaster University, 1981.

C. Richard Roberts Papers, United Church of Canada Archives, Toronto.

Thomas P. Socknat

ROBINSON, Ellen (14 March 1840, Liverpool, England—6 March 1912, Liverpool). *Education*: Moravian School, Neuweid, Germany. *Career*: private tutor, teacher, school mistress until 1889; minister, Society of Friends, 1885-1912; speaker and writer.

After many years of conducting a girls' boarding school in Liverpool, Ellen Robinson was, in 1885, recorded as a minister of the Society of Friends. Shortly thereafter she began to speak on behalf of *Priscilla Hannah Peckover's Local Peace Association Movement. By 1889 she had left teaching to become a full-time speaker and writer on peace and other social questions.

During the 1890s, Robinson was among Britain's most active pacifists. In addition to her continuous speaking engagements (as many as one hundred a year), she was vice-president of the Liverpool and Birkenhead Women's Peace Society, secretary to the National Peace Union, and a member of the National Peace Council. She also became a major figure at International Peace Congresses where her fluent knowledge of German and French, reflecting her liberal education and cosmopolitian interests, proved extremely useful.

While Ellen Robinson's pacifism undoubtedly had its origin in her Quaker faith, like many prominent Friends of her day, she was also a strong liberal in the *Richard Cobden-William Gladstone tradition. This strain of liberalism was revealed in her recognition of the connection between the expansion of the British Empire and the growing menace of British militarism. Robinson believed the injustice and oppression visited upon native peoples illustrated that the spirit of militarism rather than the spirit of Christianity and civilization moved and guided British imperialism. Another feature of Robinson's peace testimony was her warning against the attempts of Boys' Brigades and other groups to foster the military spirit among British youth.

The outbreak of the Boer War was the most momentous event of Ellen Robinson's public career. Not only did the war in South Africa fulfill her worst fears about the nature of British imperialism, it also exposed the shallowness of the British peace movement. But for all its negative effects, the war provided peace advocates with the focus and sense of urgency they had previously lacked. Robinson was a tireless and fearless public speaker against the Boer War. As a recently appointed member of the Meeting for Sufferings (executive committee for British Friends), she urged Quakers to take the lead in protesting the war, whatever the social, political, or economic consequences.

Although the condemnation of the war eventually issued by the London Yearly Meeting of Friends was less vigorous than Robinson would have liked, it was sufficient to cause many Quakers, including Robinson, to be subjected to insults, threats, and, in a few instances, physical violence. But she was never intimidated and continued to speak out against the war and the new menace of conscription. Nor did her activities cease when the Boer War ended.

For the final ten years of her life, despite advancing age and failing health, Ellen Robinson remained one of Britain's most imposing peace advocates. Increasingly, she felt that the struggle against militarism should be waged from within the existing political structure. To this end, she was an unsuccessful candidate for the Liverpool City Council in 1907, but was elected a Poor Law Guardian in the next year. She was still fulfilling the responsibilities of this office, while maintaining her lifelong stance against militarism and the growth of armaments, when she died.

Ellen Robinson's gentle manner could not subdue her passionate attachment to the principles she held dear. A lifelong feminist, she supported female suffrage and made the advocacy of high education for women her own special cause. But her greatest achievements were in helping to bring peace testimony back to a place of central importance within the Society of Friends and to bring the peace movement itself into the mainstream of Edwardian Radicalism.

Bibliography:

A. *A Word to the Working Classes on the Military Training of Their Boys* (Leonminister, 1895).

B. "Dictionary of Quaker Biography," Friends' House Library, London; *The Friend*, March 22, 1912.

Thomas C. Kennedy

ROERICH, Nicholas K. See *Biographical Dictionary of Internationalists*.

ROLIN, Henri. See *Biographical Dictionary of Internationalists*.

ROLIN-JAEQUEMYNS, Gustave Henri Ange Hippolyte. See *Biographical Dictionary of Internationalists*.

ROLAND HOLST-VAN DER SCHALK, Henriette Goverdine Anna (24 December 1869, Noordwijk, Netherlands—21 November 1952, Amsterdam). *Education*: boarding school, Arnhem; private education, Liège. *Career*: writer, journalist, editor, and political activist.

Born into an intellectual family, Henriette Roland Holst grew up in surroundings dominated by leading artists and writers. She began her own writing career in 1893, a career which made her an important contributor to Dutch poetry, drama, and letters in general in the twentieth century. Her husband, R. H. Roland Holst (1868-1938) became an artist, renowned for his decorative works and graphic art and eventually served as director of the academy of art in Amsterdam (1926-34). Among her close friends was Herman Gorter, a leading poet and political philosopher.

With her husband and Gorter, Henriette Roland Holst joined the SDAP (Dutch Labor Party) in 1897, having become a convinced Marxist. In 1902 she published *Capital and Labor in The Netherlands*. In addition, she became interested in the ideas of *Leo Tolstoy whose nonviolence was attractive to a number of Dutch intellectuals. Roland Holst, however, was not persuaded that nonviolence was a viable option for workers at the beginning of the century. Therefore, she did not fully support antimilitarism, particularly in the form of isolated, individual acts of disobedience. Instead of "down with arms," Roland Holst demanded "arm our side"—meaning the proletariat. World War I had the effect of drastically changing her view. The war, and particularly the national armies which fought it, had destroyed socialist solidarity. She became convinced of the need for nonviolent forms of social and political change.

During the war, Henriette Roland Holst opposed conscription and defended disobedience before the courts. She left the Labor party, joining a small group that formed the Revolutionary Socialist Union, a parent of the Dutch Communist party. Her writing during the war dealt with revolutionary strategies and actions and she advocated methods that were nonviolent in the proletarian search for brotherhood and freedom. Nonetheless, she continued to admire the Bolshevik social experiment, though she predicted the sad impact that militarization of the revolution would have on its mission.

In 1921 Roland Holst attended the Moscow meeting of the Third International which coincided with a bitter struggle within the young Dutch Communist party. She and Gorter ended up on the losing side. While he left the party, she accepted its ruling and their close friendship ended. In 1927, however, she finally withdrew, probably as a result of Leon Trotsky's expulsion. Roland Holst had developed an interest, meanwhile, in the religious socialism represented by *Bart de Ligt; it revived her old interest in Tolstoy. In 1930 she published a study of Tolstoy, arguing firmly for the modern applicability of his ideas.

When the Indian independence movement led by *Mohandas K. Gandhi began to attract European attention, Roland Holst found a cause which fit her ideas. She became a indefatigable European supporter, establishing a Dutch society of Friends of India, raising funds, and publicising Gandhi's actions and disseminating his ideas on nonviolence. Her bulletin, *Vrienden van India*, succeeded in arousing considerable sympathy for Gandhi whose biography she published after World War II.

After leaving politics, she devoted herself to creative writing. In recognition of her immense contribution to Dutch letters, the University of Amsterdam awarded her a doctorate, *honoris causa*, in the year of her 80th birthday, the same year she published her memoirs.

Bibliography:

A. *Gandhi* (Amsterdam, 1947); *Geweld en geweldloosheid* (1930); *Jean Jacques Rousseau* (Amsterdam, 1912); *Kapitaal en arbeid in Nederland* (Amsterdam, 1902, augmented ed., Rotterdam, 1932); *De nieuwe geboort* (Amsterdam, 1903); *Over anti-militaristische strijdmiddelen en hun gebruik* (1934); *Romain Rolland* (Amsterdam, 1946); *Social demokratie en antimilitarisme* (Leiden, 1911); *Het sociaalistische proletriaat en de vrede* (Amsterdam, 1915); *De strijd tegen het militarisme in Nederland* (n.p., 1916); *Tolstoi* (Rotterdam, 1930); *Het vuur brandde voort, levensherinneringen* (Amsterdam, 1949).

B. J. Giesen, *Nieuwe Geschiedenis, het antimilitarisme van de daad in Nederland* (Rotterdam, 1923); Gernot Jochheim, *Antimilitaristische Aktionstheorie, Soziale Revolution und Soziale Verteidigung* (Frankfort, 1977), 131-48; Gernot Jochheim, "Geweldloosheid in de proletarische revolutie," *Transaktie*, III, 3 (March, 1974), 2-9; J. P. van Praag, *H. Roland Holst, wezen en werk* (Amsterdam, 1946), K.F. Proust: *H. Roland Holst* in haar strijd om gemeenschap (Amsterdam, 1937); *Schrijvers pretenboek Henriette Roland Holst* (The Hague, 1970; 2nd ed., 1977).

J. H. Rombach

ROLLAND, Romain (29 January 1866, Clamecy, France—30 December 1944, Vézelay. *Education*: Lycée Saint-Louis, Paris, 1880-82; Lycée Louis-le-Grand, Paris, 1882-85; agrégation d'histoire and licence ès-Lettres, École Normale Superieure, 1889; docteur ès-Lettres, Univ. of Paris, 1895. *Career*: university professor, man of letters, and committed intellectual.

Romain Rolland was France's most prominent pacifist intellectual in the period between the two World Wars.

One of the beneficiaries of the Third Republic's elite education system, Rolland's first career was that of a university professor at the Sorbonne, musicologist, and art historian. He initiated his literary career as a playwright and was the key personality in the French popular theatre movement (1895-1904), writing its seminal plays, theory, polemics, criticism, and manifestoes.

Prior to World War I, Rolland attempted to be a French *Leo Tolstoy. As a youth, he had corresponded with Tolstoy and in 1911 he authored a biography of the great Russian writer. Emulating Tolstoy, Rolland mastered the genre of critical and psychological realism, took humanitarian stands on social and political issues, defended the interests of justice in the name of Christian or Kantian principles, preserved and reinvented culture, and made high forms of culture accessible to all sectors of the population, including the working class masses.

When the war broke out, Rolland found himself in Switzerland, 48 years old, too old to be conscripted. From September 1914 until the signing of the Peace Treaty in June 1919, he took a public antiwar position which was essentially moderate, humanitarian, charitable, Christian, and apolitical. The perspective of these antiwar protests was internationalist and cosmopolitan. He aimed his attack at pernicious nationalism and the unprecedented capitulation of European intellectuals to the war. Risking his literary reputation and his popularity in France and abroad, Rolland became the conscience of Europe, the man who stood ''au-dessus de la mêlée'' (''Above the Battle''), the title of his most controversial essay. In 1916 he was awarded the Nobel Prize for Literature. Antiwar dissent was his way of bearing witness against the barbarism of trench warfare and the primitiveness of contending nationalisms; he had no illusions about the practical efficacy of his stand.

The war politicized Rolland. He realized that ultimate responsibility lay not with European political leaders, but rather with the industrial and financial oligarchies which were reaping huge profits from the war. Eventually, he linked his outrage at the continuation of the war to a major critique of European capitalism and reactionary politics, both of which he connected to the international policies of imperialism. Rolland welcomed the Russian Revolution, but never became a member of the French Communist party. By 1919 he was anti-Wilsonian, anti-Leninist, anti-imperialist, and absolutely opposed to violence. He attempted to regroup the intelligentsia of the world in an intellectual's international, penning a widely circulated manifesto, ''The Declaration of Independence of the Mind,'' to publicize the cause. The watchword of Rollandism in these years was individual autonomy and complete freedom for the artist, scientist, and thinker.

In three immediate postwar works, the play *Liluli* (1919), the novella *Pierre and Luce* (1920), and the meditative novel, *Clérambault: The History of a Free Conscience During the War* (1920), Rolland depicted the social and psychological reality of the war and described his own dilemma as a pacifist intellectual. These works represented early experiments in the genre of antiwar literature. They articulated an integral pacifist position, maintaining a thoroughly religious or Kantian outlook which denied the distinction between historical means and ends and which denied the validity of just wars or justifiable forms of violence.

In a celebrated debate with the French Communist intellectual *Henri Barbusse in 1922, Rolland revealed his reasons for not affiliating with the French Communist party, discussed his theoretical and moral difficulties with Marxism as a method, and voiced alarm at the undemocratic policies of the Soviet Union. At this juncture, Rolland introduced the political philosophy of *Mohandas K. Gandhi to indicate his disagreements with Marxism-Leninism and to suggest a practical alternative to liberalism and Bolshevism.

Rolland's biography, *Mahatma Gandhi*, appeared in French in 1924 and was immediately translated into several langauges. From 1923 to 1932, Rolland harnessed his international prestige and his gifts as a writer to serve as the European popularizer of Gandhi. He presented Gandhism as a potentially powerful political philosophy, a vision of politics and morality, that allowed for individual resistance and refusal as much as it did for collective disobedience. He linked Gandhism to anti-imperialism and to a full-fledged critique of all Eurocentric world views, and predicted the beginning of the end of European colonial domination. Gandhism, he hoped, might develop into an instrument of peaceful, progressive, even revolutionary change; in the distant future, it might usher in an era of global unity and world collaboration.

Although an admirer of Gandhi and an adherent to the doctrine of nonviolent resistance, Rolland was not uncritical of the Indian leader. His personal relationship with Gandhi began with the 1924 biography and was marked by mutual esteem and a desire to debate serious ideas. Tension, however, existed from the very beginning. Rolland disagreed with Gandhi's version of nationalism, his opposition to industrial and technological progress, his austere asceticism with regard to diet and to sexuality, and to certain reactionary features of his doctrine which were fundamentally Hindu. Although they met just once, in December 1931, they differed on a wide variety of subjects, including Gandhi's role in World War I and his twenty-five year support of the British Empire, his attitude toward the organized working class, his misinformation and misperception of fascism, the practical utility of using nonviolent resistance to combat fascism, Gandhi's dismissal of the Soviet Union, and the possibilities of extending Indian national liberation in a socialist direction. After Hilter's ascension to power in March 1933, and certainly by 1934, Rolland reluctantly realized that Gandhism had not taken root in the secular West, primarily because of the religious component of its doctrine. While breaking with Gandhi's theory and practice, Rolland maintained enormous respect for Gandhi the man and for Gandhi's role as an historical personality.

In the 1920s Rolland took public positions against imperialism and fascism. In 1927 he served as honorary president (with *Albert Einstein and *Henri Barbuse) of the first large antifascist assembly held at the Salle Bullier in Paris. He also tried to mediate between pacifism and communism, arguing that the goals were the same even though the methods were different. In 1932 Rolland

and Barbusse conceived a vast united front against fascism, imperialism, and war. This effort resulted in the Amsterdam-Pleyel Movement, one of the historical antecedents of the French Popular Front.

During the same period, Rolland wrote eloquently and angrily against all forms of international fascism. He consistently took strong positions against National Socialism and he considered Hitler the world's gravest threat to peace, democracy, freedom, and stability. In the 1930s Rolland emerged as an engaged intellectual personifying the ideals and aspirations of the Popular Front era: no enemies on the left; organized military resistance to fascism; active and armed support of the Spanish Republicans; defense of the Soviet Union and the policies of collective security; opposition to the fascist leagues in France; support for politicized cultural efforts to make culture available to the organized working class.

Rolland became the cultural symbol of the Popular Front, embodying its hopes and contradictions, its utopian energies and its unrealizable program. In 1936 he became involved in a controversy with several French pacifist intellectuals including *Félicien Challaye, *George Pioch, *Victor Basch, *Michel Alexandre, and *Alain. At this time, French pacifists broke with the Popular Front over the issue of negotiating with Hitler. Rolland in three *Vendredi* articles, later collected into the brochure, *Comment empêcher la guerre* (1936), argued against appeasement and the idea of peace at any price. He insisted that the only effective way to resist fascism was through armed struggle. In short, Rolland broke with his pacifist past and urged a massive coalition between the democratic states of Western Europe and the Soviet Union against the Nazis.

Antifascism, then, was the key mediating factor in Rolland's evolution from integral pacifism, Gandhism, and revolutionary pacifism to a more favorable outlook on the Soviet Union. From 1936 until 1939, Rolland wrote increasingly pro-Soviet articles, while remaining privately alarmed at Stalin's cult of personality, at the repressive internal politics of the regime, and the early aberrations of authoritarian socialism in Russia. He vehemently denounced the Munich Accords in 1938 as a treacherous capitulation to fascism. He agonized over but did not publicly contest the Nazi-Soviet Pact of 1939. At the end of his life, his commitment to the destruction of fascism over-shadowed all other concerns.

Rolland helped to make pacifism a respectable literary subject in Europe. He was instrumental in creating and diffusing a distinctly pacifist discourse in plays, novels, biographies, protests, and journalistic writings. He took unequivocal positions against war, militarism, imperialism and fascism, and introduced and popularized Gandhi's ideas and tactics, making them comprehensible to a Western European audience. His controversies with pacifist and nonpacifist intellectuals reflected the problematics inherent in the peace movement in this era, and his evolution from Gandhism to ''fellow travelling'' indicated his capacity for historical reappraisal and penetrating self-criticism. Rolland's itinerary, including his rupture with pacifism, demonstrates how decent and thoughtful men dealt with the issue of fascism in the 1930s. Integral antifascist resistance in the Popular

Front era was incompatible with nonviolence and the politics of appeasement, but perfectly consistent with pro-Soviet sympathies, especially if one perceived the Communist International as a realistic and humanistic alternative to fascism.

Bibliography:

A. *L'Ame enchantée* (Paris, 1922-23); *Au-dessus de la mêlée* (Paris, 1915); *Clérambault: Histoire d'une conscience libre pendant la guerre* (Paris, 1920); *Comment empêcher la guerre* (Paris, 1936); *Jean-Christophe* (Paris, 1904-1912); *Journal des années de guerre* (Paris, 1952); *Liluli* (Geneva, 1919); *Mahatma Gandhi* (Paris, 1924); *Par la révolution, la Paix* (Paris, 1935); *Pierre et Luce* (Paris, 1920); *Les Précurseurs* (Paris, 1919); *Quinze Ans de combat* (Paris, 1935); *Romain Rolland and Gandhi Correspondence* (Calcutta, 1976); *Vie de Tolstoi* (Paris, 19ll).

B. René Cheval, *Romain Rolland, L'Allemagne et la guerre* (Paris, 1963); David James Fisher, *Intellectual Politics: Romain Rolland and Engagement Between the Wars* (forthcoming); David James Fisher, "Pacifism and the Intellectual: The Case of Romain Rolland," *Peace and Change*, 7 (Winter, 1981), 85-96; David James Fisher, "Romain Rolland and the Popularization of Gandhi," *Gandhi Marg*, 18 (July, 1974), 145-80; David James Fisher, "The Rolland-Barbusse Debate," *Survey*, 20 (July, 1974), 121-59; Pierre Grappin, *Le Bund 'Neues Vaterland' 1914-1916* (Paris, 1952); Pierre-Jean Jouve, *Romain Rolland Vivant* (Paris, 1920); William Starr, *Romain Rolland and a World at War* (Evanston, IL, 1956); Stefan Zweig, *Romain Rolland: The Man and His Work* (New York, 1921 [1972]).

David James Fisher

ROOSEVELT, Anna Eleanor. See *Biographical Dictionary of Internationalists*.

ROOT, Elihu. See *Biographical Dictionary of Internationalists*.

ROSMER, Alfred (23 August 1877, Paterson, NJ—6 May 1964, Paris). *Education*: Montrouge, printing license. *Career*: printer, copy-clerk, theater critic, journalist, historian, and revolutionary syndicalist.

Alfred Rosmer (born André Alfred Griot) personified the aspirations and contradictions of French revolutionary syndicalism in the twentieth century. He began his political career as an anarchist, became a Dreyfusard, and then a militant revolutionary syndicalist. He opposed the Second International and parliamentary socialism for being reformist, bureaucratic, and for muting class conflict. During the 55 years of his militant life, Rosmer developed into an astute observer of revolutionary experience. In his varied careers, Rosmer straddled narrow class and occupational distinctions, while remaining committed to individualism, free thinking, and anticlericalism. Suspicious of collectivities and organizations, fiercely internationalist, Rosmer worked for the world proletarian revolution to be achieved through a general strike and direct action by freely associating, class conscious workers. Without active class struggle, he believed, there would be no social revolution. He was not well versed either in Marxian or anarchist theory; he distrusted theoreticians who had lost contact with the working masses.

Two key figures influenced him greatly: *Pierre Monatte and Leon Trotsky. Monatte became a comrade within the French revolutionary syndicalist movement. The two collaborated on the newspapers, *La Vie Ouvrière* and *La Bataille Syndicaliste*. Together with a cluster of radical trade unionists, they developed a stand in opposition to World War I which they saw as imperialist, an inevitable outcome of capitalist rivalries. Their condemnation of the war was global and unequivocal. Rosmer criticized the Second International for abdicating international working class solidarity and for supporting the Union sacrée. He became a leading member of the Zimmerwald minority wing, calling for a new international, for a struggle against nationalism, for refusal to vote war credits, for peace, and for revolutionary combat against bourgeois society. During the war, Rosmer encountered Trotsky and shared his hope that social revolution would follow the conflict. Subsequently, Rosmer published a two volume historical work on the worker movement during the war.

An ardent supporter of the Russian Revolution, Rosmer spent much time in Moscow from 1920-24. For him, the Soviet Union was the heart of world revolution and the Bolsheviks, the makers of the true revolution. Though he saw that Bolshevism was not perfectly compatible with revolutionary syndicalism, Rosmer nevertheless joined the French Communist party. By 1924 he broke discipline and was excluded.

From 1924 until Trotsky's assassination in 1940, he sustained a leftist opposition in the Third International, opposing the Popular Front because of its political compromises with the bourgeoisie. Rosmer remained anti-Stalinist to his death based on his anti-authoritarian and anti-bureaucratic position. He never endorsed a Cold War or pro-American stance. He lived an uneasy life as a revolutionary without a revolution. Rosmer represented a generation of worker militants whose hopes were first raised, then dashed by the Russian experience.

Bibliography:

A. *Moscou sous Lénine* (Paris, 1953); *Le Mouvement ouvrier pendant la guerre* (2 vols., Paris, 1936; The Hague, 1959); *Union sacrée 1914* (Paris, 1948).

B. Colette Chambelland, *Syndicalisme révolutionnaire et communisme* (Paris, 1968); Christian Gras, *Alfred Rosmer (1877-1964) et le mouvement révolutionnaire international* (Paris, 1971).

David James Fisher

RÖTTCHER, Fritz (27 June 1879, Meschede an der Ruhr, Germany—8 August 1946, Ingwiller, Alsace, France). *Career*: pacifist writer, editor, and publisher.

Fritz Röttcher, the eldest of seven children of a Lutheran pastor, settled down at the age of twenty three as the owner of a drug store in Wiesbaden. Interest in social questions led him, as a very young man, to join the German Social Democratic party in 1899. However, since he retained ties with bourgeois democracy, his actual association with the party is unclear. As a member of the German Society for Ethical Culture, Röttcher came into contact with the peace movement and joined the Wiesbadener Gesellschaft der Friedensfreunde (Wiesbaden Society of Friends of Peace). As its secretary, he organized the third German Peace Conference in Wiesbaden in 1910. From that time, he participated regularly in German peace congresses and distinguished himself with articles on questions of pacifism that appeared in *Völkerfrieden (International Peace)*, the organ of the Deutsche Friedensgesellschaft (German Peace Society). Increasingly, his commitment to the goals of the peace movement strengthened, and in early 1914 he joined the Secretariat of the German Peace Society. In the course of his peace activities, he met Anni Mertens (a Netherlander born in Batavia in 1893), whom he married in 1918 and who participated with him in his pacifist work.

Röttcher's pacifist convictions stood the test of the First World War. Supported by the International Peace Bureau in Berne and by the Red Cross, he established a letter-exchange office within the Stuttgart Secretariat through which international contacts were maintained. The letter-exchange also benefitted numerous prisoners of war and their families. Running the exchange unavoidably confronted Röttcher with the irrational manifestations of the conduct of the war. He soon came into conflict with the government authorities, who instituted criminal proceedings against him for disseminating pacifist literature. Despite his induction into military service, he continued to attend meetings of the German Peace Society and the Zentralstelle für Völkerrecht (Coordinating Office for International Law). His continued peace activities provoked the displeasure of military officials who had him transferred to the front.

At the end of World War I, the Secretariat of the German Peace Society moved to Berlin, but Röttcher remained in Stuttgart and took charge of the Society's south German office. He established a book outlet and began publishing pacifist writings, calling his press Friede durch Recht (Peace Through Justice). In 1919 Röttcher and his wife wrote *Die Frau und der Völkerbund (Women and the League of Nations)*, and in 1920 Röttcher and Rudolf Broda became co-editors of the journal *Die Menschheit*. *Friedrich Wilhelm Foerster became one of the most important contributors to the journal and Röttcher published Foerster's *Mein Kampf gegen das militärische und nationalistische Deutschland (My Struggle Against the Militaristic and Nationalistic Germany)*. For a time *Die Menschheit* was the leading organ of the German Peace Society. In 1923 Broda emigrated to the United States and Röttcher became sole editor.

Beginning in 1923, *Die Menschheit* waged an unrelenting battle against illegal rearmament activities in Germany. In October 1923 the journal published details about rearmament and, as a result, was banned. When the journal appeared again in March 1924, it was published in Wiesbaden in the occupied Rhenish zone. This move gave the journal some protection against harrassment and prohibition, but it allowed the Prussian authorities and right-wing nationalist circles to depict it as a tool of French designs to create a separate Rhenish state. Similar charges were raised in 1926, when it became known that attempts, initiated by Röttcher, were underway within the German Peace Society to organize those who were sympathetic to the federalist political tradition represented by *Constantin Frantz and *Karl Christian Planck. In keeping with this tradition, Röttcher, who was influenced by Foerster in this regard, advocated the creation of a central European political unit based on the principle of confederation. Röttcher's acceptance of an invitation from the Carnegie Endowment for International Peace in 1923, to submit a study of German textbooks, was animated by his interest in gaining recognition within Germany for a view of its history which stressed the coexistence of several sovereign German-speaking states within a confederation.

New conflicts arose related to the continuing battle against the German foreign minister, +Gustav Stresemann, carried on in the pages of *Die Menschheit* by Foerster and *Karl Mertens. In not always accurate ways, Stresemann was charged with dishonesty in negotiating with France while Germany was secretly rearming. In early November 1928, Röttcher was arrested for publishing an article about rearmament and was held for interrogation until the end of January 1929. Even pacifists, such as *Ludwig Quidde, who generally opposed the political positions taken by Röttcher and Foerster, challenged the arrest as a flagrant violation of German law.

A break took place between Röttcher and the German Peace Society at the end of 1929, when the Society, which had become increasingly radical, decided to withdraw its support of *Die Menschheit*. The journal was able to survive only for a short time thereafter. Increasingly isolated within the peace movement, Röttcher decided to leave Germany. In 1930 he settled in Saarbrücken, in the Saar area, which was governed by the League of Nations. There he created a new existence for himself, but had to move to France in 1935 because he had voted against the return of the Saar area to Germany in the plebiscite of that year. Living in Strasbourg he obtained French citizenship, but kept in contact with other German pacifist exiles. Like them, he suffered bitter privation and had to look to the Comité de secours aux pacifistes exiles (Committee for the Relief of Pacifist Exiles), organized by *Ludwig Quidde, for assistance.

With the defeat of France by Germany in 1940, Röttcher was forced to flee from German pursuit and changed residences many times. He had the satisfaction, however, of living to see the defeat of Hitler's Germany. After the war he returned to Strasbourg, living in Alsace until his death. Röttcher was not an original thinker; his greatest contribution to the German peace movement was as a pacifist publisher.

Bibliography:

B. Hans Wehberg, "Fritz Röttcher (1879-1946). Herausgeber der Zeitschrift 'Die Menschheit,' " *Die Friedenswarte*, 47 (1947), 283-87.

Karl Holl
Trans. by William L. Hopkins

ROWELL, Newton Wesley (1 November 1867, Arva, Middlesex County, Ontario, Canada—22 November 1941, Toronto). *Education*: commercial college, London, Ontario; Chatauqua reading courses; read law and called to Ontario bar, 1891. *Career*: leader of Ontario Liberal party, 1911-17; president, Privy

Council of Canada, 1917-20; president, Toronto General Trusts Corp., 1925-34; Chief Justice of Ontario, 1936-38; lawyer, politician, churchman, and jurist.

Newton Rowell's attitudes towards public affairs were shaped largely by his Methodism and by his admiration for British parliamentary institutions. Although an enthusiastic supporter of Canadian participation in both the Boer War and World War I, he became a strong advocate of the League of Nations and liberal internationalism.

As a young lawyer in Toronto in the 1890s, Rowell became active in Liberal party politics and ran unsuccessfully as a Liberal candidate in the federal election of 1900. During the First World War, he was determined that Canada, as part of the British Empire, should do her utmost to ensure the defeat of Germany, and he devoted his great oratorical skills to recruiting drives and other patriotic endeavors. A visit to Britain and to the Canadian troops in France in the spring of 1916 convinced him that the war must be waged more effectively and he soon became an outspoken advocate of conscription for overseas service. In October 1917 he resigned his leadership of the Ontario Liberals and with other prominent Liberals from across the country, entered a coalition government led by the Conservative, Sir Robert Borden. In the new Union Government, he became president of the Privy Council and chairman of the War Committee. His strong commitment to solidarity with Great Britain even led him to support Canadian participation in the Allied intervention in Siberia, an enthusiasm shared by few of his war-weary countrymen.

Like many other internationalists in both Great Britain and the United States, Rowell viewed World War I as a righteous war that would lead to a new social order in the world. For him the Allied victory "vindicated the moral conscience of the race." After the war, he engaged in a number of activities which, in his view, would contribute to the new peaceful order. He served as the first federal minister of health and represented the Canadian government at the founding conference of the International Labor Organization (1919), where, against the representative of Canadian employers, he contended strongly for the adoption of the principle of the eight-hour day and the forty-eight hour week.

After his retirement from parliament and from active politics in 1920, Rowell became one of Canada's strongest supporters of the League of Nations. A member of the Canadian delegation to the first Assembly of the League, he was soon recognized as one of the ablest and most forceful participants. In the Assembly, Rowell urged that all ex-enemy states should be admitted to the League speedily, and he endeavoured to ensure the maximum influence for the smaller, mainly non-European members. Therefore, he opposed measures that would have increased the responsibilities of the League Council at the expense of the Assembly where the smaller nations enjoyed permanent representation. Although it appealed to the isolationist pacifist sentiments of many North Americans, few Europeans appreciated Rowell's impassioned and much publicized denunciation of the failures of European statesmen: "Fifty thousand Canadians under the soil of France and Flanders is what Canada has paid for European statesmanship trying to solve European problems."

In addresses across the country, often given under the auspices of the League of Nations Society which Rowell was instrumental in organizing (1921), Rowell tried to arouse interest in the League. To no avail, he exhorted Canadian and British politicians to exercise moral leadership in the resolution of what he viewed as the most pressing postwar issue—the reparations controversy. He believed the level of reparations demanded by France was a violation of the terms of the armistice, far beyond what Germany could bear, detrimental to the growth of world trade, including Canada's, and bound to plant the seeds of a new war.

During the 1920s the force of events compelled Rowell to abandon his conviction that a common foreign policy based on consultation could be pursued by the developing British Commonwealth of Nations. Thus it became even more desirable than before for Canada to have her own policies and a body of opinion well informed on international relations. Rowell urged the Canadian government to expand the Department of External Affairs and was one of the founders of the Canadian Institute of International Affairs (1928), serving as its president from 1932-33. A continuing interest in the Pacific was fostered by a visit to China in 1929, attendance at the conference of the Institute of Pacific Affairs in Kyoto that year, and at Yosemite in 1936.

Always the churchman, and convinced that the churches could play a large role in creating the moral climate in which international disputes could be resolved, Rowell was active in promoting the Laymen's Missionary Movement in Canada before World War I and attended conferences of the International Missionary Council before and after the war. For more than twenty years from its establishment in 1906 he represented the Canadian Methodist Church on the Board of Governors of West China Union University. The leading lay figure in the creation of the United Church of Canada (1925), he continued to be active in its councils and in 1929 chaired the church's Committee on War and Peace.

In the face of the League's evident ineffectiveness in the 1930s, Rowell reluctantly supported China in the Manchurian crisis, and later he was an early advocate of the imposition of economic sanctions against Italy for her invasion of Ethiopia. Throughout the decade, in a time when few Canadians were concerned about world affairs, he continued to be a knowledgeable and committed educator of public opinion.

Bibliography:

A. *The British Empire and World Peace* (Toronto and London, 1922).

B. Margaret Prang, *N. W. Rowell: Ontario Nationalist* (Toronto, 1975).

C. N.W. Rowell Papers, Public Archives of Canada, Ottawa.

Margaret Prang

ROYER, Clémence Auguste (21 April 1830, Nantes, France—6 February 1902, Neuilly-sur-Seine, France). *Education*: self-educated. *Career*: independent scholar, writer, and journalist.

Economist, anthropologist, naturalist, philosopher, and feminist, Clémence Royer impressed contemporaries with her intellect and boldness. Ernest Renan called her "almost a man of genius." Best remembered as the first French translator of Charles Darwin's *Origin of Species*, Royer retained a lifelong interest in analogies between nature and human society. Interestingly, the social Darwinist conviction that a struggle for existence prevailed among men as well as among animals seems to have heightened her pacifist leanings. A liberal committed to laissez faire, she viewed economic competition as a source of peaceful progress rather than a cause of war. Like Herbert Spencer, she condemned military conflict as inappropriate for present civilization, even if useful in the past. Modern wars retarded peaceful economic development. She also believed that social solidarity increased as the division of labor became more pronounced in industrial societies.

Residing in Switzerland during the late 1850s and much of the 1860s, Royer encountered numerous exiles from the Second Empire, including the republican Pascal Duprat who arranged for her to publish in the French classical economists' *Journal des Economistes*. In the *Journal* in 1866 she advocated the suppression of standing armies. She was also among the French exiles (including Jules Barni and *Ferdinand Buisson) who supported the Ligue internationale de la paix et de la liberté (International League of Peace and Freedom) founded in Geneva in 1867. That man's history exhibited wars rather than the development of a universal federation Royer attributed to the failings of hereditary monarchies. International peace thus depended upon the creation of democratic political institutions.

Convinced after 1870 that another war between France and Germany or between any major European powers would produce unmitigated disaster for the entire continent, Royer argued that peace could best be maintained by preserving ethnic diversity and an equilibrium between powers. However, her respect for the rights of major nations did not necessarily extend to non-European ones she deemed inferior; the latter might profit from adopting a "superior" culture, although war should not be the instrument for accomplishing such cultural transplants. In the feminist newspaper *La Fronde* between 1898 and 1901, Royer frequently attacked conscription, insisted that standing armies made wars more rather than less likely, damned the French army's posture during the Dreyfus Affair, and censured the British role in the Boer War. She recommended that nations join together to outlaw the right to make war. Unfortunately her resolute condemnation of war between European powers was marred by her perception of a "yellow peril": Europeans should avoid conflict with each other in order to remain strong enough to face a presumably inevitable struggle with Asians. After her death in 1902 her contribution to the pacifist cause was cited at an international peace congress in Monaco.

Bibliography:

A. *Le Bien et la loi morale* (Paris, 1881); "Considérations sur le groupement des peuples et de l'hégémonie universelle," *Journal des Economistes*, 3d ser., 46 (May, 1877), 272-83; "De la guerre et des armées permanentes," *Journal des Economistes*,

3d ser., 4 (February, 1866), 240-58; "De l'étendue et la forme des groupes nationaux," *Journal des Economistes*, 4th ser., 10 (May, 1880), 234-52; "La Nation dans l'humanité et a dans la série organique," *Journal des Economistes*, 3d ser., 40 (November, 1875), 234-49; *Origine de l'homme et des sociétés* (Paris, 1869).

B. A. Milice, *Clémence Royer* (Paris, 1926); André Moufflet, "L'Oeuvre de Clémence Royer," *Revue internationale de sociologie*, 18 (1910), 658-93.

Linda L. Clark

RUSSELL, Bertrand Arthur William (18 May 1872, Trelleck, Monmouthshire, S. Wales—2 February 1970, Penrhyndeudrath, N. Wales). *Education*: B.A. (Mathematics), Trinity Coll., Cambridge Univ., 1893, B.A. (Moral Sciences), 1894, M.A., 1897. *Career*: Trinity College fellowship, 1895, and lectureship, 1910; numerous other academic positions in the United States and the United Kingdom; Fellow of the Royal Society, 1908; Order of Merit, 1949; Nobel Prize for Literature, 1950; mathematician, author, philosopher, and peace activist.

Bertrand Russell's conversion to pacifism occurred during the Boer War (1899-1902). He claimed that a mystical experience washed him clean of Liberal imperialism and lent a strong emotional and spiritual component to the rational liberal internationalism in which he had been bred, born, and brought up. Nevertheless, Russell was essentially a pragmatic pacifist, for whom peace was of generally overriding importance, while the route to obtaining or preserving it was negotiable. He did not regard himself as an absolute pacifist, maintaining that some wars were justified, yet much of his life was dedicated to working directly for peace, and in an important sense much of his seemingly more academic work is also concerned with peace and conflict. Understanding Russell's pragmatism helps to make sense of his progression through different attitudes and suggested solutions in the course of his long life.

Russell was horrified by the outbreak of World War I, by Britain's part in it, and by what he saw as the guilt of the Liberal statesmen. Throughout he worked at whatever offered hope of an end to the war and a better system to follow. The Union of Democratic Control and the Women's International League for Peace and Freedom received his support, he campaigned for peace negotiations, and above all he devoted himself to the No-Conscription Fellowship. In these causes he wrote and spoke incessantly, and (uniquely among distinguished British academics) forewent academic position and protection to take part in the day-to-day resistance to conscription and the continuing war, incurring a fine and a prison term. His close associates at this time were a mixed bag of socialists and Quakers, and included *Clifford Allen, *Catherine Marshall, Fenner Brockway, Alfred Barratt Brown and *Edward Grubb.

In common with most British pacifists, Russell welcomed the Russian Revolution, believing it the beginning of the people's refusal to cooperate with the machinations of statesmen and militarists, and perhaps the coming of the kind of highly decentralized socialism which he had outlined in the seminal *Principles of Social Reconstruction* (1916). The entry of the United States into the war, and the failure of the peoples of the other belligerent nations to lay down arms, destroyed this hope. Yet enough optimism remained for Russell to be profoundly shocked by the reality of Soviet Russia when he went there in 1920; he saw only bureaucratic totalitarianism, suppression of excellence, attempted thought control, and gross joylessness. Not until late in his life did anything supersede his sense of this system as the ultimate threat to civilization.

Between the wars Russell joined numerous peace organizations, working for peace from a position approaching absolute pacifism. Still more important, he sought to lay the foundations of a more peaceful world through his writing. He examined power, freedom, and organization, looking always for the root causes of conflict. His work in ethics, including *Marriage and Morals* (1929) and *Conquest of Happiness* (1930), was directed to the obviation of conflict by the enlargement of people's views and objectives to encompass unselfish ends. In addition, he sought to develop the principles of an educational system that would promote peace. He did this not only in his writing, but in practice, at the school he and Dora Black ran at Beacon Hill.

Throughout the thirties, Russell continued to believe that war with Germany was to be avoided at almost any cost, a view whose expression reached its apogee in *Which Way to Peace*? (1936), a small book which Russell later refused to have reissued. The outbreak of World War II found Russell in the United States, where he remained until 1944. His pacifism did not withstand his perception of the evils of Nazism. By mid-1940 he was openly, though sadly, speaking out in support of the allied war effort. Opposition to fascism did not weaken Russell's fear of communism; indeed, the Russo-German pact of August 1939 was one of the factors leading him to despair of a peaceful solution.

What he saw as the failure of unarmed solutions in face of fascism may have contributed to the apparent readiness with which, when the war was over, Russell again contemplated and indeed advocated a policy based on weaponry. As soon as the first atomic bomb was dropped, Russell began to wrestle with the problems of the age of nuclear arms. The determining factors for him were his recognition that the bomb would rapidly develop into an even more frightful weapon, his realization that Russia would soon possess it, his conviction that it was as useless to try to conciliate Russia as it had been to appease Germany in the 1930s, and his belief in a viable world government. He concluded that Russia must be frightened into compliance before she could develop her own nuclear bomb. There is conflicting evidence (much of it from Russell's own pen) as to how far he seriously advocated going, yet for a time, indisputably, he saw the threat of nuclear war as a legitimate tool of policy.

By the early 1950s, the hydrogen bomb had been invented and Russia had atomic weapons. Now war, in Russell's view, had again become unthinkable, and on December 23, 1954, he broadcast an epoch-making talk on "Man's Peril;" from that time on he worked to combat the threat of war. He helped coordinate the protests of scientists on both sides of the Iron Curtain. Together with *Albert Einstein, he issued an appeal which led to a series of conferences of scientists from both Cold War blocs to discuss the problems caused by nuclear weapons. The first of these conferences met at Pugwash, Nova Scotia, in July 1957. Russell also moved into mass protest in the Campaign for Nuclear Disarmament (working with Canon Collins), and into civil disobedience in the Committee of 100, drawing the second jail term of his life. In the 1960s he extended the use of his immense personal prestige into international conflict situations, such as the Cuban missile crisis (1962).

Russell now perceived the dangers of United States militarism and economic imperialism to be as threatening as communism, and wholeheartedly opposed the Vietnam War. Ironically he was now often accused of favoring Soviet communism. In fact, he never ceased to speak out against infringements of civil rights, wherever occurring, but survival took priority over ideologies. He viewed the task of turning the world back from the brink of nuclear destruction as the most important of his life. He established the Bertrand Russell Peace Foundation to carry on the work for peace.

Russell's very single-mindedness was at times a liability. His attention—much greater in later life than during the period of the First World War—to goals rather than always to integrity of process sometimes led him to take disastrous shortcuts: in policy, as in his short-lived belief in the efficacy of nuclear threat; in principle, as in the one-sided focus on his Vietnam War Crimes tribunal; and in human relations, as in his mishandling of the split between the Campaign for Nuclear Disarmament and the Committee of 100. But he brought to a lifetime of work for peace integrity, unflinching realism, and personal courage, as well as his great intellect, practiced skills of writing and speaking with startling clarity, and a prestige that was far more earned than inherited. He had a vision for humanity, and he worked to preserve for it the opportunity of fulfillment.

Bibliography:

A. *The Autobiography of Bertrand Russell* (vols. 1 and 2, Boston, 1967-68, vol. 3, New York, 1969); *Common Sense and Nuclear Warfare* (London and New York, 1959); *Has Man a Future*? (London and New York, 1961); *New Hopes for a Changing World* (London, 1951; New York, 1952); *Principles of Social Reconstruction* (London, 1916; in U.S. as *Why Men Fight*, New York, 1917); *Roads to Freedom* (London, 1918; in U.S. as *Proposed Roads to Freedom* New York, 1919); *Unarmed Victory* (London and New York, 1963); *War Crimes in Vietnam* (London and New York, 1967), *Which Way to Peace*? (London, 1936).

B. Ronald W. Clark, *The Life of Bertrand Russell* (London, 1975; New York, 1976); Jo Vellacott, *Bertrand Russell and the Pacifists in the First World War* (London, 1980; New York, 1981).

C. Bertrand Russell Archives, McMaster University, Hamilton, Ontario.

Jo Vellacott

RUYSSEN, Théodore Eugène César. See *Biographical Dictionary of Internationalists*.

S

SAAVEDRA LAMAS, Carlos (1 November 1878, Buenos Aires, Argentina—5 May 1959, Buenos Aires). *Education*: Doctorate of Laws, National Univ., Buenos Aires, 1903. *Career*: lawyer, statesman, diplomat, professor, and author.

Scion of one of Argentina's leading families and son-in-law of former president Roque Saenz Peña, Carlos Saavedra Lamas devoted his life to public service. He began as Director of Public Credit (1906-7) and as Secretary of the Buenos Aires municipality (1907). He served two terms in the national legislature where he drafted the "Saavedra Lamas Law" of 1912. This law nearly excluded all foreign sugar from the country resulting in a national subsidy for the sugar producers in Tucumán province. In 1915 he headed the Ministries of Justice and Public Education.

It is, however, his diplomatic life that is most remembered. From 1932 to 1938 Saavedra Lamas served as foreign minister in the Conservative administration of President Augustín Justo. It was during this critical period in history that the world experienced the Great Depression, the rise of totalitarianism in Europe, violent warfare between Paraguay and Bolivia, and the Good Neighbor Policy of +Franklin D. Roosevelt. The Argentine foreign minister proved himself equal to this era. At the Seventh International Conference of American States, meeting in Montevideo in 1933, Saavedra Lamas introduced his famous Anti-War Treaty of Non-Aggression and Conciliation. Eventually signed by all the American republics and a number of European states, the treaty emphasized three significant principles: 1) condemnation of wars of aggression and an emphasis on the settlement of all disputes by peaceful means; 2) denial of the validity of territorial acquisitions or occupations by force; 3) prohibition of armed and diplomatic intervention. Although this Anti-War Pact was significant, it repeated many of the basic principles of other peace pacts of the era such as the Gondra Conciliation Treaty and the Kellogg-Briand Pact of Paris, neither of which Argentina ever ratified. In this light, the Saavedra Lamas Pact can be seen as an effort to prevent military and diplomatic intervention and thus a direct challenge to United States primacy in the area.

Saavedra Lamas again applied his strategy of denying the United States the leadership role in the Pan American movement in his efforts to settle the Chaco War between Paraguay and Bolivia. During the Washington Conference of 1928-29, a Commission of Neutrals was established by the United States to end the war. The absence of Argentina from this conference excluded it from the newly formed conciliation machinery. In response, Argentina established a rival commission of neutrals nominally under the auspices of the League of Nations.

Meeting in Buenos Aires in June 1935, this new grouping arranged an armistice between the warring nations. The ultimate peace terms, which were not signed until 1938 when Saavedra Lamas was out of office, gave nearly all of the Chaco region to Paraguay. It may be a matter of debate whether this award violated the Argentine foreign minister's own Anti-War Pact against recognizing territorial conquest. Critics may also argue whether Saavedra Lamas was primarily concerned with ending hostilities or reducing the United States influence in the area.

In 1936 Saavedra Lamas received the Nobel Peace Prize for his Anti-War Pact and his efforts at ending the Chaco War. In that same year he presided over the Assembly of the League of Nations. Such prominence enabled him to dominate the Inter-American Conference for the Maintenance of Peace which met in his capital city in December 1936. The Buenos Aires Conference was an important landmark in the Inter-American system because the participants were asked for the first time to consider measures against aggression from outside of the Western Hemisphere. The United States, mindful of the gathering war clouds in Europe, wanted to establish a permanent inter-American consultative committee composed of the foreign ministers from the American republics. Saavedra Lamas opposed such a formal organization because he felt it would remove the Americas from the jurisdiction of the League of Nations, and, thus, would weaken that international organization. He found a responsive cord among Latin Americans still concerned about United States intervention.

The Argentine foreign minister ridiculed the United States suggestion of a European attack as an "imaginative hypothesis." Many of the delegates to the Buenos Aires Conference felt that the United States was not as concerned with European aggression as it was with gaining economic advantage in Latin America. Saavedra Lamas opposed any direct or implied challenge to Europe in that he recognized the tremendous economic dependence Argentina, an exporting nation, had on that area of the world.

In many ways Saavedra Lamas personified the intense rivalry between the United States and Argentina. During the 1930s, as Argentina's foreign minister, he adopted a policy of universalism with an emphasis on close cooperation with the League of Nations and special ties with Europe. He saw the League and Europe as providing a balance against the United States, thus allowing for greater national self-determination. Furthermore, he constantly fought against what he called "Monroeism," that is, the United States' Pan American policies based upon the Monroe Doctrine which enabled the North Americans to dominate the Latin Americans.

After leaving the foreign ministry in 1938, Saavedra Lamas began to realize that he had been wrong about conditions in Europe. In 1940 he helped organize Accíon Argentina, a nonpartisan organization that criticized the pro-Axis neutrality of the Castillo regime. During this period of his life he turned to academic affairs as the rector of the National University (1941-43) and as a professor of economics (1943-46). He wrote many books on public education, economics, and international law.

Bibliography:

A. *Por la paz de las Américas* (Buenos Aires, 1937); *Tratado general para reforzar los medios de conservar la paz* (Buenos Aires, 1936); *La unidad económica de América* (Buenos Aires, 1941).

Paul E. Masters, Jr.

SAHLBOM, Naima (15 May 1871, Stockholm, Sweden—29 March 1957, Stockholm). *Education*: studies at the universities of Stockholm and Uppsala; Ph.D., Univ. of Neuchatel, 1910. *Career*: geologist, Helsinki, Heidelberg, Basel, and in the Department of Minerology, Swedish State Museum; peace activist.

Naima Sahlbom, an internationally known scientist, contributed a great deal to the development of petrographic and mineralogic research in Sweden. Among her many research interests was radioactivity in Swedish spring waters. Her commitment to the cause of peace, however, led her to set aside much of her scientific work, although the question of radioactivity played an important role in her later concern for peace and disarmament.

During World War I, Sahlbom took part in the International Women's Conference that was held at The Hague in April, 1915, and she joined the Women's International League for Peace and Freedom (WILPF) when it was founded in 1919. After the war she dedicated herself more seriously to studies on scientific warfare and its effects. Among other things, she carried out extensive research on poisonous gases. When the WILPF Commission on Scientific Warfare was set up in 1924, Sahlbom was asked to chair it.

In 1925 Sahlbom, together with Dr. Gertrud Woker, Professor of Chemistry at the University of Berne and co-member of the Commission on Scientific Warfare, visited the American Gas Armament Center in Maryland. Sahlbom hoped to convene a conference of experts to discuss modern methods of warfare and she launched an appeal to scientists to condemn the misuse of scientific research for war purposes and to refuse to contribute their knowledge to warfare. Her plan materialized in 1929 at the WILPF Congress in Frankfurt, when three hundred experts in economics, medicine, and military science gathered to discuss modern methods of warfare. The conference concluded that contrary to public assurances many nations were preparing for air war that would combine the use of poison gas with incendiary and explosive bombs. Civilian populations would not be spared in such a war. Only disarmament could prevent the coming holocaust.

In 1930 the WILPF Commission on Scientific Warfare, still headed by Sahlbom, prepared an appeal for a mass propaganda campaign for universal disarmament. Alluding to the Kellogg-Briand Peace Pact of 1928, the Commission adopted the slogan "War Is Renounced—Let Us Renounce Armaments." The petition, translated into 18 languages, obtained more than six million signatures and was presented to the World Disarmament Conference in Geneva in 1932. It called on governments to instruct their delegates to examine all proposals for disarmament that had been or might be made, and to take the necessary steps to achieve the goal of a world without arms.

Apart from her work on problems of disarmament, Naima Sahlbom was active in many other fields related to peace work; she served on the board of the Committee for Spanish Children; she became involved with the Relief Committee for Children in Czechoslovakia; she was a member of the Bureau of International Cooperation; and for many years, she represented the Swedish Section of the WILPF in the World Assembly for Peace. In 1946 her contributions were recognized and she was awarded the Swedish royal medal given to distinguished persons.

Bibliography:

A. *Giftgasvapnet* (Stockhold, 1925); *Radioaktiviteten hos svenska källvatten* (Stockholm, 1915).

B. Per Anders Fogelström, *Kampen för Fred* (Stockholm, 1971); Magareta Larsson, "Kvinnoföreningar i Sverige med fred pa sitt program" (Ph.D dissertation, University of Stockholm, 1971); *Svenska män och kvinnor*, 6, 465, *Svensk Uppslagsbok*, 25, 15-16.

Elisabeth Ståhle

SAITŌ Takao (18 August 1870, Izushi, Hyōgo Prefecture, Japan—7 October 1949, Tokyo). *Education*: graduated, Tokyo Semmon Gakkō (Waseda Univ.), 1894; studied at Yale Univ., 1901-4. *Career*: member (Hyōgo Prefecture), House of Representatives, 1912-49; lawyer, politician, author, and reformer.

Saitō Takao opposed Japan's military activities in the 1930s because he believed they were not serving Japan's best interests. Originally not a pacifist nor an antimilitarist, Saitō's opposition was not based on religious or philosophical principles but stemmed from practical reasons.

On four different occasions Saitō made strong antimilitary speeches in the prewar House of Representatives. After the "May 15th Incident" (1932), in which military aligned rightists assassinated both the prime minister and a major financial leader, Saitō charged the army with being irresponsible and called for a purge. Again in a House speech of January 25, 1935, Saitō scored the Japanese army for issuing pamphlets that fostered a jingoistic spirit in the people. Such propaganda, he said, caused foreigners to look upon Japan as a war-like nation with little regard for international cooperation. His declaration that Japan had no intention of beginning a war aroused enthusiastic handclapping among House members.

Following the "February 26th Incident" (1936), where several young officers led fourteen hundred soldiers in an insurrection that paralyzed Tokyo for five days, Saitō delivered a stinging criticism of the military involvement in politics. On May 7, he derided the military for its involvement in domestic politics for over an hour on the House floor. He stridently called for a purge in the army and courageously reminded the military that the political involvement of servicemen was prohibited by law. He called upon the military to avoid any national disturbance and to curb their nationalistic thoughts and intrigues. Saitō criticized the army for its use of force in carrying out their ideas and charged that the army was "trampling on the rights of the Japanese people." His speech brought thunderous applause from House members and gallery observers. The speech was widely reported in the press and political analysts called it the most important speech in the House in several years.

On February 2, 1940, Saitō again created a great furor in the House when he raised serious and penetrating questions concerning the conduct of the war in China. In an hour and a half interpellation he called for the censure of the government over the handling of the Sino-Japanese war. He denounced the government and the military for their incompetency and irresponsible behavior in the China war. Criticizing the general concept of Japan's "holy war," he strongly urged its early settlement and declared that "peace can be invited only when a country keeps its armed power in the background." Saitō's speech threw the House into pandemonium. War Minister Hata demanded a public retraction. An Army spokesman charged that Saitō had "belittled Japan's holy war and defiled the souls of hundreds of thousands of dead." Various groups called for Saitō's expulsion from the House. Under military pressure, the secretary deleted over two-thirds of Saitō's speech from the House record and the disciplinary committee asked him to resign. Saitō refused. After more than a month of turbulent political furor, Saitō became only the third member of the House to be expelled. However, in the next general election (1942) Saitō was reelected to the House in spite of intense government interference.

A passionate supporter of his country, Saitō did not question the philosophical aims of the army in China but inquired as to the cost and procedures. His critical approach toward army domination of foreign policy suggested moderation. Saitō in his ardor so criticized the lack of concrete results that such arguments were interpreted as denouncing the war itself. After his expulsion, Saitō continued to criticize Japan's aggressive war in speeches and articles. In the postwar period, he served a variety of political roles but throughout continued to urge people to cooperate and rebuild a peaceful Japan.

Bibliography:

A. *Kaiko shichijūnen* (Tokyo, 1948); *Saitō Takao seiji ronshū*, ed. by Kawami Teiichi (Hyōgo, 1961).

B. Kawami Teiichi (ed.), *Saitō Takao* (Hyōgo, 1955); Tabata Shinobu, "Hangun ni ikita daigishi Saitō Takao den," *Jidai*, I, No. 2 (August, 1971), 252-60, No. 3 (September, 1971), 246-56, No. 4 (October, 1971), 252-61.

William D. Hoover

SALOMON, Berthold. See JACOB, Berthold.

SALTER, James Arthur. See *Biographical Dictionary of Internationalists*.

SANGNIER, Charles François Marc Marie (3 April 1873, Paris—28 May 1950, Paris). *Education*: Collège Stanislas, prix de philosophie, 1891; entered École polytechnique, 1895; licencié en droit, Sorbonne, 1898. *Career*: editor,

Le Sillon, 1894-1910, *L'Eveil Démocratique*, 1905-10, *La Démocratie*, 1910-31, *La Jeune République*, 1912-39, *L'Eveil des Peuples*, 1932-39; deputy, 1919-24; author and journalist.

Marc Sangnier, scion of a distinguished family of academics and lawyers, received a bourgeois and Christian education; he displayed early his passion for organizing and his concern for ordinary people by forming, while at the Collège Stanislas, a student discussion group, La Crypte, to whose sessions workers were invited. In 1894 Le Sillon was founded by several friends from the Collège, as an organization for combatting anticlericalism and encouraging moral education; in 1902 Sangnier became director, changing its objective to democratic political action in an attempt to reconcile the Republic and the Church. But opposition from French bishops brought about in 1910 the papal condemnation of Le Sillon, Pius X being then under the influence of Charles Maurras. In 1909-10, he joined the first avowedly Catholic peace society, Ligue internationale des pacifistes catholiques (International League of Catholic Pacifists), which participated in the international peace movement.

When the war came, Sangnier, mobilized as a lieutenant of engineers, was discharged in 1918 with the rank of commandant, having won the *Croix de Guerre* and the *Légion d'honneur*. In 1914 he firmly believed in the rectitude of France's cause. But the war changed all that, and in *La Démocratie* (October 3, 1919) Sangnier, characterizing the war as a "cruel and imbecile folly," called for reconciliation between France and Germany as the only way to a permanent peace. From that time forward, his entire life was devoted to the aim of reconciliation, and, despairing of his own generation, he looked toward youth as the only hope. As he said at the founding of the Internationale Démocratique in 1921, the only way to thwart the resolve of the French Right and the German nationalists was to convert youth to faith in "the Republic, in democracy and in peace."

This same resolve motivated Sangnier to found the Ligue française des auberges de jeunesses (French League of Youth Hostels) in 1929. With its headquarters at Bierville (which Sangnier had already established as an international center) the League brought together young people from several countries, notably France and Germany, for festivals of camping and sports, religious observances and pacifist action. Resolutely opposed to racism, anti-Semitism and dictatorship, Sangnier founded the review *L'Eveil des Peuples* in 1932 as an organ for carrying on the work of the League; it flourished, with many distinguished contributors, until shut down in 1939.

Sangnier's election to the Chamber of Deputies in 1919 led him to attempt to form a Christian democratic party, based on the Jeune République, successor in 1912 to the social Christian policy of Le Sillon, but he was unsuccessful. Torn between the Catholic Right, who rejected his democratic liberalism, and the republican Left, who were suspicious of his religious orientation, Sangnier never won another election. Moreover, as the question of war or peace came to be the paramount issue for him, he called on his associates in the Jeune République to forsake internal politics and concentrate on pacifism alone. When they refused, he left the Jeune République.

From 1919 on Sangnier's devotion to pacifism was complete, and his leadership in various peace groups earned him a place as a delegate to nearly every national and international peace congress held between the wars. As a member of the Comité d'action pour la paix en Espagne (Committee of Action for Peace in Spain), Sangnier advocated mediation by the League of Nations and a plebiscite. He welcomed Munich as a last effort to save the peace, but realized that war was not the worst evil. Under Vichy he retired to Treignac, placing the presses of *La Démocratie* at the disposal of the Resistance; in February 1944, the Gestapo arrested him and all the printshop personnel, but he was freed. In November 1944 the abiding dream of Le Sillon was realized in the formation of the Movement Républicain Populaire, of which Sangnier became the honorary president.

Bibliography:

A. *Albert de Mun* (Paris, 1932); *Discours*, (10 vols., Paris, 1891-1937); *L'Esprit démocratique* (Paris, 1905); *Histoire des Auberges de Jeunesses* (1946); *La lutte pour la démocratie* (Au Sillon, 1908).

B. Madeleine Barthélemy-Madaule, *Marc Sangnier, 1873-1950* (Paris, 1973); André Darricau, *Marc Sangnier* (Paris, 1958); Jean de Fabregues, *Le Sillon de Marc Sangnier* (Paris, 1964); Georges Hoog, *Marc Sangnier au Parlement, 1919-1924* (Paris, n.d.).

Albert S. Hill

SANTOS-DUMONT, Alberto (20 July 1873, Palmira [now Santos-Dumont], Brazil—23 July 1932, Sao Paulo, Brazil). *Education*: privately tutored. *Career*: inventor, engineer, and aviator.

Known as "The Father of Aviation," Santos-Dumont had a vision: that from the one-man prototypes of the early twentieth century would develop "giant ships of the air which will carry passengers in swift flight above continents and oceans, linking the peoples of the earth into one family." When he saw his designs turned into machines of destruction in World War I, he used his international stature to protest what he believed to be the perverted use of airships as warships. Because of his protest, the French government stripped him of his Legion of Honor (awarded in 1909), and he was accused of espionage by the Allies. Cleared of the spying charges after the war, he continued to promote the peaceful uses of flight. The period of his brilliant contribution to aviation, however, was closed.

Santos-Dumont's education followed a pattern typical of his wealthy Brazilian peers. He was tutored at home, in this case on his family's coffee plantation in Sao Paulo, and then sent on a sojourn abroad. Not typical was the young man's passion for flying machines, a passion first fired in 1888 when he attended a demonstration by a professional balloonist. His enthusiasm was nurtured by his father, and when Santos-Dumont arrived in Paris in 1891, he joined an international coterie of aviators experimenting with all manner of aircraft.

During the next three decades, Santos-Dumont won international renown for his achievements in flight design and as a pilot. He was the first man to turn the internal combustion engine to practical use for aviation. In 1901, flying a dirigible airship of his own design, he won the coveted Deutsch Prize for being the first man to navigate a set time course—a course charted from St. Cloud around the Eiffel Tower and back. In addition to the judges, his feat was witnessed by thousands of spectators. He subsequently turned his attention to the development of heavier-than-air machines, and in 1906 piloted his Bis-14 to claim the Archdeacon Award. The European press proclaimed him the first man to conquer the air, a title immediately disputed by the Wright Brothers, who were conducting their experiments in heavy secrecy in North Carolina. Santos-Dumont, dismayed at the controversy, began work on a new model. His "Demoiselle", completed in 1909, was the world's first successful monoplane, the prototype of the modern airplane.

The charming, dapper Brazilian was an immensely popular figure, and his romances with heiresses, his hair-breadth escapes from repeated crashes, his Parisian dinner parties, were all recounted with relish in the international press, while more serious journals such as *Scientific American* vied for his by-line. He was generous with his designs, believing that they belonged to the world.

The outbreak of World War I and the employment of aircraft for the purposes of war horrified him. He made public his antiwar sentiments, which were widely published. The Allied Governments responded by calling him a traitor, and his hitherto adoring public dismissed his statements as the words of an eccentric. For the remainder of his life, he felt a personal responsibility for the carnage of the war, and retreated from public life, first to a villa near Paris, and after 1928, to his home in Sao Paulo.

In 1932 civil war broke out in Brazil, and the Federal Government sent planes to bomb the city of Sao Paulo, a rebel stronghold. When Santos-Dumont realized that bombs were being dropped by Brazilians on their fellow countrymen, the "Father of Aviation" made the ultimate protest of taking his own life.

Bibliography:

A. *Dans l'air* (Paris, 1904). *O Que Eu Vie O Que Nos Veremos* (Sao Paulo, 1918).

B. A. Brigole, *Santos Dumont: The Air Pioneer* (Rio de Janeiro, 1943); *Santos-Dumont: Cinquecentenario do Primeiro vôo do mais pesado que o ar* (Rio de Janeiro, 1956); Peter Wykeham, *Santos Dumont: A Study in Obsession* (New York, 1962).

C. The Museo Santos-Dumont in Petropolis, Brazil, has many of his blueprints and some papers pertaining to his flights. The Seccao Raros Livros in the Biblioteca Nacional, Rio de Janeiro, has a good collection of his publications and drawings.

Francesca Miller

SARMIENTO, Domingo Faustino (15 February 1811, San Juan, Argentina—11 September 1888, Asunción, Paraguay). *Education*: self-educated; LL.D., Univ. of Michigan, 1868. *Career*: teacher, editor, government official, diplomat and author; president of Argentina (1868-74).

Sarmiento came from a poor San Juan family. His uncle a priest, greatly stimulated his self education. In San Juan with the aid of his sister, he organized a school for young women. Exiled to Chile in 1839, he had a remarkable career in his adopted country where he founded its first normal school, edited newspapers, and drafted a basic education law.

His appointment as envoy to Chile and Peru led to his prominent participation in the Lima inter-American conference of 1864. The French invasion of Mexico and the Spanish seizure of the Chincha Islands occasioned this gathering. It was the last of a series of futile attempts to form a defensive confederation of Latin American states. As minister to the United States (1865-68), he furthered the idea of hemispheric cooperation through publishing a review, *Ambas Americas*. His study of education in the United States led to a lifelong friendship with *Horace Mann and the conviction that education was a prerequisite to national development and peace.

Known as the ''School Teacher President,'' Sarmiento induced the national and provincial governments to develop a program of universal education, making Argentina one of the most literate nations of the world. Sarmiento gave Argentina its first stable, peaceful, and constitutional government. As President, he saw the end of the Paraguayan War (1864-70), successfully opposing the partition of Paraguay when he proclaimed the principle that ''Victory gives no rights.'' He also took the initiative in the peaceful resolution, by arbitration, of the border conflict with Chile over Patagonia.

Bibliography:

A. *Obras completas*, Luis Montt and Augusto Belin Sarmiento, eds. 53 v. (Buenos Aires, 1884-93).

B. Allison W. Bunkley, *The Life of Sarmiento* (Princeton, NJ, 1952), Manuel Galvez, *La vida de Sarmiento* (Buenos Aires, 1940), Alberto Hidalgo, *Sarmiento y la cuestion de Patagonia* (Buenos Aires, 1945).

C. Sarmiento Papers, Museo Sarmiento, Buenos Aires.

Harold Eugene Davis

SASSOON, Siegfried Loraine (8 September 1886, Weirleigh, Kent, England—1 September 1967, Heytesbury, Wiltshire, England). *Education*: Marlborough Coll., Clare Coll., Cambridge Univ. *Career*: author.

Siegfried Sassoon was brought up by a brilliant and dedicated mother to a life of literary leisure. He left Cambridge without a degree and became a country gentleman, playing cricket and riding to hounds. World War I cut short this idyllic life. Sassoon joined up and was commissioned in 1915. As a soldier his daring was incredible. He was awarded the Military Cross; a recommendation for the Victoria Cross was not accepted. His escapades led him to be known as ''Mad Jack.'' Then in April 1917, while convalescing from wounds, he wrote a searing attack on the conduct of the war. He declared that although he entered the war believing that it was being fought for defense and liberation, he now saw it as a war of "aggression and conquest." He refused any longer to support the conflict, viewing it as "evil and unjust."

Sassoon expected to be court-martialed, but his standing was too high, and he was treated as crazed by shell-shock. In the hospital he met the young antiwar poet *Wilfred Owen, whom he encouraged and influenced. Sassoon's own war experiences turned him from a dilettante into a serious poet, of bitingly satirical epigrams and one exquisite lyric "Everyone Sang."

After the war he was briefly involved with the Labour party and *The Daily Herald*, but returned to the country life and played cricket, hunted, and wrote. He wrote a thinly fictionalized autobiography including *Memories of an Infantry Officer* (1930). In 1933 he married and settled in Wiltshire, staying there after his marriage broke up. He was essentially a recluse, with a few close friends. He wrote a straight autobiography, *Siegfried's Journey*, which incorporated his account of the war. In 1957 he became a Roman Catholic.

Sassoon's importance lies in the uniquely courageous nature of his protest. His age and standing made him the leader of the literary men who reacted against the war. The power of his epigrams remains.

Bibliography:

A. *Collected Poems* (London, 1961); *Memoirs of an Infantry Officer* (London, 1930); *The Path to Peace* (Stansbrook, 1960); *Siegfried's Journey* (London, 1945).

B. DNB, 1961-70, 927-28.

John Ferguson

SAUMONEAU, Louise-Aimée (17 December 1875, Poitiers, France—23 February 1950, Paris). *Education*: self-educated. *Career*: seamstress, 1901-14; journalist and socialist militant from 1899; leading member of the French Socialist party (SFIO-Section française de l'Internationale ouvrière), 1918-40; founder and secretary, Groupe féministe socialiste, 1899-1905; founder, Groupe des femmes socialistes, 1913-17 and 1924-30; editor, *La Femme Socialiste* (monthly), 1901-2 and 1912-35; editor, *Propagande et Documentation* (SFIO quarterly), 1931-36 and 1947-49.

Louise-Aimée Saumoneau was an exceptional figure in the French socialist movement during the first half of the twentieth century—a woman of the working class who rose to high office in a party that was 98 percent male and an active pacifist during the early years of the First World War and beyond.

Outspoken pacifism during the Great War brought Saumoneau to prominence and, in October 1918, earned her a seat on the Socialist party's central coordinating body, the Commission Administrative Permanente (CAP). Though she founded and led the only groups for socialist women and edited the party's journal for women, Saumoneau consistently subordinated feminist issues to the overarching goal of working-class emancipation. In the early months of the First World War, Saumoneau was one of very few French socialists to take an antiwar position. Convinced that the war had resulted from the rapacity of Europe's ruling classes, she rejected the thesis that the exigencies of a defensive war in

France justified the patriotic compromise of class collaboration in pursuit of military victory. Saumoneau became an active pamphleteer early in 1915 when she issued a series of three pamphlets under the title *Les Femmes socialistes contre la Guerre* (*Socialist Women Against the War*). She was the only French participant in the international conference of socialist women, held in Berne, Switzerland (March 25-27, 1915). Saumoneau's persistent antiwar activity led to her arrest and seven-week imprisonment in October 1915. Released by a government fearful of publicizing the pacifist cause through a trial, Saumoneau joined the Comité pour la reprise des relations internationales (Committee for the Reestablishment of International Relations) (CRRI). The CRRI was a nucleus of leading socialist and syndicalist opponents of the war who banded together in the aftermath of the first conference of European socialists from the major belligerent countries, held in Zimmerwald, Switzerland, September 5-8, 1915. The conference had repercussions far beyond the small circle of participants since it signaled and became the symbol of a pan-European movement against the war. Thus, despite its negligible support within the French Socialist party and trade unions, the CRRI played a unique role in disseminating antiwar literature and in encouraging pacifist tendencies within the party's minority faction. When the minority, led by *Jean Longuet, gained control of the Socialist party at the end of the war, Saumoneau was elected to a seat on the Commission Administrative Permanente and given special responsibility for disseminating the party's propaganda throughout France.

In 1919 Saumoneau campaigned in favor of having the French Socialist party join the Third International as a necessary step in what appeared to be the dawn of a revolutionary era throughout Europe. However, repelled by the Bolsheviks' "Twenty-One Conditions," Saumoneau refused to join the newly-formed French Communist party. She remained a leading member of the Socialist party between the two world wars and continued to address herself to socialist women through *La Femme Socialiste* and the Groupe des femmes socialistes. Saumoneau opposed rearmament in the late 1930s and in 1940 left the Socialist party which she accused of war-mongering.

Bibliography:

A. *Les Femmes socialistes-contre la Guerre* (Paris, 1915).

B. Robert Brécy, *Le Mouvement syndical en France, 1871-1921*, (Paris, 1963); Jean Maitron, ed., *Dictionnaire Biographique du Mouvement Ouvrier Français* (Paris, 1977), vol. 15; Charles Sowerwine, *Les Femmes et le socialisme* (Paris, 1978).

Ioannis Sinanoglou

SAYRE, John Nevin (4 February 1884, South Bethlehem, PA—13 September 1977, South Nyack, NY). *Education*: B.A., Princeton Univ., 1907; B.D., Episcopal Theological School, 1911; Union Theological Seminary, 1908-10; Univ. of Marburg, Germany, 1913-14. *Career*: instructor, Princeton Univ., 1911-12, 1914-15, Boone Univ., Wuchang, China, 1913; minister, Christ Church, Suffern, NY, 1915-19; teacher, Brookwood School, Katonah, NY, 1919-21; editor,

The World Tomorrow, 1922-24; executive secretary, Fellowship of Reconciliation, 1921, 1924-25, 1940-46; chair of American section, 1935-39; president, National Peace Conference, 1935-38; chair, International Fellowship of Reconciliation until 1955, and thereafter co-treasurer and secretary of American section; peace society executive.

John Nevin Sayre was a charter member of the Fellowship of Reconciliation and for many years its organizational genius. A quiet, cultivated man, yet possessing a warm humor, he served the FOR tirelessly as editor, teacher, and traveling ambassador. He created the International FOR, which was in a sense its missionary arm and foreign office. It was due to Sayre's efforts that the FOR was established in India, much strengthened in South America, and revived after World War II in Japan. Under his direction, the International FOR established training centers of reconciliation, distributed pacifist books, and sought to foster nonmilitary service for conscientious objectors. Sayre always stressed the Christian roots of the FOR, whether opposing J.B. Matthews, who preached class struggle in 1933, or Alfred Hassler, who sought a universalist body in 1955. An Anglican clergyman, Sayre was also influential in the development of the Episcopal Peace Fellowship.

Sayre's pacifism had several roots: the influence of such professors at Union seminary as Henry Sloane Coffin, George William Knox, and George A. Coe; *Norman Angell's book *The Great Illusion* (1910); Charles Raan Kennedy's play *The Terrible Meek* (1912); and personal study of the gospels. Although he presided over the White House wedding of his brother, Francis B. Sayre, later a prominent diplomat, to a daughter of +Woodrow Wilson, he broke with the president's policies and declared himself a pacifist when *William Jennings Bryan resigned as secretary of state.

During the 1920s and 1930s, few pacifists were more active than he. In 1927 Sayre traveled to Nicaragua, venturing over mountains on horseback to promote peace negotiations with the United States. He founded the Committee on Militarism in Education, an organization opposed to compulsory military training in American schools, and was a spearhead of the American Civil Liberties Union. In an essay calling for the recognition of Russia, written in 1930, Sayre linked the Soviet Union's militarism, radical collectivization, and persecution of Christians to its fear of isolation and attack. He questioned the impact of the Washington and London disarmament conferences of 1922 and 1930, pointing out in 1932 that armaments had increased since the end of World War I. Unlike some pacifists, he opposed efforts to boycott Japan. Such economic pressure, he claimed in 1937, would cause severe unemployment in America and lead to a destructive war with Japan.

In 1935 Sayre became president of the National Peace Conference, a coalition of thirty-eight nongovernmental groups. He worked hard to promote an international economic conference and in July 1938, he helped organize the Conference on World Economic Cooperation, a group devoted to reordering economic relations between nations. Within several months he led a delegation to the White

House, pleading for an intergovernmental peace conference. In 1936 he was one of the mainstays of the Emergency Peace Campaign, a body that established a No-Foreign-War crusade centering on strict neutrality, lower tariffs, and international organization based on justice.

Sayre's greatest enthusiasm, however, was reserved for "Embassies of Reconciliation," a program whereby such British pacifists as *George Lansbury and *Muriel Lester visited world leaders and appealed for a new peace conference. In 1938 Sayre claimed that denunciation of Hitler accomplished nothing, while a boycott of German goods only fostered more tension. When World War II broke out in Europe, Sayre called for a hemispheric commission of conciliation to meet continually and to offer peace terms to all belligerents. He also sought an embargo on all materials used in prosecuting war activities and the adoption of a war referendum. By February 1940, he was saying that President +Franklin Roosevelt should arrange an immediate truce and offer economic aid for postwar reconstruction. After Japan attacked the United States, Sayre remained a strong pacifist. The FOR, he said, could not support the war. While denouncing the strike at Pearl Harbor and Japan's war against China, he called Japan "an injured, angry, cornered, frightened animal." In Sayre's opinion, the United States shared much blame for the conflict: it engaged in insulting immigration practices, closed the door of economic opportunity, and was involved in dangerous naval activity on Japan's side of the Pacific.

In February 1944 *Fellowship* magazine, coedited by Sayre, published *Vera Brittain's indictment of the Anglo-American air war, "Massacre by Bombing." In endorsing her article, he called for open towns and sanctuary areas. Yet, although he found the war abhorrent, he was relieved that American and British pacifists had been allowed full civil liberties and that many churches had recognized pacifism as a legitimate Christian position. In both nations, the FOR had more members, resources, and prestige in 1945 than it had in 1939.

During the immediate postwar period Sayre traveled extensively. In 1945 he went to Puerto Rico, where he condemned its colonial status and called for a plebiscite on independence, statehood, or federation. Going to Europe in 1946, he was so troubled by the resurgent nationalism he witnessed there that he called for a federal world government, patterned on the American union. In 1947 he visited fifteen Latin American nations, covering some 14,000 miles. Upon his return, he opposed an inter-American military cooperation bill, claiming that the people there feared the United States and their own dictators more than they feared communists. On journeying to the Philippines in 1949, he personally convinced President Quirino to commute the death sentences given to seventy-four Japanese war crimes prisoners, and in the ensuing years, Sayre worked to free Japanese prisoners in other lands as well.

Even in his sixties, Sayre remained active. He regretted that the first assembly of the World Council of Churches, meeting in Amsterdam, neither sent peace delegations to the various nations nor endorsed the pacifism he found so essential to the world's survival. Yet he was never discouraged, and building on a practice he initiated before World War II, he sent "apostles of reconciliation" into as many lands as possible.

Bibliography:

A. "My Adventure in Pacifism," *Fellowship*, XXVI (May 1, 1960), 7-11.

B. "Great-Grandson of the Revolution: The Story of John Nevin Sayre," *The World Tomorrow*, 13 (May 1930), 219-222; NYT, September 16, 1977.

C. Fellowship of Reconciliation Papers, Swarthmore College Peace Collection.

Justus D. Doenecke

SCHAIRER, Erich (21 October 1887, Hemmingen, Germany—3 August 1956, Schorndorf, Germany). *Education*: studies in philosophy and Lutheran theology, Univ. of Tübingen, 1905-9; Ph.D., Univ. of Tübingen, 1913. *Career*: journalist, editor, newspaper publisher, and political writer.

After completing his theological studies, Erich Schairer served as vicar at various churches in Württemberg. In December 1911 he voluntarily left his church office and began his career as a political writer. For a short time he was secretary to the liberal politician Dr. Wilhelm Ohr. In March 1912 he became co-editor of the *Reutlinger General Anzeiger*. An admirer of Friedrich Naumann, the liberal social-political reformer, Schairer succeeded Theodor Heuss as Naumann's secretary in Berlin at the end of 1912, becoming at the same time editor of *Die Hilfe*, the organ of Naumann's National-Social Union. After a brief period at the *Neue Hamburger Zeitung* (October 1914-January 1915), Schairer was appointed the manager of the German-Turkish Association in Berlin and private secretary to its director, Professor Ernst Jäckh.

At the beginning of 1918, Schairer assumed editorship of the *Neckar-Zeitung* in Heilbronn, a post he held until November 1919, with the exception of a brief period of military service. His departure from the newspaper was accompanied by something of a scandal. After the war, Schairer steered the newspaper on to a course supporting a socialist planned economy and pacifism. An article on the antirepublican machinations of Karl Helfferich, a former imperial cabinet minister and right-wing politician, caused the conservative publisher of the newspaper to have the article scratched from the engraving plate. The paper appeared with a blank space on the front page. The upshot of the affair was that Schairer, at the beginning of January 1920, established his own weekly newspaper, the *Heilbronner Sonntags-Zeitung*, later renamed simply *Die Sonntags-Zeitung*. The four page journal became one of the most courageous newspapers in the Weimar Republic. It waged an unrelenting battle against the remilitarization of Germany, the nationalist secret societies, and the murder of republican politicians by right-wing extremists.

In 1931 Schairer resigned as the editor of the *Sonntags-Zeitung* only to resume the post in October 1932. The Nazi government forced him to sell the newspaper in February 1937. Until that time, the *Sonntags-Zeitung* carried on a cleverly concealed opposition to the Hitler regime. After the Second World War, in June

1946, Schairer first became editor of the *Schwäbisches Tagblatt* in Tübingen, and in September 1946, co-editor of the *Stuttgarter Zeitung*, a position from which he resigned on January 1, 1955.

Bibliography:

A. *Mit anderen Augen. Anthologie der Sonntags-Zeitung* (anonymous editor [Erich Schairer], Stuttgart, 1929); *Sozialisierung der Presse* (Jena, 1919).

B. Agathe Kunze, ed., *Erich Schairer zum Gedachtnis. Aus seinen Schriften, Würdigungen, Erinnerungen* (Stuttgart 1967); Will Schaber, *Der Gratgänger. Welt und Werk Erich Schairers* (Munich, 1981); Richard Schmid, "Aufgepasst, ohne Stelzen," *Stuttgarter Zeitung*, May 29, 1982.

Will Schaber
Trans. by Solomon Wank

SCHERMERHORN, Nicolaas Jacob Cornelis (1 December 1866, Avenhorn, Netherlands—23 March 1956, Apeldoorn, Netherlands). *Education*: Theology, Univ. of Leyden, 1892. *Career*: minister, Dutch Reformed Church, Beets, 1892-4; Nieuwe Niedorp, 1894-1929 and then, emeritus; antimilitarist.

Raised in the comparatively liberal atmosphere of West Friesland, Nicolaas Jacob Schermerhorn, the son of a village schoolmaster, became a crusading apostle for his radical beliefs and not a theologian. Known as an eloquent speaker, he exerted wide influence on young people and aided in the formation of a small agricultural colony which endured for 25 years. He was a follower of *Domela Nieuwenhuis, but Schermerhorn's anarchism was closely rooted in religion and spiritual values. In 1904 he published a collection of "sermons of a revolutionary" which espoused his main ideas—antimilitarism, total abstinence, and free socialism. The work assumed that the Church or organized religion was inherently opposed to the sort of freedom which Schermerhorn saw in true Christianity.

Schermerhorn joined the leaders of the International Anti-Militarist Congress which met in Amsterdam in 1904 and which founded a society. He worked actively for the Dutch section which became one of the most important in the international organization. In 1910 he became editor of its periodical *De wapens neder* and in 1920 was instrumental in organizing the third Anti-Militarist Congress which led to the creation of its headquarters in The Netherlands. While not an administrator of the group, he was among its most indefatigable public speakers and propagandists, one of the first to sign anticonscription manifestos during World War I and to defend conscientious objectors. His activities were strongly opposed by traditionalists within the Church but no formal ecclesiastical suit was ever pressed against him.

After retiring for reasons of health in 1929, he continued an active life as a speaker, often at meetings of the society of freethinkers, de Dageraad. Towards the end of his life, he left the church and associated himself with the modern humanist movement while remaining faithful to his basic ideals about the organization of a just world.

Bibliography:

A. *Vrijheid en gezag* (The Hague, 1901); *Over God, Christus en het level* (Nieuwe Niedorp, 1902); *Wat dunkt U van den Christus?, preeken van een revolutionair* (Amersfoort, 1906); *Vrijheid en persoonli jkheid* (collected works, G. Nabrink, ed., Amsterdam, 1937).

B. J. Giesen, *Nieuwe geschiedenis* (Rotterdam, 1923), 171, 209.

J. H. Rombach

SCHICKELE, René (4 August 1883, Oberrehnheim, Alsace, Germany [now in France]—31 January 1940, Vence, France). *Education*: studied at the universities of Strassburg, Berlin, Paris, and Munich. *Career*: journalist, poet, novelist, playwright, and essayist.

René Schickele's birth in Alsace to a French mother and a German father gave him a special love for and sensitivity to both the French and German languages and cultures. It made him as Thomas Mann observed, "A French mind expressing himself in the German language." Even as a student in Strassburg, Schickele edited two journals devoted to new literature inspired by Friedrich Nietzsche and Emile Zola. An assignment to Paris in 1909 as political correspondent for a Strassburg newspaper helped him to formulate his political beliefs. In 1913 he published a collection of essays, *Schreie auf dem Boulevard*, which gave expression to his belief in social humanism and to democracy on the French model.

The outbreak of war in 1914 coincided with the publication of his play *Hans im Schnakenloch*. The play reflected his divided loyalties. In it the main character, Hans, is torn between Germany and France in time of war. He seeks death by joining the French army which he expects to be defeated. In spite of his reluctance to have the play performed, it enjoyed a considerable success before it was banned in Germany and Austria on grounds that it weakened national resistance by criticizing naive patriotism and by promoting the idea that love, nonviolence, and socialism were the answers to the problems of the time.

In 1915 Schickele assumed the editorship of the pacifist-expressionist journal *Die Weissen Blätter* and in the following year moved the editorial offices from Berlin to neutral Zurich, where it became an effective mouthpiece for European antiwar sentiment. Among its distinguished list of contributors were *Romain Rolland, Charles Péguy, *Heinrich Mann, and Franz Werfel. Schickele published letters from both French and German soldiers to point out the similarity of the state of mind and the agonies on both sides of the trenches; he analyzed the orders of the day by a French general and by the German Kaiser to reveal the similarity of blind patriotism; and by joining his own poems with those of Péguy, he pointed to an idealism transcending national boundaries which was alive in both camps. He hoped for the defeat of both German militarism and French nationalism, and for a cultural revolution of the spirit through persuasion, example, and love. The goal was an expressionist Utopia, conceived of as a European cultural community.

Schickele became disillusioned when the war ended and he realized that the developing socialism was turning in the direction of a narrow state-socialism and away from the ideal of an international community. He chose to end his active role as a pacifist and devoted himself completely to his own literary development. His trilogy *Das Erbe am Rhein* (1925-31) showed, however, that he had not abandoned his ideals. In an interview in 1926 he observed once again the need for a common idea for all—"I dare say it: a religious idea!" But that was not the ideal that Europe embraced. In his last work, *Die Flaschenpost* (1937), written after he had already escaped to France in 1933, he wrote about a world in which a perfectly sane idealist can find safety only in an insane asylum, and pointed to the frightening similarity of both fascist and bolshevist methods. As a citizen of France, he strove, until his health failed, to help friends who had to escape from the new German regime.

Bibliography:

A. *Das Erbe am Rhein* (Berlin, 1925-31, Eng. trans., *The Inheritance on the Rhine*, New York, 1928-31); *Die Flaschenpost* (Amsterdam, 1937); *Hans im Schnakenloch* (Leipzig, 1915); *Schreie auf dem Boulevard* (Berlin, 1913).

B. Paul K. Ackerman, *René Schickele: A Bibliography* (Cambridge, MA, 1956); *Brockhaus Encyklpädie* (1963), 17, 621; Rainer Schickele, "René Schickele," *Books Abroad*, 15 (1941), 3; J. W. Storck, *René Schickele* (Frankfurt-am-Main, 1971); Thomas Mann, "René Schickele," *New York Times Book Review*, May 26, 1940.

Peter S. Seadle

SCHLESINGER, Therese Eckstein (6 June 1863, Vienna—5 June 1940, Blois, France). *Education*: private tutors after elementary school. *Career*: social reformer, feminist, and pacifist.

Therese Schlesinger's father was a successful liberal industrialist who provided many social benefits for his workers before the introduction of any social legislation. His reformist attitude was reflected in his daughter's early interest in women's emancipation and socialist activities. She was active in the Austrian Association of Women and wrote many articles and pamphlets on the rights of women. Her interest in the living standards of Viennese workers, aroused by a public inquiry in 1896, brought her into close contact with the socialist movement and its leading women, such as Adelheid Popp and Anna Boschek. From that time, Schlesinger dedicated herself to working for the emancipation of labor, especially women workers. She coupled this with working for the cause of international solidarity.

Schlesinger became very popular as a public speaker and journalist, and was an effective organizer. In 1902 she founded the League of Austrian Social Democratic Women and became a member of its executive committee. She took an active part in the struggle for universal suffrage which was won for men in 1907. Many of her articles appeared in *Arbeiter-Zeitung*, *Der Kampf*, and *Die Neue Zeit*, Austrian and German socialist newspapers.

Schlesinger became a well known socialist antiwar opponent before 1914.

After the outbreak of World War I, she sided with Friedrich Adler and the minority within the Austrian Socialist party that opposed the support of the war effort. She became the chief organizer of the antiwar opposition within the Austrian socialist movement. The Karl Marx Circle, which she founded in Vienna, became the core of socialist opposition to the war. The Circle issued a regular newsletter providing information about antiwar activities in various countries. The activities of the Circle were closely watched by the police and many of its members suffered imprisonment and other hardships. Schlesinger was a close friend of Friedrich Adler, the secretary of the Austrian Socialist party. After he assassinated the Austrian prime minister, Count Stürgkh, on October 21, 1916, an act intended to galvanize the opponents of the war into more intensive activity, Schlesinger courageously defended him in public. As a delegate to the third Zimmerwald Socialist peace conference in Stockholm in 1917, she suggested that the best way to end the war was through a socialist transformation of society.

At the end of World War I Austrian women received the right to vote and in 1919 Schlesinger was elected to parliament. As a government official she introduced and spoke in favor of social legislation. After the suppression of the Austrian labor movement by the clerical authoritarian government of Engelbert Dolfuss in 1934, Schlesinger kept in close touch with the underground movement until 1938. The incorporation of Austria into Hitler's Germany in that year forced Schlesinger to flee Vienna. She died ill and lonely in the small French town of Blois, shortly before Germany occupied France.

Bibliography:

A. *Die Frau im 19, Jahrhundert* (Berlin, 1902); *Die Frau im sozialdemokratischen Parteiprogramm* (Vienna, 1928); *Was Wollen die Frauen in der Politik* (Vienna, 1919).

B. Norbert Leser, ed., *Werk und Widerhall* (Vienna, 1964), 353-61; Jean Maitron and Georges Haput, eds., *Dictionnaire biographique du mouvement ouvrier international, Autriche* (Paris, 1971), 275-7.

Herbert Steiner

SCHMITT, Eugen Heinrich (5 November 1851, Znojmo, Moravia, Austria [now Czechoslovakia]—13 September 1915, Berlin). *Education*: Ph.D., Univ. of Budapest, 1889. *Career*: editor, *Die Religion des Geistes*, 1894-96, *Ohne Staat*, 1897-99; freelance writer on philosophy, religion, and nonviolence.

Born of a German father and a Hungarian mother, E. H. Schmitt was brought up by his widowed mother in Hungary. After a brilliant career at high school and university, he entered the civil service where he was employed in Budapest as a librarian in the Ministry of Justice. He soon became interested in the study of religion and began to formulate a Gnostic "religion of the spirit." This strove to combine the essential truths of all faiths which he believed had been handed down through the centuries by a long series of teachers. Schmitt gathered around him a small group of religious seekers and published a journal *Die Religion des Geistes*, which acted as its organ.

Soon after the appearance of *Leo Tolstoy's *The Kingdom of God Is Within You* in 1893, Schmitt read the work in translation and immediately became a convert to the idea of nonviolence. In mid-1894 he entered into a correspondence with Tolstoy which continued intermittently until the latter's death in 1910. In 1897 Schmitt, who had resigned from government service the previous year, founded a weekly journal, *Ohne Staat*, in order to propagate nonviolent anarchism. Around this time he also established contact with the agrarian socialist leader, István Várkonyi, and began to contribute to his newspaper *Földmivelö* and to spread Tolstoyan ideas in the countryside. Due to Schmitt's influence the program of the Independent Socialist party, founded by Várkonyi in the same year, contained anarchist elements, including a rejection of the state, and under Schmitt's guidance Tolstoyan groups were set up in some areas of rural Hungary, then the scene of widespread unrest. After the alarmed government had suppressed the agrarian socialist movement in 1898, Schmitt continued to write in favor of Tolstoyism until his departure in 1908 for Berlin where he became the guiding spirit of an esoteric circle of "Gnostics." Henceforward his interest concentrated exclusively on religion. By the time of his death in 1915 his reputation, outside a small group of followers, had dwindled.

Schmitt's importance for the study of nonviolence does not lie in the originality of his ideas, for most of these were modeled on Tolstoy's. It stems from the fact that he succeeded, however briefly, in grafting Tolstoyan nonviolence onto a political movement of the left and inspiring a section of Hungary's poverty stricken agricultural laborers to pursue their goal of radical land reform by nonviolent means.

Bibliography:

A. *Die Gnosis: Grundlagen der Weltanschauung einer edleren Kultur* (2 vols., Leipzig, 1903-7); *Der Idealstaat* (Berlin, 1904); *Leo Tolstoi und seine Bedeutung für unsere Kultur* (Leipzig, 1901).

B. Peter Brock, "Tolstoyism in Hungary," *The Slavonic and East European Review* (London), 58 (July, 1980), 345-69; Gábor Miszoglád, "Eugen Heinrich Schmitt als Theoretiker," *Acta Litteraria* (Budapest), 20, no. 3/4 (1978 [October, 1979]), 314-17; Peter Milosevits, "Eugen Heinrich Schmitts praktische Tatigkeit," *Acta Litteraria* (Budapest), 20, no. 3/4 (1978) [October, 1979]), 317-23.

Peter Brock

SCHOENAICH, Paul von (16 February 1866, Klein-Tromnau, West Prussia [now Poland]—7 January 1954, Reinfeld, Schleswig-Holstein, German Federal Republic). *Education*: gymnasium; Cadet School, 1879-83; Naval Academy, Kiel, 1883-84. *Career*: army officer; pacifist.

Baron Paul von Schoenaich was one of the few imperial German officers who in the course of their lives turned to pacifism. Descended from an old Prussian aristocratic house—the Barons of Hoverbeck—his early life resembled that of many of his peers. In 1883, after studying at Cadet School in Culm and Lichterfelde, he became a cadet in the Imperial German navy. Commissioned the following year, after completing his training at the naval academy in Kiel, he served on the cruiser ''Elisabeth'' until he left the navy in 1887 with the rank of sub-lieutenant to enter the Second Prussian Guard Dragoon Regiment in Berlin.

Except for occasional travels and service during World War I, Schoenaich spent his remaining military service of more than 30 years primarily in Berlin. During his first years in Berlin, he attended a broad range of lectures at the University of Berlin, giving special attention to studies in political economy and laying the foundation for his later efforts at land reform and his eventual turn towards Silvio Gesell's free economy theory. Prior to the outbreak of World War I, he served as an advisor to the Prussian War Ministry, dealing mainly with reforms in the cavalry service regulations and the military veterinarian system. With the coming of war in 1914, Schoenaich was named commander of the 14th Dragoon Regiment in Colmar. At the head of his regiment, he participated in battles on the western and eastern fronts, but in 1915 he was called to the directorate of the cavalry department in the War Ministry and remained in Germany for the remainder of the conflict.

Initially inspired by soldierly and patriotic conviction, and committed to a peace based on victory, Schoenaich only gradually came to doubt the political and military wisdom of the German leadership and the official German war policies. The upheavals of November 1918, especially the abdication of the Kaiser, increased Schoenaich's disillusionment about the German Imperial state and he joined the liberal bourgeois Deutsche Demokratische Partei (German Democratic Party) which supported the new republic.

His strong support of the Weimar Republic and his desire to subordinate the military to the new political leadership, placed Schoenaich in conflict with General Walther von Lüttwitz. In July 1919 (officially April 1, 1920), he retired from the military at the rank of major-general. His republican sentiments earned him the scorn and hatred of most of his aristocratic peers and fellow officers. The income from farmland in Reinfeld (Schleswig-Holstein) and his learning fruit and vegetable growing techniques assured him economic independence, and he resolved to devote himself to politics. In numerous newspaper articles, in several published books, and in speeches at public gatherings, he continually supported the Republic, the maintenance of peace, German-French rapprochement, and disarmament. As a member of the pro-republican paramilitary Reichsbanner Black-Red-Gold, he opposed the renewal of Prussian-German militarism.

In 1922 Schoenaich also became a member of the Deutsch Friedensgesellschaft (German Peace Society) (DFG). He had long criticized the Social Democrats for failing to take an antiwar position during World War I, but now he also came into conflict with his own party and with its appointed Minister of Defense Otto Gessler for deferring to the army. In 1928 he left the German Democratic party, which he had served on a national, regional, and local level. He sided with the radical West German faction of the German Peace Society surrounding *Fritz Küster, supporting both conscientious objection and the view that Germany had been solely responsible for World War I.

Interested in international alliances between the German peace movement and that of other countries, he maintained contact with retired generals in England and France, who, as he, had become pacifists. He undertook lecture tours abroad and participated in international meetings and congresses, beginning with a meeting of the Danish Women's Peace Society in the summer of 1923. The following year, he participated in a meeting of the Deutsche Liga für Menschenrechte (German League for Human Rights), to whose executive committee he belonged. In 1927-28, he appeared as a speaker at the international conference of the No More War Movement in England. In February 1929 Schoenaich, together with Fritz Küster, took over the German Peace Society, replacing the more moderate leadership of *Ludwig Quidde. As chairman, Schoenaich strove for, among other things, an alliance between pacifism and Silvio Gesell's free economy theory.

The coming to power of Adolf Hitler ended Schoenaich's organizational activity for pacifism, and beginning in March 1933, he was held "in protective custody" for several weeks. His status as a general may have spared him from worse treatment. After World War II, he helped reestablish the German Peace Society and once again assumed its leadership. For a short time he also joined the Christian Democratic Union.

Bibliography:

A. *Abrüstung der Köpfe. Ein Weg zum Inneren und äusseren Frieden* (Leipzig, 1923); *Lebende Bilder aus Sowjetrussland* (Halberstadt, 1925); *Mein Damaskus. Erlebnisse und Erkenntnisse* (Hamburg, 1925); *Mein Finale. Mit dem geheimen Tagebuch 1933-1945* (Flensburg Hamburg, 1947); *Palästina. Eine Fahrt in das gelobte Land* (Halberstadt, 1925); *Vom vorigen zum nächsten Krieg* (Berlin, 1924); *Zehn Jahre Kampf für Frieden und Recht 1918-1928* (Hamburg, 1929).

Karl Holl

Trans. by William H. Hopkins

SCHREINER, Olive Emilie Albertina (24 March, 1855, Wittebergen, South Africa—10 December, 1920, Cape Town, Union of South Africa). *Education*: self-educated. *Career*: writer, feminist, pacifist, and social reformer.

During the 1890s, Olive Schreiner, celebrated worldwide for her novels and allegories, won reknown as Cecil Rhodes' foremost British critic. She opposed his imperial and race policies in South Africa through political tracts and fictional polemics. A Cassandra among South Africans, she forecast war between England and the South African Boer republics (Transvaal and the Orange Free State) and strenuously worked to avert it. In her public addresses, political essays, and pamphlets she sought to foster British understanding of the distinct cultural traditions and human rights of South African Boers. She warned that an Anglo-Boer war would be long and devastating, costing England far more than it would gain. While her husband campaigned in England against the war, Schreiner condemned England's policies at public meetings in South African cities and towns until, interned in Hanover, her residence surrounded by barbed wire, she was no longer free to travel.

Upon the conclusion of the Anglo-Boer War, Schreiner shifted her attention to laying the groundwork for South Africa's political development. Her constitutional suggestions, contained in *Closer Union* (1909), set her at odds with prevalent South African Boer and British opinion. She viewed an egalitarian solution to South Africa's racial issues as pivotal to the nation's peaceful progress and advocated a culturally plural, federated, and democratic South African republic.

Throughout World War I Schreiner lived in England where, despite her declining health, she vigorously opposed the war. She defended conscientious objectors in a brief address published in the *Labour Leader* (1916) and drafted her fullest pacifist statement, "The Dawn of Civilization," which, in a version much truncated from her original, unfinished, and still unpublished manuscript, was posthumously published as *Stories, Dreams and Allegories* (1924). A member of the Union of Democratic Control since 1915, Schreiner endorsed its efforts to reform international diplomacy and promote public comprehension of the causes of war. She also composed addresses to women's peace groups in America and Europe, underscoring the need for a peace based on principles of racial, social, and sexual equality and transnational consciousness. In 1915 she joined a small British contingent of women who planned, together with with 50 American women, to undertake a peace mission to The Hague, a journey the British government ultimately blocked. In her short story, "Who Knocks at the Door?" (*Fortnightly Review*, 1917), Schreiner depicted the war as suicidal folly and the peace-minded individual inaudible amid the din of war enthusiasm. Though committed to international cooperation she opposed the League of Nations as counterproductive and as camouflage for traditional power politics.

Although peace advocacy was not Schreiner's primary political focus—feminism and anti-imperialism claimed priority—it was a lifelong concern that entered into all her writing. Her influential feminist treatise, *Woman and Labour* (1911), included a lengthy chapter on women and warfare, while her novel, *From Man to Man* (1924), was inspired by Schreiner's awareness that, to paraphrase her protagonist Rebecca, "the supreme moment" between herself and another living creature was not in killing or conquering it but in meeting its eye, forming her connection with its spirit.

Schreiner's emphasis on life-connection was rooted in childhood visions when meditating alone on the South African karoo. Alienated from the stern evangelicalism of her missionary parents and older siblings, and appalled by the diverse forms of human domination and brutality that she witnessed and read about, she found solace in dazzling images of human equality, compassion, and peace. Although by adolescence a freethinker, Schreiner never relinquished her spiritual intuition of the necessity for pacifism. Though she never joined any organized religion her sense of the unity and identity of all being attracted her to Buddhism. In this respect, the spiritual basis of her pacifism resembled that of a number of later British pacifists, including *Aldous Huxley and *Gerald Heard. Schreiner's regard for Eastern pacifism was strengthened during *Gandhi's *satyagraha* campaign in South Africa. She and Gandhi became mutually admiring friends.

Schreiner's goal since childhood was to become a doctor. Thwarted, she turned her pen into a scalpel and suturing needle, diagnosing and dissecting social conflicts and proposing new modes of healing them. In her search for a scientific basis for her egalitarian and pacifist outlook, she jettisoned much of Social Darwinism as biased apologia for warfare and for current forms of social authority and hierarchy. Although she admitted that drives for power, wealth, and even blood were deeply embedded in the human psyche, she insisted that no less elemental and formative were drives for intimacy and collective unity. As an environmentalist she looked to progressive social policies to favor the expansion of altruistic impulses over those fomenting war. She stressed as equally important the inner struggle for nonviolent, compassionate modes of being.

Absolute in her pacifism, Schreiner felt isolated from the growing number of relative pacifists, usually Socialists, who appeared during World War I. At the same time she found liberal pacifists, such as *Norman Angell, naive in their understanding of the complex psychosocial sources of war. As a freethinker she could not affiliate with Quakers, though in one significant ethical matter she and they were closely allied. Like the Quaker theorist, Robert Barclay (*An Apology*, 1802) Schreiner held that the soldier was not necessarily immoral. She distinguished as comparably honorable a personal witness on behalf of pacifism to which a majority of individuals might not adhere and a second-best alternative: fighting for a just cause. Accordingly, she hailed the heroic struggle of revolutionaries for freedom, be they American colonists in 1776 or militant suffragettes in 1912. Though she herself could neither resort to nor counsel violent tactics, she admired individuals, martyrs, and warriors alike (though she valued the former more) for willingly risking their lives for the sake of human rights.

In her rational case for pacifism Schreiner relied upon Utilitarian arguments akin to those of *Bertrand Russell whose wartime pacifist writing she praised. Her ethics, like Russell's, owed much to her early immersion in the writing of John Stuart Mill. Ultimately, however, Schreiner's pacifism rested upon her spiritual intuition, upon—as she called it—"a certain psychic compulsion."

Bibliography:

A. *Closer Union* (London, 1909); *Dreams* (London, 1890); *From Man to Man* (London, 1924); *Stories, Dreams and Allegories* (London, 1924); *The Story of an African Farm* (London, 1883, published initially under the psuedonym Ralph Iron); *Thoughts on South Africa* (London, 1923); *Trooper Peter Halkett of Mashonoland* (London, 1897); *Woman and Labour* (London, 1911).

B. Joyce Berkman, *Olive Schreiner: Feminism on the Frontier* (Montreal, 1979); S. C. Cronwright-Schreiner, ed., *The Letters of Olive Schreiner* (London, 1924); S. C. Cronwright-Schreiner, *The Life of Olive Schreiner* (London, 1924); Ann Scott and Ruth First, *Olive Schreiner* (London, 1980).

Joyce Avrech Berkman

SCHÜCKING, Lothar Engelbert (30 April 1873, Wollin, Germany [now Poland]—2 February 1943, Sassenberg near Warendorf, Westphalia, Germany). *Education*: Dr. jur., Univ. of Jena, 1896. *Career*: lawyer and notary in Dortmund; mayor of Husum; writer.

Lothar Schücking, descended from an old Westphalian patrician family, was elected major of Husum in 1903, shortly after finishing his law degree. He resigned his office in 1909, following frequent clashes with an autocratic county councillor. The immediate cause of his resignation was a book published by Schücking in 1908, entitled: *Die Reaktion in der inneren Verwaltung Preussens (Reactionary Traits in the Inner Administration of Prussia)*, wherein Schücking painted an unvarnished picture of the autocratic conditions in Prussia. Though the book had appeared anonymously, the name of the author was quickly known. In the summer of 1908 disciplinary measures, leading to Schücking's removal from office were started because of this book and several newspaper articles. In the ensuing trial Schücking was defended by his brother, the human rights advocate and pacifist +Walther Schücking. The trial ended with Schücking being ordered to pay a fine of 500 Reichsmark.

Beginning in 1906, Schücking wrote for left-liberal newspapers such as the *Berliner Tageblatt, Frankfurter Zeitung, März*, and *Blaubuch* about problems of communal administration, an area in which he had special qualifications. Politically Schücking leaned toward left-oriented liberalism in those years and was closely associated with Friedrich Naumann, Theodor Barth, and *Hellmut von Gerlach. As an executive member of the Deutscher Monistenbund (German Monists League) he was already well acquainted at that time with the views of organized pacifism. In the period immediately preceeding World War I, his views came closer to the ideas of socialism, a development that quickened during the war and finally led him into the socialist camp. In spite of his advanced age, Schücking volunteered for active duty at the outbreak of the war and participated in the western campaign as a captain in the Landwehr (Homeguard). The bloody, wasteful battles in which he participated on the western front turned him into a convinced pacifist, who from that time on devoted all his strength to the prevention of any future wars.

He had joined the Sozialdemokratische Partei Deutschlands (German Social Democratic Party) (SPD) shortly after the proclamation of the republic on November 9, 1918, but was disappointed in the SPD after a brief time and resigned. He criticized the party for its unwillingness to include pacifism in its political program. When, in 1928, the SPD agreed to the construction of pocket battleships, he turned his back on the party and devoted himself completely to antiwar endeavors. He worked for the local chapter of the Deutsche Friedensgesellschaft (German Peace Society) (DFG) in Dortmund which he had founded and whose president he became in 1919. He also organized a local chapter of the Deutsche Liga für Menschenrechte (German League for Human Rights) in Dortmund.

As a pacifist, Schücking argued that just as it had been possible in the middle ages to negotiate successful peace arrangements—at least on the local level—it should be equally as possible to solve the problems of the present without war. In his many articles, written mainly for *Die Weltbühne, Das Andere Deutschland* and the *Dortmunder Generalanzeiger*, he was strongly critical of German postwar conditions. He spoke out strongly against the corruption in the judiciary, against the inadequate expropriation of aristocratic landholdings, and against the glorification of war. As a member of the Republikanischer Führerbund (Organization of Republican Leaders) he advocated a republicanization of the Reichswehr (Army).

In June 1933 the National Socialist rulers denied Schücking the right to practice his profession on grounds of having worked for the Communist party. Thereupon he retired to his country estate at Sassenberg, where he devoted himself mainly to historical legal research.

Bibliography:

A. *Christoph Bernhard von Galen, Fürstbischof von Münster. Ein Charakterbild des Barock (1606-1678)* (Emsdetten, 1940); *Das Elend der preussischen Verwaltung* (Munich, 1911); *Die innere Demokratisierung Preussens. Die Demokratisierung der inneren Verwaltung* (Munich, 1919); *Ein Jahr auf Oesel. Beiträge zum System Ludendorff* (Berlin, 1920); *Die pazifistischen Grundlagen der mittelalterlichen Verfassung des Fürstbistums Münster* (Leipzig, 1924); *Die Reaktion in der inneren Verwaltung Preussens*, under the pseud. "Burgermeister XY in Z" (Berlin, 1908).

Lothar Wieland
Trans. by Susan E. Cernyak

SCHÜCKING, Walther Adrian. See *Biographical Dictionary of Internationalists*.

SCHULZE-MOERING, Georg (c. 1897—1928, Berlin). *Career*: employee, Siemens and Halske, Berlin.

Georg Schulze-Moering came from poor circumstances, received only a primary school education, worked at an exhausting job, and was always in dire economic straits. In spite of all this, he used his free time working for the peace movement with boundless energy and uninterrupted activity. Schulze-Moering became an antimilitarist out of ethical conviction and for reasons stemming from his war experiences. He joined the Weltjugendliga (World Youth League) (WJL), founded in 1919 by free-Germans, Catholics, socialists, and pacifists. The group strongly supported peace, rejecting racial hatred, man's exploitation of his fellow man, and glorification of war and violence. Schulze-Moering was honorary general secretary of the German branch of the WJL, edited its information service, and represented it in the Deutsches Friedenskartell (German Peace Cartel) (DFK). He also was honorary director of the Bund der Kriegsdienstgegner (War Resisters

League) (BdK) as well as a member of the BdK's Reichsausschuss (National Committee). Schulze-Moering seldom represented these groups as a public lecturer but rather served them behind the scenes as an organizer.

Schulze-Moering's main accomplishment was the creation of an information service financed by and serving the DFK. From the end of 1923 on, the information service provided provincial newspapers with announcements of various peace organizations. In addition, Schulze-Moering coordinated an international youth letter exchange program that had been started by the WJL. He also helped coordinate youth conferences.

Schulze-Moering worked on behalf of international understanding as well as against increasing militarism within Germany. He wrote pamphlets against government support of small calibre riflery and against compulsory labor service. He feared that either could make it easier for the government to reintroduce universal conscription. He was secretary of the Deutscher Ausschuss der Internationalen Kommission gegen die Wehrpflicht (German Committee of the International Commission against Compulsory Military Service), a coordinating agency formed by the BdK in November of 1924. In this position he helped disseminate the peace organization's "Manifest gegen die Wehrpflicht" ("Manifesto against Compulsory Military Service"), published in 1926, which demanded a ban against universal conscription. Schulze-Moering was particularly active in increasing pacifist propaganda. In June 1928 he took part in the Propagandakommission des Warschauer Weltfriedenskongresses (Propaganda Commission of the Warsaw World Peace Congress). The following month, he gave a report on the work of the BdK at an international conference of opponents of military service held in Sonntagsberg, Austria.

After his sudden death, his widow, as well as Alfred Oehmke, carried on the work of the information service of the WJL.

Bibliography:

B. *Das Andere Deutschland*, 8 (August 18, 1928); *Der Fackelreiter*, 1 (September, 1928), 377; *Friedenswarte*, 28 (October-November, 1928), 319; *Neue Generation*, 24 (October, 1928), 340.

Reinhold Lütgemeier-Davin
Trans. by Robert C. Reimer

SCHWANN, Hans (5 July 1884, Munich—end of December 1965/beginning of January 1966, Schloss [Castle] Birnbaum at Schweinfurt, German Federal Republic). *Education*: left school in 1900; business training. *Career*: businessman, editor, journalist, publisher, federalist, and pacifist.

Hans Schwann, the son of a Rhenish scholar, grew up in Zurich where he lived with his mother after his parents' divorce. At the age of 13 he attended ethical-culture courses taught by *Friedrich W. Foerster. Schwann became one of Foerster's closest colleagues and lifelong friend. In 1900 Schwann left school to begin training as a tradesman in order to support himself, his mother, and his sister. He went to Germany in 1909, living first in Nuremberg and then moving to Berlin in 1912, where he worked as a head clerk for an industrial firm (R. L. Schultze) until 1921. In order to be more independent and devote more time to cultural and political movements, above all pacifism, Schwann set up his own paper exporting business in 1921 which he managed until 1924-25.

Schwann began to write political articles for pacifist newspapers and weeklies after World War I and was soon considered one of the leading figures in the peace movement. Joining the staff of *Menschheit* in 1920, Schwann became editor of the publication in 1926 as well as an editor of Friede durch Recht (Peace through Justice), a publishing house connected with *Menschheit*. He contributed, among others, to the *Pazifist* later renamed *Das Andere Deutschland*; *Fritz Röttcher's *Menschheit*; *Georg Moenius' *Allgemeine Rundschau*; *H. V. Gerlach's *Welt am Montag*; *Johann Ohrtmann's *Deutsche Zukunft*; and *Carl von Ossietzky's *Weltbühne*. In his articles he argued for pacifism on economic as well as on cultural and political grounds. He proposed a world economy which would serve the people in place of national economies which only led to imperialism and prevented economic well-being. Under the name of "H. Tiefbauer" he wrote repeatedly on the economic misery of large parts of the German people as a result of the effects of the First World War.

In addition to his journalistic activity, Schwann also held important positions in the Deutschen Friedenskartell (German Peace Cartel), the Deutsche Liga für Menschenrechte (German League for Human Rights) (DLM), and the Deutsche Friedensgesellschaft (German Peace Society) (DFG). Schwann, agreeing with Foerster's and *Fritz Küster's evaluation of the postwar situation, supported the efforts of the Westdeutscher Landesverband (West German Regional Association) (WLV) of the DFG which brought him into opposition with *Ludwig Quidde. Along with Foerster, Schwann saw the deeper causes of the First World War in Otto von Bismarck's power politics and the Prussianization of Germany. The national arrogance and glorification of war and the military which these encouraged survived the collapse of the Hohenzollern monarchy and the November 1918 revolution to pose the threat of touching off another war. This analysis led to the conclusion that the chief task of the DFG was rooting out militarism and extreme nationalism at home. Quidde, in part because he believed that concentrating on domestic politics would generate internal strife within the DFG and weaken its influence on the German public, argued for giving priority to international efforts to prevent war, i.e. international law, compulsory arbitration, and world disarmament. The differences between Schwann and Quidde came to the fore when Schwann opposed the nationalistically inspired passive resistance to the French invasion of the Ruhr in 1923, after Germany's default on reparations payments. At a meeting of the DFK in January 1923, Schwann unsuccessfully advocated entering into negotiations with France over the issue. Because of his differences with Quidde, Schwann left the presidium of the DFG in which he had been representing the WLV.

Schwann's activities in the peace movement were influenced by the ideas of *Constantin Frantz. A leitmotiv of his writings is the de-Prussianization of

Germany by the establishment of a federal political system in which no one state would be able to dominate the others. Not only would this counteract the distortion of German politics brought about by Bismarck, but it would allow Germany to play the conciliatory role among the nations of Europe which it had played before the foundation of the Bismarckian state. In his writings and speeches Schwann carefully distinguished between federalism and particularism (separatism) and between the equating of federalist movements with separatist ones. Within a federalistically organized Germany, the Rhineland would be given back the mediating function between Germany and France which it had for so long by eliminating all Prussian influence from the region by setting up a Rhenish state patterned after Baden. Schwann advocated his federalist ideas in the pacifist-federalist publication *Menschheit* and through such organizations as the Wiesbaden Arbeitsgemeinschaft für Frieden durch Recht (Study Group for Peace Through Justice), which he co-founded in 1926, and Reichsarbeitsgemeinschaft Deutscher Föderalisten (National Study Group of German Federalists) which had joined with Benedikt Schmittmann's Reichs-und Heimatbund Deutscher Katholiken (National and Local League of German Catholics) and Ludwig Alper's Reichsbund Deutscher Föderalisten (National League of Federalists).

As part of his efforts to eliminate militarism and power politics, Schwann supported rapprochement with France and Poland, opposed illegal efforts to rebuild German military strength, and fought against propoganda denying German responsibility for the outbreak of World War I. For all of the above he was vilified by the political right. As an active DLM member he hoped to eliminate brutal transgressions of human rights in postwar Europe by exposing transgressions wherever he found them. Schwann was responsible for the DLM's publication, *Warte für Menschenrechte* (1925). He also was a strong supporter of the League of Nations. Together with Robert Kuczynski, Schwann published *Über die Reparationszahlungen Deutschlands, über den Wiederaufbau in Frankreich, über Militärkontrolle und Völkerbund (On Germany's Reparations Payments) on France's Reconstruction, on Military control and the League of Nations* (1924). Thirty thousand copies of the publication were distributed to help the DLM in its support of the League of Nations. Schwann was especially critical of Germany's policies toward the East and Poland after 1918. He knew conditions in eastern Germany and Poland well because of his business activity there before the war and his many trips to Poland after the war. From talks with leading politicians and clergymen he realized that Poles viewed Germany's refusal to recognize its eastern frontiers with Poland with concern and that German propaganda for revision of the German-Polish frontiers carried with it the danger of war. He therefore demanded recognition of the realities created by the Versailles treaty. Schwann's criticism of Germany's eastern policies were considered too shrill and insensitive to German national feelings by other pacifists, especially *Kurt Hiller.

As editor and writer for F. W. Foerster's *Die Zeit* in the years 1930-33, Schwann warned of the dangers of another war. The journal sought to enlighten the German people on the nature of and reasons for growing mistrust abroad concerning German armaments, foreign policy, and its right-wing tendencies. The journal criticized the German left for its failure to understand the intentions of nationalist and military circles and its support of nationalist propaganda on the question of war guilt, revision of the Versailles treaty, and demands for other nations to disarm. In February/March 1933, Nazis destroyed Schwann's Berlin home and his publishing office. He escaped persecution by fleeing to Paris. After the Nazis took military control of France, he fled from place to place. He spent the last years of the war in a concentration camp. After the war he again became a journalist and renewed his efforts for political agreements between Germany and France and Germany and Poland. He settled in France owing to his skepticism of the German Federal Republic's postwar policies, especially those regarding Poland.

Bibliography:

A. *Bulgariens Blutstrom* (Berlin, 1925); *Deutsche Welt-Politik im Lichte Constantin Frantz's* (Wiesbaden, 1920); *Einheitsstaat oder Föderativ-system*? (Wiesbaden, 1921); "F. W. Foersters Gedanken in ihrer Beziehung zur Lebenswirklichkeit," in *Programm einer Lebensarbeit. Eine Schrift von und über Friedrich Wilhelm Foerster* (Freiburg, Basel, and Vienna, 1961), 7-72; *Kultur und Machtpolitik* (Wiesbaden, 1920); *Das Märchen vom billigeren Einheitsstaat* (Cologne, 1929); *Wer ist F. W. Foerster?* (Berlin, 1930).

B. I.K. [Ingeborg Küster], "Abschied von Hans Schwann," *Das Andere Deutschland*, 2 (January, 1966), 6; D. Rappich, "Aus dem Leben eines katholischen Publizisten. Zum 80. Geburtstag von Hans Schwann," *Vaterland* (Lucerne), July 4, 1964.

C. Hans Schwann Papers (concerning activities in early 1920s), Deutsches Zentralarchiv, Potsdam, German Democratic Republic.

Helmut Donat
Trans. by Robert C. Reimer

SCHWANTJE, Magnus (6 March 1877, Oldenburg, Germany—9 November 1959, Oberhausen, German Federal Republic). *Education*: volksschule (primary school), training as a bookstore clerk. *Career*: antivivisectionist, ethical reformer, editor, journalist, and pacifist.

Magnus Schwantje contributed not only to the radicalization of all ethical endeavors, but also to the peace movement. In the years before 1914, during World War I, and during the Weimar Republic, he played a leading role in the political battle against militarism and chauvinism in Germany. To the rabble-rousing Pan-German watchword, "Gott strafe England" ("God punish England"), Schwantje answered in August 1914 with the greeting "Gott segne die Völker" ("God bless all nations"). In a pamphlet widely disseminated by the Deutschen Friedenskartell (German Peace Cartel) in 1925, he denounced the militaristic and antirepublican attitude of Field Marshal Paul von Hindenburg, the former head of Germany's Supreme Command in World War I, who was a candidate for president of the Republic. Until forced to leave Germany by the Nazis, Schwantje, one of the founders of the Bund der Kriegsdienstgegner (War

Resisters League), the German branch of War Resisters' International, took part in many activities of the German peace movement.

Schwantje's work for peace was marked by his vegetarianism and by his campaigns against vivisection and the sport of hunting. His involvement as editor, writer, and speaker in more than 150 cities in Switzerland, Austria, and Germany in the years before 1914, breathed life into the animal protection and vegetarian movements. He gave these movements a philosophical foundation and succeeded in attracting interest in their goals on the part of the Social Democratic party and trade unions. In 1902 he coined the phrase "Respect for Life" which he used as a motto for the radical-ethical movement. He employed this motto to express a "holy reluctance to annihilate any living creature," and designated it as a "feeling related closely to religious devotion." In contrast to the later use of the motto by *Albert Schweitzer, who interpreted the meaning of the concept as empathy and respect for the rights of other creatures, Schwantje's definition was based on a feeling of "aversion to nourishment with materials that can be made available only by killing."

Schwantje's radically ethical teaching was linked to the ethical activity of the antivivisectionist Richard Wagner, particularly to his principal work *Religion and Art*. Schwantje agreed with Arthur Schopenhauer's view that all moral actions rest upon a feeling of active sympathy for all sufferers. Inasmuch as moral rules apply to all suffering creatures, Schwantje considered "meat consumption" and killing of animals as "violation of justice." Truly ethically permeated human relationships would be prevented as long as people refused to recognize the rights of animals as well as those of humans and the need to care for the welfare of both. Since he believed animal protection to be the most useful and indespensable means of awakening empathy, he made this idea along with that of vegetarianism the center of all his ethical goals.

Schwantje's philosophy embraced support of the fight against war, against unjustified restrictions on individual freedom, and against the unjust distribution of material wealth. At the same time, he regarded it as his mission—and here Schopenhauer's influence on Schwantje's thinking is unmistakable—to oppose the delusion that the good of mankind was to be seen primarily as stemming from social and political reforms. Consequently, the Gesellschaft zür Förderung des Tierschutzes und verwandter Bestrebungen (Society for the Promotion of Animal Protection and Related Activities) (GTFB), which he founded in 1907 and whose name he changed to the Bund für radikale Ethik (Association for Radical Ethics) (BfRE) in 1919, supported the deepening of individual ethics and the moral strivings of individuals.

Schwantje also believed, however, that the various and separate ethical efforts, insofar as they strove independently of one another for their own justified aims and failed to recognize the overriding common elements of their efforts, were not in a position to alter the living conditions of people or their character. He therefore regarded his publication, *Ethische Rundschau,* the journal of the GFTB, which he founded in 1912, as a forum in which the advocates of moral reform could make clear to themselves and to the public the connection between all of their efforts and their mutual dependence. The journal supported animal protection, peace, temperance, criminal law and prison reform, land reform, conservation, school reform, protection of mothers and children, women's rights, and many other liberal political causes. Contributors included *Richard Feldhaus, *Wilhelm Foerster, *Alfred H. Fried, *Leopold Katscher, *Hans Paasche, *Adolf Richter, *Fritz Röttcher, *Rosika Schwimmer, +Hans Wehberg, and *Otto Umfrid. After the outbreak of World War I, Schwantje changed the name of the journal to *Friedens-Hefte*, until further publication was made impossible in 1915 by wartime pressures.

Schwantje was highly regarded in the peace and youth movements because of his intellectual charisma and intellectual breadth. As head of the Society for Radical Ethics he was always busy and constantly plagued by financial problems. With a membership of barely a thousand people, Schwantje had no funds with which to hire help and was forced to do everything himself. His selfless work often led to illness and exhaustion, but he never flagged in his empathy for the sufferings of others. He remained firm in his conviction that "an injustice remains an injustice even if it is universally practiced."

Schwantje's antivivisectionist writings, his numerous journal articles, and his pamphlets aroused great interest in the peace movement. This was particularly true of his *Das Recht zur Gewaltanwendung* (*The Right to the Use of Force*), published in 1922. Here he clarified the problems involved in the use of force and sought to provide radical war resisters with a coherent foundation for their position. In logical, exact, and analytically precise arguments, Schwantje, himself an opponent of the *unjustified* use of force, argued against *Leo Tolstoy's doctrine that all force is morally reprehensible and showed that pacifism is not to be equated with absolute nonviolence. The treatise became a classic discussion of the conditions under which the use of force is justified or even a moral obligation.

In September 1933, nine months after the Nazis came to power, Schwantje was arrested. The interrogator was so impressed by his writings and his courageous bearing that he released him and had his name stricken from the list of people to be sent to Dachau concentration camp. Schwantje refused an offer of a leading position in the field of animal protection under the Nazi regime. In 1934 Schwantje emigrated to Switzerland and settled in Zurich. Between 1935 and 1945 he was active as an editor for *Der Vivisektionsgegner,* a periodical published in Berne. In 1950 he returned to Germany and settled in Hamburg. Undaunted by the shabby treatment accorded him by the authorities in matters of housing, pension, and restitution for the loss of irreplaceable writings, he resumed the fight for his ideals. In 1951 he founded the Arbeitsgemeinschaft zur Verbreitung von radikal-ethischen Schriften (Study Group for the Spread of Radical-Ethical Writings). He maintained contact with other pacifists, vegetarians, and protectors of animals. He gave speeches, took part in a number of congresses, published short essays, and revised some of his earlier publications.

Schwantje's success as a moral reformer and peace leader was limited by his strong antipathy toward conflict. This aversion prevented him from publicly responding to attacks upon him or his ideas which weakened his public image. His altruism often worked against him, but his unselfishness magnifies the moral greatness of his life. The leaders of the Bund für Lebenserneuerung (Society for the Renewal of Life), which advocates an ethically structured life and vegetarianism in the Federal Republic of Germany, acknowledge Schwantje as "one of our great men" whose thoughts and writings are still valuable after the passage of half a century.

Bibliography:

A. *Friedensheldentum. Pazifistische Aufsätze aus den Jahren 1914 and 1915* (Berlin, 1919); *Gesammelte Werke, vol. I: Vegetarismus, Schriften und Notizen zur ethischen Begründung der vegetarischen Lehre* (Magnus-Schwantje-Archiv ed., Munich, 1976); *Hat der Mensch das Recht, Fleisch zu essen*? (Berlin, 1921; 3rd. rev. ed., *Sittliche Gründe gegen das Fleischessen*, Zurich, 1942); (ed.) *Die Liebe zu den Tieren. Erzählungen, Gedichte und Abhandlungen* (Berlin, 1923); *Das Recht zur Gewaltanwendung* (Berlin 1922; 2nd rev. ed., Göttingen and Hamburg, 1950); *Schopenhauers Ansichten von der Tierseele und vom Tierschutz* (Berlin, 1919); *Tierschlachtung und Krieg* (Berlin, 1928; 2nd. rev. ed., *Ehrfurcht vor dem Leben: Brüderlichkeit und Vegetarismus*, Zurich, 1950); *Uber Richard Wagners ethisches Wirken* (Berlin, 1919).

B. Wilhelm Brockhaus, "Magnus Schwantje (1877-1959). Leben und Werk." *Der Vegetarier. Zeitschift für ethische Lebensgestaltung, Vegetarismus und Lebensreform*, 1 (January, 1977, Sonderheft zum Gedenken an M. Schwantje), 4ff., Walter Schütte, "Kurzer Lebenslauf Magnus Schwantjes," in *Gesammelte Werke, vol. 1: Vegetarismus, Schriften und Notizen zur ethischen Begründung der vegetarischen Lehre* (Magnus-Schwantje-Archive ed., Munich, 1976), 10-23; H. Wehberg "Magnus Schwantje 70 Jahre alt," *Die Friedenswarte*, 47 (1947), 164-65.

Helmut Donat
Trans. by Irene Seadle

SCHWEITZER, Albert (14 January 1875, Kayersberg, Alsace, Germany [now France]—4 September 1965, Lambarene, Gabon). *Education*: Ph.D., Univ. of Strasbourg, 1899, M.D., 1913. *Career*: pastor, professor, organist and organ builder, physician, founder of Lambarene Hospital, lecturer, and author.

The roots of Albert Schweitzer's pacifism lay in the phrase: reverence for life. It was a product of his years of work on the Apostle Paul, but that one crystal phrase did not precipitate from his complex treatises until he sat on a boat moving silently upriver in the fathomless jungle of French Equatorial Africa. For most of life, reverence for life was a simple personal philosophy, not a social creed. It made him a humanitarian, but not a politically active pacifist.

After receiving his doctorate in theology at 24, Schweitzer became a pastor, professor, and soon a leading liberal theologian in the Lutheran church. At the same time he played the organ with such skill that there was a constant demand for concerts. Yet this multitude of careers failed to curb his relentless energy.

He sought a new challenge that would express the philosophy he had been writing and preaching. This was his first step toward becoming a public pacifist.

For his new challenge, Schweitzer chose to undertake medical missionary work in Africa. He studied medicine both in Paris and Strassburg, and finished his medical degree in 1913, at the age of 38. The Paris Missionary Committee had grave doubts whether to allow a person of his very liberal theology into their missionary preserve in French Equatorial Africa, but they relented when he promised to cure bodies and not souls. Schweitzer and his wife of one year promptly forsook the amenities of Europe for what was then perhaps aptly called darkest Africa. His clinic was a chicken coop, the best of the buildings at Lambarene. Disease was legion, the neighbors' customs unfamiliar, and the patients often unsympathetic with the proprieties of European culture. Schweitzer's racism became apparent. He had no doubt about the superiority of his culture, and particularly about European mores regarding property. In this he was very much a creature of his era. Yet never did frustration with these cultural differences undermine his faith in the fundamental humanity of the people about him. He became, in fact, particularly sensitive to the need to adapt the hospital routine to local habit, including permitting cooking in rooms and the live-in presence of relatives. At Lambarene Schweitzer not only discovered the phrase reverence for life, but discovered what it meant to try to live by it.

The outbreak of World War I in 1914 caught Schweitzer as a German national on French colonial soil. But he was a German only by virtue of the previous Franco-German conflict (1870-71). Culturally and linguistically he belonged to both countries, and the war excited no patriotic zeal for either. But neither did it mobilize his pacifist sentiments. He spent the first three years under house arrest in Lambarene, much of which time he spent writing his *Philosophy of Civilization*. In 1917 the government sent him and his wife back to metropolitan France, where he spent the remainder of the war in various internment camps. Conditions in these camps were poor, and though Schweitzer himself was ill, he turned his energy and his medical skill to helping others.

After the war Schweitzer spent five years in a Europe that was brimming with new found (if short lived) pacifist movements as ardent as the chauvinism of a decade before. Schweitzer imbibed none of it. After an operation and period of recovery in Switzerland, he began a series of lectures and concerts from Barcelona to Uppsala, the forerunners of many additional tours. Schweitzer spoke about the war and its consequences, but he did so in a highly philosophical manner which removed him from politics and limited the audience to the cultural elite. Perhaps his inhibited and abstract discussion of the problem of war may be attributed to his apolitical upbringing in Wilhelmine Alsace, but regardless of the reason, he never acquired the pacifist epithet. He happily accepted instead the more refined label of humanitarian.

In these years the pattern of his remaining life was set. In 1924 he finished two more books and returned to Lambarene for three years. After rebuilding the hospital, he came back to Europe to acquire an honorary doctorate in Prague, the Goethe Prize in Frankfurt, and more money for the hospital at a long series of lectures and concerts. Four times more before the Second World War he journeyed to Lambarene, returning always after a year or so to collect further honors, and give more lectures and concerts and publish still more books. In February 1939 Schweitzer, like others, sensed the imminence of a new European war and fled to Lambarene for the duration.

Late in 1948 Schweitzer returned to Europe and to what appeared to be a simple continuation of old habits on a slightly grander scale, traveling now to lecture at the Goethe festival in Aspen, Colorado. In 1951 he received the peace prize of the German book trade and in 1953 the Nobel Peace Prize, for which he was an eminently safe and saintly candidate. But then Schweitzer unexpectedly became steadily more outspoken and political in his pacifist beliefs. His friend *Albert Einstein may well have had a decisive influence on his politicalization. Schweitzer's plea for a ban on the testing of nuclear weapons in the atmosphere had a tone of moral urgency. His arguments were based less on the altruism of reverence for life than on rational self-interest. Nuclear testing must be banned, he declared in his radio broadcast from Oslo, because radiation was killing human beings and inevitably would kill everyone. It now seemed clear to Schweitzer as never before that reverence for life required an end to war which only political action could bring about. Schweitzer died at Lambarene in 1965. His final public effort, just a few months before his death, was to support a call for a cease fire in Vietnam.

Bibliography:

A. *Aus meinem Leben und Denken* (Lepzig, 1933, Engl., trans., *Out of My Life and Thought*, London, 1933); *Friede oder Atomkrieg* (Berne, 1958, Eng. trans., *Peace or Atomic War*, London, 1958); Die Lehre von der Ehrfurcht vor dem Leben: Grundtexte aus funf Jahrzehnten (Munich, 1966); *Das Problem des Friedens in der heutigen Welt* (Munich, 1954, Eng. trans., *The Problem of Peace in the World Today*, London, 1954).

B. Otto Bernd, *Albert Schweitzers Beitrag zur Friedenspolitik* (Hamburg, 1974); James Brabazon, *Albert Schweitzer: A Biography* (New York, 1975); *Brockhaus Enzyklopedie* (Wiesbaden, 1973), 17, 157-8; Madeleine Lang, *Albert Schweitzer 1875-1965* (Strasbourg, 1975); NYT, September 6, 1965.

Michael Seadle

SCHWIMMER, Rosika (11 September 1877, Budapest, Hungary—3 August 1948, New York). *Education*: eight years' formal schooling; private tutoring in music and languages. *Career*: journalist, editor, lecturer, suffragist, feminist, pacifist, first woman diplomat, pioneer advocate of world federal government; editor of *A Nö és a Társadalom (Woman and Society*, later *A Nö [Woman]*, a feminist periodical), 1907-28.

Rosika Schwimmer's life divides into three well-defined periods. From the age of twenty to thirty-seven her writing and organizing efforts were completely concentrated on mobilizing all classes of Hungarian women for the attainment of their political, economic, educational, and social rights. As a young suffragist-feminist leader, she created the movement from scratch in her country, breaking down barriers of law and custom and facing ridicule and slander. The Hungarian Feminist Association of men and women, which she founded in 1904, promoted trade unionism, land reform, feminism, suffrage, and pacifism, and never capitulated to war, communism, or fascism. Her annual European lecture tours and leadership at international suffrage congresses helped forge strong links with the leaders and movements in other countries. Under her exceptional leadership, suffrage was won in sixteen years, in 1920, one of the shortest campaigns in the history of the movement.

The second phase of her activities comprised the years of World War I, when she concentrated on ending the war through a neutral conference that would offer continuous mediation to the belligerents. In extensive lecture tours, based on the huge network of suffrage organizations in the United States and Europe, she focused on winning over President +Woodrow Wilson and European statesmen to concerted mediatory action. Her eloquent appeals galvanized a number of American peace groups into existence. They included the Emergency Federation of Peace Forces and the Woman's Peace party which later became the American Section of the Women's International League for Peace and Freedom. Her dramatic initiatives, adopted by the Hague Congress of Women (April 1915), helped make that gathering historic. As Schwimmer's hope of governmental mediation waned, she managed to win the support of the automobile magnate, Henry Ford, for the organization of an unofficial neutral conference. This led to the dramatic gesture of the Peace Ship (December, 1915), which broke through the worldwide censorship of peace news. In February 1916 the Ford Neutral Conference, composed of delegations of men and women from five of the European neutrals and the United States, met in Stockholm.

Unhappy over internal dissension and the growing emphasis on theoretical discussion, Schwimmer and some former conference members organized the International Committee for Immediate Mediation in June 1916, which sent private missions to England, Germany, and Russia. These unofficial peace efforts were followed carefully by the various governments. Their archives reveal how close Schwimmer came, in the summer of 1915, to winning a Swedish-Danish initiative for calling a conference of neutral governments. This was undermined by one of the belligerents.

When in mid-November 1918, after the dissolution of the Austro-Hungarian Monarchy, Hungary became a democratic republic, its Prime Minister, Count Michael Károlyi, appointed Schwimmer Minister to Switzerland. The appointment of a woman to a diplomatic post was unprecedented. The Allies, moreover, despite the new government's conformity to the Wilsonian ideology of 1918, continued to regard Hungary as an enemy state. Consequently, Schwimmer needed all her determination, ingenuity, and imagination to carry out her mandate to contact American and other Allied statesmen with her pleas for amelioration of Hungary's desperate situation. With the assistance of French, Italian, and American special missions she managed to send the Peace Conference numerous appeals on behalf of Hungary. Lavish Allied wartime pledges of Hungarian territory to Czechs, Serbs, and Rumanians negated her efforts.

The third phase of Schwimmer's life began with the overthrow of the Károlyi Regime by the communist dictatorship of Béla Kún. Her opposition to it and to the succeeding white terror regimes was uncompromising. Her last years spent in Hungary were filled with great hardship and physical danger until her escape to Vienna in 1920 and emigration to the United States in 1921.

Unaware of the strong postwar reactionary mood in the United States, Schwimmer was shocked to find herself slandered and blacklisted for her peace efforts. Much of the rest of her life was spent in agonizing struggles to clear her name of the most bizarre slanders. She won a libel suit against one of the patrioteer blacklisters but lost her five year court battle for American citizenship when the Supreme Court decided against her because of her refusal to promise to bear arms in defense of the Constitution of the United States (May 1929). Although she found much moral satisfaction in the eloquent and classic dissenting opinion of Justice Oliver Wendell Holmes and in the overwhelming editorial denunciation of the majority's decision, she remained stateless to the end of her life.

This last phase of her life was also marked by notable theoretical and organizational contributions to the movement to create world federal government developed in association with her closest American collaborator, Lola Maverick Lloyd. In 1937 they established the Campaign for World Government in conjunction with the award to Schwimmer of a World Peace Prize, sponsored by an international committee of her former associates in various reform movements. During 1947-48 Schwimmer was nominated for the Nobel Peace Prize by thirty-three parliamentarians from Great Britain, Sweden, France, Italy, and Hungary. She died before the award could be made. No prize was given that year.

Rosika Schwimmer was a mover and shaker. Many people swore by her, many swore at her, and some did both at different times. She possessed a universal mind, capable of broad concepts while attentive to the most minute details. Despite lifelong ill health, her immense capacity for work was legendary. She sought social, economic, and political change at national and international levels by nonviolent political means, never resorting to masochistic, self-immolating methods. Going to prison was not for her the ultimate proof of dedication. With her immense gift for attracting the widest press and public attention through dramatization of the causes she espoused, she had no need for self-mortification. An eloquent speaker—often called the Pied Piper of Hungary—she was not only able to move audiences to tears and laughter but also to sweep them into long-term political action.

Bibliography:

A. *Chaos, War or a New World Order? What We Must Do To Establish the All-Inclusive, Non-Military, Democratic Federation of Nations*, with Lola Maverick Lloyd (Chicago 1924, New York 1937, 1938, 1942); *To All Men, Women, and Organizations Who Want To Stop the International Massacre At the Earliest Possible Moment* (London, 1914); *Union Now for Peace or War? The Danger in the Plan of Clarence Streit* (New York, 1939).

B. Marie Louise Degen, *History of the Woman's Peace Party* (Baltimore, 1939); Litván György, ed., *Károlyi Mihály Levelezése, 1905-1920* (Budapest, 1978); *Report of The Hague International Congress of Women* (Amsterdam, 1915); Arthur and Lila Weinberg, *Instead of Violence* (New York, 1963); Edith Wynner, *Rosika Schwimmer, World Patriot* (New York, 1947); Edith Wynner, *World Federal Government; Why? What? How? In Maximum Terms* (New York, 1954); DAB, Suppl. IV, 724-28; NAW, III, 246-49.

C. Schwimmer-Lloyd Collection, New York Public Library, New York City.

Edith Wynner

SCOTT, James Brown. See *Biographical Dictionary of Internationalists*.

SCOTT, Rose (8 October 1847, Glendon, New South Wales, Australia—20 April 1925, Sydney). *Education*: educated at home. *Career*: foundation member, Women's Literary Society, 1889; foundation member, Womanhood Suffrage League 1891, its honorary corresponding secretary, 1891-1902; foundation member, Women's Political Educational League, 1902, its president, 1902-10; foundation member, New South Wales Peace Society, 1907, its president, 1907-17; international secretary, National Council of Women, 1896-1921; social reformer, feminist, and pacifist.

Rose Scott is most noted for her advocacy of legislation to improve the position of women and children in New South Wales in the late nineteenth and early twentieth centuries. Yet she was also a pioneer of the organized peace movement in Australia. Her devotion to the movement prior to and during the First World War was not generally known then and has seldom been acknowledged since. Contemporary newspapers lauded her efforts for and achievements in social reform but regarded her participation in the cause of international peace as an aberration. Yet she often claimed that of all the groups she founded and with which she was connected the NSW Peace Society was the one nearest to her heart.

Scott's background did not predispose her toward involvement in the peace movement. Family members on both sides had distinguished themselves in the British Army and Navy. Her father was for many years a squatter, a member of the colonial landed gentry. When he died in 1879 he left Rose—who never married—the means to live the remainder of her life in relative comfort. Her involvement in public life, let alone the peace movement, was slow to develop. Not until after she had achieved prominence through her efforts to win the vote for women did she make public pronouncements on foreign affairs. By the mid 1890s she had become an apostle of international arbitration. But she lectured only occasionally on the subject and there is no evidence that during the second (or Great) Boer War of 1899-1902 she joined either of the two groups in Australia formed specifically to oppose British and Australian participation in that conflict: the Peace and Humanity Society in Melbourne and the Anti-War League in Sydney. However she opposed the war and was typically most concerned about the plight of Boer women and children herded into British concentration camps.

The Treaty of Vereeniging in May 1902, under which Britain gave back nearly all it had fought for and won, convinced her of the futility of the conflict and undoubtedly made her more receptive a few years later to the urging of *Charles Strong that she use her ''powerful influence'' to set up a Peace Society in New South Wales.

Both the Victorian and NSW Peace Societies, formed in 1906 and 1907 respectively, were branches of the London Peace Society established in 1816. They advocated the substitution of arbitration for war in all international disputes, the simultaneous reduction of armaments, and the cultivation of international brotherhood and goodwill. The new group—the first organized Peace Society in Sydney—elected Scott as its first president. For the next ten years she was its most prominent member and driving force. Very much a nineteenth-century liberal with a strong faith in rationality and progress Scott insisted on orderly and unobtrusive methods. Although a leading feminist, she had no sympathy with the violent actions of the suffragettes in England. Although a Christian, she belonged to no denomination, had her ''own private religion,'' and was highly critical of clergymen who preached patriotism and did more to sanction war than promote peace. An internationalist, she claimed the true patriot sought to extend international friendship. An opponent of war—but not a pacifist—she approved of the use of force to compel nations to submit to arbitration and thus accepted the necessity for an international police force as well as an international court. Hostile toward party politics she many times refused an offer to become a candidate for parliament. In 1913 the London Peace Society recognized her work by electing her an honorary vice-president.

Following her lead the Society concentrated on working through established institutions to bring about change. In spite of considerable rhetoric about appealing to ordinary people the Society's principal targets were the influential, particularly politicians and political organisations, churches, the state education department, and the press. It deplored the spirit of militarism in the schools and made several approaches to the state minister of education urging the exclusion of articles in school readers glorifying war, the inclusion in the history curriculum of lessons on international arbitration, and the publication of articles on peace and arbitration in the *Educational Gazette*. It also offered to endow prizes for a school essay competition. Emphatic that the best way to bring about peace was by not preparing for war it protested against the federal government's proposal to introduce compulsory military training for boys and young men. After the scheme was implemented in 1911 it tried to obtain for conscientious objectors the same exemption from military *training* as already applied to military *service*. At the same time it tried to encourage friendly relations between Britain and Germany and persistently denied that Japan menaced Australia or Australian interests.

The First World War was a demoralising experience for the New South Wales Peace Society. It split between a pro-German group and the majority who, like Scott, believed the British cause was just and condemned Germany for invading "brave little Belgium." However it urged the Australian government to press for negotiations, protested the proposed internment of all Germans in NSW, and set up a small local distress fund. None of its efforts met with much success.

Scott's role diminished after the outbreak of war. Old age—she was almost 70—failing health, and anxiety that the Society had become too militant and strident by its association with the anticonscription coalition, the Australian Peace Alliance persuaded her to resign as president in 1917. She retired from public life in 1921 but was still elected an honorary vice-president of the NSW branch of the League of Nations Union, a body about which she had reservations and on which she was completely inactive. She died in 1925 and was one of the first in NSW to be cremated.

Although most of the NSW Peace Society's proposals had been ignored or rejected, Rose Scott's involvement was crucial in achieving even a modicum of support. She inspired loyalty and was a witty and accomplished public speaker. She was most skillful in dealing with influential people and personally led many deputations to parliamentarians and public servants. But above all her reputation preceded her and did much to make the group respectable. By the turn of the century her home (Lynton) had become the only real salon in Sydney. There she entertained politicians of all parties, clergymen of all denominations, distinguished overseas visitors, and leading men in the arts and letters. A charming, cultured, much-loved and highly-respected woman, her name had by 1900 become almost synonymous with social and political reform. But the liberalism which inspired her in the 1890s and early 1900s, when she saw implemented most of the reforms she advocated on behalf of women and children, was increasingly ineffective in the face of the militarism pervading Australian society in the years up to and during the First World War.

Bibliography:

B. Alec H. Chisholm, "The Lady of the Treasure House," *Life Digest*, (July 1, 1948); Zora Cross, "Pioneer in Fight for Woman's Suffrage: Achievements of Rose Scott", *Argus* (February 20, 1937); Miles Franklin, "Rose Scott: Some Aspects of Her Personality and Work," in F. Eldershaw (ed.), *The Peaceful Army: A Memorial to the Pioneer Women of Australia: 1788-1938* (Sydney, 1938), 90-107; Septimus Harwood, *Reminiscences of the Late Miss Rose Scott as Founder, President, and Life-Long Friend of the Peace Society, New South Wales Branch* (Sydney, 1925).

Malcolm Saunders

SELINHEIMO, Aarne (16 July 1898, Helsinki, Finland—29 October 1939, Helsinki). *Education*: high school; studies at Polytechnical Coll. *Career*: clerk; stenographer; translator; salesman; editor of peace magazines; member, boards of Finland's Peace Union and Antimilitaristic Union.

Aarne Selinheimo's father was one of the leaders of the Finnish national movement and also a governor and senator. Aarne's five brothers chose military careers, but Aarne went to the Polytechnical College to study and married a carpenter's daughter. This caused a rift between him and his parents. The rift deepened when, during the civil war of 1918, Aarne sided with the losing "Red" forces of the Revolutionary Peoples Soviet.

The civil war deepened Selinheimo's pacifism which had developed earlier. He joined Finland's Peace Union, founded in 1920, and acted for many years on its board as a close collaborator of *Felix Iversen. The Peace Union, however, proved too moderate for Selinheimo and, in 1923 with *Arndt Pekurinen, he founded the Antimilitaristic Union. Four years later Selinheimo and Pekurinen convinced the board of the Antimilitaristic Union to join the War Resisters' International. Selinheimo's knowledge of German, Swedish, and English proved valuable to the Finnish peace effort, for it enabled him to make contacts with leaders of the European antiwar movement, including *Henri Barbusse, +H. G. Wells, +Christian Lange, and *Bertrand Russell. Selinheimo was an enthusiastic Esperantist; in his opinion it could be developed into a language for the international workers' and peace movements. He founded two peace unions of Esperantists (UNUECO and FLEA), both of which remained small and exercised little influence.

Like Felix Iversen, Selinheimo invested a good deal of his own financial resources in peace work. He traveled at his own expense to European peace congresses and reported on their work in Finnish papers. He took a particularly strong interest in the conscientious objector issue, sending personal appeals to various governments and heads of state urging them to release imprisoned opponents of military service. He collected names for petitions and visited conscientious objectors who were imprisoned in Germany and Estonia. He even edited, published, and printed two antiwar papers, *Aseet pois (Weapons Away)* and *Sodanvastustaja (War Resister)*, which he sold door to door. Shortly before his death, Selinheimo worked eagerly to promote the Pan-European idea of the Austrian Count +Richard Coudenhove-Kalegri.

Unlike most other leaders of the Finnish peace movement during the interwar period, Selinheimo had close relationships with the workers' movement. He believed that the workers' movement was, in principle, a peace movement and that it formed a natural basis for peace work. He was not, however, a party politician. His writings and speeches indicated that he was primarily an anarchist, sympathetic with the ideas of Michael Bakunin and *Peter Kropotkin. Consequently, he viewed political parties and social institutions as supporters of war and violence. Because of his activism and antiwar efforts, Selinheimo gained widespread recognition as one of Finland's most prominent peace leaders.

Bibliography:

B. Kalevi Kalemaa, *Suomalisen rauhanliikkeen juuria* (Vaasa, 1981); Oskar von Schoultz, "Aarne Selinheimo kuollut," *Rauhaa Kohti*, 21 (1939), 208.

Kalevi Kalemaa
Trans. by Oliver and Rita Whitehead

SELLON, Jean-Jacques (20 January 1782, Geneva, Switzerland—7 June 1839,

Belfort, France). *Education*: private tutors. *Career*: landowner and member of the Geneva Council of State.

Jean-Jacques Sellon was born into the ruling circles of Geneva. His family descended from Huguenots who fled Nîmes during the reign of Louis XIV and became wealthy and honored in its adopted Calvinist homeland. In his youth, making the classical Grand Tour, Sellon was deeply impressed by the enlightened administration of Tuscany under the Habsburg Grand Duke Leopold, as well as by the writings of Cesare Beccaria, the criminologist. He became a crusader against the death penalty and for penal reform. These were only two among a host of progressive causes which interested him. Despite the fact that Sellon was named a chamberlain in the last years of Napoleon's Empire, he obtained a seat on the governing council of Geneva after the Bourbon Restoration in France (sitting from 1816-29) where he championed numerous reforms ranging from road and canal improvements to elimination of the death penalty.

In 1830 Sellon founded the first peace society ever created on the continent, La Société de la paix de Genève (Geneva Peace Society), presumably inspired by the English and American groups of which he read. For the remaining nine years of his life, he devoted his wealth and energies to this cause through meetings, lectures, pamphlets and a vast private correspondence. The Society offered the first cash prize for an essay on the best means to achieve peace in Europe. The award eventually went to a Zurich professor, who wrote the first essay on the subject in German in the nineteenth century.

Sellon's deep religious convictions about the inviolability of life inspired his opposition to the death penalty and his opposition to war. When the French invaded Algeria in 1830, he condemned the use of violence to further European commercial interests and demanded that a council of diplomats be convened to arbitrate conflicts in Europe. Arbitration and negotiation, argued Sellon, were the only proper means to solve disputes in the modern age; war was a relic of feudal, pre-industrial eras. Armies should be converted into worker battalions to dig tunnels, canals, and railways. War, Sellon pointed out, left only a "legacy of misery" and placed an "outrageous tax" on working people. It brought neither security for kingdoms nor prosperity for citizens.

Sellon's admiration for benevolent rule and his horror of revolution (based on the Terror and the guillotine of 1792-94) convinced him that only enlightened despotism or leadership was feasible to achieve well governed states. Thus, he focused his propaganda on European elites to arouse them "to the entirety of immorality in the art [called] war." His letters went forth to rulers, ministers, government and business leaders, eminent personalities (including Louis Napoleon), and the small British peace community.

One convert whom he failed to make was his sister's son, Camille di Cavour, who insisted on the right of oppressed peoples to wage wars of national liberation. In the correspondence and relationship between this uncle and nephew lay a permanent dilemma which haunted European peace activists throughout the century—the difficulty of urging peaceful tactics on peoples who wanted national freedom. Sellon did not grasp the force of nationalism and seemed to believe in a vague evolutionary process toward independence. Neither his loving nephew nor Joseph Mazzini, the Italian nationalist, could accept that vision.

After his death, the peace society seems to have disappeared though his daughter, Valentine de Sellon, continued writing much in the same vein as her father—against the death penalty and on behalf of peace. Four years after Sellon's death, the first international peace congress of private citizens was convened in London by British and American organizers.

Bibliography:

A. *Archives de la Société de la paix à Genève* (Geneva, 1831, 1832, 1834, 1837); *Des Institutions propres à remplacer la peine de mort et à éviter la guerre* (Jura, 1836); *Opuscules divers (1829-30) sur la peine de mort, la paix, la guerre* (Geneva, n.d.); *Rapports (et al) relatifs à la Société de la paix* (Geneva, 1830-5).

B. Geneviève Abel, comp., "Dokumente der Friedensbewegung: Verzeichnis der Schriften des Grafen Jean-Jacques de Sellon (1782-1839) über die Todesstrafe, die Friedensbewegung and andere internationale Fragen," *Friedenswarte*, 21 (1931), 309-13; Giuseppe Gallavresi, "La Centenaire d'un précurseur: Jean-Jacques de Sellon," *Revue internationale de la Croix Rouge* (May, 1931), 348-58; Albert De Montet, ed., *Dictionnaire Biographique des Genevois et des Vaudois* (Lausanne, Bridel, 1878), II, 512-15; Herbert Eulenberg, "Die Friedensfreund de Sellon (1782-1839)," *Friedenswarte*, 30 (1930), 221-22; L. Weisz, *Jean Jacques de Sellon* (Zurich, 1929); Hans Wehberg, "Graf Sellon, ein Vorkämpfer des Volkerbunds," *Friedenswarte*, 30 (1930), 354-56.

Sandi E. Cooper

SENŌ Girō (16 December 1889, Hiroshima prefecture, Japan—4 August 1961, Nagano prefecture, Japan). *Education*: attended high school briefly. *Career*: author, leader of Buddhist movements, and conscientious objector.

When Senō Girō entered the prestigious First Higher School (Dai-ichi Kōtō Gakkō) in Tokyo in 1908 after finishing his middle school at the top of his class, a bright future seemed assured for him. However, the following year he contracted tuberculosis and had to spend the next ten years in painful struggles with his illness. The illness ruined his future as an elite, but it gave him a religious faith. He became a firm believer in the Buddhist teachings of Nichiren (1222-82).

In 1918 Senō returned to Tokyo, and the following year he began religious activities under the patronage of Honda Nissei, one of the most influential champions of Nichiren's teachings in modern Japan. That same year, dissatisfied with the state of established Buddhism, Senō helped create the Dai Nippon Nichirenshugi Seinendan (Great Japan Nichiren Youth Association), an organization to revitalize Buddhism as a living force in contemporary society.

Senō's commitment to making Japan the locus where Buddhist ideals would be realized made him increasingly sensitive to the social discontent of his time as expressed in labor and peasant conflicts. When his increasingly leftist stand evoked opposition from some leaders of the Great Japan Nichiren Youth Association, Senō withdrew and created the Shinkō Bukkyō Seinen Dōmei (Youth

League for Rising Buddhism) in 1931. This League, with Senō as president, criticized not only existing Buddhist sects as being devoid of the living Buddhist spirit, but also condemned the capitalistic economic structure.

Senō's endorsement of class struggle and his advocacy of the overthrow of capitalism made him look more Marxist than Buddhist. He believed, however, that the Buddhist spirit of selfless love demanded such actions. Senō of this period, no longer a follower of Nichiren in the narrow sense of the term, wanted to restore unity and timeliness to Buddhism by a return to historical Shakyamuni, the founder of Buddhism. Buddhism was originally atheistic. It did not preach the doctrine of immortality of soul. It was not an other-worldly religion. Thus, according to Senō, struggles for improvement of people's material life was not at all incompatible with true Buddhist teachings.

Senō's Youth League for Rising Buddhism stood for internationalism and took a clear antimilitaristic stand in the period when militaristic tendencies were becoming increasingly dominant in Japan. Senō's pacifist tendencies had started early. In the midst of anti-American agitations caused by the enactment of the so-called Japanese Exclusion Act (1924) by the United States, Senō published "Nichi-Bei mondai to Nichirenshugi" ("The Japanese-American Crisis and the Nichiren Principle") to warn people of the danger of impulsive chauvinism devoid of the ability for self-criticism. He advocated a pacifism based on the realization of the mutual dependence and brotherhood of all mankind as taught by Buddhism. Senō's publications such as "Shakai henkaku tojō no shinkō bukkyō" ("Rising Buddhism on the Way to Social Revolution") (1933) and "Bukkyō to heiwa undō" ("Buddhism and Peace Movement") (1934) contained theoretical justifications for the internationalist and pacifist stands taken by the Youth League for Rising Buddhism. The stand of the League made a strong contrast with generally nationalistic tendencies manifested by the majority of Buddhist groups in prewar Japan.

Senō was arrested in December 1936 for alleged violation of the Peace Preservation Law. The arrest of other leaders of the League followed in 1937. Senō was imprisoned for over a year and obliged to refrain from public activities until after Japan's defeat. In the postwar period he participated in the peace movement as well as in the reform movement of Buddhism.

Bibliography:

A. *Senō Girō shūkyūron shū*, Inagaki Masami, ed., (Tokyo, 1975); *Senō Girō nikki*, Senō Tetsutaro and Inagaki Masami, eds., (Tokyo, 1974-75).

B. Matsune Takashi, *Senō Girō to "Shinkō Bukkyō Seinen Dōmei"* (Tokyo, 1975); Shimane Kiyoshi, "Shinkō Bukkyō Seinen Dōmei: Senō Girō," Shisō no Kagaku Kenkyū Kai, ed., *Tenkō* (rev. and enl. ed., Tokyo, 1978); Tokoro Shigemoto, *Kindai shakai to Nichirenshugi* (Tokyo, 1972); Yoshida Kyūichi, *Nihon no kindai shakai to bukkyō* (Tokyo, 1970).

Yuzo Ota

SERRATI, Giacinto Menotti (25 November 1872, Spotorno, Italy—10 May

1926, Asso, Italy). *Education*: secondary school graduate. *Career*: journalist; editor, *Lotta di classe*, 1892-93; *Avvenire del lavoratore*, 1899-1902, 1904-11, *Proletario* (New York), 1902-3, *La Lima*, 1911-12, *Secolo nuovo*, 1912-14, *Avanti!*, 1914-23, *Comunismo*, 1919-22, *Piu avanti!*, 1923-24, *Pagine rosse*, 1923-24, *Il sindicato rosso*, 1924-26, *L'Unità*, 1924-26; labor official, 1911-14.

Upon the outbreak of World War I, Giacinto Serrati had already earned a reputation as an exceptional man of the Italian Socialist party (PSI). He was both a ''new man'' who had returned recently to Italy following a fourteen year absence and an old militant of the PSI's pioneer struggles. Besides a firm belief in socialism, Serrati was distinguished by his commitment to internationalism.

From such an internationalist perspective, Serrati faced both the Italo-Turkish war of 1911-12 and World War I as an advocate of peace. No strict pacifist, Serrati nevertheless condemned the Italian government's imperialistic ventures with all of his powers. During World War I, as Mussolini's successor as editor of *Avanti!* (the PSI's nationwide newspaper), he succeeded in drawing new sections of the popular masses into the antiwar and socialist camps. Under his vigorous direction, thousands of copies of each issue of the paper reached soldiers in the trenches, as well as peasants in their villages and workers on the streets.

When, after Italy's entry into the world conflict in May 1915, the country's antiwar movement lay dazed and dispirited, Serrati spearheaded its revival with the publication and distribution of hundreds of thousands of secretly-printed copies of the ringing antiwar ''Zimmerwald Manifesto,'' which emerged from the Zimmerwald Conference of antiwar socialists in September 1915 and at which Serrati served as an Italian delegate. Moreover, as Italians in 1915-16 became steadily radicalized by their growing discomfort with the war, Serrati steadily pressed forward the ''intransigent'' antiwar line in *Avanti!* However, as Antonio Gramsci observed, Serrati's overriding concern for maintaining unity within the broad-based PSI kept him at arm's length from Lenin's leftist position of advocating outright revolution. Even after the February Revolution in Russia, *Avanti!* favored the Socialist Revolutionaries—the leaders of whom supported the Russian war effort—in the paper's coverage of the Russian scene. Not until July 1917 did Serrati announce his own sympathy for the Bolsheviks, who demanded an end to Russia's participation in the conflict.

Serrati's subsequent popularization of Lenin's antiwar position corresponded with the rapid leftward drift of Italian workers and much of the PSI through the late spring and summer of 1917. At one point, however, Serrati tried to gain the agreement of PSI and labor leaders for the creation of a network throughout the country which might coordinate socialist communications and activities, in the event of an emergency, only to be turned down. He nevertheless continued his ''intransigent'' agitation, the success of which became apparent when a touring delegation of prowar Russian socialists was greeted in Italy with cries of ''Viva Lenin!'' Moreover, such agitation was credited with instigating the three-day uprising in Turin in August 1917, which erupted around the issues of inflation and the war.

Unlike other Italian antiwar currents of the period, including that of the Vatican, the PSI under Serrati sought to rally and involve the mass of the population in antiwar activities. With close contacts among working people, Serrati felt none of the fear of "the people" which limited the appeal and the efforts of bourgeois liberals, churchmen, and others. However, for his role in arousing Turinese workers in August, Serrati was sentenced to 3 1/2 years in prison following the uprising; and, he won release only in February 1919, as a result of the Amnesty of Victory.

Serrati's later activities revolved around the heady days of Italy's *biennio rosso* (Red Biennium), the early antifascist resistance, and his adhesion—after having striven fruitlessly to preserve socialist unity— to the communist party of Italy in 1924. To the broad mass of Italian workers, however, Serrati remained largely the man who had led the most effective component of the antiwar movement of 1914-18. Upon his death in 1926, Serrati's funeral became the last important public demonstration of the Italian labor movement before the implementation of the Exceptional Laws of the fascist dictatorship.

Bibliography:

A. *Ascolta soldato! Parole simplici dedicate ai proletari in divisa* (Milan, 1920); *La bibbia e immorale*, under pseud A. Tormenti (Geneva, 1904); *Cooperazione e socialismo* (Rome, 1910); *Dottrinetta razionalista*, under pseud. A. Tormenti (Geneva, 1904); *La situazione del partito socialista* (Rome, 1925); *Storia dei Savoia*, under pseud. G. M. Parrasio (Lugano, 1901); *La vera dottrina di Cristo*, under pseud. G. M. Parrasio (Lugano, 1901).

B. A. Caracciolo, "Serrati, Bordiga e la polemica gramsciana contro il 'blanquismo' o settarismo, in *La citta futura*," in A. Carocciolo and G. Scalia, eds., *Saggi sulla figura e il pensiero di A. Gramsci* (2nd ed., Milan, 1976); T. Detti, *Serrati e la formazione del Partito comunista italiano* (Rome, 1972); A. Gramsci, "G. M. S.," in *L'Unita*, May 14, 1926; A. Gramsci, et. al, *Il testamento politico di Serrati* (Milan, 1926).

C. Giacinto Menotti Serrati Archives, Gramsci Institute, Rome.

James A. Young

SÉVERINE [pseud. of Caroline Rémy] (24 April 1855, Paris—23 April 1929, Pierrefonds, Oise, France). *Career*: journalist, anarchist activist, editor, and peace activist.

Daughter of a civil service functionary, Séverine endured an unhappy childhood and experienced the rigors of war and revolution in Paris in 1870-71. At 16, she married Antoine Montrobert, bearing a child in one year. That marriage failed and she later married Dr. Adrien Guébhard of the Sorbonne Faculty of Medicine, a liaison which also produced a child but did not last. In the early 1880s she met the anarchist editor and ex-communard, Jules Vallès, became converted to his views and collaborated with him in publishing *Le Reveil*. Under the pseudonym Arthur Vingtras, she published articles in other journals from the libertarian point of view. With Vallès' death in 1885, she became editor of

Le Cri du Peuple, writing in defense of striking miners and supporting feminists. She completed Vallès' novel, *L'Insurgé* as well.

For a short time in the late 1880s and early 1890s, Séverine abandoned her political commitments and became a supporter of the Boulanger movement as well as an anti-Dreyfusard. This apostasy ended and by 1900 she returned to principles more consonant with her earlier views, became an ardent feminist and published *Vers la Lumière* (articles defending women's suffrage). She also joined the newly formed Ligue des droits de l'homme (League for the Rights of Man) and the Socialist party, becoming a regular contributor to *L'Humanité*.

From her feminism and her deep commitment to human rights, it was a short step to involvement in the peace movement. She joined the Association de la paix et le désarmement par les femmes (Women's Association for Peace and Disarmament), participated as its delegate in national and international peace congresses, and was one of the few women elected to the Délégation permanente des sociétés françaises de la paix (Permanent Delegation of French Peace Societies), headed by *Gaston Moch before 1914. At national congresses, her biting insights' made her an *enfant terrible*, for Séverine was totally impatient with the self-congratulatory pieties which often filled hours of the peace agendas, forcing orators to face the realities of mounting military budgets and the threat of war. In one speech delivered in 1909 at the sixth national peace congress, she took all the male leadership to task for its unsubstantiated optimism about the progress of their cause. When the war came, she was far less willing to support the Union sacrée and to accept government justification that the war was one of "defense" than were most of the other peace leaders.

Her active antiwar career really began when she joined the Société d'études documentaires et critiques sur la guerre (Society for the Critical and Documentary Studies of the War) in 1916, a group founded by *Mathias Morhardt and *Georges Demartial to examine French responsibility for the war and to counteract chauvinism. After the war, she never abandoned her pacifist commitment, remaining active in the Association de la paix et le désarmement par les femmes and on the Délégation permanente. When she joined *Madeleine Vernet and *Marianne Rauze in creating the Ligue pour la reconnaissance de l'objection de conscience (League for the Recognition of Conscientious Objection), her pacifism took a more absolutist turn.

Séverine never gave up her commitments to the poor, the exploited, and the unfortunate. She struggled for the rights of indigent women in Algeria and against the execution of Nicola Sacco and Bartolomeo Vanzetti in the United States. She supported anticonscription movements, signing a petition in 1926 with *Albert Einstein, *Henri Barbusse, and others which the War Resisters' International had drafted and which asked the League of Nations to take steps against conscription around the world. She supported disarmament, urging the French government to take that part of the Versailles treaty seriously and not dwell on the war-guilt clause, and in 1927, she attacked the proposed new bill for a revised military service law. Her vision of all Europe as "ma patrie" was reflected in her articles (especially in *Le Cri des Peuples*, June 1928) and in her support of *Victor Margueritte's concept, "la patrie humaine." Until the end of her life, though largely in seclusion in the last years, she remained a member of peace societies and the Bureau international de la paix (International Peace Bureau) as well as the Association pacifiste internationale des journalistes (International Pacifist Association of Journalists).

Bibliography:

A. *Notes d'une frondeuse* (Paris, 1894); *Pages mystiques* (Paris, 1895); *Pages rouges* (Paris, 1893).

B. B. Lecache, *Séverine* (Paris, 1930); Jules Vallès, *Correspondance avec Séverine* (Paris, 1972); "Séverine," in Jean Maitron, ed., *Dictionnaire Biographique du Mouvement Ouvrier Français, 1871-1914* (Paris, 1977), XV, 160-61.

Albert S. Hill

SEWALL, May Eliza Wright (27 May 1844, Greenfield, WI—23 July 1920, Indianapolis, IN). *Education*: graduated (Mistress of Science), Northwestern Female Coll. (later absorbed by Northwestern Univ.), 1866; M.A., 1871. *Career*: teacher and school administrator in Michigan and Indiana, 1866-82; founder, Girls' Classical School, Indianapolis, 1882-1907; founder and first secretary, Indianapolis Equal Suffrage Society, 1878; chair, executive committee of the National Woman Suffrage Association, 1882-90; founder and later president, National Council of Women, 1897-99; president, International Council of Women, 1899-1904; chair, Committee on Peace and Arbitration, International Council of Women, 1904-14.

May Wright Sewall came to the international peace movement following a number of years of activity in the women's suffrage movement. In 1888 she helped found the National Council of Women and the International Council of Women and remained active in both groups for many years. During the 1890s she worked for the adoption of a manual on peace promoted by the National Council of Women for use in the schools. Its contents were designed to show that the principle of arbitration could be adapted equally to family, school, business, and relations among nations. As a leader of the International Council of Women she was particularly proud of the fact that representatives of all nations sat as equals and had the same number of votes on all issues that came before the body. In her view, by rejecting the idea that a nation's size and population would determine its voting power, the Council was rejecting the idea that might makes right. When the Hague Conference of 1899 was announced, Sewall worked to gain support for its efforts. The following year, President William McKinley appointed her to represent the United States at the Paris Exposition.

During the decade preceding World War I, Sewall became increasingly active on behalf of world peace both as a member of the American Peace Society and within women's organizations. With her powerful personality she inspired fierce loyalties on the part of some and strongly negative feelings in others. An effective platform speaker, she was also a talented organizer. Following the outbreak of

World War I she headed the organizing committee for an "International Conference of Women Workers to Promote Permanent Peace" held in July 1915 as part of the Panama-Pacific International Exposition in San Francisco. She presided over the conference and edited the published proceedings. Later that year, Sewall braved the ridicule of the press when, at the age of 71, she sailed to Europe with *Rosika Schwimmer and a number of other peace advocates on Henry Ford's peace ship, the *Oscar II*, in a quixotic attempt to set up a mediation conference and bring an end to the war. Her activities as a leader of the Women's Peace party and her continued opposition to American involvement in the war set Sewall apart as one of only a handful of leaders in the prewar peace movement who continued their efforts after 1914, when it was less respectable to espouse peace doctrines, and after 1917, when questioning U.S. involvement had become rarer still.

Bibliography:

A. (Edited volumes): *Genesis of the International Council of Women and the Story of Its Growth, 1889-1893* (Indianapolis, 1914); *Women, War, and Permanent Peace* (San Francisco, 1915); *The World's Congress of Representative Women* (2 vols., Chicago, 1894).

B. NAW, III, 269-71.

C. May Wright Sewall, scrapbooks and some correspondence, Indianapolis State Library, Indianapolis, IN.

Michael A. Lutzker

SHEPPARD, Hugh Richard Lawrie (Dick) (2 September 1880, Windsor, England—31 October 1937, London). *Education*: B.A., Trinity Hall, Cambridge Univ., 1904. *Career*: Anglican priest, Vicar of St. Martin-in-the-Fields, 1914-27; Dean of Canterbury, 1929-31; canon and preceptor of St. Paul's Cathedral, 1934-37; founder and leader of the Peace Pledge Union, 1936-37; pacifist.

Hugh Richard Lawrie Sheppard, an Anglican priest, is best remembered as a church reformer and the founder of the Peace Pledge Union, Britain's largest pacifist society during the interwar period. At the height of his career, "Dick" Sheppard was undoubtedly one of the most well-known and best liked personalities in the country. He seemed to have an extraordinary effect upon everyone he met. His sense of humor, his obvious concern for other people, his ability to instill hope in those who despaired, all this brought comfort and joy to those around him. The irony was that while he brought so much joy to others, he was himself an unhappy man. Psychohistorians would likely label him a "manic-depressive," given to bouts of elation, only to be followed by moods of dark depression. Part of his unhappiness was linked to poor health: throughout his life he experienced a variety of debilitating illnesses, but the most cruel offender was asthma. In addition, he feared that he was of no use to people, that his life was a series of failures, and near the end he was demoralized by the prospect of his marriage breaking up.

His early career was dominated by a desire to reform the Church of England.

He loved the Church but was frustrated by its stuffy and conservative posture. More specifically, he accused the Church of England of being too concerned with dogmatic and organizational matters, of being out of tune with the times and indifferent to the real spiritual and physical needs of its members. Much of what he proposed would appear modest by later standards, but at the time he was regarded within certain clerical circles as a maverick at best and a dangerous radical at worst. Sheppard's accumulated grievances against organized religion were summed up in his book, *The Impatience of a Parson* (1927). Its contents merely confirmed in the minds of his critics that he was too flamboyant and impetuous, a flashy popularizer of religion who preached a syrupy brand of Christianity.

He arrived at his pacifist beliefs rather late in life; his first major speech on the subject was delivered at Albert Hall in November 1931. Apparently, the Quaker playwright Laurence Houseman played an important role in inducing him to take up the pacifist cause. But even then Sheppard was never absolutely certain about the validity of the pacifist position, and he was somewhat hesitant in making it his only interest. He based his pacifism upon the Christian ethic: no specific Gospel text but rather the whole spirit and teaching of Christ. In October 1934, Sheppard sent his famous Peace Letter to the press in which he asked his readers that if they agreed with his pacifist conviction never to support another war, they should send him a postcard stating their agreement. The response was tremendous: he received some 80,000 cards within the first year, and eventually that figure was to reach 130,000.

Sheppard then proceeded to organize this powerful expression of peace sentiment into the largest pacifist society in modern British history: the Peace Pledge Union. In its early years the Peace Pledge Union generated much enthusiasm and optimism. The PPU attracted world famous intellectuals to its ranks, as well as members of parliament and highly respected clergymen. It developed a first-rate organization, secured ample funding, started its own newspaper (*Peace News*), and sponsored an immense amount of activity and propaganda. Part of the success of the PPU was due to the fact that pacifism and antimilitarism had already captured the public imagination in Britain during the thirties, and thus the Union's message found a receptive audience. But much of its success could also be traced directly to Sheppard. His sense of timing, his intuition of what was possible, his flair to attract publicity, his organizational talents, his reluctance to pursue reckless schemes, all this attested to a remarkable degree of competence in practical affairs. Sheppard's popularity received a further boost in October 1937, when he was asked to stand as a pacifist candidate in the Glasgow University Rectorial Election. He faced considerable opposition in Winston Churchill (Unionist), J.B.S. Haldane (Popular Front), and William Dixon (Scottish Nationalist). Yet, he won easily, something which gave him immense satisfaction. The final irony of his life was that just when he was so elated by this victory, he died suddenly in the early hours of October 31, 1937.

His public funeral, observed by thousands, brought an outpouring of genuine sorrow and sense of loss, and the numerous tributes that flowed in reflected the deep esteem and love with which he was held, not only by pacifists and Anglicans, but by all segments of British society.

Bibliography:

A. *We Say "No": The Plain Man's Guide to Pacifism* (London, 1935).

B. William Paxton, et al., *Dick Sheppard* (London, 1938); R. Ellis Roberts, *H.R.L. Sheppard: Life and Letters* (London, 1942); Carolyn Scott, *Dick Sheppard* (London, 1977); DNB, 1931-1940, 809-10; NYT, November 1, 1937.

David C. Lukowitz

SHERK, J. Harold (20 December 1903, Kitchener, Ontario, Canada—28 February 1974, Kitchener). *Education*: Chicago Evangelistic Institute, Chicago, IL, 1922-25. *Career*: teacher, Emmanuel Bible Coll., Kitchener, Ontario, 1940-44, 1946-49; executive secretary, Mennonite Central Committee, Peace Section, Akron, Pennsylvania, 1949-58; executive secretary, National Service Board for Religious Objectors, Washington, D.C., 1958-69; Mennonite minister; churchworker.

From World War II through the Korean and Vietnam wars, J. Harold Sherk was a leader in promoting Christian pacifism, working particularly to plead the case of the conscientious objector, both in Canada and the United States.

Sherk was the first secretary of the Conference of Historic Peace Churches, formed in Ontario in 1940 to represent Mennonite, Brethren, and Quaker churches in their struggle for exemption from military service. On behalf of this committee, he made many trips to Ottawa for negotiations with the Canadian government. For over a year (1941-42), Sherk served as a pastor and counselor to young men in alternative service camps in Northern Ontario and British Columbia.

In 1944 Sherk was sent to India under the auspices of Mennonite Central Committee, an inter-Mennonite agency for relief, peace, and service. There he spent two years implementing and administering what is today a million-dollar relief program.

Sherk became executive secretary and the first fulltime employee of Mennonite Central Committee—Peace Section, a resource body for peace promotion and activity in North America from Akron, Pennsylvania. Under his administration, a postwar alternative service program for conscientious objectors was initiated in the United States and a network of draft counselors established at state and local levels. He was active during the government debates on universal military conscription during the early 1950s, speaking out strongly against repressive laws, and his efforts to protect the rights of COs was evident in the 1951 U.S. military draft law.

Sherk continued his campaign in support of conscientious objection as executive secretary of the National Service Board for Religious Objectors (NSBRO) in Washington, D.C., from 1959 until his retirement in 1969. In this capacity, he counseled many young men facing the draft as well as representing the peace interests of the Mennonites to the American government. His expertise and diplomacy gained him the respect of the Washington legal community and the national Selective Service offices, even though he worked at counterpurposes with the latter.

Whether lobbying the government for military exemption for COs or whether preaching to a congregation or teaching in a classroom, Sherk's entire career was that of an apostle of peace.

Bibliography:

B. Walter Hackman, "A Peacemaker in Memoriam: J. Harold Sherk," *MCC News Service*, March 8, 1974; Dave Kroeker, "The Boys from the CO Camps Remembered Harold Sherk," *Mennonite Reporter*, April 1, 1974, p. 9; John A. Lapp, "The Peace Mission of the Mennonite Central Committee," *Mennonite Quarterly Review*, 44 (July, 1970), 281-97.

Frank H. Epp and Marlene G. Epp

SHOTWELL, James Thomson. See *Biographical Dictionary of Internationalists*.

SIEGMUND-SCHULTZE, Friedrich Wilhelm (14 June 1885, Görlitz, Silesia, Germany—11 July 1969, Soest, Westphalia, German Federal Republic). *Education*: Lic. (Ph.D.), Univ. of Marburg, 1908. *Career*: editor: *Die Eiche*, 1913-33, *Okumenische Jahrbuch*, 1934-37, *Okumenische Einheit*, 1948ff; social worker, ecumenist, writer, and peace activist.

Siegmund-Schultze was a product of the liberal German theological school associated with Adolf von Harnack and *Martin Rade, and was strongly influenced by the pre-1914 ideas of internationalism, pacifism, and social justice, based on concepts of ethical reformation of society through the churches. In the 1920s he became the leading proponent of such ideas in Germany, seeking to combat the nationalist trends. Expelled from Germany by the Nazis in 1933, he spent fourteen years in Switzerland, organizing relief measures for refugees. In 1947, he returned to Dortmund to establish an institute for social pedagogy, and after his retirement directed the Ecumenical Archive in Soest, Westphalia.

Appointed at an early age to be secretary of the Associated Council in the German and British Empires for fostering friendly relations between the two peoples, he organized the inaugural conference of the World Alliance for promoting international friendship through the churches in August 1914. After its revival in 1919, Siegmund-Schultze was one of the four international secretaries of the World Alliance, responsible for central and eastern Europe, and built up the organization as an independent group seeking to mobilize church opinion against war, and in support of disarmament, compulsory arbitration, and the League of Nations. He was active in promoting the reconciliation of disputes amongst the minority religious groups in eastern Europe, and was a leading champion of international conciliation in such matters as war guilt and revision of the Treaty of Versailles. From 1913-33, he edited *Die Eiche*, the most prominent quarterly journal in the peace movement.

From 1911 onwards he was the director of a social work settlement in the Berlin slums, which was adopted as a model in other German cities. He took a leading part in voluntary agencies concerned with social problems especially for children. From 1913-25 he was chairman of the Berlin section of the German Central Office for Youth Welfare, and from 1917-19 first director of the Berlin Municipal Youth Office. In 1925 he was appointed Honorary Professor for Youth Welfare at Berlin University. He pioneered extension courses for the unemployed and apprentices and a slum rehousing project for workers. In addition, he sought to involve pastors and students in the social reform movement by offering them the chance of first-hand practical experience in the slums. Following the Nazi take-over of power in 1933, he promoted measures of relief for German Jews, for which he was arrested and expelled.

Resident in Zurich from 1933-47, he was engaged in stimulating the refugee efforts of the international Christian community. From 1934-37 he was student advisor at the Zurich University. Depressed by the failure of the world's churches to stop the drift to war, and the inactivity of the World Alliance, he drew closer to the International Fellowship of Reconciliation, and acted on its behalf throughout the war years in Switzerland, and later in West Germany.

As a great admirer of Archbishop Nathan Söderblom, Siegmund-Schultze heartily endorsed the plans for greater collaboration between the churches, resulting in the Stockholm Conference of Life and Work in 1925. Siegmund-Schultze vigorously campaigned for German participation, but was disappointed by the rigid dogmatism and nationalism of the official German delegation. He also strongly supported the Faith and Order movement, but was later disenchanted by what he believed was the "bureaucratization" of the World Council of Churches.

A capable and forthright lecturer, Siegmund-Schultze gained a considerable following in appealing for his vision of a reformed church, peace, and social justice. At the same time, he was a stringent critic of the churches' leadership and gained the reputation of being a provocative gadfly. His lack of sympathy with both the nationalist *Deutsche Christen* and the Barthian theology of the Confessing Church was based on his continued belief in the inspirational qualities of liberal theology, evidenced in his book *The Overcoming of Hatred* (1946). He consistently argued the cause of a "better" Germany, and was bitterly disappointed by the post-1945 division of the country and the onset of the Cold War.

Bibliography:

A. *Ekklesia* (15 vols., 1934-41); *Die soziale Botschaft des Christentums* (Berlin, 1921); *Sozialismus und Christentum* (Berlin, 1919); *Die Uberwindung des Hasses* (Zurich, 1946).

B. E. Bornemann, ed., *Lebendige Ökumene* (Witten, 1965); H. Delfs, ed., *Aktiver Friede* (Soest, 1972).

C. Siegmund-Schultze Papers, Ecumenical Archive of the German Evangelical Church, West Berlin.

John S. Conway

SIEMSEN, Anna Marie (18 January 1882, Mark/Westphalia, Germany—22 January 1952, Hamburg, German Federal Republic). *Education*: Ph.D., Univ.

of Bonn, 1909. *Career*: teacher, Detmold, Bremen, and Düsseldorf, 1909-19; honorary professor of pedagogy, Univ. of Jena, 1923-32; Reichstag member, 1928-30; education official; political and educational writer.

After completing her studies in Germanistics and philosophy at the University of Bonn, Anna Marie Siemsen, the daughter of a Lutheran pastor and his wife, became a school teacher. World War I turned Siemsen and her brother *August Siemsen into sharp critics of political and social conditions in Germany. During the war she joined the Bund Neues Vaterland (New Fatherland League) and the Unabhängige Sozialdemokratische Partei Deutschlands (Independent German Social Democratic Party) (USPD), both of which were antiwar organizations. After the German November Revolution (1918), she was appointed to a position in the Prussian Ministry of Education and later held an administrative post with the technical and vocational schools in Düsseldorf. From 1920 until 1923 she was a member of the Berlin School Board. In 1923 Siemsen, along with her brother and other members of the moderate faction of the USPD, returned to the Sozialdemokratische Partei Deutschlands (German Social Democratic Party) (SPD). That same year, the Socialist government of the state of Thuringia entrusted her with the reform of state secondary schools and teacher training programs. In addition, she received an honorary professorship of pedagogy at the University of Jena. Her reform work came to an end after a few months with the federal government's dissolution of the Thuringian Socialist state government; but she retained her professorship.

Within the SPD, Siemsen was a leading representative of the left opposition. She worked on left opposition periodicals, was co-editor of the "Young Socialist Series" and, in 1926 was co-founder of the Bund sozialdemokratischer Intellektueller (League of Social Democratic Intellectuals), which was not recognized by the SPD. As an SPD member of the Reichstag (1928-30), Siemsen, in opposition to the majority of her SPD colleagues, voted against the approval of funds for the building of a new armored cruiser. Coincident with her membership in the SPD, Siemsen also belonged to the Deutschen Liga für Menschenrechte (League for Human Rights), on whose executive committee she served, and was a member of the German section of the Woman's International League for Peace and Freedom. In 1931 Siemsen left the SPD and helped found the Socialist splinter party, Sozialistische Arbeiter Partei Deutschlands (German Socialist Worker's Party) (SAPD). The increasingly Nazi dominated state government of Thuringia revoked her professorship in 1932 when she signed a protest against the dismissal of *Emil Julius Gumbel.

After the accession of the Nazis to power in January 1933, Siemsen fled to Switzerland where she was active for fourteen years as a writer and as a leading figure in various antifascist organizations. In 1946 she returned to Germany where she became a teacher of literature at the University of Hamburg and director of the Institute for Teacher Education in that city. In the postwar years, she devoted herself especially to the Sozialistischen Bewegung für die Vereinigten Staaten von Europe (Socialist Movement for a United States of Europe), whose German section later was named after her (Anna-Siemsen-Kreis). Anna

Siemsen was not only a leading pacifist, but a teacher, who in her professional activity as an educator and in her publications, strove to instill socialist and pacifist ideals in young people and women.

Bibliography:

A. *Auf dem Weg zum Socialismus. Kritik der sozialdemokratischen Parteiprogramme von Erfurt bis Heidelberg* (Berlin, 1931); *Einführung in den Socialismus* (Hamburg, 1947); *Kämpfende Menschheit* (Jena, 1929); *Parteidisziplin und sozialistische Überzeugung* (Berlin, 1932); *10 Jahre Weltkrieg* (Dusseldorf, 1947).

B. Marie Juchacz, *Sie lebten für eine bessere Welt. Lebensbilder furhrender Frauen des 19. und 20 Jahrhunderts* (Berlin [East], 1955; new ed., 1971); Werner Röder and Herbert A. Strauss, eds., *Biographisches Handbuch der deutschsprachigen Emigration nach 1933* (Munich and New York, 1980), I, 696-97; August Siemsen, *Anna Siemsen. Leben und Werk* (Frankfurt, 1951); *Geschichte der deutschen Arbeiterbewegung: Biographisches Lexikon.* Institut fur Marxismus-Leninismus (Berlin [East], 1970), 429-30.

Hans-Josef Steinberg
Trans. by Solomon Wank

SIEMSEN, August (5 July 1884, Mark/Westphalia, Germany—25 March 1958, Berlin [East], German Democratic Republic). *Education*: Ph.D., Univ. of Göttingen, 1909. *Career*: teacher, editor, political writer, and politician.

After completing his studies in Germanistics and history at the University of Göttingen, where he studied under +Max Lehmann, August Siemsen, the brother of *Anna Siemsen, became a teacher in Essen. There he joined the left-liberal Fortschrittlichen Volkspartei (Progressive People's Party). Later, under the influence of the First World War, he turned away from left-liberalism and joined first the Sozialdemokratische Partei Deutschlands (German Social Democratic Party) (SPD) and then the Unabhängige Sozialdemokratische Partei Deutschlands (Independent Social Democratic Party) (USPD). After the war he became active in workers' educational efforts. His participation in the fight of the Ruhr workers against the right-wing nationalist Kapp putschists in 1920, led to a six month prison term. In 1923 the left-wing coalition government of SPD and Kommunistische Partei Deutschlands (German Communist Party) (KPD) of the State of Thuringia called Siemsen to Jena to head the state's adult education program. He lost that position when the national army acting on executive orders of the federal government occupied Thuringia and quashed the coalition government.

In the years after his Thuringian experience, Siemsen was the chief-editor of the periodicals, *Sozialistische Erziehung* and *Sozialistische Kultur*, and he was actively involved in the executive committee of the Arbeitsgemeinschaft sozialdemokratischer Lehrer und Lehrerinnen Deutschlands (Study Group of Social Democratic [Male and Female] Teachers of Germany), the Kindefreundebewegung (Friends of Children Movement), and the Bund Freier Schulgesellschaften (League of Free School Association). From 1930 until 1932 he was a member of the Reichstag. There he represented pacifist positions by fighting especially against rearmament. He was one of eight Social Democrats who voted against the naval bill of March 20, 1931. His pacifist convictions led Siemsen from the

SPD to the Sozialistische Arbeiter Partei Deutschlands (Socialist Worker's Party of Germany) (SAPD), of which he was one of the founding members. At the first meeting of the SAPD, Siemsen was elected to the party's executive committee.

In April 1933 Siemsen fled from Nazi Germany and emigrated to Switzerland. From there he went to Argentina where, together with other German émigrés, he founded the movement Das Andere Deutschland (The Other Germany) and became editor of a periodical of the same name. The periodical exercised considerable influence among German emigrants. In 1952 he returned to the German Federal Republic. Displeased with political developments in the Federal Republic, he moved to the German Democratic Republic in 1955 and joined the communist Sozialistischen Einheitspartei Deutschlands (Socialist Unity Party of Germany) (SED). Siemsen's move to the German Democratic Republic led to a prolonged controversy between the leaders of the SPD and the SED.

Bibliography:

A. *Anna Siemsen. Leben und Werk* (Frankfurt, 1951); (ed.), *Preussen, die Gefahr Europas* (Paris, 1937); *Die Tragödie Deutschlands und die Zukunft der Welt* (Buenos Aires, 1945; Hamburg, 1947).

B. Werner Röder and Herbert A. Strauss, eds., *Biographisches Handbuch der deutschsprachigen Emigration nach 1933* (Munich and New York, 1980), I, 697; *Geschichte der deutschen Arbeiterbewegung Biographisches Lexikon*. Institut fur Marxismus-Leninismus (Berlin [East], 1970), 430-31.

Hans-Josef Steinberg
Trans. by Solomon Wank

SIGOURNEY, Lydia Howard Huntley (1 September 1791, Norwich, CT—10 June 1865, Hartford, CT). *Education*: district schools and tutors. *Career*: teacher, poet, and author.

Commonly called the "sweet singer of Hartford," Lydia Huntley Sigourney was one of the first women in America to achieve fame as a poet and moral writer. Although modern critics have not been kind to her, finding that she wrote too much, had little originality, chose morbid themes, and moralized every idea she addressed, Sigourney was widely published in the popular press.

Lydia Sigourney was not particularly active in the various antiwar organizations established during the first half of the nineteenth century. She did, however, participate in *Elihu Burritt's Friendly Address movement of 1846, designed to stave off conflict with Great Britain over the Oregon boundary dispute, and she assisted Burritt in organizing juvenile peace societies in Connecticut. More important to the cause of peace was her writing. In her autobiography she claimed that she wrote for peace all her life and to some she, along with *John Greenleaf Whittier, were the poet laureates of the American peace movement.

Although perhaps a somewhat exaggerated claim, Sigourney apparently did donate a short story, "The Farmer and the Soldier" (1833), and a book *Olive Buds* (1836) to William Watson, one of the publishers of the *American Advocate of Peace*, and to the American Peace Society. These works, and several of her other poems and stories, show a consistent, if oblique, concern with peace which can be characterized as pious, civilized, and domestic. Much of the success of Lydia Sigourney's work lay in her feminized and genteel approach, an approach which helped bring peace values to more American women than the activities of the more activist women in the antiwar movement. She argued for the elevation of peace-lovers over military heroes, questioned the conditions which created famous heroes at the cost of poor soldiers' deaths, and suggested that women would make better rulers than blood-thirsty men.

Lydia Sigourney's appeal was both personal and moral, made to impressionable children and to civilized adults. It was an appeal based on a firm, but quiet commitment to pacific values. This approach was the strength of her success and her popularity.

Bibliography:

A. *Faded Hope* (New York, 1859); *Letters of Life* (New York, 1866); *Olive Leaves* (New York, 1852); *Selected Poems* (Philadelphia, 1854).

B. Gordon Haight, *Mrs. Sigourney; The Sweet Singer of Hartford* (New Haven, 1930); Peter Tolis, *Elihu Buritt; Crusader for Brotherhood* (Hamden, CT., 1968).

C. Sigourney Collection, Connecticut Historical Society, Hartford, Connecticut.

Jane F. Crosthwaite

SILONE, Ignazio [pseud. of Secondo Tranquilli] (1 May 1900, Pescina dei Marsi, Abruzzi, Italy — 22 August 1978, Geneva). *Education*: studied at Catholic institutions to 1918. *Career*: a founder of the Italian Communist party, 1923; party organizer, 1923-29; Socialist member, Constituent Assembly, 1944-49; journalist, novelist, editor, and essayist.

Ignazio Silone traced the origins of his political radicalism to his early childhood in a village of the Abruzzi. In 1918 he interrupted his studies to engage in social and political activities and three years later, he helped to found the Italian Communist party, which he subsequently represented on several official missions to Moscow. As editor of progressive journals in the 1920s, notably *Avanguardia*, an extreme left organ that had opposed World War I, Silone participated in the diffusion of anti-Fascist literature and led the clandestine existence of organizer and agent. During imprisonment in a Spanish jail for efforts to organize Communist youth groups, he adopted the pseudonym by which he subsequently became known: Ignazio (for the militant Loyola) and Silone (for the Roman rebel, Pompaedius Silo). In 1929 Silone broke with the party in opposition to what he considered the oppression and betrayal of socialist values by the Soviet regime. A period of exile in Switzerland followed, and with it, the beginnings of what was to be a rich literary career. Acclaimed with more consistent enthusiasm abroad than in his native country, Silone has often been cited as the successor to Giovanni Verga and compared to John Steinbeck and other major figures in proletarian literature.

Fontamara (1933), Silone's first novel, represented the conscious fusion of the activist and the artist, "the painful and lonely continuation of a struggle" which the author was careful to oppose to "serene aesthetic enjoyment." The characters in *Fontamara*, peasants or *cafoni* of Southern Italy, represented a forgotten class, those who worked a backward and desolate land. After *Fontamara* Silone remained committed to the struggle for social justice through essays, pamphlets, the novel *Pane e vino* (1937), and in a diatribe against totalitarianism, "La scuola dei dittatori" ("School for Dictators") (1938).

In 1941 Silone joined the international socialist movement, arguing for a "third front" position to take effect with the destruction of fascism. To Silone, the defeat of fascism was not the sole objective of World War II; it was the prelude to the creation of a just, peaceful world order that would eliminate colonialism. Silone's vision of a new international order differed markedly from what was imposed by the two "sides" that defeated the fascists and began the Cold War. Neither the Western capitalist nor the Soviet-led communist system would eliminate the forces that produced war and social inequality. Instead, Silone argued for direct associations of free producing communities that bypassed and replaced the traditional sovereign states, the monopolies of international capitalism, and large scale national bureaucracies. The new Europe would begin by ending all colonial and imperial activities in Africa and Asia. Obviously his ideal vision, particularly his desire to eliminate the nation-states, came from a deep felt belief that such power could not be curbed by any ordinary legal association of governments such as the League of Nations. However it was a vision that had no realistic chance of success in the atmosphere following World War II.

Silone served in the Constituent Assembly when he returned from exile in 1944, representing the left wing of Italian socialism. Hoping to transform the Italian Socialist party into a party that would sever ties with both major power blocks, he remained in parliament until 1950. The rigidification of Cold War battle lines and his growing disillusionment with postwar political conflicts finally led Silone to leave politics altogether. He became convinced that his ingredients for a peaceful world would not be accepted. Silone devoted himself to cultural labors, editing *Tempo Presente*, working with the Association for Cultural Freedom, and arguing for freedom of expression and the obligation of writers to serve social needs. Silone's early vision of humanity saved by the disciplined efforts of a party gave way to the vision of salvation through individual action, a theme he developed in *Vino e pane*, published in 1955 as a revision of his earlier work, *Pane e vino*. Brotherhood and selflessness now replaced political theory and organization. In an interview published in *L'Express* (1961) he described himself as "a Socialist without party and a Christian without church."

Bibliography:

A. *Fontamara* (Paris, 1933, Eng. trans., New York, 1962); *Pane e vino* (Lugano, 1937, Eng. trans. *Bread and Wine*, New York, 1937); *La scuola dei dittatori* (Milan, 1962, Eng. trans., *The School for Dictators*, New York, 1963); *Uscita di sicurezza* (Rome, 1951, Eng. trans., *Emergency Exit*, New York, 1968); *Vino e pane* (Milan, 1955, Eng. trans., *Bread and Wine*, New York, 1962).

B. Irving Howe, *Politics and the Novel* (New York, 1957); R.W.B. Lewis, *The*

Picaresque Saint (New York, 1961); G. Sapelli, "Ignazio Silone," in Franco Andreucci and Tommaso Detti, *Il Movimento operaio italiano, dizionario biografico* (Rome, 1978), IV, 640-46.

Mirella Jona Affron

SIMON, Jules (27 December 1814, Lorient, Brittany, France — 8 June 1896, Paris). *Education*: agrégation, École normale superieure, 1835; doctorate, Sorbonne, 1839. *Career*: teacher, Caen, Versailles, and Paris; professor of Philosophy, Sorbonne, 1839-51; author and politician.

The attainment of peace was not an isolated commitment for Jules Simon. Indeed, he cannot be considered a pacifist, nor was peace the central pursuit of his life. It was a component in a comprehensive program of republicanism. Simon's advocacy of peace rested on two cornerstones: an attachment to liberalism and a conservative outlook on social relations. He condemned war, first because it led to militarization, waste, and excessive growth of the state, and second because it threatened social stability. Ideologically a descendant of the revolution of 1789, Simon feared as much the belligerency of irresponsible absolutism as the patriotic mass mobilization of Jacobinism. He was a close associate of moderate French peace activists, notably *Frédéric Passy.

The notion of liberty was the leitmotif of Simon's philosophy. It pervaded and underpinned his writings. Under the influence of rationalist thought, he restricted faith to the spiritual domain but adhered neither to positivism nor to anticlericalism. His liberal doctrine was largely the outgrowth of his espousal of freedom of thought and of conscience.

As a consequence of the revolution of February 1848, he was elected to the Constituent Assembly on April 23. He combatted the establishment of National Workshops and fought on the barricades against the insurgents in the June uprising. In the subsequent swing to the right, he failed to win reelection in 1849. On December 10, 1851, he was suspended from the Sorbonne for declining to take the oath of allegiance to the Empire.

In an important treatise entitled *La Liberté*, Simon strove to determine the extent beyond which authority should not limit liberty. Necessity being the only basis of society, authority was legitimate only if it was necessary. Man was free and subject solely to natural law. Freedom, he stated, was inconceivable without private property.

Simon secured a seat in the Corps législatif in the elections of 1863 and became a defender of basic liberal demands such as representative and responsible government, separation of powers, separation of Church and State, free trade, and freedom of thought, press, and assembly. The cause of republicanism was best served, he believed, by the expansion of education. A liberal constitution did not by itself produce enlightened voters. Opposition to the warlike activity of the government was part of the indictment of the Empire. Simon had condemned French involvement in the Crimean War and the Mexican expedition.

He now criticized the regime's intervention in Italy, its hands-off opportunism in the Austro-Prussian conflict, and its provocative stance in 1870. In December 1867 Simon spoke in favor of the abolition of standing armies and their replacement by a trained citizenry.

Upon the downfall of the Empire on September 4, 1870, he entered the Government of National Defense. He was put in charge of supplies during the siege of Paris, but wished to see the fighting brought to a halt and clashed with proponents of a *guerre à outrance*. Simon sought to convince the notables of France that the republic would serve their interests and did not constitute a popular revolution. Rather it represented "peace, order and liberty." Although he was second to none in his determination to suppress the Paris Commune, Simon came to be regarded as a representative of the left in an Assembly dominated by monarchists.

Adolphe Thiers' cabinet was overthrown on May 24, 1873, but republican constitutional laws were finally adopted in February 1875. Simon was able to form a government on December 13. His center-right administration found little room to maneuver as the conflict intensified between the clerical party and Marshal Marie MacMahon on one side, and the anticlerical Assembly under Léon Gambetta's ascendancy on the other. Simon resigned on May 16, 1877. Internal affairs being uppermost in his mind, he did not play a prominent role during the war scare of May 1875 and the Balkan crisis of early 1877.

At no time was the relationship between peace and conservative republicanism more evident to Simon than during the Boulanger affair. Drawing a parallel between Georges Boulanger and Napoleon III, he warned of the menace to liberal institutions and international peace. Under conditions of modern warfare, a conflict could be disastrous to both victor and vanquished because it would unleash social war and be a godsend for socialists.

In March 1890 Simon represented France at the Berlin conference called by Wilhelm II to discuss labor regulations. Being a laissez-faire liberal, he could hardly save it from failure, but he did contribute to the improvement of Franco-German relations through the warm talks he held with the Kaiser and Bismarck.

Bibliography:

A. *Le Devoir* (2nd ed., Paris, 1854); *Le Gouvernement de M. Thiers* (2 vols., Paris, 1878); *La Liberté* (2 vols., Paris, 1859); *La Liberté politique* (Paris, 1867); *La Politique radicale* (Paris, 1868); *Quatre portraits* (Paris, 1896); *Souvenirs du quatre septembre* (2 vols., Paris, 1874); *Souviens-toi du deux-décembre* (Paris, 1889); *Thiers, Guizot, Rémusat* (Paris, 1885); *Victor Cousin* (Paris, 1887).

B. Philip A. Bertocci, *Jules Simon: Republican Anticlericalism and Cultural Politics in France, 1848-1886* (Columbia, MO, 1978); Louis Madeline, "Les Mémoires de Jules Simon," *Revue des deux mondes*, no. 1 (January 1, 1910), 216-28; Léon Séché, Figures bretonnes. *Jules Simon, sa vie, son temps, son oeuvre, 1814-1896* (Paris, 1898); Gustave Simon, "Jules Simon: notes et souvenirs (Documents inedits)." *La Revue mondiale*, February 15, 1926, 339-49, March 1, 1926, 3-16, March 15, 1926, 113-27, April 1, 1926, 211-18, April 15, 1926, 315-22.

C. Jules Simon Papers, Archives Nationales, Paris.

Samir Saul

ŠKARVAN, Albert (31 January 1869, Tvrdošín, Slovakia, Hungary [now Czechoslovakia]—29 March 1926, Liptovský Hradok, Czechoslovakia). *Education*: M.D., Univ. of Innsbruck, 1894. *Career*: physician, translator, and protagonist of Tolstoyism.

Albert Škarvan was born in a Slovak village in northern Hungary. His Slovak national consciousness and his opposition to Magyarization were strengthened by his student years in Prague, where he began to display considerable literary talent. A turning point in his life came around 1890. After reading some of *Leo Tolstoy's works, he entered into correspondence with the master and came increasingly under the influence of his ethical teachings. When, however, on the conclusion of his training as a medical doctor at the University of Innsbruck, he was conscripted into the Imperial army, Škarvan did not at first object: he served in a military hospital until six weeks before the completion of his term. Then, on February 6, 1895, he announced his decision to refuse further service. He was arrested, tried, and sentenced to imprisonment. His account of his life in prison and of the motives leading him to make this protest was published in 1898 in a Russian version by *Vladimir Chertkov, then in exile in England. From reports of his experiences printed in several West European languages, Škarvan became well known in antimilitarist circles.

Wholly isolated from the Slovak intelligentsia which did not share his views, and now regarded by the authorities with extreme suspicion, and in addition still liable for military service, Škarvan on his release from prison left for Russia where he visited Tolstoy at Yasnaya Polyana. There he became a close friend, too, of Tolstoy's medical adviser, Dušan Makovický, a fellow Slovak who was also to become a leading exponent of Tolstoyism among the Czechs and Slovaks. Early in 1897 Škarvan was forced to leave Russia, since the government threatened to hand him over to Austria-Hungary as a deserter. Settling first in England and then in Switzerland, he was allowed in 1910 to return to his native land where he practiced as a country doctor until his death in 1926. His admiration for Tolstoy (whose *Resurrection* he translated into Slovak) remained unabated. He continued to advocate nonviolence and to regard the state as un-Christian and a form of legalized oppression. But drifting slowly away from the Tolstoyan movement he lived an intellectually lonely life, out of sympathy too with political and cultural trends among the Slovaks and Czechs.

In Slovakia today scholars have shown considerable interest in Škarvan. While disapproving his anarchist proclivities, they stress his devotion to Slovak popular culture and his belief in its ability to survive in a hostile political environment. For the peace movement his importance lies in his act of individual defiance of the Austro-Hungarian military authorities. There were in this period other conscientious objectors on the European continent but no case became so well known as Škarvan's.

Bibliography:

A. *Moy otkaz ot voennoy sluzhby: Zapiski voennago vracha* (Purleigh, U.K., 1898); "Vlastný životopis," *Prúdy* (Bratislava), 10 (September, 1926), 411-25; *Život je zápas: Vnútorná biografia Alberta Škarvana*, ed. Rudolf Chmel (Martin, 1977).

B. Štěpán J. Kolafa, "Albert Škarvan o slovenské otázce v knize 'Slováci'," *Literárny archiv 1969* (Martin, 1970), 117-94; Katarina Mičátková, "Literárna činnost' Tolstého stúpenca dr. Alberta Škarvana," *Z ohlasov L.N. Tolstého na Slovensku* (*Slovanské Štúdie*, vol. IV) (Bratislava, 1960), 185-207; Andrej Mráz, "Albert Škarvan-slovenský tolstovec," *Z ruskej literatúry a jej ohlasov u Slovákov* (Bratislava, 1955), 150-71.

Peter Brock

SKRZYŃSKI, Aleksander. See *Bibliographical Dictionary of Internationalists*.

SMILEY, Albert Keith (17 March 1828, Vasselboro, ME — 2 December 1912, Redlands, CA). *Education*: B.A., Haverford Coll., 1849, A.M., 1859). *Career*: educator, hotel proprietor, philanthropist; founder of the Lake Mohonk Conferences on International Arbitration.

Albert K. Smiley's main contribution to the peace movement centered around the series of annual conferences on arbitration he sponsored during the late nineteenth and early twentieth centuries. Together with his twin brother, Alfred Homans, Albert spent his early career in education, teaching at Haverford College from 1849 to 1852 and then later at other Quaker institutions. In 1869 he purchased the Lake Mohonk property in the mountains near New Paltz, New York and there built a resort hotel, the Mountain House. For a decade Alfred managed the hotel, but after he built his own hotel at nearby Lake Minnewaska in 1879, Albert assumed full responsibility.

The Mountain House maintained a serene religious atmosphere and its many guests were not deterred by unwritten rules against drinking and card playing. Smiley won the attention of prominent people and in 1879 President Rutherford B. Hayes appointed him to the Board of Indian Commissioners on which he was to serve until his death. In 1883 he asked a number of people interested in Indian problems to attend a conference at Mohonk. The Indian Conference became an annual event, and, in 1890, a similar series of conferences on Negro problems began. These conferences were reorganized as the Lake Mohonk Conference of Friends of the Indian and other Dependent Peoples in 1904.

The success of the conferences on Indians and Negroes encouraged Smiley to try the conference idea in connection with international peace. In 1895 fifty guests attended the first Lake Mohonk Conference on International Arbitration. The conference proved to be the first of twenty-two annual spring meetings on peace and arbitration. They had a far-reaching effect on the peace movement, bringing together peace workers from many parts of the United States and from other countries.

Smiley's secretaries sought out statesmen, educators, religious leaders, lawyers, and even generals and admirals to attend the Mohonk conferences, and the lists of members grew rapidly in length. The 1910 meeting had 300 participants. Desiring to maintain harmony at the conferences, Smiley played down the division between advocates of extreme nonresistance and individuals who maintained the right of defensive war. In fact, he discouraged discussion of such matters and even tried to limit debate on the usefulness of armament reductions. For the same reason, Smiley refused to approve or disapprove America's role in the Spanish-American war and its imperialistic aftermath. He urged the participants at the Mohonk conferences to focus on the negotiation of arbitration treaties, the establishment of a permanent world court, and recognition of the Hague Conferences as a permanent world institution.

Despite the limitations imposed by their agenda, the Arbitration Conferences were of considerable long-range importance. They helped develop a school of internationalist thought which held that successful international organization required full respect for the freedom of action of sovereign states. They also provided opportunities for exchange of opinions by people with special interests. During informal talks between sessions of the 1905 Conference +Robert Lansing, +James Brown Scott, and *George W. Kirchwey began plans for the organization of the American Society of International Law. At the last meeting of the Arbitration Conference in 1916 former President +William Howard Taft explained the proposals of the League to Enforce Peace for an international organization based on the idea of collective security, so much at variance with the more limited ideas of international organization that had been advocated at Mohonk since 1895.

Smiley helped draft a proposal that ultimately led to the creation of the Carnegie Endowment for International Peace in 1910, and served on the board of trustees of that organization until his death in 1912. It was an appropriate position for this conservative yet committed advocate of internationalism and peace.

Bibliography:

A. Calvin D. Davis, *The United States and the First Hague Peace Conference* (Ithaca, NY, 1962); Calvin D. Davis, *The United States and the Second Hague Peace Conference: American Diplomacy and International Organization, 1899-1914* (Durham, NC, 1962); Warren F. Kuehl, *Seeking World Order: The United States and International Organization to 1920* (Nashville, TN, 1969); Frederick E. Partington, *The Story of Mohonk* (Mohonk Lake, NY, 1911; 4th ed., 1961); *Reports of the Lake Mohonk Conferences on International Arbitration* (Lake Mohonk, NY, 1895-1916).

C. Papers of the Lake Mohonk Conferences on International Arbitration, Swarthmore College Peace Collection, Swarthmore College.

Calvin D. Davis

SMITH, Gerrit (6 March 1797, Utica, NY—28 December 1874, New York). *Education*: B.A., Hamilton Coll., 1818. *Career*: businessman and philanthropist.

Born to an immense fortune which he increased through intelligent business operations, reared in the kind of earnest evangelical milieu that spawned so many reformers, and blessed with a sociable, generous nature, Gerrit Smith gave freely of his wealth to every reform movement of his time. Therein lay his primary importance to the peace movement.

In 1828 Smith publicly denounced Andrew Jackson as a militarist and by 1833 he was describing the need for peace as equal in importance to the need for temperance and the abolition of slavery. Smith, however, did not join the American Peace Society until 1838. Characteristically, he did so with a $500 contribution, a very large sum for the time. He joined the Society just as *William Lloyd Garrison and others were leaving it. Smith was tempted to join this secession because he felt instinctively that the advocates of nonresistance held a superior moral position, but after some soul-searching, he remained with the American Peace Society, which he served as a vice-president from 1838 until his death.

Smith's pacifism was never absolute. Like all pacifists, he had to weigh the sin of war with that of injustice, and for Smith, the scales tipped when slavery was put in the balance. He had long been an abolitionist and began to advocate violent resistance to slavery in the 1850s. He participated in a famous rescue of a fugitive slave, though he knowingly risked bloodshed to do so; he urged the American Peace Society to send rifles to the freedom forces in Kansas; he almost certainly advised, encouraged, and financed John Brown's raid on Harper's Ferry; and he supported the Union war effort without reservation.

Smith's activities in opposition to slavery stretched his pacifist principles but not enough to deny him a place in the antebellum peace movement. Most other pacifists supported the Civil War and Smith justified his actions on the grounds that slavery was itself a form of war. In a letter to *George Beckwith, president of the American Peace Society, Smith expressed his belief that the Union struggle was a war to end war. Nevertheless, Smith, even more than most pacifists at the time, suffered a reputation for inconsistency and hypocrisy. He enjoyed the privilege of a rich patron; he could contradict the basic policies of an organization without being expelled. Too often, he contented himself with easy answers to difficult questions. Although he recognized the need for a code of international law, when it was argued that such a code would prevent the United States from "liberating" Cuba by force, he simply replied: "Away with international law!"

Smith's wealth gave him advantages but he used that wealth generously for the betterment of man. Although he never joined the nonresistant movement, he made the single largest cash contribution to their cause. *Elihu Burritt's peace publications and international peace congresses received substantial support from Smith, and Burritt once addressed Smith as the "one man in America above any other" who should have represented American pacifists to their European friends. Though Smith lacked the intellectual rigor of other pacifists, his heart was always in the right place and he put his money where his heart lay.

Bibliography:

A. *Peace Better Than War* (Boston, 1858); *Speeches of Gerrit Smith* (New York, 1855).

B. Ralph Volney Harlow, *Gerrit Smith* (New York, 1939); DAB, IX, 270-71.

C. Gerrit Smith Papers, Syracuse University.

James P. Walsh

SMITH, J. Lavell (9 April 1892, Moorefield, Ontario, Canada — 5 June 1973, Toronto). *Education*: B.A., Victoria Coll., 1921, B.D., Union Theological Seminary, 1924; D.D., Victoria Coll., 1952. *Career*: school teacher, 1912-15; military officer, 1916-19; Methodist and United Church of Canada Ministry, 1923-57; president, Canadian Fellowship of Reconciliation, 1942-45.

As a lieutenant in the Royal Army Corps during World War I, J. Lavell Smith learned first hand the lessons of war which later reinforced his embrace of pacifism under the influence of *Reinhold Niebuhr and Harry Ward at Union Theological Seminary in New York. By the late twenties Smith had become one of the most promising young ministers in the United Church of Canada and he was soon rewarded with the pastorate of the prestigious Westmount Park United Church in Montreal. Although he had already begun to renounce war publicly, it was here in Montreal's affluent suburb where Lavell Smith became known as a radical Canadian pacifist.

In 1934 he personally organized a Canadian version of *Hugh Richard Sheppard's Peace Pledge and successfully collected thousands of signatures. Shortly afterward he joined Clarence Halliday, Philip Matthews, Jack Duckworth, and other Montreal radicals in the Fellowship for a Christian Social Order to protest the build-up of Canadian armaments and to organize a Montreal chapter of the Fellowship of Reconciliation.

With the outbreak of World War II Smith quickly reaffirmed his steadfast pacifism and within a month of Canada's entry he helped to produce and circulate the "Witness Against War Manifesto," a pacifist protest by approximately seventy-five United Church ministers in radical defiance of their Church and country.

Smith's highly visible role in the "Witness Against War" controversy as well as his outspoken pacifism placed him at odds with leading members of his congregation who demanded his removal. At first a poll of the congregation indicated a majority favored his retention but in the end Smith was forced to resign. Thereafter he was appointed Superintendent of Toronto's Church of All Nations, a mission for transients and immigrants representing over fifteen ethnic communities.

Smith's move to Toronto in 1942 coincided with the consolidation and concentration of Canada's pacifist activity in that city which, in turn, enabled him to exercise national leadership. As the wartime chairman of the Canadian Fellowship of Reconciliation he launched the publication of a new journal, *Reconciliation*, and encouraged cooperation with other humanitarian groups in assisting refugees and interned Japanese-Canadians. His was also one of the few voices in Canada raised against the Allied strategic bombing of German cities.

After the war Smith was instrumental in the establishment of hostels for European refugee immigrants as well as credit unions and senior citizen homes. He also remained prominent in Toronto peace activities, the antinuclear campaign in particular. Smith came to define pacifism as the active elimination of the causes of war, whether they be the stark inequalities among peoples and nations or the manufacture of armaments, especially nuclear weapons, and to this end he endorsed the principle of civil disobedience in peace demonstrations. Throughout his career as a Christian minister he consistently publicized and interpreted current pacifist thought to a Canadian audience.

Bibliography:

B. Thomas P. Socknat, " 'Witness Against War': Pacifism in Canada, 1900-1945," Ph.D. dissertation, McMaster University, 1981.

Thomas P. Socknat

SNOWDEN, Philip (18 July 1864, Ickornshaw, Cowling, Yorkshire, England — 15 May 1937, Tilford, Surrey. *Education*: elementary school. *Career*: clerk in insurance company, 1879-86; junior exciseman, 1886-93; socialist lecturer and propagandist, 1894-1905; chairman, Independent Labour party, 1903-6, 1917-20; Member of Parliament (Blackburn), 1906-18, (Colne Valley), 1922-31; Chancellor of the Exchequer, 1924, 1929-31; House of Lords, 1931-37; Lord Privy Seal, 1931-32.

Philip Snowden was a major figure in the British Labour movement and a member of the +Ramsay MacDonald governments of 1924 and 1929. He opposed British participation in World War I, championed the cause of conscientious objectors in that war, and lost his seat in parliament as a result of his unpopular stand.

The son of a Yorkshire weaver, Snowden passed a civil service examination and won a post in the Excise Service. He might have remained a civil servant if not for a crippling illness—probably Potts Disease—which struck him in 1891. This forced him from the service by 1893 and left him crippled for life. His convalescence gave him the time to study socialism and led to his career as an Independent Labour party speaker and as editor of a socialist journal. After failing in two earlier bids for Parliament, Snowden won a seat for Blackburn in 1906 as a member of the Labour Representation Committee.

Snowden became a formidable debater in the Commons and was soon recognized as an authority on financial matters. He considered himself a socialist, as against the "Labourites" in his party. His socialism was of the moderate evolutionary sort associated with the ILP, and even more clearly with the Fabian Society, to which he also belonged. He was anti-Bolshevik and even opposed the General Strike of 1926 because he preferred the parliamentary route to change.

He became identified with several causes, most notably prohibition and women's suffrage, which he called "The Dominant Issue" in a pamphlet of that title in 1913. Snowden's opposition to war developed gradually. He opposed British participation in the Boer War (1899-1902) and was suspicious of imperialist adventures. In Parliament he opposed increases in spending on armaments in the Anglo-German naval building competition before the First World War.

Never a pacifist, Snowden seemed to be moving closer to that position by

1913, when he said in the Commons that a German invasion might be preferable to continuing huge expenditures on arms. When war came the following year he was on tour in Canada, but when he returned home he supported the antiwar position of colleagues in the ILP such as Ramsey MacDonald and *Keir Hardie. They did not — like some ILP members — claim to oppose all wars, only this one. Not an absolutist, Snowden was willing to engage in war-related work on the Liquor Control Board. But he opposed recruitment and the introduction of conscription in 1916, and supported the No-Conscription Fellowship, founded in 1914. He called public attention to the plight of conscientious objectors and to the use of the death penalty by military authorities at the front. By 1916 he called for a negotiated peace.

Snowden was critical of the Versailles peace settlement as unjust to Germany. After some initial hesitation he backed the League of Nations and said that he would support military action by the world body against an aggressor.

Bibliography:

A. *An Autobiography* (2 vols. London, 1934).

B. Colin Cross, *Philip Snowden* (London, 1966).

Donald S. Birn

SÖDERBLOM, Nathan. See *Biographical Dictionary of Internationalists*.

SORENSEN, Reginald William (19 June 1891, London — 8 November, 1971, London). *Education*: elementary school and four years of study in the order of Pioneer Preachers. *Career*: minister, Free Christian Church, Walthamstow, 1916-37; Labour Member of Parliament (West Leyton). 1929-31, 1935-50, (Leyton), 1950-64; created Life Peer, 1964; Lord-in-Waiting, 1964-68; freeman, Borough of Leyton, 1968; author; lecturer and tutor, Workers Education Association.

Reginald Sorensen was one of the leading socialist-pacifists of his generation and a founder of the Socialist Christian League. He began life in humble surroundings, the son of a silversmith of Danish ancestry, and ended it as a Lord-in-Waiting to the Queen.

After leaving school at fourteen and working as an errand boy and in an office, Sorensen joined a religious community and became a minister. He gained a religious exemption from military service in World War I, and shortly after his marriage in 1916 went with his wife to live in a community of conscientious objectors at Stanford-le-Hope, Essex.

Although holding strong pacifist principles himself and joining the Peace Pledge Union, Sorensen always recognized the sincerity of others who came to different conclusions. After 1937, he maintained that it was logical for those who believed in the use of force to rearm. This upset some in the peace movement. Sorensen felt that pacifism should not be divorced from other aspects of life and that it was one's duty to work for justice. Perhaps because he took such an active part in the community he was respected for his pacifism.

After World War I, he returned to Walthamstow where he remained a minister of the Free Christian Church, ran a general shop, and became active in local politics. He joined the Labour party and soon was able to serve on the Walthamstow Urban District Council and the Essex County Council. Sorensen's long parliamentary career began in 1929 when he was elected M.P. for West Leyton. In the Commons, he supported the Parliamentary Pacifist Group after it was founded by Labour members in 1936 and became a leading advocate of Indian independence.

An active lecturer, preacher, and writer, Sorensen chaired the National Peace Council from 1951-64. He was also active in the World Congress of Faiths, the International Friendship League, and the India League.

Bibliography:

A. *Earthquake, Wind and Fire* (London, 1958); *I Believe in Man* (London, 1970); *My Impression of India* (London, 1947); *Tolpuddle* (London, 1928).

C. Reginald William Sorensen Papers, House of Lords Records Office, London.

Moira Clark

SPAAK, Paul-Henri. See *Biographical Dictionary of Internationalists*.

STAMBOLISKI, Alexander Stoimenov (1 March 1879, Slavovitsa, Bulgaria — 14 June 1923, Slavovitsa). *Education*: secondary education completed at State Vinicultural Institute, Pleven, 1898; studied agronomy at Univ. of Halle, 1901-2. *Career*: schoolteacher, 1898-1901; assistant editor, *Zemledelsko zname* (*Agrarian Banner*), 1903-6; editor, *Zemledelsko zname*, 1906-15; leader of Bulgarian Agrarian National Union, 1907-23; member of parliament, 1908-11, 1913-15, 1919-23; prime minister, 1919-23.

Alexander Stamboliski, the most original and dynamic of the peasant leaders who inspired Eastern Europe's "Green Rising" in the era between the two world wars, sought to bring an era of peace and international cooperation to the volatile Balkan Peninsula.

In the first years of the twentieth century, Stamboliski provided the theoretical underpinnings of the Bulgarian Agrarian National Union (BANU) and emerged as its preeminent leader. As editor of the BANU's newspaper, *Agrarian Banner*, Stamboliski developed a theory of social change and an analysis of contemporary problems based on the belief that economic development and raising the standards of material and cultural life had become the central problem facing all modern societies, and that in contemporary conditions this progress could be achieved only through the state's active and purposeful intervention in economic life. Unfortunately, the dominant political institutions, political parties, and the monarchy were unsuited for this task because they were vestigial remains of preceding historical stages. As such, they were destined to be replaced by organized, economic interest groups, such as the BANU, which would set policy in an economic parliament. Stamboliski did not expect monarchs and party leaders to give up power voluntarily, and he predicted that they would strive to delude the people with the doctrine of laissez-faire in economic life and by cultivating extreme nationalism and militarism.

Stamboliski's doctrines, organizational talent, and oratorical power led to his election and that of twenty-two other BANU candidates in the 1908 parliamentary elections. In the face of strident nationalist propaganda, Stamboliski was the first prominent Bulgarian to challenge the generally held assumption that it was Bulgaria's national purpose to acquire Macedonia from Turkey and to unite all ethnic Bulgarians under a single flag. The cost of acquiring Macedonia, he argued, included placing the crushing weight of huge military spending on the backs of the poor, the militarization of society with a corresponding decline in the democratic values of free speech and popular rule, and the mortgaging of Bulgaria's independence in return for Great Power financial and diplomatic support. Macedonia was simply not worth it. Bulgaria should aim at developing her own internal economic forces, which alone could provide the foundation for genuine independence in international affairs and democracy at home. In 1911 Stamboliski opposed amending the constitution to allow Bulgaria's monarch to negotiate treaties without the approval of the National Assembly. Although unable to block the amendment, which he viewed as a significant step toward war, Stamboliski formed a coalition of Agrarians, Socialists, and disaffected liberals that made a powerful statement against it.

When Tsar Ferdinand used his new powers to organize an alliance of the Balkan states to attack Turkey in the First Balkan War, Stamboliski called on his countrymen to reject the "war-lovers," but his voice was lost in the general popularity of the campaign to liberate Macedonia and in the enthusiasm generated by military victories. However, when Bulgaria launched the Second Balkan War to enlarge its share of the spoils, it suffered a catastrophic defeat which led to a tremendous BANU electoral success, making it the largest opposition force in the National Assembly.

Stamboliski responded to the outbreak of World War I by calling for the observance of strict neutrality. Tzar Ferdinand, however, desirous of recouping the losses in the Second Balkan War, entered the war on the side of the Central Powers in the Fall of 1915. On the eve of mobilization, in a face-to-face encounter with the tzar, Stamboliski warned Ferdinand that intervention would cost him his head. As a further antiwar move, he prepared and distributed a pamphlet describing his meeting with the tzar and calling on the population to resist mobilization. After mobilization orders were published, Stamboliski was arrested, tried by a military court, and sentenced to death. Yielding to the protests of various political leaders, Ferdinand commuted the sentence to life imprisonment.

Had Ferdinand chosen the winning side, little more would probably have been heard of Stamboliski or the BANU. But Bulgaria's catastrophic defeat completed the process of radicalizing the population that the Second Balkan War had begun. In the face of growing rebellion among Bulgarian soldiers, Ferdinand turned to Stamboliski to save the situation. Releasing him from prison, he begged the Agrarian leader to use his authority among the people to stabilize the front.

Stamboliski agreed, but only on condition that Ferdinand agree to an immediate armistice. After seeing the conditions at the front, however, Stamboliski put himself at the head of the rebellious troops and proclaimed Bulgaria a republic. Poor tactics on the part of his lieutenants caused his troops to meet with defeat, and he was forced to go into hiding.

The defeat of the rebellion barely slowed the disintegration of the old regime. Within weeks Ferdinand had abdicated in favor of his young son Boris III, and a provisional government was established with a cabinet that included Stamboliski and other Agrarians. In the first postwar elections in August 1919, the BANU won a plurality, with the Communist and Socialist parties finishing second and third. Stamboliski formed a coalition government with two minor parties, and seven months later, when the BANU gained an absolute majority in the National Assembly as a result of new elections, he became prime minister in an all-Agrarian cabinet.

Stamboliski's government introduced a series of major reforms aimed at translating Agrarian doctrine into reality. Central to this project was the demilitarization of Bulgarian society. The Treaty of Neuilly imposed disarmament on Bulgaria, but Stamboliski's measures went much further. Command of the armed forces was transferred from the tzar to a civilian minister of war. Military spending was held to levels below that required by the treaty, and the resources thus freed were channeled into a vast expansion of the country's school system and into economic construction. Moreover, Stamboliski's government introduced the idea of compulsory labor service to replace traditional military conscription. Requiring a year of service from young men and six months from young women, compulsory labor service was intended to contribute directly to economic construction, to provide training in technical subjects and hygiene to its members, and to replace chauvinistic indoctrination with a stress on the dignity of productive labor. The compulsory labor service attracted attention outside Bulgaria, and established Stamboliski's reputation as a bold and original leader.

Stamboliski realized that the domestic reconstruction of Bulgaria could not be accomplished without the reconstruction of Bulgaria's foreign policy. In 1920 he undertook a hundred day tour of foreign capitals to convince Europe's statesmen that Bulgaria had renounced her past militant nationalism, and that she would faithfully live up to the terms of the peace settlement. As a result of his efforts, Bulgaria was the first of the defeated states to be admitted to the League of Nations, and the Allies also later granted her a moratorium on reparations payments.

Stamboliski's primary diplomatic goals lay in establishing good relations with his immediate Balkan neighbors, particularly with Yugoslavia. Stamboliski assured the Yugoslavs that Bulgaria had abandoned any claims on the parts of Macedonia now included within Yugoslavia's borders, and he negotiated the treaty of Niš, in which Bulgaria pledged to cooperate with Yugoslavia in stamping out Macedonian terrorism by denying terrorists sanctuary on Bulgarian soil. Stamboliski saw this treaty as a first step along the road toward a federation of

Balkan states that he believed would eventually bring both strength and stability to the peninsula.

While Stamboliski's domestic and diplomatic policies enjoyed broad popular support, they also had powerful enemies among supporters of militarism and Bulgaria's traditional "national goals." On June 9, 1923, a conspiracy including the leaders of the old parties, reserve and active military officers, Macedonian terrorists and, perhaps, the court, overthrew the Agrarian government. Many of its leaders were killed or imprisoned, and Stamboliski was murdered after undergoing brutal torture. However, attempts by successor governments to blacken his reputation failed, for he remained a national hero in the popular imagination. After World War II, the Communist regime preferred to appropriate his legend rather than confront it. Today Stamboliski is officially recognized in his own country as a progressive leader, an early martyr to fascism, and one of the greatest Bulgarians of modern times.

Bibliography:

A. *Politicheski partii ili sŭslovni organizatsii?* (Sofia, 1909); *Printsipite na Bŭlgarskiia zemledelski naroden sŭiuz* (Sofia, 1919); *Zemledelsko upravlenie: pŭrva godina* (Sofia, 1921).

B. John D. Bell, *Peasants in Power: Alexander Stamboliski and the Bulgarian Agrarian National Union, 1899-1923* (Princeton, NJ, 1977); Khristo Khristov et al., eds., *Aleksandŭr Stamboliski: Zhivot, delo, zaveti* (Sofia, 1980).

John D. Bell

STANHOPE, Philip James [First Baron Weardale of Stanhope] (8 December 1847, London? — 1 March 1923, London?). *Education*: educated privately. *Career*: Lieutenant, RN; civil engineer; Liberal Member of Parliament, 1886-1900, 1904-5.

Philip Stanhope, a younger son of the fifth Earl Stanhope, was educated privately. After serving briefly in the Royal Navy, Stanhope became a civil engineer. He began his political career in 1886 when he entered the House of Commons as a Liberal, representing Wednesbury until 1892 and Burnley from 1893 until 1900. In 1904 he briefly returned to Commons for the Harboro Division of Leicestershire, but he entered the House of Lords in 1905. Stanhope had two motivations for accepting the title of Baron Weardale of Stanhope. His health required that he either retire or substantially reduce his workload. In addition, the thin ranks of the Liberal party in the House of Lords badly needed reinforcement.

Throughout his career as a Liberal, Stanhope faithfully supported the peace movement. He was among the original members of the Interparliamentary Union, founded by *Randal Cremer and *Frédérick Passy. In 1889 he attended the first meeting of the Union in Paris and presided over its second meeting the next year in London. He strongly opposed the Boer War along with *Leonard Courtney, Sir William Harcourt, and *Arthur Ponsonby. After his retirement from Commons, Stanhope became even more actively involved in peace organizations.

In 1906 he again became president of the Interparliamentary Union, presiding over its fourteenth international conference held in London that year. He also acted as president of the British delegation of the Interparliamentary Union in 1906 and 1907. In 1910 he served as president of the Sixth National Peace Conference at Leicester, as well as of the National Peace Council.

The outbreak of World War I dealt a severe blow to Stanhope's plans for international conciliation. During the war he devoted himself to relief measures. He became president of the ''Save the Children'' fund, helping the organization raise money and thereby feed thousands of children in Russia and the Balkans.

Stanhope represented the aristocratic-radical tradition of the Liberal party — a tradition which produced such notable champions of peace as *Charles P. Trevelyan and Arthur Ponsonby. In the cause of peace, Stanhope devoted himself to the development of international institutions that would mediate disputes between nations and thus ultimately remove the necessity for armed conflict.

Bibliography:

A. *The Times* (London), March 2, 1923; *Who Was Who 1916-1928.*

Gail L. Savage

STEAD, William Thomas. See *Biographical Dictionary of Internationalists*.

STEFAN [Metropolitan of Sofia] (7 September 1878, Shiroka lŭka, Bulgaria — 14 May 1957, Bulgaria). *Education*: graduated, Samokov Seminary, 1896; graduated, Kiev Theological Academy, 1904; doctorate, Fribourg Univ., 1919. *Career*: schoolteacher, 1904-10; personal secretary to Exarch Joseph, 1910-15; Bishop of Makarianople, 1921-22; Metropolitan of Sofia, 1922-45; Exarch of Bulgaria, 1945-48; monk, 1948-57.

The Bulgarian Church leader Stefan was born Stoyan Popgeorgiev Shokov, the son of a priest in a small village in southern Bulgaria. After entering holy orders in 1910, when he assumed the name Stefan, he was appointed personal secretary to Exarch Joseph, the titular head of the Bulgarian Church, who resided in Constantinople. During the Balkan Wars, the Exarch chose Stefan to communicate his opposition to the aggressive policies pursued by Tzar Ferdinand and the dominant political parties to the clergy inside Bulgaria. When World War I began, Stefan opposed the pro-German orientation of Ferdinand and the government, and when Bulgaria entered the war on the German side in the fall of 1915 he found himself in a precarious position. For his protection the Holy Synod sent him to study in Switzerland, where he spent the war years.

After the war, Stefan returned to Bulgaria to organize aid for refugees and other war victims. He was made a bishop in 1921, and soon after was named League of Nations Commissioner for organizing Bulgarian aid for refugees of Russia's civil war. Just over a year later he was elected Metropolitan of Sofia.

While Stefan actively supported a series of humanitarian and ecumenical projects during the interwar years, he is best known for his consistent opposition to fascism and to Bulgaria's alliance with Nazi Germany, and above all for his outspoken defense of Bulgaria's Jews during World War II. Because Bulgaria's military contribution to the German war effort was quite limited, the "Jewish Question" was the key element in her relationship with Germany. During the war years Metropolitan Stefan consistently took public positions that were critical of Germany and frequently embarrassing to the Bulgarian government. In September 1942 he preached an electrifying sermon denouncing anti-Semitism, holding that the fate of the Jews was a matter for God, not man, and condemning persecutions that had already taken place. Under his leadership the Holy Synod repeatedly and publicly objected to the adoption of increasingly severe anti-Semitic laws.

The Bulgarian military cooperated in deporting the Jews from newly-occupied territories. By May 1943 the government had also decided to yield to the German demand to round up and deport the Jews inside Bulgaria to concentration camps in Poland. On the eve of the first arrests, Stefan sought an audience with the tzar, and transmitted to him a letter describing the persecution of the Jews as a mortal sin, and warning him that his soul would burn eternally in hell if he continued his present course. As the round-up continued, Stefan and other Church leaders spoke out on behalf of the Jews with considerable effect. Tzar Boris held deep religious convictions and could not lightly dismiss Stefan's warnings. Moreover, anti-Semitism had little popular support in Bulgaria, and the courage of the Metropolitan undoubtedly helped to strengthen the resolve of other prominent and influential figures who joined in public protests and demonstrations in defense of the Jews. In the end this pressure, combined with German military setbacks, prevailed. The Bulgarian government reversed itself and the Bulgarian Jews survived the war.

After the war the Bulgarian Church, asserting its independence from the Orthodox Patriarchate, elected Stefan as its own Exarch. In this position Stefan made a sincere effort to cooperate with the new, Communist-dominated regime, urging the clergy to support the government insofar as it followed "progressive" policies. But his efforts to achieve a *modus vivendi* with the Communists that would preserve a degree of Church independence were not successful. An increasingly strident antireligious campaign brought Stefan into open defiance of the regime, and in 1948, in circumstances that are still unclear, he resigned as Exarch, citing "reasons of health" as the cause, and retired to monastic life.

Bibliography:

B. Frederick B. Chary, *The Bulgarian Jews and the Final Solution, 1940-44* (Pittsburgh, 1972); Dimitur Lazov, *Ekzarkh Stefan I* (Sofia, 1947).

John D. Bell

STENWALL, Edvin (26 July 1899, Parainen, Finland — 23 June 1976, Närpiö, Finland). *Education*: examination in theology, Helsinki Univ., 1922, pastor examination, 1925; higher pastor examination, Turku Univ., 1950. *Career*: vicar of Närpiö, 1926-43; county vicar of Närpiö, 1947-70; member of Parliament,

1936-38; member of Närpiö county council, 1946-56; chairman, Närpiö Peace Union, 1929-52; journalist and publisher, 1926-39.

A carpenter's son, Edvin Stenwall joined the peace movement while studying in Helsinki in the beginning of the 1920s. He was greatly influenced by *Felix Iverson, one of the leading peace advocates in Finland. After qualifying as a pastor in 1925, Stenwall returned to his native locality and took the post of vicar in the Närpiö congregation.

Among the Swedish speaking people of Ostrobothnia peace ideas had previously found supporters. Stenwall, who had joined Finland's Peace Union, started to publish a magazine on peace issues for the Swedish speaking people, calling it *Frid på jorden* (*Peace on Earth*). It was a sister publication to the journal of Finland's Peace Union, *Rauhaa Kohti* (*Towards Peace*), and was issued under Stenwall's leadership until 1939. In that year, it took the name *Fredsposten (Peace Post*), but continued to receive some financial support from Stenwall and to publish his articles on peace subjects.

In the history of the Finnish peace movement, the Swedish speaking section occupied a prominent position and contributed to the movement's ability to activate the masses. Besides *Runar Långbacka, Edvin Stenwall was one of the best known leaders. He chaired the Närpiö's Swedish speaking peace union and the Swedish speaking section of Finland's Peace Union in Ostrobothania from 1930 to 1939. During the thirties, he also chaired Christian peace organizations.

Stenwall's peace ideals were tied to his Christian view of the world. In his preaching, he sought to counter the growing threat of war and fascism during the 1930s. Like many other peace activists in those violent years, he had to bear the pressure and threats that came from fascist and nationalist circles. The Finnish speaking fascist Lapuan liike (Lappo movement) sought to have him removed from his post, but it failed because of the support he received from Swedish speaking Finns. In 1942 Stenwall published some of his peace ideas in *Stat och moral i kristen belysning (State and Morality in a Christian Light*), a work originally designed as a service book for the synod of the church. Before his death, Stenwall completed a part of his memoirs which were published, with selected writings in 1976 under the title *Frid på jorden* (*Peace on Earth*).

Stenwall's peace advocacy may have derived from his Christianity, but it affected his social consciousness. He came to believe that the removal of social evils was one way to decrease the threat of war and violence. He believed that a Christian and activist peace movement had to participate in social action. He shared this view with *Selma Anttila, an author and one of the founders of Finland's Peace Union. Taking his social responsibilities seriously, Stenwall served as a member of Parliament and the communal council of Närpiö.

Bibliography:

A. *Frid på jorden* (Närpiö, 1976); *Stat och moral i kristen belysning* (Närpiö, 1942).

B. Kalevi Kalemaa, *Suomalaisen rauhanliikkeen juuria* (Vaasa, 1981).

C. Edvin Stenwall Papers, archives of Turku University and Närpiö congregation.

Kalevi Kalemaa
Trans. by Oliver and Rita Whitehead

STEVENSON, Lilian Sinclair (16 November 1870, Dublin, Ireland — 6 February 1960, Gerrards Cross, England). *Career*: peace activist.

Lilian Stevenson was a Victorian, a woman of wealth, with a natural dignity and grace who used her wealth and position for the service of others and the work of peace. Her father was a Presbyterian minister in Dublin. She studied art at the Slade School, and joined with Temple Gairdner, of Cairo fame, in forming the Art Students' Christian Union. This merged into the Student Christian Movement, in which Lilian Stevenson played a leading part, editing the journals *Student Volunteer* and then *Student Movement*.

She was one of those present at Cambridge in the last days of 1914 at the formation of the Fellowship of Reconciliation, and served on the committee from the first with other women such as Maude Royden, Constance Todd, Marian Ellis, and Emmeline Pethick-Lawrence. In October 1919 she helped initiate the Movement Towards a Christian International (later the International Fellowship of Reconciliation) at Bilthoven in Holland and she became the historian of the Fellowship, writing *Towards a Christian International* in 1929.

Lillian Stevenson devoted all that was left of her long life to the International Fellowship of Reconciliation. She traveled extensively in the cause of peace, often breaking the barriers by her very presence. In 1925 she visited Estonia and Latvia with delegates from Sweden and Czechoslovakia. She shared in the great conferences and acts of witness in Austria, Denmark, Germany, France, and Switzerland, and in the notable experiment of a Hostel for the Oberammergau Passion Play. She did not gloss over differences: the three principles of the Fellowship were Frankness—Respect—Faith. Her house in Buckinghamshire was a League of Nations itself — or what the League might have been — a place where people from all over the world found themselves at home. She worked for disarmament and conscientious objection. As she grew older she encouraged younger people to the work of peace.

Lilian Stevenson was called "the *grande dame* of Christian pacifism." But her dignity was innate, and she did not have to stand upon it. She was wealthy by accident, identified with a minority cause by choice, and loving by character.

Bibliography:

A. *Towards a Christian International* (London, 1929).
B. V. Brittain, *The Rebel Passion* (London 1904).

John Ferguson

STILLICH, Oskar (26 September 1872, Metschlau near Sprottau, Lower Silesia, Germany [now Poland] — 31 December 1945, Schulzendorf near Berlin). *Education*: Ph.D., Univ. of Leipzig, 1896. *Career*: lecturer in political economy, Humboldt-Hochschule (Humboldt Adult Evening School), Berlin, 1898-1933;

editor, *Schriften des Sozialwissenschaftlichen Vereins in Berlin*, 1901-2, *Volks-Hochschulblätter*, Stuttgart, 1908-9; *Die Volkshochschule. Zeitschrift für das gesamte deutsche Volksbildungswesen*, Berlin, 1909-14; political economist, political and scholarly writer, journalist, and pacifist.

The son of a grist mill owner and educated as a political economist, Oskar Stillich became a lecturer at the Humboldt Adult Evening College in Berlin. Besides teaching, he published on a wide variety of topics. In addition to many articles and essays in newspapers and journals, he wrote over sixty books and pamphlets on political science, the history of German political parties, economics, financial policy, the stock market, socialism, and social conditions. A highly respected author and speaker, Stillich was also the founder and editor of the first national journal for German adult evening schools and developed into one of the most important promoters of adult education in Imperial Germany.

As an economist, Stillich had grave concerns about the impact of World War I on the German economy. As early as 1915, he pointed out that German heavy industry and other war-related industries were profiting from the conflict. In contrast to many other German economists, he pointed out that the war-related prosperity was little more than an illusion, which sooner or later would lead to a rude awakening. Concluding that the war was decreasing, rather than increasing, the wealth of German citizens, he advocated ending the war as quickly as possible by means of a negotiated peace. To promote a negotiated settlement, he helped organize the Zentralstelle für Völkerrecht (Central Office for International Law) and, in January 1918, published *Deutschlands Zukunft bei einem Macht- und bei einem Rechtsfrieden* (*Germany's Future on the Basis of a Peace Through Might and One Based on Justice*), in which he refuted the delusions of a German world superiority that were bound up with pan-German annexationist demands.

After the war, Stillich, who for years had belonged to the Deutsche Friedensgesellschaft (German Peace Society), joined the Bund der Kriegsdienstgegner (War Resisters League). His peace activities, however, were not tied to any political party, nor did he occupy a leading position in the organized peace movement. Instead, like many other academic pacifists, he believed that his scholarly activities would help disseminate truth, and thereby promote pacifistic values. It was through his publications that Stillich influenced the Weimar peace movement. His books and articles concerning the Versailles peace settlement, which he described as hard but neither unbearable nor unfulfillable, mainly called upon Germans to make a just evaluation of the treaty. He believed that the denunciation and rejection of the Versailles treaty, promoted by the government and largely supported by the press and all political parties, was "a danger for Germany." He argued that the economic ruin facing Germany was attributable to the economic exhaustion brought about by wartime mobilization and not, as was generally assumed, by paying reparations or the surrender of land. In 1925 German nationalists sought to oust Stillich from his teaching post because of his strong criticism of the revisionist propaganda directed against the "chains of

Versailles.'' The attempt failed, however, with Stillich receiving support from both his students and several members of the Humboldt College faculty.

Stillich's critique of the nationalistic *völkisch* ideology continued throughout the Weimar period. In his anonymously published three volume *Deutsch-völkischer Katechismus (German-Völkisch Catechism)* (1929-32) he made clear, in an easily understandable question-and-answer style, the horrifying extent to which large parts of the German people were infected by völkisch-racist and nationalistic-militaristic ideologies, and revealed the political parties and associations into which the antirepublican and revanchist forces were organized.

After the coming to power of the Nazis, Stillich lost his teaching position and was banned from writing and speaking. Living on his savings, he wrote a series of essays that were published after World War II critical of National Socialism and its devastating effects on German thought and action. He argued that National Socialism was not restricted to the period of the Third Reich, but had revealed itself earlier in the mentality of numerous and influential Germans. Reduced to a skeleton, he died from the effects of prolonged malnutrition.

Bibliography:

A. *Deutschland als Seiger!* (Leipzig, 1924); *Deutschlands Zukunft bei einem Macht- und bei einem Rechtsfrieden* (Leipzig, 1918); *Deutsch-völkischer Katechismus* (Von einem deutschen Hochschullehrer, 3 vols., Leipzig, 1929-32); *Der Friedensvertrag. Eine soziologische Betrachtung über: Methoden seiner Bekämpfung, seine Gegner, seinen rechtlichen Charakter, seine materielle Erfüllbarkeit, seinen Einfluss auf die Neugestaltung der Welt* (Berlin, 1921); *Der Friedensvertrag von Versailles im Spiegel deutscher Kriegsziele* (Berlin, 1922); *Gehen wir einer Hochkonjunktur entgegen? Eine Untersuchung uber die Geschäftslage nach dem Kriege* (Berlin, 1916); *Katechismus des Friedensvertrages für Jugend und Volk. Zum Gebrauch für Volks-, Mittel- und Hochschulen, insbesondere Gymnasien, Fortbildungsschulen, Volkschochschulen und Betriebsräteschulen* (Ludwigsburg, 1922); *Die politischen Partein in Deutschland* (2 vols., Leipzig, 1908-11); *Sozialisierung der Banken* (Berlin, 1919).

B. Hans Wehberg, ''Dr. Oskar Stillich (1872-1945). Sein Kampf für eine objektive Beurteilung des Versailler Friedensvertrages,'' *Die Friedenswarte* 46, no. 5 (1946), 316ff.

C. Various unpublished manuscripts in the archive of the Institut für Zeitgeschichte, Munich.

Helmut Donat
Trans. by William Hopkins.

STÖCKER, Helene (13 November 1869, Elberfeld, Germany — 22 February 1943, New York). *Education*: Ph.D., Univ. of Berne, 1902. *Career*: feminist and pacifist activist; sex reformer; editor, *Mutterschutz*, 1905-8; *Die neue Generation*, 1908-33.

Helene Stöcker began her career in social activism as a feminist. Part of the ''left wing'' of bourgeois feminism, she first took up educational reform. In 1902 she was a founding member of Germany's first woman suffrage organization, although, unlike *Anita Augspurg and *Lida Gustava Heymann—its real motivators—Stöcker had relatively little faith that women voters would transform society. Her primary interest soon became sex reform.

Stöcker's vehicle was the Bund für Mutterschutz und Sexualreform (League for the Protection of Motherhood and Sexual Reform), which she helped found in 1905 and then served as chairperson and journal editor until she fled Germany in 1933. In 1911 she founded an international Mutterschutz (Protection of Motherhood) league. Her movement had as its practical goal the improvement of the plight of unwed mothers and their children. Ultimately, Mutterschutz aimed to reform sexual ethics, battling the hypocrisy, denial of sexuality, and the double standard which blighted the lives of women and men and made pariahs of unwed mothers. Stöcker also asserted women's right to control their reproductive functions, through contraception and abortion. Believing in the private nature of love relationships, especially when there were no children, Stöcker lived in a "free marriage" with Bruno Springer, a lawyer and fellow Mutterschutz enthusiast.

Reared in a Calvinist, pietist household, as an adolescent Stöcker rejected her family's religion, though she retained some affection for the gentle, ethical Jesus of the Sermon on the Mount. As a young woman, she came under the influence of Friedrich Nietzsche, notably his radical individualism and celebration of vital forces. Rejecting other-wordly salvation (and damnation), Stöcker propounded an ethics of concern for future generations on earth, which she grounded in eugenics and her understanding of Nietzsche. Though surely problematic, her eugenics were never racist; she wanted to improve the entire human race.

Even before World War I, Stöcker had linked the German state's worries over a declining birth rate with its need for soldiers. Her intense involvement with pacifism began during the war, which she condemned from the outset. In 1915 she attended the Women's Peace Conference at The Hague, incidentally speaking against the meeting's equal emphasis on woman suffrage when she thought ending the war should be paramount. In 1922, Mutterschutz added a pacifist plank to its program, linking its encouragement of motherhood and "incipient life" to a stance in favor of "existing, flourishing life." As it fought force and brutality in sexual life, so it now opposed the principle of brute force as embodied in state-sanctioned murder. After the war, the pages of Stöcker's journal *Die neue Generation* were filled with reports from around the world of pacifist and war resistance activities.

Stöcker never joined a political party, but belonged to several pacifist organizations, including the Women's International League for Peace and Freedom, the Bund Neues Vaterland (New Fatherland League), Internationales Friedensbüro (International Peace Bureau), Deutsches Friedenskartell (German Peace Cartel), Deutsche Friedensgesellschaft (German Peace Society), in whose central committee she served, and the War Resisters' International, which she helped found in 1921. Stöcker was clearly one of Weimar Germany's critical left-wing intellectuals, outside the confines of "official" politics.

Although Stöcker supported the idea of a general strike by unions and organized pacifists in the event of declared war, her real hope for an end to violence rested with a long-range transformation of consciousness; individuals must refuse to see themselves as potential "cannon fodder." This would not be easy, since Stöcker, influenced by Nietzsche and Sigmund Freud (some of whose early essays she published), found the ultimate roots of war and hatred in primitive human instincts. To counteract these impulses, she would bolster such contrary instincts as love liberated from hypocrisy and a concern for future generations. No doctrinaire Marxist, Stöcker considered herself a socialist and identified capitalist profits and class conflict as important sources of war. Though not an uncritical admirer of the Soviet Union, she found it an interesting experiment and traveled in that nation during the twenties.

Stöcker fled Germany after the Reichstag fire in February 1933. After a long stay in Switzerland, she arrived in the United States via the Far East in 1941, helped throughout by her pacifist connections. She was already terminally ill when she arrived in New York City.

Bibliography:

A. *Verkünder und Verwirklicher: Beiträge zum Gewaltproblem nebst einem zum ersten Male in deutscher Sprache veröffentlichten Briefe Tolstois* (Berlin-Nikolassee, 1928).

B. Gisela Brinker-Gabler, ed., *Frauen gegen den Krieg* (Frankfurt, 1980); Richard J. Evans, *The Feminist Movement in Germany, 1894-1933* (London and Beverly Hills, 1976).

C. Draft of autobiography and Papers in Swarthmore College Peace Collection.

Amy Hackett

STÖCKER, Jakob (27 September 1886, Düsseldorf, Germany—14 April 1969, Düsseldorf). *Education*: attended universities of Heidelberg, Munich, and Berlin; Ph.D., Univ. of Marburg, 1911. *Career*: journalist, *Badische Presse* (Karlsruhe), 1913, *Cottbuser Anzeiger*, 1914, *Oldenburgische Landeszeitung*, 1918-19, 1924-29, *Vossische Zeitung* (Berlin), 1920, *Bielefelder Neueste Nachrichten*, 1920-24, *General-Anzeiger* (Dortmund), 1929-33.

In May 1929 Jakob Stöcker became chief editor of the Dortmund *General-Anzeiger*, the largest German provincial newspaper. To its liberal-republican tendency, Stöcker added a pacifist one. His pacifism, like that of many others of his generation, originated in his experiences as a soldier in the First World War in which he was wounded twice. Stöcker supported those members of the liberal-bourgeois German Democratic party, such as +Hellmut von Gerlach and *Paul von Schoenaich, who were in line with antimilitarism. He opened up the columns of his paper to pacifists such as *Lothar Persius, Erik Reger, *Kurt Hiller, *Friedrich W. Foerster, *Kurt Grossmann, *Otto Lehmann-Russbuldt, *Theodore Lessing, Prince Hubertus zu Löwenstein, and *Berthold Jacob. Most of the foregoing were long-time contributors to the left-wing democratic Berlin periodical *Die Weltbühne*, edited by *Carl von Ossietzky.

Stöcker's analysis of the failures of the Weimar Republic and the growth of National Socialism was influenced by the views found in *Die Weltbühne*. Accordingly, he criticized both the government's approval of new battleships and the strong position of defense minister, General Wilhelm Groener, in the coalition cabinet of the Social Democratic chancellor, Hermann Müller (1928-30). Stöcker demanded the suppression of the radical right-wing para-military Nazi SA (Storm troops) and conservative Stahlhelm (Steel Helmet) organizations. He severely criticized the democratic parties for their discord, the dictatorial control of their executive committees, and their unimaginative parliamentary politics. He argued that a reform of Germany's proportional electoral system would help to put an end to fragmentation in parliament and to secure democratic majorities in the Reichstag. Despite his uncompromising antifascist position, Stöcker, like many others in and out of Germany, believed that the only way to prevent Hitler's dictatorial seizure of power was by including him in a parliamentary cabinet government. Three months after Hitler came to power the *General-Anzeiger* was confiscated after it published an unflattering portrait of the new chancellor by the artist Emil Stumpp. As Stöcker had gone underground several weeks earlier, he escaped imprisonment.

Stöcker spent the war years in a small town on the lower Rhine river. After the war, he tried to resume his career as a journalist but was denied a license by the British occupying authorities and later shunned by German publishers who did not esteem Stöcker's brilliant and sarcastic fight against Chancellor Konrad Adenauer and the policy of West German rearmament begun in 1950. However, he found an outlet for his pacifist views in regular freelance editorials published in the Hamburg weekly, *Die Andere Zeitung*, founded in 1955 by Gerhard Gleissberg, former chief editor of the important Social Democratic party newspaper *Neuer Vorwärts* (Hannover).

Bibliography:

A. *Männer des deutschen Schickals, Von Wilhelm II until Adolf Hitler—Geschichte in Portrats* (Berlin, 1949).

B. Kurt Koszyk, "Jakob Stöcker und der Dortmunder 'General Anzeiger' 1929-33," *Publizistik*, 8 (1963), 282-95.

Kurt Koszyk,
Trans. by Solomon Wank

STRACHEY, Giles Lytton (1 March 1880, London—21 January 1932, near Hungerford, England). *Education*: studies in History, Univ. of Liverpool, 1897-99; B.A., Trinity Coll., Cambridge Univ., 1903. *Career*: author and critic.

Lytton Strachey was a private man, not a political one, almost pathologically shy and troubled with bad health. It was not his style to lead public movements, no matter how worthy. His real claim to public notice, during his lifetime and since, has rested on his extraordinarily successful career as a biographer, essayist, and literary critic, a "debunker" of the rigidity and hypocrisy of Victorian culture—not on his work for peace. Nevertheless, during World War I, as a conscientious objector, he demonstrated his firm commitment to an uncompromising pacifism, under extremely difficult circumstances, and supported that position with his able pen.

Strachey's family had a history of service to the British empire in the military. His father, Lt. General Sir Richard, made his career in Indian administration. As a young man Strachey was indifferent rather than hostile to this part of his heritage. Before 1914 he was not particularly interested in politics, but at Cambridge he had made enduring friendships with a remarkable set of critical young intellectuals, later to be dubbed "the Bloomsbury set." Though the common interests of the group were primarily literary, aesthetic, and philosophical, some of its members were keenly interested in politics and social questions, among them +Maynard Keynes and +Leonard Woolf. When the First World War began, with the rest of his friends, Strachey was quick to deplore the militarism and crude chauvinism that swept over Britain, but he went further in his antiwar commitment. Of all his circle of friends, only *Bertrand Russell (not a "Bloomsbury") seems to have gone as far in opposing the war, joining him in absolute pacifism. Keynes, for example, despite his sympathies, was satisfied to work for the war government as an economic adviser. Strachey joined the unyielding No-Conscription Fellowship soon after its creation (Russell following later) and occasionally wrote in its service, opposing the introduction of the draft. The tone of at least one of his pamphlets was so sharp that the Liberal MP and lawyer Sir John Simon, who had resigned from the government to protest the introduction of a conscription bill, urged the NCF vigorously—and successfully—to withdraw Strachey's work as seditious.

When conscription began in 1916, the few thousand members of the NCF were put to the test. Strachey had never been healthy and had clear medical grounds for being excused from service. He chose instead to apply for conscientious objector status, as a gesture of solidarity with the other members of the NCF. In March 1916, supported by Philip Morrell, an antiwar MP, and a crowd of friends, he had his tumultuous public hearing. In an exchange celebrated at the time, when asked what he would do if the invading Huns sought to rape his sister, he said solemnly that he would interpose his own body. Somewhat later, a medical board, the first of several, excused him on the grounds that he was not physically fit for service. His politics cost him two of his regular outlets as a reviewer and critic, *The Spectator* and *The New Statesman*, but when Woolf took over *War and Peace* temporarily in the last year of the war, he was able to use that as a platform. With his characteristic tartness he wrote a number of pieces skewering the blind folly of the war against Prussian militarism that threatened to militarize Britain while killing off her young men and destroying western civilization. By the armistice, the publication of *Eminent Victorians* had made him a literary celebrity and in the remaining years of his life he was not active in politics.

Though Strachey's work in the wartime peace movement was ultimately of marginal significance, his influence in the long run as a propagandist for the cause of peace and civilization, though hard to weigh, cannot be dismissed. His writing during the war and in the 1920s held up to critical scrutiny all the ideas and values of the Victorian age that had led to the slaughter—national self-glorification, militarism and political belligerence, heroism in the service of empire, and uncritical obedience to authority.

Bibliography:

B. Michael Holroyd, *Lytton Strachey: A Critical Biography* (2 vols., New York, 1968); Thomas C. Kennedy, *The Hound of Conscience: A History of the No-Conscription Fellowship, 1914-1919* (Fayetteville, AR, 1981); DNB, 1931-1940, 835-36.

S. J. Stearnes

STRATMANN, Franziskus Maria (8 September 1883, Solingen, Germany—13 May 1971, Hochdahl-Düsseldorf, Germany). *Education*: gymnasium; Dominican Academy, Düsseldorf, 1906-13; philological studies, Univ. of Berlin, 1915-19. *Career*: Catholic priest, member of Dominican Order, 1905-71; pastoral counselor to students in Berlin, 1914-24; sometime deputy chairman and chairman, Friedensbund Deutsche Katholiken (German Catholic Peace Association), 1923-33; joint founder, Arbeitsgemeinschaft der Konfessionen für den Frieden (International Study Group for Peace), 1929.

Franziskus Stratmann's pacifism did not stem directly from his experiences in World War I, but, rather, from rational and religious considerations. He was decisively influenced by his reading of *Friedrich W. Foerster's *Weltkrieg und Weltgewissen* (*World War and World Conscience*). Even before the end of the war he joined the Catholic peace movement that was just emerging under the leadership of Magnus Jocham (1886-1923), a Catholic priest who founded the German Catholic Peace Association (FDK) in 1919. With the publication of his book, *Weltkirche und Welt Fried* (*World Church and World Peace*) (1924), Stratmann became the moving spirit of the FDK.

Stratmann's involvement in peace work met such great resistance that in 1924 he had to be relieved of his position as a pastoral worker among students in Berlin and transferred to Cologne, where he nevertheless continued to work for the peace movement. In 1926 he was appointed priest in charge of the parish of St. Maria-Victoria in Berlin with the apparent intention of obstructing his activities on behalf of the FDK. His repeated requests to be relieved of this office were not granted until 1930.

Stratmann based the legitimacy of a Catholic peace movement on the encyclicals of Popes *Benedict XV and Pius XI. The significance of papal authority as a justification for the activities of the FDK are found in the FDK guidelines which Stratmann helped to compile. In spite of this, the FDK was only just tolerated by the German bishops. The task of the FDK as seen by Stratmann was to awaken the will of Catholics to banish war by means of a radical Christianity. The FDK was to function as a catalyst, but it was not to become a mass organization. To make the FDK an effective catalyst, Stratmann endeavored to break away from traditional Catholic methods of thought and behavior. By means of theological arguments he refuted the view that a modern war, as a ''bellum justum'' in the theory of late scholastic teaching, was still thinkable. Stratmann contested the widely held view that war, as a consequence of original sin, was a part of human incompleteness, by referring to Christ's power to grant redemption.

From the beginning, Stratmann linked his work for peace with support for the maintenance of democratic institutions in the Weimar Republic. He hoped that the basic philosophy and aims of the FDK would influence the Catholic Center party. When they did not, he protested against the Center party's pro-armaments defense policy. Throughout the Weimar Republic period he stood against nationalistic and militaristic tendencies, against treason trials of antichauvinist spokesmen, and against the rearmament policy of German army leaders. He spoke out against the introduction of universal military conscription and in favor of the right to refuse to do military service. In foreign policy, he advocated reconciliation with France and Poland and a strong League of Nations. For Stratmann, the rejection of war did not mean resignation in the face of power. In order to oppose military aggression, he demanded the preparation and planning of nonviolent resistance. In doing so he called attention to *Mohandas, K. Gandhi's successful use of nonviolent resistance, to the general strike against the right-wing Kapp putsch in Germany (1920), and to the passive resistance of the German population at the time of the French occupation of the Ruhr (1923).

On July 1, 1933 the FDK was prohibited by the Nazi government. Four days later Stratmann and other leading figures in the FDK were arrested. Stratmann was to be charged with treason, but he managed to leave for Rome in November 1933. In 1938 he was deprived of his German nationality and, as his passport had expired and could not be renewed, he had to leave Rome. He managed to save himself from Nazi persecution by taking refuge in Dutch monasteries. In 1947 he returned to Germany and lived in Walberberg monastery near Bonn. He assisted in the unsuccessful attempt to revive the FDK. The organization finally was disbanded on April 1, 1951. After 1947 Stratmann's writings on the problem of war attracted little attention. This can be attributed to the abstention of German Catholicism from becoming involved in questions of rearmament and nuclear weapons.

Bibliography:

A. *In der Verbannung: Tagebuchblätter 1940-47* (Frankfurt, 1962); *Krieg und Christentum heute* (Trier, 1950); *Peace and the Clergy* (London, 1936); "Thesen zum gerechten und ungerechten Krieg" in *Atomare Kampfmittel und Christliche Ethik: Diskussionsbeiträge deutscher Katholiken* (Munich, 1960); *Weltkirche und Weltfriede* (Augsburg, 1924).

B. Karl Breitenborn, *Der Friedensbund Deutscher Katholiken 1918/19–1951* (Berlin [East], 1981); Beate Höfling, *Katholische Friedensbewegung zwischen zwei Kriegen: Friedensbund Deutscher Katholiken 1917-1933* (Waldkirchen, 1979); Dieter Riesenberger, *Die katholische Friedensbewegung in der Weimarer Republik* (Düsseldorf, 1976).

Dieter Riesenberger
Trans. by Solomon Wank

STRAUS, Oscar Solomon. See *Biographical Dictionary of Internationalists*.

STREET, Jessie (18 April 1889, Chota Nagpur, India—2 July 1970, Sydney, Australia). *Education*: B.A., Sydney Univ., 1910. *Career*: founder and president, United Associations of Women; founding member and vice-president, Australian League of Nations Union; president, Society for Cultural Relations with the USSR, 1939-48; chief organizer, Australian Women's Charter Movement; delegate, United Nations Conference at San Francisco, 1945; delegate to the United Nations Status of Women Commission and its representative on the Human Rights Commission, 1948; chair, New South Wales branch of Australian Peace Council, 1949-70; political activist, feminist, socialist, and peace worker.

Despite considerable personal wealth and links by birth and marriage with the upper class, Jessie Street dedicated her political career to promoting the cause of equality for women, equality between nations, and a classless society. She was singularly uncompromising in this task. While the development of her socialism began through a commitment to feminism, the underlying genesis of her philosophical eclecticism was a deep sense of social justice allied with the belief that greed and the profit motive are the chief causes of economic discrimination and war. This accounted for her unshakable faith in the Soviet Union which she believed lacked the need to maximize profits or exploit its citizens and could therefore genuinely proclaim a desire for peace and a lack of economic discrimination against women.

Prior to 1938, Jessie Street had been one of Australia's most prominent feminists and political activists; a leader in the equal wage movement, she was also engaged in antiwar activities sponsored by the League of Nations Union. After returning from the Soviet Union in 1938, she declared herself a confirmed socialist and dedicated her political energies to promoting greater understanding of the Russian socialist experiment through leadership in a number of Australian-Soviet friendship organizations. From 1944-46 the Women's Charter Movement afforded her the opportunity to promote her twin causes of feminism and peace. In 1945 she was Australia's only woman representative to the founding United Nations Conference in San Francisco where whe pursued a policy of transnationalism and women's rights. Subsequently she was nominated as a delegate to the United Nations Status of Women Commission (1945-48). So strong was her admiration and respect for the United Nations that she continued to attend sessions as a press representative for various minor political journals until the mid-1960s.

Anticommunist pressures within the Australian Labor party (ALP), led to Street's resignation. Her decision to leave the ALP marked a watershed in her political career. Subsequent actions underlined her conviction that socialist aims could be consolidated only by presenting a united front of socialist forces opposed to capitalism. During the height of Australian anticommunism, Street emerged as one of the nation's foremost peace leaders. As chair of the New South Wales branch of the Australian Peace Council she was one of the chief sponsors of the first Australian Peace Congress (1950), which, in spite of the virulent attacks made upon it by the press and other anticommunist forces, succeeded in placing the peace movement on a firm foundation. Immediately after the 1950 Congress, she attended the Second World Peace Conference at Warsaw and was elected to the Bureau of the World Peace Council. Her loyalty to the principles of international peace, and the hostility shown her by the Australian government, created a situation which was incompatible with her private life as a wife of a senior member of the NSW judiciary. Many establishment figures regarded her as a class traitor. She remained abroad between 1950 and 1956, devoting herself to work in the international peace organization and traveling extensively in Europe, Canada, and the United States.

After returning to Australia, Street continued her activism within the peace movement, widening her interests in the 1960s to include the cause of aboriginal rights. Although she never joined the Communist party, she remained a proponent of Australian-Soviet friendship until her death in 1970. Justice, equality, peace, and unity, the themes of the 1946 Women's Charter Conference encapsulate Lady Jessie Street's political aspirations. Although the equality she envisaged was essentially economically based so that she failed to question cultural norms as a basis of female oppression, and while, like many of her generation, she believed in the all-encompassing power of legally formalized principles, her outstanding contribution was an ability to inspire others with a grander vision of a just and peaceful world.

Bibliography:

A. *Truth or Repose*, (Sydney, 1966).

B. Jean Devanny, *Bird of Paradise*, (Sydney, 1945); Peter Sekuless, *Jessie Street: A Rewarding But Unrewarded Life*, (Brisbane, 1980); Andrée Wright, "Jessie Street, Feminist," S. Curthoys, S. Eade and P. Spearitt, eds., *Women at Work*, (Canberra, 1975), 59-68.

C. Jessie Street Papers, National Library of Australia.

Gay Mason

STRESEMANN, Gustav. See *Biographical Dictionary of Internationalists*.

STRÖBEL, Heinrich (7 June 1869, Bad Nauheim, Germany—9 January 1944, Zurich, Switzerland). *Education*: gymnasium (receiving a six-year [Einjährige] leaving certificate); private study of literature, history, and political economy. *Career*: Social Democratic political writer; editor; politician.

Heinrich Ströbel began to write for Social Democratic causes at the age of twenty. In 1892 he became a member of the editorial staff of the party newspaper in Kassel and the following year he assumed the political editorship of the socialist *Schleswig-Holsteinische Volkszeitung* in Kiel. In 1900 he joined the *Vorwärts*, the leading paper of the Sozialdemokratische Partei Deutschlands (German Social Democratic Party) (SPD). He entered politics in 1908 and was elected to the Prussian state legislature, together with six other Social Democrats. Here he was one of the most determined opponents of the antidemocratic Prussian three-class electoral system. Within the pre-World War I German Social Democratic party he represented the left center which formed the nucleus of the later Unabhängige Sozialdemokratische Partei Deutschlands (Independent Social Democratic Party) (USPD).

In July 1914 Ströbel became acting chief editor of the *Vorwärts* and helped formulate the paper's opposition toward German-Austrian policy which was leading to war. He spoke against the approval of war credits and was one of those Social Democrats who rejected the wartime policy of *Burgfrieden* (domestic truce). As early as November 1914, he asked Social Democrats to seize the initiative for peace. Afterwards, he spoke out repeatedly in the Prussian legislature against the bourgeois parties' support of territorial annexations. When the left radical opposition under the influence of Rosa Luxemburg and Karl Liebknecht, which later became the left-wing, radical-revolutionary Spartacus League, published the first number of the *Internationale* in April 1915, Ströbel was one of the collaborators. Dismissed in 1916 from the *Vorwärts*, along with other editors who supported the minority in the party, Ströbel joined the USPD the following year. Within the USPD he rejected the idea of a soviet form of government as propagated by the left wing of the party and stood for a democratic and parliamentary road to socialism. He continuously spoke out against force and was one of the sharpest critics of Bolshevism in the USPD.

After the collapse of the Hohenzollern monarchy in November 1918, Ströbel, together with Paul Hirsch of the SPD, headed the provisional Prussian state government. The following month, however, the USPD withdrew from the government and Ströbel became an editorial writer for *Siegfried Jacobsohn's *Weltbühne*. Retaining his independence of judgment, he unsuccessfully urged the reunification of the two socialist parties, which he thought was the only way to protect the republic from right-wing attempts to overthrow it. Ströbel was expelled, in July 1920, from the USPD because of his opposition to the Communist International. Returning to the SPD, he was elected to the Reichstag in 1924 and three years later helped found the left-wing theoretical journal *Der Klassenkampf*.

World War I helped to make Ströbel a pacifist. By 1915 he had begun to argue that socialist thought had to ally itself with pacifist thought and that socialists could realize their political goals only if they acknowledged pacifism. After the war he joined the Deutsche Friedensgesellschaft (German Peace Society). He wrote the lead articles for the *Pazifist*, the organ of the radical Westdeutsche Landesverband (West German Regional Association) (WLV), founded by *Fritz Küster in 1921 and later renamed *Das Andere Deutschland*. At the same time he was active in the Bund Neues Vaterland (New Fatherland League), which in 1922 became the Deutsche Liga für Menschenrechte (League for Human Rights). In his articles, Ströbel argued tirelessly for rapprochement with France and Poland, for disarmament, and for a peaceful democratic Germany. It was the latter which sparked a serious conflict within the German Peace Society. Ströbel and other WLV members saw the main danger to peace coming from the continuation of the Prussian military tradition. The chief task of the German peace movement, therefore, was to free German society and politics from the Prussian military tradition. This required refuting claims of Germany's innocence with regard to the outbreak of World War I as propagated by conservative nationalists, and rooting out the political and social forces that supported the Prussian military tradition. Other German Peace Society leaders, such as *Ludwig Quidde and *Helmuth von Gerlach, regarded the domestic concerns of Ströbel and his faction as secondary, even irrelevant. They saw the danger to peace existing on the international level. Therefore, the focus of the German peace movement's efforts should be on extending the League of Nations, solving the armaments problem and the security question, strengthening the protection of minorities, and struggling against militarism and imperialism in all countries. When Ströbel's WLV faction gained a majority at the Peace Society's general meeting in Berlin in 1929, he became a member of the new executive committee.

In September 1931 Ströbel left the SPD, which he felt was too tolerant of Chancellor Heinrich Brüning's nonparliamentary cabinet, and joined the newly formed Sozialistische Arbeiterpartei Deutschlands (German Socialist Workers Party) (SAPD). Helped by pressure from its pacifist wing, he was elected one of the party's chairmen, but left the party three months later when it became apparent that it would not make the pacifist point of view the chief plank of its platform. In 1933 Ströbel emigrated to Switzerland and settled in Zurich. He spent the last years of his life in almost complete isolation.

Bibliography:

A. *Die Aufgaben der Arbeiter-Internationale* (Berlin, 1922); *Die Bilanz der Revolution* (Berlin, 1919); *Durch zur Wahrheit* (Berlin, 1919); *Die erste Milliarde der Zweiten Billion: die Gesellschaft der Zukunft* (Berlin, 1919); Introduction to Kurt Eisner, *Schuld und Sühne* (Berlin, 1919); *Die Kriegsschuld der Rechtssozialisten* (Berlin, 1919) *Nicht Gewalt, sondern Organisation! Der Grundirrtum des Bolschewismus* (Berlin, 1921); *Die Schuld im Kriege* (Charlottenburg, 1920); *Die Sozialisierung: ihre Wege und Voraussetzungen* (Berlin, 1921); *Sozialismus und Weltgemeinschaft* (Berlin, 1923).

B. Richard Kleineibst, "Heinrich Ströbel, der Mensch und Kämpfer," *Das Andere Deutschland* 23 (June 8, 1929); Hans Wehberg, "Heinrich Ströbel 60 Jahre alt," *Die Friedenswarte* 29 (1929), 207; *Biographisches Handbuch der deutschsprachigen Emigration nach 1933*, Werner Röder and Herbert A. Strauss, eds., (Munich-New York-London-Paris, 1980); *Biographisches Lexikon des Sozialismus* (Hannover, 1960), I, 304.

Lothar Wieland
Trans. by Peter Seadle

STRONG, Charles (26 September 1844, Dailly, Scotland—12 February 1942, Lorne, Victoria, Australia). *Education*: Doctor of Divinity, Univ. of Glasgow, 1867. *Career*: Presbyterian minister (until resignation in 1883); founder and minister, Australian Church, 1885-1942; editor and peace activist.

Charles Strong is most remembered as the founder and lifelong minister of the Australian Church, which taught the promotion and practice of Christian life and regarded religion not as a definitive theological creed but as a spirit of life. Strong himself supported virtually every movement for social reform in Victoria in the late nineteenth and early twentieth centuries. Among other groups he was a member of the Anti-Sweating League and the Criminology Society, and founded the first crèche in Australia at Collingwood in Melbourne.

In addition, as *Eleanor Moore has noted, Strong was "the Father of Peace movements in Victoria." He was a fervent opponent to British imperialism and Australian involvement in the Boer War (1899-1902). In July 1900, he and another minister inspired the formation in Melbourne of the Peace and Humanity Society (PHS), possibly the first antiwar group established in Australia to oppose the Boer War. Strong took a prominent part in its activities. When the Boer War ended, the PHS disintegrated. However, in 1906 Strong and its most dedicated supporters formed the Melbourne Peace Society as a branch of the London Peace Society which had been founded in 1816. With Strong as its chairman, it advocated arbitration for all international disputes, the reduction of armaments, and the cultivation of international brotherhood and goodwill. In 1907 Strong fostered the formation of similar groups in Sydney and Adelaide.

Old age did little to reduce Strong's activities against war and militarism. When compulsory military training was introduced in Australia in 1911 he opposed it and later took a prominent part in the formation of the Victorian branch of the Australian Freedom League, a group whose parent body had been formed in Adelaide in April 1912 to fight the compulsory clauses of the Defence Act. During World War I Strong addressed his congregation about the need for women to organize themselves against the war. The result was the formation of the Sisterhood of International Peace (SIP) in March 1915, a group dedicated to bringing "the humanising influence of Women to bear on the abolition of war." In 1920 SIP became the Australian section of Women's International League for Peace and Freedom.

In 1917 Strong took an active role in the campaign against the federal government's proposal to introduce conscription for overseas military service. His hatred of war and his wariness of what was being done in the name of patriotism led him to refuse to allow the National Anthem to be sung at the conclusion of each service. Attacked by the Melbourne press over his stand on conscription and rejected by many parishioners who either resigned from the church or stopped attending services, Strong, by the end of the war, had become one of the most controversial churchmen in Australia.

The death of his wife in 1919 was a blow from which Strong never fully recovered. Yet he continued to take part in peace movement activities if only as a figurehead. In 1928 he became a vice-president of the newly-formed Victorian branch of the World Disarmament Movement and in 1940, at the age of 96, was still chairman of the Melbourne Peace Society. In 1915 he had begun the journal *Peacewards*, which was printed as a section of his monthly church magazine, *Commonweal*, and the organ of both the Melbourne Peace Society and the Sisterhood of International Peace. Strong, who edited the journal until his death in 1942, used to boast that in spite of restrictive censorship laws not one word of its was ever deleted. *Peacewards* also had the distinction of having been continuously published longer than any other purely peace journal in any country.

Strong's death meant the end of the Peace Society, his magazine, and his church. The year 1942 saw the last issue of *Peacewards*. In July 1955 the Australian Church closed and its assets were transferred to the Charles Strong Memorial Trust to promote religious liberty, social work, penal reform and rehabilitation, and international friendship.

Bibliography:

B. Colin Badger, *The Reverend Charles Strong and the Australian Church*, (Melbourne, 1971); John Barrett, *Falling in: Australians and 'boy conscription' 1911-1915*, (Sydney, 1979); Mary Colligan, "Brothers and Sisters in Peace: The Peace Movement in Melbourne 1900-18," unpublished Bachelor of Arts thesis, Monash University, 1973; Eleanor Moore, *The Quest for Peace: As I Have Known It in Australia* (Melbourne, 1949); Helen Strong and Annie Worsley, *The Australian Church and Rev. Charles Strong DD: A Memoir*, (Melbourne, 1958).

C. Strong Papers, National Library of Australia, Canberra.

Malcolm James Saunders

STURGE, Joseph (2 August 1793, Elberton, Gloucestershire, England—14 May 1859, Birmingham, England). *Education*: one year at a local day school, three years at a Quaker boarding school in Somerset. *Career*: corn miller and merchant in Gloucestershire, 1814-22, and in Birmingham, 1822-59; Birmingham alderman; activist in various reform and peace organizations.

Joseph Sturge was not an intellectual but a man of many causes. His persuasive powers flowed best not with pen and paper but rather on the platform and in the pulpit, in private societies and committees, and in face-to-face meetings with political leaders. True to his Quaker heritage, he energetically promoted reform, nonviolence, and peace.

Born to Quaker parents who traced their principles to an ancestor's friendship with George Fox, Sturge first displayed his pacifist colors in 1813 when he refused to be drafted into the militia. Shortly after the founding of the London Peace Society in 1816, he formed an auxiliary chapter at Worcester.

During the next three decades, England's isolationism allowed Sturge to turn his mind to moral issues other than war and peace. In 1826 he became secretary of the Birmingham Anti-Slavery Society and called for the emancipation of slaves in the British Empire. Following the Emancipation Act of 1833, he campaigned for an end to the apprenticeship scheme whereby slaves gradually won their freedom, and in 1836 visited the West Indies to see for himself how former slaves were being treated. Three years later, with the founding of the British and Foreign Anti-Slavery Society, he broadened his scope to include American slavery, and in a visit to the United States in 1841 addressed religious and abolitionist groups throughout the Northeast.

In 1841-42 Sturge briefly placed his zeal and respectability at the disposal of the Chartists in Birmingham, until class-conscious, physical-force leaders such as Julian Harney and Feargus O'Connor repudiated not only his attempt to reconcile middle- and working-class interests but also his program of achieving universal suffrage by "peaceable and legitimate means." Sturge then threw himself into the Anti-Corn Law movement (of which he was a charter member), temperance reform, and the movement to broaden access to education. Three times he stood unsuccessfully for Parliament: at Nottingham in 1841, at Birmingham in 1841, and at Leeds in 1849.

Peace, however, was his primary concern. The Maine boundary dispute (settled in 1842) and the Oregon question (settled in 1846) prompted him to cooperate with American "friends of peace" to urge their respective governments to take the route of arbitration rather than military conflict. Scarcely had those problems been resolved before the French revolution of 1848 aroused *francophobe* panic in Britain. Beginning in 1848 Sturge attended annual international peace conferences in Brussels, Paris, Frankfurt, London, Manchester, and Edinburgh in support of disarmament, arbitration treaties, the principle of nonintervention, and the diffusion of attitudes of peace and good-will through the press, schools, and pulpits of the major Western powers.

Just before the Frankfurt Peace Congress convened in 1850, armed conflict broke out between Denmark and the Duchies of Schleswig-Holstein. At the suggestion of a Prussian emissary, Sturge joined a fellow Englishman, Frederic Wheeler, and an American pacifist, *Elihu Burritt, in a mission of peace to the governments of the warring states. They were warmly received, but the din of nationalistic interests drowned out their proposals for neutral arbitrators, and war broke out.

Four years later a much more famous peace mission to Russia similarly ended in frustration. As the "Russo-Turkish affair" simmered in the early months of 1854, the Society of Friends in England sponsored a visit by Sturge, Henry Pease, and Robert Charleton to St. Petersburg. There they had an audience with the Russian tsar, *Nicholas II, urging him to be an "honored instrument" of Christ in maintaining the peace. Much of the English press dismissed the gesture as unpatriotic, or quixotic at best. Shortly after Sturge and his friends returned home, the Crimean War began.

Like *Richard Cobden and *John Bright, Sturge suffered much public abuse as he opposed the Crimean War. Mid-Victorian chauvinism doomed a pacifist to grief. Yet to the end of his life Sturge railed against gunboat diplomacy. In 1857 he spoke out against British repression of rebels in India and China. Fittingly, he was elected president of the Peace Society in 1858, only to die on May 14, 1859, just three days before the next annual meeting. His personal integrity and ideals far exceeded his public accomplishments.

Bibliography:

A. *A Visit to the United States in 1841* (London, 1842); *A Visit to the West Indies in 1837*, with Thomas Harvey (London, 1838).

B. Henry Richard, *Memoirs of Joseph Sturge* (London, 1864); DNB, LV, 130.

William J. Baker

STURZO, Luigi (26 November 1871, Caltagirone, Sicily, Italy—8 August 1959, Rome). *Education*: seminarian at Acireale, Noto, and Caltagirone, 1883-91; ordained, Roman Catholic Church, 1894; Doctorate in Divinity, Gregorian Univ. of Rome, 1898; diploma, Academy of Thomist Philosophy, 1898. *Career*: leader, Christian Democratic Movement in Italy; secretary, Catholic Action, from 1917; founder and first political secretary, Popular party, 1919-23; senator, 1952-1959; priest, social theorist, historian, and politician.

Following his ordination, Luigi Sturzo decided upon an academic career and became professor of philosophy and sociology in Caltagirone. He was profoundly influenced by Pope Leo XIII's publication of the encyclical *Rerum Novarum* (1891), which called for the solution of concrete social problems, and the work of Giambattista Vico which stressed the close relationship between knowing and doing. He was also influenced by the thought and work of Giuseppe Toniolo and Romolu Murri. With the passage of time, he became increasingly concerned with the issue of the Christian presence in history and its mode of operation, that is its relationship to the power structure which is the basis of human social institutions. Elected provincial councillor in 1905, he called for the formation of a national party of Catholics which would not be confessional but whose principles would be based on Christianity. Such a party emerged under Sturzo's leadership in January, 1919.

The Popular party called for decentralization, democracy, and disarmament. Sturzo remained active in this democratic mass party of Catholic orientation until the fall of 1924, when apparently acceding to the wishes of the Vatican, he left for England and exile. In 1926 the party was dissolved by royal decree, and in 1929 the Vatican signed the Lateran Accords with Fascist Italy. In London, where Sturzo was warmly welcomed by Sidney Webb, he wrote a series of sociological and historical works and closely followed international developments. In 1940 he left England for the United States.

His preoccupation with Italian affairs formed part of his broader concern for the international community of which Italy was a member. A strong antifascist, Sturzo viewed Italy's problems as symptomatic of the larger ones of Europe and the West. Prior to the emergence of Benito Mussolini and the creation of the "totalitarian" or "ethical" state, Don Sturzo had placed his trust in juridical principles convinced that the law could act as a mediating agent in international affairs. The triumph of Fascism with it bellicose nationalism led him to conclude that the judicial dimension was insufficient to maintain international peace. He subsequently determined that a sociological strata was at the base of the problem of the international community. This realization did not diminish his confidence in the reign of international law but led him to insist that such law to be effective had to be established in a framework of sociological considerations. In his *Inner Laws of Society* (1944), published in

French under the title *Essai de sociologie* (1935), he stressed that there could be no true doctrine of man that ignored the historico-sociological dimension.

Sturzo's view of international relations was profoundly influenced by both his Christian faith and the fascist experience in Italy. His view of the Christian presence in history drew inspiration from Vico. He saw Church and State form a diarchy defined as the coexistence of the two powers each limiting the other. Without the Christian presence, international relations degenerated into a blatant struggle for survival among the fittest. Nations, when confronting other nations in the international arena, proved to be motivated by the same power monism he had seen to be operative within the Fascist party. He touched upon these matters in *The International Community and the Right of War* (1930), which shed light on both the evolution of the international community as well as the historico-sociological roots of war.

The Catholic Church, it might be supposed, could serve as the direct countervailing principle to the struggle for the mastery of power. To do so it would have had to preserve its universal character untouched by the national principle. Sturzo concluded that such was not the case and, therefore, looked to the Christian and pacific nations to serve as mediating agents. The Church could function as the Church of nations not because it moved at a level above them but because it had become the basis for unity within them (here his experience with the Popular party was important) and upon which the unity of the world of nations could endure. Despite the dictatorships and the war of aggression they provoked, Sturzo remained convinced that Christian impulse remained and would serve as the perennial principle of hope, peace, and renewal.

During the Fascist years Sturzo did not lose hope and proposed the formation of a Popular party in exile which would assume the reigns of power when the dictatorship collapsed. His plans proved abortive as did his desire to return to Italy in June 1944, following the liberation of Rome. When he returned in 1946 he was less than happy with the Christian Democratic party under Alcide de Gasperi's leadership which he considered inclined toward socialism. In the Senate he refused to sit with the Christian Democrats preferring to preserve his freedom of action. His political role in Italy in the postwar period was minimal but the impact of his thought remained significant.

Bibliography:

A. *Church and State* (London, 1939); *I discorsi politici* (Rome, 1951); *Inner Laws of Society* (New York, 1944); *The International Community and the Right of War* (New York, 1930); *Italy and Fascismo* (London, 1926); *Opera Omnia* (Bologna, 1954); *Il Partito popolare italiano* (rev. ed., Bologna, 1956).

B. A. R. Caponigri, "Don Luigi Sturzo," *Review of Politics*, 14 (1952), 147-65; Francesco Piva and Francesco Malgeri, *Vita di Luigi Sturzo* (Rome, 1976); Gabriele de Rosa, *Sturzo* (Turin, 1977); N. S. Timasheff, *The Sociology of Luigi Sturzo* (Baltimore, 1962).

Frank J. Coppa

SUMNER, Charles (6 January 1811, Boston—11 March 1874, Washington, DC). *Education*: B.A., Harvard Coll., 1830, LLB., Harvard Law School, 1833. *Career*: U.S. Senator, 1851-74.

Before the Civil War, Charles Sumner was nearly as widely recognized for his advocacy of world peace and international arbitration as he was for his opposition to slavery. A cosmopolitan Harvard-educated lawyer, Sumner's career turned to politics during the mid-1840s as he became increasingly well known among New England's reformers for his general pacifism and opposition to the Mexican War. In 1851 Sumner was elected to the United States Senate, a position he retained until his death. His entry into public life took place five years earlier, however, when, as the principal speaker at Boston's Independence Day celebration, he delivered a stirring appeal against warfare of all kinds. In this "True Grandeur of Nations" address, as it came to be known, Sumner displayed the formidable forensic talents which soon made him one of the lyceum's most popular speakers, as he excoriated war in general as "monstrous and impious," as wasteful of resources and as degrading to all who participated in or prepared for it. West Point, he insisted, should be abolished. Nations should cease their military spending, and divert such funds to public education and charity. Soon, Sumner made his opposition to warfare quite specific, decrying the United States's hostilities with Mexico as acts of aggression designed to promote the extension of slavery into territory obtained by immoral means. These statements brought Sumner into cooperation with nonresistant abolitionists like *Samuel May Jr. and *William Lloyd Garrison, as well as with dissident Whig politicians who were increasingly emphatic that their party take a strongly antislavery position in the growing debate, sparked by the war, between North and South. When, for example, Sumner's boyhood friend, Congressman Robert C. Winthrop voted in favor of the bill declaring war with Mexico, Sumner published a series of letters accusing him of gross moral turpitude, a charge which opened irreparable rifts in the Massachusetts Whig party, and ultimately cleared Sumner's own pathway to the Senate.

Meanwhile, Sumner's reputation as an antiwar internationalist grew further. In 1849 he addressed the annual meeting of the American Peace Society, led by the renown Connecticut pacifist *Elihu Burritt. Here, as in all of Sumner's utterances on public affairs, he took the position that nations, like individuals, should adhere to a fixed code of God-given morality and in this case should therefore eschew violence of all forms, no matter what the provocation. He also made a strong plea for "a Congress of Nations" to adjudicate international disputes. Sumner, however, never developed sustained affiliations with the American Peace Society, and from the 1850s, until his death was deeply enmeshed instead in the narrative of violence and politics which accompanied the Civil War and Reconstruction. Though his relationships with antebellum pacifist movements were always episodic, Sumner represented an important point of interaction between such movements and the larger political culture of pre-Civil War New England.

Bibliography:

A. *The Works of Charles Sumner* (15 vols., Boston, 1870-83).

B. David Donald, *Charles Sumner and the Coming of the Civil War* (New York, 1960), *Charles Sumner and The Rights of Man* (New York, 1970).

C. Charles Sumner Papers, Houghton Library, Harvard University.

James Brewer Stewart

SUTTNER, Bertha Sophia Felicita Kinsky, Baroness von (9 June 1843, Prague, Bohemia, Austria [now Czechoslovakia]—21 June 1914, Vienna). *Education*: privately tutored. *Career*: founder and president, Austrian Peace Society, 1891; editor, *Die Waffen Nieder*, 1892-1902; pacifist journalist, author, and organizer.

Baroness Bertha von Suttner influenced *Alfred Nobel, for whom she worked briefly as a secretary in Paris in 1876, to establish the peace prize. But when the Nobel Committee awarded her the prize in 1905 it was in recognition of her many services to the cause of peace. She was the authoress of the most important antiwar novel of the period, *Die Waffen Nieder* (*Lay Down Your Arms*), published in 1889. Her commentaries on world politics from the peace point of view were widely read; she was, in fact, the first woman political journalist in the German language. She campaigned for peace in person as well as by her prolific pen and her lecture tours took her throughout Europe and to the United States. As an aristocrat, she used her position in society to conduct "unofficial diplomacy" with government leaders and representatives. She urged arbitration and peace policies in audiences with European monarchs and American presidents, and she headed the lobby of pacifist leaders at The Hague Conferences in 1899 and 1907. She established and became president of the Austrian Peace Society in Vienna in 1891, and she helped establish other peace societies and branches of the Interparliamentary Union throughout central Europe. She took a leading role in international peace congresses as a highly respected advisor and conciliator. As vice-president, she was prominent in the work of the International Peace Bureau in Berne. Other peace leaders referred to her as "our commander-in-chief." In world public opinion, Bertha von Suttner symbolized the peace movement, and she was one of the best known women of her day.

Nothing in her early life seemed to presage her role as peace movement leader. Born Countess Kinsky, the daughter of an Austrian field marshal of a distinguished aristocratic family, she was educated to live the fashionable life of the aristocracy, learning foreign languages and all the social graces and spending much time abroad. When financial difficulties arose, the beautiful young countess took the unusual course of setting out to earn her own living, becoming governess to the daughters of Baron von Suttner in 1873. She and Arthur, the son, fell in love and in the face of family disapproval eloped and went off to live with friends in the Caucasus for nine years (1876-85). The break with convention was furthered during this sojourn, as Suttner and her husband read avidly in Charles Darwin, Ernst Haeckel, Herbert Spencer, and T. H. Buckle, and embarked upon writing careers. When they finally returned to Austria as successful writers in 1885, they were free-thinkers and social idealists, committed to use their literary talents in combatting prejudice and injustice and making the world a better place to live.

Bertha von Suttner had already published eight books when she decided to write a novel revealing the anachronistic nature of the institution of war in an age of progress and scientific enlightenment. *Die Waffen Nieder* told the story of a young woman whose happiness was destroyed by the wars between 1859 and 1871. It vividly portrayed the horrors of the battlefield and the case against war formed the content of much of the dialogue. Although not a great work of literary art, it proved to be a very effective work of propaganda. It struck a responsive chord in a multitude of readers, who identified themselves with the heroine and her sorrows, were shocked by the realistic scenes of war's brutality, and moved by the sincerity of the authoress. By 1914 it had appeared in 40 editions and had been translated into 16 languages. It was considered the *Uncle Tom's Cabin* of the peace movement.

For Bertha von Suttner the novel meant more than an international reputation; it gave her a new mission in life. She had conceived of the novel when she first heard of the organized peace movement that was emerging in Europe and wanted to do it a service. But in the writing she became a committed advocate and began to work for peace not just with her pen, "but with my whole being." Bertha von Suttner was 56 years of age when the novel was published; she worked tirelessly for peace during the next 25 years until her death, despite the crushing blow of her husband's death in 1902 and the weakening of her powers as she grew older.

The foundation of her plea for peace was an empowering ethical conviction. The formulation of theories of "scientific pacifism" was left to others, notably *Alfred H. Fried, who was brought to the peace movement by reading her novel and became her closest collaborator. But the Baroness was no mere emotional advocate. Her well-informed political commentaries were satirical and witty, sometimes sarcastic, but reasonable rather than vehement. In her public addresses she was no spell-binding orator. What moved her audiences so deeply was the dominant force of her personality: before them stood a great lady, speaking with calm confidence about the future, evidently inspired by an abiding faith in humanity. The opponents of peace were not villains but misguided ones who could be brought to reason.

Bertha von Suttner assumed this role upon the world's stage at a time and place when women were not expected to take part in public life. The spectacle of a woman leading the peace forces seemed only too appropriate to the jingoists and militarists who made the Baroness the target of their attacks and abuse. She was more troubled about apathy, however, than such criticism. While the hundreds of thousands who read her novel or heard her words were moved to deplore war and to dream of peace, relatively few joined the peace societies that were seeking to bring it about. The peace organizations that she helped bring into being remained small and uninfluential, weakest of all in the German Empire, more respectable in the lands of the Habsburgs, but without any mass support.

More recent critics have faulted the Baroness for her "naive optimism," her failure to analyze the economic and psychological causes of war, and her too ready acceptance of the sovereign state and its rulers. She believed in wars of defense, and she insisted that peace societies take no political stands, since the cause of peace was above politics. She had a cause, but she was no rebel. She did not challenge the established order of society; what she did attack, relentlessly, was the assumption that war was part of that order.

Her most tangible influence upon international relations was the result of the lobby of peace leaders that she led at the First Hague Conference in 1899. *Tzar Nicholas' original call for this conference had proposed an international agreement for disarmament. The Baroness and many of her colleagues recognized that disarmament was more likely to come as the consequence of the establishment of machinery to settle international conflicts, and they worked hard to promote the cause of arbitration. The most important outcome of the Conference, aside from the precedent it set of states coming together to make peace rather than to end a war, was indeed the creation of an international court of arbitration. This was far less than the federation of Europe that the Baroness felt would be the best way to prevent war between the Great Powers, but the establishment of The Hague Court was a significant landmark on the way to international organization.

The Court was not designed, however, to arbitrate the kind of conflict of national interests that led to war in 1914. Bertha von Suttner died in June and was spared the agony of experiencing what happened when her perceptive warnings about the dangers of international conflicts in the Balkans came true. Her last words were, "Lay down your arms. Say it to many, to many." The international peace congress of 1914, in the planning for many months, was to have been held in Vienna, to honor her. One of the major events was to have been the showing of the Danish film based upon her novel. But it was not to be.

As Bertha von Suttner had been the living symbol of the peace movement, her death was followed a few months later by the collapse of that movement in the First World War. Did this mean that all her efforts had been in vain? In an age of imperialism and power politics was her quest for peace an impossible dream? To generals like the German Field Marshal von Moltke peace was not just a dream but a nightmare, a vision of a warless future when all the heroic virtues would have vanished from the earth. But it was heroic to raise the standard of peace in such an age, and it took courage and dedication to carry its banner unfalteringly in the midst of apathy and indifference and even bitter attacks. Perhaps Suttner's greatest service to humanity was to keep alive the dream of peace and to give witness through her own life to the high potential of the human spirit.

Bibliography:

A. *Die Waffen Nieder* (Dresden, 1889; English trans., *Ground Arms*, Chicago, 1892; reissued as *Lay Down Your Arms*, New York, 1971); *Memoiren* (Stuttgart, 1909; reissued as *Lebenserinnerungen*, Berlin, German Democratic Republic, 1969; English trans., *Memoirs of Bertha von Suttner. The Records of an Eventful Life* (2 vols., Boston, 1910; reissued, New York, 1972).

B. Irwin Abrams, "Bertha von Suttner and the Nobel Peace Prize," *Journal of Central European Affairs*, 22 (October, 1962), 286-307; Beatrix Kempf, *Bertha von Suttner. Das Leben einer grossen Frau* (Vienna, 1964; English trans., with complete bibliography of Suttner's writings, *Woman for Peace: The Life of Bertha von Suttner*, Park Ridge, NJ, 1973); Emil Lengyel, *And All Her Paths Were Peace: The Life of Bertha von Suttner* (Nashville and New York, 1975); Carolene E. Playne, *Bertha von Suttner and the Struggle to Avert the World War* (London, 1936).

C. Bertha von Suttner Papers, Suttner-Fried Correspondence, United Nations Library, Geneva.

Irwin Abrams

SVOLOS, Alexandros (1892, Krousovo-Monastir, Macedonia, Turkey—23 February 1956, Athens). *Education*: Doctor of Law, Univ. of Athens, 1915. *Career*: public servant, 1917-22; professor, Constitutional Law, Univ. of Athens, 1929-35, 1944-46; member, National Unity Government, 1944; parliamentary deputy, 1950-56; public affairs commentator and peace advocate.

Alexandros Svolos' contribution to the cause of peace was an integral part of his lifelong involvement with constitutional theory and political practice. In his scholarly writing Svolos attempted, in opposition to legal positivism, to develop a sociological approach to constitutional analysis that would make constitutional law responsive to changing social needs. By considering the law and the constitution as integral parts of social and political reality, Svolos broke radically with academic legalism making his scholarship a pioneering model in Greek constitutional thought. He adopted the position that through socially minded reform of constitutional law aimed at ending social injustice and political exclusion peaceful socio-political change would be possible. In two essays, "The Impact of War on Public Law" (1918) and "Two New Regimes" (1921)—i.e. the Weimar constitution and the Soviet system—Svolos pointed to the challenges of political and social change posed by World War I. In these essays, as well as in his subsequent writings on Greek law, he argued for reforms that would peacefully promote social justice and democratic principles. In this way the masses would be integrated into the political process and their demands for social welfare programs met in a manner consistent with liberal-democratic parliamentary government.

The upheavals of Greek political history from the mid-1930s onward pushed Svolos from the serenity of scholarship into political activism. In this he was prompted as well by the influence of his wife, Maria Svolos, who was a prominent feminist. Dismissed from his professorship and exiled by the dictatorship of August 4, 1936, he emerged as a leading figure of the anti-German resistance in occupied Greece (1941-44). He was elected president of the Political Committee of National Liberation (PEEA) in April 1944 and joined the National Unity government that presided over the liberation of Greece in October 1944. He held the portfolio of Minister of Finance and was responsible for the first determined measures aimed at coping with the chaotic social and economic situation. Concurrently he played a prominent role in the effort to secure a peaceful transition to democratic political life amidst the rifts created by the occupation between Left and Right. Although he resigned with the ministers of the Left on November 30, 1944, he persisted in his efforts to avert the outbreak of civil violence by insisting on the necessity of national unity. After the confrontation of December 1944, he was among the first to appeal for peace. He feared that the authoritarian and illegal measures to neutralize the role of the Communist and radical left-wing parties in Greek politics by the government would provoke the Left to violence in self-defense. In an attempt to prevent that, Svolos made domestic pacification and external peace the central themes of his newspaper, *Combat*, from 1945 until 1953.

In the period of hardened ideological intolerance and political reaction that followed the civil war, Svolos strove to reorganize and preserve the noncommunist and democratic Left as leader first of the Socialist party—Union of Popular Democracy (SK-ELD, 1945-53)—and then of the Working People's Democratic party (DKEL, 1953-56). In 1950 he was elected to the Greek parliament on a platform of peace and democratic reconstruction. He was reelected in 1956. In his last major work, *The Constitution of Greece*, he focused on the civil liberties provisions of the 1952 constitution from a comparative perspective, stressing civil liberties as one of pre-conditions of political peace. In Svolos' political thought the tragedy of peace was identified with the drama of the "Third way" for which he groped both in domestic and international politics.

Bibliography:

A. *Syntagmatikon Dikeon* (2 vols., Athens, 1934-35); *To neon Syntagma ke e vaseis tou politevmatos* (Athens, 1928); *To Syntagma tis Ellados*, with G. C. Vlachos, (2 vols., Athens, 1954-55).

B. G. Paschos, *Kratos ke politevmata sto ergo tou Al. Svolou* (Salonica, 1981); Ilias Tsirimokos, *Alexandros Svolos* (Athens, 1962); NYT, February 24, 1956.

Paschalis M. Kitromilides

SWANWICK, Helena Maria Sickert (13 June 1864 Munich, Germany—16 November 1939 Maidenhead, England). *Education*: Notting Hill High School for Girls, London; Girton Coll., Cambridge Univ., 1882-85. *Career*: journalist, *Manchester Guardian*, *Time and Tide*, *Nation*, *Observer*; editor, *The Common Cause*, 1909-12, *Foreign Affairs*, 1925-28; pacifist and feminist author.

Born to an English mother and a Danish father in Munich, and residing in England since the age of four, Helena Sickert traced her determined internationalism to family roots and upbringing. Like her brother, the painter Walter Sickert, Helena early displayed an independence of mind and analytical ability that culminated in her appointments as the editor of two political journals and as a delegate to the League of Nations.

As one of the early women students at Cambridge, she revelled in the study of ethics and politics. She passed her examinations, but like other women attending Oxford or Cambridge during the nineteenth century she received no degree. In 1888 she married Frederick Tertius Swanwick, a Cambridge mathematician. They settled in Manchester where he became a distinguished member of the university faculty. There she began to write book reviews and articles on domestic themes for the *Manchester Guardian*. Her sense of feminism sharpened as she reviewed innumerable derogatory books generalizing about women.

In 1905 the public agitation of the Pankhursts for women's suffrage inspired Swanwick to active work for the vote. Finding the militant policy of the Pankhursts' Social and Political Union (WSPU) uncongenial, however, she joined the moderate, constitutional wing of the National Union of Suffrage Societies (NUWSS) and worked closely with local Lancashire branches and with Millicent Fawcett in London. This work, which she continued until women were enfranchised, committed her to socialism because she believed that only the Labour party was willing to stake its future on political freedom for women. After four years as a speaker, writer, and organizer for the NUWSS in the Manchester area, Swanwick became the editor of its newly-founded independent weekly newspaper: *The Common Cause*. In 1912 she resigned the position after three years, because (as editor) she was not permitted to express her disagreement with the suffragettes' tactics.

Helena Swanwick's attitudes, both to the relationship between the sexes and to militancy in achieving women's suffrage, were informed by a profound pacifism that underlay her internationalism. Shortly after war broke out in 1914, she joined the Union of Democratic Control (UDC), an organization that promoted international and democratic control of foreign policy. Swanwick severed her connection with NUWSS because it supported the war effort and joined the Executive Committee of the UDC. Throughout the war she spent many lonely and exhausting days touring isolated towns and villages across Britain, urging miners and factory workers to call for the ending of hostilities through discussion instead of by combat. Her editorial experience, her loyalty, and her work for the UDC resulted in her appointment as editor of its journal, *Foreign Affairs*, from 1925 until 1928.

Ill health prevented Helena Swanwick from attending the 1915 International Women's Congress at The Hague (from which the Women's International League of Peace and Freedom emerged), but she was immediately elected to chair the British wing of this organization, the Women's International League (WIL). In this position, which she held until 1922, she worked closely with Maude Royden, Chrystal Macmillan, and *Catherine Marshall in Britain, and with *Jane Addams in the U.S.

In 1924 in recognition of her longstanding work for the UDC and the WIL, Labor Prime Minister +Ramsay MacDonald appointed Swanwick as one of the nine British delegates to the fifth Assembly of the League of Nations at Geneva; in 1929 she again represented Britain at the tenth Assembly of the League.

Convinced of the wrongness of war, Swanwick was appalled at the harsh terms of the Versailles Peace Treaty, particularly the reparations clauses, which she fully expected would provoke revolt by the defeated nations. Helena Swanwick did not believe in partial measures to prevent war. She argued passionately against a militarized police force empowered by the League of Nations. During the thirties, the WIL published several of her pamphlets analyzing the inefficacy of "pooled security" (advocated, among others, by *Norman Angell), and warning of the danger of military aviation. In *Frankenstein and His Monster* (1934) she proposed international control of civil aviation. In 1931, the year of her husband's death, Helena Swanwick received the Order of Companion of Honor (C.H.) for her work on behalf of peace and of women's enfranchisement.

Bibliography:

A. *Builders of Peace* (London, 1924); *Collective Insecurity* (London, 1937); *The Future of the Women's Movement* (London, 1913); *I Have Been Young* (London, 1935); *Labour's Foreign Policy* [Fabian Tract no. 227] (London, 1929); *The Roots of Peace* (London, 1938); *Women in the Socialist State* (London, 1921).

B. Blanche Wiesen Cook, Introduction to Reprint edition of Helena M. Swanwick *Women and War*, in the Garland Library of War and Peace (New York, 1971); LT, November 18, 1939, p. 9.

Susan Groag Bell

SZILARD, Leo (11 February 1898, Budapest, Austria-Hungary—30 May 1964, La Jolla, CA). *Education*: attended King Joseph Institute of Technology in Budapest and the Institute of Technology in Berlin; Ph.D., Univ. of Berlin, 1922. *Career*: physicist, biologist, and scientist-activist for world peace; initiator and participant, Pugwash Conference of Scientists on World Affairs; founder, Council for a Livable World.

From the early days of the Manhattan Project, where the first atomic bombs were developed for use in World War II, Hungarian-born, emigré physicist Leo Szilard insisted that scientists had a responsibility regarding the use and control of a weapon they helped unleash on the world. Beginning with his efforts to help prevent the use of atomic bombs without warning on Japan, through his leadership in the postwar "scientists' movement" to prevent military control of atomic energy in the U.S., to his speaking, writing, and lobbying campaign against the accelerating US-USSR arms race, Szilard was increasingly active in the public arena. A man of foresight and vision, with passionate concern about the fate of humankind in the nuclear age, he was a symbol of the committed scientist and a kind of one-man agency for world peace.

It was apparent early in his career that Szilard was a scientist whose interests would not be bounded by laboratory walls. As a young physicist in Germany, in the 1920s, he first evidenced a proclivity for schemes to help "save the world" when he planned an organization to take the place of the government he was certain soon would collapse. Later, in 1933, as an emigré from Nazi Germany, he provided the impetus for the establishment of an organization in England to aid refugee scientists. In 1939, when the discovery of nuclear fission brought the idea of a chain reaction closer to reality, Szilard immediately foresaw the military and political implications of nuclear energy and he became absorbed in a campaign surrounding those questions that would occupy him for the rest of his life.

Like a number of other émigré scientists, Szilard, who had settled in the United States, was obsessed with the not unreasonable fear that Germany would develop atomic bombs. His success in alerting +Franklin Roosevelt to that possibility in large measure was responsible for the president's establishment of the research committee out of which the Manhattan Project evolved. Having done pioneering work on the graphite-uranium reactor, Szilard was admitted to the Manhattan Project, and the intensity of his activities there reflected his continuing fear that the Germans would be first to have atomic bombs. However, once Germany was defeated and Japan clearly was near the end of her fighting capability, Szilard vigorously opposed the use of the weapon he had helped to devise. He played a leading role among Manhattan Project scientists who thought the bomb's use against Japanese cities would be immoral and would very likely jeopardize international control of atomic energy. After efforts to prevent the bomb's use failed, Szilard turned to the issue of atomic energy control. He was in the forefront of the scientists' movement that helped defeat the army-sponsored May-Johnson bill and secure the passage of the MacMahon Act, which provided for an atomic energy commission under civilian control.

After the war Szilard left physics for biology. Although he never explicitly expressed guilt about his role in developing the atomic bomb, his mid-life career change may in part be understood as reflecting his desire to tip the balance of his contribution to humanity in the direction of life. His political commitment assumed a heightened urgency as he observed the developing Soviet-American arms race that he had predicted and feared. He became a tireless crusader for schemes for disarmament and political resolution of the great power conflict—writing, speaking, and lobbying to mobilize influential people to help break the deadlock between the two world powers. In 1957 his idea of direct communication between Russian and American scientists materialized in the Pugwash movement, which brought together world scientists for regular conferences on international affairs. His popular collection of satiric political fantasies on war and peace, *The Voice of the Dolphins* (1961), was translated and published in six languages. In 1962 a speaking tour of major colleges and universities persuaded him of the feasibility of supporting peace candidates for the U.S. Senate through establishment of a permanent Washington lobby: the Council for a Livable World.

Regarded as exceptionally brilliant, even among his illustrious peers, Szilard was legendary for his inventiveness, originality, and individualism, as a scientist and as a human being. Nothing about him was ordinary or conventional. As a peace leader he did not fit into ready-made political categories; his mind was too restless and wide-ranging to espouse any single ideology or point of view. He relied chiefly on logic and reason in his approach to world issues and problems. Although he shared the dominant American view that the U.S.S.R. was a totalitarian dictatorship, he insisted that the only approach to the great power conflict was through negotiation, beginning with a recognition of the legitimate needs of both sides. Some of his schemes seemed bizarre and mechanical, but he held that unless a novel approach was found to break the great power deadlock each qualitative leap in the arms race would bring the world closer to mass "murder and suicide."

Szilard believed that in the long run peace depended on world government, which could be achieved by gradually weakening national loyalty. He was charged with elitism because of a preference for working through groups of "exceptional" individuals and for appealing directly to national leaders. Yet he devised the Council for a Livable World as a grass roots movement, based on citizen education and electoral politics, and the thinking behind his most provocative scheme—for the US and USSR to mine each other's cities—at bottom rested on a faith that people would not support their governments in risking annihilation for the sake of national advantage.

Bibliography:

A. *The Collected Works of Leo Szilard*: Volume II, *Leo Szilard: His Version of the Facts, Selected Recollections and Correspondence*, edited by Spencer R. Weart and Gertrud Weiss Szilard (Cambridge, 1978); Volume III, *Beyond Science: For a Livable World*, edited by Helen S. Hawkins, Gertrud Weiss Szilard, and G. Allen Greb (Cambridge, 1983); *The Voice of the Dolphins* (New York, 1961).

B. Edward Shils, "Leo Szilard: A Memoir," *Encounter*, 23 (December, 1964), 35-41.

C. Leo Szilard Papers, University of California San Diego (pending final disposition).

Carol S. Gruber

T

TAGORE, Rabindranath (6 May 1861, Calcutta, India—7 August 1941, Calcutta). *Education*: private. *Career*: writer, poet, composer, philosopher, painter, educator.

Rabindranath Tagore was born to a prominent and wealthy Brahmin family of Calcutta. His family was associated with the Brahmo Samaj, a Hindu reform movement of the nineteenth century. Tagore continued this particular tradition and added to it a plan for world peace to be brought about through a synthesis of "Eastern" and "Western" cultures.

Educated by his family after unsuccessful attempts in the formal British model schools, Tagore was encouraged to pursue his obvious talents in poetry and writing. In time he read and wrote in Bengali, English, and Sanskrit. In 1874 he published his first poem and soon his literary production included works in criticism, fiction, essays, and translations. Tagore wrote most of his major works in Bengali and was an advocate of the use of Bengali, as opposed to English, as the vehicle for the education of the people of Bengal. He argued that only through mass education could the ignorance he believed to be at the base of India's economic, religious, and social inequalities be removed. In 1901 he founded a school at Santiniketan incorporating the structure of the traditional *ashram* but also including Western educational principles.

In 1912 Tagore visited the United Kingdom and the United States. The following year, he received the Nobel Prize for Literature and in 1915 was Knighted. He used the prestige which he gained from these two honors to make another lecture tour to the United States and one to Japan in the cause of peace. He urged both countries to avoid becoming entangled in the World War. He continued to travel throughout his life in the cause of world peace advocating a synthesis of the cultures of East and West as the best means to obtain such peace.

In 1918 Tagore founded an institute, Visva Gharati, at his school in Santiniketan. This institute was an international university through which Tagore hoped his ideas on cultural synthesis would develop into an active force for peace. Although an admirer of *Mohandas K. Gandhi, whom he met first in 1915, Tagore disagreed with much that Gandhi advocated. In particular, he believed that mass nonviolent disobedience was not possible. Most people, he argued, were incapable of maintaining the degree of self-discipline necessary to prevent Gandhi's campaigns from deteriorating into violence. Tagore also believed that political independence was not as important for India as was its economic, religious, and social reform.

Tagore was the major interpreter of Indian culture for the West during the first three decades of the twentieth century. His ideas about universal brotherhood based on a union between Asian and European culture struck a responsive chord in the West. He was a unique figure in modern India, and he was an example of the cultural synthesis he hoped would replace the particularism and parochialism which he so ardently opposed.

Bibliography:

A. *My Reminiscences* (London, 1917); *The Religion of Man* (London, 1931).

B. Amiya Chakravarty, *A Tagore Reader* (New York, 1961); S. Radhakrishnan, *Great Indians* (Bombay, 1949); Sachin Sen, *The Political Thought of Tagore* (Calcutta, 1947); Edward Thompson, *Rabindranath Tagore: Poet and Dramatist* (2nd ed., London, 1948).

John C. Hume, Jr.

TAVES, Harvey W. (22 March 1926, Winnipeg, Manitoba, Canada—11 May 1965, Kitchener, Ontario). *Education*: Grace Bible Institute, Omaha, NE, 1947-48; B.A., Goshen Coll., Goshen, IN, 1951; Goshen Coll. Biblical Seminary 1952-53; Univ. of Buffalo, 1964-65. *Career*: teacher in Manitoba, 1944-47; director, Canadian office of Mennonite Central Committee, 1953-65; appointed executive director, Mennonite Central Committee, Ontario, 1965.

Throughout his life Harvey W. Taves was dedicated to a peace witness that was widely interpreted and widely applied. He was a man of innovation and ideas and was often at the forefront of creating projects and implementing programs which furthered the peace mission of the Mennonite churches. For Taves, promoting peace was not something exclusive to wartime, it meant service to humanity at all times.

For twelve years prior to his death at age 39, Taves served with the Mennonite Central Committee, first heading the Canadian office at Kitchener-Waterloo, Ontario, and in 1965, assuming leadership of the Ontario branch of the newly organized Canadian counterpart to the Mennonite Central Committee. Taves was one of the catalysts in the founding of the Mennonite Central Committee Canada. As an inter-Mennonite organization devoted to peace, relief, and service, the central committee offices provided Taves with a vehicle for the realization of many successful peace-related projects.

During the 1950s Taves sat on the executive board of the Conference of Historic Peace Churches, an organization formed in 1940 to deal primarily with the conscription issue of World War II. The peace interests of this body expanded after the war, and it became an advisory board for several projects which were largely implemented and administered by Taves from his office.

Taves became involved in the problem of civil defense which confronted Mennonites and other peace churches during the Cold War. Although he believed that Christians must shoulder responsibility in the event of disaster, Taves felt, like others, that the national civil defense program was too closely related to the military and to the defense policy of the government. Consequently, the Mennonite Disaster Service was created in Canada in 1958 as an alternative to civil defense, but with the purpose of providing aid to the victims of disaster. The new organization was managed by Taves.

Taves focused much of his work on alleviating human suffering. Summer service for young people in mental institutions and hospitals, mission programs in urban centers, a teaching and nursing unit in Newfoundland; these were all projects resulting from Taves' initiative and hard work.

Taves was also devoted to peace education. During the late 1950s he figured prominently in discussions leading to the establishment, in 1963, of Conrad Grebel College, a church college on the campus of University of Waterloo. The college's main purpose was to provide an education for young people that was undergirded by the peace commitment of the Mennonite church. Taves served as secretary of the board of Conrad Grebel for several years.

The impact of a man like Harvey Taves can best be seen in the fruits of his labors, in the many service and peace-related projects which came into being out of his dedication to peace.

Bibliography:

B. Larry Kehler, ''Harvey W. Taves Dedicated His Life to Serve his Fellowman.'' *The Canadian Mennonite* June 1, 1965, p. 7.

Frank H. Epp and Marlene G. Epp

TEN KATE, Jan Jacob Lodewijk (12 June 1850, Middelburg, Netherlands—28 May 1929, Loosduinen, Netherlands). *Education*: Military Academy, Breda, artillery officer, 1869; painting lessons in Amsterdam and Munich. *Career*: artist, specializing in peace and antiwar themes; Prix d'excellence, 1873.

Jan Jacob ten Kate, son of a Dutch Reformed minister who also wrote poetry and nephew of two well-known Romantic painters, moved from a military career to that of an artist. He first attracted public attention in 1885 with paintings of a sea rescue scene and of a group of persecuted Jewish people fleeing Russia. From that point, his paintings reflected his total commitment to peace themes and he became a well known propagandist among the leaders of the European peace movement at the end of the century.

Ten Kate attended several international congresses. He developed a correspondence with *Alfred H. Fried whom he met in 1897 at the Hamburg congress, and during the 1899 conference at The Hague, ten Kate held a private exhibition of his paintings for peace leaders who greatly admired his work. This admiration, however, did not lead to a sufficient income and he was in regular financial trouble. An effort to display his antiwar paintings in London in 1901 became a disappointment, for many in Britain viewed the topics as too pro-Boer.

Among his important works were a portrait of the Swiss founder of the Red Cross, *Henry Dunant, which still hangs in the Netherlands Red Cross headquarters and a large canvas called ''War on War,'' which contained portraits of leading peace activists meeting on a battlefield scene. ''War on War'' as well as many other smaller antiwar paintings were sent to hang in the Lucerne War and Peace Museum, established by *Jean de Bloch, but with the closing of the museum after the First World War, much of its contents were dispersed.

An attempt to obtain the Nobel Peace Prize for ten Kate did not succeed. In 1910, in cooperation with the Dutch peace society, Vrede Door Recht, he began to organize a great exhibition for the opening of the Peace Palace. As with so many of his plans, this did not materialize. A year after his death, however, a League of Nations and Peace exhibition took place in The Hague. Among the exhibits were several paintings by ten Kate who had devoted his life to publicizing the peace cause.

Bibliography:

A. *A Catalogue of the Pictures, Sketches and Drawings for the Promotion of International Peace* (Epe, 1899).

B. Alfred H. Fried, "Ein Besuch bei ten Kate," *Die Waffen Nieder* (1888), 118-20; Alfred H. Fried, "Die Maler der Friedens Idee," *Ibid.* (1899), 234-5; W. Haverkamp, "J. J. L. ten Kate" in *Boon's geillustreerd Magazine* (1902), 99-108; P. A. Scheen, *Lexikon Nederlandse beeldende kunstenaars* (1970, 2nd ed., 1981).

J. H. Rombach

TEPPER-LASKI, Kurt von (8 August 1850, Germany—5 February 1931, Berlin). *Education*: presumably military academy. *Career*: army officer, gentleman horse-racer, writer, and pacifist.

Little is known about Kurt von Tepper-Laski's early life. As a young aristocratic officer, he served with distinction in the Franco-Prussian War of 1870-71, but resigned from the army after receiving a disciplinary transfer for having refused to have a guard stand stiffly at attention before a young princess. As a private citizen, he soon gained national recognition as a steeplechase racer. For eight years in succession he won the Grand Prize of Karlshorst and became one of the most popular personalities in German and international equestrian sports.

Quaker-like in his attitude towards animals and humans, Tepper-Laski used his authority as a gentleman rider to promote peace and international causes. He worked for an agreement between France and Germany and in 1913 he helped finance a meeting in Brussels between French and German journalists. He also became an advocate of the Movement for Secession from the Church. In 1900 he helped organize, along with Bruno Wille and Wilhelm Bölsche, the Giordano Bruno League. Six years later, he participated in the founding of the peace-oriented society Deutsche Monistenbund (German Monist League), which was created by Ernst Haeckel and Wilhelm Ostwald.

Prior to the outbreak of war in Europe in 1914, Tepper-Laski made known his opposition to the German arms buildup and to Imperial foreign policy. In anticipation of a European war, he decisively spoke out against the arms bill of 1913 and forcefully challenged the Reichstag's unanimous decision to grant war credits in August 1914. When it became clear that neither the German Social Democratic party nor the Deutsche Friedensgesellschaft (German Peace Society) would stand firmly against the war, Tepper-Laski and *Otto Lehmann-Rüssbuldt decided to create an organization that would promote a rapid negotiated peace. In November 1914, together with *Albert Einstein, *Lilli Jannasch, and Ernst Reuter, they established the Bund Neues Vaterland (New Fatherland League). Tepper-Laski became the chairman of the group.

The following April, he took part in a conference of European pacifists at The Hague. Working with +Walther Schücking and influential British representatives, he sought to prepare the diplomatic ground for an end to the war. Unfortunately, the German foreign ministry refused to consider any move in this direction. A government newspaper, moreover labeled rumors about the German disposition towards peace as "foolish and malevolent inventions." In an attempt to clarify the matter, Tepper-Laski sent the paper a confidential letter in which he denounced the sabotage of peace attempts. The letter was also sent to the Chancellor of Germany and the members of the budget commission of the Reichstag. It appeared with the help of Karl Liebknecht under the title, "A Historical Document," at the end of June 1915 in the *Berner Tagwacht*.

As a result of his efforts, Tepper-Laski was arrested for "treason against the country." Although freed, he was subjected to constant official surveillance by postal authorities and was socially ostracized. At the same time, the military and the censorship officials prevented the Bund Neues Vaterland, which had developed into a resevoir of antiwar opponents, from doing any publicly effective work. Tepper-Laski increasingly held the German ruling elite responsible for the war and its prolongation. After 1918, however, he removed himself from politics for reasons of health and lived in seclusion until his death.

Bibliography:

A. *Erinnerungen* (Berlin, [1928]); *Rennsport und Engländer* (Berlin, 1915).

B. O. Lehmann-Russbüldt, "Der Republikaner Wilhelms II. Erinnerungen an Kurt von Tepper-Laski zu seinem 75. Geburtstag, " *Warte für Menschenrechte*, 5 (August 15, 1925); H. L. [Hans Leuss], "Kurt v. Tepper-Laski," *Die Welt am Montag*, 26 (August 9, 1920); Hans Wehberg, "Kurt v. Tepper-Laski 75 Jahre," *Die Friedenswarte*, 25 (1925), 275; Hans Wehberg, "Kurt v. Tepper-Laski 80 Jahre alt," *Die Friedenswarte*, 30 (1930), 275.

Helmut Donat
Trans. by Ruthann Richards

THIAUDIÈRE, Edmond (17 March 1837, Gencay, Vienne, France—1930, Asnières, Seine, France). *Education*: law, Univ. of Poitiers, 1857. *Career*: poet, creative writer, journalist, and peace activist.

A prolific author of poetry, novels, and works of philosophical morality, Edmond Thiaudière joined the peace movement in 1872 and served as secretary of the Société française pour l'arbitrage entre nations (French Society for International Arbitration) under the presidency of *Frédéric Passy for many years. In 1878 he took on the directorship of the Société d'alliance latine: L'Alouette which was founded to encourage closer ties among French, Italians, Spanish, Portuguese, and Latin American citizens for cultural and political reasons.

Among Thiaudière's more important contributions to the European peace movement was his proposal at the 1878 Peace Congress in Paris for the creation of a permanent forum for members of European parliaments. This idea, also proposed by *Eduard Loewenthal a few years earlier, was eventually realized in the creation of the Interparliamentary Union (1889). In 1878 Thiaudière was impatient with the slow, polite and, in his view, ineffective forms of propaganda which peace activists sustained. He saw the need for members of official parliamentary bodies to meet annually and find mutually acceptable ways to increase arbitration and decrease military spending. Following the creation of the Universal Peace Congress in 1889 and the establishment of the national association of French peace societies, he remained an active participant in national and international peace meetings. At the 1894 international meeting in Antwerp, he joined a small group which began active campaigning for closer liaisons with organized workers' and socialist associations. His many articles on peace questions appeared in *Les Etats-Unis d'Europe* and *La Paix par le Droit*.

Thiaudière's participation in the peace crusade reflected the personal philosophy which permeated all his writings: "think like a skeptic but act like a believer." His was a profoundly pessimistic morality and his writings, including a 10 volume work of aphorisms, revealed a healthy sense of paradox and contradiction. He was not at all surprised with the coming of war in 1914, but also never convinced that working to prevent war was the wrong thing to do. Ill health and old age reduced his activity severely in the years after World War I until his death. However, he had devoted about half a century of his life to the peace movement in Europe.

Bibliography:

A. *Un Colloque de Rois sur l'union européenne* (Paris, 1896); *La Conféderation française, forme nouvelle de gouvernement* (Paris, 1872); *La Dernière Bataille: Epophée prophetique de l'année 1909* (Paris, 1873); *Notes d'un pessimiste* (10 vols., Paris, 1886-1910).

B. Charles Richet, "Nos Grands Morts. Edmond Thiaudière," *Paix par le Droit*, 40 (Paris, 1930), 479-80; Péne Siefert, "Edmond Thiaudière et son devoir," *L'Aurore*, (August 3, 1903); "Edmond Thiaudière" in Alfred Fried, ed., *Handbuch der Friedensbewegung* (2nd ed., Berlin, 1913), II, 413.

Sandi E. Cooper

THIRRING, Hans (23 March 1888, Vienna—22 March 1976, Vienna). *Education*: Ph.D., Univ. of Vienna, 1911. *Career*: lecturer, theoretical physics, Univ. of Vienna, 1915-21, associate professor, 1921-27, professor, 1927-38, 1945-54; dean, Faculty of Philosophy, Univ. of Vienna, 1946-47; member, Austrian Academy of Sciences, 1947-76; member, Byndesrat (upper house of the Austrian parliament), 1957-63; vice-president, Austrian section of UNESCO, 1957-76; president, Austrian League of Human Rights, 1964-76.

Since the end of the Second World War, Han Thirring was the leading figure in the Austrian peace movement. As a physicist who enjoyed an international reputation for his scientific work, Thirring's voice carried special weight in the international discussion surrounding questions of disarmament. Like numerous young men of his generation, Thirring became a pacifist because of his experience as a soldier in World War I. He was inducted into the Austro-Hungarian army in 1915 and served in the military communications branch. After the war, in addition to his physics research (especially in the development of selenium cells), he committed himself with all of his energy to the peace movement both as a teacher and citizen. In 1930 he became a member of the Fédération internationale des droits de l'homme (International Federation of the Rights of Man) and was Austrian representative to the Rassemblement universal pour le paix (Universal Assembly for Peace) from 1936 to 1938. Because of his pacifist convictions, Thirring was relieved of his teaching post after Austria's incorporation into Nazi Germany in 1938.

Returning to the University of Vienna in 1945, Thirring again became active in the peace movement. He wrote numerous articles on disarmament and peace questions for Austrian, American, and other foreign newspapers and journals. His book, *Die Geschichte der Atombombe* (History of the Atom Bomb) (1947) warned of an atomic holocaust. Thirring was not satisfied solely with placing his knowledge as a physicist in the scales of the disarmament debate, but also attempted in his books *Homo Sapiens* (1948) and *Kunst des menschlichen Zusammenlebens* (*The Human Art of Living Together*) (1950) to present the psychological causes of political tensions and the possibilities for overcoming militaristic and nationalistic thinking. After the final liberation of Austria with the State Treaty of 1955, Thirring attempted to show the significance of an unarmed Austrian neutrality for disarmament in general. Corresponding with diplomats of both the superpowers and smaller nations, Thirring, despite the physical handicaps resulting from a stroke in 1968, personally campaigned for disarmament and the promotion of pacifist principles. Until his death, he was a model for the younger generation and a link between the old Austrian peace movement associated with *Bertha von Suttner and the peace activities of today's youth.

Bibliography:

A. *Atomkrieg und Weltpolitik* (Vienna, 1948); *Der Weltfriede als psychologisches Problem* (Vienna, 1946); *Die Geschichte der Atombombe* (Vienna, 1947); *Die Kunst des menschlichen Zusammenlebens* (Vienna, 1950), *Homo Sapiens, Vom National ismus zum; Weltbürgertum* (Vienna, 1948).

Fritz Fellner
Trans. by William L. Hopkins

THOMAS, Evan Welling (3 June 1890, Marion, OH—19 May 1974, Philadelphia, PA). *Education*: B.A., Princeton Univ., 1912; M.D., New York Univ., 1933. *Career*: medical faculty of New York University, professor of clinical medicine, 1948; consultant to various health organizations; after 1964, Medical

Director of the Children's Evaluation Unit, Institutes for Achievement of Human Potential; chair, War Resisters League in World War II; pacifist leader, activist, and theoretician.

During World War I, Evan Thomas was one of the band of absolutists who refused all service under military authority. Imprisoned at Fort Leavenworth for eighteen months, he and other conscientious objectors refused to obey prison regulations and, as a consequence, suffered solitary confinement. Thomas and his associates were chained to the bars of their cells in such a way that they could not sit down for eight to ten hours a day.

After his release, Thomas eventually decided on a medical career to exemplify pacifism as a constructive force. He became known as one of the leading experts on syphilis and its treatment. It might be said that he thought of his pacifist activism and his medical research and practice as two sides of the same coin.

Perhaps his short book, *The Positive Faith of Pacifism* (1942), written at the height of World War II and of his pacifist activism, best expressed Thomas' mature views. Reflecting on the origins of World War II, he asked whether the "fanaticism of a few dictators" could really be responsible for the conflict. He thought not. Instead, it was the institution of war itself which was responsible for much dictatorship, including the "totalitarian" variety. He went on to suggest that if the war continued to complete victory by one side or the other, European civilization would completely disintegrate. Responding to the contention that pacifists were merely negative, Thomas observed that there was nothing positive about being compelled to choose between the "immoral methods" of war and the authoritarianism of an "aggressive tyranny." The only hope for the world was to seek to overcome evil with good.

But how could this be done? Thomas emphasized that complete reliance could not be placed on politics, for politics necessarily tended to stress organization and organization—even for good ends—frequently stifled freedom and promoted corruption. To concentrate on politics and neglect other forms of action was to replace a stress on moral values with a "utopian fantasy."

What kind of faith was compatible with a pacifist outlook? It would, thought Thomas, embrace the notion of democracy, which rejects conformity and emphasizes compromise. One reason war was so utterly unacceptable for any end was that, as Thomas said in one of his writings, it represented "absolutism" and opposition to compromise. In modern times, democracy must include the notion of economic collectivism. But it must also spurn any tendency to make material values central. Workers' control in industry and the professions was very important. And Thomas stressed the close and organic relation between ends and means. For individuals to obey the behests of immoral organizations was to reject the faith of pacifism and surrender to "intellectual hocus-pocus" or "sheer cynicism."

How can good confront the inevitable evil of the world? If it cooperates with evil, it is denying its own being. If it uses the methods of evil to oppose evil, it intensifies the dominance of evil. Thomas thought that the way out was through the processes of nonviolent resistance. Refusal to cooperate with tyranny can never undermine the values of democracy. Once large numbers of persons support noncooperation with tyrannical rulers (often at great risk to themselves), neither foreign nor domestic tyranny could flourish. It was in this light, Thomas thought, that one had to view military conscription. Without conscription neither modern war nor tyranny would continue. While all people had to compromise at many points to make democracy work, there could be no compromise whatsoever with conscription.

According to Thomas, pacifist action was governed by values which were universal in authority because experience had proven their worth. One of the highest values was the search for truth, which was central to both science and true religion. Pacifist groups could, through their appeals to both truth and nonviolence, become the nuclei of a new and transformed society.

While never ceasing to be a pacifist, Thomas, during the latter period of his life, seemed to become uncertain about just how a world governed by pacifist values could be attained. Pacifists, moreover, were divided among themselves in terms of motivations and goals and this made for ineffectiveness. Considerations of this kind were spelled out in Thomas' resignation from the War Resisters League. In his letter of resignation, dated December 12, 1950, he still characterized war as utterly wrong morally, but did not see his "way clear" to work through either the League or any other pacifist organization. He continued to believe in nonviolent resistance but also thought that the time for it was "not yet."

In remarks at the War Registers League Executive Committee meeting on January 11, 1951, Thomas continued his comments on his resignation: "Are you going to withdraw from society or face it? . . . You can't be an anarchist rationally. It has never worked, we need organization, but organization is killing the humanity within us. I incline toward Toynbee, that we need a spiritual solution. . . . Nobody practices what they preach." There seemed to be a despairing note in his comments, a posing of dilemmas with few clues about responses or solutions.

Evan Thomas was the brother of *Norman Thomas, the socialist leader. The two were close to each other, although differing at points in their outlooks, with Norman having more confidence in the political process than Evan. Norman, moreover, gave a reluctant "critical support" to World War II after American entry, while Evan's position has been characterized by a close associate as one of "non-obstructive opposition."

Physically, Evan Thomas was a striking person. He was six feet seven inches tall and looked out at the world through piercing eyes. Despite his genuine modesty, he was a commanding figure.

Bibliography:

A. *The Positive Faith of Pacifism* (New York, 1942); *The Way to Freedom* (New York, 1943).

B. Charles Chatfield, *The Radical 'No'—Correspondence and Writing of Evan Thomas on War* (New York, 1974).

C. Some material in Swarthmore College Peace Collection.

Mulford Q. and Marjorie H. Sibley

THOMAS, Norman (20 November 1884, Marion, OH—19 December 1968, Cold Spring Harbor, NY). *Education*: B.A., Princeton Univ., 1905; B.D., Union Theological Seminary, 1911. *Career*: ordained ministry, Presbyterian Church, 1911; demitted ministry, 1931; secretary of Fellowship of Reconciliation, 1917-21; editor, *World Tomorrow*, 1918-21; associate editor, *The Nation*, 1921-22; co-executive director, League for Industrial Democracy, 1922-38; Socialist party candidate for president, 1928, 1932, 1936, 1940, 1944, 1948; chair, Postwar World Council; founder and co-chair, Turn Toward Peace; Socialist party leader and author.

At Union Theological Seminary, Norman Thomas was influenced by the Christian Socialism of Walter Rauschenbusch. Furthermore, as a young Presbyterian minister in New York City, he was moved by the economic and social suffering he witnessed. World War I galvanized his idealistic social conscience and his religious pacifism into action. He helped form the American Union Against Militarism (AUAM) to combat President +Woodrow Wilson's preparedness campaign; joined the pacifist Fellowship of Reconciliation, becoming its executive secretary and editor of its journal, *World Tomorrow*; and participated with *Roger Baldwin in the fight waged by the AUAM's Civil Liberties Bureau against the wartime suppression of civil liberties.

Thomas's brother, *Evan, was imprisoned as a conscientious objector and Evan's treatment in prison intensified Norman's hatred of war and its consequences. Moving in a politically radical direction, Thomas was part of a group of pacifist radicals including, *Kirby Page, *Devere Allen, and *A. J. Muste, who were seeking explanations of war's underlying causes. Gradually, Thomas began to question the economic institutions fostering war. This led him to support *Morris Hillquit's Socialist antiwar mayoralty campaign, to join the Socialist-organized People's Council for Democracy and Peace, and in 1918 to join the Socialist party. Political radicalization and the ease with which religious leaders supported World War I contributed to Thomas's break with organized religion. He retained, however, the moral conscience which had first brought him to the ministry; indeed, that conscience remained the dominant element in his socialism and pacifism.

Thomas rose quickly within the Socialist party in the 1920s while, at the same time, addressing issues raised by World War I. In 1923 he published a sympathetic book on conscientious objectors. Although no longer an officer in the Fellowship of Reconciliation, he continued to help edit *World Tomorrow* and to participate with his fellow pacifist radicals in the search for nonviolent methods that would bring fundamental economic and social change. As a leader of the Socialist party, Thomas spent much of his time in the early 1930s absorbed by intense party in-fighting. But through his writings and his example, he helped to keep the antiwar perspective dominant within the Socialist party. The 1934 Socialist party Declaration of Principles was written by his close associate and fellow pacifist, Devere Allen. Thomas fully supported the Declaration's call for "massed war resistance" and its threat of a general strike in case of war. In the face of criticisms from the "old guard" within the party, Thomas defended the threat as a necessary expression of the Socialist commitment to resist capitalist-inspired conflicts.

Inevitably, philosophical and practical problems developed when Thomas tried to reconcile absolute pacifism and class conflict, or to fight illegitimate coercion while developing legitimate methods of nonviolent pressure. The Spanish Civil War caused a major crisis of loyalties for Thomas and led him to drop his absolute pacifism. Criticized by his old friend *John Haynes Holmes, Thomas responded that he could not conceive of a nonviolent method of defeating Francisco Franco. Thomas's break with pacifism, while final, was less than thorough. His opposition to war—"organized murder" he called it in his last book—remained paramount. During the debates on foreign policy in the 1930s, Thomas supported U.S. neutrality legislation, except for the Spanish arms embargo. He argued that, while neutrality legislation was an incomplete answer to capitalism's wars, it was still useful for preventing American entry. International developments and Roosevelt's military build-up persuaded Thomas of the necessity for the Socialist party to take the lead in an antiwar, antipreparedeness campaign. The Keep America Out of War Committee was launched in 1938, but financial difficulties and divisions within the antiwar forces prevented its growth. The outbreak of World War II increased Thomas' fears of American involvement. As a result, he agreed to appear on programs sponsored by the newly organized America First Commitee. Thomas was able to reach large numbers with his antiwar message, but had no control over the conservative and reactionary elements that came to dominate that organization.

Between 1939 and 1941, Thomas was in the forefront of the opposition to all-out aid to the Allies, the draft, and to "armament economics." He feared that American entry into the war would turn the country fascist. After the Pearl Harbor attack, however, Thomas steered the Socialist party to a position of "critical support." He was convinced that continued opposition to the war was futile; at the same time, he wanted to prevent support from becoming approval of the capitalist system. Through the newly formed Post-War Council, Thomas actively opposed the government's internment of Japanese-Americans and sought methods to prevent World War II from leading to World War III.

In the post-World War II period, Thomas faced the dilemma of many Socialists. His deep opposition to communism and Soviet imperialism led him to domestic and international activities that sought to reduce communist influence. Thomas supported the Korean War, and his criticisms of American foreign policy were framed within a pro-Western context. Nevertheless, he opposed capitalist imperialism, Western power politics, and the American support of reactionary dictators. He was increasingly frightened by the arms race, by the militaristic mentality that pervaded the West, by the "military-industrial complex," and by violations of civil liberties in the name of anticommunism.

His writings in the postwar period argued for strengthening the United Nations and for international economic planning in order to reduce the causes of war. Horrified by the dropping of the atomic bomb on Hiroshima and Nagasaki, Thomas urged steps toward disarmament and disengagement in order to avoid a nuclear war. He was active through the Post-War Council, the National Commitee for a Sane Nuclear Policy, and Turn Toward Peace in organizing disarmament conferences, antinuclear testing demonstrations, and in helping foster alternatives to the Cold War. During his last years Thomas was absorbed in preventing thermonuclear war and in castigating American policy in Vietnam. Blind and increasingly feeble, Thomas continued to write and to speak at antiwar rallies and forums.

Norman Thomas' contributions to the peace movement do not derive from the originality of his proposed tactics or his writings. By the late 1930s, he and the Socialist party had backed off from their early threats of a general strike. His tactical strategy—whether it was his own independent campaigns or his later support for Eugene McCarthy in 1968—was mainly political. His writings warned of the dangers and insanity of war, and they justified civil disobedience when it was nonviolent, principled, and directed at unjust racial laws and military conscription. But Thomas broke no theoretical or practical ground in this area. What made him such a powerful force for world peace—what gave him his power, his courage, and his force—was his social conscience and the resulting vision of a better world. He recognized that an unjust world can not be a peaceful world, and he continually sought to alleviate domestic and international injustice. An admirer of Wendell Phillips, Norman Thomas was driven by the same kind of inner conscience. When he spoke "truth to power," he did so with an eloquence and force that gave those seeking a peaceful world new hope and inspiration.

Bibliography:

A. *America's Way Out* (New York, 1931); *Appeal to the Nations* (New York, 1947); *The Choices* (New York, 1969); *The Conscientious Objector in America* (New York, 1923); *Keep America Out of War*, with Bertram D. Wolfe (New York, 1939); *The Prerequisites for Peace* (New York, 1959); *War: No Glory, No Profit, No Need* (New York, 1935).

B. Harry Fleischman, *Norman Thomas* (New York, 1964); Bernard Johnpell, *Pacifist's Progress: Norman Thomas and the Decline of American Socialism* (Chicago, 1970); W. A. Swanberg, *Norman Thomas* (New York, 1976); Frank A. Warren, *An Alternative Vision: The Socialist Party in the 1930s* (Bloomington, IN, 1974).

C. Norman Thomas Papers, New York Public Library; Socialist Party Papers, Duke University Library.

Frank A. Warren

THOMPSON, George (18 June 1804, Liverpool, England—7 October 1878, Leeds, England). *Career*: Member of Parliament (Tower Hamlets), 1847-52; abolitionist and peace activist.

Though George Thompson was closely linked with the antislavery movement in both Great Britain and the United States, he, like other abolitionists, had strong ties to the peace movement. He was an advocate of nonresistance. No matter what the provocation, individuals, as well as nations, should not react to aggression in a war-like manner. When criticized for advocating immediate slave emancipation which would lead, it was feared, to a servile revolt, Thompson answered that it was not the slaves but the masters who were to be feared. For in all nations where slavery existed, there had been a history of wars and violence. To do away with slavery would be to curb the aggressive acts of masters; slaves, for the most part, behaved in a peaceful manner.

During visits to the United States in 1834-35 and 1851, and through voluminous correspondence, Thompson helped both the nonresistant wing of the American peace movement and the antislavery movement. After his second visit, he served as an official delegate of the American Anti-Slavery Society at the London Peace Conference of July 1851. However, on his third trip in 1863-67, Thompson, like his close friend *William L. Garrison, supported the American Civil War. That war, he believed, was a just one, for all other alternatives had failed to bring about emancipation. At the end of the Civil War, Thompson was honored by President Abraham Lincoln, who invited him to be present when the American flag was raised once again at Fort Sumter.

Thompson also worked for the peace movement in England. In 1849 he spoke in favor of international arbitration at a mass meeting in London's Exeter Hall. At that time he was a Member of Parliament from London's Tower Hamlets (1847-52). He supported the Parliamentary motion of *Richard Cobden which called on the British Government to use arbitration in international disputes. Thompson's contribution to peace continued during the Crimean War. Organized efforts to prevent the war had failed so peace groups came together in the End-the-War League. They distributed his speech "Stop the War" which had been delivered at a meeting of the British Institution in October 1855.

Born in Liverpool into a poor family of Methodist background, Thompson's oratorical skills won him many admirers. The other reform causes he worked for were the National Parliamentary Reform League (Chartists) and the Anti-Corn Law League. He was also a founder of the British India Association.

Not being independently wealthy like so many of the British reformers of that era, Thompson's devotion to worthy causes left him almost destitute in 1870.

His comrades in Great Britain and the United States raised a testimonial in his honor. Though mostly remembered for his work against slavery, Thompson was diligent in his pursuit of the cause of peace.

Bibliography:

A. *Stop the War: Speech delivered at a meeting of the British Institution, Cowper St., October 17, 1855* (London, 1855).

B. DNB, XIX, 691; *Harper's Weekly*, December 21, 1878; NYT, October 14, 1878.

Edith F. Hurwitz

THOREAU, Henry David (12 July 1817, Concord, MA—6 May 1862, Concord). *Education*: B.A., Harvard Coll., 1837. *Career*: writer, lecturer, naturalist, and day-laborer.

Although regarded as a major American writer by twentieth-century literary historians and critics, Henry David Thoreau's reputation during his own lifetime was meager. He published only two books before he died; the first went almost entirely unsold and the second was out of print by 1859. Thoreau's other books as well as his letters, poems, and twenty-volumes of journals, were published posthumously. In addition to the two books that appeared while he was alive, he also published a number of essays in contemporary periodicals; however, none was more ignored than the essay now widely known as ''Civil Disobedience,'' which ultimately linked him to an international tradition of nonviolent passive resistance.

''Civil Disobedience'' did not appear under that title until 1866. Thoreau first delivered it as a lecture in 1848 on ''The Relation of the Individual to the State'' and subsequently published it in 1849 as ''Resistance to Civil Government.'' The incident that led up to Thoreau's writing of ''Civil Disobedience'' was his arrest and jailing for one night for refusing to pay his poll tax, a symbolic action designed to protest the government's toleration and support of slavery. In the essay, Thoreau also objected to the Mexican War and insisted that the country's true patriots should not lend support to civil laws that violate the higher laws of one's conscience. He insisted that because moral law superseded civil law, it was the individual's right and duty to break the law when obedience would result in an injustice or moral wrong. Rather than be complicit in supporting an unjust government, Thoreau argued that civil disobedience could be an effective means to reform unjust laws.

''Civil Disobedience'' had little impact on the issues of his day. Thoreau vigorously opposed slavery and the Mexican War, but he never formally aligned himself with abolitionists or pacifists nor did they appropriate ''Civil Disobedience'' as a useful articulation of their positions. However, in the twentieth century, ''Civil Disobedience'' became one of the most famous essays ever written by an American. Thoreau's ideas were not original (many of the same principles are to be found in Sophocles' *Antigone*, for example) but the quality of his prose has proven inspirational to numerous individuals who share his belief that ''it is not desirable to cultivate a respect for the law, so much as for the right.'' ''Civil Disobedience'' was quoted and given international currency by *Mahatma Gandhi's campaigns of nonviolent resistance in South Africa and India, and during World War II the Danish resistance used the strategies of civil disobedience against Nazi occupation forces. In the United States the essay was quoted during demonstrations by protestors such as Upton Sinclair, *Norman Thomas, and *Emma Goldman, but the most famous American practitioner of nonviolence to invoke Thoreau was *Martin Luther King, Jr., who helped to familiarize civil rights protesters of the 1960s with ''Civil Disobedience.'' Later in the sixties activists protesting the Vietnam War and the production of nuclear weapons also quoted Thoreau as an authoritative voice from the usable past.

As useful as ''Civil Disobedience'' has been for twentieth-century activists eager to quote Thoreau in support of a particular reform movement, the essay is not representative of Thoreau's attitudes concerning the means by which reform can be achieved. He was not a pacifist. Even in ''Civil Disobedience,'' he questioned whether a ''peaceable revolution'' of the kind he described ''is possible,'' and in two important but less well-known essays, ''Slavery in Massachusetts'' (1854) and ''A Plea for Captain Brown'' (1859), he, along with many of his contemporaries, moved toward an acceptance of violence as the only effective way to end slavery in the United States.

Thoreau was neither a pacifist nor a social activist. Most characteristically he preferred nature to politics. His Transcendental values tended to be ahistorical and apolitical, and the moments when he did address himself to political issues he was often inconsistent in his attitudes. Nevertheless, he has been influential and highly quotable for readers who have read him selectively.

Bibliography:

A. The collected works in *The Writings of Henry David Thoreau* (Boston, 1906) will eventually be superseded by *The Writings of Henry D. Thoreau* (Princeton, 1971-), a more complete edition that incorporates modern textual principles.

B. Walter Harding, *The Days of Henry Thoreau* (New York, 1965); Walter Harding and Michael Meyer, *The New Thoreau Handbook* (New York, 1980); John Hicks, ed. *Thoreau in Our Season* (Amherst, MA, 1966); Michael Meyer, *Several More Lives to Live: Thoreau's Political Reputation in America* (Westport, Ct, 1977).

C. Major manuscript holdings include the Huntington Library, New York Public Library, Houghton Library, and the Pierpont Morgan Library; for a complete listing, see William L. Howarth *The Literary Manuscripts of Henry David Thoreau* (Columbus, Ohio, 1974).

Michael Meyer

THRASOLT, Ernst [pseud. of Josef Maria Tressel] (12 May 1878, Beurig near Trier, Germany—20 January 1945, Berlin). *Education*: Catholic theological seminary, Trier, ordination as a priest, 1904. *Career*: parish priest, Haag near Morbach, 1908-15; spiritual rector, St. Josefsheim orphan asylum, Berlin-Wannsee, 1918-45; editor, *Efeuranken*, 1909-13; founder and editor, *Das Heilige Feuer*, 1913-30; editor, *Vom frohen Leben*, 1921-33; permanent contributor,

Katholischen Kirchenblatt, Berlin 1932-45; priest, cultural reformer, editor, and pacifist writer.

Before World War I Ernst Thrasolt served as a priest in various places and as an editor of a periodical for young people. When war broke out in 1914, he was convinced that Germany was conducting a just war against its enemies. During the war, he was assigned the task of imparting "patriotic teachings" to German troops in Belgium, France, Latvia, and Lithuania, and he headed a mobile library unit at the front. Despite his approval of the war, his experience at the front and the defeat of 1918 turned him into a staunch opponent of war.

Before 1914 Thrasolt was well-known as a Catholic lyric poet—he won the University of Würzburg lyric poetry prize in 1911—and as one of the leading minds of the Catholic youth movement. The periodical, *Das Heilige Feuer*, strove for a religious and liturgical renewal, a reform of life and culture through a return to nature and to German ideas. After the war, Thrasolt combined cultural and religious reform with pacifism. In 1921 he established the periodical *Vom frohen Leben* and tied it closely to the Grossdeutsche Volksgemeinschaft (Great-German People's Community) led by Nikolaus Ehlen. The program of Ehlen's organization was reflected in the subtitle of *Vom frohen Leben*: "The Essential Individual Monthly Pamphlet for the German Way of Life Through Simplicity, Spirituality and Fraternity." The Grossdeutsche Volksgemenschaft took part in the peace congresses arranged by *Marc Sangnier, and Thrasolt attracted leading representatives of the German peace movement, including *Friedrich W. Foerster, as contributors to *Vom frohen Leben*. The journal soon assumed a leading role in the peace movement and most of Thrasolt's articles and essays on questions of war and peace appeared in it, many of them under pseudonyms: Hans Heiler, Christan Imboden, Bruder Minimus, Saulus, Gottschalk, Eremita, and Adam Christ.

Thrasolt firmly opposed the construction of a new armored cruiser in 1928 and throughout the 1920s he challenged the armaments industry, military training, and German fascism. He spoke before the Deutsche Freidensgesellschaft (German Peace Society) and the Deutschen Friedenskartell (German Peace Cartel), an umbrella organization for peace and antiwar groups. With *Helene Stöcker and *Kurt Hiller, Thrasolt constituted the executive committee of the Internationale der Kriegsdienstgegner (War Resisters League). His criticism of the indecisive policy of the Center party on questions of peace led him to support *Vitus Heller's Christlich-Sozialen-Reichpartei (CSRP), the only pronounced pacifist party in the Weimar Republic. Thrasolt's particular concern was the reconciliation of Germany and Poland, leading the Polish Bishop, Dr. A. Hlond, to praise the sincere and courageous peace work of the *Vom frohen Leben*.

Thrasolt's pacifism was marked more by the emotional character of his speeches and his personal example than by its analytical clarity. He demonstrated an almost anachronistic hostility toward industry and offered few solutions for the social problems he attributed to the absence of peace. Yet, he strove to understand peace not as an abstract task but as concrete social action. Consequently, he endeavored to build a Christfrieden (Christian Peace) settlement in Uckermark and beginning in 1924, published from time to time the series *Christentum und Krieg* (*Christianity and War*), which appeared as a supplement to *Vom frohen Leben*. He also published the series *Menschheitskämpfer* (*Fighter for Humanity*), which was edited by W. Hammerath.

On May 6, 1933, shortly after Adolf Hitler assumed power, the German government prohibited the publication of *Vom frohen Leben*. Reinhard Heydrich, the Gestapo chief, demanded that the Bishop of Berlin dismiss Thrasolt as a contributor to the Berlin *Katholischen Kirchenblatt*, a Catholic paper. The Bishop refused the demand. During the Nazi period, Thrasolt hid Jews in his house in Schildrow at the edge of Berlin. The Gestapo searched his residence numerous times, but no incriminating evidence ever was found. Thrasolt died in Hedwig hospital in Berlin after a serious illness.

Bibliography:

A. *Dr. Carl Sonnenschein. Der Mensch und sein Werk* (Munich/Kempten, 1930); *Geistliche Kriegslieder* (Trier, 1915); *Das Martyrologium Germaniens* (Dülmen, 1939); *In memoriam. Toten-Gedächtnislieder* (Leipzig, 1922); *Nicht Krieg! Christi Friede. Ein Sprechchor* (Berlin, 1930); *De profundis. Geistliche Gedichte* (Munich/Kempten, 1908).

B. Elisabeth Antkowiak, *Herr, meiner Halbheit mach ein Ende! Aus dem Werke Ernst Thrasolts* (Leipzig, 1962); Franz Heurich, *Die Bunde katholischer Jugendbewegung* (Munich, 1968); Walter Ottendorff-Simrock, *Es geht die Zeit sur Ewigkeit. Eine Begegnung mit Ernst Thrasolt* (Ratingen, 1959); Dieter Riesenberger, *Die katholische Friedesbewegung in der Weimarer Republik* (Düsseldorf, 1977).

Dieter Riesenberger
Trans. by Solomon Wank

TITULESCU, Nicolae. See *Biographical Dictionary of Internationalists*.

TOBAR, Carlos R. (1854, Quito, Equador—12 May 1920, Barcelona, Spain). *Education*: Doctor of Medicine and Doctor of Natural Science, Central Univ., Quito, 1878. *Career*: professor, university administrator, physician, diplomat, and man of letters.

Although Carlos R. Tobar received both a doctorate in medicine and a doctorate in natural science, he began his professional career teaching literature at the Central University in Quito. In 1880 he became dean of the School of Letters and in 1891 rector of the university. Very early in his life, Tobar established a reputation as a man of science and letters in both his native Ecuador and Spain. Tobar was equally recognized in diplomatic and political life. He was a diplomat in Chile, Spain, Argentina, and Brazil. He represented Ecuador at various international medical conferences. On the domestic front he occupied various ministries and in 1900 became vice president of the Senate. With the fall of the Eloy Alfaro government in 1912, Tobar chose self-exile and died in Spain.

While an accomplished man of many talents, Tobar did not achieve truly historical significance until after his retirement. In 1907 the United States and

Mexico convened a conference in Washington of Central American republics to deal with the problem of chronic wars and revolutions in the area. It was during this meeting that the retired Ecuadorian diplomat proposed a policy of collective nonrecognition aimed at denying legitimacy to governments that came to power by nondemocratic means. The Tobar Doctrine sought to reduce the threat of revolution and civil war in the Inter-American system by emphasizing the need for all governments collectively to seek the establishment of constitutionalism and democracy. Under this doctrine, governments would not be recognized if they came to power by any one of three applications of the use of force: 1) through internal revolt; 2) through invasion by rebels from outside the national territory; 3) through the direct intervention of neighboring states.

Because of its emphasis on ''diplomatic intervention,'' the Tobar Doctrine presented a conflict of two basic principles of the Inter-American system: 1) the promotion of representative democracy, and 2) the principle of nonintervention in the internal affairs of other nation-states. The question raised was how could representative democracy be promoted without violating the principle of nonintervention? Throughout history most Latin American states have taken an absolutist position against intervention in the internal affairs of other countries. However, at times some states have adopted a more complex view when questions of democracy were raised, willing to allow some sort of collective intervention to take place where undemocratic regimes were involved.

In 1930 the Mexican Foreign Minister Genaro Estrada directly challenged the Tobar Doctrine. Estrada declared that governments should refrain from formal acts of recognition in order to avoid judging other governments. In other words, recognition should be automatic; recognition does not bestow approval but merely acknowledges de facto control over a people and a territory. The Estrada Doctrine did not consider how a government came to power.

The Tobar Doctrine, incorporated into the Central American peace treaties of 1907 and 1923, was officially repudiated in 1934 when all the parties to the treaties recognized the Maximiliano Martínez regime in El Salvador after it came to power through the use of force. Although no longer officially accepted, the doctrine's emphasis on peaceful change still has significant support in Latin America.

Bibliography:

A. *Quand viendra la Paix* (Barcelona, 1918).

Paul E. Masters, Jr.

TOEWS, David (9 February 1870, Lysanderhoek, Trakt, Province of Samara, Russia—25 February 1947, Rosthern, Saskatchewan, Canada). *Education*: Halstead Seminary, Kansas, 1887-90, 1882-93; Winnipeg Collegiate Institute, 1896-97; Normal School, Winnipeg, 1897-98. *Career*: teacher in Manitoba and Saskatchewan schools, intermittently between 1891-1923; elder, Rosenort Mennonite Church, 1913-46; chairman and chief executive officer of the Canadian Mennonite Board of Colonization, 1922-46.

With the coming of universal military service to European states, the family of David Toews, like many other Mennonite families migrated first eastward (from Prussia to European Russia in 1869 and to Asiatic Russia in 1880) and then westward (to the United States in 1884) in search of complete exemption from military service.

These family convictions and experiences undoubtedly contributed to David Toews himself becoming a champion of conscientious objection to war service on religious grounds. During both world wars, Toews led Mennonite efforts to protect conscientious objectors (COs). There were general and specific protections in the law for Mennonite COs, but the interpretation of the law had to be clarified, administrative procedures that respected the law had to be insisted upon, and public opinion that ignored, distorted, or resisted the law had to be dealt with in the public forum. Additionally, in World War II, Toews had to negotiate alternative service under civilian direction for some 7,500 COs and had to lead appeals against judgments that seemed unfair.

Twenty thousand Mennonite emigrés of the Bolshevik revolution arrived in Canada in the interwar period under the auspices of the Canadian Mennonite Board of Colonization of which Toews was the founding chairman. Inasmuch as these people brought with them the experience of the medical corps in the Great War and more liberal attitudes generally, Toews' task, in which he also distinguished himself, required not only negotiations with governments but mediation among the Mennonite people themselves in order to arrive at the best possible common approach. He also led his people in a concerted relief action for war sufferers during World War II.

Bibliography:

B. Frank H. Epp, *Education with a Plus: The Story of Rosthern Junior College*. (Waterloo, 1975); Frank H. Epp, *Mennonite Exodus: The Rescue and Resettlement of the Russian Mennonites Since the Communist Revolution* (Altona, Manitoba, 1962).

Frank H. Epp

TOEWS, John A. (15 August 1912, Rueckenau, Molotschna, Russia—13 January 1979, Winnipeg, Manitoba, Canada). *Education*: B.A., Univ. of Saskatchewan, 1947; B.D., United Coll., 1950; M.A., Univ. of Manitoba, 1957; Ph.D., Univ. of Minnesota, 1964. *Career*: teacher, Mennonite Brethren Bible Coll., Winnipeg, 1947-67, 1976-79, president, 1956-63; preacher, writer, and church worker.

At the time of his death, John A. Toews was moderator of the General Conference of Mennonite Brethren Churches in North America, the third largest Mennonite body on the continent. He served his denomination and also Mennonites generally, as a teacher, preacher, and writer on theological and historical themes.

During World War II he became a "camp pastor" to Canadian conscientious objectors serving in alternative service camps. Young men who came into contact with Toews during this period say that through his ministry, he helped them gain a fuller historical and theological understanding of the nonresistant position for which they stood. For Toews, nonresistance was not a doctrine created only at wartime, but was an integral part of the teaching of the New Testament, vital to the Christian life.

His experience with the alternative service program prompted him to prepare a theological treatise on pacifism, *True Nonresistance Through Christ* (1955), which provided a detailed discussion on the biblical teachings against war and violence. This work was subsequently translated into the German and Japanese languages. Toews' M.A. thesis in history was a description and interpretation of the alternative service program and was published as *Alternative Service in Canada during World War II* (1959).

When his own church considered dropping the Mennonite name, Toews objected strongly on the grounds that surrendering the name might mean surrendering the doctrine of peace and antimilitarism which he believed was synonymous with Mennonitism. He considered nonresistance to be one of the most significant New Testament messages to Mennonites and Christians in general.

Bibliography:

A. *Alternative Service in Canada during World War II*. (Winnipeg, 1959); *A History of the Mennonite Brethren Church* (Fresno, CA, 1975); *People of the Way* (Winnipeg, 1981); *True Nonresistance Through Christ* (Hillsboro, KS, 1955).

B. Harold Janz, ''Toews had a vision for the church,'' *Mennonite Brethren Herald*, 18 (January 19, 1979), 12-14.

Frank H. Epp

TOLLER, Ernst (1 December 1893, Somatschin, Germany—22 May 1939, New York). *Education*: studies at universities of Grenoble, Munich, and Heidelberg. *Career*: president, Central Committee of First Bavarian Soviet Republic, 1919; commander, Red Army, 1919, political activist, dramatist, and poet.

A student in France at the outbreak of World War I, Ernst Toller returned immediately to his native Germany and joined an artillery division in Munich. His war experiences, in Alsace-Lorraine and at the front, impressed upon him the horrors of trench warfare and the inequalities within the military. Discharged for medical reasons after thirteen months at the front, Toller took up his studies in Munich in May 1916, where he nurtured his literary ambitions among the Expressionists. Haunted by images of battle, Toller began, with other young German intellectuals, to seek an end to the war. At Heidelberg he founded the ''Young Germans' Cultural and Political Union,'' dedicated to international conciliation and the elimination of poverty. Without poverty, Toller believed, there would be no cause for imperialism or for war. When this and similar societies were banned by the military authorities, Toller fled to Berlin to avoid a compulsory return to active service.

In Berlin Toller came into contact with the German workers' movement and the socialist critique of war. He followed *Kurt Eisner, the pacifist and Independent Socialist leader, to Munich where he attended Eisner's antiwar discussions. Toller joined Eisner in supporting the munitions workers' strike for peace in 1918 by speaking and by distributing pacifist passages from his unfinished play *Die Wandlung* (*Transfiguration*). Arrested after the collapse of the strike, Toller was sentenced to a year in military prison for writing a strike pamphlet.

In prison Toller read the socialist theorists and adopted their analysis of war as the inevitable outcome of capitalist economic relations. After his release and a short period in a reserve battalion, he joined Eisner in Munich in November, 1918. The Bavarian Revolution of November 7 raised Eisner to the presidency of the Bavarian Republic and Toller to the deputy presidency. After Eisner's assassination, Toller, who shared Eisner's belief that only a revolution could create a state and a society that would outlaw war, was appointed president of the Central Committee of the First Soviet Republic and was active in organizing resistance to the counterrevolution under the Communist-dominated Second Soviet Republic.

A revolutionary before he was a pacifist, as Toller explained at his subsequent trial, he renounced his vow never to carry arms and accepted the post of commander of the Red Army. He envisioned the Red Army as a purely revolutionary force, regulated by the free will and understanding of all its members, and Toller attributed its subsequent lack of discipline to the deep imprint of German militarism on the national consciousness. With the defeat of the Bavarian revolution on April 30, Toller went into hiding. Captured and tried for high treason by a court-martial, Toller was sentenced to five years fortress-imprisonment. During that time he wrote several plays that were produced in Germany. In *Masse-Mensch* (*Man and the Masses*) (1924), he reconsidered his ethical conflict over revolutionary violence and concluded that all force, in whatever cause, must be rejected. At the end of five years, Toller was released and sent over the border into Saxony.

In 1934 Toller left Germany for exile in England, and settled in America in 1936. His final two plays, *No More Peace!* (1937) and *Pastor Hall* (1939), were statements against Nazi totalitarianism and the dangerous Nazi obsession with war. On the eve of World War II, Toller committed suicide in New York City.

Bibliography:

A. *Das Bekenntnis zum Übernationalem* (Vienna, 1933); *Briefe aus dem Gefängnis* (Amsterdam, 1935, Eng. trans., *Letters from Prison*, London, 1936); *Eine Jugend in Deutschland* (Amsterdam, 1933, Eng. trans., *I was a German*, London, 1934); *Hinkemann* (Potsdam, 1924, Eng. trans., *Brokenbrow*, London, 1926); *Masse-Mensch* (Berlin, 1924, Eng. trans., *Man and the Masses*, New York, 1924); *No More Peace!* (New York, 1937); *Pastor Hall* (New York, 1939); *Das Schwalbenbuch* (Potsdam, 1924, Eng. trans., *The Swallow Book*, London, 1924); *Die Wandlung* (Potsdam, 1918, Eng. trans., *Transfiguration*, New York, 1941).

B. Thomas Bütow, *Der Konflikt zwischen Revolution und Pazifismus in Werk Ernst Toller* (Hamburg, 1975); Malcolm Pittock, *Ernst Toller* (Boston, 1979); John Spalek,

Ernst Toller and His Critics (Charlottesville, VA, 1968); W. A. Willibrand, *Ernst Toller and His Ideology* (Iowa City, 1945).

Michael Dintenfass and Polly Morris

TOLSTOY, Lev (Leo) Nikolayevich (9 September 1828, Yasnaya Polyana, Tula Province, Russia—20 November 1910, Astapovo Station, Lipetsk Province, Russia). *Education*: private tutors; studies at Univ. of Kazan, 1844-47. *Career*: writer and philosopher.

By the time he reached his fiftieth birthday, Leo Tolstoy had established himself in his homeland as one of the three greatest living Russian writers, along with Fedor Dostoevsky and Ivan Turgenev; and within another ten years his fame had spread throughout Europe and the Americas. His reputation as a literary artist rests primarily on his two great novels, *War and Peace* (1863-69) and *Anna Karenina* (1875-77). Soon after finishing the second of these he underwent a profound religious crisis that gave a new direction to his life. Paradoxically, this crisis came at the very time when Tolstoy enjoyed almost all the worldly blessings that life could offer. Only one thing was lacking: the meaning of life itself. As a product of eighteenth-century rationalism and nineteenth-century science, Tolstoy could accept no religious dogmas that he believed incompatible with reason; and yet he could make no sense out of the universe if human life was nothing more than a biochemical process that ended in death.

A careful study of the New Testament finally brought Tolstoy out of his despair and led him to create his own kind of Christian anarchism, based primarily on his interpretation of Jesus' Sermon on the Mount. In *A Confession* (1879-80), one of the five principal milestones along the path of his spiritual pilgrimage, Tolstoy described the despair that had brought him close to suicide, and then drew the conclusion that "I had erred not so much because I thought incorrectly as because I lived badly." In *What I Believe* (1882-84), he set about putting his life in order and summarized the teachings of Jesus in five commandments: (1) do not be angry; (2) do not lust; (3) do not give away future control of your actions by swearing; (4) do not resist evil; and (5) love your enemies. In *What Then Must We Do?* (1882-86) he focused the light of his new Christian convictions upon the problems of wealth and poverty, money and property, luxury and idleness. In his unduly neglected little essay *On Life* (1888), devoted to the problem of death, Tolstoy argued that our existence in this physical universe has meaning only as part of a larger spiritual life before birth and after death, in which he accepts the possibility of other physical existences, in keeping with the Buddhist conception of reincarnation. In *The Kingdom of God Is Within You* (1894), perhaps the best known and most powerful of all his philosophical works, Tolstoy's Christian anarchist principle of nonresistance led him to reject all violence and all institutions resting on violence, including governments, law courts, police, prisons, armies, and even private property and money.

During the last thirty years of his life, Tolstoy was a prophet in the genuine

Old Testament tradition, fearlessly speaking truth to power wherever it resided, whether in government or in wealth. With his typically Russian tendency to take a negative view of compromise and a positive view of maximalism, Tolstoy's powerful writings can irritate and occasionally exasperate even as they stimulate and inspire. His worldwide impact has been twofold in nature. As a literary artist he has influenced the thought and works of innumerable writers, from Finland and France to Portugal and Spain, and from North and South America to Japan. As a religious and social prophet he has influenced the personal lives of thousands of individuals all over the world, including such prominent civic and political leaders as *Ernest Howard Crosby, a former member of the New York State Legislature and a judge on the International Court, whose life was transformed by reading a copy of Tolstoy's *What I Believe*; *Thomas G. Masaryk, the founder of the Czechoslovak Republic, who recommended Tolstoy's "new modern religion" as the most effective remedy for the persistent crisis of modern civilization; two influential Bulgarian statesmen, Naycho Tsanov and Dimitur Dragiev; and the peace leaders *Albert Škarvan in Slovakia and *Eugen Šchmitt in Hungary.

While Tolstoy made no effort to found an organized movement, his teachings led great numbers of his followers to establish Tolstoyan colonies both within Russia and abroad, notably in Bulgaria but also in Holland, England, the United States, and even as far away as Chile. Most of these were short-lived and many were outright failures; but it is now known from recent émigré sources that in Soviet Russia itself, despite persecution, imprisonment, and even executions, thousands of persons continued to follow Tolstoy's teachings, and in the 1920s there existed at least a hundred Tolstoyan agricultural communes. Extant records show that as late as World War II more than 100 young Tolstoyans in the Soviet Union were shot for refusing military service.

By far the greatest follower of Tolstoy was *Mohandas K. Gandhi, the leader of the independence movement in India, who as a young man corresponded with Tolstoy during the last months before the writer's death in 1910. "Russia gave me in Tolstoy a teacher who furnished a reasoned basis for my non-violence," Gandhi wrote in 1942 in his open letter "To American Friends."

For all his great debt to Tolstoy, Gandhi differed with him in two important respects. First, he did not share Tolstoy's belief in nonresistance to evil; rather, he believed in *nonviolent* resistance to evil. Second, Gandhi was not an anarchist. Rather than doing away with the state, Gandhi believed in civilizing the state. The paradox lying at the very heart of nonviolence—which Gandhi understood but which Tolstoy's anarchistic mind could never grasp—is that its effective use against evil presupposes a government based on force. Nonviolence cannot replace that government; it can only oblige it to govern more justly—or else risk losing the support of the people it governs.

Regardless of the inconsistencies in Tolstoy's anarchism and in the bundle of disparate doctrines that have come to be known as Tolstoyism, the essence of his message is his belief that love is the fundamental law of the universe. The increasing violence of the twentieth century may ultimately come to be seen as confirming rather than contradicting Tolstoy's powerful message.

Bibliography:

A. *Tolstoy Centenary Edition*, trans. by Louise and Aylmer Maude, (21 vols., London, 1928-37).

B. William B. Edgerton, "The Artist Turned Prophet: Leo Tolstoy After 1880," in *American Contributions to the Sixth International Congress of Slavists, Prague, 7-13 August 1968*, vol. 2 (The Hague, 1968), 61-85; "K semidesyatiletiyu so dnya smerti L. N. Tolstogo. Dmitry Yegorovich rasskazyvayet ...," *Kontinent*, 27 (Munich, West Germany, 1981), 292-324; Ernest J. Simmons, *Leo Tolstoy* (Boston, 1946).

William B. Edgerton

TORRES BODET, Jaime. See *Biographical Dictionary of Internationalists*.

TOYE, Edward Harold (23 June 1884, McKellar, Ontario, Canada—3 July 1974, Toronto). *Education*: B.A. Victoria Coll., 1909, B.D., 1911. *Career*: Methodist and United Church Ministry, 1911-40; executive secretary, Religion-Labor Foundation, 1940-54.

A product of the social gospel in Canada, Edward Harold Toye devoted his long career as a United Church minister to eliminating the causes of war and industrial violence by striving to establish a harmonious working relationship between church and labor. Like other members of the Fellowship for a Christian Social Order in the thirties, Toye's radicalism increased in response to the social conditions of the depression and by the end of the decade his laborite and socialist views were challenged by the officials of Toronto's Kingston Road United Church. Their effort to have him removed as their pastor came to a head once Canada entered World War II and Toye joined a small minority of United Church pacifists in producing the "Witness Against War Manifesto," an outright refusal to support the war. Toye's pacifism seriously divided his congregation and resulted in a tense situation which finally caused him to resign from his church and the parish ministry entirely for the new field of industrial relations. Also during the war years, however, he continued to work with other pacifists on behalf of conscientious objectors in alternative service.

By 1940 Toye founded the Religion-Labor Foundation, a small organization that brought together clergymen and laymen, labor representatives and social workers, in an attempt to create a dialogue between religion and labor, the two forces whose coordination and cooperation, he believed, could promote radical social changes without violent disruptions. Labor unions, collective bargaining, and industrial strikes, he argued, were all part of the true revolutionary character of the Hebrew-Christian religion and, therefore, could be useful tools in building a just and peaceful social order as long as labor functioned within the ethical and spiritual demands of religion. It was in this vein that Toye and his associates tackled the social, economic, and moral problems of industrial society, particularly those heightened by the war.

Although small in numbers and experimental in approach, the Religion-Labor Foundation was eventually successful in mediating industrial disputes and strikes and in lobbying for special legislation to recognize and protect ethical and spiritual values in labor-management relations. As the executive secretary of the Foundation for thirteen years, Toye was personally responsible for this experimental work in applying the principles of peace and nonviolence to industrial relations.

Bibliography:

A. *Some Impressions of a Parson After Two Years in the Religion-Labor Field* (Toronto, n.d.); *Trifling with Destiny* (Toronto, 1948).

B. Thomas P. Socknat, " 'Witness Against War': Pacifism in Canada, 1900-1945," Ph.D. dissertation, McMaster University, 1981.

C. E. Harold Toye Papers, United Church of Canada Archives, Toronto.

Thomas P. Socknat

TRAVEN, B. (3 March 1890, Chicago, IL?—26 March 1969, Mexico City). *Education*: self-educated. *Career*: editor and publisher, *Der Ziegelbrenner*, 1917-21; actor, author, and novelist.

B. Traven, whose entire biography is shrouded in uncertainty, first came to prominence as an opponent of war in 1917. In that year, under the name of Ret Marut, he began to write, edit, and publish *Der Ziegelbrenner*, an antiwar periodical that enlarged in scope as Traven's understanding of the connections between war and capitalism grew. Forced to flee Germany after the demise of the Bavarian Soviet Republic, Traven took up a new life in Mexico, living as "Hal Croves" and publishing a series of novels as B. Traven, some of which contained antiwar themes.

Traven conceived of *Der Ziegelbrenner* as an antiwar counterweight to the chauvinist German press. He intended it to last only as long as the war did, but his association in Munich with leading anarchists and socialists widened his perspective. As he came to see war as the byproduct of a more fundamental evil, capitalism, he was no longer content to simply encourage his readers to end the war. Traven identified capitalism, nationalism, and militarism as the three engines that powered war, and concluded that the dissolution of the state by a revolutionary movement was the only prospect for peace. Capitalism guaranteed the complicity of the workers in war by repressing their creative energies and allowing no outlet other than the excitement and stimulation of war. With the destruction of capitalism, life-sustaining work would be replaced by life-fulfilling work and workers would be immune to war hysteria. Thus, Traven developed and propagated an anticapitalist analysis of war that explained the susceptibility of workers to war propaganda in terms of their restricted human potential under capitalism.

By 1919, Traven was using *Der Ziegelbrenner* as a forum for exposing Germany's responsibility for World War I. The war had been an offensive war, prepared for since the 1890s; the negotiations to resolve the conflicts that immediately caused the war were wrecked through manipulation of the venal press and the imperialist ambitions of the German ruling elite; even the German church had cooperated in promoting and continuing the war. Traven celebrated the anarchist philosophy of Max Stirner in his pages, and like Stirner he refused to join a party, but nonetheless he took an active role in the Bavarian revolution of 1918-19. Under the first Soviet Republic, Traven joined the propaganda committee in charge of censoring the bourgeois press in Munich, and he was involved in the planned socialization of the press. Arrested and condemned to death for high treason in May 1919, Traven escaped. Fleeing from village to village, he brought out occasional numbers of *Der Ziegelbrenner*. In his final issues, in 1921, he repudiated his own Germanness.

Traven next appeared in Mexico. There he began a long career as a novelist, writing among other books, *The Death Ship* (1926), which described the postwar plight of men who had lost their countries, and six novels describing the exploitation of Indian workers in the Mexican jungle. In the novels, as in *Der Ziegelbrenner*, Traven advocated the abolition of the state and inveighed against nationalism, militarism, capitalism, materialism, and the chauvinist press.

Bibliography:

A. *The Death Ship* (London, 1934); *The General from the Jungle* (New York, 1954); *Government* (London, 1935); *March to the Monteria* (New York, 1971).

B. Michael L. Baumann, *B. Traven: An Introduction* (Albuquerque, 1976); Rolf Recknagel, *B. Traven: Beitrage zur Biografie* (Leipzig, 1966); Armin Richter, *Der Ziegelbrenner: Das Individualanarchistische Kampforgan des Fruhen B. Traven* (Bonn, 1977); Judy Stone, *The Mystery of B. Traven* (Los Altos, CA, 1977); NYT, March 27, 1969, 47.

Michael Dintenfass and Polly Morris

TRESSEL, Josef Maria. See THRASOLT, Ernst.

TREVELYAN, Charles Philips (28 October 1870, London—24 January 1958, Wallington Hall, Northumberland, England). *Education*: Harrow; B.A., Trinity Coll., Cambridge, Univ., 1892. *Career*: politician; Liberal Member of Parliament (for Elland, Yorkshire), 1899-1918; Labour Member of Parliament (for Newcastle-upon-Tyne Central), 1922-31; secretary, Board of Education, 1908-14; president, Board of Education, 1924, 1929-31.

In Parliament, C. P. Trevelyan rapidly established a reputation for his independent and radical views which he courageously expressed in public. In part, this accounted for his eight year wait before appointment as a junior minister. As a private member, he was chairman of the Radical Russian Committee and an early and enthusiastic supporter of *E. D. Morel's Congo Reform Campaign. Though a founding member of the National Peace Council in 1904, he censured "extreme pacifists" in his pamphlet, *England & Peace* (1907) for not being "really international" and having "no logical or complete anti-militarist policy."

After his promotion to office, Trevelyan's anxiety to be seen as loyal to the Liberal leadership though not an impediment in domestic policy curbed his public criticism of Sir +Edward Grey's foreign policy. His brave resignation from the government on the outbreak of World War I, therefore, came as a surprise to many. In public Trevelyan argued that Britain could and should have remained neutral. In private he censured Grey as primarily responsible for inveigling Britain into war with Germany at the behest of France.

Together with Morel, *Arthur Ponsonby, and +J. Ramsey MacDonald, Trevelyan was a founder and leader of the Union of Democratic Control (UDC), an important antiwar organization in Britain. He was the Union's main fund raiser and a leading UDC publicist and speaker. For his ardent advocacy of a negotiated peace with Germany he was unjustly accused by the Tory press as "unpatriotic" and "pro-German." In 1916 Trevelyan sent an open letter to President †Woodrow Wilson urging him to appeal to the peoples of the belligerent powers over the heads of their governments. In 1917 he welcomed the Russian Revolution and called for a closer association between UDC members in Parliament and the Labour party. In February 1918, in the *Nation*, Trevelyan published a letter suggesting that after the war the "natural" home for radicals would be the Labour and not the Liberal party. In the "coupon" election that year he stood as an independent and only after his crushing defeat announced that he had joined the Independent Labour party. The following year he drew much unfavorable attention to himself by his vehement criticism of the Versailles Treaty as a vindictive exercise that was "militarily, economically, morally and territorially unfair to Germany." In 1922 he was reelected to Parliament as a Labour member and subsequently served twice as Minister for Education.

Born, reared, and educated in the Liberal tradition and, as significantly, a leading member of the landowning class, Trevelyan's "defection" to the Labour party stirred an enormous furor. Those who during the war said that he ought to be shot as a traitor to his country now demanded his head as a traitor to his class, describing him as a "roaring Bolshevik" and "Lenin's lieutenant." His book, *From Liberalism to Labour* (1921), was intended to explain to a wide public the reasons for his political metamorphosis. Trevelyan charged Liberals with abandoning Liberalism during the war; they had surrendered free trade, introduced conscription without consultation, and made liberty of speech and person questions of government whim. But above all else, he accused Liberal foreign policy of becoming indistinguishable from reactionary imperialism.

Trevelyan's radicalism was the source of his profound belief in the international brotherhood of all men. His stern internationalism made him a formidable "warrior for peace." Neither *John Bright nor *Richard Cobden would have despised him as a colleague in their campaigns. In the end he grew as critical of the pusillanimous leadership of the Labour party as he had been of the Liberals and resigned as a minister. After his electoral defeat in 1931, he never again entered Parliament despite many offers to do so. For the rest of his long life he, together with his wife Molly, determined to make their family home, Wallington Hall, "a resort for Socialists and internationally minded people."

No one ever had cause to doubt Trevelyan's great moral courage, but he was best cast by temperament for the role of critic. A certain impatience and contentiousness did not accord well with the practical limits that were imposed upon a British Minister by colleagues and the conventions of party government in the parliamentary system. In the late 1930s, his deep hatred of fascism and his apprehensions concerning Adolf Hitler's intentions, caused him to turn against old allies like *George Lansbury and advocate rearmament in the face of growing German aggression. He considered World War II as the necessary price to be paid to stamp out Nazism and fully supported Winston Churchill as the nation's leader.

Bibliography:

A. *The Case Against Conscription* (London, 1913); *The Case for Negotiation* (London, 1916); *England and Peace* (London, 1907); *From Liberalism to Labour* (London, 1921); *The Union of Democratic Control: Its History and Its Policy* (London, 1919).

B. A.J.A. Morris, *C.P. Trevelyan: Portrait of a Radical* (Belfast, 1977, New York, 1979); DNB, 1951-1960, 989-90; A.J.A. Morris, "C.P. Trevelyan's Road to Resignation 1906-14: The Odyssey of an Antiwar Liberal," in, S. Wank, ed., *Doves and Diplomats* (Westport, CT, 1978), 85-108.

C. C.P. Trevelyan Papers, Library, University of Newcastle-upon-Tyne.

A.J.A. Morris

TREVES, Claudio (24 March 1869, Turin, Italy—11 June 1933, Paris). *Education*: Dr. of Law, Univ. of Turin, 1890. *Career*: socialist journalist; member of the Chamber of Deputies; editor, *Il Grido del popolo*, 1896-98, *Il Tempo*, 1906-10, *Avanti!*, 1910-12; *La Liberte*, 1927-33.

From his youth, Claudio Treves was attracted to democratic socialism and began his career in 1887 as a contributor to *Il Riscatto* and other socialist journals. His fervent pacifist commitment was expressed in articles in *Università Popolare* from 1901-18, but he resigned from the society of the same name in 1915 because of his firm commitment to Italian neutrality during World War I. During the war, he supported the Socialist party position, "neither support nor sabotage."

From 1906 when he was elected to the Chamber of Deputies, Treves introduced bills on behalf of feminist, humanitarian, and pacifist causes, including those promoted by *Bertha von Suttner. He also founded and edited *Il Tempo* to further these causes. Overall, his was a reformist interpretation of Karl Marx which avoided both extremes advocated by the followers of Georges Sorel on the one hand, and Eduard Bernstein on the other.

Treves believed that socialist participation in the government was the crucial means by which the Italian Risorgimento would achieve its democratic promise. The government's declaration of war in 1911 over Libya, however, found Treves withdrawing his support and denouncing the operation as another case of "colonial madness." In 1912, on behalf of women's rights, Treves introduced a bill in parliament inspired by *Anna Kuliscioff and Gaetano Salvemini for total universal (including female) suffrage. At the same time, he campaigned vigorously against further increases in military spending. In preparation for the 1914 (Vienna) congress of the Second International, he wrote a paper on the problem of armaments. When World War I broke out, however, the meeting was cancelled. Even after Italy entered the war, Treves continued his stand for neutrality, insisting that neither the hopes of internationalism or socialism would be ruined by the conflict.

His continued antiwar position remained intact until the Italian defeat at Caporetto late in 1917. Earlier that year he had expressed the hope that there would be "no more trenches next winter" and supported the Stockholm peace initiative of the socialists. After the disaster at Caporetto, he argued the need to fight for the state and support the soldiers since the threat of German authoritarianism in an occupied Italy presented an overwhelming threat to the survival of the Risorgimento state and outweighed the justification for neutrality. In sum, the guiding premise of Treves' thought was the necessity of preserving the conditions for the growth of democracy. He even argued that the peace treaties be put to popular referenda throughout Europe and that postwar diplomatic congresses admit representatives of workers' organizations.

In 1921, when the Socialist party divided and the Italian Communist party was created, Treves remained with the socialists. In October 1922, however, he joined the United Socialist party, a reformist branch of the Italian Socialist party. When the fascists came to power, he fled into exile in Paris.

As an exile, Treves undertook to organize antifascist groups and became editor of *La Liberté*, the organ of the Anti-fascist Concentration in 1927. He advocated European federalism, arms control, disarmament, and international arbitration. His efforts to unify the badly divided Italian left in exile even led him to invite the young Communist, Giorgio Amendola, to Paris for discussions, despite his long and ferocious polemics with the Communists. For Treves, the primary goal remained the fight against "anti-democratic" fascism which denied the Risorgimento. Here his view was similar to that of Antonio Gramsci.

Treves delivered a moving memorial to his murdered friend, Giacomo Matteotti, only one month before his own death. At Treves' funeral, most of European socialism was represented to give testimony to his contributions. Humanitarianism, a principled defense of human rights, and a firm belief in internationalism and in a democratic version of Marxian socialism underlay Treves' commitment to international peace.

Bibliography:

A. *Il fascismo nella letteratura antifascista dell'esilio*, ed. by A. Schiavi (Rome, 1953).

B. G. Arfè, *Storia dell' Avanti!* (Milan, 1958); G. Arfè, *Storia del socialismo italiano* (Turin, 1965); S. Fedele, *Storia della Concentrazione antifascista, 1927-1934*, (Milan, 1976).

Franca Pieroni Bortolotti
Trans. by Sandi E. Cooper and John M. Cammett

TROCMÉ, André (7 April 1901, St. Quentin, France—5 June 1971, Geneva). *Education*: private tutoring in early years; studied science under a Catholic priest in Belgium, 1917; baccalauréat, St. Quentin, 1918; theological studies, Sorbonne, 1918-24; attended Union Theological Seminary, New York, 1925-26. *Career*: pastorates, Maubeuge, Sin-le-Noble, Le Chambon, Geneva; traveling secretary, Fellowship of Reconciliation, 1947; director, Collège Cévenol, 1948; minister and pacifist.

Andre Trocmé was born of mixed French and German lineage, in very comfortable bourgeois circumstances. Several of his brothers followed their father, a successful manufacturer of lace, into business affairs, but Trocmé's interests—derived from his strongly pious family background—led him into the Christian ministry. His humanitarian interests were revealed early. Between 1914 and 1917 he joined the Union of St. Quentin, an organization of Protestant youth, most of whom were children of laborers, which combined extreme piety with humanitarian service, such as providing food for Russian prisoners of war.

Turning from a first attraction to science, Trocmé studied theology at Paris, and then, learning of Union Theological Seminary as a center of study for the "social gospel," he went to New York in 1925. His disappointment that the seminary did not meet his own inflexible standards was assuaged by his meeting with Magda Grilli, to whom he was married in 1926 shortly after his return to France.

In 1927 Trocmé accepted his first parish at Maubeuge, but left a year later to become pastor at Sin-le-Noble, a village of miners and steelworkers in the North of France, where he ministered to the religious and material needs of the downtrodden. It was at Sin-le-Noble, too, that he began to disseminate his views on pacifism and nonviolence. His antiwar views first became manifest in 1921 when, as an army conscript in Morocco, he refused to carry arms, an act which he saw as inconsistent with the Christian faith. At Sin-le-Noble Trocmé attracted the attention of the civil authorities; a police report of February 1933 described him as having engaged in a variety of "undesirable" activities: numerous meetings and lectures in favor of peace; condemnation of the Treaty of Versailles; frequent trips abroad (probably in his capacity as secretary of the Fellowship of Reconciliation); host to young foreign pacifists; leader of a group from his congregation at a pacifist meeting in Fribourg; witness at the trial of Camille Rambaud for conscientious objection.

The national synod of the Reformed Church had forbidden the preaching of pacifism from the pulpit and Trocmé sought another pastorate where he could express his convictions with less attention from the synod. He found it in Le Chambon-sur-Lignon, in the Cévennes, where he relocated in 1934. In this village, which had been a refuge for Huguenots during the *dragonnades* of the seventeenth century, Trocmé resumed his pacifist ministry, but his ultimate aim was to establish a school which would reflect his Christian, pacifist ideals. This he accomplished in 1938, when Edouart Theis, a conscientious objector and a friend of Trocmé since university days, arrived as assistant pastor and teacher in the new Collège Cévenol.

Following several conferences with Burns Chalmers, an American Quaker working with the American Friends' Service Committee in France, at which Trocmé proposed visiting refugees in internment camps, it was agreed in 1940 that Le Chambon should serve as a sanctuary for Jews and other refugees. The whole village participated in the work of forging ration cards, falsifying identifications, and concealing refugees, but Trocmé was the moving spirit. In 1940, after the fall of France, the entire staff of the Collège Cévenol refused to take the oath of loyalty to Marshal Henri Philippe Pétain. In 1943 Trocmé, with two others, was arrested for his illegal activities, but was released after five weeks by Pierre Laval, even after again refusing to take the loyalty oath.

After 1944, when Le Chambon was liberated by de Lattre de Tassigny's troops, Trocmé resumed his ministry, and his association with the Fellowship of Reconciliation (FOR), of which he was, after 1947, traveling secretary in southern Germany, where he organized relief measures for eleven million refugees. Prior to 1950 the FOR was too preoccupied with such measures to undertake the reconstruction of the German pacifist movement, but in 1955 Trocmé, with *A. J. Muste and Clifford Masquire, visited several west German cities, and in 1956 the German FOR was reconstituted at Cologne.

Increasingly Trocmé turned his attention to conscientious objection. In 1957 he, with Henri Roser, Jean Lasserre, and Daniel Parker, formed a Comité de la resistance spirituelle (Committee of Spiritual Resistance), with support from Catholic and Protestant groups. The Committee issued cards to French soldiers in Algeria, stating that the Church takes responsibility for those who refuse to engage in acts of torture. With Roser and Lanza del Vasto, Trocmé led numerous demonstrations against nuclear warfare and in favor of legalizing CO status. After 1960 he was active in fostering the formation of peace groups in Italy. Le Chambon was the focal point for all this activity, as it had been for Trocmé's life.

Bibliography:

A. *Sans peur et sans armes* (Geneva, 1949).

B. Philip P. Hallie, *Lest Innocent Blood Be Shed* (New York, 1979).

Albert S. Hill

TRUEBLOOD, Benjamin Franklin (25 November 1847, Salem, IN—26 October 1916, Newton Highlands, MA). *Education*: B.A., Erlham Coll., 1869. *Career*: educator, publicist, editor, and peace worker.

Benjamin Trueblood was a leading figure in the American peace movement before World War I. Born into a Quaker family and educated in a Quaker college, he began his teaching career in 1869 as a professor of classics at Penn College in Iowa. From 1874 to 1879 he was president of another Quaker school, Wilmington College in Ohio. From 1879 to 1890 he was president of Penn College. Highly successful as a teacher and administrator, he nonetheless cherished the ambition of devoting all his time to peace work. Leaving the presidency of Penn College, he spent a year in Europe as agent for the Christian Arbitration and Peace Society. In 1892 he was chosen secretary of the American Peace Society, a position he held for twenty-three years. During the greater part of that time he was the only full-time salaried peace worker in the United States. Under his leadership the society's membership grew from 400 to nearly 8000, and the subscription list for its journal, the *Advocate of Peace*, from 1,500 to more than 11,000.

Trueblood represented the American Peace Society at most of the Universal Peace Congresses held by European peace leaders during his years as secretary, and he himself organized similar meetings in America. He assisted in the organization of the Lake Mohonk Conferences on International Arbitration.

Editing the *Advocate of Peace* was one of Trueblood's most important activities. He himself wrote most of its editorials and many of its articles. Although an unusually skillful writer, Trueblood added few ideas to pacifist thought. Instead he excelled at explaining the ideas of others. One of his most important scholarly endeavors was the translation of Immanuel Kant's essay *Perpetual Peace* which he first published in the *Advocate of Peace* in serial form and later as a book. In 1899 he published *The Federation of the World*, a book inspired by Kant's idea of an international state. Unlike Kant, Trueblood was convinced that an international state based on a federation model was "necessary and inevitable." He was as much influenced by William Penn and *William Ladd as by Kant. He saw in The Hague Peace Conferences, the Permanent Court of Arbitration, and arbitration treaties the beginning of the fulfillment of their proposals. He urged that The Hague Peace Conference be made a permanent institution and that the Permanent Court of Arbitration be made into a genuine world court. Trueblood lived to see the beginning of the tragedy of World War I. Stricken by a paralytic stroke, he resigned as secretary in 1915 and died in 1916.

Bibliography:

A. *Development of the Peace Idea and Other Essays*, (Boston, 1932). *The Federation of the World* (Boston and New York, 1899).

B. Merle Curti, *Peace or War: The American Struggle, 1636-1936* (New York, 1936); Calvin D. Davis, *The United States and the First Hague Peace Conference* (Ithaca, NY, 1962); Calvin D. Davis, *The United States and the Second Hague Peace Conference: American Diplomacy and International Organization 1899-1914* (Durham, NC, 1976); Warren F. Kuehl, *Seeking World Order: The United States and World Organization to 1920* (Nashville, TN, 1969); Charles M. Woodman, "Benjamin F. Trueblood - An Appreciation," *The American Friend*, Old Series, 23, 1916, 948-50; DAB, 19, 5-6.

C. Benjamin F. Trueblood correspondence in the American Peace Society Papers, Swarthmore Peace Collection, Swarthmore College.

Calvin D. Davis

TUCHOLSKY, Kurt (1 January 1890, Berlin—21 December 1935, Hindås near Goteborg, Sweden). *Education*: Dr. jur., Univ. of Jena, 1915. *Career*: editor, *Die Weltbühne*, 1926-27; journalist, lyricist, satirist, essayist, and dramatist.

The best-known of Weimar Germany's left-wing intellectuals, Kurt Tucholsky was born of a wealthy Berlin Jewish merchant family. Afforded the best in

German education, he received his law degree but never practiced law, since by that time he had already gained recognition as an essayist and journalist.

Unlike many of his generation, Tucholsky was unaffected by the 1914 war fever. When drafted into the army following completion of his studies, he obtained bureaucratic posts in the Eastern theater of war. He remained a correspondent of *Die Schaubühne*, originally a theatrical journal but now increasingly politicized and pacifist, but his wartime writings show no trace of his later antimilitarism. It was the failure of the 1918 German revolution to bring about democracy and socialism that radicalized him and sparked his hatred of the military. His 1919 series in *Die Weltbühne* (the new name of *Die Schaubühne*), entitled "Militaria," caused a scandal because of its catalog of abuses of power and position in the armed forces.

During the 1920s Tucholsky wrote scores of highly successful antimilitarist ballads and poems, which warned of the vengeance of the proletariat who had served as cannon fodder in the war. Like many other noncommunist intellectuals, he leaned toward the Communists out of disillusionment with the Republic and the Social Democratic party during the last years of Weimar. He became a prolific contributor to the Münzenberg press and film concern, an agency of the Comintern, and in 1929 he created, together with the Communist artist John Heartfield, the biting *Deutschland, Deutschland über alles*, an album of photomontage, essays, satire, and poems directed against the Social Democrats, the bourgeoisie, the judges, the bureaucrats, and, most importantly, against the army. The book lambasted military influence on public life, the multiplication of right-wing veterans' organizations, and the undiminished prestige and power of the old Imperial officer corps.

Despite his brilliance and insight, Tucholsky resembled many of his contemporaries in his failure to appreciate the Nazi danger. To the end, his target continued to be the old Imperial regime symbolized by the bullying Prussian drill-sergeant. The far more dangerous but slick and modern Nazi murderer somehow did not capture his attention. Even worse, Tucholsky tended to identify the Prussian drill-sergeant with the entire German nation. He, the great master of the German language and a lover of German literature, projected the image of one who hated everything German, an image exacerbated by the fact that, after 1924, Tucholsky lived mostly abroad. As Paris correspondent for the Berlin *Vossische Zeitung*, he returned home only for a short stint as editor of *Die Weltbühne*. Moving to Sweden in 1929, he became an official exile after the Nazi triumph in 1933. By that time he had become disillusioned with the Communists, and, because he was also ill and depressed, he refused to write. Although successful, Tucholsky was plagued by doubt, especially about the effectiveness of his work, and in 1935, he took his own life.

Bibliography:

A. *Ausgewählte Briefe, 1913-1935* (Hamburg, 1972); *Deutschland, Deutschland über alles*, Photographs assembled by John Heartfield (Berlin, 1929; Eng. trans., Amherst, 1972); *Gesammelte Werke*, (3 vols., Hamburg, 1961).

B. Harold L. Poor, *Kurt Tucholsky and the Ordeal of Germany, 1914-1935* (New York, 1965); Klaus-Peter Schulz, ed., *Kurt Tucholsky in Selbstzeugnissen und Bilddokumenten* (Hamburg, 1959); Gerhard Zwerenz, *Kurt Tucholsky* (Munich, 1979).

Istvan Deak and Monica Scorcia

TUCOVIĆ, Dimitrije (1 May 1881, Gostilje near Uzice, Serbia—20 November 1914, in battle on the Drina River front). *Education*: LL.B., Univ. of Belgrade, 1906; studied at the Univ. of Berlin, 1907-8. *Career*: member, Serbian parliament; Socialist leader and politician; editor, author, translator, and pacifist.

Dimitrije Tucović was one of the most prominent Serbian labor leaders before World War I. As a young high school graduate, he became a fervent socialist and organized a young socialist group. As a law student at Belgrade University he led a demonstration against King Milan Obrenovic (April 5, 1903) and emigrated to Austria to escape arrest. He returned to Serbia following the overthrow of the Obrenovic dynasty in the summer of 1903. In the same year, he was one of the founding members of the Serbian Social Democratic party (SSDP). He became the party's Secretary and also the editor of the party paper *Radnicke Novine (Workers' Gazette)*.

Tucović, who had studied at the University of Berlin, knew German and Austrian socialism and their leaders well. He translated many of their works into Serbian (e.g. August Bebel, Karl Kautsky, as well as Karl Marx) and corresponded with many of them. As a consequence, Tucović advocated "scientific socialism" and through him the new SSDP was strongly influenced by German Marxian Socialism. The Erfuhrt program of the German Social Democratic party set the ideological tone for its Serbian counterpart. Revisionism became one of the major divisive factors within the SSDP. One faction in the SSDP argued that the working class was too small and ideologically immature to be an independent political movement and should join the left wing of the liberal party; Tucović led the other faction, which proposed the creation of an "independent working class movement" opposing the bourgeois parties and subscribing to the principle of "scientific socialism." He argued that socialism would be effective only if both "trade unions and the political party are united." The Tucović faction was victorious at the Second SSDP Congress of 1904. Tucović also condemned the anarcho-syndicalist-terrorist wing of the party led by Sima Markovic.

Another major shift in the SSDP occurred at the tenth Congress of 1910. The previous position that the party must not forge an alliance with the peasantry or organize them, because it was itself small and immature, was rejected. It was replaced with the Tucović version that the "advance of capitalism into the countryside" opened the way for the creation of socialist organizations in villages. This was confirmed by the Eleventh Congress in 1911. The correctness of that decision was obvious during the elections held that year. The poor peasants provided the majority of 24,000 votes cast for socialist candidates.

The internationalist position of the SSDP was expressed in its efforts to promote the spirit of Balkan federation and ease rising nationalist tension among the reawakened nationalisms of Serbian, Bulgarian, and Greek states, victorious over the decaying Turkish Ottoman Empire. The First Balkan Socialist Conference was convened at the initiative of Serbian socialists in January 1910. The road to the federation was through democratic revolution. Equality among all Balkan peoples was the fundamental principle; brotherhood was the way to resolve disputes peacefully.

The SSDP led by Tucović participated at all meetings of the Second International, with the exception of the Basel Congress, due to the Balkan War of 1912. Tucović and the SSDP practiced internationalism at home as well as abroad. They were consistent in their antiwar policy regardless of whether it benefitted Serbian national interests. They regularly opposed militarism and military budgets and urged peaceful solutions during times of crisis. In 1908 Tucović criticized the Austrian Social Democratic party for its blind support of Austria-Hungary's annexation of Bosnia and Herzegovina which inflamed Serbian nationalist passions. At the same time he urged the Serbian government to seek a peaceful solution to the crisis caused by the annexation. Even though Tucović recognized that the Bulgarian attack on Serbia and Greece in 1912 was an act of aggression against which the two countries fought a defensive war, he and the SSDP still condemned the war and voted against the war budget in the Serbian parliament. Tucović's uncompromising internationalist views on the questions of nationalism, conquest, and war were clearly presented in his *Srbija i Albanija (Serbia and Albania)* (1914), in which he condemned Serbian and Montegnegrin attempts to annex Albanian territory. Tucović and the SSDP members of Parliament voted once more against the war budget when Serbia was attacked by Austria-Hungary in July 1914. However, this time Tucović reported for duty with the Serbian Army after the hostilities began and was killed in action.

Faithful to his beliefs, the SSDP continued to oppose the war effort even as the war continued. SSDP members of the parliament demanded in their "response to the statement" of the Prince Regent Alexander "immediate armistice" and "signing of the peace treaty" on July 31, 1914. They continued with their opposition to war by voting against additional war credits six more times. The Serbian socialist press continued to oppose war until the Austrians overran Serbia and banned their papers. In addition to Russian Socialist Democrats who abstained from supporting the war credits in the Russian parliament, the Serbian Social Democrats were the only member party of the Second International to vote consistently against war credits.

Bibliography:

A. *Izabrani Spisi* (2 vols., Belgrade, 1949-50); *Sabrana Dela* (10 vols., Belgrade, 1975-81); *Srbija i Albanija* (n.p., 1914, new ed., Belgrade, 1946).

B. S. Dimitrijevic, *Dimitrije Tucović* (Belgrade, 1949); S. Dimitrijevic, *Ucesce Balkanskih Socijalista u Drugoj Internacionali, 1880-1910* (Belgrade, 1966); N. Popovic,

Dimitrije Tucović (Belgrade, 1935); Radmila Milentijevic, "A History of the Serbian Social Democratic Party (1903-1919)," Ph.D. dissertation, Columbia University, 1973.

Michael M. Milenkovitch

TURATI, Filippo (26 November 1857, Canzo, Lombardy, Italy—29 March 1932, Paris). *Education*: Doctor in Law, Univ. of Bologna, 1877. *Career*: founder, Italian Socialist party, 1892; member, Chamber of Deputies, 1897-1926; leader of antifascist exile movement in Paris, 1926-32.

The founder of the Italian Socialist party and its most influential early leader, Filippo Turati was the father of Italian reformism and the dean of Italian socialism. Turati was a pacifist who made cogent arguments favoring arms reductions and who consistently opposed war in Parliament and in the pages of his widely-read review *Critica Sociale*, which he edited with his companion *Anna Kuliscioff.

Turati's early attitude towards war may be discerned in a poem he published in 1883, later to become the most popular working-class song, the *Inno dei lavoratori*: "War Against the Kingdom of War." In a famous article of 1896, he wrote that Italy could not continue its evolution towards socialism without the defeat of the Italian army then engaged in an invasion of Ethiopia.

Turati incorporated his pacifism into his reformism in a manner which aimed at theoretical and practical consistency. He argued against socialist demands that Italy disarm unilaterally on the grounds that it was simplistic and impractical. Instead, he fought in the country and in Parliament to proportion the country's armaments to its economic potential, reasoning that Italian arms spending retarded domestic reform. Italy, he believed, should give up its arms race with its wealthier neighbors and should pursue a less aggressive foreign policy, more akin to that of Switzerland or Belgium, rather than to Germany or France. He denounced the Italian military establishment for squandering Italian wealth, for perpetuating the social inequities, and for holding the prevention of revolution rather than national defense as its main goal. In line with this reasoning he tried to build a political coalition for a reduction in military expenses and a diversion of the savings to important reforms. In Parliament his attempts to reduce military appropriations failed after an agreement of 1901 to stabilize arms expenditures ran out.

After 1905 Turati's most serious challenge came from within his own group when Leonida Bissolati, the party's foreign policy expert, became convinced that Socialist theory on the improbability of a major war was mistaken. Austria-Hungary, Bissolati believed, would attack Italy and it was the duty of all Italians to defend their country, which, he argued, had made real social progress. Turati countered that Italy's strategic position ensured that it could keep out of a war if it chose to change its policies, and that reforms would give the Italians a better society to defend in case of invasion and thus strengthen the country.

The reformist split on military policy contributed to a general weakening of the Socialist party and emboldened the government to embark on a military adventure—the Libyan War of 1911-12. Turati took the lead in denouncing the war, a position which aroused great animosity and which provoked riots against him. This war led to the expulsion of the Bissolati faction and the party's takeover by the left wing attracted by Benito Mussolini's louder but more simplistic antiwar rhetoric.

When World War I broke out the Italians declared their neutrality, but a debate began between "interventionists" and "neutralists," with Turati and the Socialist party taking the lead in attempting to keep the nation out of war. The King, the Salandra government, and the war party succeeded in attaining Italian intervention with only the Socialists and a few scattered deputies voting against the decision. Turati, their spokesman, delivered a scathing denunciation of the underhanded maneuvers by which the government had subverted the peaceful wishes of the majority of Italians.

Continued Socialist moral opposition hampered the war effort. Only in 1917, when the Germans and Austrians threatened to overrun Italy after Caporetto, did Turati urge the Italians to resist in what had now become a defensive war. When the conflict ended, Turati's stand in favor of a just peace aroused the ire of nationalists and fascists, and he became a favorite target of these groups.

Turati had a prominent part in the major events of postwar Italy, finally fleeing the country for France in 1926. As the spiritual head of the Socialist movement, Turati initiated a major effort to inform the international community that fascism was an aggressive movement which would inevitably lead to another war. He made his argument in speeches given in different countries and in numerous articles, but the international community would not listen.

Bibliography:

A. *Carteggio*, with Anna Kuliscioff (7 vols., Turin, 1949-78); *Discorsi parlamentari* (3 vols., Rome, 1950); *Le Strade Maestre del Socialismo* (Naples, 1960); *Trent'anni di Critica Sociale* (Bologna, 1921).

B. Spencer DiScala, *Dilemmas of Italian Socialism: The Politics of Filippo Turati* (Amherst, MA, 1980); Giovanni Mariotti, *Filippo Turati* (Florence, 1946); Alessandro Schiavi, *Esilio E. Morte di Filippo Turati* (Rome, 1956); Alessandro Schiavi, ed., *Omaggio A. Turati Nel Centenario della Nascita* (Rome, 1957).

Spencer DiScala

TUWIM, Julian (13 September 1894, Lodz, Russian Poland—27 December 1954, Zakopane, Poland). *Education*: gymnasium, Lodz, 1904-14; studies in law and philosophy, Univ. of Warsaw, 1916-18. *Career*: literary director of various Warsaw cabarets, 1919-39; artistic director, Teater Nowy, Warsaw, 1947-50; writer and poet.

Of Jewish origin, Julian Tuwim, who spent most of his adult life in Warsaw, was Poland's leading interwar poet. In the forefront of the Skamander literary movement, of which he was a co-founder in 1920, Tuwim's works reflected the political mood of a country that had regained its independence after over one hundred years of dismemberment. His socio-political and pacifist themes, as well as his opposition to anti-Semitism and stark realism, exerted a great influence on the general and political life in Poland.

His major pacifist work, ''Do prostego człowieka'' (''To the Common Man'') (1929), called on all to ''dash your rifles to the pavement'' and pleaded with man to reject the false, patriotic ideology peddled by war mongers to cover up their greed for profit. The poem elicited strong public reaction which was renewed in 1938-39 when his pacifism was interpreted as an effort to disarm Poland and subvert her national security. In the 1930s, at the height of his creativity, his work protested against fascism and various reactionary currents prevalent in Poland's political and social life. During this period Tuwin wrote numerous political satires, pamphlets, and the poem ''Bal w Operze'' (''Ball at the Opera'') (1936), depicting a decadent and immoral society unaware of its approaching doom, which was censored and not published until 1946.

The years prior to World War II were marked by a major political campaign against Tuwim, which at its peak called for the burning of his works and his death. Although his views might have offended some political factions, basically he was not a radical. Rather the attacks were generated more by his Jewish origin than by his political writings since other ethnic Polish writers, preaching more controversial views, were not subjected to such persecutions. Surprisingly these attacks did not hurt his popularity with the reading public or his influence on the literary field.

Tuwim left Poland in 1939 and lived mainly in New York, from 1942 to 1946. World War II convinced him that old-style liberalism could not be relied upon to combat fascism and anti-Semitism and that only Communism was capable of dealing with these evils. He supported Polish-Soviet cooperation and believed in a postwar socialist Poland. His new found ideology forced him to break with the other Polish émigrées in the West. Exile raised issues of national identity which Tuwim addressed in the 1944 essay ''My żydzi polscy. . .'' (''We, the Polish Jews. . .'') which dealt with anti-Semitism and Tuwim's personal struggle to be accepted both as a Pole and as a Jew. His nostalgic longing for his homeland and an inner need to settle old scores produced the book length poem, *Kwiaty polski (Polish Flowers)* (1949), in which he presents his concept of a postwar Poland and pleads for social justice and equality for all people.

Although welcomed with honors upon his return to Poland in 1946, Tuwim's political views were compromising to the government and most of his new writings were censored. His creativity stifled by the system that he believed would introduce absolute justice, Tuwim absorbed himself in old, prewar issues and political squabbles. His new works, however, ignored the liberal, social, and pacifist themes that had dominated his earlier writings.

Bibliography:

A. *Biblia cygańska*, (Warsaw, 1933); *Czyhanie na Boga* (Warsaw, 1918); *Dzieła*, (6 vols., Warsaw, 1955-64); *Kwiaty polskie* (Warsaw, 1949); *Polski slownik pijacki* (Warsaw, 1935).

B. Magnus J. Kryński, ''Politics and Poetry: The Case of Julian Tuwim,'' *Polish*

Review, 18 (1973), 3-33; Madeline G. Levine, "Julian Tuwim: 'We, the Polish Jews...'", *Polish Review*, 17 (1972), 82-89; Janusz Stradecki, *O. Julianie Tuwimie* (Warsaw, 1964); Janusz Stradecki, *Julian Tuwim: Bibliogafia* (Warsaw, 1959); NYT, January 27, 1954.
C. Julian Tuwim Papers, Mickiewicz Museum, Warsaw.

Zofia Sywak

TZARA, Tristan (pseud. Samuel Rosenstock) (4 April 1896, Moinesti, Rumania—24 December 1963, Paris). *Education*: graduated, Lycée Mihaiu Vutеazul, 1914; mathematical and philosophical studies, Univ. of Bucharest, 1914 and Univ. of Zurich, 1915-16; chemistry studies, Univ. of Paris, 1919-20. *Career*: a founder and leader of the Dada movement; poet and essayist.

In 1916 Tristan Tzara and a group of young people from all over Europe, who had come to Zurich because they opposed war, founded Dada. It was an international movement, appearing shortly thereafter in New York, Berlin, and Paris, and it signified pure revolt. Dada was against war, militarism, nationalism, capitalism, even art, literature, and elementary logic. Its art was "antiart," out to destroy all the old values which had proven so disillusioning, as Tzara declared in *Dadaist Disgust*, one of his early manifestoes. His famous "Recipe for a Poem," which involved cutting words out of a newspaper, putting them in a bag, taking them out at random, then copying them down, was more an expression of moral revulsion than an art form. Dada demonstrations and manifestoes were intended to outrage society, and its adherents delighted in provoking riots. In Germany, some Dadaists got arrested for singing antimilitary songs in the midst of the Spartacist revolt, and the police closed down a Dada exhibition because it featured an army officer hanging in effigy with a placard around his neck that said, "Killed by the Revolution." In Paris, they caricatured General Ferdinand Foch, Georges Clemenceau, and the Pope and held a mock trial of Maurice Barrès, "guilty" of leadership of the right-wing, militarist Ligue de la patrie française (League of the French Fatherland). To the Dadaists' delight, the French public became convinced that Dada was a movement of German agents.

Leadership of Dada in Paris passed from Tzara to *André Breton, who founded Surrealism in 1924. Tzara joined the Surrealists in 1929, supporting their antiwar activities, but left in 1935 and began to write for Communist journals such as *Commune*. He joined the Association des écrivains et des artistes révolutionnaires (Association of Revolutionary Writers and Artists), and in 1935 spoke at the antifascist Congrès international des écrivains pour la défense de la culture (International Congress of Writers for the Protection of Culture). In 1936 he and Ilya Ehrenburg were delegates from the Congress to Spain to support the Spanish Republicans. In World War II, Tzara joined the Resistance and had to go into hiding when he was denounced in *Je suis partout*, Drieu La Rochelle's collaborationist journal. Tzara joined the underground writers' organization, the Comité national des écrivains (National Committee of Writers), and wrote for underground journals such as *Confluences, Le point,* and *Les Lettres françaises*. After the war, he attacked André Breton, who had spent the war years safely in the

United States, saying that Surrealism had become utterly irrelevant to the postwar world. He traveled to Yugoslavia, Hungary, Rumania, and Czechoslovakia on cultural missions for the French government. But, in 1947, he joined the Communist party, saying that, while he did not believe in socialist realism, he did believe in revolutionary, *engagé* poetry. In 1956 he condemned the French party for not speaking out against the Soviet invasion of Hungary and his last years were spent studying and writing on African art.

Bibliography:

A. *Tristan Tzara: oeuvres complètes*, texte établi, présenté et annoté par Henri Béhar (Paris, 1975).

B. Georges Hugnet, *L'Aventure dada* (Paris, 1971); René Lacôte, *Tristan Tzara* (Paris, 1952); Robert Motherwell, ed., *The Dada Painters and Poets; an Anthology* (New York, 1951); Elmer Peterson, *Tristan Tzara: Dada and Surrational Theorist* (New Brunswick, NJ, 1971); Michel Sanouillet, *Dada à Paris* (Paris, 1965).

Helena Lewis

U

UCHIMURA Kanzō (23 March 1861, Tokyo—28 March 1930, Tokyo). *Education*: B.S., Sapporo Agricultural Coll. (later Hokkaidō Univ.), 1881; B.S., Amherst Coll., 1887. *Career*: essayist; editor *Yorozu chōhō*, 1897-1903, *Dokuritsu zasshi*, 1898-1900, *Seisho no kenkyū*, 1900-30, *Mukyōkai*, 1901-2, *The Japan Christian Intelligencer*, 1926-28; evangelist.

Uchimura Kanzō is regarded as the greatest among Japan's pacifists before 1945; his ideas about war rose from a dynamic tension between his loyalty to his nation and disagreement with its expansionism. He supported his government's participation in the first war against China (1894-95), but became an absolute pacifist right before the outbreak of the Russo-Japanese War (1904-5). He remained a pacifist and inspired a whole generation of young leaders to follow his example.

War was not considered a problem by most Japanese of Uchimura's generation. Japanese tradition extolled warriors, but the people of Japan had not known largescale warfare for over 250 years. The main concern of most Japanese in the late nineteenth century was that their nation might fall prey to the European colonial powers.

Uchimura, as patriotic as any good Japanese, experienced severe crises of identity as he found his conscience required him to question his government's policies. Trained in the new Western methods of fisheries science and converted to Christianity, he worked for a period as a government official and then went to the United States for further training. There he developed an English writing style distinguished by its clarity and precision. He also adopted the liberal Bible-centered ethics of evangelical Calvinism. Returning home, his inability to work with either missionaries or Japanese cost him a number of positions and forced him to become an independent writer.

His first articles described the pain which the demise of the old order and his adoption of Christianity had caused him. These articles won him an eager following among others who shared his dilemma. His first pacifist piece was a denunciation of army atrocities in China. It resulted from his own sense of betrayal, since he had believed government propaganda about how the invasion of China would prevent further dynastic decline and so help the Chinese people.

The biting irony with which he attacked the government, gained him a position as editor of *Yorozu Chōhō* (Morning Report), which became Japan's largest newspaper. With a coterie of able writers to assist him, he commented on domestic developments and international relations. When, in 1903, the government obviously planned to attack Russia, he and his columnists resigned in protest. Some of them continued their head-on opposition to the government which led to their conviction for lese majesty and subsequent execution.

Uchimura took a different path. He had started a magazine called *Seisho no kenkyū (Study of the Bible)* in 1900 and now turned his full energies to it. This magazine and lectures on the Bible occupied his capabilities until his death. During his final decade these lectures attracted audiences of five to seven hundred a week to hear sturdy verse-by-verse exposition of the Bible. Beginning at the age of sixty-five, he also edited for two years an English-language magazine in order to acquaint Westerners with Japanese culture and his own interpretation of Christianity.

From among those who heard his lectures and read his articles emerged some of the most effective critics of Japan's militaristic policies before the war. *Yanaihara Tadao, in particular, helped design the institutions of the more international postwar society. In a nation whose aspirations they shared and whose authorities tolerated very little dissent, these men found Uchimura a charismatic leader whose transnational Christian ethic allowed them to continue their loyalty to Japan even as they questioned its military adventures.

The growth of Uchimura's pacifist ideas may be traced in his writings. In 1894 he used his English to assure Western readers that a Japanese victory in China would bring free government, religion, trade, and education to the Chinese. When the Japanese exaction of a huge indemnity from the defeated Chinese revealed the hypocrisy of the government's earlier assurance which he had passed on in English to the Westerners, he denounced the Japanese who treated the slaughter of Chinese like a "wild boar hunt." A few years later Japanese policy made war with Russia appear inevitable. He proclaimed himself an absolute pacifist and declared that if he were made prime minister, he would unilaterally disarm Japan and shame the Russians into a similar declaration. As the war clouds gathered in Europe during the spring of 1914, he published a book of essays entitled *Shūkyo to gensei (Religion and Current Events)*, in which he called pacifism the "single touchstone" by which one could test the sincerity of a faith. From that time on he referred frequently to the need for unambiguous pacifist conviction. Finally, in the optimistic twenties, he forecast in his English-language magazine a Japan with "an army and navy on police-standing," a phrase which seemed in retrospect to prefigure the postwar Japanese self-defense forces. Beginning in 1945, these and similar statements by Uchimura attracted great attention because they articulated what so many Japanese craved.

Uchimura's pacifism grew out of his Christian faith. His great accomplishment was that he could establish and retain his credibility as a loyal Japanese at the same time as he called into question the Japanese acceptance of military values. Because his patriotism left no doubt about his fealty to Japan, he could advocate the near heresy of pacifism, whereas many Christians by their shallow adoption of numerous Westernisms lost any ability to influence their fellows.

Bibliography:

A. *Uchimura Kanzō zenshu* (20 vols., Tokyo, 1932-33).

B. John F. Howes, "Uchimura Kanzō," Nobuya Bamba and John F. Howes, eds., *Pacifism in Japan: The Christian and Socialist Tradition* (Vancouver, 1978), 91-122.

C. Uchimura Kanzō Collection, International Christian University, Tokyo; Hokkaidō University, Sapporo.

John F. Howes

UDE, Johannes (28 February 1874, St. Kanzian, Austria—10 July 1965, Grundlsee, Austria). *Education*: earned four doctorates: philosophy and theology, Gregorian Pontifical Univ., Rome, 1898 and 1901 respectively; biology and economics, Univ. of Graz, Austria, 1907 and 1924 respectively. *Career*: ordained, Roman Catholic Church, 1900; assistant professor of speculative dogmatics, Univ. of Graz, 1905-17, professor, 1917-36, concurrent lectureships in sociology and ethics; author and pacifist.

Actively engaged in the struggle for world peace and the understanding of peoples, Johannes Ude was Austria's most eminent advocate of nonviolence. A Catholic priest, university professor, and a man of polymathic learning, Ude came to pacifism by way of his Christian convictions and his priestly vocation. As a chaplain and medical corpsman in World War I, he experienced personally the horrors and tragedy of the conflict, and from its beginning he spoke against the war in sermons, public speeches, and even university lectures.

Though supported and encouraged by Pope *Benedict XV, Ude discovered that his advocacy of pacifism provoked intense opposition, even enmity, from the Austrian bishops, from Austria's politicians, and from wide sections of the public. The death of Pope Benedict in 1922 left Ude without an influential patron, and the Austrian bishops moved to silence him. Bishop Pawlikowski of Graz forbade Ude to speak publicly, prevented Catholic theology students from attending Ude's lectures at the University of Graz, and persuaded the Austrian Ministry of Education, under the authoritarian Schuschnigg regime (1934-38), to remove Ude from his professorship and place him in permanent retirement.

None of these measures silenced Ude completely, though they did make it very difficult for him to publish and to speak freely. Throughout the struggle, Ude criticized the bishops, the Austrian Christian Social party, and the Austrian government, especially for the violently repressive policies—in effect, civil war—which these urged or waged against the socialist and other sections of the Austrian population. Nor did Ude spare the Nazis the voice of his conscience. Shortly after the Nazis assumed power in Austria in 1938, Ude was apprehended by the Gestapo because of his public protests against Nazi persecutions of the Jews and was expelled from Graz with a stern admonition. Though allowed to settle as an ordinary parish priest in the remote mountain village of Grundlsee, located in the Salzkammergut region, Ude continued to fight the Nazis with the weapons of the spirit. During these years he wrote, in secrecy and at great risk to his life, his major pacifist statement, *Du sollst nicht toten!* (*Thou Shalt Not Kill!*) (1948). In this work, Ude proclaimed that the gospel of unqualified love, taught by Christ and for which Christ died, excludes all killing, even that which is sanctioned by duly constituted civic authority and pronounced by it a just war. The manuscript survived only because Ude entrusted it to a faithful friend, who hid it away. Always suspicious, the Gestapo kept a watchful eye on Ude. In August 1944 he was arrested and charged with sedition of the military and with giving aid and comfort to the enemy. After many months in jail in Linz he finally was brought to trial and condemned to death. Before the death sentence could be carried out, however, the war came to an end, and in April 1945 Ude was freed.

Though now over seventy, Ude continued after the war to work for the cause of peace with unrelenting determination. Through the final decades of his life he repeatedly condemned all forms of nuclear and conventional war, urged an end to the growing arms race, and sought to build bridges of understanding between the capitalist and communist peoples of the world. Like *Albert Schweitzer, by whom he was nominated in 1956 for the Nobel Peace Prize, Ude saw the basis of both personal salvation and world peace in the principles of belief in God and man, compassion, nonviolence, and the respect for life.

Bibliography:

A. *Ethik: Leitfaden der natürlich-vernünftigen Sittenlehre* (Freiburg i.B., 1912); *Das Gebot "Du sollst nicht töten" gilt ausnahmslos* (Grundlsee, 1962); *In der Leidenschule des göttlichen Duldens* (Graz, 1924); *Die Judenfrage* (Graz, n.d.); *Du sollst nicht töten!* (Dornbirn, 1948); *Vom fünften Gebot Gottes bis zum erzwungenen Wehrdienst: Die Forderung an die Christen der Zukunft* (Vienna, 1956).

B. Käthe Moritz, *Johannes Ude: Ein Leben und Wirken im Geiste der Bergpredigt* (Salzburg-Grossgmain, 1964); Käthe Moritz, *Sein und Wirken des grossen Friedensarbeiters und Lebensreformers Johannes Ude* (Salzburg-Grossgmain, 1960; Werner Schuder, ed., *Kürschners Deutscher Gelehrten-Kalender 1966* (10th ed., Berlin, 1966), 2530-31.

Richard R. Laurence

UMFRID, Otto (2 May 1857, Nörtingen, Württemberg, Germany—23 May 1920, Lorch, Germany). *Education*: theological studies, Univ. of Tübingen, 1884. *Career*: pastor, Peterzell bei Oberndorf, 1884-91; pastor, Stuttgart, 1891-1913; vice-president, German Peace Society, 1899-1914.

Otto Umfrid's choice of a career in theology was conventional for the son of a small-town attorney, as were the initial phases of this career. Upon completing his studies in 1884, he was first assigned a church in the town of Peterzell and then, in 1891, he was transferred to Stuttgart, where he remained pastor of the St. Martin's Church until 1913.

Soon after he moved to his new parish, however, Umfrid's career became quite unconventional. He hoped to use Christian principles to soften class antagonisms in Germany and he became active in the Evangelischer Arbeiter-Verein (Protestant Worker's Association). Although he found some support for his ministry among workers within the bureaucracy of the Evangelical church in

Württemberg, he stood practically alone in his devotion to the peace movement, which also dated from the early 1890s. In 1894 he helped found a chapter of the Deutsche Friedensgesellschaft (German Peace Society) in Stuttgart. In the next several years he established dozens of local peace societies, most of them in Württemberg, where democratic political traditions created an atmosphere more favorable to pacifism than in any other area in Germany. In recognition of this fact, the German Peace Society transferred its national headquarters in 1899 from Berlin to Stuttgart, where Umfrid became vice-president and the man who ran the organization's day-to-day operations.

Like his interest in the Evangelical-Social movement, Umfrid's pacifism reflected his commitment to an activistic liberal Protestantism, whose basic tenet was the obligation of Christians to apply the ethical injunctions of their religion in the service of their fellow human beings in the realms of society and politics. The principal source of this liberal Protestantism was the work of Adolf Harnack, but more central to Umfrid's own outlook were the writings of the pantheistic Swabian theologian, *Karl Christian Planck, to which Umfrid had been exposed as a youth by his father. From the essential unity of all creation, which Planck postulated, Umfrid extracted the ethical postulates that underlay his attempts to resolve conflicts among social groups and among nations of the world. Although he was himself not a profound or original thinker, he did contribute as much as any German to the articulation of what might be called a liberal Protestant pacifism. According to this doctrine, international arbitration and arms limitation would create a political realm in which Christian morality could become the foundation of international relations.

To hold such views was not easy for a churchman in Württemberg or anywhere else in Imperial Germany, for prevailing Protestant theology held war to be either inevitable or beneficial, an inherent feature of the debased realm of secular affairs in which the observation of Christian principles remained locked in the pursuit of individual piety. Association with the peace movement accordingly implied theological confusion or treachery. Umfrid was hence the target of anonymous denunciations and was called to face the scrutiny of his consistory.

Umfrid was a courageous man, but a pathetic rather than heroic figure. In the face of all the calumny his pacifism brought him, he continued to devote his efforts to the peace movement, delivering countless lectures and composing articles and tracts for publication. Yet the products of his labors were very sparse. He and several other Protestant churchmen managed to coax only about a hundred of their colleagues into the German Peace Society. The Peace Society, of which Umfrid remained one of the driving forces, was itself hopelessly isolated and impotent in Imperial Germany. Umfrid was frequently discouraged by his lack of success and withdrew into periods of deep depression, during which he also wrote poetry.

His ill health added to the pathos. In 1908 his eyesight began to fail; in 1913 he was virtually blind and had to resign from his parish. He took some consolation in the knowledge that *Alfred Fried was nominating him for the Noble Peace

Prize in 1913 and 1914. The outbreak of war and then the news that his son had been taken prisoner on the western front plunged him into paralyzing despair, in which the only activity his nerves could sustain was to reflect on the meaning of Planck's philosophy. He died in 1920.

Bibliography:

A. *Anti-Treitschke* (Esslingen, n.d.); *Da die Zeit erfüllt ward* (Leipzig, 1917); *Europa den Europäern: Politische Ketzereien* (Esslingen, 1913); *Friede auf Erden! Betrachtungen über den Völkerfrieden* (Esslingen, 1897).

B. Walter Bredendieck, "Otto Umfrid—ein vergessener Vorkämpfer für eine Welt ohne Krieg: Zu seinem fünfzigsten Todestag," *Stimme*, 22 (1970), 394-402; Roger Chickering, *Imperial Germany and a World Without War: The Peace Movement and German Society, 1892-1914* (Princeton, 1975); Grete Umfrid, ed., *Zum Gedächtnis von Otto Umfrid* (Stuttgart, n.d.).

Roger Chickering

UNDÉN, Bo Östen. See *Biographical Dictionary of Internationalists*.

UNRUH, Fritz Von (10 May 1885, Koblenz, Germany—28 November 1970, Dietz a.d. Lahn, Germany). *Education*: Arbitur (school leaving examination), Cadet School, Plön, 1906; studies at Univ. of Berlin. *Career*: cavalry officer, antiwar dramatist, and novelist.

Fritz von Unruh, the second son of a conservative Prussian aristocrat and general, was sent to cadet school at the age of eight. Thus from an early age he was sensitized to the authoritarian drill and systematic repression of individuality endemic to military life and later described this institution as "a hell of infamy and stupidity." In 1911 he gave up his job as a cavalry officer after his play, *Prinz Louis Ferdinand*, had been banned. In 1914 he volunteered for service in the Uhlans. The horrors he witnessed in active service in the first few weeks of World War I made him into a committed pacifist. In October 1914 he wrote *Vor der Entscheidung (Faced with the Decision)* and was court-martialled for circulating the manuscript. Increasingly tormented by his own war trauma after his appalling experiences in the trenches of Verdun, he wrote the story *Opfergang (The Way of Sacrifice)* (1916) and the play *Ein Geschlecht (A Family)* (1917).

In the early years of the Weimar Republic, von Unruh was a close friend of +Walther Rathenau, *Romain Rolland and *Henri Barbusse, an established and prolific writer as well as an active figure in the republican antiwar movement. He stood for parliament in 1924 on a pacifist platform. As one of the first Germans to be invited to Paris and London after World War I, he made an important contribution to international reconciliation and understanding.

Von Unruh emigrated to Italy in 1932. A year later he saw on a newsreel in Genoa the bookburnings in Berlin. The Nazis not only burnt and proscribed his works but also stripped him of German nationality. In a speech entitled "Europa erwache!" ("Europe Awake!") made in Basel in May 1936, von Unruh passionately called for international understanding, but it served only to put him further at risk. In 1940 he and his wife were interned in France, but they managed to escape to Spain and from there to the United States.

Although belated recognition came in the shape of the Brunswick Wilhelm Raabe Prize (1947), the Goethe Prize (1948), and the Goethe Medal (1955) in Frankfurt, von Unruh's relationship to the new and quickly remilitarized Federal Republic was ambivalent. The establishment remained "distinctly cool" to the return of such an avowed antimilitarist and his work was subjected to boycotts which forced him to leave West Germany on two occasions. From his early pacifist works to his important autobiographical novel published in 1957, von Unruh remained an untiring advocate of the moral implications of individual responsibility and of social renewal.

Bibliography:

A. *Flügel der Nike. Buch einer Reise* (Frankfurt, 1925); *Ein Geschlecht* (Leipzig, 1917); *Vor der Entscheidung. Ein Gedicht* (Berlin, 1919); *Mächtig seid Ihr nicht in Waffen. Reden* (Nuremberg, 1957); *Opfergang* (Berlin, 1919); *Politea. Aufrufe, Proteste, Gedichte, Reden* (Frankfurt, 1968); *Sämtliche Werke* (Berlin, 1970 ff.); *Der Sohn des Generals. Roman* (Nuremberg, 1957).

B. Ina Götz, *Tradition und Utopie in den Dramen Fritz von Unruhs* (Bonn, 1975); Dieter Kasang, *Wilhelminismus und Expressionismus: Das Frühwerk Fritz von Unruhs 1904-1921* (Stuttgart, 1980); Alvin Kronacher, *Fritz von Unruh, A Monograph* (New York, 1946); Friedrich Rasche, *Fritz von Unruh. Rebell und Verkünder. Der Dichter und sein Werk* (Hanover, 1960).

Martin Rooney

UPHAM, Thomas Cogswell (20 January 1799, Deerfield, NH—2 April 1872, New York). *Education*: B.A., Dartmouth Coll., 1818; B.D., Andover Theological Seminary, 1821. *Career*: professor, Bowdoin Coll., Brunswick, ME, 1824-67; philosopher, psychologist, and peace advocate.

The antebellum peace movement produced many activists and enthusiasts, but it attracted only a few academics. Perhaps the most distinguished scholar to become a pacifist during this period was Thomas C. Upham. Upham was a quiet and unassuming man who avoided publicity; while concerned about political and social questions, he was always more at home in the lecture hall than on a public platform. As an author he was prolific: his publications include learned tomes and scholarly articles on philosophy, theology, and the history of religion, books of travel and verse, and one volume as well as several shorter items on the subject of peace. He supported the antislavery movement, sympathized with European liberalism, and interested himself in such causes as temperance and peace.

Upham, who came from a well-to-do New England family, studied first at Dartmouth College and then at Andover Theological Seminary where he graduated in 1821. After a short period as associate Congregational minister at Rochester, NH, he was appointed, on the basis of his brilliant academic record, to the chair of mental and moral philosophy at Bowdoin College, Brunswick, Maine, which he held until his retirement in 1867. His interest in peace was first awakened through the influence of *William Ladd, whose headquarters were in nearby Minot. Though like Ladd he become an absolute pacifist, Upham too remained essentially a moderate. He was active, however, both at his college and in the town of Brunswick, in promoting peace groups that advocated refusal of militia service as well as renunciation of all war. Upham's career continued outwardly uneventful and his reputation as a scholar grew. But as the Civil War approached, his intense abolitionism led him to waver in his pacifism, and he seems to have supported the Unionist war effort. However, when peace came he joined the Universal Peace Society (later Union), which *Alfred H. Love set up in 1866 on the basis of absolute pacifism, and served as a member of its business committee.

Upham's contribution to pacifism rests on his *Manual of Peace*, first published in 1836 and reissued in 1842 by the American Peace Society in an abridged edition. He also wrote a chapter in Ladd's volume of *Prize Essays on a Congress of Nations, for the Adjustment of International Disputes, and for the Promotion of Universal Peace without Resort to Arms* (1840). In his peace manual, Upham mustered the arguments against war as an institution and suggested a number of remedies, including international arbitration and the setting up of a congress of nations. He also stated unequivocally the Christian pacifist point of view and supported conscientious objectors—or "pacific exempts," as he called them—as well as the idea of a "teetotal" peace pledge against participation in all forms of war. At the same time, while opposing the death penalty Upham stressed he was not against civil government. Upham's work on peace was not original, but his presentation of the pacifist case was far more systematic and detailed then most attempts hitherto.

Bibliography:

A. *The Manual of Peace* (New York, 1836); *Outlines of Imperfect and Disordered Mental Action* (New York, 1840); *A Philosophical and Practical Treatise on the Will* (Portland, ME, 1834); *Principles of the Interior or Hidden Life, designed particularly for the Consideration of those who are seeking Assurance of Faith and Perfect Love* (Boston, 1843).

B. Alpheus S. Packard, *Address on the Life and Character of Thomas C. Upham, D.D., Late Professor of Mental and Moral Philosophy in Bowdoin College; Delivered at the Interment, Brunswick, ME., April 4, 1872* (Brunswick, ME, 1873).

Peter Brock

V

VAILLANT-COUTURIER, Paul (8 January 1892, Paris—10 October 1937, Paris). *Education*: Doctorate in Law, Univ. of Paris, 1912. *Career*: deputy (sitting for Paris and suburbs), Chamber of Deputies, 1919-28, 1936; editor, *le Front Rouge; la Litterature Internationale; l'Humanité*, 1926-37; writer, journalist, militant communist, and antiwar activist.

A founder of the French Communist party in 1920, editor-in-chief of its newspaper *l'Humanité* from 1926 to 1937, elected to the Chamber of Deputies in 1919, 1924, and in the Popular Front Victory of 1936, Paul Vaillant-Couturier's deep and active commitment to peace was a basic part of a political ideology which linked the quest for peace with the success of socialism. As with so many of his generation who were deeply affected by their devastating experiences in World War I, it was perhaps this conflict which acted as a crucible for the development of Vaillant-Couturier's dual dedication to peace and socialism.

Born in Paris of an artistic family, Vaillant-Couturier took a degree in history and a doctorate in law, beginning the practice of law at age twenty. Mobilized in 1914, he spent most of the war at the front; he was wounded twice, gassed once, and decorated numerous times for bravery in action, finishing the war as an officer with the Croix de Guerre and as a Chevalier of the Légion d'Honneur. His last citation was awarded the same day he was imprisoned for writing against the war. Only the armistice enabled him to escape lengthy incarceration. While serving in the army, he had, in 1916, joined the Socialist party and in 1917, along with *Henri Barbusse, *Raymond Lefevre, and Georges Bruyère, had founded the Association républicain des anciens combattants (ARAC), a veterans' organization devoted to opposition to war.

In the Chamber of Deputies, Vaillant-Couturier served, first as a Socialist and then as a Communist, on numerous committees concerned with military and veterans' affairs and was an active speaker for the rights of soldiers, veterans, and victims of war. But it was as an orator and writer for the ARAC and the Communist party that he made his greatest contribution to the antiwar movement. Throughout the hectic period immediately following the war, he campaigned vigorously for the support of the Third International by equating war with capitalism, telling striking workers that it was for the profits of capitalists that workers had died in the trenches. As an intellectual, as editor of *l'Humanité*, and as a member of the central committee, it was Vaillant-Couturier who was instrumental in developing the strong pro-peace position of the French Communist party in the interwar years. His opposition to the French military occupation of the Ruhr in 1922 was voiced in dozens of speeches and articles. Two of these articles, "Apprenticeship to Violence," printed in *le Conscrit* and another appearing in the Communist evening newspaper, *l'Internationale*, resulted in convictions for "provocation of the military to civil disobedience." For this and other political activity, Vaillant-Couturier was to be convicted five times, serving three prison terms. It was during one of these prison terms in 1929 that he was elected mayor of Villejuif, a populous working class suburb of Paris.

The rising threat of fascism strengthened Vaillant-Couturier's conviction that only socialism would bring peace. Throughout the thirties he carried his message that "fascism is war" all over the country in articles and speeches for the ARAC, for the Communist party, and, along with *Henri Barbusse and *Romain Rolland, for the International Congress Against War and Fascism (the Amsterdam-Pleyel movement). In 1935 and 1936, he campaigned vigorously for the election of the Popular Front government and was one of the earliest voices for Republican Spain.

A musician, a painter, as well as a prodigious writer, Vaillant-Couturier published dozens of books including plays, poetry, children's stories, novels, accounts of his travels to Russia and China, as well as thousands of articles in his capacity as editor or contributor to most of the left-wing publications of the twenties and thirties. A man of seemingly endless energy, he was also deeply committed to the popularization of aviation and radio, helping to found the organizations, Radio-Liberty, Cine-Liberty, and Popular Aviation.

One of the great heroes of the French left, his death at age 45 in 1937 brought an outpouring of tribute from Socialists, Communists, trade unionists, and intellectuals. A funeral procession of over one million, the largest ever seen in Paris, was a demonstration not only of respect for Vaillant-Couturier but for the determination of the French left to oppose both war and fascism.

Bibliography:

A. *Députés contres parlement*, with Raymond Lefebvre (Paris, 1919); *Enfance, souvenirs d'enfance et de jeunesse* (Paris, 1938); *La Guerre des soldats*, with Raymond Lefebvre (Paris, 1919); *Le Mealheur d'être jeune* (Paris, 1935); *Nous ferons se lever le jour* (Paris, 1947); *Une Permission de détente* (Paris, 1919); *Sabre et Toque* (Paris, 1929); *Trains rouges* (Paris, 1922); *Vers le lendemain qui chantent* (Paris, 1962).

B. Fernande Bussieres, *Paul Vaillant-Couturier ou l'histoire d'une amité* (Rodez, 1980); *La Vie ardente de Paul Vaillant-Couturier* (Paris, 1937); *L'Humanité*, October 14, 1937.

C. Paul Vaillant-Couturier material in Archives Nationales, Paris, and Archives de la Prefecture de Police de Paris.

Judith Wishnia

VALENTIN, Veit (25 March 1885, Frankfurt/Main, Germany—12 January 1947, Washington). *Education*: Ph.D., Univ. of Heidelberg, 1906. *Career*: Privatdozent (lecturer), Univ. of Freiburg/Breigau, 1910-16, professor, 1916-17; historian, political writer, and journalist.

Veit Valentin, the son of a scholar, was dismissed from his teaching post in

1917 because of his opposition to the chauvinistic, anti-Semitic, and imperialistic Pan-German League. In 1920 he became an archivist at the Reichsarchiv (National Archive) in Potsdam, and in 1933 he became its chief archivist. In June 1933 he was driven from his office by the National Socialist government and emigrated first to England and, in 1940, to the United States.

A close friend to *Ludwig Quidde, Valentin was involved in politics during the Weimar Republic as a liberal democrat and pacifist. He was a contributor to the leading pacifist periodical, *Die Friedenswarte*, the left-wing antiwar journal, *Die Weltbühne*, and the liberal newspapers, *Vossische Zeitung* and *Frankfurter Zeitung*. He participated in meetings of the Deutsche Friedensgesellschaft (German Peace Society) and belonged to the advisory political council of the Deutsche Liga für Menschenrechte (German League for Human Rights). From 1926 until 1933, he was one of the editors of *Die Friedenswarte*. In several of his historical works, he sought to strengthen the democratic foundations of the Weimar Republic against the nationalistic and militaristic Prussian tradition by pointing to the German revolution of 1848-49 as the seedbed of a German democratic tradition. This objective underlies his well-known work, *Geschichte der Deutschen Revolution 1848-1849 (History of the German Revolution 1848-1849)*, which stresses the democratic character of the revolution. He also wrote in support of the League of Nations.

Bibliography:

A. *Die 48er Demokratie und der Völkerbundsgedanke* (Monographien zum Völkerbund, Heft 2, Berlin, 1919); *Geschichte der Deutschen Revolution 1848-1849* (2 vols., Berlin, 1930-31, abbreviated Eng. trans., *1848: Chapters of German History*, London, 1940); *Geschichte des Völkerbundsgedankens in Deutschland. Ein geistesgeschichtlicher Versuch* (Berlin, 1920).

B. Paul Honigsheim, "Veit Valentin (1885-1947): Der Weg eines deutschen Historikers zum Pazifismus," *Friedenswarte*, 47, nos. 4-5 (1947), 274-82; Will Schaber, ed., *Perspektiven und Profile. Aus Schriften von Veit Valentin* (Frankfurt am Main, 1965).

Will Schaber
Trans. by Solomon Wank

VANDERVELDE, Emile Guillaume (25 January 1866, Ixelles, Belgium—27 December 1938, Brussels). *Education*: Athénée Royale d'Ixelles; Athénée Royale de Bruxelles; Doctor of Law, Université Libre (Brussels), 1885, Social Sciences, 1890, Political Economy, 1892. *Career*: member, Chambre des Représentants, 1894-1938; minister of state, 1914; member, Council of Ministers, 1916, 1935-36; minister of stewardship, 1917-18; minister of justice, 1918-21; delegate, Paris Peace Conference, 1919; foreign minister, 1925-27; minister of public health, 1936-37; president, Executive Committee (BIS) of the Socialist International, 1900-22; member (1923-38) and president (1927-33), Socialist Workers' International; president, Belgian Socialist party, 1933-38; lawyer, socialist politician, sociologist, and educator.

Emile Vandervelde's lifetime preoccupation with peace manifested itself in his parliamentary career, years of government service, and labors in the international socialist movement. As president of the Second International, he organized and coordinated the international working class response to crises which threatened to become war. In the congresses of the International, he worked to create an organized antiwar movement. Unfortunately this did not succeed. The unwillingness of most socialists to agree to specific forms of action—particularly, the military general strike—finally paralyzed socialist pacifism before 1914. On the eve of World War I up through July 29, 1914, he tried to persuade socialist leaders to agree on a single, practical attitude and policy to prevent the war but failed.

Vandervelde began working for peace early in his career. In 1889 he served as a member of the Belgian section of the International Arbitration and Peace Association and in 1895 he became a member of the Interparliamentary Union, an organization in which he remained active until his death. His commitment to peace did not preclude him from becoming a vocal public enemy of totalitarianism and fascism. His complete commitment to the Spanish republican cause led him to resign his ministerial government post, for he could not support any view of compromise with the Francisco Franco side.

+Léon Blum's statement in 1947 serves as a fitting epitaph to Emile Vandervelde: "Each time, in any country of the world, that men struggle against hatred, privilege and war; each time an effort brings us closer to peace; Emile Vandervelde lives."

Bibliography:

A. *Les Balkans et la paix* (Brussels, 1924); *La Belgique envahie et le socialisme international* (Paris, 1924); *Carnet, 1934-1938* (Paris, 1966); *Souvenirs d'un militant socialiste* (Paris, 1939).

B. R. Abs, *Emile Vandervelde* (Brussels, 1973); L. de Brouckère et al, *Emile Vandervelde, L'Homme et son oeuvre* (Brussels, 1928); J. Messinne, *Emile Vandervelde, ein grosser Belgier* (Zurich, 1948); E. Vanden Berghe, *Emile Vandervelde: sa doctrine, son action* (Courtrai, 1928); P. Van Molle, *Le Parlement Belge, 1894-1969*, 344-47; *Biographie Coloniale Belge*, 5, cols. 839-54.

C. Emile Vandervelde Papers, Institut E. Vandervelde, Brussels.

Nadine Lubelski-Bernard
Trans. by Sandi E. Cooper

VAN KIRK, Walter William (11 November 1891, Cleveland, OH—6 July 1956, Mt. Vernon, NY). *Education*: A.B., Ohio Wesleyan Univ., 1917; S.T.B., Boston Univ. School of Theology, 1920. *Career*: Methodist pastorates in Dorchester, MA, Needham Heights, MA, Lynn, MA, 1919-25; secretary, Department of International Justice and Good Will, Federal Council of Churches of Christ in America, 1925-50; executive director, Department of International Affairs, National Council of Churches of Christ in the United States of America, 1950-56, church executive.

Throughout much of his career, Walter Van Kirk was an outspoken critic of armed force. In addition to heading a variety of interdenominational commissions, he reached a wide audience through his writings and through his NBC radio broadcast, ''Religion in the News,'' which was aired weekly from 1936 to 1949. In the 1930s he opposed American naval appropriations as well as maneuvers in the Pacific Ocean. Editing a collection of Protestant pronouncements on the cause, cure, and nature of war in 1934, he boasted that pacifism was sweeping the church as it had not done for centuries.

In 1935 Van Kirk was chosen director of the National Peace Conference (NPC), a coalition encompassing some thirty pacifist and internationalist organizations. Van Kirk's reputation as administrator, news commentator, and author, as well as his openness to all factions, made him the choice of such powerful internationalists as +James T. Shotwell and +Newton D. Baker. The NPC's initial program included a national defense based solely upon protection of American soil from invasion, stricter neutrality legislation, and membership in the League of Nations and World Court. Although the organization was split over the question of a mandatory arms embargo, Van Kirk, acting in his capacity as director, asked the United States to call a world conference on economic relations. This conference, he hoped, would undo the injustices bred by World War I and prevent its sequel. Speaking that year before the Conference on World Economic Cooperation, an assembly sponsored by the NPC, Van Kirk accused the Western powers of sabotaging German democracy, criticized the blocking of economic union between Germany and Austria, and called for ''economic appeasement and political security.''

Van Kirk offered his most detailed vision of international order in 1941. It centered on the reconstitution of the League of Nations and the readmission to it of all nations, victors and vanquished, on the basis of juridical equality. As he saw dictators arising, at least in part out of economic imperatives, he sought access of all nations to raw materials on equal terms, low tariffs, and commercial and investment equality in colonial areas. While condemning Hitler as a man of demonic cruelty, he claimed that it was self-defeating for any peace settlement to throttle the vanquished.

Van Kirk was equally active in the early Cold War years. In 1945 he was adviser to the United States delegation to the United Nations in San Francisco. In 1949 he criticized the Atlantic Pact, urging the United States to rely less upon such defensive efforts and to take the offensive in a more global diplomacy. Although he favored economic aid to underdeveloped countries, Van Kirk criticized President Truman's Point Four program for bypassing the United Nations, linking aid to U.S. political and military involvement, and foolishly offering bribes to nonaligned peoples.

Van Kirk endorsed American participation in the Korean War, claiming that intervention was necessary to keep Communists from controlling the entire peninsula. In 1952 he warned against a trend toward isolationism, as seen by irresponsible broadsides against the UN, Senate failure to ratify the Genocide Convention, demands to withdraw from Korea, and congressional efforts to slash foreign aid bills. Two years later he called upon the United States to enter a Middle East mutual defense pact, to guarantee both Israel and the Arab states against attack by the other or by the Soviets. In 1955, shortly before his death, he suggested economic development of the entire Middle Eastern region, with an accompanying defusion of war tensions.

Never an absolute pacifist, Walter Van Kirk made his contribution to the cause of peace as a conciliator between the numerous factions of the organized effort. For over thirty years, he provided leadership as one of the leading Protestant experts on international affairs.

Bibliography:

A. *A Christian Global Strategy* (Chicago and New York, 1954); *Highways to International Goodwill* (Chicago and New York, 1930); *Religion and the World of Tomorrow* (Chicago and New York, 1941); *Religion Renounces War* (Chicago and New York, 1934).

B. NYT, July 8, 1956. *Who was Who in America, 1951-1960*, 874.

Justus D. Doenecke

VERESHCHAGIN, Vassili Vassilievich (26 October 1842, Tcherepovets, near Novgorod, Russia—13 April 1904, Port Arthur, Manchuria). *Education*: St. Petersburg Naval School, 1853-60; St. Petersburg Academy of Art, 1860-63; studied in Paris under J.-L. Gérôme, 1864-65. *Career*: painter, journalist, traveler, ethnologist, and writer.

Vassili Vereshchagin was a master of critical realism, specializing in battle and historical genre paintings. He chose a painting career over the navy and, in 1874, he refused a professorship at the Academy of Arts in order to remain free to travel and paint.

Vereshchagin had traveled widely through Europe and Asia. He traveled through Asia as an artist-correspondent during the Russian campaigns in Turkestan (1867-68) and in the Russo-Turkish War (1877-78). Subsequently, he settled in Munich and painted numerous pictures from his experience. Neither a Romantic, viewing war as a heroic clash of individuals, nor an adherent of art for art's sake, downgrading the importance of subject matter, Vereshchagin was committed to a didactic art which focused on suffering and death in war. His lectures and pamphlets, moreover, reveal a genuine hatred of war. Exhibiting what some have called a Tolstoyan pacifism, Vereshchagin worked in an almost photographic style of high polish and meticulous detail, clearly derived from the academic manner of his French master, J.- L. Gérôme. His settings, however, were not academic inventions but were gathered directly from his travels in central Asia and Russia.

Vereshchagin often arranged his subjects in thematic series by military campaigns, such as the French War of 1812, the Turkestan Series (1871-74), and the Balkan Series (1877-78). Individual paintings deal with such subjects as defeated troops, *After the Failure (Conquered Men*, 1868), and *After the Attack: Dressing Station Near Plevna* (1881), or the dead and wounded, *Requiem (Mass at the Battlefield)*, and *Keep-Away-I'll Take Care of Him* (1887-93). Sometimes he directly criticized contemporary events, as in *All Quiet at the Skipka Pass* (1878-79), which illustrates a half-frozen, underclothed sentry watching over a snowbound field. Graft and poor planning by the commanding officers caused the Russian soldiers to be ill-equipped at Skipka, and Vereshchagin subtly exposed this scandal.

At other times, he veiled his criticism with symbolism, as in his famous *Apotheosis of War* (1871-72) from his Turkestan series. Here, before a barren desert landscape background, is a vast mounded pyramid of human skulls, pecked and roosted on by scavenging ravens. It refers to the practice of the fourteenth century Mongol warrior, Tamerlane, who erected such gruesome trophies after his battles. But, on its frame Vereshchagin called all war into question with an inscription that read: "To all great conquerors of the present, the past and the future."

This *Apotheosis of War* was exhibited in St. Petersburg in 1874. It, and another of the series, *Left Behind*, were suppressed because of their critical nature. However, Vereshchagin had several successful one-man exhibitions in Europe and America. After World War II, his realism and didactic intentions drew the praise of the Central Committee for providing an ideological base for Soviet art. He was cited for portraying the harsh realities of war, commemorating the suffering of the people, and denouncing militarism.

Bibliography:

A. *Na voine u Azii i Europe: Vospominaniia* (Moscow, 1894).

B. A. K. Lebedew, *V.V. Vereshchagin* (Moscow, 1958); V. Saadoven, *V.V. Vereshchagin* (Moscow, 1950).

Folke T. Kihlstedt

VERIGIN, Pyotr (Peter) Vasilyevich (11 July 1858, Slavyanka, Elizavetpol Province, Russia—29 October 1924, Farron, British Columbia, Canada). *Career*: leader of the Dukhobors.

Peter Verigin was born into a family of well-to-do Russian peasants belonging to a mystical religious sect known as Dukhobors (Russian for "spirit-wrestlers"). Originally a settlement of some 4000 persons organized on principles of egalitarian, pacifist communalism, the Dukhobors were deported to the Caucasus from the Molochnaya River region, near the Sea of Azov. Here they abandoned their communalism and prospered for some 40 years under the leadership first of Pyotr Kalmykov and later of his widow Lukerya. In 1882 Lukerya took Verigin into her home with the intention of naming him as her successor.

Upon Lukerya's death in 1886, the Dukhobors, who by that time numbered twenty thousand persons, were split by a controversy over the succession, with the majority supporting Verigin and a minority supporting Lukerya's brother. The Russian authorities intervened, took the side of Lukerya's brother, and banished Peter Verigin. Even in exile Verigin managed to keep in contact with his followers, calling upon them to return to their older and stricter way of life, to abstain from oaths, military service, the use of intoxicants, and all forms of violence, to practice vegetarianism, and to hold all property in common. Following these instructions, the young Dukhobors then enrolled in the army announced at Easter 1895 that they would no longer serve. On June 29, 1895, the Dukhobors in three different settlements held a solemn public burning of all the weapons they possessed. The Russian government reacted by subjecting the Dukhobors to extremely repressive measures. *Leo Tolstoy and his followers, with the help of Quakers in England and America, convinced the Russian officials, however, to allow more than seven thousand Dukhobors to emigrate to Canada. Tolstoy completed his last novel, *Resurrection*, for the special purpose of devoting the proceeds from its sales to financing the resettlement of the Dukhobors.

In 1902 the Russian authorities released Peter Verigin from his Siberian exile and he joined the Dukhobors in Canada. Upon his arrival most of the Dukhobors recognized his authority; and during the 22 years of his leadership in Canada the group achieved a considerable degree of stability, unity, and well-being. His rule was suddenly and tragically brought to an end on October 29, 1924, when he was killed in an explosion on a Canadian Pacific train.

Peter Verigin is revered to this day by the Dukhobors of Canada as their greatest leader. The traditional virtues to which Verigin recalled his followers gave Tolstoy and his associates the mistaken impression that the Dukhobors represented a successful demonstration of the feasibility of Tolstoyan anarchism as an organizing principle for society. What the Tolstoyans failed to realize was that the nonviolent, pacifist Dukhobors actually accepted a thoroughly autocratic form of internal government, a kind of hereditary theocracy. A move away from traditional autocratic rule was taken in 1962 when John J. Verigin, the great-grandson of Peter Vasilyevich, was proclaimed leader but proposed that he be chosen instead as honorary chairman of a democratically elected Executive Committee.

Bibliography:

B. George Woodcock and Ivan Avakumovich, *The Doukhobors* (Toronto and New York, 1968).

William B. Edgerton

VERNET, Madeleine Cavelier (3 September 1878, Houlmes, Seine-Maritime, France—1949, France). *Education*: primary schools at Houlmes and Barentin; then largely self-educated. *Career*: founder and director, L'Avenir Sociale, 1906-21; journalist, educator, and peace activist.

Madeleine Vernet, born to an ardently republican family of peasants and workers, showed concern early in life for the social afflictions of the poor, the farmers of the high ground, and the textile workers of the valleys of her native Vexin. From the same background came her awareness of the maltreatment of women. To these two causes and, after 1914, to pacifism, Vernet devoted her life.

Her journalistic career began in 1904 with the publication of an article in

Pages Libres denouncing the wretched functioning of the *assistance publique*; the result was the removal of foster children from the care of her widowed mother. Moving to Paris in 1904, Vernet obtained work briefly as an *aide-comptable*; in Paris she came to know +Albert Thomas, Marcel Sembat, and *Georges Yvetot, whose anarchist views—especially their faith in individual initiative, their confidence in the value of education, and their criticism of statist socialism—attracted her notice. Her simple peasant morality, however, led her to reject their more libertarian ideas, to which she responded in 1920 in the brochure *L'Amour libre*. In this work she rejected temporary sexual unions and abortions, but advocated latitude of choice for women.

Quitting her job, Vernet founded in 1906, with the help of her mother and sister, L'Avenir Sociale, a school for children of the poor at Neuilly-Plaisance. Plagued by financial difficulties, the school survived through aid from workers' cooperatives, through subscription drives in *l'Humanité* and *La Guerre Sociale*, and from contributions from Albert Thomas and Marcel Sembat. In 1908 the school moved to Epône and during the war, renamed the Orphelinat Ouvrier, it evacuated to Etrechat in the face of the advancing German army. Returning to Epône after the Battle of the Marne (1914), the school continued under Vernet's direction until it came under the control of the Communist party after 1921.

As war approached, Vernet's pacifist attitudes—of which she was to draw a lucid picture in the novel *La Nouvelle Équipe* (1930)—were sharpened; her attempt to publish them in *Renovation* was frustrated by the printer, who feared the censor. In May 1915, ignoring the censorship, she circulated clandestinely a poem "Pour les venger," dedicated to "all our missing comrades" who have fallen, "victims of error." Other poems followed, some suppressed by the censor but all passionately opposed to war. Several appeared in 1916 on postal cards, which were widely distributed in the trenches. In 1917 and 1918, Vernet took the lead in campaigns for the defense of Lucie Colliard, *François and *Marie Mayoux, and *Hélène Brion, all teachers active in opposition to the war.

When hostilities ended, she appealed to all to continue the work for a "true peace," calling on the French—women, especially—to reach out to the Germans; education, she said, was the answer. In January 1921 *La Mère Educatrice*, a journal founded by Vernet in 1917, published an "Appeal to Women," advocating absolute opposition to war. She followed this up in May with the establishment of the Ligue des femmes contre la guerre (League of Women Against War). In 1924 the League dissolved over the issue of support for a proletarian revolution; Vernet refused to condone any war, even civil.

In 1924 Vernet joined the République Supranationale of H. -L. Follin, and in 1927, responding to an appeal of the Women's International League for Peace and Freedom, she founded the Volonté de paix, which called for complete disarmament. Disarmament and revision of the peace treaties—along with education for peace—continued to be for Volonté de paix and for Vernet herself the crucial issues through the 1930s. Vernet spoke on disarmament in several of the principal cities of France and Belgium in 1929 and 1930, and in August

1930 she persuaded the League of the Rights of Man to adopt a resolution in favor of revision. A Free Disarmament Conference, supported by the major pacifist personalities and organizations of France and abroad, and which met in 1932, was largely the work of Vernet. Furthermore, she fought vigorously from 1920 on for recognition of conscientious objection and took an active part in the defense of Eugène Guillot and other CO's. In 1928, she published *De l'objection de conscience au desarmement (From Conscientious Objection to Disarmament)*.

The Volonté de paix ceased to exist after 1936, the victim of government antagonism and internal difficulties, but Vernet remained ever active in pacifist organizations, and continued to publish until 1939, *La Mère Educatrice*, the journal of an organization, Foyer de la Mère Educatrice, she founded in 1925. In June of that year, *Jean Giono drafted a petition, calling on the French government to disarm; it was signed by many leading French pacifists, including Madeleine Vernet. It was her last defiant act before the coming of World War II.

Bibliography:

A. *Contes et chansons pour la paix* (Levallois-Perret, 1933); *Hélène Brion: une belle conscience et une sombre affaire* (Levallois-Perret, 1917); *La nouvelle equipe* (Paris, 1930); *De l'objection de conscience au désarmement* (Paris, 1928); *Le Rameau d'olivier, contes pour la paix* (Levallois-Perret, 1929).

B. Helen Vernet and Jacques Ganuchaud, *L'Oeuvre de paix de Madeleine Vernet* (Paris, 1938).

Albert S. Hill

VÉRONE, Maria (20 June 1874, Paris—23 May 1938, Paris). *Education*: École communale, Levallois; baccalaureat, École Sophie-Germaine, Paris, 1904; licence ès-lettres, École de droit, Paris, 1907. *Career*: teacher, Paris, 1894-97; journalist, *La Paix*, 1897-1900, *L'Aurore*, 1897-98; *La Fronde* (pseudonym "Themis"), 1897-1902; *Le Droit des femmes*, 1906-38; editor, *L'Oeuvre*, 1908-38, *La Bataille Syndicaliste*, 1911-12, *La France Libre*, 1916-19; lawyer, 1907-38; founder and president, Union nationale des avocates; secretary-general, Ligue française pour le droit des femmes, 1904-19, president, 1919-38; member of central committee, Ligue des droits de l'homme, 1910-18; feminist and pacifist.

Free-thinking parents introduced Maria Vérone to pacifism in her youth. By age fifteen she was active in the movement and by twenty-three she was on the staff of a pacifist newspaper. In addition to these early influences, Vérone's pacifism developed through her long-time leadership of the French feminist movement and her briefer role in the Socialist party.

Feminism was the dominant interest of Vérone's life. For thirty-four years she led the Ligue française pour le droit des femmes (French League for the Rights of Women), where she provided one of the strongest links between feminism and pacifism. In common with most French feminists of her era, such as *Hubertine Auclert, Vérone believed that the acquisition of full rights by women would naturally lead to international peace: "To suppress war, women must vote'' ran a motto of the League. Unlike some feminists, however, Vérone also worked directly for pacifism rather than waiting for peace to result from the victory of feminism. She developed a three point program for the League—equality of the sexes, pacifism, and anti-alcoholism. In support of the League's antiwar stance, Vérone established collaboration between the League and the Foyers pacifistes, worked for the adoption of arbitration in labor disputes, created a legal counseling service for French draftees, took a leading role in the renunciation of violence by French suffragists, and produced electoral literature opposing parliamentary candidates of a ''militaristic spirit.''

In May 1914 Vérone addressed the International Council of Women at Rome and urged feminists to work ''above all for pacifism.'' A few weeks later, however, she chose to support the French war effort, convinced that France was the victim of German aggression and that pacifists could defend themselves without hypocrisy. She tried to avoid breaking with friends such as Jeanne Halbwachs-Alexandre, but refused to participate in wartime pacifist activities such as *Jane Addams' Women's Peace Congress of 1915. After the war Vérone again worked for pacifism, now stressing the need for international agencies to prevent aggression, such as The Hague tribunal and the League of Nations.

Bibliography:

A. *La Femme devant la loi* (Paris, n.d.); *La Femme et la loi* (Paris, 1920); *Maria Vérone parle du féminisme* (Paris, n.d.); *Pourqui les femmes veulent voter* (Paris, 1919); *Résultats du suffrage des femmes* (Paris, 1914); *La Séparation et ses conséquences*, with Georges Lhermite, (Paris, 1906); *La Situation juridique des enfants naturels* (Paris, n.d.); *Woman Suffrage in Practice*, with Chrystal Macmillan and Marie Stritt, (London, 1913).

B. Memorial issue of *Le Droit des femmes*, June 1938.

Steven C. Hause

VIERBÜCHER, Heinrich (19 August 1893, Neuss on the Rhein, Germany—12 February 1939, Berlin). *Education*: presumably some years of business school. *Career*: secretary, union official, and speaker, Zentralverband der Angestellten in Berlin and Essen, 1918-23; salesman, 1923-24; full-time lecturer, Deutsche Friedensgesellschaft, 1924-33; head of a book shipping business, 1933-39.

Heinrich Vierbücher spent three years of World War I in Turkey, which was an ally of Germany. Until February 1916, he was employed in foundries in Constantinople (now Istanbul), and afterwards, in Damascus, presumably as an office worker in German enterprises. While in Turkey, he witnessed the mass-murder of the Armenian people by the Turks in 1915. After the war, he was one of those pacifists—*F. C. Endres, *O. Umfrid, and *A. T. Wegner were some others—who denounced that crime of genocide. Two years before Turkey joined the League of Nations, Vierbücher wrote a small book condemning the Turkish government for its slaughter of the Armenians and, simultaneously, he emphasized the responsibility of the German war government for the massacres.

After the war, Vierbücher went to work for the Zentralverband der Angestellten, (Central Union of Employees), a union of white-collar workers. In the spring of 1922, he was sent by the union to the Ruhr district, where he came into contact with the Deutsche Friedensgesellschaft (German Peace Society) (DFG) for the first time. Until that time, the DFG had seemed to him an erudite, aristocratic club. In January 1923, after hearing a speech by +Harry Kessler to the functionaries of the free union in Essen, Vierbücher decided to become an active participant in the peace movement. When the French intervened in the Ruhr in 1923, Vierbücher joined a minority of union officials who, like the pacifists of the Rhine-Westphalian industrial district, rejected passive resistance as serving extreme nationalist purposes. After the experiences of the Ruhr episode, Vierbücher gave up his union position because of political differences.

In the spring of 1924, Vierbücher became acquainted with *Fritz Küster and joined the West German branch of the German Peace Society, for whose goals he worked indefatigably. In just a few years he became one of the most eminent agitators of the postwar German peace movement. More than most other peace advocates, he knew how to speak the language of the people; just the announcement of a speech by him attracted large audiences. The charismatic, radiant personality of Vierbücher was intensified by his tall, athletic figure which concealed a delicate, sensitive character. With his countless lecture tours, which took him to all parts of Germany including the strongholds of extreme nationalism, he succeeded time and again in stimulating large numbers of people to work for peace and to establish local branches of the DFG. His presence often transformed the discouragement of DFG members in areas of diminishing peace activity into renewed commitment. Vierbücher's powers of persuasion and argumentation contributed immensely to the fact that for the first time in its history the DFG was able to establish itself firmly in the Rhine-Westphalian industrial district and to become a prominent factor in the peace movement of the Weimar Republic.

In addition to his lecture tours and organizational work, Vierbücher contributed articles to *Das Andere Deutschland*, *Die Menschheit*, and *Die Friedenswarte*—all prominent peace and antiwar periodicals. In his articles in the late 1920s and early 1930s, he warned against strong militaristic and nationalistic currents in Germany that were opposed to the preservation of peace and the Weimar Republic. His warnings were based on his contacts with right-wing and nationalist groups during his lecture tours, when he often entered into discussions with the members of such groups and was not infrequently threatened by them. To counter the fascist threat posed by the Nazis and the Stahlhelm (a right-wing veterans organization), Vierbücher called for a broad defensive front consisting of all republican and peace oriented groups. At the same time he did not remain silent about the concessions to nationalism that were being made by the German Social Democratic party. These criticisms led to his being banned in 1928 as a speaker from meetings sponsored by the Reichsbanner, a Socialist republican defense group for which Vierbücher had lectured regularly since 1924.

In 1930-31 Vierbücher was a speaker for the small Radikaldemokratische Partei (Radical Democratic Party) and in 1932-33 was chief editor of the newly founded pacifist weekly, *Alarm*, dedicated to the defense of the republic against all enemies. The paper published essays by the leading German pacifists such as +H. von Gerlach, *O. Lehmann-Russbüldt, *H. Mann, *O. Stillich and *L. Quidde. After the Nazi takeover of the German government on January 30, 1933, Vierbücher sought to escape by crossing the border into Czechoslovakia. He was caught and imprisoned, but released after a few weeks. For the next six years he was involved in the book shipping business. In 1939 a Nazi saw to it that inflammatory articles about Vierbücher's earlier pacifist activities appeared in Nazi newspapers. House searches, confiscation of material, and another arrest followed. Released on the same day, Vierbücher went home to rest and never woke up. The cause of death was given as apoplexy, but the circumstances of his death have never been clarified.

Bibliography:

A. *Was die kaiserliche Regierung den deutschen Untertanen verschwiegen hat. Armenien 1915. Die Abschlachtung eines Kulturvolkes durch die Türkei* (Hamburg-Bergedorf, 1930).

B. August Bangel, "Heinrich Vierbücher," *Das Andere Deutschland*, 10 (May, 1960), 8; F. K. [Fritz Küster], "Aus unserer Kampfzeit. Heinrich Vierbücher," *Das Andere Deutschland*, 6 (March, 1960), 8.

Helmut Donat
Trans. by Ruthann Richards

VILLARD, Oswald Garrison (13 March, Wiesbaden, Germany—1 October 1949, New York). *Education*: B.A., Harvard Coll., 1893, M.A., 1896. *Career*: reporter, *Philadelphia Press*, 1896-97; editorial writer (and later owner and president), *New York Evening Post*, 1897-1918; editor (and later owner), *The Nation*, 1897-1932 (contributing editor and writer, 1932-40); pacifist, reformer, journalist, author, and historian.

Above all, Oswald Garrison Villard was a pacifist, and his politics were first and foremost the politics of pacifism. A militant advocate of nonresistance, he remained at war with militarism throughout his long and successful career as a crusading liberal editor of the *New York Evening Post* and *The Nation* magazine. A grandson of the abolitionist, *William Lloyd Garrison, and the son of Fanny Villard, the suffragette and feminist antiwar activist, Villard always scorned those who gave only lip service to pacifism, insisting that it was not moderates but extremists and fanatics who brought success to a cause.

As a young journalist, Villard cut his pacifist teeth in opposition to the war with Spain. He denounced President William McKinley as one of "the greatest murderers in American history" for bowing to jingoistic imperialist pressures. Long before the outbreak of World War I, Villard had become one of the most outspoken pacifists in America. He was quick to join the fight against military preparedness, opposing +Theodore Roosevelt and lobbyists for the armed forces. When President +Woodrow Wilson's initial diplomacy seemed to lessen the threat of American participation in the war, Villard broke a precedent of 114 years by printing a picture of Wilson on the heretofore unblemished front page of the staid *New York Post*. He described the President as a leader who, "without rattling a sword, had won for civilization." Villard's enthusiasms were unrestrained. However, when Wilson later called for American intervention, Villard denounced him as a betrayer of principle who had thrown away a wonderful opportunity to set an example of wisdom and restraint to the world.

Villard's militant pacifism caused him to lose control of *The Post*, but he took over *The Nation* and soon turned it into a vehicle for his pacifism and his support of an array of causes designed to achieve a liberal and humane postwar world. In 1918 Villard echoed Wilson's call for a "peace without victory" and was an enthusiastic supporter of the President's fourteen point diplomacy of postwar reconciliation. He traveled to Europe to report on the work of the treaty makers in Paris and Versailles. Enraged by the bargaining and compromises that Wilson made in an effort to obtain allied acceptance of his League of Nations, Villard joined hands with long-time political enemies in the fight to defeat the treaty and what he called "a covenant with death." *The Nation* branded Wilson an international con man, who, it charged, stood discredited and condemned before the world.

Despite the uphill battles and numerous lost causes, the twenties were Villard's and *The Nation's* golden years. Villard relished adversity and he fought the postwar reaction as hard as he had fought American militarism. He and his editors defied the one-hundred percent American vigilantism during the Red Scare and he was personally stormed off a platform for advocating toleration of the Russian revolutionary government. He fought all forms of intolerance and bigotry, and was one of the first American journalists to consistently denounce Italian fascism when many others were watching Benito Mussolini with awe and admiration. As early as 1933 he toured the country warning that the rise of Hitler was a menace, not simply to Germany and the Jews, but to the entire civilized world.

Villard's consistent courage, his support for liberal, humane values as well as his outspoken pacifism weathered the postwar tide of reaction very well and he and his magazine were applauded and respected by many of the younger generation who were determined that war and repression should never again blight American life. The decade from 1925 to 1935 saw Villard's brand of liberalism, and especially his pacifism, riding the crest of a wave among the embattled liberal partisans who rallied to the support of +Franklin Roosevelt and the New Deal. Villard had modified his earlier Manchester liberalism, thus enabling him to lend enthusiastic support to the main outlines of Roosevelt's developing welfare state.

Nevertheless, as the danger of another worldwide conflagration developed in the mid-thirties, Villard's absolute pacifism seemed to many increasingly untenable. When Roosevelt began to resist neutrality legislation and stress the threat to the democracies posed by the "aggressor nations," Germany and Japan, Villard grew suspicious of the president's leadership, accusing him of dictatorial aspirations. Sometimes confused, often obstinate and driven by fear of American involvement in another war, Villard resorted to the antiwar slogans of the past and once again joined forces with a mixed bag of isolationists and political partisans opposed to the New Deal as well as Roosevelt's foreign policy.

By 1940 Villard was so intent on avoiding American involvement that he cast suspicion on the integrity of his pacifism by arguing that while the European democracies might be obliged to resist fascist aggression, the United States' obligation went no farther than moral condemnation. This led to his final break with *The Nation*, which, under the editorship of Freda Kirchwey, had long since come out in support of collective security against fascist expansion.

Villard never wavered in his belief that war and liberalism were inherently incompatible. His unquestioning acceptance of an absolute principle protected him from the anguished reflections of those, like *Reinhold Niebuhr, who reluctantly concluded that pacifism in some circumstances could have more dangerous consequences than taking up the sword. Villard was not a reflective thinker like Niebuhr, nor an analytical critic of the modern nation-state's penchant for war in the manner of a *Randolph Bourne or a Noam Chomsky. Most of his ideas were inherited and accepted on faith. His absolutism frequently seemed to rule out debate and led to failures of insight and analysis. Nevertheless, the genuine measure of his integrity and courage should not be overlooked. If he failed to recognize the need for compromise he did not believe it was his role, as a crusading journalist, to look at politics through the eyes of the politician. Villard exemplified a tradition which at its best maintained a critical stance toward centralized State power and its militaristic tendencies. This made him a staunch critic of Cold War interventionism, as well as an advocate of a freer and more humane world, until his death in 1949.

Bibliography:

A. *The Duty of the Press in Wartime* (New York, 1915); *Fighting Years: The Memoirs of a Liberal Editor* (New York, 1939); *Our Military Chaos* (New York, 1939); *Preparedness* (Washington, D.C., 1915).

B. D. Joy Humes, *Oswald Garrison Villard: Liberal of the Twenties* (New York, 1961); Stephan Thernstrom, "Oswald Garrison Villard and the Politics of Pacifism," *Harvard Library Bulletin*, 14 (Winter, 1960), 126-52; Michael Wreszin, *Oswald Garrison Villard, Pacifist at War* (Bloomington, IN, 1965); DAB, Suppl. 4, 1946-50, 149-52.

C. Oswald Garrison Villard Papers, Houghton Library, Harvard University.

Michael Wreszin

VINCENT, Henry (10 May 1813, London—29 December 1878, London). *Education*: printer's apprentice. *Career*: typesetter; political reformer; lecturer; editor, *The Western Vindicator*, 1839.

Born to a struggling silversmith, Henry Vincent earned his own livelihood from an early age. He became a printer's apprentice in his teens, and later worked as a typesetter. His interest in politics, spurred on by the French revolution of 1830, also began in adolescence, and he was elected to the Hull political union at seventeen. Dubbed "the Demosthenes of English democracy," Vincent possessed extraordinary oratorical abilities, but was also said never to have ventured "upon the dangerous ground of logic."

In the early and most spectacular period of his life, Vincent was a physical-force Chartist, who militantly exhorted his enthusiastic followers to prepare for revolution. For his activities he was imprisoned from May 1839 to January 1841 under harsh conditions. Imprisonment, and the severe repression of the Chartist movement, moderated Vincent's violent approach to politics and deepened his religious convictions, though he never abandoned the goal of workers' political rights. He began an enormously popular career of public lecturing and spoke on timely political and historical issues. Less successful were his seven attempts at a parliamentary seat from 1841 to 1852. As a lifelong teetotaller, he was an inspiration to the temperance movement. He advocated nonsectarian education for workers' improvement, sought to reconcile Chartists with religious dissenters, supported free trade, and, in a move criticized even by moral-force Chartists, joined *Joseph Sturge's middle-class Complete Suffrage Union.

Vincent's religious sympathies were with the Quakers, and he often attended their meetings, though he never formally joined the society. Appealing for universal peace in the name of God, Vincent made an emotional address to the London Peace Congress of 1851. During the American Civil War, however, he ardently defended the northern cause, claiming that it was part of a worldwide movement for liberty. In the decade following the war, he made four well-received speaking tours of the United States.

Vincent sought social justice through a confused combination of class struggle, peaceful reform, and Christian charity, but as a striking personality, he stirred his contemporaries of the Victorian reform movement.

Bibliography:

B. William Dorling, *Henry Vincent: A Biographical Sketch* (London, 1879); R. G. Gammage, *History Of The Chartist Movement, 1837-1854* (London, 1894; reprinted, New York, 1969); Eva H. Haraszti, *Chartism* (Budapest, 1978); David Jones, *Chartism And The Chartists* (London, 1975); Alexander Tyrrell, "Making the Millennium: The Mid-Nineteenth Century Peace Movement," *The Historical Journal*, 20:1 (1978), 89; DNB, XX, 358-59.

Stanley M. Max

VIRCHOW, Rudolf (13 October 1821, Schivelbein, Pomerania—5 September 1902, Berlin). *Education*: M.D., Friedrich Wilhelm Institute, Berlin, 1843. *Career*: professor of medicine, universities of Würzburg and Berlin; member, Democratic Congress, 1848; progressive liberal member of Prussian Diet, 1860s; member, German Reichstag, 1871-1902; physician, anthropologist, and liberal politician.

Rudolf Virchow is probably best known as one of Germany's most outstanding medical scientists. Besides the many contributions he made to the advancement of medical knowledge, however, he was the most vociferous advocate of democracy and international understanding in nineteenth century Germany. His medical views were intimately linked with his political and social views; they were based on a profound sense of respect for human life, for social justice and equality.

Virchow's involvement in German politics began in 1848 when he joined the extreme radical left during the revolutionary struggle for a united Germany. Besides sitting in the radical Democratic Congress which met in October 1848 at Berlin, he was also a driving force behind the Medical Reform Movement of 1848 which, among other things, sought to improve the delivery of medical care to all segments of society.

In the 1860s, Virchow reemerged in German politics as one of the founders of the left-liberal Progressive party in Prussia. As a member of the Prussian Diet, he was one of the most tenacious opponents of Bismarck in the constitutional struggle which centered on the monarchy's push for increased military expenditures. After Germany's unification in 1871, Virchow continued to fight against the growing spirit of extreme nationalism in Germany and to foster international understanding.

In pursuit of international understanding, he was a steadfast supporter of international conferences as the best means for bringing the nations closer together. Therefore, he was a familiar figure at international medical conferences which for Virchow were not only occasions for the exchange of scientific knowledge, but served a political function as well. He also regularly attended the annual meetings of the Interparliamentary Union, an international body dedicated to maintaining a dialogue between nations.

Although Virchow never became actively involved in the German peace movement which had its beginning in 1892, he frequently used his position in parliament to promote the idea of peace. As early as 1869, he introduced into the Reichstag a proposal for international disarmament. He lent his name and prestige to several unsuccessful efforts at organizing a peace society in Germany in the 1880s. He served on the liberal Parliamentary Committee for Peace and Arbitration, which sought to pressure the German government into concluding arbitration treaties with other nations. One notable result of these efforts was the arbitration clauses appended to Chancellor Leo Caprivi's commercial treaties of 1891. Virchow and his liberal colleagues also campaigned to gain support in Germany for The First Hague Peace Conference (1899). When he died in 1902, Germany not only lost her greatest physician and liberal politician, but also one of her most persistent voices against chauvinism and military expansion.

Bibliography:

A. *Krieg und Frieden* (Berlin, 1869).

B. Erwin H. Ackerknecht, *Rudolf Virchow Doctor-Statesman-Anthropologist* (Madison, WI, 1953).

Brigitte M. Goldstein

VISSCHERS, Guillaume Joseph Auguste (31 August 1804, Maastricht, Netherlands—3 June 1874, Brussels). *Education*: Dr.' jur., Univ. of Liège, 1825. *Career*: lawyer; pacifist; president, Congress of the Friends of Universal Peace, Brussels, 1848; vice-president, Peace Congresses in Paris, 1849, Frankfurt, 1850, and London, 1851; vice-president, Ligue internationale et permanente de la paix, 1867; president, Belgian section of the Red Cross, 1870; president, Conférence pour la réforme et la codification du droit des gens, Brussels; vice-president, Association pour la réforme et la codification du droit des gens (Belgium).

Guillaume Visschers belonged to the first generation of European peace activists in the nineteenth century who sought to organize leagues and congresses to popularize the cause of peace. As a humanitarian, he opposed the practice of duelling, struggled to abolish the death penalty, and worked to reform the prison systems. Moreover, he was interested in the reform of public education and served as secretary of a society to encourage elementary education in 1836. His interest in education also included vocational teaching and the teaching of the deaf, dumb, and blind. To further these concerns, he went to Birmingham and other cities in England in the early 1840s in order to study the municipally organized educational and charitable institutions at first hand. Visschers worked also to promote the interests of workers, particularly miners.

In addition to this wide range of social concerns, Visschers became involved in the mid-century peace movement and agreed to help the Anglo-American peace societies spread their ideas in Europe. Thus he helped organize the first international peace congress ever held in Europe in Brussels in 1848. Then he traveled in England with *Joseph Sturge to participate in the Birmingham and Manchester meetings of the British Peace Society. Besides serving as vice-president of three succeeding peace congresses on the Continent, Visschers joined *Edmund Potonié's peace society (founded in Antwerp, 1858) and the Paris society created in 1867 by *Frédéric Passy and *Auguste Couvreur called the Ligue internationale et permanente de la paix (International and Permanent League of Peace). In 1873 he helped organize a meeting after consulting with two American visitors, +David Dudley Field and J. B. Miles, which led to the establishment of the Association for the Reform and Codification of the Law of Nations. Visschers served in its initial executive committee until his death the following year.

Bibliography:

B. *Bibliographie Nationale*, IV, 279-281.

Nadine Lubelski-Bernard
Trans. by Sandi E. Cooper

VOLLENHOVEN, Cornelis van (5 May 1874, Dordrecht, Netherlands—29 April 1933, Leyden). *Education*: Dr. jur., Univ. of Leyden, 1898. *Career*: Ministry of Colonies, 1897-1901; professor of law, Univ. of Leyden, 1901-33.

Cornelis van Vollenhoven developed a distinguished career in two areas of law—the adat-law or customary law of the Netherlands Indies and the study of the works of Hugo Grotius. Van Vollenhoven's special contribution was the development of the idea of an international penal law involving the creation of a supranational military force. In his thesis, *Omtrek en inhoud van het internationaal recht (Scope and Content of International Law)*, (1898), described by a colleague as one of the most brilliant treatises on international law since Grotius, van Vollenhoven raised the issue of a global peace-keeping system involving enforcement of international decisions.

While +Theodore Roosevelt mentioned such a possibility and *William J. Bryan included the idea in his notions of peace keeping, it was to van Vollenhoven's credit that he developed a model treaty and a rudimentary system for its implementation. Van Vollenhoven wanted his nation to propose such an arrangement and laid forth his ideas in "De roeping van Holland" ("The Vocation of Holland"), which appeared in the journal, *De Gids* and which were further elaborated in a much discussed work, *De eendracht van het land (The Union of the Country)* (1913). The organized peace movement, concerned largely with arbitration, did not take up his proposal nor did it encourage the Dutch government to sponsor the idea. Van Vollenhoven, however, continued to pursue his vision, hoping that the third Hague Conference, planned for 1915, would discuss it. Because of the outbreak of World War I, that meeting was never held.

Throughout the war, van Vollenhoven continued publishing on the subject of sanctions for criminal states that violated the peace of nations. His major treatise, published in English as *The Three Stages of the Law of Nations* (1919), appealed to a public eager to find ways of curbing the arbitrary behavior of sovereign states. Van Vollenhoven was enormously influential in giving new impetus to the development of international law after the war.

From 1924-27, he served as presiding officer of the general claims commission between the United States and Mexico, developing a settlement which served as a model for other cases. His work, *Du droit de paix; de jure pacis (Concerning the Law of Peace)* (1932), elaborated earlier ideas and ended with a personal plea for the success of the Disarmament Conference to fulfill the promise of article II of the League of Nations treaty. He died before the failure of the conference became apparent, but his labors helped shape the peace that emerged after World War II, in particular, the shaping of the United Nations.

Bibliography:

A. *Du Droit de paix. De jure pacis* (The Hague, 1932); *De eendracht van het land* (Gravenhage, 1913); *The Framework of Grotius' Book De Jure Belli ac Pacis, 1625* (Amsterdam, 1931); *Het onbaatzuchtige in recht en staat* (Leiden, 1917); *The Law of Peace* (London, 1936); *Omtrek en inhoud van het international recht* (Leiden, 1898); *The Three Stages in the Evolution of the Law of Nations* (The Hague, 1919); *War Obviated by an International Police* (The Hague, 1915).

B. Henriette L. T. de Beaufort, *Cornelis van Vollenhoven, 1874-1933* (Haarlem, 1954); P.S. Gerbrandy, *National and International Stability* (London, 1944); "Karakterschets Professor Mr. C. van Vollenhoven," *De Hollandsche Revue*, 18 (1913), 164-71; Johanna

K. Oudendijk, ''Van Vollenhoven's 'The Three Stages in the Evolution of the Law of Nations': A Case of Wishful Thinking,'' in *Tijdschrift voor rechtsgeschiedenis*, 48, 1 (1980), 3-27; A. J. P. Tammes, *De international politiemacht* (The Hague, 1958); *Biografisch woordenboek van Nederland* (1979), I, 625-27; *Verspreide geschriften* (complete bibliography) (vol 3, Gravenhage, 1935).

J. H. Rombach

WÄGNER, Elin Mathilda Elisabeth (2 May 1882, Lund, Sweden—7 January 1949, Berg, Kronobergslän, Sweden). *Education*: high schools in Nyköping and Hälsingborg. *Career*: reporter, *Helsingborgs-Posten*, 1903-5; assistant editor, *Idun*, 1907-16; editor-in-chief, *Tidevarvet*, 1923-36; member, Swedish Academy, 1944; novelist and pacifist.

A fervent advocate of women's suffrage, Elin Wägner was a delegate from Sweden to the International Congress of Women held at The Hague in 1915. There her encounter with the Hungarian pacifist *Rosika Schwimmer and the vision of woman as peace maker had lifelong consequences for her. Ever afterward she believed the cause of feminism to be inseparably linked with the cause of peace.

She early regarded war as a manifestation of a lopsidedly masculine civilization. Complete equality of the sexes would bring about a peaceful world. Coming from a clerical family, she tended to employ Christian arguments in her pacifist message. She worked closely with groups of English Quakers and in 1936 she joined the Society of Friends.

Elin Wägner was a highly active member of the Women's International League for Peace and Freedom. After the Armistice of 1918, she traveled to war-stricken Vienna and the occupied provinces of the German Rhineland in order to study the effects of the war and to fathom its psychological impact. In personal contacts with leaders of the victorious powers she urged modifications of the Versailles treaty, in whose harsh terms she foresaw the seeds of a new world war. In the early 1920s, she witnessed the beginnings of Nazism in the Rhineland and Bavaria and was confirmed in her belief that peace must be based upon reconciliation and nonviolent action.

During the interwar years she worked tirelessly on behalf of the League of Nations and disarmament, and against the alarming growth of munitions industries, mechanized warfare, and especially the threat of poison gas. The inspiring example of *Gandhi's nonviolent resistance was a recurring theme in her articles and lectures.

In 1935, in the pages of the magazine *Tidevarvet*, Wägner raised the idea of a "Women's Non-violent Revolt against War," calling for a collective refusal by women to accept the system of bomb shelters. She led a Swedish delegation to the League of Nations with petitions and plans in hope of finding a response among the other international peace organizations represented there. The proposal was received with interest, but achieved no practical results.

With the coming of the Second World War, Elin Wägner's thinking about peace broadened into a fundamental critique of civilization, taking as its chief target the human, particularly male, arrogance which had defied technology and chosen "supremacy," "victory," and "destruction", of enemies as its guiding values. This critique was presented with philosophical acuteness and had powerful, almost prophetic, elements of what is now called ecological insight. It was formulated principally in her books *Fred med jorden (Peace with the Earth)* (1940) and *Väckarklocka (The Alarm Clock)* (1941).

As an author of fiction, Elin Wägner was both well-known and loved. She wrote some of the most widely read and enduring Swedish novels of the first half of the twentieth century, several with strong religious overtones. Among the novels having a peace motif were *Släkten Jerneploogs framgång (The Family Jerneploog's Success)* (1916), *De fem pärlorna (The Five Pearls)* (1927), and *Dialogen fortsätter (The Dialogue Continues)* (1932). In all of them women's struggle for influence in society was intertwined with the struggle for peace and reconciliation.

Bibliography:

A. *De fem pärlorna* (Stockholm, 1927); *Dialogen fortsätter* (Stockholm, 1932); *Ett nytt försvar* (Stockholm, 1924); *Från Seine, Rhen och Ruhr* (Stockholm, 1923); *Fred med jorden* (Stockholm, 1940); *Fredrika Bremer* (Stockholm, 1949); *Selma Lagerlöf* (Stockholm, 1942-43); *Släkten Jerneploogs framgång* (Stockholm, 1916); *Väckarklocka* (Stockholm, 1941).

B. Holger Ahlenius, *Elin Wägner* (Stockholm, 1936); Ulla Isaksson and Erik Hjalmar Linder, *Elin Wägner* (2 vols., Stockholm, 1977-80); *Svenska män och kvinnor* (1955), VIII, 450-52.

C. Elin Wägner Collection, Women's History Collections, A 48, Göteborg University Library.

Ulla Isaksson and Erik Hjalmar Linder
Trans. by Howard T. Lutz

WALD, Lillian D. (10 March 1867, Cincinnati, OH—1 September 1940, Westport, CT). *Education*: graduate, New York Hospital School of Nursing, 1891; Women's Medical Coll., 1892-93. *Career*: founder, Visiting Nurse Service; founder, Henry Street Settlement; author, public health nurse, social worker, social reformer, feminist, and publicist.

Lillian Wald's belief in pacifism was rooted in her experiences as a nurse, dedicated to preserving life, and as a settlement house worker in New York City. She won prominence as a propagandist for liberal reform whose success stemmed from personal charm and from contacts with the powerful in the worlds of finance and politics.

At the outset of World War I, Wald headed a committee to organize a parade of American women to protest the fighting. On August 29, 1914, more than 12,000 women, representing a broad spectrum of organizations, marched down Fifth Avenue in an expression of opposition to war. The parade was not the first evidence of Wald's dedication to peace. Two years earlier, she had resisted the pleas of social worker friends and refused to endorse +Theodore Roosevelt's presidential bid, because she could not "swallow those two battleships" advocated by the Progressives nor accept the fortification of the Panama Canal.

Wald worked against war through two organizations. The first, the American Union Against Militarism (AUAM), evolved from meetings held late in 1914 to consider the effects of war on neutral as well as belligerent nations. Originally called the Anti-Preparedness Committee, the AUAM was committed to mobilizing public opinion against militarism, which threatened democracy, and for internationalism. Eventually, it grew to 6,000 members, with Wald as its chair. In this capacity Wald worked as a lobbyist with the public and the powerful to "save the soul" of America. She addressed mass meetings, testified before Congressional committees, and unrelentingly pressured +Woodrow Wilson in person and by letter to avoid the lure of those who favored increased armaments and conscription. In 1916 the Union attained its greatest triumph when it helped avert war with Mexico by publicizing the American role in provoking a Mexican Army attack on U.S. troops at Carrizal and by demanding a conference to resolve Mexican-American problems.

With American entrance into World War I, the AUAM coalition disintegrated because of differences over the emphasis to be placed on the Conscientious Objectors' Bureau and on the Union's participation in the People's Council. Wald, fearful that she would alienate some of her powerful friends in government, resigned as chair in the summer of 1917.

The second peace group with which Wald was associated was the Women's Peace party (WPP), an organization which reflected her philosophical blending of feminism and pacifism. Questions of war and peace, she maintained, were too important to be left in the hands of men, who tended to be susceptible to calls to battle. Women, the victims of war, should have equal rights in diplomacy. While Wald did not attend the Hague Conference, she defended the WPP's proposal of continuous mediation of the war and arranged meetings with Wilson so that the concept could be explained. She did go to Zurich for the Second International Women's Congress in 1919 and returned to promote its program, including American participation in the League of Nations.

Until her death in 1940, Wald, the self-proclaimed "militant pacifist," worked for peace through disarmament. Her influence was diminished after the Red Scare of 1919-20, but she continued to speak out, to pressure friends to protest the situation in Germany, and to think internationally. As a nurse, she knew that no nation could isolate itself, for "germs know no frontier."

Bibliography:

A. *The House on Henry Street* (New York, 1915); *Windows on Henry Street* (Boston, 1934).

B. Robert L. Duffus, *Lillian Wald: Neighbor and Crusader* (New York, 1938); DAB, Supp. 2, 687-88; NAW, III, 526-29.

C. Lillian Wald Papers, Manuscript Division, New York Public Library; Lillian Wald Papers, Butler Library, Columbia University.

Doris Groshen Daniels

WALKER, Amasa (4 May 1799, Woodstock, CT—29 October 1875, Brookfield, MA). *Education*: district schools. *Career*: businessman; member, Massachusetts House of Representatives, 1848-49, 1859-62; member, Massachusetts Senate, 1849-51; Massachusetts Secretary of State, 1851-52; member, U. S. House of Representatives, 1862-63; economist, reformer and pacifist.

One of the few absolute pacifists to hold elective office, Amasa Walker served in both houses of the Massachusetts legislature and also represented Massachusetts in Congress. Best known as an economist and authority on monetary policy, he wrote a widely read treatise, *The Science of Wealth: A Manual of Political Economy* (1866). He also taught political economy at Oberlin College (which he helped found) and at Amherst College. A successful businessman until his retirement in 1840 because of ill health and a desire to study and do public service, Walker also took an active part in many of the reform efforts of his day. He helped found the Boston Lyceum, served as president of the Boston Temperance Society in 1839, supported the abolition of slavery, and championed the cause of peace.

Walker first became interested in the question of peace after reading copies of *William Ladd's *Calumet* in the early 1830s. He quickly came to the conclusion that war was not only a great calamity, but "under all circumstances, and in every degree and form sinful." Not at all sympathetic with those advocates of peace who made a distinction between offensive and defensive war, Walker urged the Massachusetts Peace Society, which he had joined, to renounce all war and avoid any temporizing on the question.

He carried on the same battle within the American Peace Society (APS), urging its leadership in 1837 to amend the constitution of the organization and soundly condemn defensive war. The following year he refused to bolt a peace convention with *George C. Beckwith and the APS leadership when women were given full membership in the convention and its committees. Joining with *William Lloyd Garrison and the more radical reformers, Walker not only remained a participant in the meeting, but introduced a resolution declaring that all human life was "inviolable and can never be taken by individuals or nations without committing sin against God." Out of the convention came Garrison's New England Non-Resistance Society. Although a supporter of the Society's strong condemnation of all war, Walker did not join, for he could not accept its extreme "no-government" position and its total rejection of state authority. He remained active in the APS and in 1843 he represented the Society, along with Beckwith, at the international peace conference held in London. Appointed vice president, he joined with 300 other delegates to share information, coordinate peace efforts, and build international public support.

During the 1840s Walker joined with *Elihu Burritt to promote a variety of peace schemes. In 1846 they established the Worcester County Peace Society to promote the cause of "Peace and Universal Brotherhood" and the principle that all war was "inconsistent with the spirit of Christianity." Walker also helped Burritt develop the idea for a League of Universal Brotherhood (LUB) that would not only be against slavery and war, but against intemperance, trade restrictions, and "everything injurious to the universal interests of man." Burritt successfully promoted the idea of the LUB in England and then brought it back to the United States. Walker served as corresponding secretary of the American branch and helped establish numerous state and local chapters. A strong supporter of the League's efforts to hold international peace conferences in Europe, Walker attended the 1849 conference in Paris and helped convince the assembled delegates to endorse Ladd's plan for a congress of nations.

In the decade before the Civil War Walker continued his association of the APS and served as one of its vice presidents. In 1859 he wrote a satire on war preparation as a method of national defense. Entitled *Le Monde; or In Time of Peace Prepare for War*, he clearly presented the pacifist case against armaments. The pamphlet was published in both the United States and England.

The coming of the Civil War presented Walker with a difficult dilemma, as it did other peace-minded abolitionists. His hatred of slavery was pitted against his principled opposition to all war. Unlike most of his antiwar contemporaries who came to see war as the lesser of two evils and fully supported the Union side, Walker remained true to his pacifist principles. He did accept the APS position that the conflict between North and South was a rebellion and, therefore, a matter of internal order outside of the cognizance of the Society. But Walker could never bring himself to support the war. Speaking to the APS in May 1863, he declared that he had no faith in armed conflict and predicted that nothing good would come from the war that "might not be obtained in a better way."

The Civil War shattered the peace movement in the United States, but Walker continued to reaffirm his antiwar commitments. Anticipating the arguments of a later generation of pacifists, he added to his principled opposition to war the argument that the enormous costs of modern warfare would ultimately lead to its abolition. Before his death he came to see war as totally unjustifiable from both a religious and a practical point of view.

Bibliography:

A. *Iron-clad War-ships; Or, the Prospective Revolution in the War System. Speech of Hon. Amasa Walker, before the American Peace Society, at its Anniversary in Boston, May 26, 1862* (Boston, 1862); *Le Monde; or In Time of Peace Prepare for War* (London, 1859); *The Suicidal Folly of the War System. An Address before the American Peace Society, at its Anniversary in Boston, May 25, 1863* (Boston, 1863).

B. Peter Brock, *Pacifism in the United States: From the Colonial Era to the First World War* (Princeton, NJ, 1968); Peter Tolis, *Elihu Burritt: Crusader for Brotherhood* (Hamden, CT, 1968); F. A. Walker, *Memoir of Hon. Amasa Walker* (Boston, 1888); DAB, 10, 338-39.

Harold Josephson

WALLACE, Henry Agard. See *Biographical Dictionary of Internationalists*.

WANG Ching-wei (4 May 1883, Canton, China—10 November 1944, Nagoya, Japan). *Education*: graduated, Tokyo Law Coll., 1906. *Career*: statesman.

As a young student in Tokyo (1904-6), Wang Ching-wei responded to the fervent revolutionary appeals of Sun Yat-sen who was mobilizing support to overthrow the corrupt and inept Manchu dynasty that ruled China. Wang lent his talents as writer and activist to Sun's cause and by the 1920s, after two decades of association with Sun, Wang was regarded as the most trusted ally of the "Father of the Republic" and enjoyed an apparently secure position in the hierarchy of Sun's Nationalist (Kuomintang) political party. When Sun died in 1925, most observers felt that Wang was his logical successor. In the scuffle for power that ensued, however, it became clear that, for all the respect he commanded, Wang lacked the one ingredient for successful political maneuvering: a strong base of military power. Accordingly, by 1927, Wang lost the political contest to a lesser disciple of Sun's, the commander of the Nationalist military academy, Chiang Kai-shek. In the years after 1927, as Chiang solidified his control over China, he awarded posts of high standing in the Nationalist government to his rival; Wang served concurrently as premier and foreign minister (1932-35). Nevertheless, decisive political authority rested with the Generalissimo and his allies.

In his position as foreign minister, Wang worked to defuse the growing tensions between his country and Japan through peaceful means such as negotiation and compromise. In doing so, Wang stressed the same Pan-Asian theme that his mentor, Sun, had championed: that China and Japan were natural brothers with a shared cultural heritage. While the paths of the two nations had diverged sharply in the twentieth century, it was not too late to reconcile differences. If that could be accomplished, the once great Asian civilization would be revitalized and Japan and China, harmoniously allied, would then be in a position to check both Western imperialism and expanding Soviet Communism and to create a prosperous "Asia for the Asians."

Wang's commitment to these ideas was severely tested by the Sino-Japanese War which erupted in 1937. While most of his countrymen were caught up in the spirit of resistance to the Japanese aggressor, Wang became the chief spokesman of the "peace faction" within the Kuomintang. His determination to find a basis for a negotiated settlement of the war was quickened by two concerns. One was humanitarian: a sensitivity to the carnage and misery caused by the fighting, including the scorched-earth tactics employed by the Nationalist armies. The other was political: Wang's growing awareness that the war was going to be a protracted struggle which would drain the energies and resources of both Nationalist China and Japan and allow the communists (Chinese, Russian, or both) to emerge the true victors in the end—a judgment validated by history.

Wang defected from the Nationalist Government and fled to Hanoi in December 1938. At the same time he made public his purpose and program in a lengthy message meant for both Chinese and Japanese audiences. The message, soon dubbed the "peace telegram," made it clear that Wang was willing to lend his name to the sensitive and dangerous task of negotiating peace with a Japan whose armies then occupied China's main cities. However, Wang warned Japanese leaders that peace was impossible unless Japan withdrew its forces from Chinese soil and instituted educational policies which would lead the Japanese people to abandon their traditional attitude of the contempt for China.

The "peace telegram" brought forth public declarations of support for Wang from both Chinese and Japanese. It eventually became clear to Wang, however, that issuing telegrams and making radio broadcasts on the theme of peace could not undercut the influence which Chiang Kai-shek commanded. Reluctantly, therefore, and well aware of the risks to the cause of peace and to his own good name as a Chinese statesman, Wang agreed to become the head of a "peace government," the so-called Reorganized National Government of the Republic of China, inaugurated in Japanese-occupied Nanking in March 1940. Wang remained the leader of this regime until his death four years later.

Wang has been condemned as traitor and puppet by both Nationalist and Communist Chinese. Many have interpreted his cooperation with Japan as evidence of political opportunism born of frustration in his long power struggle with Chiang Kai-shek. His defenders, however, argue that Wang's intentions were patriotic and selfless. He was genuinely committed to peace, they say, and, failing that, he sought to ameliorate conditions in Occupied China by undertaking the dangerous and thankless task of wartime collaboration.

Bibliography:

A. "Towards the Realization of Peace with Honour," *A Collection of Documents with a Prefatory Note*, ed. by China Institute of International Affairs, (Shanghai, 1939), No. 2, 8-13.

B. Howard L. Boorman, "Wang Ching-wei: A Political Profile," in Chun-tu Hsueh, *Revolutionary Leaders of Modern China* (New York, 1971) 295-319; John H. Boyle, *China and Japan at War, 1937-1945: The Politics of Collaboration* (Stanford, 1972).

John H. Boyle

WARREN, Josiah (1798, Boston—14 April 1874, Boston). *Education*: self-educated. *Career*: musician, inventor, editor, publisher, and utopian radical.

A musician in youth, Josiah Warren invented the lard-burning lamp in 1821. Converted to the utopian ideas of Robert Owen, he moved with his family to the Owenite colony in New Harmony, Indiana, in 1825, but returned to Cincinnati two years later as a radical individualist. There he established "equity" store, which closed in 1829. In 1833 he established a journal, *The Peaceful Revolutionist*, in which he called for an orderly, just community that would be brought into being without the use of violence. Moving to New York in 1850, he helped establish the following year Modern Times, a utopian community on Long Island.

Warren believed that the State was the embodiment of violence and tended to undermine harmony in the community. Often called the first American anarchist, his anarchism was of the "individualist" rather than the "communist" type. A community would be held together by voluntary mutual cooperation built upon the notion of a free exchange of labor time. An ardent exponent of the labor theory of value, he worked out a scheme for labor value notes which he believed would eventually supplant money. He came to believe that the weakness of Robert Owen's approach was his reliance on communal planning.

A sympathizer described the residents of Modern Times as honest and industrious. Although they had learned to "mind their own business," they also cooperated with their neighbors for the advantage of all. Law courts, policemen, crime, and jails were nonexistent. No one could gain wealth except by his own work. Presumably a society of this kind would be the model for a truly peaceful world.

Bibliography:

A. *Equitable Commerce* (New York, 1852); *True Civilization an Immediate Necessity* (Boston, 1863; New York, 1967).

B. William Bailie, *Josiah Warren: The First American Anarchist* (New York, 1972).

C. New Harmony Workingmen's Institute Library, New Harmony, Indiana.

Mulford Q. and Marjorie H. Sibley

WARBURG, James Paul. See *Biographical Dictionary of Internationalists*.

WASZKLEWICZ-VAN SCHILFGAARDE, Johanna Maria Cornelia Bertha (7 November 1850, Zoeterwoude, Netherlands—4 December 1937, The Hague). *Education*: privately educated. *Career*: peace activist.

Johanna Waszklewicz-van Schilfgaarde was born into an aristocratic family and in 1885 married a nobleman of Polish origin who had a career in the Dutch colonial military. In 1898 this woman of great organizational talent became interested in the peace movement, probably as a result of private reading which included works by *Bertha von Suttner and the Dutch author, Louis Couperus. She became Dutch vice-president of the Paris based League of Women for International Disarmament, founded by the *Princess Wiszniewska. Very shortly afterwards, desiring her own autonomy, Waszklewicz-van Schilfgaarde broke with the Princess and created an independent Dutch women's peace society which published *Vrede door Recht*, a journal that she edited.

In 1902 this group merged with the older Dutch peace society, the Algemene Nederlandse Vredebond, and she resigned her office. She continued to remain active in the peace movement until 1902, attending the Glasgow (1901) and Monaco (1902) Universal Peace Congresses as a representative of a small society founded by the English peace crusader, *William T. Stead, whom she had met during the 1899 Hague Peace Conference. During that meeting, her energetic activity and desire to see a successful outcome from the diplomatic congress led her to undertake a number of activities to build public support in The Netherlands. Personally, she entertained lavishly during the Conference in order to create an atmosphere where diplomats and private peace activists might meet. She later wrote an introduction to the Dutch translation of Bertha van Suttner's memoir of the Hague Conference. Relief for South African victims of the Boer War became her next public activity and she undertook a private journey to England in an effort to visit with government officials to protest the war. While she was not admitted to the highest offices, her trip aroused some sympathy among politicians and gave support to Britons who opposed the war. After 1902 she moved abroad, becoming a Roman Catholic in 1904 and settling in Rome. Thereafter, her interest in peace and antiwar labors became less conspicuous.

Bibliography:

A. *Frédéric Passy* (Haarlem, 1900); *Internationale ontwapening, een vrouwenzaak en een mannenbelang* (Amsterdam, 1899); *Open brief aan Felix Ortt; een woord tot de Tolstoianen en Christeli jk anarchisten* (Amsterdam, 1899).

B. "Karakterschets; Mevrouw B. Waszklewicz-van Schilfgaarde" in *De Hollandsche Revue*, 4 (1899), 30-47; Bertha von Suttner, *Den Haag en de vredesconferentie* (Amsterdam 1900).

C. A. P. van Schilfgaarde, "Collectie mevrouw B. Waszklewica van Schilfgaarde," typewritten mss. The Hague, General State Archives.

J. H. Rombach

WAYLAND, Francis (11 March 1796, New York—30 September 1865, Providence, RI). *Education*: B.A., Union Coll., 1813, D.D., 1828; LL.D., Harvard Coll., 1852. *Career*: academic philosopher.

Francis Wayland, a Baptist minister and president of Brown University from 1827 to 1855, was the most influential academic moral philosopher in mid-nineteenth century America. Although he was never active in the organized antebellum peace crusade, Wayland's *The Elements of Moral Science* (1835) and other works effectively brought pacifism to the attention of American thinkers and the academic community.

As an evangelical Calvinist and ardent Jeffersonian, Wayland wanted to develop the Scottish common sense philosophy into a moral guide for the new nation. In 1835 he published *The Elements of Moral Science*, which sold over 100,000 copies and became the principal senior year college ethics course textbook throughout the antebellum era. Wayland's philosophical views emerged partly in reaction to some of the leading problems of the period such as slavery, manifest destiny, violence, and war. In the latter part of his textbook Wayland discussed these problems by applying the law of benevolence to them. According to him, the Gospels posited an ethics of mercy and charity: individuals had an obligation to promote the happiness of others who had no reciprocal obligations to them. If people committed acts of violence, individuals had a moral duty to forgive them and rectify the situation peacefully. If individuals were deliberately injured, only their goodness could overcome the evil action. Thus Wayland used the New Testament to claim that almost all violence was contrary to the revealed will of God; neither individuals nor governments had the right to declare war. He suggested to generations of college students that Christian nations must use love and forgiveness, not violence, to solve all disputes. The social wickedness of man could only be combatted by mutual kindness, patience, justice, and benevolence.

Wayland explicated his moral philosophy more fully after 1835. During the

Mexican War he told Americans they had a responsibility to disobey the commands of government officials who were waging a war of aggression. And as southerners began attacking the moderate antislavery position Wayland took in *The Elements of Moral Science* he modified his views by arguing that bondage was a form of violence contrary to the Bible and all laws of progress. Like many other antebellum pacifists, however, his desire to end slavery overcame his nonviolent scruples. During the Civil War he supported the Union cause, believing God was using the conflict to promote emancipation. In the 1865 revised edition of his textbook Wayland ruefully admitted that armed force was sometimes necessary to combat great evils and establish justice.

America's most famous antebellum academic philosopher pictured himself as a political moderate and upholder of sound tradition and justified authority. Ironically, however, while he rejected the radical abolitionist and pacifist views of the New England Non-Resistance Society, *The Elements of Moral Science* and other essays widely publicized a similar perspective in the decades before the Civil War.

Bibliography:

A. *The Elements of Moral Science* (New York, 1835); *The Duty of Obedience to the Civil Magistrate* (Boston, 1847).

B. Francis Wayland and H. L. Wayland, *A Memoir of the Life and Labors of Francis Wayland* (2 vols. New York, 1867).

Jayme A. Sokolow

WEGNER, Armin Theophil (16 October 1886, Wuppertal, Germany—17 May 1978, Rome). *Education*: studies at the universities of Zurich and Berlin; Dr. jur., Univ. of Breslau, 1914. *Career*: editor, *Der neue Orient* and *Der Osten*, 1918-19; antiwar activist, poet, and novelist.

The son of Marie Wegner, herself a renowned women's rights activist in Silesia, Armin T. Wegner was attracted to the intellectual radicalism of *Kurt Hiller's Activist Circle in the years prior to the outbreak of World War I when both were students of *Franz von Liszt in Berlin. Because he had principled objections to the war, Wegner enlisted in 1914 as a medical orderly. Confronting horrendous experiences of death and destruction during the campaigns in Poland and Turkey, he began writing antiwar poetry and prose, which was not published until after the war because of strict military censorship. He was an eyewitness to the appalling extermination in 1915 of one third of the entire Armenian population in the Ottoman Empire, Germany's ally. Wegner secretly photographed the death camps and passed on his detailed evidence of the systematic genocide to Johannes Lepsius in Berlin. His courageous efforts to rescue the cause of the Armenians from oblivion led to his recall to Germany.

Wegner was active in the November Revolution of 1918 as a member of the short-lived Politischer Rat geistiger Arbeiter (Political Council of Intellectual Workers) where he urged the formation of a transnational peace movement based on conscientious objection. In June 1919 he founded the Bund der Kriegsdienstgegner (League of Draft Resisters) and acted as its secretary till 1922. In the early twenties he was a regular speaker at antiwar rallies and demonstrations, a prominent member of the left-wing of the Deutsche Friedensgesellschaft (German Peace Society), and an established figure in the literary world of the Weimar Republic. In his book *Fünf Finger über Dir* (1930) an account of his five month journey to the Soviet Union in 1927-28, Wegner recorded his development from anarchism to communism and described his search for a synthesis of individual and society, of Tolstoyanism and Marxism, of freedom and necessity.

Wegner's name was on the first blacklist of 71 proscribed authors drawn up by the Nazis in March 1933 and copies of his works were publicly burned by them. Following his courageous Open Letter to Adolf Hitler, in which he protested against the anti-Semitic boycotts staged in April 1933, Wegner was arrested by the Gestapo, tortured, and imprisoned. Released in December 1933, he emigrated to Positano, Italy in 1936 where he remained, suffering from isolation and an acute crisis of identity.

Although some of Wegner's antiwar books had been highly praised by authors such as *Stefan Zweig and Thomas Mann in the twenties, he failed to reestablish his reputation in divided postwar Germany. He remained in Italy till the end of his days. Despite being awarded the Order of Merit of the Federal Republic in 1956 and the Eduard von der Heydt Prize of the city of Wuppertal in 1962, his death passed practically unnoticed. Nevertheless, his antimilitarist essays and manifestoes are valuable records of the ferment and action in the aftermath of World War I. A highly emotive, nontheoretical writer, Wegner sought to make practical contributions to the struggle against militarism, chauvinism, and fascism.

Bibliography:

A. *Der Ankläger. Aufrufe zur Revolution* (Berlin, 1921); *Fünf Finger über Dir. Bekenntnis eines Menschen in dieser Zeit* (Stuttgart, 1930); *Im Hause der Glückseligkeit. Aufzeichnungen aus der Türkei* (Dresden, 1920); *Jagd durch das tausendjährige Land* (Berlin, 1932); *Der Prozess Talaat Pascha* (Berlin, 1921); *Die Strasse mit den tausend Zielen* (Dresden, 1924); *Die Verbrechen der Stunde, die Verbrechen der Ewigkeit. Drei Reden wider die Gewalt* (Berlin, 1922); *Der Weg ohne Heimkehr. Ein Martyrium in Briefen* (Berlin, 1919).

B. Hedwig Bieber, *Armin T. Wegner. Eine Bibliographie* (Dortmund, 1973); Kurt Hiller, *Leben gegen die Zeit* (Reinbek, 1969); Jurgen Serke, *Die verebrannten Dichter* (Weinheim/Basle, 1977); Martin Rooney, "Armin T. Wegner. Eine literarisch-politische Biographie," Ph.D., dissertation, University of Bremen, 1982.

C. Armin T. Wegner Papers, Schiller Nationalmuseum, Marbach am Neckar, West Germany.

Martin Rooney

WEHBERG, Hans. See *Biographical Dictionary of Internationalists.*

WEIL, Simone (3 February 1909, Paris—29 August 1943, Ashford, Kent, England). *Education*: Baccalauréat in philosophy, Lycée Victor Duruy, 1925; Lycée Henri IV, 1926-28; diplôme d'Agrégation, École normale superieure,

1931. *Career*: philosophy teacher, Le Puy, Auxerre, Roanne, Bourges, St. Quentin, 1931-34, 1935-38; factory worker, 1934-35; agricultural worker, 1936, 1941; volunteer in Spain, Republican Front, 1936; resistance worker, Marseilles, 1940-42; editor, *Free France*, London, 1942-43.

Simone Weil's pacifism developed at the time when the growing economic crisis which became the Great Depression worsened the conditions of life for European workers. As a young student, she came into contact with Marxism and the antiwar and trade union movements. Weil was among the young rationalists who followed the pacifist *Alain. In 1927-29 she worked for *Madeleine Vernet's organization, Will for Peace, and as a member of Ligue des droits de l'homme (League for the Rights of Man), she joined many others in 1929 to protest projected increases in the French military budget.

Her diploma monograph "Science and the Perception of Descartes" (1930) signaled her commitment to an ethos based on irrevocable choice, involvement, and responsibility. During the early thirities, while she taught philosophy in various parts of France, she became involved with labor and workers' organizations and in 1934 took a year's leave from teaching to work in factories. Her aim was to experience and thus, better comprehend the worker's life in order to conceive realistic means of minimizing its dehumanizing effects. Her journal entries from this time later appeared in *La Condition Ouvrière* (1951).

Despite Weil's pacifist convictions and enthusiasm for +Léon Blum's government of the Popular Front, she opposed the official position of neutrality towards the Spanish Republic as an abdication of socialist principles of solidarity with workers and peasants. In the summer, 1936, using journalist's credentials, she went to Barcelona and there joined Burruti's guerrilla forces (anarchist-syndicalist). Following an injury she returned home, disillusioned by the scope of violence and the internationalized ideological transformation of the war which Weil had initially seen as a struggle of hungry peasants and workers.

In 1938, as a pacifist writer, she supported the compromise at Munich but did not later back the Vichy collaborationist government. Between 1936 and 1939 she argued for a national policy of nonviolence. In her view, war permitted the transfer of economic rivalries onto battlefields where the worker-turned-soldier was crushed by economic and national rivalries. In "The Power of Words," she drew a parallel between Franco-German rivalry and the Trojan War based on their common absence of moral objectives. " 'The Iliad' or the Poem of Force," one of her best known pacifist essays, examined the instability of power and the dehumanizing effect of violence on both perpetrator and victim.

Weil and her parents escaped to Vichy France just days before the Germans marched into Paris. Under the anti-Semitic laws of the Vichy state, she was forbidden to teach and these years became a period of intense spiritual and religious exploration for her. She came close to conversion to Catholicism but ultimately did not convert; her identity was based on a commitment to serve God and others as an outsider and she believed in the strength of this detachment. In 1942 the family emigrated to the United States, but Weil made her way back to London, compelled by her own conviction to work for de Gaulle's Free France. Her writings from this period were later published as *L'Enracinement* (1949, translated and republished in the United States as *The Need for Roots*), the culmination of her life and thought. In her vision of a decentralized and respiritualized society, she explored ways of breaking the circle of violence and struggle for power. In the same period she also wrote a major essay criticizing French colonial policies which was not published until 1960 in *Écrits historiques et politiques*. Her analysis of colonialism as a major cause of World War II was not known until France was deeply immersed in the Algerian war.

Simone Weil's influence has been profound. She provided a political sociology which affected the ideas and methodology of many others including Raymond Aron, Hannah Arendt, Flannery O'Connor, and Albert Camus. Her essay on Descartes and later spiritual writings have helped mold Existentialism, both atheistic and religious. Theologians today value her meditations and stoical values of self-denial and concentration. Her works on the factory which included the recommendation to increase worker participation have enormous relevance. Weil was an archetypal figure of the moral and social struggles of her time. Her lasting contributions to pacifism were philosophical and intellectual, examining power and violence in an effort to free societies from the rule of force.

Bibliography:

A. *L'Enracinement; prélude à une déclaration des devoirs envers l'être humane* (Paris, 1949, reprinted in the United States as *The Need For Roots: Prelude to a Declaration of Duties Toward Mankind*, trans. by A. Wills, New York, 1953); *"The Iliad" or the Poem of Force*, trans. by Mary McCarthy (Pendle Hill Pamphlet, PA, 1956); *Oppression et liberté* (Paris, 1955, reprinted in the United States as *Oppression and Liberty*, trans. by A. Wills and J. Petrie, Amherst, MA, 1973); *Selected Essays, 1934-1943*, comp. and ed. by R. Rees (London, 1962); *Seventy Letters*, trans. and arr. by R. Rees (London, 1965).

B. Jacques Cabaud, *A Fellowship in Love* (New York, 1964); Simone Pétrement, *Simone Weil, A Life*, trans. by R. Rosenthal, (New York, 1976); Richard Rees, *Simone Weil, A Sketch for a Portrait* (Carbondale, IL, 1976); Gustave Thibon and R. P. Perrin, *Simone Weil, As We Knew Her*, trans. by E. Craufurd (London, 1953); George Abbot White, ed., *Simone Weil, Interpretations of a Life* (Amherst, MA, 1981).

C. Simone Weil Manuscripts, Bibliothèque Nationale de Paris.

Betty L. McLane

WELLOCK, Wilfred (2 January 1879, Nelson, Lancashire, England—22 July 1972, Preston, Lancashire). *Education*: one year at Edinburgh Univ., 1903. *Career*: member of Parliament, 1927-31, author, editor, and lecturer.

As a boy of ten, Wilfred Wellock joined his parents in the cotton mills. His father was an active Methodist, and he too became active in the church and began preaching early. He attended evening classes and then Edinburgh University, which he left without taking a degree. On his return to the town of Nelson in 1907, he began writing on religious and economic subjects, and took a leading part in church and socialist organizations. He published criticisms of competitive industrial society in *The Modern Review*, a Calcutta monthly, and warned Indians against following the Western mode of acquisitive aggression.

Wellock was staunch in his opposition to World War I, and during 1916 published an anticonscription broadsheet called *The New Crusader*. When summoned for the draft he not only refused alternate service but declined to exercise his exemption as a clergyman. He served over two years in prison, being released in April 1919. *The New Crusader* continued as a pacifist weekly in London, and he now joined the staff. He made a trip to Holland to aid a new pacifist paper, and later toured Germany to examine the devastating social and economic effects of the Treaty of Versailles. In 1921 he helped establish the War Resisters' International and the No More War Movement, which later merged with the Peace Pledge Union.

At this time he received from *John Haynes Holmes a pamphlet on *Mohandas K. Gandhi's struggle in South Africa. When he read Gandhi's *Indian Home Rule*, he found it echoed his own views on industrialism and the revival of crafts. Gandhi, he recognized, shared his enthusiasm for *Leo Tolstoy and John Ruskin, and he wrote a booklet on Indian independence, *India's Awakening* (1922). The Independent Labour party provided a vehicle for his spiritual idealism and political activism, and he was elected to Parliament on this ticket in 1927. There he set up a parliamentary committee on Indian affairs and through this work met many prominent Indians, including Gandhi.

During the Depression years, he simplified his way of life, supporting himself and his wife through farming, lecturing, and writing. A convinced vegetarian from his youth, he also experimented with organic gardening and developed plans for cooperative farming, some of which were put into practice in 1940 on a farm for conscientious objectors at Holton Beckering, Lancashire. Lecture tours took him abroad, to the United States and to the Soviet Union. He also visited India in 1949-50 for a World Peace Conference and toured Gandhian *ashrams*.

During the Second World War, he served on a planning committee for the Peace Pledge Union and worked out a pacifist program of social and economic reconstruction, but was disappointed when the PPU confined its efforts to war resistance. He saw the peace movement as only one aspect of a constructive spiritual regeneration which aimed at a completeness of life. Though he moved beyond the sectarian theology of his youth, Wellock remained faithful to the idealism of the Christian socialists, the artist-poet-craftsmanship school of William Morris, and a dedication to nonviolence.

Bibliography:

A. *Ahimsa and World Peace* (Madras, 1922); *A Mechanistic or a Human Society*? (Birmingham, 1944); *Gandhi as a Social Revolutionary* (Birmingham, 1950); *Off the Beaten Track* (Varanasi, 1962).

B. Martin Ceadel, *Pacifism in Britain, 1914-1945: The Defining of a Faith* (Oxford, 1980).

James D. Hunt

WEST, Daniel (''Dan'') (31 December 1893, Preble Co., OH—7 January 1971, Goshen, IN). *Education*: B.A., Manchester Coll., 1917; M.A., Cornell Univ., 1920. *Career*: public school teacher, 1919-28; director of youth work, Church of the Brethren, 1930-36; national staff leader in peace education, Church of the Brethren, 1938-59; educator and peace activist.

After his discharge in 1918 from the U.S. Army, where he would accept only noncombatant service, Dan West was associated closely, as teacher and youth leader, with young people in the Church of the Brethren, one of the historic peace churches. Using a variety of informal educational methods, he sought to make them aware of their peace heritage and to aid them in becoming active peacemakers. In 1932 he organized a movement known as ''20,000 Dunkers for Peace,'' aimed at soliciting commitments not to engage in war, especially from young people who were seeking a ''moral equivalent of war.'' West recruited volunteers to serve in work camps and peace caravans. During 1936 he visited college campuses in the interests of the Emergency Peace Campaign.

While assisting in 1937 with a relief program on both sides of the Spanish Civil War, West alerted his church constituency and others to the need for material aid programs that would relieve suffering. Looking for some practical means of providing milk for starving children, he conceived the idea of sending heifers from American farms to war-ravaged areas overseas. His proposal was first implemented when Indiana farmers in 1944 sent heifers to Puerto Rico. Soon after the end of World War II, with the cooperation of UNRRA and the volunteer help of thousands of ''sea-going cowboys,'' the Heifer Project developed rapidly and soon became international and ecumenical, at first aiding in postwar reconstruction and later assisting developing nations. West maintained a consultative relationship with the project and was honored on its 25th anniversary, two years before his death.

Although Dan West wrote several booklets and many magazine articles, he was most effective in discussion groups and as a leader in human relations and group dynamics programs. Believing that convictions should result in action, he encouraged the development of volunteer service not merely as an alternative to military service but as an expression of a peace witness. Often described as ''a practical mystic,'' West was credited by his colleagues with providing the ideological base on which others could establish and administer peacemaking programs.

Bibliography:

A. *The Coming Brotherhood* (Elgin, IL, 1938); *Brethren Community Service* (Elgin, IL, 1943); *Peace Education in Churches* (Elgin, IL., 1957); *Peace Education in Homes* (Elgin, IL., 1956); *Thinking Together* (Elgin, IL., 1948).

B. Glee Yoder, *Passing on the Gift, the Story of Dan West* (Elgin, IL., 1978).

Kenneth I. Morse

WHIPPLE, Charles K. (17 November 1808, Newburyport, MA—10 May 1900, Newburyport). *Education*: B.A., Amherst Coll., 1831, M.A., 1834. *Career*: treasurer, New England Non-Resistance Society; assistant editor, *The Liberator*; pacifist lecturer and writer.

Charles K. Whipple, an apothecary and benevolent reformer, was an avid publicist for Garrisonian pacifism and abolitionism throughout the antebellum period. One of the leading ideologues of the New England Non-Resistance Society, Whipple wrote a number of short but original works before abandoning nonresistance during the Civil War.

After the Garrisonians converted Whipple to pacifism in the early 1830s, he became an active nonresistant and a supporter of *William Lloyd Garrison and *Henry Clarke Wright in their dispute with the American Peace Society. In 1838 he left the moderate pacifists and helped organize the New England Non-Resistance Society. Quickly Whipple developed into a leading apostle of radical pacifism in Massachusetts.

Whipple's first important work was a pioneering pacifist tract for children entitled the *Dialogues between Frank and William* (1838). Here he articulated the principles of the New England radicals: the belief in Christ's love and its incompatibility with civil government, the need to return good for evil, and the renunciation of all war and preparations for it. A year later Whipple wrote a pamphlet describing a novel tactic that would have peacefully counteracted the British during the Revolution. In the *Evils of the Revolutionary War* (1839), Whipple suggested that nonviolent civil disobedience and the force of progressive world opinion would have quickly and peacefully ended the imperial dispute. Until the Civil War Whipple consistently believed nonviolent pressure was the only acceptable Christian reaction to injustice and violence.

After the early 1840s, Whipple shifted his attention to abolitionism and became an agent for the Massachusetts Anti-Slavery Society. In the year before the Civil War he wrote two pamphlets explaining a nonviolent strategy for freeing the slaves. Like other radical pacifists, Whipple admired John Brown's courage and convictions but rejected his tactics. Instead, Whipple argued that since slavery violated democratic political principles and Christian values, Americans had a duty to help chattel escape by "uninjurious means." If emancipation could not be achieved peacefully, Whipple was ready to countenance a more active form of resistance.

During the Civil War Whipple believed that only a military victory could destroy slavery and thus establish the environment for the peaceful resolution of disputes. Although he refused to aid the Lincoln government, Whipple ruefully accepted the necessity of warfare and reluctantly abandoned his pacifist principles. In common with most of the Garrisonians his abolitionism eventually took precedence over nonviolence.

Whipple was a lucid, original New England thinker who wanted pacifism to become a mode of conduct and not merely a set of abstract principles. Although his arguments were always based upon the Christian ideals of love and forgiveness, Whipple was most concerned in creating a pragmatic ethics of nonviolence. In the crucible of war, Whipple's love of freedom forced him to jettison his pacifism in order to end what antebellum pacifists considered the most heinous example of institutionalized violence in America.

Bibliography:

A. *Dialogues between Frank and William* (Boston, 1838); *Evils of the Revolutionary War* (Boston, 1839); *The Non-Resistance Principles: with Particular Application to the Help of Slaves by Abolitionists* (Boston, 1860).

B. Peter Brock, *Pacifism in the United States From the Colonial Era to the First World War* (Princeton, NJ, 1968).

Jayme A. Sokolow

WHITE, Andrew Dickson. See *Biographical Dictionary of Internationalists*.

WHITTIER, John Greenleaf (17 December 1807, near Haverhill, MA—7 September 1892, Hampton Falls, NH. *Education*: Haverhill Academy, c. 1827-29. *Career*: Quaker poet, politician, and reformer.

Although primarily known for his abolitionist activity, John Greenleaf Whittier devoted much time and energy to promoting peace and international harmony. During the 1830s he mixed abolitionism with nonresistance. At an Anti-Slavery Society Convention in 1838, he urged nonresistance against anti-abolitionist violence. In ''The Exiles'' (1840) and ''Barclay of Ury'' (1847) a Quaker refuses to be defended with violence. His antimilitarist views were further developed in his poems ''In the Evil Days'' (1850) and ''The Quaker Alumni'' (1860) where he questioned the need for West Point. Whittier also refused to write poems commemorating the Revolutionary War battles of Bunker Hill and Bennington.

The Mexican War triggered more intense antiwar activism on the part of Whittier. In *The National Era* (1847), which he helped edit, he wrote two seminal antiwar editorials, ''Dancing and Sabbath Breaking'' and ''Piety and Justice,'' which excoriated American imperialism and atrocities in a proslavery war and vilified organized religion's support of the ''unutterable horrors of war.'' Under the pseydonym José de Santillo, he wrote a battle hymn for the Mexicans which *William Lloyd Garrison printed in *The Liberator*. He remained an anti-administration critic throughout the war.

Following the Mexican War, Whittier became increasingly internationalist in outlook. He strongly supported the international peace conference movement of the 1840s and 1850s, and he paid tribute to *Elihu Burritt's efforts in organizing the 1848 Peace Congress in "The Peace Convention at Brussels."

Like so many other antebellum advocates of peace, Whittier's antiwar sentiments were severely tested by the conflict between the North and South. He detested war but thought that some blows struck for freedom and justice were warranted. Initially, he argued that disunion was preferable to a war for union and briefly supported nonresistance to southern secession. Once the Civil War started, however, he became a strong supporter of Abraham Lincoln and openly admired General William Tecumseh Sherman. Whittier's assessment of the war as an abolitionist crusade superseded his generalized aversion to violence, yet he never entirely suppressed his Quaker beliefs. In a June 1861 open letter to the Society of Friends, he urged Quakers to relieve the sufferings of the war through hospital volunteer work and assisting widows and orphans.

After the war Whittier came to regret his temporary abandonment of the Quaker peace testimony. In 1875 he told *Lydia Maria Child that the Civil War was an ignoble means to free the slaves. He declined honorary membership in the Loyal Legion, a society of union officers, and, at the age of 82, he fully embraced pacifism, declaring that war had to be abolished.

As vice-president of the American Peace Society from 1870-92 he returned to his pre-Civil War internationalist activism. In 1872 and 1873 he called for International Peace Congresses in Europe to work for peace and world harmony. He supported the arbitration peace campaign in 1887 with particular reference to Anglo-American relations. Whittier, then, played a significant role in both the antebellum and post-Civil War peace movements.

Bibliography:

A. *The Poetical Works* (Boston, 1975).

B. Augustus Taber Murray, "Whittier's Attitude Toward War," *Present Day Papers*, 2 (July 1915), 209-19; Samuel T. Pickard, *Life and Letters of John Greenleaf Whittier* (Boston, 1859); Edward Wagenknecht, *John Greenleaf Whittier: A Portrait in Paradox* (New York, 1967).

C. John Greenleaf Whittier Papers, Essex Institute, Salem, MA; Haverford College; Harvard College Library.

Peter N. Kirstein

WICHMANN, Clara Meijer. See MEIJER-WICHMANN, Clara Gertrud.

WIDEGREN, Matilda (7 August 1863, Söderköping, Sweden—2 February 1938, Stockholm). *Education*: National Training Coll. for Women Teachers, Stockholm. *Career*: assistant teacher, National Coll. for Girls, Stockholm, 1889-1904, assistant headmistress, 1904-15; librarian, National Training Coll. for Women Teachers, Stockholm, 1888-1905, teacher, 1904-23; co-founder and visiting teacher, Private Coll. for Women Teachers, Stockholm; refugee relief worker and peace activist.

Matilda Widegren taught Swedish language and was the first woman to write a grammar textbook that was used in boys' schools. In 1904 she was entrusted by the Swedish government with the task of organizing the display of the Swedish Public Educational System for the World's Fair in St. Louis, USA. Impressed by the "new school" practices in the United States, she introduced these new ideas in her own teaching. In addition, through her studies of history and literature, and also by traveling in other countries, she became convinced of the importance of giving the issues of peace and culture greater emphasis in the teaching of history. The political events in Scandinavia, resulting in the peaceful dissolution of the Swedish-Norwegian Union in 1905, strengthened her conviction that conflicts can and should be solved without violence. Gradually she became a radical pacifist and remained so throughout her life.

Widegren attended the International Women's Conference at The Hague in April, 1915 as one of the Swedish delegates. After returning to Sweden, she dedicated a considerable part of her energies to the cause of peace. (She became a full-time peace activist after 1923 when she retired from teaching.) She became head of Swedish Women's Peace Group, founded shortly after the Hague meeting, and made peace education one of the main objectives of the organization. She encouraged a form of peace research in history by leading the Swedish Women's Peace Group in the study of modern books on peace education and the search into Swedish literature for examples of peaceful cooperation and peace "heroes." In 1920 she founded, together with other peace advocates, the Peace Organization of Swedish Teachers and four years later helped organize a meeting of Nordic Teachers in Denmark which resulted in the establishment of The Nordic Teachers' Peace Organization (1925).

When the Swedish section of Women's International League for Peace and Freedom (WILPF) was founded in 1919, Matilda Widegren became its first president and remained in that post until 1934. In 1921 the WILPF International Congress decided to set up a committee on "border missions" and appointed Widegren as chair. In that capacity she traveled in areas of unrest, such as South-Jutland, Alsace, Hungary, and the Balkans, contacting key persons and others who were concerned with the problems of minorities that often sprang from the drawing up of new frontiers after World War I.

Another of Matilda Widegren's concerns was the situation of victims of war and persecution, and she dedicated much of her time to the many refugees who arrived in Sweden in the years between the two world wars. One of her last endeavors in that field was the setting up, in 1935, of the so-called "International Foyer for Refugees" in Stockholm, simple premises where refugees could come for a meal, for clothing, and also to get information and advice from a jurist. Even before that humanitarian effort, Widegren's work as a teacher and peace leader earned her the Illis Ovorum Meruere Labores, the Swedish royal award given to distinguished persons.

Bibliography:

A. *Förenta Nationerna* (Stockholm, 1931); *Fran en studieresa i Förenta Staterna* (Stockholm, 1906); *Fredskämpen Carl Lindhagen* (Stockholm, 1932).

B. Per Anders Fogelström, *Kampen för Fred* (Stockholm, 1970); Margareta Larrson,

"Kvinnoforeningar i Sverige med fred pa sitt program," Ph.D. dissertation, University of Stockholm, 1970; *Svenska män och kvinnor*, 8, 342; *Svensk uppslagsbok*, 31, 245-46.

Elisabeth Ståhle

WILSON, Thomas Woodrow. See *Biographical Dictionary of Internationalists*.

WINARSKY, Leopold (20 April 1873, Brno, Moravia, Austria [now Czechoslovakia]—22 November 1915, Vienna). *Education*: elementary school, self-educated. *Career*: upholsterer until 1898; Austrian Socialist party official; member, Austrian parliament, 1907-14.

Leopold Winarsky was the son of a poor upholsterer and was apprenticed to the same trade. Although his formal education ended early, he was an avid reader; as an adult his broad knowledge gained him wide respect. His private library became the basis of one of the most important libraries of labor and social history in Europe (Bibliothek der Arbeiterkammer in Vienna). In 1898 Dr. Viktor Adler, the leader of the Austrian Socialist party, appointed Winarsky to the party's executive committee. Having early evinced an interest in workers' education, he became the secretary of the party's Department of Education. A first-class orator, he became very popular in the labor movement. He also wrote many articles for *Der Kampf*, the theoretical journal of the Austrian Socialist party.

In 1906 Winarsky was elected a member of the Vienna city council and, after the introduction of universal manhood suffrage in 1907, he was elected to the Austrian parliament. In many parliamentary speeches and debates, he pleaded the cause of peace. He took a brave stand against militarism, and publicly criticized the oppressive conditions under which young men drafted into the Austro-Hungarian army had to serve.

Winarsky, one of the founders of the Socialist youth movement in Austria in 1894, had always been an active pacifist. He encouraged antimilitarist education among young workers, and was imprisoned several times as a result of his speeches and articles. At the Stuttgart meeting of the Socialist International in 1907, Winarsky and Karl Liebknecht founded the International Socialist Youth Organization. The two men issued an appeal to young Socialists in all countries to fight against the danger of war and to conduct an antimilitarist educational campaign. Before 1914 he wrote many antiwar articles and pamphlets. When war broke out in 1914, he was the only member of the Executive Committee of the Austrian Socialist party who led a public demonstration against the war in Vienna. Because of his antiwar opposition, Winarsky was drafted into the army even though he was a member of parliament. He died of an incurable disease in 1915.

Bibliography:

A. *Die grosse Französische Revolution* (Vienna, 1913); *Die Revolution von 1848* (Vienna, 1911).

B. Norbert Leser (ed.), *Werk und Widerhall* (Vienna, 1964), 442-6; Jean Maitron and

Georges Haupt, eds., *Dictionnaire biographique du movement ouvrier international, Autrich* (Paris, 1971), 325-6.

Herbert Steiner

WIRTH, Franz (6 July 1826, Bayreuth, Germany—16 May 1897, Frankfurt am Main, Germany). *Education*: university studies in Heidelberg and at the Polytechnical Institute in Hannover. *Career*: engineer for Bavarian state railroad; official in Bavarian telegraph office in Frankfurt; patent attorney; member, Frankfurt City Council; chairman, Frankfurt Peace Society, 1886-97.

Franz Wirth was the second son of J.G.A. Wirth, the democratic nationalist who had delivered a stirring oration at the Hambach festival in 1832. The younger Wirth inherited his father's convictions: his involvement in the peace movement was rooted in his beliefs that lasting peace was in Germany's national interest and that democratic reform of the country's political system was the essential prerequisite for such a peace.

Wirth began his career as a technical official in the Bavarian state service before he settled in Frankfurt and became a highly successful patent attorney. He also became active in politics, serving both on the city council and as a leader of the democratic Süddeutsche Volkspartei (South German People's Party). He was, in sum, the prototypical south-German democratic notable around whom the peace movement took shape in Imperial Germany at the end of the 1890s. His introduction to the peace movement came in 1886, when the Danish pacifist *Frederik Bajer recruited him to lead a peace society in Frankfurt. The organization that Wirth founded, the Frankfurter Friedensverein (Frankfurt Peace Society), proved to be one of the strongest and most durable local peace societies in the country. Wirth was also instrumental in the founding and expansion of a national peace society in Germany. He served on the committee which oversaw the establishment of the Deutsche Friedensgesellschaft (German Peace Society) in Berlin in 1892. More significantly, he became the new organization's leading activist, as he exploited his contacts among leaders of the Volkspartei to establish chapters in nearly forty cities and towns in south Germany.

Wirth's passion for the cause not only made him the single most important pacifist in Germany in the 1890s, but also led to one notable embarrassment. The development of the peace movement in Germany faced a great many obstacles. One of these was the insistence of pacifists in France and other countries on condemning the German seizure of Alsace-Lorraine in 1871. This insistence was an affront to Wirth's patriotism, which was always the central motif in his activity in the peace movement. In 1895 he lost his temper and published a tactless article, in which he counseled the French to forget about Alsace-Lorraine because they lacked the military power to retake the provinces. The recriminations that followed on both sides of the Rhine did the peace movement no good in either France or Germany. They abated only temporarily when Wirth died in 1897.

Bibliography:

A. "Die soziale Bedeutung der internationalen Friedensbewegung," *Berichte des Freien Deutschen Hochstiftes zu Frankfurt*, 11 (1895), 185-88.

B. Roger Chickering, *Imperial Germany and a World Without War: The Peace Movement and German Society, 1892-1914* (Princeton, 1975); Alexander Dietz, *Franz Wirth und der Frankfurter Friedensverein* (Frankfurt, 1911).

Roger Chickering

WISE, Stephen Samuel (17 March 1874, Erlau, Hungary—19 April 1949, New York). *Education*: B.A., Columbia Univ., 1892, Ph.D., 1901; rabbinical ordination with Rabbi Adolf Jellinek of Austria, 1893. *Career*: rabbi of B'nai Jeshurun of New York, 1893-1900; Beth Israel of Portland, Oregon, 1900-6; The Free Synagogue of New York, 1907-49; rabbi and Jewish organizational leader.

Stephen Wise was part of that pre-World War I generation which believed that war had become an outmoded form of settling international disputes, and expected that arbitration and other devices would be adopted as humanity progressed toward a more advanced civilization. But unlike many of his fellow pacifists, Wise came to support American participation in both world wars.

Prior to 1914 Wise had little formal contact with the pacifist movement, and his first public utterances dealt with the Mexican-American border conflict that spring. When the Wilson Administration accepted the offer of three Latin American nations to mediate the dispute, Wise lauded the president's statesmanlike policy. When war broke out in Europe in August 1914, Wise joined a number of reformers to found the Anti-Preparedness Committee, which later grew into the American Union Against Militarism. In 1915 and 1916, Wise and his good friend *John Haynes Holmes were outspoken in their opposition to war, and Wise almost broke with +Woodrow Wilson when the president adopted a preparedness program in 1916.

But Wise, unlike Holmes, was not an absolute and unconditional pacifist. His close personal and reform ties to Wilson, as well as his personal assessment of international affairs, led him to move away from an antipreparedness stance in early 1917, much to the dismay and anger of his colleagues in the Union against Militarism. That April, when America entered the war, Wise draped his pulpit with an American flag. He told his congregation that the United States had no choice but to fight and that he would stand with his president and his country.

Wise continued, however, his interest in peace. When he visited Europe in 1919 and saw first-hand the devastation war had wrought on people and countries, he began to doubt whether he had acted correctly. In the 1920s and early 1930s he renewed his ties with pacifist groups; even Hilter's initial persecution of the Jews did not lead him to call for American intervention in European affairs. But as Nazi depredations increased, Wise again found himself unable to sustain an absolute pacifism. Once Germany attacked Poland, Wise called for American aid to the Allies, although right up to the attack upon Pearl Harbor he expressed his hope that the United States would be able to stay out of the conflict. Furthermore, after the war Wise, like many liberals, placed his hopes for world peace in the United Nations and condemned Winston Churchill for his ''Iron Curtain'' speech.

Wise's pacifism, while undoubtedly deeply felt, was always tempered by his belief that so long as nations were imperfect, wars might result, and that even those opposed to war in principle might have to fight to defend other values.

Bibliography:

A. *Challenging Years* (New York, 1949).

B. Melvin I. Urofsky, *A Voice that Spoke for Justice: The Life and Times of Stephen S. Wise* (Albany, 1981); Carl Hermann Voss, *Rabbi and Minister: The Friendship of Stephen S. Wise and John Haynes Holmes* (Cleveland, 1964).

C. Stephen Samuel Wise Papers, American Jewish Historical Society; Wise Collection, American Jewish Archives.

Melvin I. Urofsky

WISZNIEWSKA, Marie-Gabrielle-Hortense Hugot (1836, L'Yonne, France—23 November 1903, Paris). *Education*: private. *Career*: founder, Ligue des femmes pour le désarmement international, 1896; peace activist.

With no previous involvement in French or European peace activities, Marie-Gabrielle-Hortense Wiszniewska launched appeals to a large number of well-known, well-connected, and generally upper class European and American women in May 1896 for the purpose of creating an international society to press for general disarmament. This initiative was taken quite independently of the organized peace movement that existed since 1889. Her home became the central headquarters of a huge mailing network from which manifestos and appeals to women were sent and received from all parts of the world, requesting and obtaining support. Within one year, Princess Wiszniewska collected over a thousand names and received authorization from the French government to establish the Ligue des femmes pour le désarmement international (League of Women for International Disarmament).

Her aim was to enlist women in large numbers in a crusade for mutual, general disarmament. In a letter sent to German women, she indicated that the League would not engage in immediate political work but remain concerned with ''war in general.'' The purpose of the League was based on the idea that ''it was women who could expunge hatred among nations from the human heart, [a task] left to us from past centuries.'' The major means was through the proper training of children at home in ''the love of humanity,'' a profoundly patriotic labor, she argued.

The League sustained a program of lectures, public meetings, competitions, and held its own congresses. Its first congress, conducted during the Paris Exposition of 1900, was deliberately separated from the Tenth Annual Congress of the Universal Peace Congress, a major event in the peace movement's pre-

1914 history. At the League's meeting, banners were hung posting the names of thousands of women from around the world who had supported the League's appeal. Lists of vice-presidents from 26 foreign nations and 18 separate French provincial chapters were proudly published. Wiszniewska's purpose was to focus on the universality of woman's role as "homemaker and mother" in the peace crusade and she felt that this would best be achieved separately from the male dominated "official" pacifist congress. By 1900 her society had changed its name to "L'Alliance universelle des femmes pour la paix" ("Universal Alliance of Women for Peace") and sometime the phrase, "par l'Education" was appended. Four years after its creation, it claimed to have received over 1,000,000 letters of support, worldwide.

Initially, Wiszniewska had enlisted *Sylvie Flammarion as vice-president. By 1900, Flammarion had left to found a women's peace society which enrolled only women since the Alliance had grown to contain many male honorary members and host mainly male speakers. Flammarion's society, moreover, intended to enlist working class and poor women in large numbers, if possible, which the Alliance, despite its 50 centime fee, did not do. It tended to work with socially eminent or professionally known women.

Despite its initial promise to avoid politics, Wiszniewska's society orchestrated an early and vehement protest sent to London against the South African war, raised money to aid Boer women and children, and even sent a telegram to Boer women informing them that thousands of English women were furious with their government's war policy. The Alliance also sent delegates to a great variety of French association meetings—teachers, workers, professional groups—in its quest for support, and Wiszniewska prodded the International Peace Bureau (Berne) to support women's groups in order to broaden its own base. After 1900 the society became increasingly interested in school curricula, realizing that national education could totally undo pacific maternal influences. The French Ministry of Education was prodded continuously to permit pacifist literature and speakers into the schools.

Despite a serious illness, Princess Wiszniewska worked up to the date of her death, convinced that all the world's women carried a special mission on behalf of peace. Her successor, Marya Cheliga, continued the work for some years afterwards. While the Alliance was not the first women's peace society created in Europe (*Marie Goegg had led the way in 1868 and was followed by *Eugenie Potonié-Pierre in the early 1890s), it was one which functioned continuously for a long period of time and which attracted the backing of socially prominent women.

Bibliography:

B. "Madame la Princesse Wiszniewska," *Revue Diplomatique*, 23 (September 16, 1900), special supp. 11pp; obituaries by Rufina Noeggerath in *L'Universel*, August, 1904 and *Journal des Femmes*, December, 1903.

C. Scattered letters in Bureau International de la Paix, Archives, United Nations Library, Geneva.

Sandi E. Cooper

WITHERSPOON, Frances (1887, Meridian, MS—16 December 1973, Philadelphia). *Education*: B.A., Bryn Mawr Coll., 1908. *Career*: assistant secretary, Woman's Peace Party; executive secretary, Bureau of Legal Advice, 1917-23; organizer, War Resisters League; pacifist writer and activist.

Born in Meridian, Mississippi to a political and "entirely Southern" family, Frances Witherspoon became active politically before she left Meridian to attend Bryn Mawr College. She was influenced by her father's hatred of war. A prominent attorney, Samuel Andrew Witherspoon had denounced the Spanish-American War, ridiculed +Theodore Roosevelt's foreign policy, and spent 1911 to 1915 in Congress protesting military spending and +Woodrow Wilson's efforts to invade Mexico. Frances Witherspoon shared her father's convictions and, before his death in 1915, dedicated her life to peace and social change. She was convinced that peace depended on better living conditions.

Upon her graduation from Bryn Mawr in 1908, Witherspoon became active in organizations that pursued suffrage, socialism, and peace. A Christian Socialist, she abhorred war and violence. A passionate suffragist, her early work on behalf of racial equality began when a black companion was denied service in a New York City restaurant after a suffrage parade. With her lifelong companion and co-worker *Tracy Mygatt, Witherspoon spoke endlessly on behalf of suffrage and peace. Also, they became prolific writers—of books, plays, articles, letters of protest, and (for money) book reviews for the New York *Herald Tribune*.

During World War I Witherspoon's energies were focused on peace. In 1915 she became assistant secretary of the Woman's Peace party, but when the WPP continued to support President Wilson after he armed merchant ships and the U.S. entered a state of armed neutrality, she resigned her job and intensified her antiwar work. As one of the founders and executive-secretary of the Bureau of Legal Advice, she worked to keep conscientious objectors and dissenters out of jail and out of Bellevue Hospital, where antiwar protestors were being sent for "mental observation" after the United States entered the war. Throughout the war, she counseled conscientious objectors and lobbied for decent conditions in military camps, where objectors were "barbarously treated." After the war, Witherspoon and her associates opposed the "Red Scare" activities that threatened deportation for all labor radicals and lobbied for amnesty for political prisoners, many of whom had received 20-30-year sentences.

From 1923—when the American Civil Liberties Union, founded by *Crystal Eastman, *Roger Baldwin, and *Norman Thomas as the Civil Liberties Bureau of the American Union Against Militarism, absorbed the New York Bureau of Legal Advice—Witherspoon worked most closely with the Fellowship of Reconciliation, the Women's International League for Peace and Freedom, SANE, and especially the War Resisters League. The latter, which also emerged in part out of the New York Bureau of Legal Advice, was largely organized by Witherspoon, Mygatt and *Jessie Wallace Hughan. Witherspoon's activities on behalf of racial integration, social justice, and peace continued until her death in 1973. In 1968 she mobilized the alumni of Bryn Mawr to protest the war in Vietnam, garnering sufficient support for full page ads in the *New York Times* and *Philadelphia Bulletin*. An activist to the end, she was as proud of the many public demonstrations she organized—notably a 1919 parade on Christmas Day for amnesty, featuring trumpeters and church choirs, and a 1928 Wall Street protest demanding the Marines out of Nicaragua—as she was of the many prizes and considerable recognition achieved by her voluminous publications.

Frances Witherspoon imagined a warless world of unity and security. She supported the 1968 Poor People's campaign as vigorously as she opposed the war in Vietnam and "the disastrous Anti-Ballistic Missile System." She saw the connectedness of peace with social justice in Christian terms and died optimistic that her vision, and the work of the organizations she supported and helped to found, would prevail. "It is easier now," she said, "because there are more of us."

Bibliography:

B. Ann Morrissett Davidon, "The Lives of Tracy D. Mygatt and Frances Witherspoon," *War Resisters League News* (January-February 1974), 6; Ann Morrissett Davidon, "Founding Mothers: Tracy Mygatt and Frances Witherspoon," *WIN*, 9 (July 26, 1973), 10; Nancy Manahan, "Future Old Maids and Pacifist Agitators: The Story of Tracy Mygatt and Frances Witherspoon," *Women's Studies Quarterly*, 10 (Spring 1982), 10-13.

C. Tracy Mygatt-Frances Witherspoon Papers, Swarthmore College Peace Collection.

Blanche Wiesen Cook

WITTE, Sergei Iulevich (29 June 1849, Tiflis, Russia—13 March 1915, Petrograd [now Leningrad]). *Education*: graduate, Coll. of Mathematics and Physical Sciences, Univ. of Novorossiisk, 1869. *Career*: executive director, Southwestern Railroad Co., 1886-89; chief, Railroad Dept., Ministry of Finance, 1889-92; Minister of Communication, 1892; Minister of Finance, 1893-1903; chairman, Committee of Ministers, 1903-6; railroad administrator, Russian statesman, and peace advocate.

Sergei Iulevich Witte exercised considerable influence over the course of Russian foreign policy during his illustrious career as Minister of Finance between August 1893 and August 1903. Unlike the majority of his colleagues, especially V. K. von Plehve, the bellicose Minister of Interior, Witte was deeply conscious of Russia's need for peace. The principal consideration which prompted him to reject war as an instrument of national policy was his belief that Russian finances would collapse under the strain of on-going military expenditures.

A native of Tiflis, graduate of the University of Novorossiisk in Odessa, and champion of the theories of the German economist, Friedrich List, Witte believed that the tzarist regime could survive only if it became the impetus for the rapid industrialization of Russia. An ambitious policy of public works, particularly railroad construction, stood at the heart of his program. Accordingly, Witte caused Russia to borrow heavily from bankers both at home and abroad, and his sensitivity to the concerns of creditors influenced Witte to favor a cautious foreign policy.

Both Alexander III and *Nicholas II, who succeeded his father as Tzar in November 1894, routinely consulted Witte concerning matters of international affairs. In 1897 Witte sabotaged a scheme for dismembering the Ottoman Empire when he leaked word of Russia's intentions to the British. He unsuccessfully attempted to dissuade Nicholas II from approving the seizure of Port Arthur in March 1898, preferring the peaceful penetration of China instead. Witte supported A. N. Kuropatkin, Minister of War, in encouraging Nicholas II to issue the call for an international disarmament conference, which met at The Hague in May and June, 1899.

The removal of Witte as Minister of Finance in August 1903 and his becoming Chairman of the Committee of Ministers caused Witte to lose considerable power and influence. Lacking polish and refinement, Witte irritated the sensibilities of the gentle, cultivated, and prudish Tzar, who became increasingly convinced that the Minister of Finance was seeking to destroy such cherished Russian institutions as the peasant commune. In July 1905, however, Nicholas II turned to Witte again. Witte headed the Russian delegation that traveled to Portsmouth, New Hampshire, to negotiate the Treaty of Portsmouth, which ended the Russo-Japanese War. After 1906 Witte played no active role in the formulation of Russian domestic and foreign policies.

Bibliography:

A. *The Memoirs*, A. Yarmolinsky, trans. and ed. (New York, 1921).

B. Theodore H. Von Laue. *Sergie Witte and the Industrialization of Russia* (New York, 1963).

Dan L. Morrill

WITTING, Richard (19 October 1856, Berlin—22 December 1923, Berlin). *Education*: studies in law and administration, universities of Göttingen and Berlin, 1876-79. *Career*: legal assistant, municipal court in Berlin, 1884-89; member, city council of Danzig (now Gdansk), 1889-91; Lord Mayor of Posen (now Poznan) and member of the Prussian House of Lords, 1891-1902; director, National Bank for Germany, 1902-10, chairman of the board of directors, 1911-22; deputy chairman of the board of directors, United Dramstadt and National Bank, 1922-23; member, lower house of the Prussian state parliament, 1908-13; politician, bank director, privy councillor, author, journalist, and pacifist.

The son of the Jewish silk merchant Arnold Witkowski, Richard became a Protestant as a young man and adopted the name of Witting, as did many of his brothers and sisters. He had a broad education (studying especially history, philosophy, political economy, and literature) and possessed an extraordinary knowledge about both economic life and political and administrative structures. Despite his education and knowledge, untypical of Prussian officials of his time, Witting was typical in his enthusiastic support of the authoritarian German political system whose economic ascent he promoted until the summer of 1914. The reputation he gained, especially as the Lord Mayor of Posen and as a banker, brought him general recognition. At the turn of the century, he was one of the influential advisers on German policy in eastern Europe to Prince Bernhard von Bülow, the German Chancellor. It seemed very likely that this talented, eloquent, and energetic politician would attain high rank in the German government. The outbreak of World War I, however, led Witting in a different direction.

In the July crisis of 1914, Witting recognized that the German and Austrian refusal to negotiate with the entente powers made world war inevitable. Like Prince Karl Lichnowsky, German Ambassador to England (1912-14), he became convinced that Germany would have nothing to gain and everything to lose in a world war. Increasingly, he became disillusioned with Germany's leaders and with Prussian militarism. After war broke out, he resolutely opposed the German power elite, arguing that they did not "understand how to prevent, conduct, or end the war." His personal connections with influential members of the ruling regime provided him with insight into the mentality of both military and civilian leaders, and with information that strengthened his belief that the war had been started recklessly and in a manner which had embittered the entire world against Germany, making victory impossible.

Witting's position on the war, which largely coincided with the views of *Richard Grelling and *Hans Paasche, his son-in-law, earned him the reputation as a leading figure among the democratically-minded opponents of the war who supported a rapid negotiated peace. In March 1915 he joined the Bund Neues Vaterland (New Fatherland League), and after it was prohibited, he joined the Zentralstelle Völkerrecht (Central Office for International Law), founded the following year. Through these organizations Witting sought to counter the prevailing war mentality. He sought to persuade the German leaders to put the monarchy on a democratic basis in order to keep the inevitable collapse of Hohenzollern rule as much as possible within limits. His warnings, however, went unheeded. Convinced of the instability of the Imperial system and the impossibility of its internal reform, Witting, together with Hugo Preuss, drafted a democratic constitution in the winter of 1917-18 that later became the basis for the Weimar constitution.

Although he was one of the most important co-founders of the Deutsche Demokratische Partei (German Democratic Party) (DDP) after the war, Witting soon recognized that the party did not see acknowledgement of German war guilt as a pre-condition for the intellectual, moral, and political rejuvenation of the nation or the moral and economic regeneration of Europe. While remaining a nominal member of the DDP, he moved increasingly closer to the pacifistic wing of the Unabhängige Sozialdemokratische Partei Deutschlands (Independent

Social Democratic Party of Germany) (USPD), which also was concerned with enlightening the general public about the crimes of the Imperial government in order to prevent a recurrence of those events. However, he fought against extreme leftist-oriented plans to create a proletarian socialist state. He believed that only a governmental alliance of the Sozialdemokratische Partei Deutschlands (Social Democratic Party of Germany) (SPD), the USPD, and bourgeois democracy could bring about a prosperous and peaceful German republic. Only such an alliance, he agrued, purged of the curse of guilt-laden leaders, would be capable of restraining rebellious elements and reducing the mistrust of Germany that existed in other nations.

Because of his important position in the banking business, Witting often published his political opinions anonymously, mostly under the pseudonyms of "Licinius Stolo" and, as in *Die Weltbühne*, "Georg Metzler." Along with *Friedrich W. Foerster, *Richard Grelling, and *Fritz Küster, he stressed that the future development of Germany was dependent upon public recognition of Germany's responsibility for the start of World War I. Near the end of his life, he despaired that the public would again such a recognition in the face of nationalistic propaganda which proclaimed the innocence of Imperial Germany and extolled the political and military values of prewar Prussia-Germany. He also was alarmed at the continuing hatred of Jews, derived, in his opinion, from the social classes that had held power in Imperial Germany. When the Weimar Republic was seized by an anti-Semitic wave for the first time in 1919, Witting advised German Jews to have their children learn foreign languages, go into exile, and to seek a new fatherland.

In 1923 Witting died of a heart ailment which was exacerbated, perhaps, by his feeling oppressed at what he saw as the unalterable political and intellectual character of the German ruling elite.

Bibliography:

A. *Auswärtige Politik und Diplomatenkunst. Kriegsmentalität* (Berlin, 1917); "Juden raus!" [under pseud. Georg Metzler], *Die Weltbühne*, 15 (December 4, 1919), 685-89; *Novellen* [under pseud. Richard Gabriel] (Berlin, 1899); *Das Ostmarken-Problem* (Berlin, 1907); "Die Schuld am Kriege" [under pseud. Georg Metzler], *Die Weltbühne*, 15 (February 13, 1919), 163-81.

B. Siegfried Jacobsohn, "Dank an R. Witting," *Die Weltbühn*, 20 (January 3, 1924), 17; Arthur Kronthal, "Richard Witting," *Deutsches Biographisches Jahrbuch* (Berlin and Leipzig, 1930), 395-403).

Helmut Donat
Trans. by Ruthann Richards

WITTLIN, Józef (17 August 1896, Dmytrów, Galicia, Austrian Poland—29 February 1976, New York). *Education*: gymnasium, Lwów, 1906-14; studied at the universities of Vienna, 1915-16, and Lwów, 1918-19. *Career*: secondary school teacher of Polish language and literature, Lwów, 1919-21; literary director, Municipal Theater, Lodz, 1922-23; founder and instructor, School of Drama, Lodz, 1923-24; co-editor, *Tygodnik Polski*, New York, 1941-43; script writer and broadcaster, Radio Free Europe, New York, 1952-72; writer, poet, translator, pacifist.

Józef Wittlin, a major writer of the twentieth century and a member of the post-World War I Skamander literary group (cofounded by *Julian Tuwin), was one of Poland's few determined pacifists. His experiences as an Austro-Hungarian soldier during the war led to his abhorrence of war and became the driving force for this creativity. During the war, he wrote poems, published as a collection entitled *Hymny* (1920), which depicted all of the hideousness of war and protested against nationalism, militarism, and mechanized warfare. *Hymny* appealed for peace and urged all to abandon their weapons.

During the Polish-Ukrainian struggle for the city of Lwów (1918-19), to which both sides lay patriotic claim, Wittlin's pacifism came into conflict with his Polish patriotism, a conflict which he later documented in the essay ''Ze wspomnień by łego pacyfisty'' (''Recollections of an Ex-Pacifist'') (1925). Concluding that pacifism was closely allied with sentimental patriotism while Polish pacifism was motivated by opposition to the Partitioning Powers, he discarded the precept as a solution to war.

In the ensuing years, Wittlin grappled with the problem of war and pacifism. He pondered why human beings appeared more capable of making greater sacrifices for the cause of war than for peace. Unable to answer the questions, he became absorbed in Christian thought—of Jewish origin, he converted the Catholicism—especially the Life of St. Francis of Assisi, and in translating Homer's *Odyssey* into Polish. Eventually, Wittlin reformulated his pacifist ideas; the solution to war lay with literature and art which should assume a religious function. In his view, poetry was building ''an enormous edifice of brotherhood and love,'' and was contributing to bringing about ''the radical change'' that the world badly needed.

As a final settling of his account with war, Wittlin wrote his epic masterpiece, *Salt of the Earth: Saga of the Patient Footsoldier* (1935), which was translated into thirteen languages and won the author numerous awards and worldwide recognition. *Salt of the Earth* is almost a plotless novel, a war story that has very little to do with the war itself. The book, which was to be part of a trilogy, aimed at examining and destroying the war myth. The main character, symbolically named Niewiadomski (Unknown), is an average, unknown soldier torn out of his village and caught up in the incomprehensible machinery of a war. The experiences of this simple man assume a universal significance and becomes the common experience of every man oppressed by the daily conditions of life during war. The author examined patriotism and the justification for bearing arms in defense of one's country and concluded that there is only one kind of killing and that all killing is anti-human and anti-Christian. This conclusion represents the revolution of the conflict within Wittlin between his patriotism and his antiwar feelings in favor of the renunciation of war regardless of the cost which, as World War II approached, meant self-imposed exile.

In France when World War II started, Wittlin was joined by his family and moved to New York in 1941. In exile, he continued to write and oppose all forms of dictatorship, oppression, and violence. Although he never returned to his native land. Wittlin wrote primarily in Polish and his works, which decry the brutal dehumanization of the twentieth century, the nightmare of bureaucratization, senseless slaughter and urban decay, left their mark on modern Polish literature. Having lived through two major wars, Józef Wittlin resigned himself to the fact that on this earth there will be no paradise and that one has to live within the perimeter of faith.

Bibliography:

A. *Hymny* (Poznań, 1920), *Mój Lwów* (New York, 1946); *Orfeusz w piekle XX wieku* (Paris, 1963); *Sól ziemi; Powiesc o cierpliwym piechurze* (Warsaw, 1935, Eng. trans., *Salt of the Earth*, London, 1939); *Wojna, pokój i dusza poety* (Zamość, 1925).

B. Z. Folejewski, "The Creative Path of Joseph Wittlin," *Polish Review* 9 (1964), 67-72; H. Kesten, "Joseph Wittlin—In Memoriam," *Polish Review*, 23 (1978), 69-71; *Slownik współczesnych pisarzy polskich* (Warsaw, 1964), III, 512-17; Z. Yurieff, *Joseph Wittlin* (New York, 1973); NYT, March 1, 1976, 26.

Zofia Sywak

WOOD, Alexander (3 May 1879, Glasgow, Scotland—1 April 1950, Cambridge, England). *Education*: D.Sc., Univ. of Glasgow, 1907; M.A., Emmanuel Coll., Cambridge Univ., 1909. *Career*: fellow and tutor, Emmanuel Coll., 1907-44; lecturer in physics, Cambridge Univ., 1920-40; scientist, politician, and antiwar activist.

After taking his first degree at the University of Glasgow, Alex Wood moved to Cambridge and began his long-lasting association with the Cavendish Laboratory. For over thirty years he was arguably the finest teacher of science at Cambridge University, as well as doing important work in developing science in schools. His own original work lay in the study of sound, and, though he laid no claims to being a great scientist, made important contributions to our knowledge of acoustics.

During the First World War he already took the pacifist stand, but did not share greatly in the corporate pacifist witness. He was active in the local Red Cross. After the war he took interest in politics and became a member of the Labour party. Parliament was not to be for him; he fought four elections unsuccessfully. But his contribution to the Cambridge Borough Council was unmatched, and in the last years of his life changed the lives of hundreds of people by his involvement in local housing. Meantime he was an elder of St. Columba's Church, a member of the Council of Westminster College, and a respected speaker at the Student Christian Movement.

In the last fifteen years of his life Alex Wood was increasingly involved in the peace movement. He was a founder-member of the Peace Pledge Union and became its chairman. He was vice-chairman both of the Fellowship of Reconciliation, where his Christian pacifist convictions could have full expression with others of like belief, and of the National Peace Council, where he made common cause with others of different beliefs.

Alex Wood's strength was his sturdy common sense. He stood on his understanding of Jesus Christ, and his religion was incarnational and worked out in the practicalities of this world. He acknowledged his responsibility for the atomic bomb on Hiroshima, both as a citizen of Britain and as a teacher of many of those who devised it, but he distinguished that responsibility, which is part of the human condition, from the responsibility of those who deliberately entered the project. He always insisted on the Christian's right and duty to say "No" in the name of God to activities laid by the state on its citizens, but he also insisted that those who withdrew in this way had a duty to work to change the thing from which they stood aside. Wood's influence long outlasted his passing.

Bibliography:

B. Charles Raven, *Alex Wood—The Man and his Message* (London 1952).

John Ferguson

WOOD, George Arnold (7 June 1865, Salford, England—14 October 1928, Sydney, Australia). *Education*: B.A., Owens Coll., Manchester, 1885; M.A., Balliol Coll., Oxford Univ., 1889. *Career*: first Challis Professor of Modern History, Univ. of Sydney, 1891-1928.

George Arnold Wood was undoubtedly the most prominent opponent in Australia of British and Australian involvement in the Boer War (1899-1902). A liberal and a Christian, he fervently believed that academics should be involved actively in politics and he refused to allow his chair in modern history at the University of Sydney to inhibit his opposition to the conflict. His dissent to the Boer War manifested itself in two stages. During the last few months of 1899 he debated the war via the correspondence columns of the Sydney *Daily Telegraph* with his friend and colleague, the Scottish-born professor of modern literature at the university, Mungo MacCallum. Wood rejected the doctrine of "the Empire right or wrong" and believed that the war was not in the interests of England, the Empire, or humanity at large. Having registered his dissent, Wood remained silent for two years during which he collected information about the war mainly from British newspapers.

Reports of the British practices of herding Boers into concentration camps and burning Boer farms led Wood to break his silence and to attack these wartime practices as "both sickening and atrocious." In January 1902, in collaboration with other prominent opponents of the war, notably a few Labor members of the New South Wales parliament and Archibald Stephens, editor of the *Bulletin*, he formed and became president of the Anti-War League, a group inspired by and based on the Peace and Humanity Society in Melbourne, which was established two years earlier. The League's main project was the drafting and circulation of a petition to the House of Commons urging peace terms that would provide a complete amnesty for the Boers, compensation, and a guarantee of immediate self-government to the former Boer states, the Orange Free State, and the Transvaal.

Wood quickly became the object of intense public vilification. Local patriots were outraged and letters poured into newspaper offices and the university demanding his dismissal. Several councils responded to the League's petition by consigning it either to the wastepaper basket or the public sewer. In February the university senate censured Wood on the grounds that his public utterances were partial and passionate and lent support to the enemies of the country. Reports in the local press of an article Wood had written and sent to the *Manchester Guardian* dealing with Australian public opinion on the war brought the matter to a climax. Two events saved Wood from losing his chair: a letter from Prime Minister Edmund Barton to Chancellor Normand MacLaurin, urging that Wood be accorded the right of free speech, and a private communication to the university authorities from the Labor party that it would vote against the university estimates if Wood were expelled.

The Peace of Vereeniging, signed in May 1902, ended Wood's ordeal. Though charming and companionable in private, especially to the young, Wood was uncomfortable speaking in public and unnerved by being the target for violent personal abuse. In the university he had stood alone, his few sympathizers silent, his many critics vocal. Although very much a victim of colonial jingoism, Wood was not a pacifist. His objection was to the Boer War in particular. Indeed he described himself as a "fervid Imperialist." Only his age prevented him from enlisting in the Australian forces during the First World War. It did not, however, deter him from joining a volunteer group that undertook military training at the university.

Bibliography:

A. "Australia and Imperial Politics," M. Atkinson (ed.), *Australia: Economic and Political Studies*, (Melbourne, 1920), 380-414.

B. R. M. Crawford, *'A Bit of a Rebel': The Life and Work of George Arnold Wood*, (Sydney, 1975); R. M. Crawford, "The Antipodean Pilgrimage of Arnold Wood: A Manchester Liberal and the Boer War," *Royal Australian Historical Society Journal*, 48 (March 1963), 405-26; Percival Serle (ed.), *Dictionary of Australian Biography*, II, 504-5; Gavin Souter, *Lion and Kangaroo: The Initiation of Australia 1901-1919*, (Sydney, 1976).

Malcolm James Saunders

WOODSWORTH, James Shaver (29 July 1874, Etobicoke, Ontario, Canada—21 March 1942, Vancouver, British Columbia). *Education*: B.A., Wesley Coll., Winnipeg, 1896; B.D., Victoria Coll., Toronto, 1899. *Career*: Methodist minister, 1900-18; Member of Parliament, 1921-42; pacifist, social worker, writer, and socialist political leader.

"To have peace," declared J. S. Woodsworth from his place in the Canadian parliament in September, 1939, "requires both courage and sacrifice." His life had overflowed with both; he taught peace as much by personal example as by his mastery of parliamentary politics.

Born on a farm near Toronto, Woodsworth moved to Manitoba in 1885 where his father became superintendent of Methodist missions in the Northwest—a region stretching from Lake Superior to the Pacific coast. Woodsworth came to know intimately this vast frontier—traveling with his father across the long prairie trails as far as Calgary, and, after graduating from Wesley College, Winnipeg, serving as "circuit rider" minister for two years in Manitoba. A year spent in Toronto studying theology, and a further year at Oxford, helped formulate questions about the basic truths of orthodox Methodism.

Observing the social results of industrial capitalism—from Toronto and Winnipeg to London and Glasgow—Woodsworth concluded that his church's emphasis upon personal salvation and conversion was wrong. Moving from the pulpits of middle class Methodism to a city mission he worked with the immigrant slum-dwellers in Winnipeg from 1904-13. From All People's Mission he also sent forth a stream of articles and books which made him the leading exponent of the social gospel—that creedless Protestant movement which proclaimed the need to work for the Kingdom of God "here and now."

By the time World War I broke out, Woodsworth had become an outspoken supporter of trade unionism and collective bargaining, and in politics, a democratic socialist. Believing that modern war was a product of capitalism's imperialist competition, he openly opposed conscription for Canada's armed forces and was fired from his governmental post in social work. By 1918, more than ever persuaded that war was absolutely contrary to the Sermon on the Mount, and disillusioned by his church's enthusiastic advocacy of enlistment, Woodsworth resigned from the ministry. Working for a year as a longshoreman in Vancouver, he concluded that the profit motive of capitalism produced both war and social injustice, and committed himself thereafter to replacing that system with a social democracy which would renounce militarism and in which production of goods would be for "use" rather than profit.

During a six-week general strike in Winnipeg in 1919 Woodsworth supported the workers' nonviolent demands for union recognition and wage increases. After the strike leaders' arrest, he edited the workers' paper and was himself arrested for "seditious libel." In 1921 Woodsworth was elected to the federal parliament on the platform of Winnipeg's Independent Labour party—a platform modeled on the ideas of British Fabians but adapted to the Canadian context. He retained his Winnipeg seat until his death in 1942, by which time he had acquired many sobriquets: "conscience of Canada," "saintly failure," "red rabble-rouser." A champion of the common people, Woodsworth gave much of his income and all of his energy to promoting the twin causes of socialism and peace. In the House in the 1920s, he seized every occasion to demand reduction of military expeditures and (successfully) establishment of a system of social security. Having aligned himself with the more radical of a group of farmer-progressives in the Commons, Woodsworth became the unanimous choice as leader of the Cooperative Commonwealth party (CCF) in 1933.

Composed of provincial associations of farmers, labor parties, and socialists, the CCF was not only a significant political force for social justice during the Depression, it was also the focal point for criticism of any Canadian commitment to follow Britain into another European war—war which loomed ever more ominously as the decade of the 1930s waned. Despite some wavering in the CCF ranks and amongst the party's seven M.P.'s, Woodsworth kept the party committed to nonparticipation in any "imperialist war." In the House he frequently used +John Maynard Keynes' *Economic Consequences of the Peace* to support his argument that war simply creates the causes of more war, and to demand that Canada declare its right to remain neutral in the event of another European breakdown.

When Britain declared war on Germany in September 1939, the CCF National Council met to decide whether the party would support the government's policy of Canadian participation. Woodsworth and about one-third of the Council members were defeated as the party adopted a policy of "limited" support of "the war effort." In the debate on the government's motion to declare war, Woodsworth nevertheless (with the agreement of his colleagues) rose in the House to voice his opposition. Woodsworth raked the government for its failure to do anything to help prevent the war and then reminding his colleagues that he had left the ministry during World War I, declared that he still believed in some of the principles of the New Testament. War, he pronounced, was "an absolute negation of anything Christian."

At the end of that cruel debate Woodsworth alone requested that his vote in opposition to the war be recorded. In 1940 he was, although unrepentant, re-elected with a sharply reduced plurality. Several crippling strokes, however, prevented him from resuming his place in a parliament that admired but did not heed him.

Bibliography:

A. *Strangers Within Our Gates* (reprinted, Toronto, 1972); *My Neighbour* (reprinted, Toronto, 1972).

B. Grace MacInnis, *J. S. Woodsworth: A Man to Remember* (Toronto, 1953); Kenneth McNaught, *A Prophet in Politics* (Toronto, 1963).

C. J. S. Woodsworth Papers, Public Archives of Canada, Ottawa.

Kenneth McNaught

WOOLF, Leonard Sidney. See *Biographical Dictionary of Internationalists*.

WORCESTER, Noah (25 November 1758, Hollis, NH—31 October 1837, Brighton, MA). *Career*: secretary, Massachusetts Peace Society, 1815-28; editor, *The Christian Disciple*, 1813-18, *The Friend of Peace*, 1819-28; Congregational (later Unitarian) minister, peace advocate, and writer on religion.

Among those prominent in the early years of the American peace movement Noah Worcester played the most effective role. A courteous, gentle, and unassuming man, he strove to unite all who were willing to condemn the "custom of war," whether they were absolute pacifists or supported the "lawfulness" of defensive wars. He avoided controversy wherever possible, especially when this might lessen his effectiveness as a peace leader.

Worcester was raised on a farm, but his parents respected learning and several of his ancestors had been Congregational ministers. His formal schooling ended at the age of sixteen (the degrees bestowed on him late in life being *honoris causae*). When the American Revolution broke out his father became an enthusiastic supporter, while young Noah served for nearly a year as a volunteer fifer in the Revolutionary army. In an autobiographical fragment written in 1823, he declared that he was already acquainted with the Quaker peace testimony from hearing it expounded by a neighboring Baptist preacher, but he remained unconvinced. A second encounter with pacifism came after he settled in 1782 in Thornton, NH, as village schoolmaster. Its pastor, the Rev. Experience Estabrook, was a pacifist. Estabrook had taken a liking to Worcester, encouraging his lay preaching and in 1787 recommending his ordination and succession to himself as Thornton's pastor. With a wife and growing family Worcester was forced to supplement his meager clerical salary by teaching, farming, and cobbling. His interest in the peace question was by now awakened, but he continued to believe that war was sometimes a necessary evil.

The war of 1812 effected a revolution in his thought. He had long been a supporter of the Federalist party which opposed the war against Britain on political grounds. Federalist sympathies combined with a growing conviction that war contradicted Christian principles led Worcester to speak out openly against the war. In sermons preached during the summer of 1812 in Salisbury, NH, where he acted as assistant pastor to his brother Thomas from 1810 to 1813, he refused to pray for victory and condemned the current struggle. In December 1814, at the conclusion of the war, Worcester published anonymously his *Solemn Review of the Custom of War*. In it he argued not only that international war was incompatible with the Christian religion, but that it was inhumane, unnecessary, and the result of collective delusion. He pleaded for its abolition by international agreement. He did not raise directly the subject of either defensive war or conscientious objection or personal nonresistance, for he aimed at influencing as wide an audience as possible. The pamphlet was concise, clearly written, and not marred by the diffuseness that marked much of Worcester's other writing. These qualities led to its becoming a peace classic whose impact has not been confined to the United States.

Worcester, on his appointment in 1813 as first editor of the theologically liberal *Christian Disciple*, had gone to live at Brighton, near Boston, where he remained until his death. He had already shifted from his earlier Calvinism to a Unitarian position, for which he was officially censured by his fellow ministers. On December 28, 1815 Worcester, along with several religious liberals founded the Massachusetts Peace Society at a gathering held in Boston. Worcester became its secretary: he was to run it almost single-handed. At its height the Society may have had almost a thousand members. These were drawn from evangelical clergymen, mainly Congregational, substantial merchants, bankers, lawyers, and teachers. Like Worcester himself, many of them were Federalist sympathizers.

Considering the pioneering character of this work, Worcester's achievements were substantial, especially with respect to peace propaganda. Between 1816 and 1823 the Society distributed 155,000 copies of various tracts, addresses, sermons, and reports. The main thrust of this literature was directed against war as a public institution. It also stressed the need for peace education and for the elimination of national prejudices. It opposed privateering and duelling, pleaded for the protection of the Indian population against white exploitation, and upheld the right of conscientious objection to militia service. Though activity was centered in the Boston area, branches of the Society were established throughout New England and contacts maintained with peace activists in other states as well as in Canada. *The Friend of Peace*, which Worcester edited and filled for the most part with articles written by himself, acted as the Society's mouthpiece between 1819 and 1828. In 1828, having reached the age of seventy and racked by ill health, he closed the paper down and resigned as secretary of the Society, which now merged with the American Peace Society recently founded by his disciple *William Ladd. His remaining years he devoted to study and writing: several books on peace and religion attested to his continued intellectual vitality.

The precise nature of Worcester's views on war have been disputed. But there is evidence that by the mid-1820s, if not before, Worcester had privately reached a pacifist position (though he never adopted nonresistance of the Garrisonian variety). However, he always remained anxious to draw into the peace movement men of different opinions, and he refrained from impugning the motives of those Christians who supported war. In fact few members of his Society went as far as he did in opposing war. While all this gave it a strongly conservative hue, it meant peace ideas circulated more widely than they would have done if propagated by a leader who took a more rigid line.

Bibliography:

A. *The Atoning Sacrifice, A Display of Love—not of Wrath* (Cambridge, MA, 1829); *Bible News of the Father, Son and Holy Spirit. In a Series of Letters* (Concord, NH, 1810); *Causes and Evils of Contentions Unveiled in Letters to Christians* (Boston, 1831); *Last Thoughts on Important Subjects, in Three Parts* (Cambridge, MA, 1833); *A Solemn Review of the Custom of War* (1814), reprinted in Peter Brock (ed.), *The First American Peace Movement* (New York and London, 1972).

B. Clyde W. Macdonald, Jr., "The Massachusetts Peace Society 1815-1828: A Study in Evangelical Reform," Ph.D. dissertation, Univ. of Maine, 1973; Henry Ware, Jr., *Memoirs of the Rev. Noah Worcester, D.D.*, ed. Samuel Worcester (Boston, 1844).

C. Noah Worcester papers relating chiefly to the Massachusetts Peace Society, Massachusetts Historical Society, Boston.

Peter Brock

WRIGHT, Henry Clarke (29 August 1797, Sharon, CT—16 August 1870, Pawtucket, RI). *Education*: Andover Theological Seminary, 1819-23. *Career*: minister, abolitionist, lecturer, and author of reform literature.

Although Henry Clarke Wright rejected the severe Calvinism of his boyhood, he remained deeply religious throughout his life, insisting that love and kindness could save the world as well as souls. Founding his efforts to serve his fellow human beings on religious principle, Wright addressed himself to a variety of mid-nineteenth century reform issues, particularly abolitionism and pacifism, but also temperance, education, children's rights, and women's rights.

After resigning his ministry in 1833, Wright became an agent for the American Sunday School Union and traveled through New England raising money to establish Sunday schools for southern slaves. By 1835 Wright aligned himself with *William Lloyd Garrison's efforts to achieve immediate abolitionism. During that year he also joined in Boston the Bowdoin Street Young Men's Peace Society which was affiliated with the American Peace Society. Wright's repudiation of slavery was most firmly centered in the peace principles he espoused as a leading spokesman for the New England Non-Resistance Society.

Wright's nonresistance was informed by his faith in Christ's example of love, humility, and submission. If social evils were to be eliminated, the only effective means of doing so was love rather than resistance or violence. Wright looked to the regeneration of individuals as the only way to improve society; he wanted nothing to do with reforming government because he believed that even voting and holding office were functions that were supported by a network of violence ranging from an administration's power to declare war to a police officer's sworn duty to subdue a criminal. Wright's radical nonresistance identified him as one of the chief spokesmen for the "non-government" position taken by some reformers. However, by the late 1850s, Wright, like many of his contemporaries, could not leave the issue of abolitionism entirely in God's hands; he gave his approval to John Brown's desperate raid at Harpers Ferry and eventually supported the Union in the Civil War. Slavery had to go before peace could come. Wright never completely abandoned his pacifist principles, but he was ready to suspend them for the abolitionist cause.

In addition to advocating peace principles while engaged in antislavery activities, Wright also worked to introduce pacifism to children. He believed that if he could teach children not to fight with their playmates, they would have a better chance of enjoying peace when they reached adulthood. Wright's interest in children also engaged him in an examination of women's rights and family relationships. He argued that if families fostered love and peace, then war and violence would give way to mutual respect and harmony on a social level. Social abuses, even slavery and the violence that enforced it, might eventually be eliminated as subsequent generations of children were nurtured in peace-loving families.

Viewed as an extremist in his own time, Wright nevertheless remains important for an understanding of nineteenth-century moral suasionists who rejected institutional reform in favor of individual regeneration as the primary means of ending slavery and establishing peace in the United States.

Bibliography:

A. *Anthropology: or The Science of Man* (Boston, 1850); *Human Life* (Boston, 1849); *A Kiss for a Blow* (Boston, 1842); *The Living Present and the Dead Past* (Boston, 1868); *Man-killing, by Individuals and Nations, Wrong-Dangerous in All Cases* (Boston, 1841);

Marriage and Parentage (Boston, 1854); *Six Months at Graeffenberg; with Conversations in the Saloon, on Nonresistance and other Subjects* (London, 1845).

B. Peter Brock, *Pacifism in the United States: From the Colonial Era to the First World War* (Princeton, 1968); Lewis Perry, *Childhood, Marriage and Reform: Henry Clarke Wright, 1797-1870* (Chicago, 1980); Peter Walker, *Moral Choices; Memory, Desire and Imagination in Nineteenth-Century American Abolitionism* (Baton Rouge, LA, 1978).

C. Henry Clarke Wright, diaries and papers, Harvard College Library, Boston Public Library, New York State Historical Association, Cooperstown, NY, and Western Reserve Historical Society, Cleveland, OH.

Michael Meyer

Y

YABE Kiyoshi (4 July 1884, Aizu-Wakamatsu, Japan—26 August 1935, Otsu, Japan). *Education*: B. A., Otterbein Univ., Ohio, 1912; M.A., Univ. of Chicago Divinity School, 1913, B.D., 1914. *Career*: Christian minister; education and social worker for the Brethren Church in the Otsu-Lake Biwa area.

At age 18, Yabe Kiyoshi joined the church of the Latter Day Saints and briefly attended their mission school. Following his conscience, he became deeply interested in the movement for peace and earnestly practiced the precept ''thou shalt not kill.'' Even as the war fever surrounding the approach of the Russo-Japanese conflict grew, Yabe courageously demonstrated his antiwar commitment. On evenings he stood in front of the Aizu-Wakamatsu police station and called out, ''War is a sin which disobeys God's will.'' People abusively called him a traitor and some threw stones and roof tiles, occasionally forcing him to leave.

In January 1905 Yabe was ordered to enter military service with the Sendai regiment. He courageously told the regimental commander that he would not enter the army. He announced that as a citizen he was not a person to evade the draft but, as a servant of God he could in no way kill an enemy soldier. He said that he preferred his own death rather than take the life of another. For this act of conscientious objection, Yabe was arrested, tried, and found guilty. After serving two months in prison for draft evasion, Yabe again received an induction notice. Expecting to die, he reluctantly accepted the draft and left home after a funeral-like sendoff by family and friends. However, the regimental commander allowed him to serve in the medical corps. Yabe's conscientious objection to war was not the antiwar logic of *Uchimura Kanzō or *Abe Isō nor the influence of the Friends, but rather it came directly from the Bible and rigid application of the commandment, ''Thou shalt not kill.'' Yabe's actions made him Japan's first conscientious objector.

With help from friends in the Church of the Latter Day Saints, Yabe went to the United States to study in 1906. He attended high school in Dayton, Ohio, but his studies were interrupted when he came down with scarlet fever. During his illness he experienced the divine call and decided to enter the ministry. He enrolled at Chicago University but transferred to Otterbein University after one year. While at Otterbein he joined the Christian Brethren Church. After graduation from Otterbein University he entered the University of Chicago Divinity School where he completed an M.A. and a B.D. degree.

Yabe returned to Japan in the fall of 1915 and became a missionary for the Harajuku (Tokyo) Brethren Church. He opened a mission in Otsu near Lake

Biwa. There he was a dedicated organizer of the Sunday School Movement and even started a training center for Sunday Schools. In 1923 Yabe was selected to the Board of Directors of the Japanese Sunday School Association and represented that organization at the World Sunday School Conference in Glasgow in 1924. He opened a children's kindergarten, organized summer schools for children, founded a church and served as its minister, formed a Japanese farmers' mission group, and involved himself in various social issues.

While his pacifist reputation rests largely on his conscientious objection to the Russo-Japanese War, Yabe Kiyoski remained opposed to war throughout his life. Although he concealed his fierce antiwar activities of his youth from his students and members of his church, he nonetheless exercised a strong pacifist influence over them.

Bibliography:

B. Nihon Yūwakai, *Ryōshinteki heieki kyohi* (Tokyo, 1967); Tabata Shinobu, *Nihon no heiwa shisō* (Tokyo, 1972); Tamura Teiichi, *Yabe Kiyoshi den* (Ōtsu, 1937).

William D. Hoover

YANAIHARA Tadao (27 January 1893, Imabari Ehime prefecture, Japan—25 December 1961, Tokyo). *Education*: B.A., Tokyo Imperial Univ., 1917. *Career*: employee of the Sumitomo Sōhonten, 1917-20; university teacher and later administrator at Tokyo Univ. 1920-37, 1945-57 (president, 1951-57); leader of *Mukyōkai* (''Non-church'') Christianity in Japan; scholar, writer, and evangelist.

Beginning with the invasion of Manchuria in 1931, militaristic tendencies increasingly came to dominate Japanese life and finally led Japan into war with the United States and its allies. The end result was unconditional surrender in 1945. Yanaihara Tadao was one of the very few people who consistently resisted the militaristic tendencies during the period of the so-called Fifteen Years' War. The majority of Japanese intellectuals either underwent a ''redirection'' (*tenkō*) of thought, actively endorsing the war and Japanese aggression on the Asian continent, or tacitly acquiescing in the war by remaining completely silent.

Yanaihara received an education as a future leader of Japanese society at the Dia-ichi Kōtō Gakkō, the most prestigious prewar higher school, and at Tokyo Imperial University (renamed Tokyo University after the war). He became inbued with strong patriotic feelings and with a sense of responsibility for the destiny of his nation. Thus, he could easily be attracted by *Uchimura Kanzō's *Mukyōkai* (''Non-church'') Christian movement, which, according to Yanaihara, was characterized by ''prophetic spirit and patriotism.''

Yanaihara's opposition to Japan's militarism stemmed partly from his deep scholarly understanding of colonialism and imperialism, which he made evident in *Manshū mondai (The Manchurian Problem*) (1934), an attack upon Japan's expansionist policies. Even more important, however, was the impact of his religious teacher, Uchimura Kanzō, who influenced the handful of Japanese pacifists among the non-church Christians during the Fifteen Years' War. Yanaihara's pacifism, like Uchimura's, was more concerned with bearing witness to divine truth, which, he believed, dictated nonviolence, than with organizing antiwar activities in Japan. In this sense, his pacifism was apolitical. He never tried to organize a political opposition to the war and he did not encourage his followers to refuse military service.

The publication of pacifist writings such as "Kokka no risō" ("Ideals of the State") (1937) cost Yanaihara his position at Tokyo University. As a result, his potential impact upon Japanese society declined and the sphere of his activities became severely limited. Unconcerned about his diminished audience, however, Yanaihara continued to communicate his thoughts to a small number of loyal followers who shared his sense of God-given mission. Through his personal magazine, *Kashin (Good News)* he spoke with a note of authority, reminiscent of Old Testament prophets, especially Isaiah. He identified strongly with the Old Testament prophets because, he believed, they not only spoke divine truth, but were also patriots.

Yanaihara's self-image of patriot, his hearty endorsement of the imperial institution, his abhorance of violence, and his somewhat conservative or even "authoritarian" personality—all helped to give him a degree of respectability despite his pacifism. Yet he never compromised his pacifist position. This was probably made easier because his political and patriotic pacifism was relatively harmless in the eyes of the dominant militarists. Although a consistent critic of Japan's militaristic aggression, Yanaihara was never arrested, imprisoned, or threatened for his antiwar views. Yet he was interrogated by police and had his writings censored.

In the postwar period, Yanaihara Tadao was widely acknowledged as one of the foremost intellectual and spiritual leaders of Japan. There he could give full exposition to his pacifist ideas without fear of repression.

Bibliography:

A. *Yanaihara Tadao zenshū* (29 vols., Tokyo, 1963-65).

B. Nanbara Shigeru and others, ed., *Yanaihara Tadao* (Tokyo, 1968); Wakao Fujita, "Yanaihara Tadao: Disciple of Uchimura Kanzō and Nitobe Inazō," Nobuya Bamba and John F. Howes, ed., *Pacifism in Japan: The Christian and Socialist Tradition* (Vancouver, 1978), 199-219; Yuzo Ota, "Yanaihara Tadao (1893-1961): The Man as a Pacifist," *Kyōyō Gakka Kiyō*, No. 6, The University of Tokyo, March 1974.

Yuzo Ota

YEN Hui-ch'ing (known as W. W. Yen) (2 April 1877, Shanghai, China—23 May 1950, Shanghai). *Education*: studied at St. John's Coll., Anglo-Chinese Coll., and the T'ung-wenkuan; graduated, Univ. of Virginia, 1900; received the *chinshih* degree in 1906. *Career*: teacher, 1900-6; editor, 1906-7; government official and diplomat, 1907-26, 1931-36, 1947-49; civic leader.

Born and raised in the family of an American-educated priest and in a tradition-bound Chinese society, Yen Hui-ch'ing was cultivated as an intellectual with Christian brotherly love balanced by Confucian universal humanism. Committed to peace, he abhorred war as an absolute horror. Yen's first peace efforts were joining several Chinese ministers abroad in urging domestic peace during the second revolution against President Yuan Shih-k'ai's monarchical movement. As China's minister to Germany during World War I, he tried to convince Arthur Zimmermann of the German Foreign Office to restore the leased territory of Kiaochow to China, thus forestalling and invalidating any Japanese pretext for military assault.

Upon receiving an invitation to participate in the Washington Disarmament Conference (1921-22), Foreign Minister Yen organized a special bureau in the Foreign Ministry including Sao-Ke Alfred Sze, Minister to Washington, and V. K. Wellington Koo, Minister to the Court of St. James, and +C. H. Wang, China's senior jurist, to seek peaceful recovery of Kiaochow and the Tsingtao-Tsinanfu Railway. The satisfactory outcome of the Washington Conference, resulting in the plan for the peaceful return of Kiaochow and its railway to China was mainly due to the leadership of Yen. During the short duration of the Conference, the Peking government had two cabinet crises caused by warlords. On both occasions Yen acted as premier and preserved the stability and continuity of the Chinese government.

With the dislike of war deeply rooted in his heart and naturally disposed to serving the cause of peace, Foreign Minister Yen seized every opportunity to influence even the warlords against civil war. In 1921, at a dinner by Premier Liang Shih-i honoring the victorious Marshal Chang Tso-lin of Manchuria and Marshal Ts'ao K'un of the Chihli Army, Yen stressed the futility and inconsequence of personal military power by using the Kaiser's failure as a lesson. Again in 1924, when Marshal Wu Peifu of the Chihli Army was determined to launch a decisive campaign against his former ally, Marshall Chang Tso-lin, Yen stood out against the war in the face of the warlord President Ts'ao K'un and the other cabinet members.

Yen answered the call of the Nationalist government and was entrusted with the mission of negotiating the peaceful settlement of the 1931 Manchurian Incident in the League of Nations. While in Geneva in the Spring of 1932, Yen was also appointed China's first delegate to the World Disarmament Conference which opened its sessions at the height of the Shanghai War. With the Armistice Agreement signed on May 5th and the withdrawal of the Japanese forces from Shanghai, the Great Powers lost their interest in the Sino-Japanese conflict as well as the Disarmament Conference. The League's reconciliation effort was finally wrecked due to Japan's continued aggression. After the Assembly unanimously adopted the Lytton Report to condemn Japan's Kwantung army operations and its puppet Manchukuo, Yen left Geneva for Moscow to take up his post as the new Chinese Ambassador to the Soviet Union. When Yen retired from Moscow in 1936, his protest against the Ho-Umezu Agreement, whereby China's rights in a region northeast of Peking were curtailed, fell on deaf ears in Nanking.

Yen was very much involved in civic activities which promoted peace and reforms in an age of violent chaos. During the warlord period, the National Red

Cross Society of China elected him president. Yen organized medical units to aid casualties of the civil wars. He was the first president of the Social and Political Science Association of China and served as chairman or board member of numerous civic and educational organizations. He created a foundation of Chinese and Americans for the custody and control of the Boxer indemnity fund, part of which was used to build the National Peking Library, a permanent monument to peace and Sino-American friendship. During the Shanghai battles after the 1937 Lukouchiao Incident, Yen and his China International Famine Relief Commission succeeded in raising three and one-half million dollars to cover the cost of care for some 40,000 wounded soldiers and 200,000 refugees.

Yen undertook his last significant peace mission in April 1949, when he headed a five-man delegation for the Nationalist government trying to make peace with the Chinese Communist delegation headed by *Zhou Enlai. The Nationalist government refused Mao's conditions and the Communist troops crossed the Uangtze and Yen returned to Shanghai. After the establishment of the People's Republic of China, Yen served as chairman of the Shanghai branch of the Sino-Soviet Friendship Association until his death in 1950.

Bibliography:

A. *East-West Kaleidoscope, 1877-1944: An Autobiography of W. W. Yen* (New York, 1974).

B. Paochin Chu, *V. K. Wellington Koo: A Case Study of China's Diplomat and Diplomacy of Nationalism, 1912-1966* (Hong Kong, 1981); *Biographical Dictionary of Republican China*, IV, 50-52.

Paochin Chu

YVETOT, Georges Louis François (20 July 1868, Paris—11 May 1942, Paris). *Education*: self-educated. *Career:* secretary general, Federation of the Bourses de travail; under secretary, Confederation générale de travail (CGT); printer, anarchist, syndicalist, and antimilitarist.

Elected in 1901 as the head of the anarcho-syndicalist organization of French workers, the Bourses de Travail, and as one of the leaders of the larger Confédération Générale de Travail (CGT), Georges Yvetot was to emerge in the decade before World War I as one of the most determined and articulate advocates of independent syndicalism and antimilitarism. Born in police barracks as the son of a Parisian gendarme and raised as an orphan by Catholic charities, it was as a printer that he first came under the influence of Camille Pelloutier, the anarchist founder of the Bourses. As Pelloutier's successor, Yvetot vigorously defended the position that the French working-class organizations, linking their revolutionary hopes to the worker-led general strike, must remain independent of all political parties, including the Socialist party of *Jean Jaures. A framer and signer of the syndicalist declaration of independence, the Charter of Amiens in 1906, Yvetot continued to support this position even after the leadership of the CGT began to change course and work with the Socialist party.

But it was as the syndicalist voice of antimilitarism that Yvetot made his greatest contribution. A powerful orator, nicknamed "bouledogue" because of his aggressive personality as well as his physique, Yvetot, one of the anarchist founders of the Ligue antimilitariste, carried his message to syndicalist meetings all over France. At the heart of this antimilitarism were two basic facts of French working class life. Every French male was required to spend two years in the army and it was this army which was frequently used to shoot workers who were on strike. Yvetot attacked militarism on all levels but it was to the young workers who were entering the army that he made his major appeal, asking them, even as soldiers, to maintain their antimilitary, proworking-class ideology. In 1903 he printed a manual for conscripts that portrayed the army as the school of "vice, debauchery and cowardice." He called on the young recruits to make of this "school of crime, a school of revolt." If soldiers were ordered to murder workers, they must not fire. Although he was acquitted of the charge of insulting the army with this pamphlet, Yvetot, never one to soften his message, was in and out of courtrooms and prisons throughout the prewar period, for his speeches and writings.

Until 1910 Yvetot's position, representing the more anarchist, antimilitarist faction of the loosely organized CGT, had only been vaguely discussed at policy-making national congresses. But after a number of bitter strikes where workers were killed by soldiers and the Morocco crisis made the possibility of war with Germany more ominous, the leader of the CGT, *Leon Jouhaux, initiated a strong antiwar policy. The CGT called for a general strike of all workers in case of war and in order to keep working class soldiers in touch with syndicalist positions, a program called the "sou de soldat" was given official CGT support. Copying a long-standing church practice of support for new recruits, the CGT would now ask all workers, not only to contribute a "sou" for their comrades in the army, but to make sure that recruits, through letters, meetings, books, and study circles, were the recipients of continued syndicalist propaganda which would ensure that they would never shoot other workers, be they French or German. And it was Yvetot who became the official voice of the CGT for the "sou de soldat."

The CGT support of the declaration of war in 1914 drove Yvetot into retirement from syndicalist activity. Although he was not a supporter of this prowar position, the usually fiery Yvetot, oddly enough, did not work with *Alphonse Merrheim and *Albert Bourderon who led the struggle for syndicalist support of an international peace agreement. Instead he chose to resume his work as a printer. Though nominally still an officer in the CGT, he devoted himself to heading the association of war orphans at Etretat. Although he was admired for his devotion to the orphans, among whom so many were children of the working class, this withdrawal from war politics was viewed with some hostility by syndicalists in both factions of the CGT. In the interwar period, Yvetot, leaving national office, chose to work only within the printers' syndicate and to associate himself with various pacifist campaigns. In 1939 he was one of the signers of the manifesto "Immediate Peace" and in 1942, after the British bombing of the working-class suburbs of Paris, the elderly and ailing Yvetot was persuaded to head a relief committee. This gesture, inspired perhaps by his desire to aid the always innocent victims of war, was nonetheless much appreciated by the Nazis and their syndicalist collaborators. He died shortly after assuming this role.

Bibliography:

A. *A.B.C. de syndicalisme* (Paris, 1909); *Ma Pensée libre* (Paris, 1913); *Le Nouveau Manuel du soldat* (Paris, 1908); *Moeurs militaires. La Vache à lait* (Paris, 1905); *Le Syndicalisme, les intellectuels et la CGT* (Paris, n.d.); *Le Syndicalisme revolutionnaire* (Paris, 1913); *Syndicat et syndicalisme* (Paris, 1910); *La Triple Action de la CGT* (Paris, 1913); *Vers la grève générale* (Paris, 1902).

B. Jean Maitron, *Dictionnaire Biographique du Mouvement Ouvrier Français*, XV, 345-46.

C. Georges Yvetot Material, Archives Nationales, Paris and Archives de la Prefecture de Police de Paris.

Judith Wishnia

Z

ZAMENHOF, Ludwik Lazar. See *Biographical Dictionary of Internationalists*.

ZETKIN, Clara Eissner (5 July 1852, Weidenau, Germany—20 June 1933, Arkhangel'skoe, U.S.S.R.). *Education*: Leipzig teachers' coll. *Career*: editor, *Gleichheit*, 1891-1916; head, Woman's Socialist International, 1907-14; founding member, German Communist party; member, Comintern Executive Committee, 1920-33; deputy, German Reichstag, 1920-33, Marxist revolutionary and feminist.

Clara Eissner was born to a middle-class German family of liberal views. Her feminist mother educated her to become a teacher. While in school Clara fell in love with Osip Zetkin, a Russian student who converted her to radical Marxism. In 1881 police persecution forced Zetkin to leave Germany. He settled in Paris and a year later Clara joined him in a common-law marriage that produced two sons. After Osip's death in 1889 Clara returned to Germany, where she became a leader of the Social Democratic party. Until 1914 she led organizing efforts among women. After the outbreak of World War I she broke with the party majority, which supported the government, moving closer to the Russian Social democrats who called for an immediate peace. After the Bolsheviks came to power in 1917, Zetkin spent much of her time working in Russia as an organizer of women and as a founder of the Communist International. She also was active in the Communist party of Germany and served as a delegate to the Reichstag.

Zetkin worked for peace immediately before and during World War I. As the leader of the Socialist Woman's International of the Second International, Zetkin had a platform from which to speak against war in the years 1907-1914. When war began she worked with Russians Inessa Armand, Angelica Balabanoff, and Nadezhda Krupskaia to organize antiwar protests among socialist women. Their efforts resulted in a conference held in Berne, Switzerland in March 1915. The two dozen women who attended the meeting disagreed on numerous issues, but joined in voting a resolution opposing the war.

In subsequent months Zetkin, often ill and ostracized by her own party, was able to do little more for the socialist peace movement than write plaintive letters and newspaper articles. Her impotence was symptomatic of a larger paralysis gripping the Social Democrats, who had been overwhelmed by the nationalistic fervor the war evoked.

After the Russian Revolution Zetkin, as a prominent voice in the Comintern, called for revolution and peace. She was never a pacifist, nor was international peace her chief concern, for she was a radical socialist committed to the violent overthrow of capitalism. Her career as a peace leader was short.

Bibliography:

B. Luise Dornemann, *Clara Zetkin: Leben und Wirken* (Berlin, 1973); Karen Honeycutt, ''Clara Zetkin: A Left-Wing Socialist and Feminist in Wilhelmian Germany,'' Ph.D. dissertation, Columbia University, 1975; Jean H. Quataert, *Reluctant Feminists in German Social Democracy, 1885-1917* (Princeton, 1979).

Barbara Evans Clements

ZEUTHEN, Else Marie Bengtssen (10 October 1897, Copenhagen—27 December 1975, Rungsted, Denmark). *Education*: M.A., Univ. of Copenhagen, 1921. *Career*: lecturer in English Literature, Univ. of Copenhagen, 1929-35; trustee, People's International Coll., Elsinore, 1921-75; translator of English works into Danish; politician, diplomat, and pacifist.

In 1941, during World War II and under very difficult conditions for carrying on peace work, Else Marie Zeuthen was elected chairman of the Danish section of the Women's International League for Peace and Freedom (WILPF). Despite the difficulties, she threw herself into the work of the League. Her involvement in and knowledge of social, political, and economic affairs gained in part through her marriage to a professor of political science and economics, imbued League work with a serious political attitude. She was among the group of individuals who founded The Friends of Peace Relief Work in 1944, later renamed Danish Association for International Cooperation. She was a member of the board of the Association until her death. From 1935 until 1946, she was chairman of the International Student Service, another relief agency.

In 1953 Zeuthen was elected to the Danish parliament as a member of the Liberal-Radical party. After her election, she resigned her chairmanship of the Danish WILPF, but remained a member of WILPF's International Executive Committee. From 1956 until 1961, Zeuthen was the international president of WILPF. Her overlapping involvement in politics, domestic peace work, and international peace policy was very useful to the League particularly because she frequently served as Danish delegate to the United Nations General Assembly and the European Council. In the latter body, she opposed the North Atlantic Treaty Organization Pact because she saw a better foundation for peace in the United Nations Organization.

As the international president of WILPF, her circular letters on international matters and foreign policy to WILPF sections all over the world provided strong guidance and leadership. In addition, Zeuthen wrote several articles on peace and political issues for periodicals and newspapers. All of her activities revealed her lifelong commitment to fostering international cooperation and to the work of attaining peace and freedom for all people.

Bibliography:

B. *Dansk biografisk Leksikon*, (forthcoming), *Den blaa bog* (1975), 1152; *Folketinget*, (1956) 201-02; *Magister-Staten* (1967), 653.

Ollis Klem

ZHOU Enlai (5 March 1898, Huaian, Jiangsu province, China—8 January 1976, Beijing). *Education*: Waseda Univ. (Japan), 1917-18; Nankai Univ., 1918-19. *Career*: member, Chinese Communist party (CCP) 1922-76; member, Central Executive Committee of the Kuomintang (Nationalist) party and director of the Political Department of the Whampoa Military Academy, 1924-26; member, CCP Politburo, 1927-76; premier, Chinese People's Republic, 1954-76; foreign minister, 1949-58; vice-chairman and later chairman, Chinese People's Political Consultative Conference, 1949-76.

Although a commitment to peace, or at least to the assuagement of conflict, constituted a consistent theme in his career, Zhou Enlai chose to realize this commitment from the paradoxical context of lifetime membership in a party dedicated to violent revolution. His commitment to peace was therefore always coincidental to his commitment to the seizure of power for his party and to the enhancement of his country's national interest. With this vital caveat, it can be argued that Zhou's conciliatory proclivities and skills had an equilibrating effect on domestic politics and a deradicalizing impact on Chinese foreign policy during the long period in which he played a major role on the national and international stage.

Zhou Enlai was born a member of China's traditional elite, scion of a declassé scholar-gentry family, and he bore with him the gracious manners and quiet self-assurance characteristic of his class. As a student activist in Japan and France, he discovered how to use his considerable inter-personal charm and rhetorical skill to mobilize his peers. Upon returning from France, where he was a leader in the radical student movement, he quickly acquired prominent positions in both the Kuomintang (KMT) and Chinese Communist (CCP) parties during the period of the first United Front (1924-27). He showed an early interest in military affairs, becoming the first commissar in the Nationalist army and later playing a major role in the Communist fomented urban uprisings where he demonstrated considerable organizational skill but little strategic sense. By gracefully yielding control of the CCP Military Affairs Commission to Mao Zedong at the watershed Zunyi Conference (1935), he retained his place within the elite and became Mao's invaluable collaborator.

Zhou Enlai's conciliatory impact on domestic Chinese politics was most marked in the implementation of the United Front policy, in the establishment of the government of the Peoples' Republic of China (PRC), and in his mediatory efforts during the Great Proletarian Cultural Revolution. He was the CCP's chief contact with the dissident KMT commander Zhang Xueliang when the latter kidnapped Chiang Kai-shek in 1936, and his diplomacy averted an execution and facilitated formation of the second United Front against Japan in 1937.

During most of the ensuing War of Resistance against Japan, Zhou remained in the wartime capital of Chungking as the highest CCP official in the National United Front Government, establishing broad contacts among leaders of the small bourgeois democratic parties and setting up a major Communist news and propaganda center. After the Japanese defeat, the CCP and KMT alliance disintegrated, giving rise to renewed civil war, but the Communist victory over the corrupt and overextended KMT forces was unexpectedly swift. When the CCP formed its ''new democratic'' government in 1949, Zhou played a leading role in assembling representatives of the minority parties into a showpiece parliamentary body, the Chinese People's Political Consultative Conference. Later he became chairman of that body, where he took charge of planning the economy and implementing the regime's domestic policy program. But undoubtedly Zhou played his most indispensable mediating role during the Cultural Revolution (1966-76), which he almost alone among the Party's pragmatic faction was able to survive, thanks to his alliance with Mao Zedong. In endless negotiations with contending Red Guard and elite factions during the 1966-68 period he was able to assuage internecine violence, later rehabilitating many of the victims of radical ''mass criticism.'' In the 1968-76 period, he shifted coalition partners judiciously, sometimes seeming to encourage the radicals, always maintaining a loyal demeanor toward Mao Zedong, but finally casting his lot with the ''revisionist'' Deng Xiaoping as his chosen successor. Through such subtle politicking he was able to maintain an uneasy equilibrium until his death, and although Mao and the radicals temporarily derailed his postmortem agenda, his strong bureaucratic and popular base enabled his successors to recoup power within a few months.

Zhou Enlai was the PRC's first foreign minister, and he continued to exercise dominant influence over the foreign policy process even after being replaced in this post by his protégé Chen Yi in 1958. His cosmopolitan background, ingratiating manners, and negotiating skills enabled him to parlay a large and populous but underdeveloped nation into a major role in the world arena. He is credited with intense but futile efforts to avert a direct Sino-American confrontation in Korea, and upon Stalin's death was able to negotiate a conclusion to the Korean conflict in July 1953. He participated in the Geneva Conference in April 1954, helping to work out a settlement of the Indochinese conflict following the French defeat at Dienbienphu. On June 23, 1954, French Premier Pierre Mendes-France and Zhou Enlai draw up framework of the basic agreement to be signed by representatives of France and the Viet Minh.

During the temporary adjournment of the Geneva Conference in June-July 1954, Zhou returned to Asia to hold talks with the prime ministers of India and Burma, two countries that had expressed interest in freeing themselves from tight bloc alignments and taking a more neutral position in world affairs. On June 28, Zhou joined with Prime Minister *Jawaharlal Nehru of India in issuing the *Panch Shila* (''five principles''), setting forth guidelines for relations between the two states. They included mutual respect for each other's territorial integrity and sovereignty, nonaggression, noninterference in each other's internal affairs, equality and mutual benefit, and peaceful coesixtence. It was agreed during Zhou's visits to New Delhi and Rangoon and the reciprocal visits of Nehru and U Nu to Peking that India and Burma would maintain neutrality in the Cold War and friendly relations with China, while China, in turn, agreed to refrain from aggression or the export of revolution along the Indian and Burmese frontiers.

Zhou's meetings with Nehru and U Nu paved the way for Chinese participation in an Afro-Asian Conference held in Bandung, Indonesia in April 1955. During the Bandung meetings, Zhou added further elements to the *Panch Shila* affirmations: recognition of racial equality and respect for the rights of people of all nations to choose their own way of life and their own political and economic systems. Zhou made use of his increasing contacts to conduct several extended good-will tours in the Third World in the 1950s and 1960s. An unexpected result of the Afro-Asian Conference was the initiation of an extended diplomatic encounter between China and the United States. Zhou made a public offer at Bandung to enter into negotiations with the United States which was accepted, initiating ambassadorial-level talks at Geneva in 1955. It was through this channel that Sino-American rapprochement was to begin in earnest in the 1970s, after a decade in which China had on ideological grounds taken issue not only with the United States but the Soviet Union and most other socialist countries as well. Thus, Zhou Enlai, China's pragmatic leader, contributed to the amelioration of antagonistic conditions both at home and abroad.

Bibliography:

A. *Zhou Enlai Xuanji* (Peking, 1980).

B. Kai-yu Hsu, *Chou En-lai: China's Gray Eminence* (Garden City, NY, 1968); John McCook Roots, *Chou: An Informal Biography of China's Legendary Chou En-lai* (Garden City, NY, 1978).

Lowell Dittmer

ZIMMERN, Alfred Eckhard. See *Biographical Dictionary of Internationalists*.

ZIPERNOWSKY, Anna (1863, Hungary—20 February 1923, Budapest). *Education*: self-educated. *Career*: pacifist and peace organization worker.

Anna Zipernowsky has been called the Hungarian *Bertha von Suttner. During her lifetime, Zipernowsky was one of the leading spirits behind the Hungarian peace movement. She was instrumental in the founding of the Hungarian Peace Society in 1895; as a member of the society's presidium she influenced its activities until her death. She also founded the peace section of the Hungarian Women's Association and became its president. For fifteen years Zipernowsky was a member of the council of the International Peace Bureau and participated actively in its deliberations.

Along with her husband, Károly Zipernowsky (1853-1942), who served as vice-president of the Hungarian Peace Society, she regularly took part in international peace congresses. As a member of the International Peace Bureau's council, Zipernowsky, along with *Sándor (Alexander) Giesswein (representing the absent *Frederick Bajer), attended the special meeting of the council in January, 1915. The meeting was called for the purpose of reaching agreement among pacifists on a program for restoring and preserving peace. The meeting, attended by pacifists from belligerent as well as neutral countries, also was meant to serve as witness to the possibility of overcoming national conflicts and hatreds. There could be no better witness to that possibility than Anna Zipernowsky.

Bibliography:

A. *A Békemozgalomról* (Budapest, 1909); *A Nö Szerepe a Békemozgatomban* (Budapest, 1908).

B. Alexander Giesswein, ''Anna Zipernowsky,'' *Die Frieden-Warte*, 23 (1923), 158; Alfred H. Fried, *Handbuch der Friedensbewegung* (Berlin, 1911-1913; reissued, New York, 1972), 283, 301, 421-22.

Gabor Vermes

ZWEIG, Stefan (28 November 1881, Vienna—23 February 1942, Petropolis, Brazil). *Education*: Ph.D., Univ. of Vienna, 1904. *Career*: author of numerous dramas, short stories, novellas, poems, biographies, essays, letters, articles, reviews, lectures, and translations.

Son of a wealthy Viennese textile manufacturer, Stefan Zweig was never obliged to seek employment from others but pursued a lifelong career as an independent writer, at which he was eminently successful. Enjoying the advantages of financial security, a superb humanistic education, and precocious talent, he quickly made his mark in the literary world. At age nineteen he published his first work, a volume of poetry entitled *Silberne Saiten (Silver Strings)* (1901), and the first of his many literary contributions to the *Neue Freie Presse*, Vienna's leading newspaper, whose cultural section was then under the editorship of Theodor Herzl. During the years before 1914, Zweig's writing followed a generally aesthetic direction with little involvement in political issues. World War I changed that situation dramatically. By destroying the ''world of security'' that Zweig had come to take for granted, the war was to prove a major turning-point in his life. From its beginning Zweig opposed the war inwardly. He served not at the front but as a librarian in the Imperial War Archives in Vienna. Simultaneously, he maintained an active correspondence with French pacifist *Romain Rolland and other friends abroad who, like Zweig, longed for a speedy and just termination of the conflict. In line with these feelings, Zweig published, in 1917, the play *Jeremiah*, which condemned enthusiasm for the war and called for a moral reassessment. He looked forward to the day when all would recognize the tragic folly of Europe's division into antagonistic nation-states and would agree to put aside national differences in order to forge a new and unified Europe.

After the war Zweig's literary writings increasingly reflected themes of moral earnestness and a deep concern for moderation, tolerance, and reason. In the story *Virata or the Eyes of the Undying Brother* (1922), Zweig examined the moral dilemmas an individual faces when he uses, or refuses to use, violence on behalf of a good cause. Though Zweig wrote many kinds of literary works, he is best known for his short, insightful biographies of famous writers. Of these a collection entitled *Master Builders* (1935) which includes a biography of *Leo Tolstoy, earned widespread acclaim. Other biographies included *Romain Rolland* (1921), *Joseph Fouché: Portrait of a Politician* (1929); *Marie Antoinette* (1932), *Erasmus of Rotterdam* (1934), *Mary Queen of Scots* (1935), *The Right to Heresy: Castellio against Calvin* (1936), and an unfinished manuscript on Montaigne. In each of these works Zweig examined the lives of individuals fated, as he himself, to live in times of upheaval, violence, and bigotry. He affinity was clearly for the gentler, cosmopolitan spirits—Erasmus, Montaigne, Tolstoy, Rolland—who eschewed violence and fanaticism and sought as writers and men of intellect to set reasoned argument and compassionate appeals against organized hatred and the call to arms. Forced into exile in 1934 by civil strife and the threat of a Nazi takeover of Austria, Zweig spent the remaining years of his life as a dispirited refugee. Hitler's annexation of Austria in 1938 stripped Zweig, who was Jewish, of his Austrian citizenship and rendered him stateless and vulnerable. After intermittent stays in England, South America, and the United States, Zweig took up residence in Brazil in 1941. Depressed about the spreading war, the Nazi ascendency in Europe, and the nagging uncertainty in his own life, Zweig and his second wife, Elisabeth, committed suicide together in 1942. His autobiography, *The World of Yesterday* (1944) arguably his masterpiece, was published posthumously.

A man of pacifistic sentiment and lofty moral ideals, Zweig was not by temperament a fighter or resister. His will, in fact, seemed to suffer a fundamental paralysis when it came to the question of how to act on one's beliefs. He abhorred military life, yet he had no desire to take up a militantly pacifist or other course of action and thereby risk persecution or martyrdom. He was too well-bred to get angry or even engage in polemics, but his solutions to political and social problems were formulated in terms of broad moral perspectives and attitudes, not practical plans of action. He sought personal freedom in an inner emigration and olympian detachment, "*au dessus de la mêlée*," from which he, as a writer, might articulate rational, humanitarian ideals which, he hoped, would move the public in all countries to seek greater mutual understanding and cooperation. Like Erasmus, whom he greatly admired, he placed his trust in humanistic education: in the ability of human nature, as he put it, to ennoble itself by the dedicated cultivation of reading and learning. He juxtaposed a world of intellect and culture, represented by the great authors of history, to one ruled by blind instinct and force, and he hoped—with progressively diminishing strength—that the former, in a world of good will, would somehow prevail over the latter. At last, it seems, Zweig himself gave up on these beliefs and, under the sway of dark and tormenting thoughts, took his own life. His relationship to pacifism, therefore, is ambivalent. His desire for peace was strong and beyond doubt; what he lacked was a will to act either militarily or as a firm and forceful advocate of nonviolence. What, concretely and practically, was to be done to stop the

Nazi menace? Here Zweig's voice fell into a despondent silence. Though he supported the armed cause of the Allies against Adolf Hitler, his heart was not in the fight. In the end his ideals became the victim of his despair.

Bibliography:

A. *Erasmus of Rotterdam* (Vienna, 1934, Eng. trans. New York, 1935); *Jeremiah* (Leipzig, 1917, Eng. trans., New York, 1922); *Master Builders* (Vienna, 1935; Eng. trans. New York, 1939); *Romain Rolland* (Frankfurt am Main, 1921; Eng. trans., New York, 1921); *Silberne Saiten* (Berlin-Leipzig, 1901); *Virata or The Eyes of the Undying Brother* (Leipzig, 1922; Eng. trans., New York, 1934); *The World of Yesterday* (New York, 1943). A complete list of Zweig's writings is contained in Randolph J. Klawitter, *Stefan Zweig: A Bibliography* (Chapel Hill, 1965).

B. Elizabeth Allday, *Stefan Zweig: A Critical Biography* (London, 1972); *Neue Österreichische Biographie ab 1815: Grosse Österreicher* (Vienna and Munich, 1982), XXI, 47-56; D.A. Prater, *European of Yesterday: A Biography of Stefan Zweig* (Oxford), 1972); Friderike M. Zweig, *Stefan Zweig: Eine Bildiographie* (Munich, 1961); Friderike Zweig, *Stefan Zweig* (New York, 1946); Harry Zohn, "Three Austrian Jews in German Literature: Schnitzler, Zweig, Herzl," in Joseph Fraenkel, ed., *The Jews of Austria: Essays on their Life, History and Destruction* (London, 1967), 67-82.

Richard R. Laurence

Appendix
Listing by National Affiliation

There is no satisfactory way to identify peace leaders by national status. Many moved across boundaries, while wars and treaties often moved boundaries. Some peace leaders had impact in many nations. This appendix seeks to list peace leaders under the nation with which they were most often identified. In many cases the national affiliation was their natal land, in others it was not. The listing is according to the contemporary name of each nation, not what it was called at their birth.

ARGENTINA

Juan Bautista Alberdi
Vincente Gregorio Quesada
Carlos Saavedra Lamas
Domingo Faustino Sarmiento

AUSTRALIA

Alfred M. Dickie
Vida Goldstein
Frank John Hartley
Henry Bournes Higgins
Eleanor M. Moore
William R. Morrow
Rose Scott
Jessie Street
Charles Strong
George Arnold Wood

AUSTRIA

Adolf Fischhof
Alfred Hermann Fried
Rudolf Goldscheid
Rudolf Grossman
Friedrich Otto Hertz
Franz Jaegerstaetter
Heinrich Kanner
Leopold Katscher
Karl Kraus
Rosa Mayreder
Julius Meinl
Ernst von Plener
Karl Renner

Therese Eckstein Schlesinger
Bertha von Suttner
Hans Thirring
Johannes Ude
Leopold Winarsky
Stefan Zweig

BELGIUM

Louis Bara
Auguste Marie François Beernaert
Jean-Baptiste Nicholas Coomans
Auguste Pierre Louis Couvreur
Louis Gustave De Brouckère
Émile De Laveleye
Hendrik De Man
Gustave De Molinari
Eduard Eugene Descamps
Louis Frank
Eugène Goblet D'Alviella
Hem Day
Charles Auguste Houzeau De Lehaie
Camille Jean Joseph Huysmans
Henri Marie La Fontaine
Paul Otlet
Dominique-Georges Pire
Charles Potvin
Emile Guillaume Vandervelde
Guillaume Joseph Auguste Visschers

BRAZIL

Antônio Coelho de Sá e Albuquerque
Alberto Santos-Dumont

BULGARIA

Alexander S. Stamboliski
Stefan (Metropolitan of Sofia)

CANADA

Henri Bourassa
Therese F. Casgrain
Alice Chown
Samuel F. Coffman
William B. Creighton
Arthur G. Dorland
Benjamin Eby

Robert Edis Fairbairn
Fred Haslam
Henry Magee Horricks
William Ivens
Laura Emma Jamieson
André Laurendeau
James A. Macdonald
Alexander A. MacLeod
Violet McNaughton
Agnes Macphail
Peter G. Makaroff
Jesse B. Martin
Richard Roberts
Newton W. Rowell
J. Harold Sherk
J. Lavell Smith
Harvey W. Taves
David Toews
John A. Toews
E. Harold Toye
James Shaver Woodsworth

CENTRAL AFRICAN REPUBLIC

Barthélemy Boganda

CHILE

Arturo Alessandri Palma
Gabriela Mistral

CHINA

Chang Chün-Mai
Ch'en Kung-po
Chou Fo-hai
Kuo Sung-t'ao
Miao Pin
Wang Ching-wei
Yen Hui-Ch'ing
Zhou Enlai

COSTA RICA

Alejandro Alvarado Quirós
Lúis Anderson Morúa

CZECHOSLOVAKIA

Julius Fučík
Antonin Hobza
Joseph Lukl Hromádka
Wenzel Jaksch
Thomas G. Masaryk
Vladimir Outrata
Ferdinand Peroutka
Albert Škarvan

DENMARK

Fredrik Bajer
Else Marie Zeuthen

ECUADOR

Carlos R. Tobar

ETHIOPIA

Haile Sellassie I

FINLAND

Selma Anttila
Kyösti Huhtala
Felix Iversen
Toini Elizabeth Iversen
Arvid Järnefelt
Yrjö Kallinen
Runar Långbacka
Aaku Mäki
Juho Aatto Mäkinen
Leopold Mechelin
Juho Kusti Paasikivi
Arndt Pekurinen
Aarne Selinheimo
Edvin Stenwall

FRANCE

Alain
Michel Alexandre
Emile Arnaud
Marie-Anne-Hubertine Auclert
Henri Barbusse
Victor Basch
Claude Frédéric Bastiat

Alexandre Blanc
Gabrielle Bouet
Louis Bouet
Albert H. Bourderon
André Breton
Hélène Brion
Pierre Brizon
Ferdinand E. Buisson
Marcelle Capy
Félicien Challaye
Armand Charpentier
Georges Demartial
Maria Deraismes
Gabrielle Duchêne
George Duhamel
Jacques Dumas
Gustave Dupin
Paul Eluard
Paul Henri d'Estournelles de Constant
Sébastien Faure
Sylvie Flammarion
Marcel Fourrier
Jean Galtier-Boissière
René Gerin
Charles Gide
Jean Giono
Jean-Baptiste-André Godin
Fernand Gouttenoire de Toury
Virginie Griess-Traut
Frédéric Adolphe Augustin Hamon
Gustave Hervé
Victor Hugo
Jean Léon Jaurès
Henri Jeanson
Frédéric Joliot-Curie
Andrée Jouve
Gérald de Lacaze-Duthiers
Louis Lecoin
Raymond Lefebvre
Lucien Le Foyer
Charles Lemonnier
Frédéric Jean Longuet
Victor Margueritte
Roger Martin du Gard
François Mayoux
Marie Mayoux
Victor Méric
Alphonse Adolphe Merrheim

Georges Michon
Gaston Moch
Pierre Monatte
Léon de Montluc
Mathias Morhardt
Eugenie Niboyet
Frédéric Passy
Anne-Madeleine Pelletier
Alexandre Percin
Raymond Louis Péricat
Georges Pioch
Marceau Pivert
Edmond Potonié-Pierre
Eugénie Potonié-Pierre
Pierre-Joseph Proudhon
Jules Jean Prudhommeaux
Jean-Pierre Raffin-Dugens
Marianne Rauze
Céline Renooz
Michel Revon
Charles Richet
Romain Rolland
Alfred Rosmer
Clémence Auguste Royer
Charles François Marc Sangnier
Louise-Aimée Saumoneau
Séverine
Jules Simon
Edmond Thiaudière
André Trocmé
Tristan Tzara
Paul Vaillant-Couturier
Madeleine Vernet
Maria Vérone
Simone Weil
Marie-Gabrielle-Hortense Wiszniewska
Georges Louis François Yvetot

GERMANY

Georg von Arco
Georg Arnhold
Anita Augspurg
Ferdinand August Bebel
Hans-Georg von Beerfelde
Eduard Bernstein
Friedrich Bloh
Dietrich Bonhoeffer

Elsbeth Bruck
Otto Dix
Christoph Moritz von Egidy
Richard Eickhoff
Kurt Eisner
Franz Carl Endres
Matthias Erzberger
Albert Falkenberg
Richard Feldhaus
Hermann Fernau
Friedrich Wilhelm Foerster
Wilhelm Foerster
Leonhard Frank
Ludwig Frank
Gustav Adolf Constantin Frantz
Ernst Friedrich
Hellmut von Gerlach
Amand Goegg
Georg Gothein
Richard Grelling
George Grosz
Emil Julius Gumbel
Hugo Haase
Constanze Hallgarten
Walter Hammer
Conrad Haussmann
Adolf Heilberg
Wilhelm Heile
Vitus Heller
Heinrich Herbers
Immanuel Gottlob Herrmann
Lida Gustava Heymann
Kurt Hiller
Alexander von Hohenlohe-Schillingsfürst
Heinrich Wilhelm Hopf
Berthold Jacob
Siegfried Jacobsohn
Lilli Jannasch
Arnold Kalisch
Erich Kästner
Georg Siegfried Kawerau
Friedrich Kayser
Franz Keller
Auguste Christine Kirchhoff
Richard Kleineibst
Käthe Kollwitz
Heinz Kraschutzki
Friedrich Küster

Wilhelm Lamszus
Georg Ledebour
Max Lehmann
Otto Lehmann-Russbüldt
Theodor Lessing
Franz von Liszt
Eduard Loewenthal
Heinrich Mann
Carl Mertens
Theodor Michaltscheff
Georg Moenius
Erich Mühsam
Leonard Nelson
Eduard de Neufville
Georg Friedrich Nicolai
Otfried Nippold
Walter Nithack-Stahn
Paul Hermann August Oestreich
Johann Ingwert Knut Ohrtmann
Carl von Ossietzky
Hans Paasche
Lothar Persius
Franz Pfemfert
Karl Christian Planck
Hermann Martin Popert
Ludwig Quidde
Paul Martin Rade
Erich Maria Remarque
Adolf Richter
Fritz Röttcher
Erich Schairer
René Schickele
Paul von Schoenaich
Lothar E. Schücking
Georg Schulze-Moering
Hans Schwann
Magnus Schwantje
Friedrich W. Siegmund-Schultze
Anna Marie Siemsen
August Siemsen
Oskar Stillich
Helene Stöcker
Jakob Stöcker
Franziskus Maria Stratmann
Heinrich Ströbel
Kurt von Tepper-Laski
Ernst Thrasolt
Ernst Toller

B. Traven
Kurt Tucholsky
Otto Umfrid
Fritz von Unruh
Veit Valentin
Heinrich Vierbücher
Rudolf Virchow
Armin T. Wegner
Franz Wirth
Richard Witting

GHANA

Kwame Nkrumah

GREAT BRITAIN

R. Clifford Allen
William Allen
Charles F. Andrews
Norman Angell
Walter H. Ayles
Vernon Gerald Bailey
Percy Walter Bartlett
Edmond Beales
Harold F. Bing
John Bright
Vera Brittain
Edward Benjamin Britten
H. Runham Brown
Thomas Burt
Charles R. Buxton
Noel E. Buxton
Barrow Cadbury
Cecil John Cadoux
Thomas Corder Catchpool
William J. Chamberlain
John Clarkson
Thomas Clarkson
Richard Cobden
George D. H. Cole
Leonard Henry Courtney
William R. Cremer
Frank P. Crozier
Lionel G. Curtis
William Evans Darby
Jonathan Dymond
Havelock Ellis

William Ewart
Anna Ruth Fry
Arthur Eric Gill
John Bruce Glasier
Victor Gollancz
George Peabody Gooch
John William Graham
Edward Grubb
James Keir Hardie
Henry Fitzgerald Heard
Carl Heath
Francis Wrigley Hirst
Margaret Esther Hirst
Henry T. Hodgkin
Aldous Leonard Huxley
Katherine Elizabeth Innes
Cyril Edwin M. Joad
George Lansbury
Wilfred Lawson
Muriel Lester
Emilie Rose Macaulay
George Hogarth Carnaby Macgregor
Catherine E. Marshall
Edward Miall
Alan Alexander Milne
Edmund D. Morel
Ottoline B. Morrell
Stuart Morris
Felex Stone Moscheles
John Middleton Murry
Florence Nightingale
Philip John Noel-Baker
William Edwin Orchard
Wilfred Edwards Salter Owen
Joseph Whitwell Pease
Priscilla Hannah Peckover
George H. Perris
Mark Plowman
Arthur A. Ponsonby
Hodgson Pratt
Charles E. Raven
Herbert E. Read
Henry Richard
Leyton P. Richards
Lewis Fry Richardson
Ellen Robinson
Bertrand Arthur William Russell
Siegfried L. Sassoon

Olive Emilie Schreiner
Hugh Richard Lawrie Sheppard
Philip Snowden
Reginald W. Sorenson
Philip James Stanhope
Lilian Sinclair Stevenson
Giles Lytton Strachey
Joseph Sturge
Helena M. Swanwick
George Thompson
Charles P. Trevelyan
Henry Vincent
Wilfred Wellock
Alexander Wood

GREECE

Alexander Papanastasiou
Alexandros Svolos

GUATEMALA

Lorenso Montúfar Y Rivera Maestre

HUNGARY

Albert Apponyi
Sândor Giesswein
Vilma Gluecklich
Ferenc Keměny
Eugen H. Schmitt
Rosika Schwimmer
Anna Zipernowsky

INDIA

Vinayak Narahari Bhave
Mohandas Karamchand Gandhi
Jeewatram Bhagwandas Kripalani
Jayaprakash Narayan
Jawaharlal Nehru
Sarvepalli Radhakrishnan
Chakravati Rajagopalachari
Rabindranath Tagore

ITALY

Ezio Bartalini
Alaide G. Beccari
Benedict XV

Ruggiero Bonghi
Aldo Capitini
Carlo Cattaneo
Eduardo Cimbali
Lauro de Bosis
Angelo de Gubernatis
Alma dolens
Luigi Fabbri
Gugliemo Ferrero
Edoardo Giretti
Rosalia Gwis-Adami
John XXIII
Anna Kuliscioff
Achille Loria
Errico Malatesta
Angelo Mazzoleni
Guido Miglioli
Francesco Misiano
Ernesto Teodoro Moneta
Maria Montessori
Giacinto Menotti Serrati
Ignazio Silone
Luigi Sturzo
Claudio Treves
Filippo Turati

JAPAN

Abe Isō
Gilbert Bowles
Kagawa Toyohiko
Kashiwagi Gien
Kawai Michi
Kinoshita Naoe
Kiryū Yūyū
Kitamura Tōkoku
Kōtoku Shūsui
Saitō Takao
Senō Girō
Uchimura Kanzō
Yabe Kiyoshi
Yanaihara Tadao

LIBERIA

Edward W. Blyden

NETHERLANDS

Samuel Baart de la Faille
Cornelis (Kees) Boeke
Bartolomeus De Ligt
Jacobus Den Beer Poortugael
David van Embden
Gerrit Jan Heering
Johannes B.T. Hugenholtz
Aletta H. Jacobs
Albert de Jong
Benjamin de Jong Van Beek En Donk
Henri Charles G. Jacob van der Mandere
Clara Gertrud Meijer-Wichmann
Jacob ter Meulen
Ferdinand Domela Nieuwenhuis
Louis Raemaekers
Henriette Roland Holst-Van Der Schalk
Nicholaas Jacob Cornelis Schermerhorn
Jan Jacob Lodewijk Ten Kate
Cornelis van Vollenhoven
Johanna Waszklewicz-van Schilfgaarde

NEW ZEALAND

Archibald Baxter
Ormond E. Burton
Lincoln W.A. Efford
Charles Robert Norris Mackie

Norway

Bjørnstjerne Bjørnson
Ragnar Forbech
Marie Lous-Mahr
Diderlike Møller

PARAGUAY

Manuel Gondra

POLAND

Jean de Bloch
Stanislaw Estreicher
Oskar Ryszard Lange

Alfred Nossig
Julian Tuwim
Józef Wittlin

PORTUGAL

Sebastião Magalhães Lima

RUSSIA

Pavel Ivanovich Biryukov
Vladimir G. Chertkov
Aleksandra Mikhailovna Kollontai
Peter Alekseevich Kropotkin
Pavel Nikolaevich Miliukov
Nicholas II
Jacques Novikow
Leo Tolstoy
Vassili V. Vereshchagin
Peter V. Verigin
Sergei I. Witte
Clara E. Zetkin

SOUTH AFRICA

Albert Luthuli

SPAIN

Francisco Ferrer Guardia
Pablo Iglesias

SWEDEN

Ellenor Andrea Andreen
Klas Arnoldson
Fredrik Natanael Beskow
Fredrika Bremer
Emilia Broomé
Emilia M. Fogelklou Norlind
Ellen Key
Carl Albert Lindagen
Anna Lindhagen
Alfred Bernard Nobel
Naima Sahlbom
Elin Mathilda Elisabeth Wägner
Matilda Widegren

SWITZERLAND

Pierre Ceresole
Elié Ducommun
Henry Dunant
Auguste Forel
Albert Gobat
Marguerite Gobat
Marie Goegg
Henri Golay
Hans Karl Walter von Greyerz
Robert Grimm
Jules Humbert-Droz
Rudolf Liechtenhan
Johann Wilhelm Muehlon
Emma Pieczynska-Reichenbach
Leonhard Ragaz
Albert Schweitzer
Jean-Jacques Sellon

UNITED STATES

Lyman Abbott
Jane Addams
Devere Allen
William D.D. Allen
Susan B. Anthony
Emily Greene Balch
Roger N. Baldwin
Adin Ballou
Albert Barnes
Charles A. Beard
George C. Beckwith
Harold S. Bender
Victor L. Berger
Joshua P. Blanchard
Charles F. Boss
Randolph S. Bourne
Rufus D. Bowman
Moses Brown
William Jennings Bryan
Elihu Burritt
Theodore E. Burton
Henry J. Cadbury
Samuel B. Capen
Andrew Carnegie
Carrie Chapman Catt
Elizabeth B. Chace

William E. Channing
William Henry Channing
Maria W. Chapman
Lydia M. Child
Aaron Cleveland
Ernest H. Crosby
Dorothy Day
Eugene V. Debs
Dorothy Detzer
John Dewey
David L. Dodge
Charles F. Dole
Amos Dresser
William E.B. DuBois
Charles Durkee
Crystal Eastman
Max F. Eastman
George Sherwood Eddy
Albert Einstein
Ralph Waldo Emerson
Frederick W. Evans
Harry Emerson Fosdick
Abigail Kelley Foster
Stephen S. Foster
Erich Fromm
William Lloyd Garrison
Emma Goldman
Richard Gregg
Sara Moore Grimké
Thomas Smith Grimké
Ernest Gruening
Eliza P. Gurney
Alice Hamilton
Ammon Hennacy
Morris Hillquit
Isidor B. Hoffman
Henry Holcombe
John Haynes Holmes
Julia Ward Howe
Jessie Wallace Hughan
William Jay
Reverdy Johnson
Rufus M. Jones
David Starr Jordan
Sylvester Judd
Paul Underwood Kellogg
Martin Luther King, Jr.
George Washington Kirchwey

William Ladd
Robert M. La Follette
Joshua Leavitt
Salmon O. Levinson
Frederick J. Libby
Louis P. Lochner
Belva A. Lockwood
George Logan
John Lord
Alfred H. Love
James R. Lowell
Judah L. Magnes
Horace Mann
Peter A. Maurin
Samuel J. May
Thomas Merton
Orie O. Miller
Charles Wright Mills
Charles Clayton Morrison
Wayne L. Morse
James Mott
Lucretia C. Mott
Abraham J. Muste
Tracy D. Mygatt
Reinhold Niebuhr
John H. Noyes
Kirby Page
Alice L. Park
Theodore Parker
George F. Peabody
Clarence E. Pickett
Edmund Quincy
Asa Philip Randolph
Jeannette Rankin
John Nevin Sayre
May Eliza Wright Sewall
Lydia H. Sigourney
Albert K. Smiley
Gerrit Smith
Charles Sumner
Leo Szilard
Evan W. Thomas
Norman Thomas
Henry D. Thoreau
Benjamin F. Trueblood
Thomas C. Upham
Walter W. Van Kirk
Oswald Garrison Villard

Lillian D. Wald
Amasa Walker
Josiah Warren
Francis A. Wayland
Daniel West
Charles K. Whipple
Frances Whitherspoon
John G. Whittier
Stephen S. Wise
Noah Worcester
Henry Clarke Wright

VENEZUELA

Andrés Bello López

YUGOSLAVIA

Dimitrije Tucović

ABOUT THE CONTRIBUTORS

'Layiwola Abegunrin is a lecturer in International Relations at the University of Ife, Ile-Ife, Nigeria. He received a Ph.D. in International Relations from Howard University and has published several articles on Africa and world politics.

Irwin Abrams is Distinguished University Professor Emeritus at Antioch University. He received a Ph.D. from Harvard University. His publications include articles on Bertha von Suttner and the nineteenth century peace movement. He has also written extensively about study abroad and international cultural exchange.

Mirella Jona Affron is an Associate Professor of Romance Languages at the College of Staten Island of the City University of New York. She received a Ph.D. from Yale University and is co-editor of a 1970 edition of Ignazio Silone's *Fontamara*.

Richard Allen teaches at McMaster University in Ontario and serves as a member of Ontario's Legislative Assembly. He received a Ph.D. from Duke University. His publications include *The Social Passion: Religion and Social Reform in Canada, 1914-1928* (1971).

Herbert Aptheker received his Ph.D. in History from Columbia University and is currently Director of the American Institute for Marxist Studies. He has written extensively on Black history and on the life and career of W.E.B. Du Bois. He is the editor of the *Autobiography of W.E.B. Du Bois* (1968) and the author of an *Annotated Bibliography of the Writings of W.E.B. Du Bois* (1973).

Abelardo A. Arias is currently a Foreign Service Officer serving in Bogota, Colombia. He received a B.A. degree from American University in Washington, D.C.

Ivan Avakumovic teaches History at the University of British Columbia. He earned a Ph.D. from Oxford University and co-authored *The Anarchist Prince — A Biographical Study of Peter Kropotkin* (1950).

William J. Baker teaches History at the University of Maine at Orono. He received a Ph.D. from Cambridge University. He has published numerous articles on nineteenth century British history and has more recently worked on the history of sports. Among his books is *Beyond Port and Prejudice: Charles Lloyd of Oxford, 1783-1829* (1981).

Françoise Basch is a Professor of Civilization at the University of Paris. Receiving her Doctorat d'Etat from the Sorbonne, she has published among other things *Relative Creatures* (1974) and *Femmes Victoriennes* (1978).

J. O. Baylen is Regents' Professor of History at Georgia State University. He received a Ph.D. in History from the University of New Mexico and has published over 100 articles on British and Russian history. He is also co-editor of the *Biographical Dictionary of Modern British Radicals*.

Michael D. Behiels received his Ph.D. from York University in Toronto and teaches at Acadia University. He is co-author of *The Essential Laurendeau* (1976) and has published articles in numerous scholarly journals.

John D. Bell received a Ph.D. in History from Princeton University and now teaches history at the University of Maryland, Baltimore County. Among his publications is *Peasants in Power: Alexander Stamboliski and The Bulgarian Agrarian National Union, 1899-1923* (1977).

Susan Groag Bell is an affiliated scholar with the Center for Research on Women at Stanford University. She received an M.A. degree from the University of Santa Clara and has published two books: *Women from the Greeks to the French Revolution* (1980) and *Women, the Family and Freedom: The Debate in Documents* (1983).

Wolfgang Benz teaches at the Institut für Zeitgeschichte in Munich. He received a Ph.D. from the University of Munich and has published numerous books on German history including *Süddeutschland in der Weimarer Republik* (1970) and *Einheit der Nation. Diskussion und Konzeptionen zur Deutschlandpolitik der grossen Partein seit 1945* (1978), which he co-authored.

Joyce Avrech Berkman received a Ph.D. in History from Yale University and now teaches at the University of Massachusetts at Amherst. Her publications include *Olive Schreiner: Feminism on the Frontier* (1979).

Patrick Kay Bidelman received a Ph.D. from Michigan State University and has published in the field of French feminism, including *Pariahs Stand Up! The Founding of the Liberal Feminist Movement in France, 1858-1889* (1982).

Donald S. Birn teaches History at the State University of New York at Albany. He received his Ph.D. from Columbia University and is a Council member of the Conference on Peace Research in History. He is interested in peace and internationalism in Great Britain and has published *The League of Nations Union, 1918-1945* (1981).

Louis Bisceglia teaches History at San Jose University. Since receiving his Ph.D. from Ball State University, he has published on numerous topics dealing with peace and internationalism, including *Norman Angell and Liberal Internationalism in Britain, 1931-1935* (1982).

Julia K. Blackwelder received her Ph.D. from Emory University and now teaches History at the University of North Carolina at Charlotte. She is also director of the American Studies program. Among her publications is *Battle of the Flowers: Caste, Culture, and Gender in Depression San Antonio* (1984).

Michael Bloch is a lawyer who received his M.A. and LL.B. degrees from St. John's College, Cambridge University. His publications include *The Duke of Windsor's War* (1982) as well as articles and reviews on various historical subjects.

Mal Bochner is a Program Specialist at the University of Connecticut. He received a M.Phil. from Yale University.

Jane Bond-Howard received an M.A. degree from the University of Birmingham in England and is currently a Ph.D. candidate at University College, London University. Her dissertation research is on the opposition to the First World War in the armament factories in Bourges, France.

Franco Pieroni Bortolotti is on the Faculty of Jurisprudence at the University of Siena, where he was educated. Among his publications are *Alle origini del movimento femminile in Italia (1848-1892)* (1963) and *Femminismo e partiti politici (1919-1926)* (1978).

John H. Boyle received a Ph.D. from Stanford University and teaches East Asian History at California State University at Chico. He has published *China and Japan at War, 1937-1945: The Politics of Collaboration* (1972).

Peter Brock teaches History at the University of Toronto. He received a Ph.D. from the University of Cracow and a D.Phil. from Oxford University. He has published widely on the subject of peace, including *Pacifism in the United States: From the Colonial Era to the First World War* (1968), *Twentieth-Century Pacifism* (1970), *Pacifism in Europe to 1914* (1972), and *The Roots of War Resistance: Pacifism from the Early Church to Tolstoy* (1981).

Edwin B. Bronner is Librarian and Professor of History at Haverford College and serves as curator of the Haverford Quaker Collection. He received his Ph.D. from the University of Pennsylvania and has published and edited several volumes on Quaker history, including *William Penn's "Holy Experiment"* (1962).

Robert E. Burkholder is an Assistant Professor of English at the Pennsylvania State University, Wilkes-Barre Campus. He received a Ph.D. in American Literature from the University of South Carolina and is co-author of two forthcoming books on Ralph Waldo Emerson.

Kenneth R. Calkins received his Ph.D. from the University of Chicago and currently teaches History at Kent State University. He is the author of *Hugo Haase: Demokrat and Revolutionär* (1976).

John M. Cammett teaches History at John Jay College of Criminal Justice of the City University of New York. He received his Ph.D. in History from Columbia University and is currently on the Board of Editors of *Science and Society*. Among his publications is *Antonio Gramsci and the Origins of Italian Communism* (1967).

Geoffrey Carnall is a Reader in English Literature at the University of Edinburgh. He received an M.A. degree from Oxford University and is author of *Robert Southey and His Age* (1960). He is also co-author of *The Mid-Eighteenth Century*, which is volume 8 of the *Oxford History of English Literature* (1979).

Berenice A. Carroll is Associate Professor of Political Science and Director of Women's Studies at the University of Illinois at Urbana-Champaign. She received her Ph.D. at Brown University and is author of *Design for Total War: Arms and Economics in the Third Reich* (1968). From 1972 to 1980 she served as editor of *Peace and Change: A Journal of Peace Research* and was a founding member of the Consortium on Peace Research, Education and Development (COPRED). She is also co-author of *Peace and War: A Guide to Bibliographies* (1983).

John Whiteclay Chambers received his Ph.D. from Columbia University and teaches History at Rutgers University. He is author of *The Tyranny of Change: America in the Progressive Era, 1900-1917* (1980) and is editor of *The Eagle and the Dove: The Peace Movement and U.S. Foreign Policy, 1900-1922* (1976).

Charles Chatfield received his Ph.D. from Vanderbilt University and teaches History at Wittenberg University. He is also Director of International Education at Wittenberg. He is a past president of the Conference on Peace Research in History and served as co-editor of *Peace and Change: A Journal of Peace Research*. Among his publications are *For Peace and Justice: Pacifism in America, 1914-1941* (1961) and *Peace Movements in America* (1963). He was co-editor of *The Garland Library of War and Peace* (1972-77).

Margaret Chatterjee is a Professor of Philosophy and currently Head of the Department of Philosophy at Delhi University. She earned a Ph.D. from Delhi University. Her publications include *Our Knowledge of Other Selves* (1963), *Philosophical Enquiries* (1968), and *The Language of Philosophy* (1981).

Roger Chickering teaches History at the University of Oregon and earned a Ph.D. from Stanford University. He is the author of *Imperial Germany and A World Without War: The Peace Movement and German Society, 1892-1914* (1975). He has written a forthcoming book on *The Pan-German League: A Social and Cultural Study, 1886-1914*.

Paochin Chu is Professor of History and Director of the Center for Asian Studies at San Diego State University. He received a Ph.D. from the University of Pennsylvania.

He is author of *V. K. Wellington Koo: A Case Study of China's Diplomat and Diplomacy of Nationalism, 1912-1966* (1981).

Linda L. Clark teaches History at Millersville State College. She received her Ph.D. from the University of North Carolina at Chapel Hill and has written several articles dealing with Social Darwinism in France and the education of women in France.

Moira Clark earned a Ministry of Education Teaching Diploma in England and resides in Essex. She is the daughter of Reginald Sorenson.

Robert H. Claxton is Sponsored Projects Coordinator and teaches History at West Georgia College. He received a Ph.D. from Tulane University. Among his articles are studies of climate and history and an assessment of the Guatemalan scientist-engineer, Miguel Rivera Maestre. His articles have appeared in *Technology and Culture*, *Climatic Change*, and *Sudies in the Social Services*.

Barbara Evans Clements received a Ph.D. from Duke University and teaches History at the University of Akron. She has published *Bolshevik Feminist, The Life of Aleksandra Kollontai* (1979).

Deborah P. Clifford received an M.A. degree in History from the University of Vermont and is the author of *Mine Eyes Have Seen the Glory: A Biography of Julia Ward Howe* (1979).

Catherine Ann Cline teaches History at Catholic University. She received a Ph.D. from Bryn Mawr College and is the author of *E. D. Morel: The Strategies of Protest* (1981). In addition, she has written *Recruits to Labour* (1963).

Paolo E. Coletta received his Ph.D. from the University of Missouri, Columbia, and teaches at the United States Naval Academy. Among his many works, he has written a three-volume biography of William Jennings Bryan: *William Jennings Bryan: Political Evangelist, 1860-1908* (1964); *William Jennings Bryan: Progressive Politician and Moral Statesman, 1909-1915* (1969); and *William Jennings Bryan: Political Puritan, 1915-1925* (1969).

Walter H. Conser, Jr. received his Ph.D. from Brown University and is currently teaching in the Department of Religion at the University of North Carolina at Chapel Hill.

David R. Contosta is Director of American Studies and Associate Professor of History at Chestnut Hill College. He earned a Ph.D. from Miami University, Ohio, and has written *Henry Adams and the American Experiment* (1980).

John S. Conway is Professor of History at the University of British Columbia. He earned a Ph.D. from Cambridge University and is the author of *The Nazi Persecution of the Churches* (1968).

Blanche Wiesen Cook received her Ph.D. from Johns Hopkins University and teaches History at John Jay College of the City University of New York. She was a founder of the Conference on Peace Research in History. A co-editor of *The Garland Library of War and Peace* (1972-77) and an editor of the *Bibliography on Peace Research in History* (1969), she has written many articles relating to feminism, peace research, and international relations. She is also the author of *The Declassified Eisenhower: A Divided Legacy of Peace and Political Warfare* (1981).

J. E. Cookson is Senior Lecturer in the History Department at the University of Canterbury. He earned a Ph.D. from the University of St. Andrews. His publications include *The Friends of Peace: Anti-War Liberalism in England, 1793-1815* (1982).

Frank J. Coppa teaches History at St. John's University in New York and is a member of the Columbia University Seminar on Studies on Modern Italy. He received his Ph.D.

from Catholic University and has edited and authored many books including *From Vienna to Vietnam: War and Peace in the Modern World* (1969) and *Pope Pius IX: Crusader in a Secular Age* (1979).

Sandi E. Cooper teaches History at the College of Staten Island of the City University of New York. She received her Ph.D. from New York University. She has written several articles on peace history in nineteenth century Europe and was co-editor of *The Garland Library of War and Peace* (1972-77). Active as a vice president and council member of the Conference on Peace Research in History, she also served as a past president of the Berkshire Conference of Women Historians.

Ernest Crane is retired from the teaching profession and is now serving as an Information Officer of the United Nations Association of New Zealand. He earned an M.A. degree from the University of New Zealand and published several books on the Tonga Islands. He is currently working on a biography of O. E. Burton.

John V. Crangle is chairman of the Department of History at Benedict College in South Carolina. He received his Ph.D. in History at the University of South Carolina and has published numerous articles on the British peace movement in the *Journal of Contemporary History*, *Quarterly Review of Historical Studies*, and *Indo-British Review*.

Jane F. Crosthwaite teaches in the Religion Department at Mount Holyoke College. She received her Ph.D. from Duke University and has published articles on American religious history and women in American religion.

Merle Curti is one of the pioneer historians in the field of peace research. *The American Peace Crusade, 1815-1860* (1929) and *War or Peace: The American Struggle* (1936) helped make the study of peace respectable. He was one of the founders of the Conference on Peace Research in History. After receiving his Ph.D. from Harvard University, he went on to teach at Smith College, Columbia University, and the University of Wisconsin-Madison. Besides studying the American peace movement, he has published broadly in social and intellectual history. Among his more important works are the *Growth of American Thought* (1964) and *Human Nature in American Thought* (1980). He is now Professor of History Emeritus at the University of Wisconsin.

Doris Groshen Daniels received a Ph.D. from the City University of New York and is now teaching at Nassau Community College in Garden City, New York. She has published articles on colonial Jewry and the suffrage battle in New York State.

V. N. Datta received an M.Litt degree from Cambridge University and is now Professor of Modern History and Dean, Faculty of Social Sciences, at Kurukshetra University, Kurukshetra, India. He has authored and edited numerous books on Indian history, including a *History of Kurukshetra* (1983) and *Madan Lal Dhingra and the Revolutionary Movement* (1977).

Calvin D. Davis teaches History at Duke University and received his Ph.D. from Indiana University. He is author of *The United States and the First Hague Peace Conference* (1962) and *The United States and the Second Hague Peace Conference: American Diplomacy and International Organization, 1899-1914* (1976). He also wrote the essay on ''Arbitration, Mediation, and Conciliation'' for the *Encyclopedia of American Foreign Policy: Studies of the Principal Movements and Ideas* (1978).

Harold Eugene Davis is University Professor Emeritus of History and International Service, American University. He received a Ph.D. in History from Case-Western Reserve University and has published broadly in the field of Latin American history. Among his books are *The Americas in History* (1953) and *Latin American Leaders* (1949).

He is a member of the Board of Directors of the American Peace Society and on the Board of Editors of its publication, *World Affairs*.

Hugh Davis teaches History at Southern Connecticut State University and received his Ph.D. from Ohio State University. Among his publications is an article on the American Seamen's Friend Society which appeared in *American Neptune* (1979).

Roderic H. Davison teaches History at George Washington University. He received his Ph.D. from Harvard University and during World War II worked with the American Friends Service Committee. He has written an article on "The Records of the American Peace Society" for *World Affairs* (1978).

Istvan Deak received his Ph.D. from Columbia University. He served as director of Columbia University's Institute on East Central Europe for 11 years and now teaches in the Columbia University History Department. Among his books is *Weimar Germany's Left-Wing Intellectuals: The Politics of the "Weltbühne" and Its Circle* (1968).

Charles DeBenedetti is a past president of the Conference on Peace Research in History. He received his Ph.D. from the University of Illinois, Urbana-Champaign, and now teaches History at the University of Toledo. Among his publications are the *Origins of the Modern American Peace Movement, 1915-1929* (1978) and *The Peace Reform in American History* (1980).

Merton L. Dillon received his Ph.D. from the University of Michigan and is now Professor of History at Ohio State University. Among his publications is *The Abolitionists: The Growth of a Dissenting Minority* (1974).

Michael Dintenfass received a Masters in Philosophy from the University of Warwick, England, and is working towards his Ph.D. in History at Columbia University.

Spencer DiScala is Associate Professor of History at the University of Massachusetts-Boston. He received his Ph.D. from Columbia University and has published on various aspects of Italian Socialism. Among his publications is *Dilemmas of Italian Socialism: The Politics of Filippo Turati* (1980).

Lowell Dittmer received a Ph.D. from the University of Chicago. He teaches Political Science and is Chairman of the Center for Chinese Studies at the University of California, Berkeley. He is author of *Liu Shao-ch'i and the Chinese Cultural Revolution* (1974).

Justus D. Doenecke teaches History at New College of the University of South Florida. He received a Ph.D. from Princeton University and is the author of *Not to the Swift: The Old Isolationists in the Cold War Era* (1978). He also published *The Presidencies of James A. Garfield and Chester A. Arthur* (1981).

Helmut Donat is a Ph.D. candidate at the University of Bremen, where he is also a research assistant and tutor in History. A publisher and publicist, he is co-editor of *Das Andere Deutschland. Eine Auswahl (1925-1933)* (1980) and *Friedenszeichen Lebensizechen. Pazifismus zwischen Verachtlichmachung und Rehabilitierung- Ein Lesebuch zur Friedenserziehung* (1982).

Richard Drake received his Ph.D. from the University of California, Los Angeles and teaches at the University of Montana-Missoula. Among his publications is *Byzantium for Rome: The Politics of Nostalgia in Umbertian Italy, 1878-1900* (1980). He has also published articles on Italian history in the *Journal of Modern History* and the *Journal of Contemporary History*.

Joe P. Dunn teaches History and Politics at Converse College. He received a Ph.D. from the University of Missouri and has written numerous articles on the military draft and the Vietnam war. His articles have appeared in *Military Review*, *Parameters*, *Teaching History*, and the *Naval War College Review*.

D. F. Durnbaugh is Professor of Church History at Bethany Theological Seminary, Oak Brook, Illinois. He received his Ph.D. from the University of Pennsylvania. He has authored and edited numerous books and articles on various aspects of church history including *On Earth Peace: Discussions on War/Peace Issues Between Friends, Mennonites, Brethren and European Churches, 1935-1975* (1978).

William B. Edgerton is Professor of Slavic Languages and Literature at Indiana University. He received a Ph.D. in Russian Literature from Columbia University. He served as general editor of the *Columbia Dictionary of Modern European Literature* (1980) and has written numerous articles on Tolstoy.

John Ehrenberg received his Ph.D. from Stanford University and teaches Political Science at Long Island University. He has published several articles on Lenin in such journals as *Science and Society* and *Studies in Soviet Thought*.

Klaus Ehrler is a former West German historian who lives in Prague and is associated with the Christian Peace Council.

Arthur A. Ekirch, Jr. teaches History at the State University of New York at Albany. He received a Ph.D. from Columbia University and has authored numerous books and essays on American history and American foreign policy, including *The Decline of American Liberalism* (1955), *The Civilian and the Military* (1956), and *Ideas, Ideals, and American Diplomacy* (1966).

Dewitt C. Ellinwood received his Ph.D. from Washington University and teaches History at the State University of New York at Albany. He also serves as Associate Dean of the College of Social and Behavioral Sciences. He is a specialist in European and Asian History and has published several articles on India. He co-edited and contributed to *India and World War I* (1978) and *Ethnicity and the Military in Asia* (1981).

Wolfgang Emmerich received his Ph.D. at the University of Tübingen and teaches German Literature at the University of Bremen. Among his publications are *Zur Kritik der Volkstumsideologie* (1971) and *Kleine Literaturgeschichte der DDR* (1981).

Frank H. Epp teaches at Conrad Grebel College, University of Waterloo and received his Ph.D. from the University of Minnesota. He is author of *Mennonites in Canada, 1786-1920: The History of a Separate People* (1974), and *Mennonites in Canada, 1920-1940: A People's Struggle for Survival* (1982).

Marlene G. Epp has a B.A. degree from the University of Manitoba and is a research associate at Conrad Grebel College, University of Waterloo.

Joseph J. Fahey is director of the Peace Studies Institute and teaches Religious Studies at Manhattan College in New York. He received a Ph.D. from New York University and is the author of *Peace, War and the Christian Conscience* (1981). He has also written *Reinhold Niebuhr on Human Nature and World Peace* (1977).

John D. Fair teaches History at Auburn University at Montgomery and earned a Ph.D. from Duke University. His articles have appeared in numerous journals including *The English Historical Review*, *The Journal of Modern History*, and *The Historian*. He is author of *British Interparty Conferences, A Study of the Procedure of Conciliation in British Politics, 1867-1921* (1980).

Candace Falk received her Ph.D. from the University of California at Santa Cruz and is presently editor of the Emma Goldman Papers Project at the Institute for the Study of Social Change at the University of California at Berkeley. She is author of *Love, Anarchy and Emma Goldman* (1984) and wrote the introduction to the new edition of Goldman's *Living My Life* (1983).

Fritz Fellner is Professor of Modern and Contemporary History at the University of

Salzburg, Austria. He received a Ph.D. from the University of Vienna and has written numerous articles on the outbreak of World War I, the Paris Peace Conference, and Allied planning in World War II for the postwar period. He is also the author of *Der Dreibund: Europäischen Diplomatie vor dem ersten Weltkrieg* (1960).

Elnora Ferguson teaches at Selly Oak Colleges, Birmingham, England. She earned an M.A. from Cambridge University and is co-editor of *Reconciliation Quarterly*.

John Ferguson is a classicist, theologian, and internationalist. He received an M.A. from Cambridge University and is currently President of Selly Oak Colleges, Birmingham. He has served as chairman of the Fellowship of Reconciliation and is currently chairman of the United Nations Association and co-editor of *Reconciliation Quarterly*. He has published nearly 50 books, several of them on issues of war and peace, including *The Enthronement of Love* (1950), *The Politics of Love* (1973), *War and Peace in the World's Religions* (1977).

Clinton F. Fink is a research associate at the Peace Museum, Chicago. He holds a Ph.D. in Social Psychology from the University of Michigan and is former editor of the *Journal of Conflict Resolution*. He is also co-author of *Peace and War: A Guide to Bibliographies* (1982).

David James Fisher received his Ph.D. from the University of Wisconsin-Madison. He was formerly Assistant Director of the Center for the Humanities at the University of Southern California and now is a practicing research psychoanalyst. He has written articles on Romain Rolland in *Peace and Change: A Journal of Peace Research* and in *Gandhi Marq*. He has also completed a forthcoming book entitled *Intellectual Politics: Romain Rolland and Engagement Between the Wars*.

James Friguglietti received a Ph.D. from Harvard University and teaches History at Eastern Montana College. He is co-editor of *The Shaping of Modern France* (1969) and author of *Albert Mathiez, historien révolutionnaire (1874-1932)* (1974).

John D. Frodsham teaches Comparative Literature at Murdoch University, Perth, Western Australia. He received his Ph.D. from Australian National University, Canberra, and has published numerous books and articles on Chinese literature, poetry, and society, including *The First Chinese Embassy to the West* (1974).

Larry Gara is chairman of the History Department at Wilmington College, Ohio. He received a Ph.D. from the University of Wisconsin-Madison. He has a regular column called "Prison Notes" in the peace publication *WIN* magazine. He also has published *The Liberty Line: The Legend of the Underground Railroad* (1961) and *War Resistance in Historical Perspective* (1980).

David J. Garrow received his Ph.D. in Political Science at Duke University. He teaches at City College of New York and is author of *The FBI and Martin Luther King, Jr.: From 'Solo' to Memphis* (1981) and *Protest at Selma: Martin Luther King, Jr. and the Voting Rights Act of 1965* (1978).

Adolf Gasser received his Ph.D. from the University of Zurich and is now Professor Emeritus of History at the University of Basel in Switzerland. Among his publications are *Gemeindefreiheit als Rettung Europa* (1947), and *Ausgewähte historische Schriften 1933-1983* (1983).

Frank Gerome teaches History at James Madison University. He received his Ph.D. from Kent State University and has published articles on U.S.-Latin American relations.

Perry E. Gianakos earned a Ph.D. in American Civilization from New York University. He teaches at Michigan State University. He is co-editor of *American Diplomacy and the Sense of Destiny: Events and Attitudes* (1966) and *American Civilization Since World*

War II: Evaluations of Its Character, Form and Style (1968). Among his other publications is an essay on Ernest Howard Crosby in Charles Chatfield's *Peace Movements in America* (1973).

Gerald R. Gill received a Ph.D. from Howard University and teaches at Tufts University. He is co-author of *The Case for Affirmative Action for Blacks in Higher Education* (1978) and is author of *Meanness Mania* (1980).

Shaul Ginsburg is Senior Lecturer in the History Department at Beer-Sheba University, Israel. He received a Ph.D. at the Sorbonne and is currently working on a book about Lenin's early years.

Ann Gleeson-Lindenfelder holds an M.A. degree from Carnegie-Mellon University where she is enrolled in the doctoral program in Applied History.

Maurice Goldsmith is director of the Science Policy Foundation, England. He holds a B.Sc. degree from the University of London and is editor of several journals including *Science and Public Policy*. Among his publications are *Frederic Joliot-Curie* (1976) and *Sage, A Life of J. D. Bernal* (1980).

Brigitte M. Goldstein has an M.A. and an M.Ph. from New York University. She is currently writing a Ph.D. dissertation on the peace movement in Weimar Germany entitled "Ludwig Quidde and the Politics of Peace in Weimar Germany, 1919-1930." She has taught at Rutgers University.

James W. Gould received a Ph.D. from the Fletcher School of Law and Diplomacy. He teaches History and International Relations at Scripps College, Claremont, California. He has published numerous articles on nonviolence as well as *United States and Malaysia* (1969) and *Americans in Sumatra* (1961).

John T. Grayson teaches Religion at Mount Holyoke College. He received a Ph.D. from Columbia University.

Carol S. Gruber teaches History at William Paterson College of New Jersey. She received her Ph.D. from Columbia University. She published *Mars and Minerva: World War I and the Uses of the Higher Learning in America* (1975) and is currently working on a book on "Science, Government, and Universities in World War II."

Guido Grünewald holds a Ph.D. from the University of Cologne and is a member of the Executive of the International Peace Bureau, Geneva. He is author of several books on conscientious objection and war resistance, including *Geschichte der Kriegsdienstverweigerung* (1979) and *Pazifismus der radikalen Kriegsdienstgegnerschaft: Die Internationale der Kriegsdienstgegner (IdK) 1945-1968* (1982).

Carole Haber teaches History at the University of North Carolina at Charlotte. She received her Ph.D. from the University of Pennsylvania and published *Beyond Sixty-Five: The Dilemma of Old Age in America's Past* (1983).

Amy Hackett is a fellow at the Institute for Research in History, New York City. She received a Ph.D. from Columbia University and has published several articles on women in modern Germany. Her dissertation was on "The Politics of Feminism in Wilhelmine Germany, 1890-1918."

Fred Hahn is Professor Emeritus of History from both Trenton State College and the University of Frankfurt-am-Main. He holds a Doctor of Law and Political Science degree from the University of Prague and is co-author of *The German Social Democratic Party and the Czechoslovak Republic, 1918-1927* (1981).

Alwin Hanschmidt teaches at the University of Osnabrück. He received a Ph.D. from the University of Münster. Among his publications is *Republikanisch-demokratischer Internationalismus im 19. Jahrhundert. Ideen - Formen - Organisierungsversuche* (1977).

Steven C. Hause teaches History at the University of Missouri, St. Louis. He earned a Ph.D. from Washington University in St. Louis and has published numerous articles on the women's rights movement in France in such journals as the *Catholic Historical Review* and the *American Historical Review*.

Robert C. Hersch received a Ph.D. from New York University and is currently Director of Library Services at Pembroke State University in North Carolina. He has published an article on modern weapons transfers and wrote his dissertation on "American Interest in the War of the Triple Alliance, 1865-1870."

Albert S. Hill teaches at Southeastern Massachusetts University. He received a Ph.D. from Harvard University. A specialist in French history, he has published an article entitled "A Case of Conscience: Marcel Pichon and the Ligue Scolaire pour la Paix," in *Peace and Change: A Journal of Peace Research* (1975).

Claire Hirschfield received a Ph.D. from the University of Pennsylvania and teaches History at Pennsylvania State University, Ogontz Campus. She has published articles on the Anglo-Boer War in the *Journal of Contemporary History* and *Albion*. She is also the author of *The Diplomacy of Partition: Britain, France, and the Creation of Nigeria 1890-1898* (1979).

Joan Hoff-Wilson is executive secretary of the Organization of American Historians and Professor of History at Indiana University. She received a Ph.D. from the University of California, Berkeley. She is the author of *Herbert Clark Hoover: Forgotten Progressive* (1975) and has published an article in *The Magazine of Western History* (1980) entitled "Peace Is a Woman's Job: Jeannette Rankin's Foreign Policy." She is a member of the Council of the Conference on Peace Research in History.

Karl Holl received a Ph.D. from the University of Mainz. He has held a professorial position at the University of Bremen and is a member of the State Legislature of Bremen. He is editor of *Der deutsche Pazifismus während des Weltkrieges 1914-1918. Aus dem Nachlass Ludwig Quiddes* (1979) and is co-editor of *Pazifismus in der Weimarer Republik* (1981).

John E. Hollitz teaches History at California State University, Chico. He received a Ph.D. from the University of Wisconsin-Madison and has published in the *Wisconsin Magazine of History*.

William D. Hoover is chairman of the Department of History at the University of Toledo. He received his Ph.D. from the University of Michigan. A Japanese scholar, he is working on a book dealing with "Twentieth Century Japanese Dissent to Military Solutions." He has published in the *Journal of Asian History* and is a contributor to *Great Historical Figures of Japan* (1978). A member of the Council of the Conference on Peace Research in History, he has served as the Conference's secretary-treasurer.

John F. Howes teaches at the University of British Columbia. He received a Ph.D. from Columbia University and is co-editor of *Pacifism in Japan, The Christian and Socialist Tradition* (1979).

Charles F. Howlett teaches Social Studies at Amityville Memorial High School in New York. He received a Ph.D. from the State University of New York at Albany. He is author of *Troubled Philosopher: John Dewey and the Struggle for World Peace* (1977).

Joan B. Huffman teaches History at Macon Junior College. She received a Ph.D. from Georgia State University and is a past president of the Georgia Association of Historians.

John C. Hume, Jr. received a Ph.D. from Duke University and teaches History at St. Mary's College in North Carolina.

James C. Hunt teaches History at St. Joseph's College in Maine. He received a Ph.D.

from Harvard University. Author of *The People's Party in Württemberg and Southern Germany, 1890-1914* (1975), he has also published in *Central European History* and the *Journal of Contemporary History*.

James D. Hunt is Associate Professor of Religion and Philosophy at Shaw University in North Carolina. He received a Ph.D. from Syracuse University and is author of *Gandhi in London* (1978).

Edith F. Hurwitz received an M.A. degree from Brooklyn College of the City University of New York. She is Archivist at the Jewish Historical Society of New Haven, Connecticut. She has published numerous articles on a wide variety of subjects and is the author of *Politics and the Public Conscience: Slave Emancipation and the Abolitionist Movement in Britain* (1973).

Ulla Isaksson is a Swedish writer and novelist.

John A. Jackson, Jr. works for the Library of Congress as a research analyst. He received his Ph.D. from the University of North Carolina at Chapel Hill.

Roger B. Jeans has a Ph.D. from George Washington University and teaches History at Washington and Lee University. A China scholar, he wrote his dissertation on the early years of Chang Chün-mai and has published an article on Chang Chün-mai in *Sino-American Quarterly* (1978).

Sabine Jessner received a Ph.D. in History from Columbia University and now teaches at Indiana University, Indianapolis. Among her publications is *Edouard Herriot: Patriarch of the Republic* (1974).

Harold Josephson is Director of the Center for International Studies and Professor of History at the University of North Carolina at Charlotte. He received his Ph.D. from the University of Wisconsin-Madison and is the author of *James T. Shotwell and the Rise of Internationalism in America* (1975). He is a member of the Council of the Conference on Peace Research in History and is working on a study of ex-Communists and the Cold War.

Kalevi Kalemaa has a journalists' diploma from the University of Tampere and is an author. Among his books are two studies of the Finnish peace movement, *Suomalaisen rauhanliikkeen juuria* (1981) and *Rauhanliike Suomessa, Kansanliikkeet* (1981).

Elaine Kaye has an M.A. degree from Oxford University and is a writer. She serves as honorary secretary for the Oxford Project for Peace Studies. She is working on biographies of W. E. Orchard and C. J. Cadoux.

Martha Kearns holds an M.E. degree from Antioch University in Philadelphia and teaches at that same institution. She is author of *Käthe Kollwitz: Woman and Artist* (1976).

Jerold L. Kellman did his graduate work at the University of California, Berkeley and is currently president of Gabriel House, Inc.

John Kendle holds a Ph.D. from King's College of the University of London. He is a past president of the Canadian Historical Association and teaches at the University of Manitoba in Winnipeg, Canada. Among his publications is *The Round Table Movement and Imperial Union* (1975).

Thomas C. Kennedy teaches History at the University of Arkansas, Fayetteville. He received a Ph.D. from the University of South Carolina. He has published several articles and essays on the peace movement in Great Britain and is the author of *The Hound of Conscience: A History of the No-Conscription Fellowship, 1914-1919* (1981).

Anne R. Kenney is the associate director, Joint Collection, Western Historical Manuscript Collection, State Historical Society of Missouri Manuscripts. She holds an M.A.

from the University of Missouri-St. Louis and a M.A.L.S. from the University of Missouri-Columbia. She has published three articles on the women's rights movement in France, including one in the *American Historical Review* (1981).

Folke T. Kihlstedt is Chairman of the Department of Art at Franklin and Marshall College. He has a Ph.D. from Northwestern University. He has published articles and review essays on modern architecture and on the automobile and American culture in a variety of journals, including the *Michigan Quarterly Review* and the *Journal of the Society of Architectural Historians*.

Carlyle King is Emeritus Professor of English at the University of Saskatchewan. He holds a Ph.D. from the University of Toronto and was First Chairman, Canadian Fellowship of Reconciliation, 1938-1941.

Peter N. Kirstein received a Ph.D. from St. Louis University and is now Associate Professor of History at St. Xavier College, Chicago. He is the author of *Anglo Over Bracero: A History of the Mexican Worker in the United States from Roosevelt to Nixon* (1977).

Paschalis M. Kitromilides holds a Ph.D. from Harvard University and is at present Senior Lecturer in the History of Political Thought at the University of Athens. He has published *Small States in the Modern World: The Conditions of Survival* (1979) and *Culture and Society in Contemporary Europe* (1981).

Ollis Klem is a member and former chairperson of the Danish section of the Woman's International League for Peace and Freedom. Active as an internationalist, she studied at the University of Copenhagen and has published articles on peace efforts.

Kurt Koszyk holds a Ph.D. from Munich University and teaches Journalism at Dortmund University. Among his publications are *Deutsche Presse im 19. Jahrhundert* (1966) and *Deutsche Press 1914-1945* (1972).

Tadeusz Kowalik received a Ph.D. in Economics from Warsaw University and is an associate professor at the Polish Academy of Sciences in Warsaw. A former Woodrow Wilson scholar, he has published a book on Rosa Luxemburg's economics.

Barbara S. Kraft holds a Ph.D. in History from American University and resides in Washington, D.C. She has written articles on war and peace issues and is the author of *The Peace Ship: Henry Ford's Pacifist Adventure in the First World War* (1978).

Warren F. Kuehl received his Ph.D. from Northwestern University. He is Professor of History and Director of the Center for Peace Studies at the University of Akron. Editor of the *Biographical Dictionary of Internationalists* (1983), he has written on a variety of peace and internationalist issues, including *Seeking World Order: The United States and International Organizations to 1920* (1969).

Hans Kühner-Wolfskehl received a Ph.D. from the University of Munich. He is a writer who has published numerous books on church history, art, and music.

Richard R. Laurence is Professor of Humanities at Michigan State University. He received his Ph.D. from Stanford University. His scholarly interests center on the history of the Hapsburg Monarchy and on the problems of war and peace, topics on which he has published a variety of articles.

Claire LaVigna received a Ph.D. from the University of Rochester and teaches History at the Erindale Campus of the University of Toronto in Mississauga. She has published an article on Anna Kulisioff in *Italian Quarterly* (1976) and has also published an article on feminism and the Italian Sociality Party.

John L. LeBrun received a Ph.D. in American Studies from Case-Western Reserve

University. He is currently Associate Professor of History at Kent State University-Salem Campus.

Norbert Leser holds the position of Professor of Social Philosophy at the University of Vienna, where he received a Dr. jur. degree. His publications include *Begegnung und Auftrag: Beiträge zur Orientirung in zeitgenössischen Sozialismus* (1963) and *Zwischen Reforismus and Bolschewismus: Der Autromarxismus als Theorie und Praxis* (1968).

Joseph Levitt earned a Ph.D. at the University of Toronto and teaches History at the University of Ottawa. He is the author of *Henri Bourassa and the Golden Calf* (1969) and has written numerous articles and essays on Bourassa.

Helena Lewis teaches History at Appalachian State University in North Carolina. She received a Ph.D. from New York University and has written on French Surrealism and the propaganda of French imperialism. She is currently working on a book on Elsa Triolet, the Russian born writer and heroine of the French Resistance.

Erik Hjalmar Linder is a literary historian and journalist. He holds a Ph.D. from the University of Stockholm and is working on a biography of Elin Wägner with Ulla Isaksson.

Ulrich Linse received a Ph.D. from the University of Munich and holds the position of Oberstudienrat at München-Kolleg. Among his publications are *Organisierter Anarchismus im Deutschen Kaiserreich von 1871* (1969) and *Inflationsheilige. Messianische Führer and politisch-religiöse Erneuerungsbewegungen in der Weimarer Republik* (1981).

Clara M. Lovett is currently Chief of the European Division of the Library of Congress. After receiving a Ph.D. in History from the University of Texas, Austin, she taught at Baruch College in New York, rising to the position of assistant provost. Author of several books on Italian history, including *The Democratic Movement in Italy, 1830-1876* (1981), she is also co-editor of *Women, War, and Revolution* (1980).

Nadine Lubelski-Bernard is chief research assistant at the Institut de Sociologie, Université libre de Bruxelles, where she received a Ph.D. in Political Science. Her dissertation focused on the Belgian peace movement and was titled "Les mouvements et les idéologies pacifistes en Belgique (1830-1914)."

David C. Lukowitz teaches History at Hamline University in Minnesota. He received a Ph.D. from the University of Iowa and is a member of the board of editors of *Peace and Change: A Journal of Peace Research.* He has authored several articles on British peace leaders which have appeared in such journals as the *Canadian Journal of History, Journal of Contemporary History*, and *Friends Quarterly.*

Reinhold Lütgemeier-Davin received a Ph.D. from the Gesamthochschule (Universität) Kassel. He is author of *Pazifismus zwischen Kooperation und Konfrontation. Das Deutsche Friedenskartell in der Weimarer Republik* (1982).

Howard T. Lutz teaches History at the University of Wisconsin-Eau Claire. He received his Ph.D. from the University of Minnesota and has published an article on Emilia Fogelklou in the *Friends Journal* (1978).

Michael A. Lutzker teaches History and archival management at New York University. He received a Ph.D. from Rutgers University and is president of the Conference on Peace Research in History. He has written several articles on internationalism and the American peace movement which have appeared in such journals as *Peace and Change: A Journal of Peace Research* and *Societas.*

Lyle A. McGeoch earned a Ph.D. from the University of Pennsylvania and teaches History at Ohio University. He has written numerous articles on British foreign policy, including "On the Road to War: British Foreign Policy in Transition, 1905-1906," which appeared in *The Review of Politics* (1973).

Betty L. McLane has a Ph.D. in French from the University of Illinois and has written an essay, "Les Premières Idées de Simone Weil sur la Perception," which will appear in the forthcoming book *Cahiers Simone Weil*.

Kenneth McNaught earned a Ph.D. from the University of Toronto and now teaches History there. Among his publications are *A Prophet in Politics* (1963) and *The Pelican History of Canada* (1982).

Harold G. Marcus is Professor and Chairman, Committee on Northeast African Studies at Michigan State University. He received a Ph.D. from Boston University and is editor of *Northeast African Studies*. Among his books are *A Modern History of Ethiopia and Somalia* (1972) and *Ethiopia, Britain, and the United States, 1941-1972: The Politics of Empire* (1983).

Susan Han Marsh received a Ph.D. in Political Science from the University of Chicago. She is chairperson of the Department of Political Science at Providence College in Rhode Island. She has authored numerous essays on Chinese history, including an article on Chou Fo-hai which appeared in *The Chinese and the Japanese* (1980) and more than 70 biographical sketches in the *Biographical Dictionary of Republican China* (1967-71). She is also author of *Years of Upheaval: Revolution in Modern China* (1975).

Gay Mason was educated at the University of Queensland, Australia, and now holds a teaching position there. He has published articles in *Politics* and *Refractory Girl*.

Paul E. Masters, Jr. teaches Political Science at West Georgia College. He received a Ph.D. from St. Louis University and has published many articles and reviews on global issues and international relations.

Geoffrey Matthews teaches History at Loughborough University, England, where he earned a Ph.D. He has published articles in *Contemporary Review* on the Soviet political system and the United Nations, and has authored *The Re-Conquest of Burma, 1943-1945* (1966).

Marcus Mattmüller received a Ph.D. from the University of Basel and now serves as Director of the Institute of History there. He has published *Leonhard Ragaz und der religiöse Sozialismus* (2 vols., 1957, 1968).

Stanley M. Max earned his Ph.D. from State University of New York at Albany and is now the cataloger at the Clarke Historical Library at Central Michigan University.

L. Paul Metzger is Associate Professor of Sociology at State University College, New Paltz, New York. He received a Ph.D. at the University of Wisconsin-Madison and is the author of numerous articles on the sociology of American race relations.

Michael Meyer received his Ph.D. from the University of Connecticut, where he is currently Associate Professor of English. He has written extensively on the life of Henry David Thoreau, including *Several More Lives to Live: Thoreau's Political Reputation in America* (1977).

Michael M. Milenkovitch received a Ph.D. in International Relations and Soviet Area Studies from Columbia University and now is chairman of the Department of Political Science at Lehman College of the City University of New York. He has published and edited books on Milovan Djilas and is author of *The View from Red Square: A Critique of Cartoons from Pravda and Izvestia* (1966).

Francesca Miller is co-founder and a member of the board of directors of the Institute for Historical Study in San Francisco. She received her Ph.D. from the University of California, Davis, and has written several articles dealing with Latin America. She is particularly interested in Latin American-Russian relations.

Randall M. Miller received a Ph.D. from Ohio State University and now teaches History and is director of American Studies at Saint Joseph's University in Philadelphia. He has published *"Dear Master": Letters of a Slave Family* (1978).

Sally M. Miller teaches History and is Women's Studies Coordinator at the University of the Pacific. She received her Ph.D. from the University of Toronto. Among her publications are *Victor Berger and the Promise of Constructive Socialism* (1973) and *The Radical Immigrant 1820-1920* (1974).

Dan L. Morrill teaches History at the University of North Carolina at Charlotte. He received his Ph.D. from Emory University. Among his publications is a study of "Nicholas II and the Call for the First Hague Conference," which appeared in the *Journal of Modern History* (1974). He has also published articles in *Soviet Studies* and *The Historian*.

A. J. A. Morris is Professor and Head of the School of Philosophy, Politics and History at Northern Ireland Polytechnic. He has an M.A. degree from the University of London and has published *Radicalism Against War, 1906-14: The Advocacy of Peace and Retrenchment* (1972) and *C. P. Trevelyan: Portrait of a Radical* (1977).

Hilda Morris holds a Ph.D. from the University of Cologne and writes monthly articles on foreign affairs for *The Pacifist*. She is a journalist who has also translated books from German into English.

Polly Morris is currently completing a Ph.D. degree at the Center for Study of Social History, University of Warwick, England.

Kenneth I. Morse, who is now retired, was formerly editor of the Church of the Brethren national publication *Messenger* and was a book editor for the Church of the Brethren. He has an M.A. degree from Pennsylvania State University.

J. S. Newton has a Ph.D. from the University of Durham and now teaches History at New College in Durham. He has published two articles on Edward Miall in the *Durham University Journal*.

Nobuya Bamba teaches international relations at the University of Osaka in Japan. He received his Ph.D. at the University of California. He was co-editor and a contributor to *Pacifism in Japan: The Christian and Socialist Tradition* (1978). He also authored *Japanese Diplomacy in a Dilemma, New Light on Japan's China Policy, 1924-1929* (1973).

Anthony W. Novitsky received a Ph.D. from the State University of New York at Buffalo. He teaches part-time at Canisius College in Buffalo and wrote an essay on "Peter Maurin's Green Revolution: The Radical Implications of Reactionary Social Catholicism," which appeared in the *Review of Politics* (1975).

Sulayman S. Nyang received a Ph.D. from the University of Virginia. He teaches at Howard University in the Center for African Studies. Among his publications is *Ali A. Mazrui: The Man and His Works* (1981) and a forthcoming book on *Islam, Christianity and African Identity*.

Walther G. Oschilewski is honorary professor and retired chief editor of Social Democratic cultural and political publications. Among his numerous scholarly works is *Turmwächter der Demokratie: Ein Lebensbild von Kurt Schumacher*, written with Arno Scholz (4 vols., 1952-54).

Thomas E. O'Toole received a Doctorate in Arts degree from Carnegie-Mellon University. He is now with the Office of International Programs at the University of Minnesota. Among his publications is a *Historical Dictionary of Guinea* (1978).

Donald M. Page received a Ph.D. from the University of Toronto and is currently Deputy Director of Historical Research for the Department of External Affairs in Ottawa,

Ontario, Canada. He has published bibliographies, collections of documents, and articles on Canadian foreign relations.

D. N. Panigrahi earned a Ph.D. in modern Indian History from the University of London. He is currently deputy director, Nehru Memorial Museum and Library in New Delhi. He has published numerous books on Indian history and society and is currently working on a study of the Indian National Congress and the British Raj.

Nicholas Papayanis teaches at Brooklyn College of the City University of New York. He received a Ph.D. from the University of Wisconsin-Madison. He has published numerous articles on revolutionary syndicalism and has completed a book-length manuscript on Alphonse Merrheim.

David S. Patterson is a historian with the United States Department of State. He received his Ph.D. from the University of California, Berkeley and has written several articles on American diplomatic history and the history of the American peace movement. His major work is *Toward a Warless World: The Travail of the American Peace Movement, 1887-1914* (1976). He is vice-president of the Conference on Peace Research in History.

Vratislav Pechota is an international lawyer with a particular interest in the United Nations. Educated at Charles University in Prague where he received a J.U.D. and a Ph.D., he does international consulting and teaches as an adjunct professor at the New York University of Law. Among his publications are *International Multilateral Treaties* (1965) and *The Quiet Approach: A Study of Good Offices Exercised by the United Nations' Secretary-General in the Cause of Peace* (1972).

Sherylle Petty received an M.A. degree in History from the University of North Carolina at Charlotte and teaches History, Women's Studies, and Peace Studies at Central Cabarras High School in North Carolina.

Craig Phelan holds an M.A. from Ohio State University and is working towards his Ph.D. degree at the same institution.

James M. Pitsula teaches History at the University of Regina in Canada. He received a Ph.D. degree from York University and has published in the field of Canadian social history. His articles have appeared in the *Journal of Canadian Studies* and *Saskatchewan History*.

Murray Polner was educated at Columbia University and the Union Graduate School where he received a Ph.D. He is editor of *Present Tense* magazine and is vice-president of the Jewish Peace Fellowship. He has published on a wide range of subjects, authoring *The Disarmament Catalogue* (2 vols., 1982 & 1983) and *When Can I Come Home: A Debate on Amnesty for Exiles, Anti-War Prisoners and Others* (1972).

Cyril Powles received a Ph.D. from the University of British Columbia. He teaches at Trinity College of the University of Toronto and has published articles on Abe Isō, including a contribution to *Pacifism in Japan: The Christian and Socialist Tradition* (1978).

Margaret Prang is Professor of History at the University of British Columbia. She earned her Ph.D. at the University of Toronto and is the author of *N. W. Rowell: Ontario Nationalist* (1975).

Bimal Prasad received his Ph.D. from Columbia University. He is a Professor of South Asian Studies and Chairman, Centre for South, South-East and Central Asian Studies, School of International Studies, Jawaharlal Nehru University in New Delhi. Among his publications are *Socialism, Sarvodaya and Democracy: Selected Works of Jayaprakash Narayan* (1964) and *A Revolutionary's Quest: Selected Writings of Jayaprakash Narayan* (1980).

Gary Puckrein received a Ph.D. from Brown University and is now Associate Professor of History at Rutgers University. His publications include *Little England: Plantation Society and Anglo-Barbadian Politics 1627-1700* (forthcoming).

Bogdan Raditsa is Emeritus Professor of History at Fairleigh Dickinson University. Among his publications are *Agony of Europe* (1940) and *Conversations with Guglielmo Ferrero* (1940).

Rosemary Rainbolt is technical assistant to the Director of Admissions and Financial Aid at the University of Pittsburgh. She has received an M.A. from Antioch University and is working towards a Ph.D. in Applied History and Social Science at Carnegie-Mellon University. She has published an essay on "Women and War in the United States: The Case of Dorothy Detzer, National Secretary Women's International League for Peace and Freedom," in *Peace and Change: A Journal of Peace Research* (1977).

John L. Rector received his Ph.D. from Indiana University and is now Catedrático Auxiliar de Historia at the Universidad Católica de Puerto Rico. He has published articles in *Revista Chilena de Historia y Geografía*.

Cheri Register received a Ph.D. from the University of Chicago. She has published an article on Ellen Key's social vision in *Women's Studies International Quarterly* (1982) and is author of *Kvinnokamp och litteratur i USA och Sverige* (1977).

Carl Resek holds a Ph.D. from the University of Rochester and teaches history at the State University of New York at Purchase.

Dieter Riesenberger received a Ph.D. from the University of Freiburg im Breisgau and teaches at the University of Paderborn. He is the author of *Die katholische Friedensbewegung in der Weimarer Republik* (1976).

Diego D. G. Rivero teaches at the University of Miami and is general editor of *Bibliotheca Americana*. He holds Ph.D.'s from the Universidad Nacional Autónoma de Mexico and from the University of Georgia. Among his publications are *Angola, Uma Historia, 1434-1934* (1971) and *El caso extraño de d. Antonio Urrutia de Vergara: un episodio en la visitageneral de Juan de Palafox y Mendoza* (1975).

Keith G. Robbins holds a Ph.D. from Oxford University and teaches History at the University of Glasgow. Among his publications are a biography of *John Bright* (1979) and *The Abolition of War: The Peace Movement in Britain 1914-1919* (1976).

Jo Ann Ooiman Robinson teaches History at Morgan State University. She received her Ph.D. from Johns Hopkins University. She has published several articles and essays on A. J. Muste, as well as *Abraham Went Out: A Biography of A. J. Muste* (1982).

Neville Rogers holds a Doctor of Literature from the University of London. Having taught at the University of Birmingham, Brandeis University, and Ohio University, he is now Professor Emeritus of English at Ohio University. He has published several works on Shelley and an article on Lauro de Bosis in *Rivista* (1981).

Johannes Hendrik Rombach has a Master of Law degree from University of Gröningen. He is the Assistant Keeper of Records for the City of Alkmaar. He has published articles dealing with the history of the International Red Cross.

Martin Rooney earned a Ph.D. from the University of Bremen where he is a part-time lecturer in English.

Katherine Larson Roper teaches at St. Mary's College of California. She received a Ph.D. from Stanford University and is working on a book dealing with novels of Imperial Berlin.

Richard V. Salisbury received a Ph.D. from the University of Kansas and teaches History at Western Kentucky University. He has published articles in numerous journals, including *Hispanic American Historical Review* and the *Journal of Inter-American Studies and World Affairs*.

Jonathan Sanders received a Ph.D. from Columbia University and is currently assistant director at the W. Averell Harriman Institute for Advanced Study of the Soviet Union at Columbia University.

Gerd Grønvold Saue was educated at the University of Oslo. She has worked as both a journalist and an author. She has written novels, short stories, poems, and books for children. She has also served as chairperson of the Norwegian branch of the International Fellowship of Reconciliation.

Samir Saul earned a degree of Scolarité de doctorat from the University of Montreal, where he is presently a candidate for a Ph.D. degree.

Malcolm James Saunders received a Ph.D. in History from Flinders University of South Australia. He teaches at James Cook University of North Queensland. He has published several articles on the anti-Vietnam War movement in Australia. These have appeared in *Flinders Journal of History and Politics*, *Social Alternatives*, and *Labour History*, among others.

Udo Sautter teaches History at the University of Windsor and received a Ph.D. from the University of Tübingen. He has published *Constantin Frantz Briefe* (1974) as well as several articles on Constantin Frantz.

Gail L. Savage received a Ph.D. from the University of Texas at Austin and has taught at the University of North Carolina at Charlotte. She has published articles in the *Journal of Contemporary History* and the *Journal of Social History*. She is completing a study of the influence of the English civil service on the development of social policy between the two World Wars.

Will Schaber is an essayist and editor who was educated in Germany. For more than 20 years he served as section head at British Information Services in New York. He has written several books, including *Der Gratgänger - Erich Schairers Welt und Werk* (1981).

David L. Schalk teaches History at Vassar College. He received a Ph.D. from Harvard University. Among his publications are *Roger Martin du Gard: The Novelist and History* (1967) and *The Spectrum of Political Engagement: Mounier, Benda, Nizan Brasillach, Sartre* (1979).

Stephen Jay Scheinberg received his Ph.D. from the University of Wisconsin-Madison and teaches History at Concordia University in Canada. He has published several articles on Theodore Roosevelt, Progressivism, and American economic expansion into Canada. He is a past vice-president of the Canadian Association for American Studies.

Theron F. Schlabach received a Ph.D. from the University of Wisconsin-Madison. He teaches History at Goshen College. Among his publications are *Pensions for Professors* (1963) and *Edwin E. Witte: Cautious Reformer* (1969). He has published several articles on Mennonite history.

Hanna Schnedl-Bubeniček received her Ph.D. from the University of Salzburg. She is working on a research project for the Federal Ministry for Science and Research on the Documentation of Women's Studies in Austria and teaches at the University of Salzburg and the University of Graz. Among other publications, she is co-author of *Österreichische Schriftstellerinnen 1880-1938. Eine Bio-Bibliographie* (1982).

Brigitte Schnegg received a history degree from the University of Bern, where she is a research assistant in the Historical Institute. She has published an article on the history of the women's movement in Switzerland in *Frauen der Welt* (1982), edited by Alexander Beck.

Monica Paznokas Scorcia received an M.A. in Modern European History from Columbia University and is currently employed by Pfizer Pharmaceuticals as an information analyst in the Department of Professional Information.

Michael Seadle received a Ph.D. in History from the University of Chicago. He has published *Quakers in Nazi Germany* (1978).

Peter S. Seadle teaches German at Franklin and Marshall College. He received his Ph.D. from Ohio State University.

Yvonne Sée is president of the French section of the Women's International League for Peace and Freedom, and co-representative to UNESCO for WILPF. As "Y. Vineuil" she is the author of plays, poems, and books, and translator of Rupert Brooke.

William Shank holds an M.S. degree from Columbia University. He is Associate Professor and Music Librarian at the City University of New York, Graduate School.

David A. Shannon is Commonwealth Professor of History at the University of Virginia. He received his Ph.D. from the University of Wisconsin-Madison. He is the author of *The Socialist Party of America: A History* (1955) and *The Decline of American Communism* (1959).

Dennis M. Sherman received his Ph.D. from the University of Michigan and teaches at John Jay College of Criminal Justice of the City University of New York. He has written introductions to many scholarly reprints and has authored several articles on mid-nineteenth century France in such journals as *History of Political Economy* and *The Journal of European Economic History*.

Marjorie H. Sibley received an M.A. degree from the University of Minnesota and teaches at Augsburg College in Minneapolis.

Mulford Q. Sibley teaches Political Science and American Studies at the University of Minnesota. He has a Ph.D. from the same institution. He is author of *The Political Theories of Modern Pacifism: An Analysis and Criticism* (1970) and is co-author of *Conscription of Conscience: The American Conscientious Objector in World War II* (1952).

Nicholas A. Sims earned a B.Sc. in International Relations from the University of London. He has been active in various Quaker groups studying the United Nations and Disarmament. He teaches International Relations at the London School of Economics and Political Science. He has written *Approaches to Disarmament* (1974) and has co-authored *British Writing on Disarmament from 1914 to 1978* (1979).

Ioannis Sinanoglou is executive secretary for the Council for European Studies at Columbia University, where he earned a Ph.D. in History. He has published several essays on the Russian Revolution and French reaction to it.

Nancy A. Slote is assistant editor of the Jane Addams Papers at the University of Illinois at Chicago Circle. She has an M.A.L.S. degree from the University of Chicago.

Thomas P. Socknat received a Ph.D. in History from McMaster University. His dissertation " 'Witness Against War': Pacifism in Canada, 1900-1945" is being revised for publication. He has published articles in *The Journal of Canadian Studies* and *Quaker History*. He teaches History at Queen's University in Kingston, Ontario.

Jayme A. Sokolow received a Ph.D. from New York University and is currently a staff member at the National Endowment for the Humanities. Dr. Sokolow has published *Eros and Modernization: Sylvester Graham, Health Reform, and the Origins of Victorian Sexuality in America* (1983).

Robert V. Sparks teaches at Northeastern University and received a Ph.D. from Boston

College. His dissertation was on the life of Edmund Quincy and he has published an article on Quincy in the *Historical Journal of Massachusetts* (1982).

Elisabeth Ståhle has long been active in the Women's International League for Peace and Freedom and has been vice-president of the Swedish Section of WILPF since 1975.

Kay Clontz Starnes teaches History at the University of North Carolina at Charlotte. She received her M.A. in History from the same institution.

Stephen J. Stearns teaches History at the College of Staten Island of the City University of New York. He received a Ph.D. from the University of California, Berkeley, and has published articles in the *Journal of British Studies*, *Military Affairs*, and *Peace and Change: A Journal of Peace Research*.

Frederick Joseph Stefon received a D.Ed. degree in American Educational Policy Studies from the Pennsylvania State University. He teaches History at Pennsylvania State University, Wilkes-Barre Campus. His principal area of research is Native American history and he has published articles in *Indian History* and *The Journal of Ethnic Studies*.

Hans-Josef Steinberg teaches at the University of Bremen and was formerly president of the same institution. He received his doctorate from the University of Cologne and has written numerous articles on 19th and 20th century European labor and social movements. Among his books are *Sozialismus und deutsche Sozialdemokratie. Zur Ideologie der Partei vor dem 1. Weltkrieg* (1967) and *Widerstand und Verfolgung in Essen 1933-1945* (1969).

Dale R. Steiner received a Ph.D. from the University of Virginia and teaches at California State University, Chico. He has published *Historical Journals: A Handbook for Writers and Reviewers* (1981).

Herbert Steiner received a Ph.D. from the University of Vienna and is currently director of the Archives of the Austrian Resistance Movement in Vienna.

James Brewer Stewart teaches History at Macalester College. He received a Ph.D. from Case Western Reserve University and has published *Joshua R. Giddings and the Tactics of Radical Politics* (1970) and *Holy Warriors: The Abolitionists and American Slavery* (1976).

Laura S. Strumingher is director of the Center for Women's Studies and teaches History at the University of Cincinnati. She received her Ph.D. from the University of Rochester. Among her publications is *Women and the Making of the Working Class, Lyon 1830-1870* (1979).

Andreas Studer is a Ph.D. candidate in History at the University of Berne.

Ralph Summy teaches Political Science at the University of Queensland. He has an M.A. from the University of Sydney. He has written articles on the Australian peace movement which have appeared in *Politics* and *Social Alternatives* and is co-authoring a book, *The Australian Peace Movement: From the Sudan to Vietnam and After*.

Zofia Sywak earned a Ph.D. from St. John's University in New York and is Registrar at Kean College of New Jersey. A specialist in Polish history, Dr. Sywak is a contributor to both *Poles in America: Bicentennial Essays* (1978) and the *Biographical Dictionary of Internationalists* (1983).

Takeshi Nishida teaches in the Department of Political Science, Dōshisha University, where he received his undergraduate and graduate degrees. He has written several articles on the peace effort in Japan and on modern Japanese political thought.

David P. Thelen received a Ph.D. in History from the University of Wisconsin-Madison and teaches at the University of Missouri-Columbia. He has published on the Progressive

Movement and Robert La Follette, including *Robert M. La Follette and the Insurgent Spirit* (1976).

Margaret Tims is an author and editor. Among her publications is a study of the Women's International League for Peace and Freedom, entitled *WILPF 1915-1965* (1965), and *Jane Addams of Hull House* (1961).

Melvin I. Urofsky received a Ph.D. from Columbia University. He teaches History at Virginia Commonwealth University and is chairman of the Academic Council of the American Jewish Historical Society. Among his many publications are *Louis D. Brandeis and the Progressive Tradition* (1980) and *A Voice That Spoke for Justice: The Life and Times of Stephen S. Wise* (1981).

Peter Van Den Dungen received a Ph.D. in War Studies from the University of London. He is a Lecturer in Peace Studies in the School of Peace Studies at the University of Bradford in England. He has published widely on peace history and peace research, including *Foundations of Peace Research* (1980), *The Hidden History of a Peace 'Classic': Emeric Crucé's Le Nouveau Cynee* (1980), and *The Making of Peace: Jean de Bloch and the First Hague Peace Conference* (1983).

Jo Vellacott received a Ph.D. from McMaster University. She is a writer, researcher, and part-time lecturer at the University of Toronto. She has published *Bertrand Russell and the Pacifists in the First World War* (1980).

Thanos Veremis has a Ph.D. from Oxford University. He teaches modern Greek History at Pantios School of Political Science in Athens and has published several works on military-security considerations in modern Greek history.

Gabor Vermes holds a Ph.D. from Stanford University and teaches at Rutgers University in Newark. He has contributed articles on Hungary during World War I for *Hungary in Revolution, 1918-19: Nine Essays* (1971) and *The Habsburg Empire in World War I* (1977).

Andrew Verner teaches History at Swarthmore College and holds a Ph.D. from Columbia University.

Mary Vipond received her Ph.D. from the University of Toronto. She teaches History at Concordia University in Montreal. Among her publications are several articles on English-Canadian culture in the 1920s which have appeared in *Canadian Historical Review*, *Journal of Canadian Studies*, and *Canadian Review of Studies in Nationalism*.

Joseph Frazier Wall is Rosenfield Professor and Director of the Rosenfield Program in Public Affairs at Grinnell College. He earned a Ph.D. from Columbia University. He has published several books including *Andrew Carnegie* (1970) for which he received the Bancroft Prize in American History.

James P. Walsh received a Ph.D. from Columbia University and teaches at Central Connecticut State College. He has published articles in the *William and Mary Quarterly*, *New England Quarterly*, and *American Quarterly*, among others.

Solomon Wank received his Ph.D. from Columbia University and teaches History at Franklin and Marshall College. He has written numerous articles on Austro-Hungarian and Central European History and is editor of *Doves and Diplomats: Foreign Offices and Peace Movements in Europe and America in the Twentieth Century* (1978). He is a member of the Council of the Conference on Peace Research in History and serves on the Executive Committee of *Peace and Change: A Journal of Peace Research*.

Frank A. Warren teaches History at Queens College of the City University of New York. He received a Ph.D. from Brown University. An historian of radicalism in America, he has published *Liberals and Communism: The "Red Decade" Revisited* (1966) and *An Alternative Vision: The Socialist Party in the 1930's* (1974).

John B. Weaver received a Ph.D. from Ohio State University and specializes in nineteenth century U.S. history.

Bernerd C. Weber teaches History at the University of Alabama. He received his Ph.D. from the University of California, Berkeley. In addition to writing many scholarly articles and contributing several essays to *The Discoverers: An Encyclopedia of Explorers and Exploration* (1980), he has co-authored *Letters of Ogier Ghislain de Busbecq to the Holy Roman Emperor Maximilian II* (1961).

Robert H. Whealey received a Ph.D. from the University of Michigan and teaches History at Ohio University. A student of G. D. H. Cole at Oxford in 1956-57, Dr. Whealy has published several articles on Spain and European history in such journals as the *Journal of Modern History*, *Philosophy and Public Affairs*, and the *Journal of Contemporary History*.

Stephen J. Whitfield received his Ph.D. from Brandeis University where he now teaches American Studies. He is author of *Scott Nearing: Apostle of American Radicalism* (1974).

Lothar Wieland received a Ph.D. from the University of Bremen. He has published *Belgien 1914. Die Frage des belgischen "Franktireurkrieges" und die deutsche öffentliche Meinung 1914-1936* (1983) and has collaborated on several volumes dealing with the German peace movement including *Die Friedensbewegung. Politischer Pazifismus in Deutschland, Osterreich und der Schweiz* (1983), edited by Helmut Donat and Karl Holl.

Judith Wishnia received her Ph.D. from the State University of New York at Stony Brook, where she is presently Assistant Professor of Interdisciplinary Social Science and History. Her research interests focus on the unionization of French civil service workers, women, and pacifism.

Sarah Ellen Witte teaches English at Marquette University where she is pursuing an M.A. degree.

Lawrence S. Wittner received his Ph.D. from Columbia University and teaches at the State University of New York at Albany. Among his publications are *Rebels Against War: The American Peace Movement, 1941-1960* (1969) and *Cold War America* (1974). He is a past president of the Conference on Peace Research in History.

Richard J. Wolff is Assistant Dean and Assistant Professor of History and Education at St. John's University in New York. He has a Ph.D. from Columbia University. In addition to several articles on the relationship between Italian Fascism and the Catholic Church, he is co-editor of *The State and Clergy in Interwar Europe, 1919-1945* (forthcoming).

Michael Wreszin teaches at Queens College of the City University of New York. He received his Ph.D. from Brown University and has published *Oswald Garrison Villard: Pacifist at War* (1965) and *The Superfluous Anarchist: Albert Jay Nock* (1972).

Edith Wynner is Curator, Schwimmer-Lloyd Papers, New York Public Library. She is co-author of *Searchlight for Peace Plans: Choose Your Road to World Government* (1944) and author of *World Federal Government: Why? What? How?* (1954).

Yoji Akashi received a Ph.D. from Georgetown University and currently is director of the Center for Japanese Studies at Nanzan University in Nagoya, Japan. He is author of "A Botched Peace Effort: The Miao Pin *Kosaku*, 1944-1945," which appeared in *China and Japan: A Search for Balance Since World War I*, edited by Alvin D. Coox and Hilary Conroy (1978).

James A. Young teaches History at Edinboro University of Pennsylvania. He received his Ph.D. from Case Western University. He contributed an essay on "The Consulta and the Italian Peace Movement, 1914-18" to *Doves and Diplomats: Foreign Offices and Peace Movements in Europe and America in the Twentieth Century*, edited by Solomon Wank (1978).

Yuzo Ota received a Ph.D. from the University of Tokyo and teaches History at McGill University. He wrote the essay on Kagawa Toyohiko for *Pacifism in Japan: The Christian and Socialist Tradition* (1978) and published a book on Uchimura Kanzō entitled *Uchimura Kanzō: Nihonshugi to sekaishugi o megutte* (1977).

Gordon C. Zahn is Professor Emeritus of Sociology at the University of Massachusetts, Boston, and president of Pax Christi Center on Conscience and War. He received his Ph.D. in Sociology from Catholic University. Among his books are *In Solitary Witness: The Life and Death of Franz Jaegerstaetter* (1964) and *War, Conscience and Dissent* (1967).

Elda Gentili Zappi was educated at the University of Buenos Aires and teaches at Herbert H. Lehman College of the City University of New York.

Juergen Ziechmann has a doctorate and is Professor of Educational Psychology and Curriculum Development at the University of Bremen. Among his publications is *Curriculumtheorie in der Bunder republik* (1973).

Angela Howard Zophy teaches History and is ACCESS Program Project Coordinator at the University of Wisconsin-Parkside. She received a Ph.D. from Ohio State University and has published an article dealing with labor history.

Wolf W. Zuelzer was educated at the German University of Prague and at Wayne State University. A Doctor of Medicine, he is Professor Emeritus of Pediatric Research at Wayne State University. He has written some 200 articles in medical journals and a number of essays on American politics. His books include *Selbstzerstorung der Demokratie* (1974) and *The Nicolai Case* (1982).

Urs Zwahlen is a student of history at the University of Bern.

INDEX

The location of main entries in the dictionary is indicated here by *italic* page numbers. Peace and internationalist organizations frequently modified their names over time or were referred to differently in different places. The index lists them under their most commonly used names.

ABOUT THE EDITOR-IN-CHIEF

Harold Josephson is Director of the Center for International Studies and Professor of History at the University of North Carolina at Charlotte. Author of *James T. Shotwell and the Rise of Internationalism in America*, he has also published numerous articles that have appeared in *Diplomatic History*, *The Historian*, *Mid-America*, and *American Heritage*. He is a member of the national council of the Conference on Peace Research in History and a member of the Bernath Article Committee of the Society of Historians of American Foreign Relations.